The Last King of America

The Last King of America
The Misunderstood Reign of George III

ANDREW ROBERTS

VIKING

VIKING
An imprint of Penguin Random House LLC
penguinrandomhouse.com

First published in hardcover in Great Britain by Allen Lane,
an imprint of Penguin Random House Ltd., London, in 2021.
First United States edition published by Viking, 2021.

Illustration credits can be found on pp. 734–738.

ISBN 9781984879264 (hardcover)
ISBN 9781984879271 (ebook)

Printed in the United States of America
1   3   5   7   9   10   8   6   4   2

Set in Sabon LT Std

To Robert Hardman

Political systems and constitutional arrangements which were nei-ther planned nor made but have grown up, are like living beings: dark repositories of an imperfectly known past which can never be completely obliterated. Even in new forms, occasioned by needs, dormant shapes are apt to revive – the response of the unconscious memory inherent in the organism and moulding its nature. To hunt for analogies in the past is antiquarianism; to trace continuity in its variants is history.

L. B. Namier, *Conflicts: Studies in Contemporary History*, 1942

Contents

Acknowledgements

I would like to thank Her Majesty The Queen for her kind permission to consult and publish from the papers of King George III. In April 2015, The Queen inaugurated the Georgian Papers Programme which has put over 200,000 pages of the Hanoverian papers held in the Royal Archives and Royal Library at Windsor Castle online at https://georgianpapers.com. I would like to thank Professor Arthur Burns of King's College London, the Director of this tremendously ambitious programme, for his invaluable help. As the Georgian Papers were uncatalogued and only around 15 per cent had been published before, he showed me that there is a good deal more to be said about George III. Dr Oliver Walton, the former Georgian Papers Programme Coordinator and Curator of the Historical Papers Projects at the Royal Archives, and Dr Andrew Beaumont have been founts of knowledge and advice. I would also like to thank Julie Crocker and the rest of the staff at the Royal Archives for their customary helpfulness and professionalism.

I was very fortunate to have my friend Professor Jeremy Black as my mentor during the writing of this book, a distinguished former biographer of George III in 2006 and 2020 and a great expert on the period. I've hugely enjoyed our daily emails about the King, and cannot thank him enough for his thoughts and insights. I've wanted to keep abreast with all the latest developments in George III studies, and other experts on various aspects of the King who kindly answered my queries include Dr Rachel Banke, Dr Adam Crymble, Dr Carolyn A. Day, Dr Shannon Duffy, Dr Hugh Dussek, Dr Paige Emerick, Dr James Fisher, Lady Antonia Fraser, Flora Fraser, Dr William Gibson, James Grant, Dr David Hancock, Dr Will Hay, Dr Ronald A. Johnson, Dr Brooke Newman, Dr Andrew O'Shaughnessy, Catherine Ostler, Michael Prichard, Dr Richard Samuelson, Dr Suzanne Schwarz, Dr Nancy Siegel and Dr Neil York.

For their clarifying of the truth behind 'the King's Malady', so long misdiagnosed as porphyria, I would like to thank Dr Timothy Peters, former Professor of Clinical Biochemistry and Director of Pathology at King's College London, Professor Sir Simon Wessely, President of the Royal Society of Medicine and former President of the Royal College of Psychiatrists, and Professor Peter Garrard, Honorary Consultant Neurologist at St

George's University Hospitals, for their invaluable help and advice and for making complicated medical terms comprehensible to a layman.

I was fortunate in being given several masterclasses by experts in their specialist areas, and I would like to thank John Lee for elucidating the grand strategy of the American War of Independence; Liam Fitzgerald for showing me the King's Grand Medal Case at the British Museum; Lord (Mervyn) King for explaining the concept of William Pitt the Younger's Sinking Fund; Hugh Johnson and Paul Symington for their views on Pitt's port-drinking; Hugo Vickers for his knowledge of orders and decorations; Jeremy Solel for his work on battle statistics and analysing the King's working day; Flora Fraser for her thoughts on the relations between the King and Caroline, Princess of Wales; and Mark Herman of Studiolo Designs for information about what happens when the Revolutionary War is wargamed at tournament level.

I would like to thank Brooks's Club for permission to quote from their splendid Betting Book (my own objectivity in recounting the great Fox–Pitt struggle can be judged from the fact that I am a member of both the Fox Club at Brooks's and the University Pitt Club at Cambridge); Rebecca Salter, President of the Royal Academy, and Mark Pomeroy, its Archivist, for allowing me to research the 'Royal Books' that founded it; the staff at the London Library, the National Archives, the British Library (especially Adrian Edwards who gave me a private tour of George III's library) and Kew Palace; and Lorenzo Lunesi and Oliver Walton for checking my reference notes so expertly.

Several friends in Britain and America have read the book in pre-proof form, and I would very much like to thank James Barry III (whose idea this book was), Andrew Beaumont, Michael Bishop, Jeremy Black, Richard Cohen, Paul Felton, Augusta Harris, Luke Labern, John Lee, Jerry del Missier, Richard K. Munro, Eric Petersen, Scott Syfert and Oliver Walton for all their tremendous help and advice.

Throughout the research and writing of this book I have been fortunate enough to be the Roger and Martha Mertz Visiting Fellow at the Hoover Institution at Stanford University, and I would like to thank Roger and Martha for their great friendship and generosity.

At my publishers, Stuart Proffitt, Brian Tart, Gretchen Schmid, Richard Duguid, Peter James, Alice Skinner, Sandra Fuller, Taryn Jones, Pen Vogler, Ania Gordon and Stephen Ryan have been a delight to work with as ever; Cecilia Mackay was a brilliant picture editor; Mike Athanson provided the superb maps; and Georgina Capel is generally recognized as the best literary agent in the British Commonwealth of Nations.

This book is dedicated to the royal biographer Robert Hardman, my close friend of thirty years and the best person to ask for the plural of Earl Marshal. (It's Earl Marshals.) Although the research for this book was finished before Coronavirus hit, the writing of it took place during the pandemic, so I would like to thank my son Henry for the nightly rum punches, my daughter Cassia for her sweet good nature and humour, and above all my wife Susan Gilchrist for all her wonderful love and support while sharing the lockdowns and self-isolations with me. As Charlotte was to George in Chapter 26, she is 'the Queen of my heart'.

Andrew Roberts
London
May 2021

THE HANOVERIANS

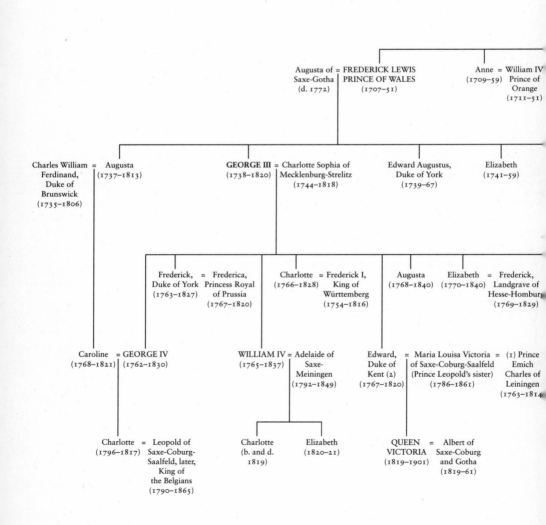

Augusta of = FREDERICK LEWIS   Anne = William IV
Saxe-Gotha   PRINCE OF WALES   (1709–59)   Prince of
(d. 1772)   (1707–51)   Orange
                                                (1711–51)

Charles William = Augusta   GEORGE III = Charlotte Sophia of   Edward Augustus,   Elizabeth
Ferdinand,   (1737–1813)   (1738–1820)   Mecklenburg-Strelitz   Duke of York   (1741–59)
Duke of   (1744–1818)   (1739–67)
Brunswick
(1735–1806)

Frederick,   = Frederica,   Charlotte = Frederick I,   Augusta   Elizabeth = Frederick,
Duke of York   Princess Royal   (1766–1828)   King of   (1768–1840)   (1770–1840)   Landgrave of
(1763–1827)   of Prussia   Württemberg   Hesse-Homburg
          (1767–1820)   (1754–1816)   (1769–1829)

Caroline   = GEORGE IV   WILLIAM IV = Adelaide of   Edward,   = Maria Louisa Victoria = (1) Prince
(1768–1821)   (1762–1830)   (1765–1837)   Saxe-   Duke of   of Saxe-Coburg-Saalfeld   Emich
                                 Meiningen   Kent (2)   (Prince Leopold's sister)   Charles of
                                 (1792–1849)   (1767–1820)   (1786–1861)   Leiningen
                                                                        (1763–1814)

Charlotte   = Leopold of   Charlotte   Elizabeth   QUEEN   = Albert of
(1796–1817)   Saxe-Coburg-   (b. and d.   (1820–21)   VICTORIA   Saxe-Coburg
          Saalfeld, later,   1819)   (1819–1901)   and Gotha
          King of   (1819–61)
          the Belgians
          (1790–1865)

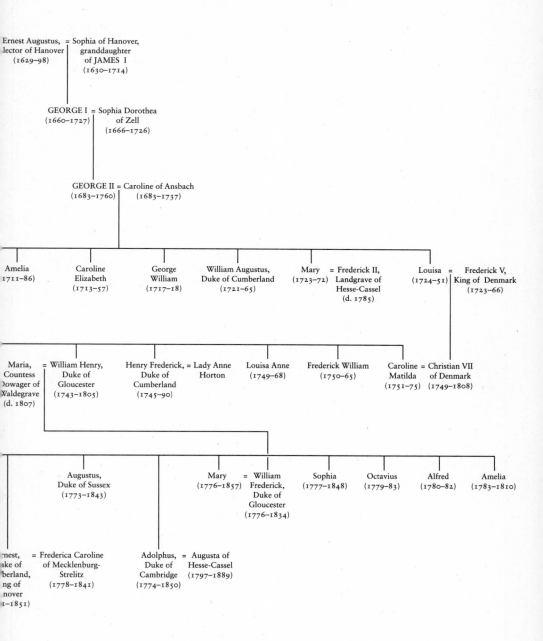

Ernest Augustus, = Sophia of Hanover,
lector of Hanover | granddaughter
(1629–98) | of JAMES I
(1630–1714)

GEORGE I = Sophia Dorothea
(1660–1727) | of Zell
(1666–1726)

GEORGE II = Caroline of Ansbach
(1683–1760) | (1683–1737)

Amelia
1711–86)

Caroline
Elizabeth
(1713–57)

George
William
(1717–18)

William Augustus,
Duke of Cumberland
(1721–65)

Mary = Frederick II,
(1723–72) Landgrave of
Hesse-Cassel
(d. 1785)

Louisa = Frederick V,
(1724–51) King of Denmark
(1723–66)

Maria, = William Henry,
Countess Duke of
)owager of Gloucester
Waldegrave (1743–1805)
(d. 1807)

Henry Frederick, = Lady Anne
Duke of Horton
Cumberland
(1745–90)

Louisa Anne
(1749–68)

Frederick William
(1750–65)

Caroline = Christian VII
Matilda of Denmark
(1751–75) (1749–1808)

Augustus,
Duke of Sussex
(1773–1843)

Mary = William
(1776–1857) Frederick,
Duke of
Gloucester
(1776–1834)

Sophia
(1777–1848)

Octavius
(1779–83)

Alfred
(1780–82)

Amelia
(1783–1810)

rnest, = Frederica Caroline
ake of of Mecklenburg-
berland, Strelitz
ng of (1778–1841)
nover
1–1851)

Adolphus, = Augusta of
Duke of Hesse-Cassel
Cambridge (1797–1889)
(1774–1850)

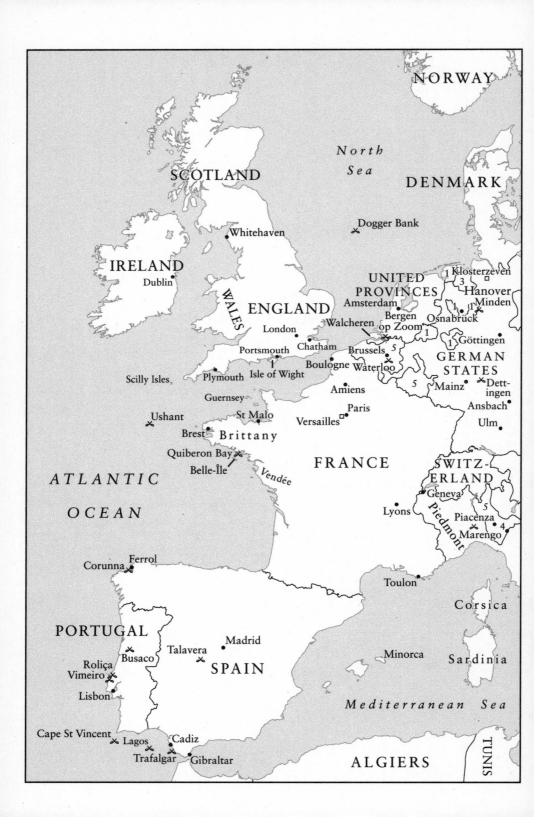

Europe in the
time of George III
—— 1763 borders
1. PRUSSIA   4. Parma
2. SWEDEN   5. HABSBURG
3. DENMARK   DOMINIONS
0   500 miles

Stockholm

Gothenburg

SWEDEN

Kronborg
Castle
Copenhagen
Zealand

*Baltic
Sea*

PRUSSIA

PRUSSIA

POLISH - LITHUANIAN
COMMONWEALTH

RUSSIAN
EMPIRE

Torgau
Hubertusburg   Leuthen
Rossbach
Jena–Auerstädt   *Silesia*

Kiev

Bohemia   Moravia

Austerlitz

Bavaria

Austria   Vienna

HABSBURG
DOMINIONS

Hungary

Venice

Bologna

MONTE-
NEGRO

*Black
Sea*

OTTOMAN

Bucharest

*ITALIAN
STATES Naples*

Rome

Constantinople

EMPIRE

*Strait of
Messina*

Sicily

Athens

Malta

Germany in the time of George III

— 1763 borders

0   100 miles

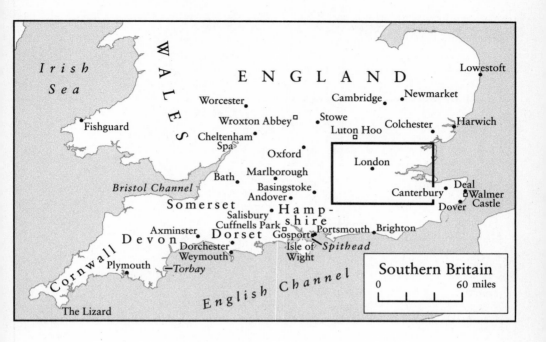

Irish Sea

WALES

ENGLAND

Lowestoft

Worcester

Cambridge
Newmarket

Wroxton Abbey
Stowe
Colchester
Harwich

Cheltenham Spa
Luton Hoo

Oxford

London

Bath
Marlborough

Deal

Basingstoke
Andover
Canterbury
Walmer Castle

Bristol Channel

Somerset

Salisbury
Hamp-
shire
Dover

Cuffnells Park
Portsmouth
Brighton

Axminster
Dorset
Gosport

Devon

Dorchester
Weymouth
Isle of Wight
Spithead

Cornwall

Plymouth
Torbay

English Channel

The Lizard

Southern Britain

0   60 miles

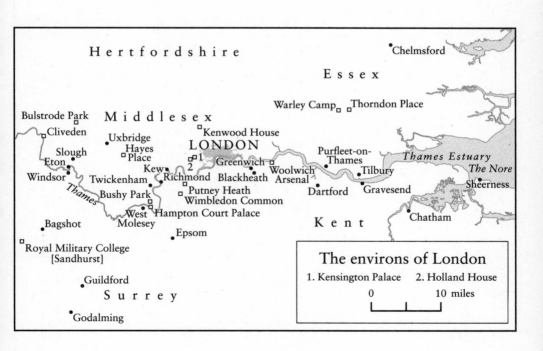

Hertfordshire

Chelmsford

Essex

Bulstrode Park

Middlesex

Warley Camp
Thorndon Place

Cliveden

Kenwood House

Uxbridge
LONDON

Thames Estuary

Slough
Hayes Place
Purfleet-on-Thames
The Nore

Eton
Kew
1
Greenwich
Tilbury

Windsor
Twickenham
Richmond
Blackheath
Woolwich Arsenal
Sheerness

Thames
2

Bushy Park
Putney Heath
Dartford
Gravesend

Bagshot
West Molesey
Wimbledon Common
Hampton Court Palace
Chatham

Royal Military College [Sandhurst]
Epsom
Kent

Guildford

Surrey

Godalming

The environs of London

1. Kensington Palace   2. Holland House

0   10 miles

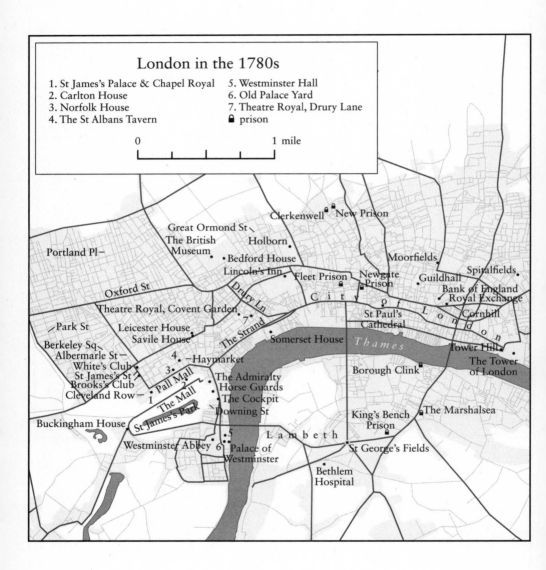

London in the 1780s

1. St James's Palace & Chapel Royal
2. Carlton House
3. Norfolk House
4. The St Albans Tavern
5. Westminster Hall
6. Old Palace Yard
7. Theatre Royal, Drury Lane
🔒 prison

0   1 mile

Clerkenwell   New Prison

Great Ormond St
The British   Holborn
Museum
Portland Pl—   Bedford House   Moorfields
Lincoln's Inn   Fleet Prison   Newgate   Spitalfields
Oxford St   Prison   Guildhall   Bank of England
Drury Ln   City of London   Royal Exchange
Theatre Royal, Covent Garden   St Paul's   Cornhill
Park St   Leicester House   The Strand   Cathedral
Berkeley Sq   Savile House   Somerset House   Thames   Tower Hill
Albermarle St—   4. —Haymarket   The Tower
White's Club   3.   of London
St James's St   The Admiralty   Borough Clink
Brooks's Club   Horse Guards
Cleveland Row— 1   2   The Cockpit   The Marshalsea
Pall Mall   Downing St   King's Bench
Buckingham House   The Mall   Lambeth   Prison
St James's Park   5   St George's Fields
Westminster Abbey   6   Palace of
Westminster   Bethlem
Hospital

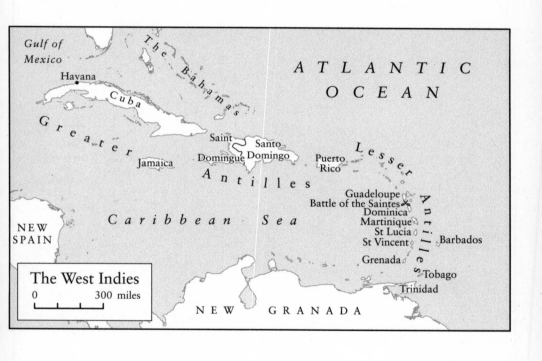

Gulf of
Mexico

The Bahamas

ATLANTIC
OCEAN

Havana

Cuba

Greater

Jamaica

Saint
Domingue

Santo
Domingo

Puerto
Rico

Lesser

Antilles

Caribbean Sea

NEW
SPAIN

Guadeloupe
Battle of the Saintes
Dominica
Martinique
St Lucia
St Vincent
Barbados

Antilles

Grenada

Tobago

Trinidad

NEW GRANADA

The West Indies

0   300 miles

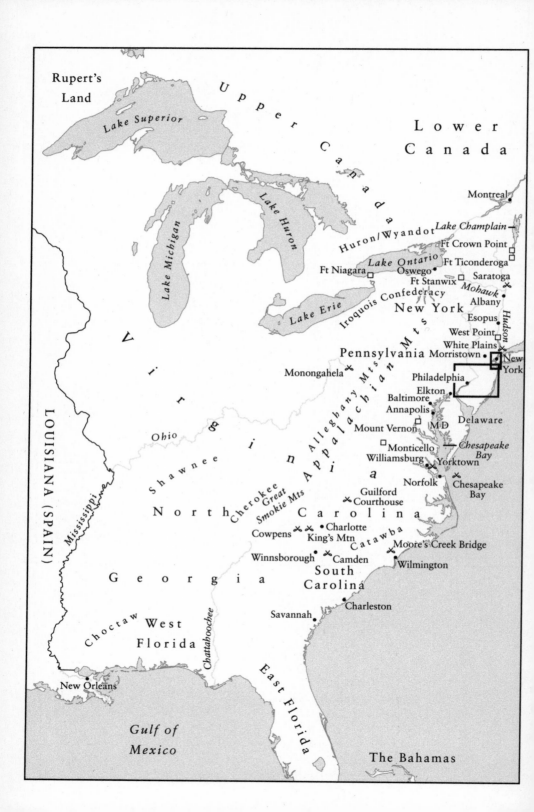

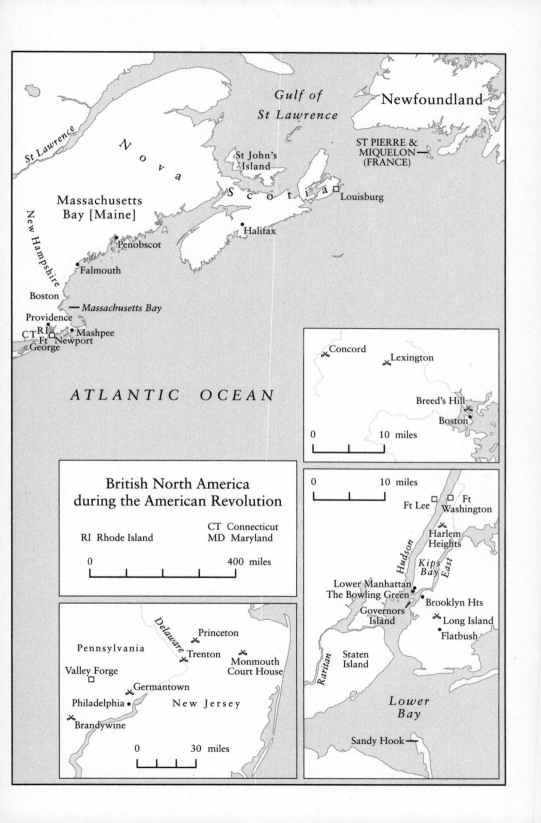

Gulf of
St Lawrence

Newfoundland

ST PIERRE &
MIQUELON ←
(FRANCE)

St Lawrence

N o v a

St John's
Island

S c o t i a

Louisburg

Massachusetts
Bay [Maine]

Halifax

New Hampshire

Penobscot

Falmouth

Boston

— *Massachusetts Bay*

Providence

CT RI
Ft Newport
George   • Mashpee

ATLANTIC OCEAN

Concord

Lexington

Breed's Hill

Boston

0   10 miles

British North America
during the American Revolution

RI Rhode Island

CT Connecticut
MD Maryland

0   400 miles

0   10 miles

Ft Lee   Ft
         Washington

Harlem
Heights

Hudson

Kips
Bay

East

Lower Manhattan
The Bowling Green

Brooklyn Hts

Governors
Island

Long Island

Flatbush

Delaware

Princeton

Trenton

Pennsylvania

Monmouth
Court House

Valley Forge

Germantown

Philadelphia •

New Jersey

Brandywine

Raritan

Staten
Island

*Lower
Bay*

Sandy Hook ←

0   30 miles

Author's Note

Eighteenth-century spelling, punctuation and capitalization were notoriously haphazard. I have generally standardized and modernized them for ease of reading, except where I feel meaning might otherwise have been lost. 'Reflexion' thus becomes 'reflection', 'sayd' is rendered 'said', 'shewing' is 'showing' and 'entir'ly' is 'entirely', while ampersands become 'and', nouns receive no automatic capitalization and so on.

Contemporary references to the 'premier', 'first minister', 'chief minister' or 'Prime Minister' in George III's reign referred to the First Lord of the Treasury, except in the case of the Chatham administration. I use the term Prime Minister even though it was not used officially until Benjamin Disraeli signed the Treaty of Berlin in 1878.

Some place names, such as Charles Town, South Carolina, have been updated as well.

The Julian calendar prevailed in Britain until 1751; I have given all dates according to the modern, Gregorian calendar.

When a word has a meaning today significantly different from the one current in the eighteenth century, I have given in a footnote the definition from the 1778 edition of Samuel Johnson's *Dictionary of the English Language* that most closely approximates to what I think the writer meant.

The modern equivalents of eighteenth-century monetary values vary wildly according to context and date, but £1 then was worth very roughly £125 today.

Introduction

As he prances on to the stage in *Hamilton: An American Musical*, singing three show-stopping numbers, King George III somehow manages to be comic yet cruel, camp yet sinister. It is a difficult feat to pull off in the theatre, but the character as portrayed in Lin-Manuel Miranda's award-winning production does it to perfection. 'You'll remember you belong to me,' a sardonic, preening, pompous monarch sings, and 'You were mine to subdue,' and 'I will kill your friends and family to remind you of my love.'

Thomas Paine, the author of the most influential pamphlet of the King's reign, *Common Sense*, published in 1776, would certainly have agreed with these lines. He described George as 'the Royal Brute of Britain' who had 'athirst for absolute power', adding 'Even brutes do not devour their young, nor savages make war upon their families.'[1]

The theme of George's tyranny saw its apogee in Thomas Jefferson's Declaration of Independence later that same year, which justified the American War of Independence through no fewer than twenty-eight intensely personal charges against the King. 'A prince, whose character is thus marked by every act which may define a tyrant,' Jefferson wrote, 'is unfit to be the ruler of a free people.'[2]

This portrait of a heartless, absolute sovereign is repeated almost every single day in America's print and online media. Even two centuries after his death, hardly a day passes in the United States without some reference to George III in different publications, where he is still held up as the template for arbitrary government. He is an equal-opportunities hate-figure, an archetypal bogeyman attacked in the same measure by Democrats and Republicans alike.

Here are just some sentences plucked virtually at random from the United States media recently: 'In America,' says the *Reno Gazette-Journal*, 'we had our own problems with the notion of absolute power enshrined in the personage of a monarch residing on some distant throne.'[3] 'The British King represented an oppressive arm of the English government,' states the *Greenfield Recorder*.[4] 'King George III didn't allow the colonists any say in the laws that governed them,' claims the *Huntingdon Daily News*.[5] The *Boston Herald* calls him a 'power-mad little petty tyrant'.[6] 'Would England have been better off if the King had not been so dictatorial?' asks the *North Augusta Star*.[7] He was 'the last authoritarian ruler America had', according to the *Eugene Weekly*.[8] 'They have a standing army inside their country and use it to take away people's liberties,' claims the *Deseret News* in reference to George's Britain.[9] 'The last dictator we had was King George III,' states the *Altoona Mirror* of a man who, according to the *Hartford Courant*, was 'a despotic monarch'.[10] The *Towanda Daily Review* meanwhile decries 'the tyrannical rule of King George III'.[11]

This daily reviling of an eighteenth-century king in the twenty-first-century American media faithfully reflects Paine's and Jefferson's claims, but also the views of the British Whig and Liberal politicians and historians of the nineteenth and early twentieth centuries, who, if anything, were even more personal in their dislike. 'In all that related to his kingly office,' declared Lord Brougham of the King, 'he was the slave of deep-rooted selfishness, and no feeling of a kindly nature ever was allowed access to his bosom.'[12] W. E. H. Lecky thought George 'ignorant, narrow-minded and arbitrary', adding that his plans for America were 'as criminal as any of the acts which led Charles the First to the scaffold'.[13] Lecky also described George as 'A sovereign of whom it may be said without exaggeration that he inflicted more profound and enduring injuries upon his country than any other modern English king.'[14] (One wonders what he could have said if he *had* wanted to exaggerate.) George Otto Trevelyan described George as 'a ruler who cherished every abuse in Church and State'.[15] Not to be outdone, his son George Macaulay Trevelyan, in his enormously influential *History of England*, castigated 'the attempt of George III to recover the powers of the Crown' and put Britain's defeat in the American War of Independence entirely down to 'the unbending stubbornness of George III'.[16]

Lord John Russell, the Liberal Prime Minister, believed that 'The project of restoring to the Crown that absolute direction and control which Charles the First and James the Second had been forced to relinquish . . . was entertained and attempted by George the Third.'[17] The Conservative Prime Minister Stanley Baldwin agreed. 'He hated the Cabinet system and he wanted to be, as King of England, the dictator of English policy,' he argued. 'He refused to submit to the Cabinet.'[18]

The historian Sir Lewis Namier diagnosed George's personality disorders as stemming from his childhood, because he had been a 'neurotic boy, bitter in soul and mentally underdeveloped'.[19] The King's biographer C. E. Vulliamy went much further, declaring that 'He abandoned his men and his principles . . . We should recognise him if we met him at a party in the underworld.'[20] Another biographer, J. C. Long, agreed, presenting George as 'sometimes seeming possessed of the Devil'.[21]

As well as his character, George's intellect has been denigrated for generations. When the Labour Foreign Secretary Ernest Bevin was asked by an American visitor why he had a gigantic portrait of King George III behind his desk, he answered: ''E's my hero. If he hadn't been so stupid, you wouldn't have been strong enough to come to our rescue in the war.'[22] Bevin's Tory wartime boss, Winston Churchill, merely thought George 'a limited man'.[23] Vulliamy described George as 'a stupid man at the end of his tether', and even as recently as 2018 a book on Lexington and Concord described the King having a 'vague, simplistic understanding of history and economics'.[24] The biographer Philip Guedalla thought him 'singularly unimpressive'; the Unitarian writer Alexander Gordon dubbed him 'George the Third-Rate', while the historian J. H. Plumb equated him with King John as 'one of England's most disastrous kings'.[25]

Ditty-writers concur: here are two humorous ones:

> George the Third
> Ought never to have occurred.
> One can only wonder
> At so grotesque a blunder.[26]
>
> Edmund Clerihew Bentley

> George the First was always reckoned
> Vile, but viler George the Second;
> And what mortal ever heard
> Any good of George the Third?
> When from earth the Fourth descended
> (God be praised!) the Georges ended.[27]
>
> Walter Savage Landor

Before mental illness came to be seen in a decent and modern way, historians regularly stigmatized George and ascribed what was called 'the King's Malady' to supposed defects in his personality. In 1941, Manfred Guttmacher linked the King's manic-depressive psychosis to his failure to establish autocratic power.[28] Plumb bizarrely believed it had been brought on by the strain of having to make love to his unattractive wife Queen Charlotte. In 1976 a biographer thought it worth asking 'whether or not it was the blight of God'.[29]

Yet now that Queen Elizabeth II has allowed over 200,000 pages of the Georgian Papers kept in the Royal Archives in the Round Tower of

Windsor Castle to be published – 85 per cent of them for the first time – it is at last possible to show that every single word quoted above about George III is completely wrong.

George undoubtedly made many errors during his sixty-year reign, and in an undated memorandum (probably written around 1766) he looked uncompromisingly at them. He wrote it, he said, so that 'the tongue of malice may not paint my intentions in those colours she admires, nor the sycophant extol me beyond what I deserve ... That I have erred is undoubted, otherwise I should not be human, but I flatter myself all un-prejudiced persons will be convinced that whenever I have failed it has been from the head not the heart.'[30]

What follows here is the true story of King George III. I hope that I have written without malice or sycophancy for 'all unprejudiced persons' to judge George objectively by the facts, unswayed by the opinions of Thomas Paine and Thomas Jefferson, Whig politicians and historians, Winston Churchill, modern websites and psycho-historians, or even by Lin-Manuel Miranda. At the end, all I request is that you ask yourself whether you have read the biography of a brute ('nay worse than brute'), a dictator and a tyrant, or rather the most unfairly traduced sovereign in the long history of the British monarchy.

I

Prince of Wales

June 1738–May 1756

Solitary trees, if they grow at all, grow strong: and a boy deprived of
his father's care often develops ... an independence and vigour of
thought which may restore in after life the heavy loss of early days.[1]
Winston Churchill, *The River War*, 1899

Prince George William Frederick of Hanover was born at Norfolk House
in St James's Square, London, between six and seven o'clock on the morning of 4 June 1738. He was the second child and first son of Frederick
Louis, Prince of Wales, and Augusta, the daughter of Frederick, Duke of
Saxe-Gotha. Born two months premature, he was privately baptized by
the Bishop of Oxford at eleven o'clock that night, in case he should die.
He was named in honour of his late great-grandfather, King George I,
whose Hanoverian dynasty had come to the throne of England just twenty-
four years earlier.

The Hanoverian dynasty has become a byword for family dysfunction.
George I had hated his eldest son George II, who had acceded to the throne
in 1727, and who in turn loathed his own eldest son Prince Frederick.
Indeed, the reason why the baby Prince George had been born in the Duke
of Norfolk's mansion house rather than in a royal palace was that George
II and his wife Queen Caroline of Ansbach so despised their eldest son
that he had escaped from them at the time of the birth of his first child.

Prince Frederick and Princess Augusta had been staying at his parents'
country residence of Hampton Court Palace when Princess Augusta's
waters broke in the middle of the night on 31 July of the previous year,
1737. Rather than have the baby born under his parents' roof, Frederick
had Augusta driven 12 miles by coach to St James's Palace to have the
baby – George's elder sister – delivered in London instead. Queen Caroline
retaliated by encouraging a rumour that her eldest son was impotent, thus
casting doubt on her own granddaughter's legitimacy. The rumour did not

take root, since it was known that Frederick kept a string of mistresses; as well as the beautiful courtesan Anne Vane, there was the daughter of a playhouse oboist, a prima donna at the opera, an apothecary's daughter from Kingston, and Grace, Countess of Middlesex, Princess Augusta's Mistress of the Robes.[2]

Queen Caroline was irreconcilable in her hatred of Prince Frederick, a consequence of his political opposition, supposed overspending and perceived unfilial slights against his parents. 'Look, there he goes,' Queen Caroline once told the courtier Lord Hervey on spotting Frederick from an upstairs window. 'That wretch! That villain! I wish the ground would open this moment and sink the monster to the lowest hole in Hell!'[3] In the German language which that generation of the royal family customarily spoke among themselves, the King called Frederick a *Wechselbalg* (changeling), but the Queen seems to have disliked him even more, telling Hervey, 'My dear first-born is the greatest ass, and the greatest liar, and the greatest canaille [blackguard], and the greatest beast, in the whole world, and I most heartily wish he was out if it.'[4]*

If Prince Frederick tried to visit his mother on her deathbed, the King ordered a courties to 'Bid him go about his business; for his poor mother is not in a condition to see him act his false, whining, cringing tricks now, nor am I in a humour to bear his impertinence; and bid him trouble me with no more messages, but get out of my house.'[5] Queen Caroline died on 20 November 1737, but not without a vicious parting shot at her eldest son. 'At least I shall have one comfort in having my eyes eternally closed,' she said of him, '– I shall never see that monster again.'[6]

When Prince George was born seven months later, Frederick's friend John Perceval, 2nd Earl of Egmont, noted in his diary that 'His Majesty took little notice of it, on account of the difference between him and His Royal Highness, only laughed and said the saddler's wife was brought to bed,' an allusion to Frederick's recent election to the governorship of the Worshipful Company of Saddlers, a City livery company.[7] The King had demanded Frederick's eviction from St James's Palace, 'as soon as ever the safety and convenience of the Princess will permit', forcing Frederick to take the lease on the Duke of Norfolk's house until 1743 when he was able to buy his own residence, Leicester House in Leicester Square.[8]†

Personality clashes, oppositional politics and vicious rows over money all combined to ensure that George grew up in an atmosphere overshadowed

---

* Hervey's diaries need to be treated with caution, however, as Anne Vane had left him for Frederick.
† On the site of today's Empire cinema.

by his grandfather's hatred of his father, a loathing that was fully reciprocated. It had been a joyous day for the King in 1737 when the House of Commons turned down a proposal to increase his son's allowance from £50,000 per annum to £100,000 per annum – the sum he himself had enjoyed when Prince of Wales – by 234 votes to 204.[9]

What made the Hanoverians' intergenerational hatreds all the stranger was that as a very young dynasty in Britain – although an old one in their native Hanover – their throne was hardly secure. The Act of Settlement in 1701 had vested the succession, after the death of the childless Queen Anne, in her second cousin Sophia, the wife of Elector Ernest Augustus of Hanover and mother of the future George I. Sophia was a niece of the deposed Charles I of England and sister of Prince Rupert of the Rhine, and the only Protestant with a reasonably direct claim to the throne.

The main purpose of the Act was to exclude Roman Catholics from the succession, so the Hanoverians essentially owed their claim entirely to their Protestantism (they were Lutherans who converted to Anglicanism when George I acceded), and to the Bloodless and Glorious Revolution of 1688 that had deposed Charles I's Catholic son James II, replacing him with the Protestant King William III, Stadtholder of the Netherlands, and his wife Queen Mary II (James II's daughter). The Revolution had thus overthrown the absolutist Stuarts in favour of a limited, constitutional monarchy, but there followed two major Jacobite (from Jacobus, Latin for James) uprisings in 1715 and 1745 as first James II's son the Old Pretender and then his grandson the Young Pretender ('Bonnie Prince Charlie') sought to recapture the throne. Yet even these grave international and domestic threats could not unify the Hanover dynasty.

For all the danger presented by his premature birth, Prince George grew into a healthy boy. He later put this down to the ministrations of his wet nurse, Mary Smith. 'She suckled me,' he wrote upon her death in 1773, 'and to her great attention my having been reared is greatly owing.'[10] In thanks he made her the royal laundress when he became king and ensured that her daughter inherited the post after her. The four-year-old Prince George was described by an MP's wife as a fat and 'lovely child'.[11] He certainly had loving parents, a welcome exception to the Hanoverian custom. 'You have a father who loves you all tenderly,' Frederick wrote to his children on one occasion, and on another he told George that he was 'a father who (what is not usual) is your best friend'.[12]

Frederick had been born in Hanover and only came to England in 1728 aged twenty-one, but he fully identified as British. This was probably another reason why his parents hated him, as George II was happiest when he was in Hanover, where he went for several months every other year. Frederick was also determined that his own children – of whom there were nine born between 1737 and 1751 – should be brought up as British. At a ball he threw for his eldest daughter Princess Augusta's third birthday at Cliveden in Buckinghamshire, the country house he leased for the summer months, Frederick commissioned Thomas Arne to compose the music for *The Masque of Alfred* about the ninth-century English monarch Alfred the Great, a piece today best known for its powerful finale, 'Rule, Britannia!'.

In sharp contrast to the philistinism of the Court of George II – Alexander Pope called him 'Dunce the Second' – Frederick and Augusta were cultured patrons of the arts. They collected Van Dyck, Rubens, George Knapton and Barthélemy du Pan, and employed William Kent to design botanical gardens at Kew (where they had a summer residence) and to reconstruct the Prince of Wales' official residence at Carlton House on the Mall. They are widely credited with having brought the rococo style to Britain. Frederick wrote French verse, visited Pope at Twickenham and knew Jonathan Swift. He supported the natural philosopher John Theophilus Desaguliers, Sir Isaac Newton's experimental assistant. Augusta promoted the painter Jean-Étienne Liotard, as well as the craft of clock- and watchmaking.[13] George therefore grew up in a highly cultured household.

A lover of music, Frederick played the cello, commissioned Handel to compose an anthem for his wedding and put on amateur dramatics at Cliveden featuring his own songs and poems, which, even if they were not particularly distinguished, still placed him on a far higher artistic plane than George I or George II. Frederick was also an early enthusiast for cricket, although his captaincy of the Surrey team probably owed more to his rank than to proficiency at the crease.

Despite being fated always to be in political opposition – such was the patronage and power available to the governments of the eighteenth and early nineteenth centuries that they rarely lost general elections – Frederick had a strong sense of what he wanted to achieve when he became king, and a natural sense of public relations. He would walk the streets un-attended by bodyguards, he would drink at the local public houses around Cliveden and he was ready to enter, in the words of one near-contemporary, 'the cottages of the poor, listen with patience to their twice-told tales, and partake with relish of the[ir] humble fare', leaving them with a few guineas as well as his friendly regards.[14]

On 27 June 1743, when George was five years old, his grandfather became the last British king to command an army in person, defeating the French at the battle of Dettingen in the War of Austrian Succession. The thirty-six-year-old Frederick's request to take part in the campaign had been ignored by his father. Instead, the King's third and favourite son, Prince William Augustus, Duke of Cumberland, was given a corps to command and was severely wounded in the leg by a musket ball. He became a national hero, but it caused bad blood between him and Frederick that would fester for years.

The situation worsened two years later when Cumberland was chosen to command the forces that put down the Jacobite rebellion of James II's grandson the Young Pretender. Once again Frederick offered to serve, but was turned down, even though every English male monarch for the past two and a half centuries (except for the boy-king Edward VI and the pacific James I) had fought on a military campaign.[15] According to the Whig MP and diarist Horace Walpole, whose father Sir Robert Walpole had been Prime Minister at the time, 'When the royal army lay before [the Jacobite-held city of] Carlisle, the Prince, at a great supper that he gave to his Court and his favourites . . . had ordered for the dessert the representation of the citadel of Carlisle in paste [pastry], which he in person, and the maids of honour, bombarded with sugar plums!'[16]

Was this levity intended to draw attention to Frederick's frustration at being forbidden to fight, or a somewhat laboured jape, or just a fun post-prandial diversion? Was it even true, given Horace Walpole's capacity for malicious invention? If it did happen, it emphasizes Frederick's enforced impotence compared to the effectiveness of Cumberland, a brother fourteen years his junior who was busy in the north saving the dynasty. Even Cumberland's brutal reprisals against the Jacobite Highlanders after his victory at the battle of Culloden in April 1746, which earned him the nickname 'Butcher', failed to dent his popularity in the Court or the country; indeed, it might even have enhanced it.

No record survives of what the seven-year-old George felt during those nerve-wracking days of the Jacobite rebellion, when the rebels marched as far south as Derby, just 130 miles from London. However, in September 1747 Frederick announced himself 'well pleased' with his son's spirited strictures against the Governor of Bergen op Zoom for surrendering his city without a fight towards the end of the War of Austrian Succession. We cannot know whether a horror of rebellion was instilled in the boy by the frantic preparations of Londoners to escape the capital should it fall to the Jacobites in 1745, but he certainly grew up in the knowledge that his ultimate accession to the throne was still threatened a full three decades after his great-grandfather had become king. Instinctive to the Hanoverian dynasty was the assumption that rebellions, if they could not be reasoned with, must be crushed by overwhelming force.

One of the reasons why Prince Frederick emphasized his own and his son's Englishness was that it served as an unsubtle critique of his Germanic father the King, but another was that so long as the Hanoverians were perceived as foreigners their occupation of the throne might be insecure. Frederick's campaign of anglicization reached its apogee when he staged a production of Joseph Addison's play *Cato* 'before a numerous court of the nobility' at Leicester House on 4 January 1749.* A paean to the liberty brought over by William III during the Glorious Revolution, it lauded 'the great William brought to bless this land . . . Of power well bounded'.[17] The cast included Frederick and Augusta's four eldest children – Princess Augusta (who was eleven), Prince George (ten), Prince Edward, Duke of York (nine) and Princess Elizabeth (seven). George played Portius and delivered a prologue specially written by his father:

> 'tis the first great lesson I was taught,
> What, tho' a boy! It may with truth be said
> A boy in *England* born, in England bred,
> Where freedom best becomes the earliest state,
> For there the love of liberty's innate.[18]

One of the other child actors in that production was the sixteen-year-old Frederick North, playing Syphax. He was the son of Francis North, Lord Guilford, one of Frederick's lords of the bedchamber (a post traditionally held by the Prince's closest friends and advisers). As George did not go to school, his playmates and friends were drawn from his own siblings and a small group of aristocratic courtiers' children, of whom Frederick North was one, despite the large age gap. The Prince and Princess of Wales' Court was a close-knit group that made its own amusements. In 1748, Lady Hervey noted that the young Prince George and the other royal children were playing 'at baseball, a play all who are or have been schoolboys are well acquainted with'.[19] She added that 'the ladies as well as the gentlemen join in this amusement'. It was a form of rounders that later became popular in America – a game that, ironically, George III played but George Washington did not.

Nine days after the production of *Cato*, Frederick wrote a political testament for his son's guidance in the event of his early death, the full title of which included a dig at his father: 'Instructions for my Son George, Drawn by Myself, for His Good, that of my Family and for that of His People, According to the Ideas of my Grandfather and Best Friend, George I'. 'To my son George,' it began:

---

* The Irish actor James Quin, who coached George during the rehearsals, would later try to take the credit for George's clarity of delivery when he gave his first Speech from the Throne.

as I always have had the tenderest paternal affection for you, I cannot give you a stronger proof of it than in leaving this paper for you in your mother's hands, who will read it to you from time to time and will give it to you when you come of age or when you get the Crown . . . I entertain no doubt of your good heart, nor of your honour; things I trust you will never lose out of sight. The perverseness and bad examples of the times, I am sure, will never make you forget them.[20]

The assumption that they had the misfortune to be living through a particularly dissolute and dissipated era was a common one, and was later to be enthusiastically adopted by George.

Although Frederick was only forty-one, the testament was written as if he were on his deathbed. 'I shall have no regret never to have wore the crown,' he wrote, 'if you do but fill it worthily. Convince this nation that you are not only an Englishman born and bred, but that you are also this by inclination, and that as you will love your younger children next to the elder born, so you will love all your other countries, next to England.'[21] Frederick also mentioned the rarity and value of finding a trustworthy friend who would tell the Prince the truth. In future years, as we shall see, George cleaved to this advice if anything too closely.

The specific policies that Prince Frederick advocated in his letter were few: they included the avoidance of war and the gradual repayment of the National Debt by keeping public spending within the revenues raised by the two-shilling (10 per cent) land tax and the malt tax. He also suggested breaking the personal union of Britain and Hanover under the British Crown, by having one of Frederick's brothers or uncles become Elector of Hanover when George became King of England. There was nothing about trying to increase the already very wide prerogatives enjoyed by the Crown under the Act of Settlement of 1689, which had sealed the Glorious Revolution. Later commentators, such as the Irish-born Whig MP Edmund Burke, came to believe that Frederick had wanted to extend Crown powers, but there is no evidence for it; indeed Frederick specified that his plan to decouple Hanover depended on gaining 'the sanction of the [Holy Roman] Empire and the authority of an Act of Parliament'.[22]

Frederick believed that reduction of the National Debt was vital, and 'if not done, will surely one time or other create such a disaffection and despair that I dread the consequences for you, my dear son'.[23] In hoping that George would be a wise man and brave prince, Frederick added, 'If you can be without war, let not your ambition draw you into it. A good deal of the National Debt must be paid off before England enters a war: at the same time, never give up your honour nor that of the nation.'[24] To this concept of intertwined personal and national honour George was to return again and again throughout his reign, probably impelled by his father's clearly heartfelt political testament.

Although only half a dozen letters from Frederick to his children survive, they all show a loving father, deeply interested in their upbringing. 'That none of you, my dear George, may ever forget your duty but always be a blessing to your family and country is the prayer of your friend and father,' reads one; another asks the boy to write more often, 'which will make me happy as nothing can do more than a prospect to say my children turn [out to be] an honour to me and a blessing to my country'.[25] 'Pray God that you may grow in every respect above me,' he wrote in another, '– goodnight, my dear children.'[26]

On 22 June 1750, George II invested the twelve-year-old Prince George as a knight of the Garter, England's oldest and grandest order of chivalry, dating back to 1348, although he possibly only did so under advice from his ministers, who recognized that one day Frederick would be king. Frederick arrived to attend the ceremony, held in the King's Chamber at Hampton Court, but was forced to watch it through an open door from the next room because his father refused to receive him. The day after the investiture, George wrote his earliest extant letter, which was to the King in well-formed script: 'Sir, I hope you will forgive me the liberty I take to thank Your Majesty for the honour you did me yesterday. It is my utmost wish and shall always be my study to deserve your paternal goodness and protection. I am with the greatest respect and submission, Sir, Your Majesty's most humble and dutiful subject, George.'[27]

Initially George's education, together with that of his younger brother Prince Edward, was undertaken by the Rev. Francis Ayscough, Clerk of the Closet, but in September 1749 Frederick's friend Lord Guilford was appointed as their governor, Ayscough then concentrating solely on their religious education. Their new tutor was the scholar-mathematician George Lewis Scott. Although Scott had been recommended to Frederick by the Tory politician Lord Bolingbroke and was later accused by Whigs of having been a Jacobite sympathizer, he had in fact been born in Hanover (where his father had held a Court appointment from George I, after whom he was named), and there was no hint of any unpatriotic allegiances.*

Between them, Frederick and Guilford laid down a programme of instruction for the two young princes that covered almost every moment of their weekdays. They awoke at 7 a.m., attended classes from 8 a.m. to

---

* At least at that point in his career; much later on Scott became a follower of Thomas Paine, a very strange political trajectory.

12.30 p.m., then enjoyed an hour of play before more lessons. After dinner at 3 p.m. there were further lessons until supper at 8 p.m., and the boys went to bed between 9 p.m. and 10 p.m. They learned Latin, mathematics, history, French, German, geography, elementary science, art and architecture, as well as dancing and fencing. On Sunday mornings there was divine service, followed by ninety minutes of instruction in the doctrines of the Church of England, from which George developed the devout Anglican faith that guided him throughout his life.

It was an unrelenting schedule, and while it offered a much better education than most of the great public schools provided, crucially the boys did not grow up in the company of children of their own age beyond a few of their courtiers' sons, with the result that George developed into a somewhat shy and introverted boy. He was not a stupid one, however. Horace Walpole and a succession of Whig historians presented George as a slow pupil who struggled with reading and writing. It is an enduring claim that still persists; a typical accusation is that George was 'apathetic, sleepy, dull and backward, unable to read properly until he was eleven'.[28] In fact his exercise books in the Royal Archives show that George was perfectly competent at reading and writing English by the age of nine and corresponded with his father in German aged twelve. By fifteen he was translating from Latin, translating classical texts including some philosophy. Around this time he also composed an essay in French on kingship from the story of Telemachus.[29]

Early in 1751, Frederick and Augusta settled the twelve-year-old George and eleven-year-old Edward at Savile House, adjoining Leicester House. It was the Hanoverian practice to give princes their own establishments early, and Savile House, built in the 1680s, was to become George's London home for the next nine years. His mini-Court there consisted of a governor, preceptor (responsible for teaching), sub-governor, sub-preceptor and treasurer, with part-time teachers for languages, fencing, dancing and riding brought in from outside. He studied algebra, geometry and trigonometry. He was the first British monarch to study science, being taught basic physics and chemistry by Scott. He was receiving a good, all-round, enlightened education.

The monarch was the head of eighteenth-century governments, which tended to be formed by factions formed around prominent individuals; there were no political parties based on delineated ideology in the modern sense. Cabinet ministers considered themselves to be directly responsible to the King rather than to a prime minister and there was no concept of a Loyal Opposition, merely the supporters of factions that were not in government, whose exclusion from power and influence was underlined by the fact that the King did not invite them to Levees and Drawing Rooms, and they were therefore consigned to the political wilderness. Honours, patronage and sinecures were reserved solely for government supporters, hence the constant jockeying for position among the factions that so characterized the politics of the era.

Neither the Whigs nor the Tories were political parties in anything approaching the modern sense of the term, in that a member of Parliament would consider himself to be not so much primarily a Whig or Tory MP as a county or borough MP, or a friend of Mr Pelham, or a Court supporter, and so on. Whigs and Tories had separate political philosophies, but it was not until the nineteenth century that MPs identified themselves through ideology as opposed to faction.

Britain had effectively become a one-party state in 1714, when soon after coming to the throne George I had expelled the Tories from all positions of authority in the country because they were suspected – in a few cases correctly, but mostly wrongly – of having Stuart rather than Hanoverian sympathies. Some three decades later, Toryism remained a political philosophy that dared not speak its name. There were fewer than a hundred Tory MPs in a House of Commons totalling 558, and almost none of any stature, since anyone of talent or ambition joined the ruling Whigs. Yet although to George I and George II Tory men were pariahs to be kept away from government, Tory measures could seep back into the body politic, albeit championed by politicians who outwardly at least still professed to be Whigs.[30] In the reigns of those two Hanoverians, neither the Whigs nor the Tories had elected leaders or had a party membership. Both reflected tendencies and traditions that went back to the Civil War period of the 1640s.

Yet Tories no longer passed their wine glasses over water jugs as they toasted the monarch at dinner, a secret code indicating that their true allegiance was to the Jacobite Pretender, who lived 'over the water' in exile in Rome. Similarly, all but the most fanatical Jacobites had long ceased toasting 'The little gentleman in the black velvet waistcoat', an equally euphemistic reference to the mole whose burrow had caused William III's horse to throw him, break his collarbone and bring about his early death from pneumonia.

Although Prince Frederick and the Leicester House Set were not Tories as such, several had Tory sympathies and they wanted to reform the system by which parliamentary elections had for decades been manipulated by the 'Old Corps' or 'Old Whig' government – also nicknamed the 'Old Gang' – that had ruled Britain since the Glorious Revolution. Whigs tended to emphasize the advantages of trade, Continental commitments to protect Hanover and sharing out jobs ('places') between themselves. Yet, for all their reformism, the various means by which the Leicester House Set intended to win and keep power looked suspiciously like those by which the Old Whigs such as Sir Robert Walpole and the Pelham family – Henry Pelham and his brother Thomas Pelham, 1st Duke of Newcastle – had ruled through an oligarchy of Whig aristocrat cousins.[31]

Prince Frederick and the Leicester House Set were attracted by the political philosophy of the septuagenarian Tory radical Henry St John, 1st Viscount Bolingbroke, who had long been Walpole and the Old Whigs' greatest ideological and parliamentary adversary. Bolingbroke had indeed been a Jacobite for a period and had been forced to live in exile until 1723, but he was a gifted intellectual who numbered Pope, Voltaire, Jonathan Swift and Thomas Gray among his friends. In the late 1720s and early 1730s, he hoped to create a political movement in which a 'Country' (that is, anti-London) party of squires and patriots would oppose what he saw as Old Whig corruption and demand a more efficient government, one that would end – or at least ameliorate – the system of jobbery, nepotism and patronage personified by Sir Robert Walpole.

Because the monarch was the head of state, and government ministers were his servants, it followed that any Prince of Wales who was estranged from him would naturally come to be seen as the leader of the oppositional faction in Parliament and the country. In his struggles with a hateful father and what he considered a corrupt Court, Frederick seemed to have one inestimable advantage on his side: time. 'The Prince of Wales gains strength in Parliament', noted the statesman and writer Lord Chesterfield in April 1749, 'in proportion as the King grows older.'[32] Frederick gathered around him at Leicester House a shadow Cabinet of Opposition politicians, who would take over the government on the death of the King. The Leicester House Set included Lord Egmont (whom Frederick intended to make Prime Minister), Robert Henley (later Lord Northington), George Bubb Dodington MP and Sir Francis Dashwood MP, who enjoyed an exaggerated reputation as a libertine.[33]

The political ideas of Lord Bolingbroke coalesced in the mid- to late 1730s, just at the time that Frederick and the Leicester House Set were looking for a political ideology to differentiate themselves from George II, Walpole and the Pelhams. For Frederick and his friends, Bolingbroke was no longer the feared and suspected Tory–Jacobite of old: having now embraced loyalty to the Hanoverian succession, he was for them an eloquent harbinger of a new concept of politics. Bolingbroke's book *The Idea of a Patriot King*, written and distributed privately in 1738 but only published in 1749, became their unofficial manifesto. Yet, for Bolingbroke's Old Whig opponents, the 'Patriot' or Country movement ideologically entwined with the Leicester House Set looked suspiciously like the Stuart absolutism that their forefathers had overthrown half a century earlier in the Glorious Revolution.

Given their subsequent influence on Prince George, as well as on his father and his father's friends, the thinking expressed in *The Idea of a Patriot King* is worth examination. Bolingbroke's condemnation of the political establishment of his age from a Country perspective has been described as 'a classical, humanistic and agrarian dread of corruption, and the sad conviction that eighteenth-century England was corrupt to the core, or very near it'.[34] Bolingbroke opposed the Whig special-interest groups that he believed were becoming increasingly dominant in politics and society. This could only be done by what he called 'a coalition of parties meeting on a national bottom'.[35] The genesis of George's attempts throughout his reign to replace the Whig oligarchs with a broadly based national coalition of patriots regardless of faction can be traced back to these ideas of the 1730s.

Contrary to the Whig imperative of minimizing royal power, *The Idea of a Patriot King* argued that the role of a constitutionally limited hereditary monarchy was important. Bolingbroke fully accepted that such seventeenth-century notions as the Divine Right of Kings had 'no foundation in fact or reason', and he believed 'a limited monarchy the best of governments'.[36] The limits on the power of the Crown, he maintained, should be 'carried as far as is necessary to secure the liberties of the people' and enough to protect the people against an arrogant (by which he meant Old Whig) aristocracy.[37] Bolingbroke's patriot king would revere the constitution, regard his prerogatives as a sacred trust, 'espouse no party' and 'govern like the common father of his people'.[38]

A key message of the book was that government by party inevitably resulted in a factionalism disastrous to the state. 'Party is a political evil,' Bolingbroke wrote, 'and faction is the worst of all parties. The king will aim at ruling a united nation, and in order to govern wisely and successfully he will put himself at the head of his people,' so that he can deliver them 'tranquillity, wealth, power and fame'.[39] These notions might sound utopian, but George took them to heart, and many of his actions as monarch can be seen as attempts to live up to the idea of a patriot king that this Tory political philosopher had prescribed for his father. Indeed, it is impossible to understand many of George's actions as king unless one recognizes the profound influence of *The Idea of a Patriot King*, the wider political assumptions of the Leicester House Set and his revered father's political testament. Many of their ideals were naive, but they were undeniably attractive compared to the Old Whigs' governing principle of relentless appeal to politicians' love of titles, money and sinecures.

The patriot rulers that Bolingbroke most admired included Henri IV of France and Elizabeth I of England, because he saw their rule as 'broad-based upon the people's will'. He argued strongly against unnecessary foreign entanglements and against the retention of a large standing army, except as a last resort and for short periods in order to foster the balance of power in Europe. An important aspect of a patriot king's rule was that upon his accession he would expel adventurers and corrupt politicians from office and replace them with honest patriots, thereby winning the support and love of a contented people. When Bolingbroke was writing in 1738 this meant ousting Walpole, who had been Prime Minister since 1721 and was to remain so until 1742. In foreign policy, Bolingbroke contended, Britain ought to look to her colonies around the globe rather than to Europe (including Hanover), where he believed the patriot king would triumphantly extend 'the right and the honour of Great Britain as far as waters roll and as winds can waft them'.[40]

In April 1749, Frederick and Egmont drew up a 'List of those who must if possible be kept out of the House of Commons', which, although never acted upon, is useful for identifying those whom the Leicester House Set saw as their chief opponents. The Old Corps stalwart Henry Pelham was 'to be obliged (if he can be made) to go up to the House of Lords'; the venal Commons influencer Henry Fox was 'to have some very profitable employment (though it should be for life) which will be inconsistent with a seat in Parliament'; the ambitious Whig orator William Pitt was 'to have likewise some profitable employment and inconsistent with a seat in Parliament'; the capable but unprepossessing George Grenville* was 'to be kept out', as were his fellow moderates William Legge and William Barrington ('but perhaps in time brought in by us'). There was another list, comprising eighteen of 'The most obnoxious men of an inferior degree', which included staunch Whigs such as Colonel Henry Conway and Lord George Sackville.[41] Frederick and Egmont understood the political landscape: their diverse list included all the impressive up-and-coming Whig politicians of the day, as identified by a clique seemingly determined to define itself by its enemies.

On 16 March 1751, Frederick was gardening at Kew when he was suddenly caught in a rain shower. He later attended the House of Lords in

---

* Spelt 'Greenville' in that and many other documents.

heavy, sodden clothes, before changing into lighter ones, went back to Kew for a walk in the garden and at last returned to Carlton House on the Mall where he reportedly rested by an open window. This seems to have triggered a pre-existing condition, and the next day he was taken ill with what the doctors correctly diagnosed as pleurisy, or inflammation of the lungs. He was blistered and bled according to standard practice, and by 26 March he seemed out of danger. On the evening of Wednesday 31 March, however, he was eating bread and butter and drinking coffee when he had a sudden coughing fit. He then laid his hand on his stomach and said, 'Je sens le mort.'[42] His valet, Schrader, is said to have called out to Princess Augusta, 'The Prince is going,' but by the time she had found a candle and arrived, Frederick was dead.[43]

A post-mortem found that the forty-four-year-old Prince of Wales had died from an 'impostume' or swelling abscess in his breast that had burst and suffocated him. This was variously attributed to a blow from a cricket ball sustained at a match at Cliveden with his sons three years earlier or to a fall the previous summer, which had been aggravated by the pleurisy.[44]

Frederick was not widely mourned; today he is best known for the Jacobite squib:

> Here lies poor Fred, who was alive and is dead.
> We had rather it had been his father,
> Had it been his brother, better'n any other,
> Had it been his sister, no one would have missed her,
> Had it been the whole generation, all the better for the nation,
> But as it's just poor Fred, who was alive and is dead,
> There's no more to be said.[45]

George was two months short of his thirteenth birthday when his father died. It dealt him a devastating blow from which he took years to recover. When Ayscough told him the news, he went pale, pointed to his heart and said, 'I feel something here, just as I did when I saw two workmen fall from the scaffold at Kew.'[46] His mother Princess Augusta was thirty-one and pregnant with a ninth child, and she now had to take on her husband's sizeable debts. She was over-protective towards George, and occasionally given to paranoiac fears about her in-laws, but she was not the strong-willed, power-obsessed, 'passionate, domineering woman' and political absolutist portrayed, with no evidence whatever, by Walpole and later Whig historians and propagandists.

Augusta was only sixteen when she had arrived in England to marry Frederick, not formally educated and speaking no English, but she learned it quickly and was a good mother and good person, and certainly did not deserve the slurs that were shortly to be directed at her. (She was even widely accused of having poisoned her husband, with no evidence.) Overshadowed by Weimar in today's imagination, in the eighteenth century Augusta's birthplace of Saxe-Gotha was well known as a centre of Enlightenment culture and science, and modern historians free of the political and misogynistic bias of Horace Walpole and others agree that she was a credit to her origins.[47] In December 1804, long after her death, George reminisced that 'his mother was a very sensible woman and entirely governed his father at the end of his life'.[48] She was now left in an impossible position, and could only appeal to the mercy of her father-in-law, writing to the King the day after her husband's death, 'I throw myself, with my children, at your feet. We commend ourselves, Sire, to your fatherly love and royal protection.'[49]

There had been no fatherly love whatever, as they both knew. 'I have lost my eldest son,' George II said at the end of the year, 'but I was glad of it.'[50] As for Frederick's burial, the King merely 'ordered the bowels to be put in a box' and three days later the undertakers had still not taken the box or the body away. 'The bowels not yet sewed up nor the body embalmed,' Egmont noted in his diary, 'a scandalous neglect. The smell is to be perceived over the whole house and descended even into Prince George's apartment.'[51] The key new relationship in British politics – that between George II and his grandson and heir apparent Prince George – therefore started off with the Prince subjected to the stench of his father's rotting corpse thanks to his grandfather's neglect.

The funeral took place in the Henry VII Chapel at Westminster Abbey on the afternoon of 13 April 1751. It was a cut-price affair, one mourner noting that 'no organ went, nor was there any anthem.'[52] George and his siblings were considered too young to attend, and, aside from Augusta, the official chief mourner at the funeral was the non-royal Duke of Somerset as the rest of the royal family and senior aristocracy, taking their cue from the King, stayed away; except for the pall-bearers there were no English lords, one lone bishop and only two privy councillors.[53] The procession was rained upon as no one had thought to erect a canopy between the House of Lords and the Abbey. Nor were there any catering arrangements, so Dodington, a friend of the Prince, and the Prince's former lords of the bedchamber were obliged to send out 'for a great cold dinner from a common tavern in the neighbourhood'.[54]

It was arranged that if the sixty-seven-year-old King died before George became eighteen, Augusta would become Dowager Princess Regent, but effective power would lie with the Duke of Cumberland and the Pelhams in a Regency Council. The King had originally wanted Cumberland to be Regent, but he was too unpopular among the Old Whig ministry. Augusta somehow gained the impression that Cumberland might launch a military coup against her regency, and over the coming years she passed on to George her intense distrust of his uncle.

George was allowed to continue to live at Savile House, and was occasionally invited to meet his grandfather at Hampton Court. These visits tended to be unhappy and unsuccessful, and on at least one occasion the King lost his temper and boxed the boy's ears so hard that, in the words of one of George's children many years later, 'The blow so disgusted him with the place that he could never afterwards be induced to think of it as a residence' – the reason why George never lived at Hampton Court as king.[55] (Indeed, when a fire broke out there in June 1770, he told a courtier that 'he should not have been sorry had it been burnt down'.)[56] The psychological impression made upon a twelve-year-old boy first by the death of a loving father and subsequently by the physical abuse at the hands of his callous grandfather naturally led George further to revere the memory of the former and despise the latter.

Three weeks after his father's death, on 20 April, George, who had automatically inherited the Duchy of Edinburgh, was created Prince of Wales. The Old Whigs recognized that George's education needed to be radically overhauled if they hoped to stay in power during the next reign. The Duke of Newcastle cashiered Lord Guilford as George's governor and replaced him first with a political supporter, Earl Harcourt. In reality, however, it was the new sub-governor Andrew Stone, Newcastle's former private secretary, who directed George's education. Half a century later, George recalled Harcourt as 'well intentioned, but wholly unfit for the situation in which he was placed'.[57] He remembered Thomas Hayter, the Bishop of Norwich, who became his preceptor, as 'an intriguing, unworthy man, more fitted to be a Jesuit than an English bishop'.[58] Although Ayscough was dismissed, Scott, whom a friend of George recalled as 'amiable, honourable, temperate, and one of the sweetest dispositions I ever knew', was confirmed as sub-preceptor.[59] Soon after his fifteenth birthday George began Latin translations, ending one piece with 'Monsieur Caesar, je vous soite [souhaite] au diable' ('Mr Caesar, I wish you'd go to the Devil').[60]

By October 1752, the notoriously miserly King's refusal to pay off Frederick's debts had left Augusta desperately short of money and extremely bitter. The King had clawed back Frederick's revenues from the Duchy of Cornwall on the basis that they belonged to the monarch's eldest son, not to that son's eldest son. George Dodington's diary records several conversations at Kew in which Augusta was openly disrespectful of the King, saying in January 1753 that 'She reckoned the King no more than one of the trees we walked by (or something more inconsiderable, which she named),' and the next month that 'The King would sputter and make a bustle' but not offer any actual financial help.[61] Of George and his tutors she said that 'she wished he were a little more forward, and less childish, at his age; that she hoped they would improve him . . . : that Stone was a sensible man, and capable of instructing in things, as well as books: that Lord Harcourt and the Prince agreed very well, but she thought he could not learn much from my Lord: that Scott, she believed, was a very good preceptor.'[62] She was unimpressed by the Bishop of Norwich.

Dodington took the view that George should not just be taught by books, but should 'begin to learn the usages, and knowledge of the world'; however, the Princess thought 'the young people of quality were so ill-educated, and so very vicious,* that they frightened her'.[63] She said of George 'that he was a very honest boy, and that his chief passion seemed to be [his friendship for his brother] Edward'.[64] She has been criticized for keeping the heir to the throne away from his contemporaries, but when one considers the schooling of the upper-class youths of the day – the regular revolts and uprisings at Eton were a case in point – she probably had good reason. The highly ambitious Dodington was worried – possibly for his own sake – that George was not being brought up to remember Frederick 'and those that were about him', but the Princess put him right, assuring him that George 'seemed to have a very tender affection for the memory of his father . . . she encouraged it as much as she could'.[65]

In November 1752 a scandal erupted at Savile House when Harcourt accused Stone of making George read supposed Jacobite tracts supporting arbitrary government, citing *The Idea of a Patriot King*. Furthermore, because he was a mathematician and Fellow of the Royal Society, Scott was suspected by Hayter of being an atheist, while James Cresset the treasurer also fell under suspicion of secret Jacobitism.[66] The King set up a committee of inquiry which did not take long to establish that there was no truth to the allegations that Stone, Scott and Cresset were all 'creatures of Lord Bolingbroke' – who had died the previous December – beyond an anonymous letter that had been written to a friend of Cumberland's. Many years later, Horace Walpole admitted to having written this himself out of hatred of Henry Pelham† for refusing him a lifetime sinecure of £1,400 per annum

---

* 'Devoted to vice' (*Johnson's Dictionary*).
† The animosity persisted even though the love of Walpole's life was the Earl of Lincoln, Henry Pelham's nephew and later the 2nd Duke of Newcastle.

that he believed was due to him as it had once belonged to his brother.[67] Walpole hoped it would damage Pelham with the King if it was believed that George was being infected with Jacobitism during Pelham's premiership, but the King and Pelham's brother Newcastle dismissed both the rumours and the letter. Harcourt and Norwich resigned, and, in Harcourt's place, James Waldegrave, the 2nd Earl Waldegrave, was appointed as George's governor and the Bishop of Peterborough was made preceptor.

Although Walpole had simply lied when he claimed that 'friends and pupils of the late Lord Bolingbroke' had co-opted George's education and were conspiring 'to overthrow the government and restore the exiled and arbitrary house of Stuart', the non-scandal had far-reaching ramifications.[68] Walpole's accusations of secret Jacobite influence, served to establish a myth that George had been indoctrinated by Tories as a believer in dictatorial Stuart theories of government, a conspiracy theory taken up by Whig politicians of the day and accepted by some Whig and Liberal historians thereafter. In a revealing self-portrait years later, Walpole wrote that he had 'a propensity to faction, and looked on the mischief of civil disturbance as a lively amusement'.[69]

The immediate upshot was that George had a new governor in Lord Waldegrave, of whom he said in 1804, four decades after Waldegrave's death, that he was a 'depraved worthless man', although it is not at all clear upon what he based that judgement.[70] Waldegrave similarly disliked George, noting in his memoirs that 'Whenever he is displeased, his anger does not break out with heat and violence, but he becomes sullen and silent, and retires to his closet, not to compose his mind by study or contemplation, but merely to indulge the melancholy enjoyment of his own ill humour.'[71] Although George might be excused for being little different from other teenagers in that regard, Waldegrave went on to say that 'Even when the fit is ended, unfavourable symptoms very frequently return, which indicate that on certain occasions His Royal Highness has too correct a memory.'[72]

It was certainly true that George, as king, retained a long memory for slights and enmities, but he also had one for kinder things such as tending ill relatives and remembering promises. Waldegrave claimed that George was 'uncommonly indolent', snobbishly and sarcastically adding that he was 'full of princely prejudices, contracted in the nursery, and improved by the society of bedchamber women and pages of the back stairs'.[73] When George was twenty, Waldegrave, who had not been his governor for two years, declared:

> His religion is free from all hypocrisy, but is not of the most charitable sort;
> he has rather too much attention to the sins of his neighbour. He ... does

not want* resolution, but it is mixed with too much obstinacy. He has great command of his passions, and will seldom do wrong, except when he mistakes wrong for right.[74]

The accusation of obstinacy would dog him throughout his life and was often deserved; but, as we shall see, on occasion it could be put to good use.

On 6 March 1754, Henry Pelham, who had been Prime Minister since August 1743, died suddenly, and was succeeded by his brother the Duke of Newcastle. An important question for the future direction of the ministry was who would succeed Pelham in the key role of Leader of the House of Commons: would it be Henry Fox, the Secretary at War, or William Pitt (later known to history as William Pitt the Elder), the Paymaster-General of the Forces? The rivalry between the two families, enthusiastically adopted by their sons Charles James Fox and William Pitt the Younger, was to continue for over half a century.

The Pitt family came from Hampshire, Cornwall and Dorset gentry. William Pitt the Elder's grandfather, Thomas 'Diamond' Pitt, acquired his nickname because of the enormous gem he brought back from India after his career as Governor of Madras. His grandson was something of an outsider as a result of his wilful, turbulent and outspoken temperament. He drank heavily as a junior officer in the cavalry, despite having contracted gout while still at Eton, excesses that he came bitterly to regret in later life. In 1754 he married Lady Hester Grenville, niece of the 1st Viscount Cobham, connecting him to the ambitious Grenville political dynasty and making him brother-in-law to Richard Grenville-Temple, 2nd Earl Temple, and to George Grenville MP.

Pitt had a natural gift for oratory, which he gladly unleashed upon the Old Whig government, deploying an array of historical allusions, witty rejoinders, hard-hitting political points and sarcasm. He spoke eloquently in favour of the vigorous prosecution of war against Spain in 1739, establishing his reputation as a popular patriot. From 1748 until Pelham's death in 1754, Pitt was a force on the government's fringe, even though on some issues, such as his support for subsidies for Hanover during the War of Austrian Succession and for peace with Spain in 1748, he demonstrated a flexibility of principle that verged on opportunism.

On entering his brother's vacant premiership, Newcastle did not want Pitt as Leader of the House of Commons, but Henry Fox would not accept the position unless he was allowed full patronage powers, which Newcastle

---

* 'Lack' (*Johnson's Dictionary*).

would not grant him. Newcastle distrusted both men: Pitt as a potential adversary and Fox as the recognized Commons spokesman for the Duke of Cumberland, a foreign-policy hawk whose influence was growing due to escalating tensions with the French in North America. Instead he appointed the former diplomat Sir Thomas Robinson, who held the post along with the secretaryship of state for the Southern Department. 'The Duke might as well send his jackboot to govern us,' complained Pitt, and joined Fox in attacking Robinson from the front bench, despite still being ostensibly in Newcastle's Cabinet. Although the Northern and Southern secretaries were theoretically equal in rank, the way that the two roles had developed historically meant that the Southern – which handled relations with France, Spain, the Mediterranean, America and the other colonies – was in practice more important than his Northern counterpart, who dealt with Germany, Holland, Russia, Scandinavia and Scotland, as well as domestic matters.

Although he was still only seventeen in the summer of 1755, George now found an interest in art, architecture, science and history that had been sparked by his father and Ayscough but had lain dormant under the uninspiring governorships of Harcourt and Waldegrave. Now someone emerged in his life who was to reignite his curiosity, and was to play a major role in George's life for the next eight years. John Stuart, 3rd Earl of Bute, was a relatively minor figure in the Leicester House Set who had first become friendly with Frederick when the Prince asked him to make up a fourth at cards on a rainy afternoon at Egham Races in Surrey, and who in 1750 was appointed one of Frederick's lords of the bedchamber.

After Frederick's death, when many of the Leicester House Set scurried across to ingratiate themselves with the Court and government, Bute continued his friendship with Augusta, who liked and trusted him. There is nothing to suggest, however, that Augusta and Bute were lovers, as Whig propagandists were soon insinuating. One of the strongest, albeit circumstantial, rebuttals is that the pious and somewhat straitlaced George came to treat Bute, who was twenty-five years his senior, as a surrogate father-figure. Given his veneration for both his mother and his late father's memory, had George even so much as suspected Bute of sleeping with his mother (a secret which it would have been impossible to conceal in their tiny Court) he would doubtless have despised them both.[75] Bute, a Scottish Episcopalian, was moreover happily married to Mary Wortley Montagu, with whom he had eloped in 1735 and had eleven children.

What actually brought Augusta and Bute together was not lust but horticulture. She created the royal botanical gardens at Kew; Bute wrote learned books on botany, shrubs and flowers, including his nine-volume *Botanical Tables*. In that gossip-driven milieu and age, it took nothing more than a connecting door at the bottom of Augusta's and Bute's respective gardens at Kew to turn a baseless rumour into what the pamphleteers and the extensive gutter press constantly retailed as undoubted fact. Yet people who were in a good position to know the truth, such as Charles Jenkinson, 1st Earl of Liverpool, never believed it. As Liverpool told Lord Glenbervie in 1808, Augusta liked Bute because he was 'the only person about her husband who was attached to her on her own account'; he had not used her to get to Frederick, but treated her as a friend in her own right.[76]

John Bute was tall, handsome and charming. It was said of him that in all high society Lord Bute had the 'finest calves'.[77] George II, who was never short of rude remarks about his son's friends, said of Bute that he would have made 'an excellent ambassador in any court where there was nothing to do'.[78] Bute was the nephew of the 2nd and 3rd Dukes of Argyll and, after attending Eton and Leiden University, was from 1737 to 1741 one of the Scottish representative peers in the House of Lords. Afterwards he returned to his large but low-income estate on the Isle of Bute in Scotland. When he appeared in London in 1746 it was said he was so poor that he could hardly afford to keep his own carriage, then considered the most basic social prerequisite for an aristocrat.

Bute was artistic and intelligent, and had a genuine interest in philosophy, mechanics, metaphysics and natural science. Later, his collection of mathematical apparatuses at his country seat at Luton Hoo in Bedfordshire was considered one of the most complete of its kind in Europe.[79] He was a cultured, discerning and tasteful man, ideally suited to be the moral tutor and mentor of a future king, but fundamentally ill-suited to the often undignified rough-and-tumble of eighteenth-century high politics. Bute also suffered from a problem that the political elite and the popular mob alike could never forgive: he was a Scot.

Bute was descended from an illegitimate branch of the Stuart kings of Scotland, and only a decade after the Jacobite rebellion there were many who still loathed and feared Scots, despite England and Wales having been in a legislative union with Scotland since 1707 and a union of the two Crowns having existed since 1603. Augusta nonetheless appointed Bute as George's tutor in the early summer of 1755, and suddenly the Prince of Wales' education turned from a boring but conscientious slog into a thing of delight. It was wrong to suggest, as Sir Lewis Namier did in 1953, that 'the boy spent joyless years in a well-regulated nursery, the nearest approach to a concentration camp,' but he had not been excited intellectually until Bute arrived.[80]

Although Frederick had been a cultured man, he had died when his eldest son was only twelve. It was thus Bute who introduced George to many of the artistic and intellectual passions of his life, and to the people who stimulated them. He arranged for the distinguished natural scientist Stephen Demainbray to teach him a course of natural and experimental philosophy in May 1755, sparking George's lifelong fascination for the natural sciences. Bute also inspired George's keen bibliophilia, reverence for scholarship, collecting addiction, love of architecture and the intellectual satisfaction that comes from having wide cultural interests. Historical debate over the extent to which the relationship between George and Bute was personal and affectionate or political and ideological underplays the extent to which it was all four, and by far the most important influence on George's life between 1755 and 1763.[81] Bute became George's teacher, mentor, counsellor and role model, in the process completely ousting Lord Waldegrave, who resigned the governorship in 1756.

Between 1756 and 1765 George wrote Bute 340 letters that survive (and it is believed that some others were destroyed).[82] 'I am conscious of my own indolence,' he wrote in March 1757. 'I do here in the most solemn manner declare that I will entirely throw aside my greatest enemy and that you shall instantly find a change.'[83] Yet he was certainly not indolent, writing fifty-page essays for Bute on such demanding subjects as the 'Original Nature of Government' and a 'Short History of England'.[84] In all, the essays that survive from George's education cover 8,500 pages, breaking down into 59 per cent history, 22 per cent law, 5 per cent classics, 4 per cent mathematics and 2 per cent philosophy, political economy and geography.[85]* George and Bute were consciously building up the necessary intellectual apparatus – including readings of Montesquieu and Hume – for George to be a monarch worthy of the Enlightenment. The essays demonstrate a good deal of reading and research, especially in George's extensive knowledge of ancient and medieval history. He did not keep a commonplace book like many of his contemporaries, but he did précis and paraphrase writers and books he admired – 500 pages for William Blackstone, 200 for Montesquieu – reshaping arguments, adding, editing and reorganizing complex texts for his own use. The Whig portrait of a lazy or ignorant student is pure fiction.

The practice of essay writing never left Bute's pupil, who continued a form of it with his political memoranda into late middle age. The (sadly

---

* These include duplicates and redrafts, as well as, in the words of their historian Jenny Buckley, 'pages of unlabelled annotations, sheets of doodles, and notes on musical scales and works'.

undated) essays of George's youth allow us to delve into the mind of the Prince of Wales in his late teenage years and early twenties, and to dispel the myth put about by Walpole and other Whig writers that George had been taught dictatorial tendencies by a sinister absolutist descendant of the Stuarts.

In fact the precise opposite is true. George's essays suggest a young man who revered the way the Glorious Revolution had brought about liberty, took William III for his role model as king and passionately agreed with his father and Bolingbroke on the personal role of the monarch in defending the people against an overweening aristocracy. Indeed, George regarded the British constitution with something approaching idolatry. 'The pride, the glory of Britain, and the direct end of its constitution is political liberty,' he wrote in one essay.[86] In another, on William and Mary's Convention Parliament of January 1689 to February 1690, he wrote that 'with all its blemishes [it] saved the nation from the iron rod of arbitrary power,' so 'Let us still remember we stand indebted for our liberty . . . to the success of 1688.'[87]

Some of the essays presented texts and arguments from other thinkers, and it is not always clear whether George agreed or was merely rehearsing their arguments the better to understand them. In one passage on the great Genoese admiral Andrea Doria, George wrote that in re-establishing self-government in the republic in 1528, 'This great action must by all free people be looked on as the most excellent and truest sign of a great man.'[88] In another essay he asserted of freedom of speech that it 'is not only the natural privilege of liberty, but also its support and preservation, every man therefore here is allowed to declare his sentiments openly, to speak or write whatever is not prohibited by the laws'.[89] There was nothing that the young George wanted more for his people than life, liberty and the pursuit of happiness.

The conclusion of another of George's essays is worth quoting for its sophisticated appreciation of the importance of the balance of powers:

> Thus have we created the noblest constitution the human mind is capable of framing, where the executive power is in the prince, the legislative in the nobility and the representatives of the people, the judicial in the people and in some cases in the nobility, to whom there lies a final appeal from all other courts of judicature, where every man's life, liberty and possessions are secure, where one part of the legislative body checks the other by the privilege of rejecting, both checked by the executive, as that is again by the legislative; all parts moving, and however they may follow the particular interest of their body, yet all uniting at last for the public good.[90]

Exchange 'prince' for 'president' and 'nobility' for 'Senate' and there is a more than passing resemblance to that jewel of the Enlightenment, the United States constitution of 1787. That is because both the Glorious Revolution and the founding principles of the United States stemmed from the concept of the social contract as expounded by John Locke, to which George fully subscribed. George valued the balance of the British constitution, and his lifelong hostility to the Whig oligarchy stemmed from his belief that the aristocracy were intent on trying to tip its delicate balance between the prince, the nobility and the representatives of the people too far in their own favour.

Further evidence that George was not brought up to be an arbitrary monarch lies in the essays he wrote on the Civil War and the Glorious Revolution, in which he emphasized how much greater was the freedom that his house of Hanover offered than the despotism of the Stuarts. The youthful George criticized Charles I who, in his words, 'had too high a notion of the regal power, and thought that every opposition to it was rebellion'.[91] Although he believed Charles' execution had been illegal, he thought it was understandable, and ultimately the fault of his being 'easily governed by his favourites'.[92]

Despite George's avowed criticism of cronyism, Bute was fast becoming precisely such a favourite. An undated letter from him to George argued of the Egyptian, Assyrian, Babylonian, Persian, Greek and Roman empires that 'the cause of their destruction' was that their princes were badly educated, whereas Bute flattered himself that 'The prospect of serving you and forming your young mind is exquisitely pleasing to a heart like mine.'[93] He warned the Prince that one day someone would whisper to him that he (Bute) had been 'your father's friend and is strongly attached to the Princess', and he added, 'I glory in my attachment to the Princess, in being called your father's friend, but I glory in being yours too.' It was a clever way of dealing with the rumours that he knew would reach George's ears were he to establish total dominance over the impressionable teenager.

It is easy to see why George should have so admired the British constitution, considering the wide powers it gave the monarchy to appoint and dismiss ministers, to prorogue and dissolve parliaments, to make war and peace, to create and advance peerages, and so on; yet he also supported the limits on royal power inherent in the House of Commons' right to refuse taxation as a restraint on royal despotism. At that time it was taken for granted that Parliament also had the right to tax Britain's colonies if necessary, so he was not taught anything different. Thomas Jefferson was later to claim that the King had received a 'Tory education', but in fact it was classically Lockeist and had at its core the rejection of absolutism.[94]

At some point in the late 1750s, George made a long précis of Charles de Montesquieu's classic Enlightenment text *The Spirit of the Laws*, originally published in 1748. By comparing Montesquieu's text with the Prince of Wales' rendition, it is possible to see where the ventriloquizing ends and George's own commentary begins; this is particularly noticeable in Book 15, which covers the issue of slavery. 'The almost universal establishment of civil slavery in the hot regions of Asia, Africa and America', George writes, 'and the abhorrence of it under the more temperate zones is apparent to everyone, but yet the causes of it have been hitherto little examined.'[95] George's own abhorrence becomes very clear in further comments he made on Montesquieu's text, and indeed goes further than Montesquieu's own opposition to the practice. 'The pretexts used by the Spaniards for enslaving the New World were extremely curious,' George noted; 'the propagation of the Christian religion was the first reason, the next was the [Indigenous] Americans differing from them in colour, manners and customs, all [of] which are too absurd to take the trouble of refuting. But what shall we say to the European traffic of black slaves, the very reasons urged for it will be perhaps sufficient to make us hold this practice in execration.'[96]

George then listed Montesquieu's reasons for the Spaniards' enslavement of non-whites, which included the expense involved in growing tobacco, the fact that American blacks looked different from them and their valuing glass necklaces higher than gold.[97] All this led George to conclude that, as to these 'arguments for an inhuman custom wantonly practised by the most enlightened polite nations in the world, there is no occasion to answer them, for they stand self-condemned'.[98] George's writings on this subject were much more than merely ventriloquizing Montesquieu, and have been described as being at the vanguard of the radical argument over slavery, since they predated even the arguments made in George Wallace's pioneering anti-slavery book *A System of the Principles of the Law of Scotland*, published in 1760. George clearly did not believe in either the classical or the modern arguments defending slavery and, at least before he acceded to the throne, was a convinced abolitionist.

In terms of British grand strategy, George's essays reflected the global maritime attitudes of Pitt rather than the Continental strategy of his grandfather. Also discernible was Bolingbroke's vision of foreign policy founded on 30,000 to 40,000 sailors manning a navy capable of defending British security in all circumstances. The Royal Navy, George wrote, should be 'equal if not superior to those of all other powers together, which must preserve [Britain] from invasion'.[99] Of course for financial reasons this would preclude having a large British standing army of the kind that could protect Hanover in time of war. 'Numerous armies and strong fortresses are inconsistent with freedom,' George wrote in the same essay, although militias were acceptable because they sprang from the people and would 'reconcile the nation to that army that shall be thought necessary'.[100] All this conformed closely to the Leicester House political agenda of the 1740s. Although George never mentioned his father once in his letters to Bute, which cover 250 printed pages, their connection with Frederick was ever present.

George's father would have been pleased that public finance was an area his son studied carefully between 1755 and 1760. As far as private finance was concerned, George wrote that a monarch 'will be feared and respected abroad [and] adored at home by mixing private economy with public magnificence'.[101] This seeming dichotomy would typify George's reign, with its marked contrast between his private parsimony, frugal meals and refusal to carpet his palaces on the one hand and the public splendour of his State Coach, silver plate and even silver furniture on the other.[102]

Bute was essentially a university don manqué, with all the advantages and disadvantages which that entailed. He could be pedantic. In the Royal Archives at Windsor is one of George's essays entitled 'Problems of Practical Geometry Useful in Fortification', with corrections by Bute that display his perfectionism.[103] Where George wrote 'Richard II succeeded his grandfather Edward III when he was eleven years old,' Bute corrected his syntax to 'Richard II was but eleven when he succeeded his grandfather Edward III.'[104] (An even more pedantic correction would have been to point out that Richard II was actually ten and a half.) Where George had written 'begged him to call his grandfather to memory', a perfectly acceptable phrase in the eighteenth century, Bute changed it to 'begged him to call to mind his grandfather'. Nor was George allowed to use ampersands, despite their being almost universally employed at the time, but was made to write out 'and' in their place.[105]* George received a far better all-round education than his contemporaries at the ancient universities, where, Edward Gibbon reminds us, undergraduates were almost completely ignored by their lazy, port-sodden dons.

Bute also instilled a keen sense of morality in George, one in which virtue and monogamy were paramount. Further refuting the notion that he was sleeping with Augusta was Bute's choice of example after example of illicit sex leading to political disaster, among them Robert of Normandy, Henri II of France, Roger Mortimer and Queen Isabella. Bute's real

---

* Today the essays can be seen on the Georgian Papers Programme website at https://gpp.rct.uk/Record.aspx?src=Catalog&id=GIII_ESSAYS.

intended target was probably George II, whose mistresses held established positions at Court, a practice that George was taught to believe produced bad governance. Augusta approved strongly of Bute's influence upon her son. 'Pursue, my worthy friend,' she wrote to Bute, 'those instructions you have begun, and imprint your great sentiments in him,' which, she went on, 'will make my son and his mother happy'.[106]

Bute's influence extended far beyond schoolwork. He appointed the Scottish-Swedish architect and polymath Sir William Chambers to give George thrice-weekly tutorials in architecture and drawing. Chambers was a leading proponent of the 'Georgian' style that is such a jewel of Britain's built environment today in such places as Belgravia, Bath, Dublin and Edinburgh. He had George read a central Enlightenment text written by his friend Julien Le Roy, *Les Ruines des plus beaux monuments de la Grèce*, on its publication in 1758. An immensely influential work, it launched the use of the colonnade in urban buildings, and George made sketches based on Le Roy's engraving of the Tower of the Winds in Athens. Chambers had worked in Rome, Paris, Gothenburg and Canton, and introduced George to Roman and Greek architecture, such as that of Palmyra and Baalbek.

The Prince of Wales has no specific powers under the British constitution, occupying a role similar to that of the American vice-president: characterized as waking up each morning and inquiring after the health of the president. He was however expected to contract a strategically useful and fruitful marriage, to which end, returning from Hanover in the summer of 1755, the King suggested that George marry Princess Sophia Caroline, the daughter of the Duke and Duchess of Brunswick-Wolfenbüttel. The prospective bride was the niece of King Frederick II 'the Great' of Prussia, whose territorial ambitions menaced Hanover. The King hoped that an alliance between the adjoining territories of Hanover and Brunswick would deter any potential invasion. As secondary considerations, Sophia was a cousin, spoke German and was nearly the same age as George.

Yet George and Augusta violently opposed the match, so much so that the King temporarily withdrew the idea. For his part, George saw it as an attempt to draw Britain closer to Hanover, which ran contrary to Leicester House policy. Augusta explained her opposition to Dodington on 6 August, calling it 'premature; the Prince wanted to mix with the world; this would prevent it: he was shy, and backward;* this would shut him up forever,

---

* 'Unwilling; averse; hesitating' (*Johnson's Dictionary*).

with two or three friends of his, and as many of hers.'[107] She also thought Sophia's mother, the Duchess of Brunswick, 'the most intriguing, meddling and also the most satirical, sarcastical person in the world, and will always make mischief whenever she comes. Such a character would not do with George . . . he was not a wild, dissipated boy, but good-natured and cheerful, but with a serious cast [of mind], in the whole . . . he was not quick, but, with those he was acquainted with, applicable and intelligent.'[108] In the event, George II had nothing immediately to fear from Prussia invading Hanover: indeed, they were about to become allies.

Since 1754, border clashes in the Ohio River Valley between the British forces protecting the thirteen American colonies and French forces pushing southwards from French Canada had been escalating. As early as 9 July 1755, a large force of British regulars and some American irregulars under General Edward Braddock was soundly defeated by French and Native American forces at the battle of Monongahela near Fort Duquesne, in present-day Pennsylvania. Braddock and twenty-seven of his officers were killed or mortally wounded in the engagement, along with over 400 troops and as many again wounded. Braddock's aide-de-camp, the twenty-three-year-old Major George Washington, had two horses shot from under him and was lucky to escape with his life.

With a conflict clearly approaching, the King and Newcastle had to choose between William Pitt and Henry Fox as war leader. They chose Fox, as much for his connection to the rising power of the Duke of Cumberland as for his own influence in the Commons. Chagrined over Fox's promotion, Pitt distanced himself from Newcastle. In October Bute, now the leading figure of what remained of the Leicester House Set through his closeness to George and Augusta, proposed an alliance with Pitt and the Grenville family against Newcastle, Cumberland and Fox. It was a smart, pragmatic move, but it took the seventeen-year-old George into active opposition against his seventy-two-year-old grandfather as the country slipped inexorably towards war.

On 13–14 November 1755, the House of Commons debated a series of treaties that the government – actively encouraged by the King – had concluded with Russia and Hesse-Cassel to protect Hanover, treaties which committed Britain to paying large subsidies to foreign countries. Pitt delivered a masterful speech in which he supported the idea of defending the 'long-injured, long-neglected, long-forgotten people of America' from the French and simultaneously denounced the payment of subsidies to defend Hanover from the same enemy.[109] He was summarily dismissed as Paymaster-General of the Forces, and thereafter Bute took to referring to him as his 'dearest friend'.[110] Fox meanwhile succeeded Robinson as Leader of the

House of Commons. The British government had readied themselves for war by sacking their one brilliant strategist, William Pitt, and promoting instead a corrupt placeman, Henry Fox. On 17 May 1756, France and Britain declared hostilities, less than a month before George attained his majority. It was a conflict that would later be described as history's first world war, and it would have global consequences lasting to this day.

2

Seizing an Empire

May 1756–October 1760

*I have already lived long enough to know you are the only man I
shall ever meet with who ... at all times prefer[s] my interest to
your own.*[1]

George, Prince of Wales, to Lord Bute, April 1760

The outbreak of Britain's war with France ignited disputes in Europe that
had been unresolved by the War of Austrian Succession between 1740 and
1748, including Austria's wish to regain the rich province of Silesia that
she had lost to Prussia. This led to the 'Diplomatic Revolution' of January
1756 by which Prussia allied with Britain and Hanover, forcing Austria to
ally with France, along with Russia, Saxony and Sweden. What became
the Seven Years War started badly for Britain, with a disastrous naval battle
against the French off Minorca on 20 May 1756, forcing the Royal Navy
to retreat to the British stronghold of Gibraltar. The humiliating fall of the
island in late June, which the French were then to hold throughout the
conflict, severely weakened Newcastle's ministry and led to the court martial and execution of the defeated admiral, John Byng. (It was this ruthless
act that prompted Voltaire's quip that the English executed their admirals
'pour encourager les autres'.)

George and Bute's attitude has been widely misinterpreted as one of
outright opposition to the war, although in fact they resisted only an expensive Continental war, and with good reason: a land war would increase
the National Debt dangerously through the commitment of British troops
and the payment of foreign subsidies to protect Hanover from France.
Instead, they strongly favoured the cheaper alternative strategy, advocated
stridently by Pitt, of waging a naval and imperial war against France's
colonies and coastline.

In anticipation of George's eighteenth birthday on 4 June 1756 – the
age at which he could rule without a regency in the event of his

grandfather's death – the Duke of Newcastle advised the King that the Prince should receive £40,000 per annum to set up his own establishment with Prince Edward at St James's and Kensington Palaces. Earl Waldegrave would head the new household as George's Groom of the Stole,* and the government entertained hopes that George could thereby be weaned off his closeness to his mother and Bute. George's answer was 'full of gratitude for the allowance', but he said of Augusta that 'Her happiness depends on their not being separated and anything so sensibly affecting his mother must prove extremely uneasy to him.'[2] He also insisted on Bute rather than Waldegrave becoming Groom of the Stole, which displeased the King and Newcastle owing to Bute's closeness to Pitt, but they eventually accepted in early October. On his birthday, Augusta gave George his father's political testament which in accordance with Frederick's wishes she had read to him routinely over the past four years.

On 1 July, George wrote Bute a letter to mark the first anniversary of his tutorship. 'I have had the pleasure of your friendship during the space of a year,' he began, 'by which I have reaped great advantage, but not the improvement I should if I had followed your advice; but you shall find me make such a progress in this summer that shall give you hopes that with the continuation of your advice, I may turn out as you wish.'[3] Of the government's tardiness in granting Bute the groomship, George complained:

> It is very true that the ministers have done everything they can to provoke me, that they have called me a harmless boy, and have not even deigned to give me an answer when I so earnestly wish to see my friend about me. They have also treated my mother in a cruel manner (which I will neither forget nor forgive to the day of my death) because she is so good as to come forward and preserve her son from the many snares that surround him.[4]

In what was possibly an oblique reference to the rumours of his mother's affair with Bute, which disgusted him, George wrote:

> My friend is also attacked in the most cruel and horrid manner, not for anything he has done against them, but because he is my friend, and wants to see me come to the throne with honour and not with disgrace and because he is a friend to the blessed liberties of his country and not to arbitrary notions. I look upon myself as engaged in honour and justice to defend these my two friends as long as I draw breath.[5]

* The term derived either from the Latin for a long vest (*stola*), implying close personal contact, or from 'stool' or a commode, implying even closer and more intimate contact as the courtier responsible for managing the prince's ablutions and excretions.

Of course there was no indication that Newcastle, Fox, the King or anyone else wanted him to come to the throne with anything but honour; this was melodramatic histrionics of a kind not unusual in a teenager but which, as we shall see, George also occasionally displayed well into middle age.

George made a series of promises 'in the presence of Our Almighty Lord' to remember the insults against his mother and never to forgive anyone who spoke disrespectfully of her; moreover, he promised Bute to 'show to the world the great friendship I have for him', especially against 'all the allurements my enemies can think of'. He ended by telling his friend and mentor:

> I hope my dear Lord you will conduct me through this difficult road and will bring me to the goal. I will exactly follow your advice, without which I shall inevitably sink. I am young and inexperienced and want advice. I trust in your friendship which will assist me in all difficulties . . . I do hope you will from this instant banish all thoughts of leaving me . . . I have often heard you say that you don't think that I shall have the same friendship for you when I am married as I now have. I shall never change in that, nor will I bear to be in the least deprived of your company.[6]

George's expressions of attachment, and his elevated, platonic male friendship with Bute, would have profound political implications over the coming years.

Such was Bute's influence over George that when the Prince of Wales formally joined the House of Lords on 13 November 1759, he wrote to ask 'whether I am not to put on my hat on taking my seat' later that day.[7] The occasion excited much interest in high society, since George lived mainly at Kew and was not seen much in London, except for occasional visits to the theatre and opera. He probably did not return to the House of Lords during his grandfather's reign, although some sources claim he attended the sensational murder trial of the 4th Earl Ferrers for shooting his steward, for which the Earl was hanged (in deference to his rank, with a silken rope).

The loss of Minorca, combined with attacks upon the government by Pitt, forced Newcastle to resign on 11 November 1756, and the Whig grandee William Cavendish, 4th Duke of Devonshire, became Prime Minister five days later, with the understanding that Pitt would be free to run the war as Southern Secretary and Leader of the House of Commons. 'My lord,' Pitt told Devonshire soon afterwards, 'I am sure I can save this country, and nobody else can.'[8] It was an outrageously egocentric claim, but it proved to be well founded. Although Pitt's energetic prosecution of the war made him extremely popular with the British people, the Devonshire–Pitt ministry was neither strong nor stable: the King disliked it on account of its perceived lack of commitment to the security of Hanover. For George and Bute, however, there was delight that Pitt might be able to pursue a more expansive 'blue water' campaign – that is, one both navalist and colonial in its outlook.

Before embarking for Europe to take command of the British forces already on the Continent, Cumberland convinced his father to dismiss Pitt and Earl Temple, First Lord of the Admiralty, together on 6 April 1757. It was an obvious misstep. Buoyed by his public reputation as a patriot – as attested by the thirteen British cities that declared him a freeman in close succession – Pitt was back in office by late June. The incident provided an object lesson in the underappreciated lobbying power of public opinion: although only one British male in twelve had the franchise, governments were obliged to keep a weather eye on the vast majority beyond the electorate.*

Pitt's dismissal also serves to overturn an enduring myth that George II was the minion of his ministers, and that one of his successor's aims was to restore those royal prerogative powers that George I and George II had allowed to fall into abeyance (it has been suggested this was because they spoke German, and were so persistently interested in the fate of Hanover). In fact, George II was a fully engaged monarch: he exercised exactly the same powers over army and Court appointments that George III would, made and unmade ministries, approved candidates and authorized expenditure at elections; he also controlled honours, bishoprics and peerages closely. He was an effective monarch conscious of his rights, quite different from the fable of a distant Hanoverian who allowed his authority to be undermined by Old Whig politicians such as Walpole and the Pelhams. That he did not often clash with his various ministries was simply because he generally supported the policies the Old Whigs pursued, not because he was in thrall to the Whig grandees themselves.[9]

In early June 1757, George somehow inferred from rumours of an Opposition alliance between the recently deposed Newcastle, Cumberland and Henry Fox that his succession to the throne itself might be in danger. Fearful of 'this fatal alliance', he wrote to Bute in a wild combination of hyperbole and paranoia that 'I will rather die ten thousand deaths than truckle at their impious feet.'[10] He added that he would only accept the crown 'with the hopes of restoring my much loved country to her ancient state of liberty; of seeing her in time free from her present load of debts

---

* The word 'democracy', under which the masses received the vote at a time when there was no statutory education, tended to be used pejoratively to describe a self-evident evil.

and again famous for being the residence of true piety and virtue'. If such hopes were lost, he proposed 'retiring to some uninhabited cavern as that would prevent me from seeing the sufferings of my countrymen and the total destruction of this monarchy; for if the government should remain two or three years in the hands of these myrmidons of the blackest kind, I imagine any invader with a handful of men might place himself on the throne and establish despotism here.'[11] Bute's more measured response was to ask Newcastle's friend the 4th Earl of Chesterfield* to try to repair relations between Newcastle and Pitt.

In one respect, however, George was not exaggerating: Britain's 'present load of debts' amounted to over £74 million in 1753, to £77.8 million in 1758 and to £82.8 million in 1759, prompting a deep concern in Parliament over the nation's creditworthiness, and reaffirming those fears in George that had been planted by Bute's teachings and his father's political testament.[12] George wrote several essays on the subject in the second half of the 1750s, which in total covered no fewer than 557 pages.[13] For the young Prince, revenue and expenditure profoundly affected national power and prosperity, and 'to know this is the true essential business of a king'.[14] The seriousness with which he and Bute approached this subject was no mere intellectual exercise; it was a blueprint for what they believed needed to be done about the economy once George became king and Bute his Prime Minister.

George's conception of economics was staunchly conservative. He dreamed not of conquering great territories such as Canada and India, but rather of redeeming the National Debt and leading a great, unleveraged trading nation which would be 'the residence of true piety and virtue'. His essays articulate his belief that the establishment of the Debt, in the reign of William III and Mary, had emerged from the cowardice of politicians in borrowing for William's wars rather than incurring unpopularity by increasing taxation, which he characterized as a willingness 'to live and die without the least regard to posterity, a way of thinking now become fatally prevalent'.[15] As he wrote elsewhere, 'The world ever produces wrong-headed individuals who would rather pay £10 imperceptibly than £4 out of their pockets at once.'[16] If there was a specific period when George conceived his low opinion of politicians for their short-termism, factiousness and pusillanimity – a general view that was to last throughout his reign and cause him a good deal of trouble – it was when he studied in detail the way the National Debt had ballooned in the six decades after the 1690s.

* Author of the posthumous *Letters to his Son on the Art of Becoming a Man of the World and a Gentleman.*

George likened the Whig governments' behaviour in allowing this to happen to 'a young spendthrift who eagerly compounds for a present convenience at the expense of any future encumbrance, however burdensome or reproachful'.[17] Economics, for George, was profoundly moral. He denounced the first national lottery, of 1694, as 'a most pernicious precedent, too often made use of since, as it serves not only to excite, but even authorize, a spirit of gaming in every man who is able to raise a few pounds, though perhaps at the expense of his morals, credit and character'.[18]

George was brought up with a horror of gambling, and Augusta and Bute kept him far from the high-stakes gaming and carousing with which eighteenth-century upper-class society was rife. He therefore had no social interaction, either as prince or later as king, with the very fast set of rich young Whig aristocrats who drank, gambled and whored at the new clubs in St James's such as Almack's (founded in 1759), Boodle's (1762) and Brooks's (1764). White's, founded in 1693, was Tory, but the Prince of Wales was not to be found there either. Although he adored horses and was a keen rider, he eschewed the fashionable race meetings of the day too. Whig aristocrats thought of George as straitlaced and boring; he thought of them as louche and godless.

When in mid-June 1757 Henry Fox unsuccessfully attempted to form an administration, Lord George Sackville refused to serve in it, earning George's admiration. 'Lord George shows himself the man of honour you have often described him to be,' he wrote to Bute.[19] This positive feeling towards Sackville, then no more than a forty-one-year-old cavalry colonel, was unimportant at the time but was to have empire-shattering consequences later on. Tall and long-faced with strong features, clear blue eyes and a melancholy look, Sackville was a proud, reserved man with a grave manner that some saw as aristocratic hauteur, though his friends thought him 'capable of genial and engaging frankness and sincerity'.[20] He was a younger son of the 1st Duke of Dorset, and his mother had been a maid of honour to Queen Anne.

Sackville had attended Westminster School and Trinity College, Dublin, when his father was Viceroy of Ireland,* then entered the army and served under both the Duke of Marlborough and the Duke of Cumberland. He had been shot in the chest at Fontenoy in 1745, a battle in which only three officers of his regiment were not killed or wounded. Cumberland had commended Sackville's 'courage and soldierly ability' during the Jacobite rebellion.[21] After his well-timed refusal of office under Fox, Sackville

* Also known since 1690 as Lord Lieutenant of Ireland, and before that as Chief Governor.

became a junior member of the Leicester House Set, and by December 1758 George was numbering him along with William Legge, General Henry Conway and the ambitious, capable George Montagu-Dunk, 2nd Earl of Halifax, as prospective ministers in the next reign.

On 29 June, following protracted negotiations to find a ministry that would have the support of both the King and the Leicester House Set, a momentous compromise was struck: George II's man Newcastle was restored to the nominal premiership, while Pitt regained the two key posts he had held previously, granting him unbridled control over the war, foreign affairs and the House of Commons. The Duke of Devonshire agreed to stay in the Cabinet as Lord Chamberlain. In a move aimed largely at placating the Duke of Cumberland, a place was found for Henry Fox as Paymaster-General of the Forces. Over the next eight years, Fox made an estimated £400,000, on top of his £3,000 per annum salary, largely from the way he was permitted to run the nation's huge wartime balances through his own private bank accounts.

On 26 July 1757, following a French invasion of Hanover, British and Allied forces under Cumberland's command were defeated by the French at the battle of Hastenbeck. On 8 September in the battle's aftermath, Cumberland was forced to sign the humiliating Convention of Kloster-zeven, an agreement which took Hanover out of the war and allowed for its partial occupation. Despite having been given full plenipotentiary powers to conclude the peace treaty, Cumberland on his return to London was publicly humiliated by his father, who remarked, 'Here is my son, who has ruined me and disgraced himself.'[22] With his reputation destroyed, and his rivals now in the political ascendancy, the disavowed Cumberland withdrew from politics for the remainder of his father's reign.

Although George did not regret his uncle's and thus Henry Fox's eclipse, he did worry that Frederick the Great might now agree a separate peace with France. 'This will certainly bring the French back to their native air,' he told Bute on 5 November, 'and enable them by putting soldiers into their ships to man a great fleet; I begin now to think that you and I my friend shall see the end of this once great and glorious country; yet I will not give way to black thoughts ... If you are but well and Providence assists us, England may yet be free and happy.'[23] Pessimism clearly came easily to the nineteen-year-old George. He added as a postscript, 'The more I think on Henry Vth['s] soliloquy, the more I admire it.' He was presumably referring to the King's speech at the end of Act IV scene 1 of Shakespeare's play:

> Upon the king! let us our lives, our souls,
> Our debts, our careful wives,

Our children and our sins, lay on the King!
We must bear all. O hard condition,
Twin-born with greatness, subject to the breath
Of every fool, whose sense no more can feel
But his own wringing! What infinite heart's ease
Must kings neglect that private men enjoy!

But George's fears were once again unfounded: the rumour about Prussia was untrue; indeed, on the very day that George wrote his letter, Frederick won one of his greatest victories over the French, at Rossbach, and a month later defeated the Austrians at Leuthen.

No sooner was Pitt in the political ascendant than George began to understand his grandfather's misgivings towards the populist hero of the hour, especially once it became clear that he no longer advocated George and Bute's preferred strategy of a minimal Continental commitment. In late June 1758, Pitt approved plans to field a 9,000-strong British expeditionary force in western Germany under Prince Ferdinand of Brunswick, his own choice to replace Cumberland. He persuaded the reluctant Bute to agree to it, but only on the basis that 'a small body should not lead to a great one'.[24] The Leicester House Set had few options but to concede: its own alternative strategy had come to nothing once its preferred expedition against Saint-Malo failed only three weeks after it began. 'I had but little hopes that these cautious g[eneral]s would choose to think any part of the F[renc]h coast fit for them to land,' George wrote to Bute on 2 July.

I am certain the K[in]g will make a push to have them sent to G[erman]y; and I can't help fearing your wavering friend [that is, Pitt] would not be against it; if this unhappy measure should be taken we shall be drawn deeper into a Continent [sic] War than ever; and when I mount the thr[on]e I shall not be able to form a m[inistr]y who can have the opinion of the people ... what a pretty pickle I should be in a future day if I had not your sagacious counsels.[25]

From having been an outspoken opponent of Continental commitments on the ground that they weakened Britain's imperial and maritime efforts, by the autumn of 1757 Pitt had become the leading advocate for deeper British military involvement on the Continent. He now spoke in open support of Frederick the Great, with whom he had formed a strong personal alliance despite their never having met. This seeming volte-face earned him George's lasting distrust, even contempt. No epithet was too rude, at least in private, when holding forth to his chief adviser whom he now consistently addressed in his letters as 'my dearest friend'. The reversionary interest* at Leicester House was overwhelmingly 'blue water' and the sense of betrayal expressed on 11 April 1758, when Britain signed a treaty promising an annual subsidy to Prussia for protecting Hanover, was total.[26] For the Leicester House Set, Pitt's perfidy threatened to realize George's nightmare of financial catastrophe. Despite Frederick the Great's undoubted brilliance as a general, he had committed Prussia to war with Austria, France, Russia and Sweden, financed by Britain, and ultimately could not possibly hope to overcome them all.

Pitt's sole concession to George and Bute had been to appoint Lord George Sackville as the 3rd Duke of Marlborough's second-in-command in the new Continental force. Sackville's secret instructions from the Leicester House Opposition were to ensure that the army was employed in the pursuit of British interests as much as those of Hanover.[27] When Marlborough died of dysentery on 20 October, Sackville took over the British contingent, and almost immediately began to clash with Prince Ferdinand and other senior officers in the Anglo-German force over victualling costs and overall strategic direction. As in any coalition force, a measure of goodwill was needed, but between Ferdinand and Sackville there was precious little – a situation not helped by Augusta and George's dislike of the Brunswick family in general.

If George despaired of the King and Pitt alike, he was also highly critical of himself at this time, promising Bute in late September that he would 'throw off that incomprehensible indolence, inattention and heedlessness that reigns within me'.[28] His supposed laziness was a theme to which he would returned regularly – describing it as his 'natural indolence' – yet nothing seems to justify it. He was still writing his long, well-researched essays. In one, he argued that the present high wage rate encouraged the poor to buy 'unnecessary things', among which he included brandy, sugar, foreign fruit, strong beer, printed linen, tobacco, snuff and tea.[29] If tea had indeed been an unnecessary commodity, it would have saved George a good deal of trouble in years to come.

George's frugality contrasted sharply with Pitt's policies. While the Great Commoner – as he had begun to be called because he was not a titled grandee – had declared that he would not 'send a drop of our blood to the Elbe to be lost in that ocean of gore', he showed no such circumspection about losing money. The year 1758 saw millions spent on an ever expanding theatre of conflict, seemingly with little resistance in Parliament. Indeed, by November, Pitt was arguing that Parliament ought not to question the

---

* A legal expression from trust law, the reversionary interest in eighteenth-century politics meant the group around the heir to the throne who would benefit when the monarch died.

expense of the army in Germany at all.[30] For George, Pitt's change of tone was astonishing: having actively opposed the expenditure of £700,000 at the opening of a parliamentary session, at the opening of the next he advocated spending £3 million. 'I cannot conceive what the great Orator wants,' George wrote sarcastically to Bute in December before Bute was due to meet Pitt, 'but am glad of his interview with my dearest friend, thinking it will either produce an explanation with regard to past conduct, or end in a rupture, either of which I prefer to uncertainty, particularly as I have in you a friend, and an able man, whose integrity and ability I should do great injustice if I did not look on them as superior to any of the politicians.'[31]

'I am certain he has given himself either up to the K[ing] or the D[uke] of N[ewcastle],' George wrote dejectedly to Bute of Pitt soon afterwards, 'or else he could not act the infamous and ungrateful part he now does.'[32] Allied with Newcastle, Pitt could afford to overrule the financial objections of the Leicester House Set, and informed Bute only after the subsidies decision had been taken. 'Indeed, my dearest friend,' George wrote to Bute, 'he treats both you and me with no more regard than he would do a parcel of children. He seems to forget that the day will come when he must expect to be treated according to his deserts.'[33]

With the King now aged seventy-five, at a time when life expectancy in no country in the world exceeded forty, it was characteristically egotistical for Pitt to treat the heir to the throne so flippantly: privately he also remarked upon George's innocence and the reclusive manner in which he lived. George's references to being treated like 'a harmless boy' and 'a parcel of children' betrayed a sensitivity over the disparity between his mere twenty years and those of all the major political figures of the age, such as Newcastle (who was sixty-five), Fox (fifty-three), Pitt (fifty), Bute (forty-five), Devonshire (thirty-eight) and Cumberland (thirty-seven).

In February 1759, George II and the Duke and Duchess of Brunswick-Wolfenbüttel renewed the suggestion that George marry Sophia Caroline, which George, Augusta and now Bute again rejected. George both believed he should be allowed to choose his own bride and did not want to marry someone to satisfy his grandfather's desire to draw the Opposition into protecting Hanover. 'The more I think of the D[uke] of Br[unswick's] letter, the more I am incensed against him,' George told Bute angrily; 'it manifestly shows a mind greatly embittered against our part of the family and a certain pride that generally attends those petty princes . . . I would never consent to take one out of that House.'[34] (In fact, George's elder sister Princess Augusta was to marry the Duke of Brunswick's heir with George's blessing five years later.)

After his twenty-first birthday on 4 June, George's hope, expressed to the King the following month, was that he would be allowed to serve in the army, as so many princes of Wales, although not including his own father, had done in the past. 'Now that every part of the nation is arming for its defence,' George wrote to the King on 20 July,

> I cannot bear the thoughts of continuing in this inactive state . . . Permit me, therefore, humbly to request of Your Majesty to give me an opportunity of convincing the world that I am neither unworthy of my high situation nor of the blood that fills my veins. Your Majesty's known valour will diffuse its influence on my head and make the presence of your grandson an encourage-ment to your people, a terror to the enemy, and joined to his own resolution may in some measure supply his want of experience in military affairs, and enable him to support with dignity the post of danger, which he esteems the post of honour.[35]

It was a good letter – once again mentioning his honour – but the King, Pitt, Newcastle and Robert Darcy, 4th Earl of Holderness, the Northern Secretary, did not reply for a week. 'The K[ing] and those he has consulted have treated [me] with less regard than they would have dared to have done any Member of Parliament,' George complained to Bute.[36]

Finally, on 27 July, the King replied from Kensington Palace, his London residence, to say, 'I received your letter which is a mark of duty to me, and have the highest satisfaction in your spirit and zeal for the defence of my kingdoms. It is my intention to give you, on a proper occasion, an oppor-tunity of exerting them.'[37] This obviously temporizing but hardly rude letter had George fulminating to Bute about 'how shuffling it is and unworthy of a British monarch; the conduct of this old K[ing] makes me ashamed of being his grandson; he treats me in the same manner his knave and coun-sellor the D[uke] of N[ewcastle] does all people.'[38] He described 'this unworthy letter', which he showed to his mother, as 'an absolute refusal', which on the face of things it was not.

George had an audience with the King three days later, which Newcastle told Holderness only lasted 'some seconds'.[39] After George had thanked his grandfather 'for his promises', the King replied that he would send for the Prince when the need arose but did not say when that might be, and George said nothing in reply. Before leaving for the audience, he had asked Bute whether it would be 'totally improper for me to go as a volunteer if the K[ing] refuses my petition, for I really cannot remain immured at home like a girl whilst all my countrymen are preparing for the field and a brother younger than me allowed to go in quest of the enemy'.[40] Of course, it was because he was the eldest brother and heir apparent that he could not be risked in battle, whereas his younger brother Edward was given the captaincy of the newly launched forty-four-gun ship *Phoenix* and was allowed to go on Channel raids.

In the government's defence, it was hard to know where they could have placed a Prince of Wales who was completely militarily untrained, although he would probably have been brave and a keen and quick learner. After a discussion with Bute, Pitt suggested various uses: George might review Guards regiments, inspect the great naval bases at Chatham and Portsmouth, or perhaps join the staff of Lord Ligonier, the seventy-eight-year-old Commander-in-Chief of the army, and report to the King on the state of national readiness in the event of a French invasion. Despite Newcastle adding his support, nothing came of any of it. George again blamed Pitt: 'I am not much surprised at this insolence of Pitt's,' he told Bute on 30 July, 'he has long shown a want of regard both of you my dearest friend and consequently of myself.'[41] But the rebuke was undeserved; it had ultimately been the King's decision to refuse George military employment, which Pitt told Bute was due to 'repugnancies hard to be eradicated in age'.[42]

The repugnance was mutual, and in early August George was already lamenting the seemingly chaotic military situation on the River Weser caused by his grandfather's commitment to Hanover, which he privately described as 'that horrid Electorate, which has always lived upon the very vitals of this poor country'.[43] There had been further contretemps between Sackville and Ferdinand, the former's criticisms of the latter being dutifully passed back to George and Bute. These were personal, tactical and strategic, the most serious being that in order to keep lines of communications open with Prussia, Ferdinand had cut the British Army off from its shortest lines of communication via Holland.

On 1 August 1759, however, Prince Ferdinand won a famous victory over the French at the battle of Minden, in what is now the North Rhine-Westphalia region of Germany. It saved Hanover and completely altered the strategic situation in the Allies' favour. But in the battle's aftermath Ferdinand alleged that the only reason why it had not been a complete rout was that Sackville, commanding the British cavalry on the right flank, refused three direct orders to press home the attack at the decisive moment. In a proclamation the following day, Ferdinand stated that had Lord Granby, Sackville's second-in-command, been in charge of the cavalry the victory would have been even more emphatic. Outraged, Sackville demanded a court martial to clear his name of what amounted to an accusation of incompetence at best, at worst cowardice. Only two years after the execution of Admiral Byng for the similar offence of 'failing to do his utmost', British commanders did not lightly call for their own court martial.

After the news of Minden arrived in London on 8 August and the capital gave itself over to wild celebration, the Leicester House Set had to face the unsettling fact that one of their number would be tried for cowardice. After Bute had received a report from Sackville of what had transpired, George initially stood by his follower, saying of Ferdinand, 'I think it is pretty pert for a little German prince to make public any fault he finds with the English commander, without first waiting for instructions from the King on so delicate a matter.'[44] Yet George II was only too happy to disgrace Sackville, and was supported enthusiastically in his determination by Pitt, more reluctantly by Newcastle. Because the officers needed to give evidence in a court martial were still on active service, the trial could not be held for six months, further poisoning the atmosphere between the Court and government on one side, and the Leicester House Set and Opposition on the other, with long-term effects that neither could have foreseen.

The victory at Minden was followed on 13 September by an even greater one in Canada, where Anglo-American forces under Major-General James Wolfe, having driven the French from the northern part of the British colony of New York, took Quebec, the capital of French Canada, in a battle on the Heights of Abraham. George II, not one known to joke much, remarked upon learning from Newcastle of Wolfe's reported mental imbalance, 'I wish to my God he would bite some of my Generals, and make them mad too.'[45] Scaling the Heights in a surprise attack at night had been an audacious, near-suicidal manoeuvre by Wolfe, but his victory opened up the British conquest of the whole of Canada. Killed during the battle (and subsequently memorialized in a portrait by Benjamin West), Wolfe became a heroic symbol of the empire.

For George, however, September 1759 would for ever hold sad memories instead. In that month, his eighteen-year-old sister Elizabeth died from appendicitis, the first of his eight siblings to predecease him. His deep-seated Christian faith helped him face these tragedies.

In November 1759 George fell in what he persuaded himself was love with Lady Sarah Lennox, the fourteen-year-old sister of Charles Lennox, 3rd Duke of Richmond, and sister-in-law of Henry Fox, who had just made her debut at Court. Horace Walpole, an aesthete who can at least be trusted in matters of beauty (if on little else regarding George), wrote that there was 'no Magdalen by Corregio half so lovely and expressive' as Lady Sarah, observing that she was 'a very young lady of the most blooming beauty, and shining with the graces of unaffected, but animated nature'.[46] George Scott had written of the eighteen-year-old George that he had 'the greatest temptation to be gallant with the ladies, who lay themselves out in the most shameful manner to draw him in', but he had hitherto resisted.[47] (There is no truth in the gossip that George had secretly married Hannah Lightfoot, the daughter of a Quaker tradesman from Wapping, by whom he was alleged to have had several children.)[48]

George initially tried to hide his feelings for Sarah from Bute. 'You have often accused me of growing grave and thoughtful,' he wrote to him in late 1759 without mentioning her by name; 'it is entirely owing to a daily increasing admiration of the fair sex, which I am attempting with all the philosophy and resolution I am capable of to keep under ... princes when once in their hands make miserable figures.'[49] He cited the Bourbon courts, and alluded (though not by name) to George II and his German mistress the Countess of Yarmouth as examples of the pitfalls and pathos of petticoat government. 'When I have said this you will plainly feel how strong a struggle there is between the boiling youth of twenty-one years and prudence.' He hoped the latter would 'ever keep the upper hand', and that, in 'a few years, marriage will put a stop to this combat in my breast', believing that 'keeping the mind constantly employed is a likely means of preserving those passions in due subordination to it.'

But he could not keep Sarah's identity secret from Bute for long. 'If I say things you think improper,' he confided in his next letter, 'impute them to the violence of my love.'[50] After identifying her, George went into raptures, saying, 'She is everything I can form to myself lovely. I am daily grown unhappy, sleep has left me, which never was before interrupted by any reverse of fortune; I protest before God I never have had any improper thought with regard to her; I don't deny having often flattered myself with hopes that one day or other you would consent to my raising her to a throne.' When he heard that the twenty-year-old George Spencer, 4th Duke of Marlborough, was flirting with her, he 'retired to my chamber where I remained for several hours in the depth of despair'.

George ended his letter with a melodramatic, adolescent flourish, telling Bute, 'Let me preserve your friendship, and though my heart should break, I shall have the happy reflection in dying that I have not been altogether unworthy of the best of friends though unfortunate in other things.'[51] Bute's reply was equally gushing, promising that he would certainly consider the matter carefully, but forewarning that when they met George must 'prepare your mind with a resolution to hear the voice of truth, for such alone shall come from me ... though death looked me in the face'.[52] Death was certainly not looking either of them in the face, but if George could write that way then so could he.

It is remarkable, given the sexual proclivities of the courts of that era, that George did not even contemplate simply making Lady Sarah his mistress, or at least attempting to. His religious piety and emphasis on personal virtue precluded the path of sexual infidelity taken enthusiastically by his father, grandfather and great-grandfather – none of whom had a strong Christian faith. Indeed, among the whole Hanoverian dynasty, from George I to William IV, stretching over more than a century, George was the only uxorious husband and pious Christian. Having heard what he called Bute's 'voice of truth' about the political impossibility of his marrying Lady Sarah, a commoner related to Henry Fox, he concluded that 'The interest of my country ever shall be my first care, my own inclinations shall ever submit to it; I am born for the happiness or misery of a great nation, and consequently must often act contrary to my passions.'[53] Here at last he was not being histrionic, as that sentiment might serve almost as a leitmotif for George's whole life and reign.

George ultimately had a lucky escape from Lady Sarah, who, after marrying Sir Charles Bunbury in 1762, became one of the great femmes fatales of the era. 'So Lady Sarah Bunbury is with child!' Lady Mary Coke, the Duke of Argyll's well-informed daughter, wrote to her sister the Countess of Stafford in 1768. 'The town is rather ill-natured upon her subject, and think it a lucky circumstance for her that this pregnancy happens at a time when she has no particular lover.'[54] Lady Sarah's illegitimate daughter was fathered by the 3rd Duke of Gordon's son Lord William Gordon, with whom she ran away to Paris soon afterwards. When she refused to marry him the following year, Lady Mary was prompted to add that she was 'void of shame or principles'.[55] Despite such scandals, some lasting fondness clearly remained between George and Sarah: in 1804, after the death of her second husband, he granted her a pension of £800 per annum for the education of her daughters.

George promised Bute never to marry an Englishwoman, who could not be of royal birth and marriageable, and during that winter he asked him 'by some method or other [to] get some account of the various princesses in Germany', using a process that 'binds me to nothing, and would save a great deal of trouble whenever I consent to enter into those bonds'.[56] He reported that he and his mother were already 'looking in the *New Berlin Almanack* for princesses, where three new ones have been found', almost in the manner of modern mail-order brides.[57] Bute misinterpreted this to mean that George wanted to marry in the summer, but was put right when George told him, 'I can never agree to alter my situation whilst this Old Man lives; I will rather undergo anything ever so disagreeable than put my trust in him for a single moment in an affair of such delicacy.'[58]

*

In mid-November, Richard Grenville-Temple, 2nd Earl Temple, Pitt's brother-in-law and a key figure in the powerful Grenville clan, threatened to resign as Lord Privy Seal on being refused the Order of the Garter, putting the entire survival of the government in jeopardy. George was furious that Temple had acted without informing him, and was still fuming days later when Temple withdrew his threat after the King reluctantly appeased him by promising the next vacant blue riband. 'I could write you volumes if I attempted enumerating the many insolences we have received from that faithless band,' George wrote to Bute of the Grenvilles, who were to loom large throughout his reign.[59] His dislike and distrust of them started early, merging with that of their cousin, William Pitt.

Admiral Edward Hawke won a great victory at the battle of Quiberon Bay in the Bay of Biscay on 20 November, where he sank, destroyed or captured seven French ships-of-the-line.* When this was added to the victories of Minden and Quebec, successes in India under Robert Clive, the capture of Guadeloupe in the West Indies in May, the defeat of a French squadron in the Bay of Lagos off Portugal in August and the capture of the fortresses at Ticonderoga, Crown Point and Niagara in North America in September, the year 1759 rightly became known as the *Annus mirabilis*, and William Pitt was hailed as the greatest war leader since Elizabeth I defeated the Armada.

One might assume that, set against such a backdrop, past mistakes might have been ignored or forgiven. Yet even in this climate of universal victory the demand for vengeance upon commanders who had allegedly underperformed did not subside. Sackville's court martial for 'disobedience of orders' began at Horse Guards in Whitehall, the British Army's headquarters, before fifteen generals on 29 February 1760. Over the next five weeks the details of what had transpired at Minden the previous August were highly disputed: the orders had gone through three generals in three languages and appeared to be contradictory; the nature of the wood that the cavalry was expected to ride through was challenged, as was the exact position of a Saxe-Gothan infantry regiment which had to get out of the way before the cavalry could move. Most contentious was the amount of time lost by Sackville's purported inaction: some accounts claimed as long as ninety minutes, others forty-five, while Sackville himself stated only eight.[60]

There were moments of drama as on the fourth day of the trial when a Colonel Sloper alleged that 'My Lord George Sackville was alarmed to a very great degree,' an imputation of cowardice which was later proved to

---

* A ship-of-the-line typically had seventy-four guns or more, although in this battle the French *Inflexible* had sixty-four.

be down to personal malice and without substance.[61] The trial was highly political: Sackville was a member of the Leicester House Set and had made enemies in both the government and the army, ostensibly through his haughtiness but also possibly because he was suspected of bisexuality (although that was not raised). The court martial found him guilty on 3 April, and declared him 'unfit to serve His Majesty in any military capacity whatsoever'.

A delighted King had Sackville's name struck off the list of privy councillors; he was also forbidden from attending Court, and the sentence was read out to every regiment in the army, with the comment that it was 'worse than death'.[62] As had been the case with John Byng's sentence three years earlier, the verdict may have satisfied certain political circles, but it met with stony-faced incomprehension from those who understood the nature of warfare and the fog of battle. Three months later, General Sir Jeffery Amherst, the Commander-in-Chief of the British Army in North America, wrote, 'I have carefully read the court-martial relating to the affair of Minden, all my garrison have studied it, and I may venture to affirm that there is not an officer in it who does not blush that such a sentence should have been pronounced by a British court.'[63]

It was an indication of how vicious and polarized the conflict between the rival courts had become that the King stated he would not exercise mercy for his grandson's friend Sackville, who would be shot by firing squad if ten generals of the fifteen voted for it – in the event, only seven did so.[64] There were plenty of other examples of these intergenerational feuds within the European nobility: Peter the Great of Russia had his son Alexis executed in 1718; Charles Emmanuel of Savoy arrested and imprisoned his father in 1731; Frederick William I of Prussia threatened to execute his son, Frederick the Great, instead imprisoning him for a time and beheading his best friend (and probable lover) Hans Hermann von Katte. With the Hanoverians such hatred ran deep, continuing for generation after generation, fuelled to a degree by the partisan cliques of British politics. The late Prince Frederick's abiding hope that this dreadful tradition might finally cease at his accession died with him.

When it was reported by Lady Yarmouth that George intended to receive Sackville at Leicester House, the Duke of Devonshire informed Bute that 'The King has forbid Lord G. Sackville the Court,' with the clear implication that George must too.[65] Augusta's Chamberlain was meanwhile given the same message, infuriating George. 'The K[ing]'s message is a true slap in the face to me . . .' he told Bute; 'my honour forces me to remain but little longer passive; my dearest friend I don't doubt sees the necessity of my taking a bolder and more resolute part; nothing but that can draw men to follow my banner.'[66] Yet for all George's talk about his honour, Bute sensibly advised him not to expend any more political capital over Sackville, who had after all been found guilty, and so George did not receive him again until the following year – when his appearance at Court caused such an outcry that Bute had to tell him to stay away until the war was over. George felt profound embarrassment, even guilt, at effectively endorsing Sackville's public shaming, and these feelings were to have significant repercussions in later years.

For all the great victories of the *Annus mirabilis*, the war was exorbitantly expensive, and George and Bute worried about the National Debt, which grew from £77.8 million in 1758 to £90.4 million in 1760. By January 1761 it was due to increase by a further £8.2 million.[67] In April 1760 George lamented in an essay on public finance that 'We can scarce expect a peace before we have increased our debt to £130 or £140 million.'[68] He fully recognized that great things could be achieved by spending money wisely, citing the Duke of Marlborough's victories in the War of Spanish Succession of 1701–14, Robert Clive's victory at Plassey in West Bengal in June 1757 and the victories in North America that led to the capture of Montreal on 8 September 1760 and of Detroit a week later, delivering large swathes of the world into British hands. Despite these gains, and while acknowledging the jubilant public sense of victory, George and Bute nonetheless remained determined, in the words of one historian, 'to lighten the burdens on posterity as much as they could, and as soon as they dared'.[69]

While the Treason Act forbade Britons even so much as to 'imagine' the death of the monarch, George and Bute constantly did just that, and when he was king George recalled to Bute how much they had been preparing for 'the hour ... which has been so long been wished for by my d[earest] friend, I mean the entering on a reformation in government', one in which 'the wicked machinations of faction' would be replaced by a virtuous commitment to 'the wellbeing of this country'.[70]

George was relatively uninterested in the actual personnel of government, beyond the overwhelming necessity of Bute becoming Prime Minister. This was pivotal, since that post controlled the main fount of government patronage. 'Whilst my dearest is near me,' George wrote to Bute on 4 May 1760, 'I care not who are the tools he may think necessary to be in [the] ministry provided the blackest of hearts [that is, Pitt] is not one of them.'[71] The reference to ministers as mere 'tools' of government gives another indication of his general view of members of Parliament.

George readily accepted that he would attract what he called 'the ingratitude of some, the pusillanimity and enmity of others', when he appointed his favourite as Prime Minister, but with 'a proper steadiness of conduct' he believed their policies would make them popular in the country: 'The game will ever be in my favour unless I fall into some of the snares youth is so often subject to.'[72] The policies that he assumed would eventually make 'his' government more popular than that of Pitt were essentially those that his father had prescribed over a decade earlier. He also proposed to accept only a fixed sum to be paid him by Parliament of £800,000 per annum for life, a reduction on the £876,988 George II received for 1759/60 and less than the £823,956 average over the 1750s. More controversially, although to George's mind merely a gesture of progress, he proposed opening government places to Tories, independents and other non-Whigs.[73] Along with the decoupling of Hanover from Britain it was a worthy programme, but George was naive to think it might be as popular as Pitt's delivery of unprecedented worldwide martial glory.

George's resentful preoccupation with Pitt, whom he described to Bute as 'the most ungrateful and in my mind the most dishonourable of men', seemed to cast a cloud over the brilliance of Britain's successes. Even while celebrating the fall of Montreal, George told Bute that 'at the same time I can't help feeling that every such thing raises those I have no reason to love,' meaning Pitt, and he added, 'I hope this nation will open her eyes and see who are her true friends, and that her popular man is a true snake in the grass.'[74] For George to see this victory, the fall of the last major French stronghold in Canada, through the narrow political prism of his own resentment of Pitt was indicative of how personal politics had become for him. It indicates solipsism as well as a lack of judgement.

An important essay written by George about the British constitution some time between mid-January and late February 1760 provides a fascinating insight into his thinking just as he was about to ascend the throne. Foremost in his thoughts were not the prerogatives of the Crown but the rights of individuals. He lambasted the trial of revenue officers without juries as 'entirely contrary to our constitution', and saw the decision to court-martial Lord George Sackville as setting a dangerous precedent for civilians serving in the militia. He criticized Queen Anne's creation of twelve Whig peers to flood the House of Lords during the anti-Tory purge of 1712 as an abuse of the royal prerogative, 'for if the power of the Lords should be annihilated, despotism would surely follow the loss of liberty'.[75] In other essays, even Oliver Cromwell – a figure rarely praised by monarchs – was offered up as 'a friend of justice and virtue', as 'Charles I had too high a notion of the royal power.'[76] John Adams himself could hardly have quarrelled with George's statement in the essay that 'The pride, the glory of Britain and the direct end of its constitution is political liberty.'[77]

George also considered the threats posed by a royal standing army, suggesting instead that local militias should be twice the size.[78] 'Every form of government has some principle to which its laws and rules of action ought to be agreeable,' the twenty-year-old wrote: 'in democracy's and aristocracy's this is virtue, in monarchy, honour; in despotism pride, avarice and sloth. The British constitution being a mixture of the three forms of government, honour and virtue ought to be equally thought of.'[79] There were plenty of times in George's reign when he was unable to live up to all the noble views of this essay – he was to advocate non-jury trials for revenue officers during the American Revolution, for example, and created several peerages on a single day in 1784 to get out of a difficult political situation – but nonetheless his belief in the vital importance of the monarchy retaining its honour stayed with him throughout his life, for good and ill.

Bute had motivated George to study hard by infusing him with the belief that, as he told him, 'You are not accustomed to serious things, and yet your temper is extremely formed for it, formed for manly ideas and even refinements in virtue.'[80] Hard work would thus 'make everything easy'. George had recognized that he had something important, worthwhile and, he believed, quite revolutionary to study for: nothing less than a moral and political regeneration of the nation that he and Bute would lead, which might redeem his father's tragically untimely death. They had a clear agenda as they contemplated power in 1760, one far removed from the Old Whig establishment's affinity for comfort and the status quo. 'If vice and faction can be got the better of,' George had told Bute in August 1758, 'this nation will again appear in her ancient lustre.'[81] The revolution would be achieved, he hoped, by 'attempting with vigour to restore religion and virtue when I mount the throne'.[82]

'If I am but steady and have your assistance,' George wrote to Bute of their political opponents in December 1759, 'we may make them all smart for their ingratitude.'[83] As well as punishing their enemies, among whom George dangerously counted Pitt, they knew they would also have to reward friends in the new reign. This would not be done in return for lickspittle support for the government, as at present, but because 'noble actions and generous sentiments shall lead to the royal favour,' while their opponents' 'prostitution of principle, venality and corruption meet their just reward'.[84] In an essay George wrote about this new political system, 'the honest citizen, the zealous patriot' would be deservedly uplifted, while 'the degenerate mercenary sons of slavery' would be forced to become virtuous.

If it all sounded somewhat simplistic, that is because it was – George offered no clear explanation of how to distinguish between the sincere, zealous patriots and the mercenary sons of slavery. Yet while it is easy to smile at the naivety (and priggishness) of the young Prince, these were not low ideals to have, however unworldly and however unattractive the whiff of self-righteousness and moral superiority – traits which he never grew out of. His youth had been disorienting – not only the death of his father when he was young, but also the enforced resignations in his household in the middle of his education – but now with Bute by his side George saw his path forward once he had acceded to the throne.

Just after 8 a.m. on Saturday 25 October 1760, George was out riding (as he started most days) between Kew Bridge and the milestone marking 6 miles from Hyde Park Corner in what was called Gunnersbury Lane when a messenger from Kensington Palace reported that the King had met with an accident there. Ordering his entourage to say nothing about it to anyone, George galloped back to Kew to await further news. He did not want to be seen anticipating too eagerly the news for which he, Bute and the Dowager Princess Augusta had been waiting so long.

3

'I Glory in the Name of Briton'

October 1760–January 1762

The accession of George the Third to the throne of these kingdoms
opened a new and brighter prospect to men of literary merit . . . His
present Majesty's education in this country, as well as his taste and
beneficence, prompted him to be the patron of science and the arts.[1]
James Boswell, *The Life of Samuel Johnson*, 1791

At 7.30 a.m. on 25 October 1760, George II drank his morning cup of chocolate, then sat on the 'closet-stool' (lavatory) in his apartment in Kensington Palace, where he suffered a heart attack, cutting his face against the edge of some furniture as he fell barely conscious to the floor. His *valet de chambre* M. Schröder heard 'a noise louder than the royal wind', followed by a sound 'like the falling of a billet of wood from the fire'.[2] He rushed in, but all the King could manage was 'Call Amelia.' By the time his daughter Princess Amelia arrived, he was dead. She wrote to her nephew at Kew addressing her letter, 'To His Majesty'. He signed his reply 'GR' – Georgius Rex – his first use of the royal initials.[3]

George's first action on receiving the news was to write to Bute, who lived nearby. 'A most extraordinary thing is [*sic*] just happened to me when on the other side of the bridge,' he told his friend.[4] He added that he had sworn all the servants to secrecy 'as they value their employments, and shall wait till I hear from you to know what further must be done'.* He then went to his mother's house to tell her the news, and having received Amelia's confirmatory message he went to Bute's neighbouring house to confer.

It was a Saturday, and the only minister in London was William Pitt,

---

* By 1804 George had completely misremembered the incident, believing that he had gone on to Kew and told his mother not to tell Bute for fear that he would use it as an opportunity 'to be placed in a political situation' (ed. Harcourt, *Diaries and Correspondence of George Rose*, II pp. 189–92).

who was standing at the door of his coach outside his house in St James's Square* about to leave for the country when he received an urgent summons from the King's mistress Amalie von Wallmoden, Lady Yarmouth, to Kensington Palace, where Princess Amelia told him the news. He summoned the Privy Council to Kensington Palace, but made his own way to Kew where he saw Bute at 10 a.m. and George at 11 a.m. George, 'with a grave and manly deportment' suited to the occasion, told Pitt that 'he felt how unequal he was to the load now come upon his youth'.[5]

There was some initial confusion about where the first Privy Council of the new reign would meet in order to sign the accession proclamation: ministers arrived at Kensington Palace but George insisted it should instead take place at Savile House. Once it was learned that there were no servants on duty there, they finally met at 6 p.m. at Carlton House, Princess Augusta's London residence. When the Prime Minister, the Duke of Newcastle, arrived for his first audience and told George that he wanted to do everything possible to contribute to 'the ease and success' of the new reign, the new King replied, 'My Lord Bute is your very good friend; he will tell you my thoughts at large.'[6] Newcastle replied that he hoped Bute was so, even though both men knew perfectly well that the other was not his good friend and never had been.

During George II's lifetime, George and Bute had drawn up a declaration to be read to the Privy Council, which therefore needed only light revisions on the day itself. George had Newcastle read it to Pitt before the formal meeting. Most of it was unremarkable, with predictable sentiments about the late King, how George was 'animated by the tenderest affection for this my native country' and how he entered 'with cheerfulness into this arduous situation' and would maintain the constitutions of Church and state, and so on.[7] But there was also a sentence that read, 'As I mount the throne in the midst of a bloody war, I shall endeavour to prosecute it in the manner most likely to bring an honourable and lasting peace.'[8] Pitt was either not listening carefully or did not spot this coded rejection of his prosecution of the war, and it was only after George had read his address to the Council that Pitt proposed it be substantially altered before it was published. He wanted 'bloody war' changed to 'expensive, but just and necessary war' and the words 'in concert with our allies' added at the end.[9]

Bute did not want these changes, not least because they seemed to imply that Britain could not make peace without the approval of Frederick the Great, but when Lord Mansfield, the eminent Lord Chief Justice, supported Pitt, Bute agreed to advise George to alter the document. George was also

---

* Chatham House, today the headquarters of the Royal Institute of International Affairs.

'very adverse to the altering [of the] declaration' but he too assented.[10] Henry Fox said that the Privy Council had known nothing about the declaration 'which had not been shown them till they came to Carlton House, not subjected to their consideration, nor without difficulty altered the next day'.[11]

King George III was proclaimed by the heralds of the College of Arms at Savile House and four other London locations on Sunday 26 October. His full title included 'King of France', a fiction dating back to the Plantagenet days when the kings of England really had ruled much of the territory of their great rival, while his Electorate of Hanover was subsumed within the words 'and so forth' at the end of his list of titles. Although Ireland was mentioned, the territories in North America, India and the Caribbean were not. Succeeding the man who was then Britain's longest-lived monarch, George was himself the youngest since Edward VI in 1547, and the public rejoicing at his accession was akin to that which had greeted Charles II's Restoration a century earlier. 'He died unlamented,' wrote Lord Chesterfield of George II, 'though not unpraised because he was dead.'[12] The Court announced that mourning for the late King would end as early as George's birthday on 4 June rather than continue for the traditional twelve months, ostensibly in order to help the silk and weaving industries. The truth was that few mourned George II, a difficult man whose successes had been largely eclipsed by his general air of unpleasantness.

When an envelope addressed to Lady Yarmouth was found in the late King's desk at Kensington Palace containing £6,000 in banknotes – other sources say £9,000 in bank bills and 1,100 guineas in cash – George ordered that it be passed on to her.[13] It was to be the last monarchical payment to a mistress for sixty years; the petticoat government which George had denounced in his essays, and which had played a part in corrupting both the Bourbon dynasty and every British reign since that of Charles I, would not infect his. When years later a minister tried to exculpate himself after a state secret had been leaked, saying, 'I can assure Your Majesty I told no one but my wife,' the King was reputed to have replied, 'I did not tell *mine*.'[14]

As Prince of Wales, George had lived a relatively private existence, but he was now the centre of his subjects' attention. They found a young man tall for the era at 5 foot 10 inches, with blue-grey eyes and light auburn hair, a high forehead, slightly protruding eyes, a large nose, thick lips, a dimpled chin and ruddy complexion. George often wore a short wig according to the fashion of the times. 'There was a noble openness in his countenance,' the Duchess of Northumberland noted in her diary, 'blended with a cheerful good-natured affability, he was fair and fresh-coloured and had now and then a few pimples out.'[15] She added that his teeth were 'extremely fine', and that he danced 'with an unparalleled air of majestic dignity'. Horace Walpole noted that, although he was 'not apt to be enamoured with royalty', he had to admit that the new King 'gives all the indication imaginable of being amiable. His person is tall, and full of dignity; his countenance florid and good-natured; his manner graceful and obliging.'[16]

George had grown greatly in confidence under Bute's direction, and had developed a good-natured demeanour by the time he acceded, replacing his childhood shyness. He had excellent manners, allowing ladies through doors first, which was not always the case with his brothers.[17] For someone often thought of as reserved, he could also be gracious: when he was nearly injured during a review after a general's horse had kicked his own, 'The King behaved exceeding well, and did everything to dissipate his uneasiness.'[18]

The realm to which George acceded in 1760 was much the same as that to which Charles II had been restored a century earlier. Britain was primarily rural, socially stratified, religiously Anglican and parliamentary, the main difference being that in 1760 the nation was at war. The Industrial Revolution would not really begin to make its mark until the 1780s, and Britain's consequent massive increase in population – it doubled in George's reign – had therefore not yet begun when he came to the throne. There were about 6¾ million English and Welsh, 3¼ million Irish and 1¼ million Scots.[19] The majority of the new King's subjects lived in villages and small towns and were employed in agriculture; the two largest cities in England were London, with 750,000 inhabitants, and the port of Bristol, with 60,000. Most of the country's commerce took place in small market towns and little ports, which went largely unsupervised by government. The quality of the harvests, which had been good before 1760 but were generally worse from then until 1780, affected the price of bread and thus intimately the material wellbeing of the population.

George stood at the apex of a social hierarchy dominated by the land-owning aristocracy and a powerful squirearchy; entry into both of their ranks usually took more than one generation, even for the families of successful tradesmen. 'The Englishman', wrote the Swiss painter Jean Rouquet in 1755, 'always has in his hands an accurate pair of scales in which he scrupulously weighs up the birth, the rank, and above all, the wealth of the people he meets, in order to adjust his behaviour towards them accordingly.'[20] As local employers and the primary consumers of small producers, and aslo as justices of the peace and members of Parliament, local squires wielded tremendous power, despite being junior in social rank to the territorial aristocracy who made up almost the entirety of the House of Lords, which in George's reign enjoyed a political a status at least equal to that of the House of Commons. The squire's ally tended to be the Church of England priest, who generally manifested a social conservatism that was a strong feature of the age.

The timing of George's accession could hardly have been better; it took place on the anniversary of the battle of Agincourt, and only a few days later Frederick the Great won another victory over the Austrians at the battle of Torgau. 'What a change!' Bute's mother-in-law, Lady Mary Wortley Montagu, the famous letter writer, socialite and poet, wrote of the alteration in the national mood. 'If nutmegs flowered in our fields, I could scarcely be more surprised.'[21] George made much of the fact that he was the first monarch since Charles I to have been born and raised entirely in England. He was a native English-speaker who had never so much as visited Germany; when his subjects said that he could probably not find Hanover on a map they were wrong, but they meant it in approbation.[22] Several commemorative medals were minted, one stating 'Entirely British' and another depicting a triumphant Britannia – 'Felicitas Britanniae' – complete with flag, lion, liberty cap and cornucopia.[23]

George had come to the throne at a glorious moment for British arms: the French and Dutch had been driven from the oceans by the Royal Navy, avenging the humiliations of the past century. Canada, India, rich sugar islands and Gorée Island, the French slave-trading centre off Senegal, had all recently been seized. The widespread celebrations of George's accession were particularly strong in Boston, capital of the King's loyal Massachusetts Bay Colony. As the proclamation was read in which Boston acknowledged 'all faith and constant obedience' to the new King 'with all hearty and humble affection', the crowd shouted 'Huzzah!', militiamen fired three volleys, cannon from the harbour fort boomed and the town was illuminated in the traditional celebratory manner by placing candles in the windows of houses.[24] The exertions Britain was making in blood and treasure to protect her American imperial brethren from incursions over the previous six years of what was then known as the French and Indian War were greatly appreciated. 'I have been here about sixteen years,' a Bostonian noted, 'and I don't know of one single man but would risk his life and property to serve King George the Third.'[25]

Someone else who hailed the new King unreservedly was Edmund Burke, the Dublin-born man of letters and aesthete who co-edited the *Annual Register*, a chronicle of significant national and world events. In its 1761 edition, he described enthusiastically how 'The virtues of a king, a native of the country he governs, has united all sects and all parties, religious and civil, in the one wish of continuing the government in him and his family.'[26] 'We were so weary of our old King, that we are much pleased with his successor,' Dr Samuel Johnson told his friend Joseph Baretti, 'of whom we are so much inclined to hope great things that most of us begin already to believe them.'[27]

Soon after his accession, George announced his plan to hand over all Crown revenues to Parliament in return for £800,000 a year for life. It turned out to be a terrible decision, and by 1769 had cost him a total of £767,770.[28] The Civil List Act of 1698 had made Parliament responsible for the great expenditures of the state such as the army, navy and National Debt, while Civil List revenues were granted to cover the cost of the royal family and civil government. But both these outgoings increased while George's income was now fixed.[29] His siblings at the time of his accession were Augusta (who was twenty-three), Edward (twenty-one), William (sixteen), Henry (fourteen), Louisa (eleven), Frederick (ten) and Caroline Matilda (nine), all of whom were growing up and needed supporting, and he had not considered what a wife and large progeny would one day require, let alone the effects of inflation in wartime.

On 31 October, George issued a proclamation 'for the encouragement of piety and virtue, and for [the] preventing and punishing of vice, profaneness and immorality'. It stated that vice had 'so fatal a tendency to the corruption of many of our loving subjects, otherwise religiously and virtuously disposed', that from henceforth 'all persons of honour, or in place of authority, will give good example by their own virtue and piety'.[30] Although his two predecessors had issued similar proclamations upon their accessions, George took his seriously. It was intended to herald not a new puritanism so much as a reign in which the King would become a model of domestic fidelity and religious piety. While he embodied such traits himself, many of those who would subsequently have to be appointed as his ministers did not, prompting accusations of hypocrisy from the Opposition. It did not help his cause that several of George's uncles and (later) sons later chose to live openly with their mistresses.

'Moral panics' had occurred previously in the 1690s and 1730s, and another had already been under way in the 1750s when Sir James Lowther MP warned that Britain was 'undone as a nation, or shall be in a few years under the heels of France thanks to the excess of gaming and diversions of all kinds'.[31] Luxury, gambling, corruption: all were assumed to weaken the moral fibre of the nation. The theory of coming French dominance because of British immorality rather broke down when the almost institutionalized immorality on display at Versailles was considered, but George's early proclamations on moral and financial probity were widely approved of. A young Boston lawyer named John Adams found in them 'sentiments worthy of a king – a patriot king'.[32]

Although Newcastle, the elderly embodiment of the Whig elite, had tendered his resignation only two days after George II's death, it was refused. He was no longer the political master he once was, but the Duke still exercised significant influence, and Bute felt, probably correctly, unready to risk a power vacuum that might hand the keys of office to Pitt. Newcastle's gradual decline had pushed Pitt to the forefront; while the latter's political and oratorical powers were at their height and his victories were still being won, Bute understandably hesitated to take on this mercurial, brilliant and ambitious dynamo as his nominal lieutenant.

It may with hindsight seem curious that the Old Corps Whigs such as the Pelham brothers and the Duke of Devonshire were so surprised to learn that George did not want them to continue to rule Britain, as they had been doing without interruption since 1714. Devonshire put this point of view rather bluntly, telling Bute that Newcastle 'had united with him the principal nobility, the moneyed men and that interest which had brought about the Revolution, had set this family on the throne, and supported them in it, and were not only the most considerable* party but the true solid strength that might be depended on for the support of government'.[33] For these reasons, Devonshire assumed, his party 'were infallibly the people that the King must trust to for the effectual support of his government'. Their sense of entitlement was palpable, but Devonshire had a point: over the coming decades the King would find it very hard to govern without the Whigs' consent.

Writing to his friend Sir Horace Mann, the British Minister (that is, ambassador) to Tuscany, Walpole conveyed the same sense:

> [The new reign] set out with great show of alteration; it soon settled into the old channel. The favourite [Bute] appeared sole minister for a day or two. The old ministers agreed to continue as they were, and though the Duke of Newcastle attempted to pretend to have a mind of retiring, he soon recollected that he had no such inclination. Mr Pitt . . . acquainted the King that he was content to manage the war, and wished to act in other things as he had done under the Duke of Newcastle in the late reign . . . Thus only the superficies† . . . is altered, not the government.[34]

In early November, not long after George had left Leicester and Savile Houses and taken up residence in St James's Palace, Newcastle began to

---

* 'Worthy of regard and attention; respectable; above neglect; important; valuable' (*Johnson's Dictionary*).
† 'Surface' (*Johnson's Dictionary*).

voice suspicions of an apparent friendliness between Pitt and Bute, whom he thought 'seem previously to concert about measures' before Cabinet meetings.[35] The sixty-seven-year-old duke sensed that his days in office might be numbered, especially after Bute told him that the King would be naming a new Cabinet in around six months' time.[36] In truth little had changed, and there was no Pitt–Bute alliance beyond Pitt needing Bute's support for his running of the war. Within the ministry, opinion was divided between those backing Pitt, who wanted to attack the island of Belle-Île off Brittany and to expand the militia, and Newcastle, who worried about the cost.

Lord Hardwicke, Newcastle's closest friend in politics, later claimed that the King and Bute exaggerated their support for the active prosecution of the war so as to drive a wedge between Pitt and Newcastle and thus hasten the fall of the government. Bute, he alleged,

> principally availed himself, with great art and finesse, of the dissensions between the Duke of Newcastle and Mr Pitt; . . . he played off one against the other occasionally, till he had got rid of the popular minister; and when that was compassed, he strengthened himself in the Cabinet by bringing in [Charles Wyndham, 2nd Earl of] Egremont and Mr [George] Grenville, and never left [off] intriguing till he had rendered it impracticable for the old Duke to continue in office with credit or honour.[37]

This probably owes more to Hardwicke's hindsight than to Bute's guile at the time, although Newcastle complained bitterly to Hardwicke on 7 November 1760 that 'I am the greatest cipher that ever appeared at Court. The young King is hardly civil to me; talks to me of *nothing*, and scarce answers me upon my own Treasury affairs . . . Is this giving me the countenance and support which is necessary for me to carry on His Majesty's business, much less what is sufficient to make me happy and easy?'[38] 'Countenance and support' referred to the King's confidence and willingness to create peerages and spend money on elections; and Newcastle's question was clearly rhetorical.

Despite being on such shaky ground, Newcastle turned down Bute's request in mid-November for an English peerage that would allow him to sit in the House of Lords for life. 'His Grace spoke out boldly that it was absolutely impossible,' noted Devonshire.[39] With the King's enthusiastic support for such an elevation it was clearly not impossible, but nonetheless it was arranged that Bute should instead be elected to the House of Lords as one of Scotland's sixteen representative peers, as he had been from 1737 to 1741. On 16 November he was formally appointed the King's Groom of the Stole, which carried with it a seat in the 'Nominal' Cabinet, a separate body from the 'Efficient' Cabinet* that wielded actual power (whose meetings he was also attending).[40] At that period, there was no such concept as Cabinet responsibility, and constitutionally ministers regarded themselves as directly responsible to the King rather than to the Prime Minister, who was merely *primus inter pares*.

On Tuesday 18 November, George delivered his first Speech from the Throne at the State Opening of Parliament. This traditionally set out the government's political agenda for the coming session, but on this occasion it was extended to include general remarks about the new reign. 'The just concern which I have felt in my own breast on the sudden death of the late King, my royal grandfather,' George began, not entirely convincingly, 'makes me not doubt but you must all have been deeply affected with so severe a loss.'[41] The speech had been drafted by Hardwicke, but George inserted some words with which he has been justifiably identified ever since: 'Born and educated in this country, I glory in the name of Britain; and the peculiar happiness of my life will ever consist in promoting the welfare of a people whose loyalty and warm affection to me I consider as the greatest and most permanent security of my throne.'[42]

Although George actually wrote 'Britain', it was reported as 'Briton' in the *London Gazette*, the *Journals of the House of Commons* and elsewhere, which makes much more sense in the context as he was speaking about himself and attempting to tell his people that their new King gloried in his Britishness, thus differentiating himself from his German grandfather and great-grandfather. (In an early draft of the speech, Hardwicke had included a reference to George being an 'Englishman', which further supports the view that George meant Briton rather than Britain.)[43] However it was spelt – and in the eighteenth century spelling was considerably more fluid than later on – it was in any case a conscious echo of Queen Anne's speech on her accession in 1702, in which she attested that 'I know my heart to

* The Efficient Cabinet consisted of the King's 'confidential servants' who ran the various government departments, whereas the Nominal Cabinet comprised not only the members of the Efficient Cabinet but also the Archbishop of Canterbury, Lord Chief Justice, Speaker of the House of Commons, Lord Chamberlain, Master of the Horse, Lord Steward and Groom of the Stole. The Nominal Cabinet met in the King's presence to hear the Southern Secretary read out the Speech from the Throne that the King delivered at the opening and closing of parliamentary sessions, and also to review all of the death sentences handed down from the Old Bailey, a practice that continued until the eighteen-year-old Queen Victoria acceded, whereupon the responsibility was passed to the Home Secretary. References to the Cabinet from now on will allude to the Efficient Cabinet, from which today's Cabinet is descended. The Nominal Cabinet still met to hear the King's speech read until February 1921, after which it was merely sent to George V at Balmoral in a box.

be entirely English,' despite her having spent much of her childhood in exile in France.

George, who spoke English without a German accent, further differentiated himself from his grandfather by announcing a moral agenda: 'It is my fixed purpose to countenance and encourage the practice of true religion and virtue.'[44] He went on to hail the victories in Canada and India, to praise 'my general' Prince Ferdinand of Brunswick and to congratulate 'My good brother and ally the King of Prussia' on his 'very considerable victories' and the Royal Navy for blockading France. As Pitt had insisted, he declared the war 'both just and necessary', adding that he was 'determined, with your cheerful and powerful assistance, to prosecute this war with vigour, in order to [achieve] that desirable object, a safe and honourable peace'.[45] As for future expenditure, 'On my part, you may be assured of a regular and becoming economy.' The speech was a success, although Henry Fox slyly noted that 'He was much admired but thought to have too much studied action and it was observed that he laid the accent on the first syllable of "allies" and "revenues", which is after the Scotch pronunciation.'[46]

Only a few days later, Bute was complaining to his friend and adviser the Sardinian Minister the Comte de Viry about the rudeness to which Pitt subjected him in Cabinet meetings, and in mid-November the King wrote to Bute to ask, rhetorically at least, 'whether I have not from the first day of my mounting the throne wished for his [Bute's] consent to get rid of those who are unwilling to do their duty' – meaning Newcastle over the issue of Bute's English peerage, and Pitt over the war – adding of the latter, 'and I plainly see if every ill humour of a certain man is to be soothed, that in less than a couple of months I shall be irretrievably in his fetters; a state of bondage that an old man of seventy odd [that is, George II] groaned [under], and that [one of] twenty-two ought to risk everything rather than submit.'[47] Believing that 'my honour is here at stake,' George felt he ought to show Pitt 'that aversion which will force him to resign', because the British people would never 'join the man who from his own ambition, pride and impracticability means to disturb my quiet and (what I feel much stronger) the repose of my subjects'.

George then returned to the melodramatic language he had used when contemplating his love for Sarah Lennox, telling Bute that if the British people turned out to be 'so ungrateful' as to support Pitt over him, 'I should then I really believe fall into the deepest melancholy which would soon deprive me of the vexations of this life.'[48] When considering George's regular use of such histrionic phraseology we should remember that sentiment and sensibility were important strands in eighteenth-century aristocratic culture, and by no means at odds with self-control. His frequent invocations of abdication or even suicide were not intended to be taken seriously. Keen to emphasize to Bute that he was not depressed, George ended his letter, 'Do not imagine that what I have here said is owing to any foreboding thoughts'; rather it was prompted only by a sense that if he did not show his subjects 'that I will not permit ministers to trample on me, that my subjects will in time come to esteem me unworthy of the crown I wear'.[49] His frustration at not being fully in power after waiting so long for it was clear; but so too was the immaturity, even paranoia, of a youth who had very little knowledge of the world, but was now preparing himself to enter into political battle with one of the most popular and accomplished figures of British history.

In one very important area George had already struck out on his own, disregarding both Pitt and Newcastle: he would find himself his own wife. He was the first unmarried monarch for a century, and soon after his accession he directed Baron P. A. von Münchhausen,* his discreet and trusted Hanoverian Minister in London, to draw up a list of potential brides. Considering how intensely political the choice of wife was – with profound strategic implications for British foreign policy during a major war – it is remarkable that George and Münchhausen managed to keep the search process secret from the Cabinet (except of course Bute). George was looking for a Protestant princess (therefore almost certainly a German) who was pleasant, bright, cultured, fertile and utterly uninterested in politics.

The initial list had six names, which on 20 November Münchhausen extended with two more: the Princess of Denmark (though she might already be engaged), and Princess Charlotte of Mecklenburg-Strelitz, a small German grand duchy near the Baltic, whom he thought probably too young at sixteen and a half. In the course of further investigations and discussions, in which the Dowager Princess Augusta was closely involved, the list was whittled down. The Princess of Anhalt-Dessau was rejected because her grandfather had married an apothecary's daughter; the Princess of Brandenburg's mother was reputed to have had an affair with a courtier; Princess Frederica of Saxe-Gotha was thought deformed and incapable of having children, but she was also suspected of being fond of 'philosophy', suggesting she had her own intellectual interests that might slide into the *verboten* areas of freethinking. The Princess of Brunswick was only fifteen. Caroline of Hesse-Darmstadt did not appeal to George

---

* A cousin of Baron Hieronymus von Münchhausen of the eponymous Syndrome.

because of 'her size', because her father was 'very near the borders of madness' and because she was 'stubborn and ill tempered'; that last characteristic also ruled out Princess Philippine of Brandenburg-Schwedt. George told Bute that he had 'melancholy thoughts of what may perhaps be in the blood' of the Hesse-Darmstadt family.[50] The stigmatizing of mental illness was standard at that time, and all that can be said in George's defence is that he would eventually be more sinned against than sinning.

After exhaustive inquiries, helped by on-the-spot investigations in Germany carried out by Münchhausen's brother Gerlach Adolph, the process of elimination left Charlotte of Mecklenburg-Strelitz. It was reported that she was not beautiful but was of good character; moreover she was not given to philosophy, and her family were neither mad nor involved in *mésalliances*. Mecklenburg-Strelitz, roughly the size of Sussex, was not important strategically, but then neither was Charlotte a niece of Frederick the Great like Princess Philippine, which was a definite advantage in George's eyes. He had come to regard the King of Prussia as a major obstacle to peace, as well as a drain on the British treasury, and felt no inclination to have him as an uncle.

It was not the strongest basis for marriage, however, as George recognized when he told Bute, 'I own 'tis not in every particular as I could wish, but yet I am resolved to fix here.'[51] It was entirely – and correctly – taken for granted that any princess to whom he proposed would automatically accept, such was the wealth and power of England compared to whichever duchy or principality his bride hailed from. That December Walpole caustically reported that because Augusta could not '[chain] up his body as she had fettered his mind' she and Bute had arranged George's marriage, and he had 'blindly accepted the bride she had chosen for him', but that was completely untrue: George had made the choice himself.[52] Because Walpole is unquestionably the most entertaining source for this period it has all too often been assumed that he was also accurate, though he was in fact driven by personal resentment, political opposition and preternatural levels of malice.

In December 1760, Bubb Dodington urged Lord Bute 'to recover monarchy from the inveterate usurpation of oligarchy'.[53] George did not see himself as fighting against some irresistible tide of democracy and universal suffrage, as some Whig historians later claimed; rather he was battling against the small cabal of aristocratic and gentry Whig families (including the Walpoles) who had helped instigate the 1688 Revolution and believed that that gave them the right to rule England in perpetuity. George would find it difficult to govern without the Old Whigs, but in order to weaken them he carefully brought the long-distrusted Tories out of their near-half-century sojourn in the political wilderness, appointing a few to positions at Court. William Petty MP, later Lord Fitzmaurice and still later the 2nd Earl of Shelburne, was appointed an aide-de-camp to the King. He was only a colonel (though a distinguished one, having fought at Minden): his appointment over the heads of several generals infuriated the Whig traditionalists in the Court, such as Charles Lennox, 3rd Duke of Richmond, who consequently resigned as a lord of the bedchamber.

When five Tories were appointed to Court in 1760 – which was still a small fraction of the total – Henry Fox said that Whigs must 'stand aghast' at the King's actions. In fact it was a sensible move, as the Tories were keen to return to respectability and conspicuous loyalty.[54] George wanted to abolish what he called 'those unhappy distinctions of party called Whigs and Tories', and finally provided Tories such as Sir William Blackstone, the leading jurist of the era, and Samuel Johnson, its leading man of letters, with the opportunity to declare their unequivocal allegiance to the Hanoverians.[55]

On 11 February 1761 George Grenville was admitted to the Cabinet, despite only previously having held the post of Treasurer of the Navy. Hard-working, intelligent, serious and mindful of government expenditure, he ought to have been just the kind of politician who appealed to the King – at least as a 'tool' – but Grenville was also tactless, verbose and obstinate over all matters of patronage, and had a tendency to bore and irritate. He owed his elevation to the fact that he was a key figure in what was known as the Cousinhood, the extended family group centred on his cousin by marriage William Pitt and his brother-in-law Earl Temple. The Grenvilles held three places in the Newcastle–Pitt ministry and six seats in Parliament (controlling a great many more besides) and represented a major political force throughout George's reign. 'Respected, but unloved' is a neat summation of the charmless George Grenville offered by one historian.[56]

On 3 March it was suggested to Newcastle by de Viry that Lord Holderness, the Northern Secretary since 1754, might exchange roles with Bute to become Groom of the Stole. That evening, Newcastle met Devonshire and Hardwicke at the Cockpit* and agreed to this suggestion, partly in the hope that Bute might become an ally against Pitt, but also because they had no real alternative. The King held an audience with Newcastle three days later at which Newcastle proposed the idea as though it had been his own. The King agreed willingly, and Pitt was not even informed of the coming change. Pitt's only supporter in Cabinet at the time was his

* A large meeting room in Whitehall, where cockfights had been held in Henry VIII's time.

brother-in-law Earl Temple, although he had assumed, perhaps unwisely, that he could trust George Grenville too.

By 10 March, George and Bute were ready for a general reshuffle of the ministry, which they intended to present to Pitt as a fait accompli. They discussed Pitt's possible resignation, Bute saying that 'his credit and popularity were much sunk' and that he would probably 'retire with some honourable pension'.[57] Since Pitt was still firmly in front-line politics a decade and a half later, long after Bute had himself retired, this was not one of his better predictions. Newcastle, who now sought peace with France and to stay on as First Lord of the Treasury, liked Bute's suggestion that even if Pitt did choose to remain in a new role as Southern Secretary, and thus in control of much of foreign policy, he would actually be overseen by Hardwicke, Devonshire and himself. Bute also discussed the reshuffle with a powerful government supporter, John Russell, 4th Duke of Bedford, the leader of the Bedford Whigs (or 'Bloomsbury Gang') which included Lord Egremont, John Montagu, 4th Earl of Sandwich, and Richard Rigby MP. Bedford was Viceroy of Ireland, and much in favour of ending the war.

News of the reshuffle leaked, and on the afternoon of 13 March Pitt demanded an interview with Bute, who claimed that the idea had been the King's. He said that he had informed Newcastle and Bedford only the day before and that he did not know whether Devonshire had known about it. This was 'a paltry untruth', in the words of one historian, and, after all Bute's high-flown talk about returning virtue and honesty to politics, also patent hypocrisy.[58] Pitt was more worried about a change of policy than of personnel, expressing his doubt to Bute as 'to His Majesty's real wish and intention' to continue the war, to which he received the answer that the King supported it, 'as long as it was practicable to carry it on'.

Lord Holderness was asked to return the seals of office as Northern Secretary, which were presented to Bute on 25 March. 'I own the scene hurt me,' George told Bute, but Holderness was promised the lord wardenship of the Cinque Ports when the Duke of Dorset died (which he did four years later) and was awarded a generous £4,000 per annum pension. The leaders of the Leicester House Set were well rewarded in the reshuffle, and the basis was established of a new political grouping in Parliament called the King's Friends, who joined the other factions already there, including the Old Whigs led by Newcastle, the Bedford Whigs, the Pittite Whigs (who tended to represent London commercial interests and the seaports) and their close allies the Grenvillite Whigs led by George Grenville.[59]

The King's Friends, a loose agglomeration of Prince Frederick's old acolytes from the Leicester House days, some old-style Tories and ambitious young men who saw the advantage of joining what looked like the winning side, were led by Bute. They had the additional and rare advantage in Hanoverian politics that there was no heir apparent around whom an Opposition could gravitate and assemble. 'There is now *no reversionary* resource,' wrote Hardwicke. 'Instead of an old King and a young successor, a young healthy King and no successor in view.'[60]

Until the reign of Queen Victoria, general elections were automatically held on the death of a monarch. The one that took place after the dissolution of Parliament on 20 March 1761 was no more nor less corrupt than any other that century. The government's placemen – civil servants, government contractors, Court officials, sinecure holders, and so on – made up roughly one-third of the 558 seats in the House of Commons. The majority of MPs throughout George's reign were independent local men of means from the minor aristocracy and upper squirearchy with a sense of public duty, for whom politics was not always their first interest in life, but who saw their role as being to support the King's ministers in Parliament unless there was an extremely good reason not to do so.[61]

The accession of a new monarch meant that general elections had to be held throughout the empire as well as in Britain. In Virginia, for example, a twenty-nine-year-old member of the House of Burgesses, George Washington, found that he had an unexpected challenger for his seat, which he won by what his biographer Ron Chernow describes as the 'ethical shortcut' of persuading the election sheriff that the first voters called upon to declaim their choice (in the era before secret ballots) should be Washington's three brothers, his brother-in-law and a close friend, thereby 'stimulating a bandwagon effect'.[62] In George III's empire, gerrymandering and influence peddling were not confined to the rotten boroughs of Westminster.

March 1761 also saw a severe breach open between the King and the Fox family. When George spoke to the pretty seventeen-year-old Lady Susan Fox-Strangways about the bridesmaids for his impending marriage to Princess Charlotte, she somehow got the completely wrong impression that he was propositioning her. Henry Fox, her uncle, immediately encouraged efforts to install Susan as the King's mistress, a not entirely ridiculous proposal considering that every king since Charles I had had at least one. What George said to her was 'I have had a great many applications from abroad but don't like them,' which she (entirely wrongly) took to mean that he would prefer an English bride, namely herself, a prospect that excited Henry Fox.[63]

Once it dawned on the King this was what was happening, he was furious. Later that year, after his wedding, he complained to Bute that:

Many who flattered themselves to make their way through some mistress to me, seeing themselves entirely disappointed by that attachment I have for her to whom I am wedded, out of rage and despair spread such reports because they will rather snarl when not in their power to bite; but I despise that malice . . . the voice of detraction and envy.[64]

He was referring to Henry Fox, whom he had disliked since at least 1757. Now he reproached himself bitterly for having ever been civil to him.[65] Any hopes that Fox might have had that either Sarah Lennox or his niece Susan might have increased his power at Court had spectacularly backfired.

When on 27 March the Duc de Choiseul, the French Foreign Minister, proposed holding discussions to end the war, a major Cabinet split developed. Pitt, who was planning assaults on Belle-Île and Dominica, did not want any serious talks to take place until their outcomes were known; in any case, he would accept peace only on the basis of Britain retaining all her territorial conquests and a European settlement that protected Frederick the Great. George, Newcastle, Bute and especially Bedford all wanted negotiations to open, but feared that Pitt would publicly denounce an over-generous peace treaty. In early June, the diplomat Hans Stanley was discreetly sent to Paris to open secret and still tentative discussions about the outlines of a settlement.

Newcastle and Pitt were much more Continentally minded than George and Bute, producing the strange situation whereby, as one historian has put it, the government 'was far more "German" and solicitous of the welfare of Hanover than the Elector of Hanover himself'.[66] The expedition against Belle-Île was launched by Commodore Edward Keppel in April, and its citadel captured on 7 June after a forty-day siege, by which time the breach between Newcastle and Pitt over peace negotiations had become virtually unbridgeable. Relations between Bute and Newcastle were little better: in late June they fell out over who was going to be the next Bishop of London, but also because, as Newcastle alleged, the King and Bute were 'more disposed to give in to and support Mr Pitt in his warlike notions and dispositions than they were formerly'.[67]

Devonshire and Hardwicke strongly counselled Newcastle to stay in office. But he already felt sidelined in important decisions about bishops. (Appointments to bishoprics were political as well as ecclesiastical since they held twenty-six seats in the House of Lords and were generally expected to support the government.) He was to feel much worse when on 1 July Bute told him that in his search for a bride the King's 'choice had fallen upon the Princess Charlotte of Mecklenburg-Strelitz', without any prior consultation with the Prime Minister. 'His Majesty had taken his final resolution,' Newcastle was told, 'and was in a great hurry to put it into execution.'[68] The Privy Council would be informed a week later.[69] It was unilateral decisions such as this, over what was in effect an issue of national strategy requiring consideration by the most senior members of the government, that persuaded some Whigs that George had a strain of absolutism to him.

Secret negotiations had been going on since June, when Bute had sent a friend, Colonel David Graeme, to Mecklenburg to ask Charlotte's mother, the Dowager Duchess Elizabeth, and her brother Duke Adolphus Frederick IV, for her hand in marriage. Graeme reported that Charlotte was 'not a beauty, but what is little inferior, she is *amiable*, and her face rather agreeable than otherwise'.[70] Some historians have described her as 'formidably ugly' and even 'hideous', but although she was not beautiful such epithets are unfair.[71] She was dark, had fine auburn hair, a nose with a little upward tilt, good teeth and a pleasant smile. (There was no truth to the rumour that she was a 'mulatto', the contemporary word for biracial.)[72] Naturally, Horace Walpole could be relied upon to be spiteful about her in his memoirs, quoting Charlotte's chamberlain Colonel Disbrowe's comment many years later, 'Yes, I do think the *bloom* of her ugliness is going off.'[73]

The distinguished surgeon Dr William Bromfeild was sent out to Mecklenburg to establish Charlotte's virginity and potential fecundity before any engagement was agreed. He undertook this delicate task with tact, and later became Surgeon to Her Majesty and Master of the Company of Surgeons.[74] Charlotte agreed to change her Lutheran denomination for Anglicanism, and no difficulty was raised about her leaving by 1 August so that she could get to London in good time for her marriage in September and the couple's Coronation shortly afterwards. However, on 29 June the Dowager Duchess died, and the obsequies delayed Charlotte's journey. It was just as well she had not come over any earlier, as on 22 July George was diagnosed as having contracted chickenpox. While he awaited her arrival, George was pleased to receive a lock of Charlotte's hair, 'which seems at candle[light] of a very fine dark colour, and very soft'.[75]* When the Privy Council was summoned on 8 July expecting to be told about the opening of peace negotiations with France after five successful but expensive years of war, they learned instead of the King's decision to marry Charlotte. They made no protest.

Princess Charlotte arrived at Harwich in Essex on 7 September after ten days at sea. Her attendants were seasick on the journey, but she was not; indeed, she had learned how to play 'God Save the King' on her harpsichord.

---

* Contrary to some accounts, this is not the lock of Charlotte's hair in the Royal Archives, which dates from 1780 (RA GEO/ADD/2/64).

'I now think my domestic happiness in my own power,' George wrote to Bute. 'I am overjoyed to the greatest degree and very impatient for that minute that joins me to her, I hope for my life.'[76] At 3 p.m. the next day Charlotte appeared at St James's Palace, where Prince Edward, Duke of York, met her and took her to the garden to meet George, the man she was going to marry only six hours later. Just as she curtsied to him, George stepped forward, raised her up and kissed her on the cheek. He then took her inside to meet his mother, his uncle the Duke of Cumberland, his brother Prince William, Duke of Gloucester, and other family members.

At 9 p.m., having lunched and dressed in her bridal gown (which she had not previously seen), Charlotte was escorted across the road to the Chapel Royal, her train carried by ten unmarried daughters of dukes and earls. Seeing her trembling as she processed, Prince Edward whispered to her in French, 'Courage, Princesse, courage,' as she did not speak English. She was given away by the Duke of Cumberland, and married by Thomas Secker, the Archbishop of Canterbury, who twenty-three years earlier had baptized George on the day of his birth. In her response in the marriage vows Charlotte said, 'Ich will,' rather than 'I do.'[77]

The new Queen later played on the harpsichord and sang before a supper that went on until 3 a.m., when the two virgins retired to bed. Throughout what was an extraordinarily stressful day for the seventeen-year-old orphan, as well as through the receptions and nuptial ball the following day, Charlotte behaved with quiet dignity and composure. She might have been George's last choice of bride on the initial list of eight, but it soon became clear that she had been the correct one, and they enjoyed an extremely close and happy marriage, at least for its first four decades. She started learning English straight away and was soon able to speak it fluently, even if her German accent was always noticeable.[78]

There were stormy scenes at Cabinet throughout mid-September as the majority of ministers continued to refuse Pitt's demands for an immediate declaration of war against Spain, even after he showed them an intercepted letter from the Spanish Ambassador in Paris making it clear that Madrid was only waiting for a Colombian treasure fleet to arrive safely at Cadiz before declaring war against Britain. 'Spain is France and France is Spain,' Pitt told them plainly.[79] Lord Anson replied that preparations to attack could not be made in time, that an intercepted letter was not sufficient evidence and that when Britain attacked the Spanish Fleet in 1718 it had been long remembered with bitterness. Anson was not perhaps the most credible advocate for this argument; back in 1743 he had personally seized over 1.3 million silver pieces-of-eight from the famed Manila Galleon.

Only Temple agreed with Pitt that the British Ambassador to Madrid,

Lord Bristol, ought to be withdrawn forthwith and war declared. Bute privately advised Newcastle and Devonshire that 'as the continuance of the war [against France] seemed unavoidable, he thought we should do what we could to hinder Mr Pitt from going out, and thereby leaving the impracticability of his own war upon us'.[80] The King supported Bute in his task of what he called 'overturning Mr Pitt's black scheme', writing, 'I thank heaven that you know him so well, that being the case his venom is not to be feared . . . I would say let that mad Pitt be dismissed, but as matters are very different from that we must get rid of him in a happier minute than the present one.'[81] Bute mentioned Grenville or Lord Egremont as potential successors to Pitt as Southern Secretary, but everyone knew that only Pitt could successfully prosecute the war.[82] When on 21 September Pitt laid his memorandum demanding the extension of the war before the King, George refused to accept it until Stanley had returned from Paris, which understandably Pitt took as a rebuff.[83]

The next day, Tuesday 22 September, George and Charlotte were crowned at Westminster Abbey.[84] They went from St James's Palace to Westminster Hall in sedan chairs rather than in gilt carriages: 'like ordinary citizens going to the theatre', wrote one biographer.[85] They entered the Abbey at 1.30 p.m. but the King was not crowned for two hours, and it was noticed that, when he entered, William Pitt received louder cheers than Their Majesties. 'What was most remarkable were the prodigious acclamations and tokens of affection shown by the populace to Mr Pitt, who came in his chariot,* accompanied by Earl Temple,' an eyewitness recounted. 'At every stop, the mob clung about every part of the vehicle, hung upon the wheels, hugged his footmen, and even kissed his horses. There was an universal huzza, and the gentlemen at the windows, and in the balconies, waved their hats, and the ladies their handkerchiefs.'[86]

The Coronation Oath that George took had first been devised for William and Mary in 1689, when the French were fully supporting James II in his hopes of invading Britain, and contained an unequivocal rejection of Roman Catholicism. George was asked a series of questions by Archbishop Secker to which he had to assent, among them:

> Will you to the utmost of your power maintain the laws of God, the true profession of the Gospel, and the Protestant reformed religion established by law? And will you maintain and preserve inviolably the settlement of the united Church of England and Ireland, and the doctrine, worship, discipline and government thereof, as by law established, within England and Ireland, and the countries thereunto belonging?[87]

---

* A light carriage, with a coach box and back seats only.

The King stood up from his throne in the Abbey, walked to the altar, laid his right hand on the Bible and answered, 'The things which I have here before promised, I will perform and keep. So help me God.' He then kissed the Bible, and was anointed King.

Those who paid ten guineas each for front-row seats in the gallery inside the Abbey got their money's worth, but, with so much going on and so many people involved, George's conformed to the long tradition of British coronations going slightly awry, mixing splendour with farce. The Sword of State had been mislaid, meaning that Francis Hastings, 10th Earl of Huntingdon, carried the Lord Mayor of London's Pearl Sword instead, and the Dean of Westminster and his clergy were left waiting outside the North Door of the Abbey for ninety minutes. Because he wanted to receive Holy Communion as an ordinary person rather than a monarch, George took off his crown beforehand, upon which the peers then confusedly followed with their coronets, even though they themselves were not receiving the sacrament. The Dean 'would have dropped the crown if it had not been pinned to the cushion', recorded the poet Thomas Gray, 'and the King was often obliged to call out and set matters right'. The 'stupid' heralds were among the officials who Gray felt 'knew nothing they were doing'.[88] No chairs were provided for the King and Queen, and there was no canopy to carry over them (there had been no dress rehearsal). The writer James Henning recorded, 'The whole was confusion, irregularity and disorder.'[89]

The service took six hours, so people had picnics sent in, and at solemn moments a clattering of knives, forks and plates and a tinging of glasses could be clearly heard. At the subsequent banquet – which had to be postponed – the Hereditary Champion rode into Westminster Hall on horseback and threw down his gauntlet as a challenge to anyone who disputed the King's right to the throne. Fortunately no latter-day Jacobites came forward. The dinner placement had been done so badly that several invited aristocrats had nowhere to sit. 'No dinner to eat, shameful expedients to defraud mob,' Lady Northumberland complained, 'instead of profusion of geese, etc., not wherewithal to fill one's belly.'[90]

'I . . . saw the Hall, the dinner, and the Champion, a gloriously illuminated chamber, a wretched banquet, and a foolish puppet-show,' Walpole reported to Sir Horace Mann. 'The heralds were so ignorant of their business, that, though pensioned for nothing but to register lords and ladies, and what belongs to them, they advertised in the newspaper for the Christian names and places of abode for the peeresses. The King complained of such omissions and of the want of precedence.'[91] George could hardly believe that the heralds had failed so badly in one of their most important jobs, to know aristocratic orders of precedence at a coronation. When he upbraided Thomas Howard, 2nd Earl of Effingham and Deputy Earl Marshal, for all the egregious mistakes of the day, Effingham apologized and solemnly promised 'that the next Coronation would be conducted with the greatest order imaginable'.[92] George found the remark so funny that he 'made the earl repeat it several times'.

One person who cut short a trip to the Continent in order to attend the Coronation was Benjamin Franklin, the celebrated Boston-born scientist, publisher, inventor and polymath, Deputy Postmaster-General of the thirteen colonies, whose father and four grandparents had all been born in Britain. Then a proud British royalist, Franklin hoped that the new monarch would protect his American colonists by not returning Canada to France in return for West Indian sugar-producing islands. 'To leave the French in possession of Canada when it is in our power to remove them', Franklin had written in April 1760 in a pamphlet entitled *The Interest of Great Britain with Regard to her Colonies*, 'seems neither safe nor prudent.'[93]

The Coronation over, the Cabinet returned to its hard-fought discussions of the peace, which they debated throughout late September. 'The King seems every day more offended with Mr Pitt,' noted Newcastle on the 26th, 'and plainly wants to get rid of him at all events.'[94] Finally, on 2 October, Pitt and Temple resigned over the refusal to declare war on Spain. It was a watershed moment for Pitt, who with only two short breaks had been in office since 1746, but was now to be out for all but two of his remaining seventeen years. When he returned his seals of office to the King three days later, George 'expressed his concern for the loss of so able a servant, and to show the favourable sense he entertained of his services he made him a most gracious and unlimited offer of any rewards in the power of the Crown to bestow'.[95] The King nonetheless received the seals 'with ease and firmness, without requesting that he should resume his office'. Pitt 'was sensibly touched with the grandeur and condescension of this proceeding', saying, 'I confess, Sir, I had but too much reason to expect Your Majesty's displeasure. I did not come prepared for this exceeding goodness. Pardon me, Sir – it overpowers, it oppresses me.'[96] He then burst into tears. George awarded him an annual pension of £3,000 for both his life and that of his eldest son, and made his wife Hester a peeress.

Pitt was succeeded at the Southern Department by Lord Egremont, a friend of Lord Bute and another brother-in-law of George Grenville. Egremont was the son of a former Tory leader in the House of Commons, adding to Whig disquiet. With the inner Cabinet now consisting of

Newcastle, Bute, Egremont, Bedford (who succeeded Temple as Lord Privy Seal) and Grenville, Bute was in a position to assume the premiership from Newcastle as soon as he felt able.[97]

In January, the King had told Newcastle that anyone who spoke against Bute 'speaks against me', but as Bute's power grew there were more and more people willing to speak against him.[98] Royal favourites had long been hated in British history, as attested by the bloody fates of Piers Gaveston, Roger Mortimer, Edmund Beaufort, William de la Pole, Cardinal Wolsey, Thomas Cromwell, David Rizzio, the Duke of Buckingham, Thomas Strafford and William Laud. It was apparent to all that Bute's position derived solely from the King's friendship, rather than from any territorial interest, wealth, ideological stance, military prowess, previous service to the state or any of the other usual prerequisites of eighteenth-century power.

A Scotsman in power only a decade and a half after the Jacobite Rebellion – especially one whose family name was Stuart – was never going to be popular with the London mob, and the widespread presumption that he owed his position to being the Dowager Princess's lover was spread yet further in November when posters appeared across the capital, presumably the work of Pitt's devotees in the City, accusing Augusta of running a 'petticoat government'.[99] The jeers 'No petticoat government!' and 'No Scotch minister!' were regularly heard on public occasions.[100] At the time, Horace Walpole did not believe the rumours of Bute sleeping with Augusta, telling his friend George Montagu that 'no petticoat ever governed less'.[101] It was only later, when he discovered that Bute had blocked him from advising the King on art and aesthetics, that he insisted on the slander's truth and claimed that he could not have been more certain of it if he had caught them in the act.[102]

For all the elegant and witty debates in the Commons chamber, eighteenth-century politics was often a brutal contact sport. Although the electorate was tiny, politics was followed closely in the taverns and coffee houses, and in street protests the mob rarely hesitated to make its anti-Catholic, anti-Scottish and anti-foreigner prejudices felt. In 1765, soldiers had to be sent to protect the Duke of Bedford's house from being burned down; later in the reign Lord North's coach was destroyed on his way to Parliament and William Pitt the Younger had to vacate Downing Street.[103] Pitt the Elder, the patriot who had brought the victories of the *Annus mirabilis*, was still the darling of the mob. Four weeks after he had forced Pitt's resignation, Bute's carriage was pelted with street dirt and filth on its way to the Lord Mayor's Banquet at Guildhall. Despite being protected by the 'one-eyed fighting coachman' George Stephenson and other burly bodyguards, Bute had to be saved by a squad of constables.[104] The coach that

Pitt and Temple arrived in, by contrast, was hailed with loud cheers, and when they entered Guildhall the huzzahing was once again louder than that for the King and Queen.

Pitt's resignation at least freed him from the obligation of remaining silent, and on 13 November he denounced the idea of making peace with France separately from Prussia. Canada, he told the Commons, 'had been conquered in Germany', by which he meant that the Prussian alliance had concentrated French power on the European Continent, weakening it elsewhere in the world.[105] For all his eloquence and public support, however, Pitt had few followers in the Commons now that he was no longer able to distribute honours and places, and Newcastle was soon noting that the King 'was in high spirits' at Pitt's seeming isolation there.[106]

Although Pitt had resigned, the threat of war with Spain remained. After General Riccardo Wall, the Spanish Prime Minister, had refused to answer the British Ambassador Lord Bristol's questions about the Franco-Spanish Bourbon alliance known as the Family Compact, the King wrote to Bute on 14 November that 'It is a sort of declaration of war, which I am convinced must now soon follow . . . This fresh enemy makes my heart bleed for my poor country. I think unless we can get rid of our expense *somewhere* it will be impossible to bear up when a new power attacks us.'[107] The underlined 'somewhere' meant Prussia and Hanover, whose subsidies George and Bute meant to cut now that Pitt was no longer in Cabinet to defend them.

None of this, however, materially affected Britain's situation vis-à-vis Spain. In December, Bristol had to be recalled from Madrid, just as Pitt and Temple had proposed back in mid-September. Eventually, reluctantly, on 2 January 1762 Britain declared war, despite half the Cabinet – Newcastle, Hardwicke and Bedford – as well as Lord Mansfield, the Lord Chief Justice, being unable to see a *casus belli* beyond the (justified) fear that Spain was about to declare war herself. Over the previous three months the pro-peace Newcastle–Bute government – fully supported by the King – had somehow managed not only to expand the scale of the war significantly but also to lose the one man who could wage it successfully.

4

Victory

January 1762–February 1763

Nothing can astonish me more than that anyone should accuse me of all people of loving foreign fashions, whom I own rather incline too much to the John Bull and am apt to despise what I am not accustomed to.[1]

George to Lord Bute, early 1762

Early in 1762, George bought Buckingham House in west London as a present for Charlotte. It had been built by John Sheffield, Duke of Buckingham, fifty-nine years earlier, and the King employed Sir William Chambers to remodel it extensively. Although George preferred living in the country, first at Kew and then at Windsor, all his children except the Prince of Wales were born in the building he rechristened the Queen's House, but which most people still referred to by its original name.* Having spent £28,000 on its purchase, George paid out a further £73,000 on its refurbishment, engaging the architect Robert Adam, a Scot who had been suggested by Bute. It contained no fewer than four libraries including an Octagonal Library, as well as a music room, a then fashionable Japanese Room and a Large Saloon for which the King had seven very large Raphael cartoons brought over from Hampton Court. There were also extensive gardens at the back of the house, where Charlotte kept a menagerie that included a zebra, two elephants and as many as eighteen kangaroos once the Royal Navy had reached Australia.

The King played an enthusiastic part in Buckingham House's decoration, and on a visit there in 1783 John Adams, by then the American Ambassador to Holland, compared it to the other great houses of England he had visited, finding 'the same taste, the same judgement, the same

---

* It was not known as Buckingham Palace until the 1820s, when John Nash redesigned it for George IV.

elegance, the same simplicity, without the smallest affectation, ostentation, profusion or meanness. I could not but compare it, in my own mind, with Versailles, and not at all to the advantage of the latter.' The Octagonal Library, in particular,

> struck me with admiration. I wished for a week's time, but had but a few hours. The books were in perfect order, elegant in their editions, paper, binding, etc., but gaudy and extrava[g]ant in nothing. They were chosen with perfect taste and judgement; every book that a king ought to have always at hand, and as far as I could examine, and could be supposed capable of judging, none other. Maps, charts, etc., of all his dominions in the four quarters of the world, and models of every fortress in his empire.[2]

It soon became clear that the King and Queen enjoyed a close and happy marriage, something of a rarity in a marital system based upon international power politics rather than personal compatibility. Their shared interests in philanthropy, music, walking, books, theatre and aspects of the sciences – botany for the Queen, horology and astronomy for the King – were fine bases for what quickly blossomed into love. They were also alike in their religious views, and both appreciated the fine arts, between them hugely increasing the Royal Collection.[3] They furnished and decorated several royal residences, indulging the King's love of architecture to the full. It may have been an arranged marriage, but George himself had arranged it, and it became a genuine love match because he adored everything about his wife except her addiction to snuff (in later life she acquired the unattractive nickname of 'Old Snuffy').[4] The writer Fanny Burney, who became a lady-in-waiting in 1786, found that the King was all fondness and tactile affection for the Queen, giving her frequent pecks on the cheek.

Charlotte was an intelligent, cultured and artistic woman, albeit one whose freedom of activity was circumscribed by being pregnant with fifteen children for over half of the first two decades of her married life. Between 1762 and 1780 there was never more than an eighteen-month interval between the births of their children. Charlotte enjoyed going to theatre and concerts, was good at needlework, read English, French and German literature and sermons with evident pleasure, and collected jewellery and furniture.[5] After her death, her private library fetched £5,615. She had a taste for fine porcelain – the Queen was among the first in England to appreciate Sèvres, and in 1765 appointed Josiah Wedgwood as Potter to Her Majesty* – and for Indian and Chinese textiles and lacquers, and she

---

* After Wedgwood had presented a tea set to Charlotte in 1760, he lost little time in making the most of royal approval for his brand (Hunt, *Radical Potter* pp. 92–3).

was also a genuinely interested amateur botanist and collector of curiosities.[6] Crucially, she was not at all interested in politics. Burney describes her attractive informality: 'When I was alone with her she discarded all royal constraint, all stiffness, all formality, all pedantry of grandeur, to lead me to speak to her with openness and ease.'[7]

The King liked regularity in his daily schedule: he rose at 6 a.m.,* shaved himself (in an age when this was often done by servants), attended chapel, dealt with correspondence that had arrived in the night (especially from the Prime Minister reporting on the events in Parliament the previous evening) and went for a short ride before an 8 a.m. cup of tea with the Queen, who took coffee. During bad weather he would ride in an indoor paddock he had built in the Buckingham House gardens. The children would be presented after a light breakfast, and afterwards he would work in his study until noon, when on Wednesdays and Fridays (and also Mondays during parliamentary sessions) he attended the all-male Levee at St James's Palace; on Thursdays and Sundays he and the Queen attended the mixed-company Drawing Rooms there.

Charles II had imported this custom of Levees from Versailles, where the Bourbons had used it as a means of personal political control. (Louis XIV would say of someone with no position, 'He is a man I never see.') Attendance was a means by which the Bourbons kept the aristocracy close – absences would be noted. Being seen by the monarch at St James's also became a way for George to keep an eye on political developments; he quite literally saw any politicians, aristocrats, soldiers, diplomats, clergymen, foreign visitors and gentry who happened to be visiting London.[8] Entry was allowed to anyone properly dressed for Court, provided they could be presented by someone known to it. The King, wearing special Levee clothes, entered the crimson and gold Presence Chamber at noon, accompanied by one or two senior members of the royal household, whereupon conversation ceased and the guests formed themselves into a large rectangle around the walls. The King began by speaking to the gentleman on his right, who, after their conversation, was free to leave.[9] Forms and customs of etiquette and precedence were strictly adhered to. The King spoke first, and was not asked questions. Nobody sat down in his presence nor turned their back on him. Levees could last four or five hours, though outside the parliamentary term they tended to be smaller, and thus shorter. Opposition MPs did not attend.

After the Levee, George would retire to his Closet, a study-cum-drawing

---

* He is said to have told the architect James Wyatt that six hours' sleep was enough for a man, seven for a woman and eight for a fool (Brooke, *King George III* p. 290).

room behind the state bedchamber, where he would confer with senior ministers and receive foreign ambassadors. Access to the Closet belonged by right to the Prime Minister, the two secretaries of state, the Leader of the House of Commons and the Secretary at War during wartime. If a person of rank asked to be invited there, the King tended to grant it, even though what they almost always wanted was a title or honour for themselves or a relative.

As at the Levee, no one sat down in the Closet: indeed some traditionalists, including William Pitt, knelt upon entering. Pitt's son, William Pitt the Younger, would later attend a three-and-three-quarter-hour audience with the King at which both men remained standing the entire time. George would therefore be on his feet for three to six hours at least four days a week, without having eaten since his light breakfast at 8 a.m. Eighteenth-century kingship, if done conscientiously, could be physically gruelling.

The Drawing Rooms observed much the same etiquette as the Levees, except that women were invited and the Queen attended too, unless she was pregnant. ('The Queen did not come out,' Lady Mary Coke noted of one Drawing Room in 1768, 'so I imagine Her Majesty is breeding, for it was not said she was ill.')[10] These meetings at St James's Palace were an invaluable way for George to stay in close touch with the country outside London, as gentlemen would attend if they could get the necessary introduction from their county Lord Lieutenant or Member of Parliament. George deluged his interlocutors with questions, generally about local economic conditions relating to the harvest and agriculture, in which he was greatly interested, so that he often knew more about the minutiae of his kingdom than most of his ministers.

George understood how important the personal touch was to his subjects, and was determined not to disappoint them. 'I find it does a man good to be talked to by his sovereign,' said Dr Johnson, and many other subjects felt the same.[11] There was a good deal of surviving belief in 'the divinity that doth hedge a king': when in August 1770 a woman asked Lord Hertford if she could kiss the King's hand to cure her infertility, George 'granted it in one of the rooms as he walked towards the Drawing Room, to the great joy of the woman'.[12] Sadly, history does not relate whether or not it worked.

Dinner, the main meal of the day, was taken at 4 p.m. back at Buckingham House. If his Levee and Closet had gone on until 5 p.m. or 6 p.m. – as they frequently did because the King insisted on speaking to everyone who attended – the rest of the family tended to wait for him. Typical fare included soup, a joint of meat (often mutton, but roast beef on Sundays) or a pie or cold sirloin, with vegetables (usually turnip or beetroot), salad, sweetbreads, oysters, fruit and macaroons.[13] Not all the royal meals were basic British fare; they would occasionally eat Italian 'Chicken Vermicelly', French pâté, pilau rice and 'Metworst of Sweetbreads' and something called 'Brounmole'.[14]

The King was virtually teetotal, and the Queen drank very little by the standards of the time. 'Nor does he ever taste a drop of wine except in hot weather when he sometimes has a cup made three parts water and one part wine,' noted the Duchess of Northumberland. 'The Queen always drinks one glass of burgundy with her dinner.'[15] The King preferred lemonade (called 'cup') to wine, and a courtier remarked that a Trappist monk could have drunk the same as the King 'without any infraction of his monastic vow'.[16] Much to the disgust of his senior equerry Colonel Philip Goldsworthy, the King drank only barley water after a hard day's hunting, and another courtier noted in 1786 that 'His Majesty has the most vigorous health, and accustoms himself to none of the indulgences which almost all his subjects regard as indispensable.'[17] He did not even have a cellar at Buckingham House, but bought wine whenever the occasion demanded, and never drank spirits. George's abstemiousness and vigorous exercise regime – he enjoyed walking long distances and rarely felt the cold – kept his weight down until late middle age, as he was conscious of the Hanoverian propensity towards obesity.

Dining was a family affair; the King and Queen did not throw dinner parties except for visiting royalty or on royal birthdays. (As Charlotte's birthday on 19 May was so close to the King's a fortnight later, she was seemingly arbitrarily accorded an official birthday on 18 January.) When Queen Victoria later invited Charles Fulke Greville, a clerk of the Privy Council, to a dinner for sixteen people at Buckingham Palace in March 1838, he recalled being a page of honour at George III's Court, when the monarch 'never dined but with his family, never had guests, or a dinner *party*'.[18]* Queen Victoria was told by her Prime Minister Lord Melbourne that George III did not hold dinner parties because 'he dined with great rapidity, was very temperate and hardly ate anything.'[19] To have invited non-family members to such dinners, Melbourne opined, 'would not have suited him and he would not very probably have made it very agreeable to others'. In the almost thirty years of their combined premierships, neither Lord North nor William Pitt the Younger ever dined with the King at home.

After dinner, the King would go back to work in his study until he rejoined the Queen at 7 p.m. when tea was served. He was conscientious

---

* Greville thought it 'a vile, vulgar custom' to toast Queen Victoria's health 'at her own table' (ed. Morrell, *Leaves from the Greville Diary* p. 343).

and meticulous, writing out letters in his own hand, and did not employ a secretary until his eyesight began to fail in 1805.* Supper was served at 10 p.m. A lesser meal than dinner, it tended to include chicken, cold mutton, buttered eggs, custard, veal and chicken broth. The Duchess of Northumberland wrote that the King and Queen's daily habits were 'very methodical and regular. Whenever it was in their power they went to bed by 11 o'clock.'[20] They slept in the same bed, which was extremely unusual for their class and time, although they had separate apartments connected by a staircase.

The King's attention to detail extended over every aspect of his life; when completing his household accounts in January 1761, for example, he even set the wages of the royal laundresses. Although he and the Queen were to gain reputations for parsimony, they could be generous if moved. When Lady Molesworth's house in Upper Brook Street burned down in May 1763, killing ten people, the King provided for the surviving children, doubling their late mother's pension and finding a house for them.[21] The King's favourite charitable cause was imprisoned bankrupts, whom he helped financially at his numerous jubilees and at other times. This underlined how seriously he took his kingly responsibilities: according to the Bible and Jewish teaching, forgiveness of debts was a defining characteristic of a jubilee.

The King and Queen went to the theatre on Thursdays (where Charlotte occasionally had to restrain George from laughing too loudly in the royal box) and to the opera on Saturdays, and were regular concertgoers. Other evenings were spent listening to music at home (they each had a band) and playing the card games vingt-et-un, 'whisk', 'Commap', piquet and reverse for minimal stakes – and for the Queen often none at all – with close friends and courtiers such as Lord Ailesbury and Lord and Lady Weymouth.[22] The couple's friends tended to be intelligent, aristocratic, practising Anglicans and happily married.

The King and Queen dined at friends' houses in London, but very rarely, and they only occasionally stayed overnight at houses in the country. Cards would not be played on Sundays, Good Friday, Christmas Day and – somewhat strangely for someone whose family was on the throne only thanks to the fall of the Stuarts – the anniversary of the execution of King

---

* An horologist and collector of timepieces, George dated his letters to the minute, which allows us to know that of the 2,050 letters for which he gave times of day between 1765 and 1801, a total of 850 were written in the morning. His busiest hours were between 8 a.m. and 9 a.m. (259 letters, or 12.6 per cent of the total) and 6 p.m. to 7 p.m. (214 letters, or 10.4 per cent). Although he wrote only 163 of these letters (8 per cent) between 11 a.m. and 2 p.m., he was often still writing them late into the evening, with 135 (6.6 per cent) between 10 p.m. and midnight.

Charles I on 30 January. The King disapproved of the St James's clubs holding masked balls during Lent.[23] He was opposed to puritanism, however, and, when Bishop Beilby Porteus of London visited him to remonstrate with him about travelling to Windsor on a Sunday, the King received him 'with his carriage at the door'.[24]

George was an extremely accomplished horseman. He loved hunting stag and hare and even in his mid-sixties would think nothing of riding 10 miles in heavy rain, rarely joining his family in their coach journeys back from hunts. He went to Epsom races occasionally and had a road built from Windsor to Ascot, where he sponsored a race. He had a keen eye for horseflesh, bought regularly but shrewdly and was careful not to pay over the odds. On being handed a long pedigree document by a dealer, he joked, 'Take it back, take it back – do just as well for the next horse you sell – what?'[25]

Music was a mutual passion of the King and Queen, especially that of George Frederick Handel, whom the King revered. George himself played the harpsichord, piano, organ and flute. He was occasionally accompanied on the keyboard by Johann Christian Bach, the great composer's son. The first performance given in England by the eight-year-old Wolfgang Amadeus Mozart was at Buckingham House on 27 April 1764: he played the harpsichord and organ for three hours, and returned several times until August 1765. Mozart dedicated six sonatas for harpsichord and violin – K10–15, in B flat, G, A, F, C and B flat – to Queen Charlotte, who had commissioned them. In 1795 Joseph Haydn was offered a summer house at Windsor by the King, in an unsuccessful attempt to persuade him not to return to Vienna.

The King also enjoyed playing backgammon: indeed at a time when many obscure court appointments were being abolished, courtiers joked that a new one, 'Backgammon Player to His Majesty', ought to be instituted for Colonel Goldsworthy and another equerry, Colonel Ramsden, who regularly had to play with George for hours.[26] Although that post was never instituted, the Court was awash with plenty of arcane and esoteric ones, such as Embellisher of Letters to the Eastern Princes, although most had a practical purpose, such as Keeper of the Fire Buckets, Keeper of the Orchard Gate, Keeper of the Ice House, Distiller of Milk Water, Keeper of the Lions, Lionesses and Leopards in the Tower, and Carrier of His Majesty's Despatches Between His Court or Residence and the Post Office.

The royal dentist was known as the Operator for the Teeth. 'I don't know whether *you* are afraid of *me*,' the King told him when he needed a tooth removed; 'but I can tell you, *I am of you*.' When the dentist bowed and said he hoped it would go well, George replied, 'Oh! I dare say, but I think it would go better with me if I had a little brandy.' 'After the operation I

presume?' asked the dentist. 'No,' the King replied, 'before, to give me courage.' A page was sent to procure some and was about to pour it into a glass
when George exclaimed, 'No, no! let the dentist do that; he makes me a
coward, let him give me courage.' The brandy was poured out and presented
by the dentist, to whom the King, smiling as he refused it, said, 'I have no
need of it, but was merely anxious to observe if your hand was steady.'[27]

Court etiquette could be strange and stifling. The lady-in-waiting Fanny
Burney told her sister Susan that it was 'something so little like common
and real life, in everybody's standing . . . so aloof from each other, that I
almost thought myself upon a stage, assisting in the representation of a
tragedy'.[28] In one of her 'court journals' written for her family in the late
1780s, under the heading 'Directions for Coughing, Sneezing or Moving
Before the King and Queen', she explained:

> In the first place you must not cough. If you find a cough tickling in your
> throat, you must arrest it from making any sound: if you find yourself chok-
> ing with the forbearance, you must choke. But not cough. In the second place
> you must not sneeze. If you have a vehement cold, you must take no notice
> of it . . . If a sneeze still insists upon making its way, you must oppose it by
> keeping your teeth grinding together; if the violence of the repulse breaks
> some blood vessel, you must break the blood vessel. But not sneeze.[29]

Those were on formal occasions, of course, and she was being slightly
satirical, and the danger of contracting a life-threatening disease was ever
present in that era.

George wore new clothes on Charlotte's birthdays, but otherwise he
dressed like a country squire with an eye more for comfort than fashion.
Yet for all their almost bourgeois taste for eating plainly and privately – in
stark contrast to the Bourbons' elaborate public rituals at Versailles – when
they decided to throw a grand celebration the British royal family could
entertain in magnificent style. The state visit of George's brother-in-law
King Christian VII of Denmark in 1768 and the installation of their
favourite son Frederick, Duke of York, as a Garter knight in 1771 were
public occasions marked with suitable pomp. George also delighted in
extravagant firework displays when the opportunity arose.

An unmistakable sign of royal magnificence was the Gold State Coach
that George commissioned from London's leading coachmaker Samuel
Butler in 1760 at the vast cost of £7,562.* Twenty-one feet long, 9 feet

---

* As it has been used for every Coronation and most State Openings of Parliament ever since,
the expense can be amortized over two and a half centuries. It can be seen today in the Royal
Mews at Buckingham Palace.

high and weighing over 4 tons, it was designed by Sir William Chambers, with ornate wooden sculptures carved by Joseph Wilton, who on Bute's advice George appointed to the new role of Sculptor to the King. The painted panels, featuring Britannia and Neptune, Apollo the god of art and Mercury the god of peace, were by Giovanni Cipriani. It was 'a vehicle not only for [the King's] person but for his political and artistic ideals'.[30] For all of its undoubted splendour as a work of art, it had drawbacks as a means of conveyance, and was not built in time for George's own Coronation. William IV complained that travelling in it was like 'tossing in a rough sea'; Queen Victoria disliked its 'distressing oscillation'; George VI described his journey to his Coronation as 'one of the most uncomfortable rides I have ever had in my life', and Elizabeth II likewise described hers as 'horrible'.[31]

Although one had to have some social standing to converse with the King at a Levee or Drawing Room, outside such formal engagements he chatted happily to people he met. 'The King and Queen, Prince Ernest and Lady Effingham walked the other day through Richmond town without a single servant,' a shocked Lady Mary Coke noted in July 1769. 'I am not satisfied in my own mind about the propriety of a queen walking in a town unattended.'[32] Other than having his profile on the coinage and his face in some prints, there was no reason why ordinary people should have recognized their monarch in an age before mass communications, and there are many, by no means implausible, stories of the King enjoying conversations with people incognito. One day while out walking in Windsor Great Park, the King met a young lad and asked him who he was. 'I be pig boy,' came the reply, 'but I don't work. They don't want lads here. All this belongs hereabouts to Georgy.' 'Pray, who is Georgy?' asked the King, presumably knowing the answer perfectly well. 'He be king and lives at the castle, but he does no good for me.' The King found him a job on one of his three farms there.[33] In another story, arriving early at the Windsor stables one morning, he asked a stable boy where the grooms were and was told, 'I don't know, sir; but they'll soon be back, because they expect the King.' Slipping him some money the King said, 'Then run, boy; run, run, run boy to the Three Tuns; they are sure to be there, for the landlord makes the best purl* in Windsor.'[34] When a woman working in a field near Weymouth told him she couldn't join her friends to go to see the King in the town as she had five children and couldn't afford the time off work, he pressed a guinea into her hand with the words,

* Hot beer mixed with gin as a morning draught.

'Then you can tell your companions that the King came to see you.'[35] Even allowing for some growth in the retelling, the basic pattern and sheer volume of these stories about George all tend to show a kindly monarch who was at ease among his people, was delighted by the opportunity of not being recognized and took pleasure in being generous.

As well as hobnobbing happily with his subjects, George enjoyed having intellectuals visit him at London and Windsor, such as the Swiss physicist and chemist Aimé Argand, the botanist John Lightfoot, the astronomers William and Caroline Herschel, the Provost of Eton College Dr William Roberts,* the painter Mary Delany (who became a good friend), the classical scholar and mythagogue Jacob Bryant,† the historian of music Charles Burney (Fanny's father) and many others. He enjoyed questioning such figures intently on their interests and particular expertise. George, though not an intellectual himself, was at ease in their company.

'All pomp is instituted for the sake of the public,' Samuel Johnson replied to critics of the expense of the Coronation. 'Magnificence in obscurity is equally vain with "a sundial in the grave".'[36] In early 1762 the King, having been told that Johnson was 'a very learned and good man', awarded him a pension of £300 per annum.‡ The King believed in supporting intellectuals: he also granted pensions from his Privy Purse to David Hume and Jean-Jacques Rousseau, the latter payment being particularly unusual in that the £100 per annum continued after Rousseau's death in 1778 to be paid to his mistress, Thérèse Levasseur.

In November 1761, George created a new position, Architect of Works, in a department within the royal household which was barely accountable to Parliament, and awarded it jointly to William Chambers and Robert Adam. In 1769 Chambers was promoted to Comptroller of the Works, and in 1782 he succeeded Thomas Worsley to become Surveyor-General too. 'If Adam the architect succeeds Worsley at the Board of Works,' the

---

* 'His Majesty takes a great interest in the welfare and prosperity of that seminary,' noted Fanny Burney (eds. Barrett and Dobson, *Diary and Letters of Madame d'Arblay* III p. 112).
† He asked the frail and mild-mannered Bryant what he had been best known for at Eton and was astonished to receive the reply, 'Cudgelling, sir.' (It was taught as a sport.)
‡ The idea came from a suggestion of the lawyer Alexander Wedderburn MP to Bute, and was not the political bribe it was later suggested to be, although in the 1770s Johnson did submit two of his political pamphlets to ministers for revision and correction. Johnson was awarded the pension secretly, and so was not publicly embarrassed by the fact that in 1755 he had defined 'pensioner' in his great dictionary as 'A slave of state hired by a stipend to obey his master'. When Johnson thanked Bute, the great lexicographer was for once at a loss for English words, writing, 'I am *pénétré* with His Majesty's goodness' (ed. Pottle, *Boswell's London Journal* p. 55).

King wrote, 'he shall think Chambers ill-used.'[37] Instead, Chambers held both jobs for seventeen years, during which time he promoted the neo-classical style now known as Georgian architecture, which is rightly regarded today as a glory of the age. In cities and country houses through-out the country, beautiful Georgian buildings emphasized symmetry and proportion with their columns, terraces, sash windows and restrained ornamentation. The neo-classical revival was already under way in the reigns of George's predecessors, of course, but thanks to his close interest in all official architectural appointments, even down to minor offices, it was to reach its apogee during his reign.

'Building, I am told, is the King's favourite study,' sneered Horace Wal-pole in January 1761. 'I hope our architects will not be taken from the erectors of turnpikes.'[38] They certainly were not; instead George bestowed architectural patronage upon the four leading architects of the day – Chambers and Adam, but also James 'Athenian' Stuart and James Wyatt – commissioning them to work at Buckingham House, St James's Palace, the White House at Kew, Richmond Lodge, Windsor Castle and in Windsor Great Park.[39] He also employed Chambers' pupil John Yenn, William Robinson, Henry Emlyn and Thomas Sandby, and the great land-scape gardener Lancelot 'Capability' Brown. Architects who made plans for the King for buildings that were not executed included John Soane, Robert Adam's brother James Adam and Thomas Wright. Four architects would dedicate books to him.

George's passion for painting and the fine arts was not far behind that for architecture. In July 1762 he bought the collection of paintings, prints, books, incunabula, coins and medals of Joseph Smith, the British Consul in Venice, in a sale negotiated jointly by James Stuart-Mackenzie, Bute's younger brother, and George's librarian, Richard Dalton.[40]* It included fifty-four paintings by Canaletto, thirty-four by Marco Ricci, twenty-eight by Sebastiano Ricci and twenty-four by Rosalba Carriera. Among the earlier Italian masters were important works by Giovanni Bellini and Raphael, and Dutch paintings such as Vermeer's *The Lady at the Virginals*, Rembrandt's *The Descent from the Cross* and others by Rubens and Van Dyck. Almost half of today's Royal Collection, comprising over 30,000 paintings and drawings, were bought by George, who also collected Wedg-wood and other porcelain, and commissioned silver and goldware – his silversmith Thomas Heming was recommended to him by Bute. He also formed collections of drawings, model ships and everything else an

---

* Visitors to the British Library can recognize Consul Smith's books in the King's Library tower by their white parchment bindings and red or green labels.

eighteenth-century gentleman of means might appreciate, albeit on a vastly larger scale. 'The accession of George III', recorded Sir Oliver Millar, the Surveyor of the Queen's Pictures in 1969, 'is a watershed in the history of the Royal Collection. Within a few months it was obvious that he was following the example of his father.'[41] No less an artist than Thomas Gainsborough called George 'a good connoisseur'.[42]

As well as buying Smith's extensive library of printed and manuscript books, in 1762 George bought and presented to the British Museum the Thomason Tracts, a collection of over 22,000 Civil War and Commonwealth-era tracts, sermons, political pamphlets and news-sheets. By the early 1770s, the King's library rivalled the Museum's, even though George II had presented it with the entirety of the old royal library. 'It is now very choice,' wrote Sylvester Douglas MP of the book collection at Buckingham House. 'The King spends most of his time in it when in town.'[43] After Richard Dalton, the next librarian was Frederick Augusta Barnard,* who was behind the acquisition of most of the King's book collection.

George allocated £2,000 per annum for Barnard to spend on books and their preservation, but was regularly to spend double that as his obsessive bibliomania took hold. Overall, his library has been estimated to have cost George £120,000 out of the Privy Purse and that did not include librarians' salaries or the cost of binding.[44] (In the seventeenth and eighteenth centuries, books were very often published unbound, allowing the purchaser to have them bound according to their personal preferences. The cost of binding was thus not a marginal element, and the King had many of his books bound beautifully by the talented John Baumgarten.) The library included 300 books about the American colonies, including volumes published in New York, Philadelphia, Newport, Charleston, Cambridge, Boston, Worcester, Connecticut and Burlington, on a very wide range of topics – exploration, flora and fauna and geographical descriptions, as well as history, government, law and taxation. Nor did George's desire for knowledge about the colonies end when they were lost; he received the *Transactions of the American Philosophical Society* from 1771 to 1801 and bought Elihu Smith's *American Poems*, the first general collection of American poetry, when it was published in 1793. His ten titles on the issue of slavery included such abolitionist classics as Anthony Benezet's *A Caution and Warning to Great Britain and her Colonies in a Short Representation of the Calamitous State of the Enslaved Negroes in the British Dominions,*

---

* For all that he was named after his godparents the then Prince and Princess of Wales, there was no truth to the widespread rumour that Barnard was the Prince's illegitimate son; it would have taken gall, even by the standards of eighteenth-century royalty, to have named one's bastard son after one's wife.

which was published in Philadelphia in 1767, and Grímur Thorkelin's *An Essay on the Slave Trade* (1788). He also owned John Eliot's Algonquin-language *Indian Bible* (1663), the first Bible to be published in North America in a tongue besides English. When the library was donated to the British Museum after the King's death, its 79,910 volumes (which included 14,460 pamphlets) and 450 manuscripts doubled the holdings there. It is today displayed in a six-storey glass tower which forms the centrepiece of the British Library at St Pancras.*

The King opened his library at Buckingham House to any scholar who asked to use it, even radical republican Dissenters such as Dr Joseph Priestley. He collected books by authors such as Voltaire, Rousseau, Frederick the Great and Edmund Burke, despite disliking or disapproving of them at one time or another. As his library grew it came to include a collection of over 800 incunabula, some given to him by the antiquary Jacob Bryant in 1782, as well as the Mainz Psalter (1457), Johann Gutenberg's second printed book,† more than thirty books printed by Caxton, the original manuscript of Dr Johnson's *Irene*, the first four folios of Shakespeare (and Charles I's own copy of the second folio), a first edition of *Paradise Lost*, 200 different editions of the Bible, six Indian manuscripts given to him by the Nawab of Lucknow in 1797 (among them the *Padshahnama*, which includes some of the finest Mughal miniatures ever made) and an enormous number of first and rare editions.[45]

The King's Topographical Map Collection included some 50,000 maps, atlases, architectural drawings and landscape watercolours, some going back to the sixteenth century, which constituted a compendium of knowledge about the geography of the world that was unrivalled at that time.[46] He placed these in the room immediately next to his bedroom in the Queen's House.[47] Today split between the British Library and the Royal Library at Windsor, the Collection's highlights include the vast Kangxi atlas of China made by the Italian Jesuit Matteo Ripa in 1719, the 'Duke's Plan' of New York, made to celebrate the capture of the city by the English from the Dutch in 1664, and the Klencke Atlas, which is the largest antiquarian atlas in the world, presented to Charles II in 1660.‡ In 1784 the King gave his patronage to the Trigonometrical Society, the precursor of the Ordnance Survey, which was to map the entire United Kingdom in great detail. He

---

* Not included in the donation were those books that the King kept at Windsor and Kew palaces, which still belong to the royal family.

† Only ten copies are extant, making it far rarer than the forty-eight extant Gutenberg Bibles; today it is the most valuable book in the Royal Collection.

‡ Over 17,000 pages of the Topographical Collection of George III can be seen at: https://www.flickr.com/photos/britishlibrary/albums/72157716220271206.

was not only the most generally cultured monarch since Charles I, but 'undoubtedly the most scientifically and cartographically interested monarch that Britain has ever had'.[48]

What is perhaps most unique about George's bibliophilia is not its breadth or the subsequent value of the collection, but rather its owner's motive in amassing it. The King was attempting to build a library of rare and valuable books and maps not for its own sake, but so that he and his scholarly subjects could use it every day.

'His Majesty ascended the throne in conquest and in glory,' Lord Bute told the House of Lords on 5 February 1762, but by then both men wanted to explore the possibilities of peace. They were supported by the Duke of Bedford who, despite being a member of the government, had moved a motion deploring the expense of the war in Germany. Robert Murray Keith, Britain's Ambassador to St Petersburg, was reporting that Russia's new Tsar, Peter III, was about to make peace with Prussia, prompting George to tell Bute that the 'sudden' Russian volte-face was 'liable to encourage that *too ambitious monarch* [he meant Frederick the Great] to breathe still stronger revenge against the Court of Vienna . . . therefore 'tis our business to force him to peace; the happy day is come that will bring that forward; my dearest friend will no doubt by his speech oblige that *proud, overbearing prince* to see he has no safety but in peace.'[49]

The Cabinet was moving towards peace, Bedford being supported by the Duke of Marlborough, Earl Gower, Lords Sandwich and Weymouth, and Richard Rigby MP, an effective wire-puller and the Master of the Irish Rolls. Newcastle, Hardwicke and Anson could not see what was to be gained by fighting on now that Canada had been taken. George Grenville was supported by Lords Egremont, Barrington and Hillsborough in wanting at least to discover what terms might be available. Yet still the victories came, and in the first three months of 1762 Rear-Admiral George Rodney and Major-General Robert Monckton took Martinique, St Lucia, St Vincent and Grenada. None of this inclined the King towards Newcastle's continued premiership, however, and in April he wrote to Bute that 'The more I know of this fellow the more I wish to see him out of employment.'[50]

Yet just as Pitt had been popular in the country, Newcastle commanded a large parliamentary following, the product of decades of placemanship and the backstairs intrigues of which the Duke was an unparalleled master. Ousting him would exact a heavy political toll within the Commons. Bute had established a small cadre of supporters, which included his brother James Stuart-Mackenzie, his private secretary Charles Jenkinson and Sir

Gilbert Elliot MP, as well as figures from the old Leicester House Set such as Lord Melcombe, Francis Dashwood, the Earl of Northumberland and Lords Egmont and Barrington. Although not an undistinguished group, it was nowhere near as large as Newcastle's following and hardly offered the appearance of an effective alternative government. Perhaps sensing this, on 7 May Newcastle suddenly resigned, giving as his reason a disagreement with Grenville over a vote of credit. In fact he had long felt ignored and sidelined by the King; George nevertheless admitted to Bute his 'great astonishment'.[51]

Newcastle had held high ministerial office since 1724, so there was a tangible sense of the last vestige of the old guard departing, especially as Hardwicke resigned with him, and Devonshire decided no longer to attend Cabinet, even though he remained Lord Chamberlain. Like Pitt, Newcastle promised the King he would loyally support the government, but almost immediately began intriguing against it. The King offered the outgoing premier a generous pension, which Newcastle refused but (as Pitt had also done) burst into tears at the kindness it reflected. 'The Pelhams can cry when they please,' remarked the hardened Henry Fox, 'and their tears are regarded accordingly.'[52]

Although they had been planning for this moment for years, when it finally came Bute was nerve-wracked, and the King had to put backbone into him. Bute was uncertain whether he even wanted to become First Lord of the Treasury, but George was adamant. 'Either the thought of his not accepting the Treasury, or of his retiring chill my blood,' George wrote to Bute in one of three letters on 19 May; 'is this a moment for despondency? No, for vigour and the day is ours.'[53] To Bute's excuse that he knew little about economics – despite the many essays he had set him on the subject – the King replied that James Oswald MP, a junior Lord of the Treasury, could take care of that side of the job.

Bute kissed the King's hands – a literal description of the ceremony by which someone became a government minister – a week later, and the following day, in another sign of royal approbation, was awarded the Order of the Garter. Bute was succeeded as Northern Secretary by Grenville. A key figure from outside Bute's friendship circle was Henry Fox, who had served as Paymaster-General of the Forces since 1757, but had been excluded from effective power during the Pitt–Newcastle coalition. In May 1762 Fox also became Leader of the House of Commons owing to his deft expertise in political management.

George disliked Fox, not just because of the Sarah Lennox and Susan Fox-Strangways imbroglios, but also for the way in which he had repeatedly exploited his offices in order to enrich himself hugely. Bute's new government possessed scant influence in the Commons, however, and short of a reconciliation with Pitt or Newcastle, Fox was the only one with genuine sway among rank-and-file MPs. For all of their earlier talk of ending corruption in public life, George and Bute were forced to turn to Fox, in return for the promise of a peerage once he had got a peace treaty with France and Spain through the House of Commons.

It was not unusual for a monarch to promote a favourite to power upon their accession. Queen Anne had promoted the Marlboroughs; George I had dismissed the Tories, and Frederick, Prince of Wales, had planned to make Lord Egmont Prime Minister. As we have seen, the reversionary interest had been a standard feature of British politics for decades, and George was certainly not unique in following it. Yet Bute was the wrong person to have appointed to the role, and he can hardly be criticized entirely for baulking at assuming the premiership both at the time and in the form in which it was finally offered to him. He was an intellectual who grasped the theory of government and could expound upon it to his pupil, but unlike Newcastle, Fox and Pitt he had never experienced the business of government, which could be tough – as he was about to discover. Unable to overcome the public perception of him as a crypto-Jacobite Scottish Svengali, he invariably provoked fervent dislike: over the next few years Bute would be 'attacked by the mob, threatened with assassination, vilified in pamphlets, prints, newspapers, songs, plays and handbills, and effectively rejected as a potential ally by all the leading politicians of the day except for the none too politically respectable Henry Fox'.[54] Nicknamed the 'Northern Machiavel', he was subjected to endless attacks in pamphlets such as the none too subtly titled *The Butiad ... being a Supplement to the British Antidote to Caledonian Poison* (1763).

The Bute ministry came to power with a commitment to discontinuing the 1758 Convention by which Britain gave £670,000 per annum in subsidies to Prussia. This at least was a policy enjoying support from Bedford and Grenville, and particularly from George, who wrote of Frederick the Great with barely concealed contempt, calling him 'cavalier', 'impertinent' and a 'subsidized monarch'.[55] In October, George even ordered Lord Halifax 'to treat the Prussians ... with that contempt which they deserve'.[56] Militarily, the Prussians certainly did not deserve contempt, and George's disdain evidently ran deeper than the conduct of war itself. Frederick's 'free-thinking' (that is, his atheism) may well have been one of the sources of George's enmity, as well as distrust over Frederick's supposed designs against Hanover, and his continuing refusal to consider making peace.

Frederick saw little point in ending a war in which he was continuing to win ever greater laurels. Additionally, on 24 June at the battle of

Wilhelmsthal, and on 23 July at Lutterberg, forces under Prince Ferdinand of Brunswick and the Marquess of Granby scored further victories over France, which were followed by the evacuation of Göttingen on 16 August and the surrender of Cassel on 1 November. Spain had also fared badly since declaring war against Britain; an Anglo-Portuguese force under Colonel John Burgoyne secured further victories at Valencia de Alcántara on 27 August and at Vila Velha in Portugal on 6 October.

The summer's other triumphs were eclipsed when Admiral George Pocock and Lord Albemarle captured Havana on 12 August 1762 following a two-month siege, providing the Royal Navy with a staging base from which to threaten the trade routes and treasure fleets of the Spanish Main. The extension of the war to Spain that Pitt had wanted and George and Bute had feared had achieved great successes, albeit at considerable financial cost and with a paralysing effect upon foreign trade. 'I was much hurt on receiving Lord Halifax's account of the appearance of success at Havana,' George told Bute in mid-August, 'as I fear lest if the Spaniards don't make haste it may defer the peace.'[57] Although it sounds a deeply unpatriotic thing for a British monarch to have written, George rightly recognized the public opprobrium that would face the government when Havana was returned to Spain as part of a peace treaty, the first drafts of which arrived in September.

On the same day that Havana fell, George and Charlotte's first child, George Augustus Frederick, was born at St James's Palace, and was proclaimed Prince of Wales a week later. When Lord Huntingdon went to inform the King of the Queen's safe delivery of a child, he originally told him that it was a girl. 'The King answered he was but little anxious as to the sex of the child so the Queen was but safe,' Lady Northumberland recorded.[58] The birth of a boy, however, and thus the continuation of the Hanoverian line and civil peace, was celebrated in Britain almost like a military victory – indeed, one of the commemorative medals that was struck to celebrate the Prince's birth also found space to mention Havana, Martinique, Cassel, Amherst, Ferdinand, Granby and Rodney.[59]

The King's hope, expressed to Bute on the day that Charlotte had landed in England, that God would 'make her fruitful' was to be more than fulfilled. Three boys – George, his eventual heir, then Frederick, Duke of York, and William, Duke of Clarence, later King William IV – were born between 1763 and 1765. A year later Princess Charlotte, the Princess Royal, was born. A year after her came Edward, Duke of Kent, then two girls, Augusta and Elizabeth (later Landgravine of Hesse-Homburg), with two years between them. A group of three boys came next – Ernest, Duke of Cumberland, later King of Hanover, Augustus, Duke of Sussex, and Adolphus,

Duke of Cambridge – who were followed by two girls with only a year between them, Mary (later Duchess of Gloucester), and Sophia. Then Octavius in 1779 and Alfred in 1780, and finally George's favourite child Amelia, born in 1783, whom Fanny Burney dubbed 'the little idol'. The King observed to his friend George Rose in March 1786 that 'Heaven ha[s] blessed me with a numerous progeny.'[60]

The King made the Duke of Cumberland a godfather to the Prince of Wales on 3 September 1762, a fitting peace offering to an uncle whose political support might be needed if the war was to be satisfactorily concluded. Over time, the two had come to a kind of détente. 'The King of Prussia had no one but himself to thank for his being not a party in the peace,' the King told his uncle, who agreed.[61]

That month, the Duc de Nivernais was accredited to London as a peace envoy, and Bedford was in turn sent to Paris as ambassador. But still the victories kept coming: on 18 September Jeffery Amherst recaptured St John's in Newfoundland from the French, and on 6 October Admiral Sir Samuel Cornish took Manila from the Spanish. Since it was feared that the peace would be unpopular because of the need to give back recently celebrated conquests, there were ructions in the Cabinet and multiple threats of resignation. At one point Lord Egremont, the Southern Secretary, was said to have allowed himself 'to fly in a passion in the Closet', demanding that Bedford be recalled if the French did not accept his terms, such an outburst being 'a circumstance not easily forgiven' by George. 'The King's answer was that his sentiment was totally different from his own; that a boy of ten years old might have as well be sent to Paris on such an errand . . . in short, he spoke daggers to him.'[62] The capture of Havana indeed proved a major problem for the government – for, as Bute told Fox, Cabinet ministers were considering refusing to give it up without a quid pro quo from Spain, such as Florida or Puerto Rico.[63]

Matters came to a head on 5 October when the Duke of Devonshire, who led the remnant of Newcastle Whigs in the government, refused a direct request to attend the next day's Cabinet, because he did not want it to be misrepresented as support for the peace terms. Devonshire claimed inadequate knowledge of the subject, an unlikely excuse in a former Prime Minister. 'This I believe is [an] unheard of step,' the King told Bute, 'except when men have meant open opposition to the Crown; this is a personal affront to my person, and seems to call for the breaking his wand,' a reference to the ceremonial white staff that lord chamberlains carried.[64]

A little later, going in his coach from Kew to London, the King overtook Devonshire and Newcastle. He was still incensed that his own Lord Chamberlain had refused to attend the crucial Cabinet meeting that agreed the final peace offer, and now assumed that Devonshire was travelling with Newcastle to organize opposition to it. (In fact, he was on his way to his country estate at Chatsworth via St James's Palace.) When Devonshire called on the King at lunchtime before going on to Derbyshire, George said that he would not receive him. Recognizing this as essentially a demand for his resignation, Devonshire asked where he should leave his wand. George replied that he would receive his orders in due course, whereupon Devonshire left the palace, telling a page, 'God bless you, it will be very long before you see me here again.'[65]

On 31 October, the King called for the Privy Council book to be brought to him, and he personally crossed through Devonshire's name. It was rare for privy councillors to be dismissed, let alone a duke who had never voted against the government and hailed from one of the families that had been prominent during the Glorious Revolution. Although the incident has been seen as the pique of a twenty-four-year-old monarch, George was in fact taking the opportunity to send a powerful message to anyone who intended to oppose the coming peace: namely, that rank would confer no protection against his wrath.

George was helped in his campaign to get the peace through Parliament by the secret service, which routinely unsealed, decoded and resealed diplomatic messages. 'By the intercepted letters of the foreign ministers,' he reported to Bute in early November, 'I see the Duke of Rutland, Lord Lincoln and Lord Coventry named as certain to resign as well as Lord Rockingham; if it should be so, I should think myself well rid of them. Force and steadiness will undoubtedly overturn this faction.'[66] Rutland, the Master of the Horse, and Lord Coventry, a lord of the bedchamber, did not in fact resign, but it was clear that the King was spoiling for action. 'The sword is drawn,' George wrote to Bute on 3 November about Devonshire's dismissal, 'vigour and violence are the only means of ending this audacious faction ... I have but one man about me, that is my d[earest] friend.'[67]

The Preliminaries of Peace ending the Seven Years War were signed at Fontainebleau on 3 November 1762, although they could not be finally ratified until the end of separate negotiations between Prussia and Austria. This forced Frederick the Great into a peace he did not yet want, and simultaneously ended the British subsidies, for which he never forgave George. The news of the signing arrived in England on 8 November, and although George was irritated that Bedford had conceded some minor details since receiving his last instructions, overall, as he told Bute, 'I wish so much [for] peace that, unless my d[earest] friend sees more reasons for altering it than I do, I think it a noble peace.'[68] The Preliminaries gave

Britain Canada, Cape Breton Island and all of Louisiana east of the Mississippi (with the freedom to navigate the river), as well as Florida, Minorca, Senegal, Dominica, Grenada, Tobago, St Vincent, all Clive's conquests in Bengal and timber-cutting rights in Honduras.

Yet, despite these enormous territorial gains, William Pitt certainly did not consider the settlement noble and neither did the London mob. They denounced the return of Havana, Martinique, Manila and other recently captured outposts, with wags likening it to the peace of God, because it 'passeth all understanding'. Despite the guns of the Tower of London being fired in celebration on 22 November, the terms were considered so generous to France and Spain that Bute was accused of being in the pay of the French.* Although much of Britain quietly accepted the peace – especially the commercial world, which welcomed the return of prosperity after so many years of war – a proportion of the populace was furious, and their hatred focused largely upon the Scottish Prime Minister, openly castigated in a contemporary pamphlet as 'le parvenu montagnard' (the upstart highlander).[69]

At the State Opening of Parliament on Thursday 25 November, a detachment of the Guards had to protect Bute's coach from being pelted on its way to Westminster. He decided to return home incognito in a sedan chair rather than a coach, but, as Rigby reported to Bedford, 'the mob discovered him, followed him, broke the glasses of the chair, and, in short, by threats and menaces, put him very reasonably in great fear; if they had once overturned the chair, he might very soon have been demolished.'[70] The King was also hissed and booed, but he took no notice and indeed went out to the theatre that same evening.[71] He wrote to commiserate with Bute about the riot and 'the wicked designs of the mob'.[72]

The State Opening had been the first outing for the new Gold State Coach, which had to stay parked in the Palace Yard at Westminster for an hour at 4 p.m. until the mob had dispersed.[73] Addressing Parliament in the House of Lords, the King commended the 'just and honourable terms' of the peace, declaring that they 'are such that there is not only an immense territory added to the empire of Great Britain, but a solid foundation laid for the increase of trade and commerce'.[74] He warned that the expenses of the war meant that 'we must expect for some time to feel the consequences of them to a considerable degree.'[75] 'It was a very noble thing,' the young Scottish lawyer James Boswell noted in his diary. 'I here beheld the King of Great Britain on his throne with the crown on his head addressing both

---

* A libel so tenacious that it was even repeated in the *Cambridge Modern History* as late as 1909.

the Lords and the Commons. His Majesty spoke better than any man I
ever heard: with dignity, delicacy and ease. I admired him.'[76]

Soon handbills were being pasted to walls mock-advertising for 'a modern Felton' – a reference to John Felton, who had murdered Charles I's
favourite, the Duke of Buckingham, in 1628. Writing to his friend and
confidant Dr Campbell on 30 January 1763, Bute complained of how the
stress of politics – 'the little infamous scenes, the black ingratitude, etc.,
etc., etc.' – had had a profound physical effect on him:

> My health is every day impairing; a great relaxation of my bowels of many
> years standing is increasing on me continually; the eternal unpleasant labour
> of the mind, and the impossibility of finding hours for exercise . . . the little
> time I get for sleep . . . In my opinion the Angel Gabriel could not at present
> govern this country, but by means too long practised and such as my soul
> abhors.[77]

Campbell prescribed rhubarb for Bute's diarrhoea – which Bute called an
'old inveterate illness' – a treatment that might have made it worse. He
was also bled for it, which is unlikely to have helped much either. In more
than a usually literal sense, Bute lacked the intestinal fortitude for the
premiership.

After the riot at the State Opening, Bute sent George the first of many
pleas that he be allowed to resign. The King replied that Bute's letter:

> gives me the greatest concern, as it overturns all the thoughts that have alone
> kept up my spirits in these bad times; I own I had flattered myself when peace
> was once established that my d[earest] friend would have assisted me in
> purging out corruption, and in those measures that no man but he that has
> the [King's] real affection can go through; then when we were both dead our
> memories would have been respected and esteemed to the end of time.[78]

Instead, he averred, 'the ministry remains composed of the most abandoned
men that ever had those offices': this was a reference to Fox and also possibly Dashwood, whose hedonistic parties in the Hellfire Caves beneath
his Berkshire estate and at the disused abbey at Medmenham in Buckinghamshire were reputed to involve his friends engaging in sexual acts while
dressed as monks.

The King pointed out that, even though he wished to 'attack the irreli-
gious' in politics, it would have 'no effect' if ministers were themselves 'of
that stamp', since 'men will with reason think they may advance to the
highest pitch of their ambition through every infamous way that their own
black hearts or the rascality of their superiors can point out.'[79] To encourage his mentor and father-figure to stay on as premier, George reminded

him of a taunt that Fox had apparently once uttered that 'We will give Lord B[ute] a Garter and a Court employment and then we may do as we please.' George did not deny that Bute was under mortal threat, writing of 'How bad are not men grown when their minds can harbour an instant the thought of assassination.'[80] In other letters he wrote at around this time, George similarly railed against 'an ungrateful, wicked people', 'the wickedest age that ever was seen' and 'ingratitude, avarice and ambition', and lamented his 'many melancholy thoughts that as daggers pierce my breast'.[81] Bute agreed to stay on as premier.

Pitt denounced the peace in a tremendous three-and-a-half-hour oration in the House of Commons on 9 December 1792. The treaty, he claimed with no small degree of artistic licence, had left Britain with 'nothing, though we have conquered everything', after which he was hailed outside in the streets by the crowd. Despite Pitt's masterful and incendiary rhetoric, in the subsequent division moved by Henry Fox, 319 MPs voted in favour of the peace and only 65 against. Walpole wrote indignantly that the 319 had surely been bribed, but beyond the jingoistic London mob many people were weary, and happy to see a victorious end to the long war. The Duke of Rutland and his son the Marquess of Granby voted for the peace, as did most of Newcastle's party, and even Hardwicke's sons deserted their father to support it.

The Preliminaries were only that, and the Fontainebleau peace was subject to revision before its formal ratification as the Treaty of Paris in 1763. When in December 1762 Bute received intelligence that the state of French public finances were significantly better than reported, suggesting that they could return to the fight, he feared the National Debt could not sustain a resumption of war. He was therefore persuaded to stop claiming Guadeloupe in order to secure final ratification. This was a greater renunciation than it might appear, for it was a very rich sugar island – indeed, there had been serious discussion in the Cabinet in 1761 about whether it was better to retain Guadeloupe or Canada. Bedford had preferred to keep the former and cede the latter to France for an extraordinarily astute reason, which was that 'I do not know whether the neighbourhood of the French to our northern colonies was not the greatest security of their dependence on the mother country, who I fear will be slighted by them when their apprehensions of the French are removed.'[82] Put plainly, if Canada were returned to France, the consequent strategic threat to the thirteen North American colonies from the French might keep them loyal to Britain.

After their victorious division on the Preliminaries, Bute and Fox exacted a wide-ranging purge of those government office holders who had been among the sixty-five opponents of peace, which was carried out with George's full approval. There is no evidence that George's actions were in any way guided by his mother; nor any grounds for Walpole's claim that on hearing the news of the vote Augusta had exclaimed, 'Now my son is really King of England.'[83] The 1909 *Cambridge Modern History* stated that the Dowager Princess 'was imbued with all the autocratic ideas of a petty German Court. She was never tired of exhorting her son to be a king,' but there is no evidence for this, and it simply does not ring true.[84] Another version (which was even to appear in school textbooks) was that his mother had told the youthful prince, 'George, be [a] King!', exhorting him to extend his personal authority at the expense of the government and Parliament.[85] Yet there is no evidence she ever said this beyond the autobiography of the Opposition MP John Nicholls who was fifteen when George acceded, and did not publish his libel until half a century after Augusta's death. As Lewis Namier argued, even if Augusta did say it, she might have been trying to encourage her son to have better table manners rather than enjoining him to overthrow the constitution. Myths about George III take a long time to expire, but the idea that he was urged to be an absolutist monarch by his mother has deserved to die sooner.

The rebels' purge was stepped up on 23 December when the Duke of Newcastle was dismissed from his three county lord-lieutenancies, and his political deputy, Charles Watson-Wentworth, the 2nd Marquess of Rockingham, was likewise sacked from his. In solidarity, the Duke of Devonshire resigned the lord-lieutenancy of Derbyshire. By mid-January 1763, George was wondering whether the punishment of the Old Whig aristocrats might have gone too far, asking Bute to take only 'what steps are necessary to ruin the Newcastle faction . . . no man should be dismissed unless others . . . declare them to be of that denomination.'[86]

By that time the King had also recognized that power within the ministry had tipped too far towards Henry Fox, not least because Bute was still hoping to resign. He disliked Fox's suggestions for army promotions, and still more his recommendations for the bench of bishops, both areas in which George guarded his powers of appointment fiercely. 'I don't think Mr Fox very likely to recommend a man that will do honour to that sacred profession,' he wrote of one proposed prebendary post.[87] When Newcastle lost power and the bishops started supporting Bute, he had wryly noted that 'even the bishops forgot their maker.'[88]

The Treaty of Paris was finally ratified by all parties on 10 February 1763; when joined five days later by the Treaty of Hubertusburg between Prussia, Austria and Saxony, the Seven Years War came to a close. 'There shall be a Christian, universal, and perpetual peace,' read the Treaty of

Paris's opening line, 'as well by sea as by land.' It secured British maritime
supremacy and the military prestige of Prussia, and was dubbed 'the disgraceful peace' in France.[89] Britain now controlled the North American
continent from Hudson's Bay in the north down to the Gulf of Mexico,
securing Canada (including the Great Lakes and Illinois Country), Nova
Scotia, Cape Breton, St Vincent, Tobago, Dominica, Grenada, the Gren-
adines, Senegal and Minorca from France, and Florida from Spain. France
regained Martinique and Guadeloupe, the strategically important St Lucia,
and fishing rights off Newfoundland and within the Gulf of St Lawrence,
as well as the fishery islands of Saint-Pierre and Miquelon. No new French
fortifications could be built on their restored territories in India, and those
at Dunkirk had to be demolished. France similarly agreed not to station
an army in Bengal – thus de facto ceding it to Britain – and de jure ceded
areas in Sumatra as well. The French presence in India was reduced to a
few trading ports, and pro-British rulers were confirmed in control of
Hyderabad and the Carnatic.

France separately ceded western Louisiana to Spain, which exchanged
Florida for Havana with Britain, and recovered the Philippines, thus protecting her Caribbean and Chinese trade routes. She agreed to dismantle
her forts in the Bay of Honduras and renounce her claims to the Newfoundland fisheries. France and Spain both accepted the Mississippi River
as the westward limit of British dominion.

Pitt was right to argue that the peace left French naval power untouched,
and that Saint-Pierre and Miquelon were important both commercially for
their £500,000 annual profit but also as a naval training ground for
France's 14,000 fishermen. Overall, however, whereas before the Treaty of
Paris Britain had been one of the major European colonial powers, after
it she was the predominant imperial one. This would, of course, store up
trouble for the future, and no one thought the peace 'perpetual'. Austria,
which had failed to regain Silesia, was now pro-French. Frederick the Great
never forgot or forgave the way he felt he had been mistreated, and would
later reject an alliance with Britain because of what he called 'the indecent,
I might almost say infamous, way in which England treated me at the last
peace'.[90] Holland sensed the coming end of her status as a great power.
France and Spain were resentful and irredeemably revanchist. 'She had
crushed her enemies,' writes one military historian of Britain, 'but lost her
friends.'[91]

The King issued a proclamation in October that added four new western
hemisphere colonies – Quebec, East Florida, West Florida and the Wind-
ward Islands – to join the thirteen North American colonies, and gave each
the right to 'call general assemblies ... as is used and directed in those

colonies and provinces in America . . . to make, constitute and ordain laws, statutes and ordinances'.[92] Thus Quebec was to have the same rights and freedoms as Massachusetts, a fact that the latter soon came bitterly to resent.

Richard Neville, the Secretary of the Paris embassy, who took the signed treaty to London for the King and Lord Egremont's approval on 15 February, later reported to Bedford that George had:

> received me most graciously, and kept me a full hour and a half in his Closet. He read over your Grace's dispatch with great eagerness; asked me questions upon many particulars of it; and, expressing a satisfaction even greater than I could have conceived, said to Lord Egremont, 'Why, my Lord, this is greater than we could have hoped for: England never signed such a peace before, nor, I believe, any other power in Europe; indeed the Duke of Bedford has done greatly.' Lord Egremont said no prince had ever begun his reign by . . . so glorious a peace.[93]

Neville reported how 'civil, nay affectionate' the King was about Bedford, and how pleased he was that Hanover's independence had been guaranteed and Britain's ancient alliance with Portugal reaffirmed.

'Spoils under the Treaty of Paris in 1763 were among the greatest ever won by force of arms,' one American historian has written.[94] The colonial administrator Lord Macartney wrote of 'this vast empire on which the sun never sets', a phrase which became legendary.[95] The glory was unquestioned, but a major question now arose about the future security of the colonies, all the more so now that those in America were no longer in any direct existential danger from France or Spain. Who was going to pay for that security?

5

The Problems of Peace

February–October 1763

A mighty empire ... will arise on this continent where she [Britain] cannot hinder its progress.[1]
Henry Laurens, Charleston, South Carolina, February 1775

As a direct consequence of the Seven Years War, Britain's National Debt soared from £55 million in 1755 to £132.6 million in 1763, by far the highest it had ever been.[2] At a time of fiscal conservatism, minimal state borrowing and determination to balance budgets, this could only mean that there had to be both a drastic cut in expenditure and an increase in taxation. The interest on the Debt alone cost the Treasury £4.7 million per annum, when the Chancellor of the Exchequer, George Grenville, was attempting to slash public expenditure as a whole from £13.5 million annually to less than £8 million.[3] It was the post-war defence budget that saw the most serious cuts: the British Army was reduced from over 120,000 men to only 48,000. The Royal Navy likewise saw drastic cuts, with officers and sailors laid up on shore and many of its warships mothballed.

Post-war demobilization was a common practice for the time: the sheer scale of European armies and navies meant that they never remained standing very long after the outbreak of peace. But Grenville's cuts went far deeper than the norm, with the result that Britain found herself obliged to defend far more with far less. Pitt, naturally, was furious; so too was Lord Egmont, First Lord of the Admiralty from September 1763, who protested vociferously. But they were in a minority. Most of the Cabinet accepted – and George in the main championed – the need to reduce the Debt in line with the fiscal assumptions of Bute, Grenville and his late father.

The government had already started to examine ways to incorporate the newly acquired territories of Canada into the empire, extend revenue and judiciary services there and generally put the empire's western hemisphere, including the Caribbean and thirteen North American colonies, into a position of financing itself, especially with regards to defence. This notion was not controversial in Britain at the time. The template the politicians and civil servants looked to was Ireland, which was not subsidized by the British taxpayer.

As they surveyed the global scene, ministers thought of the twenty-two British colonies in North and South America and the West Indies as part of a wider imperial community. The analogy commonly employed in political pamphlets and in Commons speeches was that of England as the mother country and the colonies as her children – a rather glib sentiment considering that some of the New England colonies were almost a century and a half old. Ministers certainly took it entirely for granted that it was in both Britain's and the colonies' best interests to be part of the same broad polity. The hope of some progressive imperialist thinkers, such as the writers Thomas Whately MP and Thomas Pownall MP, the former Governor of Massachusetts, was that there might be a 'grand marine dominion', focused chiefly upon the Atlantic and its surrounding seas, which would advance the mutual socio-economic development of all the English-speaking peoples living around and trading across it.[4]

Imperialism for these idealists was never a zero-sum game in which either Britain or America benefited at the exploitative expense of the other; instead it saw Britons on both sides of the Atlantic as belonging to one nation. It naturally followed from this worldview that there was an ultimate sovereign authority, from which the entire community drew rights, but to which in turn it owed obligations and allegiance. Since the 1530s this had been the constitutional concept of the Crown-in-Parliament, re-affirmed by the Restoration and the Glorious Revolution and enshrined within the Bill of Rights and Act of Settlement. From this, Parliament had for many decades possessed the right to legislate for the entire empire, and its overarching authority to do so had been broadly accepted by its North American colonists. In practice the British government seldom exercised its powers over them directly and the American provinces were governed by royal governors and directly elected assemblies.

Over a century or more, the colonies had developed their own institutions of government, houses of burgesses and other such legislative bodies, in a process that first adopted and then adapted the British structure of governance to their own purposes. The result by the mid-eighteenth century was an informal quasi-independence, with mere lip service paid to the customs and practices of the mother country. Edmund Burke dubbed this practice 'salutary neglect': the de facto devolution of autonomy from the imperial centre to its colonial peripheries.

Accepting a largely nominal status as a dominion in return for minimal

interference in local affairs seemed to many a fair compromise. American*
consumers imported the latest European fashions, read many of the same
political and scientific pamphlets, delighted in learning of the latest London
scandals through their local newspapers and held the Bill of Rights and
Act of Settlement in high esteem. In many ways they really were Britons,
with the important caveat that they were not British. Quite reasonably, the
Bute government had little expectation of problems from North America
as the world transitioned to peace.[5]

One problem with the British governmental system was that until 1768
there was no Colonial Office, so American affairs fell somewhere between
the Board of Trade and Plantations and the Southern Department, both of
which had amassed a hotchpotch of other responsibilities. The latter, for
example, covered relations with the Catholic and Muslim states of Europe,
with which American issues had nothing in common. The Southern Department also tended to concentrate on whatever was its most important crisis
at the time.

Perhaps naively, there was also an expectation in London of gratitude
for the victory in the recent French and Indian War (as the Seven Years
War was called in colonial America), which had started in clashes between
the American colonists and the French and French-allied Native Americans
that had ultimately been won by around 21,000 British regular troops as
well as some 17,000 American militiamen and large numbers of allies from
Indigenous Nations such as the Wyandot, the Catawba, the Cherokee and
the Iroquois Confederacy. An informed estimate suggests that 1,512 British
and North American colonial troops were killed in action, around 1,500
died of wounds and 10,400 died of disease in the war; perhaps a further
4,000 or so were wounded but survived.[6] These losses were overwhelmingly British: in the attack on Ticonderoga in July 1758, for example, the
total numbers of killed and wounded were 1,600 British and 334 North
American colonial. When Louisburg finally fell that month, it was to
11,000 British regulars and 200 American Rangers. Additionally, the Royal
Navy had been deployed at substantial cost and loss of life to protect
American trade from the French, Spanish and Native Americans, since the
colonies had no fleet of their own.

Pontiac's Revolt, a two-year-long conflict that began in May 1763, saw
warriors of the Ottawa, Wyandot, Potawatomi, Ojibwa and later the Delaware, Shawnee and Seneca nations engage in hit-and-fade actions in the

* Henceforth 'Americans' refers to the mainly British-descended North Americans from the
thirteen colonies that seceded, even though the formal definition also of course includes enslaved
African-Americans, Native Americans, Canadians, Spanish Floridans and others.

poorly defended back countries of Pennsylvania, Maryland and Virginia. General Amherst estimated that no fewer than 10,000 troops would be needed to garrison the military posts policing the Peace of Paris in the regions west of the thirteen colonies. They would need to keep several potentially hostile peoples in order, including 70,000 French Canadians, thousands of Spanish in Florida and around 150,000 Indigenous peoples.[7] Amherst did not want hostile Native Americans marauding through the back country; but neither did he want colonial squatters, smugglers, bandits and especially land-hungry unlicensed settlers in the then largely lawless trans-Appalachian territories, where they might turn friendly Native Americans, who had been allies in the war, into foes.[8]

With India and Canada now part of the empire, London was starting to think imperially in a way that policymakers had not been willing, able or motivated to do before. George and his ministers accepted Amherst's estimate for a twenty-battalion peacetime force in North America, a standing army that would cost £214,340 per annum to maintain. This was emphatically not intended to be used against the North American colonists, as later propaganda alleged, but rather was for their protection, which was why ministers thought that at least part of the cost should be met by the colonists rather than solely by the British taxpayer, a view the King endorsed.

Outside the government, some wise former ministers such as Newcastle, Hardwicke and Legge worried that the estimated number of troops was too large and the cost thus likely to be too high. Although the first census was not carried out until 1790, there were around 2.5 million people living in the thirteen colonies in the early 1760s, of whom 600,000 – almost one-quarter – were African-American slaves. The British government believed that if the cost of 10,000 soldiers were spread as evenly as possible across the colonies' taxpayers, it should not be too onerous. When £214,340 is divided by 1.9 million people it comes to two shillings and threepence per American colonist per annum, at a time when soldiers were paid a shilling a day. The 1763 Budget had already saddled Britain with a new £7 million loan, and Bute's new duty of four shillings per hogshead on cider production was already extremely unpopular.

In March 1763, Welbore Ellis, the Secretary at War, told the Commons that twenty battalions of regulars would be stationed in North America, and although Britain would pay the £214,340 for the first twelve months, after that 'the country who have immediate benefit shall pay them'.[9] Because defence matters fell within the imperial purview decided at Westminster and Whitehall, no attempt had been made to ask the American governors or assemblies what they thought of this idea, although they of course knew that no one ever welcomes new taxes. A tax that averaged

THE PROBLEMS OF PEACE

two shillings and threepence per person per annum for the military protection of the thirteen colonies was simply not considered likely to cause serious complaint, let alone a rebellion. The idea that the Americans might baulk at paying for their own protection – not a penny of any of George III's taxes on Americans was ever spent on anyone except Americans – did not occur to civil servants until far too late.

What the King, politicians and civil servants completely failed to recognize was that the Seven Years War had fundamentally changed the strategic situation in North America. Britain's decisive victory had at a stroke removed the French threat over the colonies; except for the 93-square-mile islands of Saint-Pierre and Miquelon off the Newfoundland coast, the nearest French territory which could pose a military threat to North America was at Saint-Domingue, present-day Haiti, 1,150 miles away. Similarly, the threat posed from the west by the hostile Indigenous Nations, even when brought together by charismatic leadership such as that of Pontiac, posed no existential danger to the thirteen colonies as a whole, however much many on the frontier may have felt threatened by them.

Most of all, by the time of the Peace of Paris of 1763 Americans were accustomed to de facto autonomy and some were ready for full statehood. 'The colonies had arrived at that point in the progress of nations when it is no longer just or practicable to govern one country with reference to the interests of another,' *The Times* correctly stated in George's obituary decades later. 'North America had become too rich, too populous, too ambitious of enterprise, too conscious of power, to remain an appendage of a distant state.'[10] The North American economy had grown at twice the rate of Britain's over the previous century.[11] The population of the thirteen colonies was doubling every quarter-century, a rate four times faster than in Britain, and their citizens were flourishing.[12] In the fifteen years before 1776, Philadelphia had more booksellers than the ten largest English provincial cities combined.[13]

In the 1688 Revolution, New England had thrown off James II's government and restored the assemblies he had suspended: as one historian has put it, 'The supremacy of Parliament had thus become associated in the colonial mind with the supremacy of the assemblies.'[14] During the recent war, the joint interest in protecting the colonies from French and Native American incursion kept arguments about taxation powers quiescent, since Britain was paying the lion's share to protect her American colonists. Once those threats were over, the assemblies were likely to make their move. The British response – either to acquiesce in the new political reality or to emphasize Westminster's historic rights – was not a decision of the King, who had no settled view on the subject until much later on.[15]

Why did so few Britons recognize the enormous potential of America, and move far earlier to try to work in concert with the thirteen colonies rather than continue to treat them as before? The advantages American society enjoyed over British – with the obvious exception of the horrific incubus of slavery – were impressive. Two-thirds of American male colonists owned land, compared to one-fifth of male Britons. Two-thirds were literate, a higher rate than in Britain, and two-thirds had the vote in their provincial assemblies.[16] Yet the massive increases in the North American population and in economic activity since 1700 had not been reflected in concomitant constitutional change. Few apart from the polymath Benjamin Franklin were sufficiently prescient to point out that the demographics alone would eventually force the empire to shift its centre of gravity across the Atlantic.

The Americans had created a new economic situation as expansive as its demographic one: North American trade with Britain engaged half of all British maritime shipping, a quarter of her exports, and in the eighteen years after 1747 the value of American exports to Britain grew from £700,000 to £1.5 million, with imports growing even faster.[17] The trade deficits built up by the colonists buying British goods were serviced by an American debt to Britain that between 1760 and 1772 grew from £2 million to £4 million. The American colonies were prosperous, as could be seen in the huge increases in the importation of British luxuries, 'from tea and tea sets to silk handkerchiefs and feather mattresses', as one historian has noted.[18] George Washington had his boots, his slippers, his coach, the glass in his windows and even his false teeth imported from London.

One of the reasons why British politicians failed to comprehend that Americans would soon be agitating for nationhood was the paradoxical one, considering the propaganda of the independence movement twelve years later, that they were not being persecuted in any discernible way. 'The colonists were the least oppressed of all peoples then on earth, politically, economically and nationally,' noted Hans Kohn in his seminal book *The Idea of Nationalism* in 1944, written when half the world knew genuine oppression. 'Politically the colonists were infinitely freer than any people on the European continent; they were even freer than Englishmen in Great Britain. The favourable conditions of frontier life had brought Milton's and Locke's teachings and English constitutional liberties to faster and fuller fruition in the colonies than in the mother country.'[19] Royal governors and colonial assemblies generally ruled Americans with the lightest of touches, and the colonists certainly paid the lightest of taxes in the empire. The average American in 1770 paid a tiny fraction of what his British cousin paid in direct taxes, and crucially all of what he did pay stayed in America.

Insofar as they thought about such issues at all, most British politicians of the time shared a strong commitment to the absolute sovereignty of the Westminster Parliament in all matters concerning the empire. British government interference in the internal affairs of the colonies had been minimal before the Seven Years War, other than enforcing the Navigation Acts which required that exports from the colonies be transported in British ships. The assumption – championed by Louis XIV's First Minister Jean-Baptiste Colbert but widely accepted – was that trade was power, because profits from it could be churned back into war materiel via taxation. So it was in the interests of all Britons – on both sides of the Atlantic – to do as little trade as possible with potentially hostile states such as France, Spain and Holland, and as much as possible with each other. This Colbertian protectionist policy would prevent foreign manufacturers and merchants from making profits that could be made by Britons and Americans instead.

Because British official circles thought in imperial not insular British terms, Britons were similarly prevented from buying all but the most expensive luxury French goods by prohibitive tariffs. The American colonists were expected, as overseas Britons, to trade within the guidelines of a policy intended to weaken France as much as possible.[20] This mercantilism was intended to be not anti-American but anti-French. In any case, the regulations were routinely flouted by mass smuggling as the profit motive and demand for cheaper, untaxed goods in the thirteen colonies had their effect.

By the time of the Peace of Paris, relations between Britain and her American colonies clearly had to be regulated. Successive attempts at reform that had been shelved during the War of Austrian Succession and the Seven Years War were now dusted off and looked at anew. The colonists' widespread ignoring of the Navigation Acts, their continued push to the west of the Appalachians (and propensity to start wars against the Native Americans, many of whom had been British allies against the French) and the tax-and-spend power of colonial assemblies vis-à-vis those of the Crown-appointed colonial governors all needed to be settled. There were huge opportunities for the empire if these were handled carefully, but great pitfalls if they were not. Yet, for reasons that were largely unconnected with what was happening in North America, Westminster now entered into a seven-year period of endemic factionalism and political strife in which the governance and taxation of Americans became a political dispute between shifting alliances of competing politicians, and genuine statesmanship was in very short supply.

After the Peace of Paris had been ratified by Parliament, Bute thanked Henry Fox for 'a spirit and generosity that I can never forget', adding, 'the vessel's safe in harbour.'[21] He moved again to resign, fearing that some of his unpopularity, over his Scottishness, the peace and now also the cider tax, was rubbing off on the King.[22] On 2 March 1763, when Bute suggested offering the premiership to Fox, George described his proposed resignation as 'the most cruel political blow that could have happened to me', asking him to stay on until the summer or 'instantly look out for some other man than Mr Fox for that mighty office'.[23] George added that Fox was 'void of principles' and that 'his own bad character comes strongly into my thoughts whenever I hear him named; 'tis not prejudice but aversion to his whole mode of government that causes my writing so openly my thoughts to my only friend.' The King believed that Bute was 'too upright' to enjoy 'his present employment, which has given him too many proofs of the baseness of the present age'.[24]

After Fox had written a paper for the King, at Bute's request, suggesting a stopgap premier – presumably himself – and mentioning Lords Gower and Shelburne as prospective secretaries of state, George wrote to Bute, as if the point still needed to be made, of 'my personal dislike to Mr Fox'.[25] He suggested his old governor, Lord Waldegrave, as better than either Gower or Shelburne, 'but he would fairly be but a chip in the porridge'.* Of the idea that James Oswald should become Chancellor of the Exchequer, the King said that 'perhaps his being born on the other side of the Tweed [that is, in Scotland] might cause some more abuse but I would willingly go through fifty times as much if I could persuade my d[earest] friend to remain.' He predicted that as premier Fox would put army commissions and even judicial appointments up for sale, and thus was someone 'I would rather see perish than at the head of [a] ministry'.[26] Only if Bute utterly refused to continue in office would 'I agree to the trying [of] Fox, but I own from the moment he comes in I shall not feel myself interested in the public affairs and shall feel rejoiced whenever I can see a glimmering hope of getting quit of him.' The prospect of losing the person to whom over the previous eight years he had been closer than anyone else besides his mother clearly terrified George.

The Opposition leaders Devonshire and Hardwicke were swiftly ruled out by George on political grounds; the Duke of Bedford's 'dirty demands' for pensions for friends rendered him likewise unacceptable; Pitt and Legge were 'obnoxious to me', and George expressed a personal dislike for Grenville and Egremont too.[27] A recent historian has described Grenville as treating the King 'like a schoolboy who had failed to do his homework', which the twenty-five-year-old was bound to resent.[28] George thought Lord

---

* An expression meaning that he would do neither good nor harm.

Halifax 'the worst man who could be in the place except Ch[arles] Townshend', whom he in turn considered 'the worst man that lives ... I would
as soon employ a common thief as him.'[29] It is not immediately apparent
quite what the brilliant, witty and ambitious Charles 'Champagne Speech'
Townshend, the First Lord of Trade, had done to merit such a judgement,
although Burke thought the whole government was like 'a tessellated pave-
ment without cement'.[30] The fact that Townshend and his mentor Halifax
were both known to be heavy drinkers and gamblers with questionable
private lives was perhaps enough to incur George's disdain. From the ease
with which he casually dismissed such men, it is clear that George held
most of the senior politicians of the day in extremely low regard. Yet over
the coming years he would eventually be forced to offer the premiership
to no fewer than three on that list of rejects.

Just as George was finally reconciled to having Fox as Prime Minister,
Fox refused it, becoming the 1st Baron Holland instead. He claimed this
was due to his wife's opposition to his taking the office, but it cannot have
escaped so assiduous and subtle a politician that the King, whose confidence he would have needed, regarded him as personifying all that was
wrong with politics. Detractors implied that Lord Holland preferred to
hold on to his post at the Pay Office, with its opportunity to siphon tens
of thousands of pounds of public money into his own accounts over the
next few years. A title for Fox could hardly be denied him after his extensive service in important roles in government, not to mention his role in
shepherding the Peace of Paris through the Commons with such large
majorities. Yet he was alienated by the award because it was not the earldom he believed he deserved.

The King conformed to the general view at Westminster that Parliament
had the legal right to tax the colonies and that the home government should
exercise its constitutional authority when required. The very first reference
he ever made to America as king was a message sent to Parliament on 14
March 1763 recommending that proper compensation be made to the
colonies for their expenses during the Seven Years War.[31] His feelings about
his American subjects thus began positively, but all his knowledge about
them was gleaned from books, maps and individuals he had met; he did
not know the country. George never visited America, just as he never visited
the rest of his dominions, including Scotland, Wales, Hanover and Ireland;
indeed he never set foot in England north of Worcester or west of Plymouth
in his entire sixty-year reign. He went often to Weymouth, but never to
Manchester, Birmingham or Leeds, where later in his reign innovation and
industry were fundamentally changing Britain. His vast topographical map

collection and his fascination with the solar system displayed an interest in things far beyond the English Home Counties where he spent almost his whole life, yet he was the first monarch since Elizabeth I who never visited the Continent of Europe. For the amount of time that George II had spent in Hanover in 1736 alone, his grandson could easily have travelled to Boston, New York and Philadelphia and back.[32]

For a man with so inquisitive a mind in so many areas to be quite so personally insular was an extraordinary lacuna: if the King had through personal experience been able to gain an inkling of America's potential and her discontents, the story of the next twenty years might well have been very different. Back in September 1749, his father had had the idea of one day settling his then four-year-old son Prince Henry on 'an island near Antigua' with the title of Duke of Virginia, but there was no thought in the early 1770s of George visiting the scene of the problem.[33] Decades later in December 1804, when he was 'in very pleasant spirits and very narrative'* at a small dinner party in Blackheath, he spoke of how his great-grandfather King George I had been 'extremely unwilling to come to England and wished to have only sent his son. But it was represented to him that if he did not come he would run the risk of losing the crown of the three kingdoms and he at last declared he would sacrifice himself for his family.'[34] In the 1770s, there was no analogous courtier or politician to suggest to George that if he did not make the journey to America he ran the risk of losing thirteen of his colonies. It is of course by no means certain that he would have been able to stave off the rebellion by doing so, but he should surely have made the effort, just as his great-grandfather had. As the Hanoverians had by 1763 been resident in Britain for less than half a century, George could have contemplated not just visiting America but moving there permanently, the carpet-bagging principle having already been established by his dynasty's relocation from Hanover.[35] Yet this seems never even to have been considered.

On 19 March 1763, on Charles Townshend's proposal, a Bill was introduced to reduce the duty on West Indies molasses, in order to help the Rhode Island rum distillers. Back in 1733, the Molasses Act had imposed a deliberately prohibitive duty of sixpence per gallon on the importation of all foreign (effectively French West Indian) molasses into Britain and the British colonies. Because the British West Indies plantations did not produce enough molasses to satisfy the huge North American demand for rum, it had led to widespread smuggling into the thirteen colonies: merchants

---

* 'Storytelling; apt to relate things past' (*Johnson's Dictionary*).

would bribe corrupt customs officials roughly a penny a gallon to under-report the quantity of molasses on board their ships by a factor of ten.*

The Molasses Act had been intended to harm not the American rum industry but the French West Indian planters. It had initially been passed for five years and was regularly extended, and after coming before the Commons' Expiring Laws' Continuance Committee on 9 March it was decided ten days later to renew it for another year, only with Charles Townshend's amendment to reduce the duty to twopence, which he had not previously cleared with Bute or with any other senior minister. This two-thirds reduction was proposed 'the more effectually to secure the payment of it'.[36] British ministers believed it was necessary to control colonial smuggling, which had become so well established in America that it was considered almost customary.[37]

Agents of the American colonies argued that the duty ought to be set at one penny, which Thomas Hutchinson, Lieutenant Governor of Massachusetts, reported to London 'would be generally agreeable to the people here, and the merchants would readily pay it'.[38] Some historians argue that had the government indeed lowered the duty on foreign molasses imported into America from sixpence per gallon to one rather than two, he would have 'upheld Parliament's sovereignty, raised a revenue, reduced smuggling, and asserted British control over the colonies', because smugglers would then have had no incentive to bribe corrupt customs officers to enter the foreign molasses as domestic.[39] Yet this is to misinterpret the coming American protestations over taxation as purely economic, which by 1763 they were not. They were, rather, proxy protests against British political control by a people who sensed they could now thrive as an independent country. The underlying issue was not taxation, or indeed representation: it was about sovereignty, independence and self-government – once Britain had made North America safe from foreign threats.

Instead of being generally agreeable to the merchants of Boston, and presenting a policy that would have saved a good deal of trouble later on, Charles Townshend made 'heavy complaints' in his speech to the House of Commons Ways and Means Committee about 'the state of our revenues in North America', which at that time amounted to less than the £7,000 it cost to collect.[40] The King's response to Townshend's surprise proposal to reduce the molasses duty by two-thirds was to complain vociferously to Bute. No lords of the Treasury had made any effort to block Townshend's motion, and George thought that ministers ought to have spoken out, because:

---

* Although they lied to the Revenue, the merchants insured the molasses for the correct amount, which is how historians were able to spot the enormous discrepancies.

this subject was new to none, having been thought of this whole winter; all ought to have declared that next session some tax will be laid before the House but that it requires much information before a proper one can be stated, and thus have thrown out this insidious proposal; I think Mr Townshend's conduct deserves the dismissing [of] him or [at] the least the making him explain his intentions.[41]

Welbore Ellis had already stated in Parliament that 'the American force [that is, the twenty battalions] was intended to be paid for a future year by America'. Townshend, for his part, knew that government policy was to wait until the tax proposals were thoroughly thought through and discussed with both Lord Egremont, the Colonial Minister, and Lord Halifax, an expert in colonial policy from his thirteen years as Trade Secretary, before they were put before the Commons. The reason why the King found the lower duty on molasses an 'insidious proposal', therefore, was not that he wanted high duties to be paid by his North American subjects, but that he knew it would now be necessary to raise duties on other goods or services with all the commercial, administrative and political difficulties that would entail.[42]

Bute, still hoping to resign, showed little interest in dealing with either the molasses issue or Townshend's insubordination. The King, who now had had six months to prepare for Bute's departure, still did all he could to persuade his favourite to change his mind. The situation would be repeated all too often later in his reign with other premiers, always with bad results. George never learned that, once a prime minister's heart was no longer in the job, he should be allowed to leave it as soon as possible.

Instead the King impressed on George Grenville that, although he would be First Lord of the Treasury and Prime Minister, Bute would continue to have the royal ear. He lamented Bute's ill-health, 'as that robbed me in government of the only friend I ever could have'. He added that he was appointing Grenville on Bute's recommendation, but that 'I would rather quit my Crown' than have the Old Whigs Newcastle and Devonshire back in power, and that Lord Holland's faction and especially Lord Shelburne 'must be treated with the greatest kindness'.[43] Similarly, the King instructed Grenville that the Tories 'must meet [with] every degree of regard', and that James Stuart-Mackenzie, Bute's brother, must stay on as Lord Privy Seal for Scotland, effectively the leading minister there. This was a humiliating series of conditions for the job, but Grenville wanted it enough to accept them all. 'Grenville was full of professions,' George told Bute, 'to which I made him not the least compliment.'[44] Grenville kissed hands as Prime Minister on 13 April 1763.

Grenville was not a good public speaker, but he was a highly competent administrator who had served under Bute as Northern Secretary from May to October 1762 and thereafter as First Lord of the Admiralty. He and George agreed on most political questions, although the King resented Grenville's constant requests for pensions and places for himself, his family and supporters.[45] He also found him prolix, and over three days in late April complained to Bute about Grenville's 'tiresome manner', 'ill humour' and 'selfish disposition'.[46] What was more he felt patronized by his Prime Minister, who was twenty-six years older and something of a self-righteous bore, constantly returning to issues the King believed had been closed.

Although George was reconciled to having Grenville as premier, he was unenthusiastic. 'Though young, I see but too much that there are few, very few honest men in the world,' was a typical complaint to Bute from this time. 'I shall therefore support those who will act for me and without regret change my tools whenever they act contrary to my service.'[47] This highly utilitarian attitude towards politicians, and the fact that he did not have another premier that he liked as much as Bute for the rest of the decade, go some way towards explaining why there were no fewer than seven different prime ministers in the first eleven years of George's reign.

Despite relinquishing the premiership, Bute was not about to yield his influence to Grenville quickly or easily; and in the first two months after his resignation the King wrote to him at least thirty-three times, putting Grenville in an almost impossible political position that he soon came to resent. Although Grenville was First Lord of the Treasury, Chancellor of the Exchequer and Leader of the House of Commons, the real influence remained in Bute's hands, and Grenville knew that he essentially served at Bute's pleasure. Bute, who had declined the office of Lord Chamberlain, went to Harrogate spa to try to cure his bowel afflictions. He retained patronage for all Scottish and most ecclesiastical offices, and Grenville had to send him the King's speeches for revision. Grenville understandably feared that the King was intending to treat him only as a functionary.

The King's willingness to employ men like Holland, Dashwood, Halifax and John Montagu, 4th Earl of Sandwich, somewhat undermined his earlier protestations about returning morality to public life, although Lord Le Despencer (as Dashwood became) who was appointed Master of the Great Wardrobe was not quite the dissipated rake that his 'Hellfire Caves' reputation suggested, and Sandwich lived quietly in non-conjugal bliss with the Drury Lane singer Martha Ray and their many children after his wife went mad. Halifax's own mistress, the former Drury Lane actress Anna-Maria Faulkner (who would later write a scandalous kiss-and-tell memoir), was rumoured to have sold government positions when he was Viceroy of

Ireland, but it did not prevent his promotion either. George morally disapproved, but he was acclimatizing himself to the ways of the aristocracy.

The King closed the parliamentary session with a Speech from the Throne on 19 April 1763, in which he praised the treaties of Paris and Hubertusburg, claiming that 'my good brother the King of Prussia . . . that great prince' approved of the latter, and he also promised 'the utmost frugality' in trying to reduce 'the heavy debts unprovided for during the late war'.[48] Little could he have guessed that these anodyne remarks presaged a series of events that would derail British politics for years, at precisely the time when its leaders should have been focused on reconciling the North American colonies to continuing the British connection.

On Saturday 23 April 1763, St George's Day, John Wilkes, the ugly, witty, vain, rakish, talented and thoroughly incorrigible MP for Aylesbury, published the forty-fifth edition of his newspaper the *North Briton* – the name intended as a satire on Bute – with an anonymous article that for all its pro forma flattery was a personal attack on the King. 'Every friend of his country must lament that a prince of so many great and amiable qualities, whom England truly reveres,' it read, 'can be brought to give the sanction of his sacred name to the most odious measures, and to the most unjustifiable public declarations, from a throne ever renowned for truth, honour, and unsullied virtue.'[49] The author added that he hoped the King would not profane St Paul's Cathedral by attending a thanksgiving service for the Peace of Paris, and that 'I wish as much as any man in the kingdom to see the honour of the Crown maintained in a manner truly becoming royalty. I lament to see it sunk even to prostitution.'

Wilkes accused the King of lying to Parliament about the advantages of the treaties of Paris and Hubertusburg, yet given that everyone knew it was his ministers who wrote the Speech from the Throne rather than the King himself, who was ultimately its target? Since 'Number 45' (as it became known) went on to attack 'the most abandoned instance of ministerial effrontery ever attempted to be imposed on mankind' and 'a weak, disjointed, incapable set' who Wilkes claimed served as the 'tools of corruption and despotism', it was clearly aiming at the Grenville Cabinet itself.

Wilkes rarely pulled his punches: previous editions of the *North Briton* had accused Princess Augusta of being Bute's mistress, the Archbishop of Canterbury of buggery and the wife of Dr William Warburton, Bishop of Gloucester, of prostitution. Given his record, it is hard to escape the conclusion that Wilkes was courting prosecution to increase his fame; indeed it is surprising that there had already been forty-four scurrilous issues of the *North Briton* published before Wilkes was finally arrested on the charge of seditious libel. In retrospect, the government ought to have ignored No. 45 as an impertinent squib by an insignificant troublemaker, who, in John Plumb's estimation, was hoping 'that his talents or his nuisance value, or both, would secure him a place and a settled political career'.[50] If that were so, then Wilkes did not understand the character of the King, who was genuinely outraged by the accusation made against his honour. There was also a wider political angle; Wilkes was a protégé of the 2nd Earl Temple, the Prime Minister's elder brother and leader of the Pitt faction in the Lords, who also opposed the Peace of Paris. The King, Grenville, Bute and both the secretaries of state, Halifax and Egremont, all agreed with the Solicitor-General, Fletcher Norton, who described No. 45 as 'a seditious and scandalous libel', and decided to bring a charge which carried a prison sentence for the writer, editor and publishers.

If Wilkes had been mentioned in the arrest warrant by name and had claimed his parliamentary privilege as an MP, the whole story might have ended there, rather than viciously poisoning the next decade of British politics. On 30 April, however, the overworked Lord Halifax made the error, because the article was unsigned, of issuing a general warrant for seditious libel, against the unnamed 'authors, printers and publishers of "the North Briton number 45"'. General warrants that allowed the authorities to arrest people without their names being specified had been used on several occasions by the Newcastle ministry, three times by William Pitt and once before by Halifax in 1762, all without any protest as to their legality; they were thus not the original invention of a tyrannical new regime, as Horace Walpole and many others later alleged.[51]

In this case, however, Wilkes and No. 45 caught the popular imagination, and allowed the King and his ministers to be presented as tyrannical, especially in America where the story was followed with a sense of increasing outrage. In truth, the King and government merely wanted their dignity and honour to be protected; they emphatically did not want powers of arbitrary mass arrest, censorship or the suspension of civil liberties, but their heavy-handedness in pursuing Wilkes allowed him to present them in the worst possible light. Had they been genuine tyrants, they would not have allowed the *North Briton* to be published in the first place.

Wilkes' personality was aptly described by the historian John Brooke as that of 'a jolly blackguard, fond of his bottle and his whore, with a taste for scholarship and good conversation, and out for what he could get'.[52] In short – except for the part about scholarship and conversation – about as distant from George's character as it was possible to get. That Dr Johnson, Edward Gibbon and James Boswell admired 'Jack' Wilkes is evidence that he possessed personal gifts far beyond his taste for obscenity and sedition, but George never saw those. All he felt was a profound contempt and dislike for the man who had repeatedly and cruelly libelled his mother and his dearest friend, and was now libelling him too.

Wilkes was arrested under Halifax's general warrant on 30 April. His house was then searched and papers were seized. He was interrogated by Halifax and sent to the Tower of London. Wilkes stated that he was only criticizing government ministers and not the King himself, despite writing that the Crown had 'sunk even to prostitution' and that the King was 'responsible to his people' for his ministers' policies.[53] The King responded by cancelling Wilkes' commission in the militia. In the raid on Wilkes' home, a blasphemous and obscene poem entitled *An Essay on Woman* (a satire on Alexander Pope's *Essay on Man*) was discovered. It had been started by Thomas Potter, the debauched illegitimate son of a former archbishop of Canterbury, but had been completed, annotated and printed by Wilkes himself.

On 6 May Sir Charles Pratt, the Chief Justice of the Common Pleas, freed Wilkes on the grounds of parliamentary privilege, since libel was neither treason, felony nor a breach of the peace; and when Wilkes sued the ministers involved in his arrest he was awarded £1,000 in damages. The case was heard in Westminster Hall, which when the verdict was delivered rang with the cry 'Wilkes and Liberty!' Pratt thereafter began encouraging juries to award large amounts in damages to the printers and publishers whom Wilkes had employed, and he argued strongly against the use of general warrants. The government was thus defeated in the courts, which again serves as a rebuttal to the notion of government tyranny. It took years for George to forgive Pratt for his rulings in the Wilkes case, but he could do nothing against Wilkes' supporter Lord Temple beyond forbidding him to attend Court, and dismissing him from the lord-lieutenancy of Buckinghamshire.

There was a happier moment on 4 June when George celebrated his twenty-fifth birthday, for which Queen Charlotte organized an elaborate party. Telling her husband that he was not to go into the gardens of Buckingham House for two weeks beforehand, or into any of the rooms on the west side of the house with views over it, she had Robert Adam create a beautiful and ornate backdrop to the garden for the fireworks and illuminations. On the evening of his birthday, she blindfolded him and led him out into the garden to show him the spectacular result. That night their guests ate a 'supper of a hundred cold dishes followed by an illuminated dessert' lit by 4,000 lamps.[54] They ate off a French rococo gilt Coronation dining service, comprising 10,000 ounces of gilt plate and 6,000 ounces of white porcelain plate, commissioned by the King shortly before his wedding at a cost of £8,783 6s 1d, but which, like his Gold State Coach, had not been ready in time for the Coronation itself.[55]

Throughout Grenville's premiership, the King and Bute explored ways to bring in various factions that might strengthen it by turning it into what was termed a 'broad-bottomed' ministry. Not all of these plans necessarily involved Grenville staying on as Prime Minister. Such discussions entailed meetings that were hard to keep private, since factional leaders who were offered positions needed in turn to sound out their supporters. Consequently news soon got out, with Grenville left feeling betrayed. In June, Bute even sounded out Newcastle, despite the humiliations heaped on him, his family and supporters only four months earlier.

On 21 August the King told Grenville he had no desire to change his ministers, whom he claimed to like, but he was worried about 'the licentiousness of the times' and in particular by the recent attempt of a mob in Croydon to save Matthew Dodd, the coachman of the celebrated courtesan Kitty Fisher, from being hanged for raping a farmer's daughter two days earlier. It had taken 150 soldiers to see the man properly hanged; the King was sure that 'if he suffered force to be put upon him by the Opposition, the mob would try to govern him next'.[56] It was absurd of George to extrapolate profound political consequences from a sordid local disturbance in Surrey, but it nonetheless indicated the extent to which he feared that the Opposition would, in the contemporary idiom, 'storm the Closet': that is, force a government on him that he did not want.

Grenville left the King just before noon and went to Lord Egremont's house in Piccadilly to recount what had happened. At the door of Egremont's dressing room he met with his doctor, who told him that the Earl had been struck with apoplexy 'and was past all hopes of recovery'.[57] Egremont died at 8 p.m. Grenville and Halifax went to tell the King, who 'lamented the loss of his servant, and spoke in very high commendation of him'.

Within three days, Bute had opened discussions with Pitt via the Lord Mayor of London, William Beckford, about which the King informed Grenville on 26 August. 'The King opened to Mr Grenville his intention of calling in Mr Pitt to the management of his affairs,' Grenville's wife wrote in a diary on his dictation, 'declaring that he meant to do it as cheap as he could, and to make as few changes as was possible.'[58] Grenville expressed 'surprise and concern' and protested at the King's volte-face – his surprise feigned, as he had known for two days that Pitt and Bute were in talks. When Grenville arrived at Buckingham House the next day, he found Pitt's coach in the courtyard and suffered the humiliation of having to sit in the lobby for over an hour while the King and Pitt negotiated his removal from the premiership. When he was finally given his audience, Grenville found the King 'a good deal confused and flustered', yet George 'took no notice of Mr Pitt's having been with him, and in less than twenty minutes bowed* to Mr Grenville, told him it was late, and, as he was going out of the room, said with emotion, "*Good morrow, Mr Grenville*", and repeated it again a second time, which was a phrase he never had used to him before.'[59] Grenville was left with the distinct impression that he was not going to remain Prime Minister for much longer.

He was wrong, however. When George offered Pitt the Southern secretaryship and lord presidency of the Council during a three-hour meeting on 28 August, the seemingly triumphant Pitt responded with a long litany of demands, which included not only appointing to every position in the government, but also awarding a peerage to Chief Justice Pratt and the Order of the Garter to Charles Powlett, 5th Duke of Bolton.[60] Under Pitt's terms, just two of Bute's close friends, Sir Gilbert Elliot and James Oswald, would be allowed to keep their places in an otherwise general clear-out. Even if the King could accept the storming of his Closet by Pitt and his men, he could not accept Pitt's other measures, which included a Prussian rapprochement and a blanket refusal to have anyone in the Cabinet who had supported the 'dishonourable, dangerous and criminal' Peace of Paris.[61] 'Well, Mr Pitt, I see (or I fear) this won't do,' the King reportedly replied. 'My honour is concerned, and I must support it.'[62] The King spoke often about his honour, sometimes overlapping it with that of the country, but here he was on solid ground: he could hardly have permitted a purge of those ministers who had supported the Peace of Paris when he himself had acclaimed it in his speech to Parliament as recently as 19 April.

George now offered Grenville 'the fullest assurances of every support and every strength that he could give him towards the carrying his business into execution'.[63] This abortive restructuring of the post-Peace government in late August 1763 would prove of greater importance than many actual changes of ministry which took place that decade. Pitt, Newcastle, Hardwicke and the other Old Whigs who would have come into office (with the notable exception of Charles Townshend) did not believe in trying to tax the American colonies, whereas Grenville and his supporters did. Had these Opposition figures formed the government in the autumn of 1763, it is unlikely that another Pitt–Newcastle coalition, with Hardwicke in the Cabinet, would have proposed the Stamp Act, which is what ignited

* The traditional signal that the audience was at an end.

Britain's smouldering tensions with her American colonies in the mid-1760s. Hardwicke's opinion on taxing America was that it was 'inexpedient' because, in his words, 'They had not been used to taxes.'[64] His son later recalled that Hardwicke 'had doubts about the *right*' of taxing America, and had no doubts 'that the colonies will be very restive' if it were tried.[65] Similarly, Newcastle had expressed misgivings about both the politics and the practice; and Pitt's stance, in 1763 at least, was likewise opposed to new American taxes. If they had been in government, these three might have been able to finance the continued protection of the colonies from the already existing British land and cider taxes, without asking for a contribution from North America.

The King was unwilling to be dictated to by Pitt, however, over who received the Order of the Garter and so on. (It was just as well that the Duke of Bolton did not get one, as he shot himself in mysterious circumstances two years later.) George told Grenville that Pitt's terms had simply been too high, and asked 'if he, Mr Grenville, would abandon him and oblige him to submit to them, rather than which he would die in the room he then stood in'.[66] George would return to such histrionic language often in his reign, just as he was to accuse several more premiers of abandoning him. Historians who have attributed 'abandonment issues' to the King because of his father's early death and his subsequent adolescent over-reliance on Bute stray into cod psychology, however. In fact his melodramatic style was of a piece with much of eighteenth-century hyperbole, and some of his premiers did indeed abandon him, including the two he most liked personally.[67]

George's disdain for Pitt and his excessive demands brought him no closer to Grenville, however. 'When he has wearied me for two hours he looks at his watch to see if he may not tire me for an hour more,' George wrote.[68] They fell out over trivia and minor slights, some of them probably imagined. Walpole invented a story that the King disliked Grenville because he had refused to part with £20,000 from the Treasury to prevent builders from developing land overlooking the gardens of Buckingham House. The King himself told Bute that Grenville had irritated him by asking for a lease on New Lodge in Richmond Park, where he liked to 'drink tea or shelter myself in riding from a shower'.[69] This might be true, but it did not happen until at least April 1764, by which time the animus was long established. Bute certainly believed that the King resented a remark Grenville had made when George proposed to abolish the post of Court Painter after the death of William Hogarth. Grenville had reportedly threatened Thomas Worsley, the Surveyor-General, that any other minister speaking directly to the King about patronage besides Grenville himself 'would not serve an hour'.[70]

Again, however, Hogarth did not die until October 1764, and so this could not have been the root cause of George's antipathy. Whatever it actually had been, and Grenville was charmless enough that it may just have been his general manner, the fact is that just as the American taxation crisis was about to break – a crisis in which, ironically, the King and Grenville saw largely eye to eye – George was saddled with a prime minister whom he profoundly disliked. This perhaps should not have mattered and maybe George ought simply to have put up with the situation, but in a relationship as intensely personal as that between monarch and first minister in eighteenth-century politics, it did matter.

By the end of the meeting on 28 August, Grenville had agreed to remain in office on condition that George would 'suffer no secret influence whatever to prevail', which the King correctly took to be a lightly coded reference to Bute. The King replied that Bute 'desired to retire absolutely from all business whatsoever, that he would absent himself from the King for a time', which 'should leave no room for jealousy against him'.[71] Paradoxically, therefore, Grenville was in a stronger position after his ousting had failed, especially as George was already starting to see beyond his attachment to Bute, who had failed to pull off the change of ministry. Before July 1763 George had written Bute at least 330 letters, but afterwards there are only nine extant, and they are addressed to 'my dear friend', rather than 'dearest'.

Years later, Charles Jenkinson said the King had become 'disgusted with a sort of loftiness and huffy manner of Lord Bute's, and had not seen him from the year 1765'.[72] That did not of course preclude the Dowager Princess Augusta from passing on Bute's thoughts and advice to her son; but the idea, which nonetheless prevailed for many years, that the King remained under Bute's backstairs influence after the autumn of 1763 was without foundation. George had emphatically dropped his mentor and was now striking out on his own, albeit with the same overall aims and principles. 'Let us not look back,' George told Grenville on 8 September about the failed coup against him, 'let us only look forward; nothing of that sort shall ever happen again.'[73]

Bute's fall from favour meant that the Grenville ministry could strengthen itself. The Duke of Bedford would return to the Cabinet as Lord President of the Council on 9 September, bringing his friends and supporters Lord Sandwich as Northern Secretary and Wills Hill, the Earl of Hillsborough, as First Lord of Trade. This rapprochement also brought across twenty more votes in the Commons. Sandwich had been only ten when he inherited his impoverished earldom in 1729. At twenty-six he became a lord commissioner of the Admiralty, and at twenty-nine he negotiated the Peace of Aix-la-Chapelle, one of the few eighteenth-century peace treaties which did not destroy the government that signed it. Sandwich* (a friend of Frederick, Prince of Wales as well as a protégé of the Duke of Bedford) had been turned out of office after 1751, since when he had preferred Opposition in Bedford's faction to serving under Bute. The King liked him personally and seemed generally willing to overlook his scandalous private life, perhaps partly because the Earl was founder of the Concerts of Antient Music and a promoter of Handel, George's favourite composer. Sandwich played the timpani when Handel visited his country seat, Hinchingbrooke House in Cambridgeshire.

On Bute's fall, Charles Jenkinson, his former private secretary and now Secretary to the Treasury,† took over as leader of the King's Friends party in Parliament. Years later he said that he had got his position because his brother had been a page to George when Prince of Wales and he would sometimes go along to the riding house, 'and that on those occasions the King used to discourse with him and conceived a kindness for him'.[74] He certainly was a far more adept political operator than Bute had been. His shrewd sense of where power and ability lay, keen ear for political gossip and capacity for swift ruthlessness were to serve George extremely well over the coming decades – even though he came to be portrayed as the King's political enforcer and became a hate-figure for the radical Whigs.

In June 1762 George received an embassy from a Cherokee chieftain, Otacity Ostenaco – 'The Man-Killer of Tomotly' – and two of his companions, who pledged friendship after the harsh war that had been fought between mid-1759 and September 1761. It was a visit that 'highlighted a wider public interest in Native Americans – both as vulgar public spectacle, and as noble savages whom Britain should both admire and protect'.[75] The Cherokees inhabited sixty settlements in the Great Smokies region at the southern end of the Appalachian mountain range, near the ever advancing Carolina frontiers. Further north, Virginia was intruding on them too. The ninety-minute meeting between George and Ostenaco on 8 July 1762 was hampered by the fact that the only person fluent in both English and Cherokee, William Shorey, had been pushed into a cold, fast-flowing stream by his wife for his drunkenness and died of 'a galloping consumption' on the voyage to England; nevertheless Lord Egremont and the Southern

---

* The inventor of the eponymous foodstuff, when he placed salt beef between two pieces of bread in order to continue working at his desk (not to gamble as is popularly believed) (Rodger, *Insatiable Earl* p. 79).
† The position that eventually became Government Chief Whip.

Department recognized the importance of the Cherokee nation as allies with whom Britain had solemn treaty obligations. There were several more pre-war and wartime agreements made between the British and the Native American tribes which the Grenville government meant to honour.

George enjoyed such encounters with visitors from faraway places. On 17 July 1774, he met Omai, the Tahitian brought to England and feted as one of Rousseau's 'noble savages'. Sir Joseph Banks introduced him to the King at Kew Palace three days after his arrival. 'The King very familiarly took him by the hand,' noted a contemporary, 'and made several very kind enquiries concerning him,' giving him an allowance and organizing his inoculation against smallpox. He also gave him 'a very handsome sword', which he was wearing six months later when Fanny Burney met him, and he enthusiastically toasted the King at dinner.[76] 'Oh, very *dood* [good] man, King George!' Omai told Burney.[77] The King's welcome helped to ensure that Omai's visit was an immediate social success. He was painted by Joshua Reynolds and stayed in England for two years before returning home with Captain Cook. George was moved to tears by a performance of the play *Omai, or A Trip around the World* when he saw it in Drury Lane in 1785.

On 7 October 1763, possibly in part as a result of the Cherokee embassy the previous year, the British government made a decision that was to become one of the major causes of the loss of the North American colonies. Severely rattled by the still-ongoing Pontiac uprising in the Ohio Valley, and conscious of the promises made to Native American tribes that had supported Britain in the Seven Years War, Lord Halifax (who for thirteen years had been First Lord of Trade and Plantations) issued a proclamation to prevent the American colonists' westward settlement. The whole continent to the west of a Proclamation Line, running from the Great Lakes down to the Gulf of Mexico and along the western slopes of the Appalachian Mountains, would be one gigantic Native American reserve where no American colonial settlement would be permitted.[78] There was even an order for settlers then on the western side of the Line 'forthwith to remove themselves'.[79]

This was a major obstacle to the expansion of American wealth and growth. Now, far from viewing the twenty battalions of British troops as being for their own protection, the colonists saw them as enforcing a new policy of boxing them into the seaboard colonies and preventing expansion from ocean to ocean. As well as maintaining good relations with the Indigenous Nations, it was the Board of Trade's express policy, as it had told George in November 1761, to keep the colonists within the British orbit,

buying British-manufactured goods along the eastern seaboard. The colonists' mass movement westwards was a 'most dangerous tendency' in the
Board's view, liable to weaken the relationship with ever more distant
Britain, and also to lead to war with the Indigenous Nations, with several
of whom Britain had treaties and mutually lucrative trade agreements
(especially in furs).[80] George had distributed large silver friendship 'peace
medals' to the chiefs of Native American allies and trading partners during
the Seven Years War and was not willing to betray them.

Yet the exponential population growth of the thirteen colonies meant
that Americans were looking to move westwards across the continent. In
the almost inevitable struggle between the American colonists and the
Indigenous Nations on the other side of the Appalachians, Britain had
attached herself to what would be the losing side for the short-term gain
of the fur trade. It was now very much in American colonists' interests that
the taxes to pay for the British troops should *not* be raised, so that the
Proclamation Line could not be policed.[81]

The first and most obvious losers from the Proclamation were those
speculators who had intended to develop the land between the Allegheny
Mountains and the Mississippi, among whom were Benjamin Franklin,
Patrick Henry, the Lee family and George Washington. In September 1763,
Washington and nine other speculators had launched the Mississippi Land
Company, with the intention of claiming 2.5 million acres in the Ohio
Valley, covering what is today Ohio, Indiana, Illinois, Kentucky and Ten-
nessee. If the British government had possessed sufficient foresight and
self-interest, they would have sought to engage with and channel the drive
westwards, rather than attempting to block it off. A society whose most
enterprising and energetic members were intent on forging their way across
a vast continent might not have concerned themselves with overthrowing
the royal government had London been facilitating such a push.

Instead, the British government put their pre-war and wartime treaty
obligations to the Native Americans, and their trading interests, before
their long-term strategic best interests. As Ron Chernow writes in his
biography of the hugely disappointed George Washington, 'It was a catastrophic blunder to confine settlers to the eastern seaboard.'[82] The tethering
of the Americans to the territory of the established thirteen colonies, all
pressed against the Atlantic Ocean, was perhaps the worst peacetime strategic error of George's reign, and in stark contrast to the inland advances
being made by Britons in Asia and elsewhere in the empire at the time. For
an empire that had only months earlier won a world war, and could now
have unleashed its colonists right across the American continent, Britain

behaved with an honourable punctiliousness towards her treaties with the Indigenous Nations that verged upon the pedantic.*

'I can never look upon that Proclamation in any other light than as a temporary expedient to quiet the minds of the Indians,' Washington wrote years later.[83] He saw the displacement of the tribes by waves of westward-heading Americans as inevitable. Washington's cynicism was warranted: while the British government rejected his Mississippi Land Company application as violating treaties signed with both the six nations of the Iroquois League and the Cherokee, in 1770 they approved a proposal for the creation of Vandalia by English investors, of much the same size and in much the same region. In 1772, writing off his investment as a total loss, Washington declared that it demonstrated Britain's 'malignant disposition towards Americans'.[84] As one historian of Washington's relationship with the Native Americans has pointed out, 'the old French and Indian barrier seemed to have been replaced by a British–Indian barrier. Washington, Jefferson, Arthur Lee, Patrick Henry, and others denounced British interference as tyranny and demanded freedom. It included the freedom to acquire and sell Indian land at will.'[85]

Despite its significance to all that would follow, the Proclamation Line found no mention in George Grenville's diaries, which instead recorded his spats with ministers over whether his private secretary's brother, Philip Lloyd, the vicar of Piddletown† in Dorset, should become Dean of Norwich. The future of the empire was at stake, but the British Prime Minister was focusing on Piddletown.

---

* Nor was the Proclamation clear about whether the 70,000 French Canadians now in the empire might be able to move south-westwards. The idea had been to try to divert American migration northwards towards Nova Scotia and southwards towards Florida, and away from the Indigenous peoples west of the Alleghenies, yet the Ohio Valley was now accessible to the French Canadians, prompting further angry remonstrances from the American colonists that these Catholic French-born new 'Britons' seemed to be better served by Westminster than they were themselves.

† Which understandably changed its name to Puddletown in the late 1950s.

6

Sugar, Stamps and Silk

November 1763–May 1765

My nature ever inclines me to be acquainted with who are my true,
and who false friends; the latter I think worse than open enemies.[1]
George III to George Grenville, February 1764

George read newspapers intently, paying £10 a month to his 'newsman' between 1763 and 1772. He generally considered the journals of the day to be 'vehicles of abuse', but recognized that he needed to know what was being said about himself and his family. He tolerated falsehoods regularly, only baulking at the utter licentiousness of writers such as John Wilkes.[2] On 14 November 1763, he mentioned the previous Saturday's edition of 'the abusive *North Briton*' to Grenville, and 'expressed great abhorrence of the scandalous manner in which Lord Egremont was treated in it'.[3] (Egremont, now dead, could not sue for libel.) Other abuse was levelled in that same issue at Grenville himself. 'The continuation of Wilkes's impudence is amazing, when his ruin is so near,' George wrote to Grenville (which he always spelt 'Greenville').[4]

The next day, on the first evening of the new session of Parliament, Grenville proposed that *North Briton* No. 45 be censured as seditious libel, and burned by the public hangman in both the Old Palace Yard* at Westminster and at the Royal Exchange. The public burning of publications had been going on since the early fourteenth century; just over 300 were committed to the flames between 1541 and the end of the practice in 1775. The House debated the issue until 2 a.m., a debate which saw a highly personal altercation between Grenville and Pitt, but, as the former's diary recorded, 'the day was very triumphant on the Court side,' with a large government majority of about 200.[5] Many MPs considered the pornographic *Essay on Woman*, which Wilkes had insouciantly attributed to

---

* Where the statue of Richard the Lionheart stands today.

a clergyman and which included some lewd paraphrasing of Christian hymns, to be blasphemous.

Lord Sandwich, who as the new Northern Secretary now had to lead the government attack in the House of Lords despite having met Wilkes socially on a number of occasions, read extracts from *An Essay on Woman* during the debate.* One peer was said to have fainted from shock. Because Sandwich was living openly with his mistress Martha Ray he was widely accused of hypocrisy: Lord Le Despencer, a former friend of Wilkes, remarked that he had 'never before heard the devil preach a sermon against sin'.[6] To make the situation more bizarre, the poem had originally been written to humiliate Dr William Warburton, the Bishop of Gloucester and Alexander Pope's literary executor and editor, whose wife had had an affair with Thomas Potter, so the Bishop tried unsuccessfully to prevent its being read out in the chamber. It also accused Lord George Sackville, whose sexuality had already been the subject of rumour, of being the lover of George Stone, the Archbishop of Armagh. Despite all this, Sandwich led the onslaught against Wilkes and read from the poem.

Although the Pope parody had not been publicly circulated by Wilkes, and there were only about a dozen copies in print, the King and his senior ministers agreed to put a motion before Parliament specifically removing parliamentary privilege for acts of seditious libel.[7] If George's attitude towards Wilkes seems personally vindictive, we should remember that effigies of his mother Princess Augusta and Bute – usually represented by a petticoat and a boot – were repeatedly jeered at and burned during the Wilkesite disturbances.† Horace Walpole gleefully noted that in the West Country, where Bute was particularly unpopular thanks to the cider tax, 'they dressed up a figure in Scotch plaid, with a blue riband [the sash of the Order of the Garter], to represent the favourite, and this figure seemed to lead by the nose an ass royally crowned.'[8] A ballad sheet published at the time showed a kilted figure with bonnet, bagpipes and cider excise bill

---

* It was untrue that Sandwich, who was gregarious, politically moderate and generally much liked, and Wilkes were especially firm friends, although they had a great many friends in common. Indeed, he was possibly the subject of a much celebrated riposte: when told that he would die either of the pox or on the gallows, Wilkes replied, 'That depends, my Lord, whether I embrace your mistress or your principles' (Rodger, *Insatiable Earl* p. 100).

† The attacks on Bute and Augusta continued for years. In John Horne Tooke's 1765 pamphlet *The Petition of an Englishman* there was a heavy-handed reference to Bute's 'erections' at Kew. The *Political Register* in May 1767 featured an equally suggestive print of the house on Kew Green built for Bute 'to study in', with a door in the garden wall opening on to the Dowager Princess of Wales' garden. As late as 1768, half a decade after Bute had fallen from favour, a frontispiece to Almon's *Political Register* showed Augusta and Bute in her bedchamber, with the royal arms in a widow's lozenge pictured over the bed.

being burned on a bonfire by labourers, with a woman looking under Bute's kilt crying 'See his arse! See his arse!'⁹ In one Wilkesite riot in St James's Park, Sir Richard Perrott narrowly prevented Bute from being attacked by a man wielding a lead-weighted club.¹⁰

On 23 November, the Commons resolved that the privilege from prosecution of its members did not extend to seditious libel. Frederick, Lord North, the Earl of Guilford's son and the King's childhood friend, pushed the motion through the Commons, and even Pitt joined the censure of Wilkes, although he pointedly opposed the waiver of privilege on constitutional grounds. Although 'greatly pleased with the success of the day', the King nonetheless felt compelled to drive home the message further still, suggesting to Grenville that he dismiss Conway from his commissions and William Fitzherbert MP as a lord of the Board of Trade, 'and any others who have equally with these gone steadily against us, and giving it out that the rest would have the same fate if they do not amend their conduct'.¹¹

After the government won another division about Wilkes in the Lords on 29 November, Grenville found the King to be 'in great spirits, and greatly pleased with the success'.¹² He was angered, however, to learn that the Duke of Cumberland had voted against the motion. When Cumberland soon afterwards suffered an apoplectic attack, George did not send to ask after him because, as he told Grenville, 'Nobody could suppose he could inquire out of regard to him.'¹³ It was a sad reflection on the state of politics during the long Wilkes imbroglio that the King did not feel he could ask after his uncle's health following a stroke without people assuming that he was hoping for the worst.

The official burning of *North Briton*'s forty-fifth issue caused a riot at the Royal Exchange. 'The mob gathered to incredible numbers and opposed it,' Grenville recorded, 'took the faggots away from the pile, and beat the constables and the Sheriff.'¹⁴ (The latter was Alderman Thomas Harley MP, a younger son of the 3rd Earl of Oxford.)¹⁵ A boot and petticoat were burned, and the crowd cheered for Wilkes, Temple and Cumberland, and then when Wilkes' publisher was put in the pillory he was hailed as a hero, rather than being pelted with horse manure and rotten food as was the custom. The King was, in Grenville's words the next day, 'much disturbed and exasperated at the outrage' against Harley.¹⁶ When a few days later the Lord Mayor of London cast his deciding vote against the City of London Common Council's motion to give official thanks to Harley, Grenville noted that 'The King seemed much hurt and offended.'¹⁷

The King was particularly offended that Lord Shelburne (who had promised he would not join the Opposition) had sided with Wilkes, telling Grenville that 'he has acted like a worthless man and has broken his word with me.'[18] On 14 December, George deliberately cut Shelburne at the Levee, speaking to the two people on either side of him but skipping him entirely. Such an action might seem small, but it was widely noticed and consigned Shelburne to the political Opposition for the foreseeable future. Shelburne's character has somewhat mystified historians; he was intelligent, but was disliked and distrusted for no reason that can be discerned, even though his nickname 'Malagrida', after a famous Spanish Jesuit, might be a clue that he was considered an ambitious intriguer. Having inherited his earldom and a vast fortune at twenty-four, Shelburne started out as a Buteite, but over the coming years he became a supporter of Bedford, later of Pitt, and later still a major figure in his own right.

On Christmas Day 1763 Wilkes fled to France to avoid imprisonment after his parliamentary immunity had been removed. He was expelled from the House of Commons for seditious libel in his absence on 19 January 1764, a move which prompted renewed rioting in London. After a fourteen-hour debate on the legality of general warrants on 18 February, the government won an adjournment motion in the Commons by just 232 to 218, with Conway, Sackville, Charles Townshend and Charles Yorke, the previous Attorney-General and Lord Hardwicke's second son, all voting with the Opposition. Members of Parliament who personally despised the reprobate Wilkes nonetheless showed their concerns about freedom of speech, and the offence against habeas corpus inherent in a government's ability to arrest people not named in a warrant. Those who spoke for the government included Lord North, the Attorney-General Sir Fletcher Norton, the Scottish lawyer Alexander Wedderburn and Lord Barrington, all of whom earned the King's approbation. On 21 February, Lord Mansfield and the Court of King's Bench found Wilkes guilty *in absentia* of publishing No. 45 and printing the blasphemous *An Essay on Woman*, and somewhat belatedly issued a warrant for his arrest. When Wilkes failed to return from France, he was outlawed by the Court of King's Bench on 1 November 1764.

Distracted by the Wilkes cause célèbre, the British government entirely missed important developments taking place across the Atlantic. In December 1763, the Virginian lawyer Patrick Henry delivered a radical speech on what was called 'the parson's cause'. It stemmed from a case brought by an incumbent Anglican clergyman, the Rev. James Maury, for the restitution of his salary from Hanover County, in which Henry (appearing for the County), denied the long-established right of the Crown to disallow Acts of colonial legislatures. In Maury's words to a friend, he claimed that Henry went further still, asserting 'that a King, by disallowing Acts of this salutary nature, from being the father of his people, degenerated into a tyrant and forfeits all right to his subjects' obedience'.[19] The Crown would have had strong grounds to appeal against the decision, not least since the judge in the case was none other than Colonel John Henry, Patrick's father. The jury's decision to award Maury just one penny in damages served as an effective signal that the Crown's veto over colonial legislation had been overturned. But with ministers' attention elsewhere, nothing was done about it.

Instead, on 9 March 1764 Grenville moved a resolution in the House of Commons stating that in order to defray the cost of stationing the battalions in America 'it may be proper to charge certain stamp duties on the said colonies and plantations.'[20] He proposed an American Revenue Act (also known as the Sugar Act) to revise the largely moribund Molasses Act of 1733 and try to raise revenue from it, stating that 'It is just and necessary that a revenue be raised in Your Majesty's said dominions in America, for defraying the expenses of defending, protecting and securing the same.'[21] The Act reduced the duty on the import of foreign molasses into the colonies, while increasing the duty on sugar imported into British possessions from the French and Spanish West Indies. It was therefore intended as a simultaneous attack on American smuggling and on French and Spanish producers. The duties were designed to raise £45,000, and were essentially ad hoc financial measures rather than part of any new ideology of proactive imperialism. All the money raised was going to be spent in the American colonies, but as Grenville told the Commons, 'We have expended much in America. Let us now avail ourselves of the fruit of that expense.'[22] The next day he noted that the King was 'highly pleased with what had passed the day before in the House ... concerning the supplies of the year'.[23] George dutifully read through every Bill before they received their three readings each in the Commons and Lords and, once passed, became Acts which required his signature for royal assent, whereupon they became law.[24] He was thus entirely conversant with the Sugar Act when he gave it his royal assent on 5 April.

By the end of 1764, the Sugar and Currency Acts had produced protest petitions from the assemblies of Massachusetts, Rhode Island, Connecticut, New York, Pennsylvania, Virginia and North and South Carolina. In a 'Memorial' addressed to the House of Lords, appended to its 'Remonstrance' to the House of Commons in December 1764, the Virginia House of Burgesses announced that it would not accept representation in an imperial Parliament, as South Carolina had already stated in September. The slogan 'No taxation without representation' would very soon resonate across the thirteen colonies, but it should not be mistaken for a literal demand for representation.

In a pamphlet entitled *The Rights of the British Colonies Asserted and Proved*, published in 1764, James Otis, a lawyer and member of the Massachusetts House of Representatives, protested against the Sugar Act. Although he asked profound questions such as 'When and where was the original compact for introducing government into any society?', Otis was not by any means ready to question the monarchy, and indeed declared that 'we have the joy to see the scepter swayed in justice, wisdom and mercy, by our lawful sovereign George the Third, a prince who glories in being a Briton born, and whom may God long preserve and prosper'.[25] Indeed, Otis is more noteworthy for how revolutionary he was not in 1764: 'We all think ourselves happy under Great Britain,' he declared. 'We love, esteem and reverence our mother country, and adore our King.'[26]

Otis' proclaimed loyalty was rather at odds with the help he was to give in organizing the Stamp Act Congress of 1765 and the non-importation movement after 1767. A close friend of the wealthy businessman John Hancock, Otis took his Britishness seriously, and complained only because he felt genuinely aggrieved by the behaviour of his fellow countrymen across the Atlantic. Brilliant but mentally unstable – a condition aggravated by a serious head injury he sustained in 1769 in a brawl with a British tax collector – Otis' moderate views might well have made him a difficult Founding Father for his comrades had he not died prematurely after being struck by lightning in 1783.

Otis had implied that the King, but not the British Parliament, might have the right to tax the colonies. George could have seen here an opportunity to separate his American Crown from his British one, in the same way that his Hanoverian electorate and Irish kingdom were discrete from Westminster. But 'The very fact that George III so thoroughly and loyally stood by the constitutional principles of the time rendered a conflict inevitable,' Sir Lewis Namier averred. 'Had he entertained any idea of power or authority apart from the British Parliament, he might have welcomed the conception of a separate sovereignty in the colonies.'[27]

Several other European monarchs of the day held different territories as belonging to them personally, quite separate from the metropolitan power and its parliament. Among these, the Emperor of Austria was separately the King of Hungary, the Elector of Saxony was also King of Poland, while the King of Piedmont was independently King of Sardinia. That George never considered pursuing the same route was a testament to his constitutionalism, albeit one that proved ultimately myopic: today this is the same arrangement that the British monarch has with the fifteen Commonwealth countries which the Westminster Parliament has no right to tax.

The publication of Sir William Blackstone's four-volume *Commentaries on the Laws of England* after November 1765 had a profound effect on the King's already highly conservative legal thinking about the constitution. George summarized the volumes in what he called a 'short abridgement', and they convinced him that the American case for self-government had no standing in English law.[28] Blackstone was the Vinerian Professor of Law at Oxford, and his first volume, *The Rights of Persons*, which covered such issues as the royal prerogative and the balanced elements of Crown, Lords and Commons in the constitution, coincided with the views that George had learned as a youth and written about in his essays for Bute. In 1770 the King insisted on Blackstone being appointed a justice of the Court of King's Bench.[29] It is ironic that Whig historians attacked George for trying to subvert the British constitution when in fact it was his unshakeable respect for it that helped him lose America.

On Thursday 10 January 1765, the King opened Parliament with a short speech in which he welcomed the forthcoming marriage of his youngest sibling Princess Caroline Matilda to King Christian VII of Denmark, and made an 'earnest recommendation' for the diminution of the National Debt.[30] As he left the House of Lords, the King 'felt the cold seize him'.[31] Over the next two days, Grenville found the King 'embarrassed and distant', then 'rather less cold but still much embarrassed', which he put down to his having held further secret dealings with the Opposition. In retrospect, this was in all likelihood the first instance of an illness that was in later years to be dubbed 'the King's Malady'. On 13 January, the royal doctor Sir William Duncan* visited him at Buckingham House and drew 14 ounces of blood, according to the standard eighteenth-century practice of bleeding bad 'humours' from patients. The illness was sufficiently serious for Duncan to visit the Prime Minister afterwards and inform him that the King had 'a violent cold, had passed a restless night, and complained of stitches in his breast'.[32]

The following day the King was too ill to receive ministers, but the day after that Grenville found him 'perfectly cheerful and good-humoured, and full of conversation'.[33] From 16 January the King was ill for ten days continuously. The rumour spread, eagerly fanned by the likes of Henry Fox and Horace Walpole, that he had contracted pleurisy and was in grave danger. 'So critical a situation made men take notice that,' wrote Walpole,

---

* When the King was asked to make the physician William Duncan a baronet on the grounds that he was an eminent Scottish apothecary, George replied, 'What, what, is that all? It shall be done. I was afraid you meant to ask me to make the Scotch apothecary a physician; that's more difficult' (eds. Ryskamp and Pottle, *Boswell: The Ominous Years* p. 143 n. 8).

'to secrete him from all intercourse with his Court, Lord Bute had placed the King at Buckingham House, a damp unwholesome spot . . . It was even said that Dr Duncan advis[ed] His Majesty to have one of his palaces in the country fitted up, and to live there for some time.'[34] Walpole also suggested to Lord Holland that the King 'wasn't likely to live a year'.[35] He blamed Princess Augusta, later claiming that 'It was too notorious to be concealed that the Princess Dowager has brought into the royal blood a humour which occasioned the deaths of several of her children and at length her own,' a slur both unfair and inaccurate since she eventually died of cancer.[36]

There are some clues to the exact nature of George's illness in 1765, which as it lasted on and off until at least early April was clearly far more serious than a normal cold or fever. One historian has claimed symptoms were still evident on 24 July, when the King was reported to have had 'a slight return of his former complaint'.[37] The lack of documentary evidence (Duncan kept no notes) may suggest that the King's physicians were uncertain of its cause. We do know, of course, that between 1788 and 1789, and then on three more occasions during his life (including his last ten years), the King was afflicted with a serious mental condition, of which 1765 may well have seen the first outbreak. If that were so, discretion might have prompted the curious silence, because the health of the monarch was usually something that was extremely well documented. Although there are over a hundred volumes of medical records and correspondence and diaries – some kept in shorthand hieroglyphics – covering the King's later attacks, there are none for 1765.

Another clue lies in the autobiography of Charlotte Papendiek, the daughter of Frederick Albert, Queen Charlotte's hairdresser and one of the three servants whom she had brought with her from Mecklenburg-Strelitz in 1761. Although Charlotte was only a baby in 1765, her family were close to the royal household and possessed intimate knowledge of their affairs. Her autobiography was not intended for publication, which lends her account greater credence. That the events took place in the year of her birth also supports her account, since she could have learned of them only from her parents, who were unquestionably first-hand eyewitnesses to what occurred. 'In this year, 1765, the King was attacked with alarming illness,' she wrote.

> The close attendance of the Princess Dowager at first appeared to proceed from the amiable motive of keeping the Queen from the knowledge of the full extent of his dreadful malady, as well as from the affection the Princess bore towards her son . . . It was not known beyond the palace that His Majesty

was mentally afflicted, but our poor Queen found this out only too soon for her peace of mind, for notwithstanding the Princess Dowager's endeavours to keep her from her proper place at her husband's side, she would not be wholly excluded, both inclination and her strong sense of duty prompting her to assert herself in this emergency. It was, however, Her Majesty's wish, as well as that of others around the King, to prevent the public from discovering the nature of his illness, and as long as it was possible His Majesty appeared on all state occasions. It was thought that he looked pale, but no idea of the real truth was then discovered and the general fear was that he showed a tendency towards consumption.[38]

Charlotte Papendiek's account was not published until the Victorian era, but even during the King's lifetime questions were being asked about whether the illness of 1765 had been of the same type as the King's Malady. Thomas Williams' biography, *A Brief Memoir of Her Late Majesty Queen Charlotte*, published in 1819, stated that 'His Majesty suffered a short indisposition, the nature of which was not announced, but has been since supposed to have been of the same kind, though slight and transient.'[39] Whereas the later attacks were ones of outspoken manic excitement, the 1765 attack was seemingly of a lesser kind: some form of mixed manic-depressive psychotic episode, on this occasion with the depressive side dominant.[40] Importantly, although his mood was pathologically exaggerated, George's thinking was not distorted. He lost track of neither time nor reality, as he did during his later attacks, and it appears was not delusional.

For more than half a century from the late 1960s, the King's malady was misdiagnosed as the disease porphyria, which it could not have been, for reasons outlined in the Appendix. This theory has nonetheless skewed all the biographies written of him between 1969 and 2016, as well as the play *The Madness of George III* and the film version that followed, which were based on this incorrect premise.

Modern medical opinion, however, has concluded that in fact the King suffered from recurrent manic-depressive psychosis. A study undertaken in 2013 using the Operational Criteria in Studies of Psychotic Illness programme confirmed that the King's symptoms in the 1788–9 episode were consistent with mania with psychosis.[41] Moreover, neurology professor Peter Garrard, from St George's Medical School at the University of London, used a computer analysis of the language of the King's letters to argue that he suffered from periods of acute mania – a hyperactive condition akin to the manic phase of bipolar disorder. Garrard and his team – Vassiliki Rentoumi, Timothy Peters and Jonathan Conlin – programmed a computer to make comparisons between the letters written when the King was mentally sound and those written when he was ill. These exposed a set of significant linguistic differences.[42]

'King George wrote very differently when unwell', reported Garrard, 'compared to when he was healthy. In the manic periods, we could see that he used less rich vocabulary and fewer adverbs. He repeated words less often and there was a lower degree of redundancy, or wordiness.'[43] The researchers also compared the possible effects of external influences which could have altered George's psychological state, such as between wartime and peacetime. They found no difference in the language he used between these periods, implying that the differences found between symptomatic and asymptomatic periods were due to endogenous mental change. 'In the modern classification of mental illness,' Garrard states, 'acute mania now appears to be the diagnosis that fits best with the available behavioural data.'

'Making retrospective diagnoses in historical figures is fraught with difficulties, especially in the field of psychiatry, but the case for bipolar disorder rather than one of the porphyria diseases, is compelling,' states Sir Simon Wessely, Regius Chair of Psychiatry at the Institute of Psychiatry, Psychology and Neuroscience in London.* Wessely believes that the porphyria diagnosis put forward by Ida Macalpine and Richard Hunter was more a reflection of some of the schisms within psychiatry in the 1960s than a convincing account of the illness of George III. He concludes, 'The evidence of elation, handwriting change, pressure of speech, disinhibited behaviour, occasional violence, disorders of thought (that is, psychosis) and so on all point toward acute mania, which is part of what we used to call manic depression, but now more often is referred to as bipolar disorder.'[44] Garrard also describes the porphyria diagnosis as 'thoroughly discredited'.[45]

These months in 1765 probably saw the first instance of George's hypomania, or bipolar affective disorder Type 1, a condition which for a long time was known as manic-depressive psychosis, and which in the eighteenth century came under the general heading of 'mania.' The 1765 attack was a classic 'prodrome' example: that is, an early, symptomatic illness, presaging worse to follow. After the second and third attacks, the likelihood of further episodes grows exponentially, especially when as in the eighteenth century there was none of the medication (chiefly lithium) now administered in order to reduce their frequency and severity. Under what

---

* The only person ever to be President of both the Royal College of Psychiatrists and the Royal Society of Medicine. He was also an adviser on the Georgian Papers Programme at King's College London.

is known as rapid cycling, patients get better but for shorter and shorter periods. Although a major life event can trigger illness or relapse, that is not a prerequisite, and nothing identifiably stressful beyond George's speech to Parliament (his ninth such) served as a trigger in this instance.

In understanding the 1765 attack there is the added problem for historians that the Queen and the doctors actively hid the King's symptoms from public view. Manfred Guttmacher speculated that:

> There were days of dejected brooding, followed by short and indefinite periods of overactivity . . . It was so mild that it incapacitated him for only a few days at a time . . . Its true nature was successfully masked from all but very few of his contemporaries . . . Sir William Duncan, the physician in charge of the case, reported . . . a slight fever . . . It persisted chronically from January to July with sporadic exacerbations. Whether a respiratory illness actually occurred as a complication is difficult to say. In all probability, the disorder was purely mental and the clinical reports were falsified.[46]

Dr Isaac Ray, superintendent of the Butler Hospital for the Insane in Rhode Island, lecturing on the King's malady in 1855, similarly surmised that 'The particulars of the first attack were studiously concealed by [the royal] family, and its true character was not generally known at the time.'[47]

A further clue can be found in a letter from Sir Gilbert Elliot, a King's Friend who by June 1804 was the 1st Earl of Minto. Nearly forty years after the event, Elliot wrote to his wife, 'I learnt a piece of history today which I did not know before: the King was ill in the *same way* in the year 1765, very early in his reign. I will show you a passage in the *Continuation* of Smollett which proves it, and which was softened down even to what it is at the instance* of government, and at a good price.'[48] The fifth volume of Tobias Smollett's *Continuation of the Complete History of England*, which was published in late 1765, states that the illness was 'not dangerous', but that the public were told so little about it that they had 'prodigious apprehensions . . . that the state of his health was precarious'.[49]

Later evidence supported Elliot's belief: John Watkins' *Biographical Memoir of his Late Royal Highness Frederick, Duke of York and Albany*, published in 1827, and John Adolphus' updated edition of his *History of England* in 1840 both allude to the 1765 episode as a precursor to the King's later mental illness. 'I did not mention the fact in former editions of this work,' Adolphus admitted in a footnote, 'because I knew that the King, and all who loved him, were desirous that it should not be drawn into notice.'[50] Some historians have claimed that the King could not have been suffering

---

* 'Importunity; solicitation' (*Johnson's Dictionary*).

from mental illness in 1765 because he was able to put his signature on a commission for judges to hold assizes in Lancaster, some financial warrants and the royal assent to the Stamp Act on 22 March.[51] Yet bipolar disorder, especially in this light and initial prodrome phase, can sometimes have extremely minor symptoms and not fully incapacitate the unfortunate sufferer. As we shall see, the King was able to sign documents at different stages even when he was under restraint in later years.

In the 1950s, the historian Sir John Plumb wrote of 'George III's dark and cloudy mind' and put the King's mental breakdown in 1765 down to the loss of Bute and his political isolation, 'together with the sexual strain of his marriage to so unattractive a woman as the Queen'.[52] Yet George's marriage was a singularly happy one, and fifteen children does not suggest a sexual problem. Plumb also believed that the King's high turnover of premiers in the 1760s was evidence that his 'eagerness to adopt at once any man senior to himself, as a father-image, is a measure of his own lack of confidence'.[53] Plumb was grasping too far: George was still only thirty-two at the end of that decade, and so most politicians of Cabinet rank were older than him. Nor, aside from Bute, were any of them credible father-figures: indeed he had described Pitt as having 'the blackest of hearts', and he certainly did not look to Lord North, only six years his senior and a childhood acquaintance, as a father surrogate. The cod psychology (and in Plumb's case misogyny) to which historians have subjected George has harmed the King's reputation for decades.

It was very unusual, perhaps unprecedented, for the King to go a full nine days without seeing his Prime Minister. When they met on 25 January 1765, Grenville wrote of himself in the third person, 'The King heard him patiently, though with a good deal of confusion and embarrassment.'[54] Confusion can cover any number of things, or symptoms. Grenville complained to his diary that there was 'not the least word in commendation or approbation to Mr Grenville', but the Prime Minister might not have understood that the King had just suffered a bout of mental as well as physical illness, as Charlotte, Augusta and Duncan seem to have kept the matter successfully under wraps at Buckingham House. When Grenville returned two days later to remonstrate about a lack of support in the Commons from the King's Friends faction, George 'received it in the same manner as the preceding day, assenting to the evil, but neither pointing out the remedy, nor enquiring into the cause of Mr Grenville's alarm, nor saying a word of approbation of his services or past conduct'.[55] Thereafter the King appears to have suffered a relapse, a condition common to his later bouts of manic depression, because although Grenville saw him very occasionally the next letter between them was not written until 5 March, when Grenville expressed joy at the King 'being so much better'.[56]

During the King's incapacity – whether mental or physical – the situation presented by American taxation rapidly worsened. On 2 February, Benjamin Franklin and three other agents representing North American colonies in London handed Grenville petitions of protest from their respective assemblies.[57] Grenville replied truthfully that, as Jared Ingersoll reported to Governor Thomas Fitch of Connecticut,

> He took no pleasure in giving the Americans so much uneasiness as he found he did – that it was the duty of his office to manage the revenue – that he really was made to believe that considering the whole of the circumstances of the mother country and the colonies, the latter could and ought to pay something, and that he knew of no better way than that now pursuing to lay such tax, but that if we could tell of a better he would adopt it.[58]

There was no sneering disregard for the colonists on the part of the British government. Richard Jackson, the agent for Pennsylvania, told Fitch that Grenville spoke 'of the colonies in general in terms of great kindness and regard'.[59] Two days after the meeting, Franklin wrote that the ministry had 'a view to make us Americans easy, which shows some tenderness for us'.[60] It suited later propagandists to try to make British decision makers out to be haughty and uncaring towards the colonists, but that was not right; they were harassed politicians who were trying to balance the books after an unusually long and unprecedentedly expensive war, and who presumed that the prosperous colonies of North America ought to make a contribution to their own defence and security.

When on 24 February Grenville visited the King 'and made a strong remonstrance . . . upon his having yielded to . . . permit Lord Rochford's chaplain to be appointed secretary to the embassy in Spain', a position Grenville wanted abolished, he recorded that George 'looked confounded'.[61]* It was not the completely trivial nature of Grenville's complaint – which should not have come anywhere near the agenda of a prime minister, let alone a monarch – that had confounded George, but his illness. The next day George was 'blooded, and kept [to] his bed with a feverish cold'.[62] It was the last time that any of his ministers saw him until 10 March.

'The King all this time continues ill,' wrote Grenville on 26 February, 'and sees none of his ministers.'[63] This seems to have been on doctors' orders, as on 5 March the King wrote to Grenville that 'the physicians, on

---

* 'To confound': 'to disturb the apprehension by indistinct words', 'to throw into consternation', 'to stupefy' (*Johnson's Dictionary*).

my naming that I feel as yet some weakness in the breast, have renewed their injunctions of not talking, and particularly on business.'[64] The most likely reason for this was that the doctors feared political business might agitate the King. This also points to his suffering from a mental rather than merely a physical illness, and to the doctors' awareness of this.

On 27 February 1765, while the King was incommunicado, George Grenville's Stamp Bill passed the Commons with a large majority. There was only one division during the Bill's entire progress and the opposition to it amounted to only around forty MPs. One of them, the Dublin-born Whig Edmund Burke, Lord Rockingham's private secretary, later said he had never heard a more languid debate.[65] The Bill passed uncontested through the Lords without a debate or division, and became law on 22 March. 'The important point that it establishes is the right of Parliament to lay an internal tax on the colonies,' a government supporter stated during the Commons debate. 'We wonder here that it was ever doubted. There is not a single Member of Parliament that will dispute it.'[66] The Stamp Act was not mentioned in any of the correspondence between George and Grenville, because the idea that revenue to offset the cost of protecting North American colonies would have to be raised there was so politically uncontroversial.

Yet the Stamp Act was a different type of tax, not an external trade regulation: most American colonists then accepted that Parliament had the right to impose the latter. It was an internal duty and therefore a new departure, one undertaken, moreover, at a politically divisive time. But neither of these points raised concerns. The Treasury had been discussing the introduction of a revenue in North America for over a decade, and did not consider it particularly radical. There had been a stamp tax in Britain for many years, which raised £300,000 per annum: the proposed extension of it into America was only expected to raise between £45,000 and £60,000, and some colonies already imposed stamp taxes on official documents of their own. Even if the tax yielded its highest estimates, it would not cover much more than a quarter of the £213,000 that it cost Britain to station approximately 10,000 soldiers in the colonies.

There were, nonetheless, several problems with the Stamp Act that had not been sufficiently thought through by the government or discussed in the debate. The tax (which applied to the certification of documents and had nothing to do with postage) fell very widely on all legal transactions and newspapers, but also on printed paper of all kinds – playing cards, pamphlets, wills, bonds, deeds, almanacs, mortgages, college diplomas – as well as on dice (on the basis that if you could afford to gamble, you could also afford to pay the tax). The tax had the great disadvantage of hitting precisely those people such as lawyers, merchants and journalists who could be guaranteed to be the most vocal in complaint. Another problem was that it had to be paid in cash, which colonial merchants disliked as there was already an adverse trade balance with England, and a shortage of specie in America.[67] Even more seriously, it would have to be collected by special revenue officers. These were soon subjected to such an extraordinary degree of violence and intimidation that it only ever actually raised £45, or 0.1 per cent of the total expected, all of which came from Georgia, the most Loyalist of the colonies.[68]

It has been argued that Parliament passed the Stamp Act so blithely because it was ignorant of and uninterested in the American colonies, and because MPs did not personally know any Americans, but this is untrue. Between 1763 and 1783, there were least fifteen people in the House of Commons who knew America intimately, among them two provincial agents, two former governors, the compiler of the laws of Maryland and five actual Americans.[69] Nor did this include the large numbers of former naval officer MPs who had been stationed in America, those merchants who traded with the colonies and many others who had close family members living there. Parliament did not pass the Stamp Act through ignorance of its American colonies, but it did dramatically misread the colonists' temperament despite the many connections.

The American historian George Bancroft concluded of the King that 'At the moment of the passing of the Stamp Act, George was crazed.'[70] Yet although he was indeed suffering a psychotic episode while the Bill was passing through Parliament, he seems to have had plenty of sane and normal interludes in which he could have lodged a complaint if he had thought the legislation would cause serious disturbances in America. However, like his Prime Minister and the rest of the government – and indeed like the royal governors in America, whose job it was to implement the new Act – he saw nothing wrong with it.

Five years later, once the Stamp Act had become the most disputed topic in British politics, Grenville tried to shift the blame on to the King. In a speech on 5 March 1770, he said, 'His Majesty, ever desirous to divide the burdens among the people equally, wished to see them divided equally in this instance.'[71] Four months later the diarist James Harris, after a conversation with Grenville, recorded that 'The Stamp Act was not enacted in haste. That the King was particularly desirous to have it, and frequently called upon him to bring it on. That he told His Majesty, it should be done . . . as it was, deliberately.'[72]* Grenville's attempt to shift the blame

* 'Deliberately': in the sense of with calm deliberation, rather than with prior intent.

was successful, yet there is no evidence for George having been 'particularly desirous' in Grenville's own diary, which recorded every instruction or opinion that dropped from the King. George tended to appoint prime ministers and then let them legislate; as an historian of the Act accurately says, 'The Stamp Act was fully Grenville's responsibility from July 1763 onward.'[73]

'The King had a good night,' Grenville wrote in his diary on 3 March 1765, 'but waked in the morning with a return of fever and pain upon his breast; he was blooded in the foot.'[74] That day Richard Rigby MP, who was head of the Duke of Bedford's faction in the Commons, wrote to the Prime Minister to say that Bedford was incapacitated by gout, but that he 'begs you to send him the latest account you have received of the King's health. What is whispered about is very unpleasant.'[75] Since there would have been no need to whisper about a mere long-running cold, it is possible that Walpole was correct and that the King was indeed 'in much danger', but not from a physical illness. If the sweating, chest pains and fever conditions were also accompanied by hypomaniacal babbling – a symptom of all his later attacks – it is obvious why the royal family might have wanted 'to secrete him from all intercourse with his Court' and also why Sir William Duncan might have wanted him taken out of London altogether. Grenville replied directly to Bedford that 'I do not wonder at all at the general concern and anxiety which those who are not informed of the exact state of the King's health express upon an occasion in which the happiness of all is so nearly concerned.'[76]

Grenville visited Buckingham House to inquire after the King on 5 March, but was not allowed to see him. 'The King sees nobody whatever, not even his brothers,' the Prime Minister was informed.[77] It is entirely possible that George or the Queen did not trust his brothers to keep private the exact nature and extent of his illness: he had recently been arguing with Prince Edward, Duke of York, over his £15,000 per annum grant. The King nonetheless later wrote to Grenville saying that he was well enough to sign essential documents, such as financial warrants. Five days later, the King had been sufficiently sharp-eyed to write to his Prime Minister about a draft American Mutiny Act (also known as the Quartering Act) that the Prime Minister wanted as a money-saving device, saying, 'Lord Halifax appears to disregard the noise that may be made here in Parliament by extending the quartering [of] soldiers in private houses in America.'[78] Grenville ignored the King on this point, but was soon proved wrong as the clause at issue had to be withdrawn when it did indeed cause a clamour in Parliament, with MPs citing the Magna Carta in defence of colonial

American liberties. It is ironic that one of Thomas Jefferson's foremost criticisms of George in the Declaration of Independence was about the quartering of British troops on American households, yet, as one historian of the original Quartering Act has observed, 'It was King George III who first raised questions about violating the colonists' privacy.'[79]

Grenville finally saw the King on 10 March and found him 'very cheerful, and his complexion clear, but a good deal thinner than before his illness. His Majesty talked very easily with him, told him he had seen nobody, and should still keep quiet for some time, and that he would send to him again soon.'[80] (Severe weight-loss was another feature common to all the King's later bipolar afflictions, which lends further credence to the 1765 illness being a prodrome of his disorder.) Never one to pass up an opportunity for patronage, Grenville asked George to agree to the appointment of Dr Thomas Dampier, the Lower Master of Eton College, to a prebendary at Canterbury, which he did.

A week later, Grenville received a peremptory, one-sentence note from the King demanding his attendance the next day at 2 p.m., which the Prime Minister noted was 'differently worded from what they usually were'.[81] At that day's Drawing Room the Queen told him that she wished 'that the King would not see his servants [that is, ministers] so often, nor talk so much upon business'.[82] Grenville nonetheless attended the following day, and found 'the King's countenance and manner a good deal estranged, but he was civil, and talked upon several different subjects.'[83] When his disorder became acute many years later, this multiplicity of conversational subjects became a recurring feature. In what appears to have been its mildest form in 1765, he merely confined himself to discussing various government appointments, albeit in a manner 'a good deal estranged'. The Queen also let it be known through the Dowager Lady Egremont that she wanted ministers to avoid discussing politics with her husband while he was ill. She understandably feared that the pressure of public affairs exacerbated whatever it was that was afflicting her husband.

On 22 March, Grenville was told by a page at Buckingham House that 'The King was not so well as he had been, and that the physicians had seen him in the morning, and desired him to keep quiet.'[84] Why should the patient need to be kept quiet if all he had was a physical rather than mental illness? One reason that the psychological aspect of the malady was not noticed by Grenville was that he was allowed to see the King only when the Queen and the doctors decided that he was in a fit state to hold an audience. The Stamp Act had to be given royal assent that day by proxy of the Lord Chancellor, but three days later George was able to have a long talk with Grenville about politics.

'The King's confinement makes a great deal of talk,' the Prime Minister unsurprisingly noted in his diary.[85] Horace Walpole speculated about how Britain would be run under a regency if the King died, a difficult proposition with George, Prince of Wales not yet three years old. 'You will shudder at the idea of such a long minority at such a time,' he told Horace Mann.[86] At the end of the month, George was taken to Richmond Lodge for a week's convalescence even further from the public eye. For all that most of George's biographers have denied that the King was mentally deranged in 1765, there is plenty of circumstantial evidence to suggest that he did indeed suffer a minor episode then, although the symptoms were not to recur for many years afterwards.

When the King unexpectedly returned to London on 3 April for a Levee, George asked Grenville to join him afterwards in the Closet, where he said that he wanted a new Regency Bill passed as soon as possible, one based on the provisions made in 1751 when his father died, but with some important differences intended as 'a means to prevent any faction or uneasiness in his family upon this subject'.[87] If George II had died before George had reached the age of twenty-one, the 1751 Regency Act provided for the Dowager Princess Augusta to rule with a Regency Council headed by the Duke of Cumberland as Vice-Regent. She would have needed its consent to dissolve Parliament or declare war. Fourteen years later, George did not wish Cumberland to hold the same powers over the new Regent, whom he wanted to be Queen Charlotte (provided that Lord Chancellor Northington, the former Robert Henley, was able to establish that the Act of Settlement could not be construed as preventing her, given that she had been born outside England). The fact that Cumberland had suffered a series of strokes which had affected his speech further undermined his suitability as Vice-Regent. (The previous October, Walpole had enthusiastically spread the rumour that the Duke had died.)[88]

Under the new Regency Act sought by the King, neither the Regent nor the members of the Regency Council – except those holding their places *ex officio*, such as the Archbishop of Canterbury and the Lord Chancellor – would be named in the Bill. Instead, George would have the power to nominate the Regent and Council secretly, giving their names to the Lord Chancellor, signed under the Great Seal. Serious problems with this scheme emerged almost immediately. Grenville and other ministers, among them Bedford and Sandwich, feared that instead of the obvious choice of Queen Charlotte, the King was intending to choose his mother Dowager Princess Augusta as Regent, and thus provide for the continued influence of Lord Bute, who they heard had seen the King the previous month.

In fact, Bute was not even consulted about the regency, and George always intended Charlotte to be Regent, but she could not yet be named as she was not twenty-one years old until 19 May 1765, and the King wanted the Act to be enshrined in law immediately. One plausible explanation for his haste is that George 'was simply a very conscientious and rather frightened young man who knew that he had been seriously ill and that he must take steps to protect his eldest son – and his country – in case his next attack should prove more serious still'.[89] The people whose influence he most wanted to negate were his brother Edward and Opposition figures such as the Duke of Richmond who delighted in amplifying the rumours and innuendo concerning Augusta and Bute, much to the King's mortification.

The Cabinet having agreed to the King's new Bill with whatever reluctance on 5 April, George sent for Cumberland on Easter Day, two days later. Uncle and nephew had not met for three years, due in large part to the Duke's opposition to the Peace of Paris, and both of them were ready for a sincere rapprochement. They discussed the Regency Bill, but also whether Hugh Percy, 2nd Earl of Northumberland, then Viceroy of Ireland, might be persuaded to replace Grenville as First Lord of the Treasury. Northumberland's eldest son, also called Hugh Percy, had married Bute's daughter Anne. Cumberland arranged to meet Northumberland, a rich landowner and patron of the arts, at the Newmarket spring meeting, ostensibly to watch the horse racing but also to discuss whether together they, the King's Friends, and the Buteites might be able to produce a workable government.

The King wanted to reunite the royal family and end the very long-running feud between his mother and Cumberland; and he was also still hoping to free himself from Grenville. When Grenville returned to London on 17 April the secret negotiations were fully under way to remove him. It was later alleged that the King wanted to be rid of him because of the series of errors over the Regency Bill, but those, in due course, only reinforced his existing intention.

Having fallen out over money with Prince Edward, Duke of York, George did not want him even to be on the Regency Council until Cumberland pointed out the irrevocable offence that this would cause. In fact, the King had already caused a good deal of offence when he chose to leave the bishopric of Osnabrück – an estate in the Holy Roman Empire with £20,000 per annum attached – vacant for two years so he could give it to another son rather than to his younger brother. It was awarded to George's second son Frederick when he was six months old. In the eighteenth century there was nothing outrageous about a baby being made a bishop at birth, but in this instance it proved a slight for which Edward never truly forgave George.

On 29 April, a motion asking the King to name the Regent was defeated by 89 votes to 31 in the House of Lords, with the Whig grandees Newcastle, Richmond, Albemarle and Rockingham among the minority. The size and eminence of the rebellion obliged the government to state that the Regent would be either Charlotte or 'one of the descendants of the late King usually resident in Great Britain', thereby ruling out Augusta. George complained vigorously to Grenville about this 'mark of disregard shown to the Princess of Wales', which it undoubtedly was.[90] 'You will want a key to all this,' Walpole wrote pithily to Lord Hertford, 'but who has a key to chaos?'[91]

In the midst of that chaos, a pro-government amendment in the Commons successfully reinserted the Princess's name without a division on 9 May, and when opposition arose from Lord John Cavendish and George Onslow it was soundly defeated by 167 to 37. The Bill received its final reading on 13 May, six days before Charlotte's birthday, whereupon the King announced that she would be Regent in the event of his death, and in the event of her predeceasing him it would pass to the Dowager Princess of Wales. It had been a bruising and embarrassing time for him and his mother, made worse by the failure of George and Grenville to be honest with one another about their suspicions and ulterior motives. The mere fact however that George thought the business worth the expenditure of so much political capital implies that whatever had ailed him over the previous months had left him intensely fearful for the future. In each of his later mental illnesses, there were forty-eight-hour or seventy-two-hour periods where his life was despaired of; if that had happened during this illness, too, his insistence upon organizing the Regency, to the neglect of all other pressing affairs of state, makes perfect sense.

On 13 May 1765, the same week that the Regency Bill passed, the Duke of Northumberland approached Cumberland on the King's explicit authority with a plan to create a new 'strong and . . . lasting administration', comprising himself as First Lord of the Treasury, Pitt as Southern Secretary and Newcastle as Lord President of the Council. The proposal set out a government in which the Grenvillites would be reduced merely to Lord Egmont (who was anyhow an old member of the Leicester House Set) as First Lord of the Admiralty.[92] Temple described the proposed new government as 'Butal-Ducal', although in fact neither Bute nor Cumberland would be more than outside supporters of it.[93] It may be doubted how much the King really admired Northumberland; when in November 1760 he had been appointed Lord Chamberlain to the Queen, George had told Bute, 'The thought pleases me much. I think him quite cut out for the nothingness of the employment.'[94]

Yet at least with Northumberland as premier he would no longer have to listen to Grenville's interminable monologues and self-interested requests for friends to be appointed to posts.

Just as the King launched this second attempted coup against Grenville, a serious crisis struck London which threatened to derail everything. On 13 May, the Duke of Bedford, the Lord President of the Council, spoke against a Bill intended to raise duties on Italian silk imports and protect Britain's silk industry from new, post-war foreign competition, which the Lords then rejected. The next morning, thousands of outraged unemployed silk weavers and other affected workers marched from Spitalfields and East London with the avowed intention of burning down Bedford House in Bloomsbury. A paving stone was thrown at the Duke's carriage on his way to the House of Lords, leaving his face bloody and bruised, although he disdained to display anything but contempt for the mob. Once the silk weavers had been joined by other poverty-stricken East Enders, Wilkesites and others protesting against the end of wartime protectionism, the scene was set for six full days of violent rioting in the capital.

On the morning of 14 May, a large number of silk weavers also marched 'very quietly and unarmed' to the royal residence at Richmond to present their grievances to the King and Queen for redress.[95] 'The King told them he would do all that lay in his power to relieve them,' recorded Horace Walpole accurately, 'and they returned pleased and orderly.'[96] Although meeting such deputations was usually the work of ministers, the King accepted petitions personally and so on this occasion he spoke to them directly. The next day the King 'pressed Mr Grenville very earnestly to see what could be done', asking him to meet the weavers' leaders, and the Queen ordered the Court to wear no silks but English ones woven at Spitalfields.[97] It was about as much as a constitutional monarch could do. That same day, a 'considerable mob' appeared outside the House of Commons, but did not attack it.[98] Cavalry and infantry were posted around Bedford House for a week, and as Sir Gilbert Elliot, the Treasurer of the Chamber, noted, 'Everything carried the appearance of a siege but little mischief was done.'[99]

On 16 May, when Grenville and Lord Chancellor Northington produced the King's speech for closing the session and proroguing Parliament the following week, George told them that in fact he only wanted it adjourned for a few days. The pair replied 'that all public business was now finished and pressed for a further explanation, but they received none'.[100] Grenville correctly guessed that he was about to be replaced, and that the King wanted to adjourn rather than prorogue Parliament so that writs could be issued for the by-elections of new ministers.* On his asking the King directly whether that was the case, George replied, 'Mr Grenville, I will speak to you another time about that. I promise I will speak to you; you may depend upon it I will speak to you,' and 'in this kind of emotion and disorder parted with him'.[101] It is important to recall that the only evidence we have for most of these meetings, and the King's apparent dismay, distress, confusion, embarrassment and so on, comes from one side only – Grenville's diary, as taken down by his wife Elizabeth Wyndham.

The next day, 17 May, with the Brigade of Guards still in Old Palace Yard protecting Parliament from the mob, government ministers visited the Duke of Bedford in Bloomsbury to show their solidarity with him as the Riot Act was read outside. Lord Halifax suggested appointing the Marquess of Granby, the successful and popular Seven Years War commander, to become Captain-General.† The post, essentially Commander-in-Chief of the army, had been vacant since Lord Ligonier had retired in 1759, but if anyone was to have it the King wanted it to be the newly reconciled Cumberland, who had held it from 1745 to 1757.

The sense of crisis and suspicion was heightened by Bedford, Halifax and Grenville telling one another that Bute had been paying the mob to riot, though without any evidence or even likelihood that this was true.

On 19 May, the day after refusing the King's offer of the captain-generalship, Cumberland went to Pitt's house, Hayes Place in Middlesex, at George's behest and spent five hours trying to persuade him to join a Northumberland ministry, since Newcastle had refused to come in without him. To appreciate the prestige that Pitt still enjoyed at Hayes six years after the *Annus mirabilis* of 1759, one might think of Winston Churchill at Chartwell or Charles de Gaulle at Colombey-les-Deux-Églises in the late 1940s. The King, desperate to dispense with Grenville, had even authorized Cumberland to agree to an alliance with Prussia if that was the price Pitt demanded for returning to his previous posts of Southern Secretary and Leader of the House of Commons.

Yet Pitt still refused, wanting to have Temple as First Lord of the Treasury. This, given Temple's well-known friendship with the pariah Wilkes, the King would not accept. It is an illustration of how limited the political gene pool had become that, notwithstanding Northumberland, the three remaining front runners for the premiership in May 1765 were the two brothers George Grenville and Richard Temple and their sister's husband

---

* MPs appointed to government posts had to stand for re-election to the Commons.
† His popularity can be gauged by the large number of public houses named after him, by veterans who bought them with the generous demobilization money he had secured for them.

William Pitt. Considering that both Pitt's son and Grenville's became Prime Minister in the next generation, while Temple's nephew and heir became Foreign Secretary, the role of the Grenville clan in George's reign can hardly be overestimated.

The next day, 20 May, amid fears that the rioters were about to be joined by a rabble peasant army from the countryside, as well as by 'a great reinforcement from the great manufacturing towns in the country', Cumberland offered senior roles to Lord Egmont, Lord Lyttelton (a former Chancellor of the Exchequer), Lord Holderness and Charles Townshend, but was refused each time, the last preferring to take his chances with Grenville. Indeed, as Sir Gilbert Elliot recorded, 'The plan of administration which the Duke of Cumberland proposed at this time was so ridiculous that the King could not help smiling at it.'[102]

There was not much else for George to smile about, and on 21 May he returned to London from Richmond as militia regiments converged on the capital to restore order. He saw Grenville, who claimed that the King was in a state of 'great disorder and agitation' over the riots, and 'Hurt with people thinking he had kept out of the way from fear, [he] said he would put himself at the head of his army, or do anything to save his country.'[103] When their conversation moved away from the plans to restore order in the capital, George admitted to Grenville 'that he had had a design to change his government, but not the part which was under his care', that is, the first lordship of the Treasury.[104]

This was untrue, as Northumberland had been offered the premiership by Cumberland, which could not have been done without the King's prior knowledge and consent. George added that some of Grenville's colleagues had been guilty of 'slackness, inability, precipitation and neglect' and denied that Bute had been behind the move. Grenville answered in a way that made it clear that he believed the King was not being truthful.[105] When George nonetheless asked him to remain in office, Grenville refused to give a commitment without consulting his supporters, and went to Bedford House – now no longer under siege – to speak with Bedford, Halifax, Sandwich and Northington about their price for staying in office, knowing now that the King had nobody with whom to replace them. Grenville stayed at Bedford House drawing up his list of demands with these Cabinet ministers and in touch with others, despite the King asking him to attend Buckingham House.

'I am surprised that you are not yet come', George wrote to Grenville at 9.15 p.m., 'when you know it was my orders to be attended this evening. I expect you therefore to come the moment you receive this.'[106] When Grenville finally appeared, he told the King that the Cabinet – not including

Egmont – collectively sought the 'strongest assurances' that Bute, his brother James Stuart-Mackenzie and Cumberland would no longer be consulted by him on public affairs. Grenville added that the Cabinet would be meeting again the next morning. 'The King in the course of the conversation repeated several times that he was an honest man, and he hoped Mr Grenville thought that he was so.'[107]

Even to have to ask this implied that George had a guilty conscience, perhaps for the untruth he had told Grenville at their last meeting. Once Grenville had departed, George's next visitor was Cumberland, who confirmed to him that Newcastle would not enter the government without Pitt, and that Pitt would not enter at all. Their discussion continued until 1 a.m., and by the time he went to bed George knew that he was effectively at Grenville's mercy. The Closet had been stormed once again, but this time from within.

7

Rockingham Repeals the Stamp Act

May 1765–December 1766

The sovereignty of the Crown I understand. The sovereignty of the British legislature out of Britain I do not understand.[1]

Benjamin Franklin on the Stamp Act, 1766

On 15 May 1765, just as the silk-weaving-cum-political crisis began, the King gave royal assent to the American Mutiny Act (more commonly known as the Quartering Act), whereby the colonies were compelled to provide for some of the accommodation, supplies and transportation of British soldiers. Many studies have claimed that the Act forced soldiers into American homes against their inhabitants' will, leading to the destruction of property, the devouring of food and drink and the sexual molestation of their wives and daughters.[2] 'A better cause for revolution would be hard to imagine,' writes one recent historian of the Act, 'except that none of these allegations were true. The Quartering Act *prohibited* British soldiers from entering private houses, and records indicate that the [British] Army faithfully complied with this stipulation.'[3] The clause that would have billeted troops in private houses was the one to which the King had objected, and it had been withdrawn in order to protect Americans' rights. Nonetheless the Act still required Americans to provide some help for the building of barracks and supplying of troops, to which the New York Assembly stridently objected.

The Act covered every American colony from Canada to the Floridas, not just the thirteen North American ones. Taking troops into homes as lodgers for payment was a practice with roots in the seventeenth century, predating George's reign, and it had been common during the recent French and Indian War. Colonial opposition to it came only in 1768, when four regiments were deployed to Boston. Although the Declaration of Independence denounced George for the practice, the Quartering Act of 1765 was in fact the first time that Parliament recognized Americans' right to privacy.

By 1775, 'it had taken [the colonists] two decades to see billeting redcoats as an example of British tyranny,' rather than as a good way of their earning extra income.[4] Nevertheless, after 1768 the sheer numbers of troops billeted in Boston was sufficient to cause friction between the inhabitants and the soldiers, especially once money, drink, sex and especially politics were all added into the mix. Unlike during the French and Indian War, the British began to be seen more as adversaries than as protectors.

Wednesday 22 May 1765 was a humiliating day for George, and one that was to colour his political outlook for the next twenty years. Grenville, who had retained his Cabinet's almost unanimous support, understood that (as in August two years previously) he was in a significantly stronger position than before the King's bungled dismissal attempt, and was determined to capitalize upon it. George rose at 7 a.m. as usual, and at noon met Grenville at Buckingham House. His emboldened premier arrived bearing a list of five demands: Lord Bute was to stay at Luton Hoo, excluded from all influence; James Stuart-Mackenzie was to be dismissed as Lord Privy Seal of Scotland; Lord Granby was to become Captain-General (at least in part to prevent Cumberland succeeding to the post); Lord Holland was to be replaced as Paymaster-General by Charles Townshend; and finally Thomas Thynne, 3rd Viscount Weymouth, was to be appointed Viceroy of Ireland in place of the Earl of Northumberland. These, Grenville insisted, were terms presented as 'absolutely *sine qua non*'.[5]

George told Grenville that he would consider these ultimata and see him again that evening. All afternoon he gave individual audiences to Northington, Cumberland (for an hour), Bedford, Granby (for another hour), Egmont (for two hours) and then to Cumberland and Northington again.[6] According to a memorandum drawn up by Sir Gilbert Elliot, most probably after a conversation with the King, 'The Duke of Cumberland, the [Lord] Chancellor [Northington] and Lord Egmont advised the King to re-establish his former ministers. They represented the impossibility of forming at that time any other administration and His Majesty after expressing the utmost reluctance at length complied.'[7] George at least persuaded Granby, who had fought at Culloden under Cumberland, to refuse the captain-generalship. The General was not prepared to embarrass his old commander or defy the King, so it was agreed that the post would stay vacant but Granby would have it upon Cumberland's death.

For the King, having stayed up until 1 a.m. the previous night, and having been ill for three months earlier that year, it had already been a marathon day, but by 11 p.m. he was ready to undergo another conversation with

Grenville, knowing by then he had no other choice but to comply. He was forced to beg that Stuart-Mackenzie be allowed to stay as Lord Privy Seal of Scotland, a post George had personally promised him for life. Grenville refused. George told Lord Egmont that he had said to Grenville, 'He saw evidently they were not satisfied with his parting with his power, but that nothing would content him but his parting with his honour too . . . As a King for the safety of his people he must submit – but . . . nothing induced him to this but the danger of the crisis.'[8]

Grenville's diary merely records how the King 'fell into great agitation upon the article relating to Mr Mackenzie, and strove in every manner possible to have saved him, going so far as to say "he should disgrace himself if he did it"'.[9] Grenville then 'begged' that the King should dismiss him instead rather than submit him to the 'cruel dilemma' he had set out. Both men knew that that could not happen. The King reportedly replied, 'Mr Grenville, I have desired you to stay in my service. I see I must yield. I do it for the good of my people.' Another account has the King telling Grenville, 'I will not . . . put my kingdoms into a state of confusion . . . You force me to break my word, and you must be responsible for the consequences.'[10]

Grenville was not even prepared to let Stuart-Mackenzie hold the post nominally, if stripped of his powers. In retrospect Grenville ought to have compromised, since now George felt that he would be dishonoured. Grenville disagreed, but failed to spot the extent to which he was making a lifelong enemy of the one person who had the power to dismiss him the moment he felt able. George had never before encountered much personal opposition to his face, but on 22 May 1765 he certainly did, and the memory of it stayed with him for years – profoundly colouring his already jaundiced view of politics, politicians and the Grenville family. That night he sent for Stuart-Mackenzie and explained the situation, in what Elliot described as 'a very affecting scene . . . between them'.[11] Never one to pass up the chance to sneer, Horace Walpole gloated that 'George the Third is the true successor of George the Second, and inherits all his grandfather's humiliations.'[12]*

Ignoring Grenville's stipulation not to consult Bute, George wrote to his 'd[earest] friend':

> I wish sometimes I were a private man that I might with my own arm defend my honour and freedom, against men whose [Old Whig] families have formerly acted with more duty to the Crown than these wretches their

---

* Walpole was probably referring to the enforced departure of his father's rival John Carteret in 1744 and George II's failure to bring him back into office in 1746.

successors . . . Every day I meet with some insult from these people; I have been for near a week as it were in a fever, my very sleep is not free from thinking of the men I daily see; patience cannot last, I incline much to putting everything to a quick upshot, that I may know who are friends, and who secret foes; indecision is the ruin of all things; excuse the incoherency of my letter; but a mind ulcered by the treatment it meets with from all around is the true cause of it.[13]

It was the letter of a man in a state of high nervous anxiety and tension, who recognized that he had been outmanoeuvred politically. Two years earlier George had told the French Ambassador, the Duc de Nivernais, that he 'was very determined not to be the toy of factions', but now it looked very much as if he had become just that.[14]

Yet the fact that the King did not write to Bute again for another eight months implies that he intended to keep, at least for the moment, his side of the bargain with Grenville. Lord Holland duly lost his post as Paymaster-General that same day, to be replaced by Charles Townshend, and Stuart-Mackenzie was replaced as Lord Privy Seal of Scotland by Lord Frederick Campbell, son of the 4th Duke of Argyll. As well as the King, the Scottish people were the losers, as Stuart-Mackenzie had championed such initiatives as the Forth–Clyde Canal, the bridge over the Tay at Perth, a daily postal service from London and a Bill to abolish fictitious voting in Scottish country elections.[15]

On 24 May, Grenville found the King understandably 'very gloomy, and with an air of great dissatisfaction', but he also had a quickened pulse, having not slept for more than two hours a night for several nights.[16] (A fast pulse and insomnia were also seen in all his later bipolar attacks.) George had acceded to all of the Cabinet's terms except for Granby, whose appointment was merely postponed, and the stress was clearly affecting his health. His sharpness of tongue was unaffected, however; when Grenville mentioned Lord Lorne's gratitude at becoming colonel of the 1st Regiment of Foot, the King replied tersely, 'It's your goodness, Mr Grenville, not mine.'[17] (George also said to Lord Sandwich of Lorne's promotion, 'When Mr Grenville made the vacancy, I let him fill it up as he pleased.') Two days later, Elliot recorded that the King 'continued at Richmond, his mind so agitated that he did not choose to take the Sacrament that day nor was there any Drawing Room.'[18] It had hitherto been unknown for the King not to attend Holy Communion on a Sunday.

While the Grenville ministry consolidated its power in London, events were moving swiftly against the Stamp Act in America. On 29 May, the twenty-nine-year-old lawyer and orator Patrick Henry, a slave owner since he was eighteen, made an impassioned speech about liberty in the Virginia House of Burgesses. He denounced the Stamp Act as the work of a dictatorship, saying that 'Tarquin and Julius had their Brutus,* Charles had his Cromwell, and he did not doubt that some good American would stand up, in favour of his country.'[19] As his biographer has pointed out, 'The speaker's implication was unmistakable, radical, even treasonous: Patrick Henry was implying that the King should be assassinated.' Before Henry could finish his speech, however, Speaker John Robinson rose from his chair and declared that he had spoken treason, whereupon Henry immediately recanted and said that he would 'show his loyalty to His Majesty King George the Third, at the expense of the last drop of his blood'.† Henry's speech had a powerful effect on one listener, however. 'He appeared to me to speak as Homer wrote,' recalled a twenty-two-year-old law student, Thomas Jefferson.[20]

When news of the Stamp Act reached Boston, the Massachusetts House of Representatives called on the other colonies to send delegates to a special congress in New York City in October, 'to consider of a general and united, dutiful, loyal and humble representation of their condition to His Majesty and the Parliament, and to implore relief'.[21] The British government responded to the danger of consolidated colonial opposition by merely observing that new taxes were never popular, and that to repeal or ameliorate this one before it even went into operation in November would establish a new principle that American colonists could not be taxed at all. As Thomas Whately MP, Grenville's Secretary to the Treasury, wrote to John Temple, the Surveyor-General of American Customs, 'To establish the right of Parliament to impose these [taxes], and to produce an American revenue, is a great and necessary measure.'[22] In truth it was neither – the £60,000 it was hoped to raise was not a vast amount, and there were other ways of approaching it – but the government were uninterested in the opposition it was provoking. The Prime Minister did not so much as mention it in his daily journal.

The government's pressure on George mounted significantly on 12 June when the Duke of Bedford, who held a deserved reputation for bluntness, had an audience in the Closet and read the King a Cabinet paper complaining that he was still consulting Bute and was not giving them 'countenance and support'.[23] 'Countenance' meant outward friendliness towards

---

* Lucius Junius Brutus overthrew King Tarquin of Rome in 509 BC and was claimed as an ancestor by Marcus Junius Brutus, who assassinated Julius Caesar in 44 BC.
† His supposed retort, 'If this be treason, make the most of it!', was invented later.

ministers at Levees and Drawing Rooms; 'support' meant agreeing to give honours and lucrative sinecures to the ministry's nominees. Bedford asked rhetorically, 'Is not the Earl of Bute representing the ministers in a bad light to the King . . . interfering at least indirectly in public counsels? Does not this favourite, by interfering in this manner . . . risk the utmost hazard to himself and, which is of more consequence, risk the King's quiet and the safety of the public?'[24] The language of the rebuke could hardly have been ruder within the social conventions of the day. The memorandum, if he ever saw it, would not have put to rest Bute's ever present fears of assassination at the hands of his enemies or the mob. Bedford issued the King with a one-month ultimatum 'to permit his authority and his favour and countenance to go together'. George told Lord Northington afterwards that although he felt 'indignation . . . at so very offensive a declaration, yet I mastered my temper and we parted with cool civility'.[25] It had of course been the King's cool civility that the memorandum had at least in part been criticizing.

Unwilling to accept being dictated to, and fearing that his prerogative rights to make his own Court, ecclesiastical and military appointments might soon be at risk, George asked Cumberland in mid-June to go back to Hayes Place to see Pitt, but Pitt's demands if anything had increased slightly. George therefore instructed Cumberland to start negotiating again, this time with Newcastle, the moderate Marquess of Rockingham and Augustus Fitzroy, 3rd Duke of Grafton instead. He appealed to the class solidarity of these aristocrats, saying to Cumberland that 'they are men who have principles and therefore cannot approve of seeing the Crown dictated to by low men'.[26] By early July, they had agreed to replace the Grenville ministry.

When Grenville returned the seals of office on 10 July, he told the King that he had no idea why he had lost his confidence. 'When he had anything proposed to him,' the King replied, 'it was no longer as counsel, but what he was to *obey*.'[27] It was as much the tone as anything Grenville actually said that the King disliked – the man rather than the measures. Over the subject of America there had been no real disagreement between them; indeed it was a complete coincidence that George eventually dismissed the Grenville ministry during the Stamp Act crisis.[28]

Grenville, who privately blamed Bute for his sacking, went resentfully into Opposition with about seventy supporters in the Commons, awaiting his chance for revenge. He recorded that in his last audience as premier 'The King's whole conduct was civil, imputing no blame, but giving no word of approbation throughout the whole conversation.'[29] Grenville advised the King against allowing the Rockingham Whigs to subvert his policies, 'and most particularly on the regulations concerning the colonies; ... he besought His Majesty, as he valued his own safety, not to suffer anyone to advise him to separate or draw the line between his British and American dominions; ... his colonies w[ere] the richest jewel of his Crown.' George had no such intention.

On 13 July, the thirty-five-year-old Charles Watson-Wentworth, 2nd Marquess of Rockingham, accepted the premiership and leadership of the House of Lords, with the septuagenarian Newcastle as Lord Privy Seal to lend authority and ballast to the ministry. Rockingham was reputed to be the richest man in England; the 300 rooms of his country seat, Wentworth Woodhouse in South Yorkshire, covered over a quarter of a million square feet. His income from rentals in Northamptonshire and Yorkshire was estimated at £24,000 per annum, to which could be added around £10,000 from his lands in Ireland.[30] The King approved of him personally because he had a loving marriage – his wife Mary advised him on politics, played the harpsichord and had a fortune of £60,000 – and was a practising Anglican. He was also a great devotee of the turf, but when the Jockey Club offered to name a race after him, he modestly suggested it be named after its founder, Anthony St Leger, instead.

Rockingham had established his independence less than three years earlier when he resigned his lord-lieutenancies in protest against Devonshire's removal from the Privy Council, but he was a strange choice for Prime Minister, having never sat in the Commons, and was the only Prime Minister since 1721 (besides Sir Robert Walpole) not to have served in anyone else's Cabinet. He had been invited to move the address at the opening of the new session in November 1753, but had refused out of shyness and lack of ambition; and his first major setpiece speech in Parliament was on the window tax instituted in May 1766 to replace the cider tax, a full ten months after he became Prime Minister.

In view of Rockingham's political inexperience, Cumberland was intended to be the mainstay and godfather of the new ministry, but from the outside since he was a royal duke. The twenty-nine-year-old Duke of Grafton, who like Cumberland and Rockingham was a leading light of the Jockey Club that ran British horseracing, took over the Northern Department. (Cabinet meetings were not allowed to clash with important racing fixtures.)

Rockingham, who enjoyed life more than he did work, and much more than he did politics, appointed Edmund Burke, the son of a Dublin attorney and an authority on aesthetics, to serve as his private secretary. Burke soon became the Rockingham Whigs' foremost thinker and propagandist, and after becoming MP for Wendover in December also started to establish himself as one of the greatest orators of the age.

In August, the King penned a long memorandum about his tribulations with the Grenville ministry, which permits us an insight into his political thinking at the time. 'My chief care shall be to state nothing but what is most exactly agreeable to truth,' he wrote, 'and not to give way to that heat which the very uncommon usage I met with might in some degree authorize.'[31] It underlines just how little the great affairs of the day had shaped his decision to be rid of Grenville. 'Whenever opposition alarmed them they were very attentive to me,' he recorded of the late government, 'but whenever released from that, their sole ideas were how to get the mastery of the Closet; no office fell vacant of ever so little value, or in the department of any other person, that they did not claim it, and declared that if not complied with they would not serve.'[32] Noting Grenville's 'insolence' over the position of Hogarth's successor, he wrote, 'Had I given way to my feelings on receiving this account he would have been instantly dismissed, but I thought it detrimental to the business of the nation to make any alteration during the sitting of Parliament.'[33] Grenville fell not over America, therefore, but as a consequence of monarchical *amour propre*.

On the morning of 14 August 1765, the Boston merchant Samuel Adams organized a well-behaved crowd in the streets of his city to listen to a series of speeches and then to burn effigies of Lord Bute and Andrew Oliver, the Boston-born stamp distributor for Massachusetts. That night, a much less orderly crowd of largely unskilled labourers systematically dismantled a building owned by Oliver and set about his home too, though the organizers prevented its being torched or looted.[34] Oliver quickly resigned his post. Twelve days later, the house of Thomas Hutchinson, the Lieutenant-Governor of Massachusetts (and Oliver's brother-in-law), was looted and burned so badly that the next morning only its frame was still standing.[35]

Far from being some English invader intent on oppressing the people of Massachusetts, Hutchinson had been born in Boston and educated at Harvard, had been elected to the Massachusetts House of Representatives where he became Speaker and had served on the Governor's Council. He became Chief Justice of the Massachusetts Supreme Court in 1760, and had written a three-volume history of Massachusetts. He and his family escaped from his house minutes before a crowd crying 'Liberty and property!' smashed down his front door with axes and smashed or stole his and his wife's porcelain, paintings, furniture, jewellery and £900 in cash, before destroying an archive of New England historical artefacts that he had spent thirty years collecting.

The mob intended to 'tar and feather' Hutchinson, but he at least escaped that brutal, twelfth-century European punishment of pain and humiliation. In the attacks on customs agents, pine tar used to waterproof ships was applied to their naked bodies, and feathers from fowls or pillows added. They were then exposed to the weather, in one case till frostbite struck. Yet even this threat failed to intimidate the stalwart Hutchinson, who became Acting Governor of Massachusetts in 1769, Governor in 1771 and a key figure in what followed. By late October, all the stamp distributors for the colonies (with the exceptions of North Carolina and Georgia) had resigned because of the extreme violence, intimidation and threats to their homes and families.

The Stamp Act Congress met at New York's City Hall (later known as the Federal Hall) from 7 to 25 October 1765, attended by twenty-seven representatives from nine colonies, who drew up a 'Declaration of the Rights and Grievances of the Colonies'. This acknowledged the supremacy of the Crown and Parliament in legislating on imperial issues, but denied Parliament's right to tax the colonies for the purpose of revenue. While declaring 'all due subordination to that august body, the Parliament of Great Britain', the delegates nevertheless concluded that 'It is inseparably essential to the freedom of a people, and the undoubted right of Englishmen, that no taxes should be imposed on them but with their own consent, given personally, or by their representatives.'[36] Since 'the people of these colonies are not, and from their local circumstances cannot be, represented in the House of Commons in Great Britain,' only colonial legislatures could give the necessary consent. The Congress left unresolved the precise constitutional difference between an internal levy, such as the Stamp Act, and an external levy, such as the customs duty on molasses. When the Sugar Act was passed in 1766 it caused little protest, and it raised over £20,000 yearly between 1766 and 1774.[37]

Opponents of the Stamp Act routinely employed the pithy and reasonable-sounding slogan of 'No taxation without representation', but just in case the British simply acceded to the implied demand, the Massachusetts House of Representatives instructed its delegates to the Stamp Act Congress that 'such a representation of the colonies as British subjects are to enjoy would be attended with the greatest difficulty, if it is not absolutely impracticable, and therefore you are not to urge or consent to any proposal for any representation, if such be made in the Congress.'[38] They therefore knew their cry to be fanciful, if not spurious, even while it served a powerful purpose as a propaganda slogan. Even though – as in the cases of Scotland and Ireland under the Acts of Union of 1707 and 1800 – a certain number of seats in the Lords and Commons could indeed have been set aside for the Americans, notwithstanding a raft of political pamphlets from the early 1770s onwards the concept of American representation at Westminster was never seriously considered on either side of the Atlantic.[39]

One of the factors that George and British politicians consistently under-estimated throughout the American crisis of the 1770s was the capacity of the colonists to act in concert with one another, despite their having ably demonstrated by the Stamp Act Congress in 1765 that they could do so. As the Act was not even scheduled to come into effect until 1 November 1765, it was already effectively moribund, especially once North Carolina's distributor resigned in November 1765, and Georgia's two months later.

As a constitutional monarch, George correctly left the next steps to the politicians, telling them, 'Whatever remains to be done on this occasion I commit to your wisdom.' The central problem with that was neatly apho-rized by an historian: 'Grenville, who was responsible for the Stamp Act but would not be responsible for its enforcement, wished it to be enforced. Rockingham, who had not been responsible for the Stamp Act but who would be responsible for its enforcement, wished it to be repealed.'[40]

George and Charlotte's third child, William Henry, Duke of Clarence, was born on 21 August 1765, but no sooner did one royal duke enter the world than another left it. The Duke of Cumberland was obese, had suffered strokes and had never fully recovered from the wound he received at Det-tingen; he died on 31 October that year aged just forty-four. His death removed the chief sponsor and supervisor of the Rockingham ministry, and the lynchpin between the King and his ministers. Although his mas-sacre of the defeated Scottish Highlanders in 1746 has deservedly led to lasting infamy, at the time he was widely mourned in England: indeed, a medal was struck depicting a grieving Britannia, with a scroll inscribed 'Culloden' at her feet.[41] Nor was his the last royal ducal death that year; on 29 December George's fifteen-year-old brother, Prince Frederick Wil-liam, died from tuberculosis.

Rockingham, Newcastle, Grafton and Conway all wanted to recruit Pitt in order to alleviate the weakening of the ministry caused by Cumberland's death. 'I had three times in vain attempted that measure, that it could never again arise from me,' George told Rockingham. 'Mr Pitt had declared to me the last time he was with me that now he must for ever retire.'[42] The King's primary desire was of course to keep out Grenville, who had re-established friendly relations with his elder brother Temple. The King was determined that 'The Family' (as he nicknamed the Grenville–Pitt clan) should not return en masse. Their power in the Commons, however, remained formidable, especially when faced with a young and inexperienced group of senior ministers (barring Newcastle) now shorn of the support of their royal patron.

By now events across the Atlantic could no longer be ignored. 'I am more and more grieved at the accounts in America,' the King wrote to Conway, the Southern Secretary, on 5 December. 'Where this spirit will end is not to be said. It is, undoubtedly, the most serious matter that ever came before Parliament. It requires more deliberation, candour, and temper* than I fear it will meet with.'[43] This was emphatically not the response of a hardliner. Thirteen days later, the New York Assembly† offered a renewed declaration of 'their faith and allegiance to His Majesty King George the Third, and of their submission to the supreme legislative power', adding that they would show 'that the rights claimed by them are in no manner inconsistent with either'.[44] At some point it would be impossible for the colonists to reconcile such allegiance to a King who firmly believed in Parliament's right to tax them with the views of the members of their own assemblies who did not.

After the death of King James II's son, James Francis Edward Stuart, the Old Pretender, on New Year's Day 1766, Pope Clement XIII finally recognized George III as the rightful King of England, rather than Charles Edward Stuart ('Bonnie Prince Charlie'), the Young Pretender, who was to live in Rome and Florence until his death in 1788. Twenty years after Culloden, the Jacobite threat was finally extinguished, and George's policy of drawing Tories back into the British polity was vindicated. His decision not to accept Pitt's return to office looked equally prescient when on 5 January Rockingham informed him that he had sent Thomas Townshend MP, a lord of the Treasury and Charles Townshend's cousin, to sound out Pitt's views on America and determine whether he might join the ministry. Pitt, suffering from gout,‡ was taking the waters at Bath; he had haughtily replied that he would give his advice only to the King or to the people, and would only join a ministry led by Temple or himself which did not contain any former Prime Minister. He thereby ruled out Newcastle. In his first (at least extant) letter to Bute in eight months, written on 10 January, George said that he had replied to Rockingham that 'they might consult who they pleased but that I had no share in the affair.'[45]

* 'Calmness of mind; moderation' (*Johnson's Dictionary*).
† The equivalent of the Virginia House of Burgesses or Massachusetts House of Representatives.
‡ An extremely unpleasant disease that causes great pain to its innocent sufferers, yet which for some unaccountable reason people persist in finding funny. As well as gout, Pitt possibly suffered from debilitating psoriasis and periods of extreme depression.

Knowing that Rockingham was considering repealing the Stamp Act because of its rejection in America, something that as a constitutional monarch he would have had to support while privately preferring its modification, George nevertheless signalled to Bute that he and his faction, which broadly commingled with that of the King's Friends, could actively oppose repeal if they so chose. On the question of whether they would be dismissed if they voted against repeal, the King told Bute, 'As to my friends differing from ministers where they think their honour and conscience requires it, that I not only think right, but am of opinion it is their duty to act so; nay I think that it is also incumbent on my dear friend to act entirely so also.'[46] The King was thus effectively encouraging Bute to rebel against his own government's policy of appeasement of the American colonists. Nor was this out of respect for the rights of MPs under the constitution; he had not previously permitted office holders to follow their consciences when he had wanted legislation passed concerning the Peace of Paris or general warrants.

'All I desire is that they will act firmly till the arduous business of the American colonies is over,' the King told Egmont, his closest ally in the Cabinet, on 11 January, 'then I can stand upon my own feet.'[47] By this he meant he would be able to form a government more to his liking, but the 'business' was to become far more arduous than he could possibly have guessed. When later that month the Cabinet decided upon full repeal of the Stamp Act, it seemed to the King to be a complete surrender to American blandishments, violence and boycotts. The government's argument explaining the clear volte-face – that Americans could not be expected to have the money to buy both the stamps and British goods – convinced few. More persuasive was the argument of Soame Jenyns, a lord of the Board of Trade, who pointed out that the colonists' argument, that people should not be taxed without their consent, was 'the reverse of the truth, for no man I know is taxed by his own consent'.[48]

George would come bitterly to regret the repeal of the Stamp Act: he had far preferred its modification to a purely nominal sum that he believed the colonists might not have bothered to contest. One of the key reasons why Rockingham wanted to repeal the Stamp Act – quite apart from its disastrous reception in America – was to bolster his attempt to bring Pitt (who sympathized with the colonists) into the government to shore it up against Grenville and Bedford's united opposition. Ultimately, partisan politics and factionalism in Westminster played as great a role in the decision to repeal the Stamp Act as the good governance of America; had Cumberland lived another six months, the government might not have repealed it at all.

Fortunately for Rockingham, the Opposition was profoundly split, between the anti-repeal Grenvillites, the pro-repeal Pittites and the Bedfordites who were divided among themselves. Shelburne's characteristically pragmatic stance was that the right to tax existed, but for fear of boycotts should not be exercised. After all, the £60,000 that the government hoped the Stamp Act would raise was dwarfed by the revenues Britain would lose through a comprehensive trade boycott.[49] In a Commons debate on 14 January, Pitt 'spoke strongly in favour of the Americans – said he condemned every measure of the late administration'.[50] After Grenville had said he supported the Stamp Act 'for the strict dependence of America', Pitt replied very strongly, 'declaring for the repeal – and said he would rather cut off his right hand than be for enforcing the S[tamp] Act'.[51]

This speech, coming from the Great Commoner and victor of the Seven Years War, had a tremendous impact in the colonies. The official notes record that Pitt 'treated Mr Grenville's arguments with great contempt, said he had *been betrayed* by all parties, said this country was ruined by factions, and wished, but scarcely hoped to see, a solid administration established'.[52] He added that, while it could not tax America, Parliament nonetheless did have 'a right to bind, to restrain America', and that its 'legislative power over the colonies is sovereign and supreme'.[53] Yet for all the drama of Pitt's declaration against the internal taxation of the colonies, how much was opportunism and rhetoric rather than conviction? When challenged about the exact meaning of some of his statements he lapsed into vague pronouncements.[54]

Grenville's reply was equally hard-hitting. 'Protection and obedience are reciprocal,' he argued.

Great Britain protects America; America is bound to yield obedience. If not, tell me when the Americans were emancipated? When they want the protection of this kingdom, they are always ready to ask it. That protection has always been afforded them in the most full and ample manner. The nation has run itself into an immense debt to give them their protection; and now they are called upon to contribute a small share towards the public expense, an expense arising from themselves, they renounce your authority, insult your officers, and break out, I might almost say, into open rebellion.[55]

The King would not have disagreed with that. Many Pittites did though, hissing at Grenville as he spoke. 'The gentleman asks when were the colonies emancipated?' Pitt replied. 'I desire to know when they were made slaves.'[56] Taxation was 'no part of the governing or legislative power' of Britain, and the Americans were 'the sons, not the bastards of England', which could 'not take money out of their pockets without their consent . . .

The gentleman tells us America is obstinate. America is in almost open rebellion. I rejoice that America has resisted.' Sir Fletcher Norton condemned this as 'the trumpet to rebellion'.

Pitt's gambit worked, and on 18 January George approved yet another approach for him to join the government, this time from Rockingham and the Duke of Grafton. Although Pitt's reply was open to other interpretations, the King took it to mean that he would take office only if the Rockingham Ministry was ended rather than merely reshuffled. Pitt demanded too much again, and George thought it impossible to bring him in. By then the Stamp Act had also become highly unpopular in Britain too, and the colonists' cause had been taken up by merchants whose goods were being embargoed. Although George still preferred modification to outright repeal, the government wanted it gone, and were prepared to stake their survival in office on it.

To lose Rockingham and have to fall back on Grenville and Bedford was not worth a Stamp Act for George, who hoped that there might be subtler ways of raising money from the colonists for imperial defence that would not provoke such an outcry. To that end, on the morning of 21 January he wrote to Rockingham from Buckingham House that William Talbot, 1st Earl Talbot, the Lord Steward of the Household, 'is as right as I can desire on the Stamp Act; strong for our declaring our right but willing to repeal, and has handsomely offered to attend the House daily and answer the very indecent conduct of those who oppose with so little manners or candour'.[57] By sending his own Lord Steward, the King was indicating that he would be encouraging the King's Friends to vote for repeal, a mere eleven days after suggesting to Bute that he did not mind if Buteites voted against it. The question thus arose: whose side was the King really on?

The ambivalent answer, explained in an audience on 30 January with his former governor, Lord Harcourt, was that 'he was strenuously for supporting and asserting the right of Great Britain to impose the tax, was against the repeal of the Bill, but thought it could perhaps be modified'.[58] When Harcourt asked whether he could make these views known to other peers before they voted, George replied that 'he would never influence people in their parliamentary opinions, and that he had promised to support his ministers'. As one historian of the King's role in the American Revolution has observed of this conversation, 'This is not the language of the would-be autocrat of legend.'[59] Nonetheless, with rumours of the King's uncertain view about repeal seeping out in Westminster, helped by Bute and possibly Harcourt too, a parliamentary crisis developed prior to the vote on 4 February in the House of Lords, where there were already a great many peers who did not believe that imperial policy should bend under duress from the American colonists.

Rockingham soon got wind of trouble, and following an audience with George on 2 February the King reported to his trusted Lord Chancellor Northington the next day that he 'called on my promise at all times of [the King] not giving up [the] administration whilst they thought they could act. By this you are fully apprised of the part they will take this day, which I believe will prove a fatal day to them. This hour is perhaps one of the most critical ever known in this country.'[60]

When the repeal of the Stamp Act was introduced in the Lords the vote ought to have been a foregone conclusion. The government had a large inbuilt majority comprising twenty-six bishops, sixteen Scottish representative peers and the large 'Household Brigade' of peers who held Court and other royal appointments, on top of the dozen or so peers who received pensions. But since Bute was now leading the opposition to repeal in the Lords it was widely assumed that the King opposed it too, and in the division on 4 February the Rockingham government was defeated on an amendment to the repeal of the Act by 63 votes to 60. After a crisis meeting of almost the whole Whig party hierarchy the next morning – including the Dukes of Newcastle, Grafton and Portland, the Marquess of Rockingham, Lords Winchelsea, Albemarle and Bessborough and General Conway, as well as the King's Friends Lords Dartmouth and Egmont – Newcastle visited the King to ask him directly whether he was for repeal or not. 'Yes, I am now,' George replied. 'I was not for it at first, but now I am convinced or think *that* is necessary.' 'Why then, Sir,' replied the Duke, '. . . I hoped Your Majesty would let your servants know your opinion upon it.' George claimed to have already done so, but added, 'But what can I say when they tell me they can't in conscience vote for the repeal?' 'Conscience, Sir,' replied the cynical old former premier, 'is too often influenced by prejudice in favour of persons and things, and that Courts have ways of letting their opinion be known.'[61]

When on 6 February the government was again defeated in the Lords, this time by 59 to 55 after Bute had spoken against repeal, Grenville took the opportunity to put forward a motion, to be debated in the Commons the next day, that the Stamp Act instead be enforced. Left now with no alternative between repeal and enforcement, and with no hope of modification being debated or becoming law, the King had no choice but to give Rockingham explicit permission to state that he favoured repeal. On Friday 7 February 1766, Grenville's motion fell by 274 votes to 134 in the Commons, an outcome which 'much enraged' its proposer, who suffered the added indignity of seeing Pitt walk out of the chamber while he was speaking.[62]

In a memorandum he wrote for himself – and for posterity – on 10 February, George recalled that 'Lord Rockingham this day came and complained to me as if he was accused of having wrong stated my opinion on the Stamp Act; I told him I had on Friday given him permission to say I preferred repealing to enforcing the Stamp Act; but that modification I had ever thought both more consistent with the honour of this country, and all the Americans could with any degree of justice hope for.'[63] The King had been consistent in desiring modification, but if it came down to either enforcement or repeal – which in the end it did – he favoured repeal. The government's victory in the subsequent Lords vote was 73 to 61 (105 to 71 including proxies), so the King's action did help waverers decide. The total of 176 votes was the largest of any Lords division in the eighteenth century, reflecting the vital importance by then of North American issues in Parliament.[64]

George wrote another, much longer memorandum the next day to justify his actions over the previous month. 'The late variety of opinions that have been reported to be mine on the Stamp Act makes it very eligible that I should, whilst fresh in my memory, put on paper the whole of my conduct during this very arduous transaction,' he began.[65] Was the memorandum a defence of his position before history (it was not published until 1927), or an aide-memoire to help future deliberation, or a salve for a guilty conscience for having performed a volte-face? Perhaps it was all three.

George was characteristically direct. 'From the first conversations on the best mode of restoring order and obedience in the American colonies,' he wrote,

> I thought the modifying [of] the Stamp Act the wisest and most efficacious manner of proceeding; first, because any part remaining sufficiently ascertained the right of the mother country to tax its colonies, and next that it would show a desire to redress any just grievances; but if the unhappy factions that divide this country would not permit this in my opinion equitable plan to be followed, I thought repealing infinitely more eligible than enforcing, which could only tend to widen the breach between this country and America.[66]

On 22 February, an Opposition amendment to prevent repeal fell by 275 votes to 167 in the Commons, with independent MPs overwhelmingly trooping into the government lobby. 'Lord Rockingham cannot nor ought not to disguise from His Majesty the pleasure he felt upon this event,' the Prime Minister wrote, adopting the customary third person, 'as he flatters himself that it is a confirmation that the opinion he had humbly submitted to His Majesty was well founded in point of public opinion.'[67] The third and final reading of the Repeal Bill passed the Commons by 250 to 122 on 5 March, whereupon it went up to the Lords, where George advised his courtiers and the King's Friends to vote for it. Despite his clear instruction, no fewer than seven lords of the bedchamber voted against it, as did Bute and the Duke of York, but none was admonished for doing so.

On 12 March Rockingham reported to the King that during the debate 'Lord Mansfield spoke with his usual eloquence and ability but rather anticipating upon the gloomy prospect of the colonies throwing off all allegiance.'[68] William Murray, 1st Earl Mansfield, was the legal luminary of the age, the most important jurist and legal reformer of the eighteenth century. A former Attorney-General and Solicitor-General, he was convinced of Parliament's legal right to tax America. Instead of heeding Mansfield's warnings, Rockingham, having met an American deputation that morning, wrote (with a sudden rash of capital letters) that he had 'now full Reason to assure His Majesty that there is the Greatest Prospect of an Advantageous System of Commerce being Established for the Mutual and General Interest of this Country, North America and the West India Islands'.[69] The King replied the next day, 'I am glad the American affair has ended this day without any great altercation,' by which he meant in Parliament rather than anything that was happening on the other side of the Atlantic.[70]

The repeal of the Stamp Act passed the Lords without division on 17 March 1766. The King replied that he was 'glad to hear the debate ended so soon this day', and when he went to Parliament to give the royal assent he was cheered in the streets.[71] In North America, the repeal was celebrated with parties, fireworks, poetry and the commissioning of a statue in New York of George dressed as a Roman emperor.[72] Two medals were struck to commemorate it in Britain, one of which depicted Pitt with the words 'The man who, having saved the parent, pleaded with success for her children.'[73]

The day after the repeal, Parliament passed the Declaratory Act, reaffirming its ancient right to legislate imperially. It was based upon the Irish Declaratory Act of 1720, an unequivocal statement of sovereignty over Ireland that was much resented by Catholic nationalists. Benjamin Franklin had told Lord Dartmouth that repealing the Stamp Act 'will be deemed a tacit giving up of the sovereignty of Parliament', and the Declaratory Act was passed to scotch any such interpretation.[74] Officially described as 'An Act for the better securing the dependency of His Majesty's dominions in America upon the Crown and Parliament of Great Britain', the Act included the statement that Parliament 'had, hath, and of right ought to have full power and authority to make laws and statutes of sufficient force and validity to bind the colonies and people of America ... in all cases whatsoever'.[75] Pitt, who had supported repeal, opposed the Declaratory Act. 'Let the sovereign authority of this country over the colonies be asserted in as strong terms as can be devised ...' he sarcastically summed up the government's position, 'that we may bind their trade, confine their manufactures, and exercise every power whatsoever – except that of taking money out of their pockets without their consent.'[76] It nonetheless passed without a division in the Commons and only five dissentient voices in the Lords.

Pitt's attacks on the ministry continued, and he even made efforts to befriend Lord Bute again. Yet with large majorities having supported repeal of the Stamp Act, Rockingham was now of no mind to negotiate with either of them. His resolve was such that, when Grafton resigned on 28 April, saying that he could not hold office in a ministry 'that set Mr Pitt at defiance', the Prime Minister remained unmoved.[77] Grafton was a cultured, liberal-minded and ultimately unambitious politician, whom the King admired chiefly because he was not grasping. When he awarded Grafton the Order of the Garter in 1769, he said that he was pleased to do it as Grafton was 'one of the very few who had received it unsolicited'.[78] Conway became Northern Secretary, and his replacement as Southern Secretary was Charles Lennox, 3rd Duke of Richmond, whom the King disliked for the *lèse-majesté* of his insulting address the previous June, and his seemingly radical politics – which the King suspected might even extend to republicanism – but whom Rockingham insisted on having in his Cabinet.

The factionalism of politics fell heavy on the King's shoulders, and it was perhaps in a moment of wistful hope for an easier life that he once again turned to Bute. On 3 May, George wrote him a long letter in which he complained about the physical and mental pressures under which he had laboured during the three years of almost continual political crises since Bute's resignation. He wanted to know whether Bute and his followers might be prepared to return to office, making clear that such an overture was conditional upon Pitt and Grenville not joining him. 'In short I am willing to take any but the men that used me so infamously last year,' George wrote; 'I will rather run any risks than submit to ... the having Mr Grenville and the late Secretaries near my person ... This will I am sure fully convince my d[ear] friend how agitated I am, indeed I can neither eat nor sleep, nothing pleases me but musing on my cruel situation.'[79] There might have been an oblique reference to his bout of mental illness of 1765 when he added, 'If I am to continue the life of agitation I have these three years, the next year there will be a Council [of] Regency to assist me.'

Despite this olive branch, Bute had no interest in returning to his old, bowel-irritating responsibilities. And at any rate, even if he had been prepared to take up office, the public was not prepared to permit him. When he went to Dover to begin a long journey abroad in 1768, a mob awaited him and he had to escape a stoning by taking a small boat far from the usual point of departure. He travelled abroad incognito, and even in England often used an alias. As late as the 1780s he was still being attacked in the popular press.

When William, Duke of Cumberland, died, George had promised his three brothers, Edward, Duke of York, Henry, the new Duke of Cumberland, and William, Duke of Gloucester, £8,000 per annum each, to come from the £25,000 per annum that their uncle had received from Parliament. By early May, Rockingham, correctly suspecting that the King was looking to replace him as Prime Minister, tried to use this as a way of remaining in office, telling the King that the vote over the royal dukes' incomes would have to be postponed on account of the pressures of other business. 'They mean to show their spite at me,' George wrote to Bute of this fairly blatant attempt to twist his arm. 'Now they will not do that unless they can be sure of continuing; how mean, how very rancorous is this.'[80]

George complained to Egmont that Rockingham 'wants now to make me break my word, which I cannot do . . . My prudence is now exhausted. I am inclined to take any step that will preserve my honour.'[81] It was always dangerous for governments when George persuaded himself that his honour was at stake.

Some historians have assumed that the King dismissed the Rockingham ministry because of disagreements over the American colonies, but there were no such issues in contention. On America the two were aligned, but Rockingham's intended replacement, William Pitt, denied that Britain even had the moral right to tax America. The real reason was that George, as usual, preferred a broad-bottomed national government to one run by Whig oligarchs such as Rockingham, Newcastle and Richmond. He was staying true to his core principle of 1760, which concentrated on never becoming the prisoner of any faction, and especially not of the 'Old Gang' Whigs. Pitt was a Whig, but the king hoped his government would be widely based.

On 7 July, George wrote to Pitt asking him to come to London so that he could have 'your thoughts how an able and dignified ministry may be formed'.[82] Pitt's reply the next day showed a deference exaggerated even by the standards of eighteenth-century Court flummery. 'Sir,' it began,

Penetrated with the deepest sense of Your Majesty's boundless goodness to me, and with a heart overflowing with duty and zeal for the honour and

happiness of the most gracious and benign sovereign, I shall hasten to London
as fast as I possibly can . . . the sooner to be permitted the high honour to lay
at Your Majesty's feet the poor but sincere offering of the small services of
Your Majesty's most dutiful subject and most devoted servant, William Pitt.[83]

All Pitt's letters to George were couched in this ludicrous style, which has
been likened to that of Uriah Heep from *David Copperfield*.[84] Was there
also perhaps an element of passive-aggression from the celebrated national
hero to a young man (albeit a king) half his age? Certainly, in every other
area of life, and especially in politics, Pitt was haughty and completely
undeferential. The King could never quite be sure that Pitt was not privately
teasing him by adopting this oleaginous language.

A day later, on 9 July 1766, recognizing that the King wanted Pitt as
Prime Minister, Rockingham returned the seals of office. 'By the last
accounts from America,' he boasted, 'the repeal of the Stamp Act had had
all the good effect that could be proposed; had been received with the
utmost duty and gratitude; and . . . everything was quiet in America and
no one mark left of disobedience or discontent.'[85] The King replied that he
was satisfied with him, which he tended to say whenever he sacked his
premiers. Newcastle complained privately of the King's 'cruel usage' of the
ministry, although George was no more cruel on this occasion than he had
been on previous ones.[86]

Newcastle confided to Charles Yorke that the King had described Rockingham's ministry as an 'administration of boys'.[87] It was true that some
of the senior ministers were very young, but ironic that he had fumed over
a similar accusation of youth when he believed Pitt had made it against
himself nine years earlier, and that he was now using it to justify giving
Pitt the premiership.

'Though the conduct I have met with makes me impossible of acquiring
any fresh attachments of a political kind,' George wrote to Bute, 'yet I am
resolved, as much as possible to make no new enemies; for it is very
unpleasant to be afterwards obliged to appear forgetting what one has
suffered.'[88] One new enemy he had made in sacking Rockingham was
Edmund Burke, who convinced himself that the King had made a secret
cabal with Bute, Egmont, Jenkinson and Northington, all of them, he
believed, virulently opposed to change and progress. Monarchs had always
taken counsel from outside the Cabinet, but there was just enough truth
in Burke's suspicion for him to construct an elaborate conspiracy theory
that was to bedevil George in later years, as we shall see.

Pitt kissed hands on 30 July 1766. Even before becoming Prime Minister,
he had declared his wish 'to dissolve all factions and to see the best of all

parties in employment'.[89] This of course was exactly what the King wanted to hear, having expressed a desire for 'an administration of the best of all parties and an exclusion to no descriptions'.[90] Despite this inclusive sentiment, Pitt wanted no ex-premiers in his Cabinet, which excluded Grenville, Newcastle and Rockingham. 'I now hope God is giving me this line to extricate this country out of faction,' George told Bute, and spoke to Pitt about 'destroying all party distinctions'.[91]

It was what Bolingbroke, Bute and Frederick, Prince of Wales, had wanted, but was it merely a fantasy? The new Cabinet hardly saw an explosion of new talent. Pitt himself had not taken the premier's traditional post of First Lord of the Treasury but became Lord Privy Seal instead, an office without portfolio and thus without onerous departmental responsibilities. This required him to be raised to the House of Lords, assuming the title of Earl of Chatham (in a nod to the naval shipyards). It was an unexpected move for the Great Commoner, which lost him some popularity both in the country and in the City of London – despite the merchants there being desperate for titles themselves. More importantly, it took him out of the Commons, leaving the government's leadership there to the chronically indecisive Conway and the brilliant but irresponsible Charles Townshend, the Chancellor of the Exchequer.

It has been claimed that the King appointed Chatham as it 'would leave more scope for the exercise of his personal authority than had existed under the Rockinghams', but this is not so, because the King hoped and expected Chatham to be a much more assertive premier than his predecessor.[92] The problem of the 1760s so far had been to find a stable ministry which had the confidence of both the King and Parliament, and Chatham's appointment finally seemed like that moment. Pitt had been a highly disruptive force in politics since his resignation in 1761, opposing Grenville and working only with the Rockinghamites over the repeal of the Stamp Act and little else of importance. He was 'too considerable to be neglected, too uncooperative to be assimilated'.[93] Now the King had given him his chance to form his own ministry, and promised him more support than he had given to anyone since Bute. It was support that Pitt would need, for by his own actions he had seen to it that Bedford, Rockingham and Grenville were all now firmly aligned against him.

The Chatham ministry was effectively the end of the King's friendship with Bute. George and Bute would have no contact for more than two decades, until an older, more reflective King wrote to the Earl on his fiftieth birthday in June 1788 and then invited him to a ball at Windsor the next year. Bute attended, despite being in frail health, and the two were finally reconciled three years before Bute's death aged seventy-eight.

The King had a great many reasons to dislike Chatham: for his betrayal over the Prussian subsidy in 1758, for his opposition to the Peace of Paris, for his extravagant demands and perhaps also for his irritating inferiority-superiority complex – 'I am with the most profound veneration, Sir, Your Majesty's most dutiful and most submissive servant,' etcetera.[94] Yet George allowed him to return to a foreign policy of traditional Whig interventionism, that of making overtures to Prussia and Russia for a northern alliance to counterbalance the Bourbon Family Compact. George dreaded the prospect of an entangling alliance with either country, but to his relief Frederick the Great rejected it outright; the projected Russian alliance foundered on Catherine the Great's demands for large peacetime subsidies and a commitment from Britain to oppose the Ottoman Empire in the wars she was planning. As well as going along with Chatham's foreign policy initiatives, the King also created three dukes on his advice – those of Northumberland, Montagu and Leinster – the only non-royal dukedoms of his entire reign.* Consolation included Chatham's reinstatement of Stuart-Mackenzie as Keeper of the Privy Seal of Scotland, where he remained until his death in 1800, thus salvaging the King's 'honour'. The three royal dukes also received their late uncle's stipend.

In December, Chatham suffered an attack of gout so severe that he had to retire to Bath, and was unable to return to London until March 1767. Pitt's debilitating physical infirmity, a condition which today would have been treatable in just a few hours, combined with an underlying mental health problem to exact a terrible toll, and he appears to have suffered some form of nervous breakdown as Prime Minister which essentially rendered him incapable of any human contact.[95] An historian of the ministry believes that Chatham suffered from 'some mental disturbance which paralysed his will and action'.[96] At home, food had to be passed to him through a hatch in the door of his darkened top-floor room, so that he did not have to interact with his servants.[97] Dyspepsia and chronic insomnia followed. It seems extraordinary that Britain should have simultaneously had both a king and a prime minister who were manic depressives, although George did not suffer an attack during the Chatham administration.

The fifty-eight-year-old Lord Chatham was the only undeniably great British statesman of George's reign until the appearance of his son and namesake William Pitt the Younger a generation later. Unfortunately for Chatham, George and ultimately Britain, by the time he was in a position to effect meaningful change as Prime Minister he lacked the ability to achieve it. The time of his greatness had been when he was Southern

---

* Wellington's in 1814 was created by the Prince Regent.

Secretary during the Seven Years War, and the lionized Pitt of memory had long since passed into the faded and feeble figure of the late 1760s. His critics now sneered at his failure to live up to his own bravado: he had been a preening egotist in the Commons, who made devastating speeches in opposition, but he proved unable to translate this into good government once in power. As premier he found himself both psychologically incapacitated and physically and politically isolated, unable to halt the drift towards separation in North America. Despite his many protestations in their defence while in opposition, as Prime Minister he found the American colonists to be an 'irritable and umbrageous people quite out of their senses'.[98]

What ought to have been the high point of his career – in power, enjoying the King's support and with much of his public reputation still intact – proved a bitter and hollow victory. Just as the government lurched into a period of uncertainty, discord and imperial crisis, it needed decisive leadership. Britain needed William Pitt, but all it had in his place was Lord Chatham.

8

'The Apple of Discord'

January 1767–June 1769

His Majesty's character, then, after all the pains which have been
taken to make him odious as well as contemptible, remains unim-
peached; and therefore cannot be in any degree the cause of the
present commotions.[1]
John Wesley, 'The Present State of Public Affairs', December 1768

When George Adams the Elder, the mathematical instrument maker and
optician, presented his book *A Treatise Describing the Construction and
Explaining the Use of New Celestial and Terrestrial Globes* to the King in
1766, 'His Majesty looked over the dedication, and said, "This is not your
writing." "No, Sire," replied Adams, "it was composed for me by Dr Johnson." "I thought so," answered the King; "it is excellent – and the better
for being void of flattery, which I hate."'[2] What Samuel Johnson had
written – but which somehow did not count as flattery in the eighteenth
century – was that when the King 'revolves the terraqueous globe', he
must, 'consider, as oceans and continents are rolling before you, how large
a part of mankind is now waiting on your determinations, and may receive
benefits or suffer evils as your influence is extended or withdrawn'.[3] Yet it
was true that George disliked flattery; when a sycophantic priest hoping
for advancement extolled him during a service in the Chapel Royal, he
complained that he wanted to hear God praised in church, not himself.

Johnson was friendly with Frederick Barnard, the King's librarian at
Buckingham House, and told James Boswell that the collection there 'was
more numerous and curious than he supposed any person could have made
in the time which the King employed'.[4] When the King heard from Barnard
that the greatest public intellectual of the day used his library regularly, he
asked to be told when next he visited. In February 1767, while Johnson was
reading in a chair close to the fire, the King came in especially to see him.
They discussed a new edition of Polybius and the libraries of All Souls,

Christ Church and the Bodleian in Oxford, and the King told Johnson what a fine writer he was. When asked later by a friend whether he had replied to this compliment, Johnson replied, 'No, sir. When the King had said it, it was to be so. It was not for me to bandy civilities with my sovereign.'[5]

Johnson modestly informed the King that he had not read as much as Bishop William Warburton of Gloucester, whereupon the King replied that Warburton's learning 'resembled Garrick's acting in its universality'.[6] The two men then discussed a controversy between Warburton and Robert Lowth, Bishop of London, over Warburton's book *The Divine Legation of Moses*. George's conclusion was sound: 'Why truly, when once it comes to calling names, argument is pretty well at an end.' Their conversation then ranged over a wide variety of topics, including Lord Lyttelton's recently published biography of Henry II, Dr John Hill's experiments with microscopes, the *Journal des Savans* and other literary journals, and whether the *Monthly Review* was better than the *Critical Review*.

It was at that point that George suggested to Johnson that he might write a literary history of Britain, and it is not impossible that Johnson's great work of 1779, *The Lives of the Poets*, was at least in part inspired by the King. George clearly made an impression. 'Sir, they may talk of the King as they will,' Johnson said to Barnard after George had left, 'but he is the finest gentleman I have ever seen.'[7] Afterwards he went further, telling his friend Bennet Langton, 'Sir, his manners are those of as fine a gentleman as we may suppose Louis XIV or Charles II.'[8]

Dr Hill's microscopes were a subject upon which George was something of an authority. True to his Enlightenment principle of trying to understand and order nature through science, over the years the King amassed an enormous collection of scientific instruments including barometers, hygrometers, microscopes and orreries, as well as models of engines and steam pumps.* Only two months after coming to the throne, he commissioned George Adams to be the Royal Mathematical Instrument Maker, and to create high-quality, often beautifully ornate scientific instruments. Between 1761 and 1762, Adams built machines to perform experiments in pneumatics, mechanics, gravity, hydraulics, magnetism, optics and electricity and with pendulums. When Adams' assistant, John Miller, gave an air-pump demonstration to show that a guinea coin and a feather fall at the same rate when there is no air, Miller provided the feather for the experiment and the King supplied the guinea. 'At the conclusion, the King

---

* The King George III Collection of early scientific instruments at the London Science Museum has no parallel, comprising over a thousand instruments which were used for demonstrations in natural philosophy from the 1750s onwards (Morton and Wess, *Public and Private Science* p. v).

complimented the young man on his skills as an experimenter,' an eyewitness observed, 'but frugally returned the guinea to his waistcoat pocket.'[9]

If only political dynamics could be ordered as precisely as gravity in a glass. During Pitt's long absences through gout and mental illness, much of the day-to-day work of running the government fell to the Duke of Grafton, 'a weak, indolent and incapable man, unwilling to take decisions without Chatham's authority'.[10] Part of this unwillingness stemmed from Grafton's belief that he was constitutionally responsible only for his own department, the Treasury, and not for those of his Cabinet colleagues, who would have resented his interference.

While the gout-stricken Chatham languished in Marlborough on the way back from Bath in late February 1767,* his ministry had to contend with Opposition attacks, in particular Grenville's opportunistic demands for a cut in the land tax. This was easy point-scoring, and could always be depended upon as a way of stirring up the independent squirearchy who comprised the majority of MPs. Grenville had not forgotten about America, though, moving a motion to be debated 'That the troops to be kept up in America should be paid by the colonies respectively for whose defence and benefit they were employed.'[11]

In a letter to Grafton on 24 February, time-stamped with his usual accuracy at 9.55 a.m., the King wrote that he thought 'Mr Grenville's conduct [over public finances] is on this occasion as abundant in absurdities as in the affair of the Stamp Act; for there he first deprived the Americans by restraining their trade from the means of acquiring wealth, and then taxed them, now he objects to the public's availing itself of the only adequate means of restoring its finances.'[12] This has been described by one historian as 'the closest that George III ever came to sympathizing with the American contention that the economic restrictions of "the old colonial system" were equivalent to taxation and that it was therefore unfair for Britain to levy actual taxes as well'.[13] The King's hindsight was somewhat rose-tinted, for at the time of the passing of the Stamp Act he had been very much in its favour. Privately he could express exasperation with his government. Charles Cadogan MP, Surveyor of the King's Gardens, told Grenville that George 'had spoken with great peevishness to the Duke of York upon the . . . disorder amongst his ministers, saying one was in bed at Marlborough, and another in town with the piles [that is, haemorrhoids], and this was the way in which he was served'.[14]

---

* Dr Henry Addington, his physician and friend, gave Chatham the worst possible prescriptions for gout – alcohol, red meat and little exercise – which he hoped would induce fits of the condition and thereby somehow make it better (Black, *George III: American's Last King* p. 92).

Chatham returned to London on 2 March, although he remained incapable of attending an audience for another ten days. 'Now you are arrived in town every difficulty will daily decrease,' George wrote to Chatham, with an unusual excess of optimism.[15] Chatham replied gushingly that he counted 'every hour till he is able to attend His Majesty's most gracious presence', adding that he lacked the words 'to convey to His Majesty his duty, submission and devotion, and how deeply he is penetrated with the exceeding condescension and transcending goodness of His Majesty'.[16] In marked contrast with George's cheery prognosis, Chatham's difficulties only increased, however: gripped by morbid depression and bouts of extreme melancholy, the Prime Minister sat in his darkened room for hour after hour, unable to interact with the outside world. Extraordinarily, after their audience of 12 March 1767, the King would not see his Prime Minister again for another two years.

George was immensely, almost unbelievably, patient with Chatham, who was unable to write, telling him on 30 April that 'I am fully persuaded of your zeal and attachment to my service, and that nothing but the weight of your disorder prevents your taking the vigorous part your heart at all times prompts you to.'[17] Pitt's colleagues, however, unsurprisingly scented blood: Conway opposed Britain's conciliatory policy towards America, and both he and Charles Townshend undermined the government over reforms to the East India Company, the private corporation that ran British interests on the Indian subcontinent. Chatham meanwhile allowed Grafton to visit him only when the King specifically requested it. At the end of May, the Duke found Chatham's 'nerves and spirits ... affected to a dreadful degree', yet still George could not insist on his resignation, as he felt Grafton was too insubstantial a figure to take over and there was no one else to whom he felt he could make an approach.[18] The combination of an absent Chatham and an indolent Grafton was considered better than having a prime minister from the Opposition, despite the fact that the situation in America was worsening once again.

The Massachusetts Assembly, having passed an Act compensating the victims of the Stamp Act riot violence, nonetheless also gave indemnity to the rioters, which was clearly at odds with the solely royal power of pardon. On 13 May, the Privy Council ordered that the whole Act be repealed, and the Governor of Massachusetts was instructed to obtain a separate Act of compensation for the victims. The King personally attended the meeting, in order to give it more force.[19] Sympathy for the Americans and the weakness of the ministry meant that normally healthy majorities in the Lords had dropped to just six, and even down to three in late May, despite George having 'made two of my brothers vote on both those days'.[20]

In Chatham's absence, Charles Townshend emerged as the most energetic minister in the ministry, with the task of trying to plug a large gap in
the public finances caused by the reduction in the land tax. In June he
proposed that a series of light duties should be imposed on American
imports of lead, glass, paper, dyestuffs, painters' colours and tea, which he
believed might raise around £40,000 per annum in North America. Townshend's proposed duties should have been uncontroversial: they were
external tariffs, collected at the seaports, unlike the internal stamp tax
collected throughout the colonies.[21] The taxes were intended to defray the
costs of civil government there, so that judges, previously reliant for their
salaries on the colonial assemblies, would be independent, thereby allowing
them to enforce the new trade regulations and duties without fear of
retribution.

The Townshend Duties passed the Commons easily, receiving royal
assent on 2 July. Chatham expressed little interest in the problem: indeed,
in a sense he had in part allowed it, since he had initially opposed having
a separate American Department that might coordinate policy and engage
with the colonial administrations. He failed to give any central direction
to the ministry, offered no vision for America's place within the empire and
contributed nothing positive to the debate. The colonial response to the
Townshend Duties over the summer of 1767 was to adopt a series of 'non-
importation agreements', effective trade boycotts that saw British exports
to the colonies fall by half. Such agreements also served the interests of
established Boston merchants, many of whom made good returns from
smuggling the goods being taxed.

'Easy credit from Britain had glutted Boston with manufactured goods
and had tripled the number of the city's shopkeepers who moonlighted as
importers,' notes one historian. 'Non-importation gave more established
merchants a chance to restrict supply, sell off inventory, and thin out the
ranks of their rivals.'[22] They were occasionally embarrassed, however, when
pro-British Loyalist newspapers printed the ships' manifests of professed
non-importers. The leading radical John Hancock, for example, was
revealed to have brought five bales of fine British linen into Boston four
months after the non-importation agreement. Any Boston importers who
refused to sign the non-importation agreement had their windows smashed
and shop signs, doors and business premises daubed with faeces (a slurry
later nicknamed 'Hillsborough Paint' after the First Lord of Trade, Lord
Hillsborough).[23] Customs agents continued to be intimidated, beaten and
hanged or burned in effigy, and officials who seized a smuggling sloop
belonging to Hancock were promptly stoned.

For a whole year, while Massachusetts was boycotting British produce and radicalization was taking hold in other colonies, Chatham remained as an hermitical First Minister. Grafton, recognizing that it was too weak to continue without Chatham's physical presence, wanted to reconstruct the ministry by bringing in one of the Opposition factions, but he failed to entice anyone before the summer recess. George wrote to Chatham on 25 June, 'I am thoroughly resolved to encounter any difficulties rather than yield to faction,' adding that if the Prime Minister could 'cast aside any remains of your late indisposition' he would 'raise the reputation of your own political life in times of inward faction even above it in the late memorable war'.[24] This was either a great compliment, showing how far the King had come round to Chatham, or else a challenge to his patriotism and sense of duty. George was certainly not above taking either approach as a means of motivating his ministers to do their job.

Chatham replied five hours later from his London house in North End to say that his health was so bad 'as renders at present application of mind totally impossible', adding in his customary flowery prose, 'May I be permitted to prostrate myself at Your Majesty's feet and most humbly implore Your Majesty's indulgence and compassion not to require of a most devoted unfortunate servant what in his state of weakness he has not the power to trace, with the least propriety, for Your Majesty's consideration, the very few words my state of nerves enables me to offer ...' He eventually got round to saying that he believed his ministry would prosper only so long as Grafton stayed on as First Lord of the Treasury.[25]

George was unconvinced, and a week later implored Chatham 'to lay before me a plan and also to speak to those you shall propose for the most responsible offices; you owe this to me, to your country, and to those who have embarked in administration with you.'[26] Within a year of becoming Prime Minister, Chatham had thrown away all the advantages he had initially enjoyed, except for the King's support, and had left the nation adrift at a critical point in its history.

On 4 September 1767, Charles Townshend, the caretaker of the Chatham ministry, died suddenly of a fever at the age of just forty-two. In retrospect, it would have been the ideal time to repeal his disastrous duties, and bury the furore along with its creator. Instead, two days later Frederick, Lord North, was appointed Chancellor of the Exchequer, and signalled his commitment to continue them. North had been a lord of the Treasury from 1759 to 1765, and was considered to be a good financier (except with regard to his own money, his management of which was a disaster). Perhaps surprisingly for someone who was later to become a byword for political failure, Lord North was a respected and popular figure in the Commons, a good debater with an agreeable, self-effacing character. 'He was a witty, fair-minded man not prone to mean-spirited or egotistical behaviour in the House,' is one historian's accurate summation.[27] Charm is a notoriously hard thing to describe, but North was clearly suffused with it. 'If they turned out Lord North tomorrow,' Edward Gibbon wrote of him in 1775, 'they would still leave him one of the best companions in the kingdom.'[28] Along with his patience and willingness to suffer (pro-government) fools gladly, his charm was an important contribution to his skill as a superb manager of the Commons.

Ungainly, sometimes unkempt and in later life increasingly heavy-set, with a tongue thought too large for his mouth and with slightly protruding eyes, North was memorably caricatured by Horace Walpole:

> Nothing could be more coarse or clumsy or ungracious than his outside. Two large prominent eyes that rolled to no purpose (for he was utterly short-sighted), a wide mouth, thick lips and inflated visage gave him the air of a blind trumpeter. A deep untuneable voice, which, instead of modulating, he enforced with unnecessary pomp, a total neglect of his person, and ignorance of every civil attention, disgusted all who judged by appearance ... But within that rude casket were enclosed many useful talents. He had much wit, good humour, strong natural sense, assurance and promptness, both of conception and elocution.[29]

Compared with Bute's slender features, North was undeniably a great deal more earthy; and Walpole's depiction would not have caused offence.

North had been christened Frederick in honour of his godfather the Prince of Wales, who had been a friend of his father the 1st Earl of Guilford. Lord Guilford had been George's tutor for two years, and Prince Frederick had presented the family with an obelisk in the grounds of the North family estate, Wroxton Abbey in Oxfordshire. Although he was six years older, North had known George since childhood. George and North even looked alike, so much so that a persistent rumour in both the press and Parliament was that Prince Frederick was North's biological father, making them half-brothers. Satirical prints often depicted the King and North dressed identically, with exact facial likenesses. That Prince Frederick himself had regularly joked about the rumour with Lord Guilford suggests it is unlikely to have been true, but, since the Countess of Guilford was dead, there was no opportunity to sue for libel.[30]

Certainly, when they grew up, North was part of George's close-knit group of friends, along with Lord Dartmouth, North's stepbrother, and Dartmouth's brother-in-law 'Jemmy' Brudenell, a King's Friend and Master of the Robes. All these had happy marriages and were believing and prac-tising Anglicans, which further attracted them to the King and Queen.

North was to be the first Prime Minister since Bute whom George genuinely both liked and admired, but their friendship was to contribute to the single greatest national disaster to befall their country since the loss of her Angevin provinces in the fifteenth century.

On 6 September 1766, Prince William Henry, Duke of Gloucester, the King's brother, had married in secret the beautiful Maria, Countess Waldegrave. He had been nineteen when he fell in love with her in 1762 while she was married to the 2nd Earl Waldegrave, George's former governor, who died the following year. Maria was the illegitimate daughter of Sir Edward Walpole (Horace Walpole's elder brother) and his mistress, Dorothy Clement, a Durham girl whose father sold brooms on the Yorkshire moors, and whom Sir Edward had 'fairly beckoned in from the top of a cinder cart'.[31]

Although Prince William's wedding to Maria was conducted in secret for fear of the King and Queen's reaction to what they would certainly consider a *mésalliance*, the society gossip Lady Mary Coke knew all about it by the following January, when she was nonetheless assured by Colonel George West, the Prince's equerry, that it was certainly not true, 'for that he was sure the Duke of Gloucester was incapable of deceiving the King'.[32] In fact Gloucester was perfectly capable of deceiving his brother for another six years, and was only finally forced to tell him the truth when he needed money.

A year after William's secret wedding, George's twenty-eight-year-old brother Prince Edward, the Duke of York, died in Monaco of unknown causes, which Walpole put down to 'his immoderate pursuit of pleasure and unremitted fatigues in travelling', neither of which should really have proved fatal.[33] He had been out of favour with the King, and had supported Bedford's faction, but nonetheless had been George's closest childhood friend. 'The King was most seriously grieved for the loss of his brother,' a contemporary observed, 'and literally almost cried his eyes out.'[34] Two months later, when George and Charlotte's fourth son was born he was christened Edward.

The Bedford faction was brought into the government in December 1767. Even though they amounted to no more than around twenty MPs in the Commons, this gave the ministry some much needed stability before the general election that had to be held before March 1768. It meant that two important faction members received Cabinet places: Thomas Thynne, 3rd Viscount Weymouth, and Granville Leveson-Gower, Earl Gower. Weymouth provides an example of how George sometimes did change his mind about people; he had once despised him for his purported indolence and a youth characterized by heavy drinking and gambling; but he subsequently came to appreciate his other qualities, and in 1789 he made him the 1st Marquess of Bath.

'Your name has been sufficient to enable my administration to proceed,' George told Chatham in January 1768.[35] Proceed, perhaps, but not to succeed. Without a leader able to appear in public or Parliament, ministers had no direction, especially over North American policy. This became yet more conspicuous in February 1768 when the Massachusetts House of Representatives adopted Samuel Adams' petition against the Townshend Acts, declaring that they infringed the rights of the King's American subjects. The motion was sent to the other colonial assemblies, in what was called the Massachusetts Circular Letter, which received a worryingly positive response.

One overdue reform that the Chatham administration did finally undertake in February was to set up a new department of state to conduct Britain's relations with her colonies, under a dedicated secretary of state. The Colonial Office was carved out of the Southern Department and given to Wills Hill, 1st Earl of Hillsborough. This was done in part to take the management of American affairs out of the hands of Shelburne, who was considered too conciliatory. As Chatham would perhaps have recognized had he been active, Hillsborough was the wrong man for the job, because he was a hardliner opposed to all concessions to the Americans. Almost as soon as he entered the new Colonial Office riots broke out in Boston in March, leading the customs commissioners there to request troops to be sent to restore order. In April Hillsborough ordered the colonial governors to direct their respective assemblies to ignore the 'dangerous and factious' Massachusetts Circular Letter or be dissolved. He also ordered Massachusetts itself to rescind it. When in July its Assembly refused this demand by a vote of 92 to 17, Governor Sir Francis Bernard prorogued it, leading to an outpouring of solidarity from many of the other colonial legislatures. Lines were hardening on all sides.

Just as the best brains in the Chatham ministry ought to have been concentrating on these issues, John Wilkes, having run out of money but still under criminal indictment in England, returned from France, announcing, 'I must raise a dust or starve in a gaol.'[36] He started raising dust by sending a letter to Buckingham House on 4 March, asking the King for a royal pardon. Unusually for someone so punctilious in his correspondence, but in this case sensibly, George did not answer. When Parliament was dissolved a week later, Wilkes stood in the subsequent general election despite having officially been declared an outlaw, hoping that if he were elected again the Chathamites, whom he had never opposed and who tended to be the most tolerant of him, might not pursue him further.

The continuing economic downturn, with its attendant high food prices, unemployment and strikes leading to rioting and unrest, boded well for Wilkes, the ultimate anti-establishment candidate. On 28 March he was elected for Middlesex, amid scenes of mass voter-intimidation by his supporters. With its large number of voters and close proximity to London, Middlesex was considered the senior county in terms of political influence. 'It is really an extraordinary event to see an outlaw and an exile,' wrote Benjamin Franklin, 'of bad personal character, not worth a farthing . . . carrying it for the principal county.'[37] Bute's and Egmont's windows were smashed by a mob wearing blue cockades in celebration of Wilkes' victory, while the Austrian Ambassador suffered the curious indignity of being manhandled from his coach and having '45' chalked on the soles of his shoes.

In the view of one historian of the Chatham ministry, Wilkes' victory 'raised fierce party conflict and gave new life to what had seemed a dying Opposition', after the exit of the Bedford faction to join the government.[38] It was true that Wilkes was immensely popular; more than twelve medals were struck glorifying him in this period, depicting No. 45, liberty caps and so on.[39]* The King carried himself with dignity during the Wilkesite troubles, even though he was regularly hooted at and booed on his way to the House of Lords to give royal assent to Bills. 'He carried himself so', Lord Holland wrote later, 'that it was hard to know whether he was concerned or not. A lord who is near him told me that after the great riot at St James's, or rather in the midst of it, you could not find out, either in his countenance or his conversation, that everything was not quiet as usual.'[40] On another occasion, when George was in the audience at the Theatre Royal, Drury Lane, and it was announced that the play to be performed the next night would be one entitled *All in the Wrong*, members of the audience hooted at him and called out, 'Wilkes and Liberty!'[41] Meanwhile, a boot and petticoat were hanged on a gibbet and paraded down Cornhill in the City of London.

George was irritated by the way Grafton had left London for Newmarket during the disturbances – or, as one newspaper put it, had escaped to 'a rural retirement and . . . the arms of a faded beauty', the celebrated courtesan Nancy Parsons.[42] Lord Chancellor Camden (the former Sir

---

* It was a sign of his popularity that medal minters knew these would sell to the public, although it did not require an earth-shattering moment for a medal to be struck – there was one for Prince Frederick's elevation to the bishopric of Osnabrück in 1764, another for the opening of the Armagh Library in 1771, and even one in 1777 celebrating the Chevalier d'Éon's transgenderism.

Charles Pratt) had decided instead on Bath. Despite these absences, the King was kept closely informed of plans to provide troops from the Guards' depots at the Tower of London, Savoy House and the Tiltyard in Whitehall should the civilian magistrates need them. If more were required, he was assured by Lord Barrington, the Secretary at War, that 'Immediate orders will be issued for that purpose.'[43] When he was warned that the mob might march on Buckingham House itself, he replied 'that he wished they would push their insolence so far; he should then be justified in repelling it, and giving proper orders to the Guards' (by which, presumably, he meant shoot to kill).[44]

Wilkes officially surrendered himself to the Court of King's Bench on 20 April, ostentatiously waiving his parliamentary immunity – which in any case had already been denied him – and was fined £1,000 and sentenced to twenty-two months' imprisonment, although the House of Lords' outlawing of him was overturned. He was spared the pillory, almost certainly because the judges knew that he would only have been feted by the crowd. At his trial Wilkes had, in the King's words to Lord North, 'declared No. 45 a paper that the author ought to *glory in*, and the blasphemous poem a mere *ludicrous production*', so George supported the government's decision to expel Wilkes from the Commons, despite his being the very recent choice of Middlesex's electors.[45]

'The expulsion of Mr Wilkes appears to be very essential and must be effected,' George wrote on 25 April, adding that he expected the House to act with 'the required unanimity and vigour'.[46] He cited the precedent of John Ward, an MP who had been expelled from the Commons in 1726 for forgery. With the food, wages and Wilkesite riots continuing, and a march of 4,000 unemployed merchant seamen in the offing, the King wanted a tough government response. 'If a due firmness is shown with regard to this audacious criminal,' he wrote to Lord Weymouth, the minister directly responsible for dealing with the disorder, 'this affair will prove a fortunate one, by restoring a due obedience to the laws. But if this is not the case, I fear anarchy will continue till what every temperate man must dread, *I mean an effusion of blood*, has vanquished.'[47] As a permanent police force was not established in England until 1829, large-scale policing had to be carried out by the army, and the King complained of the lack of troops available for magistrates 'in these very licentious days'.[48] 'Bloodshed is not what I delight in,' he told Weymouth, truthfully, 'but it seems to me the only way of restoring a due obedience to the laws.'[49]

The Wilkes issue, which had always had elements of *opéra bouffe* over the previous five years – despite the important questions it raised about freedom of speech, general arrest warrants and parliamentary immunity – descended into genuine tragedy on the morning of 10 May 1768, when a crowd numbering 15,000 gathered in St George's Fields next to the King's Bench Prison in Southwark, where Wilkes was imprisoned. There were cries of 'Wilkes and Liberty!', 'No Liberty, No King!' and 'Damn the King, Damn the Government!' The disturbances led the local magistrates to read the Riot Act and call up a troop of horse grenadiers to assemble in front of the prison, in case the crowd tried to storm it to release the prisoner. After some soldiers had chased a man who had been taunting them into the outhouse of the Horseshoe Inn, the publican's son was shot dead, possibly by mistake, whereupon the crowd's mood turned much uglier and more troops were called up. When these were pelted with stones, some of them fired their muskets and pandemonium ensued. The number of dead remains unknown, but might have been as many as seven or eight, with several dozen injured.[50]

The situation in London over the next few days was febrile. In Lady Mary Coke's account, 'a very great mob assembled in St James's Park, and they once talked of pulling down the Queen's Palace,* but fortunately they changed their minds.'[51] Posters were to be found on walls around the capital on 15 May threatening that if the King continued to persecute Wilkes, 'not all his Guards should protect him'.[52] In the middle of this political tumult, the King and Queen also had to deal with a crushing personal tragedy when that same day Princess Louisa, the King's nineteen-year-old sister, died of tuberculosis after a fever lasting thirteen days. She was the fourth of the King's eight siblings to have died in the past decade, and the royal couple went into mourning together, as violent rioting continued intermittently through the rest of May. On the 25th striking coal-heavers attacked blackleg seamen, who responded with equal violence, resulting, as the *Annual Register* put it, in 'the loss of many lives'.[53]

Violence was rife in America, too. June 1768 saw the Board of Customs in Boston attacked by mobs, leaving customs officials there demanding troops for protection. John Hancock's ship *Liberty* was seized for violating the trade laws, prompting further vicious and prolonged rioting. On 22 July, Lord Hillsborough sent the King the latest dispatches from Virginia, which he said were 'still more alarming than those from Massachusetts Bay'.[54] He warned 'that it is very probable Your Majesty may have occasion for five or six ships of war and a body of marines on very short notice and . . . that they do prepare accordingly'.

Three days later, the people of Providence, Rhode Island, gathered

---

* That is, Buckingham House.

around a 'Tree of Liberty'* which was dedicated by Silas Downer, the acting Attorney-General. Adopting a phrase first coined by the British radical Whig MP Isaac Barré, Downer proclaimed himself a 'Son of Liberty', stating that 'We cheerfully recognize our allegiance to our sovereign lord, George the Third, King of Great Britain, and supreme lord of these dominions, but utterly deny any other dependence on the inhabitants of that island than what is mutual and reciprocal between all mankind.'[55] That summer, Boston and New York merchants agreed to impose non-importation from Britain until the Townshend Duties were repealed, and on 1 October large numbers of British troops arrived in Boston. Yet neither these events nor the many protests or acts of violence in both North America and Britain succeeded in stirring Lord Chatham from his sickbed.

On 12 October 1768 Chatham finally asked the King to be allowed to resign the premiership on health grounds, employing some characteristically flowery language: 'May I be allowed at the same time to offer to His Majesty my deepest sense of His Majesty's long, most humane, and most gracious indulgence towards me, and to express my ardent prayers for His Majesty.'[56] When the King asked him to stay on (politely, if not entirely earnestly), Chatham replied two days later by asking for 'compassion', adding, 'My health is so broken that I feel all chance of recovery will be entirely precluded by my continuing to hold the Privy Seal, totally disabled as I still am from assisting in Your Majesty's councils.'[57] Chatham promised the King to support the government, but this was to be the last letter he ever wrote him, and he had a bad record of supporting governments which he did not lead.

George now had to try to reconfigure a new ministry in which the King's Friends, Tories, Bedfordites and Chathamite remnant could somehow remain in power. Although Chatham had taken no part in active politics since March 1767, Grafton had hitherto only ever thought of himself as being acting premier, since he knew he possessed none of Chatham's authority or charisma, and he now refused to do anything more than chair the Cabinet, instead of actively leading it as a normal prime minister would. North became Leader of the House of Commons, a post he held alongside that of Chancellor of the Exchequer.

In his Speech from the Throne on 8 November, George told the assembled parliamentarians, 'The spirit of faction had broken out afresh in some of the colonies, and, in one of them, proceeded to acts of violence and resistance to the execution of the laws ... Boston was in a state of

---

* Trees of Liberty were generally trees that were suitably decorated, while Liberty Poles were moveable like maypoles, erected in public places; both provided opportunities for speechifying.

disobedience to all law and government, and had proceeded to measures subversive of the Constitution, and attended with circumstances that manifested a disposition to throw off their dependence on Great Britain.'[58] The government won the Debate on the Address, and the Grafton ministry was safe, at least in the short term.

On the same day that the King opened Parliament, Charlotte gave birth to their sixth child, Augusta. While she was in labour, which lasted only ninety minutes, Dr William Hunter, assuming the King wanted another son, said, 'I think, Sir, whoever sees those lovely princes above stairs must be glad to have another.' 'Doctor Hunter,' the King replied, 'I did not think I could have been angry with you, but I am; and I say, whoever sees that lovely child the Princess Royal above stairs must wish to have the fellow to her.'[59]

On 21 November 1768, the first in a long series of anonymous attacks on George and the Grafton ministry appeared in the *Public Advertiser* newspaper, penned under the pseudonym of 'Junius'. These quickly became a sensation, not only for their elegant aphorisms and harsh personal invective, but also because they were clearly by a political insider. The wide readership of what became known as 'The Letters of Junius' speculated endlessly about their author's identity, as did their victims, and indeed it has still not been established beyond all doubt to this day who wrote them. Junius seemed to know things that only senior government figures could have, such as the statement in the Letter of 30 May 1769 that Lord Shelburne had not been supported in Cabinet over threatening France after her invasion of Corsica.

Published in the form of long letters to Henry Woodfall, the printer of the *Public Advertiser*, to whom they were delivered anonymously and untraceably, the Letters attacked Grafton, Bedford, Granby, Mansfield and many other important public figures. Three years later, almost to the day, they suddenly ceased, after sixty-nine letters had been published that had shaken the British political world, and they never resumed. A huge amount of scholarly work – known as 'Junian studies' – has gone into trying to ascertain the author's identity, made all the harder because of disputes over graphology and over whether Junius might also have been other contemporary letter writers and pamphleteers who used noms de plume such as 'Scaevola', 'Zeno', 'An Advocate in the Cause of the People' and 'A Barrister-at-Law'.

In 1908, the biographer Charles Pownall confidently claimed that his ancestor Thomas, the Massachusetts Governor and later MP, had been Junius. Half a century later, computer analysis of the stylistic patterns used

concluded that Junius was most likely the Dublin-born War Office administrator Philip Francis, a friend of Burke who was to become a radical Whig
MP from 1784 to 1806. If so, Francis' libels against the King showed
particular ingratitude: his father, the classical translator Dr Philip Francis,
had been 'kindly noticed' by the King, who had given him a £300 per
annum English pension for life, as well as a £600 per annum Irish equivalent, in acknowledgement of his scholarship.[60]

While it is important not to attribute to the writer of a deliberately
inflammatory series of anonymous letters the status of spokesman for
public opinion, the enormous and immediate success of the Letters was an
indication that Junius' views were shared by at least a part of the newspaper-
buying public, and they constituted a rare printed list of the complaints
against the King.

Junius wrote under the motto 'Stat nominis umbra' (the shadow of a
great name), which might just have been a reference to Marcus Junius
Brutus. Junius wanted Lord Chatham, who had once employed Francis
and who returned to the House of Lords in February 1769, to try to take
back the premiership from Grafton. A particular target was Lord Hillsborough, whom he accused of pushing Massachusetts towards rebellion, and
whose memoranda were described as 'strong assertions without proof,
declamation without argument, and violent censures without dignity or
moderation; but neither correctness in the composition, nor judgement in
the design'.[61] Taken together, Junius' allegations and accusations against
senior figures within the Grafton ministry seriously undermined their reputation. Those who believe that Francis was Junius – they are known as
Franciscans – explain that Junius attacked his department head Lord Barrington in public, while thanking him profusely in private for his kindness
and offers of support, because he needed to protect his cover, and anyhow
great writers can also be great hypocrites.[62]

Over the centuries, no fewer than forty-eight people have been seriously
advanced as having been Junius, comprising almost a 'who's who' of mid-
to late eighteenth-century politicians and men of letters. The list includes
Lord Shelburne (unlikely, since he was attacked in the Letters), Lord George
Sackville, General Charles Lee (who actually claimed to have been Junius
on one occasion), John Dunning MP, the Duke of Portland (on very flimsy
evidence), Colonel Isaac Barré MP, Earl Temple, Edmund Burke,* Chatham
(highly unlikely, as he was incapacitated and Junius wrote private letters

---

* Burke denied his authorship to Dr Johnson, saying, 'I could not if I would, and I would not
if I could,' which is, however, just the kind of epigram with which the Letters of Junius are
replete (ed. Everett, *Letters of Junius* p. 383).

to him), John Wilkes (to whom Junius also wrote letters), the Bishop of Hereford, Horace Walpole (both alone and in conjunction with the poet William Mason), John Kent ('a hack writer who wished to pass for Junius'), John Horne Tooke (who pretended he wrote them, despite being ridiculed in them), Lord Camden, Lord Lyttelton, Thomas Paine (who was an excise-man in Lewes at the time), Alexander Wedderburn (who was viciously attacked in them), Henry Grattan (who pointed out that he was twenty-two and living in Ireland when they were written), George Grenville (who died before they ended), William Greatrakes (Shelburne's private secretary, whose headstone reads 'Stat nominis umbra'), Philip Francis' father and Edward Gibbon.[63] Virtually the only major figure of the era who has not been promoted as Junius is King George III himself. As with Jack the Rip-per, when the Last Trump is sounded the Junius who steps forward will probably be someone whom no one has even considered.

On Monday 28 November 1768, an architect and three painters visited the King at St James's Palace to ask him to establish a new professional society for 'the arts of design', one which it was hoped would not be sub-ject to the same chronic infighting that plagued both the Society of Arts and the Incorporated Society of Artists, and which would be actuated by the belief that painting had a moral and didactic purpose.[64] They were a distinguished quartet, led by Sir William Chambers and including the Penn-sylvanian Quaker artist Benjamin West, Francis Cotes (who had painted the Queen) and the Swiss painter George Michael Moser. Less than a fort-night later, on 10 December, George approved the Instrument of Foundation of the Royal Academy, established without a charter but merely by the King's signature and with his personal support, meaning that the govern-ment would not be in any way involved in it, which remains the case to this day. 'The Royal Academy is not funded by, and thus is not subject to, the State,' records its history emphatically: 'It is private.'[65] The monarch personally approved all of the appointments,* and George III signed no fewer than 111 Royal Academy documents during his lifetime, including obscure library rules such as that 'No person shall take more than two books under the penalty of one shilling,' and that only black lead pencils were to be allowed for tracing pictures or prints. He royally ordained that the Academy's sweeper was to be paid £10 a year.[66]

Chambers drafted the first statutes, which included stipulations that there should be a maximum of forty members (today there are 127), that it should teach (which it still does) and that it should hold an annual

---

* The monarch still has to approve those of the President and Secretary today.

exhibition (which it also still does). George wrote out in his own hand a first draft of the diploma to be sent to Academicians:

> Whereas We have thought fit to establish in this our city of Westminster for the purpose of cultivating and improving the arts of painting, sculpture and architecture under [the] name and title of the Royal Academy of Arts, and under our own immediate patronage and protection, and whereas We have resolved to entrust the sole management and direction of the said society under us unto forty Academicians, the most able and respectable* artists resident in Great Britain, We therefore in consideration of your great skill in the Arts do by these presents constitute and appoint you to be one of our said Royal Academy by granting unto you all the honours, privileges and emoluments thereof according to the tenor of the institution.[67]

The Academy was initially housed in the print warehouse of the King's first librarian Richard Dalton in Pall Mall, and met about once a month. It boasted a small but active staff, and it soon hosted its first annual summer exhibition there, which the King and Queen attended, and which by 1780 generated enough income that George no longer had to subsidize it. Until then he had spent £5,116 supporting it. The first summer exhibition in May 1769 featured 136 paintings, including four by Sir Joshua Reynolds, the foremost portraitist of the day, and it soon became the leading contemporary art exhibition in London. Reynolds was appointed the Academy's first President and was knighted that April. (His close friend Dr Johnson had been completely teetotal for a decade, but on that occasion he raised a glass to celebrate.) The King did not much like Reynolds, whom he found pompous, but he recognized his pre-eminent claim, while ensuring that Chambers became Secretary of the Academy, and Benjamin West succeeded as President after Reynolds' death in 1792.

The Royal Academy was a training school for artists, with a large gold medal awarded annually for each of the three disciplines of architecture, painting and sculpture until 1772, and biennially thereafter until 1936. In 1780, the King moved the Academy into purpose-built premises designed by Chambers at Somerset House on the Strand, which also included a number of government buildings and was to be the largest single building undertaken at public expense in the whole Georgian era, being finally completed in 1796.

In 1771, George had the Academy's founder members painted by Johan Zoffany, who included himself in the bottom left of the canvas. Among the others portrayed were Reynolds, Chambers, Wilton, Giovanni Cipriani

---

* Meaning worthy of 'regard, attention' rather than of 'reverend character' (*Johnson's Dictionary*).

(who had painted the State Coach), Benjamin West and Richard Wilson (who offended the King's honour by offering to be paid in instalments, and was never asked to paint for him again). Two female artists, Mary Moser and Angelica Kauffman, were appointed Academicians at the founding, which was a radical step for the time. Kauffman exhibited no fewer than seventy-nine works at the Academy and Moser thirty-six, but disappointingly the precedent set in George III's reign was not followed, and the next female Academician to be elected was Laura Knight in 1936.

The Royal Academy became a jewel of the British Enlightenment, but it was initially controversial, and unpopular with its rivals, at least in part because of the King's patronage. The Wilkesite *Middlesex Journal* attacked George for setting it up. 'You disdain, Sir,' it complained, 'to mingle your royal favour with the vulgar, the honest, ardent wishes of the people, in support of the Society of Artists of Great Britain, and therefore instituted the Royal Academy, so that the plumes of prerogative might wave in triumph over the cap of liberty.'[68] The Academy was indeed an elite, and unashamedly so. In January 1770, Dr Johnson and Oliver Goldsmith were elected to its honorary chairs in ancient literature and ancient history respectively, with Dalton as its 'Antiquary'. As there were no duties or stipends for these posts but only a good dinner once a year, Goldsmith quipped that it was 'like ruffles to a man who has no shirt'.[69]

The King continued to take a close personal interest in the Academy's affairs for as long as he was of sound mind. In July 1791 he struck out its proposal to subscribe one hundred guineas from the Academical Fund towards a monument to Samuel Johnson in St Paul's Cathedral (the Doctor had died in 1784), not from any hostility to Johnson's memory but because he believed the money was 'only to be applicable to the purposes of the Royal Academy'.[70] He simultaneously approved James Boswell's appointment as the Secretary for Foreign Correspondence. He intervened when the painter Robert Smirke* was put up as Keeper in February 1804, writing tersely, 'Rejected. Proceed to a new Election.'[71] Smirke had been elected an Academician in February 1793, served as a Visitor (that is, teacher) in 1794 and sat on the Council in 1795 without attracting the King's ire, but by 1800 he was openly praising Britain's wartime enemy Napoleon Bonaparte and denouncing the institution of monarchy as 'the effect of a corrupt society'.[72] George has been criticized for putting politics before art, but the surprising thing was that Smirke wanted to hold office in an academy that

---

* Not to be confused with his son of the same name, himself a Royal Academician architect, who designed the British Museum, the Royal Mint and the Green Park tableau for the centenary of the Hanoverian succession in 1814.

was so intimately connected with, and indeed owed its genesis to, the very institution he professed to despise.

The King's most significant intervention in the running of the Royal Academy came in May 1803 when its General Assembly of all the Academicians clashed with the Council over who was to control its teaching arm. George wrote that 'His Majesty disapproves of the conduct of the General Body of the Royal Academy censuring and suspending some of the members of the Council, viz John Singleton Copley, James Wyatt, John Yenn, John Soane and Sir Francis Bourgeois, and therefore directs that all matters relating to these proceedings shall be expunged from the minutes.'[73] In June he wrote with similar terseness, 'His Majesty, finding that the communications made by him to the Royal Academy early in the last month has not been clearly understood, finds it necessary to convey his sentiments in a manner that will prevent any misunderstanding in future.'[74]

The King's interest in neo-classical painting stemmed in part from his love of architecture, imbibed from Chambers. In 1761 he admired a portrait by Nathaniel Dance-Holland entitled *Death of Virginia*, in which the daughter of a Roman centurion chooses death before sexual dishonour in a heavily Doric architectural setting. In 1765 George bought Holland's *Timon of Athens*, with its theme of putting self-sacrifice before financial reward and comfort, and four years later he commissioned Benjamin West to paint seven 'statement' paintings for the Warm Room of Buckingham House, mainly on the themes of heroic death and the magnanimity of victorious commanders. The King liked paintings that told uplifting stories. One of them, *The Departure of Regulus from the Senate and his Return to Carthage* (1769), showed the third-century BC Roman consul in a highly Doric senate house heroically going to his death. *The Death of General Wolfe* (1770), *The Death of Chevalier Bayard* (1772) and *The Death of Epaminondas* (1773) were all hung on one wall at Buckingham House. In 1769 George commissioned West to paint no fewer than thirty-five religious paintings for the extensive restoration of St George's Chapel, Windsor. Of the £34,187 that the King paid West between 1769 and 1801, no less than £21,705 was for pictures on religious subjects.[75]

By mid-December 1768 the situation in Boston had become so serious that two British regiments had to be sent there, and, through successive reinforcements thereafter, by the end of 1769 a total of 4,000 British troops were garrisoned in a city of 15,000 people. With nothing like enough space in barracks for that number, it became necessary to billet soldiers in private homes for payment. It has been alleged that this enormous military presence proves that the British government were intent on war as early as

1768, but, as the historian Nicholas Rodger points out, 'Police action to restore order among Englishmen was what they contemplated; it is quite anachronistic to think in terms of two different nations going to war.'[76] This situation was to last for another five years. The King wrote to Grafton in mid-December that he hoped the government's policy towards the American colonists would display the 'desire with temper to let them return to their reason, not with violence to drive them'.[77] These were not the words of a warmonger.

It is clear from the King's voluminous correspondence in the years following the Stamp Act's repeal that the problems of American taxation and the future loyalty of the North American colonists struggled to compete for his attention with what appeared to be equally pressing domestic political issues. Keeping Grenville out of power, Wilkes (who was elected a City alderman in January 1769) out of the Commons, Parliament out of the royal finances and the French out of the West and East Indies all laid claims upon the King's time, often to the exclusion of simmering issues across the Atlantic. With the benefit of hindsight, we can of course see that the King and his ministers were prioritizing their many crises unwisely. Questions over reforming the East India Company occupied more time and space than those of America, for example, but that was not surprising: the government still firmly believed that the disturbances in Massachusetts were merely the work of a small group of Sons of Liberty radicals, rather than symptomatic of a wider discontent across the colonies. It was a fundamental error, and one to which the overly optimistic royal governors of the provinces contributed, instead of attempting to redress.

In February 1769 the news arrived that the merchants of Philadelphia had adopted the same non-importation agreements that their confederates in Massachusetts and New York had already declared in protest against the Townshend Duties. Ten days after Barrington's motion on Wilkes, Lord Hillsborough submitted a list of proposals to the Cabinet intended to resolve the Townshend Duties crisis. In the King's considered responses to these, written in a detailed memorandum, it is clear that he supported Grafton's conciliatory policies over America and opposed Hillsborough's much tougher proposals.[78] George's innate conservatism can be seen in his opinion that Hillsborough's proposal to assume the powers of the Massachusetts Bay Company 'ought to be avoided as the altering [of] charters is at all times an odious measure'.[79]

Against Hillsborough's proposal that all those assemblies which denied Parliament's supremacy should be abolished, George argued that it was 'of so strong a nature that it rather seems calculated to increase the unhappy feuds that subsist than to assuage them'.[80] When royal governors met their assemblies, he suggested, they should be 'instructed to avoid as much as possible giving occasion to the assemblies again coming on the Apple of Discord'.[81] The Golden Apple of Discord was tossed by the goddess Eris into the wedding feast of Peleus and Thetis, which led to the Trojan War. George clearly did not want the same thing to happen in Massachusetts. Indeed, he was keen to avoid confrontation and to grant concessions, so long as they did not make it seem that his government was being held to ransom. He suggested that any colony that agreed to implement the Townshend Duties 'may another year be exempted from every article of it except the tea duty'.[82] And if the Virginians had not been 'so offensive the last Spring' the government would have altered the Act in their favour during the last parliamentary session. It was not really until the Boston Tea Party four years later that George's stance significantly stiffened, because from then on any concession would have been visibly wrested from Britain rather than graciously accorded.

The King's exception of tea was an important one. Whereas taxes on glass, paper and so on applied to British manufactured goods, and thus increased their cost to the colonists, tea was 100 per cent re-exported from Asia, and thus from an economic perspective entirely different.[83] Whereas Britain would be affected positively if the other Townshend Duties were repealed, no domestic industry would be helped by the abolition of the tax on tea. If one duty had to be retained in order to uphold the principle of the right to tax, it was logical to choose tea.

George's accession proclamation about returning morality to public life was always likely to be a hostage to fortune, and this was sorely tested in early June when Grafton suggested Lord Sandwich as the next Viceroy of Ireland – the King's personal representative there. After stating that it might be too much to give a Bedfordite such a prestigious post, the King added, 'besides his character is so well known in both kingdoms that it would sully [the] administration . . . [I] cannot think his constant teasing can be sufficient grounds for placing him where his private character must disgrace me and [the] administration.'[84] Grafton himself had lived openly for several years with Nancy Parsons, and had only got divorced from his wife a few weeks earlier after she became pregnant by the Earl of Upper Ossory. We do not know how he took George's censoriousness, but three weeks later he married the daughter of the Dean of Worcester.

The King was not consistent in applying his moral strictures, even in the case of the Irish viceroyalty. Sandwich's cousin and close friend Lord Halifax had held the post from 1761 to 1763, and had brazenly taken his mistress Anna Maria Faulkner (by whom he had a daughter) with him to Dublin. Nine days after George's letter to Grafton about Sandwich, he allowed the great adventuress Elizabeth Chudleigh, who had previously been involved with the 6th Duke of Hamilton and others, to be presented at a Drawing Room after she married the 2nd Duke of Kingston. The snobbish Lady Mary Coke wrote, 'I was sorry to observe that His Majesty was as civil to the lady who calls herself Duchess of Kingston as he was to any of the ladies present.'[85] Lady Mary gossiped to her sister that 'The Queen behaved more properly and only just spoke to her,' even though Chudleigh had once been a maid of honour to Augusta, Princess of Wales. Everyone else there, Coke noted, had 'shown a proper dislike for a character so composed of guilt'. Had the King known quite how guilty she was, he would probably have not received Chudleigh, because in 1776 she was convicted of bigamy in front of 4,000 spectators at Westminster Hall, after it emerged that when she married Kingston she was in fact already married to Augustus Hervey, later 3rd Earl of Bristol.

The respectability that presentation at Court bestowed occasionally placed the King in awkward situations. Peers had the right to demand an audience with the monarch, and refusing it was a serious step. When Frederick Berkeley, 5th Earl of Berkeley, presented himself at St James's Palace in 1803, the King had to tell Charles Bragge, the Secretary at War, 'He is come, having demanded an audience, to press that Lady Berkeley may be received at Court. He has done so frequently before, but you know it is impossible.'[86] Bragge did indeed know, because he had been a Lincoln's Inn barrister on the Oxford Circuit in the late 1770s when Mary Cole, a publican's daughter, had been plying her trade as a 'common prostitute' in Worcester, where she had engaged in transactions with several of his fellow barristers, 'in houses of accommodation for such temporary amours'.

In 1796 Lord Berkeley nonetheless married Mary Cole and they had seven legitimate children together, but after his death in 1810 she claimed – in order to try to legitimize the six children she already had by him – that there had been an earlier marriage between them in 1785. The House of Lords found this earlier marriage to be fictitious, so the elder illegitimate sons were disbarred from succession to the earldom. Since the eldest legitimate son refused to impugn his mother's honour by petitioning for the title, it became dormant, and remained so until 1891. However indulgent he had been towards the notorious Duchess of Kingston back in 1769, the King did not receive Lady Berkeley at court in 1803, as there was then held to be a world of difference between Kingston, the daughter of the Lieutenant-Governor of the Royal Hospital, Chelsea, who had been a maid of honour to his mother since the age of five, and a former 'common prostitute'. As so often in eighteenth-century Britain, morality was highly tempered by considerations of class.

On 27 January 1769, as Parliament prepared to discuss the expulsion of Wilkes from the Commons, George wrote to the veteran courtier Lord Hertford to express his hope that he had directed his two sons in the Commons to vote in favour, 'for I should be sorry that anyone could say that in a measure whereon almost my Crown depends, his family should not have taken an active part'.[87] There was an element of royal hyperbole in this: George's crown did not in any sense genuinely depend on whether the MP for Middlesex was disbarred from the House of Commons. Nonetheless, the Seymour-Conway brothers duly supported the motion. The Commons voted 219 to 137 in favour of Lord Barrington's motion that Wilkes be expelled from the House, a decision confirmed five days later by the Lords by 169 votes to 69. 'Nothing could be more honourable for [the] government than the conclusion of the debate this morning,' the King jubilantly told North, 'and promises a very proper end of this irksome affair this day.'[88] Yet the government had failed to spot a glaring loophole, for nothing in the constitution prevented Wilkes from simply standing in the by-election that was forced by his own expulsion. Only Grenville foresaw that Wilkes would be re-elected for Middlesex, and there was nothing the supposedly tyrannical government could do about it.

On 16 February, Wilkes was re-elected for Middlesex without opposition, whereupon he was immediately, and somewhat farcically, re-expelled from the Commons. Five weeks later, on 22 March, an anti-Wilkes delegation to the King from 130 City aldermen and City of London gentlemen was set upon and pelted by a mob, only a dozen or so coaches making it through to St James's Palace. The Duchess of Douglas told Mary Coke:

> There had been a great mob, and a hearse had been drove up Pall Mall and stopped before Carlton House. On one side was painted the young man [William Allen, the innkeeper's son] who was killed in St George's Fields with the soldier firing at him; on the other, the figure of Liberty expiring. The mob had been very insolent, calling out 'Wilkes and No King', abusing all the merchants ... upon which the Guards were sent for, but the riot continued a long time thereafter ... 'Tis shocking to see how entirely the common people have lost their respect for the royal dignity.[89]

Even though seventeen arrests were made that day, there were no convictions. To George's chagrin, London juries tended to include enough

Wilkesites to ensure acquittals. 'If there is no means by law to quell riots,' the King complained to Lord North on 31 March, 'and if juries forget they are on their oath to be guided by facts not faction, this constitution must be overthrown, and anarchy (the most terrible of all evils) must ensue.'[90] He therefore wanted 'every honest man with vigour to stand forth . . . to give elasticity to the springs of government'. Grafton was certainly not a man of vigour or elasticity, but the King told North, 'Your zeal and firmness I know I can thoroughly rely on.'

Although Wilkes' first two re-elections for Middlesex had been unopposed, in April Grafton persuaded Colonel Henry Luttrell, an Irish-born Tory and the son of the Earl of Carhampton, to stand against him. Luttrell received only 296 votes to 1,143 for Wilkes, but nonetheless the Commons resolved two days later, by a vote of 197 to 143, that 'Henry Lawes Luttrell, Esq, ought to have been returned a member for Middlesex and not John Wilkes, Esq.' The King's stance during what he called 'this unpleasant business' was to support his government, since the Commons had the right to expel one of its members for blasphemy and sedition – just as Wilkes had every right to stand yet again for the vacant Middlesex seat, which he duly did. One of Wilkes' supporters was the twenty-year-old Charles James Fox, Lord Holland's younger son, who was then a moderate Whig.*

On 1 May, the nine-member Cabinet decided to repeal all the Townshend Duties except the one on tea, which was retained by a majority of five to four when the two King's Friends ministers, Northington and Hillsborough, joined with the Bedfordites Gower and Weymouth and the independent Rochford to outvote Grafton, Granby, Camden and Conway, who had been members of Chatham's original 1766 Cabinet.[91] It has been argued that it was the King's support for retaining the tea duty in February that was 'strongly influential' within the Cabinet, but there is no direct evidence of that.[92] It was just as likely that the five ministers opposed total repeal for the reason given at the time, as a symbol of Parliament's right to tax America – the one that would cost British merchants least – and because otherwise it would look as though they were capitulating to disturbances, tarring-and-feathering, boycotts and blackmail.[93]

On 13 May, Hillsborough sent a circular letter to the governors in America announcing that all the Townshend Duties except the one on tea were being dropped as 'contrary to the true principles of commerce'.[94] He untruthfully claimed that the Cabinet had been unanimous, and failed to include the emollient phrases that they had suggested he employ to placate

* Henceforth referred to merely as Charles Fox, as he was generally called Charles James Fox only after his death, in the first instance hagiographically.

the colonists. Grafton later blamed Hillsborough for the 'unfortunate and unwarrantable' language in the letter and attributed to it the 'mischief' that the retention of the tea duty would cause.[95] Later that month, the Virginia Assembly had to be dissolved after protesting about the removal of treason trials to Westminster, even though no such trials were contemplated. The issue of the Townshend Duties had clearly not been resolved, nor the colonies placated.

9

'That Factious and Disobedient Temper'

June 1769–April 1772

> *I do not pretend to any superior abilities, but will give place to no one in meaning to preserve the freedom, happiness and glory of my dominions and all their inhabitants, and to fulfil the duty to my God and to my neighbour in the most extended sense.*[1]
>
> George III, *c.* 1766

On 3 June 1769, a little over two weeks after witnessing a solar eclipse, George and Queen Charlotte observed the Transit of Venus – a silhouette for a few minutes as it passed across the face of the sun – from the King's Observatory in the Old Deer Park at Richmond. The Observatory had been designed especially for the event by Sir William Chambers and Dr Stephen Demainbray, and had been given to him by his mother as his thirty-first birthday present; it possessed a telescope with magnification of 170. Demainbray recorded that the King 'was the first who saw the penumbra of Venus touching the edge of the Sun's disc', the exact timing of which Demainbray recorded using John Shelton's Regulator clock.[2]

This exceptionally rare astronomical event – it has only happened four times since, in 1874, 1882, 2004 and 2012 – caught the King's imagination, because as the ratio of the distances to the sun, the earth and Venus was known, it became possible to calculate the size of the sun itself, and thus the dimensions of the solar system, by observing the Transit of Venus from different places on earth at known distances apart when the three bodies were all in alignment.[3] This was one of the reasons George had donated £4,000 to the Royal Society to support Captain James Cook's expedition to Tahiti, where the event was also observed by astronomers. When the expedition returned under budget, the Royal Society used the remaining funds to commission a bust of the King from Joseph Nollekens, which stands in its entrance hall today. George was an Enlightenment monarch, for whom scientific discovery mattered deeply.

The Observatory was used four years later for one of the most important experiments of the modern world. George had actively followed John Harrison's attempts to develop a clock accurate enough to establish longitude, and allowed his prototype H-5 timepiece to be tested at the Observatory. He also ensured that the Board of Longitude paid the octogenarian Harrison the last £8,750 of his £20,000 prize money in June 1773, which was being withheld on a technicality. Harrison's son William claimed that the King had told his father, 'By God, Harrison, I will see you righted!' (although the terminology, and the use of the Almighty's name in an oath, do not ring true).[4] The Board claimed to doubt whether Harrison's chronometer met the full criteria for improving methods to fix the longitude of ships at sea, but following the further trial at the Observatory it was finally convinced that it did. Harrison gratefully presented the King with his fifth and last chronometer, accurate to within 4.5 seconds over ten weeks. So potentially important was Harrison's invention, with its ability to pinpoint longitude to within 18 miles (which of course had significant naval applications) that the King was one of only three people entrusted with a key to inspect the H-5, the others being Demainbray and Harrison himself.

On 13 March 1781 the astronomer William Herschel discovered a new planet, which initially he wished to name Georgium Sidus (George's star); sadly for the King it was instead given the classical name Uranus. The discovery overturned the fundamental conception of the solar system, which since ancient times had assumed there were only six planets. Herschel had originally come from Hanover in 1757 as a musician, but had mapped the heavens in his spare time and became a protégé of Demainbray. The King invited Herschel to an audience at Windsor on 25 May 1782, and along with the Queen he went to the Kew Observatory to inspect Saturn and Jupiter. George appointed Herschel Court Astronomer, awarding him a pension of £200 per annum and his sister Caroline, a distinguished astronomer in her own right, £50 per annum.

The position of King's Astronomer 'seems to have made him happier even than the pension', wrote someone who knew Herschel well, 'as it enables him to put into execution all his wonderful projects'.[5] The greatest of these was building five 10-foot telescopes and one gigantic telescope 44 feet long and 49 inches wide, the biggest in the world at the time, which cost George a literally astronomical £4,000. It was constructed in the field behind Herschel's home, Ivy House at Slough, near Windsor, where he lived for nearly forty years, and where he would go on to discover the existence of galaxies. On 24 August 1786, the Herschels came to Windsor to show the King and Queen a new comet that Caroline had discovered. Caroline was to discover seven more comets before 1797, and in her extraordinary ninety-seven-year life she added a new star, eight comets and more than 500 nebulae and galactic clusters (two of which bear her name) to the catalogue of those known in the universe.[6]

By 19 December 1769, the anonymous Junius felt confident enough in his thirty-fifth Letter to move on from the Grafton ministry and direct his eloquent bile against the King himself. He began with the accusation that George's 'mother and her minion', implying Bute, had 'wilfully neglected' the young Prince's studies to keep him in 'ignorance and want of education' in order 'to prolong his minority until the end of their lives'.[7] Here at least Junius clearly possessed no inside knowledge. 'We separate the amiable, good-natured prince from the folly and treachery of his servants,' Junius continued, 'and the private virtues of the man from the vices of his government.'[8] Junius was a radical Whig – pro-Irish, pro-American, pro-Wilkes and anti-Scottish – so it was not unexpected that he should blame the King for abandoning the Whigs for a coalition of outsiders, newcomers and Tories. 'When you affectedly renounced the name of Englishman,' Junius wrote in a reference to George's choice of the word 'Briton' in his first Speech from the Throne, 'believe me, Sir, you were persuaded to pay a very ill-judged compliment to one part of your subjects at the expense of another.'[9] He added that in their new-found, post-Culloden allegiance, the Scots 'have no claim to your favour'.

The next section of the thirty-fifth Letter contained a passionate defence of Wilkes, whose actions were 'not enough to entitle him to the honour of Your Majesty's personal resentment', not least because 'The rays of royal indignation, collected upon him, served only to illuminate, and could not consume . . . Are you not sensible how much the meanness of the cause gives an air of ridicule to the serious difficulties into which you have been betrayed?'[10] To imply that the monarch was 'hated or despised', as Junius did, was extremely dangerous territory for him (and by extension, his now three publishers, including Henry Woodfall).

On America, Junius criticized George's Speech from the Throne of the previous year. 'The decisive, personal part you took against [the Bostonians]', he wrote, meant that 'They consider you as united with your servants against America, and know how to distinguish the sovereign and a venal Parliament on one side, from the real sentiments of the English people on the other. Looking forward to independence, they might possibly receive you for their King; but if you ever retire to America, be assured they will give you such a covenant to digest as the presbytery of Scotland would have been ashamed to offer to Charles II.'[11] The allusion to the Stuarts' problems in getting Scotland to accept their ecclesiastical views was seditious by the standards of the time, as was what followed: 'Divided as they are into a thousand forms of policy and religion, there is one point in which [Americans] all agree: they equally detest the pageantry of a King, and the supercilious hypocrisy of a bishop.'[12]

Junius then made his other grievance against the King – that he had forsaken the Whigs – perfectly clear and unambiguous. 'It is not then from the alienated affections of Ireland or America that you can reasonably look for assistance,' he sarcastically counselled,

> still less from the people of England, who are actually contending for their rights, and in this great question are parties against you. You are not, however, destitute of every appearance of support: you have all the Jacobites, Non-jurors [that is, Dissenters], Roman Catholics, and Tories of this country, and all Scotland without exception. Considering from what family you are descended, the choice of your friends has been singularly directed; and truly, Sir, if you had not lost the Whig interest of England, I should admire your dexterity in turning the hearts of your enemies.[13]

Junius was correct that George had solicited the support of political elements beyond the Whig aristocracy, and his thirty-fifth Letter was essentially a Whiggish cry of fury and resentment, sentiments which perhaps point further to the authorship of Philip Francis. Three of the publishers of Letter No. 35 were prosecuted for seditious libel, but the juries found two of them to be innocent, and the other 'Guilty of printing and publishing only', a charge which carried no criminal penalty. Woodfall was freed on payment of £20 costs, which Junius had promised to reimburse along with all his other legal expenses.[14] If George III was a tyrant, he was one of those rare ones who obeyed the law of the land and permitted it to protect his antagonists.

By 1769 there was a consensus view about America that was generally accepted by the King, his Prime Minister and Cabinet, the majority of peers and MPs, the law officers of the Crown, the American Department of the civil service, the army and navy, and the bishops of the Church of England. It also held for much of the press, and probably also for the majority of the electorate, although their views are harder to discern in the era before opinion polling. In the words of Edmund Burke's biographer, 'The general belief was that responsible people in the colonies accepted British sovereignty; that the disturbances in America were the work of a small minority of trouble-makers; and that American resistance would collapse if confronted with a show of force. If a war proved necessary, Britain would win it quickly and easily.'[15] Not until Appeasement in the 1930s did virtually the entire British establishment get something so important so badly wrong.

Yet just as it was always likely that the American colonists would resent any restraints on their already wide degree of autonomy after 1763, so it was impossible for the British government to allow the thirteen colonies to become independent without a fight if it came to it. No imperial power simply allowed significant parts of its empire to secede unilaterally without some form of military struggle, at least not until India was accorded her independence in 1947. Ominous shadows and portents notwithstanding, there was no one in the early 1770s who predicted that by 1783 Britain would play no constitutional part whatever in the destiny of the thirteen North American colonies, not even the Founding Fathers themselves. Benjamin Franklin was bold enough to ask what might happen when, in a century's time, more Britons would live in America than in Britain; but even he elected not to venture a guess.

By 1770 the Townshend Duties had raised less than £21,000, while their cost to British business through the non-importation movement was estimated to be running at £700,000 per annum.[16] 'The annual taxes born by the people of Great Britain amounted to ten millions sterling,' Lord North told the House of Commons in a debate in 1770, 'and the number of inhabitants I supposed to be eight millions, therefore every inhabitant paid at least twenty-five shillings annually. The total taxes of the continent of North America amounted to no more than £75,000; the inhabitants were three millions, therefore an inhabitant of America paid no more than six-pence annually.'[17] (Sixpence was one-fiftieth, or 2 per cent, of the twenty-five shillings North mentioned.) It is hardly surprising therefore that the colonists wished to retain both their financial privileges and their considerable de facto powers of self-determination. (Of course North's arithmetic could be questioned: the North American population was closer to 2.5 million of whom African-American slaves constituted around 600,000, and they contributed sweat and toil but not direct taxes.)

Ultimately, the North American colonists wanted independence because they had enjoyed the benefits of de facto autonomy, which they wanted to preserve. Many, though by no means all, felt ready for nationhood, and crucially those who sought it were in a position to articulate their ambition without attracting condemnation among their fellow countrymen as a radical fringe group. Clearly however, and contrary to the powerful rhetoric that would eventually break their bonds with Britain, they did not seek independence because a tyrannical George III was crushing them under his unbearable imposition of taxation.

Taxes were in fact exceptionally light, and a true tyrant would have imposed a large administrative presence in America, ruling his down-trodden masses with a salaried bureaucracy, secret police, armed forces and so on. He would have censored the press and communications, banned demonstrations and public meetings, undertaken mass arrests, suspended habeas corpus and disrupted the Stamp Act Congress. That was how true autocracies, such as the Russian tsars and Ottoman sultans, ruled the outlying districts of their far-flung empires in the mid- to late eighteenth century, ruthlessly suppressing the first hints of rebellion with overwhelm-ing occupation forces that remained for years, even decades. Yet in the whole of Virginia in 1770, for example, there were only seventeen people (besides a handful of customs officials) who held offices from the King. In Massachusetts the number was even smaller.[18]

In his Speech from the Throne at the opening of Parliament on 9 January 1770, George told the assembled Lords and Commons that he wanted to 'recommend to the serious attention of my Parliament the state of my gov-ernment in America', where 'in some of my colonies, many persons have embarked in [sic] measures highly unwarrantable and calculated to destroy the commercial connection between them and the mother country.'[19] There was, however, little reaction to George's warning. The government was being rocked yet again by the Wilkes affair, with both Lords Chatham and Camden, the Lord Chancellor, demanding public inquiries into his grievances; another Cabinet minister, Lord Granby, resigned as Commander-in-Chief and Master of the Ordnance, declaring that he repented his previous Commons vote for Wilkes' expulsion.

When Camden had not resigned by 17 January, George dismissed him and forced the job on to Charles Yorke, the son of the former Lord Chan-cellor Hardwicke. Yorke accepted the post only with the greatest reluctance: he too had supported Wilkes in the past, and had promised Rockingham that he would not enter a government led by Grafton. The King made it clear that if he did not accept it now he would never be given the oppor-tunity again. Sensationally, Yorke died just three days later, and opinion was divided as to whether the cause of death was an aneurysm or suicide. The argument for the latter grew when it was discovered that Yorke had refused to put a seal on the patent that would have raised him to the barony of Morden, a necessary prerequisite for taking on the lord chancellorship.

The day after Yorke's death, Grafton himself asked to resign, which the King regarded as a personal 'desertion', fearing as he did that his Closet would now be stormed by Chatham, Grenville and the Rockingham Whigs. In order to pre-empt that, at 7.13 p.m. on 22 January he asked Lord North to visit him at Buckingham House, where he invited him to form an administration. 'My own mind is more and more strengthened with the rightness of the measure that would prevent every other desertion,' he told North the next day, sending Lords Weymouth and Gower to argue that there could be a First Lord of the Treasury in the Commons despite the principal Opposition politician, Chatham, being in the Lords.[20] In the fifteen months since resigning the premiership, Chatham had staged a remarkable recovery and was once more a political force, and leader of a small but determined faction. On 25 January an Opposition censure motion was defeated by 226 to 186, a relatively small margin. When Grafton resigned two days later, the King told him resentfully, 'My heart is so full at the thought of your retiring from your situation that I think it best not to say more as I know the expressing it would give you pain.'[21]

The next day, 28 January, Lord North became First Lord of the Treasury of a King's Friends ministry, while retaining both the chancellorship of the Exchequer and leadership of the House of Commons. It was an extraordinary agglomeration of senior posts for one man to hold. He always disclaimed the title of Prime Minister or first minister, correctly stating it to be unknown to the constitution, and like Grafton he claimed that he could not be held responsible for the actions of ministers in other departments.[22] Historians who argue that George attempted to accrete political power to himself tend to ignore the extent to which a series of senior politicians of the day tried to divest themselves of it, leaving a difficult vacuum.

Frederick the Great was known to scoff in the 1760s that the King of England changed his Cabinet as often as he changed his shirts. At the start of the 1770s however, George had finally found someone who had not been a faction leader and who thus had few personal enemies. Lord North, he believed, could potentially command the confidence of both Houses of Parliament, in good times and bad, for the coming decade.

North was good-natured and conciliatory, although he found dealing with the endless demands for offices and honours from people wearying, and recognized that they rarely brought genuine gratitude. 'If England and Ireland were given to this man,' he said of one applicant, Thomas Hely-Hutchinson, 'he would solicit the Isle of Man for a potato garden.'[23] Hely-Hutchinson proved him right, replying to criticism of the Prime Minister with the mealy-mouthed words, 'I am a placeman, and consequently must have a high respect for Lord North.'[24]

North himself was showered with honours (and a £5,600 per annum salary) during his long premiership. In 1772 he was elected to the chancellorship of Oxford University and received the Order of the Garter, the first bestowed upon a mere MP since Sir Robert Walpole in 1726. His family benefited handsomely too: when North's uncle Lord Halifax died in 1771, the King awarded the vacant title of Ranger of Bushy Park to North's wife Anne, a post which came with a salary and a pretty house where the Norths lived when not at Downing Street. North's father, the Earl of Guilford, who had been the only one of his governors whom George had liked when growing up, became Treasurer to the Queen in 1773, while North's half-brother Brownlow found himself on an exceptionally fast track of ecclesiastical appointments, becoming Dean of Canterbury and Bishop of Lichfield in 1771, and Bishop of Worcester in 1774.

One seemingly minor appointment to the North ministry was later to become very important. John Robinson was appointed Junior Secretary to the Treasury. He was a party manager par excellence, ever attuned to where power lay in the Commons. A stocky attorney from humble beginnings in Appleby in Westmorland, 'unadorned with any accomplishments of education or advantages of address', Robinson had got on by hard work and competence. The diarist Nathaniel Wraxall MP described him as 'coarse, inelegant and somewhat inclined to corpulency', and he used to snore loudly through debates. When awake, however, he was 'one of the most active and essential functionaries of the executive government'.[25] He worked hard, had solid judgement and knew the Commons intimately.[26]

Robinson was trusted by the King and North with much of the confidential work of politics, involving honours, patronage, secret service payments, electioneering and encouraging (and occasionally threatening) would-be supporters – the less public but no less essential aspects of keeping a government majority. It helped that Robinson had long been a close friend of Charles Jenkinson, and by 1774 they even represented the same town of Harwich. 'Mr Robinson's accurateness and expedition in executing whatever he is entrusted with can only be equalled by his zeal and integrity,' the King wrote enthusiastically in August 1775.[27]

The North ministry started well, with another censure motion being defeated three days after he kissed hands, leaving the King 'greatly rejoiced' and observing, 'Believe me, a little spirit will soon restore a degree of order in my service.'[28] Within a month the government's majority had risen to ninety-seven on a contentious Civil List vote brought by Grenville. 'The seeing that the majority constantly increases gives me great pleasure,' the King told his new premier.[29] They seemed to have rounded a corner since Yorke's shocking death and Grafton's departure, and North was able to relax, showing a keen display of wit against Grenville during debates on the public finances. North had reportedly instructed Robinson to jog him awake at the end of Grenville's speech (whether from real or feigned sleep, we know not), but he was instead roused just as Grenville announced, 'I shall draw the attention of the House to the revenues and expenditure of the country in 1689.' 'Zounds,' North expostulated to Robinson, loud enough for MPs to hear, 'you have wakened me near one hundred years too soon.'[30]

North did not of course invent the government's American policy. Some of it he inherited from Rockingham's Declaratory Act, with its insistence that Britain was supreme over her empire 'in all cases whatsoever'. It stemmed also in part at least from Chatham, who had stated in the Stamp Act repeal debate that, in the event that America continued to resist Britain's rights of taxation, he would 'compel her with every man and ship in this country'.[31] The policy North attempted to carry on was the one created by these predecessors, adapted by the dead Charles Townshend and continued by the Duke of Grafton.

On 5 March, North stated that he was willing to repeal all the Townshend Duties 'which bear upon the manufactures of this country; such as the duties upon glass, red lead, etc.', but as for that on tea, 'It is an object of luxury; of all commodities it is the properest for taxation. The duty upon it is light, and such as it can very well bear.'[32] As we have seen, this was very much George's view too. At just threepence in the pound, the tea tax was expected to bring in only £12,000 per annum, a tiny amount from nearly two million American colonists. He admitted that the duties 'had given umbrage to the Americans', but wanted to keep the tea duty, as he put it, 'as a mark of the supremacy of Parliament and an efficient declaration of their right to govern the colonies'.[33] (It was for that very reason that Americans thought it almost a patriotic act to drink smuggled tea instead.)

'I wish for harmony, but I see no prospect of obtaining it,' North told the House of Commons, referring to the colonists. 'If I thought I could appease that factious and disobedient temper which prevails, I should be glad to do it . . . I wish to be thought what I really am, to the best of my conviction – a friend to trade, a friend to America.'[34] It was ultimately a clash of two deeply held and legitimate principles, which in theory men of good faith might have resolved. North did repeal almost all the Townshend Duties, but it came too late to have the conciliatory impact he hoped for, because on the very same day that he said these words events in Boston overtook them.

After three days of provocation between the Sons of Liberty and British troops in Boston, during which soldiers were pelted with stones packed in snowballs, a private's arm was broken by a club and another had his face smashed in, their mutual antagonism finally became lethal on 5 March 1770. If anything, considering the tinderbox situation it is surprising that it was seventeen months since the troops arrived in Boston before blood was shed.[35] Captain Thomas Preston and seven redcoats of the 29th Regiment of Foot who were guarding a customs house opened fire on a crowd, some of whom were Sons of Liberty, proving yet again that the taunting of armed men by unarmed ones rarely turns out well. The five people killed would hardly count as a massacre by the standards of the American Civil War or the Indian Wars – indeed more had died during the Wilkesite riots in London in 1768 – but there and then, and in those fervid political circumstances, it was shocking.

For Samuel Adams and the Boston radicals it was a rare propaganda gift, and the 29th Regiment were dubbed 'the Vein-Openers'. The resultant murder trial was a victory for both parties, as just two of the accused soldiers were found guilty, and then only for the lesser crime of manslaughter (for which they were branded upon the hand). The decision reflected well upon the fairness of the American judicial system, and also upon the virtuoso performance of Adams' second cousin John, whose spirited legal defence saw Preston acquitted. Meanwhile, the army was withdrawn from the city to Castle William in Boston Harbor. It might have been expected that Anglo-American relations would deteriorate in the immediate aftermath of the Boston Massacre, but surprisingly they did not. The trade boycotts declined on news of the repeal of the Townshend Duties, and New York abandoned its non-importation agreement. By October even Boston had ended non-importation.

On 23 April 1770 (St George's Day) Edmund Burke published a pamphlet entitled *Thoughts on the Cause of the Present Discontents*, a broadside against what he characterized as the King's 'personal rule'. This soon became a seminal text for those Rockinghamite and other Whigs who suspected George of a secret yearning for absolute monarchy. Burke himself described his pamphlet as his party's 'creed', and it was reprinted four times before the end of the year.[36] He had already written a defence of the yearlong Rockingham ministry, *A Short Account of a Late Short Administration*, but *Thoughts* was to be a full-scale attack on the King's Friends and Court influence in politics. It was as brilliantly written as it was inflammatory. 'The power of the Crown, almost dead and rotten as prerogative,' Burke claimed, 'has grown up anew, with much more strength and far less odium under the name of influence.'[37]

Burke's main argument was that 'To secure to the Court the unlimited and uncontrolled use of its own vast influence, under the sole direction of its own private favour, has for some years past been the great object of policy.'[38] This was supposedly the policy of 'a certain set of intriguing men . . . in the court of Frederick, Prince of Wales'. Burke accused them of conspiring to bring down William Pitt during the Seven Years War and of having 'endeavoured by various artifices to ruin his character'.[39] He further claimed that the Duke of Newcastle 'seemed rather pleased to get rid of so oppressive a support, not perceiving that their own fall was prepared by his, and involved in it'.

Burke argued that the King worked through a 'Cabal' or 'Junto', although only Bute was named as a member. It supposedly had its own 'constitution, laws and policy' and would still have bedevilled politics even 'if the Earl of Bute had never existed'.[40] He wrote that incidents such as the St George's Fields Massacre had made the King's Friends 'completely abhorred by the people'.[41] 'It is this unnatural infusion of a system of favouritism', he claimed, 'that has raised the present ferment in the nation.'[42] Secret influences were ascribed to the King, who was accused – though never directly by name – of operating a 'double Cabinet' system, whereby he actually listened to another group of advisers (meaning people such as Robinson and Jenkinson) rather than the actual Cabinet, which was purely for show. Burke deftly interlaced these notions of an 'interior Cabinet', 'double Cabinet', 'secret system' and 'hidden influence' to suggest that the King really ran the government rather than Lord North, whom he else-where called 'an hireling, and the sheep are not his own'.[43]*

Burke's theory of a royal conspiracy against the constitution was fal-lacious. The King possessed enough powers under the constitution to do everything he wished, and he neither desired nor required any more. He had of course favoured some advisers over others, as all monarchs – and indeed statesmen – do, but no more than that. It would have been difficult if not impossible for the King to have created a 'double Cabinet' without others soon learning of its existence, and there would have been little point in constantly changing his ministries in the way he had throughout the previous decade if they had genuinely held no power.

In fact, the King had been openly exercising the same powers to make and unmake governments that his hero King William III had done, and which both his own grandfather and great-grandfather had exercised dur-ing the long rule of the Old Corps Whigs. Burke's attack on the King's Party and its allies was launched because the Rockinghamite Whigs, who saw themselves as the natural heirs of the Old Whigs, were finally being eclipsed, to their intense shock and frustration, and being replaced by people such as North who, though still nominally Whig, were suspected

---

* This dichotomy was quite separate from that between the 'Nominal' and 'Efficient' Cabinets, although it has often been mistaken for that by historians.

of not wanting to limit royal power enough to be true heirs of the 1688 Revolution.

Burke expressed doubts about the supposed American colonial policy adopted by this 'double Cabinet', protesting that 'Nothing can equal the futility, the weakness, the rashness, the timidity, the perpetual contradiction, in the management of our affairs in that part of the world.' He overlooked the fact that his employer Lord Rockingham's own Declaratory Act had only made that situation worse.[44] Burke's repeated references to King Charles I gave the deliberate impression that 'the present discontents' might lead to worse ones, in Britain as well as America. He even called for 'the interposition of the body of the people itself' in order to oppose the King's Friends, a suggestion which sounded suspiciously like encouraging direct action against royal authority, and he went on to refer to 'a legal remedy . . . when it is evident that nothing else can hold the constitution to its true principles'.[45]

Burke did not go into detail about what those true principles were, but a clue might be gleaned from his paean to 'the great Whig families', whose power 'was rooted in the country' where 'they possessed a far more natural and fixed influence. Long possession of government; vast property; obligations of favours given and received; connection of office; ties of blood, of alliance, of friendship . . . [and] the name of Whig, dear to the majority of the people'.[46] *Thoughts* was long considered to be a reforming, populist document, but it was also a cry of rage and pain from a propagandist of the Whig oligarchy, whose eighty years of aristocratic dominance were finally being challenged by George and his allies in Parliament. Although Burke complained that the King's revenues were 'not much short of a million annually', he was always careful to refer to George's own 'high and sacred character'.[47] He noted that his friend Wilkes was 'the object of persecution . . . for his unconquerable firmness, for his resolute, indefatigable, strenuous resistance against oppression', but he was not about to risk Wilkes' fate.[48]

In a country of eight million people but only around 300,000 electors, where great landowning families controlled most of the county parliamentary seats, occasionally renting them or selling them off to those who could afford them, and where corporations often auctioned seats to the highest bidder to augment town funds, for Lord Rockingham's private secretary to denounce the Crown for corruption was somewhat hypocritical. But its eloquence, its force and the beguiling conspiracy theory at its heart made *Thoughts on the Present Discontents* a very effective pamphlet which earned Burke the King's enmity for over twenty years.

*

On Thursday 26 April 1770, a gilded neo-classical equestrian statue of George III was officially dedicated on the Bowling Green in Lower Manhattan. It had been commissioned four years earlier after the repeal of the Stamp Act by the General Assembly of New York, which had resolved to mark 'the deep sense this colony has of the eminent and singular blessings received from him during his most auspicious reign'.[49] The ceremony was attended by Lieutenant-Governor Cadwallader Colden, members of the council and assembly, 'clergy of all denominations' and a large number of prominent local inhabitants, who heard speeches, a thirty-two-gun salute and a band playing from the ramparts of the city's fort. 'Our loyalty, firm attachment and affection to His Majesty's person was expressed by drinking the King's health,' Colden recalled, 'while the spectators expressed their joy by loud acclamations . . . and the ceremony concluded with great cheerfulness and good humour.'[50] The statue was one-third larger than life-size and mimicked the gestures and Roman costume of the statue of the Emperor Marcus Aurelius on the Capitoline Hill in Rome. It was also forged from 2 tons of lead, which six years later the King's troops would come to regret.

How could such a large crowd show its respect for a King whose soldiers had shot down five Bostonians only seven weeks earlier? Writing to the Rev. Samuel Cooper of Boston on 8 June, in his first response to the Boston Massacre, Benjamin Franklin pointed out that it was not the King whom Americans objected to, but instead the claims of:

> subjects in one part of the King's dominions to be sovereigns over their fellow-subjects in another part of his dominions . . . Let us therefore hold fast [to our] loyalty to the King (who has the best disposition towards us, and has a family-interest in our prosperity) as that steady loyalty is the most probable means of securing us from the arbitrary power of a corrupt Parliament that does not like us, and conceives itself to have an interest in keeping us down and fleecing us.[51]

In every clash that was to come, however, the King declared himself a champion of the rights of the Westminster Parliament over his American colonies.

In August 1770, the North ministry deftly avoided war with Spain over the contested Falkland Isles, where a British settlement had been first established four years earlier. Chatham and Wilkes both advocated war, but North did not, and he was supported by Samuel Johnson (by then something of a government pen-for-hire), whose *Thoughts on the Late Transactions Respecting Falkland's Islands* attacked Chatham's 'feudal gabble'.[52] The Spanish climbdown in the face of the mobilization of the

Royal Navy brought the North ministry popularity, and the King told the Prime Minister that 'every feeling of humanity as well as the knowledge of the distress war must occasion makes me desirous of preventing it if it can be accomplished, provided the honour of this country is preserved'.[53] His reign saw three major wars, but George cleaved to his father's admonitions not to go to war if at all possible. He inherited his first one and, as we shall see, was given no choice in the other two.

In 1767 rumours emerged that the King's womanizing twenty-two-year-old younger brother Prince Henry, Duke of Cumberland, had married a commoner, the painter and novelist Olive Wilmot, although he flatly denied it, as he did the paternity of their daughter. Wilmot would nonetheless later style herself Princess Olivia of Cumberland, much to the King's irritation. After the ensuing scandal, Henry was packed off to sea as an officer in the Royal Navy, but once back on shore in 1769 he reverted to type, except now he consorted with married women, including Lady Sarah Bunbury (the former Lady Sarah Lennox, George's first love) and Lady Cravan, obliging his elder brother to take him aside and talk to him severely about his behaviour. Although George believed at the time that 'the truths I have thought it incumbent to utter may be of some use in his future conduct,' a year later he was to be proved categorically wrong.[54]

In November 1769, Prince Henry had the dubious distinction of being the first member of the royal family to be seen riding openly in the company of his mistress, Henrietta Grosvenor, the wife of Richard, Lord Grosvenor, who subsequently sued him for having 'criminal conversation' (that is, adultery) with her after they were caught *in flagrante delicto*. Henry's love letters, which have been described as 'fervent but ungrammatical', were read out in court to the great embarrassment of the royal family.[55] When damages of £10,000 were added to his legal fees, the Duke had to ask the King for £13,000, which North found from the Secret Service Fund in the Civil List. 'This takes a heavy load off of me,' the King confided to his Prime Minister, 'though I cannot enough express how much I feel at being in the least concerned in an affair that my way of thinking has ever taught me to behold as highly improper.'[56]

On 1 November 1771, the King was visited by Henry at Richmond Lodge, where he asked George to go for a walk in the woods with him and read a letter that he had written to him. It explained that, having now given up Lady Grosvenor,* on 2 October the Prince had married a widow,

---

* Lord Grosvenor could not divorce his wife as he had himself been with Leicester Square prostitutes, so he settled £1,200 a year on Henrietta.

Anne Horton, the daughter of the reprobate Irish peer Simon Luttrell, 1st Earl of Carhampton.* 'After walking for some minutes in silence to smother my feelings,' the King wrote in a memorandum afterwards, 'I without passion spoke to him . . . that I could not believe he had taken the step declared in the paper.'[57] When Henry confirmed that he had, George took it upon himself to break it to their mother Augusta, who was then dying of cancer, but 'as the step was taken I could give him no advice, for that he had irretrievably ruined himself. But that it appeared to me that after such a disgraceful conduct any country was preferable to his own.' The Duke and Duchess left for Calais two days later. Always keeping her ear out for scandalous rumour, Lady Mary Coke had already been informed of 'the additional disgraceful circumstance of Mrs Horton being two months gone with child before he married her', although it is not clear whether the King knew this, and they certainly never had any acknowledged children.[58]

In the pain of discovering another *mésalliance* in the family, George unburdened himself to his beloved brother William, Duke of Gloucester. 'In any country a prince marrying a subject is looked upon as dishonourable, nay, in Germany the children of such a marriage cannot succeed to any territories,' the King wrote, 'but here, where the Crown is too little respected, it must be big with the greatest mischiefs.'[59] The exceptions to the rule of British monarchs not marrying subjects – Henry VIII (four times) and the hapless James II – would not contradict the King's view. George was also angry that, without a significant income, Prince Henry had married secretly hoping that his brother would have to subsidize this 'dishonourable' and 'disgraceful conduct' by increasing the £15,000 a year that he received from him, which Henry thought not enough for a royal duke to raise a family. 'The more I reflect on his conduct,' the King told his mother two days after the walk in the woods, 'the more I see it as his inevitable ruin and as a disgrace to the whole family.'[60] George felt there was the national interest to consider: royals who married out of love could not be used to sweeten foreign alliances, and he feared the Hanoverians would become a laughing stock among the German princes.

The King asked Henry not to allow the person he called 'Mrs Horton' to take the title Duchess of Cumberland, which his brother refused. 'I am sorry to say it seems the performance of a Newgate attorney,' wrote the King to his mother. 'I now wash my hands of the whole affair, and shall have no further intercourse with him.'[61] The Court was given to understand that anyone received by the Cumberlands would not be received by the

---

* Coincidentally the father of Henry Lawes Luttrell, who had stood against Wilkes in Middlesex in 1769.

King and Queen, thereby immediately destroying the couple's social life in England.

'You are the only friend to whom I can unbosom every thought,' George wrote to William about the Cumberland imbroglio.[62] Frail, gentle and unpolitical, William was often abroad for his health, and when he nearly died in Italy in October 1771, George dispatched three of his personal doctors to him. The news of his illness had, George told his brother on his recovery, 'possessed my mind with the greatest grief. I expected no other account but that Heaven had taken you from me, though thanks to God my mind is now at ease. I can scarcely relate what I have suffered without tears, than this has only taught me how much I love you.'[63] William told George that their brother Cumberland's marriage to Anne Horton was 'a series of follies and inconsistencies' and 'inexcusable and weak beyond measure'.[64] Yet the dear William to whom he unburdened himself over their brother's disastrous marriage had an amorous secret of his own.

When George Grenville died on 13 November 1770 and the Duke of Bedford the following January, many of their supporters drifted over to North, whose only real opposition in Parliament now came from the Rock-inghamites in the Commons and Chatham in the Lords. On 13 February 1771, the Commons approved the treaty with Spain that concluded the Falklands dispute, by which Britain kept the islands, by 271 votes to 157. 'The great majority yesterday is very creditable for [the] administration,' a delighted George told North, suspecting that war with Spain might have resulted in Chatham's return to office. Britain had also avoided what he called the 'calamity of war' over French ambitions in Holland the previous month.

On that occasion, the King explained to Sir Joseph Yorke (the British Ambassador to Holland, younger brother of the late Charles Yorke) his underlying view of foreign policy, which was based on his belief that the French 'can never be trusted'.[65] Frederick the Great, he added, was not 'a sincere friend to this country', and 'I confess my political creed is formed on the system of King William [III]. England in conjunction with the House of Austria and the [Dutch] Republic sees the most secure barrier against the [Franco-Spanish Bourbon] Family Compact, and if Russia could be added to this, I think the Court of Versailles would not be in a hurry to commence hostilities.' Although under normal circumstances this was a very sensible foreign policy for Britain to adopt – and fitted in well with her historic role as a guarantor of the European balance of power – it had already been badly damaged, if not wrecked, the previous May by the wedding of the Bourbon Dauphin Louis (later Louis XVI) to the

1. George, Prince of Wales, aged sixteen, by Jean-Étienne Liotard.

2. George's loving father, Frederick, Prince of Wales, who died when George was twelve, by Godfrey Kneller. 'Poor Fred', as he came to be known, bequeathed many of his noblest thoughts and principles to his son.

3. George's much abused but guiltless mother, Princess Augusta, by Allan Ramsay. Rumours about her love life meant that she was booed at her funeral, but George knew them to be untrue.

4. 'In the whole of high society,' a lady said of George's dearest friend the 3rd Earl of Bute, 'Lord Bute has the finest pair of calves.' Painted by Joshua Reynolds.

5. (*opposite*) George's attack on the justifications for slavery in an essay from the 1750s: 'Slavery is equally repugnant to the Civil Law as to the Law of Nature . . . The propagation of the Christian religion was the first reason, the next was the [Indigenous] Americans differing from them in colour, manners and customs, all [of] which are too absurd to take the trouble of refuting. But what shall we say to the European traffic of Black slaves, the very reasons urged for it will be perhaps sufficient to make us hold this practice in execration.'

Slavery is equaly repugnant to
the Civil Laws as to the Law of Nature;
a Slave is no Member of Society,
he cannot therefore be restrain'd
by Laws in which has no interest,
from attempting to procure liberty
by flight; the legal authority of the
Master only can prevent him.

The pretexts used by the Spaniards
for enslaving the New World were
extrem'ly curious; the propagation
of the Christian Religion was the
first reason, the next was the
Americans differing from them in
colour, manners & Customs, all
which are too absurd to take the
trouble of refuting.

But what shall we say to the
European traffic of Black Slaves,
the very reasons urg'd for it will
be perhaps sufficient to make
us hold this practice in execration.

6. George Grenville thought similarly to the King on a wide range of issues, including over the taxation of the North American colonies, but their personalities clashed.

7. William Pitt the Elder, the hero of the Seven Years War, was a recluse for most of his last premiership – due to depression brought on by chronic gout, for which his doctor prescribed alcohol as a cure.

8. The 3rd Duke of Grafton failed to heed the warning signals from the American colonies.

9. The Marquess of Rockingham repealed Grenville's hated Stamp Tax, but too late.

10. George, Queen Charlotte and their six eldest children. George, Prince of Wales, and Frederick, Duke of York, stand beside their father; William, Duke of Clarence, holds a cockatoo; Edward, Duke of Kent, plays with a dog. The Queen holds the infant Princess Augusta, while Princess Charlotte stands alongside.

11. George bought Buckingham House for Queen Charlotte in 1762, extensively renovating and adding to it. Fourteen of their fifteen children were born there.

12. The King's Octagonal Library at Buckingham House, where he kept some of his 80,000 books and where he met Samuel Johnson in 1767.

13. George founded the Royal Academy of Arts, and had its original members painted by Zoffany in 1772. Among others in this picture are Giovanni Cipriani, the American-born Benjamin West, Paul and Thomas Sandby, William Chambers and Joshua Reynolds.

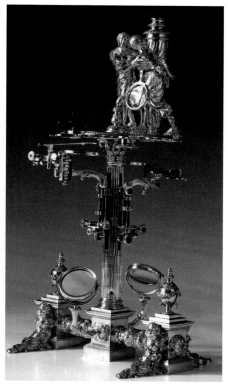

14. William Herschel's 40-foot telescope was built at Slough in 1787 with funds from George III.

15. A silver microscope commissioned by the King from George Adams *c.* 1770.

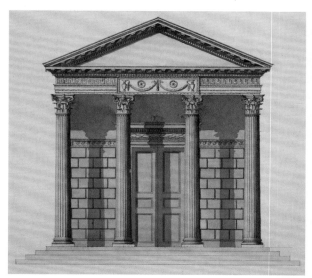

16. George's design for a neo-classical Corinthian temple at Kew, drawn as an exercise for his tutor William Chambers, *c.* 1759, when he was still Prince of Wales. The numerous compass holes down the centre, across its base and in the centre-left column suggest painstaking work.

17. John Harrison's H5 chronometer, which enabled longitude to be determined with precision for the first time. George ensured that Harrison was awarded a magnificent £20,000 prize for his invention.

18. Kew Palace, also known as the Dutch House, where George and his brother Prince Edward were educated in 1750s and where their mother the Dowager Princess Augusta lived until her death in 1772 and where Queen Charlotte died in 1819.

19. Thomas Pelham-Holles, 1st Duke of Newcastle, personified the Old Whigs whose power George wanted to reduce.

20. George's uncle, William Augustus, Duke of Cumberland, in 1758. George and his mother wrongly suspected him of plotting a coup against them.

Archduchess Marie Antoinette of Austria. As subsequent events were to prove, it was no longer safe to predicate British security upon Austria's traditional Francophobia. Just as they were to be embroiled in a debilitating struggle on the other side of the Atlantic, the British needed to rethink their foreign policy entirely.

The Wilkes affair was reignited all over again on 9 March 1771 when the government ordered the arrest of two printers for illegally publishing reports of parliamentary debates. One of them was arraigned before an alderman of the City of London, who turned out to be none other than Wilkes himself, who promptly released him without charge. 'I do in the strongest manner recommend that every caution may be used to prevent its becoming a serious affair,' the King cautioned North. He wanted debates to stay secret and that 'this strange and lawless method of publishing debates in the papers should be put a stop to,' but he did not want publishers arrested wantonly.[66] Now that the Wilkes imbroglio was entering its seventh year, he was finally learning some of its lessons.

By then the legal process was in motion, however, and when the House of Commons messenger who arrested a third printer under the Speaker's warrant was himself arrested on an assault charge, Wilkes, now acting also as a magistrate, sent it on to trial. The King accepted that 'the honour of the Commons must be supported' in this clash with the City of London, but 'As to Wilkes, he is below the notice of the House.'[67] If only that had been true. By 20 March the King was telling North that he wished Wilkes had not been ordered to appear before the House, as his cause would simply be 'given new life by some punishment inflicted on him, which will bring him new supplies, and I do not doubt he will hold such a language that will oblige some notice to be taken of him'.[68] He had at last learned another truth about Wilkes: that he thrived on publicity.

Nine days later the King was hissed at in the streets, and a rotten apple thrown at his carriage as he went to Westminster to give royal assent to some Bills. He ignored it. When a mob tried to assault the Prime Minister, George told him, 'Believe me, the spirit you showed yesterday will prevent its being often called upon; they now know you are not to be alarmed.'[69] On 1 April a large crowd assembled at Tower Hill with two carts, on which, Horace Walpole recorded, 'were figures representing the Queen Dowager and Lord Bute, attended by a hearse. The figures were beheaded by chimney-sweepers, and then burnt.'[70] Effigies of pro-government politicians then had 'their supposed dying speeches cried about the streets'. On the King's birthday, 4 June, which the Royal Academy celebrated with an illumination of his coat of arms at Somerset House, a Wilkesite mob used fireworks to 'set fire to a part thereof and endangered the palace'.[71] The King rose above all such popular manifestations of unpopularity, just as he did not allow his head to be turned by cheering crowds either.

Two days later, George escaped assassination at the hands of Jonathan Britain, an English soldier who was hanged for forgery the following year. His eve-of-execution confession, supported by his posthumously published autobiography, revealed that there had been a plot of five Irish and French Catholic extremists to burn down the Portsmouth dockyards and induce British Catholics in the British armed forces to desert and join the French. On the night of 6 June, Britain was about to step out of his cover in St James's Park and fire a pistol at George as he passed by in a sedan chair, protected only by two Yeomen of the Guard. On examining the priming pan shortly beforehand, he saw that there was not enough gunpowder, so he slunk back into the bushes, unbeknown to his intended victim.[72]

Benjamin Franklin returned from a journey in northern England to attend Court on the King's birthday. 'While we are declining the usurped authority of Parliament,' he wrote to his friend Thomas Cushing in Massachusetts, 'I wish to see a steady dutiful attachment to the King and his family maintained among us.'[73] Franklin was toying with the idea of a North American constitution in which the Crown was sovereign and the legislative role in the Americas rested with a King-in-Council that would defend colonial rights from Parliament. In 1754 he had attended a cross-colonial conference at Albany in New York, where a proposal had been presented for a colonial union, a grand council of America under the leadership of a president-general. This scheme, apparently the brainchild of Franklin and Thomas Pownall,* had come to nothing, largely as a result of the outbreak of the Seven Years War.[74]

Franklin's ideas were developed further by James Wilson of Pennsylvania in his pamphlet *Considerations on the Nature and Extent of the Legislative Authority of the British Parliament* of 1774, which argued that the King was sovereign in America but Parliament was not; this remained more or less the American colonists' position until 1776. It was largely a political stance, however, adopted in order not to frighten American Loyalists away from the revolt against Parliament. Franklin personally despised George, and in his autobiography John Adams wrote that his colleague had almost a fixation about him and would constantly bring up his 'severe resentment' of the King, even when it was neither helpful nor relevant.[75]

*

---

* Although it has also been suggested that it was originally the idea of the then First Lord of Trade, Lord Halifax.

With the marriage of Prince Henry, Duke of Cumberland, now common knowledge, the sixty-seventh Letter of Junius, published on 27 November 1771, offered a scurrilous attack on 'the King's brother-in-law Colonel Luttrell', with much salacious detail. 'We have now a better reason than ever to pray for the long life of the best of princes, and the welfare of his royal issue,' Junius wrote of the (extremely remote) prospect of Cumberland becoming king.[76] Soon thereafter the letters ceased.*

The deep and multiple embarrassments caused to George by his close family increased significantly in January 1772 when there was a coup d'état in Denmark, where his youngest sister Caroline Matilda was Queen. She had been born after their father Prince Frederick had died, and George had arranged her marriage in 1766 at the age of only fifteen to her first cousin King Christian VII of Denmark. He soon turned out to be a mentally unstable, debauched, syphilitic near moron, and in the spring of 1771 Caroline had begun an affair with Johann Friedrich Struensee, the handsome Court doctor who became the effective ruler of Denmark. Struensee's reforming programme was so opposed by the aristocracy that they overthrew him on 17 January in a coup in Copenhagen that King Christian at least seemed to support. On 28 April Struensee was mutilated, beheaded and quartered for treason, while Queen Caroline was imprisoned in Kronborg Castle in the town of Helsingør.†

The rumours of a relationship between George's sister and Struensee inevitably drew comparisons with those involving Princess Augusta and Bute; the key difference was that the former were true. George was furious about his sister's treatment, and deliberately passed by the Danish Ambassador at a Levee without a word.[77] 'Outrageous indignities to the Crown of England cannot pass with impunity,' Lord Suffolk, the Northern Secretary, told Robert Keith, the British Ambassador to Denmark, and Lord Sandwich, now the First Lord of the Admiralty, sent the Royal Navy into Danish waters with the implied threat that Copenhagen might be bombarded if Queen Caroline were not released from Kronborg.[78] The Danish government sensibly allowed her to go into exile in Celle in Hanover; she

---

* The historian and politician Conor Cruise O'Brien has speculated that this was because the King, having identified Philip Francis as Junius, bribed him 'to write no more', offering him a seat on the Bengal Council at the lucrative salary of £10,000 per annum (O'Brien, *Great Melody* pp. 279–80). This theory, for which O'Brien provided no evidence, does not stand, as it was totally against the King's nature to submit to such blackmail, and Francis was not given the seat until three years later. It was Lord Barrington, for whom Francis worked, who suggested the Bengal appointment to Lord North, and the King was still inquiring of his friend George Rose about Junius' true identity decades later.

† Immortalized by Shakespeare as Elsinore.

was not, however, allowed to take her children, the next generation of the Danish royal family, which utterly traumatized her.

George sent her regular good advice, including the injunction that it was 'detrimental to your health' to think constantly of a counter-coup in Copenhagen. 'Whenever the present horrid people that manage that kingdom are either removed by death or the intrigues of some new party,' he told her, 'it cannot avail anything in your favour. But your leading an exemplary life will by degrees turn the cry in your favour.'[79] When her support was requested for a counter-coup in April 1775, George ordered her not to give it, and she died a month later aged just twenty-three, having never seen her children again.

Three years before her daughter's death, at 6 a.m. on 8 February 1772, George's mother the Dowager Princess Augusta died of throat cancer at Carlton House. The King and Queen had visited her at least twice a week throughout his reign, and she came to them on Wednesdays. During her long illness they visited her every evening at 8 p.m., but when the night before her death the doctors advised that her end was imminent, they arrived at 7 p.m., 'pretending they had mistaken the hour. The Princess, though evidently dying, insisted on rising and dressing to receive them. After four hours' conversation she parted with them with greater warmth and affection than usual, saying she should have a tranquil night.'[80] Her husband had died more than twenty years earlier and she had led an unblemished life since, but she still remained hated by the general populace for an affair she had never had. At her funeral at Westminster Abbey on 13 February, Walpole reported, 'The mob huzzaed for joy and treated her memory with much disrespect,' such was the pervasive power of the conspiracy theory and the gutter press (and his own lies and gossip).[81] The King had to endure his mother's coffin being booed by the crowd. He was entitled to feel, as he had said to his brother, that the Crown was 'too little respected'.

When Augusta left only £7,500 in her will, it was alleged that the rest of her fortune had been bequeathed to Bute. In truth, she had paid off her husband's debts, raised nine children, built her son an observatory and been generous to her charities, often anonymously.[82] A medal was struck bearing the words 'A much injured victim'.[83] George inherited the White House at Kew, which adjoined his first country residence, Richmond Lodge, and he and Charlotte moved there in May 1772, demolishing the Lodge.

The embarrassment that Prince Henry's marriage had caused, and the (extremely well-founded) fear that others of his close relations might do the same in future, prompted the King to propose a Royal Marriages Bill on 19 February. This would prevent any descendant of George II from marrying without the prior consent of the monarch; in the absence of such consent the marriage would be invalid. It was the only piece of legislation George initiated in his entire reign besides the Regency Bill of 1765, and brought British law into line with the rest of the courts of Europe.

Some people feared that the Royal Marriages Act would cause more problems than it solved, however. A joke that went around the House of Lords was that it would be 'giving leave to the Princes of the Blood to lie* with our wives, and forbidding them to marry our daughters'.[84] Decades later Lord Melbourne, Queen Victoria's first Prime Minister, told her that the Act sent the royal dukes 'like so many beasts into Society, making love everywhere they went, and then saying they were very sorry they couldn't marry them'.[85] (It was a brave thing for Melbourne to have said: Victoria's own father, Prince Edward, Duke of Kent, had enjoyed a twenty-eight-year affair with a French lady, Madame de Saint-Laurent, before he eventually married Victoria's mother.)

Six months after the Royal Marriages Act had passed, George received a letter from his brother Prince William – to whom he had described their brother Henry's marriage to a non-royal as 'dishonourable' – informing him that he had been secretly married to Maria, the Dowager Lady Walde-grave, for six years, and that 'it would have never been made public' if she were not now pregnant. The first of their three children was born in May.

George now recognized that William's criticisms of their brother Henry had been the height of hypocrisy.[86] Much as he loved William, he could hardly treat him less harshly than he had Henry, so he told Lord Hertford, his Lord Chamberlain, 'to notify to everybody that those who go to the Duke of Gloucester must not come to Court', the only exceptions being the officers of his regiment, the 1st Foot Guards, but not their wives or daughters.[87] It was the second brother whom George had dispatched to social Siberia in less than a year.†

In January 1775, Prince William threatened to have the issue of his financial provision raised in the Commons unless he received more money from his brother, with all the public embarrassment which that would cause the royal family. 'I cannot deny that on the subject of the Duke of

---

* 'To converse in bed' (*Johnson's Dictionary*).

† In October 1772, at a dinner party of Lady Blandford's, Horace Walpole claimed that the King and Queen were intending to visit his house at Strawberry Hill to view a state bed he had recently installed. Lady Mary Coke knew that, as Walpole was the Duchess of Gloucester's uncle, such a visit was impossible, noting in a letter to her sister, 'You'll observe how distant from the truth his relation is of this affair' (ed. Home, *Letters and Journals of Lady Mary Coke* IV p. 127). This otherwise trifling anecdote illustrates how much the King's brothers' scandals reverberated through high society (and also demonstrates Walpole's compulsive mendacity).

Gloucester my heart is wounded,' George confided to North. 'I have ever loved him more with the fondness one bears to a child than a brother.'[88] He was adamant that he could not give in to the blackmail threat. Nevertheless, he added, 'Should any accident happen to the Duke I shall certainly take care of his children.' In the event he did make generous provision for Gloucester's children, both during their father's lifetime and after his death in August 1805. By then, the King had long resumed relations with his brother, initially on the basis that the Duchess's name was not mentioned in his presence, but later on he wrote to her too and allowed her to be buried in St George's Chapel, Windsor. The Duchess of Cumberland, by contrast, was never recognized by the family as even being royal.

The Royal Marriages Act effectively meant that British royals could really only marry German royals, a law that forced the Prince of Wales into an unhappy marriage and others of George's children and siblings into unmarried relationships. Three of George III's daughters remained unmarried for want of appropriate matches: at Windsor they sometimes headed their letters 'The Nunnery'. It was a sad effect of the Act, and of the King's desire that his family should not marry non-royals, that only one of George's fifteen children – Charlotte, Queen of Württemberg – enjoyed a marriage that was both happy and legal.

IO

The Boston Tea Party

June 1772–July 1774

The rebellion of the Americans was not only treason to him but treason to Parliament; treason to the ancient, providential Constitution which both he and his advisers had inherited and which it was their sacred duty to protect.[1]

John Plumb, *The First Four Georges*, 1957

The Boston Tea Party, which did so much to impel the two sides towards war, had a violent antecedent when on 9 June 1772 a gang of smugglers from Providence, Rhode Island, overpowered the crew of the revenue cutter *Gaspée* after it ran aground in Narragansett Bay, wounding the captain and setting it alight. The British commission that was dispatched to investigate could not find any locals willing to testify about who had been responsible. George supported the government's decision not to react aggressively, but even an unofficial suggestion that the commission might take colonists back to England for trial was enough for the Virginia House of Burgesses to establish a Committee of Correspondence, a proto-revolutionary organization intended, at least initially, to coordinate opposition to Britain's colonial policy.*

Four days after the *Gaspée* attack, Governor Thomas Hutchinson of Massachusetts informed the Assembly there that he and the justices of the colony's Supreme Court would no longer be paid by them, but would instead receive their emoluments directly from customs revenues, thus freeing royal officers from their dependence on the assemblymen. This was immediately denounced as 'a despotic administration of government'.[2] Samuel Adams founded a Committee of Correspondence at a Boston town

* The word 'correspondence' refers primarily not to letters passed between them, but to the eighteenth-century meanings of the word, comprising, in the definitions of *Johnson's Dictionary*, 'reciprocal adaptation of one thing to another', 'intercourse; reciprocal intelligence' and 'friendship'.

meeting on 2 November, which would prepare a statement of colonial rights, list violations and encourage the setting up of sister committees in other cities throughout the thirteen colonies. As so often in history, a revolutionary cadre was emerging – initially small-scale but zealous, interconnected, hard-working and chronically underestimated by its opponents – which ultimately wrought great change. Such disciplined cells sharing radical ideas had overthrown long-standing governments in the past – not least that of Charles I – and were often to do so again.[3]

The revolutionary cause was helped, at least in the South, by the historic judgment that Lord Mansfield handed down in the Court of King's Bench in London on 22 June 1772, in the case of *Sommersett* v *Steuart*. The slave James Sommersett, who had been bought by Charles Steuart in Boston, escaped when the two men visited London, and was freed by Mansfield on the basis, supported by William Blackstone, that slavery was contrary to English common law and precluded by Magna Carta, despite the fact that Britain was a slave-trading nation. 'The state of slavery is of such a nature that it is incapable of being introduced on any reasons, moral or political, but only by positive law,' Mansfield stated. 'It is so odious that nothing can be suffered to support it, but positive law. Whatever inconveniences, therefore, may follow from the decision, I cannot say this case is allowed or approved by the law of England.'[4] James Sommersett was freed. Although Mansfield did not extend his famous judgment to British territories overseas, the political effect in America was, as J. C. D. Clark puts it, that 'Colonial slave-owners therefore joined colonial merchant smugglers, colonial Dissenters, colonial debtors, and colonial land speculators as powerful groups with an interest in emancipation from British policy.'[5]

In August there was a major alteration in the British government's American policy when, after a Cabinet row over the issue of land grants in the Ohio Valley, Lord Hillsborough, who wanted to continue the Proclamation veto on American westward expansion, resigned. He was replaced as Colonial Secretary by William Legge, 2nd Earl of Dartmouth, Lord North's stepbrother and trusted ally, with whom he had gone on the Grand Tour for three years in 1751. In contrast with the hardline Hillsborough, Dartmouth was a noted dove on American policy. Benjamin Franklin wrote to his son William that the King was tired of Hillsborough because he 'had weakened the affection and respect of the colonies for a royal government'.[6] Dartmouth, on the other hand, he described as 'a truly good man'.[7] Dartmouth was indeed generous, good-natured, mild and devout, and was liked by the King. 'Lord Dartmouth', recalled the Duke of Grafton years later, 'was the only one who had a true desire to see lenient measures adopted towards the colonies.'[8] That was not quite true; at the time both the King and Lord North also tended towards a policy of conciliation – insofar as it was consistent with maintaining British honour.

The East India Company was the joint-stock corporation which administered Bengal and other parts of India as a commercial concern. It exerted significant influence in Parliament through its board of directors and its wide shareholder base. On 8 October, its chairman, Sir George Colebrooke MP, gave Lord North the extremely disconcerting news that the Company was on the verge of bankruptcy and in urgent need of government help. Shareholders' demand for dividends, problems with revenue collection in Bengal, the government's £400,000 per annum levy for its charter, heavy British import duties, the ravages of war and a worldwide tea glut had left the Company badly insolvent.

North understood that the Company, whose large private army was about to go unpaid, was too big to fail, at least unless Britain was prepared to cede north-eastern India to the French. With public spending running at £11.3 million for 1773, representing no less than 10 per cent of the economy (servicing the National Debt cost £4.5 million, the Royal Navy £1.8 million and the army £1.6 million), the £800,000 the Company paid in taxes on its Chinese and Indian tea represented about 7 per cent of the government's income and was indispensable.[9] North therefore told Colebrooke, and subsequently the Commons, that a committee would look into the finances of the Company and report to Parliament. Both the King and North took the attitude that the Company directors had amassed too much wealth, and were often vulgar in their nouveau-riche display of it. The King, who saw farmers as the nation's backbone, nevertheless had to say in his Speech from the Throne opening Parliament on 26 November 1772, 'It is impossible that I can look with indifference upon the prosperity of the East India Company.'[10]

In the late 1760s, the King had written a memorandum examining several of the issues concerning the East India Company's financial problems and organization, which concluded that it needed a recapitalization and a reduction in the dividend from 12.5 per cent to 9 per cent. He also thought the board of twenty-four directors ought to 'be impartially chosen for their abilities, resolution and disinterestedness' and have 'no bias but for the general good'.[11] He made twenty-three suggestions for the directorships, including Judge Elijah Impey, Laurence Sullivan (the leader of a faction on the board opposed to Robert Clive, Governor of Bengal from 1757 to 1760) and even Edmund Burke.[12] Under the King's plan, the £400,000 annual levy charged by the government for its Charter would be dropped, and the memorandum may have been the basis for the East India Company Regulating Act and the Loan Act which North's government passed in 1773, establishing a Council and a Governor-General for India.[13] These Acts gave the government a greater say in Indian affairs – George's man Impey was appointed the first Chief Justice of Bengal, for example – which was felt reasonable given that the Treasury had altogether loaned the Company some £1.4 million. When the Company threatened to refuse the loan in a bid to keep its independence in mid-May, George suggested to North a radical idea for crushing what he called 'the absurdity of the proprietors', which was to 'Continue the Bill of regulations, and as the Company do not choose to be assisted with money, pass an Act to prevent their having a dividend [for] three years. They must then come on their knees for what they now seem to spurn.'[14]

Like many Britons, the King had once been a great admirer of Robert Clive, who after his victory at the battle of Plassey during the Seven Years War had done much to establish the empire in India. George had accepted gifts from Clive (as had the Queen), and heeded his advice over India. By May 1773, however, after Clive had been on trial for fourteen months, during which unsavoury details of his administration of Bengal had emerged, George felt that the House of Commons might have been unduly lenient when it rejected a censure motion by 155 to 95. 'I own I am amazed that private interest could make so many forget what they owe to their country, and come to a resolution that seems to approve of Lord Clive's rapine,' he told North. 'No one thinks his services greater than I do, but that can never be a reason to commend him in what certainly opened the door to the fortunes we see daily made in that country.'[15] He hoped that Warren Hastings, who was to become India's first Governor-General under the new Act, might bring better administration to the ever larger parts of the subcontinent that were coming under British sway.

As well as loans, another way of helping the East India Company out of its financial difficulties was for the government to permit the sale of huge amounts of its surplus tea to North America, where an estimated three-quarters of the 1.2 million pounds of tea consumed annually was the cheaper, smuggled variety sold by the Dutch East India Company. If the American market was opened up to market forces, it was presumed, the price to American consumers would approximately halve, thereby undercutting the Dutch alternative.[16] 'Consumers would save,' as one historian has summed up the advantageous consequences, 'Parliament needn't lose quite so much on its bailout of the East Indian Company, and smugglers would be driven out of business.'[17] Under the Tea Act of May 1773,*

---

* 'An Act to allow a drawback of the duties of customs on the exportation of tea to any of His Majesty's colonies or plantations in America ... and to empower the Commissioners of the Treasury to grant licences to the East India Company to export tea duty-free'.

which was passed in the Commons in an hour and without even needing a division, British duties on the tea re-exported to America were abolished, and the Company was allowed to sell its tea directly to consignees in the American colonies. Americans would still have to pay the threepenny-per-pound import duty, but since the tea itself would be so much cheaper than its illegal alternative, no difficulties were anticipated.[18]

Once again the government had not reckoned with the radicalism of the New England merchant-cum-smuggling community, or the unpopularity of what Americans saw as Britain's licensed monopoly provider. If Americans bought the East India Company tea, it was argued, it would damage in four ways the people who were increasingly calling themselves 'the Patriots': Parliament's right to impose taxes (albeit only the import duties charged for decades) would be reinforced; merchants who depended on smuggling for their larger-margin profits would be damaged; the revenue necessary to pay colonial officials and judges would be boosted, thereby lessening the influence of provincial assemblies; and the regiments that were preventing the westward drive of the colonists into Native American territory west of the Appalachians would be further financed. It therefore fell to the Sons of Liberty to prevent the tea being sold to consumers who might want it cheaply – perhaps in such a way as to provoke British reprisals, which would in turn engender further resistance.

At the end of a royal command performance of David Garrick's play *The Irish Widow* at the Drury Lane Theatre on the evening of 11 November 1772, a cry of 'Fire!' went up. An eyewitness recalled people starting to panic, scream, faint and attempt to leap down from the galleries to the stalls. 'You may guess what confusion this would have made,' wrote Lady Mary Coke to her sister, 'but the composure of the King, who never rose from his chair or showed the least apprehension, put a stop to the general hurry.'[19] The Queen had 'started when she heard the cry of fire, but recollecting herself almost in the same moment, remained composed', especially after her husband had said to her in German, 'Madam, if there is any danger, there will be care taken of you.'[20] It turned out a gang of pickpockets had been responsible, hoping to profit from the mayhem.

Although there had been no disaster on that occasion, the previous two years had been *anni horribiles* for the King, with Prince Henry's humiliating court case and subsequent morganatic marriage, his mother's death from cancer and the public's ugly reaction, his sister Caroline's affair and subsequent exile, his favourite brother William's lies, hypocrisy about his morganatic marriage – but at least Lord North's government was secure.

Indeed, the Opposition in the House of Lords did not even bother to force a vote on the King's Speech from the Throne in any of the sessions between 1771 and 1774. At Brooks's Club in St James's Street, the unofficial head-quarters of the Whig party, one of its most prominent members, Charles Fox, wagered Mr Codrington 200 guineas on 14 March 1772 that Lord North would still be First Lord of the Treasury twelve months later.[21] His money was safe.

The King disliked Brooks's, believing it – quite correctly – to be a den of aristocratic drunkenness, high-stakes gambling and radical ideas. Its betting book provides a valuable insight into the thinking of the Whig party since the Club's founding in 1764, although the members wagered on many things beyond politics, such as who would be the next bishop of Durham; whether the beautiful Anna-Frederica Heinel would dance at the Opera House the next winter; whether the 3rd Duke of Queensberry would die before 5.30 p.m. on 27 June 1773;* whether Lord Northington would get married before Lord Cholmondeley or the Duke of Devonshire; whether Charles Fox would clear his debts;† who would become the Prince of Wales' governor; when there would be another war with France; whether any minister would be beheaded;‡ whether the Perreau brothers would be hanged for forgery;§ the future size of the National Debt; the average weight of sheep sold at Smithfield Market; whether 'a ball fired from a cannon pointed horizontally does not rise before it falls (to be decided by a demonstration)';¶ the outcomes of courts martial, horse races and by-elections, and whether Captain John Donnellan had confessed to the murder of Sir Theodosius Broughton before he was hanged.** Charles Fox and Mr Hanger even bet on which of them would get gout first, though sadly history does not record who won.

In September 1772, John Wilkes joined other important City figures in criticizing the King's commutation of capital punishment for Captain Rob-ert Jones, who had been sentenced to hang for sodomizing a thirteen-year-old boy (although surprisingly the victim's age did not seem to have played a part in Jones' conviction).[22] Friends of Jones – a fireworks expert who had also popularized the sport of figure skating – produced female prostitutes who attested to his bisexuality, as though that would alleviate the serious-ness of the crime. Jones (who was in fact an artillery lieutenant) was due

---

*   He lived until 1778.
†   He did not, as we shall see.
‡   At odds of fifty to one.
§   The 2nd Duke of Leinster lost his wager; they were.
¶   It does not, although it is not known whether the demonstration took place.
**   He did not, so Richard Brinsley Sheridan won five guineas.

to hang until, on the day of the execution, George commuted his sentence to life imprisonment, and then a month later allowed him to go into lifelong exile in the South of France.

In what has been described as the first major public discussion of homosexuality in Britain, Wilkes used the pardon to allege widespread immorality and deviancy in governing circles and the Court. Obscene verses were published about the King and Jones, and newspapers alleged that ministers had spoken in Cabinet in favour of the sodomy practised in ancient Greece and Rome.[23] In a letter to the *Morning Chronicle* George's Court was likened to that of James I (who loved to surround himself with handsome young men), and in Newcastle a radical preacher, James Murray, preached on Zephaniah, chapter 2 verse 9, where 'Moab will become like Sodom.' With his sublime disregard for the passions of the mob, George ignored the demands for Jones' death penalty to be reimposed and so spared the life of the author of *A New Treatise on Artificial Fireworks* (1765) and *A Treatise on Skating* (1772).

Nor was it the only time that George defied the vicious prejudices of the day against homosexuality and bisexuality.* In June 1766, as a favour to his theatre-loving brother Prince Edward, the King signed a document making the Little Theatre in Haymarket into the Theatre Royal, which stated that it was 'Our will and pleasure' that Samuel Foote, the flamboyant impresario, should have 'a company of comedians' act there every summer, and authorized him to charge the sums necessary to offset 'the great expense of scenes, music and new decorations'.[24] The King was a patron not just of the serious arts but of comedy too, although he did not visit the Theatre Royal until 12 June 1776, when he attended a royal command performance with the Queen, and Foote personally showed the royal party to their seats. (Foote had only one leg, which inevitably led to a good number of jokes.)

The King and Queen's presence was controversial because Foote was then involved in a war of words with Elizabeth Chudleigh, the notorious Duchess of Kingston, who had alleged in court that he was homosexual. Did the King attend that night because he did not believe the well-known rumours – Foote had two children by his mistress – or because he did not care about them? It is unlikely to have been the latter as he believed sodomy to be 'a most detestable and unnatural crime', though not necessarily a capital one, as his decision over Jones attested.[25] Whichever it was, his visible support, which included ordering a second command performance

---

* These labels of sexual identity were not recognized in the eighteenth century, when people thought and spoke in terms of actual sexual practices, such as sodomy, onanism and so on.

at the Haymarket while Foote was on trial for sodomy later that year, was unpopular with some. A poem entitled 'Sodom and Onan' published by an enemy of Foote's referred to:

> King George, inveigled by Scotch insinuation
> To pardon sodomites, and damn the nation.[26]

It was noticeable that more than a decade after Bute's fall the Earl was still credited with having influence over the King.

On 26 March 1773 Edmund Burke made a speech in the Commons that verged on the histrionic. The previous August, King Gustav III of Sweden had connived in the coup that had overthrown his kingdom's parliamentary constitution, and Burke somehow connected an innocuous line in the King's Speech at the opening of Parliament with the events in Stockholm to suggest that Britain was teetering on the edge of a similar royal takeover. In his Speech, George had spoken of 'the most real concern that the produce of the late harvest has not given us the relief which we had hoped for in respect to the dearness of corn. So far as human wisdom can provide for alleviating the distress of the poor I am persuaded your attentions will not be wanting.'[27]

It was a fairly bland statement, one that he had also made at the time of the last bad harvest five years earlier. Yet, because King Gustav had distributed free food to the masses to help establish his despotism over the Diet in Stockholm, Burke declared, 'I hope to God, sir, no such design is formed against us . . . The multitude are incapable of judging from their ignorance. Let us not deceive them, but meet them upon fair and honest ground . . . We cannot alter the decrees of Providence, notwithstanding you have been told the contrary in a cajoling speech from the throne.'[28] The King was clearly not promising better harvests, just urging cheaper bread, which was not beyond the decrees of Providence but well within the capabilities of the House of Commons. As Burke's biographer puts it, 'The idea of George III distributing sacks of flour as a prelude to establishing a personal despotism is easily dismissed as a product of Burke's overheated imagination. Yet to understand his mind, his fantasies have to be taken seriously.'[29] That they were indeed fantasies is clear from what George himself said about Gustav's coup to Sir John Sinclair at an audience a few years later: 'I never will acknowledge that the king of a limited monarchy can on any principle endeavour to change the constitution and increase his own power. No honest man will attempt it.'[30]

Gustav's coup led to a serious scare of war with France, in the light of Catherine the Great's concern that it would mean increased French influence in the Baltic. Lord Sandwich had to mobilize the Royal Navy on 24 April, whereupon the French backed down. Sandwich had established himself as a great reforming naval minister, who fought against the institutionalized inefficiencies of the Admiralty. He introduced the concept of promotion on merit, rejecting two-thirds of the petitions for promotion from members of the nobility (something that would have been politically impossible without the King's wholehearted support). George extended his belief in allowing merit to determine at least some jobs at the universities, asking Lord North to appoint Dr William Vivian to the Regius professorship of physic* at Oxford, because 'I am thoroughly resolved that these employments at both universities shall be faithfully administered, not held as sinecures, therefore the gentleman must be acquainted that he will be required to read such a number of lectures as the Heads of Houses may think necessary.'[31] Outside the universities, however, the King retained a strong regard for the precedence of birth. 'Lord North cannot seriously think that a private gentleman like Mr Penton is to stand in the way of the eldest son of an earl,' he was to write to his Prime Minister over a comptrollership for Lord Lewisham, for 'undoubtedly if that idea holds good it is diametrically opposed to what I have known all my life.'[32] North, himself the eldest son of an earl, appointed Lewisham.

Between Tuesday 22 and Saturday 26 June 1773, the King attended a review of the Royal Navy at Portsmouth, sailing past twenty ships-of-the-line, three frigates and two sloops in two lines stretching over 5 miles, and also visiting the dockyard, gun wharf and victualling yards. Despite the severe retrenchments after the Seven Years War, the navy still boasted over 300 ships and the merchant marine had around 40,000 sailors, so there was much to celebrate.[33] George's journeys to Portsmouth and back were attended by large and enthusiastic crowds; when the soldiers of the 20th Regiment of Foot had to use fixed bayonets to hold back a crowd in Portsmouth from pressing too close, he told them, 'My people will not hurt me.'[34] The King looked 'tall and full of dignity' to one spectator, 'his countenance florid and good-natured'.[35] He made similar visits in 1778, 1781, 1789 and 1794. What interested him most at this first inspection was seeing the intricate process by which the thick naval ropes were made.

The King went on to become the best-informed monarch on naval matters between the two sailor kings, James II and William IV.[36] Sandwich (whom he was to acknowledge as the best of the seventeen first lords of the Admiralty of his reign) arranged for models and plans of ships and dockyards to be sent to Buckingham House, organized tutorials in ship

---

* Changed in the twentieth century to Regius professorship of medicine.

design from the Surveyor of the Navy and invited the King to ship-launching ceremonies at Deptford. 'I give you infinite trouble,' his eager pupil told Sandwich, 'but it is a desire of being a little au fait of ship building.'[37]

Sir Hans Stanley MP, the Cofferer of the Household, was not on the dockyard trip, but he wrote to Countess Spencer soon afterwards, 'I am told his questions were all manly, sensible, and pertinent, and that he made every note and observation, from whence this expedition might be a real instruction to him, and not a mere amusement.'[38] Another benefit of the trip was that it reassured the King about his great personal popularity in the country at large, away from the hissing and booing of Wilkesite London. 'The King is exceeding delighted with his reception in Portsmouth,' wrote Sir Joshua Reynolds, who saw him shortly afterwards.[39] 'He was convinced he was not so unpopular as the newspapers would represent him to be.' The women of Godalming threw so many nosegays into the King's carriage as he passed through the town that they reached up to his knees, and all along the route 'God Save the King' was sung 'in a tumultuous manner. The King was so affected that he could not refrain shedding an abundance of tears, and even joined in the chorus.'[40] Reynolds also noted of the King's return to Kew that he 'was so impatient to see the Queen that he opened the chaise and jumped out before any of his attendants could come to his assistance. He seized the Queen, whom he had met at the door, round the waist, and carried her in his arms into the room.'[41] Alone of the Hanoverians, his marriage was a genuine love-match.

In the late eighteenth century there was a delay of anything between four and six weeks (longer on outbound journeys to America due to the prevailing winds) for news to cross the Atlantic, a length of time that was to bedevil attempts by the government in London to keep abreast of fast-moving events. After the first of three East India Company ships carrying tea arrived in Boston Harbor on 28 November 1773, events in America moved very quickly indeed. The local merchants and their workmen, supported by the populace, prevented the tea from being offloaded, which by law had to happen within twenty days of docking. If the duty was not paid by the importer within that period, customs officials had the right to seize it, in which case it would have been sold in Boston, massively undercutting the smugglers' prices. The Sons of Liberty called a meeting the next day, at which it was agreed that the tea had to be sent back to England without the tax being paid. The day after that, Thomas Hutchinson ordered a group of pickets at the docks to disperse. On 16 December he refused permission for the ships bearing the tea to leave the harbour without offloading it, as had been the compromise solution in other American ports. At 6.30 that night, the merchants' employees and other Patriots from the Boston Corresponding Committee carried out a prearranged attack upon the (curiously undefended) ships, in what humorously became known as the Boston Tea Party.

Between 100 and 150 men took part in the attack in three teams, some wearing Mohawk disguises and using soot for blackface, allowing plausible deniability in court. They raided the ships, smashed open the 342 chests containing more than 45 tons of tea and threw it overboard into the harbour, in under two hours destroying tea to the value of £9,659. The efficiency of the operation points to its having been well organized in advance by the Boston merchants who stood to lose by the halving of the tea price, rather than a spontaneous outburst of rage by ordinary citizens. An historian who has identified a hundred participants discovered that eight were employed by one radical Boston merchant alone.[42]

Many of the artisans, labourers and apprentices who participated were veterans of the Stamp Act riots of 1765, the violent confrontations with soldiers in 1770 in Boston and the beatings and tarring-and-featherings of customs commissioners.[43] Smashing open the hundreds of chests with axes and destroying 90,000 pounds of tea was hard work requiring efficiency, time and discipline, and contemporary accounts 'portray a tightly controlled, almost military operation'.[44] Some historians have described the Sons of Liberty as the 'henchmen' of the rich smuggler-merchants: 'It was essentially a private operation for the benefit of racketeers.'[45] Whatever it was, it lit a tinderbox.

As well as destroying tea, the Sons of Liberty continued their campaign of terrorizing British officials. In early 1774 they tarred and feathered John Malcolm, a Boston customs comptroller (his second experience of this punishment), using boiling tar that left him bedridden for two months. Ann Hulton, the sister of Henry Hulton, the Boston Commissioner of Customs, wrote of how Malcolm's:

> arm [was] dislocated in [the] tearing off [of] his clothes, he was dragged in a cart with thousands attending, some beating him with clubs and knocking him out of the cart, then in again. They gave him several severe whippings at different parts of the town. This spectacle of horror and sportive cruelty was exhibited for about five hours . . . They brought him to the gallows and put a rope round his neck saying they would hang him . . . [46]

Malcolm took strips of his own scorched and cracked skin back to London, some of it with tar and feathers still attached, which he would occasionally enclose in the petitions that he sent to British politicians asking for recompense. When Malcolm met the King in January 1775, he bitterly joked that he might perhaps be made a 'Knight of the Tar, that I was so tarred with that I like the smell of it'.[47]

News of the Boston Tea Party reached London on 19 January 1774. The King's initial concern seems to have been as much about the tea as about the political implications of the attack. 'I am much hurt that the instigation of bad men hath again drawn the people of Boston to take such unjustifiable steps,' he wrote to Lord Dartmouth, 'but I trust by degrees tea will find its way there; for when Quebec is stocked with that commodity it will find its way southwards.'[48] By then even Lord Dartmouth and Opposition figures such as Chatham and Rockingham were ready to condemn those responsible for the Tea Party. The King now approved of North's proposal to reintroduce a version of Hillsborough's hardline measures of February 1769, which at the time he had opposed.

The underlying assumption, not just of the King but of almost all policymakers, was that those responsible for the Boston Tea Party needed to be met with firmness, that the colonies would not unite in defending Massachusetts over such a gross provocation, and that even if they did, Britain would have the last word as she was a large empire at the height of her power. Moreover, tough action against the colonies was unusual but hardly unprecedented: Charles II had revoked Massachusetts' charter in 1684 as a result of excessive puritanism there, and James II had abolished some colonial assemblies and prohibited town meetings.

The Cabinet was thus relatively united in favour of a coercive response. Although the months after the Boston Tea Party saw different emphases from minister to minister, with Dartmouth and North recoiling from anything that might lead to what they saw as a civil war between Loyalists and Patriots in America, the underlying assumption of the ministry was that Britain had an undeniable historical sovereignty over all her North American colonies, which included the right to tax. The only people in British politics who did not believe that were the most radical elements of the Whig party. Nor was there too distinct a dividing line between the government 'moderates' Dartmouth and North and the 'hardliners' Sandwich, Suffolk and the King, since ultimately they all believed in the same end: the explicit constitutional subordination of the thirteen colonies to the mother country.

In any case, the Cabinet was not always where policy was made: of the five meetings held in 1774, two consisted of only five ministers and two of only six.[49] They were usually held to decide only one or sometimes two specific issues, rather than meeting with a long agenda. No one took minutes or followed up on what was agreed. In general, policy was made between North and the minister concerned, North informing the King afterwards. The idea that George III pushed his government towards tyrannical measures aimed at provoking a war to crush American liberty is therefore wrong in every particular.

The King and Lord North were surprisingly badly advised over what might happen if fighting did break out in America. Lieutenant-General Thomas Gage, Commander-in-Chief of British forces in America since 1763, had an audience with the King on 4 February 1774 when he was in England on leave. 'His language was very consonant to his character of an honest determined man,' George reported to North.

> He says they will be lions whilst we are lambs, but if we take the resolute part they will undoubtedly prove very meek. He thinks the four regiments intended to relieve as many regiments in America if sent to Boston are suffi-cient to prevent any disturbance. I wish you would see him and hear his ideas as to the mode of compelling Boston to submit to whatever may be thought necessary. Indeed all men seem now to feel that the fatal compliance in 1766 [that is, the repeal of the Stamp Act] has encouraged the Americans annually to increase in their pretensions [to] that thorough independency which one state has of another, but which is quite subversive of the obedience which a colony owes to its mother country.[50]

It was truly terrible advice from Gage, who knew America well and had no basis upon which to assert that the citizens would be 'very meek'.

The Boston Tea Party was seen as a latter-day Rubicon. The Cabinet met at Lord Dartmouth's house in St James's Square on the evening of 19 Feb-ruary 1774 to discuss how best to punish Massachusetts. Two warships were already on their way to reinforce a Royal Navy squadron anchored off the city, and Gage had been ordered to return to Boston immediately. The main issues under discussion were what to do about the Tea Party perpetrators, the port of Boston itself and the Massachusetts Charter of 1691. The problem, as the hardline Attorney-General Edward Thurlow informed the Cabinet, was that prosecution of the perpetrators was blocked because too much of the evidence was based on hearsay. The Cabinet decided upon four Coercive Acts – subsequently known in America as the Intolerable Acts, which is indicative of the way they were received there.

The government knew that, once the Acts were passed, they could not be repealed like the Stamp Act and Townshend Duties had been: as two American historians rightly points out, 'No government could have made the response required to meet the American demands – which, at the very least, meant the repeal of the Coercive Acts – and remained in power.'[51] The King was not directly involved in formulating the Acts, and although he supported Lord North over them, he certainly did not give direction, as is clear from his correspondence with North and his ministers at the time.[52]*

Parliament started to debate the Coercive Acts on 7 March. The first of these, the Boston Port Act, closed the harbour to all shipping from 1 June until such time as 'peace and obedience to the laws' returned and the loss of the tea was reimbursed; next, the Massachusetts Government Act suspended the 1691 Charter, made the Assembly, sheriffs and judges royal appointees and limited town meetings to one per year; third, the Administration of Justice Act allowed British customs officials to be tried in Nova Scotia if they could not get a fair trial in Massachusetts, where local juries were often the direct beneficiaries of smuggling. (George Washington hyperbolically labelled this the 'Murder Act', claiming it would legalize the wanton murder of Americans.) Lastly, a new Quartering Act would permit troops to be quartered in occupied buildings, but not billeted in private homes. Considering the immense long-term consequences of these Acts of Parliament, they passed through their three readings in both Houses with very little opposition, except among some of the more radical Whigs such as Burke and the Duke of Richmond. The Boston Port Bill passed its second reading in the Commons with no debate or division at all. 'The feebleness and futility of the opposition to the Boston Port Bill', the King told North, 'shows the rectitude of the measure.'[53]

For all the popularity of the Coercive Acts in Parliament, Britain had overreacted disastrously, however. The British government assumed that the other colonies would disown Massachusetts after the Tea Party, but this proved a profound misreading of the colonists' reaction. Many of them were already looking for grievances to justify their split from Britain, and were now being provided with plenty.

One person who spoke against the Boston Port Bill on its third reading was Charles Fox, who had shown no interest in supporting the people of Massachusetts before. In 1772, Fox had resigned his seat on the Board of Admiralty, a position which he had held for only a fortnight, to oppose the Royal Marriages Act. Five years earlier, his father Lord Holland had asked the King to advance his barony to a viscountcy, or even an earldom (like his brother the Earl of Ilchester), but as he reported to Charles, 'I saw obstinate, determined denial, without any reason given. Don't ever, Charles,

---

* As so often, the political crisis coincided with Queen Charlotte having a baby, in this case Prince Adolphus, Duke of Cambridge, who was born on 24 February 1774 and who grew to be 'the only son of George III to live above the age of four and keep all the Commandments' (Iremonger, *Love and the Princesses* p. 88). He was christened by Frederick Cornwallis, Archbishop of Canterbury and uncle to Lieutenant-General Charles Cornwallis.

make any exception, or trust as I did.'[54] Some of the quasi-republicanism of Charles Fox and his uncle, the Duke of Richmond, stemmed from their contempt for the Hanoverians (Richmond was descended from Charles II). Fox's Christian names Charles James – named after not one but all of the male Stuart monarchs – amounted to almost a baptismal rejection of George's family. North gave Fox another chance of office, appointing him to the Board of Treasury in December 1772, but when Fox threw that up too in 1774 by voting against the Boston Port Bill he made a formidable enemy of the King.

In 1773, Fox had undertaken to help Edmund Burke's disreputable brother Richard over a land speculation in St Vincent in return for a share of the expected profits, which was astonishingly not illegal for a government minister at the time. However, in the execution of the matter he had received no help from Lord North, the First Lord of the Treasury, which had left him with an acute sense of pique. It is possible that Fox used the coincidence of the Coercive Acts to make his crossing of the floor of the House of Commons look principled.

The King had spotted Fox as a troublemaker early on, not least because he had the reputation of being one of the most notorious gamblers in Brooks's Club, a failing George regarded as bad for 'morals, credit and character'.[55] The King wrote to North on 16 February 1774 – before the Coercive Acts were even agreed by the Cabinet – about Fox's insolent behaviour towards North in the Commons, saying, 'I am greatly incensed at the presumption of Charles Fox ... indeed that young man has so thoroughly cast off every principle of common honour and honesty that he must become as contemptible as he is odious, and I hope you will let him know you are not insensible of his conduct towards you.'[56] After Fox's intervention on the Boston Port Bill, North dismissed him from the ministry with the single sentence, 'His Majesty has thought proper to order a new commission of the Treasury to be made out, in which I do not see your name.'[57] This cost Fox his salary of £1,600 per annum, adding another grievance to his list.

Although the King has been much criticized by Whig historians for not spotting Charles Fox's undoubted charm and charisma, he was correct to assume that Fox kept loose company. In April 1776 it was noted in the Brooks's Club betting book that 'Mr Fitzpatrick and Mr Hanger have agreed that whenever either of them go to a bawdy house in King's Court he shall pay ten guineas for the other *toties quoties*.'* The agreement was

* *Toties quoties*: 'as often as', a Roman Catholic expression formerly used for certain plenary indulgences that could be gained several times a day.

witnessed by Fox, the 5th Duke of Devonshire and Lord Edward Bentinck, the son of the Duke of Portland. Fox was also relatively open to friends about his bouts of venereal disease.[58]*

Little wonder that the King wanted the Prince of Wales to avoid the clubs of St James's, and distrusted those aristocrats who revelled in them. Yet what he saw as Fox's licentiousness was not the only thing the King held against him. When Lord Holland died in July 1774, Fox and his elder brother Stephen, now the 2nd Lord Holland, failed to observe the customary period of mourning. 'They both went into company directly,' Lady Mary Coke recorded, 'without observing any kind of decency, and will I suppose do just the same when their poor mother breathes her last.'[59] For all Fox's personal charm and wonderful capacity for friendship, such behaviour revolted the King, who was a stickler for proprieties.

Travelling in the opposite political direction to Fox, Lord George Sackville – who in 1769 had changed his name to Germain in order to inherit the Drayton House estate in Northamptonshire and a large fortune from a widowed aunt by marriage – spoke strongly in favour of the Massachusetts Government Bill in the Commons, thus marking himself out for future political advancement. Here, too, a strong stance on the Coercive Acts might well have been masking and legitimizing a more personal impetus: Germain wanted the absolution from his Minden court-martial shame that appointment to an important government post would bring. Whether his bid for office was opportunistic or principled, it was to have incalculable consequences for George's reign and place in history.

In April 1774, Parliament passed the Quebec Act, which put the government of that province into the hands of a governor-in-council and partially returned French civil law to the 70,000 French-speakers in Canada. It also gave them the right to practise their Roman Catholicism and for their churches to gather tithes, while expanding Quebec's borders into the Ohio country. The Act was passed in order to secure French Canadians' loyalty to the British Empire in America and (a full decade after the Treaty of Paris) was long overdue, but in the current American context it could not have been worse timed.

To permit the Quebecois to retain their language, laws, customs and religion without interference from London was an intelligent, liberal

---

* In another Brooks's wager that would certainly have confirmed His Majesty's view of the Club had he known about it, 'Lord Cholmondeley has given two guineas to Lord Derby to receive five hundred guineas whenever his Lordship fucks a woman in a balloon one thousand yards from the earth.' As far as we know, the wager was never consummated. Derby's money was safe.

measure that pertains to this day and it kept French-speaking Canadians relatively content. The King supported the Act, describing the Quebecois as 'the old inhabitants whose rights and usages ought by no means to be disturbed'.[60] However, given the gathering atmosphere of mistrust in America, even in some quarters paranoia, the Act was used by Protestant clergy in the thirteen colonies to allege, entirely untruthfully, that the British had designs not only to impose Anglican bishoprics on them but Roman Catholic ones too. It was a bizarre conspiracy theory, but one that took powerful hold just as the relationship between Britain and the American colonies came under maximum strain. 'It is a pity the King of England was turned papist,' an English visitor heard colonists declare the following year.[61]

Rumour and conspiracy theories were no less influential in eighteenth-century politics than they are today. After the Quebec Act, American Patriots were busily promoting such theories, in which they did not necessarily believe, knowing that they made excellent anti-British propaganda. Because the colonies had risen against the Catholic James II, if George III could somehow be made out to be pro-Catholic it would help justify them in doing so again. Particularly in the sparsely settled backcountry, where there were few printing presses and reliable information was both rare and long delayed, anti-English conspiracy theories were widespread. 'The anti-Catholic paroxysm of the 1774–75 phase of the American Revolution', as Conor Cruise O'Brien termed it, was crucial, for if people could be persuaded that there was 'a great British and Catholic conspiracy against the freedoms and religion of American Protestants', then 'revolution became a religious duty as well as a political cause.'[62]

Whereas fewer than one-tenth of Englishmen were Dissenters, among Americans the proportion was three-quarters. Nonconformist denominations such as the Presbyterians and Congregationalists were large in number, prone to be radical and almost as intolerant of Anglicanism as they were of Catholicism and Judaism. 'As well as being a civil war,' J. C. D. Clark reminds us, 'the American Revolution contained many of the elements of a war of religion.'[63] The Enlightenment was not the only well from which revolutionaries drew their inspiration; Congregationalists and other Nonconformist Protestant sects in America often had millennial expectations of the coming revolution; indeed, as another historian has put it, 'Many of the clergy saw in the imperial crisis signs of the Second Coming of Christ and the Day of Judgement.'[64]

While it is not true that George decried the American Revolution as a 'Presbyterian rebellion', as Presbyterian preachers thereafter claimed, the religious side to the American Revolution was extremely important in so devout a society, and fears that the Quebec Act would set precedents for the rest of North America were fanned to a flame in sermons, pamphlets and remonstrances.[65] To take just one example, Paul Revere, a Boston printmaker, produced an engraving entitled *The Mitred Minuet*, featuring four fat Catholic bishops holding hands as they danced around the Quebec Act, as Satan, Lord North and Lord Bute (identifiable by his kilt and bagpipes) looked on approvingly.[66] Ironically enough, if George had kept the defeated French down and forced them to live as second-class citizens without civil and religious rights, American radicals would have been happier.

There was another factor. By extending the western and southern boundaries of Quebec to the Ohio and Mississippi rivers, the Quebec Act made it seem that Britain was putting French Canadian interests ahead of British American ones. Here was the Proclamation Line debacle all over again, only this time advancing the cause of a mainly Catholic province rather than Native Americans. It prompted many American colonists to view the Quebec Act as a fifth piece of intolerable legislation to add to the other four. 'The Finger of God points out a mighty empire to your sons,' argued the *New York Journal* in an attack on the Quebecois in July 1775: 'the savages of the wilderness were never expelled to make room in this, the best part of the Continent, for idolators and slaves.'[67]

North defended the Coercive Acts on 22 April, arguing that they were essentially reactions to provocations. 'The Americans have tarred and feathered your subjects,' he told the Commons, 'plundered your merchants, burnt your ships, denied all obedience to your laws and authority; yet so clement and so long forbearing has our conduct been that it is incumbent on us now to take a different course. Whatever may be the consequences, we must risk something; if we do not, all is over.'[68]

'I am infinitely pleased,' George told his premier on 3 May, after the Massachusetts Government Bill had passed by 239 votes to 64, despite harsh denunciations from Charles Fox, Edmund Burke, John Dunning and Colonel Barré.[69] Three days later, when the Administration of Justice Bill passed by a similar majority, he told North that it 'gives me infinite satisfaction. Perseverance and the meeting [of] difficulties as they arise with firmness seem the only means of either with credit or success terminating public affairs. Your conduct on the American disturbances is a very clear proof of the justness of that proposition.'[70] Despite Rockingham's opposition in the Lords, the Bill passed there by 43 votes to 12 on 18 May, and two days later George signed both Bills into law. Yet throughout this crisis, as over the Stamp Act, the Declaratory Act and the Townshend Duties, George was following his Prime Minister, not leading him.[71]

The passing of the Coercive Acts led to the first real criticism of the King in America. Before their enactment, many Americans believed that the King was essentially their protector, if badly advised by corrupt or evil counsellors. There had been very little direct personal criticism of him between the repeal of the Stamp Act in 1766 and the Boston Tea Party in 1773. Once he had given his formal assent to the Coercive Acts, however, he was widely seen to have failed his American subjects. Josiah Quincy Jr published a savage denunciation of him in his pamphlet *Observations on the Act of Parliament Commonly Called the Boston Port-Bill* in May 1774, which sarcastically shredded the traditional loyal expressions of Americans towards the King, arguing that they were based on an illusion.[72]

On 13 May, General Gage arrived at Boston after a speedy twenty-six-day crossing, and was commissioned as Governor of Massachusetts soon after landing. In June the previous year, a series of secret reports written for the government in London in 1768–9 by Governor Thomas Hutchinson had come into the possession of Benjamin Franklin, who made sure they were published in the American press. They were (unsurprisingly) critical of the Sons of Liberty and the Patriots, and the resultant public outcry led to a petition for his dismissal. The North government ignored these for a year, but Gage's return allowed for Hutchinson to be replaced.

Ironically enough, considering the events of the following year, Gage was greeted on his way from the docks to his swearing-in at the Assembly council chamber by several companies of the Massachusetts Militia.[73] Over the next few days, as Bostonians absorbed the news of the Port Act, which had arrived just before Gage, the mood in the city changed fundamentally. Two weeks after his landing, the Virginia House of Burgesses adopted a resolution calling for a Continental Congress, and the Maryland Assembly passed resolves in support of Boston. Of course in that febrile political atmosphere no genuine tyranny would have permitted a congress of all the thirteen colonies to gather together to plot the next moves against it, yet the British government did nothing to prevent or disrupt it.

When on 19 June the City of London petitioned the Crown to refuse royal assent to the Quebec Bill, the King wrote to North to say that he would not do so.[74] Three days later he signed the Act, going to Parliament to do so even though he could have signed it at Buckingham House, and 'was very much insulted' by a Wilkesite mob on the way, with people shaking their fists at him and yelling, 'Remember Charles I! Remember James II!' and 'No Roman Catholic King: no Roman Catholic religion! America for ever!'[75] Horace Walpole claimed that 'The King was hurt and alarmed,' and that 'when he came to the Lords he trembled, he faltered, and could scarcely pronounce his speech.'[76]

Walpole liked to impute cowardice to the King, but since no other sources mention this, and as he behaved with perfect composure on every other occasion when physical courage was required of him, such strictures can be safely ignored. Walpole's fellow gossip-monger Lady Mary Coke doubted whether even the agitation of the mob, let alone that of the King, was real. 'I suppose [they] were hired to treat His Majesty with such impertinence, for 'tis not likely that any one of them know anything of the Quebec Bill, which seems to have given them so much offence.'[77]

Within two days of landing in England on 29 June 1774, at a Levee at St James's Palace Thomas Hutchinson was presented to the King, who invited him and Lord Dartmouth to the Closet afterwards to discuss American affairs in private. (It was, as the palace official Lord Pomfret harrumphed, quite contrary to custom for such audiences to occur spontaneously.) Hutchinson, a keen amateur historian, later wrote a detailed account of their meeting in his diary.

After politely asking about his journey, and hearing an apology from Hutchinson for the way he was dressed, the King asked him how the Bostonians had reacted to the Coercive Acts. Hutchinson replied that they only knew of the Port Act by the time he had left, but that it was 'extremely alarming to the people'.[78] George commended Hutchinson, saying his conduct 'has been universally approved of here by people of all parties', adding that 'nothing could be more cruel than the treatment you met with in betraying your private letters,' although he then said to Dartmouth that 'I remember nothing in them to which the least exception could be taken.'[79] When the King asked how the letters had got to New England for publication, Hutchinson said that Benjamin Franklin had publicly stated that he had sent them. The King was curious to know about his opponents in Massachusetts, but was neither angry or vindictive; he knew the names of several of his more prominent American antagonists, including Samuel Adams, John Hancock, Samuel Cooper, James Bowdoin, Speaker Thomas Cushing and the theologian Dr Charles Chauncy. Beyond politics, Hutchinson was impressed by the King's 'knowledge of so many facts' about America.[80]

'Where is Dr Franklin, my lord?' the King asked Dartmouth, and was told he was in London. 'In such abuse, Mr Hutchinson, as you have met with, I suppose there must have been personal malevolence as well as party rage?'[81] Hutchinson replied not, and added, 'The attacks have been upon my public conduct, and for such things as my duty to Your Majesty required me to do, and which you have been pleased to approve of.' 'I see they threatened to pitch and feather you,' the King observed. 'Tar and feather, may it please Your Majesty,' Hutchinson replied, 'but I don't remember that I was ever threatened with it.'[82] The King asked what guards he had

had as Governor, only to be told that he had had none at all, because he 'hoped they only meant to intimidate'.[83] The King then asked, 'What does Hancock do now? How will the late affair affect him?' He was referring to a large excise bill over which Hancock was being prosecuted for non-payment; Hutchinson told him that Hancock had been left a large fortune by a rich uncle.

They then spoke again of Samuel Adams, who Hutchinson said was 'considered as the opposer of the government, and a sort of Wilkes in New England'.[84] 'What gave him his importance?' the King asked. 'A great pretended zeal for liberty,' Hutchinson replied, 'and a most inflexible natural temper. He was the first that publicly asserted the independency of the colonies upon the kingdom, or the supreme authority of it.' 'I have heard, Mr Hutchinson,' the King said, 'that your ministers preach that, for the sake of promoting liberty or the public good, any immorality or less evil may be tolerated?' The former Governor replied that it was not preached from the pulpit, but it was asserted by the political leaders 'that the good of the public is above all other considerations, and that truth may be dispensed with, and immorality is excusable, when this great good can be obtained by such means'. 'That's a strange doctrine, indeed,' replied the King, who of course believed in the public good, but never that the end justified the means.

They discussed the political stances of the Congregationalists and Presbyterians of Massachusetts, Hutchinson himself being a Dissenter. They then talked about the demographics of the province; Hutchinson agreed with Franklin's assessment that the population of America was doubling every twenty-five years, with most of the immigration going to the more temperate Southern states. The King asked about colonial wheat production, pasture grazing and the importation of bread corn (he had heard of maize). He was clearly interested in the colonies' long-term economic success.

The King also asked Hutchinson about the politics of New York, Connecticut, Pennsylvania and Rhode Island, the last of which he called 'a strange form of government' because all the offices were elected annually. Hutchinson agreed, saying that it did 'approach, Sir, the nearest to a democracy of any of your colonies'.[85] Connecticut, he said, was 'cautious'. The King showed a remarkable knowledge of various government officials of New England, asking, for example, whether Massachusetts' Chief Justice Peter Oliver was the brother of the previous Lieutenant-Governor Andrew Oliver.[86] (He was.)

George then asked about the Indigenous Nations of Massachusetts, whose numbers were down to a hundred Wampanoag families clustered around Mashpee. Hutchinson predicted the extinction of the indigenous peoples throughout the continent, through 'their being dispirited at their low despicable condition among the Europeans, who have taken possession of their country, and treat them as an inferior race of beings, but more to the immoderate use of spirituous liquors'.[87] After two hours of conversation, all conducted standing up, the King ended by advising Hutchinson to recover from his seasickness through a long stay at his lodgings. 'It is surprising that he should have so perfect a knowledge of the state of his dominions,' Hutchinson wrote to an American friend ten days later.[88] The last King of America could certainly not be accused of ignorance of or lack of interest in his realm.

In a letter to General Gage three days later, Hutchinson claimed that he had asked the King to offer some relief to Boston's merchants, who could not pay customs duties if shipping were banned from the port, and that he hoped the King would not require an explicit declaration of Boston's submission.[89] But did he really say that? It was not in Hutchinson's detailed contemporaneous memorandum of the conversation, of which he wrote, 'I have minuted what remained the clearest in my mind, and as near the order in which they passed as I am able.' The King's letter to North written at 9.02 on the evening of the conversation also implies not. 'I am now well convinced they will soon submit,' he wrote. He reported that Hutchinson thought that the Boston Port Bill 'was the only wise effectual method that could have been suggested for bringing them to a speedy submission, and that the change in the legislature will be a means of establishing some government in that province which till now has been a scene of anarchy'.[90]

In the event, Gage required no 'submission' from Boston, nor an admission of the validity of the Declaratory Act, but merely compensation from the city authorities to the East India Company for the destroyed tea, whereupon the King would, as Dartmouth confirmed to Gage on 6 July, restore 'its privileges as a port'.[91] Dartmouth also hoped that the Bostonians might themselves 'prosecute and bring to justice' those responsible for the Tea Party, although that was clearly never going to happen. Hutchinson later claimed the credit for the government's softer position in early July, but it is much more likely that North and Dartmouth had already decided upon it, with the King's approval, as a way of averting conflict.

Yet the day before Dartmouth wrote to Gage with his new conciliatory approach, Gage had written to Dartmouth saying that the Boston Loyalists' proposal to compensate the East India Company had been soundly rejected by a town meeting.[92] Such was the lag in cross-Atlantic communications that the conditions for conciliation had already been rejected in

Boston the day before they had left London. The obvious solution to this sometimes crippling difficulty – to send a high-ranking viceroy with pleni- potentiary powers to New York to negotiate on behalf of the British government – never seems to have been seriously considered. (Despite being the Commander-in-Chief in America, Gage had political jurisdiction over Massachusetts alone.) In those days, the tyrant to whom all were subject was not King George but distance itself.

11

'Blows Must Decide'

August 1774–April 1775

I am more and more convinced that we have both the right and the power on our side, and that though the effort may be accompanied with some melancholy circumstances, we are now arrived at the decisive moment of preserving or of losing for ever both our trade and empire.[1]

Edward Gibbon to J. B. Holroyd, 31 January 1775

In early August 1774, an anonymous pamphlet entitled *A Summary View of the Rights of British America* was published in Williamsburg, Virginia. It had been written by the local assemblyman and lawyer Thomas Jefferson, and put forward a commonwealth view of the unfolding crisis in America, arguing that Parliament was 'foreign to our constitutions and unacknowledged by our laws' and that the colonies were related to each other only through the King, 'who was thereby made the central link connecting the several parts of the empire'.[2]

Jefferson thought that the King should use his prerogative powers more rather than less, but against a tyrannical Parliament rather than against his American subjects. In his opening sentence he suggested that at the forthcoming Continental Congress, which he could not attend because of illness, 'an humble and dutiful address be presented to His Majesty, begging leave to lay before him, as chief magistrate of the British Empire, the united complaints of His Majesty's subjects in America'.[3] It concluded, 'Open your breast, Sire, to liberal and expanded thought. Let not the name of George the Third be a blot in the page of history.'[4] George bought *A Summary View* for his library.

Jefferson was in effect urging George to become a Patriot King, to rise above party for the general good, and in this case to wield a veto power over legislation that had not been used since the days of Queen Anne. The concept of the Patriot King was deeply embedded in George's ideas of kingship, as we have seen, but it was also a common and recurrent one in American political discourse – initially used to praise George, but increasingly henceforth to condemn him.[5] British Whigs noticed with dismay that, in this aspect of the royal prerogative, American radicals were proposing ways for the King to govern America without recourse to Parliament from which even the Tories shrank at home. There were some criticisms of the King elsewhere in Jefferson's pamphlet, including the complaint that he had not done enough to inhibit the slave trade: 'The abolition of domestic slavery is the great object of desire in those colonies, where it was unhappily introduced in their infant state.'[6] Because the pamphlet was initially only stated to be by 'A native, and member of the House of Burgesses' – indeed, the *London Chronicle* described the author as 'a respectable merchant of Cumberland County in Maryland' – no one knew that the author was himself a substantial slave owner. The King, of course, never owned any slaves at all.

The central argument of *A Summary View* was the same one that Franklin had held for years and which John Adams and others were now espousing: namely, that the provinces, which they were already calling 'states', were connected to Britain solely through the King, so Parliament possessed no legislative authority over America, except possibly in the regulation of some mutually beneficial trade.[7] The fact that the colonies had clearly acquiesced in parliamentary authority for over a century did not deter the Patriots from this theory, for, as one historian has put it, they 'nearly all sought to expound what the connection *ought to be* by pretending to describe it as it *was*'.[8]

There is no evidence that the King read Jefferson's pamphlet. He seemed optimistic at Court on 3 August, saying to Richard Jackson, the colonial agent for Connecticut, 'Well, matters go on well in America. They are coming right.'[9] Jackson tactfully replied, 'I hope, Sir, they will come right, but it may require some time.' Privately, Jackson was less sanguine, telling Lord Dudley at the time, 'I don't see how we can go back.' Although the King through his approachability and affability tried to ensure his interlocutors did not just tell him what they thought he wanted to hear, such was nonetheless the occupational hazard of all courts. On 6 August, Boston received the official versions of all the Coercive Acts, but, far from breaking the radicals' will, this rallied support for them, not just in Massachusetts but across New England.

With the Continental Congress due to assemble in Philadelphia in early September, peace breaking out between Russia and Turkey, and France unsettled after Louis XVI's accession in May, the King wrote to North on 24 August to suggest an early dissolution of Parliament and a snap general election, despite Parliament still having another seven months to run under the Septennial Act. 'I trust it will fill the House with more gentlemen of landed property, as the nabobs, planters and other volunteers are not ready for the battle.' He was referring to the East India Company plutocrats of whom he and his aristocratic Prime Minister privately disapproved, not so much on class grounds as because of the ruthless and often corrupt ways they had gained their Bengal fortunes.[10] (It has been alleged that 'the battle' referred to the coming struggle with America, but the context makes it clear that the King merely meant the general election.) His timing was astute: had there not been a dissolution and had Parliament lived out its full seven years, the election would have come in April 1775, the very month when the first shots of the American Revolution were fired.

Only 95 constituencies were contested out of the 314 which returned the 558 MPs, as elections were extremely expensive to fight. Some fifty-five peers controlled around 150 seats, though not nearly as many as were overseen by the country squirearchy and gentry. Forty-five MPs came from Scottish constituencies, which tended to support the government. There were forty English county constituencies that averaged 4,000 electors, with the two Yorkshire seats having 20,000 electors, whereas Rutland's two had only 800. Over three-quarters of the eighty county MPs were from the squirearchy, who also sat for most of the 405 seats of the 203 English boroughs, which were elected on a wide variety of franchises.[11] Voting took place between 5 October and 10 November. The government's campaign strategy was managed by John Robinson, and overall was very successful, despite some Wilkesite gains in London and its environs. By early November, 321 government supporters had been returned against 237 Opposition and doubtfuls; many of the latter would anyway support the government on American issues (although these had been mentioned in only a few constituencies during the campaign). North therefore had a strong new seven-year mandate. After holding a Cabinet on 3 October, he set out for his country seat, Wroxton in Oxfordshire, but was held up and robbed by a highwayman en route. He returned to London via his home in Bushy Park, reaching Downing Street at half past midnight. With remarkable sangfroid, he wrote to the King to report favourable election news, but not explaining why he was back in London early.

In September, British embassies in Europe had begun to report that some American Patriots were buying gunpowder from Europe, shipped via Amsterdam, since virtually none was produced domestically in the colonies. British Army depots in North America were accorded increased security, and an Order-in-Council prohibiting the export of arms and ammunition to the colonies was proclaimed on 19 October. A Royal Navy flotilla was dispatched to Amsterdam which persuaded the Dutch government officially to ban exports of gunpowder, while doing little to deter it in practice, generally along the established tea-smuggling routes via the French and Dutch West Indies. The only practicable way to prevent arms smuggling was through a close blockade of all American ports, but the British government recoiled from such a step in peacetime.[12] Even if the larger ports could be blockaded, policing the long coastline along which gunpowder could be smuggled in at night would require a substantial fleet of frigates, cruisers, armed brigs and schooners, of which there simply were not enough. On 1 January 1775 the Royal Navy in America numbered only twenty-four vessels, four of which were ships-of-the-line of no use in that kind of fast interception work.

Something could be done on land, however. On 1 September 1774, General Gage sent a column of 260 soldiers 6 miles outside Boston to seize 250 barrels of militia gunpowder, which was achieved without any shots fired. The arrest of ringleaders and confiscation of arms worked, as the historian of guerrilla warfare Max Boot points out, 'on numerous occasions in Italy, Ireland and Poland in the eighteenth and nineteenth centuries'.[13] 'It's easier to crush evils in their infancy than when grown to maturity,' Gage had written in March, but by early September he had to start fortifying Boston as his writ did not extend far beyond the city, and no ringleaders were arrested.[14] On 12 September, Brigadier Hugh Percy, colonel of the 5th Regiment of Foot in Boston (later 2nd Duke of Northumberland), wrote to his father in Britain, 'This country is now in as open a state of rebellion as Scotland was in the Forty-Five.'[15] He had been only three years old during the Jacobite Rebellion, but he knew a popular uprising when he saw one.

Percy seemed to be proved right by the meeting of the First Continental Congress, which convened in Philadelphia between 5 September and 26 October 1774 to coordinate the colonies' opposition to the Coercive Acts, the Quebec Act and Gage's governorship of Massachusetts. There were fifty-six delegates, including John and Samuel Adams, George Washington and Patrick Henry, and as the Congress progressed the radical elements wishing for confrontation gained sway over moderates, such as Joseph Galloway of Pennsylvania, who preferred negotiation with Britain. 'The army was never used,' points out J. C. D. Clark, 'to round up colonial leaders, break up meetings like the Continental Congress, or shut down printing presses.'[16] Instead, the most radical elements of the colonists took and retained the initiative throughout the next seven months of the crisis.

For all the Congress's opposition to Parliament, however, it was still wary about defining America's exact relationship with the King. When

New York's representative Isaac Low left for Philadelphia, the band played 'God Save the King'. At dinner on the opening night of the Congress, John Adams noted how many of the delegates and their friends drank toasts in burgundy to the 'Union of Britain and her Colonies on a Constitutional Foundation'.[17] In one of its petitions, Congress even referred to George as 'the loving father of your whole people'.[18] Yet this did not blunt the Congress's radicalism; it attacked the Quebec Act for 'erecting a tyranny there, to the great danger, from so total a dissimilarity of religion, law and government, of the neighbouring British colonies'.[19] On 9 September the Suffolk Convention of Corresponding Committees (based in Suffolk County, Massachusetts) resolved that the Coercive Acts be disregarded, a total cessation of British trade instituted, no taxes paid and forcible resistance by armed militias offered. The Congress tempered but endorsed the Resolves on 17 September.

'The die is now cast, the colonies must either submit or triumph,' George wrote to North on 11 September, weeks before news of the Congress's deliberations had even reached London.

> I do not wish to come to severer measures but we must not retreat. By coolness and an unremitted pursuit of the measures that have been adopted, I trust they will come to submit. I have no objection afterwards to their seeing that there is no inclination for the present to lay fresh taxes on them, but I am clear there must always be one tax to keep up the right, and as such I approve of the tea duty.[20]

He always had approved of it, arguing that it should not be dropped from the Townshend Duties, the issue on which Grafton had lost by one vote at the Cabinet meeting in May 1769. He saw it as a symbol of Parliament's sovereignty much more than as a revenue-raising measure. So, quite clearly, did many Americans.

On 30 September, the Royal Navy warship *Scarborough* brought a letter from Gage warning that the Massachusetts Government Act was proving unworkable through mass obstruction and evasion. It added that it was not just the mob who now formed the opposition, but also respectable men of property. Preparing for the worst, Gage requested a large-scale reinforcement of troops, and far sooner than North originally suggested. Gage further advised that the Coercive Acts be repealed before events slipped out of his control – a remarkable request from the otherwise blunt and uncompromising general. At the same time, Lord Dartmouth thought that the King should summon his own Loyalist congress, to represent the estimated one-third of Americans who were still opposed to rebellion. He proposed to appoint delegates who would design a single, federated thirteen-colony government in North America, but, just like the proposed Albany Congress of 1754, the idea was entirely overtaken by events.[21]

When Dartmouth submitted a draft reply to Gage's letter, the King commended its 'great candour', but asked for an additional paragraph to be added assuring Gage 'that, though the conflict is unpleasant, Great Britain cannot retract'. Without it, the King thought, 'I should fear he would think that there was some wavering, which the present moment I am sure cannot allow to be the case with the most gentle minds.'[22] This was almost certainly a reference to Dartmouth himself, whom Hutchinson had thought close to despair. The letter did not promise Gage any more troops, despite the now near anarchy in Massachusetts, because of 'general safety' considerations around the world. Three ships with a battalion of marines were already due to arrive in December, but beyond that Gage would have to wait until the spring for significant reinforcements.

On 14 October the First Continental Congress passed the Declaration of Rights and Resolves,* which listed its grievances and asserted that the colonists were 'entitled to a free and exclusive power of legislation in their several provincial legislatures, where their right of representation can alone be preserved, in all cases of taxation and internal polity'.[23] Declaring the Coercive and Quebec Acts 'impolitic, unjust and cruel, as well as unconstitutional', it also denounced other post-1763 laws, protested against the dissolution of assemblies and the appointment of unelected governors' councils, and described a standing army in peacetime as 'against law'.[24] It nonetheless 'cheerfully consented' to the principle of parliamentary legislation on commercial questions, if only 'from the necessity of the case' and from 'a regard to the mutual interest of both countries'.[25] Four days later it created a Continental Association, pledging the colonies to cease importing any goods from the British Empire after 1 December. Violators would be punished by boycott and public naming (and thus be in danger of tarring-and-feathering). A Second Continental Congress was announced for 10 May 1775, although it claimed it would adjourn permanently if the King replied positively to *A Petition to the King and an Address to the British People*, when it was published on 25 October. Couched in respectful terms towards George, this effectively demanded the immediate repeal of the Coercive Acts.

For how long could this purported respect for the King last? Samuel Seabury, a Connecticut-born Yale graduate and rector of Westchester, New York, published a pamphlet entitled *The Congress Canvassed, Or, An Examination into the Conduct of the Delegates at their Grand Convention*

---

* Also known as the Declaration of Colonial Rights and the Declaration of Rights.

Held in Philadelphia, in which he stated, 'As yet they acknowledge King George the Third for their king and liege lord; how long they will abide by this acknowledgement is very uncertain.'[26] He pointed out that the Congress was now 'daily encroaching on the prerogatives of his Crown', in particular by wresting command of the militias from the royal governors, forcing royal office holders to resign and closing Crown courts. When the Suffolk Resolves arrived in London in late October, Dartmouth told Hutchinson, 'Why, if these Resolves are to be depended on, they have already declared war against us.'[27]

The First Continental Congress thought nothing of promoting what one recent historian has called 'a theory of conspiracy' about the British government that was simply not supported by the facts, but is entirely explicable by the need to claim victim status for propaganda purposes.[28] On 21 October it published *An Address to the Inhabitants of the Colonies*, which listed the supposed designs of the British government against the colonies since 1763, concluding 'that a resolution is formed and now is carried into execution, to extinguish the freedom of these colonies, by subjecting them to a despotic government'.[29] The same month, Congress warned the Quebecois that 'the substance of the whole, divested of its smooth words, is that the Crown and its ministers shall be as absolute throughout your extended province as the despots of Asia or Africa'.[30] This had little effect since it was demonstrably untrue, as the civil and religious liberties guaranteed by the Quebec Act proved.

Similarly, in the hope of stirring up trouble for the British government further afield in the Americas, the Second Continental Congress warned the Jamaica Assembly of a 'deliberate plan to destroy, in every part of the empire, the free Constitution for which Britain has been so long and so justly famed'.[31] They sought to explain and justify this in curiously racial and sexual terms, telling the (all-white) Assembly, 'In the East Indies, where the effeminacy of the inhabitants promised an easy conquest, they [the British government] thought it unnecessary to veil their tyrannic principles under the thinnest disguise . . . The Americans are not enervated by effeminacy, like the inhabitants of India; nor debauched by luxury, like those of Great Britain.'

If Americans wanted to see what genuine 'tyrannic principles' looked like in the mid- to late eighteenth century, there were plenty of examples around. The decision of the Grand Council of the Austrian Netherlands to retain torture in 1766; the brutal treatment by the Spanish of those in New Orleans who wanted to return to French rule in 1768–9 and their use of hanging, drawing and quartering in Peru; the French war against the insurgent Corsican independence movement between 1768 and 1770;

Russia's killing of tens of thousands when it crushed the Pugachev peasant Cossack uprising in 1773–4; Austria's murderous response to local uprisings in Transylvania in 1784 and Bohemia in 1785; Portugal's suppression of opposition to the Marquis de Pombal: right across Europe and far beyond, contemporary governments resorted to genuine tyranny – such as mass arrests and the execution of civilians without trial – at a time when the British government were prevented by their respect for the law from arresting so much as a single participant in the Boston Tea Party.[32]

In Boston, Gage continued to sound the alarm. On 30 October, he wrote to Dartmouth that 'foreign troops must be hired' at once, because 'This province and the neighbouring ones, particularly Connecticut, are preparing for war.'[33] He warned that he could only hold the city at best, and had nothing like enough troops to enforce the Coercive Acts. 'If you will resist and not yield, that resistance should be effectual at the beginning,' he warned. 'If you think ten thousand men sufficient, send twenty, if one million [pounds] is thought enough, give two; you will save both blood and treasure in the end.'[34] Gage again urged the suspension of the Coercive Acts, but crucially he provided no indication of the relative strength of military forces. In 1775 there were only 48,000 men in the entire British Army, including the 8,000 already stationed in North America, which with its other global commitments would be nothing like enough to subdue the 2.5 million inhabitants of thirteen colonies that stretched over a thousand miles from north to south and several hundred miles inland.

Because it was sent on a merchant ship rather than a sloop, Gage's dispatch did not arrive until 18 November. It then did finally shake the government, but not in the way Gage had intended. Instead, the Cabinet resented Gage's demand for so many troops to be taken out of the United Kingdom and other imperial stations, as well as his suggestion of using the King's Hanoverian and other German troops as auxiliaries. The suggestion of 20,000 men was considered hyperbolic. Even at the great victory of Minden in 1759 there had only been 10,000 British troops; Wolfe had captured Quebec that year with 4,400 British regulars and Clive only had 750 at the battle of Plassey in 1758. For Britain to send an army of 20,000 to America seemed unthinkable, not only on grounds of expense but also because of the exposure of sending nearly half the army so far away. 'What turned us all so much against Gage', William Knox, Under-Secretary at the American Department, recalled years later, 'was his telling Governor Hutchinson that, in his opinion, the only thing to be done was to suspend the [Coercive] Acts, and, in the meantime, make preparation for enforcing them by hiring Hessians and Hanoverians, for it was absolutely necessary to make an entire conquest of the New England governments, and not less than twenty thousand men could venture to take the field.'[35] Yet, if anything, that number was a wild *under*estimation of what would be required.

North, Dartmouth and his under-secretary John Pownall drew up a memorandum suggesting that General Amherst supersede the clearly pessimistic, possibly defeatist, Gage; but according to Knox's later recall, 'Lord North showed it to the King, who stared at it, and asked who could have thought of doing so unjust and cruel a thing to General Gage.'[36] The Cabinet rejected the plan as well.

'I am not sorry that the line of conduct seems now chalked out,' George wrote to North on 18 November, having read Gage's dispatch. 'The New England governments are in a state of rebellion, blows must decide whether they are to be subject to this country or independent.'[37] Throughout the crisis over America, the King behaved with constitutional propriety, going along with his government's measures rather than driving them, although he was generally on the more hawkish side of the argument. As a modern historian has pointed out, 'It is not easy to see what other attitude a constitutional monarch could have adopted, even setting aside the improbability that an eighteenth-century ruler would be sympathetic towards rebels.'[38] Later on 18 November, George told North that Gage's plan to suspend the Coercive Acts:

> appears to me the most absurd that can be suggested ... This must suggest to the colonies a fear that alone prompts them to their present violence. We must either master them or totally leave them to themselves and treat them as aliens. I do not by this mean to insinuate that I am for advi[sing] new measures, but I am for supporting those already undertaken.[39]

George saw his role as supporting his government and ensuring that North did not show weakness to the Americans, whom he persisted in regarding paternalistically as wayward children in need of a firm hand instead of fully grown adults who now deserved their independence.

George wanted to send out Major-Generals James Gisborne, Robert Cuninghame or Alexander Mackay to America, the last 'if it is absolutely necessary to send one who has already been in that country'.[40] He fully admitted that 'It is not a desirable commission.' Putting down rebels was not as good for soldiers' reputations as defeating foreign enemies. It was perhaps one of the reasons that it was a full three months before Gage received definitive orders to take the initiative against the rebels. The government wanted to see whether the rest of the colonies really supported Massachusetts, what the Continental Congress would conclude and whether the royal governors, Loyalist Americans and moderates might be able to halt or at least slow the slide to war. They wanted to continue to pursue political solutions – the opposite of tyranny. Meanwhile, the demoralized and isolated Gage remained in post, as provincial conventions or congresses were set up in one colony after another, eight of them by December.[41]

In his Speech from the Throne at the opening of the new Parliament on 30 November – drafted in part by Pownall and Knox in conjunction with the Cabinet – George announced, 'It gives me much concern that I am obliged ... to inform you that a most daring spirit of resistance and disobedience to the law still unhappily prevails in the province of the Massachusetts Bay, and has in divers parts of it broke forth in fresh violences of a very criminal nature.'[42] His government's response would be to persevere with the Coercive Acts, and 'You may depend upon my firm and steadfast resolution to withstand every attempt to weaken or impair the supreme authority of this legislature over all the dominions of my Crown, the maintenance of which I consider as essential to the dignity, the safety, and the welfare of the British Empire.'[43] This straightforward reiteration of the status quo was as 'tyrannical' as George III ever got.

In the Debate on the Address on 5 December, a motion giving the government full support in any action in America that it thought necessary was passed by 264 votes to 73. North told the Commons that everything was in 'a state of suspense' until Congress offered terms of reconciliation.[44] After Burke had delivered a characteristically sophisticated and eloquent speech, full of highbrow sophistry and rhetorical flourishes supporting the American Patriots, his bubble was neatly pricked by one of the Tory country backbenchers, Arthur Van, who replied bluntly, 'I have no flowers, Mr Speaker, to strew; all I have to say is, that I think the Americans are a rebellious and most ungrateful people, and I am for assuring the King that we will support him in such measures as will be effectual to reduce them.'[45] Van's curt response captured the mood of the chamber better than Burke's florid oratory; one eyewitness suggested that 'the honesty of the man and his singular manner ... answered Burke better than Cicero could have done with all his eloquence.'[46]

At Brooks's on 13 December, the 2nd Viscount Bolingbroke, nephew of the author of *The Patriot King*, wagered Charles Fox £150 to £50 that the Tea Act would not be repealed in that parliamentary session.[47] It was a sign of Fox's overconfidence, or perhaps just his addiction to gambling, that he was willing to take odds of one-to-three on such an unlikely prospect.

Lord Dartmouth's suggestion that peace commissioners be sent to Philadelphia to try to settle differences was overtaken on 13 December by the news of Congress's plans to interrupt British trade. The King told North two days later that he was 'not so fond of the sending [of] commissioners to examine into the disputes; this looks so like the mother country being more afraid of the continuance of the dispute than the colonies and I cannot think it likely to make them reasonable; I do not want to drive them to despair but to submission, which nothing but feeling the inconvenience of their situation can bring their pride to submit to.'[48] He had not appreciated, as Gage certainly had by then, that the Bostonians were beyond the point at which such 'inconvenience' was going to bring them to heel.

'Nothing can be more provoking than the conduct of the inhabitants of Massachusetts Bay,' George wrote to Dartmouth on 13 December. 'Some measures must undoubtedly be adopted after Christmas to curb them, and by degrees bring them to a due obedience to the mother country, but reason not passion must point out the proper measures.'[49] With Parliament in recess, Christmas would provide the opportunity for rethinking the government's position. The King did not try to oppose government attempts at reconciliation, even at that comparatively late stage, and accepted the Cabinet policy of devising a new initiative for 1775, though personally he was inclined towards a harder line than Dartmouth's.[50]

The Cabinet continued to suffer under the delusion that the British Army and Royal Navy that had defeated France (with her population of more than twenty-five million) and Spain (nine million) only a decade earlier, and won a great empire in Canada and India, would, if necessary, similarly destroy the untrained and semi-organized militias of far fewer Americans. The crucial difference was of course that Britain had not needed to invade and occupy France or Spain in order to be victorious in 1763.

On 16 December, North produced Army Estimates (the military budget) that showed the projected annual increase of the army over the coming year to be only 400 men, and an actual shrinkage of the navy by 4,000. With hindsight, North's thinking is bizarre and must have been curious even at the time: he had assumed a continued post-war lowering of tensions in Europe, despite its being known that both France and Spain had rebuilt and significantly improved their navies since 1763. By asking for a lower naval budget for 1775, North was delivering a sort of peace dividend, even though he knew that the Patriots of New England were covertly buying gunpowder. The Estimates show that the government was absurdly overoptimistic about the ease of winning an armed struggle in America. There was undoubtedly a snobbish arrogance towards American colonials in both the armed forces and in politics and a sense of complacency conferred after the victories of the Seven Years War.

When the full list of Congress's grievances arrived in England on

23 December, the King quite rightly responded that he would recommend them to the consideration of Parliament. Benjamin Franklin, who was still in London, had not succeeded in getting many of the other American agents based in London to go to Lord Dartmouth with him, not least because a significant number believed that the claims Congress had made, and the tone in which they were couched, were unacceptably offensive.[51] The list of grievances was put before the Commons on 19 January 1775, and a week later Franklin's petition that he and the American agents be heard on the subject was rejected by 218 votes to 68.

Having left the initiative entirely with Congress, time was no longer on Britain's side. The British authorities in America knew by 20 December that the colonists were already trying to procure military supplies. A note from the customs officials at Rhode Island, which reached the Treasury and ultimately the King, reported that the Assembly there had 'very lately passed an Act for purchasing 300 barrels of gunpowder, 3 tons of lead, 40,000 flints and four brass field pieces', mostly probably from the Dutch, as there were no supplies in the colony.[52]

Yet still the British government took almost no action. In late December, despite legal advice from Thurlow that the Massachusetts rebels were now technically traitors, the King asked the Cabinet not to issue orders to Gage to take the offensive against them for another month, presumably wanting to make it clear to all Americans that Britain did not wish to precipitate conflict.[53] Why he thought hesitation would send a positive message is unclear, especially as he had so often written to North in precisely the opposite sense. At the same time, he was writing memoranda in his own hand that show how preoccupied he was with the whole matter. In one, entitled 'Proposed Regiments of Infantry', he listed the seven regiments of foot and one battalion of Guards that were intended to stay in Britain in 1775, the nine regiments to go to America and the sixteen in Ireland. Another, 'Lists of Generals', had the names of three lieutenant-generals (including Gage) and eleven major-generals, at the very bottom of which were William Howe, Henry Clinton and John Burgoyne.

The King's concern about the navy's preparedness was clear from undated notes attributed to December 1774, such as 'Worming the rigging?' relating to the Chatham dockyard.[54] 'How does ballast taken up in salt water come to be less damp than in fresh water?' he asked himself. Then, 'The stock of timber insufficient'. At Sheerness, 'Mr Hunt's composition to prevent the bite of the worm promises better than anything yet tried.' At Portsmouth, 'Timber enough for a year's consumption. No worm of consequence.' These are the private notes of a monarch who had clearly drawn the conclusion that war was the most likely outcome, and that every

aspect of the Royal Navy's preparedness needed to be checked, even while
his ministers were cutting its manpower.

On 27 January 1775, Lord North drew up orders for Gage 'to restore the
vigour of Government' in Massachusetts that clearly condoned the use of
lethal force. These were not, however, sent for another seven weeks, while
the situation deteriorated quickly. The King reported to Dartmouth on the
28th that, in the opinion of the army's most senior generals, 'should matters
become serious in that part of the globe, more activity and decision would
be requisite than they esteem the present commander possessed of.' The
King now wanted Gage to be superseded 'with all imaginable tenderness',
but he thought Jeffery Amherst should take over as Commander-in-Chief,
because 'he is respected by the colonies' and thus 'they will give more credit
to his assertions than those of any other person'.[55]

Amherst had served for five years in America and Canada during the
Seven Years War, the latter part as Commander-in-Chief there, and his
diaries from that period reveal acute military observations, as well as notes
on topography, fortifications, relations with the Native Americans, grief
over losses, his visits to towns, and so on.[56] At fifty-eight, however, he had
no wish to end his distinguished career with a campaign against his former
American allies, a sentiment which ought to have given his fellow commanders pause for thought. He refused the command, forcing the
government to shelve their plans to extricate Gage. This deeply frustrated
the King, who had believed that dispatching Amherst 'bore a prosperous
aspect of bringing those deluded people to due obedience without putting
the dagger to their throats'.[57]

With the Seven Years War so recent, there ought to have been several
possible replacements for Gage as Commander-in-Chief in America besides
Amherst, yet several were overlooked for the post for non-military reasons.
Sir William Draper had captured Manila in 1762, for example, but his wife
came from New York, and even though General Sir Frederick Haldimand
had captured Montreal in the Seven Years War, he was Swiss-born despite
being a naturalized British subject. The King told Dartmouth that the only
alternative was to 'leave the command to Gage, send the best generals that
can be thought of to his assistance, and give him private instructions to
insinuate to New York and such other provinces as are not guided by the
madness of the times what the other [that is, Amherst] would have been
entrusted to negotiate'.[58] By that, he meant Britain's offer not to tax the
colonists if they in return admitted that the right to tax existed, and offered
to pay for their own defence. The demand for the East India Company to
be compensated for the Tea Party would be dropped, and Dartmouth was

instructed to open secret talks with Franklin in order to find a peaceful solution. In case that approach failed, Lieutenant-Generals Howe, Clinton and Burgoyne were appointed to serve under Gage.

William Howe was forty-five, a moderate Whig who had fought bravely at Quebec in the Seven Years War. He was tall, handsome and aristocratic; his father was a viscount and his mother the daughter of an illegitimate half-sister of George I. His elder brother, Richard 'Black Dick'* Howe, was sombre and tight-lipped, but brave, decent, a first-class seaman and the navy's youngest admiral. After their eldest brother George had been killed in action at Fort Ticonderoga in 1758 and buried in Albany, the Massachusetts Assembly voted £250 towards his memorial in Westminster Abbey, and as a result the Howe brothers thought fondly of the Americans. As MPs they had voted against the Coercive Acts, and Richard was involved in the secret talks with Franklin.[59] Since the Seven Years War, William Howe had concentrated on developing light-infantry tactics and improving discipline and training; in the late summer of 1774 he had demonstrated to the King the value of light-infantry companies in exercises on Salisbury Plain. He was not without his eighteenth-century vices, however, and was to promote Joshua Loring to the post of Commissary of Prisoners because he was a complaisant cuckold for his wife, Elizabeth Lloyd Loring, Howe's own mistress.

As attitudes hardened and the room for compromise narrowed, the press war heated up. The American Patriot cause was championed in London by a new newspaper that reminded many of the worst aspects of the *North Briton* and the Letters of Junius. *The Crisis*, a six-page weekly journal written and edited anonymously by the radical journalist William Moore, variously described North as 'engendered in the womb of Hell', the King as plotting 'the people's ruin' and the two men together as planning 'to plunder, butcher, starve or enslave' the Americans first and then the British.[60] During its run, *The Crisis* would describe the King as 'acting like a tyrant', being 'the greatest criminal in England' and being 'a national executioner [who] for a sceptre carried a bloody knife'.[61] In its third issue it advised the King to 'Withdraw then, Sir, from America your armed ruffians, and make a full restoration of your people's rights. Let them tax themselves and enjoy their property unviolated by the hand of tyranny ... May Lord Bute, Lord Mansfield, Lord North, and your Majesty's infamous minions, who would precipitate you and your kingdom into ruin, answer with their heads (and soon) for their horrid crimes.'[62]

---

* This 'referred to both his complexion and his downcast nature' (Chernow, *Washington* p. 239).

In response, the Commons passed a unanimous motion against the 'false, scandalous and seditious libel, highly and unjustly reflecting on His Majesty's sacred person and tending to alienate the affections and inflame the minds of His Majesty's subjects against his person and government'.[63] It ordered copies of *The Crisis* to be burned by the public executioner, which took place in Westminster on 6 March; but when this was attempted the next day at the Royal Exchange in the City, it started a riot of a thousand people. Among chaotic scenes, the City marshal was pulled off his horse, and dead cats and brickbats were thrown at officials.

The printer of *The Crisis*, Samuel Axtell, was identified, convicted of sedition and fined, but Thurlow and Wedderburn the Solicitor-General thought there was insufficient evidence against Moore to charge him as the author. *The Crisis* continued to be published until October 1776.[64] By then it had called for 'another revolution', reprinted the Declaration of Independence and contrasted 'the brave, free, and virtuous Americans' with 'the most dastardly, slavish and vicious tyrant that ever disgraced a nation'.[65] Moore rarely took refuge in understatement.

Parliament declared Massachusetts to be in a 'state of rebellion' on 9 February 1775, asking the King 'to take the most effectual measures to enforce due obedience to the laws and authority of the supreme legislature'.[66] North was nonetheless still keen to avoid bloodshed, and started to draw up a wide-ranging peace plan, known as the Conciliatory Proposal. This was loosely based on Franklin's suggestion that Parliament end all tax and other import duties as a precursor to diplomacy. The King supported this idea, although on 15 February, having received secret correspondence from a Maryland Loyalist, he wrote to North, 'Where violence is with resolution repelled it commonly yields, and I own, though a thorough friend to holding out the olive branch, I have not the smallest doubt that, if it does not succeed, that when once vigorous measures appear to be the only means left of bringing the Americans to a due submission to the mother country that the colonies will submit.'[67]*

Two days later Lord Hillsborough spoke to Thomas Hutchinson complaining that 'all the languor about America was owing to Lord North's aversion to business.'[68] Lord Dartmouth, he said, 'had too much religion, was unfit for the office, wondered at his taking it' and felt that John Pownall, his former subordinate, 'was unsteady; one day all fire, another

---

* That same day, George received a credible death threat, which he nonetheless dismissed as a 'foolish anonymous letter', taking the predictably fatalistic and self-righteous stance that 'I entirely place my security in the protection of the divine disposer of all things, and shall never look to the right or left but steadily pursue the tract which my conscience dictates to be the right one' (RA GEO/MAIN/1958).

depressed and in despair'. But by far the most important and insightful remark Hillsborough made was about the relationship between the King and his ministers, which held broadly true for almost the entirety of George's reign. The King, he said, thought as Hutchinson did about America,

> but always will leave his own sentiments and conform to his ministers, though he will argue with them, and very sensibly; but if they adhere to their own opinion he will say, 'Well, do you choose it to be so? Then let it be.' And sometimes he has known him add, 'You must take the blame upon yourself.'[69]

Hillsborough's experience was a common one for George's ministers: he neither browbeat them to adopt his way of thinking nor overruled them if they were decided upon a policy, but nonetheless reserved for himself the uninhibited right later to say I told you so.

Lord North introduced his Conciliatory Proposal to the Commons on 20 February, stating that if individual colonies would 'make provision ... for contributing their proportion to the common defence ... and shall engage to make provision also for the support of the civil government and the administration of justice ... it will be proper ... to forbear ... to levy any duty, tax or assessment ... to the account of such province or colony respectively'.[70] It was a comprehensive offer of no taxation by Westminster and an attempt to restore the status quo ante the Stamp Act. It was also of course an attempt to absolve the British government of the blame for starting the looming war. If it succeeded in making any colonies think twice about secession, particularly in the South where loyalism was strongest, so much the better. North was so keen that his Proposal be welcomed in the Commons on national rather than party political grounds that he briefed the Opposition on it beforehand, and asked them to attend the sitting, which was far from common practice.

The King 'highly approve[d]' of the Proposal, because 'it plainly defines the line to be held in America, and as it puts an end to congresses it will certainly have a good effect in this country and I should hope in at least some of the colonies.'[71] Even so, the Opposition spokesmen Edmund Burke, John Dunning, Isaac Barré and Charles Fox all condemned it as contradicting earlier government stances, which of course it did, and was intended to. Government MPs were equally bemused by the seeming volte-face. 'We went into the House in confusion,' Edward Gibbon told a friend. 'Lord North rose six times to appease the storm' of MPs denouncing what they saw as relinquishing British sovereignty over America.[72] Consternation and confusion notwithstanding, it was approved by 274 votes to 88.

In March, Samuel Johnson published his ninety-one-page pamphlet *Taxation No Tyranny*, a contemptuous rejection of the Congress's Declarations and Resolves. This had been commissioned by Sir Grey Cooper, the senior Secretary to the Treasury. Although the King had been paying Johnson an annual pension of £300, the author needed little encouragement and clearly believed every word, and indeed was angry when Cooper toned it down. One sentence that Cooper permitted to remain was the question that became famous for skewering the hypocrisy of so many of the Founding Fathers who were claiming to be enslaved by Britain: 'If slavery be thus fatally contagious, how is it that we hear the loudest yelps for liberty among the drivers of negroes?'[73]

The Conciliatory Proposal was intended to be the carrot offered to Congress to come to terms, and the stick was the New England Restraining Bill, which limited those colonies' trade with the British Empire, as well as fishing rights in Newfoundland. After the Bill had passed on 6 March by 215 votes to 61, the King wrote to North that 'The languor of the Opposition arose from feeling the sense of the nation warm in favour of the proposition. The more I revolve in my mind the line adopted in the American affairs, the more I am convinced of [its] rectitude, candour, and becoming firmness, and if properly attended to must with time be crowned with success.'[74] A week later orders were finally dispatched permitting Gage to use force if necessary in Massachusetts. But by the time the Conciliatory Proposal reached America, the first shots of the war had already been fired.

On 10 April, John Wilkes, who in September 1774 had been elected Lord Mayor of London, along with large numbers of the aldermen, liverymen and popularly elected members of its Common Hall, organized a mass demonstration and march from the City to St James's Palace to present the King with a petition against the Restraining Act. Wilkes' petition claimed 'that the real purpose is to establish arbitrary power over all America' and called on the King to 'dismiss immediately and for ever' all his ministers.[75] It went on to equate the unfolding events in America with the Revolution of 1688. The King traditionally accepted such petitions while seated on the throne, and received this one with all due ceremony, but he also exercised his right of reply. It was, he said,

with the utmost astonishment that I find any of my subjects capable of encouraging the rebellious disposition which unhappily exists in some of my rebellious colonies in North America. Having entire confidence in the wisdom of my Parliament, the great council of the nation, I will steadily pursue those measures which they have recommended for the support of the constitutional rights of Great Britain, and the protection of the commercial rights of my kingdom.[76]

That much was for the public; in private, the King referred to the City petition as 'fresh insolence from the shop that has fabricated so many'.[77] He had the Lord Chamberlain write to Wilkes to say that he would no longer receive petitions from the City except in its corporate capacity. What this meant in practice was that he would accept petitions not from the radical Livery of Common Hall, but only from the established and more conservative Corporation of the City assembled in Common Council, and when he did so he was not going to sit on the throne at St James's Palace, thereby lending grandeur and legitimacy to the protests. 'I am ever ready to receive addresses and petitions,' the King explained, 'but I am the judge where.'[78]

Although the numerous petitions that were sent to the King in favour of conciliation with the Americans have been described as 'the first modern example of a popular anti-war protest movement', they were outnumbered by those favouring coercion.[79] Eighteenth-century public opinion is notoriously hard to gauge, but of the more than 100 addresses, petitions and appeals that were submitted to the King between 1775 and 1778 in England from borough and town corporations, the two universities, militia units, justices of the peace and many other groups and some individuals, those advocating coercion outnumbered those for conciliation by three to two; in terms of signatures, there were 19,854 pro-American to 18,521 against.[80]

Upper-middle-class and middle-class England were divided. When it came, Anglican churchmen, merchants with ties to the ministry and members of local government organizations tended to support the war. Dissenters, smallholders, shopkeepers, artisans and some in manufacturing tended to oppose it. London, East Anglia, Newcastle and some parts of Yorkshire were the most pro-conciliation regions, whereas support for the war was strongest in Lancashire and the West Midlands. The war was not popular – the Americans were seen as Britons, after all – but then paradoxically neither was there much full-throated opposition to it, which was deemed unpatriotic once the army and navy were fully engaged, and especially so once France and Spain became belligerents.

Gage received his orders authorizing force against the rebels on 14 April 1775; the instruction had originally been written on 27 January, but it was not dispatched until 13 March. He had been drawing British forces to Boston since December, denuding the rest of the country, and had collected thirteen battalions of infantry. At 8 p.m. on 18 April he sent a force comprising most of the 10th Regiment of Foot (between 600 and 700 men) out from Boston to capture an arms and ammunition depot 20 miles north-west at Concord, going via Lexington. Forewarned from midnight by Paul Revere, William Dawes and Dr Samuel Prescott riding from Boston shouting 'The regulars are coming out!',* the 'minute companies' of the Massachusetts militia – so called because they could grab their muskets and fall in for duty within a minute of the tocsin being sounded – started to muster.

By the morning of 19 April, the British regulars had lost the element of surprise, as church bells were ringing, signal guns were firing and drumbeats could be heard along the route. At 4.30 a.m. the British advance guard of 238 men under Major John Pitcairn met Captain John Parker's seventy-seven Massachusetts militiamen on Lexington Common.[81] 'Disperse, you damned rebels!' Pitcairn shouted. 'Lay down your arms and disperse!'[82] It was hardly language designed to evoke a positive response, but it seems to have worked, and according to some accounts the militiamen started to disperse. Then the first shot was fired: no one knows by whom, perhaps it was even discharged by accident. It was met with British volleys, which after less than a minute left eight Americans dead and ten wounded, with one soldier wounded by return fire.

At Concord three and a half hours later, the regulars discovered that most of the depot had been removed, and what was left destroyed. They dumped 500 pounds of musket balls into a pond and spiked three 24-pound cannon. An estimated 3,500 militiamen attacked the regulars on their way back to Boston along the Concord Road, many employing the hit-and-fade guerrilla tactics they had learned a decade earlier, making use of the terrain to conceal their firing positions and then withdrawing before the regulars could respond. 'We could not see above ten in a body,' a British soldier later recalled.[83] Lord Hugh Percy arrived at Lexington at 2 p.m. with two cannon and nearly 2,000 men to save the original column, but by then the expedition had cost 244 British casualties to 95 American. The American War of Independence had begun.

---

* Not 'The British are coming!', because many still considered themselves to be British.

12

'The Battle of the Legislature'

April–November 1775

Times like these call up genius, which slept before, and stimulate it in action to a degree that eclipses what might before have been fixed as a standard.[1]

Silas Deane to his wife in the summer of 1775

Boston soon came under siege by about 15,000 militiamen, mainly from Massachusetts, but also from Rhode Island, Connecticut and New Hampshire, the latter answering the Massachusetts Provincial Congress' call for assistance. The British government's fondly held belief that they might keep the colonies divided was exploded on 10 May when representatives from all the mainland colonies except Georgia* met in Philadelphia at the Second Continental Congress. That same day, the strategically important but woefully underdefended Fort Ticonderoga in New York Province near the Canadian border fell to the Americans bloodlessly, along with cannon which were then laboriously taken overland to Boston to aid the siege. On 12 May, Crown Point also fell, and at the end of May the colonial troops investing Boston were restyled the Continental Army. The county of Mecklenburg, North Carolina, passed a series of anti-British resolves and, on 20 May, what seems remarkably like a declaration of independence.[2]

On 26 May, an American ship arrived at Southampton with copies of the *Essex Gazette* of 25 April carrying an account of Concord which claimed that the British regulars had fired first. This caused some consternation in the government when it arrived in London the next day since it seemed certain that blood had been shed in Massachusetts. 'The die is now cast,' wrote John Pownall, 'and more mischief will follow.'[3] Gibbon agreed, noting, 'This looks serious, and is indeed so.'[4]

---

* The most loyalist state – named after George II in 1732 – where those delegates who were elected declined to attend the Congress, because they were divided on the action to be taken.

The King tried to remain optimistic, telling Dartmouth on the 29th that 'It is not improbable but some detachment sent by Lieutenant-General Gage may not have been strong enough to disperse the provincials assembled at Concord; but no great reliance can be given to the manner in which it will understandably be exaggerated in American newspapers, or when related by an American trader.'[5] He added that evening, 'I am far from thinking the General has reason to be displeased. The object of sending the detachment was to spike cannon and destroy military stores; this has been effected, but with the loss of an equal number of men on both sides. I therefore hope you will not see this in a stronger light than it deserves.'[6] Two weeks later, Gage's report finally arrived in London with the news that he had suffered 244 casualties, and stating that the Americans had fired first.

Howe, Clinton and Burgoyne had left London on 20 April with three more regiments, arriving in Boston on board the frigate *Cerberus* on 25 May. Before he left, Burgoyne, a moderate Whig, made a speech in the Commons saying that the army 'would inevitably be made the instrument of correction', but it would not indulge in 'the sudden and impetuous impulse of passion and revenge'.[7] Underlying British thinking throughout the various stages of the crisis had been the unchallenged assumption that they would win any war in America. The contribution the American militiamen made to the defence of the colonies in the Seven Years War had been mixed at best. After open fighting had broken out between France and England in North America in 1754, repeated calls for militia had either gone unanswered or produced ill-equipped and undisciplined men for the most part, the worst reputedly being those from North Carolina who, in the words of Sir John Fortescue, the historian of the British Army, had 'mutinied and dispersed to their homes while yet on the march to the rendezvous. The peril was great; yet the colonies remained supine.'[8] When General Edward Braddock was putting together his expedition in 1755, 'the Pennsylvanians showed an apathy and unwillingness which provoked even George Washington to the remark that they ought to be chastised.'[9] Similarly, when Brigadier John Forbes was sent to Philadelphia in 1758 to conduct operations against Fort Duquesne, 'the provincial troops allotted to him from Pennsylvania, Virginia, Maryland and North Carolina had not even been enlisted . . . He had much difficulty in shaping the provincials into soldiers, the material delivered to him being of the rawest, and destitute of the remotest idea of discipline.'[10]

The assumption of so many in the British high command in 1775 that Britain would win another war on the North American continent, though it now seems hubristic, had some foundation in experience. It was similarly taken for granted that any prolonged Royal Navy blockade would strangle the colonies, with only minimal consideration being given to the likelihood of revanchist France and Spain supporting the colonists militarily. With the notable exception of General Amherst, British decision makers badly underestimated the colonists' stamina and fighting capacity. In a debate in the House of Lords on 13 March, when Camden had argued that for geographical and demographic reasons it was unlikely that Britain could win, Sandwich replied,

> Suppose the colonies do abound in men; what does that signify? They are raw, undisciplined, cowardly men. I wish instead of forty or fifty thousand of these brave fellows, they would produce in the field at least two hundred thousand, the more the better, the easier the conquest. If they do not run away, they would starve themselves into compliance with our measures.[11]

It would be hard to beat Sandwich's words in that debate for sheer arrogance and ignorance, but they did reflect majority Cabinet and military thinking. Even as late as 1777, General James Murray, who had served with Wolfe in Quebec, believed that Washington must have been relying on recent immigrants to boost his army's fighting prowess, because a native-born American was 'a very effeminate thing, very unfit for and very impatient of war'.[12]

Both experience and prejudice thus led colonial governors and British administrators to believe that the Continental Army would inevitably be defeated in the field and the Second Continental Congress would be captured or dispersed, and that any continuing guerrilla campaign could then essentially be policed by Loyalist militias with the support of a smattering of British regulars.[13] Yet the colonists were armed with an assortment of personal weaponry (in particular, long-barrelled hunting muskets) with which they were highly adept. Around half of the military-age New England militiamen were veterans of the Seven Years War, and many of those were farmers and frontiersmen. Anyone who relied in part on his marksmanship to put food on his family's table was going to present a danger to the redcoats.[14] Lord Hugh Percy did not echo the arrogance common among his brother officers, writing that the rebels were 'men who know very well what they are about, having been employed as Rangers against the Indians and [French] Canadians and this country being much covered with wood, and hilly, is very advantageous for their method of fighting'.[15]

As well as their proficiency with firearms, the Americans also had the advantage of numbers. According to Benjamin Franklin's calculation in 1766, if a quarter of the remaining male population bore arms, and

Loyalists, pacifists and seamen were deducted, about a quarter of a million Americans could theoretically fight against the Crown. In the event, nothing like that number did, but neither did Britain field even 1 per cent of her eight million or so population. The Americans were moreover defending a country of essentially limitless space but limited resources, with no cities whose loss would be singly fatal to their cause. Knowing that the British strategy must be to try to destroy the Continental Army early on in a conventional encounter in the open field, they could refuse to give battle except on the most favourable terms, and retreat according to classic Fabian precepts.*

The problems facing the British Army in 1775 were not confined to its grand strategy in North America. With a total strength of 48,000 men it also had to maintain garrisons in Minorca, Gibraltar, Africa and the West Indies, as well as in Great Britain itself (including Ireland, which was given to periodic unrest). Extraordinarily, the overall numbers of British troops did not increase significantly until 1778, with only one new line regiment created before then. It was only once France entered the war that the British government was forced to raise thirty more regiments, bringing the army up to 110,000 men, although that included volunteer militias that were not allowed (or intended) to leave Great Britain.[16]

The logistical supply problem was immense too: because the local population tended to be hostile – with the American Loyalists providing far fewer troops than the British government had hoped for and expected – food had to be either foraged (that is, requisitioned, with all the local unpopularity that entailed) or bought (routinely at high margins), or else transported 3,000 miles over an ocean that was vulnerable to storms, colonial privateers and, later, enemy navies. Once the British armies penetrated inland, their lack of knowledge of the interior and the inescapable problems of reinforcement and supply both told against them heavily.

The army system itself was also wildly outdated. Regiments were entirely independent, and there was no uniformity of drill, discipline, uniform, training or even military doctrine. Yet because the Seven Years War had been won on that outmoded system, there had been no pressing movement for reform since 1763. The French had overhauled virtually every aspect of their military doctrine, but they had the impetus of defeat. (George kept a close eye on French military affairs, as papers in the Royal Archives attest.)[17] In Britain the King was Captain-General, an honorary rank, but remarkably, as we have seen, there was no overall commander-in-chief of

---

* Quintus Fabius Cunctator (c. 280–203 BC) is regarded as the father of guerrilla warfare for his strategic withdrawals and refusal to fight battles in unfavourable circumstances.

the British Army between 1770 and 1778. The politician who ran the army's administration and finance, the Secretary at War, did not sit in the Cabinet by right, which anyway had no concept of collective responsibility. Despite this, strategy was the responsibility of the Cabinet in general and the Colonial (sometimes called the American) Secretary specifically – a particular difficulty since Lord Dartmouth did not have his heart in the war. The Royal Navy was run completely separately by the Board of Admiralty and a First Lord who did have Cabinet rank.

Sandwich's speech of 13 March highlighted a strange paradox in the ministry's strategic thinking: whereas Sandwich, the politician in charge of Britain's navy, believed in a land campaign, Lord Barrington, the Secretary at War and thus responsible for her army, believed in defeating the Americans through a naval blockade. In letters to Dartmouth, Barrington advocated 'our marine totally interrupting all commerce and fishery, and even seizing all the ships in the ports, with very little expense and less bloodshed'.[18] A land campaign would be far more costly, he believed, due to America's geography, politics and the fact that the country was 'full of men accustomed to firearms'. He concluded, quite rightly, that it would 'cost us more than we can ever gain by the success'.

In grappling with these strategic challenges, the King taught himself about military matters. Though by no means a martial figure who delighted in warfare, George now applied himself to this new, albeit reluctant, role of wartime monarch with his characteristic conscientiousness and capacity for hard work. He read books on military matters, attended the army's summer encampment, took part in three-hour military reviews and parades, built up a large collection of military charts on which to follow the campaigns* which it is thought were hung on purpose-made mahogany stands in Buckingham House, and memorized information about enemy fortifications, the depth soundings of harbours and so on.[19] He tried to keep as up to date as possible, taking detailed notes on every aspect of the war from the number of blankets the army needed in their cantonments to the guns on each ship of the contending fleets. He once commented approvingly that the rebel newspapers he was reading still smelt of the pies around which they had been wrapped as they were smuggled across the lines, and a military band played marches every night he was in residence at Windsor.[20]

Along with Gage's report, on 10 June the government received a letter from Lieutenant-Governor Cadwallader Colden of New York, dated 3 May, announcing that civil government had broken down, a people's assembly

---

* More than 3,000 of which in the Royal Collection can be seen at militarymaps.rct.uk.

had voted to join the Congress and rebel forces had cut off the colony. 'I am not apt to be over-sanguine,' the King nonetheless wrote to Dartmouth,

> but I cannot help being of [the] opinion that with firmness and perseverance, America will be brought to submission. If not, old England will though perhaps not appear so formidable in the eyes of Europe as at other periods, but yet will be able to make her rebellious children rue the hour they cast off obedience. America must be a colony of England or [be] treated as an enemy. Distant possessions standing upon an equality with the superior state is more ruinous than being deprived of such connections.[21]

The British high command's hopes for an early decisive victory over the Continental Army were dealt a serious blow by Thomas Gage's pyrrhic victory at the battle of Bunker Hill, fought at Breed's Hill on the Dorchester Heights overlooking Boston Harbor on 17 June. Although Gage eventually captured the high ground after the Americans' ammunition ran out, 228 British soldiers were killed and 928 wounded out of the 2,300 taking part, against only 160 Americans killed, 271 wounded and 30 captured out of their 3,200 combatants.[22] These were to be the highest casualties suffered by the British in any single engagement in the war, and included ninety officers killed or wounded, an indication both of the way they led from the front and of how well the rebels picked off their targets. 'The trials we have', Gage wrote to the London Gazette, 'show that the rebels are not the despicable rabble too many have supposed them to be.'[23] His garrison of 7,000 men was enough to hold Boston, but not to attack twice as many besiegers.

'I am of the opinion that when once these rebels have felt a smart blow', the King wrote to Sandwich on 1 July, 'they will submit; and no situation can ever change my fixed resolution, either to bring the colonies to due obedience to the legislature of the mother country or to cast them off!'[24] The news of Bunker Hill cured many decision makers, including the King, of any such overconfidence.

George Washington arrived at Cambridge Common on 2 July to assume command of the Continental Army. When New York had asked the Continental Congress for advice on preparing itself for defence against the British in May 1775, Congress formed a military committee to look into the matter. The Virginian delegate Colonel Washington was its secretary and his vigorous proposal to close the Hudson to British ships impressed all who saw it. There were already several generals from New England, so a Virginian was an ideal choice for the sake of balance.[25] If anyone could be accused of disdain for American soldiers at this stage of the war, it was the Virginian aristocrat Washington rather than milords Percy and Gage.

He described the militiamen he found there as 'provincials under very little command, discipline or order' and 'exceeding dirty and nasty* people' with 'an unaccountable kind of stupidity in the lower class of these people'.[26] 'To place any dependence upon militia', he concluded, 'is, assuredly, resting upon a broken staff.'[27] He therefore considered his job primarily to be that of 'introducing proper discipline and subordination' while continuing to prosecute the siege.

On 5 July, at John Dickinson's urging, the Continental Congress, still in session at Philadelphia, published what was called the Olive Branch Petition, calling on the King to provide 'mild and just government' and asking him 'to direct some mode by which the united applications of your faithful colonists . . . may be improved into a happy and permanent reconciliation'. It vowed loyalty to the King, and humbly begged him to dismiss his 'artful and cruel' ministers.[28] This placed George in a difficult political situation, because to accept it meant recognizing the legitimacy of the body which had sent it, which would in itself be a major concession. If the King had acceded to it, he would have been overruling Parliament in precisely the absolutist manner that had long been imputed to him. 'Had he wished to do this,' an American constitutional historian states, 'he could scarcely have succeeded, and the few friends of the Americans in Parliament would have been the first to denounce the attempt as a resumption of Stuart tyranny.'[29]

The government lawyers pointed out to George that, since the Olive Branch Petition asked him to act against Parliament and the sovereign was legally 'the King-in-Parliament', he was in effect being asked to act against himself, a constitutional absurdity and one that he should not countenance. For his part, the King thought the Petition mere propaganda, a naked attempt to divide the British. He therefore refused to accept it, despite the inevitable public opprobrium that would come with rejecting a petition posing as an 'olive branch'.† 'His Majesty seemeth to have turned a deaf ear to all the supplications of his loyal colonists,' John DeHart wrote to the New Jersey Assembly in mid-November, echoing many.[30]

Yet at the same time that Congress had been agreeing the wording of its 'olive branch', John Hancock had been enunciating Congress's war aims, Thomas Jefferson had stated that the colonists were 'resolved to die freemen rather than to live slaves', it was agreed to spend £6,000 on gunpowder and

---

* 'Dirty, filthy' (*Johnson's Dictionary*).

† Furthermore, any kingdom in America could not have been a single entity because he was head of state multiple colonies, each of which considered itself an independent and individual polity, with its own constitutional particulars. Each colony individually accepting George as head of state was in some ways analogous to the Holy Roman Emperor's dominion over separate states in central Europe.

to establish a committee to coordinate military supplies, and New York was urged to raise a 3,000-man army, so George could perhaps be forgiven for his cynicism about the petition's sincerity.[31] 'I have no doubt but the nation at large sees the conduct of America in its true light,' the King wrote to North, 'and I am certain any other conduct but compelling obedience would be ruinous and culpable, therefore no consideration could bring me to swerve from the present path which I think myself in duty bound to follow.'[32]

Four days before the news of Bunker Hill arrived in London on 25 July, the King optimistically advised Dartmouth that 'The difficulties many of the colonies will suffer the next winter, and the force that will act the next campaign will I trust bring them to soberer thoughts.'[33] On 26 July, having received the news of the extremely high casualty rate at Bunker Hill, as well as of the fall of Ticonderoga and Crown Point, the Cabinet met and decided to raise the army of 20,000 men by April 1776 that Gage had been begging for since the autumn of 1774. Barrington, the person responsible for doing this, did not believe it possible, and was still convinced that the navy should be the decisive force.[34]

'The war is now grown to such a height that it must be treated as a foreign war,' North wrote to the King before the Cabinet meeting, 'and . . . every expedient which would be used in the latter case should be applied in the former.'[35] This included the use of paid foreign auxiliary troops, and the licensing of privateers to prey on American trade. The King agreed, replying that evening, 'We must persist and not be dismayed by any difficulties that may arise on either side of the Atlantic. I know I am doing my duty and therefore can never wish to retract.'[36] Brave words, but when it came to the practicalities of fulfilling Gage's increasingly desperate pleas for troops, the King agreed with Lord Dartmouth that, some Highlanders and marines notwithstanding, no major reinforcements could be sent before the spring. British strategy would thus be to hold all positions until then.

In the summer of 1775, the British Army had 10,000 men already in America (mostly in or around Boston) and Canada, or sailing there; 7,700 in Gibraltar, Minorca and the West Indies; 7,000 in Ireland, which at half its normal peacetime establishment was dangerously low; and the remaining 23,000 in the United Kingdom, the minimum number for defence and domestic control, of whom 1,500 were unfit for duty. The King was correct to say that it would be impossible to send Gage the men he needed without denuding Britain, so he took a personal lead by sending five battalions of Hanoverians of 470 men each to Minorca and Gibraltar to relieve British units there, allowing the crack 1st and 2nd Battalions of the Royal Regiment of Foot to return home, while five other battalions in Britain embarked for Boston.

The King told North that the Hanoverian battalions were 'a clear and handsome loan ... for which I claim nothing but to be reimbursed all expenses'.[37] They were to be paid the same as their British counterparts – 'I do not mean to make one sixpence by this' – and their transportation was to be covered by the navy. It was a pragmatic solution, because unlike new British recruits these German troops would not need training nor have to be placed on half-pay when no longer required. Meanwhile, the battalions worst hit at Bunker Hill were brought home to be rebuilt, their places taken by regiments stationed in Ireland, and the War Office tried to recruit at least another 5,000 men ahead of the anticipated spring campaign.

Considering that fighting the colonists had been at least a possibility since the Boston Tea Party, it was an indictment of the North ministry that an army could not be deployed in adequate numbers right away. Lords North and Barrington suggested to the King that, in the emergency, rich landowners be allowed to establish their own 'New Corps' regiments, with advanced promotions offered to anyone prepared to serve as officers. George's instinct was to veto this idea, since he feared that it would devalue the commissions of the officers in the 'Old Corps' pre-war regular units. Furthermore, New Corps units could not be expected to train and be ready to fight within twelve months, whereas new battalions in boosted Old Corps ones could do so in three. George was thus unwilling to tear up the established system of recruitment, and conducted a campaign against nepotism and patronage by the nobility and gentry.

When the Earl of Dunmore – the former Governor of Virginia – wanted to raise a regiment of Highlanders in December 1777, which would automatically make him a colonel, one of the reasons George gave for preventing it was that 'The principle on which I go is that no man is to get above one step and he quitted the army several years ago and only as a captain.'[38] Yet the rich benefactors who would be paying for these New Corps regiments understandably expected senior commissions in them for their military-aged relatives. Another example among many was that of the 4th Duke of Gordon, who attempted to raise a regiment of Highlanders on the condition that it be commanded by his brother, Lord William Gordon. The King also refused this on the grounds that the leap from retired captain to lieutenant-colonel was too great.* As a result, the regiment was not raised.†

When the King agreed in August 1775 to the formation of the 71st

---

* There might possibly have been a personal issue involved, in that Lord William had fathered a child with the married Lady Sarah Bunbury (née Lennox), the King's first amour.

† The same mistake was not made at the time of the French Revolutionary War, when the Duke raised the 92nd Regiment (subsequently the Gordon Highlanders) and put his twenty-four-year-old eldest son in command.

Regiment ('Fraser's Highlanders'), two battalions were raised by offering commissions to those officers who recruited certain numbers of men; this lowered the price of an ensigncy from around £400 to just £18. It was called 'raising regiments for rank', but the King disliked that practice also, because it lessened the value of commissions in the regular army, and the only supposed quality control over the officers was their wealth.[39] Except for the 71st, he refused to allow New Corps regiments to be raised until 1778, dangerously late in the war. In all, in the twelve months after September 1775 only 11,000 troops were raised in Britain to fight across contested territories that stretched over 1,100 miles from Falmouth in the North to Savannah in the South. The following twelve months produced only 6,882 more.[40] North explained to the King that 'the cause of Great Britain is not yet sufficiently popular' for people to want to join up in large numbers, even from a nation of eight million.[41]

Under normal circumstances, this protection of the interests of the old established officer corps would have been reasonable, but in those of a major war it was absurd. One historian has even gone so far as to suggest that without the King's 'admirable wish to fight jobbery in the army ... Great Britain might have won the American war'.[42] An early and heavy investment of the colonies with large numbers of British troops, it is argued, might have disheartened the Americans and, almost as importantly, headed off their alliance with the French that ultimately proved so fatal to British hopes of victory. Compared to those prizes, George's fears about demoralizing the Old Corps officers should have been of secondary concern.

Despite endless pleas from British commanders in North America, therefore, nothing like enough troops were ever sent. There were 50,000 serving there for a short time in 1778, but this dropped to between 30,000 and 35,000 for the rest of the war.[43] This was never enough to pursue the Americans deep into the interior, far from the ports of Savannah, Charleston and New York that could be supplied by the Royal Navy. The refusal to reinforce hampered the British Army greatly throughout the conflict, even with the support of around 11,000 Loyalists.[44] In order to fight a rebel force which numbered in the order of 35,000 at its height, and which virtually never gave fight where and when the British wanted, far more men were needed, especially as so many senior British decision makers believed that losing the thirteen colonies would cost Britain her status as a great power.

Another action that might have been taken was the 'embodiment' (that is, mobilization) of the militia to assume roles in Britain that would have freed up regular army units for immediate service in America, yet this too was not done until 1778. Neither was the Treasury willing or ready to devote the huge expenditure necessary for a full-scale war, as Pitt had been against foreign foes in the Seven Years War.

As well as moving the Hanoverian troops to Britain's Mediterranean outposts, George was useful in prevailing upon his German cousins to lend soldiers for the war, albeit at a price to the British taxpayer. In all, for the 1776 campaign alone, the British hired 18,000 German auxiliaries, who had the advantages of already being armed and well equipped. To the request for 20,000 Russians, Catherine the Great had 'thrown out some expressions that may be civil to a Russian ear but certainly not to more civilized ones', the King wrote to North.[45]* (The optics of troops from autocratic Russia fighting an American independence movement would in any case have been terrible, so he was perhaps fortunate that she refused this request.) Landgrave Frederick II of Hesse-Cassel, who had married George's aunt Mary, the daughter of George II, leased Britain nineteen regiments, and more auxiliary troops were hired from the independent German states of Brunswick-Wolfenbüttel, Mecklenburg-Strelitz, Hesse-Hanau, Ansbach, Waldeck and Anhalt. These have often been lumped together under the generic title of 'Hessians', and over the course of the war no fewer than 29,166 of them saw service in North America in one form or another, representing at their peak in 1781 some 37 per cent of the British strength there.[46] The *Soldatenhandel*, or soldier trade, was an important money earner for states such as Hesse-Cassel, where a quarter of all households were represented in the army, a ratio twice that even of Prussia.[47]

Considering that it was not primarily their war – although George's grandmother Queen Caroline had come from Ansbach – the Hessian and other auxiliaries proved good, brave and conscientious soldiers, but, as with the employment of Native Americans on the western frontier, they came at a high political price for the British. The Hessians swiftly attracted the largely undeserved reputation – fanned by colonist propaganda pamphlets – of being brutal, undisciplined and licentious, especially when in their winter quarters in New Jersey in 1777–8. Of the 18,970 Hessians mustered into British service between 1776 and 1782, a total of 535 were killed in combat, 1,309 wounded and 2,628 captured, and if one takes disease and all other causes into account, overall 4,983 were killed in a war that was not ultimately theirs.[48]

Contrary to myth, these soldiers were not mercenaries: the cost of their hiring was paid to the ruler rather than to the men themselves, who were not volunteers. The hiring of military corps in return for cash subsidies

---

* George thought Catherine rude not to have replied in her own hand.

was accepted in international law, and during the Seven Years War Britain had paid Hesse-Cassel, Brunswick and other states for auxiliaries to fight against the French.[49] This did not prevent the deployment of Hanoverian troops to safeguard the essential Mediterranean strongholds of Minorca and Gibraltar being portrayed by the Opposition in Parliament as a violation of the Bill of Rights, and in the colonies the picture was drawn of foreign mercenaries being used to trample ancient British liberties.[50]

On 31 July 1775, Lord Barrington wrote to the King to decry the figure of 20,000 reinforcements to be sent to Gage, which was being championed by John Pownall at the American Department. 'I not only fear but am confident the proposed augmentation cannot possibly be raised, and ought not to be depended on,' he said.[51] As a memorandum he sent the King the following January showed, he feared that the army was already not strong enough to protect against insurrections in Britain, sparked by what he termed 'a very levelling spirit among the people'.[52] Nor was the militia to be trusted: their calling out, he warned, 'if not done with care and judgement may create danger, instead of securing us against it'. In fact the chance of any such domestic insurrections was negligible, and many more men were needed in America, particularly when General Philip Schuyler invaded Canada from Ticonderoga in August 1775. George told North that Barrington's pessimism stemmed from his strategic outlook: 'He is diffident as to the raising recruits, but that is much occasioned from his wish to have the American war alone carried on by sea. I do not see the prospect so indifferent as he does.'[53]

On 8 August, Lord North, with his customary decency, asked the King whether Lord Chatham, who he said would be 'living but a little while longer', could alter the terms of his large state pension, to increase it to £3,000 per annum and award it to his sixteen-year-old second son and namesake William. North believed that 'such an instance of regard to his family at a time when the Crown has nothing to fear from him would have a very good effect in the public' and within the family.[54] George replied the next day:

> The making Lord Chatham's family suffer for the conduct of the father is not in the least agreeable to my sentiments, but I should choose to know him totally unable to appear on the public stage before I agree to any offer of that kind, lest it should be wrongly construed a fear of him, and indeed his political conduct the last winter was so abandoned that he must in the eyes of the dispassionate have totally undone all the merit of his former conduct . . . When decrepitude or death puts an end to him as a trumpet of sedition, I

shall make no difficulty of placing the second son's name instead of the father, and making up the pension [to] £3,000.[55]

Although of course the King could not have known it then, this turned out to be money very well spent, since it allowed William Pitt the Younger to enter politics and in time become the saviour of his country.

On 23 August, the Privy Council published a Proclamation in the King's name, effectively a reply to the Olive Branch Petition whose delivery he had ostensibly refused to accept. This stated that the colonies were in 'open and avowed rebellion' and were 'traitorously preparing, ordering and levying war against us'; as a result the King would use 'the utmost endeavours to suppress such rebellion and to bring the traitors to justice'.[56] The Proclamation has since been accused of being 'malice-laden', but in reality it was no more than a bald statement of the situation, a full four months after Lexington and Concord.[57] The remaining moderates in the Congress, such as the celebrated 'Pennsylvania Farmer' John Dickinson, a successful barrister and propagandist, felt their hopes of conciliation undermined by it, but as by then they had lost the internal struggle it was of little consequence.

The Proclamation ended the fiction that Congress was fighting against only Parliament and not the King himself. Until then, the British Army had been called 'ministerial troops' or 'parliamentary troops' by the rebels, and provincial assemblies still dated formal documents by the number of years of the King's reign, ending them with the words 'God Save the King'. Anglican churches in America even continued to employ the customary rubric of praying for the King to overcome his enemies.[58] Yet it had now become impossible for Americans to separate the once popular King from his ministers. The marker points along the road to recognition, alienation and ultimately rejection of the King had been his failure to respond to petitions, his formal Speeches from the Throne, his recruitment of auxiliaries from Hanover and his German allies, and now the Proclamation of the state of rebellion.[59] The American reaction to the dawning realization that the King was not about to overturn the North ministry's policies varied from sorrow and perplexity to indignation and resentment, the latter two emotions best reflected in the litany of remonstrances in the Declaration of Independence the following year.[60]

'The misfortune is that at the beginning of this American business there has been an unwillingness to augment the army and navy,' the King wrote to North on 26 August, starting to apportion blame only four months after Lexington and Concord, even though he himself was partly responsible. 'I proposed early in the summer the sending [of] beating [that is, recruitment] orders to Ireland, this was objected to in the Cabinet: if it had then been adopted the army would have been at least two or three thousand stronger at this hour.'[61] The King evidently believed that these extra men alone could have made a material difference in subduing a population of almost two million colonists. In the letter, he came up with two more ideas to encourage recruitment: firstly that the nobility and gentry should each give half a guinea to a parishioner to enlist in the army, and secondly that the East India Company should stop recruiting for four months, so that their recruiting sergeants could be set to work for the army instead. Neither found favour. In late September he vented his frustration with how little the City of London was doing for recruitment, which was hardly surprising with the pro-American Wilkes still Lord Mayor. 'Are the London merchants so thoroughly absorbed in their private interests', he asked North rhetorically, 'not to feel what they owe to the constitution which has enriched them?'[62]

Although General Schuyler started to besiege St John's on the Richelieu River in Canada on 6 September, that same month the New York Assembly was still respectfully petitioning the King 'that the grandeur and strength of the British Empire' depended 'essentially on a restoration of harmony of affection between the mother country and her colonies'.[63] That harmony however could not be restored without the King acting against the authority of Parliament, which he constitutionally could not and politically would not do. 'In keeping, as he saw it, with the letter and spirit of the Settlement of 1688, George III regarded himself as the executive agent for the maintenance of parliamentary authority,' writes the historian George Ditchfield. 'The King was no more able to impose a non-parliamentary policy towards the British colonies than he was to levy non-parliamentary taxation in Britain.'[64]

George fully recognized that he was fighting for Parliament's rights rather than purely for his own. On 10 September he told North that he would be surprised if the Opposition was strong in the next session, 'for I am fighting the battle of the legislature, therefore have a right to expect an almost unanimous support'.[65] For all the Whigs' insinuations that he wanted absolute power, 'all his utterances of whatever kind, show just as clearly that he was marked throughout his long life by this same innocence of any dark ambitions towards the polity over which he presided'.[66] Yet plenty of Whigs preferred to continue to see plots where there were none. 'I most heartily wish success to the Americans,' Horace Walpole wrote to his friend Horace Mann in September. 'If England prevails, English and American liberty is at an end!'[67]

The absurdly over-optimistic predictions of the royal governors, who were steadily losing control of their provinces as Gage withdrew their military defenders, dangerously misled the King and North. These were the people on whom the government relied for sound and informed counsel, yet as a letter from North to George advocating a southern campaign showed on 15 October, almost to a man they tended to be extremely oversanguine about the chances of strangling the rebellion in its cradle. 'Lord Dunmore in his last letters seems confident he could restore order in Virginia if he had the assistance of two or three hundred men,' it began, adding that Josiah Martin, who had been Governor of North Carolina since 1771, believed that:

> if he [were] properly supported and encouraged, [he] will, probably, be able in a short time to re-establish the authority of Great Britain in that colony. Lord William Campbell gives a very favourable account . . . in South Carolina, and declares his opinion that a body of two thousand men will be sufficient . . . The province of Georgia . . . will return to her duty as soon as South Carolina is brought to a submission.[68]

The British government also made the disastrous assumption early on (and even more so in 1780–81) that the Loyalist supporters of the King and Parliament would have a far more decisive effect on the war than they in fact did. Patriot zeal, organization and intimidation prevented the Loyalists – who even John Adams estimated made up around one-third of the American population, with another third Patriot and the rest neutral – from playing an effective part in the struggle, except in limited areas and for short periods.

Parliament passed the Prohibitory Act in October, which declared that the American colonies were now beyond the protection of the British Empire. It banned all trade with them, denied the Newfoundland fisheries to American colonial vessels and stated that all hostile ships were henceforth liable to seizure by the Royal Navy, just as in a state of war with a foreign country. This was intended to damage Congress's finances and to make any colonies that were hesitating over the rebellion reconsider, but John Adams was delighted, as it 'makes us independent in spite of our supplications and entreaties'.[69] Because of the lack of Royal Navy ships in American waters, it could not be properly enforced anyway.

On 23 October, Lord Rochford, the Southern Secretary, uncovered what he believed to be a plot to kidnap the King on his way to the State Opening of Parliament three days later and to hold him in the Tower of London before deporting him to Hanover. He therefore ordered the arrest of the man behind it, the New York-born Stephen Sayre, a former High Sheriff of the City of London, on charges of treason. Francis Richardson, another American and a Guards adjutant at the Tower of London, alleged that Sayre had engaged him in conversation in the Pennsylvania Coffee House on 19 October and told him of the scheme. Once the King had been kidnapped, public order was to be kept by John Wilkes and the City Sheriffs, with proclamations issued by a revolutionary council.[70] Rochford bungled the procedure of Sayre's arrest, allowing different charges for his committal to the Tower of London, and although there was corroborating evidence from Nicholas Nugent, another Guards officer, of soldiers being bribed by an accomplice, Sayre walked out of the Tower a free man five days later, with Wilkes' assistance.

The London press decided that the plot was simply too outlandish to be believed. Rochford was notoriously bad-tempered, habitually indiscreet (despite having been a diplomat) and widely thought to have abused his position by stockjobbing with inside information. The Cabinet did not stand by him in his decision to incarcerate Sayre, who was later awarded damages of £1,000 for wrongful arrest and imprisonment (though thanks to a technicality he did not receive it).[71] Yet Sayre might well have been guilty: his letters to Samuel Adams about the need for 'high convulsions', the contemporaneous distribution of leaflets calling for an uprising against Parliament, Sayre's undoubted involvement in secret arms shipments from Holland to America, and Richardson's and Nugent's sworn testimony all suggest that Rochford had in fact taken the prudent course in arresting Sayre and did not deserve the ridicule he received before he was forced to resign 'on health grounds' on 7 November.[72] Simply because the plot sounded ludicrous does not mean it was not seriously contemplated, as several more equally bizarre attempts on George's life and liberty would demonstrate.

On 26 October, 60,000 people lined the streets of London for the State Opening of Parliament, which took place earlier than usual because the King had said he wanted its 'advice, concurrence and assistance' in the war, by which he primarily meant money, admitting in his Speech that the conflict would involve an 'extraordinary burthen'.[73] He also declared that 'those who have long too successfully laboured to inflame my people in America ... now openly avow their revolt, hostility and rebellion'; he maintained that 'many' Americans were still loyal, but 'the torrent of violence has been strong enough to compel their acquiescence till a sufficient force shall appear to support them.'[74] In an uncompromising speech, he averred that:

> The authors and promoters of this desperate conspiracy have, in the conduct of it, derived great advantage from the difference of our intentions and theirs.

They meant only to amuse,* by vague expressions of attachment to the parent-state, and the strongest protestations of loyalty to me, whilst they were preparing for a general revolt.[75]

The Coercive Acts, by contrast, he said were intended 'rather to reclaim than to subdue'. He insisted that he had always been 'anxious to prevent, if it had been possible, the effusion of the blood of my subjects and the calamities which are inseparable from a state of war'.

George still hoped that his American subjects would 'discern the traitorous views of their leaders, and [that they] have been convinced that to be a subject of Great Britain, with all its consequences, is to be the freest member of any civil society in the known world'.[76] He therefore proposed 'to put a speedy end to these disorders by the most decisive exertions', after which, 'When the unhappy and deluded multitude . . . shall become sensible of their error, I shall be ready to receive the misled with tenderness and mercy.' To this end, he proposed granting 'general or particular pardons and indemnities' and returning America to 'the same protection and security as if such province or colony had never revolted'. There is no reason to doubt that these declarations were heartfelt, and they were certainly no different from those expressed in his private correspondence. At the end of the speech he made the exceptionally bad prediction that he saw 'no probability that the measures which you may adopt will be interrupted by disputes with any foreign power'.[77]

The speech elicited a large number of pamphlets and loyal addresses from all over the country praising the King for 'refusing to augment his own power in order to placate the colonists'.[78] The City of Oxford, to take one example among many, congratulated him for not being 'tempted to endanger the constitution of Great Britain by accepting the alluring offers of an unconstitutional increase of your prerogative'.[79] The Mayor and burgesses of Maidenhead thanked him for his 'paternal care'; an anonymous pamphleteer praised his 'wisdom and goodness'; the Archbishop of York thanked the Almighty 'that we have a prince upon the throne whose magnanimity and justice were superior to such temptations'.[80]

In the Debates on the Address, the government won by 176 votes to 72 in the Commons and by 76 votes to 33 in the Lords. Thomas Hutchinson, watching from the gallery, told a friend that the King's delivery had been much stronger than it appeared on the printed page.[81] When it reached Congress on 8 January 1776, however, George Washington said it had been 'full of rancour and resentment', while Abigail Adams, John Adams' wife,

---

* 'To draw on from time to time' (*Johnson's Dictionary*).

pronounced that it 'would stain with everlasting infamy the reign of George III'.[82] Today it seems hard to see why, but it certainly ended any sense of loyalty to the King on behalf of the rebels, genuine or pretended.

Between 6 and 10 November, North carried out a major – indeed fateful – Cabinet reshuffle, which nearly foundered on several occasions because of the demands made by various ministers. For his departure after the Sayre case, Lord Rochford wanted the Garter and a £2,500 pension for life; Dartmouth rejected the groomship of the Stole; Weymouth threatened to resign, and Grafton actually did.[83] On 7 November, North wrote self-pityingly to George that 'If no other way can be devised of keeping the system together, he [that is, North] is ready to give up the profits, the honours, the future expectations of his situation, and reserve only the responsibility and the fatigue of it.'[84] The King replied, 'At all events, you shall find me ready to take any steps to extricate you from difficulty. You are my sheet anchor and your ease and comfort I shall in the whole transaction try to secure.'[85]

According to William Knox, it was the King himself who solved the problem of who should take Grafton's place as Lord Privy Seal, 'by one of those minute strokes for which he is so eminent' and which 'removed all difficulty'.[86] Dartmouth was given the post, which allowed Lord George Germain (the former Lord George Sackville) to become Colonial Secretary. The reshuffle could not come too soon, because on 13 November the American General Richard Montgomery captured Montreal, forcing Sir Guy Carleton, the Governor-General of Canada, to withdraw to Quebec, just as the freezing winter set in.

The origin of the reshuffle had been the pressing need to remove the dovish Dartmouth from the key role of Colonial Secretary and replace him with the hawkish Germain, who now became unquestionably the key figure in the grand strategy of the war, more important even than Amherst, Gage or the Howe brothers. He was a thorough hardliner of the Hillsborough mould, who believed that the Stamp Act and Townshend Duties should not have been repealed, that the Canadians and Loyalists – the numbers and vigour of the latter he was consistently to overestimate, especially in the South – needed to be used early and aggressively, and that, unless a decisive military blow could be landed against the Continental Army, the war could be left to the navy. His post had only been invented in 1768, but was now the crucial one in the ministry, giving him effective parity with the other two secretaries of state, Lords Suffolk and Weymouth – not least because he had also inherited Dartmouth's role as First Lord of the Board of Trade and Plantations, with responsibility for putting the Prohibitory Act into operation.

Some found Germain haughty and withdrawn – his brothers were both depressives – but diarists refer to his good nature and equanimity. Indeed, for every contemporary writer who ascribes a particular character trait to Germain, there is another, equally close, who entirely contradicts it.[87] He has been described as 'probably the most incompetent official that has ever held an important post at a critical moment', yet he certainly did not manifest such ineptitude at the time, and some military historians vigorously dispute the assessment.[88] Certainly, many of Germain's contemporaries and colleagues rated him extremely highly, including, crucially, the King.[89] 'He has the character of a great man,' wrote Thomas Hutchinson, who for all his exiled embitterment in later life remained an honest man and a good judge of character. 'If it is possible to bring us out of our present confusion,' wrote the diplomat Sir William Hamilton, 'I am confident he will do it.'[90] 'In business he was rapid, yet clear and accurate,' noted Sir Nathaniel Wraxall. 'There was no obscurity and ambiguity in his compositions.'[91] Those who worked under him tended to agree.

Although Germain had the energy and vision to develop a strategy, as Secretary of State for the Colonies he was not actually responsible for the execution of it; that was the business of the War Office and the Admiralty. He could direct military dispositions in the colonies only because he de facto took over Barrington's War Office, but he did not get on at all well with Lord Sandwich, the other strong personality in the ministry with whom he was expected to work closely in coordinating the military and naval operations. Another problem was that it was only fifteen years since his public disgrace, and there were still a number of officers in the army who remembered it well; indeed some had been involved in it. 'The whole of his public life', his biographer notes, 'was embittered and conditioned by the national memory of his court martial and conviction in 1760 on the charge of disobedience of orders at the battle of Minden.'[92] George had allowed – indeed promoted – the return to a key role of someone whom a court martial had ruled was 'unfit to serve His Majesty in any military capacity whatsoever'.

Whatever his character attributes or failings, Germain was undoubtedly energetic and single-minded, and the King admired and trusted him, thought him ill-used after Minden and agreed with him about the hardline measures needed to force the American colonists back into line. This admiration was reciprocated. 'The more the ministers know of their master,' Germain wrote of George, 'the more will they incline to merit his good opinion.'[93] One aspect of Germain's personality that might have damaged him with the King was his widely suspected homosexuality – or at least bisexuality, as he had a wife and five children – and the unremitting attacks on him because of it. William Jackson's poem 'Sodom and Onan' in 1776 criticized George for the fact that 'Sackville, both coward and catamite / commands department honourable, and kisses hands / With lips that oft in blandishment obscene / Have been employed'.[94] In the Whig clubs of St James's, Germain was referred to behind his back as the 'Minden buggering hero', and his promotions of the handsome young civil servant and later playwright Richard Cumberland (one of his private secretaries at the Board of Trade) and the Massachusetts-born Loyalist (and later physicist) Benjamin Thompson,* who lived in his house for years, raised predictable suspicions. Many years later Richard Wellesley MP referred to 'Sir *Sodom* Thompson, Lord Sackville's *under*-secretary'.[95] If Germain was indeed bisexual, then it does not seem to have affected George's estimation of him; as with Samuel Foote and Captain Jones, he appears to have ignored the endemic prejudices of the age and supported Lord North in choosing the person thought best for the job.

A pamphlet entitled *The Character of the Late Lord Viscount Sackville*, written by Cumberland and published immediately after Germain's death ten years later, was straightforward about his strengths and limitations:

> He was of a grave and thoughtful cast, mixed but little with the world at large, and his manners and deportment had not the easy freedom of the present fashion. He talked little, and his opinions, being expressed without circumlocution or hesitation, stamped an air of forethought and reflection upon what he said ... Reserve, contracted by long exile from society, was the result of his misfortunes ... The early avocations of a military life, and perhaps a want of taste and disposition for classical studies, prevented his advances in literature so that in fact he was not so well read as people of his rank and condition ought to be ... He sometimes fell below the dignity of the subject he was speaking upon, for it was a point for him on all occasions to take the straightest road to his object rather than a circuitous one, though ever so flowery ... He was generally represented as a proud and distant man, but in fact he had no more pride at heart than every man of honour.[96]

From multiple sources the picture emerges of Germain as an unsociable, plain-spoken aristocrat with a great deal to prove because of the accusations of cowardice at the battle of Minden.

On 8 November, in the middle of the reshuffle, as Germain was being appointed, there was a successful House of Commons division.† The King told North, 'It shows the sense of the House of Commons that we must

---

* Later known as Count Rumford.
† Germain sat in the Commons; he had a courtesy title as the son of a duke.

with vigour pursue the means of bringing the deluded Americans to a sense of their duty.'[97] Germain had been involved in the strategic consultations since July. 'One decisive blow at land is absolutely necessary,' he wrote to his friend Sir John Irwin on 13 September. 'I should be for exerting the utmost force of this kingdom to finish this rebellion war in one campaign.'[98] Once he had taken over at the Colonial Office, he set to work creating a strategy for winning the war in a single campaign, one that looked relatively simple, at least in theory.

The Germain Plan was in essence to send a force under John Burgoyne to strike south from Canada towards the Hudson River. Meanwhile, General Howe – who in October 1775 had replaced the demoralized Gage as Commander-in-Chief of British forces in North America – would capture New York City, and afterwards meet Burgoyne at Albany, thereby cutting New England off from the rest of the colonies. Albany controlled much of the Hudson River where it is joined by the Mohawk River from the west. A third, southern force would capture Charleston and link up with Loyalists in the Carolinas to end the rebellion in the South. The Germain Plan had the advantage of being simple, but suffered from the huge disadvantages of both splitting limited British forces and being hard to coordinate on the ground in America, let alone from London.

The war was not unwinnable for the British, but they helped to make it so by refusing to change their basic military doctrine and almost anything fundamental at home, in terms of finances, commercial arrangements, conscription and tax levels. Had Germain possessed the concentration of powers that William Pitt had enjoyed during the Seven Years War, he might have imposed his will on the whole governmental structure, but an over-devolving of competencies between ministries was rife for the first two years of the struggle. Until 1777, for example, the responsibility for transporting men and their supplies across the Atlantic was divided between the Ordnance Board (responsible for artillery, engineers, guns and gunpowder), the Navy Board (men, horses, uniforms, tents, medicine and camp equipment) and the Victualling Board (food), the Treasury being responsible for all other supplies. This inevitably led to vast amounts of bureaucracy; Germain and Barrington even corresponded over the selection of a single doctor for Howe's command.[99] This Whitehall system of waging war had been successful in the Seven Years War at a distance of over 3,000 miles across the ocean, but this was to be much harder without a single leader like Pitt; indeed it has been described as 'an effort without parallel in the history of the world'.[100]

Even seemingly simple matters – arranging the tents for a regiment, for example, or a date of embarkation for a forty-four-man contingent of a

Guards regiment 'with four officers' servants' – required input and agreement between the Guards, the Board of Admiralty and the Secretary at War. Everything concerning the German auxiliaries was even more complicated, involving the Northern Department (as their hiring took place in Germany), the War Office and, when they reached England, the American Department (unless they were re-embarking in Ireland, in which case the Viceroy was involved).[101] Germain tried to streamline the whole system in February 1777 but started a long-running departmental turf war with Lord Sandwich. Although Barrington continued officially as Secretary at War, Germain effectively took over his department, which he ran from the Colonial Office.

'George III did not direct the war,' wrote one historian of the conflict, Piers Mackesy. 'He received ministers individually, and commented on their views; but beyond insisting in general terms on the subjugation of America, he made no attempt to steer strategy.'[102] Theoretically the King did play a role in army administration, and exercised considerable influence over which commanders were appointed, not least to prevent politicians from appointing undeserving supporters and relatives to posts. Even so, he only ever had consultative powers over which units were moved where, rather than executive ones. He saw his role not in contributing to grand strategy – although he always kept himself minutely abreast of it – but in providing boosts in morale to the nation and his ministers. His role in strategy was, as it was also in politics more widely, to 'advise, encourage and warn' the government of the day. Just as George cannot be blamed for the war breaking out, therefore, neither can he be blamed for losing it.

13

The Declaration of Independence

November 1775–July 1776

Tyrant:

1. An absolute monarch, governing imperiously.
2. A cruel, despotic and severe master.

Samuel Johnson, *A Dictionary of the English Language*, 1755

'Believe me, dear sir, there is not in the British Empire a man who more cordially loves a union with Great Britain more than I do,' Thomas Jefferson wrote to a friend on 29 November 1775.[1] Yet in the same letter he described King George as 'the bitterest enemy we have' and argued that breaking with Britain was 'now pressed upon us' by the King and Parliament. He felt particular ire that Lord Dunmore, the Governor of Virginia, had offered freedom to any slaves who escaped from their owners and joined the British colours. Some 200 joined what was called the Ethiopian Regiment, where they saw service at the battle of Great Bridge on 9 December.[2]

On 6 December, the Second Continental Congress declared its complete independence from Parliament, while overtly still claiming loyalty to George himself. 'What allegiance is it that we forget?' it asked, rhetorically. 'Allegiance to Parliament? We never owed – we never owned it. Allegiance to our King? Our words have ever avowed it – our conduct has ever been consistent with it. We condemn with arms in our hands . . . we oppose the claim and exercise of unconstitutional powers, to which neither the Crown nor Parliament were ever entitled.'[3] Later claims by various Founding Fathers that they had favoured outright independence earlier than 1776 were for the most part false, such as John Adams' statement in his *Autobiography* that Thomas Paine's ideas about independence 'had been urged in Congress a hundred times'.[4]

Adams went so far as to claim that many Congressmen were not in favour of outright independence even at the time of signing the Declaration, writing, 'I then believed and I have not since altered my opinion, that there were several who signed with regret, and several others with many doubts and much lukewarmness.'[5] Although many Patriots had indeed long wanted the thirteen colonies to become an independent nation, even in the months after the battle of Bunker Hill they only tiptoed towards it, with the moderate representatives from outside New England still not persuaded that any successor state might be federalized.

Meanwhile, the shooting war continued: American Generals Richard Montgomery and Benedict Arnold attacked Quebec in a driving blizzard on the last day of 1775, and were defeated by the British garrison under Sir Guy Carleton. Montgomery was killed, Arnold wounded, and one-third of their army in Canada were killed, wounded or captured, yet the hardy survivors were to remain encamped on the Plains of Abraham outside Quebec for the next five months. As late as 21 April 1776, Charles Turner was betting the Earl of Northington twenty-five guineas at Brooks's 'that Quebec [is] now, or will be before 1st January 1777, in the hands of the Provincial Army, supposing no peace concluded'.[6]

The year 1775 ended with the British having signally failed to strangle the rebellion in its cradle. Boston was still under siege, and the American colonists had failed to take Canada only by a slim margin; they were by no means vanquished in that theatre. Although some in the government such as Lord Barrington wanted to concentrate on blockading the colonies into eventual submission, the majority, including the King, were determined upon a land war to force the issue.

There is a saying in military circles that amateurs talk about strategy while professionals discuss logistics. George was no professional, but he was certainly concerning himself in a professional manner with the logistics of fighting a trans-oceanic conflict. The logistical problem in the winter of 1775/6 was that each British soldier in the small East Coast bridgeheads required one-third of a ton of food, which, if it could not be sourced locally, had to be shipped to him from Britain: oats, pork, salted beef, butter, oatmeal and so on.[7] George occupied himself in working on this challenge, which in turn served to spur others to action. As one junior minister noted wryly, 'I have always observed that the Admiralty can be expeditious when the King is inquisitive or anxious about their preparations.'[8]

On 1 January 1776 Lord Dunmore's fleet bombarded Norfolk, Virginia, a Loyalist town that had been captured by the rebels; the colonial militia then demolished it themselves and blamed its ruination on the British. Of the 1,331 structures that were destroyed, the British were responsible for demolishing thirty-two before evacuating, and then nineteen more in the bombardment. The American militiamen burned 863, and then a further 416 when the Virginia Convention ordered Norfolk to be razed to the ground. Yet somehow the destruction of Virginia's largest town, and its most important port, was successfully blamed entirely on the British.[9] The widespread belief in an atrocity committed in Norfolk meant that, in the words of George Washington's biographer, 'the conflict abruptly lurched toward total war.'[10] Their relative innocence at Norfolk is not of course to suggest that the British did not burn towns during the war – they had already burned 500 houses in Charlestown, Massachusetts, during the battle of Bunker Hill in June 1775, while the guns of the Royal Navy destroyed Falmouth, Massachusetts (today's Portland, Maine), in October of that year. As in all wars that encompassed a civil war, neither side had a monopoly of atrocity. But at no point did the King condone any atrocities, outrages or behaviour contrary to the then rules of war, any more than did George Washington.

On Wednesday 10 January 1776 the publication of an anonymous pamphlet ignited the first instance of outright mass republicanism among Americans. It was called *Common Sense* and the first thousand copies went on sale in Philadelphia. It proved a literary phenomenon, going through twenty-five printings in 1776 alone, and would sell 150,000 in the eventual fifty-six editions soon thereafter, and ultimately over three million copies.[11] An American historian has stated that 'with the possible exception of *Uncle Tom's Cabin*, *Common Sense* was demonstrably the most immediately influential political or social tract ever published in this country.'[12] Its author, the Englishman Thomas Paine, asserted 'that a thirst for absolute power is the natural disease of monarchy' and that 'the prejudice of Englishmen in favour of their own government by king, lords and commons, arises as much or more from national pride than from reason'.[13] It was an anti-English diatribe as much as an anti-monarchical one, written by a Briton who had arrived from England only fourteen months earlier.

The thirty-nine-year-old Paine was a former staymaker,* schoolmaster, grocer and twice-dismissed excise officer, who, as his generally sympathetic biographer admits, had 'relentlessly failed in everything personal and professional he had ever attempted'.[14] As one historian has written, Paine was 'full of rage at the ways the Old World had kept him down'.[15] Sarah, the daughter of Paine's benefactor Benjamin Franklin, wrote of him soon after he arrived in Philadelphia, 'There never was a man less loved in a place

---

* A stay being the thick rope used aboard ships; Paine was not, as is often erroneously thought, a maker of corsets.

than Paine in this, having at different times disputed with everyone.'[16] Paine's contemporaries found him 'obnoxious, self-absorbed, impetuous, conceited and disputatious', which might help to explain why he failed in politics in both the Old World and later in the New.[17] Certainly the adjectives Paine directed against King George were evidence of an unquiet mind, for by December he was describing the King as 'a sottish, stupid, stubborn, worthless, brutish man' who resembled 'a common murderer, a highwayman or a housebreaker'.[18] Calling the King sottish was particularly inaccurate in relation to someone who rarely drank alcohol and never to excess – unlike Paine himself.[19]

'Government by kings was first introduced into the world by the heathens, from whom the children of Israel copied the custom,' Paine claimed, blaming history's oldest scapegoats. 'Monarchy is ranked in scripture as one of the sins of the Jews,' he opined, 'for which a curse in reserve is denounced against them.'[20] Further, 'The hankering which the Jews had for the idolatrous customs of the heathens is something exceedingly unaccountable,' but Paine nevertheless explained it: 'The Jews, elated with success' over Gideon's victories, wanted to make him a king. What Paine called 'the evil of monarchy' was, according to his reading of the Book of Samuel, to be put down to 'the general manner of the kings of the earth, whom Israel was so eagerly copying after'.[21]

Having thus squarely blamed the Jews for the institution of monarchy, Paine then attacked George personally, describing him as 'the royal brute of Britain', the 'royal criminal', 'his Mad-jesty',* 'a full-blooded Nero' and 'Mr Guelph' (the Hanoverians' surname), and his government as 'a detestable junto'.[22] He argued that Americans had to choose between independence and slavery, which as one of his modern critics David Pryce-Jones points out was 'imagining a polarisation that sounded urgent but was factitious, quite false' since the status quo was of course neither of those things.[23]

Common Sense was written for the ordinary populace rather than for well-educated readers, and was devoid of the customary Latin tags, classical allusions and learned footnotes of many other pamphlets of the day. Most references or allusions were to the Bible, a copy of which virtually all Americans possessed and which many knew well. Paine claimed that 'censure to individuals make[s] no part' of his argument, though that was demonstrably untrue when it came to Mr Guelph.[24] In an appendix to a later edition, Paine noted of the King's most recent speech to Parliament, 'Every line convinces, even at the moment of reading, that he who hunts the woods for prey, the naked and untutored Indian, is less a savage than the King of Britain.'[25]

---

* Admittedly, an impressive prediction, considering the episode of 1765 was not known about.

Paine claimed in *Common Sense* that 'No man was a warmer wisher for reconciliation than myself, before the fatal 19 April 1775,* but the moment the event of that day was made known, I rejected the hardened, sullen-tempered Pharaoh† of England for ever; and disdain the wretch, that with the pretended title of Father of his People can unfeelingly hear their slaughter, and composedly sleep with their blood on his soul.'[26] In fact Paine had been telling people that 'kings might very well be dispensed with' since at least 1771.[27] Three months after landing in America in November 1774, he was editing a new publication, the *Pennsylvania Magazine*, and as his biographer states, 'During his next fifteen months as executive editor, Paine tried hard to steer the magazine toward the growing controversies about the position of the American colonies within the British Empire.'[28] He published in full the text of the petition of the First Continental Congress, for example. His claim of a Damascene conversion on 19 April 1775 was therefore untrue.

A timeless tactic of warfare is to be the first to define your enemy. Paine had struck first and hard. *Common Sense* unleashed a series of newspaper articles, speeches, pamphlets and letters across the colonies that now referred to the King as the 'cruellest sovereign *tyrant* of this age', a 'butcher' and 'that wicked tryanical [*sic*] brute (nay worse than brute) of Great Britain'.[29] Patriots vied with each other in condemning him in the most extreme language possible. Yet the King was not without his supporters. Charles Inglis, an assistant rector in New York City, wrote a pamphlet entitled *The Deceiver Unmasked* about Paine, although every copy was destroyed by a mob in March 1776. Undeterred, he then wrote *The True Interest of America Impartially Stated*, describing the King as 'our true and lawful liege sovereign' and warning that Paine's republicanism would 'plunge [America] into a tedious, bloody and most expensive war with Great Britain'.[30] Inglis was to be attainted for treason by the state of New York, but escaped to become Bishop of Nova Scotia.

Inglis highlighted the way Paine had sought to imply that the King was a secret Roman Catholic, writing in *Common Sense* 'that the phrase parent or mother country hath been jesuitically adopted by the King and his parasites, with a low papistical design of gaining an unfair bias on the credulous weakness of our minds'.[31] This attempt to play on American anti-Catholic bigotry was, as we have seen, widespread after the Quebec Act. 'This curious observation was introduced purely to insinuate the King is a papist,' Inglis

---

* The events at Lexington and Concord.

† The mention of George as Pharaoh ought to have reminded readers that the Jews could not be blamed for the concept of monarchy, given that the Egyptian monarchy predated theirs by centuries.

wrote, 'which has as much truth in it as to insinuate that he is a Mahometan or Gentoo [that is, Muslim or Hindu], for there is not a firmer Protestant in Great Britain than his present Majesty.' It was true, but by then the huge success of *Common Sense* – for all its anti-Semitism, absurd exaggeration, anti-Catholic bigotry and bogus claims of objectivity – meant that its aim of blackening George's name had been triumphantly achieved. The success of *Common Sense* also underlines the appallingly bad job that the royal governors and Loyalists had done in advancing the King's point of view.

On the same day that *Common Sense* was published, Lord Sandwich wrote to the King enclosing a captured rebel flag, and apologizing that he could not see the King for the next few days because he was mourning his twenty-three-year-old son William, an MP who had died of 'dissipation' in Lisbon. The navy, he said, had experienced a whole chapter of problems in preparing Admiral Sir Peter Parker's fleet for the Southern Expedition (also known as the Cape Fear Expedition) that Lord George Germain wanted in order to support the Loyalists in the Carolinas that spring, and 'the short notice we have had for such enormous demands is without precedent'.[32] The King replied at 10.33 the next morning, commiserating over Sandwich's son but rejecting the excuse about the fleet refitting: 'You call it unprecedented . . . but when such acts of vigour are shown by the rebellious Americans, we must show that the English lion when roused has not only his wonted resolution but has added the swiftness of the racehorse.'[33] George's letters sometimes show a deft turn of phrase and, if Britain had won the war, some of them might today be considered Churchillian: instead, they read as absurd and vainglorious.

The problems the fleet encountered included 'contrary winds and accidents', the delayed refit of *Bristol*, *Boreas* beached at Spithead, *Actaeon*, *Thunder* and *Deal Castle* being blown back to Plymouth (the last of them running ashore mastless) and a hospital ship and bomb vessel not even making the rendezvous. Nonetheless, Sir Peter Parker's fleet carrying Henry Clinton's army arrived off Cape Fear to spearhead the Southern Expedition on 12 March 1776. By then, however, 1,100 North Carolinian Patriots had defeated 1,800 Loyalists at the battle of Moore's Creek Bridge on 27 February, preventing them from establishing a British naval base at Wilmington. After a failed attack in late June on Sullivan's Island, which protected the estuary leading to Charleston, Parker was forced to sail away, anchoring off New York City on 2 August.

One of the progenitors of the Southern Expedition was General Charles Cornwallis, 2nd Earl Cornwallis, who had fought at Minden and had been one of the few officers to have given evidence for Germain rather than against him at his court martial. Germain encouraged Cornwallis to apply for this command, even though he had opposed both the Stamp and Coercive Acts. Cornwallis was the kind of sober, dignified family man that the King liked, a former aide-de-camp of his, as well as being the nephew of the Archbishop of Canterbury. George approved Cornwallis's appointments as the Vice-Treasurer of Ireland in 1769, Privy Councillor in 1770 and Constable of the Tower of London in 1771. He also approved Cornwallis's request to take his own 33rd Regiment with him to Cape Fear. The King was thus intimately bound up with his advancement. Cornwallis became a lieutenant-general on New Year's Day 1776.

On 4 March 1776, George Washington occupied the Heights of Dorchester above Boston, forcing Sir William Howe on the 17th to evacuate all British forces by sea to Halifax, Nova Scotia, where he awaited reinforcements from his brother, Admiral Richard Howe. Had Gage and Howe not concentrated their forces in Boston in 1775, there is at least a possibility that some provincial governors with Loyalist support might have been able to hold on to at least a few of the other twelve colonies in the earliest stage of the conflict.[34] Yet, as Frederick the Great said, 'He who defends everything, defends nothing,' and it might have been that every small British contingent across America would have been defeated piecemeal. After forcing Howe out of Boston, George Washington moved to New York City, correctly predicting that that was where the British would attack next. He constructed Forts Lee and Washington along the Hudson River, summoned troops (mainly militia) from the nearby colonies and dispatched General Israel Putnam and half of his 13,000-strong force to the Flatbush area of Long Island. He then built fortified earthworks along the Brooklyn Heights and the hills to the south of them, as well as batteries on lower Manhattan and Governors Island.

To the north, Major-General John Burgoyne's arrival in Quebec province with British troops and German auxiliaries on 6 May led to the dispersal of the American threat to Canada, General John Sullivan retreating first to Crown Point and then Ticonderoga. Nine days later, the Virginia Convention instructed Richard Lee and its other representatives to Congress to propose a declaration of independence and the formation of a confederation of colonies, while Congress itself called for all royal authority in the colonies to be 'totally suppressed'.[35]

Back in London, the King answered another petition from the Corporation of London on 23 March:

I deplore, with the deepest concern, the miseries which a great part of my subjects in America have brought upon themselves by an unjustifiable resistance to the constitutional authority of the kingdom; and I shall be ready and happy to alleviate those miseries by acts of mercy and clemency whenever that authority shall be established, and the now existing rebellion at an end. To obtain these salutary purposes, I will invariably pursue the most proper and effectual means.[36]

There is no reason to doubt him. When the Cabinet in London envisaged what resolution in America might look like, they saw the end of the rebellion through a negotiated settlement that involved first a military surrender and then a political settlement involving no taxation and a substantial degree of autonomy.[37] Later claims that George was vengeful towards his soon-to-be-former subjects were a total fabrication.

At the time, the King was having a good deal of his time taken up by a problem that plagued all eighteenth-century governments: that of office- and honours-seekers, whose importuning did not end even when a peerage had been granted, since they continued to press for a rise through its five ranks.* This constant pressure on the King came to a head in late May 1776 over an issue that seems to have caused him as much personal distress as anything Thomas Paine or the Virginia Convention were saying or doing at that time. George Montagu, 1st Duke of Montagu, had applied for the earldom of Montagu as a remainder title that he could give to his son, to which the King had agreed. George was then reminded by Lord North that he had already promised the title to the 1st Lord Beaulieu. The King could not recall making any such pledge, but Lady Beaulieu, the proud, rich and formidable septuagenarian daughter of the 2nd Duke of Montagu (by an earlier creation) and widow of the 2nd Duke of Manchester, insisted that he had.

Because it impinged upon his honour to promise the same title to two people, the row threw the King into what he told North was 'the greatest state of uneasiness I ever felt'.[38] At the moment when thirteen colonies were fast in the process of shearing off from his empire, this must have been an exaggeration of the kind that he often resorted to, yet there is no doubt that he loathed the feeling that he might be breaking his word, even to a woman who had forced her husband to join the Opposition ten years earlier and had later boycotted the Court when the Montagu dukedom had been revived. 'I cannot go to my Levee, nor see any mortal, till you have been here,' the King told North desperately. The situation was eventually sorted out by denying the duke the earldom, and in 1784 Lord Beaulieu

---

* Only Wellington managed to go through every rank from baron to viscount to earl to marquess to duke.

became the 1st Earl Beaulieu, but not – to Lady Beaulieu's great chagrin – the Earl of Montagu.

These incessant honours issues had much the same effect on North as they had on the King, and indeed two years later he begged George to be allowed to resign the premiership, 'as I really shall not be able to stand the storm and violence which the candidates for the peerage will bring upon me'.[39] The obsession with honours was a feature of the era; the 1st Marquess of Abercorn wore the blue riband of his Order of the Garter even when he went shooting. (He also insisted his maids wear white gloves while making his bed.)[40] Tending to grandees' pride and pettiness exhausted both the King and North, just as they were approaching the greatest crisis of their lives.

On 2 July, Congress approved Richard Henry Lee's resolution of independence at the Pennsylvania State House in Philadelphia, severing all ties between the thirteen colonies and Britain, and becoming a republic. Only New York did not support the resolution, because the instructions from its assembly to its delegation were delayed. In effect, of course, Congress had already been acting as what Jefferson called one of 'the powers of the earth' for almost two years: appointing agents in Europe who were ambassadors, seeking aid from France and Spain as well as an alliance with both countries, raising capital, founding an army and navy, and so on.[41] Indeed, the Declaration of Independence has recently been described as more of 'a call for help from France and Spain' than a domestic political document, although in practice it was both.[42] To set out reasons why a new nation should exist was itself a new idea. Pasquale Paoli had not bothered with it when Corsica rose against Genoa in 1755; and while the Dutch had published the Act of Abjuration against the King of Spain in 1581, that was in no sense a manifesto for a new nation in the same way as the Declaration of Independence.

Two days after the Lee Resolution passed, on Thursday 4 July 1776, Congress printed and distributed its Declaration, which had been principally written by Thomas Jefferson. Popular legend has it that John Hancock, who as President of the Congress was the first to sign it, said he had made his signature big so that 'fat old King George could read it without his spectacles', proving that not all eighteenth-century political vituperation was witty.[43]

'The Revolution was in the minds of the People,' John Adams told Thomas Jefferson in 1815, 'and this was effected, from 1760 to 1775 ... before a drop of blood was drawn at Lexington.'[44] More than a thousand pamphlets were published in that fifteen-year period, and it was largely through them that the debate moved from explicit expressions of loyalty to George to rebellion against him. In private, Adams wrote of the Declaration that there was 'not an idea in it, but what has been hackneyed in Congress for two years before'.[45] If anything, the surprise is that it had taken so long before these issues of sovereignty actually involved the sovereign himself and for him to become the focus of open criticism – especially since he had made his views on Parliament's authority over every part of the empire publicly known since November 1767.

Congress cut one-third of the Declaration, but mercifully left its preamble largely intact. The 1,458-word document falls naturally into two discrete parts. It opens with language worthy of Shakespeare and the Book of Common Prayer in its eloquent, two-paragraph justification of rebellion. The quest for self-government and the rights of man are set within a doctrine of political equality that became the foundational principle for the United States and went on to inspire millions of people all over the globe for two and a half centuries. This first section has rightly been hailed as one of the greatest documents of the Enlightenment. The second section, however, consists of twenty-eight separate ad hominem accusations against the King which, because of their centrality to the way that King George III has been viewed by history, deserve some detailed analysis.

Perhaps surprisingly, there is nothing about Parliament in the Declaration; the word does not even appear. With the British Army out of Boston and every British governor ejected from his provincial capital, de facto independence already existed, so Congress now needed to emphasize its complete de jure independence. For that it needed to abjure the King rather than just Parliament, as it was to the King, not to Parliament, that they had previously admitted allegiance. Unless it took the form of a personal attack, therefore, it would not answer the Loyalists' argument that it was possible to become independent of Britain but remain in a political condominium of some sort under the Crown. As a result, Britain and the British people are hardly mentioned either: indeed the only reference to 'our British brethren' is to the fact that because they had been 'deaf to the voice of justice and consanguinity' they must be 'enemies in war, in peace friends'.[46] The same offer was not extended to George.

Some of Jefferson's original strictures against Britain – such as that the settlement of the colonies had been 'unassisted by the wealth or the strength of Great Britain' – were excised by the committee as it was believed that these would alienate support.[47] In order to present themselves as heirs to the 1642 and 1688 revolutions, as they genuinely believed themselves to be, the American revolutionaries had to paint George as a Stuart-style tyrant, even though he was nothing of the sort. Unlike in the two English revolutions, the King was actively supporting the policy of the British government and the majority of the House of Commons.

The second section of the Declaration, which comprises more than two-thirds of the text, was therefore devoted to a series of ad hominem accusations against the King in an attempt to prove that 'The history of the present King of Great Britain is a history of repeated injuries and usurpations, all having in direct object the establishment of an absolute tyranny over these states.'[48] These charges were kept deliberately unspecific regarding places and dates, for the obvious reason that most were untrue, since George had never sought to establish any kind of tyranny over America.[49] Indeed, in terms of genuine as opposed to theoretical liberties, Britain was well ahead of North America – Dissenters could operate in Britain without licences, for example, which was not the case in all the colonies – and as the Mansfield Judgment attested, slavery was illegal in Britain and Canada.

Two trenchant defenders made their way into print shortly after the Declaration was published. John Lind, a London barrister, wrote a 132-page rejection of its charges in his *Answer to the Declaration of Congress* which tended to refute on legal grounds. Thomas Hutchinson thought in more political terms when he read the Declaration in London in August, and published *Strictures upon the Declaration of the Congress at Philadelphia* anonymously in November. The latter attempted to counter that 'most infamous paper', full of 'a great number of pretended tyrannical deeds of the King'.[50] There could hardly have been a person better placed to undertake it than Hutchinson, since he was not only Massachusetts born and bred, but had held almost all the great offices in the colony. His argument was that 'If no taxes or duties had been laid upon the colonies, other pretences would have been found for exception to the authority of Parliament.'[51] Hutchinson believed that the accusations against the King in the document were, 'with design, left obscure; for as soon as they are developed, instead of justifying, they rather aggravate the criminality of this revolt'.[52]

The twenty-eight charges against the King fall into three distinct groups as they build up steadily in rhetoric. The first through to the twelfth were complaints about the actions that the King – or, more usually, his provincial governors with his subsequent approval – had committed in order to try to check the rising tide of rebellion. The thirteenth through to the twenty-second focused on the King's support of Parliament over American legislatures, several referring to episodes that had long predated his reign.[53] The next five, from the twenty-third to the twenty-seventh, concerned the war itself – the fighting at Bunker Hill, the occupation of Boston, the burning of Falmouth and Norfolk, and so on – and were an *ex post facto* ploy to use British attempts to suppress the rebellion as a justification for the rebellion itself.[54] The last, twenty-eighth, charge was that the King had ignored Congress's two petitions to him of 1774 and 1775, even though he did not recognize the body from which they emanated.

The first charge was that 'He has refused his assent to laws, the most wholesome and necessary for the public good.'[55] Although the lack of specificity makes it impossible to be certain, this probably refers to the vetoing of colonial laws creating paper money, granting divorces, taxing the slave trade and lowering the numbers of convicts sent to America.[56] Of course some of these were highly subjective; several colonies welcomed the thousand or so convicts that were sent every year, sometimes because they were a source of cheap labour, and sometimes because people often treated over-harshly by the British penal system eventually turned into good immigrants. Flooding the colonies with inflationary paper money would hardly be 'wholesome and necessary to the public good', and large numbers of pious Americans did not support easier divorce. Moreover, the fact that the King had, on relatively rare occasions, exercised his constitutional right to veto legislation did not prove that that right was an improper one, any more than a presidential veto over legislation would today. When the United States established control over Puerto Rico after the Spanish–American War, for example, it retained the power to annul the Acts of the Puerto Rican legislature. That is what empires do.

The second charge accused George of having 'forbidden his governors to pass laws of immediate and pressing importance, unless suspended in their operation till his assent should be obtained'.[57] The law of suspension, necessary because of the distance across the Atlantic, had been in operation since 1708, and was a sensible precaution against laws being overturned months after they had gone into operation.[58] The third charge accused the King of gerrymandering representation in the colonial legislatures against the rights of 'large districts of people'. It was true that the British government had insisted on newly created townships receiving representation in New Hampshire in 1748, and required that the Scotch-Irish should be fairly represented in the Pennsylvania legislature when it was controlled by the Germans and Quakers.

The fourth, fifth and six charges referred to interference with the colonial legislatures. The Virginia Assembly had been dissolved in 1765 over the Stamp Act, and the Virginia, Massachusetts and South Carolina legislatures in 1768 over the Massachusetts Circular Letter. In 1768 the Massachusetts Governor had directed that the legislature meet at Cambridge until 1772 rather than 4 miles away in Boston, but this had been in part because Patriots such as John Hancock and James Otis had complained that they did not want to meet in a city full of British troops.[59] (It had met in Cambridge before, during smallpox outbreaks in Boston.)

All three of these charges referred to British actions after the revolutionary movement had begun its drive for independence, and none was unconstitutional under the laws pertaining at the time. Hutchinson commented from personal experience on the fifth charge – 'He has dissolved representative houses repeatedly for opposing with manly firmness his invasions on the rights of the people' – writing that it had been 'the only way to prevent their prosecuting the plan of rebellion ... Thus ... the regular use of the prerogative in suppressing a begun revolt is urged as a grievance to justify the revolt.'[60]

The sixth charge – about the 'long time' during which Massachusetts had been left without a government, and thus 'exposed to all the dangers of invasion from without and convulsions within' – drew Hutchinson's special ire. He pointed out that Massachusetts had been without a government for less than three months, and that far from the danger being an invasion 'from without', the four regiments sent to Boston had been 'to aid the civil magistrate in preserving the peace, and the convulsions within were the tumults, riots and acts of violence which this Convention was called not to suppress but to encourage'.[61] He knew all about such riots, since one had destroyed his own home.

The seventh charge, that the King had 'endeavoured to prevent the population of these states; for that purpose obstructing the laws for the naturalization of foreigners', glided over the reasons that this had indeed sometimes happened. The British government had actively encouraged immigration into Pennsylvania and the middle colonies, for example, but was alive to the danger of naturalizing foreigners as American citizens if they owned vessels. 'Colonial naturalization had become part and parcel of colonial smuggling,' one American historian has noted, and 'The check on naturalization was, therefore, intended only as a check on smuggling, rebellion and independence,' not as a check on the colonies' demographics or economy.[62] Jefferson, of course, knew this perfectly well.

The eighth charge claimed that the King 'has obstructed the administration of justice by refusing his assent to laws for establishing judiciary powers', implying that he had often refused assent to laws establishing courts and that therefore justice had been impaired.[63] Yet that had also only happened once, again in North Carolina, when the Assembly had refused to vote salaries for judges between 1773 and 1776, which could hardly be blamed on the royal governor. 'All this was fully known to Congress,' Hutchinson pointed out, 'who, notwithstanding, have most falsely represented the regular use of prerogative to prevent injustices as an obstruction to the administration of justice.'[64] Jefferson was already starting to run out of worthwhile points on his brief, yet there were twenty more charges to come.

The ninth was that the King had 'made judges dependent on his will alone for the tenure of their offices, and the amount and payment of their salaries'.[65] In most colonies, judges had been dependent on the Crown for tenure while the assemblies paid their salaries, but lately the assemblies had refused to give judges permanent salaries, preferring to vote on them from year to year in order to retain a measure of control over the judiciary, and, it was alleged, deter them from prosecuting smuggling to the full extent of the law. In 1773, the Governor of Massachusetts took over the payment of judges, which had infuriated the legislature, but Crown payment of judges had been the practice in England when the colonies were founded, and except in charter colonies such as Rhode Island and Connecticut they were always dependent on the Crown for their continuance in office. In some colonies the judges were paid by the Crown also, and Hutchinson pointed out that those colonies 'considered it as an act of favour' because it saved them from footing the bill themselves.

The tenth charge was that the King had 'erected a multitude of new offices and sent hither swarms of officers to harass our people and eat out their substance'. This was a reference to the four new Admiralty courts which the Commissioners of Customs had headquartered at Boston and which had attempted to combat smuggling.[66] Every penny of the commissioners' salaries and the costs of the Admiralty courts were paid out of customs receipts rather than by the legislatures. John Lind pointed out that the only class of people who could justifiably complain about the new courts were smugglers. Hutchinson reminded readers that when the five customs commissioners were appointed, four surveyors-general had been dismissed, and only fifteen or twenty junior staff came over from England with them, so the size and cost of the bureaucracy was much the same. 'Thirty or forty additional officers in the whole continent', jeered Hutchinson, 'are the *swarms* which eat out the subsistence of the boasted number of three millions of people.'[67]

The eleventh charge was that the King had 'kept among us, in times of peace, standing armies without the consent of our legislatures'. Once Jefferson had excised charges criticizing George over slavery from the original draft, this was perhaps the most hypocritical allegation of those that remained. Quite apart from the obvious fact that there had been no dividing line in the period from 1754 and 1756 between a time of war with the French and Native Americans and one of peace, and a standing army on the western border had been the only way of protecting the colonies, the assemblies had actually voted their thanks for what the British Army had done. The only point at which the 'consent of our legislatures' had been withdrawn was when the four battalions had arrived in Boston in 1768, another example of the Declaration using as an excuse for rebellion the actions the British had taken in trying to prevent it.

Hutchinson explained that, before Boston rose in riot and threatened rebellion, the only British troops were on the western border, defending the colonists from the Native Americans. They were not to be found on the streets of colonial America; in fact in many parts of the colonies, particularly in the South, they barely existed at all. Britain had always had the right to station troops in her colonies, so the eleventh charge, while sounding as though it had a basis in natural or actual law, in fact had none. The amount that the colonists contributed to their own defence had been only around 10 per cent of the total, yet this was Congress's response.[68] The historian John Shy has pointed out that 'Until early 1774, most Americans would have been happy to have the services of British regulars without the "consent", that is, the appropriation of funds, of their provincial assemblies.'[69]

The twelfth charge was that the King had 'affected to render the military independent of, and superior to, the civil power'.[70] All that this can refer to is the appointment of General Gage as Governor of Massachusetts in 1774. Yet in times of rebellion – and the Boston Tea Party had taken place prior to Gage's appointment – the military is often and perfectly legally made superior to the civil power. All the King had actually done was, as Hutchinson put it, 'to reduce those rebellious civil powers to their constitutional subjection to the supreme civil power'.[71] As for the King having 'affected' to render the military politically dominant, at no point did he ever suggest, wish or plan for a military government in America.*

As soon as the American Revolution was defeated, it was Britain's intention to return the civil power to its traditional primacy. If, as Jefferson alleged, George had held any desire, let alone a plan, to establish a

---

* There are sometimes inevitably crises when the military power needs to be rendered independent of the civil power, as the United States was regularly to discover during the Whiskey Rebellion, in New Orleans in the War of 1812, when habeas corpus was suspended in Maryland on the outbreak of the Civil War, during the Great Chicago Fire and the San Francisco Earthquake, during the Omaha Race Riot of 1919, in the Illinois Mormon War, during the 1934 West Coast waterfront strike, when the Roosevelt Administration interned Japanese-Americans after the attack on Pearl Harbor, on occasion during the Civil Rights struggle in the 1960s, and in several other instances. Cuba was under American martial law for years after the Spanish–American War. None of this lessened the legitimacy of the US government, any more than it did that of George III in 1774.

dictatorial tyranny over America of the totalitarian kind implied by the language of the Declaration, there would be some evidence of this. And yet, among around 100,000 pages of George's personal archive, not a single scrap of paper exists to support such a contention. Not only is there nothing to suggest such a thing, there is the exact opposite, in the form of orders that the assemblies be left unmolested and that governors treat them considerately, at least until the aggression, destruction and law-breaking of the Boston Tea Party took place. Even then the King was not hoping to establish a tyranny, simply looking for an apology, financial restitution to the victims and a peaceful return to the status quo ante.

Jefferson's thirteenth charge – that George had 'combined with others to subject us to a jurisdiction foreign to our constitution and unacknowledged by our laws' – was a reiteration of the claim that Parliament had no authority over the colonies, which was now asserted but clearly unsupported either by law or by the experience of the previous century and a half. Critics of the Declaration such as Lind and Hutchinson pointed to the numerous Acts of Parliament that the colonists had accepted in the past, and the way the Stamp Act Congress had specifically stated that Parliament had jurisdiction in every area but internal taxation. 'Why is our present sovereign to be distinguished from all his predecessors since Charles II?' asked Hutchinson. 'And then, how can a jurisdiction submitted to for more than a century be *foreign* to their constitution?'[72] As a former supreme justice of Massachusetts, he knew the law.

The modern American historian Eric Nelson has pointed out the contradiction inherent in the thirteenth charge. 'Only because Patriots remained convinced that the King possessed a constitutional prerogative power to "refuse his assent" to parliamentary Bills could they indict him for having refused to wield it on behalf of the colonies,' he writes. 'George could only be styled a "tyrant" on the supposition that he was, as a juridical matter, far more powerful than any British monarch had claimed to be for over a hundred years.'[73] George was being criticized by Jefferson for not vetoing Bills in America, even though he had not and was not vetoed to veto any in his whole reign, just as George I and George II had not.

The fourteenth charge, the King's 'quartering large bodies of armed troops among us', was not quite the same complaint as the earlier one against the existence of a standing army, so much as an objection to paying for its upkeep. Here Jefferson was on slightly stronger ground, because although until 1764 Britain had paid for barracks, in 1765 the annual Mutiny Act had included a section stating that each colony should provide for the barracks, firewood, candles and other necessities for the men stationed in it. When in 1765 the New York Assembly had refused to provide vinegar, salt and beer, it had been suspended. Hutchinson pointed out that the colonies had not complained about the quartering of British troops when they were there 'to protect the colonies against French invasion', and that the quartering provisions were similar to those in Britain. He added that the opposition to the quartering of troops was 'not because the provision made was in itself unjust or unequal, but because they were Acts of Parliament whose authority was denied'.[74]*

The fifteenth charge of the Declaration accused the King of 'protecting [his troops] by a mock trial from punishment for any murders which they should commit' on colonists. This was a reference to the temporary provision in the Administration of Justice Act of 1774 which had been passed to ensure that revenue officers and soldiers would not be judged by partisan local juries if they were accused of murder. The trial in England or a peaceful colony would not have been 'mock', of course, and the only reason for a change of venue was to obtain an impartial jury. Moreover, the sole reason why the law was passed was to avoid the need to declare martial law in a colony. Since no 'murders' had been committed since the Boston Massacre six years earlier, it was all moot anyhow, but grist for Jefferson's mill as he piled charge upon charge, possibly hoping that sheer quantity would mask the lack of logic or legal quality.

The sixteenth charge attacked the King 'for cutting off our trade with all parts of the world'. In fact the navigation and trade laws that restricted colonial commerce dated back to Oliver Cromwell in 1651, and were instrumental in placing the American colonies within the British trading bloc and outside rival ones. All this amounted to in terms of eighteenth-century trade was that the American colonies were part of the British Empire. It was much the same as the seventeenth charge, that of 'imposing taxes on us without our consent', which had of course been the most visible of the complaints since the Stamp Act, and which will be discussed later.

* On 14 December 1775, forty armed soldiers arrived at the door of William Thompson's home in Brookline, Massachusetts, with orders to seize his residence for their quartering. He told them it was 'contrary to the sacred right of every freeman to the enjoyment of his property and domestic security', and generously offered to lodge them at his expense at the nearest public house, in order to protect his family and privacy. Instead, the sergeant used his musket to break the lock of the front door and his men, with bayonets fixed, threw Thompson's family out of his house. The irony of the Declaration of Independence's denunciation of British quartering provisions cannot have been lost on Mr Thompson the following year, since it was the Continental Army troops who had violated his home. Where there were no barracks, eighteenth-century armies needed other quartering, as George Washington's officers understood just as well as the King's. Yet what happened to William Thompson was not felt to invalidate Congress's right to rule.

The eighteenth charge was 'For depriving us in many cases of the benefit of trial by jury'.[75] This was much the same as the fifteenth charge – a certain degree of repetition was inevitable as Jefferson needed numbers more than rationality – and referred to the establishment of the Admiralty and Vice-Admiralty courts which came about because of the partisan verdicts of American juries in favour of smugglers and Stamp Act violators, regardless of the evidence produced by the Crown. Yet there had been non-jury Admiralty courts in both Britain and America since 1670, and justices of the peace tended to decide excise cases without juries in the colonies too; indeed the United States was to employ non-jury trials in order to defeat smuggling until the twentieth century.[76] Hutchinson argued that juries who lived close to where the offences took place would not be impartial over a crime such as smuggling, adding that the law had changed under William III in both Britain and the colonies. 'Strange!' he wrote sarcastically, 'that in the reign of King George the Third, this jurisdiction should suddenly become an usurpation and ground for revolt.'[77]

The nineteenth charge was 'For transporting us beyond seas to be tried for pretended offences'. Although the provision for this had existed since the time of Henry VIII for treason, in fact nobody had been transported for trial in George III's reign, and this was another example of Jefferson doing something lawyers occasionally did in the eighteenth century (and later), a practice known as 'padding the brief'.

The twentieth charge was an attack on the Quebec Act, accusing the King of 'abolishing the free system of English laws in a neighbouring province, establishing therein an arbitrary government and enlarging its boundaries so as to render it at once an example and fit instrument for introducing the same absolute rule into these colonies'.[78] Far from introducing 'arbitrary government' or 'absolute rule', the Quebecois so welcomed the return of their laws and religious liberties under the Quebec Act that there were no French uprisings against British rule in Canada at any stage of the American Revolution or afterwards. If the King had genuinely been interested in introducing absolute rule into the American colonies it might fairly be expected that he would at some point have mentioned it to someone else – such as the Cabinet ministers responsible for effecting it – which he never once did.

Charge number twenty-one condemned the King 'For taking away our charters, abolishing our most valuable laws and altering fundamentally the forms of our governments', a reference to the Government of Massachusetts Act of 1774, which was the only alteration of a colonial charter during George's reign, and once again was enacted as a reaction to the rebellion rather than being an incitement of it. Notice the way that

Jefferson yet again used the plural 'charters', attempting to turn a single instance into a general rule. There had been plenty of charter alterations in earlier reigns which had not been cited as a justification for rebellion before, but Jefferson was looking for propaganda rather than intellectual consistency in the second part of the Declaration. John Lind showed in his commentary on the Declaration that in fact every single American charter in 1775 had been altered or repealed at some earlier point in history, but not by George III. If charters once granted could not be altered or repealed by the Crown, Lind pointed out, then under the terms of Virginia's original charter its inhabitants would still be 'dependent on two trading companies residing in England'.[79]

The twenty-second charge concerned 'suspending our own legislatures and declaring themselves invested with power to legislate for us in all cases whatsoever'. This again referred to the suspension of the New York Assembly, and Rockingham's ill-advised Declaratory Act, which had used the phrase 'in all cases whatsoever'. It was such a propaganda boon that Jefferson quoted it directly. 'Both the suspension of the New York legislature and the Declaratory Act were valid and constitutional exercises of Parliament's power according to the constitutional theory prevailing in England at that time,' acknowledges an American historian of that clause, however, and by no means an abuse of the King's prerogative powers.[80] That was the last of the nine Parliament-related charges.

The next group, numbering five charges, began with the twenty-third: 'He has abdicated government here by declaring us out of his protection and waging war against us.' In the original draft that the committee submitted to Congress, the King was also accused of 'withdrawing his governors', but since everyone knew that the royal governors had been driven out by Patriot mobs and militiamen, it was dropped as too ludicrous a charge. Nor had the King in fact declared the colonists out of his protection or allegiance: indeed, he was trying to compel them back into both. This clause once again gave George's acts in suppressing the rebellion as a reason for the rebellion itself.[81]

The same objection can be made to the next charge, that 'He has plundered our seas, ravaged our coasts, burnt our towns and destroyed the lives of our people,' a reference to the destruction of Norfolk (which was mainly carried out by Patriots), as well as Charlestown and Falmouth. Hutchinson replied that 'The acts of a justly incensed sovereign for suppressing a most unnatural, unprovoked rebellion are here assigned as the *causes* of this rebellion.'[82] In terms of pure chronology, the point was unanswerable.

The next charge concerned 'transporting large armies of foreign mercenaries to complete the works of death, desolation and tyranny, already begun with circumstances of cruelty and perfidy scarcely paralleled in the most barbarous ages, and totally unworthy [of] the head of a civilized nation'.[83] A glance at the conduct of the War of Independence shows that this was nonsense. For all that there were indeed examples of atrocities and town burnings in the American War of Independence – especially in the civil-war aspect of it between Loyalists and Patriots – overall the war up until July 1776 had generally been conducted according to the rules of warfare then pertaining, with prisoner exchanges, parleys between commanders, local truces for the burial of the dead, and so on. The fact that soldiers were willing to surrender at all proves that it was not conducted as 'in the most barbarous ages', when no quarter was given. Later in the conflict, Washington even offered to allow captured commanders to return to London. Nor was it fair to assume that the 12,000 German auxiliaries then on their way to America would be barbarous; they did not fundamentally behave any differently from the British or American troops.

Although even today some American historians describe George's German auxiliaries as 'military scabs' and consider him as having somehow 'cheated' by employing them, contemporaries knew that paid foreign soldiers had been used regularly in European wars for centuries, and in a rebellion against a king who was also the Elector of Hanover it was strange to complain when he used troops from Hanover and Hanover's allies to try to quell it.[84] Of course Congress employed foreigners to fight in their army too, including large numbers of French officers long before France joined the conflict. They paid Baron von Steuben and the Marquis de Lafayette, General Casimir Pulaski's Legion, Bartholomew von Heer's Provost Corps and General Armand's Independent Chasseurs. Once the French had joined the war, they too used auxiliaries and foreigners such as the Lauzun Legion, who spoke German.[85]

The twenty-sixth charge was that the King had 'constrained our fellow citizens taken captive on the high seas to bear arms against their country, to become the executioners of their friends and brethren, or to fall themselves by their hands'. By the Prohibitory Act of December 1775, American ships could be captured and their crews pressed into British service, which ran contrary to their rights under a 1708 Act that excepted American colonists from being pressed into service in the Royal Navy. This exemption (compared with British seafarers) had been guarded jealously, and while naval press gangs did operate legitimately to recapture deserters, they were often viewed suspiciously as symbols of tyrannical rule and a potential threat to individual liberties in the colonies, and this had sometimes led to local unrest. The Prohibitory Act legislation categorically rescinded the

1708 exemption, but once again it would not have been passed had the colonies not already risen in revolt eight months earlier.

'He has excited domestic insurrections amongst us,' claimed charge number twenty-seven, 'and has endeavoured to bring on the inhabitants of our frontiers the merciless Indian savages, whose known rule of warfare is an undistinguished destruction of all ages, sexes and conditions.'[86] This was a reference to Lord Dunmore's offer of freedom and weapons to those African-American slaves in Virginia who joined the British forces, as well as the treaties made with Britain's long-standing Native American allies. Lind and others did not fail to point out the inherent contradiction of complaining about freeing slaves in a document that starts with high-sounding remarks about all men being created equal.[87] Given that Congress had already tried to outbid the British for the support of the Indigenous Nations, a Congressional committee had reported in favour of using them as auxiliaries and some Stockbridge Native Americans were serving in the Massachusetts Militia, while the Massachusetts provincial government had offered an alliance to the Mohawks, this twenty-seventh charge against the King was just as hypocritical as the one denouncing the use of 'foreign mercenaries'.[88]

The twenty-eighth and final charge was that 'In every stage of these oppressions we have petitioned for redress in the most humble terms; our repeated petitions have been answered only by repeated injury. A prince whose character is thus marked by every act which may define a tyrant is unfit to be the ruler of a free people.'[89] The two remonstrances of 1774 and 1775 were not real petitions, however, but requests that the King should work against Parliament and uphold the colonies' opinion that Parliament had no jurisdiction over them. They were demands that the King act un-constitutionally. Of this clause, Hutchinson was predictably indignant:

> A tyrant, in modern language, means, not merely an absolute and arbitrary but a cruel, merciless sovereign. Have these men given an instance of any one act in which the King has exceeded the just powers of the Crown as limited by the English constitution? Has he ever departed from known, established laws, and substituted his own will as the rule of his actions? Has there ever been a prince by whom subjects in rebellion have been treated with less severity, or with longer forbearance?

He ended with a stricture on the rebels for having grasped their opportunity to become independent as soon as the threats from the French and Native Americans had receded, thanks to the British victory in the Seven Years War:

Gratitude, I am sensible, is seldom found in a community, but so sudden a revolt from the rest of the Empire, which had incurred so immense a debt, and with which it remains burdened, for the protection and defence of the colonies, and at their most importunate request, is an instance of ingratitude nowhere to be paralleled.[90]

John Adams later wrote of the Declaration, 'There were other expressions which I would not have inserted if I had drawn it up, particularly that which called the King a tyrant. I thought this too personal, for I never believed George to be a tyrant in disposition and nature . . . I thought the expression too passionate and too much like scolding, for so grave and solemn a document.'[91]

Of all the twenty-eight charges, only two really stand in terms of logic, natural law, chronology or politics – namely, the seventeenth, about imposing taxes without the colonists' consent, and the twenty-second, about Parliament being 'invested with power to legislate for us' – yet those two were so important that they went to the heart of the issue, and justified the whole rebellion on their own. The other twenty-six were a mixture of political propaganda, hypocrisy, hyperbole and *ex post facto* rationalization, tacked on to the first two paragraphs of superb prose which will justly live for as long as democracy and self-government still matter in the world.

The Declaration of Independence is simultaneously grotesquely hypocritical, illogical, mendacious and sublime. As one American historian has put it, the twenty-eight charges are 'very dull and tiresome and mean nothing much to a modern mind except that one carries away a general impression that the King must have been a horrible monster of tyranny and cruelty against an innocent child-like and loving people'.[92] So Jefferson achieved his end, and has continued to do so ever since, especially in the United States where the document has attained the status of Holy Writ.

In the original draft of the Declaration, with breathtaking gall, Jefferson had even blamed the slave trade on George, with the words 'He has waged cruel war against human nature itself, violating its most sacred rights of life and liberty in the persons of a distant people who never offended him, captivating and carrying them into slavery in another hemisphere, or to incur miserable death in their transportation thither.'[93] This staggering piece of hypocrisy had to be, as Jefferson noted, 'struck out in complaisance to South Carolina and Georgia, who had never attempted to restrain the importation of slaves, and who on the contrary wished to continue it. Our Northern brethren also I believe felt a little tender under those censures, for though their people have very few slaves themselves yet they have been pretty considerable carriers of them to others.'[94] So it was not just Southern slave owners who got the paragraph deleted, but Northern slave traders too. Forty-one of the fifty-six signatories to the Declaration owned slaves at one point in their lives, and Thomas Hutchinson wrote that he 'could wish to ask the delegates of Maryland, Virginia and the Carolinas how their constituents justify the depriving more than an hundred thousand Africans of their right to liberty and the pursuit of happiness'.[95]

Hutchinson sent the King a copy of his pamphlet with an inscription that revealed himself to be its author, expressing his intention 'to expose . . . the very criminal designs of the leaders of Your Majesty's deluded unhappy American subjects'.[96] The receipt of the pamphlet might have nonplussed George, since there is no indication that he ever actually read the Declaration of Independence. He made no reference to or even hint of it in his voluminous correspondence, even though the text was reprinted in almost every British newspaper, usually *in extenso*, as in the *London Chronicle* on 15 August.

The Declaration of Independence prompted the Patriots to start removing and destroying the King's image and insignia across the thirteen colonies, often in front of cheering crowds. Except in those relatively small areas controlled by Loyalists, the carved and painted royal coats of arms on churches, government buildings, court houses and taverns were torn down and burned. In Boston, shop signs that featured crowns and lions were thrown on to a bonfire in King Street. In Providence, the royal arms from the Colony House and Crown Coffee House were carried through the streets and burned, as was an effigy of the King in Baltimore.[97] In Philadelphia his portrait was hung upside down. Juries were no longer summoned in the King's name, which was struck from legal documents. In some places he was subjected to mock trials and executions, buried or burned in effigy.[98] In Huntingdon, Long Island, with perhaps an element of overkill, George was 'hung on a gallows, exploded and burnt to ashes'.[99]

By far the most famous act of destruction took place in New York City after George Washington had ordered the Declaration to be read at the head of each brigade of his army, formed up in hollow squares. One of his aides-de-camp noted that it 'was received with three huzzas by the troops – everyone seemed highly pleased that we were separated from a King who was endeavouring to enslave his once-loyal subjects'.[100] Directly outside Washington's headquarters stood the two-ton gilded equestrian statue of the King in Roman imperial costume, sculpted by Joseph Wilton, that had been erected at the Bowling Green in 1770, when New Yorkers had still hoped he might side with them against his ministers and Parliament.[101]

The soldiers and crowd pulled the statue down from its marble pedestal with lassos, cut off the head, took off his nose and clipped the laurels from his brow. A musket ball was fired into his dismembered head and others into the statue's torso. The ten ounces of gold leaf that had covered it was scraped off and even the crown-shaped finials on the Green's iron fence were knocked off, as one can still see today. The statue's head was then carried in a wheelbarrow to be impaled on a stake outside the Blue Bell Tavern, to the sound of 'The Rogue's March' on fife and drums. Most of the 4,000 pounds of lead in the rest of the statue was melted down to make a total of 42,088 musket balls for the Continental Army. Washington himself pronounced his disapproval of 'the appearance of riot and want of order' in the vandalism, although he doubtless appreciated the extra ammunition.[102] When New York later fell to the British, an engineer named John Montresor found the statue's mutilated head and sent it back to London, where it was put on display to illustrate the 'disposition of the ungrateful people'.[103]*

Some street and place names were demonarchized – Boston's King Street was renamed State Street and New York's King's College became Columbia, for example – although plenty stayed the same. Georgetown, Georgia and Charlotte, North Carolina, remained, for example, as did several Prince and Duke streets. For every place name stripped of its monarchical connotations in the former American colonies, of course, there were many more being created in the rest of the empire at the time, such as Prince Edward Island, Charlottetown, Charlottesburg, George Street in Sydney, Fort Charlotte, various Fort Georges, Georgetown (Penang), the Queen Charlotte Islands and many more.

It is ironic that had King George indeed been the ruthless despot that Thomas Paine and Thomas Jefferson made him out to be, Britain might have won the war. Because he was in fact a civilized, good-natured, Christian and enlightened monarch who worked entirely through the Cabinet and Parliament, and was subject to moral and ethical restraints as well as a desire to be a good Patriot King to all his subjects – including, crucially, his American ones – he did not fight the kind of scorched-earth campaign that every other contemporary despotic power would have fought. He was thus unwilling to cause chaos in the Southern states by a mass liberation and arming of the African-American slaves there, or to create havoc in the West by arming the Indigenous Nations with flintlock muskets, or to terrorize the eastern seaboard by razing Boston and Baltimore, in the way that Admiral Thomas Cochrane was to burn Washington, DC, in 1814.

---

* The horse's tail survived, and can be seen today at the New-York Historical Society. As it turned out, the statue would probably have collapsed anyway, as its twin in London's Berkeley Square did in the early years of the next century (Marks, 'Statue of King George III' p. 66).

Nor was George about to treat the American rebels in the way that his uncle, the Duke of Cumberland, had treated the Scottish Highlanders after the Jacobite rebellion. After that bloody campaign, thousands of Scots had been interned, hundreds convicted and between eighty and 120 executed, mostly by hanging or beheading but also occasionally by hanging, drawing and quartering.[104] Jacobite sympathizers in the Highlands also faced large-scale destruction of property and mass starvation. If George had condoned the slaughter of tens of thousands of innocent civilians in the same way that other European monarchs did, then the American Revolution might have died in a welter of gore and decades-long resentment. There were undoubtedly horrific outrages committed during the war, but not ones ordered or condoned by the King or any part of the British high command. It was partly because George was *not* a tyrant, therefore, that he lost the war against his own so-called tyranny.

14

The Road to Saratoga

July 1776–December 1777

Any other general in the world than General Howe would have beaten General Washington, and any other general in the world than General Washington would have beaten General Howe.[1]
The *Gentleman's Magazine* report of the battle of Germantown,
August 1778

Benjamin Franklin was credited with making the genuinely witty remark at the time of the signing of the Declaration of Independence that 'We must all hang together, or, most assuredly, we shall all hang separately.'[2] Congressman Benjamin Rush of Philadelphia similarly joked to Elbridge Gerry, a Massachusetts delegate to the Second Continental Congress, 'I shall have a great advantage over you, Mr Gerry, when we are all hung for what we are now doing. From the size and weight of body I shall die in a few minutes, but from the lightness of your body, you will dance in the air an hour or two before you are dead.'[3] In fact the British never had any intention of behaving in the way that, for example, the Spaniards had in August 1769 when they executed the leaders of the revolt against their rule in New Orleans. Thomas Gage, Sir William Howe and his brother Lord Howe, Sir Guy Carleton, Henry Clinton and Charles Cornwallis were all unanimous in their policy of trying to kill the rebellion with kindness once the military side of it was defeated. Franklin and the other signatories were in little or no danger of being hanged in the event of defeat, unless they had fallen into the hands of Loyalist partisans. Although General Gage warned Washington that captured rebels would not be regarded as prisoners of war but instead 'destined to the cord', the only hangings of rebels that took place were lynchings by Loyalist terror gangs – such as that of Captain Joshua Huddy in April 1782 – which were not authorized by the British.[4] Spies were shot when captured out of uniform on both sides, but that happened in all wars of the day, and later.

The senior British commanders in America were almost all upper-class Whigs who followed the policy of conciliation wherever possible, trying to win over hearts and minds for far longer than was genuinely practicable.[5] Indeed, the first use of that phrase appeared in a conversation that Clinton had with Lord Drummond on 7 February 1776, about the need 'to gain the hearts and subdue the minds of America' in order to find 'a path to reconciliation' which would accentuate 'the blessings of English liberty'.[6] For much of the war the British generals* continued to believe that if they adopted what Cornwallis called the 'gentlest methods which the nature of that business will admit of', the loyalty which he believed most Americans still felt might win out.[7]

The King did not approve of Lord North's policy of British generals and admirals being expected to double up as peace commissioners – 'If Lord Howe would give up being a commissioner I should think it better for himself as well as the service,' he told the Prime Minister on 13 April 1776 – but he approved of offers being made.[8] Judging by the peace attempts made by the British generals in 1776 and the instructions given to Lord Carlisle's peace commissioners in 1778, it is certain that the terms would have been generous – starting with wide autonomy and the dropping of any taxation rights over America – and very far from the 'slavery' that Washington warned his troops of in July 1776.

On 2 July, the Howe brothers arrived off New York Harbor and soon afterwards started to land 32,000 men on Staten Island, including 9,000 German auxiliaries; there they waited for more reinforcements due in early August, and for Clinton to arrive from the South.[9] Two weeks later, General William Howe sent a letter requesting a parley over peace terms, which the Americans rejected as it was addressed to 'George Washington Esq', rather than to 'General George Washington'.[10] Howe therefore readdressed the letter. That spring, Washington had characterized peace offers as intended to 'distract, divide, and create as much confusion as possible', but in fact they were genuine.[11] Although Howe's adjutant Colonel James Paterson met Washington on 20 July, and was treated politely, it was clear that Washington was not interested.

At 9 a.m. on 22 August, the British landed 14,700 men at Gravesend Bay on Long Island without opposition, a figure which by 25 August had grown to 20,000, in readiness for what would prove to be the largest engagement of the war. During the battle of Long Island on 27 August, the

* With the possible exception of Major-General Banastre Tarleton, although the level of even his personal responsibility for outrages is contested.

Americans lost 1,400 men killed, wounded or captured, against around 400 British killed or wounded.[12] Yet on the night of 29 August, Washington brilliantly took advantage of heavy fog on the East River to evacuate 9,000 troops from Long Island to Manhattan – without a single casualty, as the Royal Navy had no idea it was happening. It was the first of a series of moments in the war where Washington was permitted to escape capture with his army bloodied but essentially intact. The apparent ease with which his force had been swept aside led to unwarranted confidence in the British Army. 'The rebels have severely felt the blow,' Lord Hugh Percy wrote hubristically to Germain, 'and I think I may venture to foretell that this business is pretty near over.'[13]

When the King heard the battle report, he awarded Howe the Order of the Bath, but also jotted on his forthcoming speech to Parliament the words 'Notes of triumph would not have been proper when the successes are against subjects not a foreign foe.'[14] For all that he wanted victory, George was not about to confuse his American subjects with foreign enemies.* Had Howe captured the Continental Army in Manhattan and then taken Philadelphia, it would have discouraged French involvement and emboldened the Loyalists, and it might even have dealt a fatal blow to the rebellion. As it was, news of a French naval buildup encouraged the British to return to the practice of press-ganging in October, although astonishingly the full-scale mobilization of the Royal Navy did not begin in earnest until the following year.[15]

On 12 September, Washington decided to abandon the (largely Loyalist) city of New York, three days before 4,000 British troops successfully crossed the East River from Brooklyn at Kips Bay, after clearing western Long Island. Instead of attempting to cut off the retreating American forces in what one American historian has described as 'the coffin that was Manhattan Island', the overcautious William Howe merely secured the beachhead and allowed the Continental Army to escape again.[16] At the battle of Harlem Heights on 16 September, Washington halted Howe's slow pursuit, but had to fall back as the British advanced up the East River. Soon Howe had captured New York, which was to prove his greatest victory of the war.

On 25 September, Admiral Richard Howe wrote to Germain that his brother William 'professes his plan to be of greater compass than he feels himself equal to direct, and judges it proper that a chief officer in the character of a viceroy with unlimited powers should be chosen for the occasion'.[17]

---

* As far as the latter were concerned, back at Brooks's 'Mr Craufurd bets Mr Boothby fifty guineas that there will be a war between England and France this day twelvemonth' (Brookes's Club Betting Book).

Howe was more of a fighting soldier and tactician than a grand strategist, and he was correct in thinking that someone with a better overview of the war ought to be dispatched to New York to take control. It seems surprising that this idea had not surfaced far sooner, long before the revolutionary crisis.* After the war had broken out the viceroy should have been Germain himself, who if he had moved to New York could have cut months from the intertwined politico-military decision-making process at a stroke. Nobody promoted the idea in London, and the King was not consulted.

After a strong American defence at the battle of White Plains on 28 October, Howe missed another opportunity to capture and destroy the Continental Army, but instead withdrew to Manhattan Island to besiege Fort Washington. On 16 November the fort fell with 3,000 Americans killed, wounded or captured, as General Washington withdrew across the Hudson into New Jersey. But then, 'Through torpor and a seemingly astonishing indifference,' concludes a modern American historian, Howe 'let Washington's ragtag army flee across New Jersey and subsist unmolested south of the Delaware.'[18] On 8 December, the same day that Washington crossed the Delaware into Pennsylvania, the British entered Trenton, New Jersey, and General Clinton captured Newport, Rhode Island. Only about 3,000 men of the Continental Army remained. Yet instead of chasing Washington with his much larger force, Howe went into winter quarters in New York City on 14 December, leaving garrisons in place across southern New Jersey.

Howe wrote to Germain on 30 November with a plan (which reached London on 30 December) that was theoretically just about compatible with the Germain Plan of a march to the Hudson by Burgoyne.[19] He suggested that 10,000 men advance from New York City to Albany in upstate New York, so splitting New England from the rest of the colonies; 5,000 would be left behind in garrison. Another 5,000 would seize Providence, Rhode Island, and then go overland to Boston, of whom 2,000 would attack Connecticut from Rhode Island. Yet still Howe would send 8,000 men away to threaten Philadelphia from eastern New Jersey. To achieve all this, he asked for a reinforcement of 15,000 men. Ten days before the plan arrived in London, however, Howe changed his mind, preferring instead to take Philadelphia rather than march his forces all the way from Rhode Island to Boston.

Under Howe's new plan, 4,000 men would remain in New York City and 3,000 on the Lower Hudson, 'to cover Jersey on that side, as well as

---

* There was no viceroy in Hanover either, at least until 1811. There was, however, a rather more developed system for remote control, involving a Hanoverian Chancery in London, which was charged with liaison between George and the Hanoverian Privy Council. Sadly there was no equivalent in the thirteen colonies.

to facilitate in some degree the approach of the army from Canada', and Philadelphia would be attacked with 10,000 troops.[20] Howe's plan was ill-considered: 3,000 troops were nothing like enough both to cover New Jersey and help Burgoyne coming down from Canada. Moreover, the replacement plan did not even reach London for authorization until 23 February 1777, a full sixty-five days after he had drawn it up. If nothing else, it was an eloquent argument for the idea of a viceroy.

Certainly, the northern part of the Germain Plan seemed to be going well when on 13 October 1776 Benedict Arnold's ramshackle flotilla was defeated on Lake Champlain by Sir Guy Carleton, whose equally makeshift squadron had the advantages of better armaments and crews of actual sailors. Yet Arnold had so successfully delayed Carleton's advance that, with the onset of winter, the British could only briefly occupy Crown Point before being compelled to withdraw to Canada. Despite this achievement in winning vital time for the Revolution, Arnold was criticized for losing too many ships and men, with the result that Congress refused to promote him to the rank of major-general until the following May.

The King understood that Carleton's tardiness and the abandonment of Crown Point meant that Lake Champlain would need to be crossed all over again in the spring. 'Although he has been slow,' North offered in Carleton's defence, 'I dare say he is perfectly sure, and we may be satisfied that no misfortune is likely to happen.'[21] The Germain Plan, it was still hoped, could be put into effect belatedly in the spring of 1777, but not by Carleton. By early December it had become clear that the relationship between him and Germain, both prickly men at the best of times, had completely broken down, especially after Carleton had written Germain a characteristically brusque letter; in response Germain began to agitate for his recall.

The King recognized that the problem was personal and warned North about it, adding on 13 December that 'perhaps Carleton may be too cold and not so active as might be wished,' but 'there is great prejudice perhaps not unaccompanied with rancour in a certain breast against Governor Carleton.' He perceived that the dismissal of Carleton 'would be cruel and the exigency cannot authorize it'.[22] As with Gage, the King wanted proprieties followed before senior officers' active careers were ended without an excellent reason, so he suggested that Germain's complaints should be listened to but nothing promised to him until the rest of the Cabinet was back in London following the Christmas recess. If the Cabinet did not want to entrust Carleton with the march from Canada to Albany, his second-in-command, John Burgoyne, currently on leave in London, might be given the post instead.[23] It was a surprising choice for George to have made, not least because Henry Clinton was senior to Burgoyne, but it appears the latter had been too proud to ask for it himself.

In the list of fourteen generals for possible service in America that the King had drawn up in December 1774, there were several who had much greater experience of command than Burgoyne for the important task of capturing Albany. While not all of them would necessarily have done better than Burgoyne, none could have done much worse, and Burgoyne's name had been right at the very bottom of George's list.

'Gentleman Johnny'* Burgoyne, who was fifty-four in 1776, had led a rackety early life. His father was deeply indebted and he himself made a youthful elopement with Lady Charlotte Stanley, the daughter of the Earl of Derby. Handsome and charming, Burgoyne was a playwright, a well-connected Whig MP and an indefatigable networker. The King cannot have approved of his being also a heavy drinker, inveterate gambler, member of Brooks's and wildly unfaithful to Lady Charlotte. He had first joined the army in 1737 at the age of fifteen, but sold his commission in 1741 – most likely to cover gambling debts – and then rejoined four years later as a cornet, in the middle of the War of Austrian Succession; by the time it ended he was a captain.

Burgoyne made his name during the Seven Years War, playing a pivotal role in the introduction of so-called 'light cavalry' units, and taking part in William Pitt's celebrated 'descents' (a series of lightning raids) on the French coast. His various commands to date had been small: companies rather than regiments, and skirmishers rather than battalions. Thereafter, he had written some tracts on army discipline and artillery, and a few West End plays besides, but his appointment to senior command in such a key expedition was, as one American historian has pointed out, 'testament to the fatal flaws in the nation's governance system', since it relied too much on personality and not enough on talent.[24] Burgoyne had helped draw up the Germain Plan, and in his meetings with Germain in London he had subtly undermined Carleton to gain the command for himself.

Because New England was the seat of the rebellion, to isolate it by simultaneously striking north from New York and south from Lake Champlain, capturing all of the Hudson River crossings, would have meant that it could theoretically have been invaded from the rear across a broad front, in conjunction with British forces based in Rhode Island.[25] In the eighteenth-century geography of North America, the Hudson, Albany, Lake George and Lake Champlain were a major commercial freeway, the control of which was essential for whichever side was going to win the war.

---

* A nickname that was not used until a century after his death (Howson, *Burgoyne of Saratoga* p. xvii).

The major problem with the Germain Plan, apart from the huge distance between its constituent parts and the difficulty in their mutual communication, was that, as one American military historian has succinctly put it, 'The British had three armies . . . each isolated from the other two, and the Americans were free to concentrate against whichever one they chose. This was dispersion of force carried to the point of absurdity.'[26] It was the duty of Germain, based in Whitehall, to coordinate the activities of the three theatre commanders – Howe, Burgoyne and Clinton – and to ensure that none of them acted so independently as to damage the overall Plan.[27] In the event, the New York force was available to advance as far along the Hudson River as West Point, but no further.

In late February 1777, the Cabinet approved Burgoyne as the commander of the northern army and Carleton was allowed to stay on in Canada as Governor. It was an unsatisfactory compromise, as Burgoyne depended on Carleton for supplies but was under Howe's overall command, while Carleton rightly suspected he had been undermined by his former second-in-command, resented it and did not feel responsible for Burgoyne's success or failure. 'The choice of Burgoyne', a British historian of the war has opined, 'was the worst ministerial error of the campaign, perhaps the only avoidable one,' because his rashness led him into a trap that other, better-qualified commanders such as Henry Clinton might well have avoided.[28]

On Christmas night 1776, George Washington and Nathanael Greene recrossed the Delaware River with 2,400 men and at Trenton, New Jersey, carried out a daring surprise attack on the Hessians, who had not fortified their positions. He captured 920 of the 1,400 Hessians and killed or wounded fifty more, losing just two men to hypothermia and four more wounded.[29] Cornwallis marched to Trenton, hoping to manoeuvre Washington's force between the Delaware and the coast, but he failed to pin down the nimble Americans. By the time Cornwallis reached Trenton, Washington had not only left but had won another victory at Princeton, capturing the town's stores and moving on to Morristown.

Yet because of the severe privations in the Continental Army, and the news that parts of Pennsylvania might be wavering in their support of the rebellion, the King wrote to North on 24 February 1777 that 'The accounts from America are most comfortable.' He uncharitably put the defeat at Trenton down to 'the surprise and want of spirit in the Hessian officers', rather than to Washington's tactical genius in organizing the surprise, and wished that Howe 'had placed none but British troops in the outposts'.[30] He recognized that Trenton 'will undoubtedly rather elate the rebels who till then were in a state of the greatest despondency'.

On 23 February, William Howe's change of plan in respect of his march on Philadelphia arrived in London. Five days later Burgoyne, still in London, sent Germain a memorandum entitled 'Thoughts for Conducting the War from the Side of Canada', which covered the northern theatre of the Germain Plan. In essence it proposed an advance from Canada to Ticonderoga and then either on to the Hudson or possibly east over the Green Mountains to the Connecticut River so as to link up with the force in Rhode Island.[31] He would lead 7,000 men to the Upper Hudson by way of Lakes Champlain and George, while Lieutenant-Colonel Barry St Leger took 1,700 regulars and auxiliaries, including Native Americans, down the Mohawk River to meet him near Albany. This was to be done at speed, with Albany the objective in order to 'effect a junction with General Howe or, after cooperating so far as to get possession of Albany and open the communication to New York, to remain upon the Hudson River and thereby enable that General to act with his whole force to the southward' (that is, into Pennsylvania).[32]

Burgoyne's 'Thoughts' were open to differing interpretations. Did he expect to meet Howe on the Hudson or not? How would Burgoyne subsist in upstate New York through the winter? How would he communicate with New York? There were many risks and variables, but, as one military historian accurately put it, 'no one in the Government raised an eyebrow'.[33] Meanwhile in New York, Howe knew about the invasion from Canada, but as his plans developed in the six months after December 1776 Burgoyne's ideas 'played only a minor and sporadic part in his thinking'.[34] He did not believe that Burgoyne could reach Albany before September 1777, assuming that he was as cautious as Howe was himself, whereas in fact Burgoyne turned out to be recklessly fast.

Germain's reply to Howe, written on 3 March 1777, crucially did not specifically mention the prospect of a junction at Albany; nor did it countermand the idea of a strike against Philadelphia, even though that would make such a junction extremely difficult. Furthermore, Howe did not receive it until 8 May. The King was sent Burgoyne's 'Thoughts', but was not instrumental in formulating the Germain Plan, which had essentially been agreed between Germain and Burgoyne. Instead he interested himself in what he saw as William Howe's over-indulgence towards the Americans. 'If he and his brother will act with a little less lenity (which I really think cruelty, as it keeps up the contest),' the King wrote to his trusted adviser Robinson on 5 March, 'the next campaign will bring the Americans in a temper to accept of such terms as may enable the mother country to keep them in order ... The regaining their affection is an idle idea. It must be the convincing them that it is their interest to submit, and then they will dread further broils.'[35] He also concerned himself in naval minutiae, asking Germain a week later about the state of the armed ship *Bute*, which was meant to have sailed to America with supplies for Howe two weeks earlier, but still had not. The King wanted the Admiralty to be asked 'the real state of the ship, and what has occasioned the delay'.[36]

Germain wrote to Carleton on 26 March about the plan to take Ticonderoga and Albany, but did not mention Burgoyne's alternative of the Green Mountains-to-Connecticut option, because of Howe's decision not to base an army on Rhode Island for offensive operations.[37] Germain also supported General Barry St Leger's diversionary attack from Oswego down the Mohawk River. Because Germain also approved Howe's invasion of Pennsylvania, he must have known that Burgoyne would not be supported until much later on in his advance on Albany. Germain did not believe the Pennsylvania operations would take as long as they did, but he also knew that he and Barrington could not provide more than a fraction of the 15,000 reinforcements that Howe thought he needed.

On learning in early April that he was not going to receive the reinforcements, Howe abandoned his plan for an offensive across New Jersey, deciding that he would instead attack Philadelphia by sea. It was a curious fixation, for despite its having been where Congress met and where independence had been declared, Philadelphia was not strategically important. This obsession was to take Howe down a strategic cul-de-sac, isolating him both from the Burgoyne expedition and from New York. Blaming the Hessians' baggage train for his tardiness, Howe recognized that he was unlikely to lure Washington into a decisive battle that might end the Revolution; and in a letter to Germain on 2 April, which did not arrive in London till 8 May, he bluntly admitted, 'My hopes of terminating the war this year are vanished.'[38]

Sailing to Philadelphia would prove one of the key strategic blunders of the war. Rather than following the bold Germain Plan of trying to split New England off from the rest of the colonies, Howe preferred a more methodical campaign, closing off the Delaware to enemy shipping, and holding areas so that the Loyalists would enlist in provincial corps. Yet he did not warn either Germain or Burgoyne that from his perspective the Germain Plan was impracticable. While his dispatch strongly implied that he was not going to support Burgoyne's campaign, because he did not send it until 2 April he had already embarked his own forces long before he could receive a reply from London. He did, however, warn Carleton on 5 April that he had:

little expectation that I shall be able, from want of sufficient strength in this army, to detach a corps in the beginning of this campaign to act upon the

Hudson River consistent with the operations already determined upon. The force Your Excellency may deem expedient to advance beyond your frontiers after taking Ticonderoga will, I fear, have little assistance from hence to facilitate their approach, and as I shall probably be in Pennsylvania when that corps is ready to advance into this province . . . [Burgoyne] must therefore pursue such measures as may from circumstances be judged most conducive to His Majesty's service consistent with your orders.[39]

Howe clearly felt no obligation to help Burgoyne, but crucially he added, 'I shall endeavour to have a corps upon the lower part of Hudson's River sufficient to open the communication for shipping through the Highlands, at present obstructed by several forts erected by the rebels for that purpose, which corps may afterwards act in favour of the northern [that is, Burgoyne's] army.'[40] Was this an assurance, or a mere aspiration? In fact it could hardly have been more than wishful thinking, as the rebels were in the Highlands and on the Hudson in some force, whereas the Manhattan garrison of 4,700 had no men to spare.

On 7 April, Germain had a long interview with Henry Clinton, who was shortly to receive a knighthood as a reward for going back to New York to serve under Howe. Clinton told him plainly that an attack on Philadelphia would not force Washington to battle. Germain still believed that Howe could conquer Pennsylvania in time to allow him to deploy his army on the Lower Hudson, while Burgoyne in turn reached the Upper Hudson. Clinton disagreed, and predicted that Howe would waste the campaigning season taking Philadelphia, which he thought should be put off until the autumn at the earliest.[41] Despite such evident misgivings, Clinton did not dent Germain's optimism.

Germain sent Howe a copy of his dispatch to Carleton of 26 March, announcing that Burgoyne had orders first to capture Albany and then to place himself under Howe's command. Yet, after that, Germain never wrote to Howe about the northern army in any other of his eight successive letters to him between 3 March and 19 April.[42] Only on 18 May, when he learned that Howe was going to Philadelphia by sea rather than across New Jersey, did Germain again urge him to finish the campaign in time to cooperate with Burgoyne: 'As you must from your situation and your military skill be a competent judge of the propriety of every plan, His Majesty does not hesitate to approve the alterations which you propose; trusting, however, that whatever you may meditate, it will be executed in time for you to cooperate with the army ordered to proceed from Canada, and put itself under your command.'[43] Germain was later accused of giving orders that were too specific and allowed the commanders no room for manoeuvre; but this key order gave Howe plenty, so long as he conformed to the overall plan of coordinating with Burgoyne. If anything, Germain can be criticized not for being specific enough about the clearly defined objective of taking Albany.[44]

In any case, Howe did not receive that dispatch until mid-August, by which time he was utterly committed to taking Philadelphia, and had no troops to spare with which to aid Burgoyne, because of the lack of re-inforcements.[45] On 20 April, Howe had warned Germain that he would probably not finish his Pennsylvania operations in time to help Burgoyne, and by July he was even writing to say that he did not understand the purpose of Burgoyne's expedition, a statement which ought to have set alarm bells ringing in London. Nevertheless, Germain nonchalantly assumed that both armies were invulnerable until the autumn, when they could start concerting their efforts once Howe had captured Philadelphia and Burgoyne had taken Albany.

'By leaving them to go their separate ways he [Germain] abdicated his responsibility,' one military historian has argued, in a view shared by most others.[46] The blame for failing to reconcile the inconsistent plans of the two generals was perhaps not all Germain's; Howe had himself neglected the problems of the northern army, while Burgoyne greatly underestimated American militia strength in the region around Albany. Only Clinton, upon his return to New York, seems fully to have appreciated the strategic situation, and he was unable to persuade Howe to operate with Burgoyne.[47] Wherever the final responsibility lay, the British were entirely uncoordinated and inviting disaster.

On 15 May 1777, the Board House at the Ordnance Department at Purfleet-on-Thames was struck by lightning, prompting the King – who had long been interested in electricity – to initiate a series of experiments at the Pantheon in Oxford Street carried out by the scientist Benjamin Wilson, to establish whether pointed or rounded lightning conductors afforded better protection. When it was concluded that the rounded ones did, he had them installed on Buckingham House. He has been accused of changing them because it had been Benjamin Franklin who had invented the pointed variety five years earlier, but this is quite untrue.[48]* Sadly, Franklin himself, and some historians since, did believe the King was petty enough to endanger his own family home out of ill-will towards him. 'The

* Nor is it true that Dr John Pringle, the President of the Royal Society, resigned with the words 'The prerogatives of the President of the Royal Society do not extend to altering the laws of nature' (eds. Morton and Wess, *Public and Private Science* p. 30 n. 45).

King's changing his pointed conductors for blunt ones is ... a matter of small importance to me,' Franklin wrote to a friend that October. 'If I had a wish about it, it would be that he had rejected them altogether as ineffectual, for it is only since he thought himself and his family safe from the thunder of Heaven that he dared use his own thunder in destroying his innocent subjects.'[49]

On 26 May the Earl of Chatham, wrapped in flannel and looking old and pale, with a voice so weak he could hardly be heard in the Lords chamber, denounced the American war as unwinnable and proposed that 'Instead of exacting unconditional submission from the colonies, we should grant unconditional redress.'[50] Lord Gower replied that the war was not being fought over taxes but on the issue of who had authority over the colonies, and the Americans had been aiming at independence all along. The King thanked North for sending him a copy of:

> Lord Chatham's highly unseasonable motion, which can have no other use but to convey some fresh fuel if attended to by the rebels. Like most of the other productions of that extraordinary brain it contains nothing but specious words, and malevolence, for no one that reads it, if unacquainted with the conduct of the mother country and its colonies, [but] must suppose the Americans poor mild persons who after unheard-of and repeated grievances had no choice but slavery or the sword, whilst the truth is, that the too great lenity of this country increased their pride and encouraged them to rebel. But thank God! the nation does not see the unhappy contest through his mirror. If his sentiments were adopted, I should not esteem my situation in this country as a very dignified one, for the islands would soon cast off all obedience.[51]

This letter is illuminating for several reasons beyond the excoriation of Chatham. By then, George clearly saw the American crisis as stemming from undue leniency over the Stamp Act, and that its repeal by Rockingham and Fox was the pivotal error. It is evident that he also fully subscribed to the thin-end-of-the-wedge argument, so often dangerous in politics, that compromise in one area would encourage resistance in others, in this case thousands of miles away. If the British government were to give ground in America, he assumed, then 'the islands' – by which he certainly meant the West Indies, but perhaps Ireland too – would demand their independence as well.

Yet even Chatham's eloquence – and, as it turned out, prescience – could not harm North's dominance of Parliament. The Prime Minister easily saw off his opponent's assault, and was also able to increase the King's Civil List payments by some 12.5 per cent. George's decision back in 1761 to

sign away a good proportion of the Crown revenues to the state and thereafter try to live on £800,000 per annum had proved a disastrous one,
especially now that his family had expanded rapidly and inflation was also
taking its toll. This was despite his domestic economy, which was so well
known as to be regularly satirized in the press and in prints as cheeseparing
meanness. When the King's total debts reached £618,000 in April 1777
they were paid off without a division, but in a second resolution, to increase
the Civil List to £900,000 per annum, Charles Fox volunteered to become
a teller for the 'No' lobby, and contrasted the glories of George II's reign
with 'the corruption and patronage' which had supposedly 'overspread the
land' since then.[52] The Civil List had seen 'shameless prodigality', Fox
claimed, criticizing 'the influence of the Crown' and its 'power over the
Treasury' and even its 'rapine and plunder'.[53] This attack on corruption
and patronage of course came from the heir of the most personally corrupt
politician of the age. 'You cannot be surprised at the pleasure I feel at the
zealous support of so very great a majority of the House of Commons to
a proposition personally regarding me,' the King wrote to North. 'Indeed
I am convinced that except a desperate faction there would not be on that
subject scarce a dissentient voice.'[54] Fox's deliberate decision to lead that
faction, on an issue 'personally regarding' the King, which moreover he knew
he could not win, goes some way to explaining why George came to regard
him as an inveterate enemy who had to be kept out of power at all costs.

By the end of June, the British had been forced out of New Jersey, having
suffered 3,000 casualties. Some had been inflicted by the Continental
Army's attacks on Trenton and Princeton, but far more by guerrilla attacks
from the local militias: 'American hornets' as one rebel officer called them.[55]
For all that the Cabinet desperately wanted, in the words of one minister,
'to bring Mr Washington to a general and decisive action', the Virginian
was not about to abandon his successful Fabian tactic of hit-and-fade, and
he used both the regular Continental Army and his irregular militiamen to
harry the redcoats.[56] Militias were also putting down Loyalist uprisings,
hampering British movement and intelligence-gathering, intercepting British communications and ambushing foraging parties.

Burgoyne, meanwhile, reached Fort Ticonderoga on 1 July with over
7,850 men – 4,000 regulars and 3,200 Hessian-Brunswickers, as well as
some Loyalists and Native Americans. He laid siege and placed his artillery
above the fort, which was evacuated five days later.[57] In one of his most
egregious inventions, Horace Walpole claimed that when George heard of
the victory, he burst into the Queen's boudoir exclaiming, 'I have beat
them! Beat all the Americans!'[58] No part of it rings true, but now that

Burgoyne was only a hundred miles north of Albany there was cause for optimism.

In at least three conversations in New York on 6, 8 and 13 July, which at times became heated and acrimonious, Sir Henry Clinton, Sir William Howe's second-in-command, tried to persuade him not to sail to Pennsylvania, as he would not have time both to capture Philadelphia and to coordinate with Burgoyne on the Hudson. Clinton argued that an advance along the Hudson from New York to make contact with Burgoyne and thereby cut American communications with New England would be more likely to force Washington into battle. 'Final victory might come before winter on the Hudson,' one historian has summed up the argument Clinton made to Howe, 'whereas it could not come on the Delaware.'[59] Clinton, despite having seen Germain only weeks before and the orders to Carleton and Burgoyne too, could not persuade him. The headstrong Howe had not yet received Germain's letter of 18 May and would not yield.

Clinton warned Howe that the rebels would not fight a decisive battle in Pennsylvania, and all that could be gained was territory that could probably not be held by the Loyalists, while tethering uselessly to Philadelphia the main body of the British Army in America. Howe replied that he did not understand Burgoyne's orders, even though he had received a copy of them from Germain. He added that he doubted Burgoyne 'could penetrate, at least till very late', whereas in reality Burgoyne was by then only a few days' march from Albany.[60] Clinton pointed out that the inactivity of the main army had already allowed Washington to detach rebel forces in order to stop Burgoyne. Howe concluded their last meeting by declaring that he was sticking to his Delaware plan. Clinton was unpersuaded, believing that if Howe went via the Delaware it would be disastrous either for himself, who would be left behind in New York with 7,000 men, or for Burgoyne, with his similarly sized force on the Upper Hudson.

'If this campaign does not finish the war,' Clinton wrote anxiously to Hugh Percy on 23 July, 'I prophesy that there is an end of British dominion in America.'[61] Howe appears never to have appreciated the danger of a rebel concentration around Albany overwhelming Burgoyne, while he himself wanted to be the man who captured the enemy's capital. He also allowed a personal dislike of Clinton to cloud his objectivity. To Clinton's distress, Cornwallis supported Howe: this fuelled Clinton's perception of the Earl as manipulating Howe and leading him to disaster. Clinton described him as 'an evil genius, which had so often interfered'.[62]

When on 21 July a messenger arrived in New York from Burgoyne bearing news of the capture of Fort Ticonderoga fifteen days earlier, Howe was already on board ship and was not about to change his mind and disembark. He wished Burgoyne luck, and said that he was going to Pennsylvania anyway.[63] Howe left Clinton with vague orders to advance through the Highlands and coordinate with Burgoyne, but did not provide him with a large enough force to do that and simultaneously protect New York. Following three well-coordinated rebel attacks on his outposts just north of New York City on 22 August, Clinton was unable to withdraw from his positions and could not effect any junction with Burgoyne. On 3 August Burgoyne received Howe's discouraging letter, but instead of returning to Ticonderoga immediately he pressed on to Albany, hoping that there three weeks later he would meet St Leger, who was coming from Oswego. A further letter from Clinton warning that he could not proceed up the Hudson arrived on 10 August, but had equally little effect on Burgoyne's impetuous push south.

On 23 July, Howe sailed from New York City with 18,000 men in transport vessels. Washington detached Arnold and Daniel Morgan to assist Schuyler, but stayed north of the Delaware himself until he heard that Howe had sailed up Chesapeake Bay. Howe went first to the Delaware and then to the Chesapeake, the most time-consuming route to Philadelphia possible. He and Carleton had been responsible for the Germain Plan not being put into operation in 1776; now he was making it almost impossible to put it into operation in 1777 either, and all in a vain attempt to force the Continental Army into a decisive battle that he knew – and had admitted to Clinton – Washington would likely avoid.[64] To make matters worse, Howe had also stopped writing dispatches home – he wrote just one between 17 July and 10 October – leaving Germain entirely in the dark about events. The government learned of his evacuation of New Jersey only through private letters from other officers, and reports that came to them via France.

On 23 August, St Leger was forced to abandon the siege of Fort Stanwix before Benedict Arnold arrived, retreating first to Oswego and then to Lake Ontario. Burgoyne was now isolated in the wilder parts of upstate New York, and by early September, when he crossed to the west bank of the Hudson, he was down to 5,000 combat-ready troops.

For all Howe's evident weakness as a leader and strategist, he was a good battlefield commander, and on 11 September his force of more than 15,000 defeated Washington's 11,000 at the battle of Brandywine in Pennsylvania, turning the American right flank and forcing Washington back towards Philadelphia with 1,100 losses to 576 British.[65] Cornwallis had been able to break through the defences, but was unable to pursue the retreating Americans thanks to a fine rearguard action by Nathanael Greene's division. It would have been intolerable for Washington to have given up the new nation's capital without a fight, but although the Continental Army was pushed back, it was not broken.

'I am very melancholy notwithstanding our victory,' North wrote after receiving the news of Brandywine. 'My idea of American affairs is that if our success is as great as the most sanguine politician wishes or believes, the best use we can make of it is to get out of the dispute as soon as possible.'[66] He was already referring to it as 'this damned war', and hoped to be allowed to resign soon.[67] John Robinson told the King on 16 September that 'the anxiety His Majesty sometimes observes on Lord North's mind' was due to the Prime Minister's financial situation being precarious. His father Lord Guilford had not settled much money on North when he married and his estate was unproductive. His expenses had outstripped his income as premier, and his debts to tradesmen alone amounted to £10,000. Robinson warned George that 'the thoughts of this his situation frequently distresses his mind and makes him very unhappy'.[68] It certainly set North apart from most of his contemporaries, who saw nothing wrong with profiting personally from the public purse: Henry Fox was still enjoying a £25,000 per annum income from the unaudited balances of the War Department at his death in 1774, despite having left office in 1765.

The King wrote to North as soon as he had read Robinson's letter, offering him up to £20,000 to 'set your affairs in order'. Given the typically reserved manner of their functional correspondence (which was often written in the third person), George added a rare outpouring of emotion between the two men, writing, 'I love you as well as a man of worth as I esteem you as a minister. Your conduct at a critical minute* I never can forget, and am glad that by your ability and the kindness of Parliament I am enabled to give you a mark of my affection.'[69] Of course Parliament had no inkling that a very large amount of taxpayers' money – North decided to accept £16,000 – from the Secret Service Fund was being used to pay off the Prime Minister's private debts.† As George's relations with North turned worse over the next seven years, the premier's knowledge that he was so financially indebted to the monarch was to play a large part in them, and may to an extent explain how easily George was able to refuse North's continuing requests to resign.

On 13 September, Burgoyne crossed the Hudson near Saratoga, effectively passing the point of no return as he no longer had the supplies to get back

---

* That is, after Grafton's resignation in February 1770.
† Despite the large salaries for those in office, it is extraordinary quite how many politicians of George's reign – including Newcastle, both Pitts, William Grenville and Charles Fox (the last an inveterate gambler) – were heavily in debt.

to Canada. Six days later he suffered 600 casualties fighting Major-General Horatio Gates and Benedict Arnold at the battle of Freeman's Farm in upstate New York.[70] What Burgoyne did not know at the time was that Gates and Arnold had fallen out so badly that if he had retreated back towards Canada he would not have been harried in the way he feared. Now a message arrived from Clinton announcing that he was planning to march up the Hudson with 3,000 men in order to create a diversion, and that Burgoyne should hold his ground. Burgoyne therefore entrenched himself in a strong defensive position at Saratoga and awaited Clinton's relief, although he soon started to run short of food as swarms of militia-men from across the region converged on him, making it impossible for his foraging parties to operate, especially since his German dragoons had been badly cut up by General John Stark at the battle of Bennington back on 16 August. Burgoyne was effectively trapped.

In the event, Clinton could not leave New York City until 3 October, and although he captured Forts Clinton and Montgomery and passed West Point – which he did not try to capture – he found the going extremely tough. Eventually, he was forced to turn back south of Albany, having achieved little more than burning the town of Esopus (modern-day Kingston, New York). It had not been enough of a diversion to aid the increasingly beleaguered and outnumbered Burgoyne. Back in London, Germain still manifestly failed to appreciate the growing danger of Burgoyne's exposure. 'I am sorry the Canada army will be disappointed in the junction they expect with Sir William Howe,' he wrote to William Knox on 29 September, 'but the more honour for Burgoyne if he does the business without any assistance from New York.'[71]

Meanwhile, Howe had the satisfaction of occupying Philadelphia on 25 September, which he was to hold for nine months while his brother Richard cleared the Delaware to provide a secure supply route. The blow to rebel morale was tangible, but nothing like as devastating as the brothers had hoped. A cabal led by Colonel Thomas Conway attempted to persuade Congressmen who had been forced to flee Philadelphia for Baltimore to replace Washington with Horatio Gates, but was unsuccessful. Washington meanwhile was again defeated by Howe at the battle of Germantown, Pennsylvania, on 4 October, suffering 700 casualties and losing 400 prisoners. The Continental Army remained distinctly on the back foot in mid-December as it went into its Valley Forge winter bivouac 20 miles north-west of Philadelphia.

Washington had successfully avoided a decisive battle, and did not break camp at Valley Forge for six months. While there, he put on a production of Joseph Addison's *Cato* as part of an entertainment for the troops, the same play in which the King and North had performed at Cliveden a quarter of a century earlier. It taught the value of stoicism; and indeed, had the Continental Army's morale broken under the harsh privations of its winter cantonment, the rebellion might well have ended then and there. For all of the formidable problems Britain had faced with her lines of communication and supply, her lack of strategic discipline and her inadequate recruitment, the Americans could have lost their war for independence as a result of the ravages of weather, hunger and demoralization. As it faced the winter, the Continental Army was desperately short of almost everything a military force requires to stay in existence as a fighting force – aside from the truly exceptional leadership qualities of George Washington.

On 7 October, Burgoyne sent out a reconnaissance-in-force to try to find a weakness in the American siege line, a foray which developed into the second battle of Saratoga at Bemis Heights and resulted in 894 British casualties to just 130 for the militiamen.[72] Forced to retreat back to Saratoga itself, Burgoyne found his situation escalating rapidly from dangerous to desperate as his force of 5,700 now starving men was besieged by an enemy three times its size. In London on the same day as the battle, Germain told Knox, 'The King cannot believe that Burgoyne is advanced so far.'[73] It is likely that he was worried rather than admiring. North showed no greater understanding of the strategic situation than the isolated and beleaguered British generals on the ground, telling William Knox, 'It seems to me that if Sir Henry Clinton and General Burgoyne make themselves master of the North River, and Sir William Howe cuts off Washington from the Southern provinces, Washington must, after a little time, be reduced to fight or disband his army. In either case I flatter myself that the war seems to be taking a more decisive turn than I thought a little while ago.'[74] The American War of Independence had indeed taken a decisive turn that day, but it was not the one that North had hoped.

On 17 October, Burgoyne signed the Convention of Saratoga with General Horatio Gates. Under its terms, the British and Hessian troops under his command would surrender their arms, be marched to Boston and then be shipped home on parole. Congress later repudiated the Convention, and Burgoyne's men instead became prisoners of war in Virginia, Maryland and Pennsylvania.[75] 'The cynical and unexpected American betrayal of this promise', one historian records, 'was what turned a setback into a disaster for the British.'[76] If the troops had been redeployed back in Britain and Gibraltar, others could have been freed for service in America, but after Congress had abrogated Gates' word of honour, that was impossible. In the immediate term, the disaster at Saratoga meant that Ticonderoga,

Crown Point and the Hudson Highlands had to be evacuated, and the British now held only New York City, part of Rhode Island and Philadelphia.

The defeat unleashed a furore in London when the news arrived in early December, Fox and the Whigs blaming Germain, and the government blaming Burgoyne, whom Washington cannily allowed to return to London to cause maximum political damage and demoralization. Saratoga did not come as a total surprise to the King. Commenting on dispatches that had finally arrived from Howe, Germain had warned him on 1 December that 'Lt-General Burgoyne's situation is bad at any rate but it is to be hoped not so very bad as reported by the rebels. Sir William Howe's complaint of want of support is very unjust, but his desire of being recalled does not come unexpected.'[77] The next day, Sandwich told the King that Captain Moutray of the fifty-gun *Warwick* had arrived with 'unpleasant accounts', which 'if Your Majesty chooses to be troubled tonight' he could show the King in person at Buckingham House.[78] George did so choose, and Moutray's news was that 'General Burgoyne capitulated on the twenty-sixth of October* [agreeing terms] for himself and the remains of his army to come home by way of Boston.'[79] We do not know the King's immediate reaction to the news, and there is certainly no corroborating evidence for Walpole's outlandish claim that he 'fell into agonies on hearing the account' and tried to disguise his concern by affecting laughter, pretending 'to be so indecently merry that Lord North endeavoured to stop him'.[80]

North broke the news to Parliament on 3 December, prompting bitter attacks on Germain by Charles Fox and the Duke of Richmond. Germain later asked for a public inquiry into whether his orders to Burgoyne to march to Albany had been absolute, as Burgoyne was alleging. The King's first recorded response to the news of the catastrophe at Saratoga came at 10.30 a.m. on 4 December when he wrote to North that 'The manly, firm, and dignified part you took brought the House to see the present misfortune in its true light, as very serious but not without remedy.'[81] When Burgoyne sent Germain a dispatch which arrived on 15 December, Germain sent it on to the King with the warning that 'It was never understood that at such a distance any order could be positive; in the present case the words of the order will not bear the strict construction the General put upon them.'[82]

The King disagreed, telling North at 10.15 a.m. on Christmas Day that there ought to be a court martial to inquire 'into the defence laid by Lieutenant-General Burgoyne that his orders were positive (which I much

---

* In fact it was the 17th.

incline to). The reference ought to extend to the failure of the expedition . . . Lord George Germain may be contented with an inquiry into what bears on himself, but when my name is mentioned it should be a candid not a partial inquiry.'[83] The generals sitting on the court martial would include all of Burgoyne's rank and above who had served in America.*

Burgoyne claimed in Parliament that Germain had 'erased' two important proposals from his 'Thoughts for Conducting the War from the Side of Canada'.[84] Although the King made a memorandum in his own hand entitled 'Remarks on "The Conduct of the War from Canada"', which rejected two of Burgoyne's alternative routes, there are two other key documents – not in the King's hand – criticizing Burgoyne's plans, on which he based them.[85] Of the proposal that Burgoyne send his whole army via Connecticut by sea to join Howe, the King had already written, 'I greatly dislike that idea.'[86] Yet crucially it was not the King's duty to choose the correct route; that was a ministerial decision, one taken by Germain. Although 'the whole campaign seems to have been talked over thoroughly with the King . . . it was the duty of Germain, alone, however, to embody all the requisitions, observations, memoranda, thoughts, remarks and conversations in concise, explicit orders'.[87] That he had signally failed to do.

The Cabinet met on Boxing Day, and split evenly on whether there should be an official inquiry into the defeat at Saratoga. Lords Suffolk, Sandwich and North supported Germain in wanting both a court martial of Burgoyne and an inquiry into Saratoga, while Lords Bathurst (the Lord Chancellor), Dartmouth, Gower and Weymouth were opposed to an inquiry, with the result that Germain allowed the idea to drop. The court martial of Burgoyne would go ahead, however, which was likely to serve much the same purpose. The strains of the political struggles over the previous decade had left the Cabinet disunited, with several mutual antagonisms (although in this instance Germain's chief antagonist, Sandwich, supported him) as well as the personal and factional weaknesses seen in any Cabinet of this time. It was said of Weymouth that his taciturnity was affected to hide his drunkenness and indolence.[88] Dartmouth virtually never attended. Suffolk was disabled by gout and was little more than a figurehead in his office.[89] Bathurst had become completely defeatist, believing that peace needed to be made immediately lest Britain's West Indies possessions be lost as well.

The year 1777 ended disastrously for the British cause in America. Howe's failure to coordinate with Burgoyne had lost the war in the North,

---

* At Brooks's, James Hare wagered Mr Shirley ten guineas 'that Lord George Germain is not Secretary for the American Department at Easter next' (Brooks's Club Betting Book).

at least for the foreseeable future. Meanwhile, his own strategically futile campaign in New Jersey and Pennsylvania had left him in control of no more than the area where his army presently stood. The Royal Navy did not have enough ships to blockade the coast, support the army, prevent the Americans receiving munitions, protect British shipping against American cruisers and potentially overawe the European navies as well.[90] Worse, the French government knew this all too well. On 7 September, the King had believed that it was possible for France to be dissuaded from joining the Americans if Britain acted 'an open firm part', but by late October he was telling North that the blockade needed to be tightened and victory won before France, and possibly also Spain, entered the war.[91] He hoped that Howe would 'turn his thoughts to the mode of war best calculated to end this contest as most distressing to the Americans, and which he seems as yet carefully to have avoided. To me it has always appeared that there was more cruelty in protracting the war than in taking such acts of vigour which must bring the crisis to the shortest decision.'[92] A recent historian has interpreted this letter as the King advocating 'greater ferocity' through the use of Native Americans against the colonists, but in fact he was merely commending the blockade.[93]

It was a woeful time for British statesmanship. North was manifestly unsuited for the premiership, but no one else within the ministry was seen as capable of taking on its demands in wartime. North's Cabinet comprised himself, the son of an earl (educated at Eton and Trinity College, Oxford), the 12th Earl of Suffolk and 5th of Berkshire (Eton and Magdalen College, Oxford), the 4th Earl of Sandwich (Eton and Trinity College, Cambridge), the 3rd Viscount Weymouth (home-educated and St John's College, Cambridge), the 2nd Earl Gower (Westminster and Christ Church, Oxford), the 2nd Earl of Dartmouth (Westminster and Trinity College, Oxford) and the 2nd Earl Bathurst (Eton and Balliol College, Oxford). Whether a wider social group from which the ministerial pool could be drawn might have done better is a moot point, although it would have required a social revolution to have broken the upper-class near monopoly on political power at that time. Henry VIII might have taken advisers such as Cardinal Wolsey and Thomas Cromwell from the tradesman class, but George III had no such luxury, even if he had wanted it, and there is no indication that he did. The battle of Waterloo might have been won on the playing fields of Eton, but the American colonies had been lost there forty years earlier.

15

Global War

December 1777–June 1778

*He held fast to the belief that his task was to check a civic broil
within the Empire, when in fact he was attempting to check the
historic developments of more than a century.*[1]

Gerald S. Brown on Lord George Germain, 1952

The collapse of the Germain Plan naturally forced a fundamental strategic
re-evaluation, and George wanted the Seven Years War commander and
hero General Lord Amherst to preside over it.* He told North in December
1777 he thought it might 'in the end prove the wisest step in our present
situation to act only on the defensive with the army ... Canada, Nova
Scotia, the Floridas, New York, and Rhode Island must probably be the
stations.'[2] He nonetheless ended with heartfelt thanks to his Prime Minister: 'I shall also add that I can never forget the friendship as well as the
zeal you have shown to me.' In reply, North made a pro forma offer to
resign, but then qualified it by adding, 'I do not see that as yet the storm
is risen to a height that absolutely requires a change of hands at home, but
the consequences of this most fatal event both in America and in foreign
parts may be very important and serious, and will certainly require some
material change of system. No time shall be lost.'[3]

The reference to foreign parts was to France, and the 'material change
of system' he had in mind entailed a national government of some kind
under Lord Chatham that would carry on the war. The King rejected
North's resignation offer, and thought the idea of simply admitting defeat
in America and bringing the army and navy home quite impossible. 'I do not
think there is a man either bold or mad enough to presume to treat for the

---

* Amherst's heroic status is questioned today as he has been accused of having in 1763 retro-
spectively endorsed the delivery of two blankets and a handkerchief infected with smallpox to
Chief Turtleheart of the Lenape tribe.

mother country on such a basis [of giving America independence],' he told
North in January 1778. 'Perhaps the time may come when it will be wise
to abandon all North America but Canada, Nova Scotia and the Floridas,
but then the generality of the nation must see it first in that light; but to
treat with independence can never be possible.'[4]

Even after Saratoga, the American colonies could have lost the war for
independence, for they too had extremely serious internal problems. (Not
for nothing is one of the best histories of the conflict entitled *Almost a
Miracle*.)[5]* The King and Germain have been heavily criticized for fighting
on after Saratoga, but if they truly believed that victory was still possible
it is hard to see what else they could have done, not least since they understood, as Piers Mackesy put it, 'that the effort was proportioned to the
stakes ... And there were good grounds for their hopes. If England could
have won the command of the oceans, the game would have been in her
hands.'[6] For a number of reasons such command proved elusive: decisive
naval victories were rare in the days of fighting sail and there was only
one† in the whole War of Independence; the French had been rearming
since 1763 and, when Spain entered the war, Brest could no longer be
blockaded; Gibraltar was under permanent siege and needed resupply;
American privateers were able to play havoc with ocean communications,
and the Admiralty regularly miscalculated French plans.[7] Simply supplying
the army was the annual work of 400 ships making the long, arduous and
increasingly dangerous Atlantic crossing.[8]

Even in those dark days of the war immediately after Saratoga, the King
was still concerned that the soldiers fighting in America would have the
prestige (and thus also market value) of their commissions debased by men
back home buying cheaper ones in New Corps regiments. In December
1777 he worried that the fast-track officering of a new, thousand-strong
Manchester Regiment 'will give such general disgust to the Army and in
particular to those serving in America that it would be more disserviceable
than advantageous'.[9] Furthermore, between 1778 and 1782 no fewer than
eight British and two Hanoverian regiments were sent to southern India
to reinforce the East India Company troops in their struggle against Haidar

---

* When the American War of Independence has been wargamed at tournament level over the
past decades, the British side win about 45 per cent of the time. Those victories tend to arise
if Howe – unless he has already destroyed the Continental Army at Brooklyn Heights or in
Manhattan – puts the Germain Plan into operation by moving briskly from New York in 1777,
ignoring Philadelphia and joining with Burgoyne, thereby avoiding the surrender at Saratoga
and the entry of France and Spain into the conflict, while cutting off New England from the
rest of the colonies.

† The battle of the Saints, by which time the war had been lost on land.

Ali, the Sultan of Mysore, at a time when Howe, Clinton and Cornwallis were being starved of troops.[10]

On 6 January 1778, North passed on the news from Lord Stormont, the British Ambassador in Paris and nephew of Lord Mansfield, that 'An approaching war with France and Spain appears now almost out of doubt.'[11] Louis XVI was fully conscious of the ideological danger of supporting a republican revolt against a monarchy, but under pressure from Charles Vergennes, his Foreign Minister, and Antoine de Sartine, his Naval Minister, he could not resist trying to humble Britain after France's defeat in the Seven Years War. The warnings of his former Finance Minister, Anne-Robert Turgot, that France was still saddled with debt from that conflict and simply could not afford another one, went unheeded.

'However insidious the conduct of France may appear,' George replied to his Prime Minister, 'it is pleasant to feel we are taking all the steps that would be necessary if it should end in a war, and my mind is perfectly prepared to meet what I should certainly think a very unhappy event from the consciousness that I have scrupulously attempted to avoid and that without one single grievance France chooses to be the aggressor.'[12] It was true that the French decision was opportunistic, but in many respects it was a masterstroke, dividing France's ancestral enemy from her potentially vast empire in the west. Yet Turgot was also correct, and the enormous costs of fighting the new global struggle would break the French Treasury, eventually leading to the calling of the Estates-General, the representative assembly of the nation, for the first time since 1614. It was their subsequent refusal to disband in May 1789 that led to the French Revolution two months later, and thus subsequently to Louis XVI's decapitation. Rarely in history has opportunism been punished so condignly.

The disaster at Saratoga prompted the King to offer the American command to Lord Amherst on 12 January 1778, three years after he had turned it down the first time, and it was again refused 'with every expression of duty'.[13] George recognized that the collapsing relationship between Germain and Howe needed to be addressed immediately. 'I am persuaded that those two are so ill together', he told North, 'that the good of the service requires that either the Secretary or the General should retire.'[14] It was excellent advice, but was not heeded by North for a full four months. Amherst was given overall command of the British Army in March, with a seat in the Cabinet, but he could not use the title of Commander-in-Chief, a post that had lain vacant since Granby's resignation in 1769, in case it offended the Duke of Gloucester's *amour propre*. Amherst had to recast the entire order of battle and very soon fight a European as well as the American war, but without his position being officially recognized.

In early 1778 Lord George Germain and William Eden MP, the Under-Secretary at the Board of Trade and Plantations, undertook a major strategic reappraisal of the war. Instead of trying to capture the rebel strongholds and bring the enemy to battle, they concluded, troops should be used to hold New York, Newport, Halifax, East and West Florida, and perhaps also Charleston if it could be captured, while the navy blockaded the eastern seaboard and raided unprotected coastlines, foraging for fresh foodstuffs and livestock to vary the shipped rations. By this means Admiral Howe would have at his command a fleet which could concentrate on blockading America rather than supporting his brother's efforts on land. Although this was not a strategy that would provide a quick victory, Eden hoped that a lengthy process of attrition might bring the rebels to negotiate a peace treaty, based on a federal system in which they would have autonomy but not total independence.[15] Boxed in by British forces to the north in Canada and to the south in Florida, and shorn of New York City, the new nation might want to come to a compromise peace.

Although the Germain–Eden plan provided minimal exposure to French and American attacks, it had the disadvantages of giving the rebels much needed time to establish themselves as a functioning state, and of effectively turning the whole North American theatre of the war into something of a sideshow for at least a couple of years during what would be a global struggle against France and also eventually Spain. Independently of Germain and Eden, the King urged North to commission Lords Amherst and Sandwich to undertake a strategic review as well. He told North that Amherst believed that:

> after the disaster of Burgoyne not less than an additional army to what there is at present of forty thousand men can carry on with any effect an offensive land war, that a sea war is the only wise plan, that the preventing the arrival of military stores, clothing, and the other articles necessary from Europe must distress them and make them come into what Britain may decently consent to; that at this hour they will laugh at any proposition.[16]

On 17 January, Amherst and Sandwich put their naval-based plan to the Cabinet, a plan which was strikingly close to that of Germain and Eden. 'Canada, Nova Scotia, Rhode Island, New York and the Floridas should be secured, and if possible Philadelphia,' they stated.[17] They concluded that Britain would need 30,000 men just to protect the bridgeheads, and 45,000 if they wanted to hold Philadelphia as well.[18] These were enormous numbers for the time: as we have seen, the whole British Army was only 48,000 strong in 1775. Doubling the army and greatly enlarging the navy would require a complete reordering of the British economic system, as well as a big increase in tax revenues. As it was, it took the existential crisis of the French Revolution and imminent invasion to institute an income tax in 1797, and no British politician was willing to contemplate such a step twenty years earlier, even in order to try to save America by some kind of imperial condominium.

The Cabinet decided to send only three more battalions to North America, and adopted an amalgam of the two strategic plans, by which the army would stay on the defensive in North America except for an attack on the Carolinas some time in the future, while a repeat of the global war against France was fought along the lines of the Seven Years War.[19] The thirteen colonies would be blockaded, but there would be no coordinated land-based attempt to crush the American Revolution until victory over France had been won. Meanwhile, Philadelphia would be evacuated.

With the prospect of a parliamentary inquiry into Saratoga, and knowing himself to be an excellent party manager but no war leader or strategist, on 29 January 1778 North once again asked the King for permission to resign. He had already been Prime Minister longer than any of the nine since Sir Robert Walpole, and in a long letter written in the customary third person he pleaded that:

> The anxiety of his mind for the last two months has deprived Lord North of his memory and understanding. The promise he has made of bringing forth a proposition of peace with America, and the necessity he thinks there is ... of endeavouring to draw some of the colonies from their claim and plan of independency from Great Britain make him think it necessary to take some sort of pacific step in Parliament.[20]

Since he and his followers 'stand in the way of everything that would be effective', he suggested that another ministry could pursue a viable peace policy that would somehow keep a self-taxing and essentially self-governing America under the Crown in one form or another.

Yet so much blood had by then been shed on so many American battlefields, and Saratoga having given the colonists more than a whiff of eventual victory, it was absurd to think that the Americans would now settle for any kind of federal accommodation. North might only have been suggesting it as a pretext for leaving office, which he was to become increasingly desperate to do, but – unlike Grafton – he felt that he could not ignore the King's wishes, not least because George had just saved him from possible bankruptcy.

The King could theoretically have accepted North's resignation and appointed someone who could prosecute the war, or he could have refused it and explored the possibility of a peace commission. He did neither. Back in November 1775 he had referred to North as his 'sheet anchor'; para-doxically, rather than weakening him, Saratoga only confirmed North in that role. The King ought to have learned the lesson of Bute's continual requests to resign and let North go, but George still admired him, thought there was no one to take his place and recognized his mastery of Parliament; in any case he instinctively disliked all except scientific and medical change. He especially disliked changes that would be interpreted as having been forced upon him by Chatham, Rockingham, Richmond, Charles Fox and the Opposition, which he thought would weaken the country in a time of global war. Although he was willing to go along the peace route as it was the government's policy, he did not believe it had any hope of success and would only persuade the rebels that they were winning. In that, at least, he was probably correct.

In his reply (at 1.25 p.m. on 31 January 1778), the King attributed North's offer of resignation to his being 'inclined to despond', adding that he had 'too much personal affection for me, and sense of honour, to allow such a thought to take any hold on your mind'.[21] He wrote of 'how sincerely you are loved and admired by the House of Commons, and how universally esteemed by the public', and that North had got through 'situations still more embarrassing than the present'. To put Burgoyne's surrender down as an embarrassment rather than a catastrophe showed the King's commitment to the war, as did his statement that:

> You will remember that before the recess I strongly advised you not to bind yourself to bring forward a proposition for restoring tranquillity to North America, not from any absurd issues of unconditional submission my mind never harboured, but from foreseeing that whatever can be proposed will be liable, not to bring America back to a sense of attachment to the mother country, yet to dissatisfy this country, which has in the most handsome manner cheerfully carried on the contest, and therefore has the right to have the struggle continued until convinced that it is in vain.[22]

George then proposed to North a plan for strengthening the garrisons in Canada, the Floridas and Nova Scotia, while withdrawing all British forces from virtually all the rest of North America – he did not mention New York City – and 'without loss of time, employ them in attacking New Orleans, and the French and Spanish West India possessions'.[23] The blockade would be kept up by the Royal Navy, and 'We must at the same time continue destroying the trade and ports of the rebellious colonies and thus soon bring both contests to a conclusion,' which in America's case would be a negotiated peace.[24] This strategy – essentially the Germain–Eden plan, with an emphasis on an aggressive naval element as soon as France and

Spain declared war – would preclude land campaigns in North America until the Southern Expedition was ready many months hence.

The King was acutely aware of the unsustainable strain on resources of a war on two fronts, against both the Americans on land and the French and Spanish at sea. 'Should a French [war] be our fate,' he warned North in early February, 'if we are to be carrying on a land war against the rebels and against those two powers it must be feeble in all parts and consequently unsuccessful.'[25] Yet he also saw an opportunity for Britain in the West Indies, where France's rich and vulnerable possessions, including sugar islands that Britain had returned in the Peace of Paris, were held by only 9,000 troops. 'Success in those parts would repay us the great expenses incurred,' he told North on 31 January. This strategy might indeed prove popular, he believed, as 'This country having had its attention diverted to a fresh object, would be in a better temper to subscribe to such terms as [the] administration might think advisable to offer America.' British imports from the West Indies had amounted to £4.5 million in 1776, as against £1.5 million from the East India Company, and were a huge source of government revenue.[26] Extraordinary as it may seem today, it was possible for British policymakers to envisage the loss of trade with North America, but not with the far higher revenue-producing West Indies.

On 2 February 1778, Charles Fox delivered a crushing two-and-a-half-hour speech in support of the resolution 'That no more of the Old Corps be sent out of the Kingdom', at the end of which no minister stood up to contradict him. The debate was a gala social occasion and no fewer than sixty society ladies, including Georgiana, Duchess of Devonshire, came to watch him.* His uncle the Duke of Richmond then moved the same motion in the Lords. In the Commons, 165 members supported the motion, including some Tories such as Edward Gibbon, although the government still had 259 votes to defeat it. 'I trust that when the next committee on the State of the Nation is resumed', the King scolded North, 'gentlemen will be more ready to speak.'[27]

By early February it was clear that either Howe or Germain would have to leave his post over the Saratoga disaster, something that the King had

---

* The level of Fox's sympathy with the fortunes of the Continental Army can be gauged from the way he and his supporters frequently wore the same blue frockcoats and buff waistcoats that 'then constituted the distinguished badge or uniform of Washington and the American insurgents' (ed. Wheatley, *Historical and Posthumous Memoirs of Sir Nathaniel Wraxall* II pp. 2–3). It is rare in British history for politicians to wear the uniform of the enemy during wartime, but Charles Fox and his followers did, claiming that the blue and buff predated the American Revolution and had been worn by the Roundhead republicans in the English Civil War. This was hardly reasoning likely to appeal to the King.

known for months. North effectively dismissed Howe by accepting a three-months-old resignation threat that he had inadvisedly made the previous November.[28] The Cabinet agreed to Sir Henry Clinton being appointed Commander-in-Chief of North American operations in his stead. From the tone of North's and Germain's letters to Howe, it was clear that the government were going to blame him and Burgoyne – both Whig MPs – for the defeat.

On 6 February, the French government and the American Congress, the latter represented by Benjamin Franklin and Silas Deane in Paris, signed treaties of amity and commerce, which would automatically turn into a full-scale alliance were war to break out between France and Britain. That was a mere matter of time; France was already providing the American colonists with 90 per cent of their gunpowder.[29] A European great power had now recognized the colonies as an independent nation, which was a great boost for its legitimacy, and American Nonconformists who had formerly denounced George as a 'papist' for allowing French Canadians to observe Catholic rites under the Quebec Act were now delighted to ally themselves formally with 'His Most Catholic Majesty' King Louis XVI of France.

Ten days after the Franco-American pact had been signed, North asked the King's permission to approach Chatham to lead a national government, having heard from the Duke of Northumberland that he would be willing to try to save the situation were 'a pretty general power put into his hands'.[30] North believed Chatham was, as he put it, 'of all the Opposition, the person who would be of most service to His Majesty', not least as he had defeated the French fifteen years earlier. He continued to press the idea for a month, against George's intransigence. The King was probably right in refusing to countenance another return to power: Chatham had indeed turned around Britain's fortunes in the Seven Years War, but as his recent abortive period as Prime Minister had so painfully shown, he was too inconsistent and unwell to be entrusted with high office again.

On 20 February the British warship *Andromeda* left for America, bearing conciliatory draft Bills intended to end the war. They offered everything short of outright independence, including promises to abolish all British taxation of America, to give preference to Americans for colonial offices and even to offer seats in Parliament for Americans.[31] In the days of the revolt against 'taxation without representation', this might have been enough, but nearly three years after Lexington and Concord the *casus belli* had become a desire for outright sovereign independence. By this point, the hearts and minds of Americans were set on self-government, and it seems extraordinary that the British government did not realize it. Yet this was no glib offer on Britain's part; the peace commission was led by the aristocrat Frederick Howard, 5th Earl of Carlisle, who was a future viceroy of Ireland, and included William Eden himself.

On 13 March the French Ambassador in London officially informed Lord Weymouth, the Southern Secretary, about the Franco-American pact, and an emergency Cabinet meeting decided upon the immediate withdrawal of the British Ambassador from Paris, prior to hostilities being declared. 'I think the strange paper this day by the French Ambassador to Lord Weymouth is a manifest declaration of war,' the King wrote to Weymouth from Buckingham House at 5.40 p.m. that day. Now more than ever, he could not afford to lose his Prime Minister. 'My sole wish is to keep you at the head of the Treasury and as my confidential minister,' George wrote to North two days later. 'That end obtained, I am willing through your channel to accept any description of person that will come devotedly to the support of your administration and as such do not object to Lord Shelburne and Mr Barré, who personally I dislike as much as Alderman Wilkes, and I cannot give you a strong[er] proof of my desire to forward anything you wish than taking this unpleasant step.'[32] He wanted North to let Chatham understand that, although he would like him to support the ministry, North must continue to lead it both as premier and as Chancellor of the Exchequer. He must have known that that would be unacceptable to Chatham.

The government took another jolt when Lord Barrington, the Secretary at War, announced that he preferred to resign than be party to Burgoyne being court-martialled over Saratoga. The King told North he hoped that the Navy Treasurer (and previous War Secretary) Welbore Ellis would be appointed in his place, 'in preference to Barré, who . . . in that event will not be so near my person'.[33] His dislike of Barré, a radical who had coined the phrase 'Sons of Liberty', was palpable. North told the King on 16 March that he had heard from Eden that Chatham would be willing to join the ministry, but that 'he expects to be a confidential* minister' and 'that he must have the appearance of forming the ministry'.[34]

The King replied by characterizing Chatham as 'that perfidious man' who wanted to be a 'dictator': 'I will not object to see that great man when Lord Shelburne and [John] Dunning, with Barré, are placed already in office but I solemnly declare nothing shall bring me to treat personally with Lord Chatham . . . I entirely stick to what I wrote to you yesterday, from which I will not change one jot.'[35] In a letter written later that day, he

* In the sense of having the King's confidence.

described the Opposition as 'a set of men who would certainly make me a slave for the remainder of my days'.[36]

When George felt himself under pressure, his handwriting and syntax suffered. When angry, he wrote faster and often punctuation and grammar disappeared. In working correspondence with North he often failed to observe the niceties in the way that today one might not bother with precise punctuation in a text message. Now, in his protestations against North's continual requests for a coalition, there was something rather histrionic. On 17 March – the day that Britain formally declared war on France – he reiterated his opposition to Chatham becoming Prime Minister:

> My dear Lord, no consideration in life shall make me stoop to [the] Opposition . . . whilst any ten men in the kingdom will stand by me I will not give myself up into bondage. My dear Lord, I will rather risk my Crown than do what I think personally disgraceful . . . It is impossible that the nation shall not stand by me; if they will not, they shall have another king, for I will never put my hand to what would make me miserable to the last hour of my life.[37]

When it came to resignation threats, the King could outdo even his Prime Minister, although as the Prince of Wales was only sixteen it was rather an empty one.

Strategically, France's entry into the war changed everything. In effect Britain now had to refight the Seven Years War in the West Indies, Africa, the Mediterranean and Asia, as well as continuing the struggle in North America. Trying to quell the American rebellion took second place to defeating France, and indeed was something of a backwater in what became a global war. There was only one major British offensive in America – the capture of Savannah, Georgia – in the rest of 1778 and the whole of 1779.

Britain had already devoted too few troops to surmount the challenges there. In 1778, approximately 65 per cent of the British Army was stationed in North America; by 1780 this had dropped to around 30 per cent (although this was partly due to the vast growth of the volunteer militia units raised in the United Kingdom to defend against an expected French invasion).[38] It was felt in London that, although American independence would be disastrous, the loss of the West Indies or India to France would be catastrophic, so reinforcements were immediately taken from America to defend the Lesser Antilles. Fortunately it was not until 1780 that India became a major drain on British resources.

Had it not been for the King, the imbalance of naval forces might have been worse. When Admiral Howe requested six more ships-of-the-line for his fleet in America in mid-December 1776, the Cabinet had approved, but failed to commission any more for the Channel or Mediterranean fleets from which they would be taken. North, who was unwell with a heavy cough and not seeing anyone, wanted to wait until there was reliable evidence that the French were embarking on a new naval rearmament programme before commencing a British one, even though the French had been strengthening their fleets steadily since the Peace of Paris.[39] The Cabinet were concerned by North's insouciance, and at that point, warned by Robinson, the King stepped in. He did not want an arms race with France any more than North, but he considered an invincible Channel fleet to be a non-negotiable prerequisite for British security when fighting a major war overseas. 'The royal intervention may have been decisive,' concluded a historian of this episode, 'for the decision to commission replacements was duly taken.'[40] Yet they were only replacements, not the kind of commitment to large-scale new naval construction necessary to face multiple enemies.

As the King had foreseen, France's entry into the war opened up opportunities as well as dangers, with the possibility that naval victories might allow Britain to seize French West Indies possessions. Both the stakes and the potential winnings had been heightened greatly, and the King and Germain thought they were worth playing for, even if they tended to fill North and Clinton with dread.[41]*

The outbreak of war with France merely reinforced North's view that Chatham should be appointed Prime Minister in his place, and on 21 March he told the King that:

> this very alarming crisis is enough to employ the greatest man of business, and the most consummate statesman that ever existed, and it is infinitely more than Lord North can undertake, so that if this load of important duties is any longer entrusted to him, national disgrace and ruin will be the consequence. Whoever may come to the assistance of government must be the director and dictator of the leading measures of government. Lord North knows too well his want of ability and decision in matters of nice† importance to pretend to be equal to such a trust . . . and will forever render it fatal to His Majesty to continue at the Treasury.[42]

There were pages more of this, of which George ought to have taken notice, thereby allowing North to retire. Instead of calling for Chatham, Sandwich,

---

* Around this time, North made a joke about his generals that decades later was plagiarized by the Duke of Wellington about his troops before Waterloo: 'I do not know whether they will frighten the enemy, but I am sure they frighten me whenever I think of them' (Mackesy, *War for America* p. 180).

† 'Accurate in judgement to minute exactness' (*Johnson's Dictionary*).

Shelburne or even Germain, the King replied simply by asking 'one clear question' – albeit one loaded with overt emotional blackmail – namely, 'Are you resolved, agreeable to the example of the Duke of Grafton, at the hour of danger to desert me.'[43] George was calling in North's debt.

In less fraught circumstances, both the King and North might be suspected of melodrama – an emotion surprisingly rife among eighteenth-century grandees before the Victorians stiffened their upper lips – but the war was undoubtedly going badly and was likely to get worse. A peace offer was about to be made, and a change of government might have given it added weight in America. North's reply, after spending a night in the country with a cold, was that of course he would not desert the King, even though he 'never thought himself in any way equal to the situation', but he also warned him that 'the almost certain consequence of His Majesty's resolution will be the ruin of his affairs'.[44] Whatever else Lord North might be accused of in the whole sorry tale of the American colonies, a desire to cling to office was not one. In his letter, he begged the King 'to choose a leader for the administration out of some other quarter if not out of the Opposition'. He did not mention anyone by name, probably because there was no one obvious who could command the Commons in the way that he still did.

George persuaded himself that his honour would be imperilled if he were forced to accept Chatham, Rockingham or Fox as premier. His humiliation by Grenville in May 1765, and his father's admonition in 'Instructions for my Son George' to 'never give up your honour' meant that he sometimes mistook normal changes of ministry for a full-scale storming of the Closet. On this occasion he was right, however, because Rockingham and Fox were bent on appeasing, or even capitulating to, the rebellious colonists, although the King did not believe the war was by any means lost. It was impossible to tell from Chatham's changes of stance over America what his policy might turn out to be, assuming that he even knew himself; and of course he remained in doubtful health.

The King held out the hope that after some successful raids on her possessions in the New World, France might be forced to sue for peace and allow Britain to concentrate once more on trying to force the Americans – by then perhaps weakened economically by a long naval blockade – back into some kind of condominium arrangement within the empire. Yet North was quasi-defeatist, another reason why George ought to have accepted his resignation. 'This country', the Prime Minister told the King on 25 March, 'is totally unequal to a war with Spain, France, and America, and will, Lord North fears, be overmatched if the contention is only with the House of Bourbon.'[45] He therefore wanted 'an accommodation with America . . . as he thinks that Great Britain will suffer more in the war than her enemies'. This would be due to a financial collapse rather than battlefield defeats, but it would ultimately amount to much the same thing, and 'Great Britain will undo herself if she thinks of punishing France.' If George was adamant the war should be continued – which he was, as were the majority of the Cabinet, government and Commons – North was clearly not the man to prosecute it.

Regarding possible future peace negotiations with Benjamin Franklin in Paris – of whom the King believed that 'hatred to this country is the constant object of his mind' – George insisted to North on 26 March that 'I will never consent that in any treaty that may be concluded a single word be mentioned concerning Canada, Nova Scotia, or the Floridas, which are colonies belonging to this country, and the more they are kept unlike the other colonies the better, for it is by them we are to keep a certain awe over the abandoned colonies.'[46] This was a major shift from his stance before Saratoga, when he believed that the rebels could be defeated outright. Far from the obstinate ideologue he is often depicted as being, the King was ready to compromise, so long as British possessions to the south of Georgia and north of New England were safeguarded. On 26 March, when he had heard that Franklin opposed any peace offer that Britain might make, he told North that nonetheless 'I think it so desirable to end the war with that country, to be able with redoubled ardour to avenge the faithless and insolent conduct of France, that I think it may be proper to keep open the channel of intercourse with that insidious man.'[47]

Upon yet another request on 29 March from North to be replaced, the King asked his Prime Minister 'the three following questions, to which I expect explicit answers in writing'.[48] The first was whether the present ministry could be strengthened by taking in 'some men of talents' from the Opposition. Failing that, would North 'cooperate with me in putting vigour and activity into every department' – that is, effect a major reshuffle? Thirdly, if North resigned at the end of the parliamentary session in early June, he could 'not be surprised at my employing that short space of time in taking such steps as I may judge necessary for putting vigour into my service', such as promoting the Attorney-General, Edward Thurlow, to be Lord Chancellor. George liked and admired Thurlow, a Tory who, despite having been sent down from Gonville and Caius College, Cambridge, as an undergraduate for insolence to the Dean,* had been appointed King's Counsel. As Solicitor-General he had prosecuted Wilkes and the publisher

---

* When the Dean reprimanded Thurlow, saying that whenever he looked out of his window he saw Thurlow idling in the court, Thurlow replied that whenever he passed through the court he saw the Dean idling at his window (Gore-Browne, *Chancellor Thurlow* pp. 5–6).

of the Letters of Junius, and had resolutely opposed American independence.

'If His Majesty should really find it necessary to detain him longer than the end of the session,' North replied, referring to himself, he would 'continue, let his situation be never so weary, till His Majesty is able to arrange his servants in the manner the most agreeable to himself'.[49] Thurlow was appointed a peer and Lord Chancellor in June – a post he was to hold under four premiers on and off until 1792 – but as other arrangements of servants would almost certainly have involved Chatham and the Rockingham Whigs entering the ministry, nothing else happened and North stayed on. With Thurlow no longer in the Commons, there were few other ministers of note left there besides North and Germain who could stand up in debate to the oratorical brilliance of Fox, Burke and Richard Brinsley Sheridan. These Whigs had been greatly encouraged in their attacks by the defeat at Saratoga, but they still had to tread the difficult ground between opposition to the war and too overt a sympathy for the Americans, which would strike independent MPs as bordering on treachery – especially with Britain's traditional enemy France now in the fray.

For all that Fox and Burke tended to win the rhetorical battles, North continued to win the divisions, albeit less and less comfortably as the war progressed. He remained personally popular in the House, especially with the large numbers of independent MPs on whom all eighteenth-century governments ultimately depended, and crucially he never revealed in public or Parliament the doubts – verging on outright defeatism – that he vouchsafed to the King with such regularity. But the melodrama of 21 March did not end there, with North expostulating on 1 April that 'He will sacrifice every personal consideration to His Majesty's service, in which he will die rather than abandon His Majesty in distress.'[50] The self-pity did not let up either – 'Let me die disgraced, for that I cannot now avoid,' he wrote in May 1778. But still no radical restructuring of the ministry took place. Every time North brought up the subject of his retirement, which he did with what George must have found monotonous regularity, he also explained that he was willing to soldier on regardless of the cost to his wealth, reputation and even sanity.[51] On dozens of occasions he told the King he did not have the qualities needed in a wartime premier, but each time George took him seriously enough to discuss the terms and timing of his retirement North rowed back just enough to stay in office, only to complain again a few days or weeks later. The correspondence between them is highly reminiscent of that between the King and Bute in 1762–4 – a couple who talk endlessly about separation but can never quite bring themselves to do it.

Meanwhile, the Opposition was not without its own hyperbole. In the usually sedate House of Lords on 31 March the Duke of Richmond likened Lord Sandwich to Johan and Cornelis de Witt, Dutch politicians and brothers who had been lynched in The Hague in August 1672 for losing wars against France and England. Richmond predicted that when Sandwich lost the American war 'There would be insurrections of the people, who would put him to death. The populace would rise, and serve the noble lord as the Dutch served the de Witts; they would tear him limb from limb.'[52]

By contrast with Richmond's mere histrionics, a week later the House of Lords witnessed one of its most genuinely dramatic moments in a history that stretches back to the thirteenth century. On Tuesday 7 April, the Earl of Chatham stood up to deliver a short, almost inaudible, but emotionally powerful speech favouring conciliation with the Americans but opposing Rockingham's solution of simply accepting American independence. He had suffered a minor stroke the previous year and his doctors had advised him against speaking, but he had come on crutches, helped by his eighteen-year-old son, William Pitt (the Younger), and his son-in-law, Lord Mahon, on either side of him. During the debate, after denouncing the dismemberment of the empire that he had done so much to defend and extend, he tried to rise to speak a second time but suffered a major stroke while doing so, and in the words of Lord Camden, 'fell back upon his seat and was to all appearance in the agony of death'.[53]

Chatham had to be carried out of the chamber by his son and son-in-law, as the debate adjourned. His stroke, in Camden's words, 'threw the whole House into confusion. Every person was upon the instant upon his legs in a moment hurrying from one place to another [except] the Earl of M[ansfield], who sat almost as much unmoved as the senseless body itself.'[54] Mansfield had been a bitter political rival of Chatham since the 1750s, but he was not the only one unaffected by the tragedy. An unemotional George asked Lord North the next day, 'May not the political exit of Lord Chatham incline you to continue at the head of my affairs?'[55]

On 13 April, the French Admiral Henri d'Estaing left Toulon with eleven ships-of-the-line, a fifty-gunner, several frigates and, so British intelligence finally learned on 27 April, a full nine months of provisions, making it very likely that he planned to cross the Atlantic. He managed to pass the Straits of Gibraltar because Sandwich and Admiral Sir Augustus Keppel decided, disastrously, not to send twelve ships-of-the-line from the Channel Fleet there to engage them. Even though there were no reports of transport ships in the French Channel ports, they were so worried about a French invasion of Britain that the entire fleet was retained at home. Immediately on receiving the news, Germain demanded that North send a strong squadron to America at once to reinforce Admiral Howe 'and prevent the fatal consequences which may follow from the French having an avowed superiority at sea upon the coast of North America'. He compared the risk to Britain as 'trifling' compared to leaving d'Estaing 'at full liberty to attack us in North America or the West Indies or Newfoundland'. The King completely agreed.

The Cabinet decided to send thirteen ships-of-the-line under Rear-Admiral John 'Foulweather Jack' Byron to America, but due to errors, incompetence and operational setbacks – as well as the fact that it was fitted out for Channel service, needed different rigging and far greater provisions – the fleet was not ready to leave for weeks. An east wind that could have taken it down the Channel was missed, and rough weather prevented victualling ships from entering Spithead. The House of Commons was soon in uproar over the delays, and the King decided to go down to Portsmouth himself to try to bring forward the all-important sailing date.

On 2 May the King and his eleven-year-old daughter Princess Charlotte left Buckingham House at 6 a.m., reaching Portsmouth in seven hours, which the King in his meticulous way noted was half an hour less than on his visit five years previously. It was a warm day but without dust and dirt on the road and he found the journey from Epsom to Guildford 'extremely beautiful'.[56] At Godalming the crowds showed 'a certain degree of affection that a feeling heart is sensible of but cannot find terms to express', as the King told the Prince of Wales and Prince Frederick in a letter from Portsmouth.[57] The weather turned, and it was pouring with rain so violently on Portsea Down that Spithead could not be seen, but 'On quitting the carriage I instantly took every step necessary to quicken the sailing of part of the fleet, and trust my directions will expedite the service.' That evening he dined with Amherst, Sandwich, Admiral Thomas Pye (Commander-in-Chief at Portsmouth), Samuel Hood (Commissioner of the Portsmouth Dockyard) and eight admirals, drank a glass of champagne to toast the fleet and went upstairs to look at it through a telescope. 'After giving the gentlemen a little time for the bad custom of toasting,' he told his sons, 'I send them word five [a.m.] was a good hour to visit the Yard.'[58]

The King stayed for a week, dispatching reports back to the Cabinet, chivvying the key people at the port and personally investigating problems.[59] He told Admiral Pye that he would not leave until Byron had sailed, and that he could dispense with his attendance upon him until that happened. 'This has put great alacrity into all of them,' George reported to North on 5 May, adding, 'I have no object but to be of use; if that is answered I am completely happy ... no one is more hearty in the cause than myself.'[60] North replied that as he was being attacked in the Commons over the fleet's tardy departure, 'Your Majesty's success ... will diffuse universal comfort in this place.'[61] Yet even on that occasion the Prime Minister took the opportunity to add that 'Your Majesty's service requires a man of great abilities, and who is confident of his abilities, who can choose decisively, and carry his determinations authoritatively into execution ... combining and connecting the whole force and operations of government. I am certainly not such a man.'[62]

Although Byron's fleet finally left England on 9 June, there were still hard-fought debates within the Admiralty about whether it should winter abroad, to the detriment of Channel defence. Sandwich supported those admirals who did not want to take the risk, but the Cabinet sided with Germain. The King strongly supported Germain in thinking that as many ships as was reasonably possible ought to be sent to the West Indies and North America, thinking that the dangers of invasion were overblown.[63] The divisions in the Admiralty were profoundly personal as well as professional. Admiral Augustus Keppel, who commanded the Channel Fleet, was a Rockinghamite Whig MP, a friend and cousin of Richmond and Fox and a former minister. His brother, George Keppel, the 3rd Earl of Albemarle, had captured Havana in 1762 and had sat on Lord George Germain's court martial. Augustus Keppel was physically brave in battle and a good naval commander, although morally too weak (or too ambitious) to speak out against the execution of Admiral Byng in the Seven Years War.[64] When an important post, the lieutenant-generalcy of Marines, had been given to Sandwich's friend Rear-Admiral Sir Hugh Palliser instead of to him, it rankled badly.

One area in which the Portsmouth visit had provided 'universal comfort' for the King and Princess Charlotte was the extraordinary reception that he received from the people who turned out in their thousands to cheer him as he made his way back from Portsmouth to London. From the way that Londoners treated him – both the Whig elite who sneered at what they saw as his miserly provincialism, and the mobs that had often booed his carriage on the way to and from Parliament – George had had sometimes doubted whether he was a genuinely popular king. His behaviour and decisions would not have been affected either way, of course, as that would have been detrimental to his sense of duty, but he was understandably curious. The massive and spontaneous applause that greeted him on his return journey in May 1778 served to reassure him that he was indeed popular, outside the metropolis.

*

William Pitt, Earl of Chatham, died on 11 May 1778, removing one of the few national figures who might have led a non-North ministry. His death did not unify the Opposition, as his following was largely inherited by Lord Shelburne, and indeed his last speech had attacked Rockingham rather than North. 'Instead of an open and contemptuous enemy,' one historian writes of Shelburne, 'the Rockingham party had now to contend with a smooth but treacherous ally.'[65] The larger Opposition party was that of Rockingham, who openly supported the Americans and drank toasts to George Washington at their private dinners at Brooks's. Shelburne's faction by contrast wanted Britain to win the war, but were highly critical of the government over its cause and now its course.

The King behaved badly over Chatham's death, telling North the day afterwards that he hoped the House of Commons' unanimous vote for a state funeral and a monument in Westminster Abbey was 'a testament of gratitude for his rousing the nation at the beginning of the last war', but that if it were a compliment 'paid to his general conduct, [it] is rather an offensive measure to me personally'.[66] Winston Churchill was to write of that statement, 'George III displayed his smallness of mind by opposing the plan,' but in fact he did not prevent either the state funeral or the monument. Chatham received both, and George also approved a government measure to pay a second pension to Chatham's younger son, William Pitt.[67] The young man was not appeased, however. 'The Court did not honour us with their countenance,' William Pitt the Younger complained to his mother after the funeral, 'nor did they suffer the procession to be as magnificent as it ought.'[68] His biographer points out that the Younger Pitt 'entered public life with a healthy suspicion of the King – a suspicion he was never to lose'.[69]

The death of the 4th Earl of Holderness five days after Chatham meant that the lord wardenship of the Cinque Ports became vacant, and Lord North did not allow twenty-four hours to pass before he applied for it himself, telling the King, 'On a thousand accounts, the wardenship of the Cinque Ports has always been the favourite object of my ambition.'[70] He wanted it for life just as Holderness had held it, arguing that 'it would be a disgrace to have that office upon a less respectable footing than my immediate predecessor.' But the King disagreed, saying that while North could have the £4,000 per annum stipend – Walmer Castle was a heavy expense – it could no longer be a lifetime appointment; indeed he insisted that 'for the rest of my life I will not confer any in that mode.'[71] He was not about to award so great an honour for life to someone who might be on the verge of resigning, although four days later North told the King 'that though his earnest wish certainly is to retire, yet he is ready to continue in his present office as long as His Majesty deems it for his service that he should continue there'.[72]

For all his outward bluffness and bonhomie, North was subject to sudden fits of depression. The King's manic depression had been in remission for thirteen years, but North's much milder and easily explicable depression – given the wartime circumstances and pressures of office – came in waves, as is evident from some of his more distraught and self-lacerating letters. He was also under pressure from his father not to resign while the King was still conferring lucrative sinecures and bishoprics on their family, and the lord wardenship was after all worth £4,000 per annum, even if not for life. There was also the problem of who would lead the Commons now that the whole Cabinet except the unpopular Germain was in the Lords. He could take care of himself in debate, but it was a lonely trudge.

In order to protect Germain, the government decided not to allow Burgoyne a full-scale court martial after all, but merely a military tribunal, which refused to judge his military conduct because he was still a prisoner of war.[73] Burgoyne had allied himself with Fox by then, and was arguing that the war was unwinnable, so the King, who had initially supported holding a court martial, turned against the idea, and refused Burgoyne an audience when he was allowed back to Britain on parole. On 23 May Burgoyne used his privilege as an MP to explain his conduct to the Commons, where he blamed the entire Saratoga disaster on Germain. 'By cutting off every proposed latitude and confining the plan to only one object, the forging of a passage to Albany,' he alleged, 'the orders framed upon that plan could in no wise be understood than as positive, peremptory and indispensable.'[74] Claiming to speak for Gage and Clinton – neither of whom was present – Burgoyne accused Germain and the government of being 'obliged to cover their ignorance and inability, and screen themselves from ignominy and contempt, by throwing blame upon men who were unwise enough to act as they were instructed'. Germain was forced to challenge a supporter of Burgoyne to a duel, and the government quashed a vote for a parliamentary inquiry by 144 votes to 92.

When on 5 June the government ordered Burgoyne to return to captivity with his army in America, he ignored it under parliamentary immunity, and went off to take the waters at Bath instead. Washington had allowed Burgoyne home to deal, as he put it, with 'the painful sensibility of a reputation exposed, where he most values it, to the assaults of malice and distraction'.[75] In October 1779, when Burgoyne admitted that his health was restored, the Secretary at War wrote to him about his disobedience and neglect of duty in not returning to share captivity with his men, to which Burgoyne replied saying that it would do no good. He demanded a court martial and resigned various of his posts that did not entitle him to one. The King was so disgusted by what he described as 'so attorney-like an epistle' that he insisted Burgoyne be stripped of his regiment and the governorship of Fort William, although he continued to be paid.

In one area the French entry into the war proved positive at least: recruitment. Whereas the American war had not been popular because it was being fought against Britons' cousins, that changed once it widened to the French and later the Spanish, against whom war was considered almost a national tradition. (Battle honours on regimental standards were not awarded to British regiments that fought in America, because the King saw the Revolution as a civil war, but they certainly were for actions against France and Spain.) Although there were regular anti-war petitions sent to the King until France entered the war, after that they stopped arriving.[76] The participation rate of eligible British adult males in the armed forces (including militia) in the American War of Independence rose to between one in seven or eight, compared with one in nine or ten in the Seven Years War and only one in sixteen during the War of Austrian Succession. George also now entirely dropped his opposition to the creation of new regiments and commissions.

Partly in order to encourage recruitment in Ireland, and partly to rectify long-standing historic wrongs, the government passed the Catholic Relief Act (popularly known as the Papists Act) which the King supported and which came into force in August 1778. At the time, no practising Roman Catholic in England, Wales or Scotland could sit in Parliament or hold official public positions,* serve as an officer in the armed forces or attend university. Catholic priests and teachers were theoretically liable to life imprisonment. Marriage between Catholics was legal only if there was a Protestant ceremony too; Catholic religious clothing could not be worn in public; Catholic chapels could not toll bells; legally at least, Catholics could not inherit property or buy land, although there were various ways around that.[77] The Catholic Relief Act repealed the laws under which Catholic priests were prosecuted and teachers were imprisoned, as well as the inheritance and land laws. Lessening these religious disabilities turned out to be of limited use for recruitment in Ireland, however, where sympathy for the American rebels was strongest.

Even this mild and only partial relaxation of the anti-Catholic laws was violently opposed by Lord George Gordon MP, the youngest son of the

---

* Except for the dukes of Norfolk, who were hereditary earl marshals.

3rd Duke of Gordon, who in February 1779 set up a Protestant Association to counter them.[78] Gordon was a well-known libertine, and when he denounced the Archbishop of Canterbury as 'the Whore of Babylon' a wit commented that Gordon had finally met a whore he didn't like.[79] By contrast, the King was no anti-Catholic bigot; he stayed in the houses of prominent Catholics such as Lord Petre at Thorndon Hall in Essex, something no monarch had done since the Glorious Revolution, and, as we have seen, he supported the Quebec Act. He was, nevertheless, unwilling to countenance Catholics sitting in Parliament, believing that it would contravene his Coronation Oath to maintain the Protestant religion 'as by law established'.

'In consequence of your repeated solicitations to quit your present employment I have seriously attempted to release you,' the King told Lord North on 2 June 1778 after yet another of the Prime Minister's resignation threats, 'but am convinced still more than at any other period how detrimental it would be to the public as well as to me.'[80] He hoped the coming summer recess would 'enable you to raise your mind with vigour to take the lead again in the House of Commons, and not let every absurd idea be adopted as has too recently appeared'. He continued in a vein unseen since the fall of Bute, adding, 'I cannot help touching on another delicate point. Where can you repose your undigested thoughts more safely than in one who has ever treated you more as his friend than his minister?'[81] If indeed it was a friendship, it was to be tested to its limits as the war entered its next phase.

16

'If Others Will Not be Active,
I Must Drive'

June 1778–May 1780

*I trust in the justness of my cause and the bravery of the nation,
and you may depend on my readiness to sheath the sword whenever a permanent tranquillity can be obtained, which certainly the
present moment is not one for accomplishing.*[1]

George III to Lord North, 13 October 1778

On 13 June 1778 the Carlisle Commission made a series of offers to Congress which, if they had been made before the Boston Tea Party five years earlier, might have arrested the outbreak of war, but by now were far too late. By virtue of these offers, Parliament would give up the right to tax the colonies, Congress would retain its army (though not a navy), provincial charters and judges' tenures would be secured, political offices would be reserved for Americans, and Britain would pay off all American war debts; all Parliament would do was regulate imperial trade.[2] The offer was so generous that William Knox of the American Department feared that, if the Americans accepted it, Britain would become depopulated, because Britons would prefer to live in a country that had all the advantages of being part of the empire without any of the burdens.[3] He need not have worried. With full independence clearly within its grasp, Congress formally rejected the offer on 17 June.

When the King received the news, he told North that:

further concession is a joke. All that can be done now is to pursue the plan very wisely adopted in the spring: the providing Nova Scotia, the Floridas and Canada with troops, and should that not leave enough for New York, which may in the end be the case, we must then abandon that place. Then we must content ourselves with distressing the rebels, and not think of any other conduct till the end of the French [war] which if successful will oblige the rebels to submit to more reasonable [terms] than can at this hour be obtained.[4]

Sir Henry Clinton had taken over as Commander-in-Chief from Howe at Philadelphia on 8 May, and with no less than one-third of the British Army in America now being redeployed elsewhere, much of it to the West Indies, he had to evacuate the city.

Howe's expectation that his capture of Philadelphia – which had effectively cost Burgoyne's army in Saratoga – would be accompanied by a major rise in Loyalist activity across Pennsylvania and beyond had not been realized, and as the King had told North back in March, 'It is a joke to think of keeping Pennsylvania.'[5] So on 18 June Clinton unceremoniously evacuated the city with a 12-mile-long baggage train to protect, and led his force towards Sandy Hook, New Jersey, where they were to embark on transports to take them back to New York City. George Washington, who was being pressed not to allow Clinton to return there unscathed, broke camp at Valley Forge to pursue him.

On 28 June, having embarked half his force to New York, Clinton turned with his 9,500-strong rearguard and launched a counterstroke at Monmouth Court House. After two hours of harsh fighting in the blazing sunshine, Clinton lost more men than Washington – around 500 to 360 – but the sharp, sudden clash enabled him to disengage that night and reach his embarkation point at Sandy Hook without suffering any further interference from the 13,500-strong Continental Army.[6] On 26 July, Washington's pursuing force took up position at White Plains, effectively trapping Clinton in New York City. In the laconic estimation of Sir John Fortescue, the historian of the British Army, 'At this point, serious operations in the north come to an end.'[7] The war still had three and a half years yet to run, but in New England and the middle colonies at least, the rebels had won.

Clinton had returned just in time, because on 8 July the Comte d'Estaing's fleet appeared off Delaware, solving the mystery of where the French had been heading. On 11 July the Admiral arrived off Sandy Hook, and soon afterwards started to blockade New York from the sea, but then sailed off for Narragansett Bay for operations against Newport which the Americans were besieging by land. On 11 August, Admiral Richard Howe attempted to attack d'Estaing there but a storm dispersed them both, d'Estaing retiring to Boston. Without naval support, the Americans broke off the siege.

Since 1775, Howe had used his fleet to supply and reinforce the army, blockade American ports and occasionally raid the eastern seaboard, but d'Estaing's arrival now made much of that impossible. In July 1778, the Royal Navy had sixty-six ships-of-the-line in commission and the French had fifty-two (thirty-two of which were in Europe), but with the Spanish entry into the war in June 1779 the balance shifted decisively, and by 1782, although the Royal Navy had ninety-four, the French had seventy-three and the Spanish fifty-four.[8] 'The misfortune is we have more to defend than we have ships ready to employ,' the King told North in November 1778. 'If Parliament can adopt some mode of raising a sufficient number of men for the navy and army, I doubt not that our numberless difficulties with spirit, assiduity and attention would soon vanish.'[9] The price was now being paid for not having addressed the recruitment problem four and a half years earlier.

During the Seven Years War, the Royal Navy had blockaded Toulon and Brest, bottling up the French Navy, but that was no longer possible. From 1778, it had to protect Britain from serious French plans for a cross-Channel invasion, as well as defending the West Indian possessions. So whereas in 1778 there were forty-one British ships-of-the-line stationed in North American waters and only eight in the West Indies, by 1780 forty-one were in the West Indies and only thirteen in North America.[10]

Nor was the Channel Fleet always in the right place at the right time. On 13 June 1778, its twenty ships-of-the-line under Admiral Keppel weighed anchor, with orders to escort reinforcements for Gibraltar past Brest and to sink the French fleet if it emerged from port. Having captured a French frigate that had papers showing there were twenty-seven ships-of-the-line at Brest, and five more being built, Keppel returned to St Helen's on the Isle of Wight on the 27th to collect stores and reinforcements.

The King said that he was 'most hurt' at Keppel's return, leaving the Gibraltar convoy unprotected, and at a time when large convoys were expected in the Channel from the East and West Indies. (The King's regular use of 'hurt', 'much hurt' and 'most hurt' covered a range of emotions from annoyance to anger, but did not usually tend to imply his being upset or offended emotionally in the modern sense.) Keppel put to sea again on 9 July aboard his 104-gun flagship *Victory*, along with eighteen ships-of-the-line, to escort a Jamaican convoy in from the Lizard,* and was later joined by five more. With Spain possibly joining the struggle, the French fleet at Brest had to be neutralized by Keppel before the Spanish fleet could emerge from Cadiz to join it. 'I rather wished than expected the French would venture a general engagement with Admiral Keppel,' the King told North on 12 July, ever confident about the Royal Navy's superiority in any general action.[11]

When it was discovered on 17 July that the French fleet had been given formal orders from Paris to destroy British merchant shipping as well as naval vessels, the Cabinet had to decide whether to respond by carrying out similar reprisals on French merchant shipping. Rather than simply

---

* The most southerly point of the British Isles, in Cornwall.

issuing immediate Orders-in-Council to that effect, North wanted to call a formal Cabinet meeting, despite ministers being widely dispersed on their country estates for the summer holidays. 'It was so self-evident,' the King told North, 'there can be no reason to delay issuing the orders till a Cabinet is summoned. What is so clear ought never to be delayed for that formality.'[12] Keppel was therefore authorized to attack French merchant shipping right away, in one of the few examples of George having an immediate and decisive effect on wartime decision-making.

The first significant clash between the French and British fleets took place at Ushant off the coast of Brittany on 27 July. Keppel had twenty-nine ships-of-the-line and 1,950 guns against Admiral Comte d'Orvilliers' thirty and 2,280 guns. No ships were sunk or changed hands, but the French lost more men – 736 to 408 – and got back to safety at Brest as Keppel's fleet, with masts shot down, was largely immobilized. French hopes for an invasion in the short term were dashed, however. 'Some decisive blow is necessary to rouse the nation from a lethargy which may prove fatal,' the King had said when the fleet put out for battle. 'If unanimity and vigour is shown, Britain is capable to cope with her enemies.'[13]

Yet any such unanimity and vigour appeared in short supply as the entire naval officer corps from the Admiralty downwards – and much of Parliament – became deeply split over suggestions in an Opposition newspaper that the Rockinghamite Keppel's chance of a decisive victory had been stymied by the cowardice of his second-in-command, the pro-government Admiral Sir Hugh Palliser. When they returned to Portsmouth, *Victory* and *Formidable*, Keppel's and Palliser's flagships, were moored far apart in case their crews got into fights with each other. Keppel resigned, both men were tried at court martial and, while both were acquitted, Palliser's career was ended. This damaged Sandwich, who had taken his side throughout the debacle. At Brooks's, the betting book noted that 'Mr Fox bets Mr Hanger ten guineas Lord Sandwich is not First Lord of the Admiralty one calendar month after the decision of the court martial upon Keppel.'[14]

The King had responded to the threat of invasion by encouraging the raising of county militias. On 19 October he visited the summer manoeuvres at the huge Warley Camp in Essex, home to 11,000 men. He and the Queen stayed for two nights with their Roman Catholic friends Lord and Lady Petre at their nearby country house, Thorndon Hall. Despite the short stay, the royal visit cost the Petres the vast sum of £12,000 – although it was good for the local economy, with dairymen providing gallons of extra milk and cream, local women being taken on to work in the kitchens, and shopkeepers such as the grocers and tallow chandlers of Brentwood doing a roaring trade.[15] It ultimately paid off for Petre too; during anti-Catholic disturbances two years later, a unit of the Pembrokeshire Militia was stationed at his house 'to resist the attempts of the mobs'.[16]

There were obvious drawbacks to distributing large quantities of arms to militias, especially in those parts of the country that were still not considered wholly trustworthy by the government, such as mainly Catholic Ireland. In March 1779, some 40,000 Irish Protestant Volunteers signed up to defend Ireland from a French invasion, but as they were connected with the Opposition in the Irish Parliament who were pressing for commercial and constitutional concessions from Westminster, the North government regarded even them with hostility. Volunteer militias established in Scotland were swiftly disbanded again by Lord Suffolk. The government had no intention of warding off a French invasion only to face well-armed and well-trained Catholic or radical militias in Britain.

The King suggested that pikes should be distributed to 'the country people', but in September he was unenthusiastic about raising twenty-four companies of militia in Sussex because the Lord-Lieutenant there was the Duke of Richmond, and the King worried that it might 'enable him to bring forward his own creatures'.[17] It seems extraordinary that when the country was in the greatest danger of foreign invasion since 1688 the King was worried about the Opposition's use of militia commissions for social and political advancement, and that he was also advocating sending a large fleet to defend the West Indies. We can assume that he was not as worried about the immediate invasion threat as some other members of the government, such as Lord Sandwich.

The King was under no illusions about North's shortcomings as a war minister, however, and was becoming more testy about him. In November he wrote to John Robinson, the King's Party manager in the Commons, to complain that the Prime Minister 'must cast off his indecision and bear up, or no plan can succeed. He must be more exact in answering letters or let others do it for him; and he must let measures be thoroughly canvassed before [being] undertaken, and when adopted must not quit them.'[18] North had returned to his practice of regularly stating how unfit he was for office, while simultaneously promising to stay on for as long as the King wished. At 12.55 p.m. on 10 November he asked 'to quit the Treasury at the end of the session', telling the King from his grace-and-favour home at Bushy that 'In critical times, it is necessary that there should be one directing minister, who should plan the whole of the operations of government, and control all the other departments of administration so far as to make them cooperate zealously and actively with his designs even though contrary to their own.'[19] He asked for 'His Majesty's removing him as soon as he can, because he is certainly not capable of being such a minister'.[20]

The King, who was at Kew, wasted no time in replying; his letter to North was delivered to the demoralized Prime Minister by one of the King's Messengers.* By 2.52 p.m. on 10 November, the King had turned down North's request, reminding him that the duty 'of those in public stations must prompt them with zeal to make every effort to assist me, who have unreservedly assisted them'.[21]

North's sensible request for a centralized office with authority to coordinate the work of all departments was simply ignored. Had such a post been given to Germain or Sandwich, the war would certainly have been fought more energetically, though not necessarily to a better conclusion. Yet there were too few alternatives to North. Sandwich cared only for what interested him and was considered louche in a way that Grafton had somehow not been. As if Germain's difficult personality alone was not already a sufficient bar to his leadership, the public revelation of his probable bisexuality would doubtless have precipitated a furore. Shelburne was not trusted by anyone, with good reason. Charles Jenkinson and Robinson were excellent backroom operators, but hardly front-rank political personalities. Suffolk was politically insubstantial. Thurlow was a successful lawyer but offered little else. Amherst had no political base. The King knew that, if North fell, the Closet would be stormed by Rockingham and Fox, who were ideologically committed to giving America independence, so all the losses and cost of the previous three years of warfare would have been for nothing.

'It has ever been a certain position with me that firmness is the characteristic of an Englishman,' George wrote to North on 14 November, 'that consequently when a minister will show a resolution boldly to advance ... he will meet with support.'[22] Unfortunately, North was embarking on yet another of his depressive, passive-aggressive resignations and replied that 'He will certainly bear patiently the misery he feels from continuing in office because it is His Majesty's pleasure that he should continue there,' adding, 'he thinks it his duty once more to repeat that he is conscious and certain that he has neither the authority nor abilities requisite for the conduct of His Majesty's affairs.'[23]

The King understandably bridled at this, telling North that 'the word *authority* puzzles me, for from the hour of Lord North's so handsomely

---

* Founded by Charles II, its members were proficient horsemen and skilled in self-defence. (The last to be killed on duty was during the Napoleonic Wars.) They wore an oval gilt medal with a silver greyhound as their badge of office, and waited attentively in lobbies outside the King's study door to deliver his letters by hand at a fast pace. Couriers such as Roderick Ogg – referred to occasionally in the King's correspondence as 'Ogg the Messenger' – could easily deliver messages, wait and return with a reply in under two hours, especially in London.

devoting himself on the retreat of the D[uke] of Grafton, I have never had a political thought which I have not communicated unto him, have accepted of persons highly disagreeable to me because he thought they would be of advantage to his conducting public affairs, and have yielded to measures my own opinion did not quite approve.'[24] He therefore demanded 'an explanation in writing on what is meant to be conveyed by that word'. As the King had indeed allowed North to advise even on areas to which he did not generally allow politicians access – such as Court and Church appointments – he felt genuinely affronted. The relationship was clearly under strain. Nevertheless he ended his letter with an undaunted clarion call for bold measures to try to win the war:

> If Lord North can see with the same degree of enthusiasm I do the beauty, excellence, and perfection of the British constitution as by law established, and consider that, if any one branch of the Empire is allowed to cast off its dependency, that the others will infallibly follow the example, that consequently, though an arduous struggle, that is worth going through any difficulty to preserve to latest posterity what the wisdom of our ancestors have carefully transmitted to us, he will not allow despondency to find a place in his breast, but resolve not merely out of duty to fill his post, but will resolve with vigour to meet every obstacle that may arise, he shall meet with most cordial support from me; but the times require vigour or the state will be ruined.[25]

Ironically, given how greatly he and Burke disliked one another, George's view of the constitution and 'the wisdom of our ancestors' was positively Burkean – but written over a decade before Burke's sublime *Reflections on the Revolution in France* of 1790. Despite being encapsulated in a single unbroken sentence, the King's meaning was clear. With a divided Cabinet, a vacillating Prime Minister, the threat of invasion, an anti-war Opposition refusing to join the ministry, an Admiralty split into openly warring parties and a Spanish declaration of war expected imminently, the King at least would 'not allow despondency to find a place in his breast'.

As if the situation was not gloomy enough, on 21 December North informed the King of another credible plot to assassinate him, this time on his way to the theatre. George wanted the plot fully investigated but added with characteristic sangfroid, 'As to my own feelings, they always incline me to put trust where alone it can avail – in the Almighty Ruler of the Universe who knows what best suits his all-wise purposes.' He also pointed out a glaring flaw in the plan. 'This being the week I go to Holy Communion, I had no thoughts of going unto the play.'[26]

The year ended on a high note, however, when Colonel Archibald

21. Allan Ramsay's coronation portrait of 1762. No fewer than 179 copies were made, rendering it the most famous image of the King.

22. On 9 July 1776 the equestrian statue of George III on the Bowling Green in Lower Manhattan was pulled down by a revolutionary crowd. It was turned into 41,000 lead musket balls for the Continental Army.

23–25. (*left*) George Germain, 1st Viscount Sackville, formulated the strategic plan for fighting the war in America, but failed to ensure that it was properly executed; (*centre*) Frederick, Lord North, was a charming and good-natured peacetime prime minister, but a dismal wartime leader; (*right*) John Montagu, 4th Earl of Sandwich, was an able First Lord of the Admiralty but presided over the naval side of the American debacle.

26–30. (*top left*) General Sir Thomas Gage was overwhelmed by events in Boston, Lexington and Concord; (*top right*) General Sir John Burgoyne was outmanoeuvred and forced to surrender his army at Saratoga; (*centre*) General Sir William Howe failed to adhere to the Germain Plan and go to Burgoyne's rescue, but instead took the rebel capital of Philadelphia; (*bottom left*) General Lord Cornwallis occupied an indefensible peninsula at Yorktown and dallied there too long; (*bottom right*) General Sir Henry Clinton took over an impossible position in the final years of the war.

31. General George Washington, an inspired leader, whom George III eventually came to describe as 'the greatest character of the age'. He is here depicted with his enslaved valet and groom William Lee.

32. Thomas Paine, who described George as a 'royal brute' in his bestselling pamphlet *Common Sense* in 1776.

33. John Trumbull's painting of 1818 depicting the five-man drafting committee of the Declaration of Independence presenting their work to the Continental Congress on 28 June 1776. The Declaration's sublime language hid the fact that it was largely wartime propaganda – only two of its twenty-eight charges were true.

34. The great orator, philosopher and polemicist Edmund Burke started his career in opposition to George, but ended it as an enthusiastic ideological ally.

35. Charles Fox's open contempt for George helped to keep him out of high office for all but nineteen months in a political career of almost forty years.

36. The dissolution of Parliament in March 1784 depicted as a thunderbolt hurled by George on Pitt's behalf against Fox, Burke and North.

37. George, Prince of Wales, took friends gleefully to Windsor in November 1788 to witness his father's descent into severe bipolar disorder. Caricaturist Thomas Rowlandson denounces his lack of 'Filial Piety'.

38. Six thousand charity children occupied huge stands at St Paul's Cathedral for the national Service of Thanksgiving for the King's recovery, held on St George's Day in April 1789.

39. A letter from Queen Charlotte to George written the day after he was forcibly removed from Kew Palace in April 1801 reads, 'My dearest King . . . Our separation must be and really is equally painful to us both.'

My dearest King. Dr John Willis has made me very happy by putting into my Hands Your very Affectionnate Letter, which contains Your approbation of my Conduct which both my Inclination & Duty led me to fullfill & which will never cease but with my Life. Our Separation must be & really is equally painfull to us both & happy as it would make me & Your Children to come & see You, The Physicians assure me that such a meeting ought not to take place at present & therefore am under the painfull Necessity to deprive myself of so Satisfactory a pleasure which would prove a happiness to

Kew
April the 22d
1801.

Your tenderly attached Wife.
Charlotte

40. George, Prince of Wales, later George IV, was a mendacious, self-pitying spendthrift with a fine taste in art.

41. Queen Charlotte's hair went white overnight when her husband suffered his second bout of manic depression, as shown by Sir Thomas Lawrence in 1789.

42. In 1786 caricaturist James Gillray depicted the supposed venality of the King and Queen, who are here leaving the Treasury with gold coins pouring out of their pockets and being offered more by a sycophantic William Pitt the Younger while the Prince of Wales is bailed out by Philippe, Duc d'Orléans.

43. William Pitt addressing the House of Commons in 1793; Charles Fox can be seen wearing a hat by the Speaker's chair, seated sixth from the right.

Campbell with 3,500 men crushed a thousand rebels and captured Savannah, Georgia, in a daring amphibious attack on 29 December. A month later he seized the provincial capital, Augusta. Despite this southern success, however, and some British coastal raids on Virginia in May 1779, the coming year merely prolonged the strategic stalemate in America that had characterized the situation in the north for the second half of 1778. The Germain–Eden plan was for Clinton's main army in New York to keep the Continental Army contained, while large expeditions would be detached to recover individual provinces piecemeal. These gains would then be held and protected by the Loyalist militias as the regular army moved on. It meant that the war would take longer, but Germain and the King still saw no reason why it could not ultimately be won.

Admiral Keppel's court martial over the battle of Ushant opened in Portsmouth in January 1779, which Rockingham, Burke, Richmond and the Earl of Effingham all attended to show their support for their Whig friend and fellow MP. 'The Rockingham squadron', Horace Walpole for once accurately observed, 'treated the trial of Keppel as an affair of party rather than as a national one.'[27] Ladies even wore silk 'Keppel cockades' in their hats at the opera. When Keppel was acquitted by his fellow admirals on 11 February, the mob went on a rampage, smashing the windows of the houses of North and Germain, looting Sir Hugh Palliser's house in Pall Mall and forcing Sandwich to escape through the back garden of the Admiralty with his mistress, Martha Ray. The King offered his own guard to protect North when he went to the Commons, in order to 'prevent any riot'.[28] The next day, after the government had lost a vote which would have prevented MPs from being awarded unadvertised contracts, the King supported North further, saying, 'I am convinced this country will never regain a proper tone unless ministers as in the reign of King William will not mind being now and then in a minority, particularly on subjects that have always carried some weight with popular opinions.'[29]

When Lord Suffolk fell terminally ill in late February, the government considered moving the unpopular Sandwich to the Northern Department, filling his place as First Lord of the Admiralty with Admiral Howe. The price the Howe brothers demanded, however, was the dismissal of Germain and the award of a sinecure to Richard Howe worth £4,000 a year. The King, who liked and admired Richard Howe, was nonetheless outraged at this, telling North on 1 March, 'If Lord Howe would have come cordially into the Admiralty it might have been a popular appointment, but as he has added conditions that it would be disgraceful to grant, I am clear Lord Sandwich fills the Admiralty much better than any man in the kingdom would.'[30] After Suffolk's death on 7 March, therefore, the duties of the Northern secretaryship were taken over by Lord Weymouth, who was also Southern Secretary, creating far too much work for one person, particularly in wartime.

On 4 April, Martha Ray was murdered by an obsessed suitor, an ex-army chaplain named James Hackman, who shot her as she emerged from watching a comic opera at the Royal Opera House in Covent Garden. Although she and Lord Sandwich lived apart – his wife, Dorothy Fane, had been declared insane in 1767 – the pair made no secret of their relationship and conducted themselves as husband and wife. 'I am sorry Lord Sandwich has met with any severe blow of a private nature,' the King wrote to him, adding, 'the world scarcely contains a man so void of feeling as not to compassionate your situation.'[31] George normally preferred to ignore extramarital affairs whenever he could, but Sandwich had had nine children by Martha over sixteen years. Sandwich's nerve had already been severely shaken by the Keppel–Palliser affair, and now he had to beg Lord Bristol to postpone a censure motion against him in the House of Lords for the sake of their former friendship. Bristol did so, citing gout, an excuse that tended to elicit ready sympathy in the Upper House.

Although Burgoyne had not been allowed a court martial when he returned to England the previous year, the Commons formed itself into a Committee of the Whole House* from 22 April to 29 June to examine the conduct of the war, which soon turned into a political struggle between Sir William Howe and Burgoyne on one side (though they were mutually antagonistic over Howe's failure to come to Burgoyne's rescue) and Lord George Germain on the other as to who had been ultimately responsible for the strategy that had led to Saratoga. During the furore, the Howes' mother, the formidable Dowager Viscountess Howe, whose mother Sophia had been George I's acknowledged illegitimate half-sister, accused Germain of briefing against her sons to the newspapers, and then Germain's Under-Secretary, Christopher D'Oyly, resigned in the brothers' support.

In what appeared to be a further blow to Germain, the King chose not to cut the Howe brothers – cousins of his, albeit on the other side of the blanket – when they appeared at a Levee; Richard Howe was 'George III's favourite admiral if no one else's', and had not been responsible for the breakdown in communication between Germain and his brother William.[32] The Committee was finally adjourned at the end of the session without a vote, but the pamphlet war continued long afterwards, including the publication by William Howe of the speech he had made in the Commons in

---

* Used then as now for clause-by-clause debates on contentious Bills.

his own defence.[33] It did not answer the central question, however, of why he had abandoned the original Albany plan to go to Philadelphia instead, and without warning Burgoyne.[34]

In April 1779 France and Spain agreed to undertake an invasion of Britain, starting with two beachheads at Gosport and on the Isle of Wight. At Brooks's the next month, 'Lord Milford bets Lord Northington ten guineas to fifty guineas that the French will make an actual landing of one thousand men in Great Britain or Ireland before 1 November next.'[35] This led to a rash of bets about when, where and at what size – four thousand, ten thousand, fifteen thousand? – the invasion would take place, and how successful it would be. The French and Spanish were actually planning to land no fewer than 30,000 men, although they were having trouble agreeing upon the logistics beyond the establishment of the beachheads.

On 4 June, Lord North wrote to the King to support a suggestion from Thurlow that Lord Gower, the Lord President of the Council, take over from him as Prime Minister in a coalition government. Yet again North 'feels himself perfectly unequal to the present circumstances of the country', and urged the King to consider it seriously.[36] George simply ignored this, and a week later wrote North a clear and dignified letter which contained his thinking on the war.[37] Discussing Sir William Meredith's motion in the Commons that day to 'direct measures to restore peace', George told North of his yearning for 'the restoration of peace and solid happiness in every part of this empire', but added:

> There is no personal sacrifice I could not readily yield for so desirable an object, but at the same time no inclination to get out of the present difficulties which certainly keep my mind very far from a state of ease, can incline me to enter into what I look upon as the destruction of the Empire. I have heard Lord North frequently drop that the advantages to be gained by this contest could never repay the expense. I own that let any war be ever so successful if persons will set down and weigh the expenses they will find that as in the last [that is, the Seven Years War] that it has impoverished the state, enriched individuals, and perhaps raised the name only of the conquerors, but that is only weighing such events in the scale of a tradesman behind his counter . . . The present contest with America I cannot help seeing as the most serious in which any country was ever engaged . . . Whether the laying of a tax was deserving all the evils that have arisen from it, I suppose that no man could allege that without being thought more fit for Bedlam* than a seat in the senate,† but step by step the demands of America have risen. Independence

---

* The Bethlem Royal Hospital for the Insane.
† 'An assembly of counsellors' – that is, Parliament (*Johnson's Dictionary*).

is their object, that certainly is one that every man not willing to sacrifice every object to a *momentary and inglorious* peace must concur with me in thinking that this country can never submit to. Should America succeed in that, the West Indies must follow ... Ireland must soon follow the same plan and be a separate state, then this island would be reduced to itself, and soon would be a poor island indeed.[38]

If Britain were ever so reduced, the King believed, merchants would leave Britain for places with better economic prospects, 'shoals of manufacturers' would move to Canada, India and elsewhere, including America. (Adam Smith agreed that the collapse of Britain's Navigation Laws would signal the end of British sea power.) It therefore made sense, George thought, to act 'with firmness to make every effort to deserve success'. Instead of replying to these arguments, North wrote back feebly to say that he felt 'his own faculties of mind and body daily diminishing, and, he is sorry to say, that he thinks the difficulties of this country increasing'.[39]

On 16 June 1779, Spain formally declared war on Britain, and five days later a blockade by French and Spanish ships began the Great Siege of Gibraltar, which was to continue for the next three years, seven months and two weeks until the end of the war – ranking as one of the longest sieges of modern history. The defence by General George Eliott, its Governor, has been hailed as 'one of the great combined arms exploits of the British Armed forces'.[40] The Royal Navy was not yet the mighty machine of Nelson's day twenty years later, in terms of size, efficiency, financing, training or fighting quality, but it now had to operate simultaneously in five theatres – the Channel, Gibraltar, India, the West Indies and along the North American coastline – as well as fighting off privateers and transporting troops 3,000 miles across the Atlantic.

'The times are certainly hazardous,' the King wrote to North, 'but that ought to rouse the spirit of every Englishman to support me.'[41]* Writing to Sandwich, he remembered an earlier age when England had been under mortal threat. 'It was the vigour of mind shown by Queen Elizabeth and her subjects,' he told the First Lord of the Admiralty, 'added to the assistance of Divine Providence, that saved this island when attacked by the Spaniards. It is necessary to be active on the present occasion, and to bring the enemy as soon as possible to decisive action.'[42] He allowed himself a moment of paternal pride, telling Sandwich of Prince William, 'I am much

---

* The day after the Spanish declaration of war, Lord North's two-year-old son Dudley died. North burst into tears in the Commons, gaining great sympathy from independent MPs, although he was mocked for it by some Whigs. The King sent his condolences, of course, but did not consider it sufficient reason for North to resign.

pleased at the conduct of my little boy on his first entering the Navy. If all my servants in their different departments will be as zealous, I shall yet guide the bark* with honour out of its present difficulties.'[43] As well as the reference to his honour, there was an equally characteristic moment of self-righteousness: 'No want of exertions shall be found in me, and therefore I shall expect the same from others.' To Lord Weymouth he wrote, 'It is an hour that requires every exertion; despair should never be harboured but by those who cannot dare to examine that inward monitor who cannot disguise the truth.'[44]

On the same day that the Spanish began to besiege Gibraltar, Monday 21 June 1779, the King took the unprecedented step of summoning his ministers to Buckingham House. He wrote out the summons in his own hand, but without saying what he intended to do or say. No monarch had presided over a meeting of the Efficient as distinct from the Nominal Cabinet since the reign of Queen Anne. Germain gave his Under-Secretary William Knox an account of what the King did once they had congregated at 1 p.m. 'He desired them to walk into his library. He sat down at the head of his library table, and desired . . . all the ministers to sit down. He started by saying that Lord North had wanted to know why they were summoned, but he meant to tell them together.'[45] Germain told Knox that he 'began to think that they were going to be dismissed, and very probably they all thought the same thing'.

Instead, the King began by saying that since his accession he had tried to do his duty conscientiously to God and the British people, but that:

> There was no one action of his life that he could blame himself for but his changing his ministers in 1765, and consenting to the repeal of the Stamp Act. The minister he then brought in [Lord Rockingham] did not, he said, intend to repeal the Act until Lord Chatham and Camden made their declarations and they approved that fatal measure. Could he have foreseen the consequences, he certainly would not have passed the Act, but it was to the repeal that he imputed all the subsequent misfortunes.[46]

As for the accusations made against him by the Whigs and Congress, the King 'declared to God he had never harboured a thought of injuring the constitution, or abridging his people's liberties in the smallest instance', adding that he was 'particularly obliged to Lord North for taking up government when the Duke of Grafton deserted him'.[47]

The King went on to congratulate Lord Sandwich and the Admiralty

---

* 'Small ship' (*Johnson's Dictionary*).

on the speed of the naval rearmament programme, and Lord North and the Treasury for 'the very abundant manner in which the war in America had been supplied'. He also reminded the Cabinet that at the time of the appointment of Generals Howe, Clinton and Burgoyne 'everybody approved', as they had been 'thought the best in his service to command the troops'.[48] This was incontestably true: indeed Germain had once described the three generals in the Commons as 'the fittest men for the service in the army'.[49] Then, with characteristic melodrama, he said that it was 'His principle, and it was [his] resolution to part with his life rather than suffer his dominions to be dismembered, for he held it to be his duty to God and his people to preserve them entire at whatever hazard or inconvenience to himself. He therefore expected firmness and support from his ministers.'[50] If the government wanted to widen the 'bottom' of the ministry – that is, to take in another Opposition grouping – he would be open to the suggestion. He spoke for nearly an hour, not 'by way of speech or formal *harangue*',* Germain said, 'but as a plain narrative, delivered in conversation'.

To Lord North at 10.55 on the night of the meeting the King added, 'I hope after having so fully stated my sentiments this day to the Efficient Cabinet that I trust everyone felt how I am interested† in the present moment, and consequently will feel that they can alone hope for my support by showing zeal, assiduity and activity' in pursuing the war.[51] At the meeting, Thurlow had again raised the possibility of a coalition government under Gower, but the next day George told North, 'I own the Chancellor's language yesterday did not please me . . . It is no compliment when I say Lord Gower would be a poor substitute to Lord North.'[52] Afterwards, he wrote to Sandwich: 'I wish to hear whether, in the kind of stupor of some departments, my idea of speaking out hath not given some degree of confidence. If others will not be active, I must drive. I cannot say the Chancellor's idea of coalition met with my approbation.'[53] Later that same day he wrote again to North, 'What I said yesterday was the dictates of frequent and severe self-examination,' and with all that we know about George there is no reason to doubt it.[54] He told the Prime Minister that he believed that the 'Independency of America is still craved by the Opposition', but, he added, 'Before I will ever hear of any man's readiness to come into office, I will expect to see it signed under his hand that he is resolved to keep the Empire entire and that no troops shall be consequently

---

* A word that then did not have the connotation of hectoring. 'A popular oration' (*Johnson's Dictionary*).

† In the sense of 'concerned' (*Johnson's Dictionary*) rather than fascinated.

withdrawn from thence, nor independence ever allowed.'[55] He then considered what Great Britain should do if France and Spain attacked her. 'Whenever an attempt is made on Ireland I should think they will also make one on this island to keep men's minds in suspense and consequently try to work on the passions.'[56] He recalled of the Jacobite rebellion that 'When a few ragged Highlanders could alarm the nation, there is no doubt twenty thousand men landed in England and ten thousand in Ireland would cause great fear.'[57]

It was quite true that 6,000 Highlanders under Bonnie Prince Charlie had terrified Hanoverian England when they reached Derby in his grandfather's reign, and now he was – with equanimity, but under no illusions – facing an invasion force five times that number. The King believed, as he put it to North, 'had not Spain now thrown off the mask that we should have soon found the colonies sue for pardon to the mother country. I do not yet despair that with the activity Clinton is inclined to adopt [probably a reference to the Southern Expedition], and the Indians in the rear, that the provinces will even now submit.'[58]*

The King's idea that America was on the verge of suing for peace was quite wrong. Nevertheless he returned to it five days later, telling North of an opinion he had:

> long entertained that America, unless this summer supported by a Bourbon fleet, must sue for peace . . . but that propositions must come from them to us, no further ones be sent from hence; they ever tend only to increase the demands. I can never agree to healing over an uncured wound, it must be probed to the bottom; if it then proves sound, no one will be more ready to forget offences, but no one sees more forcibly the necessity of preventing the like mischief by America's feeling she has not been a gainer by the contest; yet after that I would show that the parent's heart is still affectionate to the penitent child.[59]

Here is further evidence that George would not have hanged Franklin, Rush, Gerry or the other signatories of the Declaration, either together or separately.

Although d'Estaing's fleet had left Boston for the West Indies, where it had captured St Vincent and Grenada by 4 July, it then double-backed to British-held Savannah, to which it helped lay siege in September and

---

* Conor Cruise O'Brien believed that the statement proves that the King had a 'relish for the use of Indians against the settlers', because he 'had long urged the use of greater ferocity in crushing the Americans' (O'Brien, *Great Melody* p. 208). No evidence was provided for the King's supposed ferocity, because there is none.

October. The Americans were now clearly being 'supported by a Bourbon fleet'. With the Royal Navy split into Keppel and Palliser camps, Richard Howe in the Opposition in Parliament and another vice-admiral ill, the greatest invasion threat since the Spanish Armada had to be met by bringing the sixty-two-year-old Admiral Sir Charles Hardy out from his governorship of the Greenwich Hospital in July. The King supported the appointment and had great faith that he would be victorious. 'I trust in Divine Providence, the justice of our cause, the bravery and activity of my navy,' he told his premier on 20 July. 'I wish Lord North would view it in the same light for the ease of his mind.'[60] Four days later he added, 'I may appear strange, but I undoubtedly wish for the action and feel a confidence in the success that never attended any other event.'[61]

Hardy sailed with thirty-nine ships-of-the-line a hundred miles off the Scilly Isles to intercept any Franco-Spanish invasion of Ireland and to help shepherd important convoys into the English Channel. Meanwhile, every ship in the navy capable of firing a gun was pressed into service, even those listed on official records as 'unfit to leave harbour', 'irreparable', 'unfit to weather a storm', and so on.[62]

Britain had only 21,000 regular cavalry and infantry to counter an invasion, and 30,000 militia, so Amherst elected not to defend the coasts but instead to concentrate his forces inland. He left garrisons at Portsmouth, Plymouth and Chatham, but otherwise there were so few troops that the whole of Cornwall was defended by a single regiment of militia. Hardy, meanwhile, was inundated with advice from everybody, ranging from the King and Lord Mulgrave, the senior naval member of the Admiralty Board, who suggested he fight immediately despite staggeringly bad odds, to others such as Lord Sandwich who suggested he stay out at sea, while others advised that he come into port.[63] One advantage of having so experienced an admiral at the helm was that he had the self-confidence to ignore them all.

The year 1779 deserves to be remembered alongside 1588 and the Spanish Armada, 1803 with Napoleon at Boulogne, and 1940 and the Battle of Britain, as a moment of imminent, existential danger for the British Isles. Yet as the King had told North on 18 July, 'I own I have not the smallest anxiety if the ships under the command of Sir Charles Hardy can bring the combined fleet of the enemies to a close action.'[64] Of that belief, Sandwich's biographer Nicholas Rodger has written that the King had 'all the qualities of leadership which his chief minister so badly needed, and in the supreme crisis of his reign he was ready, indeed eager to stake his kingdom on a battle against fearful odds'.[65] These became clearer on 15 August when the British warship *Marlborough* sighted sixty-three enemy ships-of-the-line off Plymouth Sound, carrying an invasion force of 30,000 regulars. An enemy fleet was in possession of the English Channel for the first time since William III landed to overthrow James II nine decades earlier.[66]

Hardy received the news on 17 August and sailed back as fast as he could, but he was caught in an easterly wind that made progress slow. The King wanted a battle – 'Decision is the joy of my life,' he wrote – but the Channel Fleet was still dangerously far away.[67] Thankfully, Admiral d'Orvilliers was encountering major problems of his own: he was becalmed off Plymouth, his water and provisions were low, he did not know where the British fleet was, and he had disease on board so that the number of sick equalled the healthy, and 'so many dead were going overboard that Devon gave up eating fish.'[68] He then received a change of orders, to land at Falmouth, allowing Marshal Noël de Vaux to hold Cornwall as a bridgehead. The same wind that had kept Hardy west of the Scilly Isles meant that by the 20th the French fleet was still 50 miles south-south-west of the Lizard. It was only on the 25th that d'Orvilliers finally learned of Hardy's whereabouts.

On 29 August, after a change of wind, Hardy sighted the enemy off the Scillies. There followed a long, nerve-wracking standoff, during which d'Orvilliers did not engage Hardy despite his large numerical advantage in ships, but nor, thanks to the weather, could he disembark his large invasion force on the largely unprotected Cornish coast. 'I believe this country was never in so perilous a situation as it is at present,' Charles Jenkinson wrote in early September, 'and the events of the next fortnight will probably be as important as ever were known in history.'[69] The King was fully engaged in the crisis, exchanging letters and memoranda with Sandwich on an almost daily basis. In the first week of September they discussed the 24-pounders needed to defend Torbay; the draught of a boom intended to be laid across Plymouth harbour; the speed of supply of beer for the sailors; the number of men (824) on the sick list; the danger of the fleet being attacked at anchor; 'the most amiable and promising midshipman' Prince William (it did Sandwich no harm to praise him to George); which ships had left which harbours and when; the contrasting capabilities of Admirals Keppel and Howe; and 'the present state of the victualling of the fleet'.[70] With his country in mortal danger, George was highly attentive to every detail, without seeking to distract Sandwich from his central tasks. He had been pressing the First Lord since late July to engage the enemy combined fleet, as otherwise 'the whole nation must either be so intimidated or so disgusted as to produce universal confusion'.[71]

On 4 September, when six more ships-of-the-line had joined Hardy's fleet, bringing up his strength to forty-five, the King wrote, 'I am certain he could never have wished to take so glorious a command without feeling that ardour which ought to inspire every Englishman at this hour; therefore I am certain he will be willing to meet these faithless* people. The spirit of the fleet gives me the fullest confidence that with the blessing of the Almighty, France will now severely feel that chastisement which so infamous a conduct deserves.'[72] Even though some of Hardy's ships had been at sea since May and were down to just a single week of water remaining, the King ordered Sandwich to 'acquaint the Admiral that I expect the enemy is not permitted to quit the Channel without feeling that chastisement which so base a conduct deserves'.[73] Hardy ignored all such peremptory orders, held his nerve and adopted the tactics necessary to see off the danger at a time when a naval defeat would have meant certain invasion. Fog dictated that the fleets caught sight of one another only once, and, after a suspenseful week, on 11 September d'Orvilliers returned to Brest, the sailors on the packed lower decks of his ships riddled with illness. The Channel's autumn weather meant that Britain was now safe until the spring.

No sooner was the combined fleet's retreat known than the King pressed a reluctant Lord Sandwich to dispatch ships to Gibraltar, Minorca, Jamaica and Barbados, and to try to recapture Dominica, which had fallen to the French in September 1778. 'I see the difficulties of the times but I know nothing advantageous can be obtained without some hazard,' he told the First Lord:

> I very clearly see that if we alone attend to home security that every valuable possession will be lost before any effort is made to any other tendency but making the country secure against foreign invasion ... Perhaps no man in my dominions has a mind more ready to bear up against misfortunes, but then I must feel that all that could have been done has [been]; it is by bold and manly efforts nations have been preserved not pursuing alone the line of home defence.[74]

Here too George's martial spirit might have been seen as Churchillian if the outcome had been different. George summed up his overall strategy to Sandwich on 10 September: 'We must risk something, otherwise we shall only vegetate in this war. I own I wish either to get through it with spirit, or with a crash be ruined.'[75]

Once France and Spain had joined the conflict, the King recognized that

---

* Meant in the sense of 'perfidious' (*Johnson's Dictionary*), because the French had gone to war opportunistically.

Britain's war aims had moved on from the defence of Parliament's rights under the constitution to Britain's very survival as a great power. In a letter to Sandwich from Windsor on 13 September, he argued that now d'Orvilliers was no longer a short-term threat, the West Indian squadron needed to be increased by at least seven ships-of-the-line from the Channel squadron, otherwise there would be a huge increase in the interest rates that would be charged on British debt: 'Our islands must be defended even at the risk of an invasion of this island; if we lose our sugar islands it will be impossible to raise money to continue the war and then no peace can be obtained.'[76] It was a stark reminder of how important the West Indies always were to Britain's strategic calculations.

Unlike Sandwich, Germain fully agreed with this analysis, and argued that the loss of the West Indian island of St Vincent to d'Estaing in June showed the dangers of the timidity shown by Sandwich and Amherst. They wanted to keep forces in Britain, not to send troops and ships to Jamaica to threaten the Spanish West Indies and New Orleans. In the end, the King and North had to decide between Germain and Amherst, and they went for the former, releasing four regiments for service in Jamaica in January 1780. Yet, for all of Germain's support for the King's strategic views, George recognized that he still had questions to answer over Saratoga.

When North wanted to bring Carlisle into the government, and gave him Germain's post at the Board of Trade in November, the King would not offer Germain a peerage in compensation. 'He has not been of use in his department,' he wrote of the man with overall responsibility for the war strategy, 'and nothing but the most meritorious could have wiped off his former misfortunes,' in a reference to Minden and the Germain Plan.[77] As Colonial Secretary, Germain retained control of grand strategy, however. The King could be tough on senior Cabinet ministers: when the question of an inquiry arose about the responsibility of Lord Amherst and the Ordnance Office for the lamentable state of Plymouth's readiness during the French invasion threat, George told North, 'If they can defend themselves I do not see that any evil can arise. If they have not done their duty it is right it should be known.'[78]

He was now willing to take serious risks with home defence, telling Sandwich:

We must be ruined if every idea of offensive war is to lie dormant until this island is thought in a situation to defy attacks . . . If ministers will take a firm decided part and risk something to save the Empire, I am ready to be foremost on the occasion, as my stake is the deepest; but if nothing but measures of caution are pursued and further sacrifices are made from a want to boldness, which alone can preserve a state when hard-pressed, I shall certainly not think myself obliged after a conduct shall have been held so contrary to my opinion, to screen them from the violence of an enraged nation.[79]

It was not that different a threat from the one that the Duke of Richmond had made against Sandwich the previous year. 'The King had grasped the central truth of the British situation. That the threat of invasion at home must be boldly outstared.'[80]

Although Sandwich, North and other Cabinet members besides Germain were unconvinced, their meetings rarely decided anything. No Northern Secretary had been appointed since Suffolk's death in early March, and the meetings themselves took place in ministers' homes as much as at Downing Street, a further sign of how little North saw himself as leading the government. There were long silences during meetings when the Prime Minister was depressed, and discursively general discussions from which no action emerged. As no one took any minutes, nothing was put in writing about what had been agreed, except some very generalized conclusions that were sometimes, but not always, sent on to the King by the minister of the department concerned. 'Will your Lordship . . . allow me to lament the state of our Cabinet meetings,' Sandwich remonstrated to North in mid-September, 'and to point out to you how absolutely necessary it is that you should take the lead among us, and not suffer any question . . . that is not decided and carried into execution.'[81] Yet nothing came of it, even though there were important issues to be discussed, quite aside from the war. In mid-November there were riots against customs duties in Dublin, and for two days the authorities lost control of the Irish capital.

On 19 November, Charles Jenkinson, the Secretary at War, wrote to tell the King of another attempt to replace North with Lord Gower, led by government supporters such as Thurlow, Richard Rigby, the ambitious Scottish MP Henry Dundas and others. 'I am more and more persuaded that it is the plan of the whole of this party to drive Lord North out of Your Majesty's service,' he warned.[82] They hoped to achieve this by encouraging their friends to vote against the government, and 'do everything they can by representation and intimidation' short of actually asking the King to dismiss him. What marked this coup attempt distinctly from others was that its proposed victim seems to have been entirely unconcerned about whether or not it succeeded. Five days later, however, it was clear that it had failed, and Gower resigned as Lord President of the Council, ostensibly over the government's handling of the Irish crisis, but more probably over the failure of his own premiership bid.

Gower's departure forced a reshuffle, with Lord Bathurst taking over as Lord President of the Council and Weymouth retiring from both his secretaryships of state, the Northern going to Lord Stormont and the Southern to Lord Hillsborough. 'The die is cast, and nothing is left but to fight as well as we can,' North wrote to the King. 'These crosses and these alarms are distressing, and absolutely drive Lord North to madness.'[83] He was writing about his Cabinet, not the world war, but now that the three posts the Bedfordites had vacated had been filled by the two Northites Bathurst and Hillsborough and the King's Friend Stormont,* the Prime Minister was actually in a stronger political position within the government than he had been before the attempt to oust him.

A few weeks earlier, Charles Fox had told the Commons that 'The present reign offers one uninterrupted series of disgrace, misfortune, and calamity.' Now, in the Debate on the Address on 25 November 1779, he launched the most outspoken ad hominem attack on a monarch by a parliamentarian since the Jacobite rebellion. In contrast to the glorious opening of George's reign, he claimed, there was now only 'his empire dismembered, his councils distracted, his people falling off in their fondness for his person'.[84] He equated George with the autocrat Catherine the Great, except that whereas the Tsarina's empire was 'rising into eminence', George's had 'sunk into contempt'.[85] He then compared George to Henry VI, whose family did not claim the throne by hereditary right; 'it was by revolutions that they both obtained it.' He reprised Junius' threat when he stated that George's 'claim to the throne of this country was founded only upon the delinquency of the Stuart family, a circumstance which should never be for one moment out of His Majesty's recollection'.

Fox was not alone in the vehemence of his views. Earlier that month Rockingham had written to Burke, 'I think the means of power, and the means of corrupt influence of the Crown must soon submit to be shorn. NB: I much prefer the shears to the hatchets.'[86] Whether by Fox's hatchets or Rockingham's shears, the King recognized that his powers under the constitution might not survive a defeat in America. George was unimpressed, therefore, when he received a letter from Lord North that clearly attempted to shift the blame on to him for the way the war was going.[87] 'I have never interfered in any of their departments,' North said of his

---

* The appointment of Stormont particularly pleased the King, as he had long promoted the idea of former diplomats being promoted to foreign policymaking roles, and Stormont had been an effective ambassador in Vienna, Warsaw and Paris. George valued expertise, but such was the cult of the inspired amateur in the politics of the day that of the ten Northern secretaries between 1761 and 1782, seven had no diplomatic experience, and similarly only two of the eight Southern secretaries had served abroad (Horn, *British Diplomatic Service* p. 109).

Cabinet colleagues. 'I have never clashed with their views – but promoted their interest as much as lay in my power on every occasion. I have always made common cause with them.'[88] He did not want to be the sole scapegoat.

'I am not equal in abilities to the station which I ought to hold,' North tediously lamented yet again. 'The truth of this I have often acknowledged and the consciousness of this has often made me think myself criminal in remaining where I am.' He then resorted to pure pathos:

> I have been miserable for ten years in obedience to Your Majesty's commands, but since Your Majesty has now formed your opinion that I have been a great cause of this mischief, I hope Your Majesty has determined to permit me soon to retire . . . for it is impossible to bear misery and guilt at the same time, for I must look upon it as a degree of guilt to continue in office while the public suffers and nobody approves my conduct.[89]

Of course, under the constitution they both revered, North did not actually need the King's permission to resign any more than Chatham or Grafton had.

To this searingly personal letter, George merely replied that the feeling among the City of London merchants was 'that though they might in some things have blamed [the government for] the conduct of affairs, they thought much worse of the Opposition and that consequently a change must be disadvantageous to the public'.[90] He was probably correct in thinking that the fall of North after nine years in power, four of which had been spent unsuccessfully fighting an unpopular war, would result in the Opposition storming his Closet and giving independence to the Americans. He therefore felt he had to keep his irresolute, depressed and politically damaged Prime Minister, while providing such boosts to morale as he could.

On 28 November, Jenkinson wrote to the King about North's depression: 'I look upon all this as nothing permanent, but as a disease of the mind, which goes and comes, and which as long as it lasts is very unpleasant to those who have anything to do with him.'[91] (This was a prescient summation of George's own subsequent illness.) Two days later, Jenkinson wrote again to report that he had seen John Robinson, who 'states in the strongest and most alarming manner the distracted state of Lord North's mind'.[92] Jenkinson told the King that North had threatened that he could no longer sit in the same Cabinet as Lord Thurlow, and 'There is much passion in all this.'

Relationships in any government become strained over time and in those that are losing wars can become toxic. North was understandably infuriated when he somehow saw a letter of the King's to Robinson criticizing him.[93] The King had now asked Jenkinson to keep a close eye on North. 'I cannot help feeling in the strongest manner the very disagreeable situation in which Lord North puts Your Majesty almost every day,' the Secretary at War wrote at 4.50 p.m. on 30 November, warning that he was 'convinced' there was now another Thurlow-backed plot to replace North, this time with Lord Shelburne, and that North himself seemed to be all in favour of it.[94] At 11 p.m. Jenkinson wrote again to say that North 'appeared in good spirits, but I fear his spirits are not to be relied on for any time'.[95]

Jenkinson was effectively spying on North for the King, telling him that the Prime Minister was saying openly that he was remaining in office only because the King would not let him resign. Jenkinson thought this 'detrimental to Your Majesty' because 'every public calamity will be charged hereafter to the account of Your Majesty,' which was probably North's intention.[96] Although the King has been criticized by historians for asking Jenkinson and Robinson to report on North's moods and feelings, far from being a sinister example of royal intrigue it was more likely intended to learn how to bolster him and keep him in office. Because the relationship between individual Cabinet ministers and the monarch was far more direct in the eighteenth century than later, and Jenkinson had been the leader of the King's Friends since the fall of Bute, he felt loyalty much more to the King than to North.

'Your Majesty cannot get at the bottom of the whole business too soon,' Jenkinson wrote from his house in Park Street on 1 December about a new attempt to replace North, this time with Shelburne. George responded by sending a peremptory note to the chief plotter Thurlow, ordering him 'to cast aside all private pique and animosity and cordially unite in the service of the state'.[97] It worked, and Jenkinson reported that although North was 'very much fatigued and ill' it was hoped that he would 'alter his language' when he returned to health.[98]

If North fell, he would probably have to be replaced by either Rockingham or Shelburne, both of whom wanted to end the American war, although on different terms. Rockingham would gladly allow America her independence, and would thereafter try to foster good relations in order to rupture the Franco-American alliance, whereas Shelburne still wanted some sort of negotiated imperial condominium. Horace Walpole, whose political antennae were undimmed by his clear bias, was thus correct when he noted that the King 'had nobody to put in [North's] place'.[99] George had himself told Germain back in June that 'Although he [North] is not entirely to my mind, and there are many things about him I wish were changed, I don't know any who would do so well, and I have a great regard for him and a very good opinion of him.'[100] It was a harsh thing to say to Germain, who still thought of himself as a worthy alternative, but who was widely hated and stood no real chance of becoming Prime Minister.

On 7 December at Brooks's, 'Mr Craufurd bets Mr John Crewe MP fifty [guineas] that Lord North is not [prime] minister [on] the 1st of April 1780.'[101] For John Craufurd of Dromsoy to win his wager, there would have to be a near-revolution in Parliament. Of the 558 MPs in the Commons, Rockingham had around eighty followers, Shelburne a dozen or so, Gower and Weymouth (the old Bedford group) a dozen, whereas as Prime Minister Lord North could almost always count on nearly 200. In 1780, the government payroll vote contained around fifty government officials, thirty sinecurists, twenty-five court officials, sixty-five military and naval officers, eleven contractors and eleven holders of Secret Service pensions.* In 1761 the figure had been around 250, so in reality the power of the Crown was not increasing, at least in the Commons.[102]†

Outside Parliament, the Opposition were in a much stronger position in their attacks on the government, and they concentrated on the cost of the Crown to the taxpayer and the supposed corruption surrounding the Civil List and the Secret Service Fund, as well as the King's constitutional powers. At a meeting on 30 December in the York Assembly Rooms of 600 Yorkshire gentlemen – who, Rockingham told the House of Lords, represented a total income of £800,000 a year – a petition was signed for 'Economical Reform' and an inquiry into 'the gross abuses in the expenditure of public money' in the Civil List, the reduction of 'exorbitant emoluments' and the abolition of 'sinecure places and unmerited pensions'.[103]

The leader of this 'out-of-doors' movement – meaning outside Parliament – was a landowner, the Rev. Dr Christopher Wyvill of the North Riding, who provocatively described the Yorkshire Association meeting as a 'Congress'. This was a taxpayers' rebellion against government waste, at a time of low wheat prices, high land taxes, a National Debt of £167 million and more taxation in the pipeline to pay for the war. It reflected generally straitened economic circumstances as much as any personal attack on the King, but it was directed at Crown income and expenditure

---

* Today there are eighty-five ministers, fifteen trade envoys and more than fifty parliamentary private secretaries on the so-called payroll vote in the House of Commons, totalling over 150.
† The number of MPs holding royal bedchamber appointments fell from sixteen in 1762 to eight in 1780, for example, due to what one historian has described as 'the King's concern for economy, virtue and aristocracy in the making of household appointments, and his refusal, from a sense of justice and obligation, to deprive old servants of their places when they fell out of the ranks in the Commons' (Christie, *Myth and Reality* p. 299).

and came from the normally conservative gentry. It quickly spread from Yorkshire into a wider movement until there were twenty-eight county associations and plans being made for a national assembly. The Economical Reform movement was generally in favour of peace, but somewhat contradictorily not of American independence. Its most radical members drew parallels between the English monied gentlemen in the American Congress rebelling against Crown exactions and what was going on at home.

The Yorkshire Association called for a radical overhaul of representation in Parliament, with annual elections and a hundred more county members. (Sheffield, with a population of 32,000 people, did not have a single MP to itself, for example.) A petition by Wyvill was presented at Westminster on 8 February 1780, and three days later Edmund Burke introduced into the Commons his own scheme for Economical Reform, which proposed abolishing about sixty government places, a measure that would have greatly weakened the government in Parliament.[104] Burke's speech proposing what he called his 'Plan for the Better Security of the Independence of Parliament and the Economical Reformation of the Civil and Other Establishments' called eloquently for a radical reform of the civil establishment in order to weaken the executive and covered no fewer than seventy-two columns of the *Parliamentary History*.* North described it as 'one of the most able he had ever heard'.[105]

Lord Shelburne led the Economical Reform movement in the Lords, and together he and Burke proposed abolishing several commissioners of the Board of Trade at £1,000 per annum each, three at the Board of Works and six at the Board of the Green Cloth (the officials who ran the royal household), as well as publishing the names of Civil List pension recipients, forming a committee to oversee the accounts and proposing a Contractors Bill to prevent anyone owning a government contract from becoming an MP, which would affect seventeen of them. They also wanted to abolish the colonial secretaryship, on the grounds that the war was already lost.

The King saw Economical Reform for what it clearly was – a full-scale attack on his powers and influence, albeit clothed as one on waste and corruption – and naturally watched the process of what he called 'Mr Burke's *extraordinary* Bill' closely, worried by the narrowness of some divisions in late February when the government's majority fell to as little as seven.[106] He told North that the Bill was also intended 'to circumscribe the power of the Crown to show its benevolence to persons in narrow circumstances'.[107] Fortunately for George, even at his lowest ebb North remained an astute parliamentary operator and succeeded in removing

---

* The unofficial precursor to Hansard.

many of the Bill's clauses piecemeal. It had nonetheless been a close-run thing, and it keenly underlined why George still needed him.

'I do believe that America is nearer coming into temper to treat than perhaps at any other period,' the King told North in late December 1779, 'and if we arrive in time at Gibraltar, Spain will not succeed in that attack.'[108] He was being absurdly optimistic about America but not about Gibraltar, where Admiral Sir George Rodney won a night-time sea battle off Cape St Vincent in southern Portugal on 16 January 1780, capturing six Spanish ships-of-the-line and destroying one more, temporarily relieving the besieged Rock nine days later.

At the end of January, despite the Royal Navy's success, Catherine the Great declared that Russia would protect her trade against all belligerents in the American War of Independence (principally meaning Britain) and formed a League of Armed Neutrality that was subsequently joined by Denmark in July, by Sweden in August and over the next two years by Prussia, Austria and Naples. This posed a direct threat to the British blockade of French and Spanish supplies to the United States, since the League threatened to prevent the Royal Navy from boarding vessels at will to check cargoes. Much of the navy's stores came from the Baltic, including the best timber for masts. Britain's lack of friends and allies in Europe beyond Germany was the direct result of successive governments' policy of avoiding European commitments after the Seven Years War, and it left Britain dangerously vulnerable when its various antagonists elected to band together.

'It will be asked why, when we have as great, if not a greater force than we ever had, the enemy is superior to us,' Sandwich candidly told the House of Lords. His explanation, blunt but undeniable, was that the French had:

> no other war or object to draw off their attention and resources. We unfortunately have an additional war on our hands which essentially drains our resources and employs a very considerable part of our army and navy: we have no friend or ally to assist us. On the contrary, all those who ought to be our allies except Portugal act against us in supplying our enemies with the means of equipping their fleets.[109]

In July 1782 even Portugal joined the League. After all that Britain had done to protect her oldest ally from Spain in the Seven Years War, the King was disgusted. The situation in Europe represented a failure of diplomacy by successive British governments, and made the American war even harder to fight.

In America, General Clinton had withdrawn troops from Newport on

11 October 1779 and sailed with 8,000 men to attack Charleston on 26 December, leaving the experienced German veteran General Wilhelm von Knyphausen in command of New York City. Georgia had been recovered by a relatively small force in late 1778, and the American Department in London wanted to start a more general fightback against the rebellion in the South.[110] Clinton and Cornwallis disembarked near rebel-held Charleston, the largest and richest city in the South, and besieged it from 29 March 1780, their force augmented with an extra 3,000 men in the meantime.

On 12 May, the American General Benjamin Lincoln surrendered Charleston and its 5,466 soldiers and around a thousand sailors, along with their ships, cannon, muskets and ammunition, for the loss of only 265 British casualties.[111] It was easily the greatest British victory of the war, because when New York and Philadelphia had fallen their garrisons had escaped.[112] As well as capturing a large part of the Southern rebel field army, it opened a new theatre of operations in the region; although Clinton returned to New York City, he left Cornwallis in South Carolina with 8,000 men. Had a victory on the same scale been won in the north in 1775 or 1776 it might have doomed the rebellion.

17

Disaster at Yorktown

March 1780–October 1781

Mr Elliot bets Lord George Cavendish five guineas that before 1st January 1781 the colonies will have given up their claim of independence.

Brooks's Club Betting Book, 26 December 1779

'The country that will hazard the most will get the advantage in this war,' the King wrote to Lord Sandwich on 6 March 1780. 'By keeping our enemies employed, we shall perplex them more than by a more cautious, and consequently less active, line of conduct.'[1] Yet still he and Germain could only persuade Sandwich to send six ships-of-the-line to the North American station under Admiral Thomas Graves. Sandwich's fear of an invasion of the British mainland had led to Admiral Byron being sent out too late to counter d'Estaing in America in the summer of 1779 and Admiral Rodney being delayed that autumn. It now prevented Graves from having enough ships in 1780. 'Germain and George III strove to win the initiative by boldness and surprise,' states one historian of the war, 'and to gain a local superiority in a vital theatre that would lead to victory.'[2] But the cautious Sandwich stymied all three naval expeditions to a greater or lesser degree, leaving the Royal Navy regularly outgunned in the Americas.

Writing to North on 7 March, the King emphasized how existential he believed the struggle had become now that France and Spain were involved:

I can never suppose this country so far lost to all ideas of self-importance as to be willing to grant America independence. If that could ever be universally adopted, I shall despair of this country being ever preserved from a state of inferiority and consequently falling into a very low class among the European states. If we do not feel our own consequence, other nations will not treat us above what we esteem ourselves. I hope never to live to see that day, for however I am treated I must love this country.[3]

As so often, there was an element of melodrama here, but on this occasion it was soon justified. On 6 April, John Dunning MP, a Shelburnite who sat for Calne in Wiltshire and was a fervent admirer of Burke, carried by 233 votes to 215 what became a celebrated motion in the Commons, 'That the influence of the Crown has increased, is increasing, and ought to be diminished'.[4] A large number of independent country gentlemen had trooped into the aye lobby, signalling defeat for North.

Describing it as 'a considerable majority', even though it was only eighteen in a vote totalling 448, North predictably took the Dunning motion as another opportunity to try to resign, writing, 'It is absolutely necessary that I should be permitted to retire.'[5] Yet the King replied at 7.50 the next morning that the votes could 'by no means be looked upon as personal to him [that is, North]; I wish I did not feel at whom they are *personally levelled*', that is, himself.[6] Four days later he was assuring North that his parliamentary support:

> will return, for it cannot be the wish of the majority to overturn the constitution. Factious leaders and ruined men wish it, but the bulk of the nation cannot see it in that light. I therefore shall undoubtedly be assisted in preserving this excellent constitution ... It is my attachment to my country that alone actuates my purposes and Lord North shall see that at least there is one person willing to preserve unspoiled the most beautiful combination that ever was framed.[7]

Dunning's other resolution, that 'it is competent to this House to examine into and correct abuses in the expenditure of the Civil List revenues, as well as in every other branch of the public revenue', was also passed that night. Periodic scrutiny of the Civil List was affirmed without a division. Dunning's motions were not calling for the influence of the Crown to be destroyed altogether, rather that the Opposition should be given a better chance to challenge the government in divisions and at elections.[8] Eighteenth-century politics was not about fairness but about power, and the places, pensions and peerages that underpinned that power. If their numbers could be minimized by Burke and his supporters, such as Dunning, the power of the Crown would undoubtedly wane. When the Opposition carried a further motion saying that the House had to redress the abuse, Walpole wrote, 'The blow seems to me decisive.'[9]

Yet the country gentlemen who would gladly see lower taxes and government spending did not necessarily also want annual or reformed parliaments, and they certainly did not want to embarrass the King over his household expenditure and Court appointments. For all that he was a disastrous war minister, North was a deft party manager, adept at driving wedges between radical Whigs and conservative-minded country MPs who were worried that the war was going badly. On 13 April he managed to get enough independent MPs on his side to throw out Burke's Contractors Bill. Far from being a harbinger of more responsible government, Dunning's motions were to help cause a pro-government backlash at the time of the next general election. By the autumn, it was being openly stated in Opposition circles that Charles I and George III had several despotic things in common, and that victory in America would mean an increase in monarchical powers in Britain. Charles Fox of course promoted both views assiduously.

On 24 April, the House of Commons saw its largest gathering in living memory.[10] Another motion by Dunning, that Parliament should not be prorogued or dissolved until various grievances such as Burke's Economical Reform Bill was passed, failed by fifty-one votes, confirming the King in his calm confidence. 'It is culpable for men at an hour like this to stand neuter,' he told North the next day, especially when the Opposition had 'what no one can deny is a plan of changing the constitution'.[11] He was correct in this, as the dissolution of Parliament had long been a Crown rather than Commons prerogative, and indeed the same motion – that Parliament should not be prorogued until grievances were addressed – had been passed by the revolutionary Long Parliament just before the Civil War.

It had been a worrying time for the Court and government, but the combination of Robinson's and Jenkinson's efficient organization, the King's calmness and North's parliamentary skills had seen them through. North had put in the long hours needed in the Commons, talking happily with MPs of all factions about their concerns. He could explain complicated issues simply and without any sense of apparent superiority, and even enjoyed jokes made at his own expense.[12] Though there were few victories in America, North could still win at Westminster.

In common with many conservatively minded people, the King was very conscious of the thinness of civilization's veneer. This was brought vividly home to Londoners in the vicious, week-long civil unrest known to history as the Gordon Riots, which saw the worst destruction in London between the Great Fire of 1666 and the Blitz of 1940–41. The Riots started in early June 1780 when Lord George Gordon, the MP for one of his father the Duke of Gordon's pocket boroughs, presented a petition to Parliament demanding the repeal of the Catholic Relief Act of 1778. Anti-Catholic bigotry was still a powerful force in late eighteenth-century Britain, and Gordon had claimed to the Commons the previous November that he had 120,000 people ready to support him. It was an exaggeration but, as it turned out, only by a factor of about two.

The general tendency in government – supported by the King – had been towards a limited and gradual relief of Catholic grievances, as had been seen in the Irish Catholic Relief Acts in Ireland in 1772, 1774 and 1778, as well as the English version in 1778. These had undone some – but by no means all – of the harsh restrictions on Catholic property-owning rights and education, but they were anathema to the sectarian massed ranks of Gordon's vast Protestant Association, who took an extreme anti-Catholic stance.[13]

As an MP and the son of a duke, Lord George Gordon had the right of audience with the King, which he exercised twice in early 1780. It was generous of George to have allowed it, since the previous November Gordon had said in the House of Commons that the Scots 'are convinced in their own mind that the King is a papist'.[14] As Gordon read at length from an anti-Irish pamphlet on 29 January, George excused himself, whereupon Gordon made him promise to read the rest of it. The King promised, and then went skating.[15] Gordon was barred from further entry to Court, whereupon he took to calling the King the 'ill-educated elector of Hanover'.[16]

On Friday 2 June, a crowd of around 50,000 to 60,000 people assembled in St George's Fields, Southwark, to present the Protestant Association's petition against the Act; some 14,000 of them subsequently marched on Parliament.[17] A company of dragoons was called to protect the Palace of Westminster, although a number of demonstrators still managed to force their way in and even got into the Commons chamber itself. Others broke off on the way to Westminster to damage and loot the chapels of the ambassadors of Sardinia and Bavaria, both strongly Catholic states. When the authorities did not respond to these provocations, mob rule quickly asserted itself (this was the era before any organized London constabulary).

Over the weekend of Saturday 3 and Sunday 4 June, crowds torched Roman Catholic chapels in Spitalfields and Moorfields, and William Pitt witnessed what he called 'religious mobs' setting fire to property near Lincoln's Inn; writing to his mother he condemned 'the disagreeable and disgraceful sight which such uncontrolled licentiousness permits'.[18] By then the lawlessness had spread beyond attacking Catholic buildings and people to similarly violent assaults on Scots, Irishmen and foreigners in general. The night of Monday 5 June saw general rioting across central London, and over the coming days the prisons of Newgate, Clerkenwell, the Marshalsea, the Fleet, King's Bench and Borough Clink all had their inmates released by force, and several were then burned to the ground. Langadale's distillery in Holborn was looted of its alcohol. The dangers and terrors were in no way exaggerated by Charles Dickens in *Barnaby Rudge* more than sixty years later, when he wrote that the mobs were 'sprinkled doubtless here and there with honest zealots, but composed for the most part of the very scum and refuse of London'.[19] The defence of Protestantism was merely the excuse used by many of the rioters for larceny on a grand scale right across the capital.

'This tumult must be got the better of,' the King told Lord North on 5 June, 'or it will encourage designing men to use it as a precedent for assembling the people on other occasions. If possible we must get to the bottom of it and examples must be made … My attachment is to the laws and security of my country and to the protection of the lives and properties of all my subjects.'[20] Yet the North ministry seemed paralysed by the lawlessness, even though it was taking place in the heart of the capital of a nation at war, only a year after Britain had almost been invaded.

On Tuesday 6 June, the mob started attacking the houses of judges and ministers, including those of Sir John Fielding and Sir George Savile. Downing Street was threatened by a crowd with burning torches who were beaten off by twenty dragoons using the sides of their sabres. During the invasion scare the previous year, Burke had denounced the government's refusal 'to put arms in the hands of the people at large', arguing that 'we ought to be an armed nation'.[21] Fortunately his advice had not been heeded, otherwise the Gordon Riots might have turned into a serious insurrection.

Lord North had been caught entirely unprepared, and at 9.25 p.m. on 6 June the King complained vociferously to him of 'the great supineness of the civil magistrates', and the fact that Gordon, 'the avowed head of the tumult', was still at large. 'I fear without more vigour that this will not subside; indeed unless exemplary punishment is procured it will remain a lasting disgrace.'[22] At 11.45 that night a Cabinet meeting was held at Lord Stormont's office in the Northern Department which reported to George that power should be taken out of the magistrates' hands if they declined 'to direct the soldiery to act with effect' and that 'the whole military force should be under one command,' by which it meant that of Lord Amherst. Yet the government did not declare martial law, as was clearly required by that stage, magistrates fearing legal and perhaps personal repercussions if they ordered blood to be shed.

On Wednesday 7 June, Kenwood House, the home of Lord Mansfield, the Lord Chief Justice, who had been too soft on Catholics for the rioters' taste, was partially ransacked and destroyed. Amherst sent a detachment of light horse, but they arrived too late. 'After the leaders of the rout struck the front door with hammers and iron bars, the earl and the countess escaped by a postern gate from the premises,' recorded one account,

which were speedily in the hands of the rabble … Of course the patriots were permitted to eat the contents of their enemy's larder and to drain his wine; but apart from victuals and drink they took away nothing of the judge's property. They broke mirrors, slit pictures down and across, and hurled costly furniture into the bonfires which made the gloomy square bright as daylight. One scoundrel was seen throwing a quantity of silver plate and gold coin into the flames, and as the precious metals left his hands, he thanked God that they would not be spent on masses. When the house had been thoroughly gutted and sacked, it was set on fire. The loss of his library, containing books given him by Pope or annotated by Bolingbroke, and manuscripts by his own hand, was the part of his misfortune which Lord Mansfield felt most acutely.[23]

Stormont, whose own house was under threat, told the King that it had been 'a deep laid revolt' whose 'ringleaders at least act with deliberate rage and upon a fixed predetermined plan'.[24]

Many of the rioters had started wearing the Protestant Association's blue cockade in their caps, which soon took on the distinguishing mark of desperadoes whose true goals were far removed from protecting Protestantism. On 7 June a small number of these attempted to break into the Bank of England. None other than Alderman John Wilkes led a detachment of militia, which fired on the mob to defend it, even as bank clerks used bullets made from melted-down inkwells.[25] Wilkes recorded the killing of rioters in his diary.[26] Ironically enough, one of the people that he later committed to prison for printing treasonous newspapers during the rioting was William Moore, who had been a printer of the *North Briton*.

There were rumours that the army was mutinying, that 30,000 colliers were marching on London from Northamptonshire to sack the capital and that 70,000 Scots were on their way south under the command of the Dukes of Argyll and Gordon to overthrow the government. Senior army officers were fearful that they would be prosecuted for murder if they fired on crowds without the magistrates having first read the Riot Act, but magistrates and aldermen were refusing to enter the fray to read it, and with Lord North still giving no lead there was a serious chance that the days of rioting and looting might lead to something approaching a revolution. 'Nothing is done,' worried John Robinson, 'no line fixed, the Cabinet to determine it – no Cabinet fixed.'[27] It was clearly time for the King to step in.

At an emergency Privy Council meeting on 7 June, before the news about the Bank of England reached them, George demanded that the senior law officers of the Crown come to an immediate decision as to whether troops could open fire on mobs without the Riot Act having been formally read by a justice of the peace. With the exception of Lord Bathurst, Lord

President of the Council, the King found no support, and there were even some who argued that the law prevented the use of lethal force even after it had been read, without specific orders from civil magistrates. A future Lord Chancellor, Lord Eldon, later claimed that the King told the Cabinet that if they did not take the initiative 'he should* act without their advice, and would order his horse to the door, that he might go at the head of the troops in person, and give them orders to disperse the rioters by force'.[28]

It was only when Alexander Wedderburn, the Attorney-General, arrived late at the meeting and stated categorically that in his opinion the reading of the Riot Act would not be necessary if felonies could not be prevented by means other than force that the tide turned. 'Is that your declaration of the law as Attorney-General?' the King asked. 'Yes,' replied Wedderburn. 'Then so let it be done,' said the King as he stood up and thereby ended the meeting before anyone else could object or even comment.[29] He signed an Order-in-Council, which had all the power of law, to permit the use of lethal force without the Riot Act needing to be read, and gave it to Amherst, saying that at least there was one magistrate in the kingdom who would do his duty, presumably meaning either himself or Wedderburn.[30]†

The King has been described by one historian as displaying during the Gordon Riots 'the firmness whose want was to ruin the King of France within the decade'.[31] The Order-in-Council was printed and widely distributed immediately as a royal proclamation, stating that all necessary force would be used to suppress 'such rebellious and traitorous attempts, now making against the peace and dignity of our crown, and the safety of the lives and properties of our subjects'.[32] Amherst sent an order to all army units in London stating, 'In obedience to an Order of the King in Privy Council, the military [are] to act without waiting for the civil magistrates and to use force for dispersing the illegal and tumultuous assemblies of the people.'[33] Thus legally protected, the army started to clear the streets.

There is a minute of 7 June, the first fifteen words of which are in the King's handwriting and the rest in Lord Stormont's, which was the official response to Gordon's desire for yet another audience and which reads, 'It is impossible for His Majesty to see Lord George Gordon until he has given sufficient proof of his loyalty and allegiance by employing those means which he says are in his power to quell the present disturbances and restore peace to this capital.'[34] Later that day Stormont reported to the King the repulse of the attack on the Bank of England, and added that army officers

---

*   In the sense of 'would' rather than 'ought to'.
†   Although George disliked Wedderburn personally, he was to become Chief Justice of the Common Pleas and Lord Loughborough later that month, and eventually Lord Chancellor and the 1st Earl of Rosslyn, with a well-justified reputation for being useful in a crisis.

'seem now perfectly to understand the orders they have received and I hope that these exertions if continued with vigour will re-establish government which has been shook to its basis'.[35] He added that the King's Bench, Fleet Prison, New Prison and Toll House 'are totally burnt'.

Samuel Romilly MP captured the situation well when he commented on the decision to mass 11,000 troops (including militia) in the capital as soon as possible. 'The King and his Privy Council took the most effectual way to put a stop to the enormities which were being committed,' he noted in his autobiography. 'They ordered a great number of the regiments of the militia to march straight to London, and issued a proclamation command-ing all persons to keep within their houses at night, and warning them of the ill-consequences of neglecting this injunction.'[36]

'One might see the glare of conflagration fill the sky from many parts,' Samuel Johnson reported to his friend Hester Thrale. 'The sight was dread-ful.'[37] Meanwhile, the Channel Fleet in ports along the south coast was put on high alert in case the French should use the opportunity to raid, or even to mount an invasion. 'I am convinced till the magistrates have ordered some military execution on the rioters this town will not be restored back to order,' the King told Robinson on Thursday 8 June.[38] The shooting of rioters started that day, and order in the capital was indeed soon restored. There is some debate among historians about the total death toll from the Gordon Riots, varying from around 300 via Amherst's estimate of 458 killed or wounded up to 1,000 killed.[39] The hunt for ringleaders yielded up twenty-six who were hanged, including a fourteen-year-old, Richard Roberts, 'a slender lad' who had to have weights put in his pockets 'that he might sooner be out of his pain'.[40]

The only soldier to die in the Gordon Riots was the septuagenarian General William Bedford, commander of Cumberland's artillery at Culloden, who burst a blood vessel organizing the protection of Woolwich Armoury on horseback. Lord George Gordon was arrested on the after-noon of 9 June and taken to the Tower of London to await trial for high treason, of which he was eventually acquitted.*

By 10 June 1780 the capital was back under control, although a cartoon published that day still depicted the King as a Catholic monk, complete with robes and tonsure, praying at an altar while a picture of Martin Luther peels off the wall. Behind the King was a portrait of the Pope, above a latrine where the Protestant petitions were placed 'for necessary uses' – that is, as lavatory paper.[41] Troops stayed camped in St James's Park, Hyde Park

---

* When in September 1781 he arrived at a Levee to offer the King a book, George refused to receive him or it. They did not meet again.

and the gardens of Buckingham House for several weeks afterwards, prompting radical Whig fears (real or feigned) of a military dictatorship. The West Yorkshire Militia remained at the British Museum until late July.

The immediate political outcome of the Gordon Riots was to strengthen the North government and weaken the Opposition. Charles Fox's attacks on the King now looked unpatriotic. Shelburne too was damaged by his equivocal behaviour during the upheavals: he had never been thought of as particularly trustworthy, as attested by his nickname 'the Jesuit of Berkeley Square' (where he lived). By contrast, the Dukes of Gloucester and Cumberland were reconciled with the King by their earnest offer of help during the crisis.[42] The Riots also raised the King's stock to new levels. 'Never had any people a greater obligation to the judicious intrepidity of their sovereign,' wrote Sir Nathaniel Wraxall. 'No person can doubt', he averred, that the King 'would have given on that occasion, had it been unfortunately necessary, the strongest proof of courage'.[43]

Samuel Johnson wrote to Hester Thrale, 'There has indeed been an universal panic, from which the King was the first that recovered.'[44] He and his friend Joseph Baretti both believed that had it not been for George's vigorous measures London might have been burned to the ground.[45] Eschewing the widespread conspiracy theories that the Riots had been the result of a foreign or domestic plot, James Boswell believed that 'a gradual contagion of frenzy, augmented by quantities of fermented liquors', had been to blame, but that 'London was delivered by the magnanimity of the sovereign himself.'[46] Captain Topham of the Horse Guards, who had been mobilized, told the diarist Frederic Reynolds, 'I am persuaded that the King does not know what fear is.'[47]

Charles Fox's attacks on the war did not abate, of course, and in a Commons debate he declared that as long as he lived 'he never would agree to join in a vote of thanks to any officer whose laurels were gathered in the American war.'[48] It was a remark as unfraternal as it was ungenerous, since his own brother, General Henry Fox, had served in Boston and was to command the forces in Nova Scotia.

Lord North, who as ever wanted to resign, also now wanted to try to bring Rockingham into a coalition. Talks took place between Charles Jenkinson and the Rockinghamite whip Frederick Montagu MP in late June on the possibility that the Marquess's faction might come into government on the basis of supporting the continuation of the war.[49] The King told North that he wanted Lord Sandwich to stay at the Admiralty 'whatever his private failings may be', and vetoed Montagu's proposal to give the post to Sandwich's arch-enemy Keppel. It was hoped that the

Rockinghamites would enter the government, just as 5,000 troops under the command of the Comte de Rochambeau arrived on 10 July at Newport, Rhode Island, turning what was a British stronghold into a French one.

Once it became clear in September that the Rockinghamites would not enter the government after all, John Robinson came up with the idea – which George fully supported – of dissolving Parliament a year earlier than was necessary under the Septennial Act and calling a snap election which, after the suppression of the Gordon Riots and the fall of Charleston, would doubtless secure another majority for the government. Usually, eighteenth-century governments saw out their full seven-year terms, and the Opposition were not expecting an election, nor had they made any financial provision for one, and they were accordingly surprised and disconcerted by its announcement. Breaking down the constituencies into 'pros', 'hopefuls', 'doubtfuls' and 'cons', Robinson calculated that North would win a majority of 128.[50] He then fell ill during the campaign – 'I can scarce hold my pen,' he wrote at one point.[51]

The general election was held between 6 September and 18 October 1780. The bitterest and most controversial poll was in the King's home constituency of New Windsor, where the King was so determined that Admiral Keppel should be beaten by Peniston Portlock Powney, a local landowner from Maidenhead whose father had been a friend of his father, that he spent £2,600 of his own money on the struggle.[52] 'Scarcely any individual could be more obnoxious to the King than was that naval officer,' wrote Wraxall.[53] It was alleged, probably with at least some truth, that the King personally canvassed Windsor tradesmen who were dependent on the castle's business. In his stump speeches, Keppel certainly 'complained of undue influence made use of against him', which he claimed 'was novel in its kind, and could it be proved . . . struck at the very root of the constitution'.[54]

This was not true, as the Crown was not held to be politically neutral until Queen Victoria's time (and perhaps not even then), but after Powney had won by only 174 votes to 158 the Whig Lord Edward Bentinck MP felt that the King's involvement meant that 'Keppel has good grounds to petition.'[55] Lady Sarah Lennox told her sister Susan that voters had told Keppel, 'Sir, we have the greatest respect for you, but the roof we live under must plead our excuse.'[56] Her opinion was that the King 'has hurt himself a great deal more than he has hurt the admiral in using his influence and authority to make him lose Windsor'.

Overall, the government spent £60,000 on winning the 1780 election, as well as large sums on by-elections over the next two years. The expenditure was huge, but the Whig nobility was immensely rich too, and also used to spending prodigiously. George had been saving up for this since November 1777, handing over to North monthly contributions of £1,000 from his Privy Purse, which by February 1781 totalled £40,000. On 7 December 1780, however, North's promises to candidates forced him to borrow an extra £30,000 from Henry and Robert Drummond, the King's bankers – after securing the King's prior approval for such a step, which otherwise they would not have entertained.[57] North assumed that the King's instalments together with some candidates' loan repayments, and if necessary the Drummonds' forbearance, would allow him to repay the loan and its interest.

The vast expenditure and the favourable political circumstances meant that the government lost only five seats in the election, and thus still had a majority of around 120, even after five years of unsuccessful war.

On 14 August 1780, the King wrote a long letter to George, Prince of Wales, congratulating him on his eighteenth birthday. From being a rather sweet child, the Prince had turned into an extremely unruly adolescent. He did not study, and aged fourteen had ridiculed his governor, the former politician Lord Holderness, so badly to his face that Holderness resigned. At the time the King noted that the Prince showed 'duplicity' and had the 'bad habit . . . of not speaking the truth'.[58] The King elevated the Prince's preceptor, Dr Markham, to Archbishop of York, allowing his friend Bishop Richard Hurd of Lichfield, later Bishop of Worcester, to take over as preceptor; but Hurd could not control the boy either. The heir to the throne grew up with personal charm and much aesthetic taste, but almost no other virtues. Other governors, preceptors, tutors and so on – the governess Lady Charlotte Finch, the high-minded Anglican Lord Bruce (later the 1st Earl of Ailesbury) and the sub-governor George Hotham among them – similarly failed to prevent the Prince of Wales from growing into an utterly dissipated youth.

The King and Queen must of course bear some share of responsibility for the way 'Prinny', as he came to be nicknamed, turned out; but, as the historian Philip Ziegler judges, 'though somewhat strict and formal by contemporary standards, [they were] not far from model parents.'[59] They showed overt love and affection to their children, playing with them when young and showing interest in them when they grew older. The formality was explicable because they had to maintain a dignity appropriate to their position in society, and the strictness involved the Prince not being allowed to attend the (notoriously louche) masquerades and private balls hosted by his aristocratic friends, something he greatly resented.

'No one feels with more pleasure than I do your nearer approach to manhood,' was how the King started his birthday letter to his son, 'but the parent's joy must be mixed with the anxiety that this period may not be ill spent, as the hour is now come when whatever foundation has been laid must be by application brought to maturity, or every past labour of your instructors will prove abortive.'[60] He mentioned the Queen, 'whose conduct as a wife as well as mother even malevolence has not dared to mention but in the most respectable terms', and added, 'The numberless trials and constant torments I meet with in public life must certainly affect any man, and more poignantly me, as I have no other wish than to fulfil my various duties . . . Wherefore am I to turn for comfort but into the bosom of my family? . . . Indeed I could not bear up did I not find in her a feeling friend to whom I can unbosom my griefs.'[61]

'You have not made that progress in your studies which . . . I might have had every reason to expect,' the King continued, because 'your love of dissipation has for some months been with enough ill-nature trumpeted in the public papers, and there are those ready to wound me in the severest place by ripping up every error they may be able to find in you.' George's entire attitude to kingship can be encapsulated in the next paragraph, written from one king of England to the next, with his experience of two decades on the throne:

> God has bequeathed to you enough quickness of conception . . . that you must acknowledge the truth of the position that everyone in this world has his peculiar* duties to perform, and that the good or bad example set by those in the higher stations must have some effect on the general conduct of those in inferior ones.[62]

Because the Prince had so far not set a good example, he was not given the independent income that George himself had received aged eighteen, together with his own house, mini-Court and servants. His son greatly resented this, but it prompted no alteration in his behaviour.

George asked his son and heir to choose his friends more wisely, from 'worthy characters' who wanted 'to make themselves of utility and ornament to their country'. He criticized the Prince for his lack of 'gratitude to the Great Creator' and urged him to 'Let it be the constant practice of your life at least once in every day coolly to examine your own conduct, and it will be impossible for your good heart not to check many evils that otherwise must give you many unhappy days. I own fairly that it is to that constant habit that I have often corrected myself.'[63] There was a great deal more of this – George urging his son to brush up on his 'very moderate' German, considering that he was one day going to be Elector of Hanover;

---

* 'Appropriate; belonging to any one with exclusion of others' (*Johnson's Dictionary*).

to read more history (always fine advice for everybody at all times) and to learn about the constitution, laws, finances and commerce of the country. It was meant well even if somewhat pompously expressed – 'I have ever found self-deserved approbation a much happier state than any indulgence which met with self-condemnation,' etc. – and the Prince replied with suitable thanks, but continued doing the precise opposite of all his father had implored him to do.

'I wish more and more to have you as a friend,' the King wrote on 22 November, 'and in that light to guide you, rather than with the authority of a parent.'[64] Yet by then it was too late. Prince George was already keeping a mistress, the actress Mary 'Perdita'* Robinson, who in August 1781 blackmailed him to the tune of £5,000 – which the King paid from the Secret Service Fund, making the predictably self-righteous but nonetheless truthful remark about the blackmail that 'I am happy to say that I never was personally engaged in such a transaction which perhaps makes me feel this the stronger.'[65] The Prince was soon to become a spendthrift of sociopathic proportions. Worse – which was arguably more dangerous than either his sexual or his financial incontinence – he also followed his Hanoverian genes and plunged deeply into Opposition politics, becoming the friend and almost protégé of Charles Fox.

The Prince fell in love easily, and by May 1781 was enamoured of the Countess Christiane von Hardenberg, the pretty twenty-two-year-old Danish wife of the budding thirty-one-year-old statesman Count Karl August von Hardenberg, the son of the Commander-in-Chief of the Hanoverian Army. The Count was in London to advance his hopes of becoming Hanoverian envoy there, but such was the scandal that he had to take his wife away to Brussels. 'How I love her!' Prince George wrote to his brother Frederick. 'How I would sacrifice every earthly thing to her! By Heavens, I shall go distracted! My brain will split!'[66] He complained a month later that their father 'is excessively cross and ill-tempered, and uncommonly grumpy'.[67] The idea that his own behaviour with the Countess – especially so soon after the very expensive retrieval of his love letters from Perdita – justified his father's crossness does not seem to have occurred to him. He then came up with the scheme of asking his Groom of the Stole, Charles Fitzroy, 1st Baron Southampton, who had been Queen Charlotte's Vice-Chamberlain for many years, to get the King's permission for him to go to Brussels to continue wooing the Countess. Meanwhile, the story of his second affair hit the press.

---

* So nicknamed because of Joshua Reynolds' portrait of her as Perdita, the heroine of *A Winter's Tale*.

Considering that the Prince was asking for permission to leave England in order to continue a now public affair with the daughter-in-law of the Hanoverian Commander-in-Chief, George responded with surprising calmness, asking his son to re-read the two letters of loving parental advice that he had sent him the previous August and November. 'Examine yourself and see how far your conduct has been conformable to them,' the King wrote on 6 May 1781, 'and then draw your conclusion whether you must not give me many an uneasy moment. I wish to live with you as a friend, but then by your behaviour you must deserve it.'[68] He could not resist a little homily on his own moral superiority: 'If I did not state these things I should not fulfil my duty either to my God or my country. I say as little as possible from an hope that your reason will begin to act . . . When you read this carefully over, you will find an affectionate father trying to save his son from perdition' (having already saved him from Perdita). In the event, the Prince was unwilling to sacrifice any earthly thing at all for Madame Hardenberg, and stayed in London to search for a new mistress. The Count divorced his wife and went on to become one of the greatest German statesmen of the nineteenth century, and a key figure in the defeat of Napoleon.

On 16 August 1780, General Cornwallis and Lieutenant-Colonel Banastre Tarleton's force of 2,400 British regulars and Loyalists defeated Horatio Gates' force of 3,000 Continental Army troops and militia at the battle of Camden in South Carolina, where the Americans lost over 1,000 killed or wounded to 324 British. Two days later, Tarleton defeated another rebel force under General Thomas Sumter. Gates was forced to flee over 160 miles to Hillsborough, North Carolina, and in early October was relieved of his command. He was replaced in December as commander of the rebel forces in the South by Washington's lieutenant, Major-General Nathanael Greene.[69] After Camden, Cornwallis believed that he could not pacify South Carolina unless he captured the rebel strongholds in North Carolina. He was also still chasing that mirage of a Loyalist uprising, which he now believed would follow his Camden victory.

Meanwhile, 700 miles north-west on the Hudson River, one of the great dramas of the war was played out. After a series of unforeseeable mishaps and close shaves, General Clinton's British spymaster, Major John André, was captured by the colonists, which led to the discovery of General Benedict Arnold's plans to surrender West Point, the key strategic point of the area, and the 3,000-strong garrison of which he was the commander, for the vast sum of £20,000. Arnold's Loyalist wife Peggy Shippen had been secretly passing information from Arnold to André for eighteen months.

For all Franklin's joke at the time of the signing of the Declaration of Independence, it was actually the Briton, André, who was hanged, as a spy. (He had changed out of his uniform earlier that day and was therefore not interned as a soldier.) When the King was told of this by Germain, he awarded André's mother a pension and knighted his brother. Arnold escaped, became a brigadier in the British Army and was well compensated (though not to the tune of £20,000).

Although Carl Van Doren called Arnold 'the Iago of traitors', the King understandably saw it differently, since the cause he betrayed was itself traitorous. When Arnold came to London, the King showed him great sympathy and attention, and asked him to compile a paper on grand strategy, *Thoughts on the American War*. Benjamin Franklin jeered that 'He seemed to mix as naturally with that polluted Court as pitch with tar.'[70] In March 1782 George authorized a £500 annual pension for Peggy; and in 1798, after further 'very gallant and meritorious conduct at Guadeloupe', the King granted Arnold 13,400 acres of Crown land in Upper Canada.[71]

The discovery of a plot by one of their most heroic officers dealt a heavy blow to American morale in August 1780. Although the King has been regularly lambasted for continuing the war after Burgoyne's surrender, the lowest point of the war for the Americans came three years after Saratoga, once Charleston had fallen, Gates had been routed, the Loyalists were finally gaining ground and Washington had had to put down no fewer than six mutinies over supply deficiencies in the first six months of 1781, sometimes by hanging. 'There is not a farthing in the military chest,' he wrote to General Samuel Parsons that May.[72]

On 26 September 1780, after receiving Clinton's dispatches, the King wrote to North to point out that 'Undoubtedly this island has made greater exertions to keep its station among the considerable powers of Europe than perhaps could have been expected; the number of troops sent to America has been prodigious.'[73] That was true by contemporary standards, but it was entirely inadequate for so vast a territory as North America. He then looked at the wider need for victory, telling his premier that 'The giving up the game would be total ruin; a small state may certainly subsist but a great one mouldering cannot get into an inferior situation but must be annihilated . . . We must strengthen the West Indies squadron; we must recruit Clinton's army not for conquest but to keep what he has.'[74] He entered into some explanations for why Britain might ultimately win, such as 'The French could never stand the cold of Germany, that of America must be more fatal to them; America is distressed to the greatest degree; the finances of France as well as Spain are in no good situation; this war like the last will prove one of credit . . . In short, by perseverance we may bring things to a peace. By giving up the game we are destroying ourselves to prevent being destroyed.'

Yet the rebels' fortunes were about to change. On 7 October, Colonel Patrick Ferguson's Loyalist force of 1,100 was defeated at the battle of King's Mountain in South Carolina by 1,400 sharpshooting militiamen. All of the participants in the battle were American except Ferguson himself, who was killed. It led Cornwallis to reverse his plans to invade the province. Instead he retreated from Charlotte (just over the border in North Carolina) and removed to winter quarters at Winnsborough, in upcountry South Carolina. Despite the relatively small losses incurred – 290 Loyalists killed and 163 wounded – Clinton later said that King's Mountain had been the decisive battle of the war, because large numbers of Loyalists could no longer be raised to fight, thus dooming Cornwallis's entire bite-and-hold strategy. Meanwhile Greene, perhaps the best of the American generals of the war, assumed command of 1,482 ill-clothed and under-equipped men at Charlotte on 2 December, but was soon reinforced by up to 3,000 recruits.

Britain was forced to declare war on Holland on 20 December 1780. The Dutch had been sending supplies to the American rebels before and throughout the conflict, and had recently also helped refit the ships of Captain John Paul Jones, who had attacked the British mainland at White-haven in Cumbria in 1778. Britain's isolationist foreign policy since 1763 – which the King, Bute and the Leicester House Set had pioneered – had led to a situation where it now faced three major European enemies, with no allies and most of the ostensible neutrals actively hostile over the issue of trading with America.[75] There was nothing splendid about Britain's isolation by 1780.

In one of the very few tactical defeats of British regular troops in the field during the whole war, General Daniel Morgan defeated Tarleton at the battle of Cowpens in South Carolina on 17 January 1781. Tarleton lost over a hundred killed or wounded and 830 captured out of a total of 1,100 men.[76] Morgan's brilliant double-envelopment manoeuvre, which cost him only twelve killed and sixty-one wounded from roughly equal numbers of troops, deprived Cornwallis of the light troops he badly needed for his coming campaign in Virginia.[77] It ought to have dissuaded him from marching there at all.

On 26 February 1781, the twenty-one-year-old William Pitt the Younger delivered his maiden speech in the House of Commons, supporting the second reading of Burke's Economical Reform Bill and establishing himself as a new political force. Pitt gave the speech impromptu, replying to points made earlier in the debate, which was unusual as maiden speeches were usually well-rehearsed stand-alone addresses. The motion was defeated by 233 to 190, but Pitt's speech had established him as an undoubted new political force. He was congratulated by Fox, North described it as the best speech he had ever heard and Burke perceptively remarked, 'He is not a chip of the old block: he is the old block itself!'[78]

Pitt had been bred for political leadership from the earliest age, his father nicknaming him 'the Young Senator' and 'William the Great'.[79] Asexual (to the point that he probably died a virgin), fiercely intelligent (despite, or perhaps because of, not going to school), he was incorruptible, but as chaotic with his own finances as he was masterful and punctilious with the nation's. He ate poorly and drank heavily, at least in part due to the spectacularly poor advice of his family doctor, Dr Arthur Addington, who prescribed alcohol to steady his nerves. Pitt was a curious and enigmatic figure, uninterested in anything besides politics and power (with the noteworthy exception of landscape gardening). He enjoyed strong friendships with men including William Wilberforce, Henry Dundas and George Canning, but was otherwise surprisingly shy, which was mistaken for a haughty aloofness by colleagues and opponents alike. For all his personality quirks, which fascinated his contemporaries, he had now burst on to a political scene that he would dominate with astonishing speed.

On 15 March 1781 Lord Cornwallis defeated Greene at the battle of Guilford Courthouse at Greensboro, North Carolina. His force of 1,900 men drove Greene's 4,400 under-trained militia and newly raised Continentals from the field.[80] Yet it was a pyrrhic victory for the British, who suffered 550 killed or wounded to the Americans' 260.[81] Cornwallis marched on to Wilmington, North Carolina. 'The perpetual risings in different parts of this province', he wrote of the guerrilla insurgency in the Carolinas, 'kept the whole country in perpetual alarm.'[82] The role of the guerrilla war cannot be underestimated: unable to hold down Georgia and South Carolina, Cornwallis moved his force through North Carolina and then into Virginia, until he entrenched on the shore of the Chesapeake.[83]

Clinton had intended Cornwallis to stay in the Lower South, but instead he had penetrated far into Virginia, taking Clinton's instructions as general advice rather than an explicit order. That summer, Cornwallis established a camp on the peninsula of Yorktown between the York and James Rivers, thereby placing his army in complete dependence on the Royal Navy at a time when its predominance in the theatre could no longer be taken for granted. Cornwallis's 'inability to understand sea power' had recklessly led him from Charleston to Yorktown, and to commit the second key British strategic blunder of the war, alongside Howe's Pennsylvania campaign of 1777 which had wrecked Burgoyne.[84] Another major problem was Clinton's extremely cautious troop deployments, by which 15,000 men were left defending New York whereas less than half that number could have protected the city successfully, the rest being sent to fight elsewhere.[85]

British leadership at this stage of the conflict was at best fragmented and at worst antagonistic. Clinton despised Germain and had strained relations with Cornwallis that were to deteriorate. Clinton and Admiral Mariot Arbuthnot rowed over who had been responsible for the failure to destroy the French at Rhode Island in 1780, until the Cabinet agreed to Clinton's demands for Arbuthnot's removal.[86] There was a dearth of teamwork between the generals. On 29 April, as Admiral de Grasse was taking Tobago in the West Indies, the Marquis de Lafayette, whom Washington had sent from New York to take command in Virginia, reached Richmond with a force of 3,550 men, of whom 1,200 were veteran Continentals. Over the coming months, Washington sent Lafayette whatever troops he could spare.

It might seem strange in retrospect, but the prospects for the war did not look at all bad for Britain that summer. Cornwallis commanded over 7,000 men to Lafayette's 4,500; the Americans were under severe economic pressure; they had lost more battles than they had won; the Saratoga humiliation was now nearly four years past; Franco-American relations were at a low ebb, and the French were preparing to withdraw forces from America at the end of the campaigning season; Vergennes knew the French treasury was empty and was considering inaugurating peace talks; the Spanish, wavering after the failure of their 'Great Assault' on Gibraltar in April, were engaging in tentative peace talks with Britain; General Ethan Allen was promoting a Vermont republic separate from the thirteen colonies; and Lord North had just won a general election and held a solid pro-war majority in both Houses of Parliament. The war had gone badly, but it was perfectly understandable when in June the North government, supported as ever by the King, turned down mediation offers from the Austrians and Russians on the grounds that relations between Britain and her colonies were an internal matter and had nothing to do with any outside powers.[87]

On 17 August, as Cornwallis was throwing up defensive earthworks at Yorktown,* the King began a four-day sailing visit to the fleet stationed at the Nore, near Portsmouth. Travelling with him were Lord Sandwich, the Prince of Wales and Sir Hugh Palliser. After they had departed from Greenwich an equerry, Robert Fulke Greville, noted that George was 'cheered with the joyful acclamations of many thousands from the shores . . . Every

---

* Whose positions can still be seen today, thanks to the excellent American Battlefields Trust.

village on the banks of the Thames turned out their inhabitants . . . with loud acclamations of joy.'[88] When they reached Sheerness, 'His Majesty was joyously received by a vast concourse of people, and who rent the air with their acclamations.' Outside London's environs, the King's reception again showed him that the radical press, satirical printmakers and Whig elite were not reflective of true public opinion.

The King visited ships that had fought against the Dutch at the battle of Dogger Bank earlier that month, and aboard Admiral Sir Hyde Parker's seventy-four-gun flagship *Fortitude* he 'went through every part of this fine ship. He spoke to many. He enquired much, and feelingly, and heard many an artless tale of recent turmoil from the weather-beaten tars* who had been active in the fray.' The occasion was only spoiled for Greville by the Prince of Wales' friend, the 5th Marquess of Lothian, who during the ceremony at which the fleet officers kissed the King's hand satirized and mimicked 'the manner and awkward shyness of some of these gallant men, unused to ceremonials of this nature'.[89] When Lothian extended 'his sub-sequent comments in the same strain to the Prince afterwards', Greville was disgusted, feeling that 'on an occasion like this, such ill-timed levity was unpardonable.' The Prince of Wales nonetheless acquiesced in Lord Lothian's mockery of men who less than a fortnight earlier had risked their lives in a desperate sea battle in which over a hundred sailors had been killed and nearly 400 wounded.

After dinner on 20 August, once the King had entered his cabin aboard the *Princess Augusta*, Greville, who was sharing a cabin with Lothian and a Colonel Townsend, noted that George 'frequently opened his door and looked into our cabin just as we were preparing for our cots', but said nothing. At last he called Greville into his cabin and told him that 'He was curious to know what Lord Lothian did at night with his carefully arranged wig, and his long thick pigtail, and how these were disposed of.' When Greville told him that Lothian slept with them on in order to convince him and Townsend that he wore his own hair, Lothian turned out to be listening at the door, crying out, 'It is all true, Sir.' 'The King was much diverted with the detail,' Greville recorded of his master's wig-envy.[90]

On the last night of the working tour, the King overturned convention and invited Greville to sit within two places of himself at dinner. 'He took the best possible care of me,' his devoted equerry recorded, 'and, among other things, recommended me to eat some beefsteaks which he was then eating himself and which he thought excellent.'[91] It is said that no man is a hero to his valet, but there is no record of any of the King's servants – except

---

* Abbreviation of Jack Tar, slang for a sailor.

politicians – having a bad word for him personally, and most adored him for the way that, as Greville put it, 'Nobody is so constantly happy in doing a kind act as His Majesty.'[92] One person who hated the trip, however, was the Prince of Wales, who felt 'disgusted' by his treatment by the navy hierarchy, who had focused their attention too much on the King for his taste.[93]

On 30 August, Admiral de Grasse arrived in the Chesapeake off Yorktown from the West Indies, disembarking 3,000 troops for Lafayette: the majority of the forces that Cornwallis faced at Yorktown were now French army and navy regulars.[94] De Grasse had ignored clear orders from the French Admiralty to send ten of his twenty-four ships-of-the-line home to Europe at the end of the summer campaigning season, and as a result he had the capacity to prevent the reinforcement, relief or evacuation of Cornwallis's force at Yorktown.[95] De Grasse was subsequently strengthened from Newport by additional ships, which importantly brought siege artillery.

It was now abundantly clear that the Royal Navy needed to defeat de Grasse's fleet in order to reverse the unfolding strategic situation in America; but on 5 September 1781 at the battle of Chesapeake Bay* Admiral Thomas Graves – who had taken over from Arbuthnot and who had only nineteen ships against de Grasse's twenty-eight – engaged for two hours, with 350 British sailors killed or wounded to 220 French.[96] Five British vessels were damaged and one had to be scuttled, against two French ships damaged. Hearing reports of a further French squadron on its way, Graves sailed to New York, leaving Cornwallis to his fate. The King heard a different account to Graves' self-serving one, because Admiral Samuel Hood, his second-in-command, was friendly with George's aide-de-camp General Jacob de Budé and in all wrote him 140 letters covering every aspect of the war.[97] It was an example of how the King occasionally used backstair Court connections to find out about events independently of his ministers.†

Between 14 and 26 September, Washington's and Rochambeau's troops steadily converged on Williamsburg from Baltimore, Annapolis and Elkton. The siege of Yorktown began on 28 September, Washington's 8,850 Americans and 7,800 well-equipped French regulars, plus field guns, heavily outnumbering Cornwallis's 7,400 troops. On 30 September, still awaiting reinforcement from New York, Cornwallis withdrew to the inner fortifications. Washington's bombardment of his entire position began on 9 October. Five days later, the French and Americans stormed two key

---

* Also known as the battle of the Virginia Capes or the Capes.

† The Georgian Papers Programme has recently unearthed boxes of papers showing how closely aware the King was of British espionage operations against the French Navy in Brest, for example (O'Shaughnessy, 'Understanding the American Revolution' passim).

redoubts, and a British counterattack was repulsed on the 16th. A storm thwarted a scheme to evacuate across the York River.[98] The British casualties in the siege were light at only 156 killed and 326 wounded, but with no sign of a possible evacuation by sea, Cornwallis surrendered on Friday 19 October 1781.[99]

That the same day, General Clinton and 6,000 reinforcements left New York aboard Admiral Hood's fleet, but by the time they arrived on 24 October they were five days too late. Clinton wrote to Germain, whom he blamed for losing the war because he did not send enough reinforcements, to say that Yorktown 'is a blow ... whose loss it will be now impossible I fear to repair'.[100] The decisive battle of the war had been won four years and two days after Saratoga by a combination of factors: Washington's resolve and strategic vision; de Grasse's astute insubordination; excellent Franco-American military coordination; and the failure of the Royal Navy to fulfil its historic duty of sinking French vessels regardless of numbers. But primarily it was Cornwallis's appalling foolhardiness in choosing so exposed a position as Yorktown's Neck to entrench, the very name of which ought to have suggested that it could be cut off.

'The King is excessively cross and ill-tempered,' the Prince of Wales told the Duke of York on 18 September; 'we are not upon the very best terms.'[101] Frederick replied from Hanover, where he was undergoing military training, 'For God's sake do everything you can to keep well with him. Consider he is vexed enough in public affairs. It is therefore your business not to make that still worse.'[102] It was good advice, which his elder brother resolutely ignored. Even though the King was cross, ill-tempered and vexed a month before the surrender at Yorktown, when the news arrived five weeks afterwards he was saddened but not downhearted, and – extraordinarily enough – he still believed Britain should continue with the war. When Cornwallis surrendered, later legend had it that the British military band had played an old anti-puritan ballad tune from the 1640s, entitled 'The World Turned Upside Down'.* The news of Yorktown certainly turned George's world upside down, but, characteristically for this stubborn and change-averse monarch, his first instinct was to do everything within his power to try to right it.

---

* Although there are no references to it before 1828, and only then by someone who never actually heard it played himself.

18

'The Torrent is Too Strong'

October 1781–July 1782

*He was struggling against a secession that at best could only have
been postponed. The Americans would have left us, anyhow, during the Napoleonic Wars or later, so let us not debit George with
what was inevitable.*[1]

Guy Boustead, *The Lone Monarch*, 1940

On 3 November 1781, having received General Clinton's estimation that
Cornwallis would beat Lafayette and then return to Charleston, the King
wrote confidently to Lord North, 'We shall in [a] very few days hear from
Lord Cornwallis, and he trusts Sir Henry Clinton will soon have something
decisive to communicate. I feel the justness of our cause.' He continued:

> I think success must ensue. I put the greatest confidence in the valour of both
> navy and army and above all in the assistance of Divine Providence. The
> moment is certainly anxious. The die is now cast whether this shall be a great
> empire or the least dignified of the European states. The object is certainly
> worth struggling for and I trust the nation is equally determined with myself
> to meet the conclusion with firmness. If this country will persist, I think an
> honourable termination cannot fail.[2]

The phrase 'honourable termination' implies that the King was no longer
holding out much hope for an outright victory in America, but instead
looking for a peace treaty that might fall short of outright American independence and would leave Britain with substantial holdings on the North
American continent.

On 25 November, five weeks after Cornwallis's surrender, the news of
Yorktown arrived via Falmouth at Lord George Germain's house in Pall
Mall. Germain went with the 2nd Lord Walsingham, the former Under-
Secretary of State at the American Department, in a hackney carriage to Lord
Stormont's house in Portland Place. They then went together to Thurlow's

house in Great Ormond Street. Some time after 1 p.m., all four ministers arrived at Downing Street to break the news to Lord North. Germain later told Wraxall that the Prime Minister took the news 'as he would have taken a ball in his breast'.[3] He 'opened his arms, exclaiming wildly, as he paced up and down the apartment during a few minutes, "O God! It is all over!" Words which he repeated many times under emotions of the deepest consternation and distress.'[4] The ministers considered proroguing Parliament for a few days, but as it was meeting in only forty-eight hours' time they decided to go ahead, though with a hastily rewritten King's Speech. Germain sent a dispatch to the King at Kew and went back to his office, where he received further confirmation in French accounts from Dover.

At dinner that night, Germain 'manifested no discomposure', merely noting to Walsingham when the King's reply arrived, 'I observe he has omitted to mark the hour and the minute of his writing with his usual precision.'[5] Later in the evening, Wraxall was allowed to see the letter, which no longer exists but from which Wraxall quoted from memory in his diaries. George had written that he had:

> received with sentiments of the deepest concern the communication which Lord George Germain has made me of the unfortunate result of the operations in Virginia. I particularly lament it on account of the consequences connected with it and the difficulties which it may produce in carrying on the public business or in repairing such a misfortune. But I trust that neither Lord George Germain nor any member of the Cabinet will suppose that it makes the smallest alteration in those principles of my conduct which have directed me in past time and which will always continue to animate me under every event in the prosecution of the present contest.[6]

Wraxall observed that 'Not a sentiment of despondency or of despair was to be found in the letter, the very handwriting of which indicated composure of mind ... No sovereign could manifest more calmness, dignity, or self-command than George III displayed in this reply.'[7] The King was unalterable, but he was not victorious.

As the King's Speech had originally looked forward to a positive outcome in America, it had to be speedily revised on 26 November, a process which continued until midnight. At the opening of Parliament the next day, the King told the assembled Lords and Commons:

> It is with great concern that I inform you that the events of war have been very unfortunate to my arms in Virginia, having ended in the loss of my forces in that province. No endeavours have been wanting on my part to extinguish that spirit of rebellion which our enemies have found means to

foment and maintain in the colonies, and to restore to my deluded subjects
in America that happy and prosperous condition which they formerly derived
from a due obedience to the laws. But the late misfortune in that quarter
calls loudly for your firm concurrence and assistance to frustrate the designs
of our enemies, equally prejudicial to the real interests of America and to
those of Great Britain.[8]

Thomas Paine denounced the speech for its 'snivelling hypocrisy', but in
fact it was an open avowal of the government's determination to fight on.[9]

Charles Fox delivered a tremendous philippic during the Debate on the
Address, supporting an amendment that struck out from the government's
motion all the wording that defended the war. He had no doubt about who
was ultimately responsible for Yorktown, telling the Commons:

> There was one great domestic evil, from which all our other evils, foreign
> and domestic, have sprung. The influence of the Crown. To the influence of
> the Crown we must attribute the loss of the army in Virginia; to the influence
> of the Crown we must attribute the loss of the thirteen provinces of America;
> for it was the influence of the Crown that enabled His Majesty's ministers
> to persevere against the voice of reason, the voice of truth, the voice of the
> people.[10]

He went on to contrast the state of Britain in 1763, 'when you were governed by Whig ministers and by Whig measures', with that of 1781, 'when
you are under the conduct of Tory ministers and a Tory system', observing,
'Now mark the degradation and the change! We have lost thirteen provinces of America, we have lost several of our [West Indian] islands, and the
rest are in danger. We have lost the empire of the sea, we have lost our
respect abroad and our unanimity at home. The nations have forsaken us;
they see us distracted and obstinate, and they leave us to our fate.'[11]

There was of course an element of hyperbole to all this – and a single
naval victory would soon win back 'the empire of the sea', but MPs could
not have known that at the time. Meanwhile Burke stooped from his usual
high rhetoric to say that 'Places in America seemed to undergo an excre-
mentitious evacuation, analogous to that of the human body.'[12] The way
that some of the more radical Whigs had openly welcomed the news of
Yorktown led Lord Carlisle to write to a friend, 'It is strange they should
never have learnt [that] to show exultation in a public calamity makes
them odious.'[13]

During the debate, Germain urged the continuation of the war, citing
the 'numerous Loyalists' in the colonies and warning (like the King himself)
that if Britain was defeated, 'We shall sink into perfect insignificance.'[14] He

pointed out that Britain still had over 14,000 troops in New York, 13,700 in Charleston and Savannah and several thousand more holding Nova Scotia and East Florida. Although the Yorktown army was lost, so had the colonists' lost theirs at Charleston. He argued that there was still much to fight for, especially if the French and Americans were to fall out or if Washington became a dictator; at any rate, the Newfoundland fisheries and West Indian islands still needed protection.[15]

The Opposition put down an amendment calling for 'a total change of system', that is, government, which fell by 218 votes to 129. At 8.40 on the morning after the debate, the King told North that the majority 'is very pleasing to me as it shows that the House retains that spirit for which this nation has always been renowned, and which alone can preserve it in difficulties'.[16] Of the fainthearts who saw Yorktown as more serious than that, the King opined, 'Many men choose rather to despond on difficulties than to see how to get out of them.' As for the future, he told North that he had:

> already directed Lord G. Germain to put on paper the mode that seems most feasible for conducting the war . . . that we may adopt a plan and abide by it. Fluctuating counsels, and taking up measures with[out] connecting them with the whole of this complicated war must make us weak in every part. With the assistance of Parliament I do not doubt if measures are well concerted a good end may yet be made of this war, but if we despond certain ruin ensues.[17]

Thus, only three days after he had heard that Cornwallis had capitulated with over 7,000 men, the King was determined to continue fighting, if not to outright victory then at least to 'a good end' – an 'honourable termination' – that might keep America in some kind of political relationship with Britain. Had he lost connection with any kind of military reality on the ground in America, or did he genuinely believe that yet another effort might turn British fortunes around, after six years of war? Did George see himself as a latter-day Regulus, heroically pleading with the Roman Senate not to make peace with Carthage, as depicted in the massive painting he had commissioned from Benjamin West in 1769?

Remarkably, George did not at all blame Cornwallis personally for the defeat, telling him in March 1782 that 'your conduct has so manifestly shown that attachment to my person, to your country and to the military profession are the motives of your actions,' and asking him not to resign as Constable of the Tower of London.[18] This is perhaps all the more surprising as the King understood Cornwallis's failure in detail; he bought the mapmaker Robert Scott's topographical representation of the final British dispositions at Yorktown, showing the American trenches and the impossible position Cornwallis had chosen to defend, complete with an annotation marking the 'Field where the British laid down their Arms'.[19]

Germain now accepted that his strategy had been wrecked by Yorktown, but he still believed that amphibious operations could be conducted against Rhode Island and other places along the eastern seaboard. He also thought that if New York, Charleston, Savannah, Nova Scotia and Penobscot in Maine could be held indefinitely, they could be used as bases for further military operations.[20] Like the King, he did not see Yorktown as a reason to end the war. Cornwallis, like Burgoyne, had commanded a large expeditionary force rather than the main army under Clinton in New York, and Germain rightly intuited that with the French now focusing exclusively on the West Indies, Washington's hopes of capturing that city in 1782 would come to nothing. He warned the Cabinet that if Britain simply gave up the fight, she might lose Newfoundland and Canada to the Franco-American alliance, followed by the West Indies. Britain should instead protect the trade between New York, Savannah and Charleston, while forces in East Florida mounted new operations against the French and Spanish in the West Indies. Clinton should be replaced as Commander-in-Chief, the Loyalists protected wherever possible and more ships sent to continue the blockade and attack rebel coastal towns.[21]

Henry Dundas once said that Lord North 'only wanted one quality to make him a great and distinguished statesman', before noting two: 'despotism and violence of temper'.[22] In the absence of either, North reluctantly agreed to continue the war as the King desired, Germain advised and British prestige required, but he also wanted to make separate peace offers to both the French and the Americans. Thus on 1 December the Cabinet decided to send as many warships as were necessary to gain a superiority of numbers over the French fleet there, but would not authorize reinforcing the army in New York, without which no prospect of actively continuing the war was possible. At another Cabinet meeting a week later, nothing was said about the future conduct of the war except that no more troops would be sent beyond 'what is necessary to recruit [for] the regiments [already] there'.[23]

If there had been a strong political will in Parliament to fight on, the defeat at Yorktown might have been overcome, but the independent country backbenchers had grown sick of the war and the taxes it cost them, and were no longer persuaded that it could be fought to a good outcome. There were to be five major debates on America before Parliament went into Christmas recess on 20 December, which gave the country squires plenty of opportunities to turn against the further expenditure of blood and treasure on what now looked like an unwinnable war.

As the American military historian Max Boot points out, in earlier centuries the Roman Empire would simply have sent ever larger armies to crush its enemies until Washington had been crucified (possibly literally).[24] But the eighteenth century and the British Empire were not like that, and the government had to consider a relatively new political concept – public opinion, the first reference to which occurred in Edward Gibbon's *Decline and Fall of the Roman Empire*, first published in 1776. As the Americans themselves were to discover two centuries later in Vietnam, no matter how many battles are won in the field, in a long-running guerrilla war it is the battle for opinion at home that decides how and when a war ends.

Whig newspapers had almost uniformly opposed the war since its out-set, with the *Evening Post* describing it as 'unnatural, unconstitutional, unnecessary, unjust, dangerous, hazardous and unprofitable'.[25] Much of the Secret Service Fund was spent subsidizing pro-war newspapers such as the *Morning Post*, in the same way that the French government secretly subsidized newspapers in which Benjamin Franklin was writing in Paris. After Yorktown, the hawks lost the battle for public opinion.

On 12 December a former government supporter, Sir James Lowther, sponsored in the Commons the motion that 'all further attempts to reduce the revolted colonies to obedience are contrary to the true interests of this kingdom,' which was rejected by only 220 votes to 179. Two days later, just as Germain was telling MPs that the government was unanimous in not wanting to abandon America, North ostentatiously got up from his place beside him on the front bench and went to sit on the bench behind him, leaving Germain alone. The visual metaphor was clear, and according to Wraxall 'left no room to doubt of the dissimilarity of opinion among ministers on the great question respecting America'.[26] The next day at Brooks's, Fox wagered John Crewe MP ten guineas 'that Lord George Germain goes out before Lord Sandwich'.[27] The next three wagers in the book were about the date of Sandwich's own departure from the government, with General Burgoyne guessing he would be out in two months.

Germain, who in the debate on 12 December had declared that he would never put his 'hand to any instrument conceding the independence of the colonies', offered his resignation to the King four days later.[28] He had finally been overcome by 'the general dislike to the American war among the real friends of [the] government', and complained that at Cabinet the previous day 'a total silence' had descended when the item on the agenda was 'the measures to be pursued in America'.[29] The King refused to accept his resignation, not least because he and North could not agree upon a successor colonial secretary. The King would only have someone who opposed American independence, and of the few ministers who still adhered to that policy the only logical candidate was Charles Jenkinson, who understandably did not want the job.

In a conversation with the King on 21 December, North once more advocated making peace with the rebels, although so soon after Yorktown the terms could only be unfavourable. In a draft letter to Stormont with many crossings-out and corrections that he wrote at 8 o'clock the next morning, George said that North's language 'was so extraordinary that I almost suspected that he painted his opinions in a stronger light than he felt them in hopes of staggering mine . . . he assured me that he had not said an iota that was not dictated by the strongest conviction; on which I told him that there were many unpleasant but intermediate steps to what I must ever deem *irrecoverable destruction* and to which I would never consent'.[30]

George wanted the secretaries of state, Stormont and Hillsborough, to meet before the Cabinet the next day so that they could coordinate a response if the Prime Minister once again advocated peace. He predicted 'heat and ill-humour'. The two hardliners did meet, but Stormont reported that at Cabinet 'I never saw more harmony and good humour in any meeting,' which was full of 'fair, liberal, manly discussion' about Clinton being relieved of his command.

Politics paused for Christmas, but on Boxing Day North wrote to Robinson to say that the King did not believe that even Germain's resignation would necessarily mean that the war should end. 'You see there is no great objection to changing men, but a very great one to changing measures, and that it will be expected from me *alone* [on the Commons front bench] to carry on that plan which appears to me in our present circumstances ruinous and impracticable.'[31] It is unclear how many government ministers in either House really believed the war was still winnable and how many – certainly including North but probably Stormont and Hillsborough too – did not want to be seen as unpatriotic (and disloyal to the King) by openly calling for an armistice. In an audience with North some time in January, the King made it clear how much he sympathized with Germain over the principle of not agreeing to a peace that granted America formal sovereignty. 'If you mean by his going out', the King told North, 'to relinquish that principle you must make other removes.' 'No,' replied North, 'for no one else has declared that principle.' 'Yes,' retorted the King, 'you must go further: you must remove *me*.'[32]

At an audience on 17 January, Germain, never one to procrastinate, asked the King directly if he was still the Secretary of State for the American Department. The King replied that no decision had been taken, whereupon Germain said he would stay on only if full independence were not offered during any peace negotiations with Congress, and the war was continued 'with vigour' in the West Indies against the European powers. The King told North at 7.02 p.m. that Germain felt 'he cannot with honour continue if he is not supported by his colleagues.'[33] Yet by then the only person who truly supported his stance was the King himself. When Germain saw North soon afterwards, he was told, 'Your being out of the way won't mend matters, for the King is of the same opinion.'[34]

In the first week of January 1782, North extended separate peace feelers to both France and America, in the hope that one or other of them might betray the alliance, a ploy that failed miserably when Franklin and Vergennes naturally compared the different terms he was offering them.[35] By the time Parliament reassembled on 21 January, North knew of Franklin's refusal to discuss any peace that did not include American independence. There had been six censure votes since Yorktown, with the government majority in the Commons dwindling each time. By 7 February it was down to twenty-two.

On 21 February the King wrote to North to complain that the Prime Minister had spent six weeks unable to decide whether to ask for Germain's resignation, which 'certainly has delayed the preparation for the next campaign'.[36] It perhaps seems extraordinary that the King could have genuinely thought that there might be another campaign after Yorktown, but he did.

> I shall only add that on one material point, I shall ever coincide with Lord G. Germain, this is against a separation from America, and that I shall never lose an opportunity in declaring that no consideration shall ever make me in the smallest degree an instrument in a measure that I am confident would annihilate the rank in which this British Empire stands among the European states, and would render my situation in this country below continuing an object to me.

Here was another clear abdication threat. 'Peace with America seems necessary,' North replied the same day, 'even if it can be obtained on no better terms than some federal alliance, or perhaps even in a less eligible mode.'[37] The phrase 'less eligible mode' has been described by North's biographer as his 'delicate phrase for full independence'.[38] He once again upbraided the King for not replacing him during the war: 'If I had not repeatedly laid before Your Majesty my incapacity ... I should take to myself a much greater share of the blame for what Your Majesty's service has suffered by my indecision.'[39]

Although the King wanted to fight on, the matter was about to be decided by the House of Commons and a handful of government ministers below Cabinet level. By early February, Richard Rigby, the

Paymaster-General, and Henry Dundas, the Lord Advocate of Scotland, were both refusing to attend the coming session in the Commons if Germain were not dismissed. When North finally told Germain he had to resign, Germain was credited with replying, 'You say I must go, my Lord! Very well, but pray, why is your lordship to stay?'[40] The veteran King's Friend placeman Welbore Ellis, who having been elected in 1741 was only two years off becoming Father of the House,* was persuaded to become American Secretary in return for an eventual peerage. To put someone in the American Office the King was even prepared to overlook Ellis' increasingly acrimonious relationship with his wife.†

Germain resigned on 9 February 1782. The King agreed to award him the viscountcy of Sackville as a personal sign of thanks and support, doing so in a handwritten order to the Lord Chancellor without seeking the advice of North or anyone else. Germain asked for a more superior rank in the peerage than a barony because otherwise, as he rather grandly put it, 'my own [under-]secretary,‡ my lawyer,§ and father's page¶ will all three take rank of me'.[41] Yet his elevation further infuriated those Whig peers who both opposed the war and hated Sackville. The Marquess of Carmarthen, son of the 4th Duke of Leeds who sat in the Lords under a writ of acceleration, put down a motion saying that it was insulting to the honour of the House of Lords that they were to be joined by someone 'stamped by an incredible brand and a sentence that has never been cancelled', a reference to the Minden court martial.[42] In response, George Selwyn MP condemned Carmarthen's motion as 'an unpardonable insult to the Crown'.[43] The King evidently agreed, and when he heard that the opposition to Sackville's peerage was supported by the Dukes of Devonshire, Rutland and Portland and the Earl of Derby, he ordered that Sackville's viscountcy be immediately published in the newspapers so there could be no reversal by the ministry.[44]

Undeterred, Carmarthen went further still on 18 February, moving that 'It was highly reprehensible in any person to advise the Crown to exercise its indisputable right of creating a peer, in favour of a person labouring under the heavy censure concerned in the following sentence of a court

---

* The longest continuously serving MP in the Commons.
† During one of their spectacular rows, she told her husband that after she died, 'rather than not marry at all, you would marry the Devil's daughter,' to which he replied that that would be against the law, since 'You can't marry a sister of your former wife' (ed. Bickley, *Diaries of Sylvester Douglas* I p. 94).
‡ Baron Walsingham.
§ Alexander Wedderburn, then Baron Loughborough.
¶ Baron Amherst had been page to the Duke of Dorset when he was Viceroy of Ireland.

martial . . .' and managed to get the entire text of the court martial's sentence included in the motion. In the subsequent debate, the battle of Minden was refought in the Lords chamber, with a contribution from the Earl of Southampton, who had carried Prince Ferdinand's orders to Germain. Shelburne, who had been Granby's aide-de-camp at the battle but thought Germain blameless, nonetheless opposed the peerage being bestowed. The Earl of Abingdon hyperbolically described Germain as 'the greatest criminal this country has ever known'.[45] Some peers, such as Abingdon and the Duke of Richmond, even questioned the King's right to appoint peers, an idea so unacceptable that it undoubtedly helped ensure they lost the vote by 81 to 27. Nevertheless, it marked the first time in the reign that a direct assault had been made on such a crucial aspect of the royal prerogative.

In the Commons on 20 February, a motion censuring Lord Sandwich for his running of the Admiralty saw large abstentions from normal government supporters and only ten county MPs voting with the ministry. 'Undoubtedly the House of Commons seem to be so wild at present,' the King wrote to North on 26 February, 'and to be running on to ruin that no man can answer for the event of any question. I certainly till drove to the wall do [sic] what I can to save the Empire, and if I do not succeed I will at least have the self-approbation of having done my duty and of not letting myself be a tool in the destruction of the honour of the country.'[46] George never lacked self-approbation, but even he could see that events in the Commons meant that North's days as Prime Minister were now numbered.

On 27 February, in another debate on the war, Fox described North as merely a creature 'of that infernal spirit that really governs', meaning the King.[47] It was the kind of remark that at other times would have caused outrage, but in the passion of the debate was not remarked upon. The Opposition won a vote critical of the government proposed by General Henry Conway. The next morning, North told the King 'with the utmost concern' that 'the temper of the House was so strong that nothing could resist it.'[48] He accepted that there would have to be a confidence vote in his ministry, and if he survived that 'it might be feasible to divide the Opposition, and to take in only a part, but some step of that sort appears to Lord North to be absolutely necessary'.[49] The King replied at 11.20 a.m. that he was 'much hurt' at Conway's success, and thought North needed to consult the Cabinet on the 'highly delicate' wording of the government's response to the motion. 'I am mortified Lord North thinks he cannot now remain in office,' he replied.[50] He later asked Thurlow to sound out Lords Gower and Weymouth to find out if they would join a new ministry. The King wanted the policy of any new government to be 'keeping what is in our present possession in North America, and attempting by a negotiation with any separate provinces or even districts to detach them from France, even upon any plan of their own, provided they remain separate states'.[51] Yet the idea that any of the American colonies could be split off from the rest was simply not practical politics at that stage of the war.

On 8 March the news arrived that Minorca had fallen to the Spanish a month before, further demoralizing the Cabinet and weakening the government. Gower and Grafton refused office that same day, and North suggested that Thurlow should instead confer with Shelburne and Rockingham, even though Rockingham was demanding both the immediate recognition of American independence and Economical Reform as his price for entering the ministry. In the Commons, William Pitt made an extraordinary statement for a twenty-two-year-old, when he said that in the event of his being asked to join, 'I feel myself bound to declare that I would never accept a subordinate situation,' by which he meant a non-Cabinet rank.[52]

On 9 March, North survived the confidence motion by only 226 votes to 216, whereupon he repeated to the King 'his opinion that it is totally impossible to conduct His Majesty's business any longer'.[53] After four days of intense negotiations at Westminster, Thurlow gave an account to the King of a conversation he had held with Rockingham, and at 10.46 p.m. George agreed that he wanted 'a broad bottom, not the delivering myself up to a party' (meaning Rockingham and Fox).[54]

Despite the King's long-standing and profound antipathy to Fox, the two men hardly knew each other personally: Fox did not attend either Drawing Rooms or Levees, and had never had a private audience in the Closet. If they had met in private, it is perfectly possible that Fox's personal charm might have won George over, and they might have found at least some common ground for a working relationship. Instead, their mutual suspicion – of Fox as a drunken, immoral, republican gambler and of the King as a would-be dictator – continued for many years.

On 14 March, Rockingham set out for Thurlow four conditions under which he would enter the government: that the King not veto a Bill giving America its independence; the passing of a Contractors Bill; a Bill to disenfranchise excisemen and revenue officers (who tended to vote for the government); and the passing of Burke's reform of the Civil List, which would abolish forty sinecures in the gift of the Crown and sharply reduce the pensions list. 'The whole of these demands were so strange', the King stated in a memorandum written in the Queen's handwriting on 18 March, 'that it can only be looked upon as the disinclination of Opposition to give any assistance to their country. The King feels the indignity offered to his person by such propositions, and cannot direct any further conversation to be held with the Marquess . . . His Majesty cannot offer up his principles, his honour and the interest of his good subjects to the disposal of any set of men.'[55] In fact, although the American proviso possibly affected his honour, the other three stipulations were not strange at all, but predictable attempts to tip the balance of parliamentary power towards the Whigs and away from the Crown.

Among the King's papers from this period are several undated drafts, with many crossings-out and corrections, of an instrument of abdication in George's handwriting. It was probably not intended to be used (there was no fair copy), and there was a good deal of emotional self-indulgence to it. 'His Majesty, during the twenty-one years he has sat on the Throne of Great Britain,' it began, 'has had no object so much at heart as the maintenance of the British constitution, of which the difficulties he has at times met with from his scrupulous attachment to the rights of Parliament are sufficient proofs.'[56] He next gave the reasons for his abdication, saying 'the sudden change of sentiments' in Parliament had 'totally incapacitated him from either conducting the war with effect, or of obtaining any peace but on conditions that would prove destructive to the commerce as well as the essential rights of the British nation'. Since he could be of no further use to 'his native country', he was driven 'to the painful step of quitting it for ever', presumably for Hanover. In the last sentence, 'His Majesty resigns the Crown of Great Britain and the Dominions appertaining thereto' – which did not include the Electorate – to George, Prince of Wales, 'whose endeavours for the prosperity of the British Empire he hopes may prove more successful'.

The lack of seriousness in this draft message might be judged from the fact that there was no mention of a Regency Council, which would have been needed until Prince George's twenty-first birthday in August 1783. Nevertheless, the King wrote it. For all the hints of self-pity, and his evident desire to defend himself against Whig accusations that he was undermining the rights of Parliament, it was the looming defeat in the American War of Independence that drove him to do so, as well as the humiliation involved in accepting Rockingham's circumscription of his prerogative powers.

On the morning of 18 March, North was so provoked by a meeting with the King that he sent him a letter reminding him of a key aspect of the constitution that the King so regularly said he revered. It amounted to a history lesson, recounting matters that he knew the King understood perfectly well, but of which he felt compelled to remind him. There was a motion before the House to be debated on 20 March, 'That in the present distracted state of the country, it is contrary to the interests of His Majesty to continue the management of public affairs in the hands of the present ministers'.[57] As it looked like the motion was going to pass, he told the King that:

> The torrent is too strong to be resisted; Your Majesty is well apprised that, in this country, the prince on the throne cannot, with prudence, oppose the deliberate resolution of the House of Commons. Your royal predecessors (including King William III and his late Majesty) were obliged to yield to it much against their wish in more instances than one . . . The concessions they made were never deemed dishonourable, but were considered as marks of their wisdom, and of their parental affection for their people.[58]

North told the King bluntly that he had 'persevered, as long as possible, in what you thought right', but the struggle was now over. The only people capable of forming a new ministry were Rockingham and Shelburne, and the alternative would be to have no government at all, with 'all the evils and all the dangers which are naturally to be apprehended at such a state of affairs'.[59] The next morning George replied, clearly wounded, 'I could not but be hurt at your letter of last night. Every man must be the sole judge of his feelings, therefore whatever you or any man can say in that subject has no avail with me.'

North understandably did not want to suffer the humiliation of being forced from office by a vote of no confidence, and told the King on 19 March that if he were not allowed to resign, he 'shall remain in the journals forever stigmatized upon record by a vote in Parliament for my removal, which I believe has seldom, if ever, happened to a minister before . . . Your Majesty's affairs grow worse by every hour that my removal is delayed . . . I submit the whole to Your Majesty's kind consideration, hoping that you will permit me to save myself from disgrace.'[60] Yet the King had still not heard back from Thurlow as to whether Shelburne might assume the premiership rather than Rockingham, and he replied at 11.21 p.m., 'Till I have heard what the Chancellor has done from his own mouth, I shall not take any step; and if you resign before I have decided what I will do, you will certainly forever forfeit my regard.'[61]

The next day, 20 March 1782, with Shelburne still undecided, North had a ninety-minute audience in which the King finally accepted that the ministry was at an end. 'Then, sir, had I not better state that fact at once?' said North. 'Well, you may do so,' replied the King.[62] There was a rumour that the King 'parted rudely with him without thanking him'.[63] Walpole later alleged that the King observed tersely, 'Remember, my Lord, that it is you who desert me, not I you.'[64] Whether or not sharp words were actually exchanged, George generously offered to extend the lord wardenship of the Cinque Ports for life, which North gratefully accepted.

North then set off for the Commons at once, still wearing the full Court dress and Garter sash that he was obliged to wear for his audience. There were about 400 members in the afternoon session, all expecting the fall of the ministry in that evening's debate, and as North entered there were cries of 'Order!' and 'Places!' (meaning 'Sit down!'). When he reached the government front bench he tried to rise to speak, but was shouted down as Fox put a motion that Charles Howard, the Earl of Surrey (the future 11th Duke of Norfolk), be allowed to speak on a previous motion. This was a barefaced attempt on Fox's part not to let North resign, and instead force a vote to remove him. Amid howls and yells, and what Wraxall called a clamour 'from all quarters of the most violent description', North simply ignored Fox and got up to speak.[65]

There followed a long period of procedural wrangling, with North trying to get the opportunity to resign before Fox could force him out. With the Speaker on his side, North won, and told the Commons, 'His Majesty's ministers [are] no more,' adding that he would welcome a public inquiry into his conduct of the war.[66]* Surrey withdrew his motion and the House adjourned.

It was a snowy day and waiting outside the House of Lords, 'with that placid temper that never forsook him', as Wraxall put it, North made a wry joke to those MPs who were having to wait for their coaches because they had not known the sitting would be curtailed in the afternoon. 'Good night, gentlemen,' he said, as he stepped into his coach with his friends to go home to dinner, 'you see what it is to be in the secret!'[67] One of the MPs at the dinner that night, the Scot William Adams, recorded, 'No man ever showed more calmness, cheerfulness, and serenity. The temper of the family was the same.'[68] Nothing in office became Lord North like the leaving it.†

The next day the King formally offered the premiership to Shelburne – who had opposed taxing America, but also opposed independence. He refused it, as he knew that Rockingham would not serve except as First Lord of the Treasury. So it was arranged that Rockingham would receive the seals of office on 27 March, coming into power on the understanding that American independence would be granted, a Contractors Bill passed, excisemen and revenue officers disenfranchised and the Civil List reformed, all of them conditions deeply antithetical to the King. With the support of the Commons majority, Rockingham had won their long battle of wills and successfully stormed the Closet. He had also shown that the

---

* Another version of what was heard above the uproar was 'His Majesty has come to a determination to change his ministers' (Cobbett, *Parliamentary History* XXII col. 1217).

† At twelve years and fifty-eight days, he is the sixth longest-serving British Prime Minister, and the fourth longest in terms of an unbroken period of office.

constitution worked. He could have entered office much earlier if he had dropped what George called his 'tenets', but he had not, and now came in on his own terms.

On the last day of his premiership, North sent the King a short memorandum on the 'general state' of the 1780 election account, which revealed the distressing news that far from paying down the £30,000 he had borrowed from Drummonds at 5 per cent interest, as the King assumed he had been, the entire amount was still outstanding. With an extra £3,000 needed for electoral managers in Surrey (but £1,000 expected from Lord Bute for the election of one of his sons) in fact it would be more. North blithely assumed the King would pay part of it off in a lump sum of £13,000 and then the rest 'may be rubbed off by cheques, by the £1,000 a month, out of the Privy Purse'.[69]*

The King was shocked at North's negligence and mismanagement. Relations between them deteriorated greatly thereafter, when the former premier sent George the quarterly account book of the Secret Service, which the King was furious to see went up only to April 1780. 'I cannot help saying it is a most shameful piece of neglect I ever knew,' the financially meticulous George remonstrated to North. 'No business can ever be admitted as an excuse for not doing that.'[70] He pointed out that Grafton had never let a month elapse after each quarter without submitting the account book, let alone two whole years. He could not understand how North, 'knowing for some weeks that the ministry would be changed', had not attended to this, as some of the payments to individuals were in arrears, in the case of the long-suffering 8th Earl of Northampton, a former groom of the bedchamber and presently Lord-Lieutenant of Northamptonshire, two and a half years. The King did not need to warn North that Rockingham was very unlikely to sign off nearly £20,000 of Secret Service funds to finance an opponent's very old bribes, especially when he was entering office with a public pledge to reduce the power of the Crown.[71]

It is not hard to spot a hint of self-righteousness when he told North that 'This is a natural consequence of the total change that I have been driven to. I foretold the measures that would be expected, but Lord North as well as the rest who advised my treating with the Opposition would not credit my assertions ... As to the immense expenditure of the [1780] general election it has quite surprised me, the sum is at least double of what was expended at any other general election since I came to the throne.'[72] He agreed to pay Drummonds Bank £13,000 'by degrees', but beyond that

---

* It was not until 18 April that North came up with a final figure, £32,754 – over £4 million in today's money.

'I cannot bind myself further.'[73] He told North that if as a result of Burke's Economical Reforms his Privy Purse was to receive £12,000 per annum less from the Civil List, as was proposed, 'I have no means of satisfying the remainder now unexpectedly put to my account of £19,754 18 shillings and twopence.'[74] He generously made no mention of the £1,500 interest that had accrued as a result of North's negligence. The King was astonished that the debt had not been paid off through the Secret Service Fund years earlier. He ended by saying, 'I am sorry to see there has been such a strange waste of money,' but made it clear he was not going to pick up the nearly £6,755 shortfall. This was devastating to North, who was not a rich man and who, to his great credit, had not made any money from his twelve years as premier.

Back in September 1777, the King had paid off North's £16,000 debt, telling him, 'I love you as well as a man of worth as I esteem you as a minister.'[75] Such a sentiment was emphatically now no longer the case. Legally, the King was in the right. North was responsible for the loan and had not provided any accounts or explanations for well over eighteen months while he and Robinson had been doing extremely complex and expensive deals with a large number of constituency agents and would-be MPs. (Of course the Opposition had been doing exactly the same kind of deals, albeit not with taxpayers' money.) But the debt would not have been taken on without Drummond's well-founded assumption of the King's approval, and it was done for ends that he had desired.

North sent the King all the Secret Service accounts since he had come to power in 1770, which included pensions for pro-government (or more often anti-Opposition) journalists, £2,600 for wounded soldiers in America and a £2,817 and three shilling 'loss upon sundry lottery tickets purchased at high prices to keep up the credit of the Lottery'.[76] George did not really want to be kept informed of the details of the deals themselves, which were mildly unsavoury and would undoubtedly be considered corrupt by contemporary standards. When North itemized them for the King they included such remarks as 'Tamworth: Lord Townshend's distresses obliged him to sell the seat for £4,000. Mr Courtney, the member, returned this favour to government by supporting them always with great abilities and zeal.'[77] In today's parlance this was pure and simple cash-for-votes, but was not unusual in eighteenth-century politics.

'Lord North cannot be surprised that a mind truly tore to pieces should make me less attentive to my expressions,' the King wrote on 21 April, apologizing for what he had said when North resigned. 'I certainly did and do still think the accounts ought to have been regularly given in, but I did not mean by that to express any intention of withdrawing my good opinion of him.'[78] He little knew how prophetic his phrase about 'a mind truly tore to pieces' would be. Despite this quasi-apology, North's sheer disorganization had soured the relationship between the two men, as became very clear to them the following year.

The situation became worse on 8 May when Lord Brudenell, acting as the King's go-between with Drummonds Bank, tried to pay off £7,000 of what he considered the King's £13,000 debt, but Drummonds refused to issue a receipt as they pointed out that the debt was in fact £30,000 plus interest. North wrote to the King eight days later, saying that 'having no money, and not being able to give Mr Drummond any security', he was 'endeavouring to apply the whole income of his office [as Lord Warden of the Cinque Ports] to the gradual extinction of the debt'.[79] The King took this as an admission that North was responsible for the debt, and he piled on further pressure by refusing to sign off a Secret Service payment of £3,250 for a pro-government journalist, the Rev. Henry Bate. North's resentment against the King festered and was to continue even after Drummonds had finally been paid £32,241 nineteen shillings and fourpence from the Secret Service Fund by a different ministry more than two years later.

On the morning of 27 March 1782, Rockingham kissed hands as First Lord of the Treasury, in coalition with Lord Shelburne. In a major re-organization of government that the King had been advocating for some time, and which has stood the test of time to the present day, the Northern and Southern Departments were transformed into the Home and Foreign Offices respectively.[80] Shelburne became Home Secretary and Fox became Foreign Secretary and Leader of the House of Commons. The American Department was abolished, William Knox dismissed and colonial affairs incongruously transferred to the Home Office. Thurlow stayed on as Lord Chancellor despite being a King's Friend, but apart from him the clear-out of Northites was total, with several of the people the King most disliked and despised in politics such as Fox and Dunning being honoured and promoted, and Keppel becoming First Lord of the Admiralty.

The change of regime inaugurated two years of full-scale political crisis, in which successive ministries were hastily assembled and just as hastily collapsed. The root cause was the fact that Charles Fox and the King loathed each other. Fox had recently been making the sort of jokes that all too often found their way back to the King himself. In the summer of 1782 he had taken to calling the King 'Satan', which would certainly not have amused the pious Christian monarch, and a 'blockhead'.[81] On the very day that he became Foreign Secretary, Carmarthen noted Fox stating, 'Certainly things look well but he, meaning the King, will die soon, and that will be best of all.'[82] Although the King was only forty-four, that was the age at which his father had died, and five of his eight siblings had already died before the age of fifty. Fox therefore had reason to hope. The idea that the King would still be living thirty-seven years later, long after the much younger Fox and Carmarthen were dead, would have surprised all three of them.

In accordance with his stated ambition, William Pitt refused the vice-treasurership of Ireland as he deemed it too minor, despite his father having held it in 1746. Since he was universally considered too young for Cabinet office, Pitt did not join the government. This might well have been his intention all along, recognizing quite rightly that a ministry lacking royal approval and riven by fundamental disagreements over America between the Shelburnites and Rockinghamites was unlikely to last long.

The reform of the two most important ministries, far from settling roles, brought about the ludicrous situation in which Shelburne as Home Secretary retained control over colonial (and thus American) affairs, so was responsible for the peace negotiations with the thirteen colonies, while Fox as Foreign Secretary was responsible for making peace with France, Spain and Holland. Even if the two had been on friendly terms, or at the very least in accord strategically, it still would have been difficult to coordinate the talks in Paris under such circumstances. As it was, they not only disliked one another but saw the situation in diametrically opposed ways. Fox welcomed early and complete American independence and wanted to use it as a lever to bring about peace with the European powers, while intending to be generous to the nascent American republic over frontier and trade issues. By contrast, Shelburne wanted to use the frontier and trade negotiations to persuade the former colonies to remain in some form of a loose commonwealth arrangement with Britain, in which they would be entirely self-governing domestically but would decide foreign policy matters jointly. Predictably, the King sided strongly with Shelburne.

'At last the fatal day is come which the misfortunes of the times and the sudden change of sentiments of the House of Commons have drove me to,' the King wrote to North on 27 March.[83] This sentence has been used, not least by Winston Churchill, to describe George's response to the defeat in America; but he was in fact referring to Rockingham's accession to power that same day.[84] George complained that it was the most thorough-going change of ministry in history, and that 'I have to the last fought for individuals, but the number I have saved except my bedchamber is incredibly few.'

The King asked that the outgoing ministers of the North administration should arrive at St James's Palace at 1 p.m., as 'I think it would be awkward to have the new people presented at the Levee prior to the resignations.'[85] He also told a courtier to take a message to Thomas Brudenell-Bruce, 1st Earl of Ailesbury, who was being stripped of the lord-lieutenancy of Wiltshire to make way for the 10th Earl of Pembroke, declaring, 'You know how I love Lord Ailesbury; I trust he will know this goes to my soul . . . but I trust this will not make him quit the Queen's family.'[86] To his credit, Ailesbury dutifully stayed on as the Queen's Chamberlain.

The King was forced to award no fewer than four non-royal Garters in 1782, the second-largest number for a single year of his reign, which went to the leading Whigs Shelburne, the Duke of Richmond, the 4th Duke of Rutland and Rockingham's close friend the thirty-three-year-old 5th Duke of Devonshire. While Burke, now Paymaster-General of the Forces, was pushing forward his Economical Reform package designed to curtail the King's use of patronage, he installed his son Richard and a friend, Richard Champion, as his deputies at salaries of £500 per annum. He also created a new post for William Burke, his cousin and best friend, that paid £5 a day, took the secretaryship to the Treasury for his brother Richard at £3,000 per annum and installed his acolyte Walker King in his own previous job of Rockingham's private secretary, winning salaries for family and friends that totalled over £9,000. Burke's personal debts rapidly evaporated during his tenure of office, as he did battle with the King's supposed 'corruption'.[87]

Within a few days of coming to power, the Rockingham Cabinet made strategic alterations in policy, recommending an immediate cessation of hostilities with Holland prior to signing a peace treaty. Sir Guy Carleton, now Commander-in-Chief of all British forces in North America, was given orders to withdraw the New York garrison to Halifax, Nova Scotia, to evacuate Charleston and Savannah 'using his discretion as to mode and time' and to reinforce Barbados.[88] Since New York was one of the few territorial bargaining chips the government had left, Carleton took his time, not least because he needed to ensure that the large Loyalist population there would be able to escape the victorious Patriots' wrath.

It very quickly became clear to the King that a rift was fast developing between Rockingham and Shelburne over appointments. It was Shelburne who interacted with the King on behalf of the ministry, something that Rockingham, as its head, came to resent. Having met Rockingham twice by 5 April, George confirmed that the premier was 'wanting to get all patronage into his hands, to the exclusion of Lord Shelburne . . . I said I would see how I could accommodate them both. When Lord Shelburne was with me he expressed an uneasiness lest I should yield to the importunities of Lord Rockingham which would reduce him to a Secretary of State . . . instead of a colleague.'[89] Shelburne wanted assurance on paper, so George drafted a memorandum of agreement between Shelburne and Rockingham, saying that he hoped it was 'equally civil to both'. It was an almost textbook opportunity for the King to divide and rule his new government, and he took it.

The memorandum, of which there are four versions because he kept rewriting it, noted that he had resolved on a new ministry, formed on 'a broad basis, as most conducible to heal the divisions that distract the kingdom', and that 'all ecclesiastical and civil preferments' should be jointly recommended by Rockingham and Shelburne. He somewhat mis-chievously added that, because 'the above two noblemen had accepted offices only from a view of being serviceable to their country at a perilous time,' they 'consequently must rejoice at being obliged to consult together'.[90] The King hoped that 'both will see that there is not the smallest difficulty in conducting the line of recommendations to their mutual satisfaction,' whereas of course he knew perfectly well the level of suspicion between them. By throwing the duty of recommending advancements to them both rather than splitting the duties by region, by job specification or by any other criterion, and by deliberately keeping military positions and honours off the list, the King had effectively drawn up a perfect recipe for continu-ing antagonism between them. George was not generally Machiavellian, but he could be when provoked.

Whereas Fox and Rockingham had been publicly in favour of recogniz-ing America since 1778 (and privately even earlier), Shelburne and the other former Chathamites, who now composed half the Cabinet, believed that recognition should be awarded only as an incentive to sign the peace treaty. Fox had inherited from his father a dislike and distrust of Shelburne, but it was made worse when it became clear to the Foreign Secretary – whose agent in Paris was Thomas Grenville MP, the youngest son of George Grenville – that Shelburne was conducting a parallel set of negotia-tions with Benjamin Franklin there through his agent Richard Oswald.[91] When the Rockingham–Shelburne rivalry was added to the mix, the atmos-phere in the coalition soon grew toxic. The King supported Oswald's mission, telling Shelburne, 'I was thoroughly resolved not to open my mouth on any negotiation with America,' but Shelburne's part in it now 'obliges me now and then to give a hint'.[92] Fox was soon (justly) accusing Oswald of undermining Thomas Grenville, and within two months was considering resignation.

For all that peace was being actively discussed, the war was continuing. On the same day that Rockingham and his Cabinet kissed hands with the

King in London, on 27 March 1782, the American Colonel Matthias Ogden proposed to lead a team into Manhattan to kidnap Prince William, the King's sixteen-year-old son, and Admiral Robert Digby, the Royal Navy commander of the North American station. 'The spirit of enterprise so conspicuous in your plan for surprising in their quarters and bringing off the Prince William Henry and Admiral Digby', George Washington told Ogden, 'merits applause; and you have my authority to make the attempt, in any manner and at such times as your judgement shall direct.'[93] (By contrast, Clinton flatly rejected a Loyalist plot to kidnap Washington.)

Washington's biographer Ron Chernow believes that the General hoped that the kidnapping 'might serve to dishearten George III', whereas in fact it would probably only have hardened him further – and possibly also hardened parliamentary opposition to any easy post-war Anglo-American relationship.[94] Washington had earlier approved plans to try to kidnap Benedict Arnold and Clinton himself, so he had form for this kind of escapade. Ogden intended to use thirty-six men dressed as sailors to row across the Hudson in four whaleboats on a rainy night, disable the sentries and seize the victims, although Washington made it clear to Ogden that there must be no 'insult or indignity to the persons of the prince or admiral'.[95] To Washington's annoyance, it was never even attempted. 'I am obliged to General Washington for his humanity,' Prince William – by then King William IV – told the American Ambassador years later when shown a copy of Washington's correspondence with Ogden, 'but I'm damned glad I did not give him an opportunity of exercising it towards me.'[96]

The British government's position in the peace negotiations with France was greatly strengthened on 18 May when the news arrived of the crushing victory won by Admirals Sir George Rodney and Samuel Hood on 12 April 1782 at the battle of the Saintes between Guadeloupe and Dominica.* De Grasse lost four ships-of-the-line sunk and one captured, and 8,000 men killed, wounded or captured, to just 243 British dead and 816 wounded. The decision to send Rodney out had been taken by Germain shortly before he left office, and Keppel had subsequently tried to have him recalled, but the message only arrived after the battle. The King called the Saintes 'the most complete victory that has occurred this war', and when de Grasse was brought back to Portsmouth aboard Rodney's flagship *Formidable* on 1 August, he was the first French Commander-in-Chief to be held on British soil since the reign of Queen Anne.[97]

The victory allowed some to argue that the peace negotiations should be called off altogether, but others pointed out that now that the British

---

* Named after the Îles des Saintes, north of Dominica.

Empire's position was secure in the West Indies and the French Empire's threatened, better terms could be gained. Even before the battle of the Saintes there had been British victories over France in West Africa and over Holland in India, Ceylon (modern-day Sri Lanka) and the West Indies. On 1 July 1781, as Cornwallis had been marching towards disaster in Virginia, General Sir Eyre Coote had won the battle of Porto Novo (present-day Parangipettai) during the Second Anglo-Mysore War, in which his force of 8,500 British soldiers and East India Company sepoys defeated 47,000 Mysoris. In November, Vice-Admiral Sir Edward Hughes captured the Dutch fortress of Negapatam in the Madras Province, and in 1782 he fought Admiral Pierre de Suffren, perhaps the greatest admiral in French history, in five naval battles that ensured British rule in India would survive to grow exponentially during the rest of George's reign. For all that an empire had been lost in the west, a larger and more populous one was being won in the east. It would last until 1947, far longer than British rule over the American colonies could have done even if Britain had won the War of Independence.

'The letter to Dr Franklin seems very proper,' the King wrote to Shelburne on 27 April of the peace offer Richard Oswald was about to make in Paris, 'and there does not occur to me the smallest doubt of its being perfectly safe for Lord Shelburne to send it without alteration.'[98] He advised him to 'keep Mr Oswald at Paris, which cannot fail of being a useful check on that part of the negotiation which is in other hands'.[99] Robert R. Livingston, the American Secretary of State, was therefore wrong when he wrote to John Jay on 9 May attacking in apocalyptic terms George's supposed refusal to make peace, saying, 'We believe that God has hardened the heart of Pharaoh so that he cannot let his people go, till the first-born of his land are destroyed, till the hosts are overthrown in the midst of the sea, and till poverty and distress like the lice of Egypt shall have covered the land.'[100] In fact a week later Thomas Grenville set off for Paris, also with the King's blessing, to open peace negotiations with Vergennes.

'Provided we can stay in long enough to have given a good stout blow to the influence of the Crown,' Fox wrote to his supporter General Richard Fitzpatrick MP, 'I do not think it much signifies how soon we go out after.'[101] That blow was to be delivered by Economical Reform, and recognizing the government's seriousness over it, on 28 April the King wrote to Rockingham saying that he proposed to abolish a large number of Court and government posts himself. He was thereby hoping to forestall Burke's even harsher cutting of the royal household. Some of these positions, such as Master of the Great Wardrobe, dated back to the Plantagenets, and their abolition meant that, as Wraxall noted, 'Many persons of high rank reluctantly disappeared from about the King's person and Court in consequence of Burke's Bill.'[102] These included Lord Pelham from the Great Wardrobe, the 2nd Earl of Darlington as Keeper of the Jewel Office (instituted by Elizabeth I), the 6th Earl of Denbigh as Master of the Harriers and the 4th Earl of Essex as Master of the Stag Hounds, as well as various others such as the Treasurer of the Chamber, the Cofferer of the Household, six Clerks of the Green Cloth* who ran the royal household and the Paymaster of the Pensions. Several of these people, such as Lords Pelham and Darlington, were prominent Whigs, causing more friction within the ministry.

The Master of the Horse would survive, but would be regulated under Burke's Establishment Act† of 1782, which transferred the power over the expenditure of the royal household to the Treasury. The King could not grant a pension of more than £300 per annum after the total cost of the pension list reached £90,000. It also strictly limited the amount that could be spent by the Secret Service Fund domestically. It was intended that this should prevent the accumulation of arrears on the Civil List, but these began to pile up again as soon as it was passed, with £60,000 extra needed in 1784 and £210,000 more by 1786.[103] The Act further abolished the seven-seat Board of Trade and Foreign Plantations (although it had to be brought back two years later).

George had succeeded in retaining some posts, writing to Shelburne that the Master of the Robes had to be protected, since 'he has the peculiar employment of carrying my train at the House of Peers as well as on all ceremonies of the Garter.'[104] (The idea that this might be done by someone else at those six or seven ceremonies a year was not considered.)‡ As well as cutting expenditure and clipping the King's wings politically, the Establishment Act produced one unexpected and magnificent side-effect: when it abolished Edward Gibbon's seat on the Board of Trade, he was forced to leave England for Switzerland where he completed *The Decline and Fall of the Roman Empire*.

Although cutting the number of places available to MPs was intended to weaken the power of the Crown as well as to save money, people of course still very much wanted them; indeed it was remarked that the posts were all the more prized since there were now fewer of them. The King had long believed, as he told Lord North in July 1777 when refusing Sir William Hamilton a privy councillorship, that 'the husbanding of honours

---

* Reinstated in 1815, the office was abolished in 2003.
† Also known as the Civil List and Secret Service Money Act, and only repealed in 1993.
‡ The post survived until 1837, but since then has been revived only for kings' coronations.

is the only means of keeping up their value.'[105] He had particularly strong views on peerages. 'I desire I may hear no more about Irish marquises,' he said on refusing Lord Drogheda in March 1776. 'I feel for the English earls and I do not choose to disgust them.'[106] He disliked ennobling judges, and liked to ration advances in rank within the peerage to those who already held ancient ones, because, as he had told Bute years earlier, 'I looked upon our peerage as the most honourable of any country, and that I never would hurt them by putting the juniors of them over the seniors.'[107]

As well as Economical Reform, the Rockingham ministry achieved another of its long-term goals by repealing the Ireland Act of 1720, thus granting Ireland legislative independence subject only to the Viceroy's veto rights. The Irish politician Henry Grattan had been demanding this for years, and although the Irish Parliament in Dublin was elected solely by Protestants, repeal showed that Westminster had learned something from the mishandling of America. Instead of quietening Irish nationalism, however, it actively increased demands for Roman Catholic emancipation. Some Irish Protestants, who were greatly outnumbered on the island, were willing to concede this as the price of domestic peace.

On 21 May, Fox wrote to the King about a dispatch he had just received from Thomas Grenville, indicating 'the favourable disposition of Dr Franklin towards peace with this country, even without the concurrence of France, much more without that of Spain and Holland. Mr Fox is satisfied that Your Majesty's penetration must see in a moment the incredible importance of this object'[108] – that is, not only peace, but the real possibility of shattering the Franco-American alliance. Fox's aim was to follow up Rodney's victory at the Saintes by moving Carleton's army from New York to fight in a West Indian campaign in the autumn. The King endorsed receipt of the letter at 11.03 p.m., slept on it and replied to Fox the next morning at 6.59 (characteristically not rounding it up to 7 a.m.), saying that until Oswald had reported Franklin's views to Shelburne, 'I cannot form any hope that he [that is, Franklin] is ready to conclude a peace without the concurrence of France. Peace is the object of my heart if it can be obtained without forfeiting the honour and essential rights of my kingdom. I do not think myself at liberty to hazard any opinion. I must see my way clear before me.'[109] Three days later the King told Shelburne, 'It is of the greatest importance that gentleman [Oswald] should be fully apprised of what must be obtained at the dreadful price now offered to America.'[110] The King feared that Fox's 'dreadful price' was full independence with nothing but platitudes in return.

By then, Shelburne was actively undermining the Prime Minister in whose Cabinet he sat. At the end of April he had warned George that Rockingham was 'full of complaint' about the King's 'want of confidence' in him and had said he could not continue as premier unless 'everything must go through him,' such as Weymouth's appointment as Groom of the Stole. 'I endeavoured to tranquillize him,' Shelburne reported, but nonetheless told him of 'the impossibility of his considering me as an ordinary Secretary of State', because he was also the leader of the second-largest faction in the ministry.[111] Shelburne ended by warning that Keppel wanted to remove his great enemy Sir Hugh Palliser from the governorship of the Royal Hospital at Greenwich. The Cabinet had agreed – Fox called it 'indispensable' – but Shelburne thought it might not be legal. 'The conduct towards Palliser is certainly mean,' the King replied, 'and considering the good fortune that has attended Keppel will, if it is *legal*, soon be thought *severe*, but though saying that I do not mean to break with the phalanx for such a business.'[112] If he was going to act against his opponents, he needed a more important issue than a hospital governorship.*

By 22 May, Shelburne was advising the King not to give ground to Rockingham over his proposals for peerages. 'There is less reason than ever for opening the door to English peerages at present,' Shelburne advised, 'and infinite prejudice must result to Your Majesty's affairs if you do it, till your government is perfectly settled.'[113] Shelburne thought it perfectly possible to offer Rodney one for the battle of the Saintes – indeed 'the expectations of the public seems to go very strongly to the granting him this honour' – without establishing a dangerous precedent. By contrast the Whig borough-monger Sir James Lowther MP could be kept waiting, and did not become the 1st Earl of Lonsdale for another two years.† It was small wonder that with such advice George came to appreciate that he could work with Shelburne, who, for all his backstairs machinations and general air of untrustworthiness, had once been a supporter of Bute and one of George's aides-de-camp who had seen distinguished service as a colonel in the Seven Years War. Although the King neither liked nor trusted Shelburne, he much preferred him to Fox.

On 4 June, Fox sent Thomas Grenville back to Paris with instructions to renew negotiations aimed at giving America a generous, indeed almost unconditional, offer of independence as part of a durable European peace settlement. Shelburne simultaneously dispatched Richard Oswald to negotiate the best possible terms for Britain on trade and frontiers. It did not

---

* Palliser in fact remained at Greenwich until 1796.
† The King might also have objected to the large number of mistresses Lowther had kept while married to Bute's daughter, and his practice of keeping the corpse of one of them in a glass-topped coffin in a cupboard.

take long for these mixed messages to be picked up by the Americans and French, Grenville writing to Fox warning that Oswald's interference had led to Franklin closing down communications and the French openly mocking the contradictory lines being taken by the envoys from perfidious Albion. Over the course of June, relations therefore deteriorated between the Home and Foreign Secretaries, and when on 29 June the Cabinet supported Shelburne's stance over the timing of a recognition of the United States of America, Fox threatened to resign.

That night the Cabinet met after 11.30 and continued until much later. Even though they had all been 'enjoined secrecy' about what had transpired in their deliberations, Shelburne thought there were two points which the King needed to know. The first was that Fox supported 'declaring the colonies independent without any peace'.[114] The second was that Rockingham was so ill from the new influenza epidemic sweeping Europe that Fox was conspiring to oust him. As it was, he had no need to. Just two days later, the Marquess of Rockingham was dead.

19

'America is Lost!'

July 1782–July 1783

The pattern of British history has been much distorted through the fact that, though much of it has been made by Tories, it has largely been written by Whigs.[1]

Gerald Brown, 'The Court Martial of Lord George Sackville',

1952

Rockingham died at half-past midnight on 1 July 1782. Shelburne wrote from Whitehall at 3.06 a.m. to inform the King, who replied at 7.21 a.m., noting his 'resentment' at his 'total ignorance . . . as to the desperate state of that lord'.[2] The King's next thought was about how the Prime Minister's death might affect the peace process, telling Shelburne that the victory at the battle of the Saintes 'has so far roused the nation that the peace which would have been acquiesced in three months ago would now be a matter of complaint'. If Shelburne could not persuade Fox to remain in the coalition, he suggested that William Pitt become Home Secretary – 'His abilities would make him the most creditable nomination' – as he still sought a 'broad bottom' ministry. He did not want Shelburne, with Fox still in office, to be 'the head of a party when in reality he would be the slave of it'.

At 6.09 that evening George nonetheless formally offered Shelburne the post of First Lord of the Treasury, 'with the fullest political confidence', which implied the capacity to create peerages, something he had not previously given Rockingham.[3] After perfunctory negotiations, Fox, Burke, Sheridan, Portland and Lord John Cavendish all refused to serve under Shelburne. 'How then, Sir, did he get into favour with the King?' James Boswell asked Samuel Johnson, incredulously. 'Because, Sir,' Dr Johnson replied shrewdly, 'I suppose he promised the King to do whatever the King pleased.'[4]

On 5 July 1782, Fox attended Court with his seals of office in a bag, which he surrendered to the King, who received him civilly even though the interview lasted only five minutes. George, not wanting another

ministerial crisis, asked him to reconsider, but Fox hated Shelburne, whom
he privately away from Court called 'the *second* villain' in the land, leaving
no one in any doubt that he thought George was the first.[5] He also knew
that Shelburne's administration would attempt to oppose unconditional
American independence, which he rightly considered a doomed policy.
With more spare time, Fox now took 'Perdita' Robinson as a lover, but
within a year had met Elizabeth Armistead,* who was to become his mistress for many years and eventually his wife. William Cavendish-Bentinck,
the 3rd Duke of Portland, nominally assumed control of the Rockinghamite Whigs, but he lacked charisma and was only ever the figurehead of a
faction that Fox always dominated. Immensely grand and rich, honest,
conscientious and hard-working, although perhaps not overly gifted
intellectually – George Selwyn called him 'jolter-headed' – Portland now
led the Opposition in the Lords.

Shelburne kissed hands as Prime Minister on 11 July, and the Foxite
exodus meant that he had several key posts to fill. The forty-three-year-old
Lord Grantham, a competent and intelligent former diplomat, became
Foreign Secretary. The King approved, because he liked having a Foreign
Secretary who had served abroad.[6] Thomas Townshend, an old Chathamite
and an opponent of the American war, became both Home Secretary and
Leader of the House of Commons. William Pitt was appointed Chancellor
of the Exchequer at the age of just twenty-three. The previous May, in a
ninety-minute speech he had proposed the replacement of rotten boroughs
with redrawn county constituencies. The motion had been defeated by 161
votes to 142, but his fine speech had confirmed him as a frontline political
figure, and the ministry desperately needed a talented speaker in the Commons to respond to the often brilliant hostile orations of Fox, Burke and
Sheridan. Many expressed their astonishment at his vertiginous rise – he
had made only twenty speeches in the Commons before entering the
Cabinet – but for George the dearth of other talent there, Pitt's famous
name, his obvious intelligence and mastery of financial issues, his capacity
for hard work and above all the threat of Fox justified the decision.

George was not entirely oblivious to Fox's attributes, later writing to
William Grenville that he was 'a man of parts, quickness and great eloquence', but that 'he wants application, and consequently the fundamental
knowledge necessary for business.'[7] Some historians have agreed with this
judgement, that although Fox was able to master a complicated brief very

---

* Mrs Armistead had been previously the mistress of the Earl of Derby, the Duke of Dorset
and the Prince of Wales. 'As for Mr Armistead,' states one of Fox's biographers, 'he is generally
supposed to have been a figure of speech' (Hobhouse, *Fox* p. 165).

quickly, and was capable of occasional bouts of hard work, his general approach to public business was 'slapdash improvisation'.[8] Of course in part Fox's lack of knowledge of public business was the fault of the King, who would resolutely keep him out of power for the best part of twenty years. George's real problem with Fox, however, was that he thought him 'totally destitute of discretion and sound judgement'.[9] The King's reference to 'clubs, gaming-houses, aristocratic cabals, etc.' summed up perfectly the foremost features of Fox's favourite haunt, Brooks's.

Just before Parliament rose for its summer recess, Fox attacked the new ministry vigorously. 'The mask is certainly cast off,' George noted, adding, 'it is no less than a struggle whether I am to be dictated to by Mr Fox.'[10] Lord North, who despite the humiliation of Yorktown still held a large following in the Commons, had been wooed by both Fox and Shelburne. He had remained aloof, but with Shelburne too weak to last long without a wider coalition, on 6 August the King asked North to support the ministry in order to secure a lasting peace with the Americans. This request was couched in characteristically extravagant terms. The Northites needed 'to come early and show their countenance, by which I may be enabled to keep the constitution from being entirely annihilated, which must be the case if Mr Fox and his associates are not withstood . . . It is no less than whether the sole direction of my kingdoms shall be trusted in the hands of Mr Fox.'[11] His three months' experience of Fox in office 'has finally determined me never to employ him again, consequently the contest is become personal and he indeed sees it also in that point of view'. There was no mention in George's letter of the 1780 election debt, which at that point was still accruing interest on North's account at Drummonds Bank.

North took a full six days to reply, and when he finally did it was coolly, declining to ask his 'independent country gentlemen' to return to Parliament quickly after the end of the recess in case it 'may give them some offence'. He merely offered to start 'learning their inclinations' and promised to inform the King when he knew their position. Jenkinson later told Robinson that 'a certain person is displeased at the answer that was returned'.[12] The row over the 1780 election money and the Secret Service Fund hung heavily over their relationship, and North complained to Robinson, 'There is not the most distant hint of any intention to do me justice.' With the Commons parties numbering roughly 140 MPs for Shelburne, 90 for Portland–Fox and perhaps as many as 120 for North, it was clear that his support still mattered a good deal.

On 20 August 1782, the King and Queen were devastated to lose their youngest son, 'dear little Alfred', who died at Windsor Castle shortly before his second birthday. He had been taken to Deal by the royal governess Lady Charlotte Finch in the hope that he would recover from a fever through fresh sea air and bathing, but to no avail. The Court did not go into formal mourning as Alfred was not fourteen, but the royal couple were utterly grief-stricken. The Queen gave Finch an amethyst and pearl locket, and a lock of blond hair from 'my dear little Angel Alfred'.[13]* She wrote to her brother Charles two days after Alfred's death, 'I am very grateful to Providence, that out of a family of fourteen children, it has never struck us except in this one instance, and so I must submit myself without a murmur.'[14]

The cause was probably too high a dosage of the smallpox inoculation. The King and Queen were staunch advocates of this treatment, which was spearheaded by Edward Jenner, although they believed that Providence still played a large part in medicine.[15] 'I have the pleasure to acquaint you that my dear children underwent their operation with all possible and more than expected for heroism,' Queen Charlotte had told Finch after the inoculations of Princes Augustus and Ernest in October 1775. 'I trust that same Providence which has hitherto given me uncommon success in all my undertakings, will not withhold it from me at this time, as I can say with great truth it is not begun without praying for his assistance as the greatest and best of medicines I can put my confidence in.'[16] When Edward Jenner finally perfected his vaccination technique in the mid-1790s, the King knighted him and became patron of the Jennerian Society which advanced the practice. In his enlightened way he did not allow personal tragedy to affect his rational appreciation of the great benefits of science.

The King believed that Admiral Howe's relief of Gibraltar in October 1782 further improved Britain's chances of a good peace deal with France and Spain if the Shelburne ministry stayed firm. For financial reasons, he did not want concessions made to France in East India if Britons were to 'expect any chance of putting this country again into any flourishing state'.[17] He viewed the loss of Senegal with equanimity, as 'getting rid of a climate that certainly sweeps off a terrible number of my subjects'. Writing to North on 4 November he came as close as he ever did to making a tyrannical statement: 'I have no wish but for the prosperity of my dominions, therefore must look on all who will not heartily assist me as bad men as well as ungrateful subjects.'[18]

Peace negotiations with France were bedevilled by issues over the Newfoundland fisheries, and those with America over the treatment of the

---

* Which can be seen in the Royal Archives (RA GEO/ADD/15/443a–b).

Loyalists, who were being dispossessed of their property en masse by Congress. Since it was to him that the Loyalists had been loyal, the King had their interests very much at heart, but realistically little could be done for them. George certainly absolved himself entirely from any blame for what had happened, ending a letter to Shelburne about the peace terms:

> I cannot conclude without mentioning how sensibly* I feel the dismember-ment of America from this empire, and that I should feel miserable indeed if I did not feel that no blame on that account can be laid at my door, and did not also know that knavery seems to be so much the striking feature of its inhabitants that it may not in the end be an evil that they become aliens to this kingdom.[19]

The British do not in general have the reputation of being sore losers, but this – perhaps understandably – was an exception.

Concessions were made to France over Newfoundland, and the Americans' promises over better treatment of the Loyalists were accepted (if not wholly believed), in order to secure peace agreements with both. Writing to Thomas Townshend from Windsor at 10.23 p.m. on 19 November, the King gave his permission for a messenger to be sent to Paris with a draft of the preliminary articles of the peace treaties without his having even perused them, which was utterly out of character for him. 'Parliament having to my astonishment come into the ideas of granting a separation to North America, has disabled me from longer defending the just rights of this kingdom,' he explained to the Home Secretary, thereby distancing him-self from the coming treaty. 'I certainly disclaim thinking myself answerable for any evils that may arise from the adoption of this measure as necessity not conviction has made me subscribe to it.'[20] The Preliminaries between Britain and the United States were signed at Paris on 30 November 1782, the independence of the latter to become effective de jure on the conclusion of the war with France and Spain, although of course it had existed de facto for several years already. The agreement would remain informal until the conclusion of a peace agreement between Britain and France.

The Cabinet sat for eight hours on 3 December deliberating over the peace treaties with France and Spain. Richmond, Master-General of the Ordnance, and Keppel, who had agreed to stay in office under Shelburne, refused to demand that all the territories captured by Spain – Minorca, West Florida and the Bahamas – should be returned in exchange for Gibral-tar, Puerto Rico and one of two groups of French islands, either Martinique and St Lucia or Dominica and Guadeloupe.[21] Shelburne, Pitt, Townshend,

---

* 'Judiciously, reasonably' (*Johnson's Dictionary*).

Grantham and Thurlow believed that the East and West Indies were the key to rebuilding post-war British prosperity, and a rapid peace was needed even at the expense of giving up Gibraltar, whose possession they feared would permanently bedevil British relations with Spain. Keppel, Richmond, Grafton, Conway and Camden all preferred to continue fighting rather than lose Gibraltar.

There had been Cabinet rows over the varying peace terms since mid-November. Richmond attended an audience with the King on 4 December in which, as George reported to Shelburne, 'he roundly asserted that he did not think that anything could have been a compensation for Gibraltar, which he termed "the brightest jewel in the Crown".' The King added, 'As I did not think it right to heat the coals at present, I seemed to acquiesce in opinion.'[22] This was rare for him, because his private view, as he told Shelburne a week later, was that 'I would wish if possible to be rid of Gibraltar, and to have as much possession in the West Indies as possible.'[23]

The King uncharitably suspected Richmond and Keppel's group of wanting 'to fight the peace all over again, and to form fresh cabals ... I think peace every way necessary to this country, and that I shall not think it complete if we do not get rid of Gibraltar.'[24] He had entirely missed the crucial strategic advantage that the Rock offered, and was to afford the Royal Navy in the Napoleonic Wars – indeed future ones also – of controlling entry and egress between the Mediterranean Sea and the Atlantic Ocean. To modern strategists the idea that Britain might have given up Gibraltar in exchange for St Lucia and Guadeloupe is staggering.

'I lost no time in giving the necessary orders to prohibit the further prosecution of offensive war upon the continent of North America,' the King stated in his Speech from the Throne at the State Opening of Parliament on 5 December, claiming he had 'pointed all my views and measures ... to an entire and cordial reconciliation with those colonies. Finding it indispensable to the attainment of this object, I did not hesitate to ... declare them free and independent states.'[25] He added that 'In thus admitting their separation from the Crown of these kingdoms, I have sacrificed every consideration of my own to the wishes and opinion of my people.'[26] The French diplomat Gérard de Rayneval gloated that the King's voice sounded 'constrained' when pronouncing the word 'independent', while the American merchant Elkanah Watson claimed he 'hesitated, choked' over it.[27] 'I make it my humble and earnest prayer to Almighty God that ... America may be free from those calamities which have formerly proved in the mother country how essential monarchy is to the enjoyment of constitutional liberty.'[28] The universal accuracy of that statement might be doubted, but not the sincerity with which George made it. Then, farsightedly, he said, 'Religion, language, interest, affections may, and I hope will, yet prove a bond of permanent union between the two countries.'[29]

Horace Walpole asked Lord Oxford of the King, 'if he had not observed him lowering his voice when he came to [the American] part of his speech. This showed he had not been insensible to the ignominious part Lord Shelburne had forced him to act.'[30] Wraxall thought it 'may unquestionably be ranked among the most singular compositions ever put into the mouth of a British sovereign'.[31] It was believed to have been the longest Speech from the Throne since the reign of James I, and 'Some passages seemed more suitable to the spirit and language of a moralist or of a sage than of a monarch.'[32]

George's remarks about the connection between monarchy and constitutional liberty were mercilessly satirized by Burke in the debate afterwards. 'The King', he told MPs, 'is made by his minister to fall upon his knees, and to deprecate the wrath of Heaven from the misguided American people that they may not suffer from the want of monarchy ... They are now to be protected by the prayers of their former sovereign from the consequences of its loss! Such whimpering and absurd piety has neither dignity, meaning nor common sense.'[33] Burke derided the speech in private too, calling it 'insufferable' and comparing it to 'a man's opening the door after he had left the room, and saying, "At our parting, pray let me recommend a monarchy to you."'[34] Although Fox 'joined heartily' in the ridicule, James Boswell noted in his journal that he himself 'was truly hurt that my sovereign should be so humiliated. Supped and was sober.'[35]

The King had indeed been humiliated. The war had lasted eight years, cost 43,000 lives and almost doubled the National Debt from £127 million in 1775 to £232 million by 1783. The war alone had cost £80 million, hundreds of times more than the £60,000 Britain had wanted to raise by the Stamp Act, and more than seven times the entire government budget of 1773. Some 75,000 Loyalists were forced to flee as refugees from New York alone. Britain lost half a million square miles of her empire and around two and a half million subjects. It is unsurprising that Archduke Leopold of Austria told his brother Emperor Joseph II that, shorn of her colonies, Britain now ranked alongside Denmark or Sweden among European powers. Joseph later told the French Ambassador to Vienna, 'England's position beggars description; it shows how much this nation has degenerated [to a] desperate and pitiable condition.'[36]

With vast debts, powerful enemies, no allies and even neutral powers united in hostility, the country was as humiliated as her king by the colossal disaster, the worst in British history until the loss of India in 1947, which

at least happened peacefully. 'Rarely had a British king become so personally identified with a political policy as George had been with the American
war,' writes a modern American historian, 'and rarely had such an enterprise gone so wrong.'[37] The Americans had also paid a huge price for the
war; per capita income collapsed by 46 per cent between 1774 and 1790,
and as late as 1805 per capita wealth was still around 14 per cent lower
than it had been in 1774.[38] But the colonists had won their independence
and the freedom to expand westwards, so that within a century the United
States of America had become the richest, and subsequently the most
powerful, country in the world.

The Preliminaries of the Treaty of Paris were signed on 20 January 1783,
at which point hostilities ended. Britain would recognize the United States
with borders from the Great Lakes to the Mississippi and south to the 31st
Parallel. She kept Gibraltar and retained all of her West Indian gains of
1763 except for Tobago. Spain gained most territorially – Minorca and
West Florida, but also receiving East Florida. France recovered St Lucia,
Tobago and Goree (a slave-trading post in Senegal, captured by the British),
but not enough in East India to threaten Britain there. The treaties were
not yet ratified by any of the signatories, but their outlines were now clear,
and in Britain open to parliamentary debate.

Some time in January or February 1783, the King wrote a memorandum
in his own hand, entitled 'America is lost!'[39] For many years this was
thought to be the summation of his own thoughts on the matter, with the
exclamation mark conveying his view of the cataclysm. In fact, he had
copied it from an article written by Arthur Young in his journal *Annals of
Architecture*. The article examined the effects of the defeat on Britain's
economic and trading prospects, and it is unlikely that George would have
gone to the bother of laboriously copying it out unless he had agreed with
a good number of its arguments. Young believed that the outbreak of the
American Revolution had owed much to frustrated land speculation, 'The
wars of 1744, 1756, and 1775 were all entered into, because the beggars,
fanatics, felons, and madmen of the kingdom had been encouraged in their
speculation of settling the wilds of North America.'[40]

Crucially, however, George made some changes to the original, especially
towards the end where he deleted certain of Young's remarks and added
his own. Whereas Young assumed that the rest of the British Empire was
doomed because of the American defeat, George believed that it could and
should be preserved, and indeed extended. As for the Americans, 'We shall
reap more advantages from their trade as friends than ever we could derive
from them as colonies, for there is reason to suppose we actually gained

more by them while in actual rebellion.'[41] As much as he was anguished, George may have been relieved – and he was certainly prescient.[42]

'The more I reflect on the want of sailors and soldiers to enable us to carry on with any probability of advantage the war against so many enemies,' George reflected to Lord Grantham four days after the Preliminaries were signed,

> the total indifference at least of the other European powers towards us, and the inimical conduct of those who carry on any trade, and more particularly the ingratitude of Portugal, who owes her very existence to us,* the more I thank Providence for having, through so many difficulties, among which the want of union and zeal at home is not to be omitted, enabled so good a peace with France, Spain and I trust soon with the Dutch to be concluded.[43]

It was a curious list of scapegoats – essentially, low recruitment, Austria, Russia, the City of London, Portugal, public opinion and the Opposition – but he was right about how light the peace terms had been, owing partly to Rodney's victory at the Saintes and partly to the financial strains on France and Spain. Conspicuously absent from George's list of those responsible for the defeat were any of his ministers, admirals and generals, as well of course as himself.

With the debate on the peace looming, the various factions in Parliament had to act quickly. On 10 February (possibly the 11th, accounts differ) Pitt and Fox met alone. Pitt had only one question to ask, which was whether Fox would enter the government under any circumstances, and was told that there were none if Shelburne remained in it. 'I did not come here to betray Lord Shelburne,' Pitt retorted, and the two men parted, never to meet in private again.[44]

A few days later a much more unlikely coupling came off, however, when on 14 February, St Valentine's Day, the former arch-enemies Charles Fox and Lord North formed a coalition to bring down Shelburne and Pitt. North knew – either by suspicion or more likely by a private report – that Pitt cared no more for him than did Shelburne, and would never sit in a Cabinet alongside him, for reasons that went back to North's opposition to Pitt's father. There was, therefore, some merit in North and Fox setting aside their differences in common cause against their mutual enemy Shelburne, especially as they controlled large factions in the Commons and Lords. Fox told North at that unlikely meeting that the King should not be allowed to be his own minister – that is, to act as de facto Prime Minister – to which North replied:

---

* Britain had sent expeditions to help Portugal against Spain in 1386, the 1660s and 1762.

If you mean there should not be a government by departments, I agree with you. I think it is a very bad system. There should be one man, or a Cabinet, to govern the whole, and direct every measure. Government by departments was not brought in by me. I found it so, and had not the vigour and resolution to put an end to it. The King ought to be treated with all sort of respect and attention, but the appearance of power is all that a king of this country can have.[45]

Government by departments, as Lord Hillsborough had explained to Thomas Hutchinson in 1774, meant ministers individually reporting to the King. This manner of government was now entering its twilight months.

North's stance had long been Fox's position too, except the part about respect and attention. Whether North had been pondering on the constitutional changes that needed to be made because America had been lost, or was angry that the King was demanding £22,000 from him, he was prepared to storm the Closet in alliance with his old antagonist Fox, using the Duke of Portland as their figurehead Prime Minister. He was deeply aggrieved at the way the peace had let down the American Loyalists and was opposed to Shelburne and Pitt over parliamentary reform, while his supporters and relatives wanted a return to the emoluments of office. Fox had been his nemesis in March 1782, but less than a year later now became his ally.

The debate on the peace treaties began on 17 February, during which Fox gestured presciently, 'My friendships are perpetual, my enmities are not so. *Amicitiae sempiternae, inimicitiae placabiles* . . . The American war and the American question is at an end . . . and it is therefore wise and candid to put an end also to the ill will, the animosity, the rancour and the feuds which it occasioned.'[46] That night the Shelburne ministry lost a vote on an amendment by Lord John Cavendish by 224 votes to 208. When Townshend reported it, the King did not immediately realize that this meant the government was doomed, and it was not until 5.40 p.m. the next day that he wrote to Shelburne to admit, 'On looking again at Mr Townshend's note, I find Lord John Cavendish's amendment was carried, which is an event I did not understand when I wrote this morning.'[47] It was rare for him to make such a mistake.

The debate and vote exposed the extent to which Fox and North were in alliance to bring down the Shelburne ministry. On 21 February, Pitt told the Commons that 'he could not coalesce with those whose principles he knew to be diametrically opposed to his own.'[48] After Townshend had reported to the King that another of Cavendish's resolutions had been carried by 207 votes to 190, he added that 'Mr Pitt's speech in answer to

Mr Fox was generally agreed to be one of the finest that was ever heard.'[49] A few weeks later Pitt denounced the way that 'Gentlemen talked of forgiving animosities and altering their political opinions with as much ease as they could change their gloves.'[50]

The King, replying to Townshend from Windsor, saw the Fox–North alliance as a manifest symptom of the debased era in which they lived. 'I am sorry that it has been my lot to reign in the most profligate age and when the most unnatural coalition seems to have taken place,' he told the Home Secretary, 'which can but add confusion and distraction among a too much divided nation.'[51] Later that day he told Lord Howe that the new coalition could 'tend to nothing but hurrying this country still faster to anarchy and confusion'.[52] He replied to Shelburne's request to resign that evening by observing that 'no consideration shall make me throw myself into the hands of any party; it must be a coalition of the best of all, not a narrow line, that can prevent anarchy.'[53] It is not clear whether he meant anarchy on the streets, of which there was no real prospect, or governmental anarchy, or whether it was just another example of the hyperbole to which he and his age were so prone. Piety, self-righteousness and self-pity were some of his other default positions, and in that letter he also told Shelburne, 'I am again from necessity left to extricate myself; to the assistance of Providence and the rectitude of my intentions I can alone hope for succour.'[54]

Shelburne resigned on 24 February, after losing several votes in both Houses censuring the Peace Preliminaries. The King immediately set about trying to find yet another broad-bottomed government of national unity to get the Preliminaries through Parliament and protect the Crown from further Foxite (and now also Northite) depredations against the royal prerogative. He again employed Lord Thurlow, the Lord Chancellor, to do the groundwork of negotiation, telling him that he was 'trying to counteract the most extraordinary combination that the depravity of such times as we live in could alone have given birth to'.[55] The process was not helped when Shelburne became convinced that George had betrayed him by not ordering North to support his ministry, which it was by then well beyond his power to do.[56] On Thurlow's advice he approached Pitt, who sensibly refused, because in surveying the lists of MPs he could not see his way to a Commons majority either.

In early March, George created two baronies for Shelburne's supporters – including one for Thomas Townshend, as Lord Sydney* – which was perhaps a way of reminding the political world that there were areas of

---

* After whom Sydney, New South Wales, is named.

public life in which he retained ultimate control.[57] By 4 March, however, he was forced to reconcile himself to the notion of having Fox as a Secretary of State in a Portland ministry. Even so, he still would not accept the entire Cabinet being composed of Foxites: to have a government dominated by a single faction of Whig aristocrats went against all the Patriot King principles he had learned from Bute, Bolingbroke and his father. On 7 March he asked Thurlow to approach Lord Gower to sound out whether he and Pitt might form a ministry, because 'I shall certainly still attempt to find whether there is no man willing at this crisis to stand by the Crown against a desperate faction in whose hands I will never throw myself.'[58]

In looking for an adviser who knew all the principals concerned, the King alighted on Thomas Pitt, son of the late Lord Chatham's eldest brother, and a supporter of Shelburne. There is a memorandum in the King's handwriting of a conversation between Gower and Thomas Pitt held on 7 March at Whitehall, in which Pitt had said,

> That I had ever thought the character of Mr Fox dangerous to the public peace ... That it was in vain now to talk of the Duke of Portland; it was directly Mr Fox's administration ... That as to Lord North, if anything could be wanting to render his character complete, it was such an unparalleled act of ingratitude to his benefactor and such a profligate surrender of all public principles.[59]

All of these were the King's opinions too. Despite that, Pitt thought that allowing Fox into office, whereby he would become responsible for the implementation of the Treaty of Paris, might make him swiftly unpopular. The fact that the King copied out the very lengthy memorandum is an indication of how much he agreed with Thomas Pitt's sentiments about 'the acuteness and vehemence of Fox and all the cunning and ironical arts of Lord North'.[60] When Gower suggested asking Mr Thomas Pitt himself to be Prime Minister, George replied, 'Yes, Mr Thomas Pitt or Mr Thomas Anybody.'[61]

On 9 March the King formally offered Gower the post of First Lord of the Treasury, with Jenkinson and Henry Dundas holding the two secretaryships of state. Dundas, a former Northite who was adroitly moving into William Pitt's circle, was the most powerful political figure in Scotland. A Gower ministry would probably have formed a competent if uncharismatic government, but Gower declined the opportunity because of the unfavourable parliamentary mathematics. The next day, George told Thurlow he was 'really so ill I cannot write more' about 'this sad business'.[62]

Two coming politicians who rallied to the King during these six weeks of governmental hiatus (the longest since George II's dismissal of Pitt's father in April 1757) were sons of the late George Grenville, George Nugent-Temple-Grenville, the 3rd Earl Temple, then Lord Lieutenant of Ireland, and his younger brother William Wyndham Grenville, the Chief Secretary for Ireland.[63] The latter was invited to four audiences with the King between 16 March and 1 April from which he emerged as an ally, almost a King's Friend. His timely move was to serve him well, as he was to become one of the most important statesmen in British politics for twenty of the next twenty-five years. He had never been alone with the King before, and later recalled the evident discomfort George felt at their first meeting, which did not start until 11 p.m. and went on until 1 a.m. In a striking sketch he also noted of their discussions about Portland, Shelburne, Fox and North:

> The feelings which then agitated his mind were strongly pictured in his countenance and gestures, and aggravated all the peculiarities of his manner. The quick step and disordered motion of his body, his rapid utterance, his eager and uninterrupted speech, admitted neither of pause nor answer, and shifting perpetually in unconnected digressions through every subject of his thoughts were well suited to the passions which he expressed. They served more strongly to impress his sincerity and uprightness on a hearer already prejudiced in favour of his cause. I listened with conviction to his unqualified invectives, I sympathized in his feelings, and warmly espoused his resentments.[64]

Several of these were the same symptoms that the King was to display when his mind became much more than merely 'agitated' six years later. It is just possible that Grenville knew of George's bipolar episode in 1765 during his father's premiership, although he was only eleven when his father died, and it had gone officially undiagnosed. Grenville was also writing in retrospect, knowing that the King had gone mad later, but at the very least it shows that George cared deeply about the governance of Britain. One cannot imagine George II getting into such an agitated state over which premier to choose, not least because for him the answer had almost always been Sir Robert Walpole or one of the Pelham brothers.

At the start of their conversation, the King told Grenville that he thought the present political situation was 'that the kingdom was split into parties, not as had been formerly the case – two great bodies of men acting under the different denominations of Whigs and Tories, and upon different principles of conduct – but into factions, which had avowedly no other view than that of forcing themselves, at all hazards, into office'.[65] Of North, he 'spoke in terms of strong resentment and disgust'.[66] The King interrupted his flow of thought:

by a great variety of digressions: upon the coalition . . . upon Fox, whom he loaded with every expression of abhorrence; upon the Duke of Portland, against whom he was little less violent; upon Lord North, to whose conduct he imputed all the disasters of the country; upon American independence, which seems to have been a most bitter pill indeed; upon associations and reforms,* clubs, gaming-houses, aristocratic cabals, etc., etc.; together with much inquiry into the state of Ireland.[67]

He also 'mentioned a message which he sent through Lord Ashburton to Lord Shelburne that he should consider him a disgraced man if, after their conduct towards him, he ever "supported them in government, or joined them in opposition" (these were the precise words he used to me)'.[68]

On 18 March, the King told North that 'The Duke of Portland's being at the head of the Treasury shall not be objected to by me,' but that he needed to be shown the names of the rest of the Cabinet before appointing him. North showed the letter to Portland, who asked for an audience with the King to discuss the matter further. Because of all this protracted horse-trading there had been no Prime Minister since 24 February. The Cabinet still occasionally met but without Shelburne, and various important matters – such as a mutiny of the Yorkshire Volunteers over demobilization, bread riots in Newcastle, the 'impatience' at Spithead of naval ratings expecting pay and discharge, the choice of a new archbishop of Canterbury after the death of Frederick Cornwallis (the General's uncle) and above all the peace-ratification process – were dealt with on an ad hoc basis with no central direction.

On Sunday 23 March, after a Drawing Room, Portland showed the King the list of Cabinet ministers he intended to appoint, which George noted down and which featured Fox as Foreign Secretary, Cavendish as Chancellor of the Exchequer, North as Home Secretary and Keppel at the Admiralty. When Portland refused to divulge his agenda for government, but simply asked the King to trust him, George replied that it 'was asking more than any man above forty could engage to do'.[69]

As soon as Parliament reassembled on Monday 24 March, the Foxite MP Thomas Coke of Holkham Hall in Norfolk† moved a motion, seconded by Lord Surrey, which entreated the King 'in consideration of the distracted state of the country, to condescend in compliance with the wishes

---

* Almost certainly a reference to the Yorkshire Association and Economical Reform.
† The King already had an animus against Coke, the future 1st Earl of Leicester, who the year before had appeared at Court to present a petition calling for the end of the war wearing 'country clothes' which he took as a deliberate sign of disrespect (Mansel, 'Uniform and the Rise of the *Frac*' p. 109).

of the House of Commons to appoint an administration which may be entitled to the confidence of the nation', meaning Portland's.[70] William Pitt told the King that evening that Fox and North 'threw out general insinuations of persons who advised delay' as having been to blame for the protracted crisis, probably meaning Thurlow and Pitt himself. No vote was taken, however, so the parliamentary arithmetic was not clear.*

A mutiny of the 104th Regiment of Foot, which had been formed only a month earlier, broke out in Fort George on Guernsey on 24 March, when some of the 500 Irishmen stationed there fired on their officers. Once the local militia and the 18th Regiment had surrounded the fort, the mutiny was put down, and thirty-six ringleaders were arrested. The French had attempted to invade Guernsey in January 1781 so the prospect of a mutiny there was profoundly worrying, as was that of disloyal Irishmen in the British Army. The King told General Conway that the 104th would be transported back to England and broken up in disgrace, but it was yet another indication of the need for a fully functioning government.[71]

On 28 March, George sent Thurlow to approach Lord Gower again, warning about 'the step I have so often hinted to you' – by which he meant abdication.[72] An indication that it might not have been a completely idle threat is contained in one of two long draft messages from the King to the House of Commons in the King's handwriting, undated but most probably written on 28 March. Taken together they composed his political testament, but they called for two very different outcomes. The first was deliberately designed to inflame the populace against the Portland–Fox–North coalition, which made no mention of giving up the crown. The second contained much the same sentiments, but also announced his abdication.[73]

'When His Majesty mounted the throne now above twenty-two years,' the King's first draft message to the Commons began, 'he had the pleasing hope that being born in this kingdom, he might have proved the happy instrument of conciliating all parties, and thus collecting to the service of the state the most respectable and most able persons this nation produced.'[74] The mention of his English birth was a clear reference to first Speech from the Throne – 'Born and educated in this country, I glory in the name of Briton' – and this appeal for non-partisan politics owed its origins in part to the idea of the Patriot King. 'Of this object he has never lost sight,' the document continued, 'though sad experience now teaches

---

* Horace Walpole claimed that members of Brooks's were wagering how long the reign would continue, but this is not substantiated by the club's betting book, which as we have seen did not shy from recording bets of a sensitive nature.

him that selfish views are so prevalent that they have smothered the first of public virtues, attachment to the country, which ought to warm the breast of every individual who enjoys the advantages of this excellent constitution, and the want of which sentiment has prevented that unanimity which must have rendered Britain invulnerable, though attacked by the most powerful combinations.'

The message then moved to an even more blatant popular appeal:

> The inclination of His Majesty to alleviate the distresses of his people, added to the change of sentiments of one branch of the legislature which rendered the real object of the war impracticable, made him undertake the arduous task of obtaining the blessings of peace, become more difficult by the resolution above alluded to, he therefore rejoiced when the Preliminary Articles were concluded.

This sentence – which was hardly true, as he had in fact left London for Windsor without even reading the text of the Preliminaries – laid the blame for the loss of territory in the Paris Peace Treaty squarely on those MPs who had supported the pro-peace motion of 27 February 1782, which he had always seen as having hamstrung the government's negotiating stance.

He went on to explain how he had attempted to form a new ministry of the best men to negotiate the peace treaties, but 'this patriotic endeavour has proved unsuccessful, by the obstinacy of a powerful combination that has long publicly manifested a resolution of not entering into public service unless the whole executive management of affairs is thrown entirely into their hands.' He did not need to mention Fox and the radical Whigs by name, but neither did he spare Pitt and Gower, adding, 'At the same time, want of zeal prevents others from standing forth at this critical juncture.'[75]

Next came an argument that George was to use powerfully later on in his reign, that 'His Majesty from obedience to the oath he took at his coronation will never exceed the powers vested in him, nor on the other hand ever submit to be the tool of a party.' This reference to his devout Anglicanism, as well as the earlier one to his desire to alleviate his people's distress, was clearly designed to engender popular support, which he called for explicitly in the last sentence: 'He must therefore end this conflict which certainly puts a stop to every wheel of government, and call upon those who feel for the spirit of the constitution to stand forth to his assistance.' It was a call to arms, which if published could have led to violent Crown-and-Church riots and attacks on Parliament and MPs.

Yet the second draft of George's proposed message to Parliament was potentially even more inflammatory. 'I cannot at the most serious, as well as most painful moment of my life,' it began, 'go out of this great assembly without communicating to you my intentions, not asking for your advice.'[76] He then largely reiterated the argument of the first message, but instead of calling for 'assistance', he announced, 'I am therefore resolved to resign my Crown and all the dominions appertaining to it to the Prince of Wales,' while he would 'retire' to Hanover, 'the original patrimony of my ancestors'.[77]* He added, 'I trust this personal sacrifice will awaken the various parties to a sense of their duty and that they will join in the support and assistance of the young successor.'

In an effort to differentiate himself further from the wily, unpatriotic, partisan politicians whom he was ostensibly addressing, the King added a paragraph explaining that 'You may depend on my arduous attention to educate my children in the paths of religion, virtue and every other good principle that may render them, if ever called in any line to the service of Great Britain, not unworthy of the kindness they may hereafter meet with from a people whom collective[ly] I shall ever love.' His concluding lines played on similar emotions: 'May I to the latest hour of my life, though now resolved for ever to quit this island, have the comfort of hearing that the endeavours of my son, though they cannot be more sincere than mine have been for the prosperity of Great Britain, be crowned with better success.'[78]

Both messages were melodramatic and sensationalist, and if either – especially the second – had ever actually been delivered by the King in a Speech from the Throne in Parliament it would have been political dynamite. Was it a genuine abdication threat, a document to be used as a threat against the Opposition, one to be used by Thurlow as a threat against Pitt and Gower, or perhaps even a genuine manifesto, to be unleashed *in extremis* to inflame the populace? Was it a manifesto for a royal coup against Parliament of the kind that King Gustav of Sweden had pulled off in 1772? In short, was George genuinely contemplating tyranny?

A much more likely explanation, one that fits in with everything else we know about George III, was that it was a self-indulgent and characteristically self-pitying private expostulation written to make himself feel better at the time, as well as perhaps look better in the light of history. The documents were preserved in the archives, implying that he wanted his side of the story told. Whatever else can be said, the two messages seem heartfelt and persuasive, potentially explosive and – for all the occasional marathon sentences – sufficiently well written to refute those detractors who doubted his intelligence and literary ability.

---

* One account from this period has him actually asking the artist Benjamin West to accompany him to Hanover (ed. Greig, *Faringdon Diary* VI p. 2212).

On 29 March the King told a delegation of American merchants that they were welcome to attend his Levee the following week, something that would have been unthinkable even a month or so earlier. The next day he once more asked both William Pitt and Lord Gower to become Prime Minister, but was again refused. He noted the latter in particular showed 'no seeds of gratitude'.[79] Parliament met again on 31 March and agreed to give the King more time.

The next day George finally bowed to the parliamentary mathematics and opened realistic negotiations for Portland to become Prime Minister. Given that he resented Portland for not revealing his legislative agenda, hated Fox in general and deeply regretted the loss of Thurlow (whose lord chancellorship went into abeyance), it was unsurprising that he had no confidence in the new Portland ministry. Nor did he bother hiding this fact, telling Lord Temple on 1 April that it was 'the most unprincipled coalition the annals of this or any nation can equal. I have withstood it till not a single man has come to my assistance,' but he now feared the crisis 'would affect public credit* if it continued much longer'.[80] He ended by saying, 'I intend this night to acquaint that *grateful* man Lord North' – with the word grateful underlined to emphasize the sarcasm – that he could form a government with Fox.

'I do not mean to grant a single peerage or other mark of favour,' George told Shelburne, for 'these cannot be called matters that regard the conduct of public affairs.'[81] Of course he knew perfectly well that they could hardly be called anything else. 'I trust the eyes of the nation will soon be opened as my sorrow may prove fatal to my health if I remain long in this thralldom,' he told Temple in what might have been an unconscious reference to his 1765 illness:

> I trust you will be steady in your attachment to me and be ready to join other honest men in watching the conduct of this unnatural combination, and I hope many months will not elapse before the Grenvilles, Pitts, and other men of abilities and character will relieve me from a situation that nothing but . . . preventing the public finances from being materially affected would have compelled me to submit to.[82]

Ironically, George now hoped to rely on the children and nephews of the same members of 'the Family' that he had so derided to Bute twenty years earlier. Meanwhile Dundas, Jenkinson and Robinson, though they had served North when he was Prime Minister, saw their first loyalty as being to the King, and stayed out of the ministry. In supporting North, then

---

* That is, the rate at which the government could sell bonds.

Shelburne and later Pitt, Robinson was nicknamed 'Jack Renegado the Rat-Catcher', but this was unfair; he had not been a renegade to George as leader of the King's Friends faction in the Commons.[83]

On 2 April 1783, the Fox–North coalition finally succeeded in storming the Closet. For George it was like May 1765 all over again, with the added humiliation of the loss of the American colonies. The new government was a very strange combination, considering the Foxites' philippics against North over the twelve years of his premiership. Edmund Burke had even drawn up articles of impeachment against North in 1779. Many thought the coalition particularly unprincipled and cynical, even in an age of outlandish political manoeuvrings. Fox's nephew Lord Holland wrote in his memoirs that a minister had told him that 'he had always foreseen the coalition ministry could not last, for he was at Court when Mr Fox kissed hands, and observed George III turn back his ears and eyes just like the horse at Astley's [riding school], when the tailor* he had determined to throw was getting on him.'[84]

As soon as he came to power, Portland asked the King for a dukedom for Lord Hertford (General Conway's elder brother) and a marquessate for Earl Fitzwilliam, who was Rockingham's nephew and a vocal supporter of Wilkes and the Americans. 'I declined entering on that subject,' the King wrote in a memorandum.[85] Hertford, a courtier whom the King liked, eventually received a marquessate, albeit a decade later; meanwhile Fitzwilliam – who had already been appointed to the splendid-sounding but actually junior post of Custos Rotulorum of the Soke of Peterborough – got nothing.

George would occasionally interest himself in the minutiae of peerage warrants. In a letter to the Duke of Grafton of October 1766, he said of a proposed viscountcy for the unmarried 6th Baron Maynard, 'I perceive the continuation of the barony to Sir William Maynard [a distant cousin, the 4th baronet] and his male heirs in default of that lord's male descendants is omitted, therefore I have proposed returning it . . . and ordering a fresh one.'[86] He had spotted a lacuna in the document that had been missed by Grafton, Shelburne, the Lord Chancellor, and their advisers in the College of Arms. Some historians ascribe this to an obsessive personality, and George was indeed a stickler for detail, but in this case it was a crucial one that was to decide whether the barony died out in 1775 or went on to be inherited by Sir William Maynard's son Charles, as indeed happened.

Of course peerages had never been solely the reward for a lifetime's service to the state in politics or the military. In the earlier part of the reign,

---

* The phrase 'to ride like a tailor' meant to ride badly.

Leicester House politicians received peerages for their loyalty; Henry Fox's was given as a reward for leading the Commons for Bute; Chatham received his earldom for forming a ministry; Hillsborough and Germain were awarded their titles as consolations for being forced out of the American secretaryship in 1772 and 1782 respectively, and whomever was made Lord Chancellor or Lord Chief Justice automatically received one, so that they could sit in the Upper House. But having always been political to a greater or lesser degree, the award of peerages was about to become intensely *party* political.

George had deployed his powers of refusal earlier – Rockingham's premiership had seen only two new peerages – but that had been rapier-like compared with the sabre-slashes that faced the Fox–North coalition. Although the King generally wanted requests for peerages to go through the Prime Minister, in practice as we have seen many people petitioned him directly, and incessantly, taking up much of his time and correspondence. The applicant virtually never admitted to wanting the honour for himself, of course, but was making the request because it would acknowledge royal approval of his work for his county, or his family's loyal support for the government, or his service in the household, and so on.

There were periods where few peerages were created – there was only one between 1767 and 1776, for example – but even then the backlog meant that nine were created in May 1776 alone, simply to fulfil the many promises that had been made over the years. Until 1782, peerages regularly went to Opposition politicians – such as to Lords Camden, Radnor, Beaulieu and Foley, and to others who were unpolitical – but that now changed. In early April 1783 it was assumed that Lord North – who held only a courtesy title, as his father was the peer – would be translated to the Upper House, for example, but George had other ideas for his former friend. 'The King was playing a waiting game,' writes one historian, 'and being less than candid with ministers.'[87] He did not want to provoke a crisis, but he did want the political world to recognize that support for the Fox–North coalition would be a definite block on getting oneself ennobled. For even North himself to be forced to remain in the Lower House was a prominent advertisement of the coalition's failure to extract peerages from 'the Fount of Honour'.

George teasingly agreed to create Irish peerages for the Fox–North coalition, so as not to seem intransigent, but these did not confer the right to sit in the House of Lords at Westminster and so were deemed of much lower status. His refusals also meant that the government were short of speakers and supporters in the House of Lords, where they had only Loughborough and Stormont who could sway the chamber, since Portland himself was an unimpressive orator. George believed, quite correctly, that Fox could not force him to create new peerages, as the country gentlemen in the Commons would not support such a constitutional overreach.

One person who quickly found himself to be unpopular was Edmund Burke. He had become Paymaster-General again – and, to his chagrin, not in the Cabinet. He almost immediately embarrassed the government by restoring two senior clerks, Messrs Powell and Bembridge, to their former positions despite there being a £70,000 shortfall in their public accounts.[88] Pitt's motion that the documents relating to the scandal be opened to public scrutiny only fell by 161 votes to 137.[89] From having been the proponent of Economical Reform and transparency, in public office Burke again became what looked to many observers like a defender of sleazy practices.

The Whigs now fell victim to their own legislative success, as Burke's Establishment Act the previous year had abolished scores of sinecures and places that could no longer be awarded in return for supporting the government. In September 1783, Charles Jenkinson pointed out the irony to Robinson: 'They are now sensible that the King is personally stronger and themselves weaker by the operation of Mr Burke's Bill.'[90] Many of the lucrative controllerships, commissionerships, clerkships and other places that had traditionally kept backbenchers supportive over the years now simply no longer existed.

The coalition quickly recognized that there was nothing to be gained, and much to lose, from antagonizing the King. 'Mr Fox hopes that Your Majesty will not think him presumptuous or improperly intruding upon Your Majesty with professions,' read a letter from the Foreign Secretary of 16 April,

> if he begs leave most humbly to implore Your Majesty to believe that both the Duke of Portland and he have nothing so much at heart than to conduct Your Majesty's affairs, both with respect to measures and to persons, in the manner that gives Your Majesty most satisfaction, and that, whenever Your Majesty will be graciously pleased to condescend even to hint your inclinations upon any subject, that it will be the study of Your Majesty's ministers to show how truly sensible they are of Your Majesty's goodness.[91]

Fox, who not long before had regarded him as 'infernal' and 'Satan', saw the advantage of being on the right side of the only person who could bestow the peerages and honours that oiled the wheels of government. For his part, the King had not received so oleaginous a letter since those of Lord Chatham. Even so, he was not about to be charmed by Fox, and this obvious peace-offering was merely marked 'No answer' by a monarch who otherwise rarely failed promptly to answer every letter he was sent. The following month the Duchess of Manchester reported to her Rockingham Whig husband the 4th Duke, who was Ambassador to France, that the King's 'looks and manner strongly mark his dislike to all his present Court – he is certainly endeavouring to work a change as soon as he can.'[92]

On 15 April, the Continental Congress approved the preliminary articles of the Peace of Paris and hostilities with America ceased, although the final treaty did not go into effect until September, and New York City was not evacuated until late November. After a Cabinet meeting on 18 April had agreed the definitive treaties with France and Spain too, Fox wrote to the King offering to explain 'this very great business' orally. The King replied, 'I do not mean to call on Mr Fox for further explanations on this subject: unnecessary discussions are not to my taste, and the Cabinet having ... approved of the projects, I do not propose to give myself additional trouble with regard to them.'[93] It was virtually the only intemperate letter the King ever wrote to Fox; the rest were formal and polite. The war had been lost and the King felt there was no point in dwelling further on the humiliation involved, especially in the company of someone who had opposed it from the beginning and more or less openly sided with the enemy. Fox had essentially got the same peace terms as Shelburne had negotiated, which Fox himself had denounced and voted against as leader of the Opposition. He now had to propose them to Parliament, but such is politics.

In the process of ending the war in North America, George Washington organized a meeting with Sir Guy Carleton on 6 May 1783 for the purpose of reclaiming the slaves the British had freed and returning them to their servitude. ('If by chance you should come at the knowledge of any of them,' he had written about four of his own escaped slaves to Daniel Parker, the American in charge of recapturing them, 'I will be much obliged by your securing them, so that I may obtain them again.')[94] Carleton instead issued 3,000 freedom certificates to help protect the runaway slaves still in New York against the slave catchers rife in the city. When Carleton told Washington he had already shipped 6,000 people from New York to Nova Scotia, many of whom were former slaves, Washington expostulated, 'Already embarked!'[95]

Worse was to come for Washington when Carleton told him that Britain refused to renege on her promise of freedom for former slaves, and that 'the national honour' meant that the promise 'must be kept with all colours'. All former slaves in New York would sail to freedom before the city was evacuated.[96] The King later gave 'his royal approbation' to this decision in 'the fullest and most ample manner'.[97] Although in 1776 Washington had roused his soldiers with talk about fighting supposed 'slavery' in the political sense, when it came to actual slavery the King had a far better record than the rebel.

On 3 May 1783, less than a year after Prince Alfred had died of smallpox, the King and Queen's four-year-old son Octavius died aged four, just ten days after he and his sister Princess Sophia had been inoculated with small-pox. Both Charlotte Papendiek and Louisa Cheveley (who nursed Octavius) attributed his death to a chill, though Papendiek added that he suffocated at the end, which may well have been as a result of respiratory complica-tions of the disease.[98] 'Had you known what a sweet child he was,' the King told the Prince of Wales and Prince Frederick, 'you would have felt his death as severely as I did.'[99] Octavius was evidently a favourite, keenly devoted to his father and vice versa. George had often remarked, 'There will be no Heaven for me if Octavius is not there.'[100]

The tragedy brought a brief respite in the King's struggle against his government after Portland – who had also lost an infant child – expressed his reluctance to bother the King with signing Bills two days later. The King replied the next morning, 'The Duke of Portland's reluctance at sending me the commission for passing the Bills I look upon as an instance of his delicacy. I believe he has been in the situation it has pleased the Almighty to place me now, and therefore can judge the state of my mind; but the real trust I have in Divine Providence, and the balm I feel in religion, so far supports me that I am able to sign any warrants.'[101] On 7 August 1783, George and Charlotte's last child, Princess Amelia, was born. The Queen was thirty-nine, and had given birth to fifteen children over twenty-one years. Since there had been none in 1781 or 1782, Amelia might have been something of an afterthought.

When, on 7 May, Pitt proposed parliamentary reform, he was supported by Fox but opposed by North, signalling the first major split in the Portland ministry. Pitt wanted measures to combat bribery at elections, disenfran-chise rotten boroughs and increase the representation of London and the counties, but he was defeated heavily, by 293 votes to 149. Afterwards, Pitt wrote to his mother to say that he could not speculate on how long the coalition would remain in power, because 'the same fixed averseness . . . still continues.' He did not need to refer to the King by name, adding, 'You may easily guess where.'[102] Pitt always considered himself a Whig rather than a Tory, but his beliefs – that an ideal world was unattainable, sedition needed to be suppressed ruthlessly, the constitution should be defended, taxes should be low and government limited, while defence spending was a sound investment – later became the principles of the new Tory party growing up among his followers.

One member of the royal family who had welcomed the Fox–North coalition was the Prince of Wales. This was not out of any sense of political conviction, with which he was never much afflicted, but simply, as he had once said of the Rockingham ministry, because 'The new administration seems to wish me better than the former one.'[103] As he would turn twenty-one on 12 August, important decisions needed to be taken about his future establishment and income. Writing to the King from Downing Street on 15 June, Portland proposed that the Prince should have an income of £100,000 a year, of which £12,000 would come from the Prince's own Duchy of Cornwall and the rest from the taxpayer.[104] The Prince's debts, however, had now reached £29,000 and, for their discharge, the Prime Minister wrote, 'there is no resource but in the great liberality of Your Majesty who may direct them to be included in the arrears of Debt which Parliament was apprised of at the opening of this session by Your Majesty's most gracious Speech from the Throne.'[105] This was a barely veiled way of saying that if he could not pay his son's debts off himself (and Portland already knew perfectly well that, as a result of Burke's reduction of the Civil List, he could not) he must throw himself publicly on Parliament's mercy. The King sniffed a Foxite plot, either to embarrass him politically or to sting him financially, and he reacted with fury.

George's letter to Portland from Windsor Castle at 10.59 a.m. on 16 June has been described as 'the strongest in language' of any letter George wrote to one of his premiers.[106] 'It is impossible for me to find words expressive enough of my utter indignation and astonishment at the letter I have just received,' he wrote.[107] He described the £100,000 per annum that the government wanted to settle on the Prince as 'so lavish an idea and the more so when my subjects are so much loaded with taxes', and proposed that the Prince instead receive £50,000 plus the Duchy revenues, which was all that his father and subsequently he himself had received from George II. (He never seems to have quite grasped the concept of inflation.) He was moreover angry that 'I am to be saddled with the whole odium of this measure, and the expense at the same time ultimately to fall on me who am not from my numerous progeny in a position to bear it, though I had been assured that no part was to be paid by me, and in addition I am pressed to take £29,000 of debts on myself that I have not incurred,' all as the result of his son's 'shameful extravagance'.[108] Unless:

> all expenses are thrown on the Prince of Wales, I cannot proceed in this business, and shall think myself obliged to let the public know the cause of the delay and my opinion of the whole transaction. I cannot conclude without saying that when the Duke of Portland came into office, I had at least

hoped he would have thought himself obliged to have my interest and that of the public at heart, and not have neglected both to gratify the passions of an ill-advised young man.

The King believed that his son's excessive spending had been encouraged by the great Whig families, who had played the card game Faro for high stakes with Prince George at Brooks's and Almack's Clubs, raced with him at Newmarket and caroused with him at their houses in London and the country. On this latter point, George singled out Charles Fox in particular, who he believed had identified the Prince of Wales as the monarch who would one day make him Prime Minister.

'I cannot in conscience give my acquiescence to what I deem a shameful squandering of public money,' the King told Portland, 'besides an encouragement of extravagance and likely to prevent the Prince of Wales at a proper time wanting to marry.'[109] The King knew his son well enough by then to know that if Prince George had a large private income, it would be much more difficult to persuade him to marry a German Protestant princess for dynastic purposes than if he had a pecuniary motive to do so.

Portland was stung by the King's response, and a compromise was finally found in which Prince George received £50,000 a year out of the Civil List (£62,000 including the Duchy of Cornwall), while Parliament voted him a one-off payment of £60,000 to pay off his debts and refurbish the vast Carlton House, which had lain empty for eleven years since the death of Princess Augusta and which the King gave him for his twenty-first birthday present. Its frontage spanned much of Pall Mall and it had direct access to St James's Park at the back.* Sir William Chambers was appointed as the architect for its renovation.

The King hoped that the financial settlement would put his son on an even keel financially, and the Prince solemnly promised his father 'not to exceed my income'.[110] The King's generosity turned out to be a disastrous error; by the end of the year the Prince had sacked Chambers and appointed in his place his friend Henry Holland, who discarded any pretence at keeping to a budget. The entrance area alone would cost £6,500, a doorcase and alcove £9,000, two chimneypieces £2,000 and a single chandelier £1,050.[111] Walsh Porter, another socialite aesthete friend who was brought in for the renovations, wrote to the Prince, 'Sir, I know full well, by observation, that the word "no" forms no part of Your Royal Highness's vocabulary.'[112]

'The Prince', George had written in one of his essays for Bute in the

---

* It occupied the entire space from where the Institute of Contemporary Arts is today down to Marlborough House.

1750s, 'will be feared [and] respected abroad and adored at home by mixing private economy with public magnificence.'[113] He had managed to do this himself, but his son knew nothing whatever about economy either private or public, and all this magnificence was being created in places the public could not see. An alphabetical list of the names of just a few rooms gives a sense of Carlton House's opulence, which, although it was undoubtedly gorgeous, was paid for by the Prince's creditors. There were the Admirals Room, Armoury, Blue Velvet Closet, Blue Velvet Room, Bow Room, Chinese Drawing Room, Circular Room, Colonnade Room, Corinthian Room, Council Chamber, Crimson Drawing Room, Gothic Conservatory, Gothic Dining Room (one of three dining rooms), Grand Staircase, Great Drawing Room (one of four drawing rooms), Music Room, Picture Salon, Rose Satin Drawing Room, State Bedchamber and Throne Room, and dozens more. An 1816 inventory listed over 450 pictures.

Despite the number of rooms available to him, the Prince tended to stay in his bedroom for much of the day, where visitors would find him, according to Nathaniel Wraxall, 'rolling about from side to side in a state approaching to nudity'.[114] Robert Smirke, who designed the British Museum, thought Carlton House 'overdone with finery', while Antonio Canova dismissed it as 'an ugly barn'.[115] When he became king, George IV would tear it down entirely in favour of another vanity project. Its chimneypieces were salvaged and installed in the remodelled Buckingham Palace, while many of its finer doors went to Windsor. The only vestiges visible to the general public today are the columns of the portico, which were reused for the National Gallery in Trafalgar Square, against the wishes of its architect William Wilkins.

The controversy over the Prince's allowance, in which Fox had fully supported the Prince against the King, underscored for George how much Fox had been dissembling in his gushing letter in April. On 19 July a minor complication over the sixth article in the Spanish Peace Treaty – whether the Mosquito Shore* was included in the concept of the *Continent Espagnol* – prompted George to write to Fox damningly that for 'Every difficulty in concluding peace this country has alone to blame itself: after the extraordinary and never-to-be-forgot vote of February 1782, and the hurry for negotiation that ensued, it is no wonder our enemies, seeing our spirit so fallen, have taken advantage of it.'[116] As Fox had himself spoken and voted in the debate of 27 February 1782 that demanded peace with America, this was a blatant criticism.

---

* On the Caribbean coast of Honduras and Nicaragua, named after the Meskito natives, not the insects.

Despite this provocation, the reply was measured: 'Mr Fox entirely agrees with Your Majesty in regretting that there should remain any seeds of dispute in the definitive treaty.'[117] Three weeks later, when Fox asked 'whether it would be agreeable to Your Majesty to receive a minister from the United States', the extent to which the loss of the American colonies still rankled was clear in the King's reply:

> I can never express its being agreeable to me; and indeed I should think it wisest for both parties to have only agents who can settle any matters of commerce; but so far I cannot help adding that I shall ever have a bad opinion of any Englishman who would accept of being an accredited minister for that revolted state, and which certainly for years cannot establish a stable government.[118]

In point of fact, the United States had already established a remarkably stable government, especially given the circumstances of recent war and revolution.

Lord Thurlow invited William Pitt to dinner on 19 July, three days after the parliamentary session ended, to sound him out about taking part in an attempt to overthrow the coalition. He ventured that it would be impossible for the King ever to be reconciled to the Foxites after the business of the Prince of Wales' allowance, and tried to ascertain how committed Pitt truly was to parliamentary reform. Although Pitt's enemies were keen to make him out to be a pawn of the Court, he recognized that he needed to avoid that impression if he were to win the respect of the Commons and the country. His report to his cousin and close ally Earl Temple of his discussion with Thurlow showed how conscious he was of this, evidence of his political maturity at only twenty-four.

Thurlow, and by extension the King, hoped to play on Pitt's youthful ambition and manoeuvre him into believing that, if he wanted George to dismiss the coalition, he would be beholden to the Crown afterwards. This might have worked with many young men, but not with the most impressive statesman of the age since his own father. As is clear from his letter to Temple, Pitt explained to Thurlow that if the King wanted to be rid of the coalition it would have to be on Pitt's terms:

> Lord Thurlow's object was to insinuate that a change was not so necessary to the King; and to endeavour to make it (if it should take place) rather our act than his, and on that ground to try whether terms might be imposed that could not otherwise . . . I stated in general that if the King's feelings did not point strongly to a change, it was not what we sought. But if they did, and

we could form a permanent system consistent with our principles, we should not decline it.[119]

He had not fallen for Thurlow's gambit. Pitt then reminded him 'how much I was personally pledged to parliamentary reform on the principles I had publicly explained, which I should support on every seasonable occasion', adding that he saw it 'as out of the question any measure being taken of extending Crown influence'. He concluded unequivocally, asking that the King 'be fully apprised of the grounds on which I should necessarily proceed'.[120] The King's bluff had been called; Pitt was to be a full and equal partner in bringing down the Fox–North coalition once the Peace of Paris was safely ratified. As one of his biographers has written, 'He was ambitious but patient, confident in his own abilities, certain that he had something to offer and daring to expect a lot in return.'[121] He was exactly what the King needed.

20

'On the Edge of a Precipice'

August 1783–May 1784

The wheel of fortune turned at last in George III's favour; he
became the first Hanoverian sovereign to achieve popularity.[1]
Sir John Plumb, *The First Four Georges*, 1956

The definitive Treaties of Paris were signed with France, Spain and America on 3 September 1783 and that with Holland the following May. All the various clauses now went into effect, save one: the Americans initially reneged on their promise to compensate the dispossessed Loyalists.[2] When the texts arrived in London on 7 September, the King wrote to Fox at 7.30 a.m. about the difficulties of reconciling properly with France and Holland, remarking, 'In states as well as in men, where dislike has once arose, I never expect to see cordiality.' It might well have been a none too subtle warning that, although they were capable of working together now, Fox could not expect a thawing in their personal relations, especially after their disagreements over the Prince of Wales' income. Commenting on Portugal's decision to join the League of Armed Neutrality, the King added, 'Nothing can be more avowed than the desertion of the Court of Lisbon; but after Britain has so much lowered herself, can one be surprised that courts treat her accordingly.'[3]

The King was even blunter to Lord North at 5.44 p.m. the same day. Telling him that he had just signed the warrant for the heralds to proclaim the Peace on 9 September, George wrote:

Indeed I am glad it is on a day I am not in town, as I think this completes the downfall of the lustre of this empire. But when religion and public spirit are quite absorbed by vice and dissipation, what has now occurred is but the natural consequence. One comfort I have, that I have alone tried to support the dignity of my Crown and feel that I am innocent of the evils that have occurred, though deeply wounded that it should have happened during my reign.[4]

The pain was palpable, as was the self-righteousness that blighted the King's otherwise fine character. It was of course also wildly unfair to write such a thing to the Prime Minister who had striven so hard, albeit unsuccessfully, to support the dignity of the Crown for twelve arduous years.

When in late November the British Army and Royal Navy evacuated New York in compliance with the Paris terms, the Loyalists moved to Britain, Canada, the Bahamas, the West Indies (especially Jamaica) and Sierra Leone. The new British Empire in India was partly won by the efforts of first- and second-generation Loyalists, such as Benedict Arnold's sons; Freetown in Sierra Leone was founded by 1,200 African-American Loyalists; the first serious proposal to colonize Australia came from an American Loyalist. A British visitor to Upper Canada in 1785 marvelled at the wheat, corn and potatoes being grown along the St Lawrence River, on the Bay of Quinte and on the Niagara Peninsula. 'The settling [of] the Loyalists is one of the best things [that] George III ever did,' he noted.[5]

During the war, the King had asked Benjamin West (another American Loyalist) what he thought George Washington would do if the Americans won; in response West predicted that 'he would retire to a private situation.' 'If he does that,' the King replied, 'he would be the greatest man in the world.'[6] On 23 December 1783, Washington did indeed resign his commission as Commander-in-Chief of the Continental Army and returned to his farm at Mount Vernon. When Washington gave up the presidency in March 1797, the King similarly described him as 'the greatest character of the age'.[7] It redounds well on George's own character that he could say such a thing.* In turn, when President Washington wrote to George III on 7 June 1796 to introduce Rufus King as Minister Plenipotentiary of the United States, he opened by addressing him as 'Our great and good Friend', adding his hope that the King would 'give full credence to whatever he shall say to you on the part of the United States; and most of all when he shall assure you of their friendship and wishes for your prosperity, and I pray God to have your Majesty in his safe and holy keeping'. As the Declaration of Independence had eloquently put it, 'Enemies in war, in peace friends.'[8]

Parliament opened on 11 November 1783 with a King's Speech that welcomed the definitive treaties 'after so long and so expensive a war', but also included the vague yet ominous sentence that 'The situation of the East India Company will require the utmost exertions of your wisdom to

---

* In 1807 George bought John Marshall's five-volume *The Life of George Washington*, complete with maps of his battlefields.

maintain and improve the valuable advantages derived from our Indian possessions, and to promote and secure the happiness of the native inhabitants of those provinces.'[9] The night before the session opened, Fox read the proposed speech to government supporters at the Cockpit but North was not present, and he did not attend Parliament for the first fortnight. Fox had also appointed friends to minor government positions without asking North beforehand, in breach of the coalition agreement. Understandably, when Jenkinson and Robinson began to spread the rumour that Fox was plotting 'to get rid of the Duke of Portland and Lord North', it received some credence.[10]

At noon on 13 November – the same day that Pitt rebuffed an offer from Fox to enter the government to help shore it up – the King saw John Robinson out riding in Kensington. He overtook him and said that he was pleased that Robinson's gout had improved, 'for you are always the same, you do not change with the times. You are always steady.'[11] From George, there was scarcely a higher compliment. Before riding off, the King called over his shoulder, 'These are bad times indeed.'[12] When Pitt, Thurlow, Jenkinson and Temple arrived in London for the new session, each was invited to a separate audience with the King. All of them, and Robinson too, were waiting for the Fox–North coalition to overreach itself after the treaties had been signed.

The perfect opportunity now seemed to present itself. On 18 November, Charles Fox introduced a Bill into the Commons whose main feature was that the charter given in 1600 by Queen Elizabeth I to the East India Company would be wound up and the Company's Court of Directors would be replaced with a seven-man, government-appointed Commission headed by the Whig oligarch William Wentworth-Fitzwilliam, 4th Earl Fitzwilliam, Rockingham's nephew and heir. The government of British India would be placed under the Commission's direction for seven years before the power of nomination to it passed to the King. All of India's commerce would be controlled by eight assistant directors, responsible to the commissioners. In essence, Fox was proposing the nationalization of the East India Company.

There was something to be said for regulating and modernizing the governance of the Company, as the idea of a private commercial enterprise running Britain's growing Indian possessions for profit was starting to seem extraordinary even to eighteenth-century minds, and the corruption endemic in the Company was an acknowledged public shame. In May 1782, Dundas had carried a motion for recalling Warren Hastings, the de facto Governor-General of India since 1772, on the grounds of profoundly corrupt practices, although nothing came of it after a meeting of more than

a thousand Company shareholders reiterated that Parliament had no jurisdiction over what it did in India.[13]

The East India Bill proposed far more far-reaching change than mere
regulation and modernization. Burke, who had helped frame the Bill, privately called it 'the Magna Carta of Hindustan'. Opposition came from
the effect it would have not so much on India as on Westminster, for it
would effectively put the enormous wealth of the subcontinent into the
hands of Fox's seven friends led by Lord Fitzwilliam who it was feared
would use it to influence Westminster elections and augment their own
power. Even if Fox lost office, the seven commissioners and eight assistant
directors would continue to rule India for seven years. It was in effect a
Brooks's takeover of the wealth of a subcontinent. In the words of the Tory
MP Charles George Perceval, it would be 'erecting an aristocratical power
in this country destructive to the sovereign'.[14] Constitutionalists complained that the King's exclusion from the takeover for seven years
'appeared to be an implicit denial of the King's role as head of the
executive'.[15]

The sense that this was an unwonted power grab by Fox and his friends
was a central plank in the opposition to the Bill. Lord Midleton, who was
one of the proposed commissioners, admitted that he was startled by the
riskiness of the plan. Privately, Fox admitted the Bill was 'vigorous and
hazardous', but he was an inveterate gambler and was now playing for the
highest stakes.[16] Yet even though the Bill was seconded by Colonel George
North, Lord North's son, the two Northite Cabinet ministers, Loughborough and Stormont, had not been informed beforehand of the details,
beyond the somewhat anodyne statement in the King's Speech. Loughborough was soon reporting that North was 'seriously alarmed' by the
implications of the Bill's provisions, against which fourteen of the twenty-
four Company board directors vigorously protested, as did a larger
majority of its Court of Proprietors of larger shareholders.[17] The City of
London, which disliked government interference with the rights of a char-
tered company, criticized the Bill strongly, petitioned against it and ordered
its sponsored MPs to vote it down.

The King, unlike much of the British elite, had no significant financial
interest in the East India Company, although he recognized its importance
to the British economy, as the events leading to the Boston Tea Party ten
years earlier had shown.[18] He knew that abuses of power took place in
India and had supported both the censure of Clive of India and Lord
North's failed Regulating Act in 1773. He had also opposed what he called
'the fleecers of East India', and believed that the Company needed 'a continual inspection from Parliament' to 'save it from destruction'.[19] He was

therefore no reactionary opposed to change in the governance of the sub-continent, but he wanted regulation rather than nationalization.

'The Company is ruined and Parliament turned into ridicule,' he had told North in May 1778, 'unless Mr Hastings is instantly removed from his situation.'[20] He had based his views on a report by Sir Philip Francis and was later to come to revise them, but by 1783 he could also see the obvious political danger of all the power and wealth of the Company falling into the hands of Fox and Burke. Even the large amount that the King and North had spent securing the 1780 election would be dwarfed by the amount that the commissioners would be able to deploy in future elections if they ran India.

The Company had begun to behave like a territorial power since before the Seven Years War, ruling Bengal, annexing territory, forming alliances with neighbouring princely states, collecting taxes, fighting military campaigns, administering justice and doing invaluable work in denying East India to the French, Spanish and Portuguese. Yet, for all its burgeoning power, the Company's finances were often precarious, especially in the mid-1760s. In 1772, many prominent investors had lost out when the share price collapsed, including Edmund Burke.

Fox's unfavourable statements about the Company's finances when he presented his Bill on 18 November, essential though they were in the case for nationalization, meant that its shares fell from £138 on the morning of his speech to £120 two days later, and continued to drop thereafter.[21]* The pound had been weak since the Dutch had sold British securities heavily early in the year, and bullion reserves were extremely low as a result of the war, so this new shock worried investors. By the 1780s, Company stock was held by large numbers of investors such as retired army officers and small tradesmen, who valued the high regular dividends, precisely the kind of people whose electoral support Fox could not afford to lose; yet soon printed handbills started to appear blaming Fox for the fall in the share price. For all the roiling of the markets, however, the various stages of the East India Bill passed in the Commons by very large majorities ranging from 106 to 114.

Fox wanted to rush the Bill through Parliament before opposition to it could coalesce, announcing that the second reading would be on the 27th, giving the Opposition only nine days to mobilize, which they signally failed to do. In a complex speech during the second reading, Pitt mistakenly focused on the technical and financial aspects of the Bill, rather than on its constitutional, patronage and charter-rights aspects, and lost some of

---

* They had been issued at £100 in 1657, and had reached £276 in 1769.

his listeners in the details.[22] He was later to make up for it rhetorically, calling the Bill 'among the most desperate and alarming attempts at the exercise of tyranny that ever disgraced the annals of this or any other country'.[23]

Fox pressed on, keen to get the Bill passed before Christmas because afterwards around a hundred independent MPs would start coming to London to attend Parliament who could not be relied upon to support such a huge increase in government power. Burke spoke passionately in favour of the Bill on 1 December, and two days later it passed by 229 votes to 120. With the royal veto not having been exercised since Queen Anne in 1708, it was clear to opponents of the Bill that it needed to be killed in the Lords.

On the same day as Burke's speech, Thurlow and Temple wrote the King a memorandum advising him that the Bill would 'take more than half royal power and . . . disable His Majesty for the rest of the reign'.[24] If peers were told of the King's opposition to the Bill, however, especially 'in a manner which would make it impossible to pretend a doubt of it', it might be defeated and afterwards the King would be 'at perfect liberty to choose whether he will change [the government] or not'.[25] Using Thomas Villiers, 1st Earl of Clarendon, who had been Shelburne's Chancellor of the Duchy of Lancaster, as one intermediary and Count John von Alvensleben, the Hanoverian minister in London, as another, secret contact was established with Pitt. Meanwhile, John Robinson was deputed to take Pitt through the parliamentary numbers and to persuade him that with the King's enthusiastic support he could survive as Prime Minister until a general election. 'Everything stands prepared for the blow,' the senior East India Company executive Richard Atkinson wrote to his old friend Robinson on 3 December, 'if a certain person has courage to strike it', meaning Pitt rather than the King.[26]

Burke's allegations about the existence of a 'double Cabinet' were not true when he made them in *Thoughts on the Present Discontents* in 1770, but for some three weeks in December 1783 they briefly were, albeit only for a specific purpose. Thurlow, Robinson, Temple and Jenkinson composed this secret cabal, with Atkinson and the rich former East India Company official John Johnstone acting for them 'out of doors'.[27] Jenkinson was accused of having 'ratted' on Lord North after a decade's service to him, an unfair criticism since he was always the leader of the King's Friends first and foremost, and they considered that North had himself ratted on the King by joining forces with Fox.[28] Whig satirists decried Robinson as 'the potent spirit of the black-browed *Jacko* . . . who worketh the works of darkness!'[29] But if the King was going to trust anyone to help him pull off what has been described as 'a daring coup which was as dangerous and reckless as any of the political decisions that Fox had made', Jenkinson and Robinson were the cool-headed, calculating men for the job.[30]

In 1766, the King had told the Duke of York in relation to the repeal of the Stamp Act that 'I do not think it constitutional for the Crown personally to interfere in measures which it has thought proper to refer to the advice of Parliament.'[31] But now, with the coalition attempting to take over the East India Company's gigantic potential for patronage only a year after having abolished scores of places in the Establishment Act, the King saw a massive shift taking place in political power in Britain, away from the monarchy and towards the Whig elite that he had tried to oppose with varying success ever since ascending the throne. Dundas described the Fox–North coalition as 'an insolent aristocratic band'; the *Quarterly Review* was later to characterize the supporters of the India Bill as 'the grand and leading party of the aristocracy'.[32] One modern historian has pointed out that the King 'had to struggle against the close oligarchy of Whig nobles that had encircled and enchained the throne'.[33]

Since George saw it as his duty to uphold the authority of the Crown vis-à-vis the other branches of the executive, he thought himself perfectly justified in using his prerogative powers in its defence, short of actually vetoing the Bill as Queen Anne might have done. He had good precedents in his great-grandfather's wholesale dismissal and proscription of the Tories in 1714, and his grandfather's open opposition to both the Pension Bill in 1730 and the Habeas Corpus Bill in 1758, neither of which was vetoed.

Whig historians have used the words conspiracy and plot for what was in fact the oldest of parliamentary manoeuvres: an Opposition trying to dislodge a government. It had to be done in secret so as not to warn the coalition, but that is usual in politics too. The sources are largely silent about exactly how the operation was conducted, since almost everything was done orally, but it is clear that Pitt would need to be the new premier and that the King would have to support him steadfastly. They also realized that if the attempt failed it would leave Fox in a far more powerful position than before, having first stormed the Closet and then defended an attempt to eject him from it. The royal prerogative might be damaged, perhaps fatally. Nor could Pitt appear to have his fingerprints on the scheme, as it would inevitably detract from the reputation he had built for himself of disinterested probity.

The extent to which it was successfully kept secret was shown by Robinson in drawing up electoral lists of every constituency, and which MPs might be brought over, at his home on Sion Hill, not going into town to attend meetings in Dundas' house in Leicester Square and pleading gout to explain to government supporters his absence from the Commons. He worked late into the night on his 'complete revision of the canvass' of both the Commons and Lords, which he did 'with alacrity and pleasure'.[34] Letters between Robinson and the other plotters were entrusted only to servants, never to the post office, and Robinson acted largely through Atkinson. Robinson even spent Christmas Day at Lothian's Hotel in Albemarle Street, writing letters and discussing appointments in the future Pitt ministry. When his role eventually became clear, his old chief and friend Lord North never spoke to him again.

The reason why the King had to turn to the twenty-four-year-old Pitt was primarily that all the other major figures from previous Cabinets were politically damaged by the American calamity, and Shelburne's arrogance told against him. Someone from a new generation was needed, untouched by the military debacle yet connected by his name to the great days of Britain's recent past. Pitt's extreme youth also meant that the coalition did not suspect him or view him as a credible threat. It was Dundas who was instrumental in persuading him to strike, armed with Robinson's minute analysis of the likely future voting figures.

On 8 December, the East India Bill passed its third reading in the Commons by 208 votes to 102. The next day it received its first reading in the Lords, 'without a word of objection or obstruction from either side of the House', as an unsuspecting Duke of Portland reported to the King from Downing Street at 9.40 that night.[35] This is the last piece of communication in the King's correspondence for a whole week, a suspiciously long period of time for such a diligent curator of his own archive, who often kept half a dozen of the most important letters he received each day. There must be at least the suspicion that George did not want the extent of his personal involvement in the coup to be laid bare. On 10 December, Pitt met Temple, Thurlow and Gower and agreed to take on the premiership when the time was ripe. But he could not meet the King in person in case the government got wind of what was afoot.

On the afternoon of 11 December, the King authorized Lord Temple to inform individual peers privately that he disapproved of the East India Bill, and he might even have written out the exact wording of the authorization, though no such document survives. General Burgoyne later alleged that George had told Temple:

I think the Bill unprecedented, unparliamentary, and subversive of the constitution, as introducing a fourth power which does not belong to it [that is, the seven-man India Commission]. If the Bill passes, I am no more a king. I shall look upon those who support the Bill not only as not my friends, but as my absolute enemies.[36]

These words sound unlike George – except perhaps for the last sentence – but probably do convey the gist of his feelings.

Being an 'absolute enemy' of the King was a serious business in late eighteenth-century politics, meaning no possible social advancement for oneself or one's family, as well as the possibility – amply demonstrated after the Peace of Paris in 1763 – of losing any posts and sinecures one already held. Ministries came and went, but there had only been two monarchs in the past fifty-six years, and to oppose the known wishes of a healthy king of forty-five was effectively career suicide for an ambitious junior bishop, peer hoping for a rise in rank, Scottish representative peer who wanted an English peerage too, former royal office holder on an annual pension or county magnate who valued his lord-lieutenancy. A good number of peers also held shares in the East India Company. The King was playing his trump card, since even those at the apex of society – perhaps especially them – did not want to cross the line from political critic to enemy of the monarch. Whigs who later denounced the King as acting unconstitutionally by allowing his name to be invoked in the Lords were being hypocritical; as we saw in Chapter 7, this was precisely how Rockingham had repealed the Stamp Act.

At midnight on Wednesday 17 December, Portland reported to the King that the East India Bill had fallen on its second reading in the Lords by 95 votes to 76, including proxies. A large number of courtiers and bishops – and even Lord Stormont, the Lord President of the Council – had voted against the Bill. In the debate, Lord Fitzwilliam said that 'his mind, filled and actuated by the motives of Whiggism, would ill brook to see a dark and secret influence exerting itself against the independence of Parliament, and the authority of ministers', clearly meaning the King. There is a list in the King's handwriting which corresponds to the fifty-seven peers (that is, not including proxies) who voted 'Content' on 17 December: it was a veritable blacklist of political opponents, headed by his two surviving brothers, the Dukes of Gloucester and Cumberland.[37] (The Prince of Wales had abstained.) Extraordinarily, only a few months after the greatest military catastrophe since the fifteenth century, George had rebounded sufficiently to be able to dismiss a ministry with a working majority led by Charles Fox, who had opposed the American war.

'We are beat in the House of Lords,' reported Fox, 'by such treachery on the part of the King and such meanness on behalf of his friends . . . as one could not expect from either him or them.'[38] He swiftly proposed a successful motion in the Commons stating that the use of the King's name, 'with a view to influence the vote of the members, is a high crime and misdemeanour, derogatory to the honour of the Crown, a breach of the fundamental privileges of Parliament, and subversive of the constitution of this country'.[39] Pitt denounced this clear attack on his cousin Temple as 'frivolous and ill-timed', but 153 MPs disagreed with him and only 80 agreed.[40] Fox then turned on Pitt himself:

> Boys without judgement, without experience of the sentiments suggested by the knowledge of the world, or the amiable decencies of a sound mind, may follow the headlong course of ambition thus precipitately, and vault into the seat while the reins of government are placed in other hands.[41]

He of course meant the King's. By contrast, when Boswell heard the result in Edinburgh, he wrote to Dr Johnson, 'News has come by express that the House of Lords has made a noble stand against Mr Fox's East India Bill, which would have overwhelmed the Crown. This rejoiced my Tory soul.'[42]

After waiting throughout 17 December for the Portland ministry to resign on the defeat of their leading legislative measure, and receiving no hint that they were going to – they still after all had a large Commons majority – George wrote to Lord North from Buckingham House at 10.43 p.m. on Thursday the 18th, 'Lord North is required by this to send me the seals of his department, and to acquaint Mr Fox to send those of the foreign department . . . I choose this method as audiences on such occasions must be unpleasant.'[43]* He also wrote to Stormont to 'express to him my sorrow at his being out of my service', a courtesy he did not extend to anyone else in the coalition.[44]

On Friday 19 December, William Pitt kissed hands as First Lord of the Treasury. The Commons chamber roared with laughter when a friend of his, Richard Pepper Arden MP, announced that there would be a by-election at Appleby because its sitting member 'has accepted the office of First Lord of the Treasury and Chancellor of the Exchequer'.[45] The idea of giving so much responsibility to someone so young seemed absurd to many people, though not perhaps to a man who had acceded to the throne aged twenty-two. Pitt was the first premier who was younger than George, and it had been a brave decision to appoint him. Winston Churchill deemed it 'certainly the most outstanding domestic action of his long reign'.[46]†

---

* 'Must be' in this case meaning 'invariably are' rather than 'ought to be'.
† Pitt is still today the premier with the least parliamentary experience before his appointment, having sat in the Commons for only two years and 345 days. The second shortest is Lord Bute, having attended the Lords for only five years and thirty-four days.

Temple took on both secretaryships of state and the leadership of the House of Lords until somebody else could be found, and Gower went back to his old post as Lord President of the Council. Because there were no other Cabinet ministers in the Commons, Pitt also took on the role of Leader of the House. He had to find people to fill the places made vacant by the sixteen peers and thirty-two commoner ministers who had immediately resigned and followed Fox and North into Opposition, but most immediately he had to find the money needed to govern the country without a Commons majority. He could not dissolve Parliament and call a general election because an unpopular but financially necessary Land Tax Bill needed to be passed, and he also needed to renew the Mutiny Act* before it lapsed on 25 March. He did not have the votes to do either.

The Land Tax Bill had been held over by Fox and North until after the East India Bill had passed, but now it was pressing. On 19 December, Fox persuaded the Commons to postpone its third reading until the following Monday, 22 December, the same day as a debate in which Temple's actions would be denounced as unconstitutional, possibly leading to his impeachment. A deal was done between Pitt and Fox via Earl Spencer whereby the House would pass the Land Tax Bill in return for an assurance that there would be no early dissolution – that is, before the Mutiny Act was passed three months later. Pitt also offered Fox a place in his new ministry, but was told plainly on Sunday the 21st that he was not interested.[47] 'We are so strong that nobody can undertake without madness,' Fox told a friend, 'and if they do, I think we shall destroy them almost as soon as they are formed.'[48] The Commons then passed a resolution of Fox's once again stating that the reporting of the King's views was 'a high crime and misdemeanour' and that any minister supporting dissolution was 'an enemy to his country'.[49]

Pitt unsurprisingly struggled to find recruits for what looked like an utterly doomed government with no hope of a Commons majority. The Duke of Grafton and Lords Camden and Cornwallis and even Viscount Sackville (the former Lord George Germain) refused office. Shelburne also refused. Mrs Crewe, a prominent Whig hostess, nicknamed it the 'Mince-Pie Administration', since it would clearly not last beyond Christmas. 'What was it that induced Pitt to stay at the helm,' one historian has asked, 'especially during the weekend of 19–22 December when the cause looked so hopeless?'[50] The answer was the King, who depended on Pitt completely to save him from what would undoubtedly have been a vengeful coalition.

Paradoxically, Pitt was saved from the humiliation of not being able to

---

* Which was passed annually from 1689 to 1879, and effectively provided the legal basis for the existence of the British Army.

form a ministry at all by Temple's shock resignation on Sunday 21 December, after holding his three senior posts in the government for only three days. It was the only moment in Pitt's entire career when he was kept awake all night by worry, in this case at the prospect of having to carry on alone. There has been a lively debate, both contemporaneously and since, as to why Temple went so soon.[51] One explanation was that he panicked after hearing that Pitt had decided against dissolution, meaning that Fox would have time to impeach him.[52] Dundas subscribed to this theory, calling Temple a 'damned dolter-headed coward' and an 'uncharged blunderbuss'.[53]

Another theory was that Pitt asked Temple to resign in order to protect his nascent government from accusations of unconstitutionality stemming from Temple's bandying of the King's name around the House of Lords before its division on the East India Bill. Rather than acting out of panic or fear, Pitt protected both his ministry from disintegration and his cousin from severe embarrassment or worse. Thomas Pitt wrote to a friend that Temple, whose brother William Grenville was his son-in-law, 'wisely in my opinion (not timidly) declined being the Lord Strafford* of the day to stand as adviser of the Crown upon personal questions of crimination . . . by an angry House of Commons governed by a desperate faction . . . He is going to Stowe† to enjoy a little quiet.'[54] The King initially thought Temple had betrayed the government and himself, but came to appreciate his strategic self-sacrifice a year later, raising him as the 1st Marquess of Buckingham, and two years later conferring upon him the Order of the Garter.

With Temple gone, by 5 p.m. on the 22nd Pitt had senior posts with which he could persuade the nonetheless reluctant Lord Sydney, the Marquess of Carmarthen and the Duke of Rutland to join his ministry, which he now believed might survive; but as he told Temple, 'for how many days or weeks remains to be seen'.[55] Sydney became Home Secretary; Carmarthen, the heir of the 4th Duke of Leeds, who had held no post before and was only thirty-two, became Foreign Secretary; Rutland initially agreed to be Lord Privy Seal, but then went to Dublin as Viceroy of Ireland in February. Once the Duke of Richmond, who cared more for parliamentary and administrative reform than for his family connections to Fox, agreed to stay on in the post of Master-General of Ordnance – albeit initially refusing to sit in Cabinet – the outlines of a Pitt ministry could finally be discerned. 'To one on the edge of a precipice every ray of hope must be pleasing,' the King wrote to Pitt at 10.46 a.m. on 23 December, inviting him to an

---

* King Charles I's adviser the Earl of Strafford had been impeached by Parliament and executed in 1641.
† His magnificent country seat in Buckinghamshire.

audience at 1 p.m. 'I therefore place confidence in the Duke of Richmond, Lord Gower, Lord Thurlow, and Mr Pitt bringing forward some names to fill up an arrangement.'[56] When the King listed people, he tended automatically to do so in order of rank; in this case with Gower's earldom senior to Thurlow's barony. In practice Gower as the leading Bedfordite was able to bring over more people than Richmond, the renegade Rockinghamite.

Parliament went into recess on Christmas Eve, saving Pitt from any humiliating votes in the Commons before it reconvened on 12 January. By Boxing Day, Pitt had managed to cobble together enough ministers to form a government, albeit very much a minority one. He had not wanted to include George's favourites such as Thurlow and Earl Howe, as he did not want to be taken for the King's puppet, but with so few alternatives he had to accept the former as Lord Chancellor and the latter as First Lord of the Admiralty. At least Thurlow had served under three previous premiers in the post, and Howe was a naval hero. Other friends of the King such as Charles Jenkinson and John Robinson were only appointed to the government some years later. From the very outset, and despite his young age, Pitt made it clear that he was going to be the leader, prime spokesman and driving force of his ministry, as North, Portland and Grafton had never been, for as Dundas said of him, 'This young man does not choose to suffer it to be doubtful who is the effectual minister.'[57] Although the *Morning Herald* was stating, 'The cloven foot of absolute monarchy begins to appear,' in fact there was no such danger.[58]

During the Christmas recess Jenkinson and Robinson set about what they did so well, offering patronage in return for support, and by the time the Commons reassembled on 12 January the Opposition's seventy-three majority had been whittled down to thirty-nine. Jenkinson believed a dissolution and election would produce a healthy government majority if it could hold firm and avoid too much humiliation in the Commons before the Mutiny Act was passed in late March. The King personally asked the 2nd Duke of Newcastle, son of his first premier, to support Pitt, and the Duke obediently ordered the six MPs under his control to vote with the government. The King also wrote to the Duke of Marlborough to solicit his support for the new ministry:

> The times are of the most serious nature. The political struggle is not as formerly between two factions for power, but it is no less than whether a desperate faction should not reduce the sovereign to a mere tool in its hands. Though I have too much principle ever to infringe the rights of others, yet that must ever equally prevent my submitting to the executive power being in any other hands than where the constitution has placed it.[59]

George argued that his cause was 'that of the constitution as fixed at the [Glorious] Revolution, and to the support of which my family was invited to mount the throne'. Marlborough replied by claiming disingenuously that he had supported the East India Bill – as had all but one of the five MPs he influenced – only because he thought it had increased rather than diminished the Crown's power, but he promised that he would try to help in the future.

Having been switched off entirely during the coalition, suddenly the spigots of the Fount of Honour were fully opened for Pitt. Thomas Pitt, Henry Thynne, Edward Craggs-Eliot (a West Country borough-monger), Sir James Lowther (ditto for Westmorland and Cumberland) and the Duke of Northumberland all received baronies, and more were promised, hugely incentivizing the would-be recipients for a Pittite victory in the forthcoming election. 'All the powers of the Crown have been let loose without reserve,' complained Portland bitterly.[60] 'They are crying* peerages about the streets in barrows,' wrote Horace Walpole to the Countess of Upper Ossory.[61] (Her husband's Irish title had been created only in 1751, and for precisely the same political services that Walpole now denounced.)

The King well understood the power of honours; in 1772 he had enlarged the Order of the Bath, and he created the Order of St Patrick in March 1783 to reward and encourage support in the Dublin Parliament. He extended the permitted number of Garter knights in 1786, and then again in 1804. The lust for stars and sashes and also enamel to hang around one's neck has never been absent in British politics, but it was particularly powerful in the eighteenth century, when proud statesmen would beg pathetically for them from a monarch who privately despised them for it, while fully appreciating the power it gave him. George now permitted Pitt to use the honours system in order to shore up his support in Parliament to a degree not seen before in his reign. In all, nearly a hundred peerages were created during Pitt's premierships, entirely reconfiguring the Upper House. Peerages were created in every year except 1795 and 1800.

When Parliament reconvened on 12 January 1784, Fox proposed instituting a committee to report on the state of the nation, and in the ensuing debate he implied that Pitt was merely the creature of 'secret influences', clearly implying the King. Pitt denied this vehemently, but Fox had the votes – 232 to 193 in one division, and 196 to 142 in another. The King told Pitt that these divisions gave him 'much uneasiness, as it shows the House of Commons much more willing to enter into any intemperate resolutions of desperate men than I could have imagined. As to myself, I am

---

* 'The hawkers' proclamation of wares' (*Johnson's Dictionary*)

perfectly composed, as I have the self-satisfaction of feeling I have done my duty.'[62] George's secret influence was increasingly anything but: he even offered to dine in London if Pitt found it helpful for him to be within easy reach.

With the Opposition demanding that the King's name not be used to influence votes, and Pitt having promised not to dissolve Parliament until after the Mutiny Bill was passed, in a debate on 16 January Fox went so far as to insist that the King had a duty to appoint ministers only from the dominant party in the Commons. On this, the Opposition majority fell to twenty-one. Pitt spotted that Fox had overreached himself with the independent country members, who did not want to see far-reaching constitutional change that further limited the powers of the Crown. In February 1779, the King had reassured North, 'I am convinced this country will never regain a proper tone unless ministers as in the reign of King William will not mind being now and then in a minority.'[63] Five years later, he was taking the same attitude, but now North was on the receiving end and Pitt was the beneficiary.

Even with the King's unfeigned support, Pitt was finding it hard to govern, and on 26 January his replacement India Bill, by which the Crown rather than the government would make the appointments to the Indian Commission, fell by 222 votes to 214, leaving the whole issue in abeyance. The King had deemed the defeat of the coalition's India Bill to be a good enough reason to dismiss it, but he did not extend the same judgement to Pitt's. Instead, he summoned the Cabinet to Buckingham House, where, Carmarthen noted, 'in a well-conceived speech of some length, and in different parts of which he appeared much agitated', the King 'declared a fixed and unalterable resolution on no account to be put bound hand and foot into the hands of Mr Fox; that rather submit to that he would quit the kingdom for ever'.[64]

By the end of April, petitions were pouring in from the various counties and boroughs which supported the King's exercise of the royal prerogative over the choice of ministers. Their signatories eventually numbered over 50,000. Robinson and Atkinson's hand can be seen behind several of these, but once they gained momentum there was no further need for central direction. The petitions were received by the King with a good deal more alacrity than the City of London's remonstrations during the American war had been. 'Since the debate centred so much on the personal integrity of the King,' writes an historian, 'the response in the country was determined by its inherent loyalty to the monarchy.'[65]

A letter to General Richard Grenville MP, Prince Frederick's governor, of 13 February illustrates the King's view of the Crown as one of the bulwarks against the Commons establishing too much power vis-à-vis the Lords, Crown and people. He denounced:

> the present strange phenomenon, a majority not exceeding thirty in the House of Commons thinking that justifies the stopping of supplies when the House of Lords by a majority of two to one and at least that of the People at large approve of my conduct and see as I do that not less is meant than to render the Crown and the Lords perfect cyphers, but it will be seen that I will never submit.[66]

The way to discover the genuine views of the people – or at least that small proportion of them who were enfranchised – was through a general election, which for the King could not come soon enough.

Support for the government outside Parliament – and especially opposition to Fox's India Bill – was growing. On 28 February, none other than John Wilkes presented Pitt with the Freedom of the City of London at the Guildhall, for his support for 'the legal prerogative of the Crown, and the constitutional rights of the people'.[67] It was a hugely symbolic event, emphasizing that the City of London, which had been opposed to the Crown through much of the 1760s and 1770s, now (since the Whigs' East India Bill and the end of the American war) embraced it, led by the living embodiment of that former opposition, Wilkes himself. On his return from the triumphant Guildhall ceremony, however, Pitt's carriage was attacked outside Brooks's in St James's Street – still the citadel of Whiggery – by club servants wielding broken-off sedan poles as bludgeons, supported by Brooks's members cheering and throwing missiles from the windows of the Great Subscription Room. Pitt escaped with some difficulty to a nearby house and then crossed the street to the largely Tory White's Club to recuperate.

The King was predictably infuriated by this assault on his Prime Minister. 'I was much hurt at hearing ... of the outrage committed the last night under the auspices of Brooks's against Mr Pitt,' he wrote in commiseration, 'but am very happy that he escaped without injury. I trust every means will be employed to find out the abettors of this.'[68] When Fox was accused of having personally orchestrated the attack, he retorted that he had a perfect alibi: 'I was in bed with Mrs Armistead, who is ready to substantiate the fact on oath.'[69]

On 1 March, the Opposition majority shrank to just twelve on a motion for another Commons address to the King, and five days later came the end of Fox's attempt to postpone supply – which Pitt had successfully managed to portray as an attempt to refuse it altogether. Fox's motion to postpone the Mutiny Bill until after the King had made a formal reply to the Commons address was carried by a single vote, 191 to 190.[70] The next day the Commons went into committee on the Mutiny Bill, which both sides recognized had to pass as a matter of patriotic duty. The same House of Commons that had been elected in 1780 had almost come around to supporting the Pitt ministry, in much the way that it had previously supported those of North, Rockingham, Shelburne and Portland – a total of five successive ministries in just four years, illustrating the fluidity of MPs' allegiance and the relatively small part ideology played in politics.

The Mutiny Bill passed, Parliament was dissolved on 25 March and electioneering began in earnest. Pitt stood on the defence of the King's rights to choose his own ministers and opposition to Fox's India Bill, while Fox highlighted the unconstitutionality of the royal 'coup' in dismissing the coalition. Speaking at an election meeting in York on 25 March, Lord Fauconberg – a King's Friend in both the political and personal sense – told the audience that the central issue facing voters was 'Is George III or Charles Fox to reign?'[71]

In the county seats, which were generally less open to government manipulation, Pitt won forty-eight seats to Fox's twenty-nine; in the open boroughs he won 125 to 96. Old enmities were forgiven (if not entirely forgotten), and astonishingly the government's electoral fund funnelled no less than £2,000 towards the electoral expenses of one John Wilkes. Against Robinson's election fund and organization, the Foxites had to depend on the combination of ancestral wealth and Georgiana, Duchess of Devonshire reputedly selling her kisses. Fox sought to call in debts of past gratitude, whereas Pitt could promise future favours, and in politics the former rarely outweigh the latter.

The 1784 general election is often described as the most dramatic of the eighteenth century.[72] More seats were contested than normal; in the spendthrift election of 1768 there had been seventy-eight unsuccessful candidates for the 558 seats, and ninety-two in 1780, but in 1784 there were 107.[73] Although there was a good deal of influence, vote-buying and so on, as there was in every general election of the period, public opinion is believed to have played a far larger role in 1784 than usual. It was completely different from the 1780 contest, when North had possessed both the resources of the government and the prestige of the sovereign.

Fox's vociferous criticism of the Crown, which verged on republicanism, his naked power-grab over India, the cynicism of his alliance with North and perhaps a vestigial resentment of his support for the Americans during the recent war all helped contribute to a landslide victory for Pitt. By 4 April, the King was already noting 'the list of members returned which seems on the whole more favourable than even the most zealous expected'.[74]

The next day, Pitt came top of the poll at Cambridge University. 'I cannot refrain from the pleasure of expressing to Mr Pitt how much his success at Cambridge has made me rejoice,' George told him. 'I shall only add that as yet the returns are more sanguine than the most sanguine could have expected.'[75] By 26 May the King was congratulating Pitt on his magnanimity in victory, for 'employing only a razor against his antagonists, and never condescending to run into that rudeness which, though common in the House, certainly never becomes a gentleman'.[76]

For all that he liked to speak of himself as the representative of 'the People', to many Fox looked like the spokesman of an out-of-touch, unpatriotic Whig elite, and his friends were badly punished at the polls. In all, the Whigs lost eighty-nine seats, their MPs were dubbed 'Fox's Martyrs' (a reference to the famous sixteenth-century *Foxe's Book of Martyrs*) and the Northites were similarly trounced. Fox himself only just scraped home at Westminster, then one of the most populous constituencies in the country, with 6,233 votes to Sir Cecil Wray's 5,998. That was nonetheless enough for the Prince of Wales to celebrate with a riotous party at Carlton House on 17 May – timed to coincide with the King going past in the Gold State Coach to open Parliament – where nine large marquees were erected in the garden. Guests were entertained with four bands and served by the Prince's household whom he had pointedly, and expensively, dressed in the Whig and the Continental Army's blue and buff livery. Thomas Orde-Powlett MP recorded the Prince of Wales vomiting in public later that evening, which was a not unusual sight. Three years later he witnessed the Prince of Wales at another ball:

> Lo! At twelve o'clock in reeled H.R.H. as pale as ashes, with glazed eyes set in his head, and in short almost stupefied. The Duchess of Cumberland made him sit down by her, and kept him tolerably peaceful till they went down for supper, when he was most gloriously drunk and riotous indeed. He posted himself in the doorway, flung his arm round the Duchess of Ancaster's neck and kissed her with a great smack, threatened to pull Lord Galloway's wig off and knock out his false teeth, till some of his companions called for his carriage.[77]

Stories of the Prince's behaviour had a habit of finding their way back to the King – indeed, the 7th Earl of Galloway was one of the King's lords of the bedchamber. George was naturally worried to hear about this kind of behaviour on the part of the son who was only a heartbeat away from the throne.

The election was a personal triumph for Pitt, but also for the King: Crown prerogatives had been at the centre of the campaign and his dismissal of the Whig ministry the previous December had now been vindicated. The sheer extent of the victory became apparent to all on 28 May when the Opposition attempted to amend the address of thanks for the King's Speech and lost by 282 votes to 114. Thomas Jefferson might have thought that George was 'unfit to be the ruler of a free people', but the British clearly disagreed.

So had it been, as the Whigs alleged, unconstitutional for the King to dismiss the Fox–North coalition despite its Commons majority?[78] William Grenville stated in his unpublished autobiography that his brother Lord Temple's 'indiscretion' had been in breach of 'strict constitutional principles'.[79] 'George III's actions were constitutionally dubious and certainly shabby,' writes one of Lord North's biographers, 'but neither consideration probably troubled him much.'[80] In fact, if the King had thought that he had acted unconstitutionally it would likely have troubled him a good deal, but he knew there was nothing dubious or shabby about exercising his right to dismiss one ministry and appoint another. He believed that the whole balance of politics and the constitution was being undermined by the East India Bill, which was an attempt to nationalize an extraordinarily rich corporation by the Whig oligarchy for its own ends, an unacceptable abuse of power.[81] If Fox wanted to change the constitution by weakening the Crown, as his own statements at the time indicate, then George had every right to dismiss him. 'At the time,' the constitutional expert Lord Lexden has recently pointed out, 'the monarch possessed an unfettered right to choose his first minister and to assist him in assembling a parliamentary majority out of the independents and self-styled King's Friends who then dominated the House of Commons.'[82] Another historian has argued that the coalition of Fox and North was so unnatural that it effectively deprived the King of a genuine choice of ministers, and 'was tantamount to a breach or breakdown of the constitution, and justified him in using the means to free himself'.[83] In the absence of a written constitution, the fact that the King succeeded in his risky enterprise, and was vindicated by the 1784 election result, was justification enough for his actions.

During the first twenty-three years of his reign to December 1783, George had appointed no fewer than nine premiers, one of whom – Lord North – had been in power for twelve years, over half the time. For the next twenty-nine years he was to have only five. When he had come to the throne at twenty-two, the King had taken a decade to learn how politics truly worked, as he fought a generally losing battle against the Whig oligarchy in the 1760s. The following decade and longer had been lost to the American crisis. By 1784, he was finally in a position where he could relax somewhat, with a masterful Prime Minister who was a genuine ally. Pitt had the old Whiggish suspicion of royal influence, and certainly did not wish to see it extended, but then crucially neither did George. There was little personal intimacy between the two men, as George had enjoyed for a time at least with Bute and North. What the King and Pitt had instead was a good deal of mutual respect, admiration and trust. They also shared the conviction that Fox had to be kept out of office at all costs. Pitt trod gently in areas where he knew that he and the King differed, and the King let Pitt have his way in areas such as financial, economic and administrative reform.

If George had died in 1783, history might perhaps have regarded him in the same vein as the other unloved Hanoverian monarchs. In retrospect we can see that it was the royal 'coup' of 1783 that put Britain in such a strong position when the Bastille fell six years later, installing the administration that was to fight the French Revolutionary and Napoleonic Wars – something that Charles Fox never wanted to do. As for 'the Mince-Pie Administration' that was supposed not to last much beyond Christmas, it was still in office seventeen Christmases later.

21

Alliance with Pitt

May 1784–October 1788

I never put pen to paper without wishing to convey in the most
explicit manner the sentiments of my heart.[1]

George to Lord Grenville, July 1800

A series of five concerts were held in Westminster Abbey between 26 May and 5 June 1784 to commemorate the centenary of the birth of George Frederick Handel, which due to their scale and grandeur have been described as 'the most important single event in the history of English music'.[2] (Handel was actually born in February 1685, which was not discovered until afterwards.) Organized by Lord Sandwich and the Concerts of Antient Music, with Joah Bates as musical director, it was an extraordinary occasion. Thomas Wyatt designed wooden galleries in the Abbey to accommodate an audience of 4,500, and there were no fewer than 525 performers. The first concert began with the piece written for the coronation of the King's grandfather, but which has since become synonymous with George III: *Zadok the Priest*. The King told the composer and musicologist Charles Burney that he had long been 'very fond of old music, particularly of [Arcangelo] Corelli. I don't like the present compositions. They are too quick and hurrying.'[3] He loved the music of Handel so much that he became the first monarch to attend a public concert since 1708.

At the end of the fifth concert in the Abbey, the King stood up to order that the Hallelujah Chorus from *Messiah* be played again, starting a tradition that continues to this day.* A spectator recorded the moment with pardonable euphoria as 'The triumph of Handel, the Commemoration, and of the musical art', and recounted how the musicians and singers 'seemed to ascend to the clouds, and unite with the saints and martyrs

---

* Some ascribe the tradition to George II supposedly standing during the first London performance in 1743.

represented on the painted glass in the west window, which had all the appearance of the continuation of the orchestra'.[4] Sandwich's biographer has described it as a moment of 'national reconciliation, a healing of wounds opened by war and politics'.[5] Before his death in 1759, Handel had told Charles Burney of George, 'While that boy lives my music will never want a protector.'[6] Certainly, when Burney produced a lukewarm report of the Abbey concert, the King wrote a paragraph-by-paragraph critique of Burney's text to Joah Bates, complaining that 'A real admirer of Handel cannot help finding it is only a mask and not the sentiments of the heart.'[7] Bates had the report altered before publication to reflect the King's enthusiasm for Handel's music, which a modern historian has described as 'a dynastic soundtrack, associated with the patronage of his grandfather George II, with state occasions and – through its public and charitable use – with British identity as Protestant, manly and civic minded'.[8]

On 16 June 1784, when Alderman John Sawbridge, a London MP and republican former Lord Mayor, proposed a committee to investigate parliamentary reform, he was supported by both Pitt and Fox. The King made the profoundly Tory observation to Pitt that 'without the greatest caution it may give birth to greater evils than those attempted to be cured'.[9] He did nothing to prevent Pitt from promoting his reform agenda, however, knowing that the Prime Minister did not have enough support for it in Parliament.

There has been a long historical debate over the true nature of the relations between the King and Pitt, with some arguing that the young premier 'held the whip hand over the King',[10] others that George 'yielded to [Pitt's] superior intellect',[11] or that 'with some inward groans, he resigned himself to an alliance on equal terms'.[12] Some argue that Pitt 'was never a royal puppet, but his chief value in royal eyes was that he was the only man who could stand against Fox'.[13] Conor Cruise O'Brien even believed that the events of 1783–4 had 'drained the King's authority and left Pitt the master'.[14] In fact, the relationship between King and premier was not the antagonistic one often portrayed, nor was it one by which royal powers and prerogatives declined.[15] On the two occasions when boundaries were crossed, it was Pitt not George who did so and on both it was the Prime Minister who had to retreat, exploding any theories that Pitt was George's master. It was not a relationship of equals, as the King had the right to dismiss Pitt at will, nor of personal friendship – that had not worked out well for George in the past – but instead the one for which the constitution was developed, of partners and allies. Although it is sometimes said by historians that the King and Pitt had little in common, in fact both their minds were attracted to logical, mathematical solutions to practical problems such as those of finance, and both were unwavering patriots. This allowed them to work together for nineteen years and to weather some of the greatest perils that Britain has ever faced, especially in the late 1790s.

George found it hard to like his cold and aloof premier, but more importantly he admired him, and Pitt always treated the King with deference, though never in the unctuous, saccharine terms that his father had employed. Although the King did not agree with Pitt over the Whiggish issues of Catholic emancipation and parliamentary reform, there was much they did agree upon, aside from keeping Fox out of office. They generally saw eye to eye on foreign policy, at a time when Britain was often at war and sometimes in existential peril. They also agreed on economic issues, and the King admired the way that by April 1785 Pitt was able to announce that the success of his Sinking Fund* meant that the government expected a £1 million surplus, which would be spent paying down the National Debt. This was exactly the kind of thing that George's father Prince Frederick had enjoined him to do in his political testament. In short, the King and Pitt respected each other, and moreover needed each other.

On 17 July 1784, the King expressed his hope that Pitt's new East India Act would be helpful in 'correcting those shocking enormities in India that disgrace human nature, and, if not put a stop to, threaten the expulsion of the Company out of that wealthy region'.[16] A month later the Act placed the Company under a small, government-appointed board of 'Commissioners for the Affairs of India', whose President essentially became the minister for superintending the Company's activities. This arrangement effectively remained in place until Company rule was abolished in 1858 after the Indian Mutiny. Whigs argued that it was almost indistinguishable from the Fox–Burke Bill of the previous year.

General Lord Cornwallis went out as Governor-General of India in February 1786 and fought the Third Anglo-Mysore War successfully between 1789 and 1792. George was little involved in Indian affairs, even though it was during his reign that large parts of the subcontinent came under British rule. He followed Cornwallis's military exploits with admiration, rejoiced in the defeat of the pro-French Tipu Sultan in 1799 and approved of Pitt's Act, but Indian affairs took up little of his time and remarkably little of his correspondence.

*

---

* Interest payments on the 3 per cent Consols (perpetual bonds) issued by the British government accounted for around one-half of its revenue. To reduce the National Debt, Pitt established a Sinking Fund into which monies were paid to repurchase government debt but could be used for no other purpose, and were thus outside the reach of a potentially spendthrift Cabinet.

By contrast, George was drawn deeply into the potentially disastrous situation that developed during the summer of 1784 over the Prince of Wales' debts and love life. On 6 July, the Prince wrote from Carlton House to his brother Frederick in Hanover, telling him that he was about to leave England and join him there, begging him not to tell anyone. At the time even ambassadors and ministers, to say nothing of the heir to the throne, had to obtain the monarch's permission before travelling abroad. Prince George told Frederick that he had four reasons for wanting to leave England: to escape his creditors because 'the enormous expense' of building and refurbishing Carlton House had left him heavily in debt; 'partly the wish of travelling for the sake of dissipation'; *the very very unpleasant situation I am in at home*'; and lastly the pleasure of seeing his brother. He added that he intended to inform their father in a couple of days, and wrote (quite untruthfully), 'Luckily he cannot prevent me.'[17] 'Though I respect him and use* him with all possible duty, deference, and respect,' Prince George told his brother, 'I think his behaviour is so excessively unkind that there are moments that I could hardly ever put up with it.' He claimed that the King ignored him at Court, or merely spoke about the weather.

The Prince of Wales was being characteristically dishonest: the main reason why he wanted to go to the Continent was that Maria Fitzherbert, a twice-widowed Roman Catholic six years his senior, and the love of his life – insofar as he was capable of loving someone besides himself – had gone there to escape him. He had earlier staged a mock suicide attempt in order to extract a promise of engagement from her, stabbing himself and inflicting the lightest of flesh wounds, but this had not been enough to keep her in the country. When the King heard about his son's intentions to leave England, he generously said that he would make a contribution towards paying off his son's debts, 'if he would give up the idea of a plan so highly improper'.[18]

Prince George ignored this olive branch, and continued his preparations for leaving on 3 September, but since he did not know how to travel light the news reached his father without difficulty. The day before the proposed journey, the King ordered his son 'as his father and sovereign . . . not to leave the realm without having obtained my particular leave', which both knew would not be forthcoming.[19] The King then asked Lord Southampton, who had been the Queen's Vice-Chamberlain for twelve years and his trusted emissary, to tell the Prince that he was not angry with him but merely wanted to be told the truth.†

---

* 'Treat' (*Johnson's Dictionary*).
† Southampton had troubles that year with his own son, who eloped to Gretna Green with the daughter of the Bishop of Exeter.

Father and son knew that under the Royal Marriages Act of 1772 it would be illegal for Prince George to marry Maria Fitzherbert. 'He cried by the hour,' Charles Fox's nephew Lord Holland wrote of the Prince's reception of the King's order not to leave England, 'rolling on the floor, striking his forehead, tearing his hair, falling into hysterics, and swearing that he would abandon the country, forgo the Crown, sell his jewels and plate, and scrape together a competence to fly with the object of his affections to America.'[20] As the mock suicide had shown, the Prince had even more of a taste for melodrama than his father.

On 31 August, the King wrote to Lord Thurlow about the constitutional position regarding the Prince's threat – which was now characteristically supported by Charles Fox. The Prince intended to live in Paris on the support of Louis XVI's cousin the Duc de Chartres (the future Philippe Duc d'Orléans),* despite Britain having been at war with France only two years previously. 'If there is no power of detaining him I have reason to know no arguments will avail and every mischief that can in future disturb the quiet of this kingdom as well as of my family may with reason be apprehended,' the King told the Lord Chancellor. 'If a young man sets out with a determination to hear no advice but the dictates of his unruly passions . . . every absurdity and impropriety may be expected, and the machinations of France know well how to take advantage of such a disposition.'[21] The King sent Colonel George Hotham, the Prince's Treasurer, to Brighton to forbid him to leave the country.

On 10 September, the King told Pitt that he had ascertained from Lord Southampton that the Prince's debts 'are supposed to amount to £100,000, which in one year and without gaming seems hardly credible'.[22] The following January he was told that in fact they had reached the staggering sum of £147,293, largely owing to the rebuilding and refurbishing of Carlton House: the Prince, he learned, had never deigned to ask what his builder, upholsterer, jeweller or tailor were proposing to charge him before he commissioned them. Extravagant spending of borrowed money had become an uncontrollable addiction for the Prince of Wales, and the King saw that because the Duc de Chartres was a major creditor there were serious national security implications in the future King of England being heavily in hock to the French. The Prince privately believed the situation was the King's fault, because he had not been given a sufficient income from the Civil List. To his father he claimed that most of the debt was the result of having to buy 'objects which, in general, have been deemed necessary'.[23]

When the King asked that the Prince give a fuller explanation of the

---

* The Prince and Duc had also shared a mistress, Grace Elliott.

debts, as well as 'a reasonable security against the continuation of his extravagance', the Prince realized that he would have to reveal just how much he was subsidizing Mrs Fitzherbert, and promptly refused. The King relayed all this to Pitt, who, as Chancellor of the Exchequer as well as Prime Minister, was intimately bound up in the crisis – indeed it was Pitt who helped draft many of the King's tough but fair letters to the Prince.

Nor was the Prince the sole source of George's money worries at that time. In September 1784, Lord North informed his banker that, as his annual income did not exceed £2,500, 'It is therefore absolutely out of his power to make an arrangement to discharge the [1780 election] debt owed to Mr Drummond.'[24] An incensed George told Robinson, 'This crowns the rest of that lord's ill behaviour to me and shows that in every line I have equal reason to complain of him.'[25] George nonetheless undertook to pay off the whole debt, and by October 1787 he had managed to remit the full £32,241 nineteen shillings and fourpence, but not before he had written to Henry Drummond to tell him that 'It was not owing to inaccuracy in me, but the most barefaced fraud on the part of Lord North.'[26] Both the King and North come out badly from the affair.

On 20 May 1785, James Boswell attended a Levee where the King talked to him about the hot-air balloon in which James Sadler had flown from West Molesey in Surrey over London to the Thames Estuary two weeks earlier, saying that 'he supposed experiments made in them could not be very exact, as the people must be so frightened that they could not give full attention.'[27] He told Boswell 'that there is a point of time when the balloon gets so high, so far above the earth, that no noise is heard; and being in a quiet atmosphere, all is silence. "This", he said, "frightens them much. A very natural sensation." '[28] The King went on to ask Boswell when his *Life of Johnson* would be published, and asked him how Johnson (who had died the previous December) 'was so much master of the literature of the age, and yet for the last thirty or five-and-thirty years of his life was never known to study', whereupon Boswell let the King in on Johnson's secret, that 'He read very few books all through.'[29]

John Adams was understandably not much looking forward to his audience with the King as the first American Minister (effectively ambassador) accredited to the Court of St James's. As a leading revolutionary and one of its foremost intellectuals, he had been one of those principally driving the move for independence in the First Continental Congress in 1774, had proposed George Washington as Commander-in-Chief the next year and had helped Thomas Jefferson draft the Declaration of Independence the year after that. 'It is not to be expected that I should be cherished and beloved,' Adams suspected of his coming embassy, especially as he would be arriving directly from Paris, where he was indeed cherished and beloved by a French nation delighted at Britain's humiliation.[30] There was a good deal for Adams and Lord Carmarthen, the Foreign Secretary, to negotiate when he arrived: there were still British troops on the United States' frontiers, and the Americans had not fulfilled their obligations under the Treaty of Paris to stop persecuting Loyalists, or to allow British merchants to recover American pre-war debts in pounds sterling.

At 1 p.m. on 1 June 1785, Adams went first to Carmarthen's office in Cleveland Row, and then together with him across the road to St James's Palace.[31] He was naturally a great object of attention at the Levee, surrounded by government ministers, Anglican prelates and European ambassadors. 'I went with his Lordship through the Levee-room into the King's Closet,' Adams wrote the next day to John Jay, the American Secretary of State.[32] 'The door was shut and I was left with His Majesty and the Secretary of State alone. I made the three reverences, one at the door, another about half way and a third before the presence, according to the usage established at this and all the northern courts of Europe.' The three small bows were indeed customary, but it was still a decent mark of respect for the King from the envoy of an independent republic which had just wrested itself so dramatically away from his dominions.

Adams handed the King his credentials and then made a formal 245-word statement that he had memorized, about Congress's 'unanimous disposition and desire to cultivate the most friendly and liberal intercourse between Your Majesty's subjects and their citizens, and of their best wishes for Your Majesty's health and happiness'. He ended by saying:

> I shall esteem myself the happiest of men if I can be instrumental in recommending my country more and more to Your Majesty's royal benevolence and of restoring an entire esteem, confidence and affection, or in better words, the old good nature and old good humour between people who, though separated by an ocean and under separate governments, have the same language, a similar religion and kindred blood.[33]

It was a noble sentiment – and no small achievement to recall it word-perfectly.

George responded in kind. Adams reported to Jay that George had 'listened to every word I said with dignity but with an apparent emotion', and 'was much affected and answered with more tremor than I had spoken with'. Although Adams told Jay he could not vouch for every word of the King's response, he remembered him replying in a clear voice:

Sir, the circumstances of thy audience are so extraordinary, the language you have now held is so proper and the feelings you have discovered so justly adapted to the occasion, that I must say that I not only receive with pleasure the assurance of the friendly dispositions of the United States, but that I am very glad that the choice has fallen on you to be their minister. I wish you, Sir, to believe, and that it may be understood in America, that I have done nothing in the late contest but what I thought myself indispensably bound to do by the duty which I owed to my people. I will be very frank with you. I was the last to consent to the separation; but the separation having been made, and having become inevitable, I have always said, and I say now, that I would be the first to meet the friendship of the United States as an independent power. The moment I see such sentiments and language as yours prevail, and a disposition to give to this country the preference, that moment I shall say, let the circumstances of language, religion and blood have their natural and full effect.[34]

This was gracious and evidently heartfelt, but there was also some diplomatic pleasantry to it. The King had not in truth been by any means 'the first to meet the friendship of the United States', and indeed the exact opposite was closer to it. But all that was now in the past.

The historic part of the meeting over, the King moved on to some teasing badinage with Adams, asking with 'an air of familiarity, and smiling, or rather laughing', whether the rumours were true that Adams had not been 'the most attached of all your countrymen to the manners of France'.[35] They were indeed true, but Adams was too professional to imply any Anglophilia or Francophobia. 'I threw off as much gravity as I could,' he reported to Jay, 'and assumed an air of gaiety and a tone of decision as far as was decent, and said, "That opinion, Sir, is not mistaken. I must avow to Your Majesty I have no attachment but to my own country."' The King replied 'as quick as lightning', saying, 'An honest [man] will never have any other.'[36] On that note of mutual respect and approbation, the audience concluded, and Adams later referred to the King as 'the most accomplished courtier in his dominions'.[37]

On taking his leave as Ambassador three years later, in February 1788, Adams wrote to John Jay again about his final audience with the King. Of the 3,225 claims made by Loyalists for compensation for the expropriation of their property, 2,291 awards had been granted, so the King began by asking for the remaining ones to be expedited, saying, 'Mr Adams, you may with great truth assure the United States that whenever they shall fulfil the Treaty on their part, I, on my part, will fulfil it in all its particulars. As to yourself, I am sure I wish you a safe and pleasant voyage, and much comfort with your family and friends.'[38] After the formal part was over, 'His Majesty was then pleased to ask me many questions about myself and my family, how long I had been absent from them, etc., which were intended I suppose to be very gracious and flattering.' It was not easy for the King to receive the successful revolutionary, but he did what was required of him, and more.

One of Britain's most pressing tasks after the end of the American war was to repair her relations with various European countries, which had left her so dangerously isolated. When Lord Carmarthen became Foreign Secretary in December 1783, he hoped for 'dissolving that unnatural and, for us, fatal alliance which has so long subsisted between Austria and France'.[39] It was anything but unnatural, in fact, since Louis XVI's wife Queen Marie Antoinette was Austrian. Carmarthen wanted to divert France away from challenging Britain again by having Austria threaten France's northern and eastern borders, yet any pro-Austrian policy of the Pitt government would run directly counter to George's (as Elector of Hanover) of befriending Prussia and opposing Austria. When Lord Carmarthen proposed a more aggressive policy against the League of Armed Neutrality in the Baltic in July 1784, the King told him, 'Till I see this country in a situation more respectable as to army, navy and finance, I cannot think anything that may draw us into troubled waters either safe or rational.'[40] It was sound advice, and Carmarthen acted upon it.

Carmarthen worked hard for an Austrian alliance in the summer of 1784, with Pitt's support, believing it to be Britain's best chance of recovering what he called the nation's 'weight and influence on the Continent' in the aftermath of the American debacle.[41] Yet the King undermined the Anglo-Austrian entente, because of what he viewed as the Holy Roman Emperor Joseph II's expansionism at a potential cost to Hanover. It was a classic constitutional conundrum, and if a general European war had broken out before the French Revolution it might potentially have led to a difficult clash between the King and the Pitt ministry.

On 23 July 1785, the League of Princes (Fürstenbund) was founded whereby the rulers of Prussia, Hanover and Saxony signed a public treaty regarding the Holy Roman Empire which contained several anti-Austrian secret articles. Over the next few months, a large number of other princes also joined, including the rulers of Mainz, Hesse-Cassel, Baden, Brunswick, Saxony-Gotha and Saxony-Weimar.[42] The League was intended to defend the status quo against Joseph II's perceived desire to discard the Imperial Constitution. The League also wanted to prevent Duke Charles IV Theodore of Zweibrücken, the Elector Palatine, exchanging Bavaria, where he could not pass on the title to lands to his seven illegitimate children, for the Austrian Netherlands (modern-day Belgium), where he could, an exchange Emperor Joseph also wanted as it would make Austrian borders more rational, contiguous and defensible. The League of Princes recognized that possession of the recalcitrant Netherlands only weakened Austria, whereas holding Bavaria would strengthen her.

As well as being an early signatory as Elector of Hanover, George was an enthusiastic supporter of the League. He no longer believed, as he had in 1759, that Hanover was 'that horrid Electorate, which has always lived upon the very vitals of this poor country'.[43] Since then, he had warmed to the place – though not so much that he ever visited it, as his grandfather had done biannually throughout his reign. Nevertheless, in the 1780s George talked about 'mein deutschen Vaterland' and 'ma patrie germanique', educated three of his sons at the Georg-August University Göttingen (named for George II) and, when he toyed with the idea of abdication, it was to Hanover that he imagined retiring.[44]

Keen to remain on good terms with Austria, however, Carmarthen and the British Foreign Office were constantly forced to explain to Vienna that the Elector of Hanover and King of England were two separate entities. Despite their best efforts to demonstrate a distinction, everyone recognized that Britain would be profoundly affected by Hanover joining an anti-Austrian bloc in northern Germany, which the historian Tim Blanning describes as an 'indirect alliance between Great Britain and Prussia'.[45] This was all the more remarkable as Frederick the Great was still alive, having never truly forgiven either George or Bute for leaving him stranded at the end of the Seven Years War.

The Hanoverian dynasty, Protestant since Martin Luther, had long been opponents of the Catholic Habsburgs and were politically wedded to the fragmented status quo of the Holy Roman Empire which kept them from being subsumed by the Austrian Empire to their south. George was no different in this from his forefathers, and although he and his Hanoverian Privy Council were suspicious of Prussian motives – Hanover had Prussian lands to both her east and west – by 1785 he saw the advantage of a princes' league spearheaded by Hanover and Prussia that would oppose Austrian hegemony in Germany, in part by preventing the Bavarian Exchange.

Carmarthen complained to Thurlow and Sydney on 7 August that he had been kept 'totally in the dark' by the King over the negotiations regarding the League, adding that he had found it almost impossible to persuade the Austrians 'that Hanover and England are not entirely synonymous'.[46] Pitt admitted to Carmarthen that he had no knowledge of the Hanoverian government's activities. The effect of all this was to convince the Austrians that British ministers were either lying about the separation between London and Hanover, in which case they were too untrustworthy to negotiate with, or they were telling the truth, in which case they were too impotent for the negotiations to be worthwhile.[47]

Pitt nonetheless did protest at the way in which the King had joined the League without the Cabinet's permission, writing on 6 August in his usual respectful terms:

> The influence which Your Majesty's engagement respecting your Electoral dominions may have on the general state of the Continent and of Your Majesty's relative situation with foreign powers must also eventually affect the interests of this country. In this point of view Your Majesty will pardon me the presumption of adding that if you should think proper to direct any more particular information to be given in respect to the Treaty in question, it would be of essential advantage in enabling your confidential servants to submit to Your Majesty's wisdom any opinion, either as the line to be pursued or the language to be held on the part of Great Britain with the different powers of Europe at this important crisis.[48]

A good deal of understatement can be detected, but the thrust of Pitt's remarks was clear.

George replied to Pitt uncompromisingly, saying that if Austria did not have designs 'contrary to the Germanic constitution', the League 'cannot give umbrage; but the times certainly require this precaution'.[49] This was the high-water mark of the King's involvement in foreign policy, though of course Pitt was not to know that at the time. With several other important issues to concentrate upon – Ireland, parliamentary reform, the Sinking Fund and a comprehensive Anglo-French commercial treaty – Pitt did not want to fall out with the monarch who had so recently put him into office; and especially not over Hanover, when there was little prospect of an Austrian alliance anyway. George was after all merely attempting to defend the status quo within the Holy Roman Empire. He was acting as a German prince, which he had always been, but which he had made little or no effort to be during the 1760s and 1770s.

It might seem strange that, only four years before the outbreak of the French Revolution, Austria should have been deemed to be the principal threat to European peace. Even after the creation of the League of Princes, the balance of power was to be further affected in 1787 when Austria tried to divide up the European provinces of the Ottoman Empire, and then by the formation of a Triple Alliance by Britain, Prussia and Holland in 1788 in opposition to the Franco-Austrian bloc. When it came a year later, the

French Revolution did not break upon a placid Europe, but rather upon one full of roiling jealousies and mutual suspicions.

On 15 December 1785, George, Prince of Wales, married Mrs Fitzherbert in the drawing room of her house in Park Street, Mayfair. He had told her that the King had promised him he could marry her if he gave up his future Electorate of Hanover to the Duke of York. Mrs Fitzherbert's political senses could not have been particularly strong for her to accept this very obvious lie at face value. Her uncle and brother witnessed the Anglican 'ceremony', conducted by the Rev. Robert Burt, who was promised £500 and a future bishopric when the Prince acceded to the throne. (In the end he received the cash, but not the bishopric.)

That same night at Windsor, the King and Queen met the author Frances 'Fanny' Burney, the daughter of Charles Burney. She was the author of the successful satirical social novels *Evelina* and *Cecilia*, which the royal couple had enjoyed. When Queen Charlotte asked her to become Second Keeper of the Queen's Robes, at £200 per annum and a £100 per annum pension for life, she unknowingly did historians a huge service. Although her acceptance blighted Burney's subsequent professional writing career, her diaries and correspondence from June 1786 when she took up the post until her retirement five years later provide an invaluable insight into the royal family's domestic life and the King's conversational style. She combined a novelist's eye for anecdote and telling detail with an historian's respect for accuracy, and since her diaries were published posthumously, there could be no element of self-interest in her admiration for the King and Queen. Her diaries include scores of pages of dialogue with the King, in which he emerges as a sympathetic, emotionally intelligent and likeable person. She gave everyone nicknames: the King was 'The Oak', the Queen 'Magnolia', and so on, and her sister Susan's codename for the Prince of Wales was 'Gonerillo', possibly a combination of Goneril and gonorrhoea.

Although she was stultifyingly bored with the robing side of her duties, Burney made herself useful in other ways too, such as mixing the Queen's snuff and reading to her. She responded well to the kindness shown by the Queen, who in the words of one of Burney's many biographers 'pays impromptu visits to Fanny's sickbed, gives her gifts of a writing box, inkstand, china and books, discourses at length with her on many subjects, and allows her unexpected treats, usually visits to her friends or family'.[50]

At their first meeting, Burney recorded that the royal couple were distraught over the illness of their fifteen-year-old daughter Princess Elizabeth. The King said she had been blooded twelve times in the past fortnight, had lost 75 ounces of blood and had undergone blistering. 'He spoke of her illness with the strongest emotion,' wrote Burney, 'and seemed quite filled with concern for her danger and sufferings.'[51] (Having been blooded himself at least four times, and possibly more during his first bipolar episode twenty years earlier, George knew what it was like; and having lost Alfred and Octavius in the previous three years, he and Charlotte fully understood the dangers of childhood illnesses. Elizabeth survived, and lived to the age of sixty-nine.) As for his own health, the King told Burney that 'The fault of his constitution was a tendency to excessive fat, which he kept, however, in order by the most vigorous exercise and the strictest attention to a simple diet.' When complimented on his self-denial, he said, 'No, no. 'Tis no virtue. I only prefer eating plain and little, to growing diseased and infirm.'[52] When they discussed *Evelina*, which had initially been published anonymously, the King asked, 'What entertainment you must have had from hearing people's conjectures before you were known! Do you remember any of them?' When she told him that Giuseppe Baretti, the literary critic, had laid a wager that it had been written by a man, as no woman 'could have kept her own counsel', she recorded of the King that 'This diverted him extremely.'[53] There was a good deal of laughter during this first encounter, and when she admitted she had not written much recently, he said, 'I believe there is no constraint to be put upon real genius; nothing but inclination can set it to work. Miss Burney, however, knows best. What? What?'[54] This verbal tic would often be used at the end of a joke, as would the words, 'Hey? Hey?' Burney herself explained that 'What? What?' was intended to signify 'What say you?' even if little time was given to answer.

On another occasion, the royal couple met Burney at the home of a mutual friend, the artist Mary Delany, whose pictures adorned every wall, so the King talked about art, and then about the encyclopaedic four-volume *General History of Music* written by Fanny's father, some possible connections between the tone-deafness of Princess Amelia's Lady of the Bedchamber Lady Isabella Finch and the Duke of Marlborough's colour-blindness, the drawings of Lady Diana Beauclerk and the King's preference for sermons that were 'plain and unadorned'. His tone in Burney's diaries was inquisitive, gently teasing and immensely good-natured, preferring to let others speak rather than himself.

'She speaks English almost perfectly well,' Burney wrote of the Queen,

> with great choice and copiousness of language, though now and then with foreign idiom, and frequently with a foreign accent. Her manners have an easy dignity, with a most engaging simplicity, and she has all that fine high breeding which the mind, not the station, gives, of carefully avoiding to

distress those who converse with her, or studiously removing the embarrassment she cannot prevent.[55]

The Queen occasionally came out with charming epigrams, as in that same
conversation when she offered, 'I am always quarrelling with time! It is so
short to do something, and so long to do nothing.'[56] The King then added,
'Time always seems long when we are young, and short when we begin to
grow old,' which, sadly, is equally true.

'The King', Burney concluded in a letter to her father the next day,

> has, in private, the appearance of a character the most open and sincere. He
> speaks his opinions without reserve, and seems to trust them intuitively to
> his hearers, from a belief they will make no ill-use of them. His countenance
> is full of inquiry, to gain information without asking it, probably from believ-
> ing that to be the nearest road to truth. All I saw of both was the most perfect
> good humour, good spirits, ease, and pleasantness.[57]

Fanny Burney was no lickspittle monarchist; she hailed from the intellectual world of literary London where freethinking and neo-republicanism
thrived, and was close to radical Whigs such as Burke and Sheridan. She
had nothing to gain by praising the royal couple in a private letter. These
were her true feelings. 'Their behaviour to each other speaks the most
cordial confidence and happiness,' she continued. 'The King seems to
admire as much as he enjoys her conversation, and to covet her participation in everything he either sees or hears. The Queen appears to feel the
most grateful regard for him, and to make it her chief study to raise his
consequence with others, by always marking that she considers herself . . .
the first and most obedient of subjects.'[58] In her first encounter with them,
Burney was left 'equally charmed both with their behaviour to each other
and to myself'.[59]

In another conversation at Mary Delany's house in Windsor on 19
December, the King said of the atheist Voltaire, 'I think him a monster, I
own it fairly.'[60] He referred to the equally freethinking Jean-Jacques Rousseau, who had died in July 1778, 'with more favour, though by no means
with approbation'. Although he had once given Rousseau a pension,
George had by now recognized the danger that the *encyclopédistes* posed
to religion and perhaps also to monarchy, but it seems that his antipathy
was based as much on Rousseau's character, as he told anecdotes 'all charg-
ing him with savage pride and insolent ingratitude'.[61] Burney summoned
up the courage to tell the King that she had heard from her father that
Rousseau had been grateful for his pension and had placed the King's
portrait over the chimney of his Paris garret.

George's love for the theatre was a natural topic of conversation. 'I am an enthusiast for her,' he said of the actress Sarah Siddons. 'I think there was never any player in my time so excellent – not Garrick himself, I own it!' Inevitably they soon got around to Shakespeare, when the King said something that has led to his being denounced as a philistine. 'Was there ever such stuff* as [the] great part of Shakespeare?' he asked Burney. 'Only one must not say so! But what think you? What? Is there not sad stuff? What? What?'[62] Burney agreed, but added that the sad stuff – by which they probably meant bad acting parts, rather than unhappy moments – was 'mixed with such excellences that . . .' 'Oh,' the King interrupted, laughing good-humouredly, 'I know it is not to be said! But it's true. Only it's Shakespeare, and nobody dare abuse him.' He then 'enumerated many of the characters and parts of plays that he objected to' – sadly Burney did not record which these were – before finishing with 'But one should be stoned for saying so!'†

Thomas Jefferson spent six weeks in England in 1786, including a week in April touring a succession of English gardens. At the King's garden at Kew he admired and made two diagrams of the Archimedes screw for raising water, designed by the engineer John Smeaton, which he thought might prove useful at his house Monticello in Virginia. 'The mechanical arts in London are carried to a wonderful perfection,' he noted.[63] As well as machinery, the King and Jefferson shared interests in architecture, gardening, music, science and country life, and were family men who disliked ostentation. Yet the twenty-eight accusations of tyranny in the Declaration of Independence would have been too personal to permit the two men to get on when they finally met.

Thirty-five years later Jefferson claimed to have attended a Levee some time in the summer of 1786, at which he alleged that George had treated him badly. He gave no date for this meeting in his autobiography, claiming that 'On my presentation as usual to the King and Queen at their Levees [sic], it was impossible for anything to be more ungracious than their notice of Mr Adams and myself. I saw, at once, that the ulcerations in the narrow mind of that mulish being left nothing to be expected on the subject of my attendance.'[64] Adams' grandson further claimed that the royal couple turned their backs on the two Americans, and this public insult 'was not lost upon the circle of his subjects in attendance'.[65]

---

* 'That which fills anything' (Johnson's Dictionary).

† In this at least Horace Walpole would have agreed with the King, as he thought the Bard, though a genius, 'undoubtedly wanted taste'.

Although Jefferson probably did meet the King, since he recorded the tips he paid the 'porters at St James's Palace on my being presented' at the Levee, and newspapers of the day record him going there, nothing else rings true about his account.[66] He claims that Queen Charlotte was at the Levee, which no women attended, nor does his very full contemporaneous list of ceremonial visits – thirty-five in all – refer to the Queen. Adams made no mention of the incident in his voluminous reports to John Jay, even though such rudeness would have had profound diplomatic and even commercial implications. As we have seen, the King had greeted Adams cordially before, and would do so again afterwards. The two countries were at the time negotiating a trade treaty that the King wanted as much as the Americans.

If 'the circle of his subjects' witnessed this public rebuff, why is there no mention of it in any other contemporary diary, newspaper or piece of correspondence, including Jefferson's own? Moreover, if the King had not wanted to meet Jefferson, he would not have permitted him to be introduced at Court, and it appears extremely unlikely that he did so merely to turn his back on him.

A far more likely explanation is that this part of the Francophile and Anglophobic Jefferson's autobiography ought to be treated with the same reserve and scepticism as his claims about George's tyranny in the Declaration of Independence. 'The *Autobiography* of Thomas Jefferson cannot stand as a statement of historical truth,' states one historian of the Levee, which he dates to 17 March 1786, so even the season was recorded wrongly in Jefferson's autobiography.[67] Quite why Jefferson might have expected courtesy from the man he had famously libelled as a tyrant is in any case uncertain. When the British diplomat George Hammond was appointed Britain's first Ambassador to America in September 1791, Hammond's secretary wrote to him of Jefferson's 'decided and rancorous malevolence to the British name'.[68] This probably explains Jefferson's account of the incident better than anything George III said or did at the Levee. The following year, George bought Thomas Jefferson's new book, *Notes on the State of Virginia*.

At least Jefferson was only interested in character assassination: on Wednesday 2 August 1786, Margaret Nicholson, a former domestic servant who had been jilted by her lover and then fallen on hard times, approached the King with a petition as he alighted from his carriage for a Levee at the garden door of St James's Palace. She presented it with her right hand and, as George took it, with her left hand she drew a knife which she thrust straight towards his heart, but hardly penetrated his clothing.

The King started back in surprise as she made a second stab, which brushed against his waistcoat before she was overpowered by an attendant. 'The fortunate awkwardness of taking the instrument with the left hand made her design perceived before it could be executed,' the King reported a few hours later.[69] It turned out that the weapon was only an old, thin, ivory-handled dessert knife. If it had been long and sharp, the King recounted, 'Nothing could have been sooner done, for there was nothing for her to go through but a thin linen, and fat.'[70]

Fanny Burney, who was not present, recounted that, as soldiers and courtiers surrounded George protectively, Nicholson was:

> seized by the populace, who were tearing her away ... when the King, the only calm and moderate person then present, called aloud to the mob, 'The poor creature is mad! Do not hurt her! She has not hurt me!' He then came forward and showed himself to all the people, declaring that he was perfectly safe and unhurt; and then gave positive orders that the woman should be taken care of, and went into the palace and had his Levee.[71]

In fact, the King did not know if she was deranged, but had said that in order to prevent her being lynched.* 'There is something in the whole of his behaviour on this occasion that strikes me as proof indisputable of a true and noble courage,' Burney concluded, 'to feel no apprehension of private plot or latent conspiracy – to stay out, fearlessly, among his people, and so benevolently to see himself to the safety of one who had raised her arm against his life – these little traits, all impulsive, and therefore to be trusted, have given me an impression of respect and reverence that I can never forget.'[72]

After the Levee, the King rode to Windsor to tell the Queen what had happened. 'Here I am safe and well as you see!' he told her. 'But I have very narrowly escaped being stabbed!'[73] When the eldest two princesses burst into tears, 'The King, with the gayest good humour, did his utmost to comfort them, and then gave a relation of the affair with a calmness and unconcern that, had anyone but himself been his hero, would have been regarded as totally unfeeling.'[74] Burney made the sage political point that 'If that love of prerogative, so falsely assigned, were true, what an

---

* Nicholson was not the first lunatic to approach the King; in 1778 Rebecca O'Hara broke the window of his sedan chair at St James's as he climbed out. He asked her what she wanted but she gave an 'impudent answer' and told him her name was 'Queen Beck', after which she was arrested and taken to an asylum (Poole, *Politics of Regicide in England* pp. 58–9). After papers had been found in Nicholson's dwelling in which she claimed to be the rightful heir to the throne, and Pitt had personally witnessed her claiming to be both a virgin and the mother of Lords Loughborough and Mansfield – who were both older than her – she was sent to Bethlem Royal Hospital, where she died in 1828.

opportunity was here offered to exert it!'[75] If the King had really, as Burke and Fox alleged, been a secret absolutist, he would have taken the opportunity to strengthen himself politically, as Napoleon did after the assassination attempt on himself in December 1800. Yet that evening all George did was walk on the north terrace of Windsor Castle with his wife and children before the crowds, and no other attendant but a single equerry. At the concert that evening, the princesses kept bursting into tears, and the Queen held out her hand, saying to her husband, 'I have you yet!'[76] The outburst of relief and affection on the part of the populace led George to tell Richard Grenville that he 'had every reason to be satisfied with the impression it has awakened in this country'.[77]

Six days afterwards, virtually the entire population of Kew turned out on the Green to cheer the King and Queen. 'I shall always love little Kew for this!' the Queen told Burney.[78] The shock had been widespread, but it was not, as Burney had thought, 'an attack, in this country, unheard of before'.[79] In fact William III, George I and George II had all been the subject of Jacobite assassination plots, although there had been no actual attempts since the Gunpowder Plot of 1605, whereas on the Continent Henry IV of France and William the Silent of Holland had been assassinated. Marie Antoinette told William Eden, who was in Paris negotiating the free-trade deal with France, how shocked Louis XVI had been by the news.[80] In France they dealt with deranged assassins differently: when the madman Robert Damiens had tried to stab Louis XV in 1757 with a knife as ineffectual as the one Margaret Nicholson had used, he was tortured, drawn and finally quartered by horses in the Place de Grève in Paris.

The celebrations for the King's survival continued for several days, with official addresses read and large crowds cheering him wherever he went. The Queen cried during the address of Dr Joseph Chapman, the Vice-Chancellor of Oxford University, in the Sheldonian Theatre, using her fan to dry her tears as they rolled down her cheeks. Fanny Burney had a somewhat wryer response to the 'very ridiculous' sight of the dons coming up to kiss the King's hand:

> Some of the worthy collegiates, unused to such ceremonies, and unaccustomed to such a presence, the moment they had kissed the King's hand, turned their backs to him and walked away as in any common room; others, attempting to do better, did still worse by tottering and stumbling, and falling foul of those behind them; some, ashamed to kneel, took the King's hand straight up to their mouths; others, equally on their guard, plumped down on both knees and could hardly get up again; and many, in their confusion, fairly arose by pulling His Majesty's hand to raise them.[81]

The King and Queen kept rigidly straight faces when protocol was broken or when amusing incidents took place during public events, although Burney's diary makes it clear that they often had a good laugh in private afterwards.

Pitt reshuffled his government in late August 1786, promoting personal supporters such as George Canning and William Huskisson. Henry Dundas already had control of Indian and Scottish affairs, and the Duke of Rutland ran Ireland. A key position, the presidency of the Board of Trade, was assumed by Charles Jenkinson, who also became Chancellor of the Duchy of Lancaster and was elevated to the peerage as Lord Hawkesbury.* Pitt had originally kept him at arm's length because Jenkinson had been leader of the King's Friends in the Commons since the fall of Bute, and he did not want to seem beholden; but with the ministry stable he needed to keep it balanced too, and he had fallen out comprehensively with Thurlow, who now opposed all change and reform on principle.

The Anglo-French commercial treaty negotiated by William Eden (later Lord Auckland)† was signed on 26 September 1786, reducing many duties. Although the commercial treaty was good for British trade, it became unpopular in France and encouraged the discontent that was bubbling under the surface of the Ancien Régime. In the course of the negotiations, the French had asked George III, not unreasonably, to surrender the title of King of France, but the British delegation insisted on retaining it, and instead referred to Louis XVI as 'Le Roi Très Chrétien'.[82] There seems to have been no reason for George to lay claim to a country more than three centuries after the end of the Hundred Years War, except perhaps that it irritated the French, but in fact it was later to prove a useful bargaining chip.

The British monarchy was very unlike the French in many aspects, but a particular one was the way that George identified with farmers and the agricultural sector of the British economy. Even if in origin the King's nickname of 'Farmer George' was meant pejoratively, it served only to increase his popularity in a country that, though on the cusp of the Industrial Revolution, was still overwhelmingly rural.

At the end of a letter to Lord Sydney in June 1785, the King wrote that during the summer months, 'I certainly see as little of London as I possibly can, and am never a volunteer there.'[83] As a progressive farmer of his own

---

* George was good at rewarding loyalty: in 1796 Hawkesbury became the 1st Earl of Liverpool, and his son would be the third-longest-serving Prime Minister in British history.
† In whose honour the city in New Zealand was named.

land, George recognized the vital importance to social and political calm of increasing agricultural production faster than the growth in population, and he took great personal interest in the new innovations, modern agricultural techniques and scientific farming methods that were being followed. His reign coincided with what has been described as a period of 'agricultural enlightenment', in which increased knowledge led to an unprecedented increase in production, in a country that was quickly industrializing by 1780.[84]

In 1787 George contributed a long article on crop rotation – under the pseudonym Ralph Robinson, the name of one of his shepherds at Windsor – to the leading agricultural journal of the day, Arthur Young's *Annals of Agriculture and Other Useful Arts*. Entitled 'On Mr Ducket's Mode of Cultivation', the article recommended:

> a medium between the old and the drill husbandry ... an employment of clover, turnips, and rye, as fallow-crops, and as intermediate ones between wheat, barley, oats and rye, changing these occasionally according to the nature and state of the land. Of these intermediate crops, those which serve only to fill up the winter-interval are of the greatest use for winter and spring food, and what these take from the ground is amply resupplied by the dung and treading of the cattle that feed on them; thus his ground, although never dormant, is continually replenished by a variety of manure, and thus unites the system of continued pasture with cultivation.[85]

It is unlikely that George II (let alone Louis XVI) would have written about manure in a published article, even under a nom de plume.

When Young, whom the King ensured was appointed the first Secretary of the Board of Agriculture, was invited to Windsor, George met him on the terrace with the words 'I consider myself as more obliged to you than to any other man in my dominions.'[86] Unsurprisingly after this, Young recalled the King as 'the politest of men'. On another occasion, George took him on a two-and-a-half-hour tour of the three farms he had 'disimparked' of 1,222 acres at Windsor, discussing grass, sheep, crop systems, the Board of Agriculture, hogs, cattle and of course manure. 'I found fault with his hogs,' Young recalled. 'He said I must not find fault with a present to him.'[87] They were German and the Queen had given him them. 'The value of the intention, Mr Young,' said the King, somewhat romantically despite the subject at hand, 'is better than a better breed.'[88] He even gave Young advice on magazine editing, telling him to shorten his paragraphs 'as there are many, Mr Young, who catch the sense of a short paragraph, that lose the meaning of a long one'.

Wise words indeed.

One area in which George led innovation was by introducing merino sheep into Britain from Spain, a breed prized for their finer wool while still producing good mutton. Sir Joseph Banks, the naturalist and polymath who was President of the Royal Society from 1778 to the end of the King's reign, became George's unpaid chief scientific shepherd.[89] A small flock of merino was delivered as a present from the Spanish Prime Minister to Kew and Richmond Gardens in 1788, along with several Spanish shepherds and a letter asking for a set of horses in return.[90] The flock flourished, and were soon fetching high prices at sales, especially the young rams. A Society for the Improvement and Extension of the Merino Breed of Sheep throughout the Kingdom was established in 1810, chaired by Banks. Banks also superintended the King's gardens at Kew, where exotic plants were sent from around the world.

George has been belittled as a 'hobby farmer', but in fact he ran his farms as serious commercial enterprises, and at a respectable profit.[91] He took hundreds of pages of handwritten notes on every conceivable subject regarding agriculture, and with a particular interest in varieties of cabbage, then a staple crop.[92] While Marie Antoinette and her friends were dressing up as shepherdesses on her pretend farm in the Trianon gardens at Versailles, therefore, 'Farmer George' was writing about cabbages, crop rotation and manure, introducing new strains of sheep into England and pioneering modern practices that might increase the supplies of food that were all that stood between the peasantry and penury. In a still largely rural country, his keen interest in the way that the majority of people made their living was another reason for his widespread popularity.

In a statement to the House of Commons on 30 April 1787, Charles Fox officially denied the rumour that had been swirling about London that the Prince of Wales had secretly married Maria Fitzherbert. He told MPs that it 'proved at once the uncommon pains taken by the enemies of his Royal Highness to propagate the grossest and most malignant falsehoods with a view to depreciate his character and injure him in the opinion of his country'.[93] He went on to characterize it as 'a tale in every particular so unfounded, and for which there was not the shadow of anything like reality'. After Mrs Fitzherbert read the speech in her newspaper over breakfast the next morning, she never forgave Fox. The following day, Fox was privately informed that the Prince had indeed lied to him, and realized that the heir to the throne was just as prepared to deceive his friends as he was his family.

In mid-January, the Prince had not attended Queen Charlotte's birthday celebrations at Windsor because, as Fanny Burney noted in her diary, of 'the coldness then subsisting between him and His Majesty' on account of his refusal to tell George the truth about the full extent of his debts.[94] By the summer of 1786, those debts stood at £269,878,* having almost doubled in eighteen months – and were now equivalent to more than one-quarter of the United Kingdom's annual non-military expenditure.[95] The Prince asked the King and Pitt for an increase of £40,000 a year to his income, but they understandably feared this would simply allow him to borrow more. After much correspondence, characterized by mistrust and resentment on both sides, a deal was done whereby the Prince received an extra £10,000 per annum from the Civil List (that is, the King) to take him up to £73,000 per annum while Parliament assumed £161,000 of his debts and donated another £60,000 so that Carlton House could be completed (which it never was). The rest would be paid off by instalments from his income, theoretically at least. The King added the private rider that 'His Majesty thinks proper to add that while the Prince of Wales remained unmarried,† he does not conceive any increase of income can be necessary to enable him to support an establishment suitable to his rank and station.'[96] The pressure to provide an heir for the Hanoverian dynasty was clear.

The Prince's profligacy reflected painfully, and unfairly, upon his parents. A cartoon captioned 'A New Way to Pay the National Debt' published by James Gillray, one of several caricaturists of genius of the day, showed the King and Queen leaving the Treasury with gold coins pouring out of their pockets and being offered bags more by a sycophantic Pitt near a blind and limbless veteran.[97] It also depicted a ragged and poverty-stricken Prince of Wales being bailed out by the Duc d'Orléans (the former Duc de Chartres). The satire was made the crueller by the news bills affixed to the Treasury wall, one reporting, 'Fifty-four malefactors executed for robbing a hen-roost'. In fact, however, the Treasury had done very well out of the thrifty George and Charlotte, rather than the other way around. The problem was not a greedy King and Queen but a profoundly profligate Prince of Wales, who had finally realized that the only way out of his money troubles was to marry legally.

The Prince visited his parents at Buckingham House on 21 May 1787 and promised not to incur any more debts, at least 'as far as is in human power to foresee events'.[98] The King told his son 'that he had lost his character [that is, reputation] but might retrieve it if he would not live with such scoundrels'.[99] He was thinking of the Prince's Clerk of the Dishclouts (chief cook), who had somehow become an influential figure at Carlton

---

*   Nearly £34 million in today's money.
†   The Fitzherbert marriage was not legal under the Royal Marriages Act. If it had been, George IV could not have acceded under the Act of Succession because Mrs Fitzherbert was Roman Catholic.

House. Three days later it was announced in the House of Lords that an 'additional allowance' would be allotted to the Prince 'out of His Majesty's Civil List, in order to remove every possible doubt of the sufficiency of his Royal Highness's income to support amply the dignity of his situation, without occasioning any increase to the annual expense of the public'.[100]

The public reconciliation between the Prince and his parents was satirized in another Gillray print entitled 'Monstrous Craws at a New Coalition Feast' that was published in the window of Samuel Fores' Piccadilly print shop later that week. It depicted the King as a greedy peasant woman feasting on gold guineas alongside the Queen and a now well-dressed Prince of Wales, seated outside the Treasury. The labels on the Prince's ladles are marked '£60,000' and '£10,000'. Although prints such as these seemed to threaten the dignity of the Crown, in fact the ability to satirize and ridicule the royal family – in a way that was prosecuted in contemporary France – actually strengthened the British monarchy by 'helping to give visual articulation and practical example to the notion of the British nation as a formidable fortress of freedom'.[101]

Foreign visitors often expressed astonishment at the way that, as one French-born American put it, 'The English do not spare themselves, their princes, their statesmen, and their churchmen, thus exhibited and hung up to ridicule, often with cleverness and humour, and of course a sort of wit.'[102] It was true, and among the writers, satirists and poets who attacked George III in one way or another were numbered John Wilkes, Horace Walpole, 'Junius', Benjamin Franklin, Richard Brinsley Sheridan, Paul Revere, George Cruikshank, James Gillray, Thomas Paine, William Blake, Thomas Rowlandson, Charles Churchill, Tobias Smollett, Edmund Burke, Peter Pindar and Lord Byron. Censorship of prints had ended in Britain in 1695 and no prosecutions were brought against engravers during George's reign, though he undoubtedly understood their political influence, and when outside London he would have the latest prints by such giants of the genre as Gillray, Rowlandson and Isaac Cruikshank (father of George Cruikshank) bought surreptitiously and delivered to him.[103]

What the satirists seemed to hate the most was hypocrisy. On 1 June the King issued a royal proclamation, 'For the Encouragement of Piety and Virtue, and for the Preventing and Punishing of Vice, Profaneness and Immorality', which exhorted the public to abjure 'loose and licentious' publications – essentially pornography – although it did not have the force of law. William Wilberforce MP and Bishop Beilby Porteus of London supported the movement, but the problem, as caricaturists and others did not fail to point out to devastating effect, was that while the King and Queen did indeed personify domestic piety and virtue, virtually the entirety of their male relations emphatically did not. When a similar proclamation was made five years later, Gillray produced a print entitled 'Vices Overlook'd in the New Proclamation' which depicted Avarice represented by the King and Queen, drunkenness by the Prince of Wales, gambling by the Duke of York and debauchery by Prince William and his mistress Dora Jordan.[104] Although the King and Queen were careful rather than avaricious, the point Gillray was making about double standards was a fair one.

The King was pious and hoped such proclamations might do some good. He profoundly believed in the active involvement of the Almighty in daily life and thanked Divine Providence for, among many other things, Lord North's survival from a fever in 1777, the escape from French invasion in 1779, victory over the coalition in the constitutional crisis of 1783–4, his survival of the Nicholson and other assassination attempts, the peaceful conclusion of the Nootka Sound crisis of 1790, Princess Charlotte's survival of a miscarriage in 1798 and Thomas Grenville's survival of shipwreck in the Elbe estuary in 1799.[105] Comforting as his Christianity was for him on those occasions, it of course made American independence and his own bouts of lunacy all the harder to explain to himself. Had the Almighty turned against him in allowing these things to happen? If so, what had he done to deserve them? But if they were the result of God's displeasure at British society's licentiousness, these proclamations against vice seemed to be a sensible response, however much satirists might carp.

On 10 May 1787, Edmund Burke brought forward articles of impeachment against Warren Hastings, the former Governor-General of Bengal. There were twenty-two in all, supplied by Hastings' arch-nemesis Sir Philip Francis, who had sat on his council and against whom he had fought a duel seven years earlier.* The trial began in February 1788 and lasted more than seven years, featuring no fewer than 148 court sittings, many of them held in the enormous medieval Westminster Hall. Fashionable London fought for tickets and 300 Guardsmen had to be deployed to ensure order. Pitt supported the impeachment, even though Fox hoped that it would result in his ministry looking corrupt by association. The King and Thurlow were opposed to it privately, but could not afford to be seen supporting the defendant.

A problem for the royal family was that Warren Hastings' wife had given some diamonds to the Queen, prompting the accusation that the King had been bribed.[106] Hastings had also presented an ivory bed to

---

* It was fought over sex rather than money or politics. Hastings shot Francis, who survived because the gunpowder was old and damp and the bullet of small calibre.

Charlotte, and two Arab horses to the King himself. After a Covent Garden performer had gained widespread publicity by swallowing large stones on stage, caricatures were drawn of the King and Queen swallowing diamonds.* Some detractors, including Burke, alleged that the King was personally associated with the more corrupt aspects of British (and Company) rule in India: in fact his sympathy for Hastings and his disapproval of Burke's and Dundas' attacks on him stemmed from his views about what was possible in administering Bengal. As he put it, 'I do not think it is possible to carry on business in that country with the same moderation that is suitable to a modern European nation.'[107] He also understood the importance of keeping the French, Spanish, Portuguese and Dutch out of the subcontinent as much as was practicable. The impeachment bedevilled British politics until April 1795, when Hastings was acquitted and the East India Company gave him a £4,000 per annum pension and a £50,000 loan to help pay off his £70,000 legal fees.

One of the reasons the King privately bemoaned the trial was the opportunity it gave for loquacity on the part of orators such as Burke, Sheridan, William Windham MP and Fox, all of whom opposed Hastings. He abhorred politicians who spoke for too long, and told Pitt after a Commons debate in March had gone on until 6 a.m., with discourses on the technical issue of whether the Speaker should leave the Speaker's chair during debates on an India Bill:

> It is amazing how, on a subject that could be reduced into so small a compass, the House would hear such long speaking. The object of the Opposition was evidently to oblige the old and infirm members to give up the attendance, which is reason sufficient for the friends of government to speak merely to the point in future, and try to shorten debates, and bring, if possible, the present bad mode of mechanical oratory into discredit.[108]

Pitt's own clipped, factual, even terse style of oratory appealed to him far more.

In April 1788, to pursue his other career of ironbridge-building, Thomas Paine returned to live in England. There, instead of being arrested for libel and treason, he was feted by Whig grandees such as Charles Fox, Lord Lansdowne and the Duke of Portland, who had presumably missed his pun on 'nobility' as 'no-ability' in *Common Sense*. Paine was at that time

---

* The Queen's actual attitude to jewels can be seen in an exchange when Fanny Burney asked her 'how well she had liked' her crown jewels when she first saw them in 1760. 'But how soon was that over,' the Queen replied. 'Believe me, Miss Burney, it is the pleasure of a week – a fortnight at most – and to return no more!' (eds. Barrett and Dobson, *Diary and Letters of Madame d'Arblay* III p. 88).

being paid $800 per annum by the United States government for 'secret services' (largely propagandizing) and was also given a 300-acre farm at New Rochelle, New York, which had been expropriated from a Loyalist, Frederick Devoe. 'So war-profiteering was a consummation of Paine's vaunted pursuit of liberty,' concludes one historian.[109]

On 30 July 1768, Lieutenant James Cook had received his orders for a journey to Australia, then called New Holland, where he landed at Possession Island on 22 August 1770 and promptly claimed the entire eastern coast in the name of George III. Cook had been instructed by the King:

> to observe the genius, temper, disposition and number of the natives, if there be any, and endeavour by all proper means to cultivate a friendship and alliance with them, making them presents of such trifles as they may value, inviting them to traffic, and showing them every kind of civility and regard; taking care however not to suffer yourself to be surprised by them, but to be always upon your guard against any accidents.[110]

The King was extremely interested in Cook's expedition, and personally contributed £4,000 to the Royal Society to help fund the scientific side of the voyage, overseen by Sir Joseph Banks. The celebrated scientist later commended the King's 'paternal eye' in the establishment of a botanical garden in Calcutta in 1786, and wrote that George was 'accustomed to appreciate the benefits applicable to the different parts of his extensive empire'.[111] George particularly appreciated the possibilities of cross-pollination, sending Pacific plants to the botanical garden he set up in St Vincent in the West Indies in the mid-1780s, and a flock of his merino sheep to New South Wales in 1804, among other examples.

Nearly two decades later, on 17 April 1787, as Captain Arthur Phillip was about to set off with his First Fleet to establish the colony of New South Wales in Australia, he was given similar instructions by the King to establish relations with the local Eora indigenous tribe, and to 'endeavour by every means possible to open an intercourse with the natives, and to conciliate their affects'.[112]* Phillip was moreover directed to punish anyone who sought to 'wantonly destroy them'. These were not unique orders, but a template of those adopted for other expeditions, which, however they may have turned out – Phillip began kidnapping Eora tribesmen for information in 1789 – had at least begun with an intention in London of opening a dialogue with the local inhabitants of Australasia and the South Seas, and learning about their terrain, inhabitants, flora and fauna. The establishment of Botany Bay, meant

---

* 'Passions': 'circumstances' (*Johnson's Dictionary*).

as a destination for the transportation of British convicts after 1788, was not helped the following year when three convicts chose to be hanged rather than to be transported there. The King found it 'shocking that men can be so lost to every feeling of gratitude not to feel the mercy being shown them in sparing their lives'.[113] They were prevailed upon to change their minds, and in public at the Old Bailey, so as not to derail the entire transportation scheme.

In late May 1788, Sir William Dolben, an independent MP, moved a Bill to improve conditions for slaves on the Atlantic middle passage between Africa and the Americas. He was not proposing to abolish the slave trade, only to limit the numbers of slaves allowed in a vessel relative to its tonnage. It was passed by 56 votes to 5 in a thin House of Commons, but when it went up to the Lords in early June, Lords Thurlow and Hawkesbury (the former Charles Jenkinson) spoke against it. The opponents of the Bill challenged the evidence that Dolben had presented, and even at one point attempted to argue that soldiers in tents were sometimes worse off than the slaves crossing the Atlantic.[114] After two days' debate in the Lords, when it looked like the Bill might fall, Pitt told the Cabinet that he would resign unless it passed. Thurlow and his supporters amended it, and it eventually became law only hours before the session closed on 11 July.

As we saw in Chapter 1, George believed that slavery was morally wrong, yet he did nothing to hasten its abolition. When in the 1750s Montesquieu had summarized the reasons for the Spanish instigation of slavery in the Americas, he included the argument that 'Sugar would be too dear if the plants which produce it were cultivated by other than slaves.'[115] In his précis of *The Spirit of the Laws*, George had referred to 'The impossibility of cultivating the American colonies without them [slaves], or if that is not quite the case, the produce of these colonies as sugar, indigo, tobacco, etc., would be too dear.'[116] George placed great emphasis on the West Indian colonies during the Seven Years War and the American War of Independence; it is likely that he thought the commercial ramifications of the abolition of slavery there would lead to the collapse of the Caribbean economies and therefore of the revenues from them, and that he placed what he saw as British national interest above the moral imperative of ending the heinous institution of slavery, and thus also the transatlantic slave trade. His innate conservatism and hostility to radical change of any kind might also have played a role. By not directly involving himself in the debate on either side, however, he was essentially supporting the status quo, and must be judged by history accordingly.

The King's only comment on the Dolben Bill concerned the inaccuracies in its drafting that had also delayed its passing, using the racing analogy to Lord Sydney, 'It is not the courser* that sets out most violent,† but he that can support his speed and with most certainty at the goal.'[117] The statutes that ended the British slave trade, the Foreign Slave Trade Act and the Abolition Act, were given royal assent by George in 1806 and 1807 respectively. His acquiescence in the existence of the trade before then, however, and his own lack of campaigning for its abolition, has been held against him. Equally, he said and did nothing in its favour, and it was ultimately his signature that ended the trade. The institution of slavery itself was not abolished in the British Empire until thirteen years after his death.

When in April 1792 William Wilberforce put forward his motion for the gradual abolition of slavery he was strongly supported by both Pitt and Fox, and it passed in the Commons by 238 votes to 85. The opposition came in the House of Lords, and because three of the principal anti-abolitionists were Thurlow, Hawkesbury and Sydney, and Prince William also spoke against the measure (delivering what the Prince of Wales considered 'a most incomparable speech'), it has long been assumed that the King was opposed as well. In fact, he stayed entirely neutral on the issue, while another of his sons, Prince Augustus, was a committed abolitionist.[118] Wilberforce's son Samuel, later Bishop of Oxford, recalled three-quarters of a century later, 'There had been a time when George III had whispered at the Levee, "How go on your black clients, Mr Wilberforce?" but henceforth he was a determined opposer of the cause.'[119]

Samuel Wilberforce claimed that the King's stance was predicated upon the belief that it would 'encourage Paine's disciples' if slavery were abolished, and although he produced no evidence to substantiate it, that is not implausible.[120] The French Revolution had broken out, and the fear that allowing some worthy reforms might open the floodgates for more dangerous ones was probably the reason why the King did not embrace the greatest moral crusade of the age.[121] Although it is fourth hand, there is also some evidence that the King disliked the methods used by the abolitionists to promote their cause, such as sugar boycotts and public petitions. Lord Malmesbury noted that Lord Loughborough had been told by Pitt that privately 'The King did not like the measure, and . . . still less the manner in which it was supported by addresses and petitions, a method he (Pitt) also disliked, as it was a bad precedent to establish.'[122]

Remarkably, the King's devout Christian faith did not force him to put into practice his 1750s views on slavery's monstrous evil, any more than it did many other churchgoers of the day. He expressed no misgivings, for

* Swiftest racehorse.
† Fastest.

example, about the Society for the Propagation of the Gospel's practice of branding the letters SPG on to West Indian slaves.[123] 'Part of the opposition to abolitionism derived from the continued conviction that slavery was compatible with Christianity,' explains the historian Jeremy Black, 'and also that it was sanctioned by its existence in the Bible, notably the Old Testament, an argument that indicates the range of views that could be squeezed from Christian teaching and the Christian heritage.'[124] Although George passionately opposed slavery in private in the 1750s, he did nothing to help abolish it when it became a practical political possibility forty years later, and that is a moral blot on his reign.

As he approached his fiftieth birthday, George became even more reflective than usual, and in the spring went so far as to contact the seventy-five-year-old Lord Bute for the first time since their friendship broke down in the summer of 1766. 'Every day makes me more a philosopher,' he wrote, explaining that now he made the 'attempt to keep my desires within a narrow compass, that my disappointments may be fewer'.[125] He told his former mentor that he was now 'full of diffidence in one's attempts and therefore not surprised when they prove abortive'. He did not make it clear whether he was referring to America, his family or something else, but it might well have been the abortive efforts that he and Bute had made back in the early 1760s to end corruption in politics, dish the Whigs and lead a moral regeneration of Britain.*

On 11 June 1788, a week after his fiftieth-birthday celebrations, the King reviewed the Duke of York's Regiment on Wimbledon Common. He returned to Kew with agonizing stomach cramps, which people put down to the heat and which he himself initially dismissed as 'a pretty smart bilious attack'.[126] He was compelled to go to bed as his stomach pains were so great. 'I am what one calls one cup too low,' he told Pitt, 'but when thoroughly cleared I hope to feel equal to any business that may occur.'[127] Sir George Baker, President of the Royal College of Physicians and for years his senior physician, diagnosed his colicky abdominal pain and obstructive jaundice as 'Concretions of the gall duct' (cholelithiasis) and advised him to rest at Kew.[128] Baker had made his name by accurately diagnosing 'the Devonshire Colic' arising from the use of lead in cider-making. Then, early in July, Fanny Burney recorded, 'the King's indisposition occasioned the

---

* In 1789 he invited the Bute family to a ball at Windsor, which they attended despite the Earl's failing health. When Bute died in 1792, the King told his son the 4th Earl that his father's 'attachment to my person was most sincere and immovable', and he approved the Dowager Countess of Bute's request that two other sons continue to live in his grace-and-favour house in Richmond Park (RA GEO/MAIN/6932).

plan of his going to Cheltenham, to try the effect of the waters drunk on the spot'.[129] Between 12 July and 16 August he stayed near Cheltenham at Lord Fauconberg's house. The King and Queen took the smallest possible entourage, and appreciated the rest. 'Never did schoolboys enjoy their holidays equal to what we have done our little excursion,' the Queen wrote to Prince Augustus.[130] They attended the Three Choirs Festival at Worcester, visited Richard Hurd at his bishop's palace there and toured local country seats such as Croome Court, Matson House and Woodchester Park where the King's father had once stayed. When they passed through Cotswolds towns, vast crowds came out to welcome them, reportedly over 50,000 people on one occasion.

The King drank the waters at the Spa in the mornings (Burney thought the taste 'very unpleasant'), walking with his family through Cheltenham unaccompanied by any bodyguards, despite only two years earlier having been the target of an assassination attempt.[131] He chatted happily with other people taking the waters, although when he asked Lady Cecilia Leeson when she had last heard from her Irish fiancé, David La Touche, she gave the 'natural and simple', but hardly courtly, answer, 'Well, what's that to you?'[132] On his return to Windsor, he thanked Fauconberg and said that the waters had done him good, but a month later he felt pain in his face and was stricken with insomnia.

Lieutenant-Colonel Robert Fulke Greville, the King's equerry from 1781 until 1797 and a Northite MP for New Windsor, began keeping a journal in October 1788 which is the principal source, along with Fanny Burney's diary, for the darkness that was about to descend over the King and the Court. He was the third son of the 1st Earl of Warwick* and soon became the King's favourite equerry, but by 1788 he was thoroughly bored by the tedium of much of Court ritual.[133] (Greville's brother Charles was one of the early lovers of Emma Hamilton, before she married their uncle and later had her notorious affair with Lord Nelson.) It was Greville who was on duty on the night of 16 October when the King suffered what was thought to be a spasmodic bilious attack ascribed to not changing out of wet stockings. Baker was summoned to Kew, and recorded finding the King 'sitting up in his bed, his body being bent forward. He complained of a very acute pain in the pit of the stomach, shooting to the back and sides and making respiration difficult and uneasy'.[134] Baker gave the King a purgative to relieve the bowels, and laudanum† for the pain.

---

* Burney's nickname for him in her diaries was 'Colonel Wellbred'.
† A solution of opium dissolved in alcohol for ingestion by the droplet. It was not as potent as synthetic opioids like heroin, though nonetheless dangerous and highly addictive in large doses.

'Those around him perceived a change in his manner and in his temper,' noted Greville, 'and thought His Majesty had become more peevish than he used to be. He now talked much more than usual, and spoke to everybody on a strange variety of subjects. His incessant talking became at last so remarkable that it was thought necessary to recommend His Majesty to be a little more silent.'[135] When Baker suggested this, the King thanked him for his advice but then promptly ignored it. Increasing evidence of acute manic depression – which at the time was called 'mania', 'frenzy' and 'hysteria' – led Baker to consult his fellow surgeon William Heberden, but crucially no doctors with any experience of mental illness. In the coming weeks they embarked on an excruciatingly painful series of standard treatments of analgesics, sedatives, scarification (scratching and cutting the skin), emetic tartar (antimony potassium tartrate, a powerful emetic which causes vomiting) for mania, blistering (forming pustules on the skin by deliberately raising the cuticle) and purgatives for depression, as well as venesection (recurrent bloodletting).

Unsurprisingly, these made the situation worse and indeed some had life-threatening side effects.[136] It is not known whether arrogance or ignorance explains the refusal of Baker and Heberden to seek specialist advice from any physicians of mental illness (then known as mad-doctors). Snobbery might have been the explanation; at that time doctors were not countenanced unless they had a medical qualification from Oxford or Cambridge, however expert their training might have been elsewhere in Britain or overseas.[137] As the two doctors persevered with traditional treatments for fevers, however, the King slipped further and further into outright manic psychosis.

22

The King's Malady

October 1788–February 1789

The dear and excellent King had been praying for his own restor-ation![1]

Fanny Burney's diary, New Year's Day, 1789

'The look of his eyes, the tone of his voice, every gesture and his whole deportment represented a person in a most furious passion of anger,' Sir George Baker noted on 22 October 1788, and he informed William Pitt of the King's 'agitation of spirits nearly bordering on delirium'.[2] One of the extraordinary features of the bipolar attacks from which the King suffered was that they occasionally disappeared as suddenly as they had arrived, and – against Baker's advice – on 24 October he held a Levee at St James's Palace, as he put it to Pitt, 'to stop further lies and any fall of the stocks' (the rumours about his health having weakened the financial markets).

The next day the royal family decamped to Windsor, even though the Queen had wanted to stay in London closer to the doctors. They moved into the Queen's Lodge, as the state apartments in the castle were consid-ered too draughty. When the King spoke to Fanny Burney that day, it was 'with a manner so uncommon that a high fever alone could account for it: a rapidity, a hoarseness of voice, a volubility, an earnestness – a vehemence, rather – it startled me inexpressibly; yet with a graciousness exceeding even all I ever met with before – it was almost kindness!'[3]

'The King was prevailed upon not to go to chapel this morning,' Burney noted on 26 October.

I met him in the passage from the Queen's room: he stopped me, and conversed upon his health near half an hour, still with that extreme quickness of speech and manner that belongs to fever; and he hardly sleeps, he tells me, one minute all night; indeed, if he recovers not his rest, a most delirious fever seems to threaten him. He is all agitation, all emotion, yet all benevolence and goodness, even to a degree that makes it touching to hear him speak. He assures everybody of his health; he seems only fearful to give uneasiness to others, yet certainly he is better than last night. Nobody speaks of his illness, nor what they think of it.[4]

Baker called again during a concert on the 27th. 'During the whole music he talked continually,' he recorded, 'making frequent and sudden transitions from one subject to another; but I observed no incoherence in what he said, nor any mark of false perception ... He was lame; complained of rheumatic pain, and weakness in the knees, and was continually sitting and rising.'[5]

Part of the horror of the situation was that the King knew that he was not behaving normally, and yet could not prevent it; from the very outset he was a confused and helpless spectator at his own catastrophic degeneration. 'The King is very sensible of the great change there is in himself,' noted Burney, 'and of [the Queen's] disturbance at it. It seems, but Heaven avert it! a threat of a total breaking up of the constitution.' Lord Ailesbury was present when the Queen declared in her post-chaise carriage that she was confident that God would not inflict more suffering on the family than they were able to bear, and the King put his arm around her waist and said, 'Then you are prepared for the worst.'[6] Burney also recorded that the King told his friend Lady Effingham in a hoarse voice, 'My dear Effy, you see me, all at once, an old man.'[7] The pathos of the situation was somewhat relieved in the early period of the illness by his love for his wife, for as he told Burney, 'The *Queen* is my physician, and no man can have a better; she is my *friend*, and no man *can* have a better.'[8] She saw 'there was a hurry in his manner and voice that indicated sleep to be indeed wanted.'[9]

Blistering was painful, but not as bad as the practice of 'cupping', which the doctors began at the end of October. A barbaric practice akin to torture, it involved the application of heated glass vessels to the skin which stuck and drew blood to the surface, after which incisions were cut to drain away the supposedly infected blood, which, as we now know, was in fact perfectly healthy. The notes in the memorandum book of the King's apothecary Robert Battiscombe show how often this measure was adopted: on 30 October: 'Cupped His Majesty.' 1 November: 'Cupped His Majesty again.' 4 November: 'Cupped His Majesty again.' 5 November: 'Applied blister to the head. Sat up in the night with the King.'[10] The blistering of the King's feet left them sore and suppurating, and made the prescribed hot baths much more painful. He had leeches applied to his temples, to take off the 'evil humour', while all the time his real – psychotic – illness remained entirely undiagnosed.[11]

'Our King does not advance in amendment,' wrote a worried Burney on 1 November; 'he grows so weak that he walks like a gouty man, yet has such spirits that he has talked away his voice, and is so hoarse it is painful to hear him. The Queen is evidently in great uneasiness.'[12] She was bursting into tears a good deal. '"How nervous I am!" she cried,' as Burney recorded on one occasion. '"I am quite a fool! Don't you think so?" "No, ma'am!" was all I dared answer.'[13] At one point the King was walking with a stick, yet later on that same day he went out hunting. The next day, despite being 'so far from well' in Burney's estimation, he discussed matters with the Adjutant-General 'with great acuteness and precision'.[14]

'We are all here in a most uneasy state,' noted Burney on 3 November. 'The King is better and worse so frequently, and changes so, daily, back-wards and forwards, that everything is to be apprehended, if his nerves are not some way quieted. I dreadfully fear he is on the eve of some severe fever. The Queen is almost overpowered with some secret terror. I am affected beyond all expression in her presence, to see what struggles she makes to support serenity.'[15] Charlotte's 'secret terror' was possibly her knowledge that 'the King's Malady' that she had successfully covered up in 1765 had now reappeared, twenty-three years later, in a far worse way. Although Dr William Heberden found him 'greatly disturbed' that day, the King was able to write a perfectly normal letter to Pitt to say he could sign warrants, but not read dispatches. It turned out to be the last letter he wrote for four months. 'The Queen in deep distress,' Burney noted on 4 November, 'the King in a state almost incomprehensible, and all the house uneasy and alarmed.'[16]

'Oh, dreadful day,' wrote Burney on 5 November. It had started out reasonably well when the King went out in his post-chaise with the Princess Royal, but then he gave so many orders to the postilions and got into and out of the carriage twice 'with such agitation' that Burney felt 'fear of a great fever hanging over him'.[17] When Baker arrived he found 'an entire alienation of mind'.[18] Of course all this had a profound effect upon the Court. 'A stillness the most uncommon reigned over the whole house,' wrote Burney. 'Nobody stirred; not a voice was heard; not a step, not a motion.'[19] She could see from his attendants that the King was 'in some strange way worse', and now the Queen had been taken ill too, probably from worry and nervous exhaustion.[20] She decided that for the first time in their marriage she could no longer share a bed with him, and would not do again for several months.

On 3 November the Prince of Wales temporarily moved to Windsor Castle from the Brighton Pavilion, the brand-new palace he was building at vast expense on the south coast. He was privately very excited by the hope that he would soon become king, and if not then certainly Prince Regent, whereupon he could install Charles Fox as premier. Fox would clear his huge backlog of debt and he could then marry whomsoever he liked, rather than a German princess. Acting on his own authority, he began to interfere in the running of the household, leading to a *sotto voce* power struggle with the Queen, the outlines of which can be glimpsed in the pages of Fanny Burney's diary.

At dinner on 5 November – as Burney heard from the flirtatious Colonel Stephen Digby, the Queen's Vice-Chamberlain – the King 'had broken forth into positive delirium, which long had been menacing all those who saw him most closely, and the Queen was so overpowered as to fall into violent hysterics. All the princesses were in misery, and the Prince of Wales had burst into tears.'[21] The Prince's sisters rubbed his temples with Hungary water to prevent him from fainting. 'I thank Heaven there is but one of my children who wants courage,' the King ranted, speaking of his eldest son, who later had to be blooded so alarmed was he by his father's attack.[22]

The Queen told Lady Harcourt that at dinner that night the King's eyes were like 'nothing but blackcurrant jelly, the veins in his face were swelled, the sound in his voice was dreadful; he often spoke until he was exhausted, and the moment he could recover his breath began again, while the foam ran out of his mouth'.[23] The Prince of Wales would years later regale his mistress Lady Jersey's dinner guests with the scene, especially the moment when the King had seized him by the collar and thrust him violently against a wall.

The King slept in the Queen's dressing room next to her bedroom that night, but at one o'clock in the morning 'His Majesty found an opportunity of getting out of his bed, and taking a candle he opened the Queen's apartment, and coming gently to the bedside, he opened the curtains and looked in.' The Queen and her lady-in-waiting, Miss Goldsworthy,* 'were much surprised' at this. 'The King looking earnestly at the Queen, said "I will confess the truth, I thought you had deceived me, and was not here." He then expressed satisfaction at not being deceived, and with little persuasion he returned to his own room.'[24] 'My poor royal mistress!' Burney wrote after rushing to the Queen's bedroom because of the disturbance. 'Never can I forget her countenance – pale, ghastly pale she looked . . . her whole frame was disordered.'[25] Battiscombe agreed, noting that 'Miss Goldsworthy sat up with the Queen – who was in the utmost consternation all night.'[26]

From then on, the Queen kept her bedroom door locked, and the King was moved to a lady-in-waiting's apartment on the ground floor, from which there was only one (guarded) exit. The next morning the Queen was

---

* Daughter of the King's senior equerry, Colonel Philip Goldsworthy.

in 'a perfect agony of grief and affliction', worried that it might all happen again.[27] As Burney noted, 'The fear of such another entrance was now so strongly upon the nerves of the poor Queen that she could hardly support herself.'[28]

The Queen hated the way that her husband's descent was presented in the newspapers, which were full of all manner of lurid and baseless inventions. She wanted the editor of the *Morning Herald* in particular 'called to account' and asked Fanny Burney to burn the paper in the grate. One of the most common stories – that the King shook hands with an oak tree in Windsor Great Park 'with the most cordiality and regard' in the belief that it was the King of Prussia – seems to have been entirely invented for a book entitled *A History of the Royal Malady with Variety of Entertaining Anecdotes*, supposedly written by 'A Page of the Presence' but in fact by the hack writer Philip Withers. (If it had been the late Frederick the Great he had thought he had met, of course, it is doubtful he would have greeted him with such cordiality.)

In furtherance of his plans for a regency, on 6 November the Prince of Wales sent for one of his own doctors, the society physician Richard Warren, to come to Windsor immediately. When the King refused to see him, Warren stood outside with the door ajar and listened to his conversation with Baker. Warren refused to report his diagnosis to the Queen, but only to the Prince. He concluded that the King would never recover, and encouraged further blistering of the King's scalp and legs, intended to drive the 'evil humours' in his brain down to his legs, where they would apparently leave his body.[29]

On 7 November the King became so ill that it was feared he would die.[30] On the 8th, Fanny Burney noted, 'From this time, as the poor King grew worse, general hope seemed universally to abate, and the Prince of Wales now took the government of the house into his own hands ... From this time commenced a total banishment from all intercourse out of the house, and an unremitting confinement within its walls.'[31] The Prince expelled from Windsor Jean André de Luc, the Queen's Swiss-born reader, without explanation and in the most humiliating way possible, by getting Mr Humphreys the doorkeeper to hand him his overcoat and refuse him readmittance. The Prince quickly turned the Queen's Lodge into a secure compound, with almost all of the people closest to the King and Queen, such as the Duchess of Ancaster and Lady Effingham, denied access.[32] Fortunately for historians, Burney and Greville were interned inside; while communication with the outside world was limited, they continued to keep their diaries.

This restriction of access only meant that false news stories abounded, even though the truth was shocking enough. On 9 November there was a widespread rumour in London that the King had died, whereas in fact that day there had been, in Greville's words, 'Great agitation and much incoherence in thought and expressions', including rambling statements about religion and repeated requests to see the Queen.[33] As was common for him at this time, George slept for only two hours that night. On 18 November, the government started to issue daily bulletins about the King's health, signed by his doctors, who now included Sir Lucas Pepys, who tended to side with Baker and Heberden in being optimistic about the eventual outcome, against the Prince's Whig doctor Dr Warren, who displayed unrelenting pessimism almost throughout. (One thing they all agreed upon, however, was to charge extortionate per diem fees.)

William Pitt visited Windsor on 10 November, determined that the crisis should not result in his replacement as Prime Minister by Fox. He was told by the Prince of Wales that there was 'more reason to apprehend durable insanity than death', although the latter was a real possibility.[34] If the King was incapable of governing there would obviously have to be a regency, but Pitt wanted Parliament to control its nature, and was particularly intent on restricting the Prince Regent's prerogatives – that he should make no royal household appointments, grants of Crown property nor any other appointments that would be 'for the Crown's pleasure', and above all that he should not have the power to create peerages. By contrast, Fox thought the Prince Regent ought to be given all of the King's constitutional powers immediately.

A full-scale political crisis thus developed in which historical precedents were mined, and both parties' newspapers and pamphleteers traded blows. Constitutional arguments were bandied backwards and forwards; addresses were sent to Parliament – which was itself in uproar – and a dissolution was expected daily. From having argued eloquently in favour of the sovereignty of Parliament over the Crown during the crisis arising from the dismissal of the coalition in 1783 and in the general election of 1784, Charles Fox now suddenly completed a total volte-face on the issue. The Commons, where he was now in the minority, should not, he said, decide on what type of regency Britain should have. This allowed Pitt to pose as the defender of both the King and the rights of Parliament.

One problem for Pitt was that if he wanted to pass a Bill limiting the powers of the regency during the King's lifetime, how could it be made into an Act of Parliament without George being able to give it his royal assent? An arrangement was suggested by which the Great Seal would be placed 'in commission', whereby Acts would not need the royal assent and thus the Great Seal would not have to be affixed to them, but the legality of this seemed vague for lack of precedents.[35] A closely related problem for Pitt was that Lord Thurlow subtly changed sides as the King's illness progressed, going over to the Opposition in the hope of keeping his post in a Fox ministry. This created a dangerous moment for Pitt since the Lord Chancellor played the key role in adjudicating on constitutional issues, especially where there was little historical precedent to use as a guide. No king of England had gone mad before, at least clinically.* Thurlow only returned to the Cabinet fold when the King's health started to improve.

On 12 November, Greville noted that the King's 'constant rambling of thought continued, yet still at times recollecting persons around him by name . . . He now talked about Eton College, of the boys rowing, etc. . . . violent perspiration. He called to have the windows opened and complained of burning . . . agitated to a great degree.'[36] Although his pulse was racing at 130 beats per minute, later he became perfectly collected, despite not having slept for twenty-nine hours. Three days later, he was still distracted and speaking very fast. He asked Colonel Goldsworthy to request Eton College to give the boys a day's holiday to celebrate his recovery, and ordered the Dettingen Te Deum† to be sung in churches, and that the Queen be warned not to be frightened when the castle's cannon were fired at noon. Goldsworthy rightly did none of those things. Yet the King was still able to joke about his own verbosity, declaring, 'I speak in the third person as I am getting into Mr Burke's eloquence – saying too much on little things.'[37]‡

On 19 November, the King talked virtually non-stop for nineteen hours, sometimes incoherently, sometimes sensibly. He refused to be shaved or eat dinner, though he eventually relented over both, but then changed his mind again when he was half shaved, which Greville thought produced 'a singular appearance as he had not been shaved for upwards of a fortnight'.[38] 'One is grimly amused to note that His Majesty was as interesting in his ravings as in his sanity,' wrote the Countess of Warwick in an introduction to Robert Greville's diaries when they were published in 1930. He discussed his horses and stables, signed promissory notes to his attendants

* Madness in royal houses was not particularly unusual in the eighteenth century, however. King Philip V of Spain, a manic depressive, briefly abdicated in 1724; Queen Maria I of Portugal was declared insane in 1792; King Christian VII of Denmark (George's brother-in-law) suffered from paranoia, self-mutilation, hallucination and such frequent masturbation that it frightened his doctors; King Gustav IV of Sweden's increasingly erratic behaviour led to a coup in 1809; and in Russia there were serious questions about the mental health of both Tsar Peter III (who was assassinated in 1762) and Tsar Paul (who suffered the same fate in 1801).
† 'The King Shall Rejoice' had been composed by Handel to celebrate George II's victory in 1743.
‡ Frances, Countess of Warwick rated that remark 'a bit of ironic wit which Charles James Fox would have danced with joy to have thought of impromptu in the House of Commons' (ed. Bladon, *Diaries of Robert Fulke Greville* p. vii).

(one of whom, Mr Spicer, got one for £50 per annum for life, with reversion to his wife and daughter), Lord Hawkesbury and Thurlow, whom he described as 'grum', meaning sour and surly.

Yet the very next day the King was almost normal, and 'sensible of having been very much out of order and that still he stood in need of attention and care'.[39] It was almost worse that he had so many lucid moments, because during them he knew that he had lost his mind and would soon do so again. He asked Greville to get his children to show themselves at the windows of the Lower Lodge across the garden, which on 24 November was allowed by the doctors, who in a complete volte-face now suspected that the King might benefit from seeing his much loved daughters, even at a distance. The result was distressing. As the princesses walked out on to the lawn, they were startled to see their father 'struggling at the windows, making efforts to open them, gesticulating at his daughters and banging in frustration on the pane. But how could this be their father, this pale and haggard man wearing a nightgown and nightcap in the middle of the day?' A witness recorded that 'they all seemed more dead than alive when they got into the house.'[40]

The King told another equerry, General Jacob de Budé, about some of the 'phantoms of his delusion during his delirium' of 22 November, including that there had been a Noah's Flood-scale deluge and that he had seen Hanover through Herschel's telescope.[41] 'He fancies London is drowned and orders his yacht to go there,' Lord Sheffield reported to William Eden. 'He took Sir George Baker's wig, flung it in his face ... and told him he might star gaze.'[42] The next day the King ordered builders at Kew and gardeners at Richmond to be paid £184 in back-wages: it was a remarkably accurate estimate since the account books were kept from him and he had made the calculation in his head, showing that his capacity for mental arithmetic at least was not affected by his derangement.[43] He also gave lots of orders regarding colts that needed shodding, and for carriages to be moved from place to place. Yet the same day Greville recorded that the King spoke 'indecently', which he never did when sane.[44]

Charles Fox, who had been suffering from dysentery on holiday in Bologna when he heard of the King's illness, raced back to England. Leaving Mrs Armistead in Lyons to enable him to travel faster, he arrived in London on 25 November. 'He has hurt himself by travelling from Bologna at a great rate when he was much out of order,' wrote Lord Sydney, 'in hopes to have been in at the death.'[45] He conferred with the Prince of Wales, who was already introducing friends into the King's bedroom to amuse them and so that the accounts of his father's lunacy were widely confirmed in high society. 'Think of the Prince of Wales introducing Lord Lothian into the King's room when it was darkened,' William Grenville told his brother George Grenville, Marquess of Buckingham, in a coded letter, 'in order that he might hear his ravings at the time that they were at the worst.'[46] He added that 'no pains are spared to circulate all sorts of lies, in order to depress people's spirits,' contrasting this with the opinion of one of the King's surgeons, Dr Hawkins, who thought that he would soon recover.[47] Thomas Rowlandson published a print which he entitled 'Filial Piety!' of the Prince of Wales in a drunken frolic taking gleeful friends, including Sheridan, into the startled King's bedroom.

Dr Hawkins was over-optimistic; the King was severely mentally ill and would be for months. He could be 'violently agitated and very angry' with Dr Warren, whom he advanced on and shoved away when Warren tried to feel his pulse; when Colonel Manners, another equerry, and Greville stopped him, 'He retired from Dr Warren pale with anger and foaming with rage.'[48] Immediately afterwards he could be caring and considerate, however, as when he asked to dine with Greville and drew up a bill of fare. 'These gleams of constant kindness which floated towards me from his troubled mind', Greville wrote, 'I received with melancholy gratitude.'[49] At dinner at 3 p.m. that day, the King 'was perplexed, contriving, agitated and loquacious'.[50]

Greville thought 'the general conduct of the physicians has not been so decided or firm as the occasion of their attendance has required. They appear to shrink from responsibility and to this time they have not established their authority though pressed by every attendant.'[51] This was partly because they had no training in mental illness and really had no idea what to do; even if they had had such training, the state of medical knowledge about madness was strictly limited. Some of the beliefs about it verged on the medieval: the Comte d'Artois suggested via the 3rd Duke of Dorset that the King should drink 'the blood of a jackass . . . after passing a clear napkin through it two or three times'.[52] Someone else suggested adding rams' brains to the asses' blood. Lord Hervey suggested the doctors 'communicate the Itch [that is, scabies] to him', whose eruptions all over the body would supposedly 'carry off the disorder'.[53]

Pitt and Thurlow arrived at Windsor on 25 November for discussions with the doctors, on the same day that the Prince of Wales ordered that his father should never be attended by more than two people at a time at two-hour relief. He further added that no one else should go in or out except clergymen for evening prayer, and that his father should not leave his bedchamber and the adjoining room. The King gave the page who delivered this news 'a smart slap on the face'.[54] That same evening, he called for the page, 'took him by the hand, and asked his pardon twenty times'.[55]

He woke up that night and 'talked incessantly and incoherently, but in good humour and high spirits, and at times laughed a good deal'.[56]

Finally, on 27 November, after six weeks of his mental affliction, Pitt and the Queen overruled the doctors and introduced a specialist to see the King. The seventy-four-year-old Dr Anthony Addington was the Pitt family physician but he had also attended 'to maladies of the mind' at an asylum near Reading, from which he had lately retired.[57] Fortunately, he was better at advising on the King's condition than he had been about Lord Chatham's gout, correctly predicting that as the attack had not been preceded by a pronounced period of melancholy he would improve within a year. The times were fraught for the doctors; Burney noted that every day as fears grew for the King's life they received death threats, 'so prodigiously high ran the tide of affection and loyalty'.[58] On his way from Windsor to London, Baker's carriage had been stopped by an angry mob demanding to know the latest news, and when told it was bad 'they furiously exclaimed, "The more shame for you!"'[59]

On 28 November the *Morning Post* published the expected new Cabinet with all their posts, including Portland as premier, Fox and Stormont as the secretaries of state and places for Sheridan, Cavendish and Burke. The certainty of a change of ministry was so much taken for granted that some Whigs started falling out among themselves over who should get which post. That same day, a Privy Council meeting at the Queen's Lodge agreed that the King should be removed from Windsor to Kew, despite his strong preference for the former.[60] The reason for the removal, which set back the King's recovery at least in the short run, was that Kew was more easily accessible from the doctors' London homes than Windsor, and also that he could be kept out of sight while taking exercise in the garden at Kew, whereas the Queen's Lodge garden at Windsor could be seen 'from the tops of houses'.[61] Neither was a good enough reason for taking him out of his familiar environment, and the Queen was firmly against the idea, but she was overruled by the Privy Council. The meeting was held out of fear that when he recovered the King might take vengeance on those involved in the decision, so responsibility needed to be spread as widely as possible. This fear of the King's retribution for his treatment was not entirely fanciful; he was keeping a diary of his conversations during his illness, which regrettably has not survived. Whether it was destroyed by him when he regained his mental equilibrium, or by others to prevent further embarrassment, is not known. Charlotte Papendiek, one of the Queen's attendants, saw it at one point, and noted that he had forgiven her husband Christopher, a royal page, for the two occasions on which he had offended him.

We have Charlotte Papendiek to thank for recording something that the

King said after a visit from Lord North, by then in poor health and nearly blind himself, which has since become famous but is often misquoted. 'He might have recollected me sooner,' the King said of his former premier after he had left.

> However, he, poor fellow, has lost his sight, and I my mind. Yet we meant well to the Americans; just to punish them with a few bloody noses, and then make bows* for the mutual happiness of the two countries. But want of principle got into the army, want of energy and skill in the First Lord of the Admiralty, and want of unanimity at home. We lost America. Tell him not to call again; I shall never see him.[62]

This statement has often been quoted as the King's considered view on the American War of Independence – to the extent that 'A Few Bloody Noses' has even been used as the title of a book – even though he was clinically insane when he said it.[63]

Despite the journal he was keeping, some of the junior courtiers and orderlies took the opportunity of the King's lunacy to tell him some harsh home truths, as they would never have dared do when he was sane, forgetting that temporarily losing his mind did not mean that he would also lose his memory. Henry Compton, a page of the backstairs, told the King that his father, Frederick, Prince of Wales, 'had been a man devoid of principle; that many people around the country had been totally ruined, some even having committed suicide, from the Prince of Wales not having paid his debts'.[64] 'All this, the King observed, was rather too much to tell a sovereign, although it might be and no doubt was true.' Charlotte Papendiek noted that the King 'never forgot it, nor could he ever bear the sight of Compton'.[65] Yet he kept his job after the King finally regained his sanity, despite having taunted a man afflicted with severe mental illness.

The King's removal from Windsor to the Queen's Lodge at Kew on 29 November was a traumatic experience that caused him to suffer a relapse, as Charlotte had predicted. 'In what a confusion was the house!' recorded Burney of the botched operation. 'Princes, equerries, physicians, pages – all conferring, whispering, plotting, and caballing, how to induce the King to set off!'[66] The Queen left quietly at 10 a.m. 'Drowned in tears, she glided along the passage,' Burney recalled, 'and got softly into her carriage with two weeping princesses, and Lady Courtown,† who was to be her lady-in-waiting during this dreadful residence.'[67]

---

* This has been generally misquoted as 'laws' rather than the far more courtly 'bows'.
† Mary, Countess of Courtown, was the wife of James, 2nd Earl of Courtown, the Treasurer of the Household.

When the King was told he was leaving Windsor, he refused to get out of bed. The senior groom of the bedchamber was General William Harcourt, the future 3rd Earl Harcourt, a war hero who had captured the American General Charles Lee in New Jersey in 1776. Now he begged the King to get up and make ready for the journey. 'He became very angry and hastily closed the bedcurtains, and he hid himself from us,' wrote Greville.[68] The four doctors then entered the room and threatened to force him to go to Kew, whereupon he reluctantly dressed, but he was not moved until 5 p.m., 'in order to prevent his being seen by any crowd', and not before he had walked the rooms of the castle to check that the Queen really had gone.[69]

'The poor King has been prevailed upon to quit Windsor with the utmost difficulty,' wrote Burney. Harcourt and Goldsworthy had told him that he would be able to spend more time with the Queen if he did so, but in the end only the threat of force persuaded him to make the journey. The royal household lined the passages of the castle, 'eager to see him once more, and almost all Windsor was collected round the rails, etc., to witness the mournful spectacle'.[70] The King shared his carriage with Goldsworthy, Harcourt and Greville, escorted by a detachment of cavalry. 'Why am I taken from a place I love best in the world?' he asked Greville with what his equerry described as 'affecting sensibility'.[71] When he saw a crowd bowing respectfully in the Home Park, he cried out, 'These good people are too fond of me.'[72] Goldsworthy had unknowingly misled the King into thinking that he could see the Queen that evening. Burney could not sleep that night, as the King's 'indignant disappointment haunted me'.[73]

The whole of the ground floor of the Queen's Lodge* that looked out towards the garden was set aside for the King, although he was not allowed to go into every room. The doctors, equerries and pages each occupied a mess room, and the family lived upstairs. The room allocation had been 'written thus with chalk by the Prince [of Wales]', who had sent most of the other attendants to the nearby Dutch House.† The three younger princesses were lodged at Princess Elizabeth's house on Kew Green.

On 30 November the King tried to escape, and ran off down the corridor in a bid to see his family. When he was caught he refused to eat his meal or swallow his medicine, and was 'turbulent and violent towards one of his pages'.[74] The entirely predictable result of his enforced move from Windsor was, as Greville noted on 1 December, that 'the unfavourable

---

* Also known at different times as Kew House, Kew Lodge and the White House. The Lodge was largely demolished in 1881 but visitors today can see a door in the Page's Waiting Room that once led to the apartments where the King was confined.

† Also known at different times as the Royal Nursery, Prince's House and today Kew Palace.

symptoms of his disorder have increased, rather than diminished,' and his language was 'blended not infrequently with indecencies'.[75] When two days later the King was only allowed to walk for a quarter of an hour in the garden in front of the house, he refused to go out at all, although 'At times he was mischievously jocose and at which time he burnt two wigs belonging to one of his pages.' Moments of clarity kept returning, as when he drew an architectural plan of the house 'with tolerable accuracy', sketching proposed alterations to it, and saying to a page, 'Pretty well for a man who is mad.'[76] That night he was 'obliged to be kept in his bed', presumably by physical restraints.[77] Greville concluded, 'Altogether this has been the worst day His Majesty has experienced.'

The treatment of the King entirely changed on 5 December when the Cabinet, finally recognizing the failure of the seven doctors who had so far been consulted (not including Addington), finally decided to call in the Rev. Francis Willis, who had run an asylum in Greatford, Lincolnshire, for three decades. Willis had trained as a priest but then received a medical degree from Oxford, after which he had been Vice-Principal of Brasenose College. He brought along his three sons, John, Thomas and Robert, who, despite attending five-year medical courses in Edinburgh, were not licensed as doctors as they had not received medical degrees from Oxford or Cambridge. His illness had not dimmed the King's sense of humour; when he first met Willis he asked him if he were a clergyman or a doctor. Willis replied, 'Sir, Our Saviour himself went about healing the sick,' whereupon the King said, 'Yes, but he had not seven hundred pounds a year for it.'[78]

The King had complained of the low quality of his doctors' knowledge and advice, which was taken by them as itself evidence of insanity (which it certainly was not). The seven doctors regarded Willis as an interloper; they despised the psychiatric school of medicine, which they considered akin to quackery.[79] They were all members of the Royal College of Physicians; Baker was currently its President and Sir Thomas Gisborne and Sir Lucas Pepys were future presidents. It is likely that they also saw Willis as a threat to the fees they were receiving, especially once he had predicted soon after arriving at Kew that under his treatment the patient would recover. He immediately started to reduce the various sedatives, emetics and purgatives that were being prescribed, instead ensuring that the King received good nutrition. It was as well that Willis was brought in when he was: in the opinion of Professor Timothy Peters, the foremost modern expert in the King's illness, until then 'The King showed no evidence of improvement, and it is likely that continuing the various surgical remedies would have led to a fatal outcome.'[80]

Willis instead tried to keep the King calm through establishing moral control over him and making him obedient. He believed in cleanliness, tidiness and above all activity for his patients, what is today called 'directive psychotherapy'.[81] Visitors to Greatford saw patients ploughing and threshing – working hard, despite paying Willis from five to twenty-five guineas a week for their treatment. They all dined together and Willis tried to draw his patients into normal conversation. These techniques, approved of today but frowned upon in the late eighteenth century, led to criticism, especially once the Whigs had correctly identified Willis as standing between themselves and power. William Eden, Lord Auckland, was fairly typical in describing Willis as 'not much better than a mountebank, and not so far different from those that are confined in his house'.[82] Similarly, Georgiana, Duchess of Devonshire, described him as 'a boastful, sanguine man, violently with the administration'.[83] The Opposition poet Peter Pindar wrote squibs about him.

Willis nonetheless used advanced methods to deal with the King's acute bipolar disorder, which were far more humane than the near-tortures imposed by the traditional doctors, and which ultimately worked. Yet when his patients, including the King, got violently out of control, he did employ gags and the 'strait-waistcoat' (that is, straitjacket), where today tranquillizing drugs would be used. He had three of his attendants accompany the King by day, and two by night. On the night of 5 December, when the King was agitated and attempted to push Willis, but not strike him, he was told that he must control himself and was shown the strait-waistcoat for the first time, whereupon the King 'began to submit'.[84] Willis admitted to Greville that its use was intended to have patients 'broke in, as horses in a manège'.[85] Once Willis had gone, wrote Greville, 'the poor dear King, overcome by his feelings, burst into a flood of tears and wept bitterly.'[86] He started a habit of rolling up handkerchiefs, sometimes as many as forty or fifty times a day

Separate committees of the Lords and Commons interrogated the doctors in December, which revealed their high degree of ignorance of the prognosis and treatment of mental illness.[87] On 10 December a particularly bitter debate raged in the Commons on the regency issue, with the Whigs adopting the negative prognosis of Warren and the ministry the much more positive ones of Willis and Addington. Pitt declared that the government needed to look in detail at historical precedents, evidently stalling for time in the hope that the King's health might improve, under Willis' prognosis.

When Parliament discussed the limitations on the power of a regent, the Whigs suggested that Pitt was demanding so many powers that he should be nicknamed 'King William the Fourth', and that, whether or not the doctors were putting straight-waistcoats on the King, Pitt was certainly trying to force the Prince of Wales into a political one.[88] 'I think it certain that in about a fortnight we shall come in,' Fox told a friend on 15 December. 'At any rate the Prince must be regent, and of consequence the ministry must be changed.'[89] He added that 'The King himself (notwithstanding the reports which you may probably hear) is certainly worse, and perfectly mad. I believe the chance of his recovery is very small indeed, but I do not think there is any probability of his dying.'[90] In the vote the next day, Pitt's majority was down to sixty-four in an unusually full House of 472. There were plenty of MPs who supported Pitt as premier but not restrictions on the regency, even though the two stances seemed contradictory. Politicians were looking to the future.

On 19 December, Willis gave the King some contemporary plays by Colley Cibber and Samuel Foote, but someone else also gave him *King Lear*, 'imprudently' in Greville's view.[91] On Warren's insistence, John Willis took all these books back to the library as the King played happily with his spaniel Flora. The next day the King had to be straitjacketed from 5 a.m. to 2 p.m. after he had become completely ungovernable. 'His legs were tied and he was secured down across his breast,' recorded Greville, 'and in this melancholy situation he was when I came to make my morning enquiries . . . I can but grieve, and hope for the best.'[92] It produced profusive sweating and a pulse of 140. That day the King gave further indication that he was far from recovery when, Greville recorded, he said the Queen 'was now in no favour, he called Mr Pitt a rascal, and Mr Fox his friend'.[93] The last sentiment was proof positive that the King was not in his right mind.

Constant, violent mood swings continued for days thereafter. 'With what joy did I carry, this morning, an exceeding good account of the King to my royal mistress!' wrote Fanny Burney on 22 December. The same day that the King later 'took against' a painting by Zoffany, which Greville called *The School of Florence*,* and it had to be removed for its protection.[94] On 23 December George had to stay in his straitjacket all night. On Christmas Day, he hid some of his bedclothes under the bed, took off his nightcap, put a pillowcase around his head, and put the pillow in bed with him which he called Prince Octavius, who he said had been born that day. The pathos was palpable; Octavius had died five years earlier at the age of four. When the King realized that it was Christmas Day and he had not been allowed to go to church, 'Suddenly, in an instant, he got under the sofa, saying that as on that day everything had been denied him he would there converse with his Saviour, and no one could interrupt them.'[95] Charlotte Papendiek remarked

---

* Probably *The Tribuna of the Uffizi* (1772–8), which had been commissioned by Queen Charlotte. At 4 foot by 5 in a heavy frame, it would have been hard to take off the wall.

in her autobiography, 'How touching, and how truly sad!' He was later straitjacketed on three separate occasions, lying on his sofa.

The daily public bulletins on the King's health are of limited use to historians, as they never mentioned restraints or controls, which the Queen censored. On Boxing Day, for example, which Willis' attendants said had been the worst they had seen the King, she had the word 'disturbed' changed to 'less calm'.[96] Later that day, George played backgammon with Dr Willis and, although he spoke incoherently, he moved the pieces correctly. The next day, he was able to talk 'very collectedly and sensibly' of the changes in the 1st Regiment of Foot Guards (later the Grenadier Guards) that would be necessitated by the death of General Cox, which Greville, who had commanded it in 1777, was in a good position to judge.

One thing that brought 'a sense of shame' to the King once he had recovered was the way that, in Greville's words, 'In his more disturbed hours he has for some time past spoke much of Lady Pembroke,' plotting to escape with her.[97] Lady Elizabeth Spencer, daughter of the 3rd Duke of Marlborough, had walked at the head of the countesses at the Coronation, in Walpole's words, 'the picture of majestic modesty'.[98] In 1756 she had married the 10th Earl of Pembroke, who was made a lord of the bedchamber in 1769. The historian Lewis Namier suggested that, because the King criticized the Queen during his malady and spoke of his desire to marry Lady Pembroke, he was expressing repressed Freudian truths and was secretly in love with her. This is unlikely because the King was very much in love with his wife, as shown by his constant efforts to see her.

Lady Pembroke had been treated abominably by her husband in 1762, when he returned from the war and ran off with an MP's daughter named Kitty Hunter, by whom he had a son.* After a reconciliation with his clearly very forgiving wife, he then did the same thing six years later in Venice, when he seduced a woman on her wedding day, with whom he had a daughter. Relations between the King and Lady Pembroke were only ever, as she told him after he recovered, 'like the most affectionate sister towards an indulgent brother'.[99] Yet during his period of insanity, in Greville's hearing, 'He talked much of Lady P[embroke] lately. Now at times he calls her Esther, sometimes Queen Elizabeth.'[100] The biblical Esther, King Ahasuerus' wife, saved the Jews but wreaked a terrible revenge on her enemy Haman, and she cropped up regularly in George's ravings. He also called Lady Pembroke 'Minerva', the Roman goddess of wisdom, and took to kissing the queen of hearts whenever that card turned up at piquet.

---

* The poor boy was baptized Augustus Retnuh Reebkomp, the middle and surname being Hunter backwards and Pembroke in anagram.

On 28 December, the Queen visited her husband for only the second time since his arrival at Kew. Originally only intending her visit to last a quarter of an hour, she stayed for fifty-five minutes. 'He sat down by her while he spoke to her and often kissed her hand,' Willis told Greville afterwards, 'and he cried frequently.'[101] They spoke in German, which the Willises could not understand. Later that day, Willis told the Privy Council that the King was improving rapidly, but then on 30 December he had to be straitjacketed again, while the next day he became 'more calm and collected than he has been for some time'.[102] These wild fluctuations flummoxed everyone; he was hardly ever worse than on the morning of New Year's Eve, yet hardly ever better than that same evening.

As it was in the Whigs' interest that the King's sanity should be considered a lost cause, exaggerated stories circulated in London's political and social circles. It was said that 'he busied himself with writing letters to foreign courts on fictitious issues,' and that he had taken to 'showing his backside to his attendants to prove that he was not suffering from gout'.[103] He was supposed to have hoodwinked Baker into releasing him from his straitjacket, only to cuff him and empty the contents of the royal chamber pot over him. Alleged incidents from his holiday at Cheltenham included trying to run a race against a horse, and asking a Mr Clements if he had run away with Lady Sarah Bunbury when he, the King, was in love with her.[104] None of this was true.

On New Year's Day 1789, the King talked about Lady Pembroke, sang a song called 'I Made Love to Kate' and was kind to two attendants before striking a third. He then played piquet 'tolerably well'.[105] The next day the Queen altered a bulletin to read, 'The King continued mending,' which Dr Warren refused to sign, leading to a loud and angry altercation with Willis. It was only after three redrafts that a compromise wording could be agreed.

Although Francis Willis' name has been blackened by Whig historians,* those who knew Willis held a very different opinion of him. Papendiek described him as 'an upright, worthy man, gentle and humane in his profession, and amiable and pious as a clergyman'.[106] Fanny Burney similarly thought him 'a man of ten thousand; open, honest, dauntless, light-hearted, innocent and high-minded'.[107] From the contemporaneous diaries, correspondence and other evidence it is clear that the story of sadistic torturing of the King by the Willis family as put forward in the 1960s was simply untrue: he was only put in the straitjacket when he was on the verge of violence, and was taken out of it as soon as possible. The surprise is that

---

* And also by the mother-and-son team of Ida Macalpine and Richard Hunter, who came up with the now demolished porphyria theory (see the Appendix).

he was given so few drugs to tranquillize him; on rare occasions he was prescribed a little laudanum.

As well as singing songs and playing cards and backgammon, the King found that studying Latin was useful in calming himself, which Willis encouraged. Three years later he told Fanny Burney, 'I ... have myself sometimes found, when ill or disturbed, that some grave and even difficult employment for my thoughts has tended more to compose me than any of the supposed usual relaxations.'[108] He found it therapeutic to spend hours taking watches apart and putting their mechanisms back together again, while carefully writing out the sequence of watchmaking actions.[109] Today, we can see that these forms of behavioural therapy were helpful in reasserting some semblance of order in his mind.

In mid-January 1789, Willis was interviewed by the Solicitor-General, the Pittite Sir John Scott, later 1st Earl of Eldon, with the result that more influence was given to him and the Queen over the King's care, to the detriment of Baker, Warren and the other doctors. Yet the very day after Willis had stated that George was improving and would recover, Greville recorded that after an 'unquiet and restless night' the King 'could not be controlled or kept quiet in his bed, and ... recourse was obliged to be had to the waistcoat'.[110] He perspired heavily under the 'restlessness and coercion', and later on 'talked much of Lady Pembroke as usual – much against the Queen – and dwelt on [a] variety of subjects, with great inconsistency and incoherence'.[111]

The King's struggles against Willis included telling him 'that he was born not to be dictated to, but to command'.[112] It is instructive that virtually the only haughty and snobbish – though in this case not factually incorrect – remark we know to have fallen from his lips came while he was certifiably mad. On 13 January, the King slept for seven and a half hours, much longer than he did even when healthy, but awoke 'quarrelsome'. When playing cards with Dr Henry Revell Reynolds, he wrote on one knave, 'Sir Richard Warren Bart [Baronet], First Physician to the King', and on another, 'Sir George Baker, Bart, Second Physician to the King and First Physician to Charlotte late Queen of Great Britain'. He added on both, in reference to Lady Pembroke, 'Oh dear Eliza ever love thy prince, who had rather suffer death than leave thee.'[113] In one of his bouts of raving he said he would leave the country and exclaimed 'in great joy', without reference to anything and for no apparent reason, 'Victoria, Victoria.'[114]

The enmity between Drs Willis and Warren became evident when they were asked by a parliamentary committee on 13 January whether they had come under any pressure to alter their bulletin accounts of the King's health. Warren claimed that Willis had 'made a very unwarranted use of the name of a great person [meaning the Queen] concerning a report on His Majesty's health which he [had] wished to change', whereupon Willis said, 'I have once or twice refused to sign the certificate as His Majesty was better than the certificate implied.' The fraught politics of the situation was similarly evident in answers to questions such as 'Has the public been in any measure deceived by accounts sent to St James's?' Warren replied that 'Dr Willis has written letters to the Prince of Wales expressing His Majesty to be much better than I apprehended His Majesty to be at that time,' whereas Willis said of the public, 'I have done my utmost to prevent their being deceived,' clearly implying that Warren had not.

In July 1777 the King had introduced what became known as the Windsor uniform, when he moved his country residence there from Kew. The colour was dark blue with red collars and cuffs, reflecting his father Frederick, Prince of Wales' hunting uniform.[115] A scurrilous rumour later sourced its colours of red and blue to the King's 'compliment' to the 'very handsome' Lady Pembroke, as they were her family's livery, but that claim was baseless.[116] The uniform was worn by members of the royal family, courtiers and 'all the men who belong to His Majesty and come into his presence at Windsor', by which was meant members of the King's Friends who were invited to wear it by the King.[117] George was by no means modish, but in this respect at least he appears to have adopted a fashion that had become common practice among members of royal families in the Holy Roman Empire, Sweden and Prussia.

From around 1787 the uniform had begun to be worn away from Windsor, and by people not employed or personally sanctioned by the King.[118]* By then, George himself wore it as his normal dress, including on grand occasions. Some aristocrats such as the Marquess of Downshire had themselves painted wearing it, while others, such as Lord Dorchester, asked the King's permission to wear it. Hostile Whigs such as Lord March meanwhile sneered at it, thinking it 'humiliating' to dress 'like a livery servant'.[119] During the regency crisis of 1788, when politicians split largely along party lines as to which doctor they believed, society ladies made their political views known by wearing either the red and blue of the Windsor uniform or the blue and buff of the Foxite Whigs.[120] Some of the latter even took to wearing what were called 'regency caps' at dinner parties.

Although the King 'was in wild laughing spirits all this evening, good-humoured, but much deranged' on 15 January 1789, he was 'most violent

---

* The uniform is still worn today by members of the royal family and a very few others when at Windsor Castle.

and abusive' until almost noon on the 16th. Yet by 1 p.m. he was able to see the Queen and three of the princesses for an hour, when he 'behaved with the greatest propriety and affection to the whole party', after which the King and Queen played piquet.[121] As soon as they had gone, however, he started raving to his pages that they needed to pack for Windsor and that the Queen had permitted Lady Pembroke to come to him. He put a broad blue ribbon around the neck of his little dog Badine, remarking on its colour. (It is possible that he was awarding it the Order of the Garter.) Then he said he wanted the 1st Duke of Montagu to convene all the bishops at Windsor, as he believed that in William Paley's book *Moral Philosophy* of 1785 it stated that nature allowed men more than one wife. Montagu was a curious choice for the convenor of a theological conference, as he was Master of the Horse, but it displays a steadfast reverence for ecclesiastical law that the King intended to obtain the permission of Anglican prelates before he committed bigamy.

There was a good deal of pathos in the King's situation, for as Greville recorded, 'He is at times, and probably oftener than he appears to be, sensible of his unhappy situation.' After being given one emetic he felt so sick that he knelt down and 'He prayed that God would be pleased either to restore him to his senses, or permit that he might die directly.'[122] It was what Greville called 'a transient gleam of wisdom from our dear afflicted King'. These constant changes of mental state in part explain the wildly inconsistent rumours that escaped from Kew about him. As a friend wrote to William Eden in mid-January, 'There is no circle into which one goes, where one person does not tell you that the King ... will meet his Parliament in a fortnight; and some other contradicts him flatly by asserting that both his body and mind are in the most desperate situation.'[123]

Although the Queen had asked for no public or private observance of her official birthday on 18 January, the King knew the day and insisted upon seeing her, but was prevented. He struck one of Willis' men and picked up a chair to throw at another. It was small wonder that Queen Charlotte's hair turned entirely grey in these months of constant crisis, and some of the symptoms she exhibited, such as sudden bursts of unexplained lachrymosity, suggest that she was on the verge of a nervous breakdown.

The next day, 19 January, the King was allowed to go for a walk outside the royal compound. It went badly: at one point he tried to enter the Pagoda in Kew Gardens, grabbing a key from one of his attendants, which was 'not easily taken [back] from him'. He refused to go any further and instead 'sat down and afterwards lay extended on the grass'.[124] His attendants had to carry him home on their shoulders for a mile, and then straitjacket him for several hours after he became abusive. The following day the House of Commons formally placed the care of the King under the Queen, which signalled a victory for her and Willis over the Prince of Wales and Warren.

On 22 January, the King was 'loud in song', but later he hit out at two attendants and became 'so unmanageable that recourse was had to the waistcoat'.[125] He told Willis that 'he was not afraid of death, but that he was afraid of him'.[126] Yet the next day the Queen joined him on a walk. That evening, Greville recorded that the King had 'amused himself in *arranging a regency*. Who puts these kinds of things in his head I cannot conceive.'[127] The fantasy Regency Council was to include the Archbishop of Canterbury, the Lord Chancellor, the Lord President, the Prince of Wales and the Duke of York: not, in fact, the worst arrangement that could be devised, although it excluded Pitt, who the next day the King referred to as 'a boy' who had been too afraid to 'step forward at the close of Lord Lansdowne's* administration'.[128] Even in the depth of his lunacy, therefore, the traumatic political experiences of late 1783 were powerful enough to break through his confusion.

On 24 January, after the King had struck his attendant Mr Spicer on the cheek and cut his face, which bled 'a good deal' on to his waistcoat, Willis displayed to him a new, purpose-built restraining chair which was attached to its own stand to prevent it being knocked over. This the King 'eyed with some degree of awe', wryly nicknaming it his 'Coronation Chair'.[129] The next day he made another escape attempt in Kew Gardens – 'making a run, he attempted to get over the pales,' but was caught.[130] On 26 January, violent and abusive, he twice had to be confined to the chair in his straitjacket.[131] He believed he could see 'Eliza' over his left shoulder. It might seem surprising, under the circumstances, that the very next day he was allowed to walk in Richmond Gardens, where he once again tried to run away, 'but was soon overtaken and stopped'.[132]

'To what sudden fluctuations of good and bad,' wrote Greville, 'of calm and turbulence, does this afflicting illness doom our interesting and unfortunate patient!!'[133] The faithful equerry was irritated that Willis – with the Queen's permission and connivance – constantly put the best possible gloss on the King's condition. A typical example came on 28 January when the King attacked one of Willis' men in the evening, pulling his hair and beginning a scuffle, yet the following day's bulletin stated that the King had passed the day 'without irritation'.[134] By 30 January, the King believed that Willis' men were going to murder him – paranoia is a common symptom of bipolar disorder. The next day he sang some of Handel's choruses to the

---

* Shelburne had become the 1st Marquess of Lansdowne in 1784.

Queen, 'and commented on their different advantages of composition'.[135] By then, Willis had nine attendants working at Kew, three in the room with him day and night.

In America, George Washington, who was about to be inaugurated President in April, showed commendable sympathy over his former adversary's condition. 'His situation', he wrote to a friend, 'merits commiseration.' Gouverneur Morris reported to Washington from Paris the rumour that the King 'conceived himself to be no less a personage than George Washington at the head of the American Army. This shows that you have done something or other which sticks most terribly in his stomach.'[136] It was another untrue story: if anything it is notable how *little* the American catastrophe arose during his ramblings, with the notable exception of when Lord North visited, which was always likely to trigger memories of it.

On 2 February, Fanny Burney, who felt cooped up in Queen's Lodge, was out walking in Kew Gardens when she saw the King. The doctors' orders were that courtiers should stay out of sight as much as possible, so she turned round and 'ran off with all my might'.[137] Behind her, she could hear the hoarse voice of the King calling out, 'Miss Burney! Miss Burney!', but she kept on running, as did the King, attendants and the Willises, even after she heard people calling out, 'Stop! Stop! Stop!'[138] Not until she heard an attendant shouting, 'Dr Willis begs you to stop! . . . It hurts the King to run,' did she do so. 'Why did you run away?' asked the King when he caught up with her, with 'something still of wildness in his eyes'.[139] He then put both his hands round her shoulders and kissed her cheek, as the Willises looked on, smiling. They then walked together, during which she noticed that 'Everything that came uppermost in his mind he mentioned; he seemed to have just such remains of his flightiness as heated his imagination without deranging his reason, and robbed him of all control over his speech, though nearly in his perfect state of mind as to his opinions.'[140]

The King told Burney that he was as well as he had ever been in his life; asked her about herself; told her 'I am your friend'; complained volubly about his pages; asked after her father's final volume of his history of music; told anecdotes about Handel; attempted to sing some of the airs and choruses of Handel's oratorios; talked about his friendship with Mary Delany; asked after several politicians including Lord Grey de Wilton, Sir Watkin Wynn and the Duke of Beaufort, and showed her a list of a new Cabinet he intended to appoint, which she thought 'The wildest thing that passed'.[141] When the Willises 'grew quite uneasy at his earnestness and volubility', they parted. The encounter left Fanny thinking 'inexpressibly thankful to see him so nearly himself'. Greville agreed that it was 'among the very best days he has passed'.[142]

The following day the King was allowed to shave himself for the first time since October, despite still giving away imaginary pensions to his attendants. That evening, the Queen and princesses sang 'Rule, Britannia!' and 'Come Cheer Up my Lads'* with him, played piquet and read the life of Handel to him. 'In truth,' wrote Greville in his diary, 'it partook more of the jollity at an election than the etiquette of a Court.'[143] The next day George played the flute for the first time in months.

On 5 February, unable to put it off any longer, Pitt was forced to introduce the Regency Bill in the Commons, vesting the powers of the Crown in the Prince of Wales when the regency was declared, except for those of creating peerages or granting offices. Burke spoke on the second reading, accusing Pitt and the government of conduct 'verging on treason, for which the justice of their country would, he trust, one day overtake them and bring them to trial'.[144] Pitt replied that Burke's 'peculiarly violent tone of warmth and of passion' made a reply unnecessary, and tellingly no one came to Burke's defence.† During the clause-by-clause consideration of the Bill, Burke made a remark that was to dog him for months afterwards when he asked rhetorically, 'Did they recollect that they were talking of a sick king, of a monarch smitten by the hand of Omnipotence, and that the Almighty had hurled him from his throne, and plunged him into a condition which drew down upon him the pity of the meanest peasant in his kingdom?'[145] After several days' debate, Pitt had a majority of forty-six for a Regency Council chaired by the Queen to advise the Prince Regent. Yet Parliament still waited upon the doctors before putting the Bill into effect.

The King's recovery came in the nick of time. He was allowed to use a knife and fork for the first time on 6 February, and he walked to the Kew Observatory to meet Stephen Demainbray, who had inherited his father's post as Superintendent of the Observatory. There were still signs of eccentricity; that same day he drew up the insignia for a new Order of Minerva for literature and science, with a straw-coloured ribbon and star of sixteen points; the motto was to be the Latin for 'Learning improves character.' Greville suspected to himself that Willis' policy of restricting the ability of rival doctors such as Pepys and Reynolds to see the King, while encouraging him to see Demainbray, Sir Joseph Banks, his watchmaker Benjamin Vulliamy and even the shepherd of his merino sheep, was about power and access rather than best medical practice. Greville noticed on 7 February that the King's 'usual singular expression' of 'What! What! What!' had

---

* Also known as 'Heart of Oak', the official march of the Royal Navy.
† The author owns an undated letter from Pitt to an unnamed peer saying, 'I return Burke's letter which is like other rhapsodies from the same pen, in which there is much to admire, and nothing to agree with.'

reappeared for the first time since the illness began.[146] Horace Walpole mentioned this to Sir Horace Mann just five days later, showing how quickly news circulated.

On 8 February, the King pretended that he was lame in order to go out in his open phaeton carriage, but Baker and Pepys told Willis he was 'shamming', and they were proved correct when he then walked to Richmond Gardens, quarrelling with Willis as he went. By 10 February there were over-sanguine accounts in London that he was fit to reign again, which Greville thought absurd, not least because that day the King had told John Willis that because he had prorogued the last Parliament, the one that was presently sitting was illegal.

While the King and his usual party were walking in Kew Gardens on 11 February, the head gardener offered to give Dr Willis a basket of exotic fruits, whereupon the King said, 'Get another basket, Eaton, at the same time, and pack up the Doctor in it and send him off at the same time.'[147] Two days later he told his apothecary Charles Hawkins 'of his having played Lord Chatham, Lord Lansdowne and Lord Bute against one another', which was not exactly true, as he had tended to be a strong partisan of the last. He was still talking about 'Queen Elizabeth' with a wink, meaning Lady Pembroke rather than Good Queen Bess, and told Hawkins that he intended to travel to Göttingen in Hanover with him.[148] This was clearly not a man who was mentally well, yet Willis was reporting to Thurlow that the King was now 'in a state of convalescence'.[149] By then his pulse was down to 64 and he weighed 12 stone 3 pounds.

The official bulletin proclaimed a continued state of improvement on 15 February, and indeed the King did talk 'calmly and consistently' to Warren.[150] But then he suddenly burst into tears for no reason, and was still offering pensions of £80 per annum to his servants. He even played cards with the Queen on a Sunday, which he would never have done when sane. The positive official news about his health brought a sudden influx of visitors to Kew – the Dukes of Richmond, Atholl and Buccleuch, Lords Cathcart and Essex, Henry Dundas and many others, all arriving to assure the Queen how loyal they had been during the crisis and convey how happy they were about the King's recovery. Fox sniffed an establishment cover-up, writing to Portland and the Prince of Wales that he had 'no belief in the King's recovery, but I dare say some of our friends are a good deal alarmed'.[151] He was not entirely wrong; the Queen, Pitt and Willis were indeed tending to exaggerate both the rate and the extent of the King's recovery, presumably in order to forestall a regency.

The philanthropist Hannah More, who knew Drs Baker and Pepys well, wrote to her sister on 16 February to say that they had told her the King was much better, and 'Even Dr Warren confesses that his royal patient is reviving.'[152] She added that while walking in Kew Gardens the King had told some workmen who were burning rubbish, 'Pray put out that fire directly; don't you see it smokes Mrs Boscawen's house?' Yet that same evening Dr Dundas, one of the royal surgeons, told Greville of several things the King had done which he would not have done when sane, including kissing ribbons that had connections to Lady Pembroke, giving a compass to Dundas to guide Dr Willis over Lincoln Heath (even though Willis was in the room), saying of a portrait of himself, 'Did you ever see such a hog?', and giving Dundas a velvet bag that he said 'was to make him a nightcap'.[153]

On the 16th, the King got up no fewer than five times in the night, but Willis did not tell Warren and Pepys that before they signed a bulletin the next morning formally announcing that he was officially 'in a state of amendment and . . . convalescence'. Greville was convinced 'that the dear King was by no means well that day when the joyful news of his convalescence was announced to the public', and he blamed Willis for effectively bouncing the other doctors, who had seen much less of their patient than him, into unwarranted optimism.[154]

The King met Lord Thurlow with Willis' permission on 17 February, by which time the Lord Chancellor had deserted the Whigs and returned to the government camp. It was decided that he should not agitate the King by talking about domestic politics, so instead he brought him up to date about foreign affairs over the previous four months: Emperor Joseph II's failure to capture Belgrade in October; 'the troubles of France' (Louis XVI's decision to summon the notables* in November); and the character of the new King Charles IV of Spain who had acceded in December. George told Thurlow 'that the last time he had seen him he had made himself appear worse to him than he really had been', which Thurlow and Greville correctly thought 'improper' and not like the sane monarch at all.[155] That day, Fox wrote to General Richard Fitzpatrick MP, the son of the 1st Earl of Ossory and one of his closest friends, whose sister had married Fox's brother, 'I rather think, as you do, that Warren has been frightened.'[156] He was still assuming the Regency Bill would pass its third and final reading in the Lords in a matter of days; but, even as he wrote, his high hopes of returning to office were being dashed by the Queen, Pitt, Thurlow and Willis.

On 18 February, Colonel Digby told Fanny Burney that 'nothing now remain[ed] of the disorder, but too much hurry of spirits'.[157] The King

---

* The senior house of the Estates-General, the nobility.

walked again in Richmond Gardens arm in arm with the Queen, who received Lords Uxbridge, Beaulieu, Bulkeley and De La Warr and the Bishop of London. The Prince of Wales and the Duke of York arrived to see the King, but the Queen and Willis prevented them from doing so. George was the first king since the reign of Edward III in the fourteenth century to have a family of grown-up sons ranging from the Prince of Wales, twenty-seven, to Prince Adolphus, fifteen.[158] Yet the two eldest were now being prevented from seeing their father in case he said or did something that might confirm Fox's suspicions. The next day, the bulletin announced that 'His Majesty continued to advance in recovery,' allowing Thurlow to inform the House of Lords that it would be unnecessary and inappropriate to proceed with the Regency Bill. The King's malady had lasted for four months, but was it truly over?

23

Recovery, Revolution and War

February 1789–May 1794

An unspotted life, which, at length, has vanquished all the hearts of all his subjects.[1]

Fanny Burney's diary, 15 August 1789

'Happily every morning now is ushering in with cheering accounts,' Colonel Robert Greville wrote on 20 February 1789.[2] Yet there were indications that George was still suffering from the manic depression that had so darkened the past four months. Sir George Baker was still seeing 'some shades'; the King was still speaking of his Star of Minerva, the new order of chivalry he wanted to institute in honour of the Countess of Pembroke, and Greville continued to find him 'somewhat hurried' on their walks, a classic symptom. When Greville noticed the King getting his facts wrong, he nonetheless thought it 'more just to consider them as mist disappearing fast before sunshine'. It was vital for the government that the King should appear as well as possible: 'The Opposition would be ready enough to talk of a relapse,' the Duke of Marlborough wrote on 12 March, 'were he to get a bad cold even.'[3]

The King still deeply resented the lie that his equerries Generals Harcourt and Goldsworthy had told him at Windsor that he would be able to see more of the Queen if he moved to Kew. In truth he had been largely separated from her and their children for three months. 'Harcourt told me to trust to his honour,' George told Greville, 'and I have not forgot that.'[4]* The King also displayed coolness towards Goldsworthy 'for not executing his orders in the beginning of his illness', even though these instructions had clearly been deranged.[5]

---

* Harcourt's career continued unimpeded, however; he was later promoted to Master of the Robes, and became the first Governor of the Royal Military College at Sandhurst when it was founded in 1801. Goldsworthy became a general in 1793.

The King understandably wanted to take his recovery slowly, especially once Lord Thurlow reassured him that William Pitt had the political situation under control. 'Believe me I have no child's play before me,' the King said, 'but all will do well by degrees.'[6] Yet that evening he still called Dr Dundas 'David' and told him he was 'still the knave of hearts', and imitated Dr Gisborne's voice. Greville reached for another weather metaphor to explain how long the disease might still be noticeable: 'The tail of the cloud sprinkles thin, but long after the storm has passed, and when it is seen but in the distance.'[7] The King was still occasionally being giving emetic tartar hidden in his whey, asses' milk and bread and butter to make him vomit, but his own pages now dressed him in the morning, rather than Willis' attendants.

Light, drop-leaf tables designed for occasional use were called Pembroke tables after the connoisseur 9th Earl of Pembroke. As the King was putting up the leaf of one on 22 February he said to Dr Reynolds, 'with a significant smile', and to Greville's deep dismay, 'This is called a *Pembroke* table.'[8] He also discussed changing the motto of the Minerva Star, which Baker and Greville took to be another reference to Lady Pembroke. Yet, despite these clear indications that the King was still ill, the bulletins reported uninterrupted progress to a full recovery, adding that steps were underway to restore him to his full political powers. Thurlow met him for eighty minutes on 22 February and reported himself 'mightily pleased'.[9]

On 23 February, the King joked to Fanny Burney about their race in Richmond Gardens: 'I am quite well now. I was nearly so when I saw you before – but I could overtake you better now!'[10] He and the Queen finally met the Prince of Wales and Prince Frederick for over half an hour in the Queen's apartment, where they deliberately avoided discussing politics. On his way to see his sons, the King had wiped his eyes with a handkerchief, telling his pages that 'It was a maxim of his ancestor of the House of Brunswick never to shed a tear.'[11] However stiff his upper lip in public, however, he cried copiously when he met them. He did not know how close they had come to dethroning him during the crisis.

Sir William Fawcett, the Adjutant-General, told Lord Cornwallis in India that the promotions the princes had intended to impose on the army included four new field marshals, among whom were the two princes themselves and the Duke of Gloucester. There were also going to be no fewer than thirty-one new generals, twenty lieutenant-generals, a dozen major-generals and many colonels. Ten new aides-de-camp were going to be appointed, most for political reasons. Now, of course, none of this would take place, and as one of his correspondents told Lord Auckland, 'All the ladies may burn their regency caps ... the cheapest of which cost seven guineas.'[12] Although the King forgave both his sons, the public did not, and the Prince of Wales' coach was occasionally mobbed, pelted and hissed at when it appeared on the streets.

The King's forgiveness did not extend to the entire royal household. William Douglas, 4th Duke of Queensberry, an old Leicester House friend, was forced to resign as a lord of the bedchamber, a post he had held since the King's accession, for supporting the Opposition during the crisis. It had been noted, as Nathaniel Wraxall put it, that the Prince of Wales and Prince Frederick had spent a lot of time at Queensberry House in Piccadilly, 'where plentiful draughts of champagne went round to the success of the approaching regency'.[13] The Queen and Pitt insisted on his resignation for this 'ratting' and the Duke went into self-imposed exile in Italy, where he conceived a taste for opera, especially prima donnas and dancers.*

The King saw Pitt for ninety minutes on 24 February. 'He had no anxieties on the reflection of what had passed during his illness,' he told his Prime Minister, 'as his recovery reminded him how much he owed to God Almighty.'[14] Pitt later advised the Archbishop of Canterbury that George had asked many questions about public affairs, talked calmly and reasonably, and 'in every respect appeared to him to enjoy the most perfect self-possession'.[15] George later wrote to Pitt to say that for the rest of his reign he would 'only keep that superintending eye which can be effected without labour or fatigue'.[16] If Pitt assumed from this that the King was now going to take a back seat in public affairs, however, he was mistaken, and over the next decade would discover that George's superintending eye could in fact effect a good deal without fatigue.

Large crowds had congregated daily across the country awaiting the latest bulletins brought by the London mail coach, and on 27 February they erupted with joy when the *London Gazette* announced that no further ones needed to be issued. As he walked along the Thames at Windsor that day, the King was hailed from a boat by people shouting, 'God bless Your Majesty, long life and health to you. We are glad to see you abroad again.'[17] A charmed George raised his hat and bowed to them. On 2 March, for the first time since the illness struck, no doctors visited him, and he made his first official tour, to the new workhouse at Richmond, of which he was a benefactor. The master there, with staggering ineptitude, asked whether he

---

* The Duke was very grand; he once rang for a footman but did not speak or look at him, and when at length the servant asked if His Grace wanted anything, the Duke replied, 'God damn you, am I obliged to tell you what I want?' (ed. Bickley, *Diaries of Sylvester Douglas* I pp. 404–5).

would like to see their mad-house, and even brought up the subject of straitjackets. Yet the King went along 'without the least agitation, and no unpleasant consequence occurred'.[18] Soon afterwards he ate cheesecake at a pastry shop in Richmond and listened to an eleven-year-old Welsh harpist at Colonel Fitzwilliam's house. But in general he was still kept away from crowds in case he became unnerved.

On 3 March, Charlotte rejoined him in their bed. Francis Willis left Kew that day. The King gave him a gold watch, and a grateful Parliament awarded him a pension of £1,000 per annum for twenty-one years. The King also recommended that Willis' son Thomas be given the first vacant prebendary position that became available at Worcester Cathedral, telling Pitt, 'I have seen so much of him, that I can answer for his principles being such as will do credit to my patronizing him.'[19]

True to form, Thomas Paine proposed to mark the King's recovery with a demand that he should now 'consider yourself as more properly the servant than the sovereign of your people'.[20] In fact the King had always considered himself to be both, as had the British people, and this was reflected in massive national celebrations to mark his recovery. The Queen and princesses went up to London to see the general illumination of the city, with images of the King, Providence, Health and Britannia all much in evidence in 'elegant devices'.[21] In Greek Street, Josiah Wedgwood displayed an Etruscan-style transparency of Hygeia, the goddess of health, restoring the sovereign to Britain. Sir Joseph Banks produced one of the King being recrowned 'by the genius of Physic', which also featured the buxom Hygeia, and at the Bank of England there was a transparency of Britannia 17 feet high seated in her chariot, attended by cherubs representing Peace and Plenty, with the King's profile atop.[22] The convalescing King went to the window at the Queen's Lodge to see a painted transparency by the Italian ornamental painter Biagio Rebecca which Fanny Burney thought 'magnificently beautiful'.[23]

Across the country, landowners invited tenants and neighbouring farmers to their country seats to enjoy dinners, bonfires and lots of alcohol.[24] Subscriptions were launched for the poor, and debtors and prisoners were given porter (a dark beer made from brown malt) and roast beef. It was a bad time to be an ox, a large number of which were roasted on spits in villages across the land. The extent of the celebrations was a source of immense national pride, gleefully reported even in the press: every householder in Lewes was given beer money; in the Potteries the partying lasted three days; and in the village of Brassington, Derbyshire, the locals somehow drank their way through 200 gallons of ale. In one part of Teesdale every cottage 'blazed with light' within a 2-mile radius.[25] There were marches of charity clubs, workmen and sometimes entire villages, often to the singing of 'God Save the King', a tune that theatre orchestras played over and over again by popular demand. When a crowd got the impression that the transparency of the King in one inn appeared to show him in a straitjacket, the mayor had to intervene to stop the inn from being destroyed entirely after all of its windows were smashed. More than twenty medals were struck to celebrate the recovery of the King's health, one depicting Francis Willis and the words 'Britons rejoice. Your King's restored'.[26]

The King returned to Windsor on horseback on 14 March, surrounded by a large party of gentlemen, along roads full of cheering crowds. 'All Windsor came out to meet the King,' recorded Burney. 'It was a joy amounting to ecstasy.'[27] She cried all day on witnessing 'A scene so reversed'. Later in the month she wrote to a friend that the King 'little before knew the general loyalty and attachment of the nation. The nation knew it not, indeed, itself.'[28]

The Service of Thanksgiving at St Paul's Cathedral on 23 April 1789, St George's Day, was the first held since George I's accession in 1715. (The Peace of Paris ending the Seven Years War had been thought too controversial.) It was entirely George's idea, first articulated in the last week of February when he was still recovering. Ministers were initially doubtful, mainly because of the lack of precedent, and even after it had been agreed the Archbishop of Canterbury tried to dissuade George from attending, fearing it might prove too great a strain. The King replied by joking, 'My Lord, I have twice read over the evidence of the physicians on my case, and if I can stand that, I can stand anything.'[29] He wanted there to be 'an affecting though highly proper act of devotion' and it needed to be in public.

Three regiments of foot guards lined the 2-mile route from St James's Palace to Temple Bar, to hold back the cheering crowds which packed the streets. Public buildings and private houses were decked out with bunting, candles and illuminations, flags flew from church steeples from Westminster to Cheapside. When the King and Queen's carriage arrived at noon, a rocket was fired from Queen Anne's statue outside the Cathedral to signal the cannon at the Tower of London to boom their salute. The archbishops at the west door then processed with the royal family past the assembled Lords and Commons, ambassadors and all the senior Anglican clergy. The royal princesses and many women in the congregation wore bandeaux of Indian gold muslin in their wigs with 'God Save the King' inscribed in gold lettering.

The King personally chose the psalm, the lesson (Isaiah 12) and the anthem for the three-hour ceremony to thank Almighty God 'for the signal interposition of his good providence in removing from His Majesty the late illness with which he has been afflicted'.[30] Beilby Porteus, the Bishop of London, preached the sermon, observing that the King represented 'everything that is dear and valuable to us, as men, as Britons, and as Christians'. In the Te Deum, the Cathedral choir was joined by a chorus of 6,000 charity children. 'More than any other state occasion since the rebuilt cathedral had opened,' states the history of St Paul's, 'that of 23 April 1789 was marked not by triumphalism but spontaneous, widely felt rejoicing that the King could resume his reign.'[31] As a friend wrote to William Eden, 'Foreigners cannot upbraid us for not giving magnificent and splendid spectacles.'[32]

The future war hero Captain Sidney Smith noted that the King cried briefly during the service, 'but he covered his face with his handkerchief, and soon recovered himself.' Smith thought it natural that he was so affected 'at being the centre to which the blessing and prayers of thousands flowed'.[33] Smith thought the King looked three stone lighter than before the malady struck, while Lady Louisa Stuart, Lord Bute's great-niece, reported to Lady Portarlington, 'The King looked better than I expected him ... rather thin and older than he was, but on the whole very well.'[34]

The occasion of course had its political element; William Pitt was acclaimed rapturously by the crowd, and on the return journey the crowd threw off the horses of his carriage and drew it all the way back to Downing Street. His biographer records the day as 'in truth his triumph as much as the King's'.[35] By total contrast, Charles Fox sat back in the seat of his carriage hoping to avoid recognition, but once he was spotted at Temple Bar 'the Man of the People' was hissed all the way to St Paul's.[36] The Prince of Wales and Duke of York, who refused to wear the Windsor uniform even on that of all days, were exposed to catcalls on their journeys both to and from the Cathedral. They chatted to each other throughout the service, and one eyewitness claimed that they ate biscuits during the sermon.[37]* The Prince's estrangement from his parents led his mother to note plaintively in her diary that month that 'The P[rince] of Wales came today about 4 [p.m.] to his apartment at the Castle, dined at the White Heart [sic] but never came to see us.'[38]

The King's recovery prompted no fewer than 756 congratulatory addresses from corporations and organizations all around the country, more than double the total number of petitions received by Parliament on the cider tax in 1763, John Wilkes in 1769, the attempted repeal of the

---

* The Prince of Wales should not have; he was already 16 stone and nicknamed 'the Prince of Whales'.

Catholic Relief Act in 1780, Economical Reform in 1780, parliamentary reform in 1783 and support for Pitt in 1784.[39] On this measure, around twice as many Britons cared more that their King had recovered from insanity than about almost all the great political issues that had taken up so many hours of agonized debate and acres of newsprint over the previous generation.

On 1 May the most magnificent royal ball of the King's reign was held in celebration of his recovery at Windsor Castle by the Queen, who invited the married guests, and by the Princess Royal, who invited the unmarried ones. 'The supper exceeded anything of the kind ever given in this kingdom,' recorded the *Annual Register*. Two hundred and twenty-eight guests assembled in the ballroom at 8 p.m., with the royal family and many others wearing the Windsor uniform. The senior royal ladies wore long purple trains. Other ladies again wore bandeaux around the front of their headdresses featuring the words 'God Save the King', 'and many of them had beautiful medallions of His Majesty, some plain, some in pearl, and some set in diamonds', reported the *Annual Register*.[40] Dancing began at 10 p.m., by which time the King and Queen, six princesses and the Prince of Wales, as well as the Dukes of York, Cumberland and Gloucester, had been conversing 'in the most affable manner with every person in the room'.* The King left the ball soon after welcoming everyone, not wanting to exhaust himself.

For all the public friendliness and reconciliation, however, the Queen continued to resent the behaviour of Princes George and Frederick during her husband's illness, and none of their friends were invited to the Buckingham House parties. The Prince of Wales forbade his friends from attending the ball thrown by White's Club to celebrate his father's recovery on 21 April, and he and Prince Frederick publicly sold their tickets to it. Indeed, when the Duke of York fought a duel against Colonel Charles Lennox, later the 4th Duke of Richmond, that same month, Charlotte showed no concern for her son's fate and was courteous to Lennox at a ball shortly afterwards. No sooner was the King better than the Duke of York was writing to him to insist that 'The allowance, Sir, that you have made for us from your Civil List . . . is by no means adequate to the necessary expenses which our situation in life obliges us to incur.'[41] Five days later, Prince William chimed in: 'I think it my duty not to incur the risk of

---

* The somewhat inane affability of the Duke of Gloucester's conversation may be divined from his remark on another occasion to Edward Gibbon, who had completed his *Decline and Fall of the Roman Empire*, 'Another damned, thick, square book! Always scribble, scribble, scribble! Eh! Mr Gibbon?' (Beste, *Personal and Literary Memorials* p. 68). Sadly this phrase is still constantly attributed to George, who in fact much admired Gibbon's work.

deceiving Your Majesty by giving expectations that I can live within the present income and at the same time maintain the character and mode of living inseparable from the relation I bear to your Majesty.'[42] George's sons were clearly not inclined to think that his fragile condition was any reason to spare him from their wretched importunings.

On Willis' suggestion and as part of his convalescence, the King Queen and with their three eldest daughters went to Weymouth, a seaside town in Dorset, for an extended summer holiday, something they enjoyed so much they made thirteen further visits there over the next sixteen years (public business keeping them away only in 1790, 1793 and 1803). They stayed at Gloucester Lodge in Gloucester Row, the Duke of Gloucester's house there, eventually buying it. While at Weymouth, they walked on the Esplanade, visited local country houses, gave a ball on their wedding anniversary and generally led the lives of substantial country gentry, with the exception that they kept a Royal Navy frigate on permanent call in case they wanted to go sailing. In a sign of how relaxed he was at Weymouth, George did not always put the time on the letters he wrote there.

On their way to Weymouth, he was greeted by acclamation at Winchester before 'countless multitudes', and 'God Save the King' was sung to an orchestra on the steps of Romsey Town Hall. On the way to Lyndhurst, 'Carriages of all sorts lined the roadside – chariots, chaises, landaus, carts, wagons, whiskies, gigs, phaetons – mixed and intermixed, filled within and surrounded without by faces all glee and delight.'[43] The King stopped for five days' hunting in the New Forest, where there was an ancient law that the monarch must be presented with two milk-white greyhounds and crowds assembled to watch the ceremony, performed by green-clad forester buglers.

The King had been sane for over four months by now, but people still took the opportunity to celebrate his recovery wherever he went. The throng outside one of the country houses in which he was staying were so keen to watch him dine that they broke down the palings and hedges to get a better view. The royal couple later passed under 'a magnificent arch' at Salisbury that was festooned with flowers and mottoes such as 'The King Restored', and crowds were in 'a rapture past description'. Blandford in Dorset saw much the same, and there were even larger crowds at Dorchester. When the King made a contribution to the restoration of the spire of Salisbury Cathedral and was asked what name should be put in the record, he merely replied 'Oh! A gentleman of Berkshire.'[44]

Weymouth Lodge was situated directly in front of the beach. When the royal family walked out from it in the evening, 'an immense crowd attended them – sailors, bargemen, mechanics, countrymen; and all united in so

vociferous a volley of "God Save the King" that the noise was stunning.'[45]
Of course, gawping crowds attend many spectacles of celebrities, all the
more so of royalty, and always have done, but this extravagant exhibition
of loyalty was exceptional. There were times in the past when his coach
had been booed by the crowds – indeed, there would be again – but at this
point in his reign he was immensely popular.

Fanny Burney recorded the first time that the King bathed at Weymouth,
enjoying 'the soft air and soft footing upon the sands' at seven o'clock on
the morning of 8 July. 'The King bathes, and with great success,' she wrote;
'a machine follows the royal one into the sea, filled with fiddlers, who play
"God Save the King" as His Majesty takes his plunge!'[46]* The King, wearing a blue serge bathing costume, did not know that musicians had been
concealed in a second bathing machine. (The scene was touchingly evoked
by Thomas Hardy in 1880 in his historical novel *The Trumpet-Major*.) As
the historian Janice Hadlow points out, the medical opinion of the day
'considered sea-bathing a stimulant to sluggish bodily function. Bathing,
for Willis and his patients, did not mean swimming, but immersion, or
"dipping", below the waves, aided by professional attendants.'[47]

It clearly worked. 'His Majesty is in delightful health, and much-
improved spirits,' Burney reported to her father on 13 July. 'The loyalty of
all this place is excessive:† they have dressed out every street with labels
of "God Save the King"; all the shops have it over their doors; all the children wear it in their caps, all the labourers in their hats, and all the sailors
in their voices, for they never approach the house without shouting it
aloud.'[48] Bargemen wore 'God Save the King' cockades in their hats, women
even had it in large girdles round their waists. It was painted in large gold
letters on most of the bathing machines and in every shop and most of the
houses in Weymouth as well as in the neighbouring village of Melcombe
Regis (which had been a royal borough since 1280). The contrast between
the crowds Fanny Burney reported in Weymouth and those in Paris the
next day, 14 July 1789, could hardly be more marked.

The second great crisis of George's reign – fully the equal of the American
War of Independence – was about to occur, when the storming of the
Bastille precipitated a series of events that would lead to the French Revo-
lution, the Terror, the Revolutionary Wars and ultimately the Napoleonic
Wars. In retrospect, we can see that the King recovered in the nick of time

---

* Bathing machines were roofed and walled wooden carts which were rolled into the sea to
give people the privacy of changing into their swimming costumes.
† In the sense of 'exuberant' (*Johnson's Dictionary*).

to lead his country through the challenges thrown up by these events. Had he stayed in the grip of his malady a few days longer and the regency had been established, George told the Duke of Gloucester, 'No power on earth should have prevailed on him to resume the government,' with the result that the vacillating, unpopular Prince Regent and neo-republican Charles Fox would have been in power when Europe collapsed into anarchy and military dictatorship, rather than the solidly anti-revolutionary George and Pitt.[49] Fox actually welcomed the storming of the Bastille, writing to Richard Fitzpatrick, 'How much the greatest event it is that ever happened in the world! And how much the best!'[50]*

Fox was to be disappointed by the lack of echo in Britain for what was taking place in Paris. The more the French insulted their monarch, the more the British revered theirs, almost as an anti-Gallic reaction; and just as Britain celebrated her King being saved from lunacy, so France underwent a revolution which led to the execution of her own king and shortly afterwards to the collective tragedy known as the Terror which took the lives of 50,000 innocent people.

Although the Revolution Society, a radical organization in London, congratulated the French National Assembly on the fall of the Bastille, most British political opinion was critical of events in France, and was to become increasingly more so as they got more bloody. The Revolution added to the upsurge in the King's popularity, already so noticeable in the summer of 1789. By 1794 caricaturists such as Isaac Cruikshank, in 'John Bull Humbugg'd alias Both Ear'd', were conflating the mythical and actual personifications of Britain in a single image.[51] Whereas 'God Save the King' had only been played in ten formal performances in London theatres between 1745 and 1781, it was played more than ninety times on such occasions between 1786 and 1800; over the following two decades it supplanted 'Rule, Britannia!' to become the established national anthem.[52]

The King and Queen embarked on a 40-mile tour in the West Country on 13 August 1789 that took them through wildly cheering crowds from the Deanery at Exeter to the Robert Adam-designed seat of Lord Boringdon at Saltram House† near Plympton.[53] There were bonfires, fireworks and illuminations along the route. When they finally left Weymouth on 14 September, it was to salutes fired from the seventy-four-gun *Magnificent* and the frigate *Southampton*.

---

* On the day of the fall of the Bastille, the King was signing instruments making the lawyers John Lloyd and John Mitford MP (later the 1st Baron Redesdale) judges in Carmarthen, Pembroke and Cardigan, and considering whether they should be made King's Counsel too (ed. Aspinall, *Later Correspondence* I p. 432).

† Which Nikolaus Pevsner regarded as the most impressive country house in Devon.

Fanny Burney left the royal employ in July 1791, after five years of valuable service to Queen Charlotte, years which have proved even more valuable to historians.* She was able to say goodbye to the Queen, whom she described throughout her diaries as 'kind', 'sweet', 'gracious', spirited and perceptive, but she was too overcome to take her farewell of the King, even though he had come to see her for that purpose.[54] It might well be that no man is a hero to his valet, but on the last day of her service she wrote of George, 'His kindness, his goodness, his benignity, never shall I forget – never think of but with fresh gratitude and reverential affection.'[55]

By mid-October 1789 the French Revolution had already started to devour its own children. Lord Carmarthen, now the 5th Duke of Leeds, wrote to the King to say that the ultra-liberal Duc d'Orléans wished to see him, adding that the Marquis de la Luzerne, the French Ambassador, had 'seemed particularly anxious that Your Majesty should be apprised that the Duke's coming was not in the nature of a flight but with the consent of the French King, and by no means in consequence of any danger arising to the Duke's person from the unsettled situation of affairs in France'.[56] George was unconvinced, telling Leeds that he thought it was more likely to be as a result of 'some personal uneasiness at his own safety'.[57] That such a fear was justified was proved when Orléans was stopped at Boulogne by a mob of fishwives and held in custody for several days by the local magistrates. He nonetheless finally reached London and saw the King at Windsor on 25 October, bringing a message of friendship from his cousin Louis XVI.

Orléans also told Leeds that the King of France wished – perhaps somewhat opportunistically under the circumstances – 'to continue and even improve the system of friendship and good understanding which so happily subsisted at present between the two kingdoms of Britain and France, that it could never be in the interest of them to quarrel and that by coming to a fixed and determined system not only of peace but of intimate and substantial union and friendship, the two kingdoms would not alone derive advantage, but all Europe must gain'.[58] He then made the personally disastrous decision to return to France, where he subsequently changed his name to Philippe Égalité and voted for the execution of Louis XVI, but nevertheless followed his cousin to the scaffold ten months later. This had the effect of wiping out at a stroke of the guillotine's blade the £75,000

---

* Lord Macaulay considered Fanny Burney's account of the King's illness of greater importance to the historian than any equal portion of Pepys or Evelyn (eds. Barrett and Dobson, *Diary and Letters of Madame d'Arblay* VI p. x).

that the Prince of Wales owed Orléans, although it by no means cleared his liabilities.

Another of the King's relations who was heavily in debt was his brother, Henry, Duke of Cumberland, who when he died on 18 September 1790 left his wife Anne destitute. She turned to the Prince of Wales, who asked Pitt to intercede with the King, but George replied that 'after a full consideration of the circumstances of the case, there were no grounds for increasing his offer of £4,000 a year.' The Prince of Wales likened the attempt to help his aunt to trying 'to whip blood out of a post'.[59] Although she sold her late husband's effects and threw 'fashionable card parties' for profit, she found she could not afford to run Cumberland House* in Pall Mall on her income. She attempted to sell the Duke's furniture to the King for £8,450, before he politely pointed out that it belonged to him already.†

For all that he was abstemious and frugal in private, and unwilling to bail out the sister-in-law whose marriage he had opposed, George did not mind spending huge sums on his own palaces, firmly believing that monarchy required grandeur. In the two decades after 1791, during which time Britain was almost constantly at war, he spent £168,000 renovating Windsor Castle, £50,000 on Buckingham House and around half a million pounds on a new gothic castle at Kew. The Office of Works simply took the money for these out of the Treasury.[60] In the 1790s, the King was also spending £14,000 per annum, a quarter of the Privy Purse, on patronage of the arts.[61] The commissioning of James Wyatt at Windsor saw a revolution in architectural style in Britain, in which he was at the forefront.[62] He had reigned long enough to patronize not only neo-classicism but now also the Gothic Revival that followed it. His concentration on architectural detail was extraordinary: when on holiday in Weymouth he would write to Wyatt about the alterations and improvements at Windsor, in areas that a contemporary noted 'had escaped the vigilance of those employed upon the spot ... The localities of the late King's memory are said to have been such as almost to exceed belief.'[63] In September 1804 he sent comments to Wyatt that detailed brackets and door cases at Windsor, the precise place where Handel's bust should go and how to fit a harpsichord into the Music Room.

*

* Which stood where the Royal Automobile Club does today.
† The Duchess died in genteel poverty in Trieste in December 1808. Her high-rolling sister Lady Elizabeth Luttrell, who had once been painted by Gainsborough, had an even unhappier end: having persuaded a bankrupt hairdresser to marry her for £50 in order to escape her gambling debts, she was convicted of pickpocketing in Augsburg and condemned to clean the streets chained to a wheelbarrow, which she did before later committing suicide by poison (Gattey, 'Farmer' George's Black Sheep p. 184).

On Thursday 21 January 1790, a deranged ex-soldier named John Frith threw a stone at the King's coach as he passed Carlton House on his way to open Parliament, which smashed a window but left the King unharmed. Frith was under the delusion that he was St Paul and possessed 'Christ-like powers' (which apparently included being able to throw a stone at a moving coach with remarkable accuracy). Frith believed that Lord Amherst, who had forced him to retire from the army, had sent 'supernatural agents' to whisper in his ear, and that such was the moon's pull towards him that when it was in the south it made it dangerous for him to sleep near large buildings.[64] As with Margaret Nicholson, the King urged leniency. When Cruikshank drew a caricature entitled 'Frith the Madman Hurling Treason at the King', he depicted Edmund Burke as Frith, but in fact the grim reality of the French Revolution was finally causing Burke to appreciate the true value of the monarchy. The Revolution was the most momentous event to befall European monarchy since the English Civil War, and many people in Britain were terrified, especially when the King came into personal danger.

June 1790 saw Pitt win another general election victory, with 340 government seats to 183 for the Opposition, a result that underlined Fox's unpopularity since the regency crisis. Pitt's hand was strengthened both within his government and with respect to the King. The victory was so convincing that the Opposition did not bother to call for a vote on the King's Speech in November. It also strengthened the government's voice abroad, and on 27 July the Duke of Leeds brokered the Treaty of Reichenbach between Prussia and Austria, which lowered the rivalry between the two countries. It was the latest in a series of British foreign policy successes – the demise of the League of Armed Neutrality in 1783 and the success of the League of Princes in 1785 among them – which in the words of the historian Linda Colley 'did much to obliterate the memory of the American defeat and swell George's popularity'.[65]

Considering the ways in which Edmund Burke had opposed the King over the years, George nonetheless treated him with remarkable generosity at a Levee held on 3 February 1791. The previous November Burke had published *Reflections on the Revolution in France*, which in elegant prose denounced everything that had happened there since the fall of the Bastille. ('Read it,' the King told a friend. 'It will do you good! Do you good! Every gentleman should read it.' He himself bought two copies, the second edition of the English edition and its French translation.)[66] Burke's wife Jane proudly reported to her brother-in-law the conversation at the Levee. 'You have been of *use to us all*,' the King told Burke, 'it is a general opinion, is it not so, Lord Stair?'[67] After the 6th Earl of Stair, a former diplomat, had agreed, Burke replied, 'Your Majesty's adopting it, Sir, will make the opinion general.' At this the King added, 'I know it is the general opinion, and I know that there is no man who calls himself a gentleman that must not think himself obliged to you, for you having supported the cause of the gentlemen.' Jane added, 'You know the tone at Court is a whisper, but the King said all this loud, so as to be heard by everyone at Court.' Three months later, James Burges, the Under-Secretary at the Foreign Office, wrote to Burke about his pamphlet *Letter to a Member of the National Assembly*, 'I have this morning had an opportunity of knowing, from the best authority, that His Majesty has perused it with much attention, and that he has expressed very great satisfaction at the whole of it, particularly those parts that related to Rousseau, Mirabeau, and the new organization of the Courts of Justice.'[68]

In a direct reply to Burke's *Reflections*, in March 1791 Thomas Paine published in Paris *The Rights of Man*, which, among other more high-flown political ideas, concentrated upon George's supposed despotism. 'The Revolution in France is certainly a forerunner of other revolutions in Europe,' Paine wrote in a textbook example of sedition. Pitt's government moved successfully to indict him, meaning that he could no longer return to the country he so loathed. He did have a taste of true despotism, however, when the French revolutionaries arrested him in December 1793 and put him in the notorious Luxembourg Prison. He survived that ordeal, however, and by 1797 was plotting a French invasion of Britain, paying for a thousand pairs of boots for French troops out of his book royalties, and proposing a toast that the *tricolore* might float over the Tower of London.[69] Although George spent half an hour reading *Rights of Man* in the Windsor bookshop of Charles Knight, where his morning walk often took him, he did not buy it, and was not offended with Knight for stocking it.[70]

Despite the Revolution, which was still in its pre-Terror phase, George's eighteen-year-old son Augustus, Duke of Sussex, was living in Hyères in the South of France, for his health. His father wrote to him on 8 March 1791 encouraging him to pursue his studies while he was there, and making the wise observation about the pleasure principle that:

> Employment will make you with more pleasure enjoy those of relaxation. There is no greater wisdom than so to economize amusements that they shall continue such during life, which, if too much sought after, naturally must sooner or later become irksome. Besides, if the mind be not constantly in the habit of serious employment it will lose its energy, and those powers a man may have been blessed with will entirely vanish.[71]

Small wonder that as well as all the books that concentrate on his madness, there is also an excellent one entitled *The Wisdom of George III*.[72]

Both the King and Pitt showed considerable wisdom over the two international incidents that followed hard upon one another in the ensuing years, the Nootka Sound* crisis with Spain of May 1789 to June 1791, and the Ochakov† crisis with Russia from March 1791 to January 1792. Either of these essentially petty disagreements could easily have drawn Britain into an unnecessary and irrelevant war with powers that, unlike Revolutionary France, posed no existential threat to Britain. Pitt's rigid concentration on the most important element in Britain's grand strategy – building up the nation's strength to oppose regicide France – was fully supported by George, even though there were a good number of provocations and frustrations along the way, as well as accusations of weakness from the Opposition. The Duke of Leeds' resignation over Ochakov allowed Pitt to replace him with the talented and loyal William Grenville, and Thurlow's opposition over Nootka undermined his standing with George, which was already shaky after his opportunistic behaviour during the regency crisis.

The King told William Grenville that he was 'much affected' by Louis XVI's failure to get further from Paris than Varennes-en-Argonne in his attempt to escape France on 21 June 1791, but Britain avoided either supporting or opposing the moves promoted by Austria and Prussia to free Louis and Marie Antoinette in September.[73] When France declared war against Austria in April 1792 and Prussia in July, after which those countries invaded France, Britain remained neutral. The King and Pitt agreed ideologically with Burke about the evils of the Revolution, but Britain was not about to launch a crusade to try to destroy republicanism in France. She was not under any immediate threat, and was suffering from a period of economic downturn after a series of bad harvests.

On 3 August, Burke published his pamphlet *An Appeal from the New to the Old Whigs*, which acknowledged his split with Charles Fox over the French Revolution and tried to detach moderate Whigs from his former ally, whose opinions he contended were now almost identical to those of Thomas Paine. A copy was sent by Burke to the King via their mutual friend John Douglas, Bishop of Salisbury, who reported that the King wanted Burke to know that he had read it *'with great satisfaction'*.[74] After Burke had had dinner with Bishop Douglas at Windsor, the two men strolled on the Terrace, where the King met them; he gave Burke a gracious reception and they spoke about the plight of Louis XVI.

For all that the King accepted that Britain ought to remain neutral in

---

* On the west coast of Vancouver Island, claimed by Spain under the papal bull of 1493.
   † A fortress on the Black Sea near Odessa, captured by Russia in 1788.

the war, his neutrality unsurprisingly leaned heavily towards the two monarchies. When in April 1792 Charles-Maurice de Talleyrand, the French statesman, proposed visiting London to discuss an alliance, the King told William Grenville that Talleyrand and his fellow emissary had 'no credence', and Grenville should treat them with 'the contempt their characters entitle them to'.[75] The next month he added that 'from the commencement of the Revolution more acts of barbarity have been committed than by the most savage people.'[76]

Fox and his followers profoundly disagreed with this stance, and by April they had established the Association of the Friends of the People, an organization of Whigs openly supportive of the French revolutionaries. Its ranks included parliamentarians such as Charles Grey,* George Tierney, the Earl of Lauderdale, Richard Brinsley Sheridan and Sir Philip Francis. The Association hoped to build on the Economical Reform movement and inspire a public clamour for fundamental constitutional reforms. Already the rising industrial towns were seeing groups of tradesmen, shopkeepers and others joining corresponding societies to exchange radical ideas, and in April 1792 the London Corresponding Society became a public body.

By then, the Sheffield Society for Constitutional Information already claimed 2,000 members, and soon Manchester, Birmingham, Liverpool and Norwich all had similar organizations. Some bodies were able to publish manifestos and propaganda pamphlets numbering a hundred thousand copies. A Revolution Society already existed in Norwich, although it claimed merely to want 'to do away such institutions and imposts' that impeded national efficiency, without specifying exactly which ones it meant.[77] Once moderate parliamentary reformers had abandoned the Society for Constitutional Information owing to its growing radicalism, it was successfully infiltrated by the republican Horne Tooke and other supporters of Paine. Pitt and the government became increasingly concerned that the revolutionary fervour across the Channel was taking seed at home.

The disrespect shown to the King and Queen in popular prints peaked in 1792, with grotesque caricatures drawn by Richard Newton and published by the radical William Holland, depicting them as bourgeois, ignorant and unregal.[78] After the assassination of Gustav III of Sweden in March 1792, Gillray published a cartoon entitled 'Taking Physick', of the royal couple disturbed on their privies by Pitt running in crying, 'Another monarch done over!' and George replying 'What? Shot? What? what? what? Shot! shot! shot!'[79] The Queen was depicted as looking both distraught and ugly. One of the cruellest satirists of George was the West

* Later Lord Howick and later still the 2nd Earl Grey, after whom the tea is named.

Country cleric John Wolcot, who wrote doggerel poetry under the nom de plume Peter Pindar, which made the King out to be mean, haughty, impatient and incompetent. Late in life, Wolcot admitted that in fact the King had been 'an excellently good man, but also a clever man'; he had attacked him because 'That is a matter of mere business ... if I had written against a bad man, though all might have been very true, nobody would have purchased.'[80] It was only after Louis XVI had been guillotined that these caricaturists discovered a new sense of respect.

In response to the publication of the second part of Thomas Paine's *Rights of Man*, the government issued a royal proclamation in the King's name on 21 May 1792, condemning 'tumultuous meetings and seditious writings', although not caricatures. It was written by Pitt but read in draft form by the Opposition leader Portland, and even by Fox. Local magistrates enforced it to differing degrees across the country. While it was clearly an attack on free speech as we would recognize it today, there was no such concept in eighteenth-century England; indeed the First Amendment to the United States Constitution had been adopted only six months earlier. Moreover, in what was tantamount to wartime, Paine's statements on monarchy were plainly seditious, arguing as they did that the hereditary system everywhere produced monarchs 'below the average of human understanding ... one is a tyrant, another an idiot, a third insane ... It requires some talents to be a common mechanic; but to be a king requires only the animal figure of a man – a sort of breathing automaton.'[81] The Prince of Wales delivered his maiden speech in the House of Lords in support of the proclamation, the French Revolution having now drawn him closer to the King, doubtless in the realization that a violent British revolution would depose (and possibly dispatch) him just as quickly as it would his father. The Gordon Riots less than a decade earlier had shown that a London mob was capable of quite as much anarchic viciousness as any Parisian one.

Richard Newton's reaction to the proclamation came in a print in which Pitt was depicted sitting on the King's shoulders while a half-demented George spews out, 'Guards! Encampments! Proclamation! Spies! Spa Fields* Bastile! Bristol Bastile! Birmingham Bastile! Manchester Bastile! Informers! Confinement! Dungeons! Racks! Tortures! No Lenity! No Mercy! No Bribery! Not even Petticoat influence shall prevail!!!'[82] When George Canning became the Under-Secretary for Foreign Affairs later in the war, he gave Gillray a pension of £200 per annum on condition that he stopped caricaturing the royal family, which he accepted.[83]

---

* A place in Islington where radicals sometimes met.

'Criticism and ridicule ultimately strengthened, rather than undermined, the monarchy's position,' argues one historian of the relationship between George and the caricaturists. 'The license with which the satirists were able to treat the royal person actually helped create the image of a monarch who was endearing in his display of human foibles. George increasingly became identified with the bumbling, well-meaning John Bull.'[84] The modern cartoonist Peter Brookes agrees, suggesting that leaving Richard Newton unpunished 'was probably a good move on the monarch's part, because if people were allowed to laugh occasionally at their masters, they do not cut off their heads'.[85]

By 16 May 1792, Pitt was able to announce a £6 million increase in revenues, as the result of his introduction of the Sinking Fund nearly a decade before. The King did not involve himself in the minutiae of Pitt's financial reforms, but he admired what he was doing to promote confidence and prosperity. So when Thurlow in the House of Lords publicly attacked Pitt's plans for a further reduction in the National Debt, and Pitt demanded in mid-June that the King must choose between his Prime Minister and Lord Chancellor, the King felt compelled to agree to Thurlow's dismissal, though it was 'a decision . . . revolting to my feelings'.[86] Thurlow had a short temper, opposed everything and proposed nothing, and even the King admitted that 'the good Chancellor is rather famous for loving delay'.[87]

In a debate on Cabinet responsibility in February 1932, the future British premier Stanley Baldwin expressed his belief that the dismissal of Lord Thurlow, whom he described as 'the last minister to claim that he had a right to the King's ear as Lord Chancellor and Keeper of the King's Conscience',* marked the beginning of the concept of collective Cabinet responsibility. 'There was a very great principle at the back of that struggle,' Baldwin believed.[88] Several other factors had been working in favour of Cabinet responsibility for some time, however, including the growing size and complexity of government, increasing allegiance to parties, the importance of public opinion as expressed through the burgeoning press, Pitt's expectation that government should be conducted through himself as one of the only Cabinet ministers in the Commons, and the King's own ageing and illness. Thurlow's departure left Pitt undisputed master of the Cabinet, the person to whom all the other ministers reported. This was a key moment in the development of the British constitution, when Cabinet ministers started for the first time to regard their colleague the Prime

* A position held by a bishop from William the Conqueror to Henry VIII, and thereafter by the Lord Chancellor.

Minister not just as the leading figure in the government, but also as the person to whom they felt immediately responsible, in place of the King.

The King had already shown his approval of Pitt in December 1791 when he offered him the Order of the Garter, but he selflessly declined it and suggested it go to his elder brother, the 2nd Earl of Chatham instead. When Lord North died the following August, the King was able to award Pitt a fine gift, the lord wardenship of the Cinque Ports, which came with Walmer Castle and £4,000 per annum. It was the first emolument that Pitt had ever accepted from the King, a full nine years after becoming Prime Minister. 'I never love throwing favours on enemies,' the King told Dundas that September, 'and love rewarding steady friends.'[89]

On 10 August 1792, a mob stormed the Tuileries Palace in Paris; three days later Louis XVI was sent to the Temple prison. Lord Gower, the British Ambassador, was immediately recalled. The September Massacres in Parisian prisons between 2 and 6 September finally persuaded Charles Fox to criticize the French Revolution, more than three years too late in the opinion of the King and Burke. The French victory over the Prussians, Austrians, Holy Roman Empire and French royalist armies led by the Duke of Brunswick at the battle of Valmy on 20 September turned the tide of the war, and on 22 October Frankfurt fell to the French Army. General Dumouriez subsequently invaded what is now Belgium on 3 November, defeated the Austrians at the battle of Jemappes three days later and marched into Brussels on the 13th. In what almost amounted to a Blitzkrieg victory, by 2 December the victorious French had seized control of all the Channel ports, as well as Antwerp and Namur.

The threat to Britain was now palpable. On 19 November, the French Convention (legislature) proclaimed universal revolution in all lands and Pitt's ministry waited apprehensively to see how many Britons would heed its call. Within a fortnight the *Sheffield Register* had recorded a public procession to celebrate Valmy, and poster-sized broadsheets of the London Corresponding Society were appearing on walls and dockyards demanding the immediate 'free and equal representation of the People in Parliament'. They warned that if George III opposed their demands he would suffer the same fate as Charles I, stating that 'he had never been shaved (pruned or cut off) so unpleasantly at last!' along with a line from Ecclesiasticus, 'Let them perish that oppress the people.'[90]

On 11 December the King of France was arraigned before the Convention. Thomas Paine wrote a pamphlet entitled *On the Propriety of Bringing Louis XVI to Trial*, which pointed out that such a court case might reveal how much money George had paid to the Landgrave of Hesse – whom he described as 'a detestable dealer in human flesh' – for his auxiliaries during the American War of Independence.[91] It was hardly a state secret that the British had paid for Hessian auxiliaries in a war that had ended nearly a decade earlier, but the Hessians had been an important element in Brunswick's army at Valmy, doubly earning Paine's vitriol.

By early January 1793 it was expected that the French government, effectively the Committee of Public Safety, dominated by the ultra-radical Jacobin faction, would soon declare war against Britain. On the 6th of that month the King wrote to the Earl of Chatham suggesting it was 'the intention of the faction in France to come to acts of hostility', adding, 'I confess I am of opinion that in the actual state of things it seems the most desirable conclusion of the present crisis.'[92] The official news of the execution of Louis XVI on 21 January reached London on the morning of the 23rd. The King had already told Pitt that once it had arrived he would call an emergency Privy Council to order the expulsion of the French Ambassador, the Marquis de Chauvelin. He also cancelled his Drawing Room at St James's Palace. Despite Louis XVI having been the ruler of Britain's main enemy, George felt genuine horror at the news. It also seemed to have greatly affected the Prince of Wales, who wrote to his father at 6.30 that evening, thanking him for giving him the colonelcy of the 10th Dragoons and adding, probably with more sincerity than usual,

> Allow me, Sir, to seize this earliest opportunity of pouring forth at your feet the effusions though but faintly expressed of a truly grateful heart . . . and permit me to assure Your Majesty that in whatever situation of life you may deign to place me, there is no one existing who, both in heart and mind, can be more truly or more sincerely devoted and attached to your sacred person than myself.[93]

The death of Louis XVI had a powerful effect on British public opinion, reminding people of what they had long taken for granted about their own King and leading to a renewed surge of affection for him. A good deal of Pittite and establishment propaganda used the King's image and attributes, especially what one historian has listed as his 'accessibility, paternal benevolence, domestic virtues, and a responsible custodial role in politics', which seemed appealing to a nation staring in horror at the now literally headless state across the Channel.[94] Sermons emphasized these virtues, and 'Church and King' clubs and societies sprouted up to counter radical ones, putting out loyal prints and pamphlets of their own, eventually on a massive scale. The concepts of the King as the father of his people, a cornerstone of the constitution and a guarantor of social stability were all the more powerful because they were fundamentally true. Few but the Paineite radicals failed to contrast Britain's constitutional monarchy favourably with that of Jacobin despotism.

The French Convention declared war on Britain on 1 February 1793, arresting British subjects and seizing British ships that were still in French ports. The government had not wanted war, but all the major decision makers – including the King, Pitt, Dundas and William Grenville – saw French control of Belgium as a danger to national security to be prevented at all costs. The King told Grenville that the French declaration was 'highly agreeable . . . as the means adopted seems well calculated to rouse such a spirit in this country that I trust will curb the insolence of these despots and be a means of restoring some degree of order to that unprincipled country, whose aim at present is to destroy the foundations of every civilized state'.[95]

Just as he had been when he recovered from illness, George was now again the subject of an outpouring of patriotic support. The French regicide and declaration of war; the increasing savagery of the Revolution from the September Massacres to the Terror; George's own homeliness and piety; and his obvious commitment to victory: together served to help Britons forget his relative unpopularity in the early part of his reign and see him as the Patriot King. Furthermore, his weaknesses had turned into strengths: his carefulness with money that had once been portrayed as meanness now looked patriotically frugal; his insistence on Pitt as Prime Minister and refusal to countenance Fox seemed to be inspired political foresight; and his piety contrasted well with France's abolition of Christianity. The same boring, penny-pinching, bourgeois, pious monarch that the caricaturists had so despised and satirized in the 1760s, 1770s and 1780s now looked decent, patriotic and dependable.

'His Majesty relies with confidence on the firm and effectual support of the House of Commons,' the government proclaimed on 12 February, 'and on the zealous exertions of a brave and loyal people in prosecuting a just and necessary war.'[96] In his name, it asked MPs to oppose the 'aggrandizement and ambition on the part of France which would be at all times dangerous to the general interests of Europe, but are peculiarly so when connected with the propagation of principles which lead to the violation of the most sacred duties and are utterly subversive of the peace and order of all civil society'.[97] The support of the Commons would be crucial during the war; for all that Pitt's Sinking Fund had helped to redeem a large part of the National Debt by 1793, the government still had to borrow £4 million immediately, issue a further £5 million in bonds and find £800,000 for foreign subsidies.[98] (In 1795 Prussia alone was to drain £1.2 million out of the Treasury.) As well as public money, there would be private calls on wealth; on 17 April the King appealed for public generosity to help French Roman Catholic priests, 'refugees in our British dominions', who

44. George III in military uniform during the Napoleonic Wars, painted by William Beechey in 1799.

45. A satirical print of the King and Queen dressed as a farmer and his wife watching in astonishment as two geese suck a cow's udder. The King's interest in progressive agriculture, on which he wrote well-informed articles for journals, earned him the nickname 'Farmer George'.

46. Gillray's satirical depiction of the attack on George's coach on his way to open Parliament on 29 October 1795. Here it is Charles Fox, Richard Sheridan and the radical Whigs who make up the mob stoning the coach.

47. The greatest statesman and orator of the era and saviour of his country: William Pitt the Younger. His relationship with George was mutually supportive and respectful but never intimate.

48. The King on holiday at Weymouth in 1797, depicted by James Gillray. He visited fourteen times between 1789 and 1805.

49. George's bathing machine at Weymouth continued in use until 1916. A string quartet played from an adjoining machine as the King went swimming.

50. George taking the waters at Cheltenham, thought to be the last likeness drawn of him from life.

51. James Gillray contrasting George as the King of Brobdingnag and Napoleon as Gulliver, in 1803. When George describes Napoleon as 'one of the most pernicious little odious reptiles that nature ever suffered to crawl upon the surface of the earth', he was not, from the British perspective, being satirical.

The KING of BROBDINGNAG, and GULLIVER.

52. Gillray depicting George's dismissal of Lord Grenville's 'Broad-Bottomed' ministry in 1807 over the issue of Catholic emancipation, which George believed contradicted his Coronation Oath.

53. William Grenville was the last Whig Prime Minister for over twenty years.

54. The 3rd Duke of Portland moved ideologically towards George during his long career in politics.

55. Spencer Perceval, the last Prime Minister George appointed, was assassinated in 1812.

56. Robert Jenkinson, 2nd Earl of Liverpool, became the longest-serving Prime Minister in British history.

57. The Royal Family promenading on the North Terrace of Windsor Castle, in 1783.

58. Massive nationwide celebrations for the King's Golden Jubilee on 25 October 1809 took place days before George succumbed to his final, decade-long bout of lunacy.

59. Deaf, blind, suffering from manic depression and latterly also senility, and unvisited by his family, the King lived at Windsor for ten long years before his death.

were fleeing what he described as 'the dreadful persecutions of the French clergy'.[99]

The King took a close interest in everything military during the war, from the appointment of commanders-in-chief to the size of war pensions. In general, he supported the classic military strategy of limiting Britain's Continental commitment, concentrating instead on naval blockades and the use of expeditionary forces to harry the enemy. It was hoped that concurrent attacks in the West Indies would cripple France economically and hasten her defeat. 'No one can conceive to what an expense any inland motion will arise,' he wrote of the plan to attack Toulon in late 1793, an operation that nearly led to disaster for the Royal Navy at the hands of a newly promoted twenty-four-year-old artillery general, Napoleon Bonaparte. George supported aiding the French royalists only if it did not weaken the expeditionary force that was being sent to Flanders under Prince Frederick, Duke of York. There was jubilation in Britain when Prince Frederick's two-month siege of Valenciennes ended with its surrender in late July. George boasted to Dundas that in one engagement his son Ernest had 'saved his life by killing a French chasseur and fairly cutting his way through the enemy'.[100]

'Our line seems perfectly clear,' the King wrote to Grenville in June. 'The war being once begun, the expense already entertained, France must be greatly circumscribed before we can talk of any means of treating with that dangerous and faithless nation.'[101] He was making it obvious from the outset that he would not support any negotiated peace within the foreseeable future, a position he would steadfastly maintain. 'Now is the hour to humble France,' he told Dundas after he had heard of the capture of Tobago in April 1793, 'for nothing but her being disabled from disturbing other countries, whatever government may be established there, will keep her quiet.'[102] The next day he expressed his hope that other Caribbean islands might fall, telling Chatham, the First Lord of the Admiralty, 'Now we have been obliged to take part in the war, I trust it will not be concluded till we have thoroughly reduced the power of France.'[103]

Despite such clear and uncompromising rhetoric from the King, Prince William, Duke of Clarence, embarrassed both his father and the government by making a speech in the House of Lords in favour of opening peace negotiations. He had served in the navy creditably during the American war, which as well as coarsening his language earned him the nickname 'the Sailor King' when he succeeded to the throne in 1830. Apart from constantly being in debt and contracting venereal disease in 1788, he had been no great worry to his father and had been loving and supportive during the King's illness. In 1790 he had left the Royal Navy and lived quietly at Clarence Lodge and then Bushy House with his mistress, the actress Dorothea 'Dora' Jordan and their ten children, which by the late 1790s the King, mellowing with years, had learned to accept. 'Hey, hey, what's this,' he joked to his son. 'You keep a mistress they say.' 'Yes, sir.' 'Well, well; how much do you give her?' 'One thousand a year, sir.' 'A thousand, a thousand; too much, too much! Five hundred quite enough! Quite enough!'[104] By September 1797, Prince William had managed to rack up debts of £46,543, which his father dutifully helped to pay down, although they were not entirely paid off until William's accession more than three decades later.

Attacking the government over the war was of course unacceptable for a royal duke, and one minister called it 'a matter of scandal and discomfort'.[105] Clarence evidently took no heed, and three years later proposed himself to the King (unsuccessfully) for the post of First Lord of the Admiralty.[106]

On the evening of Saturday 10 August 1793, the King heard from Lord Grenville that Marie Antoinette might be put on trial for her life, although the Foreign Secretary said that he hoped her value as a hostage might prevent her execution. 'I am sorry though not surprised that the cruel wretches who have possessed themselves of power in France have ordered the unhappy Queen Mother to be tried,' the King replied the next morning, 'the result of which can be most easily conceived. To a man who looks on the conduct of those savages with the rational eye Lord Grenville does, it must be equal surprise as with me what lengths Divine Providence will permit them to go.'[107] When the news arrived of her guillotining, the King and Queen cancelled a Drawing Room that day and their trip to Covent Garden in the evening. With the rest of the Court, they wore black in mourning.

The King now threw himself into much the same anti-invasion measures that had occupied him in 1779. In August 1793 the *True Briton* newspaper described a visit he and Charlotte had paid to the militia and the way in which they, 'in sitting down at a table with the soldiers of a regiment to witness the happiness which their bounty diffused, must excite the warmest affection of every heart. The King, during the repast, carried several of the soldiers' children in his arms to the Queen, by whom they were tenderly caressed.'[108] The contrast with the situation in France, and the condition of the French royal family, could not have been more stark.

24

The Whale and the Wolf

May 1794–December 1798

If it was the King's 'obstinacy' which lost us America, has not the same quality of the royal character since made us ample amends? If his pertinacity of error afflicted us with misfortunes from 1775 to 1783, was not his inflexibility in a good cause, from 1793 to the hour when he dropped the reins of government, a memorable instrument of our salvation?[1]

The Times obituary of George III, 1820

General Joseph Souham's victory over Prince Frederick, Duke of York, at the battle of Tourcoing (on what is today the Franco-Belgian border) on 18 May 1794 hurt George personally. Any hopes that the King entertained at the time of the fall of Valenciennes that his son might be another successful Hanoverian conqueror, like his grandfather George II, were dashed. Luckily, the news of the defeat had not arrived when on 19 May the Queen's actual (as distinct from official) birthday was celebrated at Buckingham House. Twenty-eight different dishes were served at the dinner, including *soupe à la Reine*, plovers' eggs, and ornamented Westphalian ham. It went on until four o'clock in the morning, and although the Queen stayed in bed late the next day, the King was out riding by 9.30 a.m.

George had given up stag and hare hunting in 1789, although he rode with the harriers until he started losing his eyesight in 1805. He had hunted stags regularly and bravely, suffering two major falls, one near Salt Hill in Berkshire, and another when his horse threw him into a millpond near Blackwater in Hampshire, whereupon he 'disappeared under the water'.[2] On the latter occasion, his equerry Major William Price 'instantly dashed in, and laying hold of the King, supported him, not however before he had swallowed some water and was become a little confused'. The King nonetheless remounted and rode home. It was not unusual for him to ride for 30 or 40 miles while chasing stags.

Coming back from a stag hunt one evening, the King narrowly missed being held up by highwaymen. 'His Majesty took a post-chaise and four from Uxbridge after a long and late chase,' recalled Colonel Greville years later. 'In the coach was His Majesty, the Duke of Cambridge, his [Hanoverian] aide de camp [the Baron von] Wangenheim, and myself. Another carriage with some of the sportsmen followed us soon after from Uxbridge, and was stopped by highwaymen on Langley Brown* a very short time after His Majesty had passed it.'[3] The King would sensibly hide his favourite watches when travelling by coach, even on journeys as short as the 15 miles from Windsor to Bagshot.

On 1 June 1794, Earl Howe won a decisive victory at Ushant off the Brittany coast known in Britain as the Glorious First of June, in which six French ships-of-the-line were captured and one sunk. The King attended the thanksgiving service at St Paul's Cathedral. When he suggested that Howe be awarded one of the vacant Orders of the Garter, Pitt said that he wanted the Duke of Portland to join his ministry and needed to offer it to him instead. In the haggling that followed, it was arranged that Howe, who had served as First Lord of the Admiralty for five and a half years, be offered a marquessate and the next available Garter, with the currently vacant one going to Portland. In the event, Howe declined the marquessate but accepted the Garter in 1797. Portland brought his faction, which supported a crackdown on extreme radicalism and revolutionary activity, into Pitt's ministry in July.[4]

By then the King had unexpectedly added a European kingdom to his empire, when on 17 June 1794 the Corsicans recognized him as their sovereign. Since the execution of Louis XVI, the island's leading political figures Pasquale Paoli and Carlo Pozzo di Borgo had broken from France with the help of a Royal Navy fleet under Admiral Samuel Hood. The island adopted a democratic constitution with a unicameral legislature that was considered extremely enlightened for its day. 'Sir Gilbert Elliot has created a new kingdom in this era of republicanism,' Lord Auckland, Elliot's son-in-law, wrote to a friend the following month about the new Viceroy. 'Whether it will be more profitable to King George than it was to King Theodore is another question.'[5] The difference proved marginal: the German adventurer Theodore von Neuhoff had been King of Corsica for just eight months in 1736; when Britain evacuated the island for strategic reasons in October 1796, George III's reign had lasted twenty-eight months.

At 4.30 a.m. on 15 August 1794, the King, Queen and their youngest

---

* Langley Park, about halfway on the 9-mile journey from Uxbridge to Windsor.

children set off for Weymouth in four postcoaches-and-four (that is, with sixteen horses in all). They breakfasted at Hertford Bridge, Hampshire, and were cheered by townspeople as they went through Bagshot, Basingstoke, Andover and Dorchester. They were also applauded while they lunched at the Bishop's Palace at Salisbury. On the way from Salisbury, Harnham Hill was covered with well-wishers too. They reached Weymouth at 4.12 p.m., having covered 113 miles in less than twelve hours, including two stops. The Royal Dragoons and the Buckinghamshire Militia paraded for them and the battery of the Volunteer Weymouth Artillery Company fired a salute, as did *Southampton* out in the harbour. The King and Colonels Greville and Goldsworthy dined in their travelling boots, 'a liberty which we took only by command, and by [the] example which His Majesty set us'.[6]

Over the next six weeks of holiday before their return to Windsor on 27 September, the King took the spring water at Upwey; rode to the ancient mound of Maiden Castle; played cards most nights; walked almost daily on the Esplanade; went to church a good deal (spotting a recycled sermon from a book he had been reading to the princesses that same morning); bathed in the sea for an hour between 6 a.m. and 8 a.m. on about half the days; visited several sheep farms; heard 'God Save the King' played innumerable times by some shockingly bad bands; attended the manoeuvres of volunteer yeomanry corps and various militia units; sailed along the coast several times in *Southampton* and her small squadron (noticing on one occasion that its commanding officer was 'incapable of duty from intoxication'); visited two pink-eyed albino brothers from Chamonix in their caravan; walked on the sands of Chesil Beach (then known as the Chisel Bank and Pebbly Beach); and watched several 'very tolerably acted' plays at Weymouth's Theatre Royal, including the great comic actor John Quick reprising the role of Tony Lumpkin in Oliver Goldsmith's *She Stoops to Conquer*, which Quick had played in the first performances twenty-one years earlier.

At other times in the holiday he also witnessed seven French prisoners of war being put ashore by the privateer *Resolution*; used a telescope to view the coastline eastwards as far as the Isle of Wight and westwards across Lyme Bay to Devon; lunched at the Portland Arms where Greville noted that 'The wine was not delivered out with a sparing hand' and as a result Lords Walsingham* and Clermont had 'begun to feel the powerful effects of conviviality'; watched a convoy of sixteen East India ships and

---

* After an equally convivial dinner with the Prince of Wales the same night, Greville noted, 'Poor Lord Walsingham totally overcome by it. They left him, stripped and laid out on a couch aboard the *Minotaur*, under the care of Admiral MacBride, who promises to return him safe to his friends on shore tomorrow' (ed. Bladon, *Diaries of Robert Fulke Greville* p. 305).

its Royal Navy escorts sail up the Channel; walked around Lulworth Cove; received local people at the Weymouth Assembly Rooms; visited the architecturally innovative 'commodious and airy' dragoons' barracks at Poundbury Camp in Dorsetshire; celebrated his wedding anniversary with a ball at Gloucester Lodge; held discussions with local farmers about the optimum amount of manure to use per acre; called only one Privy Council and held only one audience with a foreign envoy (the Spanish Ambassador, Bernardo del Campo); saw 'a very remarkable goose' on the Esplanade that followed its master like a dog, flying after him if the pace got too quick and waiting patiently when he stopped; but only went hunting thrice, hare coursing with the 4th Earl Poulett's pack of hounds.[7]

Although the King was not well travelled within his kingdoms, he and the Queen enjoyed visiting homeowners at their country seats, particularly in the West Country, and by the end of the reign these had included the Marquess of Bath at Longleat (where 17,000 people came to see them and George planted an oak tree that still stands today), Lord Digby at Sherborne Castle, Lord Mount Edgcumbe at Cotehele (who was raised to an earldom during the visit), Lord Dorchester at Milton Abbey, the Earl of Morley at Saltram House, George Rose at Cuffnells, the Earl of Ilchester at Redlynch and the owners of Croome, Paultons,* Northerwood Lodge, Carne House, Lulworth Castle and Stourhead.[8] They enjoyed the history and architecture of these houses, as well as the chance to honour the hosts, present themselves to local people and, in the King's case at least, inspect the livestock on the home farms.

While riding near the village of Monkton in Kent on 21 August, the King reportedly saw a peasant woman out pushing a wheelbarrow containing three babies – two of them her own, the other a cousin's – returning home after a hard, hot day 'gleaning† in the fields'.[9] He stopped to talk to her, whereupon her cousin arrived carrying a large bundle of wheat on her head. He gave the women a guinea, and 'they resumed their journey with the greatest cheerfulness' (a guinea was about three weeks' earnings for a female agricultural worker). On another occasion he walked alongside a farmer driving sheep, and discussed land and livestock prices with him. The man asked if he had seen the King, observing, 'Our neighbours say he's a good sort of man, but dresses very plain,' to which the King replied, 'Aye, as plain as you see me now.'[10]

On Saturday 13 September there was a full-blown invasion scare at Weymouth, with warning signals fired from the *Southampton* and rumours

---

* Today the home of Peppa Pig World.
† 'Glean': 'Gather what the reapers of the harvest leave behind' (*Johnson's Dictionary*).

of four 'strange ships' on their way. The town guard and local militia were assembled, the land-based signal gun fired and the naval squadron beat to quarters, to stand ready for a French attack. A cannon was even dragged 'with much alacrity' through the streets to defend the entrance of the town from Portland Sands. 'Nothing could be more cool and collected than His Majesty during this time,' recorded Greville in his diary, as the King approved the troop deployments and then went to the Assembly Rooms to take the waters.[11] The alarm turned out to have stemmed from miscommunication from Sir James Saumarez's fleet returning from a raid on Cherbourg. Two weeks later there was a scare of a different kind, when the Queen's diary recorded 'news of a plot being discovered against the [King's] life which was to be effected by a poisoned arrow'.[12] In fact it was more of a dart, to be fired from an airgun, but no less potentially lethal for that, and members of the London Corresponding Society seem to have been implicated.[13]

Although Britain joined the Alliance of St Petersburg with Russia and Austria on 28 September, by October the military situation on the Continent looked extremely bleak. The French were on the Rhine and also threatening Holland, leading to discussions in London over strategy, especially how to get the German powers to coalesce more effectively. Lord Auckland believed that the Continent, and thus Hanover, should be abandoned altogether, and Britain ought to concentrate on fighting solely a naval war. Earl Fitzwilliam and the Portland Whigs in the ministry wanted a strategy based on supporting the French émigrés. The King preferred to attack France from three directions, a plan which was not reliant on Prussia.[14] Pitt and Grenville agreed with the King that France needed to be distracted from attacking Holland by encirclement from Austria, Spain and Sardinia, in concert with French royalist émigré risings in her eastern and north-western provinces. They accepted that Prussia and the other German powers (besides Hanover) could no longer be relied upon, and this was proved correct on 25 October when the Prussians withdrew from the war altogether.

In November, the Cabinet respectfully advised the recall of the thirty-one-year-old Duke of York from the Continental campaign, where he had been unsuccessful, although on his return in February the King promoted him to the rank of field marshal. Variously calling Prince Frederick 'my dearest son' and 'my valuable second son', his favouritism extended to blaming Britain's coalition partners Holland and Austria for the defeat in Flanders, forgiving the Duke for his opportunism during his 1788–9 malady and generally turning a blind eye to his gambling away the Osnabrück bishopric revenues, as well as the generous income of £40,000 per annum he had received upon marrying Frederica, the Princess Royal of Prussia, in 1791.[15]

The King sent Lord Grenville a memorandum on 1 December informing him that the Allies needed to learn from the new French strategy and tactics, and to try to keep Austria in the war through subsidies. 'To foresee evils is the lot of few,' he wrote, 'to profit by experience the advantage of all who have any claim to sense.'[16] How far this was a conscious reflection on the course of the war in America is impossible to say.

In fact much of the French success was owed to a strategy it could adopt only because of the *levée en masse*, the mobilization of virtually its entire adult male population, which was not something that Britain was able to do in the eighteenth (or nineteenth) century. Britain therefore continued to conduct a succession of small amphibious attacks for the next fourteen years rather in the manner of Pitt the Elder's 'descents' during the Seven Years War, before landing a serious expeditionary force in the Iberian peninsula, first under Sir John Moore and later Sir Arthur Wellesley. Yet it was unlikely that even a much larger force, under a better commander than the Duke of York, would have enjoyed much success in Holland, where the French General Charles Pichegru was received with acclaim upon entering Amsterdam on 19 January 1795.

The first Catholic Relief Act of 1778 had been followed up by British legislation in 1791 that allowed British Catholics to practise their religion without penalty. Similar legislation had been passed in Ireland in 1778 and 1782, and in 1793 the Protestant Parliament in Dublin passed the Irish Catholic Relief Act, granting the rights to hold certain civil offices and military ranks, sit on juries, vote in elections on the same property basis as Protestants and attend Trinity College, Dublin. The King personally welcomed a deputation of Irish Catholics, whereupon £2,000 was raised for a statue of him in Dublin.

In mid-December 1794 the 4th Earl Fitzwilliam, a Portland Whig and Lord Rockingham's nephew who had broken with the Foxite Whigs over the French Revolution, accepted the viceroyalty of Ireland, despite his belief (not shared by the King) that Catholic emancipation was the best way of binding the Irish peasantry to Britain, and thus obviating the danger of a French invasion. Fitzwilliam had inherited his uncle Rockingham's estates, and was one of the richest men in Britain. He had been offered the post in August when he had not told Pitt or Portland of his plans, but on arriving in Ireland he dismissed several senior Protestant office holders, known as the Dublin Castle Gang, who remonstrated with Pitt. Supported by Burke, Fitzwilliam then raised Catholic expectations of further concessions, supporting Henry Grattan's Bill in the Dublin Parliament for further emancipation beyond the 1793 Act.

Although the King believed profoundly in religious liberty and toleration, he did not believe in religious equality, and expressed his 'greatest astonishment' to Pitt about Fitzwilliam's behaviour.[17] He instanced Germany, where all religions were permitted, 'yet each respective state has but one Church establishment . . . and those holding any civil employment must be conformists. Court officials and military commissions may be held also by persons of either of the other persuasions, but the number of such is very small.'[18] Any larger, he was implying, and there might be Protestant–Catholic discord in the government, which historically had led to problems, in England as well as Ireland.

The King was angry that Fitzwilliam was actively 'overturning the fabric that the wisdom of our forefathers esteemed necessary' and 'after no longer [a] stay than three weeks in Ireland, venturing to condemn the labour of the ages' – by which George essentially meant that of his hero, William III, who had established the Protestant Succession in Britain and entrenched the Protestant Ascendancy in Ireland. Phrases about the wisdom of our forefathers and the labour of the ages were profoundly Burkean and could have been lifted from the *Reflections on the Revolution in France*, even though Burke himself – who died in July 1797 – was an adviser and supporter of Fitzwilliam.

In the light of the traumatic later events, it is worth noting that the King, who had consulted Lord Chief Justice Kenyon about the Coronation Oath, explicitly warned Pitt that 'the subject is beyond the decision of any Cabinet of ministers . . . without previous concert with the leading men of every order in the state.'[19] If Pitt wanted Catholics to sit in the Dublin or Westminster Parliaments, the King was saying, he would need to find far broader support than just the Pittites in Cabinet and the Rockinghamite Whigs, not least among churchmen. Such a reform needed to be a national rather than merely factional change.

Fitzwilliam's viceroyalty ended on 25 March 1795, after he had spent only seven weeks there. The resultant crisis rocked the Pitt ministry, and by 1797 the Society of United Irishmen paramilitary organization, which wanted radical parliamentary reform, had around 150,000 members. Religious tension was rising and there was attendant agrarian crime. Fitzwilliam was succeeded by the 2nd Earl Camden, son of the Chathamite judge, who pursued a pacification policy which confiscated 50,000 muskets and 70,000 pikes from potential rebels, quantities of arms which implied that a full-scale uprising was in the air.

*

At the end of 1794, Prussia and Spain had opened separate negotiations for peace with France, but the Royal Navy had seized the Seychelles, Martinique, St Lucia and Guadeloupe (although the last was later recaptured). Ceylon was also taken in February 1796. In his speech opening Parliament on 30 December 1794, the King recommended 'a vigorous prosecution of the just and necessary war in which we are engaged'. He described the struggle in Manichean terms, calling for 'the deliverance of Europe from the greatest danger with which it has been threatened since the establishment of civilized society'.[20] The next day Pitt's great friend William Wilberforce moved an amendment to the King's Speech advocating the negotiation of peace with France on 'just and reasonable terms', and the King cut him at the next Levee he attended. George did not believe any peace with regicides would last, but would only 'place us in the most unpleasant situation of an armed neutrality' and might necessitate the return of valuable West Indian gains.[21] Although some thought George a reactionary for his opposition to peace, these were powerful arguments.

A bad harvest in 1795 was to trigger a considerable downturn in the economy, leading to bread riots in Coventry, Nottingham, Birmingham and elsewhere. The result, perhaps predictably, was that the war became increasingly unpopular, and no number of strategic victories on faraway islands would prove a satisfactory substitute for food in empty British stomachs. 'The King has also given orders', the Queen told the Prince of Wales, referring to one of the royal economy drives at Windsor, 'to have no other bread served to the household and even to his own table than brown bread, and it is hoped that this will encourage others to do the same.'[22] George also experimented with potato bread, 'which proves to be remarkably good'. Smart London society ridiculed his frugality, but it was popular with the people, and foreigners noted that the King lived on a far less grand scale than much of the nobility, and of course far less than his eldest son.

The appointment of the Duke of York as Commander-in-Chief of the British Army in February 1795 seemed at the time like the typical nepotism of the day, especially in light of his defeat at Tourcoing, but in fact Prince Frederick had turned out to be one of the greatest administrators in the history of the British Army, introducing professional, merit-based training and a new promotions structure. 'No one man did more to improve the army than York,' writes the military historian Richard Glover, 'yet there are few of whom historical judgement has been more gross.'[23] (Today, York is principally remembered in the nursery rhyme in which he marches 10,000 men up and then down a hill.)

Just as France had learned from the Seven Years War, so Britain learned lessons from her defeat in the American War of Independence. When war broke out against Revolutionary France in 1793, there was a Commander-in-Chief in charge of the forces, while the Secretary at War concentrated on finances and administration. Strategy resided in the hands of an actively engaged Prime Minister surrounded by a group of equally energetic service ministers.

After the experience with the American Loyalists, far less reliance was placed on local groups such as the French and Dutch royalists. Light-infantry tactics had been advanced significantly as a result of what had been learned in America, and the logistics of supply over long distances also improved. Ten years of neglect of discipline and training, political interference in officer selections and a failed recruitment policy were tackled. By the start of the Peninsular War in 1808, the British Army had been transformed from one of the least to one of the most feared of France's enemies. George played a central role in this transformation by supporting his son's reforms; indeed, so entrenched was reaction in the War Office that it had taken a royal duke supported by a monarch to overcome it.[24]

Prince Frederick's promotion prompted his elder brother the Prince of Wales, who had no military experience whatsoever, to demand from Henry Dundas, now Secretary at War, that he be made a lieutenant-general or even a full general. He complained on 1 March 1795 that his lack of rank was 'a stigma . . . too heavy to be any longer endured' and one he would 'no further suffer in silence'.[25] He suggested somewhat fancifully to the King that they could fight battles together, like Edward III and the Black Prince at the battle of Crécy. The King replied to this on the Prince's wedding day on 8 April, patiently explaining that while his younger sons' lives could be risked doing their military duty, 'You are born into a more difficult one, and which I shall be most happy if I find you seriously turn your thoughts to; the happiness of millions depend on it as well as your own.'[26] Disappointed, the Prince applied himself instead to designing uniforms for his own 10th Prince of Wales' Own Regiment of light dragoons, which included leopard-skin sabretaches and oversized gold epaulettes.[27]

The Prince of Wales had travelled to visit his parents at Weymouth on 23 August 1794, to tell them that he had written to Mrs Fitzherbert to inform her that their nine-year 'marriage' was over and he was now ready to wed legally. He needed to: by that October his debts would be approaching £550,000.* Parliament had already paid off half a million pounds of his debts over the years, and he was now asking for another half-million, at a time when Pitt was having to consider introducing a tax on incomes for the first time in British history. In return for this vast bail-out, the Prince

---

* Nearly £69 million in today's money.

told his parents, he was willing to undergo marriage to his first cousin Princess Caroline of Brunswick, the daughter of the King's elder sister Augusta. The King was happy, telling him that 'It was the only proper alliance,' but the Queen was not, having heard that Caroline was not 'well behaved'.[28] She was quite right about that.

By the following year the Prince's debts had somehow ballooned to £630,000, and bankers would now no longer make loans even to the heir apparent.[29] Pitt proposed that the Prince's annual income increase from £72,000 to £121,000 upon his marriage, with a one-off payment of £77,000, nominally for 'wedding expenses' but in practice to pay the most insistent creditors. Pitt also created a sinking-fund scheme intended to deal with the Prince's debts over the next twenty-seven years. This measure was something he could not bury in the public accounts or otherwise disguise, and there was considerable unrest over it among the government's backbenchers at a time when an infantryman was paid a shilling a day (£18 five shillings a year).

The first time that Princess Caroline of Brunswick met her future husband was on 5 April 1795 at the apartment of Prince Ernest, Duke of Cumberland, at St James's Palace, where she was lodging before the wedding three days later. The Prince of Wales has been described by a royal biographer as 'corpulent ... sentimental, self-indulgent. Petulant and easily led. He was, above all, a dandy ... and it was this dandyism which was responsible for his instant repulsion at the sight of his intended bride.'[30] Unfortunately, Caroline had not properly attended to her *toilette de propreté* when the couple embraced for the first time, and James Harris, Lord Malmesbury, a diplomat who had been sent to Brunswick to escort the Princess to England, recorded that the Prince 'said barely one word, turned round, retired to a distant part of the apartment, and, calling me to him, said, "Harris, I am not well; pray get me a glass of brandy."'[31] For her part, Caroline said that her betrothed was very fat, and not at all like his portraits.

The wedding three days later at the Chapel Royal at St James's Palace scarcely went better. 'What is the matter, my Prince?' Caroline asked her husband more than once in French. 'You have such a sad face on.'[32] The matter was that he was drunk, and as she later recalled, 'Judge what it was to have a drunken husband on one's wedding day, and one who passed the greatest part of his bridal night under the grate, where he fell, and where I left him.'[33] It has been described by Sarah Bradford as 'The most famously disastrous marriage night on record.'[34] Caroline might have been coarse, noisome, pleasure-seeking and money-grubbing, but she was a paragon compared to her husband. Miraculously, they fulfilled Parliament's needs by conceiving a child in the three weeks during which they cohabited after the wedding. The birth of Princess Charlotte of Wales on 7 January 1796 was fortuitous, as her parents almost certainly had sex only once.

The King was delighted with his granddaughter Charlotte, drank her health, ordered his equerries to bumper to the same and called her 'his little beauty'. Princess Elizabeth wrote two days after the birth, 'He says there never was so perfect a little creature and everybody here was delighted to see him in such ecstasies of joy.'[35] Three days after the birth the Prince of Wales altered his will to leave everything he owned to 'my wife, the wife of my heart and soul', Maria Fitzherbert.[36] A month later, despite the extra money from Parliament, he was reduced to begging the King to stop the bailiffs from entering Carlton House to remove his furniture.

In the summer of 1793 Prince Augustus, Duke of Sussex, contracted a secret marriage in the Hotel Sarmiento in Rome to Lady Augusta Murray, the daughter of a Scottish peer, the 4th Earl of Dunmore. She was considerably more attractive than her nickname 'Goosy' implies, and in December the couple underwent another 'ceremony' in London, at which the Duke signed himself Mr Augustus Frederick on the wedding certificate. He had not been physically strong enough to join the army or navy like his brothers, so instead he had travelled extensively in Europe for three years, writing lively and intelligent letters home to his father, who paid off his debts.

When in Italy, the twenty-year-old fell under the influence of Lady Augusta, who was about five years older – Lady Dunmore claimed not to know her daughter's exact birthdate – and by January 1794 they had had a son. Once the King learned of the marriage, he had it declared illegal under the Royal Marriages Act. In late 1795, Augustus wanted his father to expunge the annulment, both to make his wife happy and because there was 'an unfortunate child, who was doomed to misfortune from the very hour he was conceived'.* Augustus told his father that 'even a heart of stone would be moved by his plight' (that is, his son's illegitimacy). But George and Lord Chancellor Loughborough were not about to alter the terms of the Act, not least because it had been passed in order to discourage precisely the kind of behaviour in which Augustus had indulged. George therefore continued to display a 'heart of stone' towards his son and would-be daughter-in-law, knowing that if he let one person off, the Act would immediately lose its supposed power as a deterrent.

At least George and Charlotte's eldest daughter, the thirty-one-year-old Princess Charlotte, the Princess Royal, did not cause the family any

---

* Augustus Frederick d'Este was doubly unfortunate, as he was the first person to be diagnosed with multiple sclerosis (a century after his death, on the evidence of his diaries).

embarrassments and complications. She was married to the forty-two-year-old Prince Frederick, Hereditary Prince of Württemberg,* in the Chapel Royal at St James's Palace on 18 May 1797. The Queen, Princess Charlotte herself and all her sisters were in tears, and the King and Duke of Clarence were seen frequently to wipe tears from their eyes too.[37] Charlotte was the only one of George's daughters to marry before the Regency, and the King never saw her again, although they corresponded regularly. George had tried to prevent the marriage, fearing it would not be happy, but it turned out to be so (even though there were some difficult diplomatic moments, such as when Charlotte's stepdaughter Catherine married Napoleon's youngest brother Jérôme). Only three of the King's six daughters married – Charlotte, Elizabeth and Mary – but none had children who lived into adolescence. The other three – Augusta, Sophia and Amelia – led an even more intensely sheltered and stultifying existence than most aristocratic women of the period, and saw virtually no one outside the family and Court, to their immense frustration.

Major-General Thomas Garth, George's ugly, gouty but charming equerry, probably married, in secret and of course illegally, Princess Sophia, who privately bore a son some time around July 1800, named Thomas Ward.[38] The baby was baptized in Weymouth parish church on 11 August 1800 and immediately put out for adoption.

The twenty-eight-year-old Colonel Charles Fitzroy of the 1st Foot Guards, second son of Lord Southampton, became an extra-equerry to the King in January 1801. He had seen action at the sieges of Valenciennes and Dunkirk as well as in the Dutch campaign of 1799. The King's youngest and favourite daughter Amelia was seventeen when she fell in love with him. Everyone in the family knew the secret except for the King. 'George III with all his solid and very considerable abilities was not gifted with keen observation in domestic matters,' wrote Amelia's biographer. 'Even before his physical blindness came upon him, things could go on under his eyes without his perceiving them.'[39] He had been a devoted father, crawling under the furniture in his palaces to play with his children when they were infants, but once they grew up he and the Queen were sometimes baffled by the way the princes and princesses wanted to lead lives independent of them.

Holland having been overrun by the French and a pro-French puppet Batavian Republic established in its place in early 1795, the question arose in Cabinet of whether or not to subsidize Prussia to re-enter the war. By 8

---

* The Prince was so fat that Napoleon, who made him a king in 1806, said that God had created him to discover how far skin could stretch.

April the whole Cabinet except Lord Grenville had agreed to the subsidy; Grenville himself did not offer to resign, but asked instead for his formal dissent to be mentioned in the report that was sent to the King. This was the first time that a Cabinet minister had done this, and it happened only three other times in Pitt's premiership.[40] 'Lord Grenville will easily understand that I must ever look on a difference of opinion between my ministers on a material question with sorrow,' the King told his Foreign Secretary the next day, 'but far be it from me to wish that any of them should ever for unanimity concur in appearance when not dictated by conviction. Lord Grenville may therefore rest assured that his dissent on the present occasion will not in the least diminish my opinion of him.'[41] Grenville was swiftly proved right, as on the 16th it was discovered that Prussia had come to terms with France at the Peace of Basel eleven days earlier, subsequently forcing Hanover, Saxony, Bavaria and Hesse-Cassel to make peace as well. This left the King in the curious position of being at war with France as King of England but at peace as Elector of Hanover.

On 27 June, some 4,000 British troops under General Sir John Doyle landed at Quiberon Bay to support a French royalist uprising in Brittany. 'Violent as the wish may sound,' Fox wrote in a letter that to some eyes would have verged upon the treasonous, 'I would much rather hear that they were all cut to pieces than that they gained any considerable success, for in the latter case the war may be prolonged to the utter destruction of both countries and to the total extinction of all principles of liberty and humanity in Europe.'[42] Fox got what he wished for, as the British regiments were badly mauled by Revolutionary forces under the French General Lazare Hoche, and the joint operation suffered around 5,000 dead and 6,332 captured.

By late October, opposition to the war had become so voluble that when the King drove to the State Opening of Parliament on the 29th a large crowd, fired by both economic distress and radical agitation, shouted, 'No War! No Pitt! Down with George!'[43] The *Annual Register* recorded that at 2 p.m. 'The Earl of Chatham, Duke of Gloucester, etc., were hissed, and the Duke of Portland was very much hooted. About twenty minutes afterwards the King left Buckingham House and was violently hissed, hooted and groaned at the whole way, but no violence was offered until he arrived opposite the Ordnance Office, when a small pebble, or a marble, or perhaps a bullet, broke one of the windows.'[44] As he entered the House of Lords, he told the Lord Chancellor, 'My Lord, I have been shot at!'[45]

It was initially believed that an airgun had been fired from a bow window of a house adjoining the Ordnance Office. 'Some stones were thrown at the State Coach, and one of the windows was perforated, apparently by a bullet from an airgun,' recorded Lord Eldon's biographer in 1844. Eldon noted that the King's unnamed attendant – either Lord Westmorland, the Master of the Horse, or Lord Onslow, a former Treasurer of the Household – started in fright at the shot hitting the window of the State Coach. '"Sit still, sir," said the King: "let us not betray any fear of what may happen."'[46] On entering the Lords chamber, George read his speech 'with extraordinary firmness and spirit', in the words of Charles Abbot, a newly elected MP.[47] Afterwards he told well-wishers, 'My lords, you are supposing this and proposing that, but there is One who disposes of all things and in Him I trust.'[48]

More stones were thrown at the carriage on its return from Parliament to St James's Palace, one striking the woodwork between the windows as it passed opposite Spring Gardens Terrace. 'That is a stone,' the King observed calmly of one missile that smashed through the glass, 'you see the difference from a bullet.'[49] When he found it lodged in his cuff, he gave it to Lord Onslow, saying, 'My Lord, keep this as a memorandum of the civilities which we have received.'[50] Later that day, after disrobing, George took another coach ride from St James's back to Buckingham House, whereupon 'the mob surrounded the carriage and prevented it from proceeding, crying out "Bread! Bread! Peace! Peace!"' until the Guards were brought up.

The *Annual Register* stated that the King displayed 'cool magnanimity' by going out a second time 'in the midst of the wildest commotions of the multitude, thereby exposing himself, almost without guards, to their fury, and then it was that His Majesty's person was most imminently in danger'.[51] (By contrast, the Prince of Wales stayed away until night-time.) 'I doubt not that I shall sleep,' the King told the Queen that evening, 'and only wish the man to sleep as well who made the attack on me.'[52] The next day, once news of it had appeared in the newspapers, Queen Charlotte was cheered at Covent Garden Theatre, where 'God Save the King' was played six times.

It was clear that the incident had had little effect on him. Not so Pitt, who had personally witnessed what he called 'the disagreeable and disgraceful sight which such uncontrolled licentiousness permits' during the Gordon Riots in 1780, and was steadfastly determined to prevent the mob from ever becoming the major force in British politics in the way that it had in France.[53] He took the opportunity of the violence to introduce the Treasonable Practices Bill and the Seditious Meetings Bill in November, which prohibited meetings of more than fifty people without first giving notice to a magistrate, and which was planned to last for three years. The former explicitly mentioned the attack on the King's coach in its preamble.

Corresponding Societies had by then extended from London to

Sheffield, Manchester, Leeds, Derby, Nottingham, Stockport, Leicester, Birmingham, Newcastle, Edinburgh, Stirling and Dundee.[54] They were radical, but by no means all republican; even so, the government did not want to take the risk of being without legal protection should it need to put down a genuine revolution. When it went too far and tried to arraign four prominent radicals (including the extreme radical Horne Tooke) citing the Treasonable Practices Act, the defendants were acquitted; indeed no one was ever imprisoned under it.

George's attitude towards the government's desire for peace negotiations with France in January 1796 has been described as 'resentful compliance'.[55] The King opposed it on moral as well as on practical grounds. Not only would it jeopardize relations with allies such as Russia and Austria, and discourage the royalist Catholic uprising in the Vendée region of western France, but above all it would also encourage 'the downfall of that horrid fabric,* established on the avowed foundation of the dereliction of all religious, moral and social principles'.[56] He had written to Grenville in September 1792 of the French Revolution 'destroying all religion, law, and subordination . . . without the smallest inclination after this destruction to build up anything', and his letters were peppered with references to 'those savages', 'that perfidious nation' and 'that unprincipled country'.[57] But on such key matters Pitt, Grenville and Dundas had learned to coalesce before engaging with him, in the hope of denying him alternative policies. 'Though I own I cannot feel the utility of it,' the King told Dundas that month, 'I do not in the least mean to make any obstinate resistance to the measure proposed.'[58] It was a relatively gracious acceptance of the power of the triumvirate that then dominated the Cabinet.

As so often, George could not resist adding an element of self-righteousness to his argument, reminding Grenville that 'My mind is not of a nature to be guided by the object of obtaining a little applause or staving off some abuse: rectitude of conduct is my sole aim.'[59] It was true, but such rectitude would have been more attractive if pointed out by others rather than by the King himself. Since the Thermidor Coup of July 1794, the French Directory (government) was much less extreme than it had been under Maximilien Robespierre. Nonetheless, in later discussions with Pitt, George still described peace negotiations with the victorious French as 'humiliating', and reached for his time-honoured hyperbole in saying they would 'for ever close the glory of this country'.[60] He was more convincing when he argued that they would also be helping to establish the Directory as France's legitimate government. George's consistent opposition

* 'Edifice' (*Johnson's Dictionary*).

to peace (including, as we shall see, in 1802–3) certainly contributed to France's eventual defeat, as Britain's long-term commitment made a crucial contribution to the wearing-down of her enemy. The statistics are telling: whereas Austria was at war with France for 108 months, Russia for 55 months and Prussia for 58 months between 1792 and 1815, Britain was a belligerent for no fewer than 240 months, giving France virtually no respite, especially in the steady strangulation of her overseas empire and trade.

In the first week of February 1796 there were intense Cabinet discussions about subsidizing Austria to fight France, and encouraging Russia and Prussia with the promise of naval support rather than cash. The immediate aim was to liberate Holland, but the negotiations became increasingly byzantine because they also had to consider the changing situations (and mutual antagonisms) among the major powers, as well as among some minor ones such as Sardinia and Naples. Grenville had to consider issues such as Prussian indemnities in Westphalia, the old canard of the Bavarian Exchange, and the Duchy of Milan's desire for territory at the expense of Sardinia. 'I always choose to act on simple principles,' the King wrote to Grenville on 9 February 1796; 'Italian politics are too complicated paths for my understanding.'[61] This modesty (with its added implication of moral superiority) should not be taken at face value: the King perfectly understood what was at stake. Unfortunately, soon after Pitt began secret peace negotiations through the Swiss Minister on 19 March, the twenty-six-year-old General Bonaparte assumed command of all French forces in Italy, and embarked on a campaign famed for its strategic, tactical and logistical genius that over the next eighteen months was to unify northern Italy under French control and knock Austria out of the war.[62]

By May, the Prince of Wales was already referring to his wife Princess Caroline as 'the vilest wretch this world was ever cursed with, who I cannot feel more disgust for from her personal nastiness* than I do from her entire want to principle'.[63] She in turn complained about the way that he had insinuated his *maîtresse-en-titre*, Frances Villiers, Countess of Jersey,† into the position of one of her ladies of the bedchamber. Caroline was undoubtedly vulgar, tactless and slatternly, but George was a lecherous, spoilt, vain would-be bigamist. They have been described with some understatement

---

* 'Dirt, filth' (*Johnson's Dictionary*).
† A position Villiers had by this point taken from Maria Fitzherbert, but in 1807 had to yield to Isabella Ingram-Seymour-Conway, Marchioness of Hertford, who in turn had to pass it on to Elizabeth, Marchioness Conyngham.

as 'an ill-suited pair', but if one good came from it at least perhaps their marriage saved two other people from being unhappy.[64]

'Only private persons can live happily married, because they can choose their own mates,' Duke Charles of Brunswick, Caroline's father, had once said. 'Royalty must make marriages of convenience, which seldom result in happiness. Love does not prompt these alliances, and these marriages not only embitter the lives of the parties to them, but all too frequently have a disastrous effect upon the children.'[65] None of this, of course, offered his son-in-law the Prince of Wales any consolation. Longing for a separation from Caroline, the Prince lamented that 'he had rather see toads and vipers crawling over his victuals than sit at the same table with her!!!'[66]

Among many others, the *True Briton* newspaper pointed out that the Prince was 'incorrigible. A total disregard to the opinions of the world seems to mark every part of his conduct ... We have long looked upon his conduct as favouring the cause of Jacobinism and democracy in this country, more than all the speeches of Horne Tooke and all the labours of the Corresponding Society.'[67] By contrast, the Princess was being cheered at the opera – for her marital travails. The King wrote to the Prince on 2 June, clearly agreeing with the *True Briton*: 'You seem to look on your disunion with the Princess as merely of a private nature, and totally put out of sight that as heir apparent of the Crown your marriage is a public act wherein the Kingdom is concerned.'[68] He then turned to the couple's separation, which was already being discussed, 'The public must be informed of the whole business, and being already certainly not influenced in your favour, the auspices in the first outset would not be promising.'

The King also warned his son that Parliament would have 'the right to secure out of your income the jointure settled on her in case of your death'. He admitted that Caroline bore some share of the blame 'in the choice of conduct she has adopted' but he felt that 'if you had attempted to guide her she might have avoided those errors that her uncommon want of experience and perhaps some defect of temper have given rise to.' He therefore begged the Prince to look again 'at the evils that may accrue to you in persisting in an idea that may lead to evils without bounds, and if more cannot be effected, have that command on yourself that shall, by keeping up appearances, by degrees render your home more respectable and at the same time less unpleasant'.[69]

The Prince replied the same day, complaining of an attack in *The Times* and somewhat self-defeatingly enclosing the *True Briton* article. He urged the King of 'the absolute necessity of speaking to your ministers to prevent any further attacks of so atrocious a nature, and Your Majesty will probably think they ought to insist upon an apology from the editors'.[70] It was a sign of how accurate the *True Briton* had been in ascribing to the Prince 'a total disregard' for anyone's opinion that he thought his father would ask Pitt to threaten to suppress newspaper reports and demand that editors apologize for writing what everyone knew was essentially the truth. The Prince had the gall to warn his father, 'Your Majesty must now see that the interests of us all are so intimately blended that we must either stand or fall together.'[71]

On 5 June the King replied, 'You know there is so great a jealousy of any infringement of what is called the liberty of the press, that it is a chord that must be touched with great delicacy.'[72] He had learned as much from the Wilkes imbroglio. Later that month George told his son 'the secret advice I am called upon as a sovereign and father to give you', that if Lady Jersey were to resign as a lady of Princess Caroline's bedchamber and was not invited to Carlton House again, the Princess of Wales might agree to a reconciliation.[73] The King made it clear this was desirable, but the Prince demanded a formal separation. That is what ensued, and it was to last for a quarter of a century until Queen Caroline's death. When in June 1821 a courtier announced, 'Sir, your bitterest enemy is dead,' George IV replied, 'Is she, by God!'[74] The courtier then had to explain that he was referring to Napoleon.

Spain, which had been in the French bloc since her peace with France of July 1795, declared war on Britain on 5 October 1796. France and her allies the Batavian Republic and now Spain had 40 per cent more ships-of-the-line than the Royal Navy, and rejected secret peace-feelers through Lord Malmesbury, especially a proposal to restore the Low Countries to Austria. Pitt, against the wishes of the King, wanted to return to peace negotiations with the French Directory in mid-November. 'I think no question in geometry more fully to be proved than that this is of all moments the worst to make peace,' the King told Henry Dundas on the 17th, 'and that if we will but steadily pursue the war, France will soon be obliged to sue for peace, and the one who seeks it must ever be obliged the most to lower his demands.'[75] Although he never vetoed the search for peace, George was relieved when the French, who were winning victory after victory under Bonaparte in Italy, once again broke off negotiations a few weeks later.

In mid-December, a 15,000-strong French expedition to Bantry Bay in south-west Ireland under the French General Lazare Hoche and the Irish revolutionary Wolfe Tone failed, largely owing to the bad weather. Despite martial law being introduced in Ireland to counter the United Irishmen, there were fears of further expeditions and a massive run on English provincial banks. By February 1797 Britain's balance of payments had fallen into serious deficit due to the war, the heavy foreign subsidies and having to pay for foreign grain because of bad harvests. Pitt therefore took the emergency measure of suspending cash payments by the Bank of England by leaving the Gold Standard, hoping that there would be enough flexibility in the money supply to stimulate an eventual recovery. As well as halting the outflow of bullion, he increased bond issues and printed banknotes. Confidence in the Bank's paper money wavered momentarily but then returned, and for the rest of the war the British government was able to borrow at several percentage points lower than the French.

Pitt did all this while consulting the King, but not much in person. 'Lord Westmorland says the King never sees his ministers but on Levee or Drawing Room days or when there are Hanging Cabinets* at Buckingham House (unless when there are intrigues and secret negotiations on ministerial arrangements going forward),' recorded the Tory junior minister Sylvester Douglas MP, later Lord Glenbervie, in his diary. 'He does not believe Pitt has ever seen the King in private ten times.'[76] This was in marked contrast to George's regular meetings with Bute, and even North, earlier in his reign.

Pitt was about to go through the most difficult period of his long premiership. On 22 February a force of 1,400 French troops landed in Fishguard in Pembrokeshire on the Welsh coast, under the command of an Irish-American colonel named William Tate. They were captured within two days by a much smaller local militia force under Lord Cawdor, in what was to be the last invasion of the British mainland to date. 'I suppose the predatory attack and landing in Pembrokeshire will rather add to the dismay of the timid,' the King wrote to Pitt on the 26th. 'But I trust a little firmness will soon restore that cool firmness which used to be the natural attendant of Englishmen.'[77]

That same month, a naval victory off Cape St Vincent under the admirals John Jervis and Horatio Nelson, and General Ralph Abercromby's capture of Trinidad, led Pitt to believe he would get better terms for peace than previously expected, even though Napoleon was then marching towards the Tyrol and Vienna. After receiving another memorandum from Pitt in favour of peace negotiations on 9 April, George said that he wanted to wait for solid news from Austria, fearing that making peace with France 'must forever close the glory of this country, and reduce Austria to a small state ... besides fixing the present wicked constitution of France on solid

---

* Cabinet meetings that the King attended to decide whether to inflict capital or lesser punishments on felons sentenced to execution.

ground of more extent and preponderancy in the scale of Europe than the most exaggerated ideas of Louis XIV ever presumed to form'.[78] He pointed out that, if France kept the Low Countries as well as the left bank of the Rhine, 'one may talk of balances of power, but they cannot exist.' Once again, he was proved right. At the time of the League of Princes he had wanted a weak Austria, but those days were long gone.

When Pitt told him on 10 April that the Cabinet unanimously 'though reluctantly' had approved renewing peace talks, George replied:

> I shall certainly not with less sorrow acquiesce in the measure, as one thought by the ministers of necessity, not choice; and Mr Pitt will, I am certain, not be surprised that the opinion which encouraged me to withstand the difficulties of the war is personally not changed. But I am conscious that if that remains a single one, I cannot but acquiesce in a measure that from the bottom of my heart I deplore, and should the evils I foresee not attend the measure, I shall be most happy to avow that I have seen things in a blacker light than the event has proved.[79]

He had opposed peace talks ever since Pitt had suggested them the previous autumn, but he allowed himself to be overruled. 'The die being now cast,' he told Pitt, 'we must look forward.'

On 16 April, sixteen ships of the Channel Fleet at Spithead near Portsmouth mutinied, followed by fifteen ships at Plymouth ten days later. The day after the Spithead mutiny broke out, the King told Earl Spencer, the First Lord of the Admiralty, that Spencer was 'perfectly right in proceeding thither accompanied by two other members of the Board of Admiralty, and trust that this early determination will soon enforce due subordination'.[80] He also trusted that 'attention will be shown to any neglect that may have given due reason of discontent.' The King watched closely as Spencer and Earl Howe, who had only just stepped down from the command of the Channel Squadron, dealt with the problem. The mutineers made it clear that they would go back to work immediately if the French navy left port, but in the meantime they wanted concessions including higher pay – sailors' pay had not increased since 1652 and the past thirty years had seen rising inflation – and the abolition of the tradition whereby ships' pursers took one-eighth of the men's meat rations.

Spencer and the Admiralty responded to these grievances by accepting most of them, issuing a royal pardon for the Spithead mutineers and beginning legislation to enact the reforms. This moved too slowly for the sailors, who began to lose confidence in Spencer and renewed their action on 7 May. The King wrote to Pitt on 9 May about 'the very outrageous mutiny' at Spithead, agreeing to support the Cabinet in whatever it decided to do on 'the present very distressing occasion'.[81] Howe went down to Portsmouth to reassure the sailors that the legislation had passed, and after the removal of some unpopular officers, the crisis was over.

However, on 12 May further mutinies broke out on several ships at the Nore, off Sheerness in the Thames Estuary. By contrast with the strike at Spithead, the Nore mutineers demanded that the King dissolve Parliament and make peace. They were led by Richard Parker, who was elected – or at least emerged – as 'President of the Delegates of the Fleet', and who threatened to blockade the port of London and sail the fleet to France. (The latter threat had little support among his followers.) Spencer wrote to the King on 23 May saying he was 'concerned to find that so extravagantly mutinous a spirit should exist in the minds of the seamen at the Nore'.[82] George replied that he thought 'further concessions would render impracticable' the process of pacification there.

That same day, the Duke of Portland wrote to warn of 'symptoms of disorder and outrage having appeared in a part of Ireland ... where that spirit had been thought to have been totally subdued and extirpated', and three days later the Duke of York wrote that artillerymen based at Woolwich were demanding higher pay, and that Cornwallis was being sent there to negotiate, accompanied by the 7th Light Dragoons.[83] On 26 May, orders had to be given at Gravesend and Tilbury for the forts there to open fire on the Nore fleet if it tried to take possession of the naval vessels moored nearby at Long Reach. Mutineers fired on two ships which tried to leave the anchorage at the end of May and held up merchant shipping in early June. There was even a fear that the newly married Princess Royal and Prince Frederick might be seized by the mutineers on their way to Württemberg, so they were diverted to Harwich and given three frigates for protection.[84]

Careful handling by the Pitt government gave it the upper hand by mid-June, and in the end Parker and twenty-eight of his confederates at the Nore were hanged, twenty-nine imprisoned, nine flogged and others transported. 'I entirely coincide with Earl Spencer as to the propriety of ordering the sentences,' the King wrote about four marines about to be hanged at Plymouth, 'as the cases require exemplary punishment.'[85] He approved all the government's punishments, including several counts of solitary confinement for six months at the start of longer sentences. Since the security of the nation rested almost entirely on the navy, it had been a nerve-wracking time.

A preliminary peace was signed between France and Austria at Leoben on 18 April. This, together with the recent naval mutinies, censure motions pending in Parliament from Fox and Lord Moira, growing disorder in Ireland and occasional panic-selling of stocks and securities in the City, prompted Pitt yet again to renew contact with the Directory, which on 11 June demanded official British recognition of the French Republic as a precondition for negotiations. In a Cabinet meeting four days later, Pitt, Loughborough, Cornwallis, Chatham, Dundas and the 1st Earl of Liverpool (the former Charles Jenkinson, Lord Hawkesbury) wanted to accept, whereas Grenville, Portland, Windham and Spencer were sceptical of negotiations and opposed to any official recognition. According to Windham's diary, Grenville argued 'that we were at a period at which nothing but firmness could save us', and that otherwise the government would not last a year.[86] Unsurprisingly, given his earlier stance, the King supported the latter group, and persuaded them not to resign but to fight on inside the Cabinet. During the American war the King's principled stance had not been helpful; now it helped to keep up the pressure on France.

Over the summer, Pitt tried hard to persuade a reluctant King of the advisability of holding peace negotiations with the French in Lille, but these were officially broken off after the coup of 18 Fructidor (4 September) brought in a new Directory government led by Paul Barras that was committed to continuing the war. Then on 22 September Pitt told the King that an agent of the Directory had agreed to an immediate cessation of hostilities, at which point Britain would receive the former Dutch colonies of the Cape of Good Hope and Ceylon. All the British had to do to effect this sensational breakthrough was pay a bribe of £1.2 million for Ceylon or £2 million for both places. No one was named as the recipient, but the Directory's Foreign Minister was the notoriously corrupt Talleyrand.

'Such a business should be conducted with the utmost secrecy,' wrote Pitt, who knew that the cost of the coming military and naval campaign was projected to cost £2 million anyway, without any certainty of winning the two key nodal points of the Indian Ocean and southern Africa. He certainly thought the bribe 'worth trying in these extraordinary times'.[87] The King agreed, replying from Windsor that it was 'absolutely necessary to say as little as the novelty of the occasion will permit'. Nothing came of the scheme, and Britain was eventually to gain the entire coastal area of Ceylon by the Peace of Amiens in 1802 and the Cape of Good Hope by the Anglo-Dutch Treaty of 1814, without enriching Talleyrand by a sou.

The King wrote regularly to stiffen Pitt's resolve, even on financial matters only tangentially connected to the war. On 15 December, for example, after Pitt's Assessed Taxes Bill inaugurating the income tax passed one of its readings by 175 votes to 50, he argued that Pitt should not accept any modifications in its committee stage, 'For experience has fully taught me that when government have from too much candour greatly weakened the effect of any proposition, it never renders it more palatable, and constantly destroys the value of it.'[88] George did not like the idea of taxing incomes per se: 'No one can dissemble that the occasion requires heavy contributions, but the cause is so great. It is to save everything that is dear to men, and must therefore be met with firmness.' As during the American war there was during this even longer contest something Augustan in George's phraseology which utterly belies his reputation among Whig historians of being an inarticulate Hanoverian oaf.

The King welcomed the income tax Bill passing its third reading by 198 votes to 71 on 5 January 1798 by telling Pitt that it was 'a new mode of taxation that may be of great utility to the finances of the country' and doubting that its alterations in the committee stages had improved it.* Back in December he had already said, 'I believe the mode adopted is the most equal that could have been devised.'[89] Characteristically, he continued, 'Sometimes, unfortunately, right gives way to expedience. When it does, I am ever hurt; for, as a plain man, I think right and wrong ought never to be blended for any momentary purpose, and try to inculcate that principle as much as possible.'[90]

As well as the 10 per cent top rate of tax for all annual incomes over £200, Pitt also asked all 'persons of affluence' for a one-off voluntary contribution to the Treasury of one-fifth of their annual income; he himself gave £2,000.[91] George made the huge contribution of £20,000, or one-third of the entire Privy Purse, to encourage the aristocracy and gentry to give generously, and he and Pitt leaned heavily on government ministers to donate similarly. The King wanted Pitt to know that:

> My income is certainly, in proportion to the greatness of the country, inadequate to my station . . . I have some debts, of which the sum borrowed for the late elections makes the most considerable part, which I am by instalments paying off . . . I have no other fund in the world. I never drew a shilling from my Electorate when in its greatest prosperity, but regularly paid off the debts that were incurred in the Seven Years' War . . . I am sorry to say the King of England is not so rich a man, and that every shilling paid from his Privy Purse must fall on the indigent; for if he has not the means, his workmen and the poor cannot but feel it to their sorrow.[92]

Contributions were made public and thus quickly became a measure of the donor's patriotism (and in turn likelihood of receiving an honour).

---

* Income tax was introduced only as a temporary measure, and was abolished in March 1816. The everlasting infamy of its reintroduction in peacetime rests with Sir Robert Peel in 1842.

When the lists were closed in February 1799, a total of £2.2 million had been contributed.

The Whig Club's celebration of Charles Fox's birthday on 24 January 1798 was held in the Crown and Anchor Tavern in the Strand, where the London Corresponding Society had been meeting since 1793. Reputedly 2,000 people turned up to hear the 11th Duke of Norfolk give the chief toast of the evening, 'to drink our sovereign's health, the Majesty of the People!'[93] For so publicly replacing the King as the object of the Loyal Toast, Pitt recommended that Norfolk be dismissed not only from his lord-lieutenancy of the West Riding of Yorkshire, but also from his colonelcy of the 1st Regiment of the West Riding Militia, which was done immediately. Fox therefore knew precisely what he was doing when at another meeting of the same club in the first week of May he also proposed the toast to 'Our sovereign, the People'.[94] Pitt told the King that those ministers he had consulted about this deliberate act of crypto-republicanism believed that 'Mr Fox's name should be erased from the list of privy counsellors.'[95] George replied that same evening that he would like the book to be brought to Buckingham House so that he could personally scratch it out himself.

For all these largely symbolic acts of aggression and counter-aggression, on occasion eighteenth-century politics could also descend to the use of lethal force.* On the afternoon of Sunday 27 May 1798, William Pitt had to fight a duel near the gibbet on Putney Heath against the Foxite MP George Tierney, whom he had accused of 'a desire to obstruct the defence of the country' in his opposition to an emergency Bill to increase naval manpower.[96] Both men missed with their first shot, and Pitt then fired another shot into the air before their seconds concluded that satisfaction had been given. As Pitt reported to his mother with characteristic sangfroid, 'The business terminated without anything unpleasant to either party.'[97] The King confined himself to telling his Prime Minister:

> I trust what has happened will never be repeated. Perhaps it could not have been avoided, but it is a sufficient reason to prevent its ever being again necessary. Public characters have no right to weigh alone what they owe to themselves; they must consider also what is due to their country.[98]

To have lost William Pitt at a time when Britain was facing the threats it was in 1798 would have been for the country a terrible self-inflicted wound.

---

* Sixty-nine people were killed and ninety-six wounded in duels during George's reign, but only three duellists were found guilty of murder in those sixty years (Hopton, *Pistols at Dawn* p. 251).

One can understand why George was profoundly opposed to duels and intervened twice to prevent their taking place. He also personally ordered a Captain de Lancey's name to be struck off the army officers' list after he behaved badly in a duel with a Major Chapman of the same regiment.[99]

Quite apart from the chance of Pitt getting shot, George was also concerned about his Prime Minister's health, writing to him about it thrice in consecutive letters in May 1798. He asked whether a bout of illness was 'some inclination to gout', which doubtless prompted unhappy memories of the many months in the late 1760s when Pitt the Elder had been incapacitated by it. He advised Pitt to take the waters at Cheltenham and then Bath 'without delay ... for the allowing bile or unformed gout to undermine a constitution may lead to the most fatal consequences', which he hardly needed to tell the son of Lord Chatham.[100] Pitt's particular problem was alcohol: he was known as a 'three-bottle man' for his reputed daily consumption of port which he had apparently been advised by Dr Addington to take medicinally, with no better result than when he had prescribed it for Pitt's father.*

Pitt's continuing health was vital, not least because on 19 May Napoleon set sail from Toulon with a large army to a destination as yet unknown. Four days later a United Irishmen uprising was foiled in Dublin, but the revolt quickly spread to Wicklow, Wexford and further afield. Henry Dundas wrote to the King on 2 June advocating the sending of regular troops to Ireland, 'considering the danger of the rebellion extending itself so far as to place the harbours of Cork and Waterford in the possession of the rebels, and consequently of France'.[101] The King replied at 7.59 a.m. the next day, noting that 'I sincerely lament the necessity of sending this additional force to Ireland,' because it meant that the troops could not be used on active service elsewhere, but 'that as the sword is drawn it [will] not be returned into the sheath until the whole country has submitted without condition; the making any compromise would be perfect destruction'.[102]

On 10 June, with the prospect of full-scale civil war in Ireland, the King suggested that Lord Camden be removed as Viceroy because he was 'too much agitated at the present hour, and totally under the control of the Irish privy councillors'.[103] He wanted him replaced by Cornwallis and for it to be done 'instantly'.[104] Cornwallis arrived in Dublin ten days later. The King's instructions were straightforward: 'Lord Cornwallis must clearly

---

* Bottles were smaller at 350ml to 500ml, and alcohol by volume around 16 per cent against today's 20 per cent, but it was still a substantial daily dosage for Pitt's frail frame.

understand that no indulgence can be granted to the Catholics farther than has been, I am afraid unadvisedly, done in former sessions, and that he must by a steady conduct effect in future the union of that kingdom with this.'[105]

The King reminded Pitt once again that 'No country can be governed where there is more than one established religion.'[106] He was personally tolerant, as when he visited Thomas Weld's chapel in Dorset; and speaking at a Levee in February 1797 he had criticized the French expulsion of the Jesuits thirty-three years earlier, saying that children educated by them 'had never learned from their Jesuit preception [instruction] any of the dangerous moral principles imputed to them'.[107] Yet Pitt could not have failed to spot the steely determination not to allow Catholics to enter Parliament, at least in the near future, that was inherent in the King's letter.

Although George reigned in Ireland as King of Ireland and not of Great Britain, in practice it was not perceived as the 'sister kingdom' of political rhetoric so much as a pseudo-colony. There were tight restrictions over the Dublin Parliament's actions, with Westminster in ultimate control. The Viceroy had all the political powers of the Crown, including the right to veto legislation. Irish commercial access to the British colonies was restricted in order to prevent competition with English, Scottish and Welsh goods.

The Irish Rebellion was led by a colourful galère including the Jacobin Lord Edward Fitzgerald, the adventurer Wolfe Tone, the idealistic dreamer Robert Emmet, an assortment of village priests and, as one historian put it, 'a sprinkling of small squireens'.[108] Having learned the lesson of the American Revolution, the British Army actively harassed and arrested Irish leaders, and put down the revolt early and vigorously. It was much easier to contain an enemy on a small nearby island than in thirteen very distant colonies, of course, and there was a sense that the English officers also had less fellow feeling for the Irish Catholic peasantry than their fathers had had with the gentleman-planters such as Washington and Jefferson.

At the battle of Vinegar Hill and in the streets of Enniscorthy on 21 June 1798, around 13,000 British regulars under General Gerard Lake defeated around 18,000 United Irish militiamen, killing between 400 and 1,200 for the loss of a hundred redcoats. Some guerrilla activity continued afterwards, and Emmet even marched on Dublin Castle on 23 July, but the back of the rebellion had been broken. Although Cornwallis had arrived too late to command at Vinegar Hill, he coordinated the campaign after 22 August when the French General Jean-Joseph Humbert landed in County Mayo with a thousand men and established the 'Republic of Connaught', which encouraged around 5,000 local rebels to rise up. The 'Republic' was swiftly put down. Cornwallis also led the response on 12 October when

Wolfe Tone attempted to land with 3,000 men in County Donegal; Tone was captured in the ensuing engagement and committed suicide before his execution. The 1798 Rebellion convinced the King and Pitt that the Dublin Parliament had to be abolished and replaced by a legislative union of the kingdoms, as had been the case with Scotland since 1707.

After it transpired that Napoleon's destination was Egypt, Admiral Sir Horatio Nelson caught up with the French fleet and destroyed it in an exceptionally daring action in Aboukir Bay at the battle of the Nile on 1 August 1798, where no fewer than nine French ships-of-the-line were captured and two destroyed. The King celebrated by attending a breakfast on board the *St Fiorenzo* off Portsmouth, a thirty-eight-gun frigate originally called *Minerve* that the French had scuttled off Corsica but which the British had managed to refloat. The King was later to 'rump' (that is, turn his back on) Nelson at a Levee because of the admiral's flagrant infidelity to his wife Fanny with Sir William Hamilton's wife Emma, but that was all in the future; for now, Nelson had won the greatest naval victory of the reign so far.

The King told Grenville that the news of the battle of the Nile was 'an event not only adding additional lustre to the British navy, but highly essential to the safety of the Neapolitan dominions', whose Bourbon rulers were under threat from Napoleon.[109] He gave his 'fullest concurrence' to Pitt's move to capitalize upon it by concluding alliances with Naples and Turkey. When Nelson's dispatch arrived on 2 October – a full two months after the battle – the King wrote to Lord Spencer, who the next year was made a Garter knight, of 'the degree of joy I have felt on this occasion' of 'the success of this brave admiral', which he said, 'electrifies Austria and Naples [and] it may save Italy'.[110] George nonetheless thought it 'out of the question' that Nelson should have a barony, for the same reason that he had earlier declined a baronetcy, because he was too poor. Instead, he suggested that Nelson 'should have a handsome pension settled on him'.[111] As we have repeatedly seen, the King was a stickler for proper form, and here alert to the danger to the class system of having titled indigents. He was persuaded by Pitt and Spencer to change his mind, however, so Nelson became Baron Nelson 'of the Nile' (which did not imply a landed estate) while receiving £2,000 per annum for the lifetime of himself and his next two male heirs, should there be any.

Writing from Hanover on 28 October, Prince Adolphus reported that the '361' transport vessels that had conveyed Napoleon to Egypt had been destroyed in the battle – a wild exaggeration – 'and that Buonaparte has been forced to retreat from Cairo to Rosetta [modern-day Rashid on the

Nile Delta]. I hope in a very short time we shall have the account of this General being taken with all his men.'[112] Even better news, though no more accurate, was imparted by Lord Grenville on 14 December, that Napoleon had been shot dead by an assassin from Tripoli, and all the French in Cairo massacred. 'So strange an end of Bonaparte's life and that of his army must in the opinion of every religious mind appear the interposition of Divine Providence against that wicked nation,' the King replied, 'and ought to rouse every European power to step forth in defence of everything that is dear to man.'[113] A few days later the report was authoritatively contradicted.

Although the news of the Nile victory had indeed electrified the Kingdom of Naples, by mid-December the French had overrun the half of it on the Italian peninsula, capturing Naples itself, and were only prevented from invading the Sicilian half by the Royal Navy. The navy's successes also included the capture of Minorca and Honduras from Spain. The war was now one between the British whale, invulnerable at sea, and the French wolf that was seemingly invulnerable on land. Finally, on Christmas Eve 1798, Britain was able to sign a treaty with the Russians that was to form the nucleus of a second coalition against France. The wolf would be challenged again.

25

'The Corsican Tyrant'

January 1799–February 1801

It is the duty of ministers as much as possible to prevent any alter-ations in so essential a part of the constitution as everything that relates to religion.[1]

George III to Lord North, 1772

For all that he wanted union with Ireland, the King never visited. Similarly, despite the fact that the Industrial Revolution was well under way by 1780 and was fundamentally to alter Britain by the end of his reign forty years later, he never went down a mine or visited an iron foundry. The closest he got to such things were single visits to a pin factory at Gloucester, a china works at Worcester and a carpet-weaving works at Axminster, and he did not say anything remarkable on those occasions, any more than he did about anything concerning the social, economic and commercial changes the Industrial Revolution was effecting in his kingdom.[2]

In June 1799, Pitt decided that he did not have enough Cabinet support to pass a Bill limiting the slave trade. Lord Liverpool wrote to Prince William, Duke of Clarence, saying that he believed it was because of 'the King's determination that any business of this sort should never be made a Cabinet measure'.[3] This should not be interpreted as the King opposing abolition; he objected merely to its being a government initiative which ran the risk of breaking up the Pitt ministry if it failed. One historian of the slave trade has speculated that it was possible that Pitt might have retreated on his Bill because the King opposed abolition, but no evidence is presented for this construction, and since George rarely if ever held back in giving his views it seems equally likely that if he had indeed opposed the limitation of slavery he would have told Pitt so plainly.[4]

On 9 November 1799, Napoleon seized dictatorial power in the Brumaire Coup, overthrowing the corrupt and incompetent Directory and replacing it with a Consulate of three, with himself as First Consul. George described this to Grenville as a 'shameless revolution', predicting that the new regime could not 'hold long' and that Britain should continue to oppose any peace that would reinforce 'French principles'.[5] A few weeks later on Christmas Day, however, Napoleon offered peace in a letter to both George III and Emperor Francis II of Austria. George's views on France had been established long before Napoleon even attained a lieutenancy, so his response to the latest peace offer was predictable. On New Year's Day 1800 he wrote to Grenville, 'I am perfectly easy that every one of my ministers must view this in the same light I and he [Grenville] do, namely that it is impossible to treat with a new, impious, self-created aristocracy, and I have too good an opinion of my subjects at large to doubt that . . . they must see it in the same light.'[6] Later in the same letter he referred to 'the want of common civility of the conclusion of the Corsican tyrant's letter'.

Pitt answered Napoleon's offer on 3 February in one of the greatest speeches of his career, stating that because the 'system of revolution' still controlled France, peace negotiations would only give the Consulate 'rest and breathing-time' but would destroy the nascent anti-French alliance. 'As a sincere lover of peace,' he declared, 'I will not sacrifice it by grasping at the shadow, when the reality is not substantially within my reach.' The King was extremely gratified that Pitt's majority that day was 201.

On 15 May 1800, James Hadfield, a former soldier, fired a pistol at the King at close range at the Theatre Royal, Drury Lane. George was entering the royal box to watch Colley Cibber's *She Would and She Would Not*, starring Dora Jordan (the Duke of Clarence's mistress) and Michael Kelly. The bullet struck the pillar of the box furthest from the stage, and was later found flattened on the floor. 'Never shall I forget His Majesty's coolness,' Kelly wrote in his memoirs about the moment when Hadfield was apprehended. 'The whole audience was in an uproar. The King on hearing the report of the pistol retired a pace or two, stopped, and stood firmly for an instant, then came forward to the front of the box, put his opera-glass to his eye, and looked round the house without the smallest appearance of alarm or discomposure.'[7] He even 'slept as quietly as usual during the interval'.[8]

With some alacrity and considerable presence of mind, Richard Brinsley Sheridan, the Foxite playwright MP who happened to be present, hastily penned a verse to 'God Save the King', which Kelly sang at the end of the performance:

> From every latent foe,
> From the assassin's blow,

> God save the King!
> O'er him Thine arm extend,
> For Britain's sake defend
> Our father, prince and friend,
> God save the King!

George was gratified at the huge applause this elicited, again ascribing his narrow escape to Divine Intervention. Although he had only recently written to Pitt, 'It is impossible to calculate the improprieties of Mr Sheridan,' on this occasion he was appreciative.[9] Lady Holland was impressed that the King displayed what she called 'the utmost sangfroid', and noted: 'He told a person that he observed the fiddlers expected a second shot as they covered their heads with their cremonas.'[10] A medal was struck to celebrate the King's survival, featuring the eye of Providence above a burning altar. Lord Chief Justice Kenyon called off Hadfield's treason trial once it became clear that he was insane, a decision which led ultimately to the passing of the Criminal Lunatics Act 1800 and the Treason Act 1800.

Unfortunately, news of the assassination attempt unleashed a spate of further incidents by other people over the following months and years. One Joseph North had to be imprisoned for being 'extremely troublesome' at royal palaces. Another unnamed individual was arrested at Windsor Castle on 9 June 1800 for posing an unspecified 'danger', and like Hadfield was declared insane. John England, a drawing master, tried to get into a Levee, and when turned away came back with a knife; he was subsequently consigned to the Bethlem Hospital. Richard Neale, a chair painter, went to Buckingham House to tell the King that Jesus Christ had told him that George was his father. He was sent to an asylum, but after his release he returned to Buckingham House in November 1802, demanding to be made Lord Mayor of London. John Stickes had been causing trouble at royal palaces for two years before he was committed to an asylum that same month. In January 1801, Palmer Hurst struggled with constables at Buckingham House, after telling them that he needed to warn the King about William Pitt, and also to take the princesses to the theatre. John Dunlop declared his 'fixed and deep enmity against the King' before he was committed to Bethlem, which is also where Catherine Kirby went in June 1801 after she threw stones at the King.[11] None of these may have posed a mortal threat, but, for all that the authorities knew, any one of them might have. On 31 August 1801, Urban Metcalf, a twenty-five-year-old lace and garter seller (and a former inmate of two lunatic asylums), threw a penknife at the King at Weymouth Theatre, which embedded itself in a door; he then sprinted along a bench and tried unsuccessfully to enter the royal box.

Although the King behaved with calm and composure, the incident understandably left the Queen and the princesses 'greatly frightened'.[12]

Napoleon's audacious crossing of the Alps in the early summer of 1800, culminating in his victory over the Austrians at the battle of Marengo on 14 June, destroyed the hopes of the Pitt ministry that France might be forced into peace talks by the threat of a second coalition of European powers. Two weeks later, as the news of Marengo was arriving in London, the King told Pitt:

> No disaster can make me think the treating for peace either wise or safe whilst the French principles subsist. An armed neutrality is the only thing that can be obtained, and that I look upon as most fatal, for no confidence can be placed in the present French government. My opinion is formed on principle, not on events, and therefore is not open to change.[13]

To his credit, Pitt politely concealed any indignation he might have felt on receiving these regular letters which intimated the moral superiority of his monarch.

When it was clear by mid-July that Austria was planning to enter into separate negotiations with France, Grenville wrote to tell the King that the Cabinet were unanimous on 'a readiness to treat conjointly with Austria for a general peace on reasonable terms'.[14] It seemed as if Pitt was now willing to 'grasp at the shadow' of peace after all. Grenville added that he 'does not see the possibility of our compelling the enemy, by our separate exertions, either to destroy the present usurpation in France, or to restore tranquillity and independence to the Continent of Europe'.[15] George replied that he 'cannot find words adequate to the uneasiness I feel at the unanimous minute of the Cabinet', but he accepted the inevitability of negotiations, taking solace in Grenville's statement that if 'any Continental power would continue the war ... this country ought to persevere'.[16]

George did insist that any terms must secure for Britain the majority of her acquisitions, particularly in the West Indies and at the Cape of Good Hope. He also wanted the negotiator to be Thomas Grenville, William's younger brother, rather than the more malleable Lord Malmesbury, the veteran of earlier failed negotiations. Grenville duly travelled to Lunéville as Britain's special envoy to the Franco-Austrian peace talks, but once there was promptly sent home by Napoleon. George was perfectly sanguine at this turn of events. 'I have not the smallest doubt of the good sense of the country at large,' he told Pitt in November, 'and that however the weight of taxes may be felt, that everyone judges that in the present state of France no secure peace can be made, and that consequently the continuance of the war is highly necessary.'[17]

Although the King had acquiesced in the peace talks, he made it clear that he would not be bounced into approving any military operation for which he had not been shown detailed plans. On 24 July, for example, the Cabinet authorized an 'immediate' attack on the Spanish naval base of Ferrol near Corunna, 'with a view of destroying the enemy's squadron and arsenals'.[18] It would involve much of the Channel Fleet and 12,000 troops, as well as assaults on Cadiz and Tenerife. The expedition had been planned in the Admiralty for months, but the King had not been told anything about it until he received the Cabinet report at Windsor that evening, after spending the day reviewing troops near Bagshot.

'Not having before heard of an expedition against Ferrol and on what ground of supposed success it is to be undertaken,' George replied to Dundas at 10.15 the following night, 'nor what force will remain in this country after the sending so large a force out of it, I cannot give any answer till I have received the data on which to form an opinion.'[19] It was a sharp reminder to Dundas and Pitt that the King did not consider himself to be a rubber stamp, especially over the sort of large-scale military operations that would denude Britain of many ships and troops, even if only temporarily. Pitt was privately frustrated, instructing Dundas to explain to the King how important the attack was and that Britain would still be left with plenty of troops for her defence, but if the King was still opposed he would be 'begging His Majesty to find servants whose judgements he can trust more than ours'.[20] Sensibly, Dundas did not transmit this implied resignation threat, recognizing that this was merely a frustrated Prime Minister letting off steam. Instead, Pitt wrote to the King himself, to report that he was:

> highly sensible of Your Majesty's condescension and goodness in graciously attending to the considerations which Mr Dundas and himself felt it their duty to lay before Your Majesty. From the same motive Mr Pitt ventures to rely on Your Majesty's indulgence in humbly representing that if the attack on Ferrol should be found practicable, it is of the utmost importance from the advanced season of the year that it should be executed without loss of time.[21]

Pitt added that the commanders on the spot, General Sir James Pulteney MP (George's former aide-de-camp) and Admiral Sir John Jervis (now Lord St Vincent), should be trusted with the final decision. The King confined himself to pointing out to Dundas that 'considering the great waste of men in the various expeditions we have attempted [in] this war and particularly in that to Holland the last autumn, it is no wonder I asked for more explanation before I gave my consent to this proposition.'[22] George was correct: the expeditions to Toulon (1793), Holland (1794), Quiberon Bay (1795), Belle-Île (1795), Corsica (1796) and Holland again (1799) had all ended in failure. Despite being a great sea power, Britain would not master amphibious operations until much later in the war, aside from the recapture of Minorca in 1798. The attack on Ferrol on 25–26 August 1800 proved yet another failure, although only light losses were sustained, and attacks planned for Cadiz and Tenerife were called off in consequence. Pitt was undoubtedly a great war leader in many respects, but no significant victories were won on land during his premiership, and he did not have his father's success in coastal 'descents'.

During that difficult period of French ascendancy, George had a fine feel not only for military possibilities, but also for how the Crown should present itself, insisting that his family set an example of abstemiousness during the string of bad harvests of the late 1790s and early 1800s. Queen Charlotte wrote to her brother, Duke Charles II of Mecklenburg-Strelitz, on 8 January 1801 giving an insight into life at Windsor during the food shortages. 'We eat only rice and a single piece of bread a day,' she confided, 'and the very word cake is unknown at present. Everyone is cooking for the poor.'[23] It was not a regime that the Prince of Wales followed, of course, but it was appreciated by the public, and the mention of cake might also serve to underline the differences that had always existed between the frugal British Court and that of Versailles before 1789, however badly misquoted Marie Antoinette might have been. Five days after that letter, the King proclaimed a national twenty-four-hour fast, which he himself observed faithfully.

Yet, however frugal he was, the King still faced mounting debts, and in June 1800 he asked Pitt for formal recognition of the difference between his personal property and liabilities and those of the Crown, so that he could provide for his children. This was something for which Pitt had been pressing, and which should in truth have been resolved forty years earlier. Neither of them welcomed the various occasions (and the reputational damage that ensued) whenever the King was forced to ask Parliament to meet the shortfalls that arose as the costs of government (as opposed to the King's personal expenditure) expanded well beyond the scope of Crown income, especially in wartime. Pitt's acute financial brain worked out a fair settlement, and even persuaded the King to pay tax, which was popular nationally amid the straitened circumstances.

The King and Pitt were thus on good terms before the latter opened a series of Cabinet discussions on Catholic emancipation in September and

October 1800, without informing George he was doing so. There were three formal aspects to emancipation: altering the Test Acts so as to allow Catholics admission into Parliament and the high judicial, military and other offices still closed to them; commuting the tithes that Roman Catholics had to pay to the Protestant Church of Ireland; and allowing state payments to Catholic (and also Dissenting Protestant) clergy.[24] It was not just over Catholicism that the King had supported the status quo; in the late 1780s he had also staunchly opposed the repeal of the Test and Corporation Acts that banned Dissenters from Parliament, as Pitt knew well.

In the Cabinet discussions in the autumn of 1800, several ministers pointed out the fundamental problems they saw in Pitt's proposals. 'Opponents of emancipation saw no reason,' as one of his biographers has put it, 'during a war and at a time when the threat of revolution was still taken seriously, to enfranchise a mass of unruly and unpropertied Irish peasants who professed obedience to a pope, a foreigner.'[25] Others opposed it because they disliked sweeping constitutional change, respected the status and privileges of the Established Church, wanted to retain basic qualifications for public offices or were simply bigoted against Roman Catholics.

A recent (Catholic) historian of the emancipation struggle has described George accurately as 'a decent, amiable, certainly not intolerant man, with good Catholic friends and compassionate towards unfortunate Catholic refugees'.[26] This is right; a decade earlier, during one of their Weymouth holidays, the King and Queen visited Thomas Weld, a Roman Catholic (father of the future Cardinal Thomas Weld), at his country house Lulworth Castle.* It was formally illegal to build Roman Catholic chapels, but Weld was, and hoped to get at least tacit approval for it from the King. With a wink, the King 'proposed that his friend was actually building a free-standing family mausoleum', which was a perfectly legal endeavour.[27] Weld afterwards wrote to Lord Arundel, who had also built a Catholic place of worship on his estate, 'I think the King's seeing the chapel in that public manner must be a kind of sanction to it.'[28] Despite this, George was completely averse to any relaxation of the constraints on Catholics holding offices, shared the anxieties about Irish enfranchisement and had not forgotten the Gordon Riots, evidence of how toxic and dangerous this issue could quickly become. Lord Liverpool, who had been Secretary at War during the Riots, believed that 'a strong spirit of fanaticism still prevails in

---

* The visit was a great success until Weld's sister was seen barefoot and bare-legged giving food to the poor. Although of course he approved of her charity, the King remarked of her dress sense, 'God might be served as well with stockings and shoes on as without them' (Fraser, *King and the Catholics* p. 46).

this country', which as a result of Catholic emancipation 'might break out into the most dangerous excesses'.[29]

George had told Pitt in May 1800 that the Act of Union with Ireland, due to come into force on 1 January 1801, was:

> one of the most useful measures that has been effected during my reign, one that will give stability to the whole Empire, and from the want of industry and capital in Ireland be but little felt by this country as diminishing its trade and manufactures. For the advantages to Ireland can only arise by slow degrees, and the wealth of Great Britain will undoubtedly, by furnishing the rest of the globe with its articles of commerce, not feel any material disadvantage in that particular from the future prosperity of Ireland.[30]

The measure had cost some £1.5 million, a score of Irish peerages and several peerage promotions to persuade Irish parliamentarians to vote themselves out of existence, but the cost was thought well worth it.

Yet as Pitt's biographer William Hague has put it, 'Catholic opposition was neutralized by the implication (but not specific commitment) that their emancipation would inevitably result' – and the King had not been told of Pitt's and the Irish Secretary Viscount Castlereagh's intimations to Irish Catholic decision makers that union would soon be followed by emancipation.[31] If he had known about them he would not have endorsed them, and he certainly would not have felt himself personally bound by them.

The King's views on emancipation could have come as no surprise to Pitt. When in 1794 the Portland Whigs had imposed Earl Fitzwilliam as Lord Lieutenant of Ireland, George had objected to his radical pro-Catholic policies so much that Pitt had been forced to make him quit Dublin after only a matter of weeks. In January 1799, the King had threatened to prevent the Act of Union going through if Catholics received any new privileges beyond fair toleration, and he had already opposed Protestant taxpayers subsidizing the Irish Catholic Church.

Pitt has been justly criticized for bringing forward Catholic emancipation in January 1801 without first consulting the King. But, even if he had, the reaction would almost certainly have been the same. Principles were involved. George's objection was ultimately bound up with his Coronation Oath, a solemn promise he felt he had made to God on that day, and therefore simply not susceptible to the hopes or promises of prime ministers, however loyal, long-standing and talented. To fail to appreciate that is to fail to understand the King's nature, which is why Pitt's biographers and other historians have searched for alternative reasons why he might have brought up the doomed issue. Was Pitt exhausted after seventeen years at the helm? Did he want to retire for a few months? Perhaps he believed that the King would indulge him, as he had when he was allowed to bring forward parliamentary reform as a private member (rather than as Prime Minister) in 1785. Other reasons why Pitt might have desired to leave office have been suggested, including 'scarcity of food, Cabinet dissension, Pitt's bad health, and his supposed desire to avoid making a necessary peace'.[32] The historian Norman Gash supposed that Pitt 'could no longer carry on a disastrous war and was unable to make a satisfactory peace'.[33]

Of course, there was another, less imaginative interpretation: namely that Pitt might have believed that Catholic emancipation was the morally correct thing to do, and that it needed to be achieved to smooth the application of the Act of Union. But none of these theories have any evidence to support them, and as his industrious involvement with other war issues suggests that Pitt was still committed to governing, perhaps he simply misjudged his own ability to overcome the King's opposition as he had over the subject of peace negotiations in 1796, 1797 and 1800. But, in that, Pitt had led a united Cabinet, whereas there was now precious little consensus for Catholic emancipation, which was actively opposed by several of its most influential members, among them Westmorland, Loughborough, Portland and Liverpool, as well as a large majority of the House of Lords.[34]

As the nineteenth century dawned, another medal was struck depicting the King, with the words 'Who Reigns in the Hearts of His People'.[35] But did the King continue to reign in the hearts of his Irish subjects, whose Catholic majority had not been consulted about the planned union? Some might have preferred it to continued rule under an exclusive Protestant Ascendancy, but such sentiment did not exactly equate to embracing the new national dynamic. And many assumed that there had been an unspoken quid pro quo when Ireland's governance was merged with that of England and Scotland, as 100 Irish MPs would now sit in the House of Commons, bringing its membership up to 658, roughly the size it has remained ever since, except for 1885–1945 when it was larger.

On New Year's Day 1801, the United Kingdom of Great Britain and Ireland came into being. George held the best-attended Privy Council meeting of his reign so far at St James's Palace, as the Union Flag was hoisted over the building. There was an artillery salute at the Tower of London and bells rang across the city. The previous November, the Privy Council had considered the titles 'Emperor of the British Isles' and 'Emperor of the British and Hanoverian Dominions', but George thought that 'his true dignity consisted in being known to Europe and the world by the appropriated and undisputed style belonging to the British Crown'.[36] So he remained merely a king, and it would be his as-yet-unborn granddaughter, Victoria, who was eventually elevated from a royal title to an imperial one.

At a meeting in Downing Street on 25 January 1801, the Cabinet adopted Catholic emancipation as government policy, as well as an increase in state support for the Irish Presbyterian clergy. It still remains something of a mystery how these measures could have been adopted considering the number of ministers who opposed them, to say nothing of their further opponents outside the Cabinet, foremost among them John Moore, the Archbishop of Canterbury, his brother-in-law Lord Auckland and Henry Addington, the Speaker of the House of Commons.* At dinner with Lord Castlereagh after the meeting, Pitt seemed convinced that he could win over the King, and the next day Castlereagh unwisely revealed the Cabinet decision to John Fitzgibbon, 1st Earl of Clare, the staunchly Protestant Lord Chancellor of Ireland, who unsurprisingly took the news badly.

Clare had been such a vocal and hardline opponent of the 1798 rebellion – he had even suggested Wolfe Tone be hanged without trial – that when he died in 1802 dead cats were thrown at his funeral procession in Dublin.[37] On either 25 or 26 January 1801, one or more of Lords Lough-borough, Westmorland, Auckland or Clare informed the King of what the Cabinet had decided, before Pitt had had a chance to break it to him.[38] (There has been much debate about who told the King, but it hardly mattered because, having not been privy to any promises that may have been made to the Irish, overt or covert, he would have reacted with indignation and anger whoever it was.) At the Levee on 28 January, George approached Henry Dundas, and in what was reported to be 'a loud voice and agitated manner' designed to attract the maximum attention possible, he angrily demanded, 'What is the question which you are all about to force upon me? What is this Catholic emancipation which *this young lord, this Irish Secretary* has brought over, that you are going to throw at my head?' Before the unsuspecting Secretary at War could defend Castlereagh, George added fiercely, 'I will tell you, that I shall look upon every man as my personal enemy who proposes that question to me . . . I hope *all* my friends will not desert me.'[39] Dundas was taken completely unawares, and did his best to smooth the situation over, attempting to draw the King aside for a private discussion. But George had meant his remark to be heard as publicly as possible and to be reported in political circles. 'I am sorry Your Majesty should see the matter in that light,' Dundas replied. 'You know I have always done so,' said the King, truthfully.[40]

Sylvester Douglas, who had recently been created 1st Baron Glenbervie,

* The son of Anthony Addington, the Pitt family doctor who had attended the King in 1788.

was attending the Levee and later wrote in his diary that the King had spoken 'loud enough for me to have heard if I had listened', and that afterwards Dundas repeated to him the King's phrase, 'I must say that I shall consider every man who supports that measure as my personal enemy.' William Wilberforce, in his own diary, recorded the King using much the same language. [41] Glenbervie himself felt that the Quebec Act of 1774 and the Irish Catholic Relief Act of 1793 had already breached the Coronation Oath, which 'showed that this objection is now too late'.[42]

In the Closet afterwards, the King spoke kindly of Glenbervie's late father-in-law Lord North, asked about his last years and learned that his daughters had read Latin to him when he was blind, even though they themselves had not understood it. The King then took the opportunity of praising Pitt, observing that he 'was apt to put off laborious or disagreeable business to the last, but then, when forced to it, got through it with extraordinary rapidity, but that this sort of irregular mixture of delay and hurry was the chief cause of his ill-health'.[43] He added later, 'Mr Pitt, as to the facility and happiness of his language, was very unlike his father, who was a very bad writer.' He believed that Pitt and the 2nd Earl of Chatham inherited their obstinacy from their mother's side: Lady Hester's brother George Grenville, he recalled, 'never could be reasoned out of or driven from any point; that Lord Grenville takes up his opinions entirely from himself and never will listen to arguments against them'.[44] The King added, 'nobody now possesses that easy natural flow of genuine good-natured wit which distinguished [Lord North], and forced a smile from those against whom it was exercised . . . He believed Mr Pitt had nothing of that talent.' Speaking of the late Edmund Burke, who 'had spoken till the House would no longer hear him', the King observed that 'Mr Pitt has the same fault and that it is attended with the same effect.'[45] With hindsight, his comments sound all too clearly as if he was preparing himself for the coming clash.

After the altercation at the Levee, Dundas immediately warned Pitt that his hope of presenting the King with a fait accompli had obviously and spectacularly failed. It would not have been lost on Pitt and Dundas that the language the King had used about 'personal enmity' was the same that he had used to destroy the Fox–North coalition over the East India Bill. Nor was Dundas the only government minister to feel the King's ire; as Pitt wrote to his brother Chatham on 5 February, 'The King's language to more than one of his ministers was so strong and unqualified on this subject as to show even then (what has since been more fully confirmed) that his mind was made up to go to any extremity rather than consent to the measure in question.'[46]

George conscientiously consulted with the senior legal experts on the issue. Although Lord Eldon, the Attorney-General, and Lord Kenyon, the Lord Chief Justice, both opposed emancipation personally, they advised the King that allowing it would not technically be breaking his Coronation Oath to maintain the Anglican Church as 'established by law', because the change in the law would have been *a priori* approved and passed by Parliament. However, Lord Loughborough, who outranked them both as Lord Chancellor and as 'Keeper of the King's Conscience', disagreed. It is claimed that Loughborough even showed the King a private letter from Pitt about what was contemplated, which was sharp practice but hardly unknown in the politics of the day.[47]*

George required little convincing that if he permitted Catholic emancipation he would be breaking his Coronation Oath; and this made his decision to reject it a matter of personal honour. At the age of sixty-three, he still possessed the same unshakeable faith and sense of duty as had been impressed upon him by his beloved father when he was just eleven. George understood that the very reason the Hanoverians sat upon the British throne was that they were Protestants, and he considered himself to be the personification of a religious and moral bulwark against Catholic emancipation. The wording of the question in the Oath – 'Will you to the utmost of your power maintain the laws of God, the true profession of the Gospel, and the Protestant reformed religion established by law?' – has been used ever since, including by the present Queen.[48] 'Where is that power on earth to absolve me from the due observance of every sentence of that Oath . . .?' the King asked his chief equerry Major-General Thomas Garth. 'I had rather beg my bread from door to door throughout Europe than consent to any such measure.'[49]

He was certainly not about to be swayed by mere politicians about an issue of conscience such as this. When Dundas later attempted to argue that the Oath affected him only as an executive and not as a lawmaker, he replied in full John Bull manner, 'None of your Scotch metaphysics!'[50] As one of his biographers put it in 1940:

> To give his assent to anything that would tend to improve the position of a body most bitterly opposed to the very things he had sworn to defend, seemed to him the vilest apostasy. His fervent sincerity on this issue cannot be questioned. Nor should his courage and tenacity of purpose in this and many other conflicts be summarily dismissed as mere obstinacy.[51]

---

* It did not win him the King's respect; when Loughborough died as the 1st Earl of Rosslyn in January 1805, the King reputedly said, 'Is he dead? Is he dead? Then he has not left behind him a greater rogue in my dominions' (Vulliamy, *Royal George* p. 308). It was a harsh summation for the man who had supported him so staunchly during the Gordon Riots.

George was anxious about the effect that emancipation might have on the union with Ireland, since the majority of Irish Catholics were national-ists. 'English government ought well to consider', he had written in 1795, 'before it gives any encouragement to a proposition which cannot fail sooner or later to separate the two kingdoms.'[52] As had been seen with the Bantry Bay and Fishguard expeditions, there were crucial strategic reasons during an existential war with France not to lose control over an island only 12 miles at its closest point from the British mainland – half the width of the English Channel. Ireland had been described as a pistol pointed at the heart of England, and he had reason to believe that if he were to grant Catholic emancipation he might very well be pulling the trigger. Moreover, scores of Irish Catholic MPs sitting at Westminster and likely voting with the radical Whigs would undoubtedly upset the whole structure of British politics.

The King's views on Catholic emancipation has been denounced as reactionary, of course, but it accurately reflected those of a majority of Britons at the time. When a pro-emancipation petition signed by ninety-nine senior Irish Catholics was delivered to Parliament, including all the Catholic peers of Ireland as well as representatives of the Irish gentry and the mercantile and professional classes, it was rejected by 336 votes to 124 in the Commons and by 178 votes to 49 in the Lords.

On 29 January 1801, the day after the Levee at which he had spoken so forcefully to Dundas, the King asked Henry Addington to try to per-suade Pitt to drop the measure. Addington had been one of Pitt's closest friends since they were undergraduates at Cambridge together, the person in whom he had confided that he had given up the prospect of marrying Eleanor Eden, Lord Auckland's daughter, and in whose house in Berkshire he had recuperated after an illness in 1800. The King told Addington that he had 'very strong apprehensions ... that the most mischievous measure is in contemplation to be brought forward in this first session' by Lord Castlereagh, 'no less than the placing the Roman Catholics of the kingdom in an equal state of rights to sit in both Houses of Parliament and hold offices of trust and emolument with those of the Established Church. It is now suggested by those best informed that Mr Pitt favours this opinion,' as did Henry Dundas and William Grenville. He told Addington he had 'certainly not disguised to them my abhorrence of the very idea, and my feeling it as a duty, should it ever come forward, publicly to express my disapprobation of it, and that no consideration could ever make me give my consent ... I as well as several of my predecessors have been obliged to swear the support of [the Established Church] at our coronations.' The King pointed out that the Oath had been dictated not by the monarchs themselves, but 'by the wisdom of the Parliament of England'.[53] Every other European state had an established Church, he continued. 'I wish he would open Mr Pitt's eyes as to the danger arising from the mere agitating so improper a question ... unhinging every political tie our forefathers have thought sacred ... indeed it is exactly following the steps of the French Revolution where every consideration of religion has been destroyed.'[54]

Addington spoke to Pitt as the King had asked, and reported the conversation back to him for over four hours between 8 p.m. and midnight at Buckingham House on 30 January. As a letter to Chatham of 5 February made clear, Pitt was under no illusion that Addington himself would be his likely successor if he resigned over the issue of Catholic emancipation, because the King could trust him to continue other Pittite policies. In such a situation, Pitt might well have believed that he could still exercise control over the government through his friend.

On 31 January, Lord Auckland reproached Pitt indignantly for his secrecy over the measure. 'Will it convert disaffection to loyalty?' he rhetorically asked of the Irish Catholics. Pointing out that it needed to pass all three parts of the constitution, he added, 'God avert the effect which it may possibly have on one of them,' meaning the King.[55]

'The knowledge of Your Majesty's general indisposition to any change of the laws on this subject would have made this a painful task to him,' Pitt wrote to the King from Downing Street that day, in the customary third person, 'and it is become much more so by learning from some of his colleagues ... the extent to which Your Majesty entertains, and has declared, that sentiment.'[56] Yet, Pitt argued, the admission of Dissenters and Catholics to public offices and of Catholics to Parliament (from which Dissenters were not excluded) was 'highly advisable, with a view to the tranquillity and improvement of Ireland, and to the general interest of the United Kingdom'. He said that there would be 'no danger to the Established Church, or to the Protestant interest in Great Britain or Ireland', because Catholics were no longer 'politically dangerous'.

The King replied the next day succinctly and unambiguously, and in as friendly a way as he could manage to his premier of more than seventeen years:

> I should not do justice to the warm impulse of my heart if I entered on the subject most unpleasant to my mind without first expressing that the cordial affection I have for Mr Pitt, as well as high opinion of his talents and integrity, greatly add to my uneasiness on this occasion; but a sense of religious as well as political duty has made me, from the moment I mounted the throne, consider the Oath that the wisdom of our forefathers has enjoined the kings

of this realm to take at their coronation, and enforced by the obligation of instantly following it in the course of the ceremony with taking the Sacrament, as so binding a religious obligation on me to maintain the fundamental maxims on which our constitution is placed, namely, the Church of England being the established one, and that those who hold employments in the state must be members of it, and consequently obliged not only to take oaths against popery, but to receive the Holy Communion agreeable to the rites of the Church of England.[57]

Pitt's proposal, therefore, amounted to 'no less than the complete overthrow of the whole fabric' of 'our happy constitution'. He added, 'My opinions are not those formed on the moment, but such as I have imbibed for forty years, and from which I never can depart,' and thus 'I fear from his letter we can never agree.' Crucially, George did not see the irreconcilable difference on emancipation as a reason for Pitt to resign. 'If those who unfortunately differ with me will keep this subject at rest,' he wrote, 'I will on my part . . . be silent also.'[58]

On 2 February the King opened Parliament with a Speech from the Throne that made reference to the new union with Ireland, but not to Catholic emancipation. 'The King looked particularly well,' noted Glenbervie, 'and read his speech with particular energy and clearness, much beyond what has been usual with him for the last ten or fifteen years.'[59] Lord Auckland told Glenbervie that while the King was robing in the House of Lords beforehand, he said to the 11th Duke of Norfolk, who was a supporter of emancipation, in the hearing of other peers, 'I believe, my Lord, you have a very fine old place at Arundel.' The Duke, who was extensively rebuilding the castle (and who later became known as the Architectural Duke), answered that indeed he had. 'I hear', added the King, 'you are making considerable alterations in it.' 'I am,' replied Norfolk. 'Take care', added the King, 'not to meddle with the foundations.'[60] This was said, according to Auckland, 'looking significantly to some of the other lords'. George knew where the foundations of his dynasty lay, and he was not disposed to meddle with them.

William Pitt the Younger resigned the premiership over the issue of Catholic emancipation on 3 February 1801, with a letter which stated that he had to 'consider the moment as now arrived when . . . it must be his first wish to be released, as soon possible, from his present situation'.[61] Addington accepted the post two days later, resigning as Speaker on 10 February. 'My dear Addington,' the King told him, 'you have saved your country.'[62] 'It was one of the most dramatic and unusual appointments to the premiership,' notes the historian Stephen Parkinson, 'a Speaker of the House of Commons who had never served in government and who had barely spoken in Parliament except from the chair suddenly transferred to the highest office in the land.'[63] Addington was a mild-mannered, perfectly pleasant man who had been an esteemed Speaker for twelve years, and Pitt seems to have assumed that he would be able to return to the premiership whenever he wanted.

The King both liked and trusted Addington, who was a diligent and popular MP for Devizes but no orator and indeed a poor debater. He had trained as a lawyer and was the first middle-class Prime Minister, unrelated to the aristocracy by blood or marriage.[64] The Foxites hated the fact that someone from the professional classes had invaded their preserve, and snobbishly referred to him as 'the Doctor' because of his father's profession. By contrast, the King got on with all classes of people, and knew that historically the monarchy had called upon people outside the upper classes to serve as ministers, such as Cardinal Wolsey and Thomas Cromwell. William Wilberforce said of Addington that he was a man of 'pure and upright intentions, and of more religion than almost any politician'.[65] This naturally appealed to the King.

Because the change of government was friendly, his brother Chatham staying on as Lord President of the Council, there seemed no hurry for Pitt to return the seals of office or for Addington to kiss hands formally or even to name a new ministry. In this curious manner, Pitt continued as almost a co-premier until he had delivered his Budget on 18 February. Addington did not mind, as he was finding his feet and appointing his ministry. 'One was de jure Prime Minister, the other de facto,' wrote Addington's biographer; 'their ministers had no idea whether they were in or out of office.'[66]

It was during this strange political limbo that the King fell ill on 15 February with a chill and cramp that affected his whole body, and within a week all of the old symptoms of the malady – hoarseness, constipation, biliousness, nausea – had suddenly reappeared. No one could be in any doubt that madness would now follow, although it took a little time. George was still able to show Lord Eldon a passage on the Catholic emancipation issue from Blackstone's Commentaries on 20 February, for example. Because traumatic experiences can be a trigger for hypomanic attacks, the Duke of York might have been right when he said in a debate in the House of Lords nearly twenty-five years later that 'The agitation of it [Catholic emancipation] has been the cause of a most serious and alarming illness to an illustrious personage.'[67]

Although he had resigned as Speaker, Addington did not officially kiss hands as Prime Minister until 17 March. For six weeks, therefore, there were effectively two governments, and on three occasions there were even Cabinet meetings at which both sets of ministers were present; indeed on one afternoon there occurred what one historian has described as 'surely the most extraordinary Cabinet meeting ever held', because there were sitting around the same Cabinet table two prime ministers, two lord chancellors and two secretaries of state for war.[68] Since they were all in the same party, and were friends and often relations, no constitutional crisis arose, although the Prince of Wales soon stirred things up by sending for each set of ministers separately, while intriguing with Fox and the Whigs behind all of their backs.[69]

All this would have been strange enough in peacetime, but Britain was fighting a full-scale war against one of the greatest conquerors in history. Moreover Napoleon now commanded what he ominously entitled the Army of England, just as the army that had conquered Italy had been the Army of Italy and the one which took Cairo had been the Army of Egypt. Furthermore, any outside hope of an early second coalition against France collapsed when he signed the Treaty of Lunéville with Austria on 9 February 1801, which brought France up to the Rhine, virtually demolished the Holy Roman Empire, created a new French state in Italy called the Kingdom of Etruria and recognized the pro-French puppet Batavian (Dutch), Cisalpine (northern Italian), Helvetian (Swiss) and Ligurian (Piedmontese) Republics. Against this protean force on the Continent, Britain had two governments, and a King who was heading for another severe bout of bipolar disorder.

George's last communication with Addington, written in his clearly legible hand, was on 17 February from Buckingham House, informing him that he had not been downstairs that day and was taking Dr James's Fever Powder for his cold. After that he wrote nothing until 10 March. He asked to meet Addington at noon on the 18th, but by 22 February he was too seriously ill for visitors. On 18 February he wrote to 'My dear Pitt', saying, 'As you are closing, much to my sorrow, your political career, I cannot help expressing the joy I feel that the Ways and Means [Committee]' had agreed his Budget without debate.[70] He clearly considered Addington to be not a stopgap premier until Pitt chose to re-enter Downing Street, but Pitt's successor. This was understandably the way Addington saw the situation too.

At 4.30 p.m. on 20 February the King spoke normally to Glenbervie at an audience, and remarked to the new Attorney-General, the aptly named Edward Law, 'It is good that you have not before been in Parliament; you will have no words to eat. The less you pledge yourself, the less inconvenience you will bring upon yourself.'[71] By the next day, he had to be confined, and he told Thomas Willis, who had been called upon as his octogenarian father Francis had retired, 'I have prayed to God all night that I might die, or that he would spare my reason ... If it should be otherwise, for God's sake keep me from your father and a regency.'[72] The next day he was delirious.

26

'A Fearful Experiment'

February 1801–September 1804

Our separation must be and really is equally painful to us both.[1]
Queen Charlotte to George III, 22 April 1801

George was once again a helpless spectator of his own condition as he slipped in and out of severe manic depression. 'My bodily health is reasonably good,' he was able to tell Addington shortly before 22 February 1801. 'I have, I trust, good common sense, and I believe a good heart, but my nerves are weak . . . Your father said twelve years ago that quiet was what I wanted, and that I must have.'[2]

On 23 February, his delirium was so strong that it was very difficult to persuade him to go to bed.[3] The next night his pulse rose to 130 beats per minute. 'This makes in favour of his mental derangement,' wrote Lord Malmesbury, 'and proves it to be only the effect of delirium in consequence of fever, but it puts his life in very great danger. [Political] Opposition very active.'[4] That same day, Charles Fox moved from his home in St Ann's Hill, Chertsey, to lodge at Lord Fitzwilliam's house in central London to be close to the political events as they unfolded, with a renewed chance to bring down the government with the help of the Prince of Wales. Yet that same day, 24 February, at 4 p.m. the King was able to sign the repeal of the Brown Bread Act, which had been passed during the winter shortages two months earlier and had prohibited the baking of expensive types of bread. Lord Eldon, one of the two lord chancellors, told Malmesbury that when he gave his royal assent the King 'was in the perfect possession of his understanding'.[5]

On 28 February, Addington told his friend Charles Abbot, who was soon to become Speaker of the House of Commons, that the King was being prescribed tree bark and port wine. He himself had suggested sleeping on a pillow of warm hops, something that his father believed to be a cure for insomnia.[6] Tartar emetics were reapplied, the fever was starved and a few days later the King had hot vinegar applied to his feet. On 2 March all the King's doctors, including his physician-in-ordinary, Thomas Gisborne, believed that he would die that day, and the Queen and Prince of Wales were summoned.[7] 'The King's fever increased last night,' read the doctors' bulletin, 'and has not since abated.'[8] Thomas Willis and his brother John were the only optimists, but at 10 p.m. George fell into a deep six-hour sleep, from which he woke 'with the fever abated, and better in every respect'.[9]

The Prince of Wales refused to accept the improvement, however, and told the 4th Earl of Darnley that 'the King's mind was completely deranged, whatever his bodily health might be'.[10] This struck Malmesbury as 'most unfeeling language. If true, it little became him to say so – but it is not.'[11] Malmesbury added that nothing was being concealed from the Prince about his father's health.

The King was able to feed himself on 3 March, and a joyful crowd congregated outside Buckingham House.[12] The next day he asked Thomas Willis to write an account of his convalescence for Addington, Eldon and Pitt: 'Tell him [Pitt] I am now quite well – quite recovered from my illness; but what has *he* not to answer for who is the cause of my having been ill at all?'[13] The King – who had no more actual insight into the cause of his attacks than his doctors – clearly believed that anxiety could bring them on, and now blamed Pitt's pursuit of Catholic emancipation for his malady. Malmesbury suspected that Pitt and Lord Spencer did indeed feel guilty, writing in his diary on 25 February that 'Pitt, though too haughty to confess it, feels also a great deal.'[14]

Pitt, replying to Willis, asked him 'to tell His Majesty that during his reign he would *never* agitate the Catholic Question; that is, whether *in* office or *out* of office'.[15] Willis wrote back to Pitt, 'After saying the kindest things of you, he exclaimed "Now my mind will be at ease." '[16] He added that, although George was not yet completely well, he probably soon would be. A month after resigning the premiership over Catholic emancipation, Pitt had therefore agreed to pursue it no further.

Although he was well enough to play piquet with the Queen on 6 March, George still had the nervous habit of rolling up handkerchiefs. This attack also had a bad effect on his already diminishing eyesight; within four years he would be virtually blind. But he improved enough for the public bulletins to be discontinued on 11 March, and at 10 a.m. on 13 March he wrote his first letter to Addington for several weeks, in which he 'cordially' approved the Cabinet minutes.[17] The next day he felt well enough to receive Pitt's seals of office, as well as those of Dundas, Grenville and William Windham. Portland stayed on, and Addington assumed the role of Chancellor of the Exchequer as well as the premiership, just as Pitt had before him.

Historians have almost unanimously characterized the Addington ministry as dull and uninspiring. Lady Malmesbury called it 'the Dumplin' Ministry', while the Pittite MP George Canning dubbed it 'the Goose Administration', vividly adding that it was 'wretched, pusillanimous, toad-eating [that is, toadying]'.[18] Another Pittite MP, John Hookham Frere, liked to tell the story of the Tory peer who, on reading out the names of Addington's Cabinet to Frere's father, then rubbed his hands with satisfaction and said, 'Well, thank God we have at last got a ministry without one of those confounded men of genius in it.'[19] Yet George himself was delighted with the new government, which he knew he could trust not to spring unpleasant surprises such as Catholic emancipation upon him. 'The King cannot find words sufficiently expressive of His Majesty's cordial approbation of the whole arrangements which *his own Chancellor of the Exchequer* has wisely, and, His Majesty chooses to add, most correctly recommended,' he wrote to Addington.[20] The words he underlined hinted at a proprietorial sense that the King felt for the new ministry. Addington had been an MP for less than seven years, and remains the Prime Minister with the third-shortest parliamentary service (after Pitt and Bute) before attaining the premiership.

Despite the King's apparent recovery, the Willises stayed on, deciding which duties he could and could not undertake, and even playing a strange quasi-political role because ministers knew that George must not be over-taxed. Astonishingly, on 18 March Addington asked Thomas Willis to inquire of the King whether Britain could make peace with France. The eventual answer was yes, but Willis recorded in his diary that 'It was some time before I could get the King to write the answer which I was anxious for.'[21]

The Willises blistered the King's legs and gave him powerful emetics so that he would not be, as they put it, 'hurried' or 'extravagant', or have 'wrong ideas' at Court.[22] When the King showed understandable resentment at this, they argued that it might mean a relapse, thereby justifying their continued presence (and concomitant fees). When on one occasion John Willis attempted to persuade the King that his verbal abuse of him and his brother was 'a proof of the remnant of the disorder', George replied 'that it was no proof, for that he had abused him ever since his former illness'.[23] This Willis took as indication that they needed to continue their treatment.

The King had recovered just in time to be aware of Prussia's invasion of Hanover on 3 April, a move that had been encouraged by Napoleon and Tsar Paul I of Russia. Prussia had joined the anti-British Second League of Armed Neutrality, whose vessels Britain had embargoed on 14 January, and this was her revenge. Hanover surrendered without a fight, and the twenty-seven-year-old Prince Adolphus managed to flee to England. The invasion only increased the pressure on Britain to come to a general settlement with France in which Hanover could be returned to the King.

Glenbervie was told that at a Privy Council meeting on 14 April 'the King was quite calm and collected and, though pale and sallow, much better than at the last Council'.[24] George had joked to Lord Eldon, whose elopement* with Elizabeth Surtees while he was still at Oxford had persuaded him to enter the law rather than take holy orders, 'You may tell her that if it had not been for her, you might probably have been at this time a country curate.'[25] Instead he was the 1st Baron Eldon and Lord High Chancellor of Great Britain.

William Huskisson MP, another Pittite junior minister, who was delivering his seals as Under-Secretary at War after six years, told Glenbervie about what seemed at the time to be a temporary arrangement because of the King's illness, but was in fact already in the process of becoming an important constitutional change in the power and responsibility of the Prime Minister, perhaps the most important before recent times. 'The King's present plan is not to give audiences to as many of the ministers as please ... ', Huskisson explained, 'and seldom to see any of them but Addington.' Instead the King was going 'to do business with the others by letter, or through Addington'.[26]

Pitt had already begun this innovation, but Glenbervie was still shocked by it. 'This is the notion of a Prime Minister as known formerly sometimes under the French government,' he wrote. 'But I question if the other ministers will submit to such an inferiority and whether Addington is equal to so uncommon a situation. I doubt also, for various reasons, whether the public will approve of it.' Yet Addington, for all the snobbish sneers about him, did carry off this new role as the sole conduit between the King and his government, after which the constitution had subtly altered for ever. Few at Westminster besides Huskisson and Glenbervie noticed that something fundamental had happened in British politics.

The Prince of Wales visited the King on 15 April, and reported that his father 'continually and repeatedly talked of himself as a dying man, determined to go abroad to Hanover, to make over the government to the Prince'.[27] Was this true or merely the Prince's wishful fantasy? With his usual unerring ability to cause the maximum amount of mischief at the worst possible time for his father, he now formally embraced the cause of Catholic emancipation. He was moreover heavily in debt once again.

---

* Classically done, with the aid of a ladder.

Four days after the Prince's visit, the King was taken to the White House in Kew, where he was kept in close confinement for a month by the Willises, with the full support of the Queen, even though he was not exhibiting any apparent symptoms of lunacy. 'Sir,' he told Thomas Willis, 'I will never forgive you whilst I live.'[28] (Parliament did, however, and the family were eventually paid £10,000 for their services.) Having essentially been kidnapped, while at Kew the King was not allowed to see his family but he was still permitted to sign Acts of Parliament, correspond with his ministers and create an English peerage for the Irish peer Alleyne Fitzherbert, Lord St Helens. He was clearly not mad, but neither was he allowed to live a normal life.

The King's sanity during his enforced, month-long captivity at Kew between 19 April and 19 May can be judged from the variety of subjects of his handwritten letters. They included sending St Helens to Moscow to congratulate Tsar Alexander I on his accession; congratulating the Secretary for War and the Colonies, Lord Hobart,* on General Sir Ralph Abercromby's defeat of the French Army of Egypt on 21 March (observing, 'It will effect that kind of consternation in France which may occasion some great event');[29] agreeing to the plans of the Lord Chamberlain, the 1st Marquess of Salisbury, for renovating the Duke of Kent's apartments in Kensington Palace; giving advice to the new Viceroy of Ireland, the 3rd Earl of Hardwicke ('Whilst on the one hand he shall treat the Irish with civility, he must not get too familiar with them and must show them that the season of jobs [that is, system of jobbery] is at an end');[30] and accepting Lord Castlereagh's resignation as Keeper of the Signet, and conferring it upon Charles Abbot ('who will certainly prove a very useful servant of the Crown').[31] All this was done while he was at least theoretically sufficiently insane to be under confinement by the Willis brothers. On 10 May in a letter to Hardwicke he scathingly referred to Ireland as 'that uncivilized island', but this owed more to the political and military situation there in the aftermath of the 1798 Rebellion than to any medical problem of his own. Indeed, the rest of the letter was extremely composed and measured, suggesting that Church of Ireland bishops should reside in their dioceses and that cathedral choir services should be performed with punctuality and decorum.[32] The evidence of these letters demonstrates that a sane King was being held by his mad-doctors with the full knowledge and acquiescence of both the royal family and the government.

Because he was not allowed to correspond with his family, the extraordinary situation developed whereby to send a note to Prince Adolphus he

---

* In whose honour the capital of Tasmania was named.

had to write to the Foreign Secretary Robert Jenkinson, Lord Hawkesbury (son of Lord Liverpool), in Whitehall, even though Adolphus was 'but two rooms off' in the same house as him.[33] Thomas Willis later admitted that they were 'unwilling to forsake the task we had undertaken where great credit was at stake and the completion of which was confidently seen'.[34] The great credit was the public acclaim that he was expecting to receive for 'curing' the King, just as his father had, and he regarded this extended period of convalescence as an essential part of the treatment.

'The reports of the King are still very uncomfortable,' wrote Lord Glenbervie on 28 April. 'The Duke of Clarence it seems tells everybody he meets at Hampton, Kingston, etc., that he is stark mad, that he had very nearly killed a page the other day, that he attempted to ride away from his attendants.'[35] None of these accusations rings true for the 1801 bipolar episode. On receiving the news on 30 April from Lord Hawkesbury that Admiral Nelson had won a great victory at the battle of Copenhagen earlier that month, George replied, 'Lord Hawkesbury may easily conceive what a balm to my heart so essential a piece of news as that he has just sent me must prove.'[36] He fully acknowledged 'the honour that must accrue to the British arms'. At least at this time the King was clearly not 'stark mad'.

In order to escape his terrible predicament, the King effectively went on strike in mid-May, telling Eldon 'as a gentleman and a king' that he now refused to sign any official documents until he was freed from the Willises, before he walked across the lawn to the Dutch House to congratulate the Queen on her birthday.[37] His illness, he told the Lord Chancellor, had taught him one positive advantage, 'namely, the means of knowing his real from his pretended friends'.[38] To one of the true friends, Bishop Hurd, he wrote, 'I have most wonderfully escaped the jaws of death.'[39] He took great solace from the collapse of the Second League of Armed Neutrality and the defeat of the French in Egypt, writing that 'the hand of Divine Providence seems to stretch forward to protect this favoured island, which alone has stood forth constantly in opposition to our wicked neighbours'.

Without his signature on parliamentary Bills and financial warrants, the government would grind to a halt, so the King's strike worked. Once the Willises had finally left, he made Prince Frederick solemnly swear to him that they would never be allowed back. His illness had once again had a pronounced physical effect on him. 'I found him very much altered indeed,' Glenbervie noted in early July, 'and instead of that fulness and roundness of limbs and countenance, an emaciated face and person with his clothes hanging upon him. But his complexion is clear, and those about him say he has got flesh and strength much beyond what he had a month ago.'[40]

On 13 June the King gave Addington a lifetime lease on White Lodge in Richmond Park which had been built for George II and long occupied by Lord Bute. It was a sign of great royal favour and Addington lived there for the next three reigns until his death in 1844. After he had written to thank the King profusely (referring to his 'perpetually animating the obligations of duty by the strongest sentiments of reverential attachment and gratitude'), George replied by saying something that he could never have said to Pitt, whose assertive genius over seventeen years had been exhausting, however little he saw of him: 'The King is highly gratified at the repeated marks of the sensibility of Mr Addington's heart, which must greatly add to the comfort of having placed him with so much propriety at the head of the Treasury. He trusts their mutual affection can only cease with their lives.'[41] The King respected Addington's conservative views and moral probity, and, as usual with his friends, his Anglicanism and happy marriage, in this case with eight children.

Addington's biographer Philip Ziegler believes that George 'admired Pitt and sincerely liked him but it was not comfortable for a king, let alone a Hanoverian, to deal always with someone who was obviously the greater man. With Addington he could revert to the avuncular and slightly condescending affability which he found came most easily when dealing with his subjects.'[42] Unfortunately, as with Lord North, someone the King liked was not necessarily the best leader of a wartime government. As George Canning's cruel rhyme put it, 'Pitt is to Addington as London is to Paddington,' at a time when Paddington was a village of only 300 houses north of the capital.[43]

The Capitulation of Alexandria of August 1801, which saw the surrender of all remaining French forces in Egypt, led to a rare instance of the King eating his words, but characteristically doing so in a generous and open-hearted way. Together with Grenville and Windham he had opposed Abercromby's expedition, which Pitt and Dundas had nonetheless championed. Dining at Dundas' house in Wimbledon shortly afterwards, George toasted him with madeira on the victory. 'In my opinion when a person has been perfectly in the wrong,' the King said in the presence of the Queen, Prince Adolphus, the Dundas family and their guests, 'the most just and honourable thing for him to do is to acknowledge it publicly.'[44] The campaign allowed the King to present the Rosetta Stone, which was surrendered by the French under the terms of the Treaty of Alexandria, and which was to play the central role in the understanding of Egyptian hieroglyphics, to the British Museum, where it is still the single most visited item today.

France and Britain were both now exhausted after eight years at war, and Napoleon wanted to concentrate on the domestic reforms necessary to bolster his regime. On 1 October, Lord Hawkesbury and the French negotiator Louis-Guillaume Otto agreed peace preliminaries in Hawkesbury's office at Downing Street. The 3 per cent Consols leaped from 59 to 68 on the news and the price of wheat fell by ten shillings a quarter, even without the terms being divulged. Otto's carriage had its horses removed and he was pulled in triumph through London by the celebrating crowd.

Under the terms, which were not significantly altered when the definitive treaty was signed at Amiens on 27 March 1802, Britain restored all of her maritime conquests except for Trinidad and Ceylon to France, Spain and Holland; France evacuated Naples, and recognized Portuguese and Ionian independence; Egypt was restored to Turkey, and Britain promised to restore the naval stronghold of Malta to the Knights of Malta, who had run it for centuries before Napoleon arrived there on his way to Egypt in 1798. A secret clause restored Hanover to George. Napoleon had won a breathing space in which to reorganize French society and administration fundamentally, of which he took great advantage.[45]

Houses were illuminated across London celebrating the peace, and Addington was briefly the most popular man in Britain. 'I do not think you are right,' the King told him some months later, 'but I have now made up my mind to your peace and I'll support you like a man.'[46] Charles Fox of course welcomed the peace, telling his constituents on 10 October 1801, 'We have not, I acknowledge, obtained the objects for which the war was undertaken – so much the better – I rejoice that we have not. I like the peace the more on this very account.'[47] When Charles Grey, the future premier, complained about this unpatriotic language, Fox admitted, 'The truth is, I am gone something further in hate to the English government than perhaps you and the rest of my friends are, and certainly further than can with prudence be avowed. The triumph of the French government over the English does in fact afford me a degree of *pleasure* which it is very difficult to disguise.'[48]

When Glenbervie saw the King at the Privy Council meeting to proclaim the cessation of hostilities, he thought that he was looking much better than he had in May, but noted, 'I believe the King very much dislikes the Peace. Addington I thought extremely out of spirits.'[49] Shortly afterwards, when the King was returning from a day's hunting and saw Addington's carriage, they rode in it together and the King confided, 'I own this has been painful to me, as it must have been to you, but I considered whether it was possible to do anything more without Continental assistance, and saw plainly it was not, and also that there was no hope of gaining such assistance.'[50] It was true; the Austrians and Prussians were in no state to challenge Napoleon, and neither was the new Tsar of Russia, Alexander I, who had only come to the throne in March 1801 on his father Paul I's assassination.

Even so, the King was not yet reconciled to the idea of long-term peaceful coexistence with regicidal, atheist and now, under Napoleon, arriviste France. 'If ministers think they can *win* me over to their opinion as to a peace with these fellows by stipulations about Hanover,' he told Lord Gower at the end of October, 'they are mistaken.'[51] 'Do you know what I call the Peace?' the King asked Malmesbury at Windsor presciently in late November. 'An *experimental Peace*, for it is nothing else. I am sure *you* think so and perhaps do not give it so *gentle* a name, but it was *unavoidable*. I was abandoned by everybody, Allies and *all* . . . Had I found more opinions like mine, better might have been done.'[52]

Someone who shared the King's opinion of the peace was William Pitt, but in September he fell seriously ill and had to retire to Walmer Castle for a rest cure. After leaving office he had suffered stomach pains and vomiting, and now his doctor recorded Pitt's 'severe morning sickness and absolute dislike to all food, with all the unpleasant symptoms of aggravated debility . . . the nerves seriously affected . . . and the whole system deranged'.[53] It was worryingly like his father's illness, but Pitt put it down merely to a change in the weather and 'a little over-exercise in shooting', even though he had suffered similar gastrointestinal pains for four out of the past five years, with each bout worse than the last.[54]

On 16 November 1802, a daring plot to assassinate the King was foiled, and all its conspirators arrested. Its leader, Colonel Edward Despard, had once served bravely alongside the young Horatio Nelson in the San Juan expedition in Nicaragua in 1780. An Irishman of good family, he had nonetheless become disappointed by his lack of promotion since then and had fallen into revolutionary politics at the time of the Spithead and Nore mutinies. He was driven not by Jacobin ideology, however, but rather, in the estimation of the historian Sir Charles Oman, by 'injured vanity and rancorous megalomania', having been 'ignored by ministers and flouted by under-secretaries' after years of being the most important Briton in Belize.[55]

In mid-1802, Despard put together a gang of desperadoes and malcontents who, fortunately for the King, included Private Thomas Windsor of the 3rd Battalion of the Grenadier Guards, who turned government spy. He informed the Home Office that the State Coach was going to be attacked as the King got into it at St James's Palace just before it picked up its cavalry escort on its way to Westminster for the Opening of Parliament. The plan was for the front two horses to be shot as the coach was rushed from both sides. A second scheme was to prime the ceremonial/ornamental cannon behind the Admiralty and to fire it point-blank at the coach as it came up the Mall.[56] Despard was then going to attack Parliament, while the 1st and 3rd Battalions of the Grenadiers mutinied at the Tower of London, and a third group attacked the Bank of England. Coaches leaving for the country would be stopped, and the semaphores used for communication with the garrisons at Dover and Portsmouth destroyed. Apart from generally de-stabilizing the country, the ultimate aim of the plot seems to have been to steal the gold in the Bank.

Beyond the murder of the King, the desperate plan could never have come off, as neither the Grenadiers nor the thousands of troops stationed at Windsor, Chatham, Colchester, Canterbury and elsewhere were rebels. Thanks to Private Windsor, the Home Office thoroughly infiltrated the conspirators for at least four months before arresting about thirty of them at the Oakley Arms in Lambeth a week before the State Opening. Despard was easy to spot because he was 'the only person there with the appearance of a gentleman'.[57]

The prosecution case at the Old Bailey was undertaken by the young Attorney-General, Spencer Perceval, a talented Pittite. Four conspirators turned King's evidence, thereby saving their own necks. The landlady of the Flying Horse Tavern had overheard Despard saying of the King's assas-sination, 'I have weighed the matter well, and my heart is callous.'[58] Admiral Nelson appeared as a character witness for Despard, but he had not seen him since 1780. After Despard refused to deny the existence of the plot, the jury took only twenty-five minutes to convict him. Luckily for Despard, the King's heart was not as callous as his: he and six other co-conspirators were spared the drawing and quartering traditionally meted out to traitors and were merely hanged in the traditional manner. Despard met his end on the gatehouse roof of the Horsemonger Lane Gaol in Southwark on 21 February 1803, and more than 20,000 people came to watch. When he learned that Despard had refused to see a clergyman before his execution, George lamented, 'It is melancholy that a man should appear so void of religion at so awful a moment.'[59]

On 4 February 1803 the King spoke at length to Louis-Guillaume Otto during a Drawing Room about Jean Soulavie's recently published *Mémoires historiques et politiques du règne de Louis XVI*, which blamed the out-break of the French Revolution on Louis' summoning of the Estates-General in May 1789. He then 'talked a great deal about the sect of modern phil-osophers and the mischief they have done', mentioning Voltaire and the mathematician and polymath Jean le Rond d'Alembert, co-editor with

Diderot of the *Encyclopédie*, saying 'that he wondered that men who devoted themselves to learning and science should grow worse men as they proceeded in acquiring knowledge'.[60] He discussed the pre-Revolutionary administrations of the Duc de Choiseul, the Duc d'Aiguillon and René de Maupeou, all of whom had failed to stave off the catastrophe.

Of the Estates-General itself, the King opined that 'It might be wrong to banish them, but it was unwise to recall and reinstate them,' which was surely correct, albeit with the benefit of nearly fourteen years' hindsight.[61] George recalled that Frederick the Great 'on his accession had been urged to repeal a tax which had been unpopular and the imposition of which was represented as a very bad measure. He answered that he thought it was, that he should never have imposed it, but that finding it in force he should not repeal it.'[62] If Otto was reminded by this discussion of the Stamp Act and Coercive Acts, he was too much of a diplomat to mention it.

More than twenty different medals were struck to celebrate the Peace of Amiens when it was signed on 27 March 1802, although it was not perceived as either a resounding victory or the definitive end to the struggle. As Sheridan quipped, all men were glad of the peace, but none were proud of it. Some prominent Pittites such as George Canning and Spencer Perceval opposed it outright. They pointed out how much Britain had been obliged to cede, including important strategic points such as the Cape of Good Hope, and that, if Malta were evacuated as the treaty stipulated, the Royal Navy would be severely weakened in the central Mediterranean; yet all that Napoleon had lost was southern Italy and the Ionian Islands. The First Consul soon wrecked the spirit of the treaty by annexing Piedmont in September, then Parma and Piacenza in October. Pitt supported the Peace initially, but soon started to criticize it, although he never went so far as explicitly to join the Opposition.

On 26 March, Malmesbury predicted to the Duke of York, 'Peace, Sir, in a week, and war in a month.' York obviously passed this quip on to George, because when the King saw Malmesbury at a Drawing Room on 11 April he told him, 'You are a great prophet; I believe your prediction will be true . . . The first half of it is already fulfilled, and I expect the other will not fail.'[63] He added that 'he was never more embarrassed than to know how to make up his mind on this measure of peace . . . He hoped he had done right, but he was sure it was a fearful experiment.'[64] Malmesbury noted that the King said 'all this and a great deal more to the same effect . . . *almost* loud enough for the persons round us to hear, and certainly so to those who were good listeners'. Since eavesdropping on the King's conversation was one of the incentives for attending the Drawing Rooms, most people were good listeners there.

In late June 1802, Addington called a general election, at which the Opposition failed to make any breakthroughs. At a Levee in September, the King complimented Addington and Eldon 'and said it was a comfortable thing to see his two sheet anchors so sound'.[65] In October he even permitted Castlereagh to enter the Cabinet as President of the Board of Control. After seventeen years of struggle, revolution, war and three bouts of lunacy, the King seemed to have found an easy contentment at last.

Then in November it was discovered that, despite Parliament's settlement of the Prince of Wales' debts on his marriage in 1795, he had incurred vast new ones, and his creditors were pressing. At a time when only 3 per cent of families enjoyed an annual income of £200 or more, the Prince had an income of £108,000 per annum, yet still had incurred debts of £146,000, which Robert Gray, his Treasurer of the Duchy of Cornwall, described as 'really alarming'.[66] Gray discovered that the Prince owed £23,000 to the builders of the Brighton Pavilion and £14,000 to those of Carlton House, £17,000 to jewellers, £9,000 to tailors, £7,500 to lacemakers, £4,800 to clockmakers, over £2,000 to coachmakers and over £5,000 to hatters, drapers, hosiers, glovers, breeches tailors and bootmakers. He had allocated £11,000 for his stables, but had overspent that by £9,000 on two coachmen, a post-chaise man and postilion, six helpers, twelve saddle horses, four curricles and coach horses, a saddle-horse groom and six helpers, seven footmen and several other servants. Four huntsmen and a helper also looked after five horses and sixty hounds. Nor had the Prince felt under any obligation to slow down his rate of exotic acquisitions for his properties, buying furniture from Paris and even sending a Dr Garrett off to China to buy 'sundry prohibited articles consisting of pictures of their customs (and particularly the Emperor's Court), armour of all kinds, mandarin dresses, flags . . . lanterns etc., etc.', on which he spent £984 (including the bribes for customs officials).[67]

Although Addington was prepared to be just as understanding as Pitt had been over the Prince's debts, the King was disgusted by his son's incontinent overspending, and the subsequent negotiations were fraught. (Today, the Prince's profligacy would be recognized as a chronic case of Buying Derangement Syndrome and treated psychologically.) Yet again, the taxpayer footed the bill, and in February 1803 it was agreed that Parliament would pay the Prince an extra £60,000 for three years, in return for a solemn promise from him to prioritize debt-reduction over continued spending. The politicians involved must have realized that this commitment was as worthless as all his earlier ones.

As 1802 drew to a close, Prince George was not the King's only family embarrassment. At Christmas, Prince Edward, Duke of Kent, had to be withdrawn as Governor of Gibraltar when his efforts to instill discipline in the troops stationed there provoked a mutiny. He had been a good regimental commander, but was not considered bright. Like his brothers, he was in debt by his late teens and had frequently lied to his father about it. When the truth eventually became known, the King had settled the debts and packed him off to Geneva, where, like most of his brothers at one time or another, he lived openly with a mistress. His failure as Governor of Gibraltar was not allowed to affect his status any more than Prince Frederick's defeats had. On his return from the Rock, Prince Edward was made a field marshal.

By late January 1803, it had become apparent to the King that although Napoleon had kept to the letter of the Peace of Amiens, he had comprehensively violated its spirit by significantly extending French hegemony in Switzerland, Italy and Germany. Britain was meanwhile violating the letter of the Peace herself by not evacuating Malta, and both countries were rearming. As he told the Foreign Secretary Lord Hawkesbury on 28 January, George opposed leaving Malta because of 'the manifest views France nourishes of fresh expeditions to the East'.[68] He was highly suspicious of Napoleon's intentions, on 9 February writing again to Hawkesbury that 'If any curb can be placed to the views of the First Consul it must be by a firm though temperate language ... The King shall see with pleasure its occasioning any moderation in the councils of the Tuileries, though he does not expect it.'[69]

In a speech to Parliament on 8 March, George declared that, given the 'very considerable military preparations' that were under way in the French and Dutch invasion ports, the government 'judged it expedient to adopt additional measures of precaution for the security of his dominions', including the mobilization of the militia and the raising of another 10,000 men for the navy, both of which were approved by Parliament three days later.[70] Napoleon was infuriated by these pre-emptive moves, which he regarded as a *casus belli*, claiming that his own build-up in the Channel ports was merely the prelude to an expedition to Louisiana.

On 11 March, Napoleon threatened Lord Whitworth, the British Ambassador to Paris, with the military occupation of the whole of Holland, and two days later at a reception at the Tuileries Palace he publicly derided the King's speech to Parliament, concluding, 'If they [the British] are the first to draw the sword, I will be the last to sheathe it.'[71] Britain's mobilization of the militia, a purely defensive force, was not the first drawing of the sword, and since later that year French, Belgian and Dutch ports were teeming with invasion vessels, there is a strong sense that Napoleon resented being caught in the act. Yet Charles Fox believed that if war returned, as he told Charles Grey on 15 March, 'it is entirely the fault of our ministers and not of Bonaparte.'[72]

By early 1803 the long friendship between Pitt and Addington was foundering. Pitt was far more sceptical about Amiens than Addington; moreover he was frustrated by how many more of Addington's supporters than Pittites the ministry now contained, and although he could not go into open opposition and still retain the King's support, he disagreed with Addington over slavery, Catholic emancipation and franchise reform. In March, they discussed the possibility of Pitt's return to office, but negotiations broke down because Addington did not see why he should relinquish the premiership. He reshuffled his government and caused insult by appointing George Tierney, the man with whom Pitt had fought the duel, as Treasurer of the Navy. On 20 April, Addington took copies of the correspondence that he had exchanged with Pitt to the King, which George angrily refused to read on the (perfectly foreseeable) grounds that he had not been told about the discussions, and that premiers were appointed by him rather than by each other: in no uncertain terms he made it clear that he would not accept 'the Crown being put into commission' in such a way.[73] So instead of getting the King on his side by this underhand move, Addington had only managed to irritate him.

The Peace of Amiens finally collapsed on 17 May 1803, when Addington placed embargoes on all French and Dutch ships in British ports by Orders-in-Council. Full-scale hostilities were renewed the next day. Writing to his ally Lord Lauderdale the following February, Charles Fox did not blame politicians such as Castlereagh for having driven 'the Doctor [Addington] into the war. I always thought it was the K[ing] and the K[ing] alone, and I think so still.'[74] In reality, many other factors had been at play; George was correct in thinking that the peace had only offered a temporary respite from an unfinished conflict, and neither side had ever truly believed in it as a lasting resolution. Napoleon had used the time to increase and consolidate French power over western Europe in a way that Britain found threatening. Britain had meanwhile refused to relinquish Malta, an island of real strategic importance.

Nor had the peace brought the economic blessings hoped for at the time of the preliminaries; there was still no upturn in exports, especially not to France; naval officers disliked being on half-pay; income tax had been extended to incomes over £60 per annum, starting at threepence in the pound (1.25 per cent) but rising to a shilling in the pound (5 per cent) for incomes over £150. These amounts might sound minuscule to today's taxpayer, but they were then considered a monstrous imposition on a free-born Briton's privacy and property.

On 26 June, Gillray published one of his best-known prints, entitled 'The King of Brobdingnag and Gulliver', depicting the King in military uniform holding a tiny Napoleon in the palm of his hand, looking at him through a microscope-cum-opera glass and saying, 'My little friend Grildrig* . . . I cannot but conclude you to be one of the most pernicious little odious reptiles that nature ever suffered to crawl upon the surface of the earth.'[75] When the King was shown the print he did not disagree with its sentiments, but merely commented on the bag-wig he was shown wearing, saying, 'Quite wrong. Quite wrong. No bag with uniform.'[76]

For all that Napoleon was depicted as harmless in the caricature, one of the immediate results of the return to war was his seizure of Hanover. George denounced it as 'the most unheard of act of injustice', but he could hardly have been surprised, and fortunately all the royal linen, silver furniture and horses of the royal stud farm had already been safely evacuated to England.[77] A large number of Hanoverian troops were also able to make their escape. They subsequently fought bravely in the King's German Legion, which distinguished itself in many battles of the Peninsular War and at Waterloo.

The renewal of hostilities prompted the Prince of Wales to attempt once more to become a general, not because he felt any genuine martial calling but because, as he told Addington on 18 July, 'I feel myself exposed to the obloquy of being regarded by the country as passing my time indifferent to the events which menace, and insensible to the call of patriotism.'[78] This was a problem he might have considered twenty years earlier, when he had chosen to wear the uniform of the Continental Army as a political-cum-fashion statement while British soldiers were fighting the colonial insurgency. 'Hanover is lost,' the Prince wrote to his father, 'England is menaced with invasion, Ireland is in rebellion, Europe is at the foot of France.' Therefore, he argued, he should be called upon to command troops in battle, despite his total lack of either training or aptitude.[79] 'Should the implacable enemy so far succeed to land,' the King nonetheless replied, 'you will have an opportunity of showing your zeal at the head of your regiment.'[80] That was as far as George would go. When the Duke of York, the Commander-in-Chief of the army, sided with their father on the issue, the Prince banned him from Carlton House.

On 7 December, without warning, the Prince took the unconscionable step of publishing in the *Morning Chronicle* his entire private correspondence with his father and brother about his hoped-for military employment. What little trust that still existed now evaporated, and the King thereafter referred to the Prince as 'the publisher of *my* letters'.[81] There was the further

---

* The name given to Gulliver in Brobdingnag.

suspicion that the Prince had written the letters in such a self-consciously literary way – 'Europe is at the foot of France' was not his usual style – because he had always had their publication in mind. From then on, the King and Queen feared that anything they wrote to him might subsequently also appear in print. George publicly visited the Princess of Wales at her home in Blackheath to show his support for her, and he had nothing whatever to do with his son for almost a year. As late as the following September he told a friend that he could never forgive the betrayal, 'because it was impossible to forget it'.[82]

On 26 and 28 October, George reviewed 27,000 members of the Corps of London and Westminster Volunteers in Hyde Park. An estimated half a million spectators turned up on each of the days. 'They are not supposed to form above a tenth part of the volunteer force of the kingdom,' Lord Auckland told a friend. 'Add to all this the army, the militia, and all the other preparations ... Surely nothing is more to be wished than that an attempt should be made on this country, and nothing is more unlikely in my opinion.'[83] He added that the King was in 'fine health'. Auckland was correct about the numbers; by December 1803, some 380,000 Britons had enrolled in one kind of volunteer unit or another. Local militias – known as Fencibles – were being raised, armed and trained all over the country; it was no doubt hoped they would perform as well as the minutemen of Massachusetts. Small defensive forts known as Martello towers, which the King thought 'capital things', were swiftly constructed along the south coast and around the Channel Islands.

Napoleon believed that in order to invade Britain all he needed was forty-eight hours of good weather in the Channel, and that he would do so with an army that had already been regularly proven in battle. (It was to be proven again very often in the years to come.) 'Should his troops effect a landing,' George wrote to his old and trusted friend Bishop Hurd,

> I shall certainly put myself at the head of mine, and my other armed subjects, to repel them: but as it is impossible to see the events of such a conflict, should the enemy approach too near to Windsor I shall think it right the Queen and my daughters should cross the Severn, and shall send them to your episcopal palace at Worcester.[84]

The plan was for the King, Addington and Charles Yorke, the Secretary at War, to move to Chelmsford if Napoleon landed in Essex, or to Dartford if he landed in Kent. (Napoleon had planned on the latter.) 'The King is prepared to take the field in case of attack,' the courtier Thomas Dodd wrote, saying that his campaign bed and military equipment 'are ready and he can move at half an hour's notice'.[85]

Glenbervie reported that when discussing the anticipated French invasion, George was 'quite keen on the subject and angry if any suggests that the attempt may not be made'.[86] Yet there must be some doubt about how much good it would have done to have a king who was utterly unversed in strategy giving military orders on campaign, and fighting against one of the greatest generals in the history of warfare. George would probably have relied heavily on Lord Cornwallis, hoping he would have made a better fist of things than he had in Virginia a quarter of a century earlier. Meanwhile, the Bank of England's gold was to be taken to Worcester Cathedral in thirty wagons, escorted by volunteer troops, while its account book went to the Tower of London; the cannon-making foundries at the Woolwich Arsenal were to be moved inland via the Grand Junction Canal; the Privy Council was to adopt emergency powers; trading at the Stock Exchange would be suspended; the press would be muzzled and 'suspected persons will be immediately arrested.'[87] It might not have been enough to stave off a Napoleonic occupation, but at least preparations were being made.

On Christmas Day, Addington received intelligence that Napoleon was about to leave Paris and head straight to Brest for an invasion of Ireland, with another force destined for England to follow shortly afterwards from Boulogne. 'The French were slaughtering oxen at Bordeaux', Addington told Speaker Abbot, 'for the immediate victualling of their fleet.'[88] It was true that the Grande Armée had arrived in Boulogne and in several ports along the French, Belgian and Dutch coasts, practising manoeuvres and waiting for a fair wind, but the reports regarding Napoleon himself were wrong, as he had stayed at the Tuileries. There were nonetheless nearly 2,000 transport vessels ready between Brest and Antwerp – many of them constructed during the Peace of Amiens – and Napoleon even had a medal struck to be awarded to the Army of England after its victory. Had the Grande Armée successfully landed in force, Napoleon would probably have been in London within a week. At this moment of grave national peril, George suffered another major relapse.

In mid-January 1804, as with all his earlier attacks, the King's malady coincided with his contracting a cold, this one attributed to his not changing quickly enough out of wet clothes after hunting. Courtiers initially suggested that he had 'symptoms of gout', but that did not fool observers such as Lord Malmesbury, who knew that George took a great deal of exercise, and ate and drank very moderately.[89] At the ball for the Queen's official birthday at St James's Palace, Lord Glenbervie saw the King walking with a crutch, but he otherwise 'seemed to be in good spirits'.[90] For

Malmesbury, however, 'his manner struck me as so unusual and incoherent that I could not help remarking it to [the former Home Secretary] Lord Pelham, who ... told me ... that it was too plain the King was beginning to be unwell. Lord Pelham, who played [cards] that evening with the Queen, added that her anxiety was manifest, since she never kept her eyes off the King during the whole time the party lasted.'[91] By the end of the month the gout story had collapsed, and it was clear the King had relapsed into his malady once again.

Lord Eldon suggested in late January that so as not to be overlooked from the upper windows in Grosvenor Place – from where the King's eccentric behaviour had already been sighted and reported to the newspapers – he would walk him two or three times around the parts of the gardens at Buckingham House that were out of view. He listened to the King telling him about every ministry of his reign – historians' gold which Eldon did not bother to record – during which 'there was not the slightest aberration' in his conversation.[92] When he got back into the house, however, 'His Majesty, laying down his hat and cane, placed his head upon my shoulder, and burst into tears; and, after recovering himself, bowed me out of his room in his usual manner.'

On 12 and 13 February the King's life was again in danger. He had developed a high fever, was talking incessantly and suffered a form of paralysis. By the 16th, complete derangement had descended.[93] Addington called on John and Thomas Willis, who only agreed to attend with the Cabinet's express sanction, but when they arrived at Buckingham House the Dukes of Kent and Cumberland physically barred them from seeing the King. They had promised their father that, if he should fall ill again, no one from the Willis family should be permitted to treat him. The whole royal family then residing in London – including the Queen and her nine children – signed a letter to that effect, which was presented to the Cabinet. Only one person refused to sign – the Prince of Wales, who declined to give an opinion on the matter. ('Many people about the Court', Glenbervie noted of the Prince, 'ascribe the King's present attack to the publication of that correspondence.')[94] Addington instead turned to Dr Samuel Simmons of St Luke's Hospital for Lunatics, who moved the King to the Dutch House at Kew.[95]

'The probability of a very formidable invasion,' Pitt told Malmesbury on 19 February, 'and the dangerous state of the King's health, placed the country in a state of difficulty and danger dissimilar to any former one, and required from all those who were called on to act in public a very different mode of reasoning and acting than at any past period.'[96] He would therefore support Addington, even though it was against both his instinct and his interests, at least for the immediate future. Although the King had a 'long interval of reason and composure' the next day, he also had to be straitjacketed at one stage. 'He submits cheerfully to the restraints which he believes to be necessary,' Addington told his ally Charles Abbot, 'greatly preferring Simmons to the Willises.'[97]

The King went in and out of bouts of mania for the rest of February and March. As before, the Whigs put the worst possible construction on the doctors' bulletins, and the Tories the best. Writing to a friend on 2 April, the Foxite MP Thomas Creevey wrote that 'the regal function will never more be exercised by him, and the Doctor [Addington] has most impudently assumed these functions in doing what he has done.'[98] Later that month, Pitt was ready to bring down the Addington ministry, and wrote to the King to warn him on 21 April. He said that he had long abjured joining the Opposition, but he had felt for a year that while Addington stayed as premier 'every attempt to provide adequately and effectually for the public defence, and for meeting the extraordinary and unprecedented efforts of the enemy, will be fruitless.'[99] Lord Chatham had once said during the Seven Years War that only he could save the country, and now his son felt the same way.

On 24 April the Pittites, Grenvillites and Foxites defeated the government by 256 votes to 204 on Fox's motion censuring Addington's defence measures. The next day, the King, who was still convalescing at Kew and far from wholly well, asked Pitt whether he would be interested in returning to the premiership. By 27 April the King was telling Eldon, 'I am persuaded Mr Pitt will never form any engagements, or enter into any connection, which will be injurious either to the rights of my subjects or to the royal prerogative. *I feel sure of this* and I also feel *my Coronation Oath safe in his hands*.'[100]

On 29 April, having almost lost his majority in the Lords, not least because the Prince of Wales had ranged his supporters there against him, Addington decided to resign. George offered his loyal minister a dissolution of Parliament, but they both knew that the invasion crisis made a general election impractical. By the time he presented the Budget on 30 April – in which he took out a £16 million loan and raised £7 million in new taxes for national defence – Addington understood that his ministry was effectively at an end.

Pitt set out his ideas for a national government to the King on 2 May, 'endeavouring to unite in his service as large a proportion as possible of the weight of talents and connections, drawn without exception from parties of all descriptions, and without reference to former differences and divisions . . . to rescue Europe from the state to which it is reduced'.[101]

A national coalition of the brightest and best in politics was what the King had always wanted, but it had finally taken the danger of imminent invasion to achieve it.

In the first written correspondence between George and Pitt since February 1801, the King stated, 'It cannot but be lamented that Mr Pitt should have taken so rooted a dislike to a gentleman who has the greatest claim to approbation from his King and country,' meaning Addington. He reminded Pitt that Addington had stepped forward 'when Mr Pitt and some of his colleagues resigned their employments' to support King and country 'when the most ill-digested and dangerous proposition was brought forward by the enemies of the Established Church'.[102] Pitt can be forgiven for having seen the events of February 1801 in a very different way.

George was determined to extract a categoric promise from Pitt, writing with severity that 'The King can never forget the wound that was intended at the palladium* of our Church establishment, the Test Act, and the indelicacy, not to call it worse, of wanting His Majesty to forgo his solemn Coronation Oath.' He said he would not be satisfied unless Pitt stated in the Commons 'that the smallest alteration of that law would be a death wound to the British constitution'. And there was one person he would not have in the government, however broad-bottomed it was. 'The whole tenor of Mr Fox's conduct since he quitted his seat at the Board of Treasury, when under age,'† George continued, 'and more particularly at the Whig Club and other factious meetings, rendered his expulsion from the Privy Council indispensable, and obliges the King to express his astonishment that Mr Pitt should [for] one moment harbour the thought of bringing such a man before his royal notice.'[103]

Pitt replied the next day, claiming that he had no 'sentiments of personal dislike' for Addington, just for 'his public conduct'.[104] As for Catholic emancipation, he repeated that he was to 'feel it both a personal and public duty to abstain from again pressing that measure on Your Majesty's consideration', an allusion to the idea that the issue had triggered the King's illness in 1801. His suggestion of Fox, he said, was a pragmatic measure to prevent the Opposition adopting the anti-war stance that it had over the American war.

After Dr Simmons had given his permission, Pitt had a chance to explain his thinking when he saw the King at Kew for three hours from 11 a.m. on 7 May, the first time they had met in the three years since he had

---

* 'A safeguard' (*Shorter Oxford Dictionary*).

† Fox was twenty-three when he joined the Treasury but there were no age limits for ministerial office; he had become an MP at nineteen, when the legal age was twenty-one, although the Midhurst constituency his father had bought for him did not seem to mind.

resigned. According to the diary of George Rose MP, a future Paymaster-General who was also a friend of both men, Pitt was received by the King 'with the utmost kindness and cordiality. He congratulated His Majesty on his looking better than on his recovery from his last illness, to which His Majesty replied, "That was not to be wondered at, as he was then on the point of *parting* with an old friend, and he was now about to *regain* one." '[105] It was generous of George to refer to Pitt as his friend, which both men knew was never truly the case.

In the discussion, the King acquiesced in having Grenville back and made no objection to Lord Spencer, though he did not think him the best choice for First Lord of the Admiralty. However, 'On Mr Fox's name being suggested the King digressed a good deal, but returning to the matter he said he could not possibly take him into his Cabinet . . . the King was quite immovable respecting him.'[106] Pitt asked whether he objected to Fox being given an appointment abroad as an ambassador, to which the King said, 'Not at all,' probably feeling that if he had to be employed, the further away the better.

Pitt agreed to try to form a government on that basis. Whether he accepted the King's veto on Fox because he knew he could not override it, or because it privately suited him (as he could not control Fox), or because he feared that forcing Fox on to the King might precipitate another attack of madness, or from some mixture of the three, we cannot be sure.[107] In any case, Fox showed no interest in serving under his arch-enemy of twenty-one years. The King's refusal to contemplate him was later bitterly denounced by the radical Whig politician and writer Henry Brougham as 'the capricious, the despicable antipathy of that narrow-minded and vindictive prince against the most illustrious of his subjects'.[108] Yet Fox's hostility even to fighting Napoleon was more than sufficient reason on its own for his exclusion from a wartime ministry. The King was also angered by the Prince of Wales' open opposition to the government. 'It is not without *astonishment* he sees by *The Times*', he wrote to Pitt on 9 May, 'that the Opposition meeting was held at Carlton House.'[109]

Although Fox generously gave Grenville permission to enter the ministry without him, the latter feared it would be too much dominated by Pitt, and refused. At 3.30 p.m. that day, Pitt visited Buckingham House to report on Grenville's decision. He said with 'indignation' that he would 'teach that proud man', meaning his cousin Grenville, 'that in the service and with the confidence of the King, I can do without him.'[110] Grenville did not unite with Fox or try to bring down Pitt's ministry, although his hitherto friendly personal relationship with his cousin had undoubtedly finished by the end of the year.

On 10 May 1804 Addington returned the seals of office to the King, who gave them to Pitt when he came back to Buckingham House to kiss hands later that day. George did not like losing his agreeable middle-class premier, and four days later wrote fondly to 'his truly beloved friend', but he recognized along with everyone else that, with Napoleon's Grande Armée on the Channel coast, Pitt was the only person for the role of war leader.[111] It was extraordinary that all the negotiations and correspondence concerning the change of government took place at a time when the King was occasionally insane enough for Dr Simmons to confine him in a strait-jacket. The Prince of Wales rightly commented on 'so extraordinary a circumstance as a King of England whilst exercising his regal powers being kept under any personal restraint'; the King was sent 'the secret boxes' of military and diplomatic intelligence, to which only he and the Prime Minister had keys, even though he was still in the daily care of Simmons and his attendants. Even in late June, the King had to organize audiences with his Prime Minister at times that did not clash with his two-hour consultations with his mad-doctors.

Two stories did the rounds about the King's bout of madness in 1804, both possibly apocryphal, but told to Lord Glenbervie by the well-connected Mary Berry in late June. In the first, the King was going to the State Opening of Parliament and told the courtiers in the coach on the way that he intended to surprise parliamentarians by beginning his speech, 'My lords and peacocks.'[112] In the other, when the list of convicts due for hanging was sent to him by Lord Pelham, he returned it with the names of Dr Simmons and another doctor added, saying, 'Yes, the names of two rascals who deserve hanging more than all the others.' What is uncontested is that he was fully sane when he was given the doctors' report on his illness on 7 July, and sent it on to Charlotte with a note that read, 'To be deposited with the former ones with the Queen of my heart.'[113] He often wrote to her without the usual eighteenth-century royal formalities, calling her 'Dearest Charlotte' and signing himself 'your loving husband'.

On 16 May 1804, Napoleon was declared Emperor by the Senate and Tribunate, just as Pitt was trying to cobble together a third coalition involving Austria and Russia with which to oppose him. With Britain still under the immediate threat of invasion, anything that might distract Napoleon's attention eastwards was desperately needed. An almost equally difficult diplomatic task was to try to effect a reconciliation between the King and the Prince of Wales, which finally took place on 12 December. Pitt hoped that the Prince would induce Lord Moira and his Whig faction to join his government, which needed strengthening. All through the summer there had been rumours about the King's health, but he carried off a speech to Parliament successfully on 1 August. Lord Glenbervie had an hour's conversation with him and General Harcourt on the terrace at Windsor on 19 August. Glenbervie found the King 'thinner, paler, and with a more shrivelled countenance' than after his recovery in 1801, and 'his clothes hung loose upon him as on that occasion, and I thought his eyes looked opened quite round with a glare that one could not look at without uneasiness, but I did not perceive any particular stutter, confusion or impediment in his words.'[114] The King did almost all the talking:

> There was nothing in what the King said of men and things which did not appear to me sensible and rational and indeed arising from the reflections of an able man, but they were matters on which it was impolitic to suppose he would have opened himself so freely and so copiously either to General Harcourt or me, much less to both together, if he had been in perfect possession of himself. It was the case of *dicenda tacenda locutus*.*

Ignoring boundaries is a common feature of bipolar disorder, but nothing that the King said to Glenbervie and Harcourt that day actually shows evidence of mental derangement or manic depression. He told Glenbervie that 'he believed there never was an honester man than [Glenbervie's late father-in-law] Lord North and none for whom he ever felt a greater regard; that he was also a true and zealous friend to that main part of our constitution, the Church of England,' and that he believed North 'had never been happy after his junction with a person who had very different sentiments'.[115] This was a clear reference to Charles Fox, but these sentiments were hardly 'impolitic' or secret. In his monologue, the King blamed Lord Auckland for having effected the 'junction' between North and Fox in 1782. The twenty-one months that Fox had spent in office between March 1782 and December 1783 had clearly traumatized the King so much that he was still bringing it up over twenty years later.

The King went on to say that 'he did not believe the Catholic question was the real reason of [*sic*] Pitt's resignation,' but that he had 'private reasons' too.[116] This had also already been the subject of public discussion. He added that 'Mr Addington had done a great service in coming into office when he did, but that his retreat when it took place had become equally necessary', and that after a number of 'inefficient measures', which he did not enumerate, only Lord Hobart wanted to continue in office with him.[117] On one occasion, Addington had apparently told the King 'that the country could not be saved but by his continuing in office', and the King

---

* 'He chatted about anything and everything' (Horace).

replied, 'I am not entirely of that opinion,' a wonderfully understated put-down. He then recalled a malicious remark by the Hanoverian Minister that 'The world in general allowed Mr Addington to be possessed of integrity and diligence but that he was as generally thought to want* one as material a quality – talents.'[118] As Addington was now in Opposition, this was hardly 'impolitic' either.

The King proceeded to describe Isaac Corry, the Chancellor of the Irish Exchequer, as 'a person of no consequence' and the impeachment of Sir Warren Hastings as 'disgraceful to the country'.[119] He stated that all intelligence sources were warning that the invasion would take place under the great French commander Marshal Jean Lannes† by the end of the month, but that he personally did not believe it. The King described Francis Jackson, then British Minister at Berlin, 'very slightingly' as 'one of the toad-eaters of the late Duke of Leeds'.[120] He also passed on the piece of gossip that George Boulton Mainwaring, the newly elected‡ MP for Middlesex, was not the real son of his supposed father the previous MP William Mainwaring; instead his mother 'had given [him] the name of Mainwaring to disguise this circumstance'.[121]

Sadly, with the King still in full flow, Glenbervie suffered a sudden and severe attack of rheumatism – he blamed the silk lining of his thin Windsor uniform – and contrary to all etiquette had to 'steal off the terrace' shivering and with his teeth chattering.[122] At some point in the conversation – at least as it was recalled by Glenbervie twelve years later – the King repeated the genuinely scandalous gossip that Charles-Louis-Napoléon Bonaparte,§ the youngest son of King Louis of Holland and Josephine's daughter Hortense de Beauharnais, was in fact the natural child of Emperor Napoleon himself. George was thus accusing Napoleon of sleeping with his own stepdaughter and cuckolding his brother, but in the circumstances of the day even that does not imply manic depression: the (completely untrue) rumour was then widely current, even in print.[123]

This fourth bout of madness did tragically break one vital bond for the King. On returning from their Weymouth holiday in September, George and Charlotte separated as a couple and never slept together again. 'He never mentions her with disrespect,' noted Lord Auckland, 'but he marks unequivocally and by many facts that he is dissatisfied with her.'[124] It was

---

* In the sense of 'lack'.
† Although it was misspelt 'l'Arne' in Glenbervie's diaries, it was undoubtedly Lannes from other internal evidence, and there was no General l'Arne.
‡ But shortly to be deposed for electoral fraud in March 1805, and then reinstated in February 1806.
§ The future Emperor Napoleon III.

possible that he had been informed that she had supported the Willises' 'kidnap' of him in April 1801, and he was certainly angry about the way she had come to take the Prince of Wales' side in some of the money quarrels with their son. For her part, fear of his suddenly descending into abusive and ungovernable lunacy was more than she could have been expected to bear for ever, even if he occasionally still called her the Queen of his heart. From then on, she lived at Frogmore and Kew and he at Windsor. They continued attending official functions together, but no longer felt the need to coordinate their arrivals and departures.

This terrible illness, and probably to some extent the Prince of Wales' suborning of his mother, had succeeded in splitting the only happy marriage of the five Hanoverian monarchs. Lord Hobart observed that it was melancholy 'to see a family that had lived so well together for such a number of years completely broken up'.[125] He added that John Willis had told him 'that things would never be quite right' – it was not an unfair diagnosis of the effects of bipolar disorder on a family, especially when aggravated by the extreme narcissism and opportunism of its eldest son.

27

Tory Spring

October 1804–October 1809

*Who remembers the Duke of Portland and the Earl of Liverpool?
Yet these men, together with a blind King, helped to defeat the
greatest politico-military ruler of the century.*[1]

John Brooke, *George III*, 1972

By the autumn of 1804, the King could read print by candlelight only
through powerful spectacles. He could hardly distinguish people from
across the room, a major disability in a political world where personal
contact and recognition at Levees and Drawing Rooms was vital. After his
bout of illness in 1788–9 these had been reduced to one a week, and he
ended them altogether when cataracts were diagnosed in June 1805. To
handle his correspondence he then took on a private secretary, Colonel Sir
Herbert Taylor, who became devoted to him. That October George lost
the sight of his right eye altogether, yet an operation was considered too
dangerous. 'At sixty-six we may still give seasonable advice,' the King wrote
to Lord Hawkesbury, 'but the activity of execution is better done by the
vigour of youth.'[2]

He could still ride, however, and it was while out riding with George
Rose at Rose's country house, Cuffnells Park in Hampshire, on 31 October
1804 that the King said 'that he had no taste for what was called the fine
wild beauties of nature. He did not like mountains and other romantic
scenes, of which he had sometimes heard much.'[3] It was a remarkable
statement, and perhaps explains why he left the Home Counties rarely and
England never. For someone with such wide intellectual curiosity, he seem
to have had none at all for personal experiences, especially travel.

During another ride earlier that month, Rose had tried to suggest to the
King that Charles Fox was now 'a determined Tory' and that his inclusion
in Pitt's ministry 'would not be attended with any danger', provocative
remarks to which he received no response.[4] This was understandable; Fox

was still a radical Whig, and unlike Pitt and Addington and their supporters could not by any means be described as a Tory – that is, someone who defended the status quo of Church, Crown and state and now wanted a vigorous prosecution of the war against Napoleonic France. Rose was proved comprehensively wrong soon afterwards, when Fox and Grenville agreed to bring forward Catholic emancipation in the next session, not least in order to embarrass Pitt. The King considered that the best way to strengthen the government against them was not to approach Whigs such as Lord Moira and George Tierney to join Pitt, but instead to try to entice Addingtonian Tories back into government.

On 12 December 1804, ten days after Napoleon had crowned himself Emperor, and under pressure from him, Spain declared war on Britain. Pitt needed to strengthen his government in anticipation of the still-imminent invasion of Britain, and wrote to the King from Bowling Green House, his villa on Putney Hill, on 17 December, saying he wanted to bring in the Addingtonians. George replied from Windsor the next day 'to express his joy' at the idea, suggesting that Addington himself could receive a pension for life for having been Speaker for twelve years.[5] On Christmas Day, Pitt told his brother, 'Though we should certainly have strength enough to stand our ground, our majority would not be such as to meet difficult questions with advantage, or to prevent much possible embarrassment to the public service, as well as uneasiness to the King's mind.'[6]

Before an accommodation could be arranged, however, George hoped to take the custody and upbringing of his eight-year-old granddaughter Princess Charlotte out of the hands of the Prince of Wales. She saw little of her mother, and the second in line to the throne was being brought up in what George saw as the morally louche, religiously compromised and politically Oppositionist Carlton House. For all that the Prince wanted to fight for his custody of her, Lord Liverpool wrote to Auckland that 'It will, however, be carried into execution, for none of the King's servants doubt of His Majesty's right on this occasion.'[7] In a later letter Liverpool added that 'The child will rejoice that she is taken out of the custody of her father.'[8] He expected there to be an Order-in-Council, organized by Liverpool's son Lord Hawkesbury, the Home Secretary, after which the Princess would be taken to Windsor by Lady Elgin and the Bishop of Exeter appointed as her preceptor.

Precedents were checked by the government law officers, especially that of 1718 in which a majority of judges had decided that George I had the right of guardianship of his grandchildren. 'There is no lady in the Prince of Wales's house proper to have the care of his daughter,' Liverpool told Auckland.

The lady with whom he is most connected [that is, Maria Fitzherbert] is highly improper on many accounts – from the nature of her connection with His Royal Highness, and from her [Roman Catholic] religion; and it would be a very extraordinary circumstance if . . . the King should not exercise his lawful prerogative in preserving from such a connection his granddaughter and the heiress of his kingdoms.[9]

Yet there was still a good deal of concern about the state of the King's mind. On 23 December, Glenbervie encountered Thomas Erskine in the street; Erskine was a radical lawyer and friend of Fox who had defended Paine and Tooke. He said that 'he knew the King to be still insane,' and had 'said last Friday he should in the spring invade Hanover in person, at the head of the Blues and the Staffordshire Militia'.[10] That was almost certainly untrue, but Erskine was on stronger ground when he argued that the Prince of Wales could not be forced to yield the custody of Princess Charlotte to someone 'whose state of mind is such that if he were a common tradesman or private individual a Commission of Lunacy would certainly take out of his hands the management of his own affairs and the custody and education of his children'. In early 1805 Charlotte was nonetheless moved with a new governess to Windsor, where the Princess of Wales was welcome to visit whenever she wanted. 'It is quite charming to see the Princess and her child together,' the King wrote in February, 'of which I have been since yesterday a witness.'[11]

On 14 January 1805, to the King's great delight, Henry Addington entered the Pitt ministry, taking the title of Viscount Sidmouth and the position of Lord President of the Council, and bringing in about thirty MPs who would shore up the government in the Commons. The Addingtonian 4th Earl of Buckinghamshire (formerly Lord Hobart) became Chancellor of the Duchy of Lancaster. Portland's conservatism since the French Revolution meant that the King now liked and trusted him, and he continued to sit in the Cabinet as a minister without portfolio. When the King delivered his Speech from the Throne the next day, he needed a document printed in a very large font; it was to be the last he ever read to Parliament in person.

Only three days later, the King and Pitt had their worst falling out since Catholic emancipation, when John Moore, the Archbishop of Canterbury, died. George had always taken his position as Supreme Governor of the Church of England extremely seriously, promoting intelligent, orthodox and genuinely pious clerics to bishoprics, although it did not hurt if they came from the upper classes too (the proportion of bishops related to peers increased during his reign, especially during the second half).[12] He also balanced Oxford and Cambridge* graduates as bishops, and promoted Tories as well as Whigs.

On Moore's death, Pitt badly overreached himself by nominating as his successor George Pretyman, Bishop of Lincoln and Dean of St Paul's Cathedral since 1787, who had been Pitt's tutor at Pembroke College, Cambridge, then later his private secretary, friend and confidant. George had objected to Pretyman taking on the two senior posts at the age of only thirty-six, and thought he had been promoted by Pitt quite high enough already. Furthermore, he had already provisionally offered the archbishopric to Charles Manners-Sutton, Dean of Windsor, Bishop of Norwich and a grandson of the 3rd Duke of Rutland, who had published sermons George admired and was a former Dean of Peterborough. Manners-Sutton had a higher standing in the Church than Pretyman, and George possessed far greater knowledge and interest in this area, not least because he was a devout Anglican, as we have seen, and Pitt had no discernible religious faith.†

Pitt protested about the King's stance in a sharply worded letter of 22 January, stating:

> how much his feelings are wounded and his hopes of contributing to Your Majesty's service impaired by Your Majesty's apparent disregard of his recommendation ... Your Majesty's refusal to comply with his request can hardly be understood by himself, and will certainly not be understood by the public in any other light than as a decisive mark of Your Majesty's not honouring him with that degree of weight and confidence which his predecessors have enjoyed and without which Your Majesty must be sensible how impossible it is ... that he can conduct Your Majesty's affairs with advantage.[13]

Soon after this clear resignation threat, and knowing that Manners-Sutton lived nearby, the King rode over to his house and asked him to absent himself from a dinner party he was giving for a brief audience. 'My Lord Archbishop of Canterbury, I wish you joy,' he told the surprised and delighted Dean. 'Not a word. Go back to your guests.'[14] By congratulating Manners-Sutton on his elevation, the King had forestalled any further

---

* Although he was the first Hanoverian monarch to visit Oxford, in 1785, he never visited Cambridge, only 50 miles from London.

† It was to Manners-Sutton that the King made one of his most celebrated jokes. 'I believe Your Grace has a large family,' he said. 'Better than a dozen?' 'No, Sir,' Sutton replied, 'only eleven.' 'Well,' quipped the King, 'is not that better than a dozen?' (Ayling, *George the Third* p. 178).

action by Pitt on behalf of Pretyman. 'If a private secretary of a first minister is to be put at the head of the Church,' George later told Lord Malmesbury, 'I shall have all my bishops party men and politicians.'[15] For the King, who disliked and shunned most politicians but admired and enjoyed the company of bishops, that was a prospect too terrible to contemplate. Manners-Sutton served with some distinction until 1828, establishing the National Society and the Indian episcopate, and presiding over the christening of the future Queen Victoria.*

On 18 May 1804, the same day that he was proclaimed Emperor, Napoleon had created the marshalate of France and on 2 December had crowned himself in a magnificent coronation that had been celebrated in Notre-Dame. On 23 April 1805, St George's Day, George administered a deliberate rebuff to these imperial pretensions by emphasizing the ancient rather than arriviste nature of his own crown when he created no fewer than six Garter knights – the Dukes of Beaufort and Abercorn, and the Earls of Winchilsea, Dartmouth, Chesterfield and Pembroke. Invitations to the Garter Ceremony at Windsor were sent to all ministers and ambassadors, and chivalric aspects going back to the Order's founding in 1348 were emphasized at the King's express wish, for, as one historian has put it, 'a calculated royal, aristocratic and British riposte, intended to parry the pretensions of a mushroom emperor and his parvenu state honours system'.[16] The ceremony cost the Office of Works some £11,000.

On 27 June, the King brought Pitt and Sidmouth together at Buckingham House, where he saw first the former and then the latter in order to effect a genuine reconciliation. 'The King told Lord Sidmouth that Mr Pitt and Lord Sidmouth should talk matters over together,' Charles Abbot wrote in his diary, 'and not have any go-betweens.'[17] Despite the King's best efforts, no reconciliation took place, because Pitt was having difficulty finding government places for Sidmouth's supporters, including his brother Hiley Addington, and on 3 July both Sidmouth and Buckinghamshire resigned from the government.

All this took place at the same time that the King was informed that, having lost the sight in his right eye, another cataract was now forming in

---

* On Pitt's death it was discovered that Pretyman had been one of six men who had lent him £12,000 in October 1801 to get the ex-premier out of financial difficulties; he was the only one of Pitt's friends to petition Parliament for repayment for that and other debts owed (Ehrman, *Consuming Struggle* p. 834). In 1813, when he was offered the bishopric of London, he turned it down as he considered the duties too onerous. Although the King could not have known any of this in 1805, his sense of who would make the better primate was considerably sounder than that of his Prime Minister.

the left. 'He bore the news with a most perfect composure,' recorded Abbot. On 22 July while on holiday at Weymouth, leeches had to be applied to his eye, apparently with some success. He still rode, albeit at walking pace and with a groom, and attended plays.[18] Years earlier, Herschel had noted that 'The King has very good eyes, and enjoys observations with the telescopes exceedingly,' but those days were now long gone.[19] Princess Sophia told Lady Glenbervie that 'before he lost his sight the King had scarcely ever read any novels, with the exception of Fielding. They are now his chief amusement. One of his daughters reads them to him for two hours every evening, and when they meet with anything that reminds him of any of Fielding's he is particularly pleased.'[20]

He was nonetheless understandably 'very low' at Weymouth, and the weather was bad too. Always abstemious and now nearly blind, the King lost his appetite. 'Supper is set out but that is merely a matter of form,' it was reported.[21] It was to be his last visit to the place where he had spent many happy summer holidays with his family before its fracturing. The death of the King's last surviving brother, Prince William, Duke of Gloucester, on 25 August further underlined his advancing years. The Prince of Wales came to visit, but Creevey recorded that when he returned to London 'he was very indiscreet in talking at his table about the King's infirmities,' and 'described the King as so blind that he had nearly fallen into some hole at Lord Dorchester's'. Because there was a pro-government MP present, Creevey butted in to say, 'Poor man, Sir!' in 'a very audible and serious tone', upon which the Prince 'immediately took the hint and stopped'.[22]

On 24 July, upon receiving news that Austria was about to join the Third Coalition – which it did on 9 August – Napoleon ordered the Grande Armée to strike camp in Boulogne and march on the exposed Austrian stronghold of Ulm in Bavaria. The invasion threat to Britain was finally over, but the military threat to Austria and Russia was now very real, especially as the Russian Army was ten days' march behind the Austrian one. Pitt had wanted to draw the Prussians into the Third Coalition too, but they had demanded Hanover in return, which of course he could never offer; for that reason, he did not keep the King fully informed of the negotiations.[23] Such an omission would have been impossible any earlier in the reign, but as Colonel Taylor wrote at the end of a letter from the King to Pitt on 15 September, 'His Majesty's sight will not allow him to add more, as though he gains some ground, he can neither read what is written to him nor what he writes.'[24] Because of Grenville's stance on Catholic emancipation, George still did not want to accept him into the government, despite his hawkishness in foreign policy, and eventually Pitt gave up asking. Instead, he said he would try to bring George Canning and Charles

Yorke into the Cabinet, and reported to his friend the 3rd Earl Bathurst on 27 September, after seeing the King, that:

> The resolution seems decidedly taken to risk all chances rather than consent (before the moment of actual necessity) to take any step towards a junction of any sort with the Opposition. The objections seem now to be as deeply rooted against Grenville as even against Fox ... I should not, however, despair of overcoming this sentiment ... if the scene opening on the Continent should lead (as is perhaps possible) to [Grenville's] taking a different line on foreign politics from the other branch of [the] Opposition; but this is so doubtful a chance that one cannot at all count upon it, and we must therefore prepare to fight the best battle we can with our own strength.[25]

On Sunday 20 October 1805, the fortress city of Ulm fell to Napoleon after a lightning French campaign, a devastating catastrophe that led to 20,000 infantry, 3,300 cavalry, seventeen generals and fifty-nine field guns passing into French hands and dealt a crushing blow to the Third Coalition. At the same time that the Austrian soldiers were laying down their arms, however, 1,200 miles to the south-west at Cape Trafalgar off the coast of Spain, Admiral Nelson was about to go into action aboard *Victory*, the same flagship in which Keppel had fought at Ushant and Jervis at Cape St Vincent. The next day, the battle of Trafalgar saw no fewer than twenty-one French and Spanish ships-of-the-line captured and one destroyed, for the loss of 458 British killed and 1,208 wounded against nearly 7,000 Frenchmen and Spaniards killed or wounded. One of the Britons who lost his life was Nelson himself. George shrewdly observed to Nelson's brother that it was precisely the death that the Admiral would have wanted. From a rough parity in numbers of ships-of-the-line in 1800, this and her other naval victories, along with a major building programme, meant that Britain now had a one-third advantage over France and her allies, and Spanish maritime power was broken.[26] However successful Napoleon was on land, Britain was now safe from invasion for the rest of the war, and was to enjoy naval hegemony for over a century.* The King wrote to Pitt on 11 November 1805 'expressing ... the joy he feels at the good news' of

---

* One of the few who failed to see the implications of Trafalgar was Thomas Paine, who even in February 1806 was writing to Napoleon that he hoped he would not forget that 'he owes the project of a descent [invasion] to an American citizen', namely himself (Keane, *Tom Paine* p. 441). Paine had been chosen as a member of the provisional government of occupation that Napoleon hoped to establish in London. If Trafalgar had gone the other way, it is not hard to envisage him celebrating the guillotining of a second monarch after Louis XVI. Instead, by the time of his death in June 1809, Paine had so alienated his friends and supporters that only twelve people attended his funeral.

Trafalgar, and giving his consent for Nelson to be buried in St Paul's Cathedral, 'which the brilliancy of the victory seems to call for'.[27] All eight admirals who acted as Nelson's pall-bearers wept, another mark of the open emotionalism of the era, before the Victorians emphasized the stiff upper lip.*

However much success Britain enjoyed at sea, however, the Third Coalition could not prevent Napoleon from capturing Vienna on 14 November, and then winning a devastating victory at Austerlitz on 2 December, the anniversary of his coronation. Two days later, and thus long before the news reached England, Lord Castlereagh, the Secretary for War and the Colonies, presented the King with a plan to encourage Prussia to join the coalition with a large British force under General Sir George Don, which would disembark on the Elbe to link up with the Swedes and Russians. George approved the plan, not least because it might afford some chance of regaining Hanover. Pitt had left London for Bath on 7 December to take the waters for his stomach ulcers, and the King insisted that he stay there until he recovered. The first rumours of Austerlitz, as related by Castlereagh to the King on 20 December, were of an Allied victory, what the King called 'the successful result of the arduous contest' in Moravia.[28] It was therefore all the harder when the truth finally reached London on 2 January 1806. 'Roll up the map of Europe,' Pitt is supposed, probably apocryphally, to have said. 'It will not be wanted these ten years.'[29] The news of Austerlitz was certainly the death knell for the alliance that Pitt had worked so hard to create and sustain, and also perhaps that of the Prime Minister himself. Lord Malmesbury certainly thought that the news of Austerlitz 'accelerated his end'.[30] All Charles Fox said of the battle was 'These are wonders indeed but they are not *much* more than I expected.'[31] At least General Don's expeditionary force was able to re-embark without loss.

The death of William Pitt on 23 January at the age of forty-six, probably of a peptic ulceration of the duodenum, shook British politics to its core. His last words were 'Oh my country! How I leave my country!'[32] (Although decades later Benjamin Disraeli was told by an elderly House of Commons doorkeeper that they were 'I think I could eat one of Bellamy's pork pies.')[33] Pitt had become known, in Canning's phrase, as 'The pilot who weathered the storm', which, though accurate, owed much to the support the King had given him over his eighteen years and 243 days as Prime Minister. In working himself into an early grave, Pitt had given his life for his country just as much as had Nelson three months earlier, and, although he would

* Although monarchs did not attend non-royal funerals (and would not until Queen Elizabeth II attended Winston Churchill's), the Prince of Wales went with his father's consent.

not live to see it, his strategy of generously financing wide Continental alliances would be vital in the eventual defeat of Napoleon Bonaparte.

In January 1806, George moved into the King's Apartments at Windsor Castle, a set of twelve rooms in the Upper Ward overlooking the North Terrace. He transferred his belongings from St James's Palace, and was never to live anywhere else, or even to visit Kew again. He initially hoped that the ministry would not collapse completely upon Pitt's death, and that a new premier might be able to carry on with much the same ministers, as when Addington had succeeded Pitt in 1801, and vice versa in 1804. The day before Pitt's death, George told William Henry Fremantle MP, a young Grenvillite, that he would consult Grenville, though not Charles Fox, if a new ministry were needed. On Pitt's death, the King asked Lord Sidmouth whether he would serve under Lord Hawkesbury, to whom he awarded the now vacant lord wardenship of the Cinque Ports, but Sidmouth was too proud to accept. It was clear that no Pittite could survive long as premier with the combined Foxites, Grenvillites and Addingtonians in Opposition, so the Duke of Portland advised the King to consult Grenville, who once again refused to go in without Fox.

With characteristic radical Whig incivility towards the King, Thomas Creevey later summed up the situation thus: 'When Pitt died, and Old Nobbs* sent for Grenville to make the government, the latter would not listen to any prejudice against Fox, but made the Crown divide the government between them.'[34] It was a tribute to the shade of William Pitt the Younger that the only possible successor to his ministry was a national government, or a 'Ministry of all the Talents',† as its supporters somewhat hyperbolically described it. Once again, the King was forced to accept ministers he neither liked nor wanted, as had been the case in 1763, 1765, 1782 and 1783.

The King called on Grenville to form a government on 27 January. 'There are to be no exclusions,' George told him, meaning that he would accept Fox in the Cabinet and allow for Eldon to be dismissed as Lord Chancellor.[35] Grenville observed that the King had been 'very gracious' at their meeting.[36] That same day a motion was put in the Commons that Pitt, 'that excellent statesman', should be accorded a state funeral in Westminster Abbey and the erection of a memorial there. Fox spoke and voted against it, on the basis that Pitt had supported 'a system of government' in

---

* A common nickname for an elderly carthorse.
† The phrase came from a speech of Canning's in which he said that a combination was needed of 'all the talents, wisdom and ability of the nation' (Ziegler, *Addington* p. 251).

which 'the invisible influence' of the Crown was unacceptably great.[37] This infuriated the leading Pittites – Hawkesbury, Canning, Portland, Perceval and Castlereagh – who were already angry with the Addingtonians for having weakened Pitt's government by their resignations the previous July. Fox did at least vote in favour of Parliament paying off Pitt's debts of £40,000,* a large amount considering his lack of vices beyond alcohol. (He had been improving his country home, and allowed his builders and servants to rob him in the process: Pitt was as careless of his own finances as he was prudent with those of the nation.)

Grenville planned his ministry over the next three weeks. When Eldon came to Windsor to deliver the Great Seal on 7 February, the King asked him to put it down on a sofa, as he did not want physically to take it from him. 'Yet I admit you can't stay when all the rest have run away.'[38] Grenville kissed hands as premier on 11 February. Fox became Foreign Secretary. Sidmouth was installed in a backseat role as Lord Privy Seal, partly to ensure royal support and partly because he controlled about thirty votes (Canning joked that 'Mr Fox has got the Doctor, as people must have the measles once in their life').[39] The ministry did not by any means represent 'all the talents' of British politics, since it contained no Pittites, who were arguably the most talented politicians of the day and undoubtedly the coming men. Among Hawkesbury, Perceval, Canning and Castlereagh alone there were three future premiers, and the last was perhaps the greatest Foreign Secretary in British history.

When the King received his new Foreign Secretary in the Closet, a place where Fox had only set foot once in the previous twenty-three years, he freely admitted, 'Mr Fox, I little thought you and I should ever meet again in this place. But I have no desire to look back upon old grievances, and you may rest assured I never shall remind you of them.'[40] Fox replied, equally graciously, by bowing and replying, 'My deeds and not my words shall commend me to Your Majesty.'[41] The King later said that Fox treated him 'frankly and yet respectfully', contrasting him with another (sadly unnamed) minister, 'who, when he came into office, walked up to him in the way that he should have expected from Buonaparte after the battle of Austerlitz'.[42]

Fox wanted to initiate peace negotiations with Napoleon right away. On 20 April the King reluctantly agreed, but insisted that Britain 'prove to Europe in general that the government of this country is resolved to assert its dignity and its established rights, and upon no account to submit to restrictions upon its political relations which France in its arrogance may wish to impose'.[43] Although Fox started off committed to finding a route

---

*   Around £5 million in today's money.

to peace, by July his dream had died, and shortly afterwards he fell mortally ill. Talleyrand and Lord Yarmouth conducted negotiations, but they foundered once it became clear that Napoleon was intent on conquering Britain's Neapolitan ally in Sicily, if he could find a way across the Straits of Messina. He plainly had no intention of returning Hanover; indeed on 15 February he had persuaded Prussia to occupy the electorate.

Charles Fox died on 13 September, aged fifty-seven, only eight months after his arch-rival Pitt. A post-mortem revealed a hardened liver, thirty-five gallstones and seven pints of transparent fluid in his abdomen. Although he had lost an estimated £200,000* over a lifetime's hard gambling, upon his death he left only £10,000 in debts. Lord Holland claimed that the King 'had watched the progress of Mr Fox's disorder. He could hardly suppress his indecent exultation at his death.'[44] His wife Lady Holland claimed in her journal that the King received the news from Lord Howick (Charles Grey, later 2nd Earl Grey) 'in the coldest possible style, and did not express even sorrow for the event'.[45] Both these accounts were untrue. In fact, as Mary, Duchess of Gloucester, who was in the room at the time, later related to the future Whig Prime Minister Lord John Russell, what the King actually said to Sidmouth was 'Little did I think I should ever live to regret Mr Fox's death.'[46] Another rendering was 'I never thought I should have regretted the loss of Mr Fox as much as I do.'[47] The King also inquired after Mrs Fox when speaking to other ministers.

Charles Fox was one of the few British politicians of whom it can be genuinely said that there endured a cult of personality after his death, a testament to his considerable charisma and capacity for friendship.[48]† But in his long rivalry with Pitt, which had started in 1783, there can be no doubt who triumphed professionally, as measured by their respective terms in office. Fox was Foreign Secretary for three short periods, in 1782, 1783 and 1806, for a total of nineteen months. By contrast, Pitt served as Prime Minister and Chancellor of the Exchequer for more than eighteen and a half years, and during the last was also Leader of the House of Commons. Pitt too enjoyed a posthumous cult of personality with dozens of Pitt Clubs established around the country, of which the University Pitt Club in Cambridge is today the sole survivor.

On 14 October, the French defeated the Prussians at the twin battles of Jena and Auerstädt, meaning that Napoleon could remove Hanover from the control of the King of Prussia. In 1810 he transferred it to the

---

* About £25 million in today's money.
† A Fox Club set up by his friends to commemorate him on his death still meets at Brooks's Club twice a year.

three-year-old Kingdom of Westphalia, ruled over by his youngest brother Jérôme. Charles-William, Duke of Brunswick, died of the wounds he received at Auerstädt, so George brought his penniless widow, his elder sister Augusta, back to England in a frigate and settled her in Blackheath with a pension for herself and her three sons.

Charles-William and Augusta's daughter, Caroline, Princess of Wales, was having a torrid time in 1806 even before her father's heroic death. Rumours of her various love affairs led to the accusation that a three-month-old boy she had adopted in 1802, William Austin, was in fact her illegitimate son. Her private life had a serious public aspect, because under the 1352 Treason Act anybody having carnal knowledge of the Princess was – theoretically at least – liable to the death penalty. Rumours abounded, and at one point the Cabinet even discussed whether it was true that one of her lovers carried around with him a bag containing some of her pubic hair.[49] The King was forced to undertake what was euphemistically called 'The Delicate Investigation' into her love life, which was conducted in secret by four of the most important men in the land – Grenville the Prime Minister, Spencer the Home Secretary, Lord Chancellor Erskine (the former Mr Thomas Erskine) and Lord Chief Justice Ellenborough. These eminences heard detailed and deeply embarrassing testimony, such as that from one of her footmen that 'The Princess was very fond of fucking,' a statement that her sympathetic biographer, Flora Fraser, suggests 'may well have been born of personal experience'.[50]

The Delicate Investigation found that, although Princess Caroline's behaviour had not encouraged a 'very favourable interpretation', there was 'no foundation whatever' to the rumour about Austin. The King continued to treat her kindly, visit her occasionally at Blackheath and ensure that she had at least occasional access to her daughter, over the Prince of Wales' objections, threats and obstruction.[51] In later years she undoubtedly did have affairs, including with her secretary Bartolomeo Pergami, who as an Italian owed no fealty to the British Crown and was thus not committing treason by sleeping with the next queen.

With Pitt dead, the Grenville ministry saw no reason to continue to abide by the late premier's promise to the King not to pursue Catholic emancipation. In March 1807 they introduced the Army and Navy Service Bill, which, buried among its proposals, included an extension of the provisions of the Irish Catholic Relief Act of 1793 to high military and staff officers. Howick admitted in Parliament that he 'had not sufficiently attended to the difference between it and the Irish Act', which is extraordinary considering the known sensitivities of the King. It has been suggested that in fact the Cabinet had tried to 'smuggle' and 'juggle' the issue past the blind King, but just because he himself could not read the small print of parliamentary Bills, it did not mean that Colonel Taylor could not read it to him.[52] 'The King is most determined and averse to the admission of Catholics into the high military offices in the army,' noted Abbot.[53] Sidmouth was prepared to resign over the issue, leaving Grenville to decide whether to keep him in the Cabinet or lose around thirty Addingtonian votes in the Commons.

On 12 March the Duke of Portland told the King that in order to stymie the Bill further in the House of Lords, 'I must take the liberty of saying that it will be absolutely necessary that Your Majesty's wishes should be so distinctly intimated that no doubt may exist respecting them.'[54] The irony was delicious: it had of course been Portland's own ministry that was brought down by precisely those methods over the East India Bill in December 1783, actions that the Whigs at the time (and their historians ever since) denounced as outrageously unconstitutional. Portland, whom George now saw as a friend, was essentially offering himself as an alternative premier to Grenville, just as Pitt had presented an alternative to Portland himself a quarter of a century before.

Portland had been a sound Home Secretary during the wartime emergency from 1794 to 1801, hostile to seditious publications, radicalism, parliamentary reform and Catholic emancipation alike. The King would have preferred Hawkesbury, the son of his old ally Charles Jenkinson, as premier, but the tired, sixty-eight-year-old Duke was the only person around whom the highly ambitious and competitive Pittites could seemingly coalesce, because none of them would tolerate one of their own number promoted except himself.

On 15 March, the Talents ministry was forced to abandon the Catholic Emancipation Bill because of opposition in the Lords. The King had now entirely lost his trust in Grenville, and two days later he demanded that he never again raise the issue. 'With a view to the prevention of all future mistakes', he asked the Cabinet for a written promise.[55] This was too humiliating a climbdown for them to accept, and after Grenville had refused, the King replied, 'I must look about me.'[56] When Lord Erskine warned him that he 'stood on the edge of a precipice' if he dismissed Grenville, implying that there would be a strong radical reaction, George replied, 'Sir, you are an honest man, and I am very much obliged to you,' then peremptorily bowed to signal that the audience was over.[57] The King had experienced some genuine precipices in his time – principally those from the time of Grenville's father's ultimatum of 1765 and Fox's threats of 1783 – and he knew that this was not one of them.

George felt, with good reason, that he had been misled over the extent of the concessions the ministry had planned to extend to Catholics in the armed forces, and he appreciated that with Fox's death the initiative had tipped away from the Grenvillites and towards Pitt's former supporters, who now identified themselves with increasing openness as Tories. Sheridan recognized this too, and observed of Grenville's actions, 'He had known many men knock their heads against a wall, but he had never before heard of a man collecting bricks and building a wall for the express purpose of knocking out his own brains against it.'[58] Whig legend puts down the 1807 episode as 'a stab in the back by the Crown', but in fact the wound was both self-inflicted and easily avoided.[59]

On 24 March, Grenville surrendered the seals of what turned out to be the last Whig ministry of the King's reign. George had at last, after forty-seven years on the throne, achieved what he and Bute had set out to do when he acceded, and expelled the Whig oligarchy, albeit employing a Whig duke to do it. 'The favourite maxim of the late reign', *The Times* was to write years later in the King's obituary, 'was represented to have been the rigorous exclusion of the great Whig families from power.'[60] For Portland was merely a figurehead, as he had been in his previous premiership in 1783: the real power was with the younger ministers who would dominate the next generation. These were Tories such as George Canning, who now became Foreign Secretary, Lord Castlereagh (Colonial Secretary), Lord Hawkesbury (Home Secretary) and Spencer Perceval (Chancellor of the Exchequer and Leader of the House of Commons) and the arch-Tory Lord Eldon, who returned as Lord Chancellor. The Portland ministry on 29 April then obtained a dissolution of Parliament (the second in eight months) and won a good majority in the subsequent general election, confirming what the King had known all along, that he had not been anywhere near the edge of a precipice.

On 13 July 1807, George outlived the last Stuart pretender, Cardinal Henry of York, who had styled himself King Henry IX but so half-heartedly that George paid him a £2,000 per annum pension out of the Secret Service Fund after the French had sacked his home in Frascati in 1799. It had been a handsome gesture, and one that was more than reciprocated when Henry bequeathed King James II's crown jewels to the Prince of Wales, together with the magnificent fifteenth-century Book of Hours once owned by King Jan Sobieski of Poland.[61] As the cardinal was childless, the Stuart threat finally died out, sixty-two years after the Jacobite uprising of 1745.*

---

* The extent to which the Hanoverians were still conscious of their Stuart predecessors can be gleaned from a remark of George's second daughter, who said in 1828 that 'I was ashamed to hear myself called Princess Augusta, and never could persuade myself that I was so, as long

Intelligence reports that Napoleon was planning to invade Denmark in July led George reluctantly to approve the plans of Lord Mulgrave, the First Lord of the Admiralty, to send a flotilla to Copenhagen to stiffen Danish resistance. Canning ideally wanted an alliance to ensure that the large Danish fleet there, which it was feared could be used to invade Ireland, did not fall into French hands. Three days later, Castlereagh told the King that the Royal Navy needed to prevent the Danes from reinforcing Zealand, and that Copenhagen might have to be attacked by land if they did not agree to the anti-Napoleonic alliance. The King was profoundly worried about Britain's reputation if she pre-emptively attacked a neutral country, and Portland had to work hard to persuade him of the necessity. Once intelligence arrived that Napoleon had signed a treaty at Tilsit with Tsar Alexander I committing the Russian Navy against Britain and closing Russian ports to British ships, the King was convinced, and the fleet set sail. Tragically it arrived before Napoleon's own impossible demands reached Denmark, otherwise an Anglo-Danish alliance might have been possible and no blood shed.[62]

Privately, the King believed the British bombardment of Copenhagen from 2 to 5 September to be 'a very immoral act', even though it swiftly led to the Danish surrender.[63] When he met Francis James Jackson, the British special envoy to Copenhagen, who had witnessed the shelling of the city, he asked him on which floor of the Danish palace the Crown Prince Regent of Denmark (later King Frederick VI) had met him. When Jackson told him it had been on the ground floor, George replied, 'I am glad of it for your sake, for if he had half the spirit of George III he would have infallibly kicked you downstairs.'[64]

Major-General Sir Arthur Wellesley MP, who had distinguished himself fighting in the Mahratta Wars in India, became Chief Secretary for Ireland in the Portland ministry, after extracting a promise from the Duke of York that it would not affect his chances of being sent abroad to fight the French. The King had known about Wellesley as a successful soldier, but had formed a low opinion of his elder brother, the politician and colonial governor Richard Wellesley, not just because of his French mistress but also because as MP for Windsor he had neglected his constituents. When in August 1804 Pitt had asked for a knighthood for Arthur, the King agreed, but insisted that two other people took precedence over 'Brigadier-General

---

as any of the Stuart family were alive; but after the death of Cardinal York [*sic*], I felt myself to be really Princess Augusta' (ed. Jennings, *Croker Papers* I p. 406).

Welsley', thus getting both Major-General Wellesley's rank and surname wrong, a rare gaffe for him.[65]

In late July 1808 the thirty-nine-year-old Wellesley was sent out to Portugal to fight the French, which he did successfully at the battles of Roliça and Vimeiro on 17 and 21 August. The King and the Duke of York thought that the overall command of the British expeditionary force there should not be entrusted to someone so young, but instead should go to the fifty-seven-year-old General Sir Hew Dalrymple, the Governor of Gibraltar, and his second-in-command Sir Harry Burrard. In this plan, which was adopted, even the Quartermaster-General, George Murray, would be senior to Wellesley. This decision was swiftly proved to be spectacularly ill-advised when the humiliating terms of the Convention of Cintra, negotiated by Dalrymple and Burrard (and reluctantly countersigned by Wellesley), reached the King and government on 4 September. They allowed the French General Junot, who had been defeated by Wellesley, to return to France with his army and booty intact, and even aboard Royal Navy vessels.

When George Canning received the report about the Convention he told the King that he had hoped that it might be a forgery. 'Although the King can hardly bring himself to believe that any British officers could, under the circumstances in which Sir Hew Dalrymple and Sir Arthur Wellesley were placed, think of agreeing to such a convention . . .' the King told Canning, 'His Majesty has observed with regret that Sir Hew Dalrymple's letter appears, from its style, genuine. The King can never sanction such a proceeding if unfortunately it should have any existence.'[66] Wellesley was acquitted of personal responsibility at the subsequent Committee of Inquiry, which effectively ended the careers of both Dalrymple and Burrard. The King was told of the heroic death of Sir John Moore at the battle of Corunna on 16 January 1809, and later approved Parliament raising a memorial to someone 'whose valuable and distinguished services cannot be too strongly marked'.[67]

On 26 March 1809, Castlereagh recommended Wellesley as the commander of a new expeditionary force to Portugal. 'In agreeing however to so young a lieutenant-general holding so distinguished a command,' the King replied, 'while his seniors remain unemployed, His Majesty must desire that Lord Castlereagh will keep in view that if the corps in Portugal should be further increased hereafter, the claims of senior officers cannot with justice be set aside.'[68]

In his stubborn insistence on respecting the traditions of hierarchy and seniority in the army, the King had almost missed the special qualities of the greatest British soldier since the Duke of Marlborough. Although Wellesley had won the battles of Roliça and Vimeiro before the Convention of Cintra, the King ought also to have noticed the much larger battles such as Assaye and the siege of Seringapatam which Wellesley had won in India, but he considered military fame easier to win on the subcontinent than in Europe. Even when Wellesley had further proved his worth by boldly capturing Oporto and forcing Marshal Soult out of Portugal in May 1809, the King was reluctant to authorize his extension of operations into Spain the next month, where a quarter of a million French troops were stationed. It went ahead, however, and after Wellesley's victory at the battle of Talavera on 28 July the King bestowed a peerage on him, as Baron Wellington. Yet the battle also prompted the King to tell Portland that he 'deeply laments that success, however glorious, has been so dearly bought'.[69] That was an expression of the King's humanity – the British had lost one-quarter of their force and suffered more casualties than the French – rather than a criticism of Wellington's command.

Writing to Castlereagh in early October, George admitted that after Sir John Moore's death at the battle of Corunna:

> he could never look with satisfaction to the prospect of another British army being committed in Spain, under the possible recurrence of the same difficulties. It was also this impression which prompted the King to acquiesce in the appointment of so young a lieutenant-general as Lord Wellington . . . of whose zealous services and abilities he has the most favourable opinion, and whose subsequent conduct has proved him deserving of the confidence reposed in him.[70]

As with Dundas over Egypt, the King was willing to admit when he was wrong. After Wellington's victory over Marshal Masséna at the battle of Busaco on 27 September 1810, Hawkesbury (now the 2nd Earl of Liverpool) told the General, 'I never saw the King more entirely satisfied than he has been in the later operations of the army.'[71]

Before then, however, a scandal had erupted that caused the King great pain, when in March 1809 his favourite son, Prince Frederick, Duke of York, was forced to resign as Commander-in-Chief of the British Army over 'the Duke and the Darling Scandal'. Frederick's embittered former mistress, Mary Anne Clarke, had been caught selling army commissions. Although he had not personally profited, and probably did not know the full extent of the corruption, it was credibly alleged that the Prince had turned a blind eye to at least some of it. The Commons examined the issue for seven weeks, and interviewed Clarke, who went into ever more lurid detail about the Duke's private life as she sought to implicate him in her crimes. By the end of the exhaustive and hugely embarrassing investigation, the only completely incontrovertible evidence that emerged was that she had tried to blackmail him and he had defied her.[72]

The King told Lord Eldon that he deplored the fact that Frederick 'should ever have formed any connection with so abandoned a woman as Mrs Clarke, but His Majesty never will allow himself to doubt for one moment the Duke of York's perfect integrity and his conscientious attention to his public duty', telling Perceval that 'There is no evidence . . . that the Duke of York knew anything of Mrs Clarke's nefarious practices.'[73] Unfortunately there was such evidence, but the King convinced himself that it was forged, whereas two witnesses from the Post Office, three from the Bank of England, almost the entire press corps and several senior ministers including the Chancellor of the Exchequer Spencer Perceval thought otherwise.

For all the Whig talk about the unacceptable and increasing powers of the Crown in Dunning's famous motion of 1780, the King's favourite son was forced to resign from a post he had held for fourteen years, even though the government won the divisions on the matter in the Commons, by 364 votes to 123 in one case, and 294 votes to 199 in another. Despite this, a succession of indignant speeches by prominent MPs including William Wilberforce made York's position untenable. The King had again yielded to public opinion, and acted according to its wishes rather than his own.

On 17 August, the Duke of Portland had an apoplectic seizure on the journey from his seat at Bulstrode to London and, since he made only a partial recovery, on 6 September he decided to resign as soon as the King and Cabinet could decide upon a successor. The Cabinet drew up a long minute to the King on 18 September, arguing that overtures should be made to the Whig leaders William Grenville and the 2nd Earl Grey (formerly Lord Howick) rather than to Sidmouth. 'The King went through a long and methodized discussion of the minute in all its parts,' Canning told Abbot, 'with a strong and clear expression of his own sentiments upon it, extremely averse to the proposed overture, but consenting to take it into consideration, and to speak to each of his ministers upon it at the next Levee day, before he gave his answer.'[74]

The government was then further and entirely unnecessarily weakened by the resignations of both George Canning and Lord Castlereagh from the Cabinet, so that they might fight a duel against one another. Canning had entreated the King and Portland to dismiss Castlereagh from the War Office over the Clarke scandal and a botched expedition to the Dutch island of Walcheren; when Castlereagh found out and challenged him to a duel over what he regarded as his ungentlemanly behaviour, Canning replied that he accepted 'cheerfully'.[75] He ought not to have been quite so cheerful, as he had never fired a pistol before.

The two men met on Putney Heath at 6 a.m. on 21 September and fired at each other from twelve paces. Both missed on the first shot, but on the second attempt Castlereagh struck Canning in the thigh. When informed of this by Portland, the King replied that while 'the Duke must be sensible that as it is His Majesty's duty not to countenance in any manner such transactions, it must be equally his wish to abstain . . . from any comment except an expression of the sincere concern with which he must ever view this event.'[76] In private, of course, the King was just as fascinated as everyone else by what had happened, and as Canning reported to William Huskisson:

> Instead of avoiding (as I imagined he would) the subject of the duel altogether, as one on which it was not proper for him to talk, or to seem informed, he began immediately to enter into all the particulars of that event. The situation of the wound (which he made me point out to him on his royal thigh), the time I received the challenge, when Charles Ellis* heard of it, how I held my pistol, etc., etc., confessing all along great abhorrence of the custom of duelling.[77]

The King wrote to Castlereagh about what had led to the duel, denying that Canning had ever accused Castlereagh of 'want of zeal or efficiency' to him.[78]

With Portland still incapacitated, on 30 September Spencer Perceval told Abbot:

> The King had been very unwilling to have the overture made to Lord Grey and Lord Grenville, and had agreed to it only upon the representation that, if such a junction could be formed, it would for a time prevent the Catholic question from being brought forward as a government measure, which otherwise might be again attempted if the present administration should be wholly overthrown, and their successors come into power by main force. The King did not see why he should be required to abandon the *fixed* principles of his *whole life*, because these two lords would not abandon their principles recently taken up. He thought that they might be required to give a pledge that they would not stir the question. *Mr Pitt had given him such a pledge in writing*, and had repeated it verbally again to the King in his Closet, adding, that (for private reasons of his own)† he would also oppose it whenever and by whomsoever brought forward.[79]

---

* The MP who acted as Canning's second.
† Probably so as not to trigger a mental collapse in the King.

Offered roles in government on such a basis, both Grey and Grenville naturally declined, as the King almost certainly intended.

Having ascertained from Spencer Perceval that he would not raise the issue of Catholic emancipation, George appointed him Prime Minister on 4 October 1809. Four weeks later, following a second seizure, the Duke of Portland died. Perceval's purely Tory administration had the necessary support in Parliament, and Perceval himself was the son of the 2nd Earl of Egmont, a King's Friend and First Lord of the Admiralty, so he was someone George had known for many years and with whom he was personally comfortable. Perceval was also an evangelical Protestant, who quite literally regarded Napoleon as the Antichrist in human form, having written a pamphlet to that effect entitled *Observations Intended to Point out the Application of a Prophecy in the Eleventh Chapter of the Book of David to the French Power*.[80] It extended even to the belief that Napoleon's fall had been foretold in the Bible and that the world was going to end in 1926. Such outlandish fervour did not seem to worry the King, who approved of Perceval's faith.

There was a neat symmetry in that George's father had singled out Perceval's father as a future Prime Minister back in the 1740s; Perceval's was to be the last government that George himself was ever to appoint. The King had no idea, of course, that in making Spencer Perceval Prime Minister he was also sending him to his death.

28

King Lear Redux

October 1809–January 1820

In the perplexity of nations, the throne of the King of England was
the only one unshaken, and its stability was the work of his virtue.[1]
The *Manchester Guardian* obituary of George III, January 1820

On 25 October 1809, nationwide celebrations began to commemorate the start of the King's fiftieth year on the throne. 'Nothing could be better than its effect in London,' wrote the moderate Whig politician and future Prime Minister Lord Palmerston, noting that the crowds forced all coachmen and servants to doff their hats to the illuminated crown over Admiralty Gate, which stood at the other end of the Mall from Buckingham House.[2] George was the longest-reigning King of England since Edward III in the fourteenth century, and his country was resisting Napoleon more successfully than any other power. Indeed, Britain had vanquished France at sea, and was striking heavy blows against her in Egypt, Portugal and now Spain.

To mark his jubilee year, George donated £6,000 to his favourite charities, including the Society for the Relief of Prisoners Confined for Small Debts, and he released all imprisoned debtors to the Crown and contributed to a scheme to improve prisons.* He also granted a free pardon to all deserters from his fleets and armies, and to everyone confined for military offences. Paroled prisoners of war were released from military prisons.[3] There were also mass promotions in the navy – five admirals, ten vice-admirals, ten rear-admirals.[4]

No fewer than 650 public events – parades, receptions, luncheons, bonfires, firework displays, illuminations and the like – took place in England alone; there were many more across the rest of the United Kingdom and

---

* George was a great admirer of the philanthropist and prison reformer John Howard, and after he had offered to lead a subscription for a statue in his honour, which Howard respectfully declined, the King declared, 'His virtues will live when every statue has crumbled into dust' (Wright, *George III* p. 85). Howard nonetheless became the first civilian to have a monument in St Paul's Cathedral, in 1796.

in the empire beyond. A book entitled *An Account of the Celebration of the Jubilee* was later published, which gathered up local reports from towns and villages up and down the country. These usually took the form of festivities with food, ale and fireworks, laudatory speeches by local worthies and appearances by the nobility and gentry, along with music, dancing and general revelry. There were also, in most cases, gifts to the poor of food and money. This report from the village of Blisworth in Northamptonshire is typical of scores of others:

> The morning was ushered in with the ringing of bells, a flag was displayed at the top of the church, and a fat sheep roasted whole. A great number of women were provided with cake and tea in the street, and at five o'clock the sheep was distributed among the poor people, with bread and beer, in equal portions to each family. A supper was afterwards provided at the Grafton Arms, where several of the respectable inhabitants assembled, and harmony and convivial mirth crowned the festivity of the day.[5]

Volunteer regiments paraded; employers threw celebratory free dinners for their employees (Lord Ailesbury gave one for 6,000 people); mayors and towns competed in displaying patriotic and local pride; statues were raised (equestrian ones for the richer neighbourhoods); bands played; it was a paid holiday; and there were civic banquets (denounced by *The Times* for their lavishness, to little effect). Leeds set up a Bible society, and Oswestry used the occasion to inaugurate its street lighting.[6] Jubilee obelisks were raised at Broughton-on-Furness and Windsor. A Jubilee Tower was built on Moel Famau in Wales. A song was sung in Dundee:

> For under him we sit and crack,*
> In peace and unity compact,
> Whilst every nation's on the rack
> That does nae like our Geordie.[7]

In Stoke D'Abernon in Surrey, to take a typical example, Mr Vaillant the rector gave 'a very appropriate and excellent discourse' after which 'he entertained the farmers with a dinner, and in the evening presided at a supper, given by a subscription of the inhabitants to the poor of the parish, who with one heart and voice drank the King's health, and sang "God Save the King" till a late hour.'[8]

The King had a bust made of him by Madame Tussaud† and no fewer

---

* 'Boast' (*Johnson's Dictionary*).
† The wax cast in Kew Palace today was made in 1996 from the original mould kept at Madame Tussaud's.

than fifteen different commemorative medals were struck, featuring such statements as 'The 50th year he has govern'd & preserved an affectionate & loyal people' and 'Britons rejoice'. The jubilee also saw the start of the practice of making commemorative china and ceramics for royal occasions, which was later to become an enormous industry.

Of course there were dissenters. Radical politicians such as Sir Francis Burdett MP complained that the jubilee was 'a clumsy trick to thrust joy down the throats of the people'.[9] The radical intellectual Leigh Hunt sneered in his *Examiner* newspaper at 'that foolish multitude' who celebrated the jubilee in their deluded monarchist ignorance, but he did not deny that a very large number of people were indeed enjoying themselves.[10] The journalist William Cobbett asked sarcastically whether the contemporaneous illuminations in Madrid for Joseph Bonaparte's rule as King of Spain meant that his rule was popular too. Nobody took much notice of the naysayers, however; people just enjoyed the day and toasted their King's half-centenary. It was in any case perfectly possible to be patriotic and anti-establishment, like the protester in London who wanted prices to return to their pre-inflation levels and carried a placard on jubilee day that read 'Be Britons on the 25th but riot on the 26th'.[11]

At about half-past two on the morning of 31 May 1810, Prince Ernest, Duke of Cumberland, rushed into his valet's room in St James's Palace covered in blood and crying, 'Neale, Neale, I am murdered!'[12] He had been struck four times with his own regimental sabre, twice to the head, and so deep that his brain could be seen pulsating in his skull. His right thumb had been almost severed. Another valet, an Italian called Joseph Sellis, had savagely attacked him while he slept, for reasons that are still unclear, and then retreated to his bedroom to cut his own throat with a razor.

Spencer Perceval told the King later that morning that 'from the last intelligence he has received of His Royal Highness the Duke of Cumberland, he appears to be going on as well as, considering the nature of his calamity, can be expected'.[13] The King replied that his son's 'preservation under so horrid an attempt has indeed been most providential'. Cumberland underwent brain surgery the following day, which was successful.

The inquest jury brought in a unanimous verdict of suicide on Sellis, but that did not prevent Whig scandalmongers and pamphleteers spreading rumours that the unpopular Tory Duke* had committed crimes including incest, rape, sodomy and murder, although there was not a word of proof

---

* Roger Fulford wrote that Ernest stood out 'from the pages of history as a shapeless lump of filth' (Fulford, *Royal Dukes* p. 230).

for any of it.[14] According to the Whig papers, Cumberland and Sellis had been lovers until Neale arrived; Cumberland was being blackmailed by Sellis over another affair, and Cumberland had fathered a child with Mrs Sellis. In March 1813, the Duke sued Henry White's newspaper the *Independent Whig* for criminal libel; White was sentenced to fifteen months in Newgate and a £200 fine. This did not silence the rumours, however, and twenty years later he had to sue the writer Josiah Phillips, who fled the country after being sentenced to six months' imprisonment. Ernest became King of Hanover in 1837, and according to one of many historians of nineteenth-century royal scandals, 'He is often still thought of as the king who got away with murder' – completely unfairly, as Sellis had locked the door from the inside.[15]

On the same day that the King received the terrible news about the murderous attack on his son, the royal physician Sir Henry Halford also brought him news from Augusta Lodge in Kew of the consumption afflicting George's favourite daughter, the twenty-six-year-old Princess Amelia, whose prognosis was now very bleak. He had been receiving almost daily reports from Halford and Princess Mary about how much she slept, when she drank chicken broth, when her head was 'cupped', her baths, fainting fits and so on, and his replies betray his constant state of anxiety. 'There is no object nearer to my heart,' he wrote to Amelia on 4 June, 'no blessing for which I pray more fervently than that you may be restored to me and to your family in the full enjoyment of your health.'[16]

Despite being separated from Queen Charlotte, the King was still generous to her. When she found herself short of money in June, she ended a letter, 'I will not detain Your Majesty any longer with such an unpleasant epistle but throw myself entirely upon your goodness, being convinced you always will be just and kind.'[17] George ensured that Perceval raised the money she needed, on this occasion by directing the Receiver of Gibraltar's payments into the Privy Purse, as well as the proceeds from shipwrecks known as the Droits of Admiralty. Such preciseness prevailed until the end of his sanity, allowing him to be 'just and kind' to the one and only true love of his life.

By October 1810, Amelia was so ill that the desperate King was asking for reports from Halford thrice a day. An historian has noted, '[George] had more than once expressed his apprehension that his mind would not be equal to the shock that her death, which he knew to be inevitable, must cause him.'[18] The strain indeed turned out to be more than his mental equilibrium could bear. On Wednesday 24 October, the day before his fiftieth year on the throne was completed, the King started to feel symptoms of stress and agitation, brought on by catching a cold. Before this final attack he had only been mentally afflicted for a total of about twelve months, but now he was never to be sane again.

One of the shocking aspects of George's last period of mental illness was that the royal doctors had seemingly not bothered to read any of the learned books on the subject that had been published since the last attack in 1804. When they were questioned on this by the parliamentary committees, their ignorance of the latest medical literature on the subject was exposed as woeful. No fewer than four major works on insanity and its treatment had been published between 1806 and 1809, yet Halford, Matthew Baillie, Sir William Heberden, Henry Dundas and Henry Reynolds had not read any of them.[19]

Halford, who was to be the longest-serving President of the Royal College of Physicians – from 1815 to 1844 – was doctor to four monarchs, including Queen Victoria. 'So suave was his bedside manner', wrote a medical historian, 'that some aristocratic women were said to prefer dying with Sir Henry than living with lesser physicians.'[20] This time the doctors brought in four specialists in mental illness to try to treat the King. Three of the four mad-doctors – Samuel Simmons, Robert Willis and Thomas Monro (the latter from Bethlem Hospital) – were fellows of the Royal College of Physicians. The fourth was Robert Willis' brother John. This was despite the promise the royal family had given not to consult the Willises again.*

'We are in the most embarrassing, as well as the most distressing, case imaginable,' Perceval wrote to Speaker Abbot from his home in Ealing on 29 October.

> The continued and calamitous situation of the Princess Amelia has, at length, so worked upon the King's mind that it is extremely doubtful whether it will be possible for him to sign that commission for the prorogation of Parliament ... I saw His Majesty myself about half past twelve o'clock. His conversation was so hurried, and, though not unconnected or irrational, so unlike his ordinary manner that I certainly should not have thought it proper to have taken his signature or his pleasure to any Act.[21]

Two days later the doctors reported that George's conversation was 'quiet, but silly'.[22]

---

* A ditty of the day went:

> The King receives three doctors daily –
> Willis, Heberden and Baillie:
> Three distinguished clever men,
> Baillie, Willis, Heberden;
> Doubtful which more sure to kill is,
> Baillie, Heberden or Willis.

(*British Medical Journal* Vol. 1 No. 2769
24 January 1914 p. 213)

When Lord Eldon saw the King on 1 November he concluded he was 'quite incompetent to sign the commission' to prorogue Parliament, so they decided to adopt the precedent of November 1788, and Speaker Abbot simply adjourned it for a fortnight. The next day, 2 November 1810, Princess Amelia died from tuberculosis and erysipelas. The King was not told at the time, but when it was gently broken to him two days later, Abbot recorded, he 'did not seem to feel or take much notice of it. The next day he spoke of it as an event that had happened.'[23] He had been such a loving and devoted father that his words now confirmed for everyone the view that he had lost his mind completely.* The King was not informed of the stipulation in Princess Amelia's will that all her possessions were to go to Colonel Charles Fitzroy. 'Nothing but the cruel situation I am placed in of being the daughter of the King', she had written, 'and the laws made by the King respecting the marriages of the royal family prevents me being married to him, which I consider I am in my heart.'[24] Fitzroy refused to accept anything from the bequest.

The King's condition worsened in early November, and for over a week he had to be strapped into a straitjacket every day. 'I feel that I am going to be ill in the former way,' he had told Halford and Baillie, 'and I request of you two that you will not be induced, on any account, to represent me as recovered till you are satisfied that I am perfectly so. By permitting me to go abroad† on the last occasion [that is, in 1804], before that was the case, the physicians were the cause of my doing a great many absurd and foolish things.'[25] It was a brave thing to say, as he knew the restraints under which he would soon be placed.

Between 23 and 26 November, the King's fever was so bad that he nearly died, yet when on the 28th and 29th Doctors Halford, Heberden and Robert Willis were questioned by the Privy Council, while all agreed that he could not undertake any public business, all three said that they were very confident he would recover, although they readily admitted that this opinion was based upon the evidence of his previous illnesses. None would conjecture about how long the illness would last, but all three agreed that he was improving. Nonetheless, as a result of the *Report of the Lords of the Privy Council Examination of the Physicians Attending His Majesty*, on 19 December Spencer Perceval told the Prince of Wales that he intended to introduce a Regency Bill into Parliament.

On Christmas Eve the King was again expected to die, but soon

---

* Something else that was considered prima facie evidence of his insanity was his idea of instituting an order of chivalry solely for women.
† 'Out of the house' (*Johnson's Dictionary*).

afterwards was able to speak sensibly to Eldon and Perceval about the war, and also to play a harpsichord that used to belong to Handel, which was to give him great solace in this last phase of his life. On 27 December, George made a joke while refusing Lord Grey's request to make his brother-in-law, the brewer and radical MP Samuel Whitbread, a privy councillor. 'No, no. It must *not* be,' he said. 'What would the world think if they were to read over an alehouse, "The Right Honourable Sam Whitbread's entire [that is, full-strength beer] sold here"?'[26]

Perceval explained the Regency Bill to the King on 29 January 1811. It would essentially be William Pitt's Bill of 1788, which had included restrictions on the power of the Prince Regent, but these would lapse after twelve months if the King was still incapacitated. George responded reasonably, even asking about the public credit considering he had not been signing Treasury warrants.[27] '[The King] then dwelt upon his own advanced age of seventy-two,' Perceval told Speaker Abbot. 'That it was time for him to think of retirement. That he must still, however, be "King"; he could not part with that name, but *otium cum dignitate*,* etc., was most suitable to his age.'[28] He added that 'He should always be at hand to come forward if he was wanted,' but overall seemed to be impatient to turn over his prerogatives to his son. On 2 February, the third reading of the Regency Bill made Prince George the Prince Regent (he was sworn in the following day) and gave the Queen control over the King's person, assisted by seven councillors headed by the Archbishop of Canterbury, who would receive quarterly reports from John and Robert Willis and Samuel Simmons on the (ever more dwindling) chances of the King's recovery.

The Whigs, who had so often been disappointed in their hope of dislodging the Tories by the King's recoveries in 1789, 1801 and 1804, scented office once more. But as Henry Brougham had written to Thomas Creevey in 1810, 'His death or idiocy would have been in the nature of a *quo warranto*† . . . If a regency had been got up for a short time, with the present men as its ministers, I am confident Eldon, Perceval, etc. . . . would have licked the dust before the P[rince] to good purpose.'[29] Sure enough, on 1 February 1811, the soon-to-be Prince Regent had made it known that, as far as the government was concerned, it was not his 'intention to make any change at present'.[30] The Prince Regent did hold talks with Grey and Grenville, but in the end decided to keep Perceval as Prime Minister, partly because he had gone cool on Catholic emancipation, partly because of the

---

* Leisure with dignity.
† A writ or legal action requiring a person to show by what warrant an office or franchise is held, claimed, or exercised.

Whigs' opposition to the Peninsular War, where Wellington was winning victory after victory, but mainly because, as his biographer put it, 'his inertia and dislike of political exertion inclined him to leave things as they were.'[31]

It came as a devastating blow to some Whigs that the Prince was now betraying them after being their champion over the decades – even to the point, as we have seen, of holding Opposition meetings at Carlton House – for they had allowed their hopes to rise on the assumption of his trustworthiness. They had been jockeying among themselves for positions in the new Whig government, calling each other 'Mr Under-Secretary' and so on. The Prince of Wales became Prince Regent at the start of February, but by then Creevey was telling his wife that Whitbread believed the Prince 'was playing a false, hollow, shabby game'.[32] Later he added, 'The folly and villainy of this Prinny is certainly beyond anything,' while also denouncing his vast profligacy, an aspect of the Prince's character which had somehow escaped him in the days when he used to dine at the Brighton Pavilion.

On 1 February, Lord Glenbervie was regaled with stories of the new Prince Regent by Barbara St John, the sister of the Dowager Countess of Essex and daughter-in-law of the 2nd Viscount St John. A close friend of Maria Fitzherbert and part of the Carlton House Set of twenty years earlier, she told Glenbervie about the viciousness of the Prince Regent, including 'several instances of his brutal cruelty to animals'.[33] Conscious of his new status, at a Carlton House dinner the Prince Regent now ordered that Maria Fitzherbert be sat 'according to her rank', which meant far away from him. One of those collaterally damaged by the Prince Regent's assumption of power was his daughter Princess Charlotte, when he decreed that the fifteen-year-old was not allowed to see any 'company' (that is, men) at her mother's house at Blackheath and imposed a social boycott on anyone who visited there.[34] He did not re-establish guardianship of her, but at least ordered that she spend the summer at Windsor with her grandmother.

On 8 February, the Queen visited the King for the first time since he had fallen ill. 'He received me very kindly, and talked much of his family with great affection,' she reported.[35] At Windsor, he played backgammon, and had Boswell's *Life of Johnson* read to him. He even seems to have been reconciled with the Prince Regent, and was delighted when the Duke of York was reappointed as Commander-in-Chief on 29 May, after two years and two months in disgrace.[36] Because he expected to recover as he had in the past, he did not see the need for the Willis brothers to stay, but they did so. Increasingly the King kept to his apartment, talking to Lord North and other long-dead people, inspecting military parades and carrying out religious ceremonies in his mind.[37]

On 1 June, Robert Willis took over the King's daily care, and maintained his father's calming – and occasional restraining – methods, which remained the basis of George's treatment for the rest of his life. The King's pages were replaced by the Willises' attendants, who were at least trained in dealing with mental illness. In mid-July he suffered a sudden violent relapse, and had to be straitjacketed again. He could not sleep, refused to eat and began talking again about 'Eliza' (Lady Pembroke). On 21 July, Perceval told Abbot that there was 'No apprehension of any immediate danger to the King's life, but the ravings were very wild; sometimes the King talked as if he were conversing amongst the dead with persons long since gone, such as Perceval's father, or at another time some old Hanoverian minister; sometimes also conceiving himself to be shut up in Noah's Ark as an antediluvian.'[38]

'Of the King's mind there are no hopes, even at Windsor,' the 7th Viscount Bulkeley told Lord Auckland in August, 'but his body may last a great while.'[39] It was true; there were many more years for the King to live, but once senile dementia took hold in 1812 and he failed to recognize his family they visited him less and less. In June 1812 the Queen visited him for a quarter of an hour, but never again. In the doctors' report to the House of Commons of January 1813, Halford and John and Robert Willis were far more pessimistic than they had been in 1810, not least because it was considered that after so long a bout of insanity it was very unlikely that the patient could now recover. Even Robert Willis, usually the most optimistic of the King's doctors, attested that recovery was 'extremely improbable' and that his health was 'worse at present than it has been at any stage since his attack'.[40]*

As he entered his dotage, George grew a long white beard, talked incessantly and played the harpsichord. He needed less and less restraint, and events in the outside world stopped mattering to him. He did not know of the assassination of Spencer Perceval on 11 May 1812 by a disappointed office seeker in the lobby of the Commons. (The Prince Regent once again failed to advance his old Whig friends, but appointed the 2nd Earl of Liverpool, who served until 1827.) At one point in his madness, the King uttered the poignant words, 'I must have a new suit of clothes and I will have them black in memory of George III.'[41] He often spoke of himself as 'the late King', and once observed, 'He was a good man.' As in his earlier

---

* The doctors all continued to charge huge fees, however, and by the time the King died, the amount spent on them since January 1812 totalled £271,691 and eighteen shillings (nearly £34 million in today's money.)

illnesses, he would weep and then laugh uncontrollably for no reason. He would tie and untie handkerchiefs and nightcaps, and button, unbutton and rebutton waistcoats. He would occasionally reminisce lucidly about events such as the Seven Years War and the Treaty of Amiens. He played the flute, and took comfort from it. In November 1811 Dr Baillie told the Prince Regent that the King had 'had a long conversation with Princess Amelia as if she was in the Room with him, and gave her a minute account of all the particulars of her funeral'.[42]

The King did not know of Napoleon's first abdication in April 1814, or of the way that the Princess of Wales was excluded by her husband from London's celebrations with the Tsar of Russia and King of Prussia. When she moved to Italy that summer, the Prince Regent gave the toast, 'To the Princess of Wales's damnation and may she never return to England.'[43] Similarly, the centenary celebrations of the Hanoverian succession in Hyde Park in August passed the King by, as did his being declared King of Hanover at the Congress of Vienna, and he was equally unaware of the battle of Waterloo.* Finally, the wars against France were over: Britain and France had been at war or skirmishing for forty-nine years of the King's seventy-seven years, but thereafter they were to be friends and long-term allies.[44]

'The King is not better in mind, nor worse in body,' Speaker Abbot recorded in 1816; he 'sits almost constantly in a loose gown, and lets his beard grow, which is milk white; talks incoherently; often speaks as if his son Octavius were still alive'.[45] In 1817 George went totally deaf. Blind and deaf, he was thankfully therefore not aware of the death on 6 November of his beloved granddaughter, Princess Charlotte of Wales, who had married Prince Leopold of Saxe-Coburg-Saalfeld but died of postpartum haemorrhage after fifty hours of agonizing and unsuccessful labour. In 1818, the King became so immobile that he had to be put in a wheelchair to get from his bed to his harpsichord, on which he would still play music, despite no longer being able to hear it. On 17 November 1818, Queen Charlotte died at Kew Palace, whereupon the care of the King's person was invested in Frederick, Duke of York, who did not visit him either.

With no legitimate Hanoverian heir beyond themselves, George's sons had to try to provide one, and they used the opportunity to try to increase their incomes from Parliament. 'By God!' the Duke of Wellington declared. 'They are the damnedest millstone about the necks of any government that

---

* When George IV claimed to have led a cavalry charge at the battle of Waterloo, and asked Wellington to confirm it, the Duke diplomatically replied, 'I have often heard Your Majesty say so' (Christie, *Wars and Revolutions* p. 312).

can be imagined. They have insulted* – *personally* insulted – two-thirds of the gentlemen of England.'[46] For all that, once he had broken up with his long-term mistress, Prince Edward, Duke of Kent, married Princess Maria Louisa Victoria of Saxe-Coburg-Saalfeld (Prince Leopold's sister), and on 24 May 1819 they provided the country with an heir, Princess Victoria of Kent, the future Queen Victoria. The Prince only just managed it in time, dying suddenly eight months later, the first of the King's adult sons to die. By that time the King was Britain's oldest monarch, and was to remain so until Queen Elizabeth II.

At 8.38 p.m. on Saturday 29 January 1820, at the age of eighty-one, King George III of Great Britain and Ireland, King of Hanover and Duke of Brunswick-Lüneburg, died painlessly of pneumonia in his apartment at Windsor Castle, overlooking the North Terrace where he had enjoyed so many promenades with his family in happier times. He had been on the throne for fifty-nine years and ninety-six days. 'All of us, except the very old . . .' noted *The Times* in its obituary two days later, 'were born beneath the sceptre of George III.'[47] It continued in words that stood radically athwart the negative evaluation of historians, noting of Britain that:

> Under the guidance of George III, she held fast by the laws and religion of her ancestors, and escaped the vortex of the French Revolution, on the edge of which she stood. She gained an empire in the heart of Asia more extensive than that which had been torn from her in the west . . . The mass of our maritime and commercial power has been reinforced by many accessions. Ceylon, the Mauritius and the Cape of Good Hope are master links in that unbroken chain which moors the peninsula of India to this island.[48]

The day after the King's death, the Royal Navy officer Edward Bransfield claimed Antarctica in his name, making George the only person to have had not one (Australia) but two continents so claimed, far more of the earth's surface than anyone else in history, as well as (initially at least) the planet we now know of as Uranus. Despite its humiliation in America, as George's reign closed the British Empire was the largest in the history of the world.[49]

In his will, drawn up in 1808, he left Queen Charlotte all his property at Richmond, Kew, West Sheen and Surrey, and all their contents and land.[50] Princess Mary and Princess Amelia (who in the event predeceased him) would inherit them on the Queen's death, while Augusta Lodge in

---

* By their constant sexual advances to wives and daughters; *Johnson's Dictionary* defines such 'insult' as 'The act of leaping upon anything'.

Kew was left to Princess Augusta, and property at Weymouth to Princess Sophia. The houses on Kew Green inhabited by the Dukes of Cambridge and Cumberland were left to them. He bequeathed his magnificent libraries at Windsor Castle and Buckingham House to the Prince of Wales, who gave them to the nation once he could not find a purchaser rich enough to buy them.

The King's funeral on the evening of 16 February broke with royal precedent, because he had chosen to be buried in St George's Chapel at Windsor rather than in the Henry VII Chapel at Westminster Abbey. He was the first monarch to be buried at Windsor since Charles I, and the tradition has survived to this day. Over 30,000 people came to pay their respects. Frederick, Duke of York, was the chief mourner, as the Prince Regent was (genuinely) ill with pleurisy.*

More than ten medals were struck to record the King's death; one simply recorded 'Pater Patriae' (Father of his Country).[51] Shops closed throughout the country, and people of every social class wore mourning, even the poorest. (Eton pupils donned black coats for the funeral, which they continue to wear today.) A book published in 1820 about the funeral procession was entitled *The Castle, the Tomb of the Patriot Monarch of Britain*. George would have been happy with that sobriquet. The Patriot King was what his father had urged him to be, and what all his life he had considered himself to be, glorying in the name of Briton.

---

* He recovered in time for his coronation. Whereas George III's coronation had cost £9,430 to stage, George II's £8,720 and George I's £7,287, King George IV's cost the taxpayer £238,000 (Strong, *Coronation* p. 372). When George IV died in 1830, by contrast with his father, *The Times* obituary stated that 'There never was an individual less regretted by his fellow-creatures than this deceased king. What eye has wept for him? What heart has heaved one throb of unmercenary sorrow? ... If he ever had a friend – a devoted friend in any rank of life – we protest that the name of him or her never reached us.'

Conclusion

The Nobility of George III

His whole conduct both in public and private ever since he began his reign, the uniform tenor of his behaviour, the general course both of his words and actions, has been worthy of an Englishman, worthy of a Christian, and worthy of a king.[1]

John Wesley, 'The Present State of Public Affairs',
December 1768

I wish some of my violent countrymen could have such an opportunity as I have had. I think they would be convinced that George the Third has not one grain of tyranny in his composition, and he is not, he cannot be, that bloody-minded man they have so repeatedly and illiberally called him. It is impossible; a man of his fine feelings, so good a husband, so kind a father, cannot be a tyrant.[2]

Pennsylvanian Quaker Samuel Shoemaker,
after meeting the King in October 1784

The tragedy is that the American colonies never received a tour from him – if a royal tour had been a conceivable undertaking in the eighteenth century the leaders of the colonies might have understood him better. Perhaps Americans will soon come to see the true George III without bias and traditionally held opinions.[3]

Prince Charles, 1972

The people who knew George III best loved him the most, which is not always the way with public figures. 'A noble sovereign this is, my dearest Susan,' Fanny Burney wrote to her sister in August 1786, 'and when justice is done him, he will as such be acknowledged.'[4] His equerry Robert Fulke Greville was utterly devoted to him, and his private secretary Herbert Taylor reported, 'It is impossible to be with our good King without finding every hour fresh cause to love and admire him.'[5] He was personally virtuous (if over-inclined to remind everybody of it), a pious Christian, honest, humane and in the last third of his life immensely stoical in the face of a truly horrific recurring illness.

George had been a shy, modest boy who at the age of twelve was plunged into history's limelight when his beloved father died suddenly and unexpectedly. He was watched carefully and judged constantly at Court in the knowledge that one day he would be king. He went through adolescence without a father-figure until the arrival in his life of Lord Bute when he was a highly impressionable seventeen-year-old. Bute was very publicly but falsely accused of sleeping with George's mother, who preferred his brother Edward to him. His grandfather the King disliked George, boxed his ears and allowed the stench of his beloved father's decomposing corpse to pervade his living quarters. Until he actually acceded, George had shared his mother's fear that his uncle the Duke of Cumberland would usurp him. George can perhaps be forgiven if this traumatic adolescence led him in later life to value stability as much as he clearly did.

Once he was king, any paranoia he felt about Cumberland evaporated, and he ruled conscientiously and well. We can see from his meticulous memoranda, with their carefully numbered drafts and long handwritten copyings-out, how seriously he took the business of government. He certainly wanted to rule through a wider group of ministers than the same families who had run Britain almost uninterruptedly since the Glorious Revolution. The Whig leaders of the 1760s and 1770s tended to be the sons and grandsons of the grandees who had put William and Mary on to James II's throne in 1688, political dynasties who felt a natural entitlement to rule Britain even a century later.

The Whigs despised George in part because he made the Tory party respectable again. Having ingested the Tory concept of the Patriot King from his father and Lord Bolingbroke, the King appointed Tories into the government and the royal household for the first time since the first Jacobite rebellion of 1715, supported their foreign policy (one that was sceptical of Continental and Hanoverian commitments), invited them to his Levees and Drawing Rooms, and awarded them knighthoods and peerages. By the 1790s, although politicians such as William Pitt the Younger and the Duke of Portland still nominally styled themselves as Whigs, they were in fact indistinguishable from Tories, and were thoroughly separated politically from true Whigs and radicals such as Charles Fox. In the successor generation, Pitt's followers threw off the Whig label altogether.

In an era of faction, George's striving for non-party government and his deliberate broadening of those who held office unsurprisingly prompted much Whig propaganda against him. Horace Walpole, one of the most gossipy diarists of his reign, many of whose waspish and prejudiced remarks have been given credence by generations of historians, claimed that George had a plan 'to raise the standard of prerogative', and Edmund Burke similarly accused him of trying 'to secure to the Court the unlimited and uncontrolled use of its own vast influence'.[6] Many historians have since agreed with them that the leitmotif of his reign was 'an attempt to restore royal power' rather than to maintain the constitution, writing of his 'personal government' of 'secret influence', contrived as 'an exercise in benevolent despotism' and that he was 'before everything an electioneer ... at home in the darkest corners of the political workshop'.[7] One of the aims of this book has been to show how false such accusations really are.

Unlike Charles I, to whom such judgements might apply rather better, George did not believe in the Divine Right of Kings, but he did believe in the near-divinity of the British constitution. 'I most devoutly pray to Heaven', he wrote to William Pitt the Younger in May 1793, 'that this constitution may remain unimpaired to the latest posterity as a proof of the wisdom of the nation and its knowledge of the superior blessings it enjoys.'[8] All George actually wanted to do was to preserve the constitutional status quo that he had inherited from his grandfather and pass it on to his son, an archetypal conservative attitude. 'What I have never been able to find', Sir Lewis Namier told the Academy of Arts in a lecture on George III in 1953, 'is the man arrogating power to himself, the ambitious schemer out to dominate, the intriguer dealing in an underhand fashion with his ministers; in short, any evidence for the stories circulated about him by very clever and eloquent contemporaries.'[9] If such evidence existed, it should not be too hard to find among the 4,453 letters in the King's early correspondence edited by Sir John Fortescue, or the 4,304 later ones edited by Arthur Aspinall, let alone in the more than 200,000 pages recently put online by the Georgian Papers Programme. Yet it is simply not there, and the reason is that the King was not attempting relentlessly 'to raise the standard of prerogative' but was a monarch who understood his extensive rights and duties under the constitution.

Part of the reason George so lauded the constitution was that the discretionary powers it gave him were wide. But they were also limited, as he fully accepted. He was forced to remove Bute as Prime Minister in 1763, to appoint Rockingham premier in 1765, Sandwich as Secretary of State in 1770, Shelburne as premier in 1782, to dismiss Thurlow as Lord Chancellor in 1792, to appoint Charles Fox as Foreign Secretary on three separate occasions, all against his wishes, and plenty of other similar instances. Namier also pointed out that 'most of his letters merely repeat approvingly what some minister, big or small, has suggested,' which is what a constitutional monarch does.[10] In February 1775, at a critical moment in the American crisis, Lord Hillsborough told Thomas Hutchinson, the former Governor of Massachusetts:

> The King himself thinks as you do but always will leave his own sentiments and conform to his ministers, though he will argue with them, and very sensibly; but if they adhere to their own opinion he will say, 'Well, do you choose it to be so? Then let it be.' And sometimes he had known him add, 'You must take the blame upon yourself.'[11]

Of course there were significant moments when he didn't agree with them, and manoeuvred to oust them. This was because George saw himself as the ultimate custodian of the national interest, which could not always be entrusted to factional politicians whom he saw as always to some extent out for themselves, while he himself reliably was not. If George III had held dictatorial tendencies, he would at some point in the half-century of his reign have vetoed a parliamentary Bill of which he disapproved, but he never once did, despite having the constitutional right to do so.

'I never will acknowledge that the king of a limited monarchy can on any principle endeavour to change the constitution and increase his own power,' George said of King Gustav III of Sweden's royal coup in Stockholm in 1772. 'No honest man will attempt it.'[12] It was true that he wanted to protect the royal prerogative from incursions by the aristocratic Whig oligarchy, but crucially he never sought to add to it. Had he dealt with Wilkes arbitrarily, as the Bourbons had treated the Marquis de Sade, for example, and many others, that would have been tyranny. As it was, George and his government were closely trammelled by a body of laws that they could not circumvent and which constantly frustrated them. The British system also ensured that Wilkes – who could have aspired to be the British version of Danton or Robespierre – instead pursued that most haut-bourgeois of ambitions, to become Lord Mayor of London, and wound up defending the Bank of England during the Gordon Riots.

In fact, far from increasing, as John Dunning's famous motion in the House of Commons claimed in 1782, the influence of the Crown in politics waned from the 1780s onwards, for a large number of reasons. The Crown was poorer, because of the terrible deal the King struck over the Civil List in 1761; the Opposition took increasing interest in the working of the Secret Service Fund; the power of Opposition parties generally and public opinion both increased; Cabinet ministers, now reporting to a prime minister rather than directly to the King, became collectively more confident; the influence of the Lord Chancellor declined; there was a need for serious retrenchment after the American war and during the French Revolutionary and Napoleonic Wars; and of course royal influence was diminished by the King's serial bouts of ill-health.

It was George's same desire to preserve the status quo, rather than to behave in an authoritarian or absolutist manner, that was evident in the American colonies, where his intentions have been just as badly misinterpreted as in Britain, very often by the same Whig politicians and historians.* George wanted his British and American subjects alike to enjoy life, liberty and the pursuit of happiness. He was not seeking to extend British power in America, let alone tyrannize his subjects there; indeed if George was a tyrant then so were all the British kings and queens of America since Queen Elizabeth I, and the word loses its meaning. In eighteenth-century English 'tyrant' meant 'an absolute monarch, governing imperiously' and 'a cruel, despotic and severe master'[13] – and George was neither. Before the Americans revolted, no newspapers were closed; no popular meetings were banned; no arrests were made without trial; no troops were put out on the streets (except latterly in one city, Boston, and even then only once the unrest had already begun). The cry of 'No taxation without representation' was essentially meaningless as a revolutionary slogan, ever since on 19 October 1765 the Stamp Act Congress had passed its fourth resolution, 'That the people of these colonies are not, and from their local circumstances cannot be, represented in the House of Commons in Great Britain', wording close to what South Carolina's Assembly had voted in September 1764.[14] By rejecting the idea of representation – which Britain was later willing to offer, even to the point of reserving American seats in the House of Commons – all that the Stamp Act Congress really wanted to assert was that there should be no taxation by Westminster at all, under any circumstances.† As the modern American historian Timothy Breen has pointed out, 'No evidence survives showing that the King or his ministers contemplated a complex plan to destroy American rights. Although they may have

---

* One historian whose history was resolutely Whiggish was Winston Churchill who, speaking on 22 February 1919 at a dinner held by the English-Speaking Union in Piccadilly's Criterion Restaurant in honour of George Washington's birthday, declared to much laughter, 'George Washington was an English gentleman, who fought against a German king and defended his country by the aid of men of British blood against a very considerable number of Hessian and Hanoverian mercenaries' (ed. Rhodes James, *Winston S. Churchill: His Complete Speeches* III p. 2672). Churchill can perhaps be forgiven for playing to his audience only three months after the end of the Great War, but that does not make what he said about George III remotely true.
† The citizens of Washington, DC, have been taxed without representation in Congress since 1790, so it is not simply George III who can be blamed for the practice, which he at least offered to redress.

struck contemporary critics as being incompetent, stubborn and vindictive, they possessed neither the will nor the ability to carry out this ambitious design.'[15]

True tyrannies in the third quarter of the eighteenth century acted very differently from the way that King George did in the thirteen colonies. The Spanish crushed an uprising against their rule in Louisiana in 1768 with mass executions. In Poland, which was partitioned between Austria, Russia and Prussia in 1772, liberty was entirely extinguished. The Russians' campaign of savage executions and reprisals in the regions affected by the Pugachev uprising against Catherine the Great in 1773–4 ended when Pugachev himself was beheaded and dismembered in Moscow in January 1775, something that George III would never have done to Jefferson, Adams, Washington or even Thomas Paine. As was seen in Chapters 12, 13 and 14, the British were for a long time desperate for a peaceful solution to the crisis, even after the bloodshed at Lexington and Concord. Yet by then many, perhaps even most, North Americans no longer believed that they needed the formal British connection to thrive, and indeed had concluded – thanks to the Proclamation of 1763 – that if they were to expand westwards they must throw it off.

The fundamental reason why the American colonies broke away was that by the end of the Seven Years War they had developed to such a stage of political maturity that they could thrive as an independent state. Freed by Britain from their fear of the French and Native American threats by the triumphant conclusion to that war, they saw their chance and took it. That they did this was in fact a tribute to the Americans' understandable and by then perfectly reasonable desire for independence from their mother country; they were not driven by a desire for greater 'liberty' and 'freedom' as individuals, which they already enjoyed far more than almost any community on the planet at the time. Taxes were a tiny fraction of what British citizens were paying at the time, and the colonial press was 'the freest in the world'.[16]

George hit upon the essential truth about the American Revolution – that taxation was the excuse, but not the underlying reason for it – in June 1779, when he told Lord North, 'Whether the laying of a tax was deserving all the evils that have arisen from it, I should suppose no man could allege that without being thought more fit for Bedlam than a seat in the Senate, but step by step the demands of America have risen. Independence is their object.'[17] This was certainly so by 1779, but for the activists among the colonists it had been since the 1760s. To bring the moderates and Loyalists and faint hearts over to their cause, they concentrated their arguments on taxes and the rights of assembly, arguments that could tend in only one direction.

Provoking George and his governments into retributive reactions, they ensured that the centre ground was vacated on both sides of the Atlantic, and room for compromise lost – against the wishes, for a long time, of many loyal colonists.

It was thus the genius of the American Founding Fathers to excite their countrymen to replace a perfectly valid political legitimacy deriving from the sovereignty of Crown and Parliament with their own form of legitimacy, which was equally valid but incompatible with the first. But though they wanted independence and their own sovereignty, the colonies did not break away so that they could instate an essentially different balance within their constitutional framework. The Americans' decision under Article Two of the United States Constitution to invest the president with powers almost identical to those of the British monarch can be regarded as an unintended homage to the political system they were ostensibly rejecting. In *Common Sense*, Tom Paine had promised Americans that they would have the 'power to begin the world over again', but instead of a grand social revolution they undertook a conservative political one, investing their head of state with the power to appoint judges, issue pardons for federal offences, sign legislation into law or veto it, serve as Commander-in-Chief, commission army officers, convene the legislature in special sessions, receive ambassadors, ensure that the laws are faithfully executed, and appoint Supreme Court justices and Cabinet officials (albeit with Senate confirmation), all just like the British monarch. Even when they overthrew monarchy for ever, Americans rejected Paine's ideas of radical democracy and instead retained governors in state constitutions. In 1787, in the words of one historian, 'the delegates to the Federal Convention wrote a republicanized version of Bolingbroke's patriot king into the very heart of the frame of government they proposed to secure the American union.'[18] Then, as the powers of British monarchs withered over the next two centuries, those of the American presidents persisted, indeed in almost all areas were strengthened or expanded.

George III did what any patriot king would have done during the American Revolution, which was to support his governments in their belief that Parliament had the right to impose tax on the colonies in order to contribute to their own protection. If he had opposed that, he would rightly have been denounced as a dictator, riding roughshod over the elected legislature at Westminster. The right to tax America was generally accepted in Britain at the time by the King, but crucially also by the Prime Minister, the Cabinet, the vast majority of peers and MPs, the law officers of the Crown and the American Department of the civil service; moreover, it was confirmed in two general elections in 1774 and 1780 to be the view of the British electorate.* 'The general belief was that responsible people in the colonies accepted British sovereignty,' writes Edmund Burke's biographer; 'that the disturbances in America were the work of a small minority of trouble-makers; and that American resistance would collapse, if confronted with a show of force. If a war proved necessary, Britain would win it quickly and easily.'[19] Not until the policy of Appeasement in the 1930s did virtually the entire British establishment get something so important so completely wrong, yet for George to bear the principal blame for that is quite wrong.

There is a good deal of irony in the idea that Thomas Jefferson, Edmund Burke, Charles Fox and later many Whig historians insisted that George was trying to subvert the British constitution when in reality it was his fundamental respect for the concept of Crown-in-Parliament that helped bring about the American Revolution. Governor Thomas Hutchinson of Massachusetts believed that even 'If no taxes or duties had been laid upon the colonies, other pretences would have been found for exception to the authority of Parliament,' and in this he was probably correct.[20] Certainly the pretences for rebellion that Jefferson grasped at in the Declaration of Independence were, on close examination by Hutchinson and others such as John Lind, extremely flimsy, as attested in Chapter 13. The Declaration's very hyperbole reveals most of it as a propaganda document, rather than a coherent case for independence. It needed to be an ad hominem attack on the King because, if it were simply directed against the British Parlia-ment, it would not answer the Loyalists' argument that it was possible to become independent of Britain but remain in a Commonwealth under the Crown. A more honest declaration, aspiring to historical truth rather than wartime propaganda, might instead have begun, 'When in the course of human events one people becomes sufficiently powerful and self-sustaining to dissolve the legitimate bands which have connected them with another three thousand miles away, and to assume among the powers of the earth the separate and equal station, they will.' Yet with a military struggle ahead, and needing a rallying cry that would portray the enemy head of state as an evil tyrant, truth became the first casualty of the American War of Independence, as it is in most wars.

History is so full of examples of peoples who have freed themselves from tyranny and won self-government that the phenomenon is almost commonplace. The Israelites were oppressed by the Egyptians, the Gauls

---

* The reason why historians reached the conclusion that George was a driving force behind the Coercive Acts was that in 1867 W. B. Donne published only the King's side of the corre-spondence with Lord North, not both. Only when the letters to the King are read in conjunction with those from North does it become clear that the King was following, sup-portively, initiatives from the government, and not the other way around.

by the Romans, the Dutch by the Spanish, the Italians by the Austrians, the Greeks by the Turks, and so they fought for their independence. The American Revolution was all the more impressive because it was undertaken *without* George III having been a tyrant and the United States is a greater country even than it realizes: its foundation was born not of a banal and commonplace struggle against a despot, but of a much rarer demand for self-government from a benevolent monarch. The American colonists' story is one of a desire for independence so strong that they broke away from someone who for contemporary propaganda purposes they needed to portray as a tyrant, but who ought today a mature republic can finally to recognize as a benign ruler. The Americans deliberately decided to abjure his light-touch, untyrannical government and leave what would soon become the largest empire on earth.[21] The American Revolution is a testament not to George III's tyranny, which was fictitious, but to Americans' yearning for autonomy.

Within that yearning, there is another irony, perhaps a hypocrisy, which we should never forget. In August 1776, George Washington wrote to the soldiers of the Continental Army, 'The hour is fast approaching on which the honor and success of this army and the safety of our bleeding country depend. Remember, officers and soldiers, that you are freemen fighting for the blessings of liberty – that slavery will be your portion and that of your posterity if you do not acquit yourselves like men.'[22] These were stirring words, using hyperbole suitable to the military circumstances, yet his ultimate opponent in Britain never had the slightest intention of imposing slavery on American colonists, nor anything like it. The King wanted only, and quite legitimately, as for all his subjects, that they should make a contribution to the cost of their own defence. As we have seen, Washington, Jefferson and their colleagues were at best enabling of slavery. George, by contrast, was the monarch who in his essays in the 1750s recognized its evil, and – although he did not actively advocate abolition himself or recognize that Christianity imposed a moral duty to oppose the system altogether – he never owned or traded slaves and he gave royal assent to the Act of Parliament that abolished the slave trade in 1807.

The loss of the American colonies was the greatest geostrategic catastrophe to befall Britain between the loss of the Angevin lands in France in the fifteenth century and the fall of France in 1940. George has been criticized by American historians for fighting the War of Independence and by British ones for losing it. In September 1782, George told Lord Shelburne, 'Posterity may not lay the downfall of this once respectable empire at my door.'[23] In fact posterity has done precisely that. But little more than a year later, on 2 November 1783, in his 'Farewell Orders to the Armies of the United States' on stepping down as Commander-in-Chief of the Continental Army, George Washington expressed his unfeigned 'astonishment' at their victory, describing it as 'little short of a standing miracle'.[24] His judgement is an acknowledgement that Britain can hardly be blamed for attempting to fight the war, however badly it was undertaken. It was not, as some military historians have argued, 'unwinnable', although given the distances involved and the small sizes of the armies compared to the vastness of the thirteen colonies, there was, to use a sporting term, a significant home-field advantage.[25] Nonetheless, the British held every major American city at some stage of the war or other, including Boston, New York, Charleston and Philadelphia. Of the twenty-six major battles of the war, the British won fifteen, the Americans eight and three were drawn, but it was the Americans who won the engagements that mattered most, including Trenton and Princeton (which kept the Continental Army in being), the three at Saratoga (which forced Burgoyne's surrender), King's Mountain (which prevented a Loyalist rising in the South), Cowpens (where the British field army in South Carolina was shattered) and finally Yorktown. If a few engagements had gone differently – if the Continental Army had been routed or captured in one of its many close scrapes in New York and New Jersey early in the conflict or if Washington had been unlucky crossing the East River or retreating through Manhattan or attacking Trenton, as he easily might have been – the war could have been won by the British.

Fighting it was a risk that the King and his ministers were therefore perfectly justified in taking. But, as the Afghan Wars and Boer Wars were also to show, it was hard for an empire to fight long insurgencies far away overseas when the struggle had to be defended against a highly critical Opposition in the House of Commons. Perhaps as early as Burgoyne's surrender at Saratoga, and certainly once the French and Spanish joined the conflict, the American part of the war was lost. It was tragic that it limped on for another three years, but that is often the nature of warfare. More soldiers died after the battle of Gettysburg in the American Civil War than before it; Germany should have surrendered at the failure of the Ludendorff Offensive in July 1918; millions died in the ten months after Operation Overlord in June 1944 and Operation Bagration in the same month.

For Britain to have won the American War of Independence after the French and Spanish joined the Americans would have needed a completely different approach, one that the King and the British commanders in America were temperamentally unwilling to adopt. It would have required total war at home, with mass conscription on the Continental model and vastly increased taxation, as well as a scorched-earth policy in America. And it is not clear that even those tactics would have been enough. The American historian Max Boot points out that all the senior British commanders of the war – Sir Henry Clinton, Sir Thomas Gage, Lord Cornwallis, Sir John Burgoyne, Sir William Howe and his brother Richard, Lord Howe – were upper-middle- and upper-class Whigs who followed the policy of conciliation wherever possible, trying to win hearts and minds. Cornwallis believed for much of the war that, if the British adopted what he called the 'gentlest methods which the nature of that business will admit of', the Loyalism to which he believed most American still ascribed might have won out.[26] In this he was utterly mistaken.

Although Russia, Austria, Prussia and Sweden filled their armies' ranks through conscription, no one in Britain, including the King, so much as considered endangering British liberties by relying on it. Conscription was not even introduced to counter the much more existential threat posed by Napoleon twenty years later. Continental tyrannies could call up legions of men by government fiat, but not the limited monarchy of George III. Even the 'embodiment' (mobilization) of British militia units to take over roles in Britain and free up regular army units for service in America was not undertaken until 1778. Neither was the Treasury willing or ready until then to devote the huge expenditure necessary for total war, as it had been against foreign foes in the Seven Years War.

Here is a third irony – had King George III been the ruthless despot he was made out to be by Thomas Jefferson in the Declaration of Independence, Britain would have had a much better chance of winning the war. If the British generals had been willing to cause social chaos in the South by arming the slaves, or to wreak havoc in the West by arming a Native American alliance, or to raze Boston and Philadelphia in the way that Admiral Cochrane was to raze Washington, DC, in 1814, or to treat American prisoners as the Duke of Cumberland had treated Scottish Highlanders in 1745, then the war might have gone differently. The British both precipitated the revolution and lost the American War of Independence in part because George III was *not* a tyrant.

But he was still the head of government, and throughout the entire period from 1770 to 1782 Frederick, Lord North, was his choice as Prime Minister. Everyone who knew North also liked him, but that was no qualification: North disliked responsibility and for most of the conflict did not want to be Prime Minister. He even once wrote to the King, 'Upon military matters, I speak ignorantly, and therefore without effect.'[27] That sentence alone should have disqualified him as a leader in a time of war. And yet the King still kept him on. There is a long list of British wars in which unimpressive war leaders have been replaced by more vigorous statesmen – Pitt the Elder replacing Newcastle, Palmerston elbowing aside Aberdeen, Lloyd George forcing out Asquith, Churchill succeeding Chamberlain – yet Lord North remained in office for five years after the disaster at Saratoga, a decision which was without question the King's.

But it was North, Hillsborough, Germain and the other Cabinet ministers actually running the war who must take principal responsibility for Britain's defeat in America. George was certainly at fault for permitting the return to office of Germain, putting his membership of the Leicester House Set ahead of the explicit recommendation of the Minden court martial. For all his impressive qualities, Germain was partly responsible for the failure of his eponymous Plan that was Britain's only comprehensive strategy for winning the American war, by not enforcing closer cooperation between the generals in the field. Similarly, George bears personal responsibility for letting footling objections over New Corps enlistment override the desperate need for mass recruitment in the opening stage of the conflict. Most of the blame, however, must lie with the generals and admirals in America itself – Burgoyne pressing on to Saratoga when he should have turned back, William Howe letting Washington escape from New York and later moving to take Philadelphia rather than carry out Germain's Plan, Cornwallis establishing himself in a deeply vulnerable position at Yorktown and Graves' abandonment of him there.

It is certainly true that George went along with the measures that provoked American resistance after the Boston Tea Party, but he did not inspire or formulate them; indeed he was more constitutionally scrupulous in loyally supporting but not directing his government over America than in any other aspect of his reign. He was doubtful about the Stamp Act and wanted it modified, but even so he exerted pressure to see it repealed when asked to do so by his Prime Minister Lord Rockingham. His reaction on hearing of the Boston Tea Party was one of hurt rather than anger. 'At each moment of crisis, right up to the outbreak of war,' writes one of the most respected of the historians of the King's actions, 'his hopes were centred on a political solution, and he always bowed to his Cabinet's opinions even when sceptical of their success. The detailed evidence of the years from 1763 to 1775 tends to exonerate George III from direct personal responsibility for the American Revolution.'[28] The worst charge that can be levelled at George was that he neither foresaw the American victory nor accepted it sooner. While virtually no one else in London did either, before Saratoga in October 1777, his subsequent stubbornness in the face of reality wasted money and lives. For it seems obvious with hindsight that the Americans had not lost 25,674 military dead – America's second-costliest war per capita after the Civil War – in order to fall short of complete independence. The British had lost an estimated 43,000 men killed, including German auxiliaries and those fighting the French and Spanish at sea.

What would the world have been like if events had taken a different course, as they could so easily have done at many junctures? The Introduction to this book quoted the great Foreign Secretary Ernest Bevin saying that George III was his hero because the loss of the American colonies allowed the United States to come to the rescue of the mother country 170 years later. But a world in which the American Revolution never took place could have been one in which a united British–American global empire would have been far too powerful for Kaiser Wilhelm II to threaten war in 1914, so no Bolshevik Revolution, no Adolf Hitler, no Cold War. British and Canadian Liberals joining with Northern abolitionists might have voted to abolish slavery in the 1830s or 1840s, sparing the United States its Civil War. The country that did the most to split Britain from her North American colonies – France – was also the one that would have benefited most from the First and Second World Wars not taking place, but such is history's iron law of unintended consequences. In his biography of George Washington, Joseph Ellis posits another tantalizing 'What if', namely the possibility of Britain adopting the 'principle of shared or overlapping sovereignty between the home government and peripheral states [that] eventually became the political framework for the British Commonwealth and before that the federal idea at the core of the American Constitution. By embracing it in 1775 the British government would have prolonged American membership in the British Empire until well into the next century and avoided the American Revolution.'[29]

But there are other possible scenarios too. In 1838 Lord Melbourne told the nineteen-year-old Queen Victoria that George III had been 'deeply hurt' by the loss of the American colonies, which she 'observed was no wonder; I said I thought it was *his* fault. Lord M said most likely it was; but that it was impossible any longer to keep up the great colonial policy, namely that they should exclusively trade with England and make nothing for themselves.'[30] About the second of these Melbourne was probably right: even if nimble British statesmanship had somehow warded off a declaration of independence in the mid-1770s it is highly likely, at the rate America was developing, that it would have come by the time of the Napoleonic Wars anyway. The alternative would have been a reverse takeover as the centre of gravity shifted towards the economic superpower of America, and perhaps by the end of the nineteenth century it would have been Britain which was forced to declare her secession rather than be part of an American-dominated empire.

*

Besides his supposed responsibility for the loss of America, in no area has George been so assailed as in his supposed lack of intelligence. Melbourne put the Whig case against him to Queen Victoria, including the dreadful and absurd slander that 'George III didn't like clever men.'[31] In fact, as this book attests, he constantly and actively sought out the company of the most intelligent men and women of the day, among them Samuel Johnson, Stephen Demainbray, Charles and Fanny Burney, Mary Delany and so many others. He paid for the world's largest telescope for the greatest astronomer of the day, William Herschel, and his sister Caroline Herschel described George as 'The best of kings, who is the liberal protector of every art and science'. He founded the Royal Academy, still the premier institution for artists in the United Kingdom.[32] His cultural activities and his patronage of the arts stretched extraordinarily widely, and his extensive correspondence shows him to have been anything but unintelligent. It was George who set up electrical experiments at the Pantheon, ensured John Harrison was paid for measuring longitude, laboriously worked on thousands of pages of essays for Bute exploring such topics as constitutional theory, political economy and moral philosophy, paid a pension to Rousseau and discussed Voltaire and the *encyclopédistes* with Monsieur Otto during the Peace of Amiens. We know from Lord Glenbervie that 'The King spends most of his time in [his library] when in town.'[33] It numbered 65,250 books and 19,000 tracts and pamphlets and over 4,000 maps, which were presented to the British Museum after his death.[34]

John Brooke correctly identified George as having 'good claims to be considered the most cultured monarch ever to sit on the throne of Great Britain'.[35]* He invited Mozart to perform at Buckingham House, encouraged the British taste for Handel and tried to persuade Haydn to live in England, played the flute, harpsichord and piano, appointed Sir Joseph Banks as Royal Botanist, gave Sir William Chambers, Robert Adam and James Wyatt important posts in public architecture, commissioned Capability Brown to landscape his gardens, promoted the scientific aspects of Captain Cook's voyages, supported the manufacture and designs of Josiah Wedgwood and Matthew Boulton, promoted vaccination despite losing at least one child to smallpox post-inoculation, established a bookbindery at Buckingham House, promoted the painters Allan Ramsay, Benjamin West and Thomas Gainsborough (who described him as 'a good connoisseur'), was himself a competent architectural draughtsman, assembled the world's

---

* It is a matter of debate whether George IV had a better taste in art and culture than his father, but worth pointing out that George III actually paid his artists, architects and musicians in full and on time, and did not dun them like his son did, forcing composers such as Haydn to apply to Parliament for payment years later.

finest collection of scientific instruments and enjoyed disassembling and reassembling intricate clocks and watches.[36] How many other 'brutes' or 'wretches' appointed a Mathematical Instrument Maker to His Majesty (George Adams the Younger) or an Historical Painter to His Majesty (Benjamin West)?

For all his wide Enlightenment interests and tastes, the boundaries of George's curiosity were sharply drawn, however, and did not extend to visiting his Scottish, Irish, Welsh, Asian, North American, Hanoverian or even northern English lands. In his whole reign, the longest of any king in British history, he only once met another ruling monarch, and even then the visit of his brother-in-law King Christian VII of Denmark to Britain in 1768 was more familial than political. He felt that his vast topographical map collection was enough to familiarize himself with his empire. Travel is a strange lacuna in his interests, even considering the discomfort of it in the eighteenth century.

George's physical courage in the face of danger was, however, another admirable part of his character. Whether when he was held up by highwaymen, or during multiple assassination attempts, or during the Gordon Riots, or when his country was in imminent danger of invasion in 1779 and again in 1804, he displayed great personal bravery. And physical assaults were not the only kind of attack on him. In the late eighteenth and early nineteenth centuries Britain enjoyed a golden age of satire, wit, pamphleteering, poetry and caricature, and despite his demonstrably generous artistic patronage George III became the butt of almost all of them.[37] In their articles, cartoons and poems he was variously depicted by these talented writers and artists – several of whom genuinely loathed him – as blind, childish, trivial, a fiddler, uneducated, King James I, King Charles I, a cypher, a fool, the Emperor Nero, Lord Bute's dupe, King Edward II, Caligula, a knave, the Pope, Nebuchadnezzar, a puppet, a cannibal, a dragon, a tailor, a dunce, a dog, a monk, a usurper, greedy, mean, a ghost, a Pharaoh, and of course a madman, even though he was none of these, except on occasion the last.[38] He bore most of it with excellent humour, even privately buying many of prints that lampooned him, but he understandably drew the line when Wilkes accused his mother of sleeping with his friend and mentor Lord Bute, and when he himself was accused of lying to Parliament, both of which he knew to be untrue.

George's own family relations were mixed. He was a loving husband who (under great duress of circumstances) separated from his wife and was hated by his son and heir. The Hanoverians have been likened to ducks in that they trampled on their offspring, but by any objective analysis George was far more the victim than the villain of what has been rightly described as 'perhaps the most scandalous royal family in British history'.[39] He was the first king since Edward III in the fourteenth century to have a large family of adult sons, and, while every family has the odd black sheep, George's had flocks of them, who often caused him great anxiety and frustration. Yet the only blame that truly sticks to him in the litany of his scandalous brothers and children might be in passing the Royal Marriages Act, the circumstances of which were described in Chapter 9. Of the five people whom George loved most in the world – Queen Charlotte, his brother William, Duke of Gloucester, his son Frederick, Duke of York, his son Octavius and his daughter Amelia – the last two died young, Frederick betrayed him during his illness and William lied about his marriage. An illness also explains his rift with his eldest son, although in this case it was the Prince of Wales' chronic case of Compulsive Buying Disorder, as seen throughout the second half of this book.

It may have been the death of his beloved favourite daughter Princess Amelia or perhaps the behaviour of otherwise trusted ministers over Catholic emancipation which triggered George's final descent into madness. The moments that gave him the most anguish and tipped him over the edge into manic-depressive episodes were not those commonly assumed to be low-water marks of George's performance as monarch. There were no episodes between the repeal of the Stamp Act in 1766 and the Treaty of Paris that ended the American war in 1783, for example, even though Britain was fighting a multi-front war for several years with no allies. Nor did the stress of having his Closet stormed by the Whigs in 1782 and his expelling them the following year bring on an episode. Similarly, the serious invasion threats of 1779 and 1797 left him robust and ready. Rather than the madness of George III we ought to consider his extraordinary mental fortitude in moments of high danger and drama.

George bore his five descents into lunacy stoically, especially considering the horror that he knew he was going mad during four of them. The disease he suffered from could not have been porphyria* as Alan Bennett's play and subsequent film make out, which is the explanation most people still believe today. In fact the King was a manic depressive who suffered a prodrome attack of bipolar disorder in 1765 that was successfully covered up, as shown in Chapter 6, and thereafter endured four full-scale attacks, the fifth one lasting a decade.

In an age that thankfully no longer stigmatizes mental illness, we can appreciate how dreadful it must have been for George to have known that

---

* See the Appendix.

he was slipping into lunacy but unable to do more than spectate, and how monstrous it was that he was treated as if he were mad on many occasions when in fact he was not. Nor should the Rev. Francis Willis and his sons any longer be stigmatized as near-torturers in the way they have been, because they were in fact far more advanced in occupational therapy and other modern techniques than the King's other, in many cases woefully ignorant and hidebound, doctors.

George's recovery from his 1788–9 bipolar attack only five months before the outbreak of the French Revolution was fortuitous indeed. During the upheaval that followed the fall of the Bastille, Lord Auckland remarked that as long as the King stayed sane 'the tranquillity of this country is on a rock'.[40]

Plato once said that not being tempted by power should be one of the primary qualifications for wielding it. Cincinnatus was called from his plough, George Washington from his farm. George III took this to the limit, so despising political ambition that he often preferred prime ministers such as Grafton and North who did not appear to want the position. Talking to Glenbervie at a Drawing Room during Addington's unremarkable premiership in March 1802, George said that 'he never could form any idea of what is called a heaven-born minister. He said the two or three instances we had seen of men born with such extraordinary talents as to be able to conduct public business ... had made everyone aspire to the same sort of reputation and success, but that for one who can fly thousands must be content to climb.'[41] George was unlucky in the paucity of great political and administrative ability in his reign. Besides the two Pitts there was no one of real historical moment in his whole fifty years as head of government – and even then he got only the tail-end of the Elder Pitt, when he was no longer the giant he had once been.

George certainly deserves much credit for spotting the Younger Pitt; appointing and resolutely supporting a twenty-four-year-old prime minister was a brave move even in the circumstances of the eighteenth century. Pitt was respectful, businesslike and professional with the King, though never personally close. Bute, North and Addington were personally friendly with George, but neither George nor Pitt wanted that kind of relationship. Pitt was aloof, socially awkward, an economic wizard, celibate if not asexual, and a genius. George was none of these things, and evidently found the gulf between their characters too difficult to cross. After Pitt had offered opponents concessions to his Finance Bill which watered down the original measure in March 1797, the King told him, in an acute piece of self-analysis, 'My nature is quite different. I never assent till I am convinced what is proposed is right ... then I never allow that to be destroyed by afterthoughts which on all subjects tend to weaken, never to strengthen, the original proposal.'[42] That might be true, but it was not necessarily politically skilful. Three years later he spoke to Pitt in similar terms: 'My opinion is formed on principle, not on events, and therefore is not open to change.'[43] This adamantine inflexibility did not work against the American colonists, but it was precisely what his country needed in a later conflict. George believed that the French Revolution was a sinister development in modern politics long before the clatter of the first tumbril and the swish of the first guillotine blade, while opponents rapturously hailed the fall of the Bastille, saying as Charles Fox did, 'How much the greatest event it is that ever happened in the world! And how much the best!'[44] Only six years after losing the American War of Independence, Britain proved herself robust enough to withstand the shocks of the French Revolution and the subsequent twenty-three years of war with France, in part due to George's stewardship. 'The times may be difficult,' he told Pitt in 1795, 'but with energy cannot fail of success.'[45]

Despite his wide and deep intellectual interests, George was not typical of the Enlightenment in that he was profoundly religious, deeply traditional in his personal morality and insistent on social conventions, all qualities which repelled the Whigs. In politics, he distrusted metaphysical abstractions quite as much as Edmund Burke.[46] He was not, however, by any means a secret Tory or crypto-Jacobite as was often said in the early years of his reign. He was intellectually as well as politically conservative, believing that, although sometimes there were improvements in human affairs, nonetheless there was no such thing as inevitable progress, and it was 'highly necessary to avoid all novelties. We know that all wise nations have stuck scrupulously to their ancient customs.'[47] When Lord Eldon became Lord Chief Justice of the Common Pleas, he asked the King whether he could stop wearing his heavy long wig when not engaged on official functions, arguing the precedents of judges under James I and Charles I, who did not wear them. George replied that, given that precedent, Eldon would have to grow a beard, concluding, 'No, no, I will have no innovations in my time.'[48] That was the essential nature of his conservatism: no innovations. Reform would always risk giving birth to greater evils than it aimed to cure; it was admirable not to 'change with the times'.

Yet, for all that, George was not a reactionary. 'To obviate future evils', he told Lord Shelburne in reference to Irish policy in May 1782, 'is as material as to remove those of the present hour.'[49] This was his attitude to crime and punishment too. He did not baulk at the way British law dispensed condign punishment, although as the 'Fount of Justice' he took his duty of dispensing mercy very seriously, and with the exception of the Gordon Rioters he personally reviewed every capital case before execution was pronounced. On occasion he did show clemency by commuting sentences. When General Conway's secretary James Sampson stole £900 in banknotes in 1768, however, and attempted to burn down Conway's house to destroy the evidence, the King was unmoved to mercy. 'Now I am sure that when this man is condemned, Conway will be teasing me to pardon him,' the King was reported as saying, 'but I am determined to hang him.'[50] While three others on capital charges for rape and sheep stealing had their executions commuted by the King to transportation, Sampson was hanged at Tyburn.

Notwithstanding his eighteenth-century views on punishment generally, George was a supporter of the penal reform movement that started around 1770. He almost always accepted judges' recommendations for transportation for life instead of hanging, which was the standard penalty for a remarkably wide number of offences – the theft of anything valued at more than £2, arson in the dockyards, forgery, damage to property, regular poaching, burglary and scores of other crimes. The King contributed to the relief of debtors at a time when bankrupts were (self-defeatingly for their creditors) regularly imprisoned.

The concept of honour is central to understanding George III, and he would not allow his own to be compromised. 'Never give up your honour nor that of the nation,' his father had told him in his posthumous political testament, and the lesson, well received, remained with him throughout his life.[51] Whenever George saw it threatened, he became immensely obstinate and determined. Two examples of many will suffice. When George promised James Stuart-Mackenzie the Lord Privy Seal of Scotland for life, he felt his honour compromised when he was forced by Grenville to dismiss him from the post in 1765, and it soured his relationships with both Grenville and his successor Rockingham, who did not reinstate Stuart-Mackenzie. Then in 1801, when Pitt the Younger tried to bounce George into emancipating the Roman Catholics, he again perceived that his personal honour was at stake because it would force him to break his Coronation Oath. For him these were moral issues.

'The interest of my country ever shall be my first care, my own inclinations shall ever submit to it,' he wrote to Lord Bute after having decided to give up his pursuit of the beautiful but wildly unsuitable Lady Sarah Lennox in the winter of 1759; 'I am born for the happiness or misery of a great nation, and consequently must often act contrary to my passions.'[52]

George's sense of his kingly duty to oppose factionalism and act solely out of the national interest was to lead him into some of the most difficult moments of his reign in peacetime. Cynics have sneered at his naivety in wanting his governments to contain what he called 'the best and ablest men the kingdom might produce', but was that really so low an aspiration?[53] He easily convinced himself that his opponents were hypocrites, who acted solely out of narrow factional, class or financial self-interest. The assumption that one's own side has a monopoly of virtue and is ethically superior to one's opponents has been a very common one in history, and George was undoubtedly guilty of it. It made the compromises he sometimes had to make with the Whig aristocrats into genuine moments of self-disgust for him, although many of them, such as the Marquess of Rockingham and the Duke of Portland, were among the most altruistic politicians in British history.

George's sense of duty had a profound effect upon the monarchy. The historian Sir Roy Strong draws attention to 'a radical recasting of the role of the Crown, one which used to be assigned to the reign of Queen Victoria but which modern scholarship rightly attributes to George III'.[54] When we look at the reign of Elizabeth II, with its leitmotif of hard work, conscientiousness, Christian piety, abstemiousness, philanthropy and uxoriousness, we indeed see George III's practices reflected quite as strongly as Queen Victoria's. It was George who bought what is now Buckingham Palace, invented the royal walkabout (on Windsor's North Terrace), inspired the jubilee commemoration industry, commissioned the Gold State Coach, made Trooping the Colour an annual ceremony, moved the family's resting place from Westminster Abbey to Windsor, and much else besides. 'Strong tenacity of view and of purpose,' wrote the courtier Lord Esher in 1912, 'a vivid sense of duty . . . a curious mingling of etiquette and domestic simplicity, and a high standard of domestic virtue were marked characteristics of George III and of Queen Victoria.'[55] They were clearly also the templates for King George V, King George VI and the present Queen.

Lord Esher also pointed out that the King 'was essentially British in character and sentiment . . . Of all sovereigns who have ever reigned in England, none so completely represented the average man among his subjects. The King's blameless morals, his regular habits, his conservative instincts and narrow obstinacy, were characteristics which he shared with the people he ruled.'[56] Esher went too far – not all eighteenth-century Britons were characterized by blameless morals – but otherwise he was right. As *The Times* obituary of the King put it, 'We mean George III no dishonour – we do him none – by saying that the familiar name of "John Bull" was applicable specifically to the whole constitution of his mind and habits. He was an Englishman all over – but an Englishman worthy to be at the head of a nation of English.'[57]

'Kings are the servants, not the proprietors, of the people,' wrote Thomas Jefferson in 1774. 'Open your breast, Sire, to liberal and expanded thought. Let not the name of George the Third be a blot in the page of history.'[58] It is not. In *Hamilton*, Lin-Manuel Miranda's George III is presented as a cartoonish pantomime villain, desperate for affection. In one of the production's best – and unquestionably its funniest – songs, 'You'll be Back', George delivers the delightfully deranged line to his 'sweet submissive subjects' that 'when push comes to shove, I will send a fully armed battalion to remind you of my love'. Having read this book, do you think that is how George III should be seen?

Well-meaning, hard-working, decent, dutiful, moral, cultured and kind, yet cursed to lose his mind no fewer than five times and also to preside over the loss of the American colonies, George III is one of the most tragic monarchs of British history, as well as being the most underestimated and misunderstood. 'I shall have no regret never to have wore the crown,' his father had written to him in his posthumous political testament, 'if you do but fill it worthily.'[59] George III more than filled the role of King of Great Britain worthily; he filled it nobly.

Appendix

The Misdiagnosis of 'The King's Malady' as Porphyria

From the mid-1960s until 2010 it was generally believed that 'the King's malady' from which George III suffered in 1765, 1788–9, 1801, 1804 and 1810–20 was the inherited metabolic disorder porphyria. This was a consequence of a theory vigorously promoted by Dr Ida Macalpine and her son Dr Richard Hunter in a number of articles such as 'The "Insanity" of George III: A Classic Case of Porphyria' (*British Medical Journal*, 1966). and in their book *George III and the Mad-Business* (1969).

Their theory gained lasting popular traction in large part from its repetition in Alan Bennett's play *The Madness of George III* of 1991, and the subsequent movie adaptation *The Madness of King George* of 1994,* in both of which porphyria was presented as the concluding diagnosis of the King's malady. Nicholas Hytner's film version added the rather caustic observation at its end that the condition was hereditary, which only further serves to undermine the diagnosis since no British royals, either before or since, have suffered from porphyria.

It is now clear that the porphyria theory was wrong. It was based on a large number of misconceptions and a highly selective use of evidence; it contained factual errors and flawed reasoning, and involved the ignoring or downplaying of evidence that contradicted the authors' thesis. Macalpine and Hunter had no clinical experience in diagnosing or treating porphyria, and presented an intellectually disingenuous case that the illness was physiological rather than psychological. This was a thesis that broadly aligned with various other theories they had expressed regarding mental illness in general, but crucially it did not fit the facts of George III's actual condition.

A meticulous examination in 2010 of Macalpine and Hunter's work undertaken by Drs Timothy J. Peters of the University of Birmingham and

---

* It is a myth that the title of *The Madness of George III* was changed for the film version so that moviegoers would not think they had missed the first two parts. The director Nicholas Hytner has stated that he wanted to insert the word 'King' into the title, making the 'III' superfluous.

D. Wilkinson of the University of London, who checked it against the original records and reports of the King's doctors, resulted in the complete rejection of the previous porphyria theory. In their article entitled 'King George III and Porphyria: A Clinical Re-Examination of the Historical Evidence' in the *History of Psychiatry* journal, Peters and Wilkinson pointed out crucial errors in each of Macalpine and Hunter's four major contentions – muscular weakness, cataracts, abdominal pains and discoloured urine – which together had identified porphyria as the cause of the King's malady.[1] For ten years, Peters was Professor of Clinical Biochemistry and Director of Pathology at King's College London, where he established a porphyria diagnostic and treatment centre.

Far from the King showing muscular weakness and peripheral neuropathy during his attacks, as Macalpine and Hunter had claimed, Peters and Wilkinson showed that he was able to go riding, feed himself, play complex card games and the flute and hold a pencil to sketch architectural drawings. What Macalpine and Hunter ascribed to neuropathic weakness, such as the King lying down on the ground after being told he could not climb the Kew Pagoda on 19 January 1789 (as recounted in Chapter 22), was in fact a simple refusal to obey his doctors' orders.[2] Earlier on the day of the Pagoda episode he had walked at least a mile, and the next day he walked in the garden for eighty minutes. The evidence presented by Macalpine and Hunter for the muscular weakness seen in porphyria did not support their contention even circumstantially. Willis noted on 15 February 1789 that the King walked four hours a day in the garden, a detail Macalpine and Hunter omitted.

Macalpine and Hunter attempted to link the cataracts George developed in his eyes to porphyria, but there is no connection between them. They also attempted to argue that the King's vocal hoarseness was a further proof of porphyria. Hoarseness ('dysphonia') is indeed symptomatic of porphyria, because vocal paresis is a sign of bulbar muscle weakness, yet they completely ignored the alternative (and much more compelling) explanation attested to in contemporary accounts that the King may have been hoarse because he talked incessantly for extraordinarily long periods of time. 'He has talked away his voice,' Fanny Burney noted on 1 November 1788, for example, 'and is so hoarse it is painful to hear him.'[3] On 18 and 19 November, Robert Fulke Greville recorded the King talking 'for nineteen hours without scarce any intermission', and in January 1812 he spoke for twenty-five hours without stopping.[4]

Also untrue are Macalpine and Hunter's claims that abdominal pains, a central symptom of porphyria, were a regular feature of the King's malady; in fact, such discomforts although debilitating were transient. Their claim that George suffered abdominal discomfort for 'many weeks' of his

1788–9 attack is not supported by any of the contemporary evidence – Robert Fulke Greville's detailed diary, John Willis' medical notes or any of the accounts by those who saw the King during that time, despite their large numbers of references to all his other ailments. From the fifty-two volumes of the Willises' papers in the British Library, the forty volumes of other doctors' papers in Lambeth Palace Library and a large number of papers in the Royal Archives, historians know about his pulse, his night sweats, his leg pains, his stool colours and consistencies, the quantity of urine passed and any number of other such details.[5] If the King had suffered persistent abdominal pain, these doctors would undoubtedly have noted that too.

The colour of the King's urine might have been a key indicator had he suffered from porphyria, as patients do pass the discoloured purple-blue water that gives the disease its name. Despite Macalpine and Hunter claiming that the King did this six times, noting that on one occasion 'it left a bluish stain on the vessel after it had been poured away', close examination of the historical evidence completely undermines this too.[6] In one instance, they claim that Sir Henry Halford's diary in the Royal Archives, which states on 14 January 1812, 'Bluish 8 and 9', meant that the King passed eight or nine ounces of bluish urine. In fact the actual reference in the diary when checked against the Willis Papers makes it clear that the word is not 'bluish' but rather 'between'; and the '8 and 9' simply refers to the time at which the King was given his medicine.[7]

Neither is it certain that urine leaving a blue stain on the vessel must necessarily be the result of porphyria, given the nature of the purgatives, drugs and medicines that he was being given at the time, which we know included gentian, aloes and senna, and emodin cathartics.[8] The King's urine and stools were not collected separately; there was a basin for their collection which was produced for the doctors' inspection the following morning. Foodstuffs such as beetroot could have had a discoloration effect, and Peters and Wilkinson explained that the King passed bluish urine the day after he had been administered therapeutic gentian. Macalpine and Hunter wilfully ignored all these alternative explanations.

In fact, there are far more mentions of the King's urine being 'pale' and 'clear' than any of the colours that might imply porphyria.[9] Nonetheless, Macalpine and Hunter kept this key fact from the porphyria experts whom they consulted, and it does not appear in their published work – an omission which Peters and Wilkinson rightly believe 'amounted to sharp practice'.[10] Similarly, the King's pale stools – which were variously described by his doctors as 'straw-coloured', 'pale', 'white' and 'ash-coloured' – undermine Macalpine and Hunter's diagnosis of porphyria. 'There is no support for the claim by Macalpine and Hunter that the acute porphyrias are accompanied by jaundice,' state Peters and Wilkinson, who describe a citation to that effect as 'either woefully ignorant or deliberately dishonest'.[11] The more that one investigates Macalpine and Hunter's methods – especially their twisting of the words of professional porphyria experts and giving them insufficient evidence on which to base diagnoses which might run contrary to their predetermined view – the more one is forced towards the latter rather than the former conclusion.

Notes

Introduction

1. Paine, *Common Sense* passim   2. *Annual Register 1776* p. 263   3. https://eu.rgj.com/story/opinion/columnists/2020/11/05/america-theres-pendulum-not-guillotine-pat-hickey/6176427002/   4. https://www.recorder.com/Count-every-vote-37154825   5. https://www.huntingdondailynews.com/opinion/read_and_comment/huntingdon/article_7971ecec-9cfe-5ae1-92a7-537e7119cc30.html   6. https://www.bostonherald.com/author/howie-carr/   7. *North Augusta Star* 20 May 2020   8. https://www.eugeneweekly.com/2020/05/21/critical-to-democracy/   9. https://www.deseret.com/authors/matthew-brown   10. https://www.altoonamirror.com/opinion/letters-to-the-editor/2020/06/trump-positioning-himself-for-kingdom/ and https://www.trib-pub.com/gdpr/courant.com/   11. https://www.thedailyreview.com/opinion/columns_editorials/by-choice-we-are-blinded/article_71b95570-2ffd-56ca-a17a-78e397064721.html   12. Brougham, *Historical Sketches* I p. 6   13. Lecky, *History of England in the Eighteenth Century* III p. 14   14. Ibid.   15. Trevelyan, *Early History of Charles James Fox* p. 521   16. Trevelyan, *History of England* pp. 547, 552   17. ed. Russell, *Correspondence of John, Fourth Duke of Bedford* III p. xxix   18. Hansard Vol. 261 col. 532 8 February 1932   19. Namier, *England in the Age of the American Revolution* pp. 84–5   20. Vulliamy, *Royal George* p. 310   21. Long, *George III* p. 15   22. Reeves, *Daring Young Men* p. 36   23. Churchill, *History of the English-Speaking Peoples* III p. 132   24. Vulliamy, *Royal George* p. 309; Daughan, *Lexington and Concord* p. 161   25. Vulliamy, *Royal George* p. 306; Black, *George III: America's Last King* p. 418; Cook, *Long Fuse* p. 18   26. Bentley, *More Biography* p. 2   27. ed. Sidgwick, *Shorter Poems of Walter Savage Landor* p. 24   28. Christie, 'George III and the Historians' p. 206   29. Andrews, *King Who Lost America* 155   30. RA GEO/MAIN/15673

1. Prince of Wales

1. Churchill, *River War* I p. 37   2. Smith, *Early Career of Lord North* p. 39   3. Brooke, *King George III* p. 16   4. Ibid. p. 15   5. ed. Sedgwick, *Hervey's Memoirs* p. 237   6. Brooke, *King George III* p. 15   7. Historical Manuscripts Commission, *Manuscripts of the Earl of Egmont* II p. 489   8. Brooke, *King George III* p. 17   9. Ayling, *George the Third* pp. 16–17   10. RA GEO/MAIN/1614 George III to Lord Bristol 8 July 1773   11. Brooke, *King George III* p. 18   12. Wright, *George III* p. 16   13. ed. Marschner, *Enlightened Princesses* passim   14. Doran, *Lives of the Queens of England* I p. 423   15. Black, *George III: Majesty and Madness* p. 11   16. ed. Holland, *Horace Walpole: Memoirs of the Reign of King George the Second* I p. 72   17. *Poetical Essays* in *The Gentleman's Magazine and Historical Chronicle* Vol. 39 (1769) p. 207   18. Simms, *Three Victories and a Defeat* p. 466   19. Lepel, *Letters of Mary Lepel* pp. 139–40   20. RA GEO/MAIN/54227–54232   21. Young, *Poor Fred* pp. 173–4   22. Ibid. p. 175   23. Ibid. p. 173   24. Ibid.   25. Ibid. p. 171   26. Ibid.   27. BL Add MS 32684 f. 78   28. Cook, *Long Fuse* p. 9   29. For reading and writing in English: GEO/MAIN/54226; for German: GEO/MAIN/54129, GEO/MAIN/54236; for French: GEO/ADD/32/267–268; for Latin: GEO/ADD/32/2211–2250, GEO/ADD/32/2484–2485, GEO/ADD/32/2251–2270, GEO/ADD/32/2271–2298, GEO/ADD/32/

2299–2326, GEO/ADD/32/2327–2352, GEO/ADD/32/2353–2375, GEO/ADD/32/2376–2423   30. Sack, *From Jacobite to Conservative* passim   31. Ayling, *George the Third* pp. 30–31   32. Ibid. p. 26   33. ed. Newman, 'Leicester House Politics' p. 85   34. Liddle, '"Patriot King, or None"' pp. 953–4   35. ed. Hassall, *Patriot King* p. xiv   36. Ibid. pp. xvii and 57   37. Ibid. p. xviii   38. Ibid. p. xix   39. Ibid. pp. xix and xxi   40. Ibid. p. xxii   41. ed. Newman, 'Leicester House Politics' pp. 169–70   42. Young, *Poor Fred* pp. 216–17   43. Ayling, *George the Third* p. 31   44. Ibid.; Marples, *Poor Fred and the Butcher* p. 113; Edwards, *Frederick Louis* p. 184; Young, *Poor Fred* pp. 217–19   45. Young, *Poor Fred* p. 223   46. De-la-Noy, *King Who Never Was* p. 217   47. See in particular ed. Marsden, *Wisdom of George the Third* pp. 14–28; ed. Marschner, *Enlightened Princesses* pp. 1–33   48. ed. Bickley, *Diaries of Sylvester Douglas* I p. 406   49. Edwards, *Frederick Louis* p. 185   50. De-la-Noy, *King Who Never Was* p. 218   51. Ayling, *George III* p. 31; ed. Newman, 'Leicester House Politics' p. 200   52. Range, *British Royal and State Funerals* p. 178 n. 143   53. Walters, *Royal Griffin* p. 219; Ayling, *George the Third* p. 31   54. Walters, *Royal Griffin* p. 219   55. Jesse, *Memoirs of the Life and Reign of King George the Third* I p. 11   56. ed. Home, *Letters and Journals of Lady Mary Coke* III pp. 242–3 n. 1   57. ed. Harcourt, *Diaries and Correspondence of George Rose* II p. 188   58. Ibid.   59. Ibid.   60. RA GEO/ADD/32/2376–2423   61. eds. Carswell and Dralle, *Political Journal of George Bubb Dodington* pp. 199, 203   62. Ibid. p. 178   63. Ibid.   64. Ibid. p. 179   65. Ibid.   66. Brooke, *King George III* p. 35   67. ed. Sedgwick, *Letters from George III to Lord Bute* pp. xxxviii–xli   68. Walpole, *Memoirs of the Last Ten Years of the Reign of George the Second* I p. 264   69. ed. Hodgart, *Horace Walpole: Memoirs and Portraits* p. 82   70. ed. Harcourt, *Diaries and Correspondence of George Rose* II p. 188   71. Waldegrave, *Memoirs from 1754 to 1758* p. 9   72. Ibid.; Trevelyan, *Early History of Charles James Fox* p. 459 n. 2   73. Waldegrave, *Memoirs from 1754 to 1758* pp. 9, 63   74. Ibid. pp. 8–9   75. Brooke, *King George III* p. 48   76. ed. Bickley, *Diaries of Sylvester Douglas* II p. 10   77. White, *Age of George III* p. 46   78. ed. Everett, *Letters of Junius* p. xxv   79. Morton and Wess, *Public and Private Science* p. 17   80. Namier, 'George III: A Study in Personality' pp. 617–18   81. Bullion, 'Prince's Mentor' pp. 34–5; Brooke, *King George III* pp. 26–44   82. Brewer, 'Misfortunes of Lord Bute' p. 4 n. 6   83. ed. Sedgwick, *Letters from George III to Lord Bute* p. 4   84. Holly, 'Long a Dispute amongst Antiquarians' passim   85. Buckley, 'The Essays of George III' passim   86. Brooke, *George III* p. 56   87. RA GEO/ADD/32/1281–1327, 1263–1264 f. 1292   88. RA GEO/ADD/32/273–319 f. 291   89. RA GEO/ADD/32/706–912, 1071–1077 f. 822   90. Ibid. ff. 815–16   91. RA GEO/ADD/32/195–205 f. 200   92. RA GEO/ADD/32/152–194 f. 183   93. ed. Sedgwick, *Letters from George III to Lord Bute* pp. lii–liii   94. ed. Boyd, *Papers of Thomas Jefferson* X p. 309   95. RA GEO/ADD/32/706–912, 1071–1077, f. 870   96. RA GEO/ADD/32/906–912, 1071–1077, f. 873   97. Montesquieu, *Spirit of the Laws* p. 234   98. RA GEO/ADD/32/706–912, 1071–1077, f. 874   99. RA GEO/ADD/32/706–912, 1071–1077 f. 825   100. Ibid.   101. Ibid. ff. 818–19   102. ed. Marsden, *Wisdom of George the Third* p. 7   103. RA GEO/ADD/32/1919–1924   104. RA GEO/ADD/32/70–125 ff. 71, 78   105. RA GEO/ADD/32/914–917, 929–936, 957–995 esp. ff. 914–16   106. ed. Sedgwick, *Letters from George III to Lord Bute* p. 4n.   107. eds. Carswell and Dralle, *Political Journal of George Bubb Dodington* p. 317   108. Ibid. pp. 317–18   109. Brooke, *King George III* p. 50   110. Ditchfield, *King George III* p. 57

2. Seizing an Empire

1. ed. Sedgwick, *Letters from George III to Lord Bute* p. 43   2. Brooke, *King George III* p. 51   3. ed. Sedgwick, *Letters from George III to Lord Bute* p. 2   4. Ibid. pp. 2–3   5. Ibid. p. 3   6. Ibid. pp. 3–4   7. Ibid. p. 33   8. ed. Brooke, *Horace Walpole: Memoirs of the Reign of King George II* III p. 1   9. Ditchfield, *George III* pp. 52–3; Thomas, *George III: King and Politicians* p. 2   10. ed. Sedgwick, *Letters from George III to Lord Bute* p. 6   11. Ibid.   12. Bullion, '"To Know This"' pp. 431–2, 436   13. RA GEO/ADD/32/1087–1684, 1692–1697, 2008–2009   14. RA GEO/ADD/32/1194, 1220–1232 f. 1226   15. RA GEO/ADD/32/1328–1449 f. 1371   16. Ibid. f. 1398   17. Ibid. ff. 1367–8   18. Ibid. f. 1402   19. ed. Sedgwick, *Letters from George III to Lord Bute* p. 7   20. Brown, 'Court Martial of Lord George Sackville'

p. 318   21. Fraser, 'Trial of Lord George Sackville' p. 49   22. ed. Hodgart, *Horace Walpole: Memoirs and Portraits* p. 74   23. ed. Sedgwick, *Letters from George III to Lord Bute* pp. 7–8   24. Ibid. p. 11 n. 1   25. Ibid. pp. 10–11   26. Simms, *Three Victories and a Defeat* p. 467   27. Brown, 'Court Martial of Lord George Sackville' p. 323   28. ed. Sedgwick, *Letters from George III to Lord Bute* p. 14   29. RA GEO/ADD/32/259–260 f. 259   30. ed. Sedgwick, *Letters from George III to Lord Bute* p. 19 n. 2   31. Ibid. pp. 17–18   32. Ibid. p. 19   33. Ibid. p. 18   34. Ibid. p. 23   35. Brooke, *King George III* p. 67   36. ed. Sedgwick, *Letters from George III to Lord Bute* p. 26   37. BL Add MS 32893 ff. 316, 318, 347, 349, 407–10   38. ed. Sedgwick, *Letters from George III to Lord Bute* pp. 26–7   39. BL Add MS 32893 ff. 408ff   40. ed. Sedgwick, *Letters from George III to Lord Bute* p. 27   41. Ibid.   42. Ibid. p. 28   43. Ibid.   44. Ibid. p. 29   45. Henderson, *Letters and Poems* p. 60   46. Hibbert, *George III* p. 30; ed. Jarrett, *Horace Walpole: Memoirs of the Reign of George III* I p. 43   47. Brooke, *King George III* p. 70   48. Clarke, *Life and Times of George III* p. 23; Hamilton, *Secret History of the Court of England* I pp. 3, 6   49. ed. Sedgwick, *Letters from George III to Lord Bute* p. 37   50. Ibid. p. 38   51. Ibid. pp. 38–9   52. Brooke, *King George III* p. 71   53. ed. Sedgwick, *Letters from George III to Lord Bute* p. 39   54. ed. Home, *Letters and Journals of Lady Mary Coke* II p. 304   55. Ibid. III pp. 31–2   56. ed. Sedgwick, *Letters from George III to Lord Bute* p. 39   57. Ibid. p. 40   58. Ibid.   59. BL Bute Papers Add MS 32899 f. 33   60. Fraser, 'Trial of Lord George Sackville' p. 49; Brown, 'Court Martial of Lord George Sackville' p. 321 n. 12; Mackesy, *Coward of Minden* pp. 114–20   61. Fraser, 'Trial of Lord George Sackville' p. 51   62. Brown, 'Court Martial of Lord George Sackville' pp. 319, 333   63. Fraser, 'Trial of Lord George Sackville' p. 48   64. Mackesy, *War for America* p. 49   65. BL Bute Papers Add MS 36796   66. ed. Sedgwick, *Letters from George III to Lord Bute* p. 43   67. Bullion, '"To Know This"' p. 436   68. RA GEO/ADD/32/1328–1449 f. 1448   69. Bullion, '"To Know This"' p. 437   70. ed. Sedgwick, *Letters from George III to Lord Bute* p. 167   71. Ibid. p. 45   72. Ibid. pp. 36–7   73. Bullion, '"To Know This"' p. 444   74. ed. Sedgwick, *Letters from George III to Lord Bute* p. 47   75. Thomas, '"Thoughts on the British Constitution"' p. 361   76. Black, *George III: America's Last King* p. 12; Plumb, *American Experience* p. 52   77. Plumb, *American Experience* p. 52   78. Thomas, '"Thoughts on the British Constitution"' p. 362   79. Ibid.   80. ed. Sedgwick, *Letters from George III to Lord Bute* p. liii   81. Ibid. p. 11   82. Ibid. p. 13   83. Ibid. p. 35   84. Brooke, *King George III* p. 65

3. 'I Glory in the Name of Briton'

1. *Annual Register 1792* Part II p. 7   2. Borman, *King's Mistress* p. 267   3. Hadlow, *Royal Experiment* p. 1   4. ed. Sedgwick, *Letters from George III to Lord Bute* p. 48   5. Brooke, *King George III* p. 74   6. Ibid.   7. Ibid. p. 75   8. Ibid.   9. ed. Newman, 'Leicester House Politics' p. 215   10. ed. Sedgwick, *Letters from George III to Lord Bute* p. 49 n. 2   11. BL 1st Lord Holland Add MS 51439 f. 3   12. Harris, *Life of Lord Chancellor Hardwicke* III p. 221   13. Clarke, *Life and Times of George III* p. 25; Ayling, *George the Third* p. 68n   14. ed. Home, *Letters and Journals of Lady Mary Coke* III p. 112 n. 1   15. ed. Greig, *Diaries of a Duchess* p. 35   16. ed. Pink, *Letters of Horace Walpole* p. 111   17. ed. Home, *Letters and Journals of Lady Mary Coke* II p. 134   18. Ibid. IV p. 108   19. Watson, *Reign of George III* pp. 10, 13   20. Ibid. p. 36 n. 2   21. Wright, *George III* p. 24   22. ed. Everett, *Letters of Junius* p. xxv   23. Eimer, *British Commemorative Medals* p. 107   24. Taylor, *American Revolutions* p. 11   25. Ibid.   26. *Annual Register 1761* p. 305   27. ed. Chapman, *Letters of Samuel Johnson* I pp. 133–4   28. Ditchfield, *George III* p. 54   29. O'Shaughnessy, *Men Who Lost America* p. 46   30. *Annual Register 1760* pp. 241–3   31. Simms, *Three Victories and a Defeat* p. 364   32. Liddle, '"Patriot King, or None"' p. 957   33. eds. Brown and Schweizer, *Devonshire Diary* pp. 54, 60   34. ed. Pink, *Letters of Horace Walpole* pp. 110–11   35. Winstanley, 'George III and his First Cabinet' p. 681   36. BL Newcastle Papers Add MS 32914 f. 171   37. ed. Albemarle, *Memoirs of the Marquis of Rockingham* I p. 6; Winstanley, 'George III and his First Cabinet' p. 683   38. Yorke, *Philip Yorke, Earl of Hardwicke* III p. 310

39. ed. Sedgwick, *Letters from George III to Lord Bute* p. 49   **40.** Winstanley, 'George III and his First Cabinet' p. 681   **41.** ed. Hall, *250 Royal Speeches* p. 1   **42.** BL Add MS 32684 f. 121   **43.** Rodger, *Insatiable Earl* p. 98; Yorke, *Philip Yorke, Earl of Hardwicke* III p. 263   **44.** ed. Hall, *250 Royal Speeches* p. 1   **45.** Ibid.   **46.** BL 1st Lord Holland Add MS 51439 f. 10   **47.** ed. Sedgwick, *Letters from George III to Lord Bute* pp. 49–50   **48.** Ibid. p. 50   **49.** Ibid.   **50.** Ibid. pp. 53, 54, 55   **51.** Ibid. p. 55   **52.** ed. Jarrett, *Horace Walpole: Memoirs of the Reign of George III* I p. 45   **53.** eds. Carswell and Dralle, *Political Journal of George Bubb Dodington* p. 407   **54.** BL 1st Lord Holland Add MS 51439 f. 14   **55.** Butterfield, 'George III and the Constitution' p. 21 n. 1; Clark, *From Restoration to Reform* p. 224   **56.** Jupp, *Lord Grenville* p. 8   **57.** BL Newcastle Papers Add MS 32920 f. 61   **58.** Winstanley, 'George III and his First Cabinet' p. 685   **59.** Barnes, *George III and William Pitt* p. 7   **60.** Yorke, *Philip Yorke, Earl of Hardwicke* III p. 317   **61.** RA GEO/ADD/26/1   **62.** Chernow, *Washington* pp. 128–9   **63.** Hibbert, *George III* p. 37   **64.** ed. Sedgwick, *Letters from George III to Lord Bute* p. 77   **65.** Ibid. p. 6   **66.** Simms, *Three Victories and a Defeat* p. 471   **67.** BL Newcastle Papers Add MS 32926 f. 187   **68.** ed. Russell, *Correspondence of John, Fourth Duke of Bedford* III p. 18   **69.** Ibid.   **70.** Hedley, *Queen Charlotte* p. 12   **71.** Plumb, *First Four Georges* p. 95; Pares, *George III and the Politicians* p. 65   **72.** Hilton, 'The "Mulatto" Queen' passim   **73.** Ayling, *George the Third* p. 84   **74.** Kelly, *Mr Foote's Other Leg* pp. 224–5   **75.** ed. Sedgwick, *Letters from George III to Lord Bute* p. 61   **76.** Ibid. p. 62   **77.** Chisholm, *Fanny Burney* p. 138   **78.** eds. Barrett and Dobson, *Diary and Letters of Madame d'Arblay* II p. 337   **79.** eds. Ward et al., *Cambridge Modern History* VI p. 419   **80.** BL Newcastle Papers Add MS 32928 f. 259   **81.** ed. Sedgwick, *Letters from George III to Lord Bute* p. 63   **82.** BL Newcastle Papers Add MS 32928 f. 325   **83.** Ibid. f. 303   **84.** For more on the Coronation, see RA GEO/MAIN/15754–15757, the King's regalia RA GEO/MAIN/15762–15763 and instructions for those attending RA GEO/MAIN/15765–15766   **85.** Brooke, *King George III* p. 85   **86.** ed. Thomson, *Faithful Account* p. 73   **87.** Fraser, *King and the Catholics* p. 54   **88.** Strong, *Coronation* p. 394   **89.** Ibid. p. 407   **90.** ed. Greig, *Diaries of a Duchess* p. 37   **91.** ed. Pink, *Letters of Horace Walpole* p. 120   **92.** Ibid.   **93.** Isaacson, *Benjamin Franklin* pp. 200–210   **94.** eds. Ward et al., *Cambridge Modern History* VI p. 419   **95.** *Annual Register 1761* p. 44   **96.** Ibid. p. 45   **97.** eds. Ward et al., *Cambridge Modern History* VI p. 426   **98.** BL Newcastle Papers Add MS 32917 f. 92   **99.** ed. Jarrett, *Horace Walpole: Memoirs of the Reign of George III* I p. xxv   **100.** ed. Stuart Wortley, *Prime Minister and his Son* p. 25; ed. Newman, 'Leicester House Politics' p. 227   **101.** ed. Jarrett, *Horace Walpole: Memoirs of the Reign of George III* I p. xxv   **102.** For Walpole's allegations see ibid. pp. xiv, xvi, xxviii, xxxvii and xlvi   **103.** Brooke, *King George III* p. 100   **104.** Brewer, 'Misfortunes of Lord Bute' p. 5   **105.** ed. Le Marchant, *Horace Walpole: Memoirs of the Reign of George III* I p. 76   **106.** Black, *George III: America's Last King* p. 61   **107.** ed. Sedgwick, *Letters from George III to Lord Bute* p. 69

4. Victory

1. ed. Sedgwick, *Letters from George III to Lord Bute* p. 77   **2.** ed. Butterfield, *Diary and Autobiography of John Adams* III p. 150   **3.** ed. Roberts, *George III and Queen Charlotte* passim   **4.** Robins, *Trial of Queen Caroline* p. 20   **5.** ed. Marsden, *Wisdom of George the Third* p. 6   **6.** Ibid. pp. 6–7   **7.** Chisholm, *Fanny Burney* p. 138   **8.** ed. Home, *Letters and Journals of Lady Mary Coke* IV p. 119 n. 2   **9.** Ritcheson, 'Fragile Memory' p. 8   **10.** ed. Home, *Letters and Journals of Lady Mary Coke* II p. 205   **11.** Brooke, *King George III* p. 296; ed. Croker, *Life of Samuel Johnson by James Boswell* III p. 27   **12.** ed. Home, *Letters and Journals of Lady Mary Coke* III p. 272   **13.** https://www.telegraph.co.uk/royal-family/2020/02/08/gourmand-george-iii-fraternised-enemys-cuisine/   **14.** Simms, *Three Victories and a Defeat* p. 559   **15.** ed. Greig, *Diaries of a Duchess* p. 199   **16.** Hibbert, *George III: A Personal History* p. 54   **17.** eds. Barrett and Dobson, *Diary and Letters of Madame d'Arblay* III p. 46   **18.** ed. Morrell, *Leaves from the Greville Diary* p. 343   **19.** ed. Esher, *Girlhood of Queen Victoria* II p. 94   **20.** ed. Greig, *Diaries of a Duchess* pp. 78–9   **21.** ed. Home, *Letters* *and Journals of Lady Mary Coke* IV p. 417 n. 2   22. ed. Marsden, *Wisdom of George the Third* p. 235   23. ed. Home, *Letters and Journals of Lady Mary Coke* II p. 191   24. ed. Esher, *Girlhood of Queen Victoria* II p. 260   25. Vulliamy, *Royal George* p. 308   26. eds. Barrett and Dobson, *Diary and Letters of Madame d'Arblay* III pp. 222, 259   27. Lindsay, 'The London Dentist of the Eighteenth Century' p. 13   28. Chisholm, *Fanny Burney* p. 137   29. Ibid. pp. 137–8   30. ed. Marsden, *Wisdom of George the Third* p. 6   31. https://www.telegraph.co.uk/news/2018/01/07/queen-horrible-coronation-coach-journey-not-comfortable/   32. ed. Home, *Letters and Journals of Lady Mary Coke* III p. 114   33. Brooke, *King George III* p. 297   34. Vulliamy, *Royal George* p. 308   35. Brooke, *King George III* p. 297   36. ed. Greene, *Samuel Johnson: Political Writings* p. 293   37. Lord Brougham, quoted in *London Quarterly Review* Vol. 79 December 1846–March 1847 New York p. 276   38. ed. Wright, *Letters of Horace Walpole* III p. 107   39. Watkin, *Architect King* p. 28   40. RA GEO/MAIN/27–28   41. Millar, *Later Georgian Pictures* I p. xi   42. Black, *George III: Madness and Majesty* p. 36   43. ed. Bickley, *Diaries of Sylvester Douglas* I p. 265   44. Brooke, *King George III* p. 306; Brooke, 'Library of King George III' passim   45. eds. Heard and Jones, *George IV: Art and Spectacle* p. 192   46. https://www.apollo-magazine.com/the-topographical-collection-of-king-george-iii/   47. Barber, 'George III's Papers' passim   48. ed. Marsden, *Wisdom of George the Third* p. 335   49. ed. Sedgwick, *Letters from George III to Lord Bute* p. 81   50. Ibid. p. 94   51. Ibid. p. 101   52. Ayling, *George the Third* p. 92   53. ed. Sedgwick, *Letters from George III to Lord Bute* p. 109   54. Brewer, 'Misfortunes of Lord Bute' pp. 3–4   55. Simms, *Three Victories and a Defeat* p. 474   56. Ibid.   57. ed. Sedgwick, *Letters from George III to Lord Bute* p. 130   58. ed. Greig, *Diaries of a Duchess* p. 48   59. Eimer, *British Commemorative Medals* p. 109   60. Black, *George III: America's Last King* p. 145   61. ed. Sedgwick, *Letters from George III to Lord Bute* p. 134   62. ed. Russell, *Correspondence of John, Fourth Duke of Bedford* III pp. 132–3   63. Ibid. p. 133   64. ed. Sedgwick, *Letters from George III to Lord Bute* p. 143   65. Ibid. p. 152   66. Ibid. pp. 154–5   67. Ibid. p. 156   68. Ibid. p. 160   69. Lovat-Fraser, *John Stuart, Earl of Bute* p. 1   70. ed. Russell, *Correspondence of John, Fourth Duke of Bedford* III p. 160   71. Ibid. pp. 159–62   72. ed. Sedgwick, *Letters from George III to Lord Bute* pp. 167, 171   73. ed. Russell, *Correspondence of John, Fourth Duke of Bedford* III p. 160   74. ed. Hall, *250 Royal Speeches* pp. 2, 3   75. Ibid. p. 3   76. ed. Pottle, *Boswell's London Journal* p. 49   77. ed. Sedgwick, *Letters from George III to Lord Bute* p. lxii   78. Ibid. p. 166   79. Ibid.   80. Ibid. p. 169   81. Ibid. pp. 167–9   82. BL Newcastle Papers Add MS 32922 ff. 449–51   83. eds. Ward et al., *Cambridge Modern History* VI p. 423   84. Ibid.   85. Nicholls, *Recollections and Reflections* p. 13; Thomas, *George III: King and Politicians* p. 3   86. ed. Sedgwick, *Letters from George III to Lord Bute* p. 187   87. Ibid. p. 188   88. Thomas, *George III: King and Politicians* p. 8   89. eds. Ward et al, *Cambridge Modern History* VI p. 347   90. Ibid. p. 422   91. Mackesy, *War for America* p. 1   92. McCurdy, *Quarters* p. 76   93. ed. Russell, *Correspondence of John, Fourth Duke of Bedford* III pp. 199–200   94. Atkinson, *British are Coming* p. 6   95. ed. Marshall, *Oxford History of the British Empire* II pp. 7–8

5. The Problems of Peace

1. Simms, *Three Victories and a Defeat* p. 587   2. ed. Wood, *American Revolution* II p. 824; Ditchfield, *George III* p. 120; Atkinson, *British are Coming* p. 8   3. Tucker and Hendrickson, *Fall of the First British Empire* p. 87   4. Christie, 'British Politics and the American Revolution' p. 208   5. Banke, 'Bute's Empire' pp. 3–7   6. Clodfelter, *Warfare and Armed Conflicts* p. 122   7. Middleton, *Colonial America* p. 442   8. ed. Wood, *American Revolution* I p. xx   9. Bullion, 'Security and Economy' p. 499   10. *The Times* 31 January 1820 p. 2   11. Lowry, *Case for Nationalism* p. 119   12. ed. Wood, *American Revolution* I p. xix   13. Atkinson, *British are Coming* p. 9   14. Morgan, *Birth of the Republic* p. 13   15. Thomas, 'George III and the American Revolution' p. 17   16. Atkinson, *British are Coming* p. 9   17. ed. Wood, *American Revolution* I p. xx   18. Ibid.   19. Kohn, *Idea of Nationalism* p. 272   20. Christie, 'British Politics and the American Revolution' p. 212   21. ed. Ilchester, *Letters to Henry Fox*

p. 172   22. BL Holland House Papers Add MS 51379 ff. 14–41   23. ed. Sedgwick, *Letters from George III to Lord Bute* pp. 196–7   24. Ibid. p. 198   25. Ibid. p. 199   26. Ibid. p. 200   27. Ibid. pp. 229, 208   28. Bunker, *Empire on the Edge* p. 20   29. ed. Sedgwick, *Letters from George III to Lord Bute* pp. 201, 195   30. Burke, *Works and Correspondence* II pp. 62–3   31. Adolphus, *History of England* I p. 113   32. Black, *George III: America's Last King* p. 209   33. ed. Newman, 'Leicester House Politics' p. 193   34. ed. Bickley, *Diaries of Sylvester Douglas* I p. 406   35. See O'Connell, *Revolutionary* pp. 73–4 for a counterfactual based on this outcome   36. ed. Sedgwick, *Letters from George III to Lord Bute* p. 201   37. Ayling, *George the Third* p. 119   38. Beer, *British Colonial Policy* p. 279 n. 3   39. Bullion, *Great and Necessary Measure* p. 1   40. Ibid. p. 40   41. ed. Sedgwick, *Letters from George III to Lord Bute* pp. 201–2   42. Bullion, *Great and Necessary Measure* p. 40   43. ed. Sedgwick, *Letters from George III to Lord Bute* pp. 209–10   44. Ibid. p. 210   45. Bullion, *Great and Necessary Measure* p. 51   46. ed. Sedgwick, *Letters from George III to Lord Bute* pp. 231, 233   47. Ibid. p. 220   48. Hall, *250 Royal Speeches* p. 3   49. Black, *George III: America's Last King* p. 77   50. Plumb, *First Four Georges* p. 102   51. ed. Jarrett, *Walpole: Memoirs of the Reign of George III* II p. 62   52. Brooke, *King George III* p. 145   53. Rudé, *Wilkes and Liberty* pp. 17–36   54. ed. Marsden, *Wisdom of George the Third* p. 238   55. Ibid. pp. 238–9   56. ed. Smith, *Grenville Papers* II p. 193   57. Ibid.   58. Ibid. p. 195   59. Ibid. p. 196   60. Ibid. pp. 198–9   61. Ibid. p. 105   62. ed. Yorke, *Philip Yorke, Earl of Hardwicke* III p. 526   63. ed. Smith, *Grenville Papers* II p. 200   64. Langford, 'Old Whigs, Old Tories' p. 114   65. Ibid. p. 115   66. ed. Smith, *Grenville Papers* II p. 197 n. 1   67. See Sir Lewis Namier's works on George III for the abandonment trope   68. Brooke, *King George III* p. 108   69. ed. Sedgwick, *Letters from George III to Lord Bute* p. 237   70. ed. Fortescue, *Correspondence* I p. 164   71. ed. Smith, *Grenville Papers* II p. 201   72. ed. Bickley, *Diaries of Sylvester Douglas* I p. 285   73. ed. Smith, *Grenville Papers* II p. 205   74. ed. Bickley, *Diaries of Sylvester Douglas* I p. 285   75. Oliphant, 'Cherokee Embassy to London' p. 2   76. ed. Ellis, *Early Diary of Frances Burney* I pp. 333–5   77. Ibid. II p. 131   78. Ellis, *His Excellency* p. 55   79. Lowry, *Case for Nationalism* p. 120; Taylor, *American Revolutions* pp. 62, 510   80. Calloway, *Indian World of George Washington* p. 180   81. Draper, *Struggle for Power* p. 200   82. Chernow, *Washington* p. 137   83. Ellis, *His Excellency* p. 55   84. Ibid. p. 56   85. Calloway, *Indian World of George Washington* p. 184

6. Sugar, Stamps and Silk

1. ed. Smith, *Grenville Papers* II p. 267   2. RA GEO/MAIN/5430   3. ed. Smith, *Grenville Papers* II pp. 222–3   4. Ibid. p. 161   5. Ibid. p. 223   6. Rae, 'John Wilkes' p. 266   7. Rodger, *Insatiable Earl* pp. 102–3   8. ed. Le Marchant, *Horace Walpole: Memoirs of the Reign of George the Third* I p. 280   9. Donald, *Age of Caricature* p. 55   10. Brewer, 'Misfortunes of Lord Bute' p. 6   11. ed. Smith, *Grenville Papers* II pp. 229, 166   12. Ibid. p. 230   13. Ibid. p. 490   14. Ibid. p. 232   15. Ibid.   16. Ibid. p. 235   17. Ibid. p. 237   18. Ibid. p. 236   19. Fontaine, *Memoirs of a Huguenot Family* p. 421   20. ed. Donne, *Correspondence of King George the Third with Lord North* I p. lxxxviii   21. ed. Wood, *American Revolution* II p. 825   22. ed. Newman, 'Leicester House Politics' pp. 234–8   23. ed. Smith, *Grenville Papers* II p. 495   24. Wright, *George III* p. 85   25. ed. Wood, *American Revolution* I p. 48   26. Ibid. p. 91   27. Namier, *England in the Age of the American Revolution* p. 37   28. RA GEO/ADD/32/999   29. Black, *George III: America's Last King* pp. 110–11   30. ed. Hall, *250 Royal Speeches* p. 4   31. ed. Smith, *Grenville Papers* II p. 116   32. Ibid. p. 115   33. Ibid. p. 116   34. ed. Jarrett, *Horace Walpole: Memoirs of the Reign of George III* II pp. 98–9   35. Green, *Madness of Kings* p. 190   36. ed. Jarrett, *Horace Walpole: Memoirs of the Reign of George III* II p. 98   37. Guttmacher, *America's Last King* p. 75; Knollenberg, *Origin of the American Revolution* p. 277   38. ed. Kassler, *Memoirs of Charlotte Papendiek* pp. 13–14   39. Williams, *Brief Memoir of Her Late Majesty Queen Charlotte* p. 28n   40. Guttmacher, *America's Last King* p. 75   41. Peters, 'Royal Medical Entourages' p. 63   42. Rentoumi et al., 'Acute Mania of King George III'   43. Ibid.   44. Wessely email to the author on 8 November 2020;

also https://georgianpapers.com/2018/11/20/the-madness-of-george-iii-revisited-sir-simon-wessely-on-georges-illness/ **45.** Rentoumi et al., 'Acute Mania of King George III' **46.** Guttmacher, *America's Last King* p. 75 **47.** Ray, *Insanity of King George III* p. 4 **48.** ed. Minto, *Life and Letters of Sir Gilbert Elliot* III p. 350 **49.** Knollenberg, *Origin of the American Revolution* p. 276 **50.** Adolphus, *History of England* I p. 175 **51.** Knollenberg, *Origin of the American Revolution* p. 276 **52.** Plumb, *First Four Georges* pp. 104–5 **53.** Ibid. p. 106 **54.** ed. Smith, *Grenville Papers* III p. 116 **55.** Ibid. **56.** Ibid. p. 6 **57.** ed. Wood, *American Revolution* II p. 826 **58.** Bullion, *Great and Necessary Measure* p. 4 **59.** Ibid. p. 3 **60.** ed. Labaree, *Papers of Benjamin Franklin* XII p. 67 **61.** ed. Smith, *Grenville Papers* III p. 119 **62.** Ibid. **63.** Ibid. **64.** Ibid. p. 7 **65.** ed. Donne, *Correspondence of King George the Third with Lord North* I p. lxxxviii **66.** ed. Wood, *American Revolution* II p. 826 **67.** Beeman, *Varieties of Political Experience* p. 83 **68.** Atkinson, *British are Coming* p. 8 **69.** Namier, *England in the Age of the American Revolution* pp. 229–32 **70.** Cook, *Long Fuse* p. 18 **71.** BL Egerton Papers MS 221 f. 34 **72.** Thomas, 'George III and the American Revolution' p. 18 **73.** Bullion, *Great and Necessary Measure* p. 107 **74.** ed. Smith, *Grenville Papers* III pp. 19–20 **75.** ed. Tomlinson, *Additional Grenville Papers* p. 247 **76.** Ibid. p. 248 **77.** ed. Smith, *Grenville Papers* III p. 121 **78.** Ibid. p. 11 **79.** McCurdy, *Quarters* p. 95 **80.** ed. Smith, *Grenville Papers* III p. 121 **81.** Ibid. pp. 121–2 **82.** Ibid. p. 122 **83.** Ibid. **84.** Ibid. p. 123 **85.** Ibid. p. 124 **86.** ed. Lewis, *Yale Edition of the Correspondence of Horace Walpole* XXII p. 288 **87.** ed. Smith, *Grenville Papers* III p. 126 **88.** Jarrett, 'Regency Crisis of 1765' p. 291 **89.** Ibid. p. 284 **90.** Ibid. **91.** ed. Wright, *Letters of Horace Walpole* II p. 393 **92.** ed. Albemarle, *Memoirs of the Marquess of Rockingham* I pp. 191–2 **93.** ed. Smith, *Grenville Papers* III p. 64 **94.** ed. Sedgwick, *Letters from George III to Lord Bute* p. 164 **95.** Ditchfield, *George III* p. 65 **96.** ed. Jarrett, *Horace Walpole: Memoirs of the Reign of George III* II p. 142 **97.** ed. Smith, *Grenville Papers* III pp. 163–4 **98.** ed. Jucker, *Jenkinson Papers* p. 368 **99.** Ibid. **100.** Ibid. p. 369 **101.** Ibid. p. 368 **102.** Ibid. p. 370 **103.** ed. Smith, *Grenville Papers* III p. 177 **104.** Ibid. **105.** Ibid., pp. 177–80 **106.** Ibid. p. 40 **107.** Ibid. pp. 181, 183

7. Rockingham Repeals the Stamp Act

1. ed. Sparks, *Works of Benjamin Franklin* IV p. 207 **2.** McCurdy, *Quarters* p. 250 n. 3 **3.** Ibid. p. 3 **4.** Ibid. p. 4 **5.** ed. Smith, *Grenville Papers* III p. 184 **6.** Ibid. pp. 43–4, 184–5 **7.** ed. Jucker, *Jenkinson Papers* p. 371 **8.** Brooke, *King George III* p. 119 **9.** ed. Smith, *Grenville Papers* III p. 187 **10.** ed. Jucker, *Jenkinson Papers* pp. 371–2 **11.** ed. Russell, *Correspondence of John, Fourth Duke of Bedford* III p. 284 **12.** Langford, *Polite and Commercial People* p. 363 **13.** ed. Sedgwick, *Letters from George III to Lord Bute* pp. 240–41 **14.** Black, *George III: America's Last King* p. 71 **15.** ed. Schweizer, *Lord Bute: Essays in Reinterpretation* p. 131 **16.** ed. Smith, *Grenville Papers* II pp. 188–9 **17.** Ibid. p. 189 **18.** ed. Jucker, *Jenkinson Papers* p. 372 **19.** Kidd, *Patrick Henry* pp. 51–2 **20.** Chernow, *Washington* p. 138 **21.** ed. Wood, *American Revolution* I p. 331 **22.** Bullion, *Great and Necessary Measure* p. 5 **23.** Brooke, *King George III* p. 120 **24.** Ibid. **25.** Ibid. p. 121 **26.** RA GEO/MAIN/104 12 June 1765 **27.** ed. Smith, *Greville Papers* III p. 213 **28.** Thomas, 'George III and the American Revolution' p. 19 **29.** ed. Smith, *Grenville Papers* III pp. 215–16 **30.** Guttridge, *Early Career of Lord Rockingham* p. 10 **31.** RA GEO/MAIN/164–173 f. 164r **32.** Ibid. f. 169(2)v **33.** Ibid. f. 170r **34.** Ferling, *John Adams* p. 46 **35.** Ibid. **36.** ed. Wood, *American Revolution* I p. 331 **37.** Egnal, *Mighty Empire* p. 5; Namier, *England in the Age of the American Revolution* p. 231 n. 2 **38.** Namier, *England in the Age of the American Revolution* p. 231 n. 2 **39.** Clark, *From Restoration to Reform* p. 235 **40.** Brooke, *King George III* p. 126 **41.** Eimer, *British Commemorative Medals* p. 110 **42.** ed. Sedgwick, *Letters from George III to Lord Bute* pp. 242–3 **43.** Black, *George III* p. 209 **44.** ed. Wood, *American Revolution* I pp. 625–6 **45.** ed. Sedgwick, *Letters from George III to Lord Bute* p. 243 **46.** Ibid. p. 242 **47.** RA GEO/MAIN/297 **48.** Tuchman, *March of Folly* p. 158 **49.** Ibid. **50.** RA GEO/MAIN/304 f. 304r **51.** Ibid. ff. 304v–304(2)r **52.** Ibid. f. 304(2)r **53.** ed. Wood,

American Revolution I p. 363   54. Langford, 'Old Whigs, Old Tories' pp. 115 and n. 45   55. Harvey, *Few Bloody Noses* pp. 69–70   56. Ayling, *George the Third* p. 137   57. RA GEO/MAIN/323   58. ed. Smith, *Grenville Papers* III p. 353   59. Thomas, 'George III and the American Revolution' p. 22   60. Brooke, *King George III* p. 129   61. ed. Bateson, *Narrative of the Changes* pp. 49–50   62. RA GEO/MAIN/350–351 f. 350r   63. RA GEO/MAIN/353   64. Thomas, *George III: King and Politicians* p. 9   65. RA GEO/MAIN/354 f. 354r   66. Ibid.   67. RA GEO/MAIN/365   68. RA GEO/MAIN/375 f. 375(2)r   69. Ibid. f. 375(2)v   70. RA GEO/MAIN/376   71. RA GEO/MAIN/381(2); Thomas, 'George III and the American Revolution' p. 24   72. Atkinson, *British are Coming* p. 8   73. Eimer, *British Commemorative Medals* p. 110   74. ed. Wood, *American Revolution* I p. 331   75. Avalon Project, Great Britain: Parliament – The Declaratory Act; March 18, 1766 (yale. edu)   76. eds. Taylor and Pringle, *Correspondence of William Pitt* II pp. 372–3   77. Brooke, *King George III* p. 131   78. ed. Anson, *Autobiography and Political Correspondence of Duke of Grafton* p. 241   79. ed. Sedgwick, *Letters from George III to Lord Bute* pp. 248, 249   80. Ibid. p. 249   81. RA GEO/MAIN/428   82. RA GEO/MAIN/454   83. RA GEO/MAIN/455   84. Brooke, *King George III* p. 138   85. Bateson, *Narrative of the Changes* p. 79   86. Browning, *Duke of Newcastle* p. 316   87. BL Newcastle Papers Add MS 32976 f. 325   88. ed. Sedgwick, *Letters from George III to Lord Bute* pp. 253–4   89. RA GEO/MAIN/174–175 f. 174r   90. ed. Sedgwick, *Letters from George III to Lord Bute* p. 251   91. Ibid. p. 253; eds. Taylor and Pringle, *Correspondence of William Pitt* III p. 21   92. O'Brien, *Great Melody* p. 116   93. Brooke, *Chatham Administration* p. xi   94. RA GEO/MAIN/111   95. John Cannon in *ODNB* George III   96. Brooke, *Chatham Administration* p. xii   97. Ayling, *George the Third* p. 149   98. Williams, *Life of William Pitt* I p. 236

8. 'The Apple of Discord'

1. ed. Telford, *Letters of John Wesley* V p. 376   2. Watkins, *England's Patriot King* p. 509   3. Morton and Wess, *Public and Private Science* p. 26   4. ed. Croker, *Life of Samuel Johnson by James Boswell* III p. 19   5. Ibid. p. 22   6. Ibid. p. 23   7. Ibid. p. 26   8. Ibid. p. 27   9. Morton and Wess, *Public and Private Science* p.22   10. Brooke, *Chatham Administration* p. xii   11. RA GEO/MAIN/593   12. RA GEO/MAIN/592   13. Thomas, 'George III and the American Revolution' p. 20   14. ed. Smith, *Grenville Papers* IV p. 214   15. RA GEO/MAIN/615   16. RA GEO/MAIN/616   17. ed. Fortescue, *Correspondence* I p. 470   18. ed. Anson, *Autobiography and Political Correspondence of Duke of Grafton* pp. 136–9   19. BL Newcastle Papers Add MS 32982 ff. 68–70   20. RA GEO/MAIN/645 f. 645r   21. Fisher, 'Twenty-Eight Charges against the King' p. 258   22. Crain, 'Tea and Antipathy' pp. 134–5   23. ed. Wood, *American Revolution* II p. xviii   24. RA GEO/MAIN/660   25. RA GEO/MAIN/661   26. RA GEO/MAIN/665   27. Lawson, *Imperial Challenge* p. 133   28. Brooke, *King George III* p. 155; ed. Norton, *Letters of Edward Gibbon* II p. 66   29. ed. Jarrett, *Horace Walpole: Memoirs of the Reign of George III* IV p. 143   30. Smith, *Early Career of Lord North* pp. 30, 37–8   31. Gattey, 'Farmer' George's Black Sheep p. 9   32. ed. Home, *Letters and Journals of Lady Mary Coke* I p. 116   33. ed. Hodgart, *Horace Walpole: Memoirs and Portraits* p. 185   34. Brooke, *King George III* p. 271   35. Black, *George III: America's Last King* p. 92   36. Brooke, *King George III* p. 147   37. ed. Sparks, *Works of Benjamin Franklin* VII p. 400   38. Brooke, *Chatham Administration* p. xiv   39. Eimer, *British Commemorative Medals* p. 112   40. Trevelyan, *Early History of Charles James Fox* p. 204   41. Ibid. p. 206 n. 1   42. Jesse, *Memoirs of the Life and Reign of King George the Third* I p. 433   43. ed. Fortescue, *Correspondence* II p. 20   44. ed. Smith, *Grenville Papers* IV p. 268   45. RA GEO/MAIN/765   46. Ibid.   47. Jesse, *Memoirs of the Life and Reign of King George the Third* I p. 432   48. RA GEO/MAIN/770 f. 770(2)   49. Jesse, *Memoirs of the Life and Reign of King George the Third* I p. 437   50. Ayling, *George the Third* p. 156   51. ed. Home, *Letters and Journals of Lady Mary Coke* II p. 261   52. Ibid. p. 262   53. *Annual Register 1768* p. 114   54. RA GEO/MAIN/792   55. ed. Wood, *American Revolution* I p. 525   56. RA GEO/MAIN/824   57. RA GEO/MAIN/830   58. ed. Everett, *Letters of*

Junius p. 142 n. 2   59. ed. Home, *Letters and Journals of Lady Mary Coke* II p. 402   60. ed. Smith, *Grenville Papers* III p. xxiii   61. ed. Everett, *Letters of Junius* p. 25   62. Ibid. pp. 378–81   63. Ibid. pp. 382–7   64. Saumarez Smith, *Company of Artists* pp. 11, 176   65. Ibid. p. 180   66. Royal Academy RAA/GA/7/1   67. Ibid.   68. Saumarez Smith, *Company of Artists* pp. 148–9   69. Ibid. p. 155   70. Royal Academy RAA/GA/7/2   71. Ibid.   72. Hoock, *King's Artists* p. 191   73. Royal Academy RAA/GA/7/2   74. Ibid.   75. Watkin, *Architect King* p. 15   76. Rodger, *Command of the Ocean* p. 331   77. Thomas, 'George III and the American Revolution' p. 26   78. O'Shaughnessy, *Men Who Lost America* p. 21   79. ed. Fortescue, *Correspondence* II p. 84   80. Ibid.   81. Ibid. p. 85   82. Ibid.   83. Thomas, 'George III and the American Revolution' p. 27   84. Rodger, *Insatiable Earl* p. 115   85. ed. Home, *Letters and Journals of Lady Mary Coke* III p. 90   86. ed. Bickley, *Diaries of Sylvester Douglas* I pp. 400–401, https://gpp.rct.uk/Record.aspx?src=CalmView.Catalog&id=GIII_PRIV%2f3   87. RA GEO/MAIN/858   88. RA GEO/MAIN/863   89. ed. Home, *Letters and Journals of Lady Mary Coke* III p. 48   90. RA GEO/MAIN/877   91. ed. Anson, *Autobiography and Political Correspondence of Duke of Grafton* pp. 229–30   92. Ditchfield, *George III* p. 124; Thomas, 'George III and the American Revolution' pp. 27–8   93. Ditchfield, *George III* p. 124; Thomas, 'George III and the American Revolution' pp. 27–8   94. Labaree, *Boston Tea Party* p. 41   95. ed. Anson, *Autobiography and Political Correspondence of Duke of Grafton* pp. 229–35

9. 'That Factious and Disobedient Temper'

1. RA GEO/MAIN/15673; Blanning, *Culture of Power* p. 345; Atkinson, *British are Coming* p. 562; Brooke, *King George III* p. 158   2. RA GEO/MAIN/895   3. Morton and Wess, *Public and Private Science* pp. v, 28–9   4. Sobel, *Longitude* p. 147   5. eds. Barrett and Dobson, *Diary and Letters of Madame d'Arblay* III p. 18   6. Robertson, *Enlightenment* p. 71   7. ed. Everett, *Letters of Junius* p. 136 n. 1   8. Ibid. p. 137   9. Ibid. pp. 137–8   10. Ibid. pp. 139, 141   11. Ibid. p. 142   12. Ibid. pp. 142–3   13. Ibid. p. 143   14. Ibid. p. 305   15. Lock, *Edmund Burke* I p. 352   16. ed. Wood, *American Revolution* II p. xviii   17. Harvey, *Few Bloody Noses* p. 103   18. Bunker, *Empire on the Edge* p. 19   19. ed. Hall, *250 Royal Speeches* p. 6   20. RA GEO/MAIN/932   21. Namier, 'King George III: A Study in Personality' p. 618   22. Lecky, *England in the Eighteenth Century* V p. 283; Valentine, *Lord North* I p. 295; Donoughue, *British Politics and the American Revolution* p. 36 n. 1   23. Valentine, *Lord North* I p. 294   24. Ibid.   25. ed. Wheatley, *Wraxall Memoirs* I p. 428   26. Ibid. pp. 428–30   27. John Cannon in *ODNB* John Robinson   28. RA GEO/MAIN/939   29. RA GEO/MAIN/948   30. ed. Bickley, *Diaries of Sylvester Douglas* I p. 238   31. Brooke, *King George III* p. 189   32. Cobbett, *Parliamentary History* XVI col. 945   33. ed. Wood, *American Revolution* II p. xviii; Cobbett, *Parliamentary History* XVI col. 853   34. ed. Wright, *Debates in the House of Commons* I pp. 487–9   35. Harvey, *Few Bloody Noses* p. 103   36. Lock, *Edmund Burke* I p. 274   37. ed. Morley, *Thoughts* pp. 7–8   38. Ibid. p. 9   39. Ibid. p. 13   40. Ibid. pp. 24–5   41. Ibid. p. 22   42. Ibid. p. 25   43. eds. Copeland et al., *Burke Correspondence* II p. 435   44. ed. Morley, *Thoughts* pp. 34–5   45. ed. Langford, *Writings and Speeches* II p. 311   46. ed. Morley, *Thoughts* p. 13   47. Ibid. p. 39   48. Ibid. p. 48   49. Marks, 'Statue of King George III' p. 61   50. Ibid.   51. ed. Willcox, *Papers of Benjamin Franklin* XVII pp. 163–4   52. Johnson, *Thoughts on the Late Transactions* p. 37   53. RA GEO/MAIN/1037   54. ed. Donne, *Correspondence of King George the Third with Lord North* p. 34   55. John Cannon in *ODNB* George III   56. RA GEO/MAIN/15900   57. GEO/MAIN/15948–15949   58. ed. Home, *Letters and Journals of Lady Mary Coke* III p. 483   59. RA GEO/MAIN/15938   60. RA GEO/MAIN/15934   61. RA GEO/MAIN/15944   62. RA GEO/MAIN/15939–15940 f. 15939   63. Ibid.   64. Brooke, *King George III* p. 277   65. RA GEO/MAIN/1082   66. RA GEO/MAIN/1119   67. Rudé, *Wilkes and Liberty* p. 159   68. RA GEO/MAIN/1147   69. RA GEO/MAIN/1157   70. ed. Le Marchant, *Horace Walpole: Memoirs of the Reign of George the third* III pp. 350–51   71. Colley, 'Apotheosis of George III' p. 96   72. Ritcheson, *British Politics and the American Revolution* p. 37   73. ed. Willcox, *Papers of Benjamin Franklin* XVIII p. 253   74. Beaumont, *Colonial America*

and the Earl of Halifax ch. 6   75. ed. Butterfield, *Diary and Autobiography of John Adams* II p. 150   76. ed. Woodfall, *Letters of Junius* II p. 307   77. Black, *George III: America's Last King* p. 28   78. Tillyard, *A Royal Affair* p. 247   79. Ibid. p. 265   80. ed. Home, *Letters and Journals of Lady Mary Coke* IV p. 34 n. 1   81. eds. Doran and Steuart, *Last Journals of Horace Walpole* I p. 17   82. Ayling, *George the Third* pp. 213–14   83. Eimer, *British Commemorative Medals* p. 114   84. Lascelles, *Life of Charles James Fox* p. 44   85. ed. Aspinall, *Later Correspondence* II p. xxxviii   86. Brooke, *King George III* p. 277   87. ed. Home, *Letters and Journals of Lady Mary Coke* IV pp. 133, 142   88. RA GEO/MAIN/1936

10. The Boston Tea Party

1. Plumb, *First Four Georges* p. 124   2. Morgan, *Birth of the Republic* p. 55   3. Hoffer, *True Believer* passim   4. Poser, *Lord Mansfield* p. 296 n. 80   5. Clark, *From Restoration to Reform* p. 238   6. ed. Willcox, *Papers of Benjamin Franklin* XIX p. 243   7. Ibid., XX p. 308   8. ed. Anson, *Autobiography and Political Correspondence of Duke of Grafton* pp. 266–7   9. Bunker, *Empire on the Edge* p. 135   10. *London Gazette* 24–8 November 1772   11. GEO/ADD/32/1698–1699   12. Ibid.   13. Ditchfield, *George III* p. 117   14. RA GEO/MAIN/1557   15. RA GEO/MAIN/1573   16. Crain, 'Tea and Antipathy' p. 135; ed. Wood, *American Revolution* II p. xx   17. Crain, 'Tea and Antipathy' p. 135   18. Black, *George III: America's Last King* p. 212   19. ed. Home, *Letters and Journals of Lady Mary Coke* IV p. 145   20. Ibid. pp. 145–6   21. Brooks's Club Betting Book   22. Sainsbury, *John Wilkes* p. 96   23. Clark, *Scandal* p. 44   24. Kelly, *Mr Foote's Other Leg* p. 240   25. BL Add MS 75839   26. Kelly, *Mr Foote's Other Leg* p. 332   27. ed. Langford, *Writings and Speeches* II pp. 71–2   28. Lock, *Edmund Burke* I p. 341   29. Ibid. pp. 341–2   30. BL Add MS 38222 f. 91   31. RA GEO/MAIN/1377   32. ed. Fortescue, *Correspondence* V pp. 134–5   33. Dancy, *Myth of the Press Gang* p. 18; eds. Fischer and Nordvik, *Shipping and Trade* pp. 40–41   34. Atkinson, *British are Coming* p. 2   35. Ibid. p. 3   36. O'Shaughnessy, *Men Who Lost America* p. 29   37. Rodger, *Insatiable Earl* p. 200   38. BL Add MS 75688   39. Black, *George III: America's Last King* p. 146   40. Black, *George III: Majesty and Madness* p. 29   41. Ibid. p. 18   42. Crain, 'Tea and Antipathy' p. 136   43. Carp, *Defiance of the Patriots* p. 135   44. Ibid. pp. 130–31   45. Arnold-Baker, *Companion to British History* p. 30   46. Hulton, *Letters of a Loyalist Lady* p. 71   47. Hoock, *Scars of Independence* p. 55   48. Donoughue, *British Politics and the American Revolution* p. 30   49. Winstanley, 'George III and his First Cabinet' p. 680   50. RA GEO/MAIN/1733   51. Tucker and Hendrickson, *Fall of the First British Empire* p. 357   52. RA GEO/MAIN/1765, 1769, 1770, 1773, 1776, 1780, 1799, 1805, 1811, 1817, 1820, 1822   53. RA GEO/MAIN/1776   54. ed. Russell, *Memorials and Correspondence of Charles James Fox* I p. 136   55. RA GEO/ADD/32/1328–1449 f. 1402   56. RA GEO/MAIN/1750   57. Ayling, *Fox* p. 47   58. Black, *Pitt the Elder* p. 8   59. ed. Home, *Letters and Journals of Lady Mary Coke* IV p. 372   60. Fraser, *King and the Catholics* p. 24   61. Taylor, *American Revolutions* p. 85   62. O'Brien, *Great Melody* p. 93   63. Clark, *From Restoration to Reform* p. 232   64. ed. Wood, *American Revolution* II p. 591   65. Phillips, *Cousins' Wars* p. 244   66. Bunker, *Empire on the Edge* p. 278   67. Miller, *Origins of the American Revolution* p. 266   68. eds. Simmons and Thomas, *Proceedings and Debates* IV p. 276   69. RA GEO/MAIN/1817   70. ed. Fortescue, *Correspondence* III p. 104   71. Namier, *King George III: A Study in Personality* p. 514   72. Liddle, '"Patriot King, or None"' pp. 963–4   73. Breen, *American Insurgents, American Patriots* p. 72   74. RA GEO/MAIN/1842   75. ed. Home, *Letters and Journals of Lady Mary Coke* IV p. 367   76. eds. Doran and Steuart, *Last Journals of Horace Walpole* I pp. 359–60   77. ed. Home, *Letters and Journals of Lady Mary Coke* IV p. 367   78. ed. Hutchinson, *Diary and Letters* I p. 158   79. Ibid. p. 159   80. Ibid. pp. 175, 195   81. Ibid. pp. 163–4   82. Crain, 'Tea and Antipathy' p. 132   83. ed. Hutchinson, *Diary and Letters* I p. 164   84. Ibid. p. 167   85. Ibid. p. 172   86. Ibid. p. 173   87. Ibid. p. 174   88. Ibid. p. 159 n. 2   89. Donoughue, *British Politics and the American Revolution* p. 163   90. RA GEO/MAIN/1846   91. TNA PRO CO 5/763 ff. 394–6   92. ed. Carter, *Correspondence of General Thomas Gage* I pp. 358–60

11. 'Blows Must Decide'

1. ed. Norton, *Letters of Edward Gibbon* II p. 58 2. ed. Wood, *American Revolution* II p. 85 3. Ibid. p. 91 4. Chernow, *Washington* p. 171 5. Liddle, '"Patriot King, or None"' passim 6. ed. Wood, *American Revolution* II p. 101 7. Hedges, 'Telling Off the King' p. 166 8. Lewis, 'Jefferson's *Summary View* as a Chart of Political Union' p. 37 9. Donoughue, *British Politics and the American Revolution* p. 170 10. RA GEO/MAIN/1861 11. Thomas, *George III: King and Politicians* pp. 10–11 12. Baugh, 'British Naval Failure' p. 223 13. Boot, *Invisible Armies* p. 64 14. Ibid. 15. Bunker, *Empire on the Edge* p. 326 16. Clark, *From Restoration to Reform* p. 236 17. ed. Adams, *Works of John Adams* II pp. 363–4 18. O'Shaughnessy, *Men Who Lost America* p. 26 19. Lowry, *Case for Nationalism* p. 124 20. RA GEO/MAIN/1870 21. Bunker, *Empire on the Edge* p. 321 22. Donoughue, *British Politics and the American Revolution* p. 206 23. ed. Wood, *American Revolution* II p. 237 24. Ibid. p. 832 25. Langford, 'Old Whigs, Old Tories' p. 111 26. ed. Wood, *American Revolution* II p. 265 27. Bunker, *Empire on the Edge* p. 330 28. Armitage, *Declaration of Independence* p. 50 29. Ibid. 30. Ibid. p. 51 31. Ibid. 32. Black, *Eighteenth Century Europe* p. 334 and passim 33. BL Add MS 73550 f. 76 34. Ibid. 35. ed. Billias, *Manuscripts of Captain Howard Vincente Knox* p. 257 36. Ibid. 37. RA GEO/MAIN/1917 38. John Cannon in *ONDB* George III; Thomas, 'George III and the American Revolution' p. 29 39. RA GEO/MAIN/1918 40. RA GEO/MAIN/1917 41. Donoughue, *British Politics and the American Revolution* p. 212 42. ed. Hall, *250 Royal Speeches* p. 9 43. Ibid. 44. Bunker, *Empire on the Edge* p. 334 45. ed. Hutchinson, *Diary and Letters* I p. 316 46. Ibid. p. 317 47. Brooks's Club Betting Book 48. RA GEO/MAIN/1924 49. Donoughue, *British Politics and the American Revolution* p. 216 50. Thomas, 'George III and the American Revolution' p. 30 51. Donoughue, *British Politics and the American Revolution* p. 158 52. RA GEO/MAIN/1927–1928 53. Ferling, *Almost a Miracle* p. 28 54. RA GEO/MAIN/1931 55. Donoughue, *British Politics and the American Revolution* pp. 228–9 56. ed. Webster, *Journal of Jeffery Amherst* p. xiii 57. Donoughue, *British Politics and the American Revolution* p. 229 58. Ibid. 59. Hoock, *Scars of Independence* p. 71 60. Crain, 'Tea and Antipathy' p. 138 61. Sainsbury, *Disaffected Patriots* p. 85 62. York, 'George III, Tyrant: The Crisis as Critic of Empire' p. 434 63. Ibid. p. 435 64. Ibid. p. 445 65. Ibid. p. 458 66. ed. Wood, *American Revolution* II p. 379 67. RA GEO/MAIN/1958 68. ed. Hutchinson, *Diary and Letters* p. 378 69. Ibid. 70. Donoughue, *British Politics and the American Revolution* p. 248 n. 2 71. RA GEO/MAIN/1963 72. ed. Norton, *Letters of Edward Gibbon* I p. 61 73. ed. Wood, *American Revolution* II p. 496 74. RA GEO/MAIN/1979 75. Sainsbury, *Disaffected Patriots* p. 84; ed. Stevenson, *London in the Age of Reform* p. 66 76. Donoughue, *British Politics and the American Revolution* p. 264 77. ed. Stevenson, *London in the Age of Reform* p. 66 78. Sainsbury, *Disaffected Patriots* p. 92 79. O'Shaughnessy, *Men Who Lost America* p. 24 80. Phillips, *Cousins' Wars* p. 243 81. Mitchell, *Decisive Battles of the American Revolution* pp. 23–4; Ferling, *Almost a Miracle* pp. 30–31; Daughan, *Lexington and Concord* p. 264 82. Boot, *Invisible Armies* p. 65 83. Ibid. p. 66

12. 'The Battle of the Legislature'

1. ed. Smith, *Letters of Delegates to Congress* I p. 567 2. Syfert, *First American Declaration of Independence?* passim 3. Mackesy, *War for America* p. 2 4. ed. Norton, *Letters of Edward Gibbon* II pp. 70–72 5. Donoughue, *British Politics and the American Revolution* p. 272 6. Cook, *Long Fuse* pp. 220–21 7. Hoock, *Scars of Independence* p. 72 8. Fortescue, *History of the British Army* II p. 267 9. Ibid. p. 270 10. Ibid. pp. 333–4 11. Donoughue, *British Politics and the American Revolution* p. 253 12. Mackesy, *War for America* p. 30 13. Mackesy, 'British Strategy in the War of American Independence' p. 547 14. Anderson, *Crucible of War* p. 288 15. Boot, *Invisible Armies* p. 67 16. Marston, *American Revolution* p. 17 17. RA GEO/ADD/35/12 18. Barrington, *Political Life of William Wildman, Viscount Barrington* pp. 148–57 19. https://www.rct.uk/about/news-and-features/george-iiis-collection-of-military-maps-

published-online#/ 20. O'Shaughnessy, *Men Who Lost America* p. 29 21. Donoughue, *British Politics and the American Revolution* p. 275 22. Marston, *American Revolution* p. 29; eds. Dupuy and Dupuy, *Collins Encyclopedia* p. 775; Mitchell, *Decisive Battles of the American Revolution* p. 34; Ferling, *Almost a Miracle* p. 59 23. *London Gazette* 22–25 July 1775 24. eds. Barnes and Owen, *Private Papers of John, Earl of Sandwich* I p. 63 25. Palmer, *George Washington's Military Genius* pp. 57–60 26. Boot, *Invisible Armies* pp. 67–68 27. Ibid. p. 68; Chernow, *Washington* pp. 195–8 28. ed. Wood, *American Revolution* II p. 771 29. Morgan, *Birth of the Republic* p. 70 30. Ferling, *Almost a Miracle* p. 113 31. Ibid. p. 38 32. RA GEO/MAIN/2051 33. Donoughue, *British Politics and the American Revolution* p. 278 34. Barrington, *Political Life of William Wildman, Viscount Barrington* pp. 148–50 35. RA GEO/MAIN/2056 36. RA GEO/MAIN/2057 37. RA GEO/MAIN/2063 38. RA GEO/MAIN/2690 39. Conway, *British Isles and the War of American Independence* p. 15 40. Ibid. 41. RA GEO/MAIN/2075 42. Brooke, *King George III* p. 182 43. Boot, *Invisible Armies* p. 79 44. Ibid. p. 600 n. 58 45. RA GEO/MAIN/2211 46. Marston, *American Revolution* p. 20; Black, *Military Strategy* p. 98; Atwood, *Hessians* pp. 254–7 47. Lockwood, *To Begin the World Over Again* pp. 195–6 48. Atwood, *Hessians* p. 255 49. Ibid. pp. 22–3 50. Langford, 'Old Whigs, Old Tories' p. 113 51. Barrington, *Political Life of William Wildman, Viscount Barrington* p. 150 52. Ibid. p. 156 53. RA GEO/MAIN/2076 54. RA GEO/MAIN/2065 55. RA GEO/MAIN/2066 56. Hoock, *Scars of Independence* p. 77 57. Ferling, *Almost a Miracle* p. 113 58. O'Shaughnessy, *Men Who Lost America* p. 26 59. Liddle, '"Patriot King, or None"' p. 966 60. Ibid. p. 967 61. RA GEO/MAIN/2076 62. RA GEO/MAIN/2190 63. Keane, *Tom Paine* p. 105 64. Ditchfield, *George III* p. 110 65. RA GEO/MAIN/2179 66. Fryer, 'George III: His Political Character and Conduct' p. 70 67. ed. Cunningham, *Letters of Horace Walpole* VI p. 250 68. RA GEO/MAIN/2196–2198 ff. 2196–2196(2) 69. French, *First Year* p. 568 70. Sainsbury, *Disaffected Patriots* p. 100 71. Roberts, *Splendid Isolation* p. 7 72. Sainsbury, *Disaffected Patriots* p. 102 73. ed. Hall, *250 Royal Speeches* p. 9 74. Ibid. 75. Ibid. 76. Ibid. 77. Ibid. 78. Nelson, *Royalist Revolution* pp. 63–4 79. Ibid. p. 64 80. Ibid. 81. O'Shaughnessy, *Men Who Lost America* p. 25 82. Ferling, *John Adams* p. 142 83. RA GEO/MAIN/2217 84. RA GEO/MAIN/2214 85. RA GEO/MAIN/2216 86. ed. Billias, *Manuscripts of Captain Howard Vincente Knox* p. 256 87. Mackesy, *War for America* p. 51; O'Shaughnessy, *Men Who Lost America* pp. 173–5 88. Mackesy, *War for America* passim 89. Ward, *War of the Revolution* p. 878 90. Mackesy, *Coward of Minden* p. 251 91. Ibid. p. 252 92. Brown, 'Court Martial of Lord George Sackville' p. 317 93. Mackesy, *War for America* p. 23 94. Mackesy, *Coward of Minden* p. 255 95. Ibid. p. 256 96. Cumberland, *Character of the Late Lord Viscount Sackville* pp. 3–4, 9, 11 97. RA GEO/MAIN/2221 98. Baugh, 'British Naval Failure' p. 222 99. Valentine, *Lord George Germain* p. 115 100. Mackesy, *Coward of Minden* p. 252 101. Spector, *American Department* pp. 79, 85 102. Mackesy, *War for America* p. 23

13. The Declaration of Independence

1. eds. Boyd, *Papers of Thomas Jefferson* I p. 269 2. https://www.nationalgeographic.com/history/article/forgotten-first-emancipation-proclamation 3. ed. Ford, *Journals of the Continental Congress* III p. 410 4. ed. Adams, *Works of John Adams* II p. 507; Keane, *Tom Paine* p. 555 n. 52 5. John Adams to William Plumer, 28 March 1813, in ed. Adams, *Works of John Adams* X p. 20 6. Brooks's Club Betting Book 7. Mackesy, *War for America* p. 66 8. eds. Barnes and Owen, *Private Papers of John, Earl of Sandwich* III p. 26 9. Atkinson, *British are Coming* pp. 190–93 10. Chernow, *Washington* p. 214 11. Brookhiser, *Give Me Liberty* p. 72 12. Jordan, 'Familial Politics' p. 295 13. ed. Wood, *American Revolution* II p. 657 14. Nelson, *Thomas Paine* p. 14 15. ed. Wood, *American Revolution* II p. 647 16. Nelson, *Paine* p. 140 17. Ibid. p. 141 18. Keane, *Tom Paine* p. 143 19. Pryce-Jones, *Treason of the Heart* p. 6 20. ed. Wood, *American Revolution* II p. 660 21. Ibid. pp. 661–2 22. Ibid. p. 680 23. Pryce-Jones, *Treason of the Heart* p. 7 24. ed. Wood, *American Revolution* II p. 651 25. Ibid. p. 693 26. Ibid. p. 675 27. Keane, *Tom Paine* p. 71 28. Ibid. p. 95 29. Liddle, '"Patriot

King, or None"' p. 968   30. ed. Wood, *American Revolution* II p. 714   31. Ibid. p. 743   32. RA GEO/MAIN/2326   33. RA GEO/MAIN/2329   34. Black, *Military Strategy* p. 99   35. ed. Wood, *American Revolution* II p. 834   36. [Anonymous], *George the Third, his Court, and Family* I pp. 439–40   37. Black, *Military Strategy* p. 100   38. RA GEO/MAIN/2424   39. RA GEO/MAIN/2926–2928   40. Cannon, *Aristocratic Century* p. 177   41. Armitage, *Declaration of Independence* p. 33   42. Ferreiro, *Brothers at Arms* p. xvii   43. http://www.john-hancock-heritage.com/john-hancock-signature/   44. ed. Cappon, *Adams–Jefferson Letters* II p. 455   45. Lowry, *Case for Nationalism* p. 116   46. *Annual Register 1776* p. 264   47. Armitage, *Declaration of Independence* p. 162   48. *Annual Register 1776* p. 262   49. Armitage, *Declaration of Independence* p. 53   50. ed. Wood, *American Revolution* II p. 772   51. Ibid. p. 775   52. Ibid. p. 781   53. O'Shaughnessy, *Men Who Lost America* p. 28   54. Fisher, 'Twenty-Eight Charges against the King' p. 261   55. *Annual Register 1776* p. 262   56. Fisher, 'Twenty-Eight Charges against the King' p. 301   57. *Annual Register 1776* p. 262   58. Fisher, 'Twenty-Eight Charges against the King' p. 266   59. Ibid. p. 274   60. ed. Wood, *American Revolution* II p. 785   61. Ibid. p. 786   62. Fisher, 'Twenty-Eight Charges against the King' pp. 277–8   63. *Annual Register 1776* p. 262   64. ed. Wood, *American Revolution* II p. 788   65. *Annual Register 1776* p. 262   66. Fisher, 'Twenty-Eight Charges against the King' p. 282   67. ed. Wood, *American Revolution* II p. 789   68. Fisher, 'Twenty-Eight Charges against the King' p. 283   69. Shy, *Toward Lexington* p. 140   70. *Annual Register 1776* p. 263   71. ed. Wood, *American Revolution* II p. 789   72. Ibid. p. 790   73. Nelson, *Royalist Revolution* p. 65   74. ed. Wood, *American Revolution* II p. 791   75. *Annual Register 1776* p. 263   76. Fisher, 'Twenty-Eight Charges against the King' p. 288   77. ed. Wood, *American Revolution* II p. 793   78. *Annual Register 1776* p. 263   79. Fisher, 'Twenty-Eight Charges against the King' p. 293   80. Ibid. p. 294   81. Ibid. p. 295   82. ed. Wood, *American Revolution* II p. 796   83. *Annual Register 1776* p. 263   84. O'Connell, *Revolutionary* p. 125   85. Marston, *American Revolution* p. 20   86. *Annual Register 1776* p. 263   87. Fisher, 'Twenty-Eight Charges against the King' p. 297   88. Ibid. p. 298   89. *Annual Register 1776* p. 263   90. ed. Wood, *American Revolution* II p. 800   91. ed. Adams, *Works of John Adams* II p. 514; Fisher, 'Twenty-Eight Charges against the King' p. 299   92. Fisher, 'Twenty-Eight Charges against the King' p. 258   93. Bicheno, *Rebels and Redcoats* p. 11   94. Ibid.   95. ed. Wood, *American Revolution* II p. 781   96. Ibid. p. 866   97. Jordan, 'Familial Politics' p. 307   98. Atkinson, *British are Coming* p. 350   99. Lowry, *Case for Nationalism* p. 115   100. ed. Ford, *Correspondence and Journals of Samuel Blachley Webb* I p. 153   101. Brookhiser, *Alexander Hamilton* p. 27   102. Chernow, *Washington* p. 237   103. Atkinson, *British are Coming* p. 350   104. Hoock, *Scars of Independence* p. 78

14. The Road to Saratoga

1. *Gentleman's Magazine* No. 48, August 1778   2. ed. Sparks, *The Works of Benjamin Franklin* I p. 408   3. ed. Butterfield, *Letters of Benjamin Rush* II p. 1090   4. Hoock, *Scars of Independence* pp. 78, 336   5. Boot, *Invisible Armies* pp. 70–71   6. Ibid. p. 70   7. Wickwire and Wickwire, *Cornwallis* p. 174   8. RA GEO/MAIN/2372   9. Fortescue, *History of the British Army* III p. 180   10. Lewis E. Lehrman in *Greenwich Time* 3 July 2013   11. Chernow, *Washington* p. 239   12. Marston, *American Revolution* p. 42; Mitchell, *Decisive Battles of the American Revolution* pp. 53–8; Ferling, *Almost a Miracle* p. 134   13. ed. Bolton, *Letters of Hugh, Earl Percy* p. 71   14. BL Add MS 37833 f. 99   15. Conway, *British Isles and the War of American Independence* p. 14   16. Ferling, *Almost a Miracle* p. 567   17. Valentine, *Lord George Germain* p. 146; Historical Manuscripts Commission, *Report on the Manuscripts of Mrs Stopford-Sackville* II p. 9   18. Ferling, *Almost a Miracle* p. 567   19. Black, *War for America* p. 127   20. Ibid.   21. RA GEO/MAIN/2478   22. RA GEO/MAIN/2488   23. Ibid.   24. Ferling, *Almost a Miracle* p. 192   25. Mackesy, 'British Strategy in the War of American Independence' p. 549   26. Willcox, 'Too Many Cooks' p. 56   27. Ibid. p. 57   28. Mackesy, *War for America* p. 113   29. Mitchell, *Decisive Battles of the American Revolution* pp. 76–9; Ferling, *Almost a Miracle* p. 175   30. RA GEO/MAIN/2519   31. Black, *War for America* p. 127; Willcox, 'Too Many Cooks' p. 57 n. 2   32. Nickerson, *Turning Point of the Revolution* pp. 86–7   33. Willcox,

'Too Many Cooks' p. 61   34. Ibid.   35. BL Add 37833 f. 137   36. ed. Billias, *Manuscripts of Captain Howard Vincente Knox* p. 128   37. Black, *War for America* p. 127   38. Willcox, 'Too Many Cooks' p. 63   39. Black, *War for America* p. 128   40. Willcox, 'Too Many Cooks' p. 64   41. Ibid. p. 66   42. Ibid.   43. Black, *War for America* p. 126   44. Ibid.   45. Anderson, *Command of the Howe Brothers* pp. 256–7   46. Willcox, 'Too Many Cooks' p. 67   47. Black, *War for America* pp. 127–8   48. Isaacson, *Benjamin Franklin* p. 264   49. Goodwin, *Benjamin Franklin in London* pp. 270–71   50. Turberville, *House of Lords in the Eighteenth Century* p. 354   51. RA GEO/MAIN/2564   52. Ayling, *Fox* p. 58   53. ed. Wright, *Speeches of the Right Honourable Charles James Fox* I p. 79   54. RA GEO/MAIN/2551   55. Boot, *Invisible Armies* p. 69   56. Spring, *With Zeal* p. 14   57. Mitchell, *Decisive Battles of the American Revolution* pp. 94–6; Ferling, *Almost a Miracle* p. 215   58. eds. Doran and Steuart, *Last Journals of Horace Walpole* II p. 42   59. Willcox, 'Too Many Cooks' p. 68   60. Ibid. p. 69   61. Ibid. pp. 70–71   62. Ibid. p. 74   63. Ibid. p. 76   64. Mackesy, 'British Strategy in the War of American Independence' p. 549   65. Mitchell, *Decisive Battles of the American Revolution*, pp. 109–10; Ferling, *Almost a Miracle* pp. 247–50   66. BL Add MS 34414 ff. 309–10   67. Mackesy, *War for America* p. 153   68. RA GEO/MAIN/2622   69. RA GEO/MAIN/2624   70. Ferling, *Almost a Miracle* p. 232; Mitchell, *Decisive Battles of the American Revolution* pp. 124–8   71. ed. Billias, *Manuscripts of Captain Howard Vincente Knox* p. 139   72. Mitchell, *Decisive Battles of the American Revolution* pp. 128–31; Ferling, *Almost a Miracle*, pp. 237–8   73. ed. Billias, *Manuscripts of Captain Howard Vincente Knox* p. 139   74. Ibid.   75. Allen and Braisted, *Loyalist Corps* p. 11   76. Harvey, *Few Bloody Noses* p. 6   77. RA GEO/MAIN/2667   78. RA GEO/MAIN/2669   79. RA GEO/MAIN/2670   80. eds. Doran and Steuart, *Last Journals of Horace Walpole* II pp. 80–81   81. RA GEO/MAIN/2673   82. ed. Fortescue, *Correspondence* III p. 514   83. Ibid. p. 521   84. Clark, 'Responsibility for the Failure of the Burgoyne Campaign' p. 542   85. RA GEO/MAIN/2523–2524   86. Fonblanque, *Right Hon. John Burgoyne* pp. 486–7   87. Clark, 'Responsibility for the Failure of the Burgoyne Campaign' p. 543   88. ed. Le Marchant, *Horace Walpole: Memoirs of the Reign of George III* II p. 176, III p. 136, IV pp. 236–7   89. Roberts, *Splendid Isolation* p. 7   90. Syrett, *Royal Navy in American Waters* pp. 90–91   91. BL Add MS 37834 f. 3; Gruber, *Howe Brothers* p. 271   92. ed. Donne, *Correspondence of King George the Third with Lord North* II p. 84   93. O'Brien, *Great Melody* p. 209 n. 1

15. Global War

1. Brown, 'Court Martial of Lord George Sackville' p. 336   2. RA GEO/MAIN/2673   3. RA GEO/MAIN/2672   4. RA GEO/MAIN/2750   5. Ferling, *Almost a Miracle*   6. Mackesy, *War for America* pp. 512–13   7. Ibid. p. 513   8. Ferling, *Almost a Miracle* p. 565   9. RA GEO/MAIN/2674   10. Marston, *American Revolution* p. 19   11. RA GEO/MAIN/2736   12. RA GEO/MAIN/2737   13. RA GEO/MAIN/2750   14. RA GEO/MAIN/2747   15. Mackesy, *War for America* pp. 154–5   16. RA GEO/MAIN/2750   17. RA GEO/MAIN/2760   18. Mackesy, *War for America* p. 155   19. ed. Fortescue, *Correspondence* IV p. 22; RA GEO/MAIN/2764   20. RA GEO/MAIN/2769–2771   21. RA GEO/MAIN/2774   22. Ibid.   23. Ibid.   24. Ibid.   25. RA GEO/MAIN/2784   26. Mackesy, *War for America* p. 184   27. RA GEO/MAIN/2779   28. Ferling, *Almost a Miracle* p. 266   29. Boot, *Invisible Armies* p. 78   30. RA GEO/MAIN/2787   31. Hoock, *Scars of Independence* p. 243   32. RA GEO/MAIN/2818   33. Ibid.   34. RA GEO/MAIN/2823   35. RA GEO/MAIN/2824   36. RA GEO/MAIN/2822   37. RA GEO/MAIN/2829   38. Mackesy, *War for America* p. 17   39. RA GEO/MAIN/2533   40. Mackesy, *War for America* p. 172   41. Mackesy, 'British Strategy in the War of American Independence' p. 554   42. RA GEO/MAIN/2840–2841   43. RA GEO/MAIN/2842   44. RA GEO/MAIN/2843–2844   45. RA GEO/MAIN/2849   46. RA GEO/MAIN/2854   47. Ibid.   48. RA GEO/MAIN/2860   49. RA GEO/MAIN/2864   50. RA GEO/MAIN/2873   51. RA GEO/MAIN/2952–2954   52. *Parliamentary Register of the House of Lords* IX 356; Roberts, *Splendid Isolation* p. 8   53. Turberville, *House of Lords in the Eighteenth Century* p. 374   54. Ibid.   55. RA GEO/

MAIN/2895 56. ed. Aspinall, *Correspondence of George, Prince of Wales* I p. 25 57. Ibid. 58. Ayling, *George the Third* p. 176 59. Mackesy, *War for America* p. 199; RA GEO/ MAIN/2944–2945 60. RA GEO/MAIN/2947 61. RA GEO/MAIN/2949 62. Ibid. 63. Mackesy, 'British Strategy in the War of American Independence' pp. 555–6 64. Mackesy, *War for America* p. 203 65. Lock, *Edmund Burke* I p. 427 66. RA GEO/MAIN/2962 67. Churchill, *History of the English-Speaking Peoples* III p. 163 68. Ehrman, *Years of Acclaim* p. 65 69. Ibid. 70. RA GEO/MAIN/2973 71. RA GEO/MAIN/2974 72. RA GEO/ MAIN/2980 73. O'Shaughnessy, *Men Who Lost America* p. 160; Mackesy, *War for America* p. 238 74. Cook, *Long Fuse* p. 311 75. Ibid. p. 310 76. Ditchfield, *George III* pp. 126, 128 77. Fraser, *King and the Catholics* pp. 4–5 78. Ibid. p. 6 79. Ibid. 80. RA GEO/ MAIN/3003 81. Ibid.

16. 'If Others Will Not be Active, I Must Drive'

1. RA GEO/MAIN/3094 2. Donoughue, *British Politics and the American Revolution* p. 9 n. 2; Black, *War for America* pp. 160–61 3. Mackesy, *War for America* p. 188 4. RA GEO/ MAIN/3051 5. ed. Fortescue, *Correspondence* IV p. 74 6. Mitchell, *Decisive Battles of the American Revolution*, pp. 142–6; Ferling, *Almost a Miracle* pp. 303–6 7. Fortescue, *History of the British Army* III p. 257 8. Dull, *French Navy* p. 365 9. RA GEO/MAIN/3114 10. Conway, *War of American Independence* p. 158 11. RA GEO/MAIN/3034 12. RA GEO/ MAIN/3038 13. BL Add MS 37834 f. 5 14. eds. Sebag-Montefiore and Mordaunt Crook, *Brooks's* p. 184 15. *Annual Register 1778* p. 237 16. Conway, *British Isles and the War of American Independence* p. 295 n. 157 17. ed. Fortescue, *Correspondence* IV p. 418 18. Mackesy, *War for America* p. 24; BL Add MS 37834 f. 39 19. RA GEO/MAIN/3108–3110 ff. 3109, 3110 20. Ibid. f. 3109 21. RA GEO/MAIN/3112 22. RA GEO/MAIN/3116 23. RA GEO/MAIN/3115 24. RA GEO/MAIN/3116 25. Ibid. 26. RA GEO/MAIN/3160, 3161 27. eds. Doran and Steuart, *Last Journals of Horace Walpole* II p. 237 28. Ayling, *George the Third* p. 263 29. RA GEO/MAIN/3233 30. RA GEO/MAIN/3262 31. Mackesy, *War for America* p. 283 32. Rodger, *Command of the Ocean* p. 429 33. O'Shaughnessy, *Men Who Lost America* p. 160 34. ed. Billias, *Washington's Generals and Opponents* pp. 57–8 35. Brooks's Club Betting Book 36. RA GEO/MAIN/3404 37. Robson, *American Revolution* p. 83 38. RA GEO/MAIN/3372 39. Ibid.; RA GEO/ MAIN/3380 40. eds. Dupuy and Dupuy, *Collins Encyclopedia* p. 784; Russell, *Gibraltar Besieged* pp. 33, 123, 194, 207 41. RA GEO/MAIN/3386 42. eds. Barnes and Owen, *Private Papers of John, Earl of Sandwich* III p. 20 43. Ibid. 44. Mackesy, *War for America* p. 264 45. ed. Billias, *Manuscripts of Captain Howard Vincente Knox* p. 260 46. Ibid. 47. Ibid. 48. O'Shaughnessy, *Men Who Lost America* p. 83 49. Ibid. 50. ed. Billias, *Manuscripts of Captain Howard Vincente Knox* p. 261 51. RA GEO/MAIN/3400 52. RA GEO/ MAIN/3402 53. eds. Barnes and Owen, *Private Papers of John, Earl of Sandwich* III p. 26 54. RA GEO/MAIN/3402 55. Ibid. 56. Ibid. 57. Ibid. 58. Ibid. 59. RA GEO/ MAIN/3417 60. RA GEO/MAIN/3451 61. RA GEO/MAIN/3452 62. Mackesy, *War for America* p. 295 63. Rodger, *Command of the Ocean* p. 341 64. RA GEO/ MAIN/3449 65. Rodger, *Insatiable Earl* p. 260 66. Mackesy, *War for America* p. 290 67. Ibid. p. 293 68. Ibid. p. 294 69. Simms, *Three Victories and a Defeat* p. 629 70. RA GEO/ MAIN/3494, 3496, 3497, 3498, 3499, 3500, 3503–3504, 3505, 3508, 3510–3511 71. Rodger, *Insatiable Earl* p. 259 72. RA GEO/MAIN/3499 73. RA GEO/MAIN/3501 74. RA GEO/MAIN/3520 75. eds. Barnes and Owen, *Private Papers of John, Earl of Sandwich* III p. 144 76. ed. Fortescue, *Correspondence* IV p. 433 77. Mackesy, *War for America* p. 302 78. RA GEO/MAIN/3598 79. ed. Fortescue, *Correspondence* IV pp. 433–4 80. Mackesy, *War for America* pp. 307–8 81. BL Add MS 70990 f. 32 82. RA GEO/MAIN/ 3595–3596 f. 3595 83. RA GEO/MAIN/3607 84. Cobbett, *Parliamentary History* XIX cols. 1116–28 85. ed. Wheatley, *Historical and Posthumous Memoirs of Sir Nathaniel Wraxall* II p. 20 86. O'Brien, *Great Melody* pp. 209–10 87. See Mackesy, *War for America* p. 22 88. RA GEO/MAIN/3602–3603 f. 3603 89. Ibid. 90. RA GEO/MAIN/3608 91. RA GEO/

MAIN/3613   92. RA GEO/MAIN/3619   93. O'Shaughnessy, *Men Who Lost America*
p. 33   94. RA GEO/MAIN/3620   95. RA GEO/MAIN/3621   96. RA GEO/MAIN/
3624   97. RA GEO/MAIN/3624, 3627   98. RA GEO/MAIN/3637   99. eds. Doran and
Steuart, *Last Journals of Horace Walpole* II p. 305   100. ed. Billias, *Manuscripts of Captain
Howard Vincente Knox* p. 267   101. Brooks's Club Betting Book   102. Christie, *Myth and
Reality* p. 300   103. Brooke, *King George III* p. 189   104. O'Brien, *Great Melody* p. 212   105.
Cobbett, *Parliamentary History* XXI p. 72   106. RA GEO/MAIN/3751   107. RA GEO/
MAIN/3720   108. RA GEO/MAIN/3654   109. Brewer, *Sinews of Power* p. 177   110.
Mackesy, 'British Strategy in the War of American Independence' p. 551   111. Mitchell, *Decisive
Battles of the American Revolution* p. 159; Ferling, *Almost a Miracle* p. 422   112. Rodger,
Insatiable Earl p. 278

17. Disaster at Yorktown

1. eds. Barnes and Owen, *Private Papers of John, Earl of Sandwich* III p. 243   2. Mackesy, *War
for America* p. 513   3. RA GEO/MAIN/3738   4. Namier, *Personalities and Powers* p. 76   5.
RA GEO/MAIN/3762   6. RA GEO/MAIN/3763   7. RA GEO/MAIN/3769   8. Foord, 'Waning
of "The Influence of the Crown"' p. 484   9. Mackesy, *War for America* p. 360   10. Ibid.   11.
RA GEO/MAIN/3784   12. Leonard and Garnett, *Titans* pp. 65–6   13. Black, *George III:
America's Last King* p. 244   14. Castro, *Gordon Riots* p. 18   15. eds. Haywood and Seed,
Gordon Riots p. 251   16. Hibbert, *King Mob* p. 29   17. Conway, *British Isles and the War of
American Independence* p. 252   18. Turner, *Pitt the Younger* p. 8   19. Dickens, *Barnaby Rudge*
ch. 49 p. 355   20. ed. Fortescue, *Correspondence* V p. 71   21. ed. Copeland et al., *Burke Cor-
respondence* IV pp. 122–3   22. RA GEO/MAIN/3830   23. Jeaffreson, *Pleasantries of English
Courts and Lawyers* pp. 77–84   24. RA GEO/MAIN/3835   25. eds. Weinreb and Hibbert,
London Encyclopaedia p. 325   26. Williamson, *Wilkes* p. 216   27. Mackesy, *War for America*
p. 361   28. Twiss, *Lord Chancellor Eldon* I pp. 293–4   29. Hibbert, *King Mob* p. 91; Castro,
Gordon Riots p. 114   30. Mackesy, *War for America* p. 361 n. 1   31. Ibid. p. 361   32. *General
Evening Post* 8–10 June 1780   33. Hibbert, *King Mob* p. 92   34. RA GEO/MAIN/3837   35.
RA GEO/MAIN/3836   36. ed. Romilly, *Romilly Memoirs* I p. 125   37. ed. Croker, *Life of
Samuel Johnson by James Boswell* VII p. 327   38. BL Add MS 38564 f. 17   39. eds. Weinreb
and Hibbert, *London Encyclopaedia* p. 325   40. Brumwell, *Turncoat* p. 230   41. British
Museum Print 5680   42. eds. Heywood and Seed, *Gordon Riots* p. 158   43. Hibbert, *King
Mob* p. 91 n. 1   44. ed. Croker, *Life of Samuel Johnson by James Boswell* VII p. 329   45. Castro,
Gordon Riots p. 115   46. ed. Croker, *Life of Samuel Johnson by James Boswell* VII p. 329   47.
Hibbert, *King Mob* p. 91   48. O'Shaughnessy, *Men Who Lost America* p. 40   49. Ibid. p.
38   50. RA GEO/ADD/26/2   51. Christie, *End of North's Ministry* p. 34   52. Namier and
Brooke, *History of Parliament* I p. 211   53. ed. Wheatley, *Historical and Posthumous Memoirs
of Sir Nathaniel Wraxall* V p. 161   54. Conway, *British Isles and the War of American Independ-
ence* p. 306   55. Ibid. p. 306 n. 215   56. eds. Ilchester and Stavordale, *Life and Letters of Lady
Sarah Lennox* p. 317   57. Christie, 'George III and the Debt on Lord North's Election Account'
p. 715   58. Ayling, *George the Third* p. 220   59. Ziegler, *King William IV* pp. 12–13   60. ed.
Aspinall, *Correspondence of George, Prince of Wales* I p. 33   61. Ibid. pp. 33–4   62. Ibid. p.
34   63. Ibid. p. 35   64. Brooke, *King George III* p. 244   65. RA GEO/MAIN/4290   66.
Brooke, *King George III* p. 245   67. ed. Aspinall, *Correspondence of George, Prince of Wales* I
p. 73   68. Brooke, *King George III* p. 246   69. Ferling, *Almost a Miracle* pp. 439–40; Mitchell,
Decisive Battles of the American Revolution, pp. 164–6   70. Brumwell, *Turncoat* p. 321   71.
Ibid. p. 329   72. ed. Fitzpatrick, *Writings of George Washington* XXI p. 55   73. RA GEO/
MAIN/3972   74. Ibid.   75. Roberts, *Splendid Isolation* pp. 4–7   76. Mitchell, *Decisive Battles
of the American Revolution* pp. 175–8; Ferling, *Almost a Miracle* p. 487   77. Mackesy, 'British
Strategy in the War of American Independence' p. 539   78. Ehrman, *Years of Acclaim* p. 52   79.
Linda Colley in *The Times* 30 May 1996   80. Mitchell, *Decisive Battles of the American Revolu-
tion* p. 180   81. Ferling, *Almost a Miracle* p. 499   82. ed. Ross, *Cornwallis Correspondence* I
p. 80   83. Harvey, *Few Bloody Noses* p. 7   84. Willcox, 'British Road to Yorktown' p. 35;

Ferling, *Almost a Miracle* p. 568   85. Boot, *Invisible Armies* p. 79   86. Willcox, 'British Road to Yorktown' p. 4   87. Mackesy, 'British Strategy in the War of American Independence' p. 556   88. ed. Bladon, *Diaries of Robert Fulke Greville* p. 34   89. Ibid. p. 40   90. Ibid. pp. 44–5   91. Ibid. p. 46   92. Ibid.   93. Ibid.   94. Clark, *From Restoration to Reform* p. 238   95. Mackesy, 'British Strategy in the War of American Independence' p. 557   96. Ferling, *Almost a Miracle* pp. 527–8   97. https://www.rct.uk/collection/georgian-papers-programme/de-bude-papers; Ambuske, 'Admiral and the Aide-de-Camp' passim   98. Mitchell, *Decisive Battles of the American Revolution* p. 198; Ferling, *Almost a Miracle* pp. 529–37   99. Mitchell, *Decisive Battles of the American Revolution* p. 205   100. Ferling, *Almost a Miracle* p. 541   101. Brooke, *King George III* p. 247   102. Ibid.

18. 'The Torrent is Too Strong'

1. Boustead, *Lone Monarch* p. 286   2. RA GEO/MAIN/4339   3. ed. Wheatley, *Historical and Posthumous Memoirs of Sir Nathaniel Wraxall* II p. 138   4. Ibid. p. 139   5. Ibid. p. 140   6. Ibid. p. 142   7. Ibid.   8. ed. Hall, *250 Royal Speeches* p. 12   9. Keane, *Tom Paine* p. 223   10. Cobbett, *Parliamentary History* XXII p. 705   11. Simms, *Three Victories and a Defeat* p. 662   12. Ferling, *Almost a Miracle* p. 542   13. Mackesy, *War for America* p. 460   14. Ferling, *Almost a Miracle* p. 542   15. O'Shaughnessy, *Men Who Lost America* p. 200   16. RA GEO/MAIN/4350   17. Ibid.   18. RA GEO/MAIN/4563   19. https://www.rct.uk/collection/734069   20. Black, *Military Strategy* p. 102   21. Mackesy, *War for America* p. 462   22. Rodger, *Command of the Ocean* p. 332   23. RA GEO/MAIN/4362   24. Boot, *Invisible Armies* p. 75   25. Lutnick, *American Revolution and the British Press* p. 59   26. ed. Wheatley, *Historical and Posthumous Memoirs of Sir Nathaniel Wraxall* II p. 160   27. Brooks's Club Betting Book   28. *Parliamentary Register* V p. 118.   29. RA GEO/MAIN/4372   30. RA GEO/MAIN/4377   31. Christie, *End of North's Ministry* p. 274   32. ed. Billias, *Manuscripts of Captain Howard Vincente Knox* p. 276   33. RA GEO/MAIN/4402   34. ed. Billias, *Manuscripts of Captain Howard Vincente Knox* p. 276   35. Ferling, *Almost a Miracle* p. 543   36. RA GEO/MAIN/4406   37. RA GEO/MAIN/4409–4410   38. Valentine, *Lord North* II p. 292   39. RA GEO/MAIN/4409–4410   40. eds. Doran and Steuart, *Last Journals of Horace Walpole* II p. 396   41. ed. Wheatley, *Historical and Posthumous Memoirs of Sir Nathaniel Wraxall* II p. 177   42. O'Shaughnessy, *Men Who Lost America* p. 202   43. Lowe, 'Peerage Creations and Politics' p. 597   44. O'Shaughnessy, *Men Who Lost America* p. 202   45. Valentine, *Lord George Germain* p. 457   46. RA GEO/MAIN/4478   47. Mackesy, *War for America* p. 468   48. RA GEO/MAIN/4479   49. Ibid.   50. RA GEO/MAIN/4480   51. RA GEO/MAIN/4482   52. Turner, *Pitt the Younger* pp. 38–9   53. RA GEO/MAIN/4492   54. RA GEO/MAIN/4502   55. RA GEO/MAIN/4512   56. RA GEO/MAIN/4555   57. RA GEO/MAIN/4521–4522   58. RA GEO/MAIN/4515–4516   59. Ibid.   60. RA GEO/MAIN/4518   61. ed. Donne, *Correspondence of King George the Third with Lord North* II p. 415   62. Ibid. p. 416   63. Thomas, *Lord North* p. 132   64. eds. Doran and Steuart, *Last Journals of Horace Walpole* I p. 221   65. ed. Wheatley, *Historical and Posthumous Memoirs of Sir Nathaniel Wraxall* II p. 242   66. Ferling, *Almost a Miracle* p. 545   67. ed. Wheatley, *Historical and Posthumous Memoirs of Sir Nathaniel Wraxall* II p. 247; Valentine, *Lord North* II p. 316   68. ed. Russell, *Memorials and Correspondence of Charles James Fox* I p. 295   69. RA GEO/MAIN/4635   70. RA GEO/MAIN/4654   71. Christie, 'George III and the Debt on Lord North's Election Account' p. 718   72. RA GEO/MAIN/4654   73. Ibid.   74. Ibid.   75. RA GEO/MAIN/2624   76. RA GEO/MAIN/4650–4651   77. RA GEO/MAIN/4641–4642   78. ed. Donne, *Correspondence of King George the Third with Lord North* II p. 427   79. ed. Fortescue, *Correspondence* VI p. 27   80. RA GEO/MAIN/4756   81. Christie, *Myth and Reality* p. 139   82. ed. Browning, *Political Memoranda of Francis, Fifth Duke of Leeds* p. 66   83. RA GEO/MAIN/4562   84. Churchill, *History of the English-Speaking Peoples* III p. 174   85. RA GEO/MAIN/4562   86. RA GEO/MAIN/4553   87. Lock, *Edmund Burke* I pp. 508–9   88. RA GEO/MAIN/4583   89. RA GEO/MAIN/4599   90. RA GEO/MAIN/4605   91. Brooke, *King George III* p. 232   92. RA

GEO/MAIN/4602   93. O'Connell, *Revolutionary* p. 289   94. Chernow, *Washington* p. 425   95. Ibid.   96. ed. Fitzpatrick, *Writings of George Washington* XXIV p. 91   97. RA GEO/MAIN/4764   98. RA GEO/MAIN/4692   99. Ibid.   100. eds. Giunta et al., *Emerging Nation* III p. iv   101. ed. Russell, *Memorials and Correspondence of Charles James Fox* I p. 316   102. ed. Wheatley, *Historical and Posthumous Memoirs of Sir Nathaniel Wraxall* II p. 287   103. Keir, 'Economical Reform' pp. 370–71   104. RA GEO/MAIN/4621–4622   105. RA GEO/MAIN/2591   106. RA GEO/MAIN/2360   107. ed. Sedgwick, *Letters from George III to Lord Bute* p. 231   108. RA GEO/MAIN/4774   109. Ibid.   110. RA GEO/MAIN/4781   111. RA GEO/MAIN/4701–4703 f. 4701   112. RA GEO/MAIN/4704   113. RA GEO/MAIN/4775   114. RA GEO/MAIN/4831–4832

19. 'America is Lost!'

1. Brown, 'Court Martial of Lord George Sackville' p. 336   2. RA GEO/MAIN/4831–4832 f. 4832   3. RA GEO/MAIN/4836   4. ed. Croker, *Life of Samuel Johnson by James Boswell* VIII p. 163   5. Ayling, *George the Third* p. 296   6. eds. Berman and Gibson, *Lantern of History* p. 74 n. 26   7. Christie, *Myth and Reality* p. 135   8. Ibid. p. 136   9. Ibid. p. 137   10. RA GEO/MAIN/4859   11. RA GEO/MAIN/4910   12. Christie, 'George III and the Debt on Lord North's Election Account' p. 715   13. RA GEO/ADD/15/443a–b   14. https://geor gianpapers.com/2018/11/23/in-gods-hands-inoculating-the-royal-children-against-smallpox/#_ endref1   15. Esfandiary, 'In God's Hands' passim   16. RA GEO/ADD/15/8157   17. ed. Fortescue, *Correspondence* VI p. 126   18. RA GEO/MAIN/5045   19. ed. Fortescue, *Correspondence* VI p. 154   20. RA GEO/MAIN/5058   21. RA GEO/MAIN/5080   22. RA GEO/MAIN/5090   23. RA GEO/MAIN/5101   24. Ibid.   25. Cobbett, *Parliamentary History* XXIII pp. 203–7   26. ed. Hall, *250 Royal Speeches* p. 13; eds. Lustig and Pottle, *Boswell: The Applause of the Jury* p. 34 n. 8   27. O'Shaughnessy, *Men Who Lost America* p. 43; Cook, *Long Fuse* p. 374   28. ed. Hall, *250 Royal Speeches* p. 13   29. Ibid.   30. eds. Doran and Steuart, *Last Journals of Horace Walpole* II p. 476   31. ed. Wheatley, *Historical and Posthumous Memoirs of Sir Nathaniel Wraxall* II p. 394   32. Ibid. p. 395   33. Ibid.   34. Cook, *Long Fuse* p. 374; O'Brien, *Great Melody* p. 426   35. eds. Lustig and Pottle, *Boswell: The Applause of the Jury* p. 34   36. Blanning, '"That Horrid Electorate"' p. 314   37. Grant, *John Adams* p. 7   38. Clark, *From Restoration to Reform* p. 242   39. RA GEO/ADD/32/ 2010–2011   40. https://www.rct.uk/collection/georgian-papers-programme/america-is-lost   41. https://georgianpapers.com/wp-content/uploads/2017/01/RA-GEO_ADD_32_2010_ Raw-Transcripton-1.pdf   42. Holly, '"Long a Dispute amongst Antiquarians"' passim   43. ed. Fortescue, *Correspondence* VI p. 222   44. Turner, *Pitt the Younger* p. 43   45. ed. Russell, *Memorials and Correspondence of Charles James Fox* II p. 38   46. Brooke, *King George III* p. 237   47. ed. Fortescue, *Correspondence* VI p. 243   48. ed. Cobbett, *Parliamentary Record* IX p. 349; Ehrman, *Years of Acclaim* p. 103   49. RA GEO/MAIN/5220   50. *Parliamentary Register* XV p. 536   51. RA GEO/MAIN/5220   52. RA GEO/MAIN/5225   53. RA GEO/MAIN/5229   54. Ibid.   55. RA GEO/MAIN/5238   56. Norris, *Shelburne and Reform* pp. 266–70   57. Lowe, 'Peerage Creations and Politics' p. 604   58. RA GEO/ MAIN/5269   59. RA GEO/MAIN/5272   60. RA GEO/MAIN/5273   61. Fitzmaurice, *Shelburne* II p. 256   62. RA GEO/MAIN/5277   63. Jupp, *Lord Grenville* p. 33   64. BL Fortescue MSS 'Commentaries' ch. 1 pp. 58–9   65. ed. Buckingham, *Court and Cabinets* I p. 189   66. Ibid. p. 190   67. Ibid. p. 192   68. Ibid. p. 193   69. RA GEO/MAIN/5379–5380 f. 5380   70. RA GEO/MAIN/5355–5356   71. RA GEO/MAIN/5359   72. RA GEO/ MAIN/5369   73. https://georgianpapers.com/2017/01/22/abdication-speech-george-iii/; RA GEO/MAIN/5367   74. ed. Fortescue, *Correspondence* VI p. 315   75. Ibid.   76. RA GEO/ MAIN/5367   77. Ibid.   78. Ibid.   79. RA GEO/MAIN/5379–5380 f. 5380(2)   80. RA GEO/MAIN/5386   81. BM Add MS 34523 ff. 371–3   82. RA GEO/MAIN/5386   83. Rodger, *Insatiable Earl* p. 305   84. ed. Russell, *Memorials and Correspondence of Charles James Fox* II p. 28   85. RA GEO/MAIN/5385   86. RA GEO/MAIN/519   87. Lowe, 'Peerage Creations and Politics' p. 606   88. Keir, 'Economical Reform' pp. 372–3   89. Downs,

'George III and the Royal Coup of 1783' p. 65   90. Lowe, 'Peerage Creations and Politics' p. 606   91. RA GEO/MAIN/5432   92. Black, *George III: Madness and Majesty* p. 55   93. RA GEO/MAIN/5442   94. Chernow, *Washington* p. 440   95. Ibid. p. 441   96. ed. Fitzpatrick, *Writings of George Washington* XXVI p. 404   97. Chernow, *Washington* p. 442   98. Hadlow, *A Royal Experiment* p. 294; https://georgianpapers.com/2018/11/23/in-gods-hands-inoculating-the-royal-children-against-smallpox/#_endref1   99. Brooke, *King George III* p. 265   100. Ibid.   101. RA GEO/MAIN/5463   102. TNA Chatham Papers 30/8 Vol. 12 f. 297   103. Brooke, *King George III* p. 247   104. Plumb, *First Four Georges* p. 137   105. RA GEO/MAIN/5514   106. ed. Fortescue, *Correspondence* VI p. xii   107. RA GEO/MAIN/5520   108. Ibid.   109. RA GEO/MAIN/5525   110. Brooke, *King George III* p. 249   111. eds. Heard and Jones, *George IV: Art and Spectacle* ch. 5   112. Ibid. p. 80   113. RA GEO/ADD/32/818–819   114. Tillyard, 'George IV's Wretched Reputation' p. 38   115. Ambrose, *Prinny and his Pals* p. 95   116. RA GEO/MAIN/5567   117. RA GEO/MAIN/5569   118. ed. Russell, *Memorials and Correspondence of Charles James Fox* II pp. 140–41   119. Historical Manuscripts Commission, *Report on the Manuscripts of J. B. Fortescue Preserved at Dropmore* I p. 215; Rose, *William Pitt and National Revival* p. 134   120. Historical Manuscripts Commission, *Report on the Manuscripts of J. B. Fortescue Preserved at Dropmore* I p. 216; Rose, *William Pitt and National Revival* p. 135   121. Turner, *Pitt the Younger* p. 278

20. 'On the Edge of a Precipice'

1. Plumb, *First Four Georges* p. 141   2. Harvey, *Few Bloody Noses* p. 7   3. RA GEO/MAIN/5615   4. RA GEO/MAIN/5617   5. Taylor, *American Revolutions* p. 326   6. ed. Greig, *Farington Diary* I p. 278; Ellis, *His Excellency* p. 139   7. Chernow, *Washington* p. 757   8. *Annual Register 1776* p. 264   9. ed. Hall, *250 Royal Speeches* p. 14   10. Downs, 'George III and the Royal Coup of 1783' p. 67   11. Christie, *Myth and Reality* p. 169   12. Connell, '"Potent Spirit"' p. 292   13. Bernstein, *Dawning of the Raj* p. 161   14. BL Add MS 38567 f. 166   15. Kelly, 'British Politics 1783–4' p. 63   16. BL Add MS 37816 f. 138   17. Kelly, 'British Politics 1783–4' p. 63   18. Ditchfield, *George III* p. 115   19. Brooke, *King George III* p. 251   20. RA GEO/MAIN/3355   21. Kelly, 'British Politics 1783–4' p. 64   22. Ibid. p. 66   23. Wilbur, *East India Company* p. 295   24. Buckingham, *Court and Cabinets* I pp. 288–9   25. Brooke, *King George III* p. 252   26. O'Brien, *Great Melody* pp. 330–31; Laprade, 'Public Opinion and the General Election of 1784' p. 226   27. O'Brien, *Great Melody* p. 331   28. Ibid. p. 332   29. Connell, '"Potent Spirit"' p. 292   30. Baker, *Life in Caricature* p. 79   31. RA GEO/MAIN/361   32. Cannon, *Aristocratic Century* p. 5; *Quarterly Review 1830* p. 311   33. Boustead, *Lone Monarch*, frontispiece   34. Connell, '"Potent Spirit"' p. 304   35. RA GEO/MAIN/5673   36. BL Northington Papers Add MS 38717 f. 142   37. RA GEO/MAIN/5675   38. BL Add MS 47570 f. 156   39. Black, *George III: America's Last King* pp. 257–8   40. Turner, *Pitt the Younger* p. 50   41. Ibid.   42. eds. Lustig and Pottle, *Boswell: The Applause of the Jury* p. 172   43. RA GEO/MAIN/5683   44. RA GEO/MAIN/5685   45. Hague, *William Pitt the Younger* p. 146   46. Churchill, *History of the English-Speaking Peoples* III p. 197   47. Kelly, 'Pitt–Temple Administration' p. 160   48. ed. Russell, *Memorials and Correspondence of Charles James Fox* II p. 221   49. Brooke, *King George III* p. 255   50. Kelly, 'Pitt–Temple Administration' p. 161   51. See Ehrman, *Years of Acclaim* p. 130; ed. Aspinall, *Later Correspondence* I pp. xxvii–xxviii; Smith, 'Earl Temple's Resignation' pp. 91–7; Turner, *Pitt the Younger* pp. 51–2; Hague, *William Pitt the Younger* p. 150   52. Kelly, 'Pitt–Temple Administration' p. 157   53. ed. Aspinall, *Later Correspondence* I p. xxvii   54. Kelly, 'Pitt–Temple Administration' p. 160   55. Ibid.   56. Stanhope, *Life of Pitt* I Appendix p. iii   57. Ayling, *George the Third* p. 307   58. Ditchfield, *George III* p. 73   59. RA GEO/MAIN/5709   60. Cannon, *Fox–North Coalition* p. 156   61. ed. Lewis, *Yale Edition of the Correspondence of Horace Walpole* XXXIII p. 430   62. Stanhope, *Life of Pitt* I Appendix p. iv   63. RA GEO/MAIN/3233   64. Brooke, *King George III* p. 256   65. Kelly, 'British Politics 1783–4' p. 72   66. BL Add MS 70597   67. Colley, 'Apotheosis of

George III' p. 104   68. Stanhope, *Life of Pitt* I Appendix pp. ix–x   69. Hobhouse, *Fox* p. 164   70. Kelly, 'British Politics 1783–4' p. 73   71. Brooke, *King George III* p. 259   72. Turner, *Pitt the Younger* p. 57   73. Laprade, 'Public Opinion and the General Election of 1784' p. 227   74. Black, *George III: America's Last King* p. 267   75. Stanhope, *Life of Pitt* I Appendix p. xii   76. Ibid.   77. Ayling, *Fox* pp. 155–6   78. See Cannon, *Fox–North Coalition* p. xiii; Christie, 'George III and the Historians' p. 221   79. BL Fortescue MSS 'Commentaries' ch. 2 pp. 42–3   80. Whiteley, *Lord North* p. 218   81. Downs, 'George III and the Royal Coup of 1783' p. 71 n. 58   82. Lexden in *Conservative History Magazine* Vol. II Issue 7 Autumn 2019 p. 71   83. John Cannon in *ODNB* George III p. 30

21. Alliance with Pitt

1. BL Add MS 58861 f. 116   2. Mackerness, *A Social History of English Music* p. 127   3. Rodger, *Insatiable Earl* p. 312   4. Ibid. p. 313   5. Ibid.   6. *Monthly Review* No. 159 1842 p. 29   7. RA GEO/ADD/32/2428   8. Head, 'Remarks on the Preface' passim   9. RA GEO/MAIN/5842   10. Davies, *Influence of George III on the Development of the Constitution* p. 45; Hunt, *Political History of England* p. 229; Melville, *Farmer George* II p. 258   11. May, *Constitutional History of England* I p. 88   12. Woods, *History of the Tory Party* p. 306   13. Wrong, *History of England* p. 189   14. O'Brien, *Great Melody* p. 455   15. Barnes, *George III and William Pitt* p. 476 and Conclusion   16. Stanhope, *Life of Pitt* I Appendix p. xiii   17. ed. Aspinall, *Correspondence of George, Prince of Wales* I p. 148   18. RA GEO/MAIN/16462   19. RA GEO/MAIN/16467   20. Brooke, *King George III* p. 319   21. RA GEO/MAIN/16462   22. RA GEO/MAIN/5879   23. Brooke, *King George III* p. 320   24. Christie, 'George III and the Debt on Lord North's Election Account' p. 723   25. Ibid.   26. RA GEO/MAIN/5905   27. eds. Lustig and Pottle, *Boswell: The Applause of the Jury* p. 297   28. Ibid.   29. Ibid. p. 299   30. Grant, *John Adams* p. 9   31. McCullough, *John Adams* p. 335   32. eds. Giunta and Hartgrove, *Emerging Nation* II p. 642   33. Ibid. pp. 647–8   34. Ibid.   35. Black, *George III: America's Last King* p. 341; ed. Adams, *Works of John Adams* VIII pp. 255–7; ed. Cappon, *Adams–Jefferson Letters* II p. 27   36. eds. Giunta and Hartgrove, *Emerging Nation* II p. 648   37. Jesse, *Memoirs of the Life and Reign of King George III* II pp. 51–8   38. eds. Giunta and Hartgrove, *Emerging Nation* III p. 731   39. BL Add MS 35531 f. 39   40. RA GEO/MAIN/5849   41. BL Keith Papers Add MS 35532 f. 353   42. Blanning, '"That Horrid Electorate"' p. 311   43. ed. Sedgwick, *Letters from George III to Lord Bute* p. 28   44. Watkin, *Architect King* p. 19   45. Blanning, '"That Horrid Electorate"' p. 313   46. BL Egerton Papers MS 3498 ff. 211, 245   47. Blanning, '"That Horrid Electorate"' pp. 331–3   48. RA GEO/MAIN/6061   49. RA GEO/MAIN/6062   50. Farr, *World of Fanny Burney* pp. 100–101   51. eds. Barrett and Dobson, *Diary and Letters of Madame d'Arblay* II p. 317   52. Ibid. p. 318   53. Ibid. p. 321   54. Ibid. p. 323   55. Ibid. p. 337   56. Ibid. p. 336   57. Ibid. pp. 337–8   58. Ibid. p. 338   59. Ibid.   60. Ibid. p. 342   61. Ibid.   62. Ibid. p. 344   63. ed. Boyd, *Papers of Thomas Jefferson* IX pp. 369–97, 445   64. ed. Ford, *Autobiography of Thomas Jefferson* p. 94   65. ed. Adams, *Works of John Adams* I p. 420   66. Ritcheson, 'Fragile Memory' passim; see also https://www.monticello.org/site/research-and-collections/london#footnoteref8_2zel7qu   67. Ritcheson, 'Fragile Memory' p. 8   68. Chernow, *Washington* p. 657   69. eds. Barrett and Dobson, *Diary and Letters of Madame d'Arblay* II p. 415   70. Ibid. p. 416   71. Ibid.   72. Ibid.   73. Ibid. p. 414   74. Ibid. p. 415   75. Ibid. p. 416   76. Ibid. p. 417   77. Black, *Hanoverians* p. 139   78. eds. Barrett and Dobson, *Diary and Letters of Madame d'Arblay* II p. 435   79. Ibid. p. 416   80. ed. Auckland, *Journal and Correspondence of Lord Auckland* I p. 152   81. eds. Barrett and Dobson, *Diary and Letters of Madame d'Arblay* II p. 466   82. ed. Auckland, *Journal and Correspondence of Lord Auckland* I p. 167   83. RA GEO/MAIN/6025   84. Fisher, '"Farmer George"?' passim   85. Ayling, *George the Third* p. 207   86. Edwards, *Fanny Burney* p. 105   87. ed. Betham-Edwards, *Autobiography of Arthur Young* p. 322   88. Ibid. p. 323   89. Carter, *His Majesty's Spanish Flock* p. 115   90. ed. Bladon, *Diaries of Robert Fulke Greville* pp. 71–3   91. Rempel, 'Carnal Satire and the Constitutional King' p. 4   92. Fisher '"Farmer George"?' passim; https://www.

historyextra.com/period/georgian/george-iii-food-german-cabbage-tastes-how-influence-british-cuisine/　93. ed. Wright, *Speeches of the Right Honourable Charles James Fox* III p. 325　94. eds. Barrett and Dobson, *Diary and Letters of Madame d'Arblay* III p. 164　95. Brooke, *King George III* p. 320–21　96. ed. Aspinall, *Correspondence of George, Prince of Wales* I p. 225　97. Donald, *Age of Caricature* p. 68　98. Brooke, *George III* p. 321　99. Fulford, *George the Fourth* p. 37　100. *London Chronicle* 24–26 May 1787 p. 497　101. Rempel, 'Carnal Satire and the Constitutional King' p. 6　102. ed. Hibbert, *Louis Simond* p. 28　103. Jones, *Cartoon History of the Monarchy* p. 40　104. Donald, *Age of Caricature* p. 99　105. Black, *George III: America's Last King* p. 189　106. Clark, *Scandal* p. 94　107. Wilbur, *East India Company* p. 298; Ditchfield, *George III* p. 135　108. Stanhope, *Life of Pitt* I Appendix pp. xxii–xxiii　109. Pryce-Jones, *Treason of the Heart* p. 8　110. Navy Records Society, *Publications of the Navy Records Society* LXV p. 348.　111. Black, *George III: America's Last King* p. 332　112. Lockwood, *To Begin the World Over Again* pp. 330–31　113. Black, *George III: America's Last King* p. 332　114. See Ehrman, *Years of Acclaim* p. 395 n. 3　115. Montesquieu, *Spirit of the Laws* p. 234　116. RA GEO/ADD/32/873　117. RA GEO/MAIN/6450　118. Brooke, *George III* p. 355　119. Wilberforce, *Life of William Wilberforce* p. 103　120. Ibid.　121. Black, *Slavery* p. 159　122. ed. Malmesbury, *Diaries and Correspondence of James Harris* II p. 464　123. Black, *Slavery* p. 105　124. Ibid. p. 160　125. Bullion, 'Prince's Mentor' p. 54　126. Stanhope, *Life of Pitt* I p. 483　127. Ibid. II Appendix p. 1　128. Peters, 'Royal Medical Entourages' p. 50　129. eds. Barrett and Dobson, *Diary and Letters of Madame d'Arblay* IV p. 1　130. Ayling, *George the Third* pp. 329–32　131. eds. Barrett and Dobson, *Diary and Letters of Madame d'Arblay* IV p. 11　132. ed. Auckland, *Journal and Correspondence of Lord Auckland* II p. 236　133. ed. Bladon, *Diaries of Robert Fulke Greville* p. vi　134. Brooke, *George III* p. 323　135. ed. Bladon, *Diaries of Robert Fulke Greville* p. 79　136. Peters, 'Royal Medical Entourages' p. 50　137. Ibid. p. 65

22. The King's Malady

1. eds. Barrett and Dobson, *Diary and Letters of Madame d'Arblay* IV p. 214　2. Brooke, *George III* p. 324　3. eds. Barrett and Dobson, *Diary and Letters of Madame d'Arblay* IV p. 120　4. Sinclair-Stevenson, *Blood Royal* p. 131　5. Brooke, *George III* pp. 324–5　6. Wright, *George III* p. 325　7. eds. Barrett and Dobson, *Diary and Letters of Madame d'Arblay* IV p. 122　8. Ibid.　9. Ibid. p. 123　10. Davenport, *Faithful Handmaid* p. 121　11. Ayling, *George the Third* p. 334 n. 1　12. eds. Barrett and Dobson, *Diary and Letters of Madame d'Arblay* IV p. 121　13. Ibid.　14. Ibid. p. 123　15. Ibid. p. 125　16. Ibid. p. 126　17. Ibid. pp. 126–7　18. Macalpine and Hunter, *George III and the Mad-Business* p. 25　19. eds. Barrett and Dobson, *Diary and Letters of Madame d'Arblay* IV p. 129　20. Ibid. p. 130　21. Ibid. p. 131　22. Ibid.　23. ed. Harcourt, *Harcourt Papers* IV pp. 21–3　24. RL RCIN 1047014 p. 4　25. eds. Barrett and Dobson, *Diary and Letters of Madame d'Arblay* IV p. 133　26. Davenport, *Faithful Handmaid* p. 22 n. 11　27. eds. Barrett and Dobson, *Diary and Letters of Madame d'Arblay* IV p. 140　28. Ibid. p. 135　29. Peters, 'Royal Medical Entourages' p. 50　30. ed. Auckland, *Journal and Correspondence of Lord Auckland* II p. 118　31. eds. Barrett and Dobson, *Diary and Letters of Madame d'Arblay* IV pp. 152, 154　32. Ibid. p. 163　33. RL RCIN 1047014 p. 5　34. Macalpine and Hunter, *George III and the Mad-Business* p. 30　35. Turner, *Pitt the Younger* p. 106　36. RL RCIN 1047014 pp. 6–7　37. Ibid. p. 13　38. Ibid. p. 19　39. Ibid. p. 21　40. Fraser, *Princesses* p. 116　41. RL RCIN 1047014 p. 27　42. BM Add MS 34428 ff. 308–9　43. RL RCIN 1047014 pp. 30, 83　44. Ibid. pp. 28–9　45. ed. Ross, *Correspondence of Charles, 1st Marquis Cornwallis* I p. 407　46. Buckingham, *Court and Cabinets* II p. 12　47. Ibid.　48. RL RCIN 1047014 p. 34　49. Ibid. p. 32　50. Ibid. p. 33　51. Ibid. p. 35　52. Black, *George III: America's Last King* p. 279　53. RL RCIN 1047014 p. 228　54. Ibid. p. 38　55. Ibid. p. 39　56. Ibid.　57. ed. Auckland, *Journal and Correspondence of Lord Auckland* II p. 246　58. eds. Barrett and Dobson, *Diary and Letters of Madame d'Arblay* IV p. 184　59. Ibid. p. 186　60. Ibid. p. 173　61. Ibid. p. 184　62. Papendiek, *Court and Private Life* II pp. 20–21　63. Harvey, *Few Bloody Noses*, preface　64. ed. Kassler, *Memoirs of*

Charlotte Papendiek pp. 146–7   65. Papendiek, *Court and Private Life* II p. 21   66. eds. Barrett and Dobson, *Diary and Letters of Madame d'Arblay* IV p. 189   67. Ibid. p. 188   68. RL RCIN 1047014 pp. 42–3   69. Ibid. p. 41   70. eds. Barrett and Dobson, *Diary and Letters of Madame d'Arblay* IV p. 193   71. RL RCIN 1047014 p. 46   72. Ibid.   73. eds. Barrett and Dobson, *Diary and Letters of Madame d'Arblay* IV p. 195   74. RL RCIN 1047014 p. 50   75. Ibid.   76. Ibid. p. 54   77. Ibid. p. 55   78. ed. Malmesbury, *Diaries and Correspondence of James Harris* IV p. 311   79. Trench, *Royal Malady* pp. 93–4   80. Peters, 'Royal Medical Entourages' p. 50   81. Ibid. p. 51; Trench, *Royal Malady* p. 94   82. ed. Auckland, *Journal and Correspondence of Lord Auckland* II p. 257   83. Trench, *Royal Malady* p. 93   84. RL RCIN 1047014 p. 58   85. Ibid. p. 146   86. Ibid. p. 59   87. Peters, 'Royal Medical Entourages' p. 49   88. ed. Auckland, *Journal and Correspondence of Lord Auckland* II p. 246   89. ed. Russell, *Memorials and Correspondence of Charles James Fox* II pp. 299–300   90. Ibid. p. 300   91. RL RCIN 1047014 p. 65   92. Ibid. p. 68   93. Ibid. p. 69   94. eds. Barrett and Dobson, *Diary and Letters of Madame d'Arblay* IV p. 212   95. ed. Kassler, *Memoirs of Charlotte Papendiek* p. 147   96. RL RCIN 1047014 pp. 80–81   97. Ibid. pp. 84–5   98. ed. Cunningham, *Letters of Horace Walpole* III p. 158   99. RA GEO/MAIN/6528   100. RL RCIN 1047014 p. 115   101. Ibid. p. 87   102. Ibid. pp. 89–91   103. Derry, *Regency Crisis and the Whigs* p. 8   104. Ibid.   105. RL RCIN 1047014 pp. 94–5   106. ed. Kassler, *Memoirs of Charlotte Papendiek* p. 147   107. eds. Barrett and Dobson, *Diary and Letters of Madame d'Arblay* IV p. 215   108. Ibid. V p. 75   109. RA GEO/MAIN/15794–15797; RL RCIN 1047014 p. 210   110. RL RCIN 1047014 p. 112   111. Ibid. pp. 112, 114   112. Ibid. p. 114   113. Ibid. p. 112   114. Ibid. p. 118   115. Mansel, *Dressed to Rule* p. 57   116. ed. Home, *Letters and Journals of Lady Mary Coke* II p. 231 n. 2   117. Mansel, 'Uniform and the Rise of the *Frac*' p. 116   118. Mansel, *Dressed to Rule* p. 58; Mansel, 'Uniform and the Rise of the *Frac*' p. 116   119. Mansel, 'Uniform and the Rise of the *Frac*' p. 116   120. Mansel, *Dressed to Rule* p. 58   121. RL RCIN 1047014 pp. 123, 124, 125   122. Ibid. pp. 123, 124, 128   123. ed. Auckland, *Journal and Correspondence of Lord Auckland* II p. 270   124. RL RCIN 1047014 p. 137   125. Ibid. p. 143   126. Ibid.   127. Ibid. p. 144   128. Ibid. pp. 148–9   129. Ibid. pp. 148, 151   130. Ibid. p. 150   131. Ibid. p. 153   132. Ibid. p. 157   133. Ibid. p. 158   134. Ibid. p. 162   135. Ibid. p. 167   136. Chernow, *Washington* p. 570   137. eds. Barrett and Dobson, *Diary and Letters of Madame d'Arblay* IV p. 243   138. Ibid. p. 244   139. Ibid. p. 245   140. Ibid. p. 246   141. Ibid. pp. 246–50   142. RL RCIN 1047014 p. 170   143. Ibid. p. 173   144. Lock, *Edmund Burke* II p. 218   145. Ibid.   146. RL RCIN 1047014 p. 183   147. Ibid. p. 191   148. Ibid. pp. 196–7   149. Ibid. p. 197   150. Ibid. p. 199   151. Ayling, *Fox* p. 164   152. ed. Roberts, *Memoirs of the Life and Correspondence of Mrs Hannah More* II p. 342   153. RL RCIN 1047014 p. 207   154. Ibid.   155. Ibid. pp. 205–6   156. ed. Russell, *Memorials and Correspondence of Charles James Fox* II p. 302   157. eds. Barrett and Dobson, *Diary and Letters of Madame d'Arblay* IV p. 261   158. Brooke, *George III* p. 351

23. Recovery, Revolution and War

1. eds. Barrett and Dobson, *Diary and Letters of Madame d'Arblay* IV p. 311   2. ed. Bladon, *Diaries of Robert Fulke Greville* p. 235   3. ed. Auckland, *Journal and Correspondence of Lord Auckland* II p. 302   4. ed. Bladon, *Diaries of Robert Fulke Greville* p. 236   5. Ibid. p. 245   6. Ibid. p. 237   7. Ibid. p. 238   8. Ibid. p. 241   9. Ibid.   10. eds. Barrett and Dobson, *Diary and Letters of Madame d'Arblay* IV p. 263   11. ed. Bladon, *Diaries of Robert Fulke Greville* p. 244   12. ed. Auckland, *Journal and Correspondence of Lord Auckland* II p. 292   13. ed. Wheatley, *Historical and Posthumous Memoirs of Sir Nathaniel Wraxall* V p. 243   14. ed. Bladon, *Diaries of Robert Fulke Greville* p. 247   15. ed. Auckland, *Journal and Correspondence of Lord Auckland* II pp. 295–6   16. Stanhope, *Life of Pitt* II Appendix p. x   17. ed. Bladon, *Diaries of Robert Fulke Greville* p. 252   18. Ibid. p. 256   19. Stanhope, *Life of Pitt* II Appendix p. xi   20. Keane, *Tom Paine* p. 287   21. eds. Barrett and Dobson, *Diary and Letters of Madame d'Arblay* IV p. 269   22. Rogers, *Crowds, Culture, and Politics in Georgian Britain* pp. 185–6   23. eds. Barrett and Dobson, *Diary and Letters of Madame d'Arblay* IV p. 269   24. Rogers,

Crowds, Culture, and Politics in Georgian Britain pp. 184–5 25. Ibid. p. 187 26. Eimer, *British Commemorative Medals* p. 124 27. eds. Barrett and Dobson, *Diary and Letters of Madame d'Arblay* IV p. 271 28. Ibid. p. 275 29. Brooke, *George III* p. 343 30. eds. Keene, Burns and Saint, *St Paul's* p. 353 31. Ibid. p. 367 32. ed. Auckland, *Journal and Correspondence of Lord Auckland* II p. 316 33. Ibid. p. 318 34. ed. Stuart Wortley, *Prime Minister and his Son* p. 220 35. Ehrman, *Years of Acclaim* p. 665 36. *The Times* 24 April 1789 37. *Public Advertiser* 24 April 1789; Hibbert, *George III* p. 301; eds. Keene, Burns and Saint, *St Paul's* p. 369 38. RA GEO/ADD/43/2 ff. 13–14 39. Colley, 'Apotheosis of George III' p. 122 40. *Annual Register 1789* p. 252 41. ed. Aspinall, *Later Correspondence* I p. 417 42. Ibid. 43. eds. Barrett and Dobson, *Diary and Letters of Madame d'Arblay* IV p. 290 44. Wright, *George III* p. 109 45. eds. Barrett and Dobson, *Diary and Letters of Madame d'Arblay* IV p. 295 46. Ibid. p. 296 47. Hadlow, *Royal Experiment* p. 418 48. eds. Barrett and Dobson, *Diary and Letters of Madame d'Arblay* IV p. 298 49. Brooke, *George III* p. 342 50. Ayling, *Fox* p. 167 51. Donald, *Age of Caricature* p. 161; Colley, 'Apotheosis of George III' p. 102 52. Colley, 'Apotheosis of George III' pp. 103–4 53. RA GEO/ADD/43/1 54. Farr, *World of Fanny Burney* p. 100 55. eds. Barrett and Dobson, *Diary and Letters of Madame d'Arblay* IV p. 491 56. ed. Aspinall, *Later Correspondence* I p. 446 57. Ibid. 58. Ibid. p. 448 59. Gattey, 'Farmer' George's Black Sheep* p. 176 60. Crook and Port, *History of the King's Works* IV pp. 345–6, 375 61. Watkin, *Architect King* p. 27 62. Ibid. ch. 5 63. Ibid. p. 31 64. Poole, *Politics of Regicide in England* p. 92 65. Colley, 'Apotheosis of George III' p. 106 n. 35 66. Lucas, *Art of Living* p. 156 67. ed. Copeland, *Burke Correspondence* VI p. 239 68. Ibid. pp. 252–3 69. Keane, *Thomas Paine* p. 436 70. Clark, *Thomas Paine* pp. 230, 231 n. 57 71. ed. Aspinall, *Later Correspondence* I p. 521 72. ed. Marsden, *Wisdom of George the Third* passim 73. BL Add MS 58856 f. 52 74. ed. Copeland, *Burke Correspondence* VI pp. 308–9 75. Ayling, *George the Third* p. 360 76. BL Add MS 58856 f. 156 77. Butterfield, 'Charles James Fox and the Whig Opposition' p. 300 n. 25 78. Donald, *Age of Caricature* p. 146 79. Ibid. 80. Craig, *Memoirs of Her Majesty Queen Charlotte* p. 555 81. Paine, *Rights of Man* pp. 173–4 82. Baker, *Life in Caricature* p. 1 83. Hill, *Mr Gillray* pp. 67–8 84. Morris, *British Monarchy and the French Revolution* p. 191 85. *The Times* 29 September 2007 86. Black, *George III* p. 297 87. Duffy, *The Younger Pitt* p. 50 88. Hansard Vol. 261 col. 533 8 February 1932 89. BL Add MS 40100 f. 59 90. Donald, *Age of Caricature* pp. 148–9 91. Keane, *Tom Paine* p. 361 92. ed. Aspinall, *Later Correspondence* I p. 642 93. Ibid. p. 649 94. Turner, *Pitt the Younger* p. 187 95. BL Add MS 58857 f. 87 96. ed. Coupland, *War Speeches of William Pitt the Younger* p. 52 97. Ibid. p. 25 98. Turner, *Pitt the Younger* p. 278 99. Watkin, *Architect King* pp. 15–16 100. BL Add MS 58857 f. 105 101. Lascelles, *Life of Charles James Fox* p. 255 102. Dundas Papers Add MS 40100 f. 79 103. ed. Aspinall, *Later Correspondence* II p. 46 104. Ziegler, *William IV* p. 80 105. ed. Bickley, *Diaries of Sylvester Douglas* I p. 59 106. ed. Aspinall, *Later Correspondence* II p. 486 107. Ibid. p. 73 108. Morris, *British Monarchy and the French Revolution* p. 170

24. The Whale and the Wolf

1. *The Times*, 31 January 1820 p. 2 2. ed. Bladon, *Diaries of Robert Fulke Greville* pp. 269–70 3. Ibid. p. 266 4. Turner, *Pitt the Younger* p. 103 5. ed. Auckland, *Journal and Correspondence of Lord Auckland* III p. 223 6. ed. Bladon, *Diaries of Robert Fulke Greville* p. 285 7. Ibid. pp. 277–360 8. Black, *George III: America's Last King* pp. 134–6, 282 9. ed. Bladon, *Diaries of Robert Fulke Greville* p. 294 10. Wright, *George III* p. 108 11. ed. Bladon, *Diaries of Robert Fulke Greville* pp. 335–6 12. RA GEO/ADD/43/3f 13. Black, *George III: America's Last King* p. 357 14. Jupp, *Lord Grenville* p. 174; Historical Manuscripts Commission, *Report on the Manuscripts of J. B. Fortescue Preserved at Dropmore* II p. 649 15. Brooke, *King George III* pp. 352–3 16. Historical Manuscripts Commission, *Report on the Manuscripts of J. B. Fortescue Preserved at Dropmore* II p. 648 17. Stanhope, *Life of Pitt* II Appendix p. xxiii 18. Ibid. Appendix pp. xxiii–xxiv 19. Ibid. Appendix pp. xxiii–xxv 20. ed. Hall, *250 Royal Speeches* pp. 19–20 21. Ayling, *George the Third* p. 397 22. Wright, *George III* p. 86

23. Glover, *Peninsular Preparation* p. 40   24. Ibid. passim   25. RA GEO/ADD/43/3f   26. RA GEO/MAIN/39076–39077   27. eds. Heard and Jones, *George IV: Art and Spectacle* p. 38   28. Brooke, *King George III* pp. 346–7   29. John Cannon in *ODNB* George III   30. Sarah Bradford in the *Daily Telegraph* 16 March 1996   31. ed. Malmesbury, *Diaries and Correspondence of James Harris* III p. 217   32. Fraser, *Unruly Queen* p. 61   33. Ibid. p. 62   34. Sarah Bradford in the *Daily Telegraph* 16 March 1996   35. Brooke, *King George III* p. 349   36. ed. Aspinall, *Correspondence of George, Prince of Wales* III p. 133   37. Morris, *British Monarchy and the French Revolution* p. 170   38. Fraser, *Princesses* pp. 190–92, 264   39. Childe-Pemberton, *Romance of Princess Amelia* p. 69   40. Aspinall, 'Cabinet Council' p. 217   41. Historical Manuscripts Commission, *Report on the Manuscripts of J. B. Fortescue Preserved at Dropmore* III p. 50   42. Reid, *Charles James Fox* p. 314   43. ed. Aspinall, *Later Correspondence* II p. 414 n. 2   44. *Annual Register 1795* p. 38   45. Ibid.   46. Twiss, *Lord Chancellor Eldon* I p. 293   47. ed. Colchester, *Diary and Correspondence of Charles Abbot* I pp. 2–3   48. Ibid.   49. Ibid.   50. Ibid.   51. *Annual Register 1795* pp. 38–9   52. Brooke, *King George III* p. 364   53. Turner, *Pitt the Younger* p. 8   54. Ayling, *Fox* p. 194   55. Turner, *Pitt the Younger* p. 195   56. Ayling, *George the Third* p. 398   57. Dobrée, *Letters of George III* pp. 215–19; ed. Aspinall, *Later Correspondence* II p. 73   58. Turner, *Pitt the Younger* p. 195   59. BL Add MS 58859 f. 47   60. Ayling, *George the Third* p. 400   61. Historical Manuscripts Commission, *Report on the Manuscripts of J. B. Fortescue Preserved at Dropmore* III pp. 173–4   62. ed. Berkey, *Disruptive Strategies* pp. 117–37   63. Brooke, *King George III* p. 349   64. Ibid.   65. Fraser, *Unruly Queen* p. 15   66. Ibid. p. 90   67. ed. Aspinall, *Later Correspondence* II p. 482 n. 2   68. RA GEO/MAIN/16710–16711, GEO/MAIN/39199–39200   69. RA GEO/MAIN/16710–16711, GEO/MAIN/39199–39200   70. ed. Aspinall, *Later Correspondence* II p. 483   71. Ibid. p. 482   72. RA GEO/MAIN/39223   73. RA GEO/MAIN/39252   74. Fraser, *Unruly Queen* p. 454   75. ed. Aspinall, *Later Correspondence* II p. 517   76. ed. Bickley, *Diaries of Sylvester Douglas* I p. 124   77. ed. Aspinall, *Later Correspondence* II pp. 545–6   78. Stanhope, *Life of Pitt* III Appendix p. iii   79. Ibid. Appendix p. vi   80. ed. Aspinall, *Later Correspondence* III p. 563   81. Stanhope, *Life of Pitt* III Appendix p. vii   82. ed. Aspinall, *Later Correspondence* III p. 576   83. Ibid. pp. 576–7   84. Ibid. p. 578 n. 1   85. Ibid. p. 596   86. ed. Baring, *Diary of the Right Hon. William Windham* pp. 367–8   87. Stanhope, *Life of Pitt* III Appendix pp. viii–ix   88. Ibid. Appendix p. x   89. Ibid.   90. Ibid. Appendix p. xi   91. Ehrman, *Consuming Struggle* p. 107   92. Stanhope, *Life of Pitt* III Appendix p. xii   93. *Annual Register 1798* II p. 6   94. Ayling, *Fox* p. 200   95. ed. Aspinall, *Later Correspondence* III p. 59   96. Hague, *William Pitt the Younger* p. 425   97. Stanhope, *Life of Pitt* III p. 131   98. Ibid. Appendix p. xiv   99. Hopton, *Pistols at Dawn* p. 81   100. Stanhope, *Life of Pitt* III Appendix pp. xiv, xvi   101. Aspinall, *Later Correspondence* III pp. 70–71   102. Ibid.   103. Stanhope, *Life of Pitt* III Appendix p. xv   104. Ibid.   105. Ibid. Appendix p. xvi   106. ed. Aspinall, *Later Correspondence* III p. 78 n. 4   107. ed. Bickley, *Diaries of Sylvester Douglas* I p. 125   108. Oman, *Unfortunate Colonel Despard* p. 1   109. ed. Aspinall, *Later Correspondence* III p. 132   110. Ibid. p. 134   111. Ibid. p. 135   112. Ibid. p. 151   113. Ibid. p. 173

25. 'The Corsican Tyrant'

1. Brooke, *King George III* p. 261   2. Black, *George III: Madness and Majesty* p. 68   3. BL Add MS 38416 f. 312   4. Anstey, *Atlantic Slave Trade* pp. 304, 332   5. BL Add MS 58861 ff. 61 and 64   6. ed. Aspinall, *Later Correspondence* III p. 308   7. Jesse, *Memoirs of the Life and Reign of King George III* III p. 235   8. Eimer, *British Commemorative Medals* p. 134   9. Stanhope, *Life of Pitt* III Appendix p. xviii   10. ed. Ilchester, *Journal of Elizabeth, Lady Holland* II p. 81   11. Poole, *Politics of Regicide in England* pp. 129–31   12. Ibid. p. 133   13. Stanhope, *Life of Pitt* III Appendix p. xxi   14. ed. Aspinall, *Later Correspondence* III p. 374   15. Ibid. p. 375   16. Ibid. pp. 375, 376   17. Stanhope, *Life of Pitt* III Appendix p. xxii   18. ed. Aspinall, *Later Correspondence* III p. 382   19. Ibid. p. 384   20. Ibid. p. 383 n. 1   21. Ibid. p. 385   22. Ibid. p. 386   23. Hedley, *Queen Charlotte* p. 207   24. Willis, 'William Pitt's Resignation in 1801' p. 238 n. 2   25. Turner, *Pitt the Younger* p. 211   26. Fraser, *King and the Catholics* p. 53

27. Ibid. pp. 46–7   28. Ibid. p. 47   29. ed. Bickley, *Diaries of Sylvester Douglas* I p. 157   30. Stanhope, *Life of Pitt* III Appendix p. xx   31. Hague, *William Pitt the Younger* p. 454   32. Willis, 'William Pitt's Resignation in 1801' p. 240   33. Gash, *Lord Liverpool* p. 37   34. Turner, *Pitt the Younger* p. 214   35. Eimer, *British Commemorative Medals* p. 135   36. ed. Aspinall, *Later Correspondence* III p. 435 n. 2   37. Fraser, *King and the Catholics* p. 58   38. ed. Auckland, *Journal and Correspondence of Lord Auckland* IV pp. 114–15   39. Willis, 'William Pitt's Resignation in 1801' pp. 252–3   40. ed. Bickley, *Diaries of Sylvester Douglas* I p. 147   41. Ibid.; Wilberforce, *Life of William Wilberforce* III p. 7   42. ed. Bickley, *Diaries of Sylvester Douglas* I p. 147   43. Ibid. p. 149   44. Ibid.   45. Ibid. p. 150   46. Ashbourne, *Pitt* p. 310   47. Yonge, *Life and Administration of Robert Banks, Second Earl of Liverpool* I pp. 44–5   48. https://www.royal.uk/coronation-oath-2-june-1953   49. Pellew, *Life and Correspondence of the Right Honble Henry Addington* I p. 286   50. Fraser, *King and the Catholics* p. 57   51. Boustead, *Lone Monarch* p. 287   52. Brooke, *King George III* p. 368   53. ed. Aspinall, *Later Correspondence* III p. 476   54. Ibid. p. 477   55. ed. Auckland, *Journal and Correspondence of Lord Auckland* IV pp. 123, 124   56. Stanhope, *Life of Pitt* III Appendix p. xxiv   57. Ibid. Appendix pp. xxviii–xxix   58. Ibid. Appendix pp. xxix–xxx   59. ed. Bickley, *Diaries of Sylvester Douglas* I p. 153   60. Ibid.   61. Ehrman, *Consuming Struggle* p. 509   62. Ayling, *George the Third* p. 413   63. Parkinson, 'Call for the Doctor' p. 12   64. Ibid. p. 10   65. Ibid. p. 11   66. Ziegler, *Addington* p. 104   67. Fraser, *King and the Catholics* p. 49   68. Aspinall, 'Cabinet Council' p. 149   69. Ziegler, *Addington* p. 104   70. Stanhope *Life of Pitt* III Appendix p. xxxii   71. ed. Bickley, *Diaries of Sylvester Douglas* I p. 184   72. Brooke, *King George III* p. 370

26. 'A Fearful Experiment'

1. Historic Royal Palaces MS HC 8SF087   2. ed. Colchester, *Diary and Correspondence of Charles Abbot* I p. 243   3. ed. Malmesbury, *Diaries and Correspondence of James Harris* IV p. 15   4. Ibid. p. 17   5. Ibid.   6. Stanhope *Life of Pitt* III p. 302   7. ed. Malmesbury, *Diaries and Correspondence of James Harris* IV p. 25   8. Ibid.   9. Ibid.   10. Ibid. p. 31   11. Ibid.   12. Ibid. p. 26   13. Stanhope *Life of Pitt* III pp. 302–3   14. ed. Malmesbury, *Diaries and Correspondence of James Harris* IV p. 21   15. Stanhope, *Life of Pitt* II p. 416   16. Ibid. III pp. 304–5   17. ed. Aspinall, *Later Correspondence* III p. 510   18. Ziegler, *Addington* p. 103   19. Festing, *John Hookham Frere and his Friends* p. 27   20. ed. Aspinall, *Later Correspondence* III p. 510 n. 2   21. Brooke, *King George III* p. 371   22. Ibid.   23. Ibid. p. 372   24. ed. Bickley, *Diaries of Sylvester Douglas* I p. 220   25. Ibid.   26. Ibid.   27. Brooke, *King George III* p. 375   28. Ibid. p. 372   29. ed. Aspinall, *Later Correspondence* III p. 524   30. Ibid. p. 530   31. Ibid. p. 531   32. Ibid. p. 533   33. Ibid. p. 519   34. Macalpine and Hunter, *George III and the Mad-Business* p. 126   35. ed. Bickley, *Diaries of Sylvester Douglas* I p. 227   36. ed. Dobrée, *Letters of King George III* p. 256   37. ed. Harcourt, *Diaries and Correspondence of George Rose* I p. 354; Brooke, *King George III* p. 373   38. Ibid.   39. Jesse, *Memoirs of the Life and Reign of King George III* III p. 338   40. ed. Bickley, *Diaries of Sylvester Douglas* I p. 236   41. ed. Aspinall, *Later Correspondence* III p. 555 and n. 2   42. Ziegler, *Addington* p. 128   43. Parkinson, 'Call for the Doctor' p. 13   44. ed. Bickley, *Diaries of Sylvester Douglas* I p. 233   45. Roberts, *Napoleon the Great* chs. 12 and 14   46. Holland, *Memoirs of the Whig Party* I p. 185   47. *The Times* 12 October 1801   48. ed. Russell, *Memorials and Correspondence of Charles James Fox* III p. 349; Smith, *Lord Grey* p. 86   49. ed. Bickley, *Diaries of Sylvester Douglas* I p. 258   50. Ibid. p. 268   51. ed. Malmesbury, *Diaries and Correspondence of James Harris* IV p. 61   52. Ibid. pp. 62–3   53. Hague, *William Pitt the Younger* p. 501   54. Ibid.   55. Oman, *Unfortunate Colonel Despard* p. 21   56. Ibid. p. 16   57. Ibid. p. 18   58. Ibid. p. 16   59. BL Add MS 33115 f. 120   60. ed. Bickley, *Diaries of Sylvester Douglas* I p. 314   61. Ibid. pp. 314–15   62. Ibid. p. 315   63. ed. Malmesbury, *Diaries and Correspondence of James Harris* IV p. 69   64. Ibid. p. 70   65. ed. Bickley, *Diaries of Sylvester Douglas* I p. 338   66. Smith, *George IV* p. 90   67. Ibid. pp. 89–90   68. BL Loan 72/1 f. 107   69. Black, *George III: America's Last King* pp. 390–91   70. ed. Aspinall, *Later Correspondence* IV pp. 82–3   71. Mikaberidze, *Napoleonic Wars* p. 155   72. Mitchell, *Charles James Fox* p. 202   73. Turner, *Pitt the Younger*

pp. 239–40   74. BL Add MS 47564 f. 197   75. Baker, *Life in Caricature* p. 15   76. Hill, *Mr Gillray* p. 130   77. BL Loan 72/1 f. 105; Black, *George III: America's Last King* p. 326   78. RA GEO/MAIN/39900–39907   79. RA GEO/MAIN/42365   80. RA GEO/MAIN/39922   81. Ayling, *George the Third* p. 425   82. ed. Harcourt, *Diaries and Correspondence of George Rose* I p. 168   83. ed. Auckland, *Journal and Correspondence of Lord Auckland* IV p. 184   84. Brooke, *King George III* p. 380   85. GEO/MAIN/46128–46130   86. ed. Bickley, *Diaries of Sylvester Douglas* I p. 361   87. ed. Colchester, *Diary and Correspondence of Charles Abbot* I p. 471   88. Ibid. p. 469   89. ed. Malmesbury, *Diaries and Correspondence of James Harris* IV p. 285   90. ed. Bickley, *Diaries of Sylvester Douglas* I p. 361   91. ed. Malmesbury, *Diaries and Correspondence of James Harris* IV p. 286   92. Twiss, *Lord Chancellor Eldon* I p. 423   93. ed. Colchester, *Diary and Correspondence of Charles Abbot* I p. 479   94. ed. Bickley, *Diaries of Sylvester Douglas* I p. 365   95. Black, *George III: America's Last King* p. 175   96. ed. Malmesbury, *Diaries and Correspondence of James Harris* IV p. 288   97. ed. Colchester, *Diary and Correspondence of Charles Abbot* I p. 481   98. ed. Maxwell, *Creevey Papers* I p. 25   99. Stanhope, *Life of Pitt* IV Appendix p. iii   100. ed. Malmesbury, *Diaries and Correspondence of James Harris* IV p. 297   101. Stanhope, *Life of Pitt* IV Appendix p. v   102. Ibid. Appendix pp. viii–ix   103. Ibid. Appendix pp. ix–x   104. Ibid. Appendix p. xi   105. ed. Harcourt, *Diaries and Correspondence of George Rose* II pp. 121–2   106. Ibid.   107. Turner, *Pitt the Younger* p. 290   108. Russell, *Memorials and Correspondence of Charles James Fox* I pp. 42, 53   109. Stanhope, *Life of Pitt* IV Appendix p. xiii   110. Ehrman, *Consuming Struggle* p. 661   111. Black, *George III: America's Last King* p. 390   112. ed. Bickley, *Diaries of Sylvester Douglas* I p. 384   113. Brooke, *King George III* p. 377   114. ed. Bickley, *Diaries of Sylvester Douglas* I pp. 395, 387–8   115. Ibid. p. 388   116. Ibid. p. 389   117. Ibid.   118. Ibid. p. 390   119. Ibid. p. 392   120. Ibid. p. 393   121. Ibid. p. 394   122. Ibid. p. 387   123. Ibid. II p. 150   124. Brooke, *King George III* p. 379   125. ed. Auckland, *Journal and Correspondence of Lord Auckland* IV p. 214

27. Tory Spring

1. Brooke, *George III* p. 380   2. BL Add MS 58861 f. 64   3. ed. Harcourt, *Diaries and Correspondence of George Rose* I p. 183   4. Ibid. p. 181   5. Stanhope, *Life of Pitt* IV Appendix p. xx   6. Turner, *Pitt the Younger* pp. 260–61   7. ed. Auckland, *Journal and Correspondence of Lord Auckland* IV p. 219   8. Ibid. p. 224   9. Ibid. pp. 225–6   10. ed. Bickley, *Diaries of Sylvester Douglas* I p. 413   11. Fraser, *Unruly Queen* p. 150   12. Black, *George III: America's Last King* p. 132   13. Turner, *Pitt the Younger* p. 261   14. Ayling, *George the Third* p. 188   15. ed. Malmesbury, *Diaries and Correspondence of James Harris* IV p. 383   16. Colley, 'Apotheosis of George III' p. 111   17. ed. Colchester, *Diary and Correspondence of Charles Abbot* II p. 5   18. ed. Auckland, *Journal and Correspondence of Lord Auckland* IV pp. 244–5   19. Lubbock, *Herschel Chronicle* p. 118   20. ed. Bickley, *Diaries of Sylvester Douglas* II p. 76   21. ed. Marsden, *Wisdom of George the Third* p. 235   22. ed. Maxwell, *Creevey Papers* I p. 63   23. Turner, *Pitt the Younger* pp. 269–70   24. Stanhope, *Life of Pitt* IV Appendix p. xxvii   25. Turner, *Pitt the Younger* p. 268   26. Clark, *From Restoration to Reform* pp. 128–9; Rodger, *Command of the Ocean* pp. 542–3   27. Stanhope, *Life of Pitt* IV Appendix p. xxvii   28. Ibid. Appendix p. xxviii   29. Ehrman, *Consuming Struggle* p. 822   30. ed. Malmesbury, *Diaries and Correspondence of James Harris* IV pp. 347–52, 354 n.   31. Mitchell, *Charles James Fox* p. 218   32. Ehrman, *Consuming Struggle* p. 829   33. Ehrman, *Years of Acclaim* p. 829 n. 2   34. ed. Maxwell, *Creevey Papers* I p. 119   35. Ayling, *Fox* p. 225   36. Jupp, *Lord Grenville* p. 346   37. Ibid. p. 348   38. Twiss, *Lord Chancellor Eldon* I p. 512   39. Ziegler, *Addington* p. 254   40. Brooke, *King George III* p. 381   41. Jesse, *Memoirs of the Life and Reign of George III* III pp. 373–4   42. Twiss, *Lord Chancellor Eldon* I p. 510   43. BL Add MS 51457 f. 34   44. Holland, *Memoirs of the Whig Party* II p. 49   45. ed. Ilchester, *Journal of Elizabeth, Lady Holland* II p. 182   46. Pellew, *Life and Correspondence of the Right Hon*ble *Henry Addington* II p. 435   47. Ayling, *Fox* p. 228   48. Dinwiddy, 'Charles James Fox and the People' p. 342   49. Sarah Bradford in the *Daily Telegraph* 16 March 1996   50. Fraser, *Unruly Queen* p. 171   51. ed. Aspinall,

Correspondence of George, Prince of Wales V p. 404   52. John Cannon in *ODNB* George III   53. ed. Colchester, *Diary and Correspondence of Charles Abbot* II p. 97   54. ed. Aspinall, *Later Correspondence* IV p. 526   55. BL Add MS 58863 f. 146   56. Wilberforce, *Life of William Wilberforce* III p. 307   57. Ayling, *George the Third* p. 442   58. ed. Maxwell, *Creevey Papers* I p. 85   59. John Cannon in *ODNB* George III   60. *The Times* 31 January 1820 p. 2   61. https://www.rct.uk/collection/search#/13/collection/1142248/the-sobieski-hours   62. Rodger, *Command of the Ocean* p. 549   63. Muir, *Wellington* p. 219   64. Twiss, *Lord Chancellor Eldon*, I p. 393   65. Stanhope, *Life of Pitt* IV Appendix p. xviii   66. ed. Aspinall, *Later Correspondence* V p. 121   67. Ibid. p. 175   68. Ibid. pp. 246–7   69. Ibid. p. 324   70. ed. Londonderry, *Memoirs and Correspondence of Viscount Castlereagh* I p. 19   71. ed. Wellington, *Supplementary Despatches* VI p. 618   72. Glover, *Peninsular Preparation* p. 41   73. ed. Aspinall, *Later Correspondence* V pp. 205–6   74. ed. Colchester, *Diary and Correspondence of Charles Abbot* II p. 217   75. Hopton, *Pistols at Dawn* p. 237   76. ed. Aspinall, *Later Correspondence* V p. 368   77. Bew, *Castlereagh* pp. 268–9   78. ed. Londonderry, *Memoirs and Correspondence of Viscount Castlereagh* I p. 18   79. ed. Colchester, *Diary and Correspondence of Charles Abbot* II p. 211   80. Roberts, *Napoleon the Great* p. 431

28. King Lear Redux

1. Colley, 'Apotheosis of George III' p. 121   2. ed. Malmesbury, *Diaries and Correspondence of James Harris* II p. 175   3. 'A Lady', *An Account of the Celebration of the Jubilee* pp. 15–16   4. Ibid. p. 15   5. Ibid. p. 118   6. Colley, 'Apotheosis of George III' pp. 116–17   7. Baker, *Life in Caricature* p. 10   8. 'A Lady', *An Account of the Celebration of the Jubilee* p. 156   9. Hansard Series 1 Vol. XV col. 121   10. Colley, 'Apotheosis of George III' p. 122   11. Ibid. p. 126   12. Van der Kiste, *George III's Children* p. 88   13. ed. Aspinall, *Later Correspondence* V p. 601   14. Van der Kiste, *George III's Children* p. ix   15. Curzon, *Scandal of George III's Court* p. 156   16. ed. Aspinall, *Later Correspondence* V p. 607   17. RA GEO/MAIN/36555-36556   18. Yonge, *Life and Administration of Robert Banks, Second Earl of Liverpool* I p. 339   19. Peters, 'Royal Medical Entourages' p. 55   20. Porter, *Greatest Benefit to Mankind* p. 349   21. ed. Colchester, *Diary and Correspondence of Charles Abbot* II pp. 280–81   22. Ibid. p. 282   23. Ibid. pp. 283, 287   24. Child-Pemberton, *Romance of Princess Amelia* p. 200   25. ed. Bickley, *Diaries of Sylvester Douglas* II p. 109   26. Ibid. p. 108   27. ed. Colchester, *Diary and Correspondence of Charles Abbot* II p. 313   28. Ibid. p. 314   29. ed. Maxwell, *Creevey Papers* I p. 119   30. ed. Colchester, *Diary and Correspondence of Charles Abbot* II p. 314   31. Smith, *George IV* p. 141   32. ed. Maxwell, *Creevey Papers* I pp. 142, 145   33. ed. Bickley, *Diaries of Sylvester Douglas* II p. 121   34. ed. Maxwell, *Creevey Papers* I p. 175; Fraser, *Unruly Queen* pp. 220–24   35. Brooke, *King George III* p. 384   36. Ibid. pp. 383–4   37. https://georgianpapers.com/explore-the-collections/collections/papers-of-george-iii/medical-papers-relating-to-george-iii/   38. ed. Colchester, *Diary and Correspondence of Charles Abbot* II p. 343   39. ed. Auckland, *Journal and Correspondence of Lord Auckland* IV p. 368   40. Peters, 'Royal Medical Entourages' p. 63   41. Tillyard, *Royal Affair* p. 331   42. RA MED/16/3/35-67   43. Fraser, *Unruly Queen* p. 250   44. Page, 'George III and the Seventy Years War' passim   45. ed. Colchester, *Diary and Correspondence of Charles Abbot* II p. 581   46. ed. Maxwell, *Creevey Papers* I p. 277   47. *The Times* 31 January 1820 p. 2   48. Ibid.   49. O'Shaughnessy, *Men Who Lost America* p. 361   50. RA GEO/MAIN/17502-17506   51. Eimer, *British Commemorative Medals* p. 157

Conclusion

1. ed. Telford, *Letters of John Wesley* V p. 376   2. Jasanoff, *Liberty's Exiles* p. 118   3. Brooke, *King George III* p. ix   4. eds. Barrett and Dobson, *Diary and Letters of Madame d'Arblay* III p. 11   5. Brooke, *King George III* p. 379   6. Smith, *Horace Walpole* p. 22; Burke, *Works and Correspondence* I p. 314   7. Vulliamy, *Royal George* p. 306; Brooke, *King George III* p. 86;

O'Brien, *Great Melody* pp. 112, 187; O'Shaughnessy, '"If Others Will Not be Active"' p. 4; Butterfield, 'George III and the Constitution' passim   8. TNA 30/8/103 f. 494, William Pitt the Younger's PM papers   9. Namier, *Crossroads of Power* p. 140   10. Namier, 'George III: A Study in Personality' p. 619   11. ed. Hutchinson, *Diary and Letters* p. 378   12. BL Add MS 38222 f. 91   13. *Johnson's Dictionary*   14. Namier, *England in the Age of the American Revolution* p. 231 n. 2   15. Breen, *American Insurgents* p. 260   16. Brookhiser, *Give Me Liberty* p. 66   17. ed. Fortescue, *Correspondence* IV p. 351   18. Liddle, '"A Patriot King, or None"' p. 969   19. Lock, *Edmund Burke* I p. 352   20. ed. Wood, *American Revolution* II p. 775   21. Brookhiser, *Give Me Liberty* p. 72   22. *Congressional Record: Proceedings and Debates of the 81st Congress, Second Session, Appendix*, Vol. XCVI Pt 15 p. A-4229   23. RA GEO/MAIN/4971; Fortescue, *Correspondence* VI p. 29   24. ed. Fitzpatrick, *Writings of George Washington* XXVII p. 223   25. Bicheno, *Rebels and Redcoats* p. 168   26. Wickwire and Wickwire, *Cornwallis* p. 174   27. Ritcheson, *British Politics and the American Revolution* p. 198   28. Thomas, 'George III and the American Revolution' p. 31   29. Ellis, *His Excellency* p. 89   30. ed. Esher, *Girlhood of Queen Victoria* I pp. 397–8   31. Ibid. II p. 236   32. Lubbock, *Herschel Chronicle* p. 124; Cecil, *Young Melbourne* p. 213   33. ed. Bickley, *Diaries of Sylvester Douglas* I p. 265   34. Black, *George III: America's Last King* p. 169; Brooke, 'Library of King George III' p. 33   35. Brooke, *King George III* p. xv   36. Angelo, *Reminiscences of Henry Angelo* I p. 354; ed. Marsden, *Wisdom of George III* p. 331   37. Carretta, *George III and the Satirists* passim   38. Ibid. pp. 381–2   39. Sack, *From Jacobite to Conservative* p. 135   40. Ayling, *George the Third* p. 460   41. ed. Bickley, *Diaries of Sylvester Douglas* I p. 318   42. ed. Aspinall, *Later Correspondence* II p. 548   43. Stanhope, *Life of Pitt* III Appendix p. xxi   44. Lecky, *History of England in the Eighteenth Century* V p. 453   45. ed. Aspinall, *Later Correspondence* II p. 416   46. Steven Hayward in *Claremont Review of Books* Fall 2019 p. 65   47. ed. Dobrée, *Letters of King George III* p. 82   48. Twiss, *Lord Chancellor Eldon* I p. 340   49. ed. Fortescue, *Correspondence* VI p. 23   50. ed. Home, *Letters and Journals of Lady Mary Coke* II p. 240   51. Young, *Poor Fred* p. 173   52. ed. Sedgwick, *Letters from George III to Lord Bute* p. 39   53. ed. Fortescue, *Correspondence* VI p. 288   54. Strong, *Coronation* p. 354   55. ed. Esher, *Girlhood of Queen Victoria* I p. 8   56. Ibid. p. 7   57. *The Times* 31 January 1820 p. 3   58. Chernow, *Washington* p. 171; Meacham, *Thomas Jefferson* p. 48   59. Young, *Poor Fred* p. 173

Appendix

1. Peters and Wilkinson, 'King George III and Porphyria passim   2. Ibid. p. 5   3. eds. Barrett and Dobson, *Diary and Letters of Madame d'Arblay* IV p. 121   4. ed. Bladon, *Diaries of Robert Fulke Greville* pp. 89–90; Peters and Wilkinson, 'King George III and Porphyria' pp. 6–7   5. For doctors' records, see https://georgianpapers.com/explore-the-collections/collections/papers-of-george-iii/medical-papers-relating-to-george-iii/. For the contemporary attitude to mental health see https://georgianpapers.com/event/mental-health-and-the-georgian-world-the-madness-of-george-iii/ and also https://georgianpapers.com/2019/12/09/the-madness-of-george-iii-revisited-reflections-on-mental-health-in-the-georgian-world/   6. Macalpine and Hunter, *George III and the Mad-Business* p. 174   7. Willis Papers BL Add MS 41700 f. 72; RA Halford Papers GEO/ADD/15/874   8. Peters and Wilkinson, 'King George III and Porphyria' p. 11   9. Ibid. p. 12   10. Ibid.   11. Ibid. p. 7

Bibliography

Archives

Lord Auckland	British Library
General Jacob de Budé	Royal Archives
3rd Earl of Bute	British Library
Henry Cavendish	British Library
1st Earl of Chatham	National Archives
Colonial Office	National Archives
Sir Henry Dundas	British Library
East India Company	British Library
Lord Egmont	British Library
Lord Egremont	National Archives
Charles James Fox	British Library
King George III	Royal Archives
King George IV	Royal Archives
Charles Grenville	British Library
George Grenville	British Library
Richard Grenville	British Library
William, Lord Grenville	British Library
Robert Fulke Greville	Royal Archives
Sir Henry Halford	Royal Archives
1st Earl Hardwicke	British Library
Warren Hastings	British Library
Lord Hobart	British Library
1st Lord Holland	British Library
Thomas Hutchinson	British Library
1st Earl of Liverpool	British Library
2nd Earl of Liverpool	British Library

1st Duke of Newcastle	British Library
Lord North	Bodleian Library
Lord Northington	British Library
William Pitt (the Younger)	National Archives
John Robinson	British Library
War Office	National Archives
William Windham	British Library
Dr Francis Willis	British Library
Dr Robert Willis	British Library

Books

Place of publication is London unless otherwise stated

'A Lady', *An Account of the Celebration of the Jubilee* 1809

ed. Adams, Charles Francis, *The Works of John Adams* 10 vols. Boston 1850

Adkins, Roy and Lesley, *Gibraltar: The Greatest Siege in British History* 2017

Adolphus, John, *The History of England from the Accession of George III to the Conclusion of Peace in 1783* 3 vols. 1840

——, *Memoirs of the Reign of George III to the Conclusion of the Peace in 1783* 3 vols. 1802

Aiken, John, *Annals of the Reign of George the Third* 2 vols. 1815

ed. Albemarle, George, Earl of, *Memoirs of the Marquis of Rockingham and his Contemporaries* 2 vols. 1852

Alden, John R., *A History of the American Revolution* New York 1969

——, *Stephen Sayre: American Revolutionary Adventurer* Baton Rouge 1983

Allen, Thomas B., and Braisted, Todd W., *The Loyalist Corps: Americans in the Service of the King* Takoma Park, Md. 2011

Ambrose, Tom, *Prinny and his Pals: George IV and his Remarkable Gift of Friendship* 2009

Anderson, Fred, *Crucible of War: The Seven Years' War and the Fate of Empire in British North America 1754–1766* New York 2000

Anderson, Troyer Steele, *The Command of the Howe Brothers during the American Revolution* 1936

Andrews, Allen, *The King Who Lost America: George III and Independence* 1976

Angelo, Henry, *Reminiscences of Henry Angelo* Vol. I 1828

[Anonymous], *The Laws of Honour; or a compendious account of the ancient derivation of all titles, dignities, offices etc* 1714)

——, *An Address to the People of the United Kingdom of Great Britain and Ireland on the Threatened Invasion* 1803

——, *George the Third, his Court, and Family* 2 vols. 1824

ed. Anson, W. R., *Autobiography and Political Correspondence of Augustus Henry, Third Duke of Grafton* 1898

Anstey, R., *The Atlantic Slave Trade and British Abolition 1760–1810* 1975

Armitage, David R., *The Declaration of Independence: A Global History* Cambridge, Mass. 2007

———, *Foundations of Modern International Thought* Cambridge 2012

Arnold-Baker, Charles, *The Companion to British History* 1996

Ashbourne, Lord, *Pitt: Some Chapters of his Life and Times* 1898

ed. Aspinall, Arthur, *The Later Correspondence of George III* 5 vols. Cambridge 1962–70

———, *The Correspondence of George, Prince of Wales* Vol. I 1963

Atkinson, Richard, *Mr Atkinson's Rum Contract* 2020

Atkinson, Rick, *The British are Coming* 2019

Atwood, Rodney, *The Hessians: Mercenaries from Hessen-Kassel in the American Revolution* 1980

ed. Auckland, Lord, *The Journal and Correspondence of William, Lord Auckland* 4 vols. 1861–2

Ayling, Stanley, *George the Third* 1972

———, *The Elder Pitt: Earl of Chatham* 1976

———, *Fox: The Life of Charles James Fox* 1991

Bailyn, Bernard, *The Ideological Origins of the American Revolution* Cambridge, Mass. 1967/1992

———, *The Ordeal of Thomas Hutchinson* Cambridge, Mass. 1974

Baker, Kenneth, *George III: A Life in Caricature* 2007

Balderston, Marion, and Syrett, David, *The Lost War: Letters from British Officers during the American Revolution* New York 1975

Bargar, Bradley D., *Lord Dartmouth and the American Revolution* Columbia, SC 1965

ed. Baring, Mrs Henry, *The Diary of the Right Hon. William Windham 1784–1810* 1866

ed. Barnard, Frederick Augusta, *Regiae Catalogus* 5 vols. 1820

Barnes, D. G., *George III and William Pitt 1783–1806* New York 1965

eds. Barnes, G. R., and Owen, J. H., *Private Papers of John, Earl of Sandwich 1771–1782* 4 vols. 1932

eds. Barrett, Charlotte, and Dobson, Austin, *Diary and Letters of Madame d'Arblay 1778–1840* 6 vols. 1904–5

Barrington, Shute, *The Political Life of William Wildman, Viscount Barrington* 1814

ed. Bateson, Mary, *A Narrative of the Changes in the Ministry 1765–1767* 1898

Beaumont, Andrew D. M., *Colonial America and the Earl of Halifax 1748–1761* oxford 2015

Beeman, Richard R. *The Varieties of Political Experience in Eighteenth-Century America* Philadelphia 2004

Beer, George Louis, *British Colonial Policy 1754–1765* New York 1907

ed. Beloff, Max, *The Debate on the American Revolution 1761–1783* 1949

Belsham, William, *Memoirs of the Reign of George III to the Session of Parliament Ending AD 1793* 4 vols. 1795

Bemis, Samuel Flagg, *John Quincy Adams and the Foundations of American Foreign Policy* New York 1949

Bentley, Edmund Clerihew, *More Biography* 1929

ed. Berkey, David L., *Disruptive Strategies: The Military Campaigns of Ascendant Powers and their Rivals* Stanford 2021

eds. Berman, Ric, and Gibson, William, *The Lantern of History: Essays in Honour of Jeremy Black* 2020

Bernstein, Jeremy, *Dawning of the Raj: The Life and Trials of Warren Hastings* 2000

Beste, Henry Digby, *Personal and Literary Memorials* 1829

ed. Betham-Edwards, Matilda, *The Autobiography of Arthur Young* 1898

Bew, John, *Castlereagh: Enlightenment, War and Tyranny* 2011

Bicheno, Hugh, *Rebels and Redcoats: The American Revolutionary War* 2004

ed. Bickley, Francis, *The Diaries of Sylvester Douglas (Lord Glenbervie)* 2 vols. 1928

ed. Billias, George Athan, *The Manuscripts of Captain Howard Vincente Knox* Boston 1972

——, *George Washington's Generals and Opponents* New York 1994

ed. Bindman, D., *The Shadow of the Guillotine: Britain and the French Revolution* 1989

Black, Jeremy, *Pitt the Elder* 1992

——, *British Foreign Policy in an Age of Revolutions 1783–1793* Cambridge 1994

——, *Eighteenth Century Europe 1700–1789* 1999

——, *War for America: The Fight for Independence 1775–1783* 2001

——, *The Hanoverians* 2004

——, *George III: America's Last King* 2006

——, *Slavery: A New Global History* 2011

——, *Military Strategy: A Global History* 2020

——, *George III: Majesty and Madness* 2021

eds. Black, Jeremy, and Woodfine, Philip, *The British Navy and the Use of Naval Power in the Eighteenth Century* 1988

ed. Bladon, F. McKno, *The Diaries of Colonel the Hon. Robert Fulke Greville* 1930

Blanning, Timothy, *The Culture of Power and the Power of Culture: Old Regime Europe 1660–1789* Oxford 2002

ed. Bolton, Charles K., *Letters of Hugh, Earl Percy, from Boston and New York 1774–1776* Boston 1902

Boot, Max, *Invisible Armies: An Epic History of Guerrilla Warfare from Ancient Times to the Present* 2013

Borman, Tracy, *King's Mistress, Queen's Servant: The Life and Times of Henrietta Howard* 2010

Boswell, James, *Life of Johnson* 10 vols. 1835

Boustead, Guy M., *The Lone Monarch* 1940

ed. Bowring, John, *The Works of Jeremy Bentham* Vol. X 1843

ed. Boyd, Julian P., *The Declaration of Independence: The Evolution of the Text as Shown in Facsimiles of Various Texts by its Author, Thomas Jefferson* Princeton 1945

——, *The Papers of Thomas Jefferson* 42 vols to date Princeton 1950–

Breen, T. H., *American Insurgents, American Patriots: The Revolution of the People* New York 2010

Brewer, John, *Party Ideology and Popular Politics at the Accession of George III* 1976

——, *The Sinews of Power: War, Money and the English State 1688–1783* 1989

British Medical Association, *Porphyria: A Royal Malady* 1968

Brooke, John, *The Chatham Administration 1766–1768* 1956

——, *King George III* 1972

ed. Brooke, John, *Horace Walpole: Memoirs of the Reign of King George II* Vol. III New Haven 1985

Brookhiser, Richard, *Alexander Hamilton: American* New York 1999

——, *Give Me Liberty: A History of America's Exceptional Idea* New York 2020

Brooks's Club, *Memorials of Brooks's* 1907

Brougham, Henry, *Historical Sketches of Statesmen Who Flourished in the Time of George III* 2 vols. 1839

eds. Brown, Craig, and Cunliffe, Lesley, *The Book of Royal Lists* 1982

Brown, Gerald Saxon, *The American Secretary: The Colonial Policy of Lord George Germain 1775–1778* Ann Arbor 1963

Brown, Peter, *The Chathamites* 1967

eds. Brown, Peter D., and Schweizer, Karl W., *The Devonshire Diary: William Cavendish, Fourth Duke of Devonshire. Memoranda on State of Affairs 1759–1762* 1982 Camden Society Series 4 Vol. 27

ed. Browning, Oscar, *The Political Memoranda of Francis, Fifth Duke of Leeds* 1884

Browning, R., *The Duke of Newcastle* New Haven 1975

Brumwell, Stephen, *Turncoat: Benedict Arnold and the Crisis of American Liberty* 2018

Bryant, G. J., *The Emergence of British Power in India 1600–1784* Woodbridge, Suffolk, 2013

Buchanan, John, *The Road to Charleston* Charlottesville 2019

Buckingham and Chandos, Duke of, *Memoirs of the Court and Cabinets of George III* 4 vols. 1853–5

Bullion, John L., *A Great and Necessary Measure: George Grenville and the Genesis of the Stamp Act 1763–1765* 1982

Bunker, Nick, *An Empire on the Edge: How Britain Came to Fight America* 2015

Burke, Edmund, *Thoughts on the Causes of the Present Discontents* 1770

——, *Reflections on the Revolution in France* 1790

——, *The Works and Correspondence of the Right Honourable Edmund Burke* Vols. I and II 1871–2

Butterfield, Herbert, *The Whig Interpretation of History* 1931

——, *George III, Lord North and the People* 1949

——, *George III and the Historians* 1957

——, *Charles James Fox and Napoleon* 1962

ed. Butterfield, Lyman Henry, *Letters of Benjamin Rush* Vol. II Princeton 1951

——, *Diary and Autobiography of John Adams* Vols. II and III Cambridge, Mass. 1961

Calloway, Colin G., *The Indian World of George Washington: The First President, the First Americans, and the Birth of the Nation* New York 2018

Cannon, John, *The Fox–North Coalition: Crisis of the Constitution 1782–4* 1969

——, *Aristocratic Century: The Peerage of Eighteenth-Century England* 1984 ed. Cappon, Lester J., *The Adams–Jefferson Letters* Vol. II Chapel Hill, NC 1961

Carp, Benjamin, *Defiance of the Patriots: The Boston Tea Party and the Making of America* New Haven 2010

Carretta, Vincent, *George III and the Satirists from Hogarth to Byron* Athens, Ga. 1990

eds. Carswell, John, and Dralle, Lewis Arnold, *The Political Journal of George Bubb Dodington* Oxford 1965

ed. Carter, Clarence Edwin, *The Correspondence of General Thomas Gage with the Secretaries of State 1763–1775* 2 vols. 1931–3

Carter, H. B., *His Majesty's Spanish Flock: Sir Joseph Banks and the Merinos of George III of England* 1964

Castro, Paul de, *The Gordon Riots* 1926

Cecil, Lord David, *The Young Melbourne* 1939

Chaldecott, J. A., *Handbook of the King George III Collection of Scientific Instruments* 1951

ed. Chapman, R. W., *The Letters of Samuel Johnson* Vol. I 1952

Chernow, Ron, *Alexander Hamilton*, New York 2004

——, *Washington: A Life* 2010

Childe-Pemberton, William S., *The Romance of Princess Amelia* 1910

Chisholm, Kate, *Fanny Burney: Her Life 1752–1840* 1999

Christie, Ian R., *The End of North's Ministry* 1958

——, *Myth and Reality in Late Eighteenth-Century British Politics* 1970

——, *Wars and Revolutions: Britain 1760–1815* 1982

Churchill, Winston S., *The River War* Vol. I 1899

——, *A History of the English-Speaking Peoples* Vol. III 1957

Clark, Anna, *Scandal: The Sexual Politics of the British Constitution* 2004

Clark, Dora, *British Opinion and the American Revolution* New York 1966

Clark J. C. D., *From Restoration to Reform: The British Isles 1660–1832* 2014

——, *Thomas Paine: Britain, America, and France in the Age of Enlightenment and Revolution* 2018

ed. Clark, Lorna J., *The Diary of Lucy Kennedy (1790–1816)* Durham, NC 2015

Clarke, John, *The Life and Times of George III* 1972

Clodfelter, Micheal, *Warfare and Armed Conflicts: A Statistical Encyclopedia of Casualty and Other Figures, 1492–2015* 2017

Cobbett, William, *Cobbett's Parliamentary History of England* 36 vols. 1806–20

ed. Colchester, Charles, Lord, *The Diary and Correspondence of Charles Abbot, Lord Colchester* 3 vols. 1861

Colley, Linda, *In Defence of Oligarchy: The Tory Party 1714–1760* 1982

——, *Britons: Forging the Nation 1707–1837* 1994

Congressional Record: Proceedings and Debates of the 81st Congress, Second Session, Appendix Vol. XCVI pt 15 1950

Conway, Stephen, *The War of American Independence 1775–1783* 1995

——, *The British Isles and the War of American Independence* Oxford 2002

Cook, Don, *The Long Fuse: How England Lost the American Colonies 1760–1785* New York 1995

Cookson, J. E., *The Friends of Peace: Anti-War Liberalism in England 1793–1815* 1982

eds. Copeland, Thomas, et al., *The Correspondence of Edmund Burke* 10 vols. 1958–78

ed. Corbett, Julian S., *Private Papers of George, Second Earl Spencer, 1794–1801* 4 vols. 1913–14

Cordasco, Francesco, and Gustave Simonson, *Junius and his Works: A History of the Letters of Junius and the Authorship Controversy* Fairview, NJ 1986

A Correct Copy of the Evidence Taken before a Committee of the House of Commons upon the Conduct of His Royal Highness the Commander in Chief 1809

ed. Coupland, R., *The War Speeches of William Pitt the Younger* 1916

Craig, W., *Memoirs of Her Majesty Queen Charlotte of Great Britain* 1815

ed. Croker, John Wilson, *The Life of Samuel Johnson by James Boswell* 10 vols. 1839

——, *Memoirs of the Reign of George the Second, from his Accession to the Death of Queen Caroline, by John, Lord Hervey* 2 vols. 1848

Crook, J. Mordaunt, and Port, M. H., *The History of the King's Works 1768–1851* Vol. IV 1973

Cumberland, Richard, *Character of the Late Lord Viscount Sackville* 1785

ed. Cunningham, Peter, *The Letters of Horace Walpole Earl of Orford* 9 vols. 1891

Curties, Captain Henry, *A Forgotten Prince of Wales* 1912

Curzon, Catherine, *The Scandal of George III's Court* 2018

Dalrymple, William, *The Anarchy: The Relentless Rise of the East India Company* 2019

Dancy, J. Ross, *The Myth of the Press Gang* 2015

Daughan, George C., *Lexington and Concord: The Battle Heard round the World* New York 2018

Davenport, Hester, *Faithful Handmaid: Fanny Burney and the Court of King George III* 2003

Davies, A. M., *The Influence of George III on the Development of the Constitution* 1921

Davies, J. D. Griffith, *George the Third* 1936

De-la-Noy, Michael, *The King Who Never Was: The Story of Frederick, Prince of Wales* 1996

Derry, John W., *The Regency Crisis and the Whigs 1788–9* 1963

——, *English Politics and the American Revolution* 1976

Dickens, Charles, *Barnaby Rudge* 1927

Ditchfield, G. M., *George III: An Essay in Monarchy* 2002

ed. Dobrée, Bonamy, *The Letters of George III* 1935

Donald, Diana, *The Age of Caricature: Satirical Prints in the Reign of George III* 1996

ed. Donne, W. Bodham, *The Correspondence of King George the Third with Lord North from 1768 to 1783* 2 vols. 1867

Donoughue, Bernard, *British Politics and the American Revolution: The Path to War 1773–75* 1964

Doran, Dr John, *Lives of the Queens of England of the House of Hanover* Vol. I 1855 eds. Doran, John, and Steuart, A. Francis, *The Last Journals of Horace Walpole during the Reign of George III from 1771–1783* 2 vols. New York 1910

Draper, Theodore, *A Struggle for Power: The American Revolution* New York 1996

Duffy, Michael, *The Younger Pitt* 2000

Dull, Jonathan, *The French Navy and American Independence* Princeton 2015

eds. Dupuy, R. Ernest, and Dupuy, Trevor N., *The Collins Encyclopedia of Military History* 1993

Edwards, Averyl, *Frederick Louis, Prince of Wales 1707–1751* 1947

——, *Fanny Burney* 1948

Egnal, Marc, *A Mighty Empire: The Origins of the American Revolution* Ithaca, NY 1988

Ehrman, John, *The Younger Pitt: The Reluctant Transition* 1983

——, *The Younger Pitt: Years of Acclaim* 1984

——, *The Younger Pitt: The Consuming Struggle* 1996

Eimer, Christopher, *British Commemorative Medals and their Values* 2010

ed. Ellis, Annie Raine, *The Early Diary of Frances Burney 1768–1778* 2 vols. 1907

Ellis, Joseph J., *His Excellency: George Washington* New York 2004

Ernst, Joseph, *Money and Politics in America 1755–1775* Chapel Hill, NC 1973

ed. Esher, Viscount, *The Girlhood of Queen Victoria: A Selection from Her Majesty's Diaries between the Years 1832 and 1840* 2 vols. 1912

ed. Everett, C. W., *The Letters of Junius* 1927

Farr, Evelyn, *The World of Fanny Burney* 1993

Ferling, John, *John Adams* Knoxville, Tenn. 1992

——, *Almost a Miracle: The American Victory in the War of Independence* Oxford and New York 2007

Ferreiro, Larrie D., *Brothers at Arms: American Independence and the Men of France and Spain Who Saved It* New York 2016

Festing, Gabrielle, *John Hookham Frere and his Friends* 1899

Fischer, David Hackett, *Paul Revere's Ride* New York and Oxford 1994

eds. Fischer, Lewis R., and Nordvik, Helge W., *Shipping and Trade 1750–1950* Pontefract 1990

Fitzgerald, Percy, *The Royal Dukes and Princesses of the Family of George III* 2 vols. 1882

——, *The Good Queen Charlotte* 1899

Fitzmaurice, Lord Edmond, *Life of William, Earl of Shelburne* 2 vols. 1875

ed. Fitzpatrick, John C., *The Writings of George Washington* 39 vols. Washington, DC 1931–44

Fliegelman, Jay, *Prodigals and Pilgrims: The American Revolution against Patriarchal Authority 1750–1800* New York 1982

Fonblanque, Edward B. de, *Political and Military Episodes in the Latter Half of the Eighteenth Century Derived from the Life and Correspondence of the Right Hon. John Burgoyne* 1876

Fontaine, James, *Memoirs of a Huguenot Family* New York 1845

ed. Ford, Paul Leicester, *Autobiography of Thomas Jefferson 1743–1790* Philadelphia 2005 ed. Ford, Worthington, *Correspondence and Journals of Samuel Blachley Webb* New York Vol. I 1893

——, *Journals of the Continental Congress 1774–1789* 34 vols. Washington DC 1904–37

Foreman, Amanda, *Georgiana, Duchess of Devonshire* 1998

Fortescue, Sir John, *History of the British Army* Vol. III 1902

ed. Fortescue, Sir John, *The Correspondence of King George the Third from 1760 to December 1783* 6 vols. 1927–8

Fraser, Antonia, *The King and the Catholics: England, Ireland and the Fight for Religious Freedom 1780–1829* 2018

Fraser, Flora, *The Unruly Queen: The Life of Queen Caroline* 1996

——, *Princesses: The Six Daughters of George III* 2004

——, *George and Martha Washington* 2015

French, Allen, *The First Year of the American Revolution* Boston and New York 1934

Froude, J. A., *The English in Ireland in the Eighteenth Century* 3 vols. 1881

Fulford, Roger, *Royal Dukes* 1933

——, *George the Fourth* 1949

eds. Garlick, Kenneth, and Macintyre, Angus, *The Diary of Joseph Farington* Vols. I, IV and VI 1979

Gash, Norman, *Lord Liverpool* 1984

Gattey, Charles, *'Farmer' George's Black Sheep: The Lives and Loves of George III's Siblings* 1985

eds. Giunta, Mary A., and Hartgrove, J. Dane, *The Emerging Nation: A Documentary History of the Foreign Relations of the United States under the Articles of Confederation 1780–1789* Vols. II and III 1996

Glover, Michael, *General Burgoyne in Canada and America* 1976

Glover, Richard, *Peninsular Preparation: The Reform of the British Army 1795–1809* 1963

Goodwin, George, *Benjamin Franklin in London* 2017

Gore-Browne, Robert, *Chancellor Thurlow* 1953

Grant, James, *John Adams: Party of One* New York 2006

Green, Vivian, *The Madness of Kings: Personal Trauma and the Fate of Nations* 1993

Green, William, *Annals of George the Third* 2 vols. 1808

ed. Greene, Donald J., *Samuel Johnson: Political Writings* New Haven 1977

Greene, Jack P., *Negotiated Authorities: Essays in Colonial Political and Constitutional History* Charlottesville 1994

ed. Greene, Jack P., and Pole, J. R., *A Companion to the American Revolution* Oxford 2003

ed. Greig, James, *The Diaries of a Duchess: Extracts from the Diaries of the First Duchess of Northumberland (1716–1776)* 1926

——, *The Farington Diary* 8 vols. 1922–8

Gruber, Ira, *The Howe Brothers and the American Revolution* 1972

Guttmacher, Manfred S., *America's Last King: An Interpretation of the Madness of George III* New York 1941

Guttridge, G. H., *The Early Career of Lord Rockingham 1730–1765* Berkeley, Calif. 1952

——, *English Whiggism and the American Revolution* Berkeley, Calif. 1963

Hadlow, Janice, *A Royal Experiment: Love and Duty, Madness and Betrayal – The Private Lives of King George III and Queen Charlotte* New York 2014

Hague, William, *William Pitt the Younger* 2004

ed. Hall, John, *250 Royal Speeches from 1760 to 1882* 2011

Halsband, Robert, *Lord Hervey: Eighteenth-Century Courtier* 1973

Hamilton, Lady Anne, *Secret History of the Court of England* 2 vols. 1903

ed. Harcourt, Edward William, *The Harcourt Papers* Vol. IV Oxford 1880

ed. Harcourt, Leveson Vernon, *The Diaries and Correspondence of the Right Hon. George Rose* 2 vols. 1860

Harding, Nick, *Hanover and the British Empire 1700–1837* 2007

Hardy, Thomas, *The Trumpet-Major* 1880

Harris, George, *The Life of Lord Chancellor Hardwicke* Vol. III 1847

Harvey, Robert, *A Few Bloody Noses: The Realities and Mythologies of the American Revolution* Woodstock, NY 2003

ed. Hassall, A., *Letters on the Spirit of Patriotism and on the Idea of a Patriot King* 1917

Hay, William Anthony, *The Whig Revival 1808–1830* 2005

——, *Lord Liverpool: A Political Life* 2018

eds. Haywood, Ian, and Seed, John, *The Gordon Riots: Politics, Culture and Insurrection in Late Eighteenth-Century Britain* 2012

Heard, Kate, *High Spirits: The Comic Art of Thomas Rowlandson* 2013

eds. Heard, Kate, and Jones, Kathryn, *George IV: Art and Spectacle* 2019

Hedley, Olwen, *Queen Charlotte* 1975

Henderson, John, *Letters and Poems by the Late Mr. John Henderson with Anecdotes of His Life by John Ireland* 1786

Hibbert, Christopher, *King Mob: The Story of Lord George Gordon and the Riots of 1780* 1959

——, *George III: A Personal History* 1998

ed. Hibbert, Christopher, *Louis Simond: An American in Regency England* 1968

Hill, Draper, *Mr Gillray: A Caricaturist* 1965

Historical Manuscripts Commission, *Report on the Manuscripts of J. B. Fortescue Preserved at Dropmore* Vols. I–III 1892–9

——, *Report on Manuscripts in Various Collections* Vol. VI 1909

——, *Report on the Manuscripts of Mrs Stopford-Sackville* Vol. II 1910

——, *Manuscripts of the Earl of Egmont* Vol. II 1923

Hobhouse, Christopher, *Fox* 1947

ed. Hodgart, Matthew, *Horace Walpole: Memoirs and Portraits* 1963

Hoffer, Eric, *The True Believer* 1951

eds. Hoffman, Ronald, and Albert, Peter J., *Arms and Independence: The Military Character of the American Revolution*, Charlottesville, 1984

Hoffman, Ross J. S., *The Marquis: A Study of Lord Rockingham 1730–1782* New York 1973

Holland, Lord, *Memoirs of the Whig Party* 2 vols. 1852–4

ed. Holland, Lord, *Horace Walpole: Memoirs of the Reign of King George the Second* Vol. I 1847

ed. Home, James, *The Letters and Journals of Lady Mary Coke* 4 vols. 1970

Hoock, Holger, *The King's Artists: The Royal Academy of Arts and the Politics of British Culture 1760–1840* Oxford 2003

——, *Scars of Independence: America's Violent Birth* New York 2017

Hopton, Richard, *Pistols at Dawn: A History of Duelling* 2007

Horn, D. B., *The British Diplomatic Service 1689–1789* 1961

House of Commons Journal 1788–9 Vol. 44

House of Lords Journal 1788 Vol. 38, 1810 Vol. 48

Howson, Gerald, *Burgoyne of Saratoga* New York 1979

Hulton, Ann, *Letters of a Loyalist Lady* Cambridge, Mass. 1927

Hunt, Tristram, *The Radical Potter: Josiah Wedgwood and the Transformation of Britain* 2021

Hunt, William, *The Political History of England from the Accession of George III to the Close of Pitt's First Administration* 1905

ed. Hutchinson, Peter Orlando, *The Diary and Letters of His Excellency Thomas Hutchinson* 2 vols. 1883

ed. Hutton, J., *Selections from the Letters and Correspondence of Sir James Bland Burges* 1885

eds. Ilchester, Countess of, and Stavordale, Lord, *The Life and Letters of Lady Sarah Lennox* 1904

ed. Ilchester, Earl of, *Journal of Elizabeth, Lady Holland* 2 vols. 1908

——, *Letters to Henry Fox, Lord Holland* 1915

Iremonger, Lucille, *Love and the Princesses* 1958

Isaacson, Walter, *Benjamin Franklin: An American Life* 2003

James, W. M., *The British Navy in Adversity* 1926

ed. Jarrett, Derek, *Horace Walpole: Memoirs of the Reign of King George III* 4 vols. 2000

Jasanoff, Maya, *Liberty's Exiles* New York 2011

Jeaffreson, John Cordy, *Pleasantries of English Courts and Lawyers* New York 1876

ed. Jennings, Louis J., *The Croker Papers* 3 vols. 1884

Jesse, John Heneage, *Memoirs of the Life and Reign of King George the Third* 3 vols. 1867

Johnson, Samuel, *Thoughts on the Late Transactions Respecting Falkland's Islands* 1771

——, *Taxation No Tyranny* 1775

——, *Dictionary of the English Language* 2 vols. 1778

Jones, Michael Wynn, *A Cartoon History of the Monarchy* 1978

ed. Jucker, Ninette S., *The Jenkinson Papers 1760–1766* 1949

Jupp, Peter, *Lord Grenville 1759–1834* Oxford 1985

ed. Jupp, Peter, *The Letter-Journal of George Canning 1793–1795* 1991

ed. Kassler, Michael, *The Memoirs of Charlotte Papendiek 1765–1840* Durham, NC 2015

Keane, John, *Tom Paine* 1995

eds. Keene, Derek, Burns, Arthur, and Saint, Andrew, *St Paul's: The Cathedral Church of London 604–2004* 2004

ed. Kehervé, Alain, *Mary Delany (1700–1788) and the Court of George III* Durham, NC 2015

Kelly, Ian, *Mr Foote's Other Leg* 2012

Kemp, Betty, *King and Commons 1660–1832* 1957

ed. Kennedy, John Pendle, *Journals of the House of Burgesses of Virginia 1761–65* 1907

Kidd, Thomas S., *Patrick Henry: First among Patriots* New York 2011

A King's Purchase: King George III and the Collection of Consul Smith 1993

Knollenberg, B., *Origin of the American Revolution 1759–1766* New York 1960

Kohn, Hans, *The Idea of Nationalism* 1961

Labaree, Benjamin Woods, *The Boston Tea Party* New York 1964

ed. Labaree, Leonard W., *The Papers of Benjamin Franklin* Vol. XII 1967

Langford, Paul, *The First Rockingham Administration 1765–1766* 1973

——, *A Polite and Commercial People: England 1727–1783* Oxford 1989

ed. Langford, Paul, *The Writings and Speeches of Edmund Burke* Vol. II Oxford 1981

ed. Laprade, William T., *Parliamentary Papers of John Robinson 1774–1784* 1922

Lascelles, Edward, *The Life of Charles James Fox* 1936

Lawson, Philip, *George Grenville: A Political Life* 1984

——, *The Imperial Challenge: Quebec and Britain in the Age of the American Revolution* Montreal 1989

ed. Le Marchant, Denis, *Horace Walpole: Memoirs of the Reign of King George the Third* 4 vols. 1845

Lecky, W. E. H., *History of England in the Eighteenth Century* Vols. III 1882 and V 1887

Leonard, Dick, and Garnett, Mark, *Titans: Fox vs Pitt* 2019

Lepel, Mary, *Letters of Mary Lepel, Lady Hervey* 1821

Lepore, Jill, *These Truths: A History of the United States* 2018

Lewis, Sir George, *Essays on the Administrations of Great Britain from 1783 to 1830* 1864

ed. Lewis, W. S., *The Yale Edition of the Correspondence of Horace Walpole* 48 vols. New Haven 1937–83

Lind, John, *An Answer to the Declaration of the American Congress* 1776

Lock, F. P., *Edmund Burke* 2 vols. Oxford 1998 and 2006

Lockwood, Matthew, *To Begin the World Over Again: How the American Revolution Devastated the Globe* 2019

ed. Londonderry, Charles Vane, Marquess of, *Memoirs and Correspondence of Viscount Castlereagh* Vol. I 1848

Long, J. C., *George III: A Biography* 1960

Longford, Elizabeth, *Wellington: Years of the Sword* 1969

Lovat-Fraser, J. A., *John Stuart, Earl of Bute* Cambridge 1912

Lowry, Rich, *The Case for Nationalism* New York 2019

Lubbock, C. A., *The Herschel Chronicle* Cambridge 1933

Lucas, F. L., *Art of Living: Four Eighteenth-Century Minds: Hume, Horace Walpole, Burke, Benjamin Franklin* 1959

eds. Lustig, Irma S., and Pottle, Frederick A., *Boswell: The Applause of the Jury 1782–1785* 1982

——, *Boswell: The English Experiment 1785–1789* 1986

Lutnick, Solomon, *The American Revolution and the British Press* Columbia, Mo. 1967

Macalpine, Ida, and Hunter, Richard, *George III and the Mad-Business* 1969

McCullough, David, *John Adams* 2001

——, *1776* 2005

McCurdy, John Gilbert, *Quarters: The Accommodation of the British Army and the Coming of the American Revolution* Ithaca, NY 2019

Macfarlan, R., *The History of the Reign of George the Third* 1770

McKelvey, James Lee, *George III and Bute: The Leicester House Years* Durham, NC 1973

Mackerness, E. D., *A Social History of English Music* 1964

Mackesy, Piers, *Statesmen at War: The Strategy of Overthrow 1798–1799* 1974

——, *The Coward of Minden: The Affair of Lord George Sackville* 1979

——, *The War for America 1775–1783* 1993

McLynn, Frank, *1759: The Year Britain Became Master of the World* 2004

ed. Mahon, Lord, *Secret Correspondence Connected with Mr Pitt's Return to Office in 1804* 1852

Maier, Pauline, *From Resistance to Revolution: Colonial Radicals and the Development of American Opposition to Britain 1765–1776* 1973

ed. Malmesbury, 3rd Earl of, *Diaries and Correspondence of James Harris, 1st Earl of Malmesbury* 4 vols. 1844

Mansel, Philip, *Dressed to Rule: Royal and Court Costume from Louis XIV to Elizabeth II* 2005

Manwaring, G. E., and Dobrée, Bonamy, *The Floating Republic: An Account of the Mutinies at Spithead and the Nore in 1797* Barnsley 2004

Marples, Morris, *Poor Fred and the Butcher: Sons of George II* 1970

ed. Marschner, Joanna, *Enlightened Princesses: Caroline, Augusta, Charlotte and the Shaping of the Modern World* 2017

ed. Marsden, Jonathan, *The Wisdom of George the Third* 2005

Marshall, P. J., *Problems of Empire: Britain and India 1757–1813* 1968

——, *'A Free though Conquering People': Eighteenth-Century Britain and its Empire* Aldershot 2003

——, *The Making and Unmaking of Empires: Britain, India, and America c. 1750–1783* Oxford 2005

ed. Marshall, P. J., *The Oxford History of the British Empire* Vol. II Oxford 1998

Marston, Daniel, *The American Revolution 1774–1783* 2002

ed. Maxwell, Sir Herbert, *The Creevey Papers* 2 vols. 1904

May, Henry F., *The Enlightenment in America* Oxford 1976

May, T. E., *The Constitutional History of England* Vol. I 1891

Meacham, Jon, *Thomas Jefferson: President and Philosopher* New York 2014

Melville, Lewis, *Farmer George* 2 vols. 1907

Middlekauff, Robert, *The Glorious Cause: The American Revolution 1763–1789* New York and Oxford 1982

Middleton, Richard, *Colonial America: A History 1565–1776* Oxford 2002

Mikaberidze, Alexander, *The Napoleonic Wars: A Global History* Oxford 2020

Millar, Oliver, *The Later Georgian Pictures in the Collection of Her Majesty the Queen* 2 vols. 1969

Miller, John C., *Origins of the American Revolution* 1945

——, *Triumph of Freedom 1775–1783* 1948

ed. Minto, Lady, *Life and Letters of Sir Gilbert Elliot, 1st Earl of Minto* Vol. III 1874

Mitchell, Joseph B., *Decisive Battles of the American Revolution* 2004

Mitchell, Leslie G., *Charles James Fox* 1992

ed. Mitchell, L. G., *The Writings and Speeches of Edmund Burke* Vol. VIII 1989

Montesquieu, Charles de, *The Spirit of the Laws* 2020

eds. Moots, Glenn A., and Hamilton, Phillip, *Justifying Revolution: Law, Virtue and Violence in the American War of Independence* Norman, Okla. 2018

Morgan, Edmund S., *The Birth of the Republic 1763–89* 2013

ed. Morley, Henry, *Edmund Burke: Thoughts on the Present Discontents, and Speeches* 1884

ed. Morrell, Philip, *Leaves from the Greville Diary* 1929

Morris, Marilyn, *The British Monarchy and the French Revolution* New Haven 1998

——, *Sex, Money and Personal Character in Eighteenth-Century Politics* New Haven and London 2014

Morton, Alan Q., and Wess, Jane A., *Public and Private Science: The King George III Collection* Oxford 1993

Mowl, Timothy, *Horace Walpole: The Great Outsider* 1996

Muir, Rory, *Wellington: The Path to Victory 1769–1814* 2013

Mumby, Frank Arthur, *George III and the American Revolution* 1923

ed. Murray, John, *The Autobiographies of Edward Gibbon* 1896

Namier, Sir Lewis, *The Structure of Politics at the Accession of George III* 1929

——, *Additions and Corrections to Sir John Fortescue's Edition of the Correspondence of King George III (vol.1)* Manchester 1937 https://transcribegeorgianpapers.wm.edu/files/original/c7675f7a49e12b2ffocc25aa5501e8ff.pdf

——, *Personalities and Powers* 1955

——, *Crossroads of Power: Essays on Eighteenth-Century England* 1962

——, *England in the Age of the American Revolution* 1966

Namier, Sir Lewis, and Brooke, John, *The History of Parliament: The House of Commons 1754–90* Vol. I 1964

Navy Records Society, *Publications of the Navy Records Society* Vols. LXIII and LXV 1928

Nelson, Craig, *Thomas Paine* 2007

Nelson, Eric, *The Royalist Revolution: Monarchy and the American Founding* Cambridge, Mass. 2014

Nicholls, John, *Recollections and Reflections, Personal and Political, as Connected with Public Affairs, during the Reign of George III* 1822

Nickerson, Hoffman, *Turning Point of the Revolution or Burgoyne in America* Boston and New York 1928

Norris, John, *Shelburne and Reform* 1963

ed. Norton, J. E., *The Letters of Edward Gibbon* 3 vols. 1956

O'Brien, Conor Cruise, *The Great Melody: A Thematic Biography and Commented Anthology of Edmund Burke* 1992

O'Connell, Robert L., *Revolutionary: George Washington at War* New York 2019

O'Gorman, Frank, *The Rise of Party in England: The Rockingham Whigs 1760–82* 1975

Oman, Sir Charles, *The Unfortunate Colonel Despard and Other Stories* 1922

O'Shaughnessy, Andrew Jackson, *The Men Who Lost America: British Leadership, the American Revolution, and the Fate of the Empire* 2013

Ostler, Catherine, *The Duchess Countess: The Woman Who Scandalised a Nation* 2021

Pain, Nesta, *George III at Home* 1975

Paine, Thomas, *Common Sense* 1986

Palmer, Dave R., *George Washington's Military Genius* 2012

Papendiek, Charlotte, *Court and Private Life in the Time of Queen Charlotte* 2 vols. 1887

Pares, Richard, *King George III and the Politicians* 1970

eds. Pares, Richard, and Taylor, A. J. P., *Essays Presented to Sir Lewis Namier* 1956

Parliamentary Archives, Houses of Parliament Committee Report, *Touching the Present State of His Majesty's Health* 13 January 1789

——, House of Lords Committee Report, *Touching the Present State of His Majesty's Health* 11 December 1788, 20 December 1810

——, House of Commons Committee Report, *Touching the Present State of His Majesty's Health* 11 December 1788, 17 December 1820

Parliamentary Register, or, History of the Proceedings and Debates of the House of Commons Vols. V, IX and XV 1802–20

Parliamentry Register, or, History of the Proceedings and Debates of the House of Lords Vol. IX 1778

Pellew, George, *The Life and Correspondence of the Right Honble Henry Addington, First Viscount Sidmouth* 3 vols. 1847

Pemberton, W. Baring, *Lord North* 1938

Peterson, Merrill D., *Thomas Jefferson and the New Nation* 1970

Philbrick, Nathaniel, *Valiant Ambition: George Washington, Benedict Arnold and the Fate of the American Revolution* 2016

——, *In the Hurricane's Eye: The Genius of George Washington and the Victory at Yorktown* 2018

Phillips, Kevin, *The Cousins' Wars: Religion, Politics, and the Triumph of Anglo-America* 1999

Picard, Liza, *Dr Johnson's London* 2004

Pindar, Peter [John Wolcot], *Ode upon Ode; or A Peep at St James's* 1787 ed. Pink, M. Alderton, *The Letters of Horace Walpole* 1938

Plumb, J. H., *The First Four Georges* 1957

——, *The American Experience* 1989

ed. Pocock, J. G. A., *Three British Revolutions 1641, 1688, 1776* Princeton 1980

ed. Pool, Bernard, *The Croker Papers* 1967

Poole, Steve, *The Politics of Regicide in England 1760–1850* 2000

Porter, Roy, *The Greatest Benefit to Mankind: A Medical History of Humanity* 1999

Poser, Norman S., *Lord Mansfield: Justice in the Age of Reason* 2013

ed. Pottle, Frederick A., *Boswell's London Journal 1762–1763* 1951

Powell, David, *Charles James Fox: Man of the People* 1989

Prochaska, Frank, *The Eagle and the Crown: Americans and the British Monarchy* 2008

Pryce-Jones, David, *Treason of the Heart: From Thomas Paine to Kim Philby* 2011

Range, Matthias, *British Royal and State Funerals* 2016

Ray, Isaac, *Insanity of King George III* New York 1855

Reeves, Richard, *Daring Young Men: The Heroism and Triumph of the Berlin Airlift June 1948–May 1949* 2010

Reid, Loren, *Charles James Fox: A Man for the People* 1969

ed. Rhodes James, Robert, *Winston S. Churchill: His Complete Speeches* Vol. III New York 1974

Ritcheson, Charles R., *British Politics and the American Revolution* Norman, Okla. 1954

Roberts, Andrew, *Napoleon the Great* 2014

ed. Roberts, Jane, *George III and Queen Charlotte: Patronage, Collecting and Court Taste* 2004

Roberts, Michael, *Splendid Isolation 1763–1789* 1970

ed. Roberts, William, *Memoirs of the Life and Correspondence of Mrs Hannah More* Vol. II 1835

Robertson, Ritchie, *The Enlightenment: The Pursuit of Happiness 1680–1790* 2020

Robins, Jane, *The Trial of Queen Caroline* New York 2006

Robson, Eric, *The American Revolution 1763–1783* 1955

Rodger, N. A. M., *The Insatiable Earl: A Life of John Montagu, 4th Earl of Sandwich* 1993

——, *The Command of the Ocean: A Naval History of Britain 1649–1815* 2004

Rogers, Nicholas, *Crowds, Culture, and Politics in Georgian Britain* 1998

ed. Romilly, John, *Memoirs of the Life of Sir Samuel Romilly* 3 vols. 1840

Rose, John Holland, *William Pitt and National Revival* 1911

ed. Ross, Charles, *Correspondence of Charles, 1st Marquess Cornwallis* Vol. I 1859

Rubinstein, Hilary L., *Catastrophe at Spithead: The Sinking of the Royal George* 2020

Rudé, George, *Wilkes and Liberty* 1962

Russell, Jack, *Gibraltar Besieged* 1965

ed. Russell, Lord John, *Correspondence of John, Fourth Duke of Bedford* Vol. III 1846

——, *Memorials and Correspondence of Charles James Fox* 4 vols. 1853–7

Ruville, Albert von, *William Pitt, Earl of Chatham* 1907

eds. Ryskamp, Charles, and Pottle, Frederick A., *Boswell: The Ominous Years 1774–1776* 1963

Sack, James J., *The Grenvillites 1801–1829* 1979

——, *From Jacobite to Conservative: Reaction and Orthodoxy in Britain c.1760–1832* Cambridge 1993

Sainsbury, John, *Disaffected Patriots: London Supporters of Revolutionary America 1769–1782* 1987

——, *John Wilkes: The Lives of a Libertine* 2006

Saumarez Smith, Charles, *The Company of Artists: The Origins of the Royal Academy of Arts in London* 2012

Schuyler, Robert Livingston, *Parliament and the British Empire* New York 1929

ed. Schweizer, Karl W., *Lord Bute: Essays in Reinterpretation* Leicester 1988

Scott, H. M., *British Foreign Policy in the Age of the American Revolution* 1990

eds. Sebag-Montefiore, Charles, and Mordaunt Crook, Joe, *Brooks's 1764–2014: The Story of a Whig Club* 2013

ed. Sedgwick, Romney, *Letters from George III to Lord Bute 1756–1766* 1939

——, *Lord Hervey's Memoirs* 1963

Shy, John, *Toward Lexington: The Role of the British Army in the Coming of the American Revolution* Princeton 1965

ed. Sidgwick, J. B., *The Shorter Poems of Walter Savage Landor* Cambridge 1946

eds. Simmons, R. C., and Thomas, P. D. G., *Proceedings and Debates of the British Parliaments Respecting North America 1754–1783* Vol. IV New York 1985

Simms, Brendan, *Three Victories and a Defeat* 2007

eds. Simms, Brendan, and Riotte, Torsten, *The Hanoverian Dimension in British History 1714–1837* Cambridge 2007

Sinclair-Stevenson, Christopher, *Blood Royal: The Illustrious House of Hanover* 1979

Smart, William, *Economic Annals of the Nineteenth Century* 1910

Smith, C. D., *The Early Career of Lord North, the Prime Minister* 1979

Smith, E. A., *Lord Grey 1764–1845* 1990

——, *George IV* 1999

ed. Smith, Paul, *Letters of Delegates to Congress 1774–1789* Washington, DC Vol. I 1976

Smith, Warren Hunting, *Horace Walpole: Writer, Politician and Connoisseur* New Haven 1967

ed. Smith, William James, *The Grenville Papers* 4 vols. 1852–3

Sobel, Dava, *Longitude* 1998

ed. Sparks, Jared, *The Works of Benjamin Franklin* Vols. I, IV and VII Boston 1844

Spector, Margaret M., *The American Department of the British Government 1768–1782* New York 1940

Spring, Matthew H., *With Zeal and Bayonets Only: The British Army on Campaign in North America 1775–1783* Norman, Okla. 2008

Stanhope, Earl, *Life of the Right Honourable William Pitt* 4 vols. 1861–2

ed. Stavordale, Lord, *Further Memoirs of the Whig Party, 1807–1832, with Some Miscellaneous Reminiscences, by Henry Richard Vassall, 3rd Lord Holland* 1905

ed. Stevenson, John, *London in the Age of Reform* 1977

Strachey, Lytton, *Queen Victoria* 1921

Strong, Roy, *Coronation: A History of Kingship and the British Monarchy* 2005

ed. Stuart Wortley, Mrs E., *A Prime Minister and his Son: From the Correspondence of the 3rd Earl of Bute and of Lt.-General the Hon. Sir Charles Stuart, K. B.* 1925

Sutherland, Lucy, *The East India Company in Eighteenth-Century Politics* 1952

Syfert, Scott, *The First American Declaration of Independence?* Jefferson, NC 2013

Syrett, David, *Shipping and the American War 1775–1783* 1970

——, *The Royal Navy in American Waters 1775–1783* 1989

ed. Syrett, Harold C., *The Papers of Alexander Hamilton* 27 vols. New York 1987

Taylor, Alan, *American Revolutions: A Continental History 1750–1804* 2016

Taylor, Joseph, *Relics of Royalty, or Remarks, Anecdotes and Amusements of His Late Most Gracious Majesty, George III* 1820

eds. Taylor, William, and Pringle, John, *Correspondence of William Pitt, Earl of Chatham* Vols. II and III 1838–9

ed. Telford, John, *The Letters of the Rev. John Wesley* Vol. V 1960

Thackeray, Francis, *A History of the Right Honourable William Pitt, Earl of Chatham* 2 vols. 1827

Thomas, Peter D. G., *British Politics and the Stamp Act Crisis: The First Phase of the American Revolution 1763–1767* 1975

——, *Lord North* 1976

——, *John Wilkes: A Friend to Liberty* 1996

——, *George III: King and Politicians 1760–1770* 2002

ed. Thomson, Richard, *A Faithful Account of the Processions and Ceremonies Observed in the Coronation of the Kings and Queens of England* 1820

Tiedemann, Joseph S., *Reluctant Revolutionaries* Ithaca, NY 1997

Tillyard, Stella, *A Royal Affair: George III and his Troublesome Siblings* 2006

Tomalin, Claire, *Mrs Jordan's Profession* 1994

Tomline, George, *Memoirs of the Life of the Right Honourable William Pitt* 2 vols. 1821

ed. Tomlinson, John R. G., *Additional Grenville Papers 1763–1765* Manchester 1962

Trench, Charles Chenevix, *The Royal Malady* 2003

Trevelyan, George Macaulay, *Lord Grey of the Reform Bill* 1920

——, *British History in the Nineteenth Century and After* 1937

——, *The History of England* 1944

Trevelyan, George Otto, *The Early History of Charles James Fox* 1880

——, *George III and Charles Fox: The Concluding Part of the American Revolution* 2 vols. 1912

Tuchman, Barbara, *The March of Folly* New York 1984

Tucker, Robert W., and Hendrickson, David C., *The Fall of the First British Empire* Baltimore 1982

Turberville, A. S., *The House of Lords in the Eighteenth Century* 1927

Turner, Michael J., *Pitt the Younger: A Life* 2003

Twiss, Horace, *The Public and Private Life of Lord Chancellor Eldon* 3 vols. 1844

Urban, Mark, *Fusiliers: Eight Years with the Redcoats in America* 2007

Valentine, Alan, *Lord George Germain* Oxford 1962

——, *Lord North* Norman, Okla. 2 vols. 1967

Van der Kiste, John, *George III's Children* 1999

Van Tyne, Claude Halstead, *The Loyalists in the American Revolution* New York 1902

ed. Varvicensis, Philopatris, *Characters of the Late Charles James Fox* 1809

Vulliamy, C. E., *Royal George* 1937

Waldegrave, James, Earl, *Memoirs from 1754 to 1758* 1821

ed. Walker, Ralph S., *James Beattie's London Diary 1773* 1946

Walpole, Horace, *Memoirs of the Last Ten Years of the Reign of George the Second* Vol. I 1822

——, *Letters of Horace Walpole, Earl of Orford to Sir Horace Mann* 2 vols. Philadelphia 1844

Walters, John, *The Royal Griffin: Frederick Prince of Wales 1707–51* 1972

eds. Ward, A. W., et al., *The Cambridge Modern History* vol. VI Cambridge 1909

Ward, Christopher, *The War of the Revolution*, ed. John Richard Alden, New York 1952

Wardle, G. L., *A Circumstantial Report of the Evidence and Proceedings upon the Charges Preferred against His Royal Highness the Duke of York in the Capacity of Commander in Chief* 1809

Watkin, David, *The Architect King: George III and the Culture of the Enlightenment* 2004

Watkins, J., *The Life and Times of 'England's Patriot King' William the Fourth* 1831

Watson, J. Steven, *The Reign of George III 1760–1815* Oxford 1960

ed. Webster, J. Clarence, *The Journal of Jeffery Amherst* Toronto 1931

eds. Weinreb, Ben, and Hibbert, Christopher, *The London Encyclopaedia* 1983

ed. Wellington, Duke of, *Supplementary Despatches, Correspondence and Memoranda of Field Marshal Arthur, Duke of Wellington* 15 vols. 1858–72

ed. Wheatley, Henry B., *The Historical and Posthumous Memoirs of Sir Nathaniel William Wraxall 1772–1784* 5 vols. 1884

White, Reginald James, *The Age of George III* New York 1968

Whiteley, Peter, *Lord North: The Prime Minister Who Lost America* 1996

eds. Whiteman, Anne, et al., *Statesmen, Scholars and Merchants* 1973

Wickwire, Franklin and Mary, *Cornwallis and the War of Independence* 1971

Wilberforce, Samuel, *Life of William Wilberforce* Vol. III 1838

——, *Life of William Wilberforce* 1868

Wilbur, Marguerite, *The East India Company* 1945

Wilentz, Sean, *No Property in Man: Slavery and Antislavery at the Nation's Founding* Cambridge, Mass. 2018

ed. Willcox, William B., *The Papers of Benjamin Franklin* Vols. XVII–XX 1973–6

Williams, Basil, *The Life of William Pitt, Earl of Chatham* 2 vols. 1966

Williams, Thomas, *A Brief Memoir of Her Late Majesty Queen Charlotte* 1819

Williamson, Audrey, *Wilkes: A Friend to Liberty* 1974

Wills, Gary, *Inventing America: Jefferson's Declaration of Independence* New York 1978

Wilson, Kathleen, *The Sense of the People: Politics, Culture and Imperialism in England 1715–1785* Cambridge 1998 eds. Wimsatt, William K., and Pottle, Frederick A., *Boswell for the Defence 1769–1774* 1960

ed. Wood, Gordon, *The American Revolution: Writings from the Pamphlet Debate 1764–1776* 2 vols. 2015

ed. Woodfall, Henry, *Letters of Junius* 2 vols. 1772

Woods, Maurice, *A History of the Tory Party* 1924

Wright, Christopher, *King George III* 2005

ed. Wright, J., *The Speeches of the Right Honourable Charles James Fox in the House of Commons* 6 vols. 1815

——, *The Letters of Horace Walpole* 4 vols. Philadelphia 1840

——, *Sir Henry Cavendish: Debates in the House of Commons 1768–1771* 2 vols. 1841

Wrong, E. M., *History of England* New York 1927

ed. Wyndham, Henry Penruddocke, *The Diary of the Late George Bubb Dodington* 1784

Yonge, Charles, *The Life and Administration of Robert Banks, Second Earl of Liverpool* 3 vols. 1868

Yorke, Philip C., *The Life and Correspondence of Philip Yorke, Earl of Hardwicke* 3 vols. Cambridge 1913

Young, George, *Poor Fred: The People's Prince* 1937

Ziegler, Philip, *Addington* 1965

——, *King William IV* 1971

Articles and theses

Ambuske, Jim, 'The Admiral and the Aide-de-Camp' *Georgian Papers Programme* https://georgianpapers.com/2017/05/03/the-admiral-and-the-aide-de-camp/

Andrews, Stuart, 'Pitt and Anti-Jacobin Hysteria' *History Today* September 1998

Aspinall, A., 'The Cabinet Council 1783–1815' *Proceedings of the British Academy* Vol. 38 No. 149 1952

Attwood, Bain, 'Captain Cook's Contested Claim' *History Today* Vol. 70 Issue 8 August 2020

Banke, Rachel, 'Bute's Empire: Reform, Reaction and the Roots of Imperial Crisis' University of Notre Dame, Indiana PhD thesis 2017

Barber, Peter, 'George III's Papers and Acquisition of his "Geographical Atlas"' *Georgian Papers Programme* https://georgianpapers.com/2016/04/20/george-iiis-papers-and-acquisition-of-his-geographical-atlas/

Baugh, Daniel A., 'The Politics of British Naval Failure 1775–1778' *American Neptune* Vol. LII 1992

Black, Jeremy, 'Hanover and British Foreign Policy 1714–60' *English Historical Review* Vol. 120 No. 486 April 2005

Blanning, T. C. W., '"That Horrid Electorate" or "Ma Patrie Germanique"? George III, Hanover, and the *Fürstenbund* of 1785' *Historical Journal* Vol. 20 No. 2 June 1977

Brewer, John, 'The Misfortunes of Lord Bute: A Case-Study in Eighteenth-Century Political Argument and Public Opinion' *Historical Journal* Vol. 16 No. 1 March 1973

Brooke, John, 'The Library of King George III' *Yale University Library Gazette* Vol. 52 No. 1 July 1977

Brown, Gerald S., 'The Court Martial of Lord George Sackville, Whipping Boy of the Revolutionary War' *William and Mary Quarterly* Vol. 9 No. 3 July 1952

Buckley, Jenny, 'The Essays of George III: An Enlightened Monarch?' *Georgian Papers Programme* https://georgianpapers.com/explore-the-collections/virtual-exhibits/the-essays-of-george-iii-an-enlightened-monarch-a-virtual-exhibition-by-jenny-buckley/

Bullion, John L., ' "To Know This is the True Essential Business of a King": The Prince of Wales and the Study of Public Finance 1755–1760' *Albion* Vol. 18 No. 3 Autumn 1986

——, 'Security and Economy: The Bute Administration's Plans for the American Army and Revenue 1762–1763' *William and Mary Quarterly* Vol. 45 No. 3 July 1988

——, 'The Prince's Mentor: A New Perspective on the Friendship between George III and Lord Bute during the 1750s' *Albion* Vol. 21 No. 1 Spring 1989

——, 'George III and Empire' *William and Mary Quarterly* Vol. 51 No. 2 1994

Burns, Arthur, 'The Abdication Speech of George III' *Georgian Papers Programme* https://georgianpapers.com/2017/01/22/abdication-speech-george-iii/

Burns, Arthur, and Fitzgerald, Liam, 'Commemorating the Death of George III: A Reflection on the 200th Anniversary of his Death' *Georgian Papers Programme* https://georgianpapers.com/2020/01/29/commemorating-the-death-of-george-iii-a-reflection-on-the-200th-anniversary-of-his-death/

Burns, Arthur, and Wulf, Karin, 'The Madness of George III Revisited: Reflections on Mental Health in the Georgian World' *Georgian Papers Programme* https://georgianpapers.com/2019/12/09/the-madness-of-george-iii-revisited-reflections-on-mental-health-in-the-georgian-world/

Butterfield, Herbert, 'Charles James Fox and the Whig Opposition in 1792' *Cambridge Historical Journal* Vol. 9 No. 3 1949

——, 'George III and the Constitution' *History* Vol. 43 No. 147 1958

Christie, Ian R., 'George III and the Debt on Lord North's Election Account 1780–1784' *English Historical Review* Vol. 78 No. 309 October 1963

——, 'Was There a "New Toryism" in the Earlier Part of George III's Reign?' *Journal of British Studies* Vol. 5 No. 1 November 1965

——, 'British Politics and the American Revolution' *Albion* Vol. 9 No. 3 Autumn 1977

——, 'George III and the Historians – Thirty Years On' *History* Vol. 71 No. 232 1986

ed. Christie, Ian R., 'George III and the Southern Department: Some Unprinted Royal Correspondence' *Camden Miscellany* XXX 4th Series Vol. 39 1990

Clark, Jane, 'Responsibility for the Failure of the Burgoyne Campaign' *American Historical Review* Vol. 35 No. 3 April 1930

Colley, Linda, 'The Apotheosis of George III: Loyalty, Royalty and the British Nation 1760–1820' *Past and Present* Vol. 102 No. 1 February 1984

Connell, Andrew, ' "The Potent Spirit of the Black-browed *Jacko*": New Light on the Impact of John Robinson on High Politics in the Era of the American Revolution

1770–84' *Bulletin of the Institute of Historical Research* Vol. 86 No. 232 May 2013

Cox, T. M., et al., 'King George III and Porphyria: An Elemental Hypothesis and Investigation' *Lancet* Vol. 366 No. 9482 July 2005

Crain, Caleb, 'Tea and Antipathy: Did Principle or Pragmatism Start the American Revolution?' *New Yorker* 20 December 2010

Dent, C. E., 'Royal Malady' *British Medical Journal* Vol. 1 No. 5587 February 1968

Dinwiddy, J. R., 'Charles James Fox and the People' *History* Vol. 55 No. 185 1970

Downs, Murray Scott, 'George III and the Royal Coup of 1783' *Historian* Vol. 27 No. 1 November 1964

Duff, Stella F., 'The Case against the King: The *Virginia Gazettes* Indict George III' *William and Mary Quarterly* Vol. 6 No. 3 July 1949

Esfandiary, Helen, 'In God's Hands, Inoculating the Royal Children against Smallpox' *Georgian Papers Programme* https://georgianpapers.com/2018/11/23/in-gods-hands-inoculating-the-royal-children-against-smallpox/

Fisher, James, '"Farmer George"? Notes on Agriculture' *Georgian Papers Programme* https://georgianpapers.com/2017/01/19/farmer-georges-notes-agriculture/

Fisher, S. G., 'The Twenty-Eight Charges against the King in the Declaration of Independence' *Pennsylvania Magazine of History and Biography* Vol. 31 No. 3 1907

Foord, Archibald S., 'The Waning of "The Influence of the Crown"' *English Historical Review* Vol. 62 No. 245 October 1947

Fraser, David, 'The Trial of Lord George Sackville' *History Today* Vol. 24 No. 1 January 1974

Fryer, W. R., 'George III: His Political Character and Conduct 1760–1784: A New Whig Interpretation' *Renaissance and Modern Studies* Vol. 6 No. 1 1962

Good, Cassandra, 'Illuminating the Virtuous King George III' *Georgian Papers Programme* https://georgianpapers.com/2018/12/03/illuminating-the-virtuous-king-george-iii/

Head, Matthew, 'Remarks on the Preface to the Account of the Musical Performance in Commemoration of Handel' https://georgianpapers.com/2017/01/18/remarks-preface-account-musical-performance-commemoration-handel-george-iii/

Hedges, William L., 'Telling Off the King: Jefferson's *Summary View* as American Fantasy' *Early American Literature* Vol. 22 No. 2 Fall 1987

Hift, Richard J., Peters, Timothy J., and Meissner, Peter N., 'A Review of the Clinical Presentation, Natural History and Inheritance of Variegate Porphyria: Its Implausibility as the Source of the "Royal Malady"' *Journal of Clinical Pathology* Vol. 65 No. 3 March 2012

Hilton, Lisa, 'The "Mulatto" Queen' *The Critic* February 2020

Holly, Nathaniel F., '"Long a Dispute amongst Antiquarians": How a King's Understanding of History Changes Our Understanding of a King (and History)' *Georgian Papers Programme* https://georgianpapers.com/2017/01/20/long-dispute-amongst-antiquarians-kings-understanding-history-changes-understanding-king-history/

Jarrett, Derek, 'The Regency Crisis of 1765' *English Historical Review* Vol. 85 No. 335 April 1970

Jordan, Winthrop D., 'Familial Politics: Thomas Paine and the Killing of the King, 1776' *Journal of American History* Vol. 60 No. 2 September 1973

Keir, D. L., 'Economical Reform 1779–1787' *Law Quarterly Review* Vol. 50 1934

Kelly, P., 'The Pitt–Temple Administration 19–22 December 1783' *Historical Journal* Vol. 17 No. 1 March 1974

——, 'British Politics 1783–4: The Emergence and Triumph of the Younger Pitt's Administration' *Bulletin of the Institute of Historical Research* Vol. 54 1981

Kuypers, Jim A., and Althouse, Matthew T., 'John Pym, Ideographs and the Rhetoric of Opposition to the English Crown' *Rhetoric Review* Vol. 28 No. 3 2009

Langford, Paul, 'Old Whigs, Old Tories, and the American Revolution' *Journal of Imperial and Commonwealth History* Vol. 8 No. 2 1980

Laprade, W. T., 'Public Opinion and the General Election of 1784' *English Historical Review* Vol. 31 No. 122 April 1916

Large, David, 'The Decline of "the Party of the Crown" and the Rise of Parties in the House of Lords 1783–1837' *English Historical Review* Vol. 78 No. 309 October 1963

Lewis, Anthony M., 'Jefferson's *Summary View* as a Chart of Political Union' *William and Mary Quarterly* No. 5 No. 1 1948

Liddle, William D., '"A Patriot King, or None": Lord Bolingbroke and the American Renunciation of George III' *Journal of American History* Vol. 65 No. 4 March 1979

Lindsay, Lilian, 'The London Dentist of the Eighteenth Century' *Proceedings of the Royal Society of Medicine* Vol. 20 No. 4 1927

Lowe, William C., 'George III, Peerage Creations and Politics 1760–1784' *Historical Journal* Vol. 35 No. 3 September 1993

Macalpine, Dr Ida, and Hunter, Dr Richard, 'The "Insanity" of George III: A Classic Case of Porphyria' *British Medical Journal* Vol. 1 No. 5479 8 January 1966

Macalpine, Ida, Hunter, Richard, and Rimington, C., 'Porphyria in the Royal Houses of Stuart, Hanover and Prussia' *British Medical Journal* Vol. 1 No. 5583 6 January 1968

McDougall, Donald J., 'George III, Pitt and the Irish Catholics 1801–1805' *Catholic Historical Review* Vol. 31 No. 3 October 1945

Mackesy, Piers, 'British Strategy in the War of American Independence' *Yale Review* No. 52 1963

Mansel, Philip, 'Monarchy, Uniform and the Rise of the *Frac*' *Past and Present* No. 96 August 1982

Marks, Arthur S., 'The Statue of King George III in New York and the Iconography of Regicide' *American Art Journal* Vol. 13 No. 3 Summer 1981

Millar, Oliver, 'The Queen's Pictures' *Horizon* 1963

Namier, Sir Lewis, 'George III: A Study in Personality' *History Today* Vol. 3 No. 9 September 1953

ed. Newman, Aubrey N., 'Leicester House Politics 1750–60' *Camden Miscellany* 4th Series Vol. 23 1969

Newman, Brooke, 'Uncovering Royal Perspectives on Slavery, Empire, and the Rights of Colonial Subjects' *Georgian Papers Programme* https://georgianpapers.

com/2019/01/21/uncovering-royal-perspectives-on-slavery-empire-and-the-rights-of-colonial-subjects/

Norris, John M., 'The Policy of the British Cabinet in the Nootka Crisis' *English Historical Review* Vol. 70 No. 277 1955

O'Donnell, Angel Luke, 'America is Lost!' *Georgian Papers Programme* https://georgianpapers.com/2017/01/23/america-is-lost

——, 'Further Thoughts on "America is Lost!"' *Georgian Papers Programme* https://georgianpapers.com/2017/01/19/thoughts-america-lost/

Oliphant, John, 'The Cherokee Embassy to London, 1762' *Journal of Imperial and Commonwealth History* Vol. 27 No. 1 1999

O'Shaughnessy, Andrew, '"If Others Will Not be Active, I Must Drive": George III and the American Revolution' *Early American Studies* Vol. 2 No. 1 Spring 2004

——, 'Understanding the American Revolution from George III's Archives' *Georgian Papers Programme* https://georgianpapers.com/2017/08/03/american-revolution-george-iii-archives/

Page, Anthony, 'George III and the Seventy Years War 1744–1815' *Georgian Papers Project* https://georgianpapers.com/2019/01/03/george-iii-and-the-seventy-years-war-1744-1815/

Parkinson, Stephen, 'Call for the Doctor: The Under-rated Premiership of Henry Addington 1801–04' *Conservative History Journal* Vol. 2 No. 8 Autumn 2020

Pelling, Madeleine, and Wulf, Karin, 'Women and History: Power, Politics and Historical Thinking in Queen Charlotte's Court' *Georgian Papers Programme* https://georgianpapers.com/explore-the-collections/virtual-exhibits/women-and-history-power-politics-and-historical-thinking-in-queen-charlottes-court/

Peters, Timothy J., 'King George III, Bipolar Disorder, Porphyria and Lessons for Historians' *Clinical Medicine* Vol. 11 No. 3 June 2011

——, 'Royal Medical Entourages: Analysis of the Roles of Doctors during the Episodes of Madness of King George III' *Court Historian* Vol. 24 No. 1 2019

Peters, Timothy J., and Beveridge, Allan, 'The Madness of George III: A Psychiatric Reassessment' *History of Psychiatry* Vol. 21 No. 1 2010

——, 'The Blindness, Deafness and Madness of King George III: Psychiatric Interactions' *Journal of the Royal College of Physicians of Edinburgh* No. 40 2010

Peters, Timothy J., and Wilkinson, D., 'King George III and Porphyria: A Clinical Re-examination of the Historical Evidence' *History of Psychiatry* Vol. 21 No. 1 2010

Rae, W. F., 'John Wilkes', *Fortnightly Review* Vol. 4 NS July–December 1868

Rempel, Lora, 'Carnal Satire and the Constitutional King: George III in James Gillray's *Monstrous Craws at a New Coalition Feast*' *Art History* Vol. 18 No. 1 March 1995

Rentoumi, Vissiliki, Peters, Timothy, Conlin, Jonathan, and Garrard, Peter, 'The Acute Mania of King George III: A Computational Linguistic Analysis' *Plos One*, March 2017 https://journals.plos.org/plosone/article?id=10.1371/journal.pone.0171626

Ritcheson, Charles R., 'The Fragile Memory: Thomas Jefferson at the Court of George III' *Eighteenth-Century Life* Vol. 6 Nos. 2–3 1981

Rowe, Michael, 'George III and the "German Empire"' *Georgian Papers Programme* https://georgianpapers.com/2017/01/22/george-iii-german-empire/

Schwarz, Suzanne, 'Slave Trade, Slavery and Abolition in the Royal Archives, c. 1785–1810' *Georgian Papers Programme* https://georgianpapers.com/2017/01/23/georgian-papers-programme-slave-trade-slavery-abolition-royal-archives-c-1785-18101/

Schweizer, Karl W., 'William Pitt, Lord Bute and the Peace Negotiations with France May–September 1761' *Albion* Vol. 13 No. 3 Autumn 1981

——, 'The Cabinet Crisis of August 1761: Unpublished Letters from the Bute and Bedford Manuscripts' *Bulletin of the Institute of Historical Research* Vol. 59 No. 140 November 1986

Siegel, Nancy, 'Mommy Dearest: Britannia, America, and Mother–Daughter Conflicts in Eighteenth-Century Prints and Medals' in eds. George W. Boudreau and Margaretta Lovell, *A Material World: Culture, Society, and the Life of Things in Early Anglo-America* University Park, Pa. 2019

Smith, Anthony, 'Earl Temple's Resignation' *Historical Journal* Vol. 6 No. 1 1966

Thomas, P. D. G., 'George III and the American Revolution' *History* Vol. 70 No. 228 February 1985

——, '"Thoughts on the British Constitution" by George III in 1760' *Bulletin of the Institute of Historical Research* Vol. 60 No. 143 1987

Tillyard, Stella, 'George IV's Wretched Reputation' *BBC History Magazine* February 2020

York, Neil, 'George III, Tyrant: *The Crisis* as Critic of Empire 1775–1776' *History* Vol. 94 No. 4 October 2009

——, 'Natural Rights Dissected and Rejected: John Lind's Counter to the Declaration of Independence' *Law and History Review* Vol. 35 No. 3 August 2017

Wessely, Sir Simon, 'From an Enlightenment King to Enlightened Princes: Mental Illness and the Royal Family' https://www.huffingtonpost.co.uk/professor-sir-simon-wessely/george-iii_b_14497230.html?guccounter=1&guce_referrer_us=aHR0cHM6Ly93d3cuZ29vZ2xlLmNvbS88&guce_referrer_cs=sqKJ-Xx41gHrRvGQov9maA

Willcox, W. B., 'The British Road to Yorktown: A Study in Divided Command' *American Historical Review* Vol. 52 No. 1 1946

——, 'Too Many Cooks: British Planning before Saratoga' *Journal of British Studies* Vol. 2 No. 1 1962

Willis, Richard, 'William Pitt's Resignation in 1801' *Bulletin of the Institute of Historical Research* Vol. 44 No. 110 1971

Winstanley, D. A., 'George III and his First Cabinet' *English Historical Review* Vol. 17 No. 68 October 1902

List of Illustrations

Photographic acknowledgements are given in parentheses.

1. George, Prince of Wales, 1754, by Jean-Etienne Liotard. The Royal Collection. (*The Royal Collection Trust; copyright © Her Majesty Queen Elizabeth II, 2021/Bridgeman Images*)

2. Prince Frederick Louis, Prince of Wales, *c.* 1730–50, circle of Godfrey Kneller. Hartwell House, Aylesbury, Buckinghamshire. (*National Trust Photographic Library/Bridgeman Images*)

3. Augusta of Saxe-Gotha, Princess of Wales, *c.* 1760, by Allan Ramsay. (*© Crown Copyright. UK Government Art Collection*)

4. John Stuart, 3rd Earl of Bute, 1773, by Joshua Reynolds. National Portrait Gallery, London. *Stefano Baldini/Bridgeman Images.*

5. Extract from an essay in the King's hand, 1750s. The Royal Archives (RA/ GEO/ MAIN/32/873 fol 295–296). (*The Royal Archives; copyright © Her Majesty Queen Elizabeth II, 2021*)

6. The Right Hon. George Grenville MP, *c.* 1767, by Joshua Reynolds. Petworth House, West Sussex. (*National Trust Photographic Library/Bridgeman Images*)

7. William Pitt the Elder, 1st Earl of Chatham, 1772, after Richard Brompton. (*Copyright © National Portrait Gallery, London*)

8. Augustus Henry Fitzroy, 3rd Duke of Grafton, *c.* 1770, by Nathaniel Dance-Holland. Private collection. (*Philip Mould Ltd, London/ Bridgeman Images*)

9. Charles Watson-Wentworth, 2nd Marquess of Rockingham, *c.* 1768–86, by the studio of Joshua Reynolds (detail). The Royal Collection. (*Royal Collection Trust; copyright © Her Majesty Queen Elizabeth II, 2021/Bridgeman Images*)

10. George III, Queen Charlotte and their six eldest children, 1770, by Johann Zoffany. The Royal Collection. (*Royal Collection Trust;*

Index